SCIENTIFIC COMPUTING

An Introductory Survey

Second Edition

Michael T. Heath

University of Illinois
at Urbana-Champaign

McGraw Hill

Boston Burr Ridge, IL Dubuque, IA Madison, WI New York
San Francisco St. Louis Bangkok Bogotá Caracas Kuala Lumpur
Lisbon London Madrid Mexico City Milan Montreal New Delhi
Santiago Seoul Singapore Sydney Taipei Toronto

To Mona

McGraw-Hill Higher Education

A Division of The **McGraw-Hill** *Companies*

SCIENTIFIC COMPUTING: AN INTRODUCTORY SURVEY, SECOND EDITION

Published by McGraw-Hill, a business unit of The McGraw-Hill Companies, Inc., 1221 Avenue of the Americas, New York, NY 10020.

This book is printed on acid-free paper.

5 6 7 8 9 0 FGR/FGR 0 9 8 7 6 5

ISBN 0-07-239910-4
ISBN 0-07-112229-X (ISE)

General manager: *Thomas E. Casson*
Publisher: *Elizabeth A. Jones*
Developmental editor: *Melinda Bilecki*
Executive marketing manager: *John Wannemacher*
Project manager: *Joyce Watters*
Production supervisor: *Kara Kudronowicz*
Coordinator of freelance design: *Michelle D. Whitaker*
Freelance cover designer: *Rokusek Design*
Senior supplement producer: *Audrey A. Reiter*
Media technology senior producer: *Phillip Meek*
Compositor: *Interactive Composition Corporation*
Typeface: *10/12 Computer Modern*
Printer: *Quebecor World Fairfield, PA*

Cover images: The cover images show results from a numerical simulation of the solid rocket booster for the U.S. Space Shuttle. Shown is a cutaway view of the forward segment at a sequence of four times shortly after ignition. Colors show stress in the solid propellant (purple to red), isosurfaces of gas temperature (blue to red), and cones indicating gas velocity (black to beige). Visualization produced by Robert Fiedler and John Norris from data produced by Amit Acharya, Prasad Alavilli, Xiangmin Jiao, Ali Namazifard, and Dennis Parsons, all of the Center for Simulation of Advanced Rockets at the University of Illinois, of which the author is Director.

Library of Congress Cataloging-in-Publication Data

Heath, Michael T.
Scientific computing : an introductory survey / Michael T. Heath .— 2nd ed.
p. cm.
Includes bibliographical references and index.
ISBN 0-07-239910-4 — ISBN 0-07-112229-X
1. Science—Data processing. 2. Numerical analysis—Data processing. I. Title.

Q183.9.H4 2002
519.4′0285—dc21

2001031265
CIP

INTERNATIONAL EDITION ISBN 0-07-112229-X

www.mhhe.com

About the Author

Michael T. Heath is Professor and Fulton Watson Copp Chair in Computer Science at the University of Illinois at Urbana-Champaign, where he is also Director of the Computational Science and Engineering Program and Director of the Center for Simulation of Advanced Rockets. He received a B.A. in Mathematics from the University of Kentucky, an M.S. in Mathematics from the University of Tennessee, and a Ph.D. in Computer Science from Stanford University. Before joining the University of Illinois in 1991, he spent a number of years at Oak Ridge National Laboratory, first as Eugene P. Wigner Postdoctoral Fellow and later as Computer Science Group Leader in the Mathematical Sciences Research Section. His research interests are in numerical analysis—particularly numerical linear algebra and optimization—and in parallel computing. He has been an editor of the *SIAM Journal on Scientific Computing*, *SIAM Review*, and the *International Journal of High Performance Computing Applications*, as well as several conference proceedings. He was named an ACM Fellow by the Association for Computing Machinery in 2000, and was elected a member of the European Academy of Sciences in 2002. His teaching awards at the University of Illinois include the William L. Everitt Award for Teaching Excellence in the College of Engineering and the Campus Award for Excellence in Graduate and Professional Teaching.

Contents

Preface

This book presents a broad overview of numerical methods for students and professionals in computationally oriented disciplines who need to solve mathematical problems. It differs from traditional numerical analysis texts in that it focuses on the motivation and ideas behind the algorithms presented rather than on detailed analyses of them. I try to convey a general understanding of the techniques available for solving problems in each major category, including proper problem formulation and interpretation of results, but I advocate the use of professionally written mathematical software for obtaining solutions whenever possible. The book is aimed much more at potential users of mathematical software than at potential creators of such software. I hope to make the reader aware of the relevant issues in selecting appropriate methods and software and using them wisely.

At the University of Illinois, this book is used as the text for a comprehensive, one-semester course on numerical methods that serves three main purposes:

- As a terminal course for senior undergraduates, mainly computer science, mathematics, and engineering majors
- As a breadth course for graduate students in computer science who do *not* intend to specialize in numerical analysis
- As a training course for graduate students in science and engineering who need to use numerical methods and software in their research. It is a core course for the interdisciplinary graduate program in Computational Science and Engineering sponsored by the College of Engineering.

To accommodate this diverse student clientele, the prerequisites for the course and the book have been kept to a minimum: basic familiarity with linear algebra, multivariate calculus, and a smattering of differential equations. No prior familiarity with numerical methods is assumed. The book adopts a fairly sophisticated perspective, however, so a reasonable level of maturity on the part of the student (or reader) is advisable. Beyond the academic setting, I hope that the book will also be useful as a reference for practicing engineers and scientists who may need a quick overview of a given computational problem and the methods and software available for solving it.

Although the book emphasizes the use of mathematical software, unlike some other software-oriented texts it does not provide any software, nor does it concentrate on any specific software packages, libraries, or environments. Instead, for each problem category pointers are provided to specific routines available from publicly accessible repositories and the major commercial libraries and packages. In many academic and industrial computing environments such software is already installed, and in any case pointers are also provided to public domain software that is freely accessible via the Internet. The computer exercises in the book are not dependent on any specific choice of software or programming language.

The main elements in the organization of the book are as follows:

Chapters: Each chapter of the book covers a major computational problem area. The first half of the book deals primarily with algebraic problems, whereas the second half treats analytic problems involving derivatives and integrals. The first two chapters are fundamental to the remainder of the book, but the subsequent chapters can be taken in various orders according to the instructor's preference. More specifically, the major dependences among chapters are roughly as follows:

Chapter	Depends on	Chapter	Depends on	Chapter	Depends on
2	1	6	1, 2, 3, 5	10	1, 2, 5, 7, 9
3	1, 2	7	1, 2	11	1, 2, 7, 9, 10
4	1, 2, 3	8	1, 2, 7	12	1, 2, 7
5	1, 2	9	1, 2, 5, 7	13	1

Thus, Chapters 7, 8, 12, and 13 could be covered much earlier, and Chapters 3, 4 and 6 much later, than their appearance in the book. For example, Chapters 3, 7, and 12 all involve some type of data fitting, so it might be desirable to cover them as a unit. As another example, iterative methods for linear systems are contained in Chapter 11 on partial differential equations because that is where the most important motivating examples come from, but much of this material could be covered immediately following direct methods for linear systems in Chapter 2. Note that eigenvalues are used freely throughout the remainder of the book, so there is some incentive for covering Chapter 4 fairly early unless the students are already familiar with the basics of this topic.

There is more than enough material in the book for a full semester course, so some judicious omissions will likely be required in a one-term course. For example, Chapter 13 on random numbers and stochastic simulation is only peripherally related to the remainder of the book and is an obvious candidate for omission (random number generators are used in a number of exercises throughout the book, however). The entire book can be covered in a two-quarter or two-semester course.

Examples: Almost every concept and method introduced is illustrated by one or more examples. These examples are meant to supplement the relatively terse general discussion and should be read as an essential part of the text. The examples have been kept as simple as possible (sometimes at the risk of oversimplification) so that the reader can easily follow them. In my experience, a simple example that is thoroughly understood is usually more helpful than a more realistic example that is more difficult to follow.

Software: The lists of available software for each problem category are meant to be reasonably comprehensive. I have not attempted to single out the "best" software available for a given problem, partly because usually no single package is superior in all respects and partly to allow for the varied software availability and choice of programming language that may apply for different readers. All of the software cited is at least competently written, and some of it is superb.

Exercises: The book contains many exercises, which are divided into three categories:

- *Review questions*, which are short-answer questions designed to test basic conceptual understanding
- *Exercises*, which require somewhat more thought, longer answers, and possibly some hand computation
- *Computer problems*, which require some programming and often involve the use of existing software.

The *review questions* are meant for self-testing on the part of the reader. They include some deliberate repetition to drive home key points and to build confidence in the mastery of the material. The longer *exercises* are meant to be suitable for written homework assignments. Some of these require manual computations with simple examples, while others are designed to supply details of derivations and proofs omitted from the main text. The latter should be especially useful if the book is used for a more theoretical course. The *computer problems* provide an opportunity for hands-on experience in using the recommended software for solving typical problems in each category. Some of these problems are generic, but others are directly related to specific applications in various scientific and engineering disciplines.

Changes for the Second Edition. Each chapter now begins with a motivational discussion and one or more illustrative examples, which are then followed by discussions of existence, uniqueness, and conditioning of solutions for the given type of problem. The intent is to enhance the student's understanding of why the problem is important and how to recognize a "good" or "bad" formulation of the problem before considering algorithms for solving it. The major algorithms are now stated formally and numbered for easy reference. The bibliography has been brought up to date and the historical notes slightly expanded. The discussion in Chapter 1 on forward and backward error and the relationship between them has been expanded and clarified. Most of the material on the singular value decomposition has been moved from Chapter 4 to Chapter 3, where its applications fit more comfortably. The coverage of eigenvalue algorithms in Chapter 4 has been expanded to include more motivation and details, especially on QR iteration, as well as some additional methods. The treatment of constrained optimization in Chapter 6 has been expanded substantially. The chapters on differential equations have been slightly reorganized and the coverage of spectral methods expanded. Chapter 12 on the fast Fourier transform has been reorganized and streamlined by deleting some extraneous material.

I would like to acknowledge the influence of the mentors who first introduced me to the unexpected charms of numerical computation, Alston Householder and Gene Golub. I am grateful for the bountiful feedback I have received from students and instructors who have used the first edition of this book. Prepublication reviewers for the first edition were Alan George, University of Waterloo; Dianne O'Leary, University of Maryland; James Ortega, University of Virginia; John Strikwerda, University of Wisconsin; and Lloyd N. Trefethen, Oxford University. Reviewers of the first edition in preparation for the second edition were Thomas Coleman, Cornell University; Robert Funderlic, North Carolina State University; Thomas Hagstrom, University of New Mexico; Ramon Moore, Ohio State University; Mark Pernarowski, Montana State University; Linda Petzold, University of California at Santa Barbara; and Brian Suchomel, University of Minnesota. I thank all of these reviewers for their invaluable suggestions. In addition, I particularly want to acknowledge my colleagues Joerg Liesen, Paul Saylor, and Eric de Sturler, all of the University of Illinois, each of whom read some or all of the revised manuscript and provided invaluable feedback. I would like to thank Melchior Franz and Justin Winkler for helpful advice on typesetting that was crucial in enabling me to prepare camera-ready copy. Finally, I deeply appreciate the patience and understanding of my wife, Mona, during the countless hours spent in writing and revising this book. With great pleasure and gratitude I dedicate the book to her.

Michael T. Heath

Book website: `www.cse.uiuc.edu/heath/scicomp`

Notation

The notation used in this book is fairly standard and should require little explanation. We freely use vector and matrix notation, generally using upper-case bold type for matrices, lower-case bold type for vectors, and regular type for scalars. Iteration and component indices are denoted by subscripts, usually i through n. For example, a vector $\boldsymbol{x}$ and matrix $\boldsymbol{A}$ have entries x_i and a_{ij}, respectively. On the few occasions when both an iteration index and a component index are needed, the iteration is indicated by a parenthesized superscript, as in $x_i^{(k)}$ to indicate the ith component of the kth vector in a sequence. Otherwise, x_i denotes the ith component of a vector $\boldsymbol{x}$, whereas $\boldsymbol{x}_k$ denotes the kth vector in a sequence.

For simplicity, we will deal primarily with real vectors and matrices, although most of the theory and algorithms we discuss carry over with little or no change to the complex field. The set of real numbers is denoted by $\mathbb{R}$, n-dimensional real Euclidean space by $\mathbb{R}^n$, and the set of real $m \times n$ matrices by $\mathbb{R}^{m\times n}$. The analogous complex entities are denoted by $\mathbb{C}$, $\mathbb{C}^n$, and $\mathbb{C}^{m\times n}$, respectively.

The transpose of a vector or matrix is indicated by a superscript T, and the conjugate transpose by superscript H (for Hermitian transpose). Unless otherwise indicated, all vectors are regarded as column vectors; a row vector is indicated by explicitly transposing a column vector. For typesetting convenience, the components of a column vector are sometimes indicated by transposing the corresponding row vector, as in $\boldsymbol{x} = \begin{bmatrix} x_1 & x_2 \end{bmatrix}^T$. The inner product (also known as dot product or scalar product) of two n-vectors $\boldsymbol{x}$ and $\boldsymbol{y}$ is a special case of matrix multiplication and thus is denoted by $\boldsymbol{x}^T\boldsymbol{y}$ (or $\boldsymbol{x}^H\boldsymbol{y}$ in the complex case). Similarly, the outer product of two n-vectors $\boldsymbol{x}$ and $\boldsymbol{y}$, which is an $n \times n$ matrix, is denoted by $\boldsymbol{x}\boldsymbol{y}^T$. The identity matrix of order n is denoted by $\boldsymbol{I}_n$ (or just $\boldsymbol{I}$ if the dimension n is clear from context), and its ith column is denoted by $\boldsymbol{e}_i$. A zero matrix is denoted by $\boldsymbol{O}$, a zero vector by $\boldsymbol{0}$, and a zero scalar by 0. A diagonal matrix with diagonal entries $d_1, \ldots, d_n$ is denoted by $\text{diag}(d_1, \ldots, d_n)$. Inequalities between vectors or matrices are taken to apply elementwise. The subspace of $\mathbb{R}^m$ spanned by the columns of an $m \times n$ matrix $\boldsymbol{A}$, i.e., $\{\boldsymbol{A}\boldsymbol{x} : \boldsymbol{x} \in \mathbb{R}^n\}$, is denoted by $\text{span}(\boldsymbol{A})$.

The ordinary derivative of a function $f(t)$ of one variable is denoted by df/dt or by $f'(t)$. Partial derivatives of a function of several variables, such as $u(x, y)$, are denoted by $\partial u/\partial x$, for example, or in some contexts by a subscript, as in u_x. Notation for gradient vectors and Jacobian and Hessian matrices will be introduced as needed. All logarithms are natural logarithms (base $e \approx 2.718$) unless another base is explicitly indicated. We use the symbol $\approx$ to indicate approximate equality in the ordinary sense and reserve the symbol $\cong$ specifically for least squares approximations.

The computational cost, or *complexity*, of numerical algorithms is usually measured by the number of arithmetic operations required. Traditionally, numerical analysts have counted only multiplications (and possibly divisions and square roots), because multiplications were usually significantly more expensive than additions or subtractions and because in most algorithms multiplications tend to be paired with a similar number of additions (for example, in computing the inner product of two vectors). More recently, the difference in cost between additions and multiplications has largely disappeared (indeed, many modern microprocessors can perform a coupled multiplication and addition with a single `multiply-add` instruction). Computer vendors and users like to advertise the highest possible performance, so it is increasingly common for every arithmetic operation to be counted. Because certain operation counts are so well known using the traditional practice, however, only multiplications are usually counted in this book. To clarify the meaning, the phrase "and a similar number of additions" will be added, or else it will be explicitly stated when both are being counted.

In quantifying operation counts and the accuracy of approximations, we will often use "big-oh" notation to indicate the order of magnitude, or dominant term, of a function. For an operation count, we are interested in the behavior as the size of the problem, say n, becomes large. We say that

$$f(n) = \mathcal{O}(g(n))$$

(read "f is big-oh of g" or "f is of order g") if there is a positive constant C such that

$$|f(n)| \leq C|g(n)|$$

for all n sufficiently large. For example,

$$2n^3 + 3n^2 + n = \mathcal{O}(n^3)$$

because as n becomes large, the terms of order lower than n^3 become relatively insignificant. For an accuracy estimate, we are interested in the behavior as some quantity h, such as a step size or mesh spacing, becomes small. We say that

$$f(h) = \mathcal{O}(g(h))$$

if there is a positive constant C such that

$$|f(h)| \leq C|g(h)|$$

for all h sufficiently small. For example,

$$\frac{1}{1-h} = 1 + h + h^2 + h^3 + \cdots = 1 + h + \mathcal{O}(h^2)$$

because as h becomes small, the omitted terms beyond h^2 become relatively insignificant. Note that the two definitions are equivalent if $h = 1/n$.

Chapter 1

Scientific Computing

1.1 Introduction

The subject of this book is traditionally called *numerical analysis*. Numerical analysis is concerned with the design and analysis of algorithms for solving mathematical problems that arise in many fields, especially science and engineering. For this reason, numerical analysis has more recently also become known as *scientific computing*. Scientific computing is distinguished from most other parts of computer science in that it deals with quantities that are *continuous*, as opposed to discrete. It is concerned with functions and equations whose underlying variables—time, distance, velocity, temperature, density, pressure, stress, and the like—are continuous in nature.

Most of the problems of continuous mathematics (for example, almost any problem involving derivatives, integrals, or nonlinearities) cannot be solved exactly, even in principle, in a finite number of steps and thus must be solved by a (theoretically infinite) iterative process that ultimately converges to a solution. In practice one does not iterate forever, of course, but only until the answer is approximately correct, "close enough" to the desired result for practical purposes. Thus, one of the most important aspects of scientific computing is finding rapidly convergent iterative algorithms and assessing the accuracy of the resulting approximation. If convergence is sufficiently rapid, even some of the problems that *can* be solved by finite algorithms, such as systems of linear algebraic equations, may in some cases be better solved by iterative methods, as we will see.

Consequently, a second factor that distinguishes scientific computing is its concern with the effects of approximations. Many solution techniques involve a whole series of approximations of various types. Even the arithmetic used is only approximate, for digital computers cannot represent all real numbers exactly. In addition to having the usual properties of good algorithms, such as efficiency, numerical algorithms should also be as reliable and accurate as possible despite the various approximations made along the way.

1.1.1 Computational Problems

As the name suggests, many problems in scientific computing come from science and engineering, in which the ultimate aim is to understand some natural phenomenon or to design some device. *Computational simulation* is the representation and emulation of a physical system or process using a computer. Computational simulation can greatly enhance scientific understanding by allowing the investigation of situations that may be difficult or impossible to investigate by theoretical, observational, or experimental means alone. In astrophysics, for example, the detailed behavior of two colliding black holes is too complicated to determine theoretically and impossible to observe directly or duplicate in the laboratory. To simulate it computationally, however, requires only an appropriate mathematical representation (in this case Einstein's equations of general relativity), an algorithm for solving those equations numerically, and a sufficiently large computer on which to implement the algorithm.

Computational simulation is useful not just for exploring exotic or otherwise inaccessible situations, however, but also for exploring a wider variety of "normal" scenarios than could otherwise be investigated with reasonable cost and time. In engineering design, computational simulation allows a large number of design options to be tried much more quickly, inexpensively, and safely than with traditional "build-and-test" methods using physical prototypes. In this context, computational simulation has become known as *virtual prototyping*. In improving automobile safety, for example, crash testing is far less expensive and dangerous on a computer than in real life, and thus the space of possible design parameters can be explored much more thoroughly to develop an optimal design.

The overall problem solving process in computational simulation usually includes the following steps:

1. Develop a mathematical model—usually expressed by equations of some type—of a physical phenomenon or system of interest
2. Develop algorithms to solve the equations numerically
3. Implement the algorithms in computer software
4. Run the software on a computer to simulate the physical process numerically
5. Represent the computed results in some comprehensible form such as graphical visualization
6. Interpret and validate the computed results, repeating any or all of the preceding steps, if necessary.

Step 1 is often called *mathematical modeling*. It requires specific knowledge of the particular scientific or engineering disciplines involved as well as knowledge of applied mathematics. Steps 2 and 3—designing, analyzing, implementing, and using numerical algorithms and software—are the main subject matter of scientific computing, and of this book in particular. Although we will focus on Steps 2 and 3, it is essential that all of these steps, from problem formulation to interpretation and validation of results, be done properly for the results to be meaningful and useful. The principles and methods of scientific computing can be studied at a fairly broad level of generality, as we will see, but the specific source of a given problem and the uses to which the results will be put should always be kept in mind, as each aspect affects—and is affected by—the others. For example, the original problem formulation may strongly affect the accuracy of numerical results, which in turn affects the interpretation and validation of those results.

A mathematical problem is said to be *well-posed* if a solution exists, is unique, and depends continuously on the problem data. The latter condition means that a small change in the problem data does not cause an abrupt, disproportionate change in the solution; this property is especially important for numerical computations, where, as we will see shortly, such perturbations are usually *inevitable.* Well-posedness is highly desirable in mathematical models of physical systems, but this is not always achievable. For example, inferring the internal structure of a physical system solely from external observations, as in tomography or seismology, often leads to mathematical problems that are inherently ill-posed in that distinctly different internal configurations may have indistinguishable external appearances.

Even when a problem is well-posed, however, the solution may still respond in a highly sensitive (though continuous) manner to perturbations in the problem data. In order to assess the effects of such perturbations, we must go beyond the qualitative concept of continuity to define a quantitative measure of the sensitivity of a problem. In addition, we must also take care to ensure that the algorithm we use to solve a given problem numerically does not make the results more sensitive than is already inherent in the underlying problem (the Hippocratic oath, "do no harm," applies to numerical analysts as well as physicians). This requirement will lead us to the notion of a *stable* algorithm. These general concepts and issues will be introduced in this chapter and then discussed in detail in subsequent chapters for specific types of computational problems.

1.1.2 General Strategy

In seeking a solution to a given computational problem, a basic general strategy, which occurs throughout this book, is to replace a difficult problem with an easier one that has the same solution, or at least a closely related solution. Examples of this approach include

- Replacing infinite-dimensional spaces with finite-dimensional spaces
- Replacing infinite processes with finite processes, such as replacing integrals or infinite series with finite sums, or derivatives with finite differences
- Replacing differential equations with algebraic equations
- Replacing nonlinear problems with linear problems
- Replacing high-order systems with low-order systems
- Replacing complicated functions with simple functions, such as polynomials
- Replacing general matrices with matrices having a simpler form

For example, to solve a system of nonlinear differential equations, we might first replace it with a system of nonlinear algebraic equations, then replace the nonlinear algebraic system with a linear algebraic system, then replace the matrix of the linear system with one of a special form for which the solution is easy to compute. At each step of this process, we would need to verify that the solution is unchanged, or is at least within some required tolerance of the true solution.

To make this general strategy work for solving a given problem, we must have

- An alternative problem, or class of problems, that is easier to solve
- A transformation of the given problem into a problem of this alternative type that preserves the solution in some sense

Thus, much of our effort will go into identifying suitable problem classes with simple solutions and solution-preserving transformations into those classes.

Ideally, the solution to the transformed problem is identical to that of the original problem, but this is not always possible. In the latter case the solution may only approximate that of the original problem, but the accuracy can usually be made arbitrarily good at the expense of additional work and storage. Thus, primary concerns are estimating the accuracy of such an approximate solution and establishing convergence to the true solution in the limit.

1.2 Approximations in Scientific Computation

1.2.1 Sources of Approximation

There are many sources of approximation or inexactness in computational science. Some approximations may occur *before* a computation begins:

- **Modeling:** Some physical features of the problem or system under study may be simplified or omitted (e.g., friction, viscosity, air resistance).
- **Empirical measurements:** Laboratory instruments have finite precision. Their accuracy may be further limited by small sample size, or readings obtained may be subject to random noise or systematic bias. For example, even the most careful measurements of important physical constants—such as Newton's gravitational constant or Planck's constant—typically yield values with at most eight or nine significant decimal digits, and most laboratory measurements are much less accurate than that.
- **Previous computations:** Input data may have been produced by a previous computational step whose results were only approximate.

The approximations just listed are usually beyond our control, but they still play an important role in determining the accuracy that should be expected from a computation. We will focus most of our attention on approximations over which we do have some influence. These systematic approximations that occur *during* computation include

- **Truncation or discretization:** Some features of a mathematical model may be omitted or simplified (e.g., replacing derivatives by finite differences or using only a finite number of terms in an infinite series).

- **Rounding:** Whether in hand computation, a calculator, or a digital computer, the representation of real numbers and arithmetic operations upon them is ultimately limited to some finite amount of precision and thus is generally inexact.

The accuracy of the final results of a computation may reflect a combination of any or all of these approximations, and the resulting perturbations may be amplified by the nature of the problem being solved or the algorithm being used, or both. The study of the effects of such approximations on the accuracy and stability of numerical algorithms is traditionally called *error analysis*.

Example 1.1 Approximations. The surface area of the Earth might be computed using the formula

$$A = 4\pi r^2$$

for the surface area of a sphere of radius r. The use of this formula for the computation involves a number of approximations:

- The Earth is modeled as a sphere, which is an idealization of its true shape.
- The value for the radius, $r \approx 6370$ km, is based on a combination of empirical measurements and previous computations.
- The value for π is given by an infinite limiting process, which must be truncated at some point.
- The numerical values for the input data, as well as the results of the arithmetic operations performed on them, are rounded in a computer or calculator.

The accuracy of the computed result depends on all of these approximations.

1.2.2 Absolute Error and Relative Error

The significance of an error is obviously related to the magnitude of the quantity being measured or computed. For example, an error of 1 is much less significant in counting the population of the Earth than in counting the occupants of a phone booth. This motivates the concepts of *absolute error* and *relative error*, which are defined as follows:

$$\text{Absolute error} = \text{approximate value} - \text{true value},$$

$$\text{Relative error} = \frac{\text{absolute error}}{\text{true value}}.$$

Some authors define absolute error to be the absolute value of the foregoing difference, but we will take the absolute value (or norm for vectors and matrices) explicitly when only the magnitude of the error is needed. Note that the relative error is undefined if the true value is zero.

Relative error can also be expressed as a percentage, which is simply the relative error times 100. Thus, for example, an absolute error of 0.1 relative to a true value of 10 would be a relative error of 0.01, or 1 percent. A completely erroneous approximation would correspond to a relative error of at least 1, or at least 100 percent, meaning that the absolute error is as large as the true value.

Another interpretation of relative error is that if an approximate value has a relative error of about 10^{-p}, then its decimal representation has about p correct significant digits (*significant digits* are the leading nonzero digit and all following digits). In this connection, it is worth noting the distinction between precision and accuracy: *precision* refers to the number of digits with which a number is expressed, whereas *accuracy* refers to the number of *correct* significant digits (i.e., relative error) in approximating some desired quantity. For example, 3.252603764690804 is a very precise number, but it is not very accurate as an approximation to π. As we will soon see, computing a quantity using a given precision does not necessarily mean that the result will be accurate to that precision.

A useful way to express the relationship between absolute and relative error is the following:

$$\text{Approximate value} = (\text{true value}) \times (1 + \text{relative error}).$$

Of course, we do not usually know the true value; if we did, we would not need to bother with approximating it. Thus, we will usually merely *estimate* or *bound* the error rather than compute it exactly, because the true value is unknown. For this same reason, relative error is often taken to be relative to the approximate value rather than to the true value, as in the foregoing definition.

1.2.3 Data Error and Computational Error

As we have seen, some errors can be attributed to the input data, whereas others are due to subsequent computational processes. Although this distinction is not always clear-cut (rounding, for example, may affect both the input data and subsequent computational results), it is nevertheless helpful in understanding the overall effects of approximations in numerical computations.

Most realistic problems are multidimensional, but for simplicity we will consider only one-dimensional problems in this chapter; extension of the definitions and results to higher dimensions is straightforward, usually requiring only replacement of absolute values by appropriate *norms* (see Section 2.3.1). A typical problem in one dimension can be viewed as the computation of the value of a function, say $f\colon \mathbb{R} \to \mathbb{R}$, that maps a given input value to an output result. Denote the true value of the input by x, so that the desired true result is $f(x)$. Suppose that we must work with inexact input, say $\hat{x}$, and we can compute only an approximation to the function, say $\hat{f}$. Then, using the standard mathematical trick of adding and subtracting the same quantity so that the total is unchanged, we have

$$\begin{aligned}
\text{Total error} &= \hat{f}(\hat{x}) - f(x) \\
&= (\hat{f}(\hat{x}) - f(\hat{x})) \quad + \quad (f(\hat{x}) - f(x)) \\
&= \text{computational error} \quad + \quad \text{propagated data error}.
\end{aligned}$$

The first term in this sum is the difference between the exact and approximate functions for the *same* input and hence can be considered pure *computational error*.

The second term is the difference between exact function values due to error in the input and thus can be viewed as pure propagated *data error*. Note that the choice of algorithm has no effect on the propagated data error.

Example 1.2 Data Error and Computational Error. Suppose we are without access to a computer or calculator, and we need a "quick and dirty" approximation to $\sin(\pi/8)$. First, we need a value for π to determine the input. We briefly consider the classic approximation $\pi \approx 22/7$ remembered from school days, but decide it would be too much work to convert to the desired decimal fraction format, and we settle instead for the simple "biblical" approximation $\pi \approx 3$, so that our actual input is 3/8. To compute the function value, we remember from calculus that a good approximation for small arguments is to use the first term in the Taylor series expansion, which for $\sin(x)$ is simply x. Our final result is therefore

$$\sin(\pi/8) \approx \sin(3/8) \approx 3/8 = 0.3750.$$

The first of the foregoing approximations—using a perturbed input $\hat{x} = 3/8$ instead of the true value $x = \pi/8$—induces propagated data error: even if we evaluated the sine function exactly, we would obtain an incorrect result because we used an incorrect input. The second approximation represents a computational error, even though our "computation" in this case consisted of merely copying the input! (Computational errors are often such "errors of omission," though usually not this extreme.) In the notation introduced earlier, we used a truncated mathematical expression $\hat{f}(x) = x$ instead of the true function $f(x) = \sin(x)$, which means that we would have obtained an incorrect result even if we had used the correct input. Our overall accuracy is determined by a combination of these two approximations.

Later, having gained access to a calculator, we determine that the correct answer, to four decimal digits, is

$$\sin(\pi/8) \approx 0.3827,$$

so that the total error is

$$\hat{f}(\hat{x}) - f(x) \approx 0.3750 - 0.3827 = -0.0077.$$

Observing that the correct answer for the perturbed input is

$$f(\hat{x}) = \sin(3/8) \approx 0.3663,$$

we see that the propagated data error induced by using inexact input is

$$f(\hat{x}) - f(x) = \sin(3/8) - \sin(\pi/8) \approx 0.3663 - 0.3827 = -0.0164.$$

The computational error caused by truncating the infinite series is

$$\hat{f}(\hat{x}) - f(\hat{x}) = 3/8 - \sin(3/8) \approx 0.3750 - 0.3663 = 0.0087.$$

The sum of these two errors accounts for the observed total error. For this particular example, the two errors have opposite signs, so they partially offset each other; in other circumstances they may have the same sign and thus reinforce each other instead. For this specific input, the propagated data error and computational error are roughly similar in magnitude, differing by a factor of about two, but either source of error can dominate for other input values. Using the same approximations for π and $\sin(x)$, propagated data error would dominate for much smaller inputs, whereas computational error would dominate for much larger inputs (Why?). To try to reduce the total error, we could use a more accurate value for π, which would reduce propagated data error, or a more accurate mathematical representation of $\sin(x)$ (e.g., more terms in the infinite series), which would reduce computational error.

1.2.4 Truncation Error and Rounding Error

Computational error (that is, error made *during* a computation) can be subdivided into truncation (or discretization) error and rounding error:

- *Truncation error* is the difference between the true result (for the actual input) and the result that would be produced by a given algorithm using exact arithmetic. It is due to approximations such as truncating an infinite series, replacing derivatives by finite differences, or terminating an iterative sequence before convergence.
- *Rounding error* is the difference between the result produced by a given algorithm using exact arithmetic and the result produced by the same algorithm using finite-precision, rounded arithmetic. It is due to inexactness in the representation of real numbers and arithmetic operations upon them, which we will consider in detail in Section 1.3.

By definition, then, computational error is simply the sum of truncation error and rounding error. In Example 1.2, the input was rounded, but there was no rounding error during the computation, so the computational error consisted solely of truncation error from using only one term of the infinite series. Using additional terms in the series would have reduced the truncation error, but would likely have introduced some rounding error in the arithmetic required to evaluate the series. Such tradeoffs between truncation error and rounding error are not uncommon.

Example 1.3 Finite Difference Approximation. For a differentiable function $f: \mathbb{R} \to \mathbb{R}$, consider the finite difference approximation to the first derivative,

$$f'(x) \approx \frac{f(x+h) - f(x)}{h}.$$

By Taylor's Theorem,

$$f(x+h) = f(x) + f'(x)h + f''(\theta)h^2/2$$

for some $\theta \in [x, x+h]$, so the truncation error of the finite difference approximation is bounded by $Mh/2$, where M is a bound on $|f''(t)|$ for t near x. Assuming the error in function values is bounded by ϵ, the rounding error in evaluating the finite difference formula is bounded by $2\epsilon/h$. The total computational error is therefore bounded by the sum of two functions,

$$\frac{Mh}{2} + \frac{2\epsilon}{h},$$

with the first decreasing and the second increasing as h decreases. Thus, there is a tradeoff between truncation error and rounding error in choosing the step size h. Differentiating this function with respect to h and setting its derivative equal to zero, we see that the bound on the total computational error is minimized when

$$h = 2\sqrt{\epsilon/M}.$$

A typical example is shown in Fig. 1.1, where the total computational error in the finite difference approximation, along with the individual bounds on the truncation and rounding errors, for the function $f(x) = \sin(x)$ at $x = 1$ are plotted as functions of the step size h, taking $M = 1$ and using a computer for which $\epsilon \approx 10^{-16}$. We see that the total error indeed reaches a minimum at $h \approx 10^{-8} \approx \sqrt{\epsilon}$. The total error increases for larger values of h because of increasing truncation error, and increases for smaller values of h because of increasing rounding error.

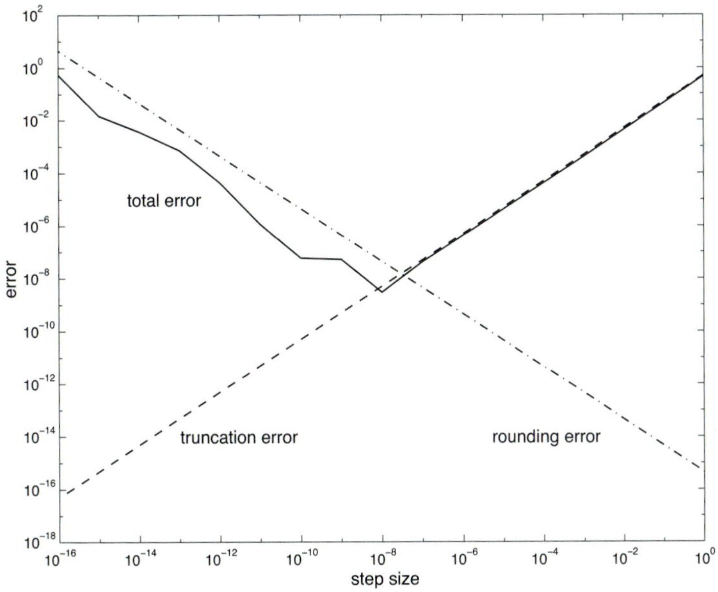

Figure 1.1: Computational error in finite difference approximation for given step size.

The truncation error could be reduced by using a more accurate finite difference formula, such as the centered difference approximation (see Section 8.6.1)

$$f'(x) \approx \frac{f(x+h) - f(x-h)}{2h}.$$

The rounding error could be reduced by working with higher-precision arithmetic, if available.

Although truncation error and rounding error can both play an important role in a given computation, one or the other is usually the dominant factor in the overall computational error. Roughly speaking, rounding error tends to dominate in purely algebraic problems with finite solution algorithms, whereas truncation error tends to dominate in problems involving integrals, derivatives, or nonlinearities, which often require a theoretically infinite solution process.

The distinctions we have made among the different types of errors are important for understanding the behavior of numerical algorithms and the factors affecting their accuracy, but it is usually not necessary, or even possible, to quantify precisely the individual types of errors. Indeed, as we will soon see, it is often advantageous to lump all of the errors together and attribute them to error in the input data.

1.2.5 Forward Error and Backward Error

The quality of a computed result depends on the quality of the input data, among other factors. For example, if the input data are accurate to only four significant digits, say, then we can expect no more than four significant digits in the computed result regardless of how well we do the computation. The famous computer maxim "garbage in, garbage out" carries this observation to its logical extreme. Thus, in assessing the quality of computed results, we must not overlook the possible effects of perturbations in the input data within their level of uncertainty.

Example 1.4 Effects of Data Error. Suppose we want to predict the population of some country ten years from now. First, we need a mathematical model describing changes in population over time. Assuming that both births and deaths are proportional to the population at any given time yields the simple model

$$P(t + \Delta t) = P(t) + (B - D)P(t)\Delta t,$$

where $P(t)$ denotes the population at time t, Δt is some time interval (say, one year), and B and D are the birth and death rates (for example, the net growth rate might be $B - D = 0.04$, or 4 percent per year). We could just use this discrete model for a fixed time interval Δt, or we could take the limit as $\Delta t \to 0$ to obtain a differential equation

$$dP(t)/dt = (B - D)P(t),$$

whose solution is the familiar exponential growth law

$$P(t) = P(0)\exp((B - D)t).$$

In either case, the model is obviously only an approximation to reality; for example, we have omitted immigration and any effects of limited capacity. Though we will ignore such modeling errors for purposes of this illustration, their presence in almost all real scientific problems should temper our expectations regarding achievable accuracy in subsequent computations. To use either the discrete or continuous model for our population projection, we need to know the current population and the birth and death rates. It is notoriously difficult to count everyone in a census without missing anyone, so the starting population is known with only limited accuracy. Accordingly, the starting population would usually be expressed in "round figures" (i.e., with only a few significant digits) to indicate the level of uncertainty in its value. This should not be thought of as a rounding error because the resulting value is just as likely to be correct as the more precise value, since the discarded digits were dubious or meaningless anyway. Similarly, the birth and death rates, which represent averages taken over many discrete events, are also known with only limited accuracy.

These uncertainties in the input for our model necessarily imply some degree of uncertainty in the resulting population projection. Consequently, we can think of our model as relating a fuzzy region in input space with a fuzzy region in output space (namely, the set of all possible results for all possible combinations of inputs within their regions of uncertainty). In implementing our model, we may incur some computational error (truncation error or rounding error), but as long the result produced remains within the fuzzy region of output space corresponding to the uncertainty in the input data, the result can hardly be faulted. Another way of saying this is that *any* result, however obtained, that is the exact result for some input that is equally as plausible as the one we actually used is as good an answer as we have any right to expect.

We now formalize these notions, again focusing on one-dimensional problems for simplicity. Suppose we want to compute the value of a function, $y = f(x)$, where $f: \mathbb{R} \to \mathbb{R}$, but we obtain instead an approximate value $\hat{y}$. The discrepancy between the computed and true values, $\Delta y = \hat{y} - y$, is called the *forward error*. One way to assess the quality of the computed result is to try to estimate the relative magnitude of this forward error, which may or may not be easy, depending on the specific circumstances. In general, however, analyzing the forward propagation of errors in a computation is often difficult for reasons we will see later. Moreover, worst-case assumptions made at each stage often lead to a very pessimistic bound for the overall error.

An alternative approach is to consider the approximate solution obtained to be the exact solution for a modified problem, then ask how large a modification to the original problem is required to give the result actually obtained. In other words, how much data error in the initial input would be required to explain *all* of the error in the final computed result? More formally, the quantity $\Delta x = \hat{x} - x$, where $f(\hat{x}) = \hat{y}$, is called the *backward error*, whose relative magnitude we try to estimate in *backward error analysis*. From this perspective, an approximate solution to a given problem is good if it is the exact solution to a "nearby" problem (i.e., the relative backward error is small). Indeed, if the nearby problem is within the uncertainty in the input data, then the computed solution $\hat{y}$ might actually be the "true" solution for all we know (or *can* know, given the uncertainty in the input), and therefore can hardly be faulted.

These relationships are illustrated schematically (and not to scale) in Fig. 1.2, where x and f denote the exact input and function, respectively, $\hat{f}$ denotes the approximate function actually computed, and $\hat{x}$ denotes an input value for which the exact function would give this computed result. Note that the equality $\hat{f}(x) = f(\hat{x})$ is due to the choice of $\hat{x}$; indeed, this requirement *defines* $\hat{x}$. In Section 1.2.6 we will quantify the relationship between forward error and backward error.

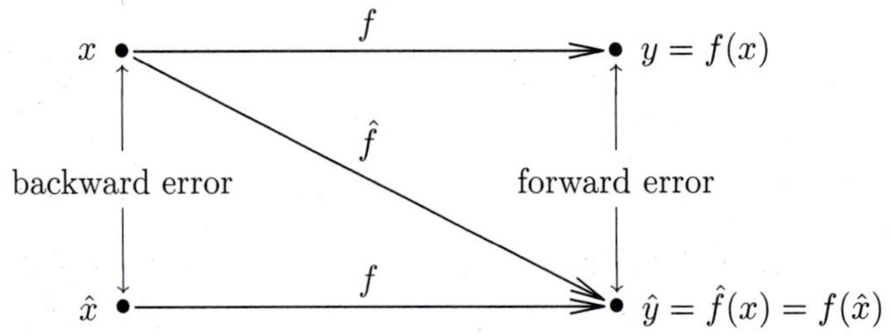

Figure 1.2: Schematic diagram showing forward and backward error.

Example 1.5 Forward and Backward Error. As an approximation to $y = \sqrt{2}$, the value $\hat{y} = 1.4$ has an absolute forward error of

$$|\Delta y| = |\hat{y} - y| = |1.4 - 1.41421\ldots| \approx 0.0142,$$

or a relative forward error of about 1 percent. To determine the backward error we observe that $\sqrt{1.96} = 1.4$, so the absolute backward error is

$$|\Delta x| = |\hat{x} - x| = |1.96 - 2| = 0.04,$$

or a relative backward error of 2 percent.

Example 1.6 Backward Error Analysis. Suppose we want a simple approximation to the cosine function $y = f(x) = \cos(x)$ for $x = 1$. The cosine function is given by the infinite series

$$\cos(x) = 1 - \frac{x^2}{2!} + \frac{x^4}{4!} - \frac{x^6}{6!} + \cdots,$$

so we might consider truncating the series after, say, two terms to obtain the approximation

$$\hat{y} = \hat{f}(x) = 1 - x^2/2.$$

The forward error in this approximation is then given by

$$\Delta y = \hat{y} - y = \hat{f}(x) - f(x) = 1 - x^2/2 - \cos(x).$$

To determine the backward error, we must find the input value $\hat{x}$ for f that gives the output value $\hat{y}$ we actually obtained, that is, for which $\hat{f}(x) = f(\hat{x})$. For the cosine function, this value is given by

$$\hat{x} = \arccos(\hat{f}(x)) = \arccos(\hat{y}).$$

Thus, for $x = 1$, we have

$$y = f(1) = \cos(1) \approx 0.5403,$$

$$\hat{y} = \hat{f}(1) = 1 - 1^2/2 = 0.5,$$

$$\hat{x} = \arccos(\hat{y}) = \arccos(0.5) \approx 1.0472,$$

$$\text{Forward error} = \Delta y = \hat{y} - y \approx 0.5 - 0.5403 = -0.0403,$$

$$\text{Backward error} = \Delta x = \hat{x} - x \approx 1.0472 - 1 = 0.0472.$$

The forward error indicates that the accuracy is fairly good because the output is close to what we wanted to compute, whereas the backward error indicates that the accuracy is fairly good because the output we obtained is correct for an input that is only slightly perturbed. We will next see how forward and backward error are related to each other quantitatively.

1.2.6 Sensitivity and Conditioning

An inaccurate solution is not necessarily due to an ill-conceived algorithm, but may be inherent in the problem being solved. Even with exact computation, the solution to the problem may be highly sensitive to perturbations in the input data. The qualitative notion of *sensitivity*, and its quantitative measure, called *conditioning*, are concerned with propagated data error, i.e., the effects on the solution of perturbations in the input data.

A problem is said to be *insensitive*, or *well-conditioned*, if a given relative change in the input data causes a reasonably commensurate relative change in the solution. A problem is said to be *sensitive*, or *ill-conditioned*, if the relative change in the solution can be much larger than that in the input data. Anyone who has felt a shower go from freezing to scalding, or vice versa, at the slightest touch of the temperature control has had first-hand experience with a sensitive system in that the effect is out of proportion to the cause.

More quantitatively, we define the *condition number* of a problem to be the ratio of the relative change in the solution to the relative change in the input. A problem is ill-conditioned, or sensitive, if its condition number is much larger than 1. Using the notation from our earlier example of evaluating a function, we have

$$\text{Condition number} = \frac{|(f(\hat{x}) - f(x))/f(x)|}{|(\hat{x} - x)/x|} = \frac{|(\hat{y} - y)/y|}{|(\hat{x} - x)/x|} = \frac{|\Delta y/y|}{|\Delta x/x|}.$$

We recognize the numerator and denominator in this ratio as the relative forward and backward errors, respectively, so this relationship can be rephrased

$$|\text{Relative forward error}| = \text{condition number} \times |\text{relative backward error}|.$$

Thus, the condition number can be interpreted as an "amplification factor" that relates forward error to backward error. If a problem is ill-conditioned (i.e., its condition number is large), then the relative forward error (relative perturbation in the solution) can be large even if the relative backward error (relative perturbation in the input) is small.

In general, the condition number varies with the input, and in practice we usually do not know the condition number exactly anyway. Thus, we often must content ourselves with a rough estimate or upper bound for the maximum condition number over some domain of inputs, and hence the relationship between backward and forward error becomes an approximate inequality,

$$|\text{Relative forward error}| \lessapprox \text{condition number} \times |\text{relative backward error}|,$$

which bounds the worst case forward error but will not necessarily be realized for all inputs. Based on this relationship, the condition number enables us to bound the forward error, which is usually of most interest, in terms of the backward error, which is often easier to estimate.

Using calculus, we can approximate the condition number for the problem of evaluating a differentiable function $f\colon \mathbb{R} \to \mathbb{R}$:

$$\text{Absolute forward error} = f(x + \Delta x) - f(x) \approx f'(x)\Delta x,$$

so that

$$\text{Relative forward error} = \frac{f(x+\Delta x) - f(x)}{f(x)} \approx \frac{f'(x)\Delta x}{f(x)},$$

and hence

$$\text{Condition number} \approx \left| \frac{f'(x)\Delta x / f(x)}{\Delta x / x} \right| = \left| \frac{x f'(x)}{f(x)} \right|.$$

Thus, the relative error in the output function value can be much larger or smaller than that in the input, depending on the properties of the function involved and the particular value of the input.

For a given problem, the *inverse problem* is to determine what input would yield a given output. For the problem of evaluating a function, $y = f(x)$, the inverse problem, denoted by $x = f^{-1}(y)$, is to determine, for a given value y, a value x such that $f(x) = y$. From the definition, we see that the condition number of the inverse problem is the reciprocal of that of the original problem. Consequently, if the condition number is near 1, then both the problem and its inverse problem are well-conditioned. If the condition number is much larger or smaller than 1, however, then either the problem or its inverse, respectively, is ill-conditioned.

We recall from calculus that if g is the inverse function $g(y) = f^{-1}(y)$, and x and y are values such that $y = f(x)$, then $g'(y) = 1/f'(x)$, provided $f'(x) \neq 0$. Thus, the condition number of the inverse function g is

$$\text{Condition number} \approx \left| \frac{y\, g'(y)}{g(y)} \right| = \left| \frac{f(x)(1/f'(x))}{x} \right| = \left| \frac{f(x)}{x f'(x)} \right|,$$

which is the reciprocal of the condition number of the original function f.

Example 1.7 Condition Number. Consider the function $f(x) = \sqrt{x}$. Since $f'(x) = 1/(2\sqrt{x}\,)$, we have

$$\text{Condition number} \approx \left|\frac{x f'(x)}{f(x)}\right| = \left|\frac{x/(2\sqrt{x}\,)}{\sqrt{x}}\right| = \frac{1}{2}.$$

This means that a given relative change in the input causes a relative change in the output of about half that size. Equivalently, the relative forward error is about half the relative backward error in magnitude, as we saw for this same problem in Example 1.5. Thus, the square root problem is quite well-conditioned. Note that the inverse problem, $g(y) = y^2$, has a condition number of $|y\,g'(y)/g(y)| = |y(2y)/y^2| = 2$, which is the reciprocal of that for the square root, as expected.

Example 1.8 Sensitivity. Consider the tangent function, $f(x) = \tan(x)$. Since $f'(x) = \sec^2(x) = 1 + \tan^2(x)$, we have

$$\text{Condition number} \approx \left|\frac{x f'(x)}{f(x)}\right| = \left|\frac{x(1+\tan^2(x))}{\tan(x)}\right| = \left|x\left(\frac{1}{\tan(x)} + \tan(x)\right)\right|.$$

Thus, $\tan(x)$ is highly sensitive for x near any integer multiple of $\pi/2$, where its value becomes infinite. For example, for $x = 1.57079$, the condition number is approximately 2.48275×10^5. To see the effect of this, we evaluate the function at two nearby points,

$$\tan(1.57079) \approx 1.58058 \times 10^5, \qquad \tan(1.57078) \approx 6.12490 \times 10^4,$$

and see that indeed the relative change in the output, which is approximately 1.58, is about a quarter of a million times larger than the relative change in the input, which is approximately 6.37×10^{-6}. On the other hand, the inverse function $g(y) = \arctan(y)$ has a condition number of $|y\,g'(y)/g(y)| = |y(1/(1+y^2))/\arctan(y)|$. For $y = 1.58058 \times 10^5$, this condition number is about 4.0278×10^{-6}, which is the reciprocal of that for the tangent function at the corresponding value for x. Thus, $\arctan(y)$ is extremely *insensitive* at this point.

The condition number we have defined is sometimes called the *relative* condition number because it is defined in terms of relative changes, or relative errors, in the input and output. This is usually most appropriate, but it is undefined if either the input x or output y is zero. In such cases, the *absolute* condition number, defined as the ratio of the absolute change in the solution to the absolute change in the input, $|\Delta y|/|\Delta x|$, is an appropriate measure of sensitivity. Such a situation arises, for example, in *root finding*: given a function $f\colon \mathbb{R} \to \mathbb{R}$, we seek a value x^* such that $f(x^*) = 0$ (see Chapter 5). Evaluating the function $f(x)$ near such a root x^* has absolute condition number

$$\frac{|\Delta y|}{|\Delta x|} \approx |f'(x^*)|,$$

and the inverse problem of determining the root, i.e., finding an input value x^* for x that yields $y = f(x^*) = 0$, has absolute condition number $1/|f'(x^*)|$, provided $f'(x^*) \neq 0$.

1.2.7 Stability and Accuracy

The concept of *stability* of a computational algorithm is analogous to conditioning of a mathematical problem in that both have to do with the effects of perturbations. The distinction between them is that stability refers to the effects of computational error on the result computed by an algorithm, whereas conditioning refers to the effects of data error on the solution to a problem. An algorithm is *stable* if the result it produces is relatively insensitive to perturbations due to approximations made *during the computation.* From the viewpoint of backward error analysis, an algorithm is stable if the result it produces is the exact solution to a nearby problem, i.e., the effect of perturbations during the computation is no worse than the effect of a small amount of data error in the input for the given problem. By this definition, a stable algorithm produces *exactly* the correct result for *nearly* the correct problem. Many—but not all—useful algorithms are stable in this strong sense. A weaker concept of stability that is useful in some contexts is that the algorithm produces *nearly* the correct result for nearly the correct problem.

Accuracy refers to the closeness of a computed solution to the true solution of the problem under consideration. Stability of an algorithm does not by itself guarantee that the computed result is accurate: accuracy depends on the conditioning of the problem as well as the stability of the algorithm. Stability tells us that the solution obtained is exact for a nearby problem, but the solution to that nearby problem is not necessarily close to the solution to the original problem unless the problem is well-conditioned. Thus, inaccuracy can result from applying a stable algorithm to an ill-conditioned problem as well as from applying an unstable algorithm to a well-conditioned problem. By contrast, if we apply a stable algorithm to a well-conditioned problem, then we will obtain an accurate solution.

1.3 Computer Arithmetic

As noted earlier, one type of approximation inevitably made in scientific computing is in representing real numbers on a computer. In this section we will examine in some detail the finite-precision arithmetic systems that are used for most scientific computations on digital computers.

1.3.1 Floating-Point Numbers

In a digital computer, the real number system $\mathbb{R}$ of mathematics is represented by a *floating-point* number system. The basic idea resembles *scientific notation*, in which a number of very large or very small magnitude is expressed as a number of moderate size times an appropriate power of ten. For example, 2347 and 0.0007396 are written as 2.347×10^3 and 7.396×10^{-4}, respectively. In this format, the decimal point moves, or *floats*, as the power of 10 changes. Formally, a floating-point number system $\mathbb{F}$ is characterized by four integers:

β	Base or radix
p	Precision
$[L, U]$	Exponent range

Any floating-point number $x \in \mathbb{F}$ has the form

$$x = \pm \left(d_0 + \frac{d_1}{\beta} + \frac{d_2}{\beta^2} + \cdots + \frac{d_{p-1}}{\beta^{p-1}} \right) \beta^E,$$

where d_i is an integer such that

$$0 \le d_i \le \beta - 1, \quad i = 0, \ldots, p-1,$$

and E is an integer such that

$$L \le E \le U.$$

The part in parentheses, represented by a string of p base-β digits $d_0 d_1 \cdots d_{p-1}$, is called the *mantissa* or *significand*, and E is called the *exponent* or *characteristic* of the floating-point number x. The portion $d_1 d_2 \cdots d_{p-1}$ of the mantissa is called the *fraction*. In a computer, the sign, exponent, and mantissa are stored in separate *fields* of a given floating-point *word*, each of which has a fixed width. The number zero can be represented uniquely by having both its mantissa and exponent equal to zero or by having a zero fraction and a special value of the exponent.

Most computers today use binary ($\beta = 2$) arithmetic, but other bases have also been used in the past, such as hexadecimal ($\beta = 16$) in IBM mainframes and $\beta = 3$ in an ill-fated Russian computer. Octal ($\beta = 8$) and hexadecimal notations are also commonly used as a convenient shorthand for writing binary numbers in groups of three or four binary digits (*bits*), respectively. For obvious reasons, decimal ($\beta = 10$) arithmetic is popular in hand-held calculators. To facilitate human interaction, a computer usually converts numerical values from decimal notation on input and to decimal notation for output, regardless of the base it uses internally. Parameters for some typical floating-point systems are given in Table 1.1, which illustrates the tradeoff between precision and exponent range implied by their respective field widths. For example, working with the same 64-bit word length, the Cray system has a wider exponent range than does IEEE double precision, but at the expense of carrying less precision.

The IEEE standard single-precision (SP) and double-precision (DP) binary floating-point systems are by far the most important today. They have been almost universally adopted for personal computers and workstations, and also for many mainframes and supercomputers as well. The IEEE standard was carefully crafted to eliminate the many anomalies and ambiguities in earlier vendor-specific floating-point implementations and has greatly facilitated the development of portable and reliable numerical software. It also allows for sensible and consistent handling of exceptional situations, such as division by zero.

System	β	p	L	U
IEEE SP	2	24	-126	127
IEEE DP	2	53	$-1,022$	$1,023$
Cray	2	48	$-16,383$	$16,384$
HP calculator	10	12	-499	499
IBM mainframe	16	6	-64	63

Table 1.1: Parameters for typical floating-point systems

1.3.2 Normalization

A floating-point system is said to be *normalized* if the leading digit d_0 is always nonzero unless the number represented is zero. Thus, in a normalized floating-point system, the mantissa m of a given nonzero floating-point number always satisfies

$$1 \leq m < \beta.$$

(An alternative convention is that d_0 is *always* zero, in which case a floating-point number is said to be normalized if $d_1 \neq 0$, and $\beta^{-1} \leq m < 1$ instead.) Floating-point systems are usually normalized because

- The representation of each number is then unique.
- No digits are wasted on leading zeros, thereby maximizing precision.
- In a binary ($\beta = 2$) system, the leading bit is always 1 and thus need not be stored, thereby gaining one extra bit of precision for a given field width.

1.3.3 Properties of Floating-Point Systems

A floating-point number system is finite and discrete. The number of normalized floating-point numbers in a given floating-point system is

$$2\,(\beta - 1)\,\beta^{p-1}\,(U - L + 1) + 1$$

because there are two choices of sign, $\beta - 1$ choices for the leading digit of the mantissa, β choices for each of the remaining $p - 1$ digits of the mantissa, and $U - L + 1$ possible values for the exponent. The 1 is added because the number could be zero.

There is a smallest positive normalized floating-point number,

$$\text{Underflow level} = \text{UFL} = \beta^L,$$

which has a 1 as the leading digit and 0 for the remaining digits of the mantissa, and the smallest possible value for the exponent. There is a largest floating-point number,

$$\text{Overflow level} = \text{OFL} = \beta^{U+1}(1 - \beta^{-p}),$$

which has $\beta - 1$ as the value for each digit of the mantissa and the largest possible value for the exponent. Any number larger than OFL cannot be represented in the given floating-point system, nor can any positive number smaller than UFL. Floating-point numbers are not uniformly distributed throughout their range, but are equally spaced only between successive powers of β.

Example 1.9 Floating-Point System. An example floating-point system is illustrated in Fig. 1.3, where the tick marks indicate all of the 25 floating-point numbers in a system having $\beta = 2$, $p = 3$, $L = -1$, and $U = 1$. For this system, the largest number is $\text{OFL} = (1.11)_2 \times 2^1 = (3.5)_{10}$, and the smallest positive normalized number is $\text{UFL} = (1.00)_2 \times 2^{-1} = (0.5)_{10}$. This is a very tiny, toy system for illustrative purposes only, but it is in fact characteristic of floating-point systems in general: at a sufficiently high level of magnification, every normalized floating-point system looks essentially like this one—grainy and unequally spaced.

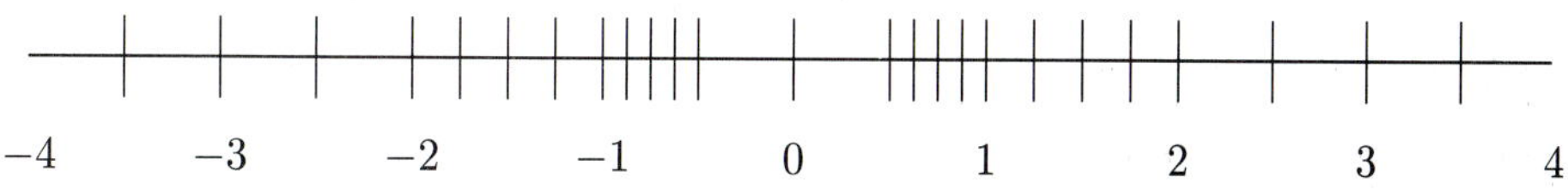

Figure 1.3: Example floating-point number system.

1.3.4 Rounding

Real numbers that are exactly representable in a given floating-point system are called *machine numbers*. If a given real number x is not exactly representable as a floating-point number, then it must be approximated by some "nearby" floating-point number. We denote the floating-point approximation of a given real number x by $\text{fl}(x)$. The process of choosing a nearby floating-point number $\text{fl}(x)$ to approximate a given real number x is called *rounding*, and the error introduced by such an approximation is called *rounding error*, or *roundoff error*. Two commonly used rounding rules are

- *Chop*: The base-β expansion of x is truncated after the $(p-1)$st digit. Because $\text{fl}(x)$ is the next floating-point number towards zero from x, this rule is also sometimes called *round toward zero*.
- *Round to nearest*: $\text{fl}(x)$ is the nearest floating-point number to x; in case of a tie, we use the floating-point number whose last stored digit is even. Because of the latter property, this rule is also sometimes called *round to even*.

Rounding to nearest is the most accurate and unbiased, but it is somewhat more expensive to implement correctly. Some systems in the past have used rounding rules that are cheaper to implement, such as chopping, but rounding to nearest is the default rounding rule in IEEE standard systems.

Example 1.10 Rounding Rules. Rounding the following decimal numbers to two digits using each of the rounding rules gives the following results

Number	Chop	Round to nearest	Number	Chop	Round to nearest
1.649	1.6	1.6	1.749	1.7	1.7
1.650	1.6	1.6	1.750	1.7	1.8
1.651	1.6	1.7	1.751	1.7	1.8
1.699	1.6	1.7	1.799	1.7	1.8

A potential source of additional error that is often overlooked is in the decimal-to-binary and binary-to-decimal conversions that usually take place upon input and output of floating-point numbers. Such conversions are not covered by the IEEE standard, which governs only internal arithmetic operations. Correctly rounded input and output can be obtained at reasonable cost, but not all computer systems do so. Efficient, portable routines for correctly rounded binary-to-decimal and decimal-to-binary conversions—`dtoa` and `strtod`, respectively—are available from `Netlib` (see Section 1.4.1).

1.3.5 Machine Precision

The accuracy of a floating-point system can be characterized by a quantity variously known as the *unit roundoff*, *machine precision*, or *machine epsilon*. Its value, which we denote by ϵ_{mach}, depends on the particular rounding rule used. With rounding by chopping,

$$\epsilon_{\text{mach}} = \beta^{1-p},$$

whereas with rounding to nearest,

$$\epsilon_{\text{mach}} = \tfrac{1}{2}\beta^{1-p}.$$

The unit roundoff is important because it bounds the *relative error* in representing any nonzero real number x within the normalized range of a floating-point system:

$$\left|\frac{\text{fl}(x) - x}{x}\right| \le \epsilon_{\text{mach}}.$$

An alternative characterization of the unit roundoff that you may sometimes see is that it is the smallest number ϵ such that

$$\text{fl}(1+\epsilon) > 1,$$

but this is not quite equivalent to the previous definition if the round-to-even rule is used. Yet another definition sometimes used is that ϵ_{mach} is the distance from 1 to the next larger floating-point number, but this may differ from either of the other definitions. Although they can differ in detail, all three definitions of ϵ_{mach} have the same basic intent as measures of the relative granularity of a floating-point system.

For the toy illustrative system in Example 1.9, $\epsilon_{\text{mach}} = 0.25$ with rounding by chopping, and $\epsilon_{\text{mach}} = 0.125$ with rounding to nearest. For IEEE binary floating-point systems, $\epsilon_{\text{mach}} = 2^{-24} \approx 10^{-7}$ in single precision and $\epsilon_{\text{mach}} = 2^{-53} \approx 10^{-16}$ in double precision. We thus say that the IEEE single- and double-precision floating-point systems have about 7 and 16 decimal digits of precision, respectively.

Though both are "small," the unit roundoff should not be confused with the underflow level. The unit roundoff ϵ_{mach} is determined by the number of digits in the mantissa field of a floating-point system, whereas the underflow level UFL is determined by the number of digits in the exponent field. In all practical floating-point systems,

$$0 < \text{UFL} < \epsilon_{\text{mach}} < \text{OFL}.$$

1.3.6 Subnormals and Gradual Underflow

In the toy floating-point system illustrated in Fig. 1.3, there is a noticeable gap around zero. This gap, which is present to some degree in any floating-point system, is due to normalization: the smallest possible mantissa is 1.00..., and the smallest possible exponent is L, so there are no floating-point numbers between zero and β^L. If we relax our insistence on normalization and allow leading digits to be zero (but only when the exponent is at its minimum value), then the gap around zero can be "filled in" by additional floating-point numbers. For our toy illustrative system, this relaxation gains six additional floating-point numbers, the smallest positive one of which is $(0.01)_2 \times 2^{-1} = (0.125)_{10}$, as shown in Fig. 1.4.

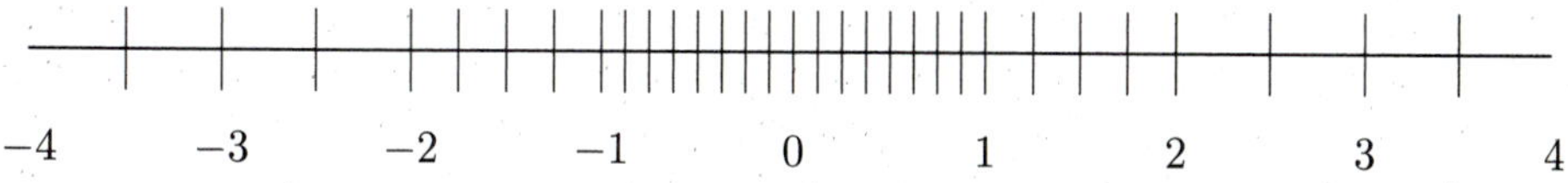

Figure 1.4: Example floating-point system with subnormals.

The extra numbers added to the system in this way are referred to as *subnormal* or *denormalized* floating-point numbers. Although they usefully extend the range of magnitudes representable, subnormal numbers have inherently lower precision than normalized numbers because they have fewer significant digits in their fractional parts. In particular, extending the range in this manner does not make the unit roundoff ϵ_{mach} any smaller.

Such an augmented floating-point system is sometimes said to exhibit *gradual underflow*, since it extends the lower range of magnitudes representable rather than underflowing to zero as soon as the minimum exponent value would otherwise be exceeded. The IEEE standard provides for such subnormal numbers and gradual underflow. Gradual underflow is implemented through a special reserved value of the exponent field because the leading binary digit is not stored and hence cannot be used to indicate a denormalized number.

1.3.7 Exceptional Values

The IEEE floating-point standard provides two additional special values to indicate exceptional situations:

- `Inf`, which stands for *infinity*, results from dividing a finite number by zero, such as 1/0.

- NaN, which stands for *not a number*, results from an undefined or indeterminate operation such as $0/0$, $0 * \texttt{Inf}$, or $\texttt{Inf}/\texttt{Inf}$.

Inf and NaN are implemented in IEEE arithmetic through special reserved values of the exponent field.

Whether Inf and NaN are supported at the user level in a given computing environment depends on the language, compiler, and run-time system. If available, these quantities can be helpful in designing software that deals gracefully with exceptional situations rather than abruptly aborting the program. In MATLAB (see Section 1.4.2), for example, if Inf and NaN arise, they are propagated sensibly through a computation (e.g., $1 + \texttt{Inf} = \texttt{Inf}$). It is still desirable, however, to avoid such exceptional situations entirely, if possible. In addition to alerting the user to arithmetic exceptions, these special values can also be useful as flags that cannot be confused with any legitimate numeric value. For example, NaN might be used to indicate a portion of an array that has not yet been defined.

1.3.8 Floating-Point Arithmetic

In adding or subtracting two floating-point numbers, their exponents must match before their mantissas can be added or subtracted. If they do not match initially, then the mantissa of one of the numbers must be shifted until the exponents do match. In performing such a shift, some of the trailing digits of the smaller (in magnitude) number will be shifted beyond the fixed width of the mantissa field, and thus the correct result of the arithmetic operation cannot be represented exactly in the floating-point system. Indeed, if the difference in magnitude is too great, then the entire mantissa of the smaller number may be shifted completely beyond the field width so that the result is simply the larger of the operands. Another way of saying this is that if the true sum of two p-digit numbers contains more than p digits, then the excess digits will be lost when the result is rounded to p digits, and in the worst case the operand of smaller magnitude may be lost completely.

Multiplication of two floating-point numbers does not require that their exponents match—the exponents are simply summed and the mantissas multiplied. However, the product of two p-digit mantissas will in general contain up to $2p$ digits, and thus once again the correct result cannot be represented exactly in the floating-point system and must be rounded.

Example 1.11 Floating-Point Arithmetic. Consider a floating-point system with $\beta = 10$ and $p = 6$. If $x = 1.92403 \times 10^2$ and $y = 6.35782 \times 10^{-1}$, then floating-point addition gives the result $x + y = 1.93039 \times 10^2$, assuming rounding to nearest. Note that the last two digits of y have no effect on the result. With an even smaller exponent, y could have had no effect at all on the result. Similarly, floating-point multiplication gives the result $x * y = 1.22326 \times 10^2$, which discards half of the digits of the true product.

Division of two floating-point numbers may also give a result that cannot be represented exactly. For example, 1 and 10 are exactly representable as binary floating-point numbers, but their quotient, $1/10$, has a nonterminating binary expansion and thus is not a binary floating-point number.

In each of the cases just cited, the result of a floating-point arithmetic operation may differ from the result that would be given by the corresponding real arithmetic operation on the same operands because there is insufficient precision to represent the correct real result. The real result may also be unrepresentable because its exponent is beyond the range available in the floating-point system (overflow or underflow). Overflow is usually a more serious problem than underflow in the sense that there is *no* good approximation in a floating-point system to arbitrarily large numbers, whereas zero is often a reasonable approximation for arbitrarily small numbers. For this reason, on many computer systems the occurrence of an overflow aborts the program with a fatal error, but an underflow may be silently set to zero without disrupting execution.

Example 1.12 Summing a Series. As an illustration of these issues, the infinite series

$$\sum_{n=1}^{\infty} \frac{1}{n}$$

has a finite sum in floating-point arithmetic even though the real series is divergent. At first blush, one might think that this result occurs because $1/n$ will eventually underflow, or the partial sum will eventually overflow, as indeed they must. But before either of these occurs, the partial sum ceases to change once $1/n$ becomes negligible relative to the partial sum, i.e., when $1/n < \epsilon_{\text{mach}} \sum_{k=1}^{n-1}(1/k)$, and thus the sum is finite (see Computer Problem 1.8).

As we have noted, a real arithmetic operation on two floating-point numbers does not necessarily result in another floating-point number. If a number that is not exactly representable as a floating-point number is entered into the computer or is produced by a subsequent arithmetic operation, then it must be rounded (using one of the rounding rules given earlier) to obtain a floating-point number. Because floating-point numbers are not equally spaced, the absolute error made in such an approximation is not uniform, but the relative error is bounded by the unit roundoff ϵ_{mach}.

Ideally, x **flop** $y = \text{fl}(x \text{ op } y)$ (i.e., floating-point arithmetic operations produce correctly rounded results); and many computers, such as those meeting the IEEE floating-point standard, achieve this ideal as long as x op y is within the range of the floating-point system. Nevertheless, some familiar laws of real arithmetic are not necessarily valid in a floating-point system. In particular, floating-point addition and multiplication are commutative but *not* associative. For example, if ϵ is a positive floating-point number slightly smaller than the unit roundoff ϵ_{mach}, then $(1+\epsilon)+\epsilon = 1$, but $1+(\epsilon+\epsilon) > 1$. The failure of floating-point arithmetic to satisfy the usual laws of real arithmetic is one reason that forward error analysis can be difficult. One advantage of backward error analysis is that it permits the use of real arithmetic in the analysis.

Rounding error analysis is usually based on the following *standard model* for floating-point arithmetic:

$$\mathrm{fl}(x \;\texttt{op}\; y) = (x \;\texttt{op}\; y)(1+\delta),$$

where $|\delta| \le \epsilon_{\mathrm{mach}}$ and op is any of the standard arithmetic operations $+, -, \times, /$. Rearranging, we see that this model can be interpreted as a statement about the relative forward error:

$$\frac{|\mathrm{fl}(x \;\texttt{op}\; y) - (x \;\texttt{op}\; y)|}{|(x \;\texttt{op}\; y)|} = |\delta| \le \epsilon_{\mathrm{mach}}.$$

It can also be interpreted as a statement about backward error. For example, for $\texttt{op} = +$,

$$\mathrm{fl}(x+y) = (x+y)(1+\delta) = x(1+\delta) + y(1+\delta),$$

which means that the result of floating-point addition is exact for operands x and y that are each perturbed by a relative amount $|\delta|$.

Example 1.13 Rounding Error Analysis. Consider the simple computation $x(y+z)$. In floating-point arithmetic we have

$$\mathrm{fl}(y+z) = (y+z)(1+\delta_1), \quad \text{with } |\delta_1| \le \epsilon_{\mathrm{mach}},$$

so that

$$\begin{aligned}
\mathrm{fl}(x(y+z)) &= (x((y+z)(1+\delta_1)))(1+\delta_2), \quad \text{with } |\delta_2| \le \epsilon_{\mathrm{mach}} \\
&= x(y+z)(1+\delta_1+\delta_2+\delta_1\delta_2) \\
&\approx x(y+z)(1+\delta_1+\delta_2) \\
&= x(y+z)(1+\delta), \quad \text{with } |\delta| = |\delta_1+\delta_2| \le 2\epsilon_{\mathrm{mach}}.
\end{aligned}$$

As before, this bound can be interpreted in terms of forward error (discrepancy between computed and desired result) or backward error (perturbations of operands) and may be quite pessimistic. For example, δ_1 and δ_2 may be of opposite sign and hence offset each other, yielding a much smaller overall error than expected from worst-case analysis. Similar analyses of more complicated computations generally lead to error bounds containing correspondingly larger multiples of ϵ_{mach}. Fortunately, ϵ_{mach} is so small that in practice it is extremely rare for the sheer volume of computation alone to degrade results seriously.

1.3.9 Cancellation

Rounding is not the only necessary evil in finite-precision arithmetic. Subtraction between two p-digit numbers having the same sign and similar magnitudes yields a result with *fewer* than p significant digits, and hence it is always exactly representable (provided the two numbers involved do not differ in magnitude by more than a factor of two). The reason is that the leading digits of the two numbers cancel (i.e., their difference is zero). For example, again taking $\beta = 10$ and

$p = 6$, if $x = 1.92403 \times 10^2$ and $z = 1.92275 \times 10^2$, then we obtain the result $x - z = 1.28000 \times 10^{-1}$, which, with only three significant digits, is exactly representable.

Despite the exactness of the result, however, such cancellation nevertheless often implies a potentially serious loss of information. The problem is that the operands are often uncertain, owing to rounding or other previous errors, in which case the relative uncertainty in the difference may be large. In effect, if two nearly equal numbers are accurate only to within rounding error, then taking their difference leaves only rounding error as a result.

As a simple example, if ϵ is a positive number slightly smaller than the unit roundoff ϵ_{mach}, then $(1+\epsilon) - (1-\epsilon) = 1 - 1 = 0$ in floating-point arithmetic, which is correct for the actual operands of the final subtraction, but the true result of the overall computation, 2ϵ, has been completely lost. The subtraction itself is not at fault: it merely signals the loss of information that had already occurred.

Of course, the loss of information is not always complete, but the fact remains that the digits lost to cancellation are the most significant, leading digits, whereas the digits lost in rounding are the least significant, trailing digits. Because of this effect, computing a small quantity as a difference of large quantities is generally a bad idea, for rounding error is likely to dominate the result. For example, summing an alternating series, such as

$$e^x = 1 + x + \frac{x^2}{2!} + \frac{x^3}{3!} + \cdots$$

for $x < 0$, may give disastrous results because of catastrophic cancellation (see Computer Problem 1.9).

Example 1.14 Cancellation. Cancellation is an issue not only in computer arithmetic, but in any situation in which limited precision is attainable, such as empirical measurements or laboratory experiments. For example, determining the distance from Manhattan to Staten Island by using their respective distances from Los Angeles will produce a very poor result unless the latter distances are known with extraordinarily high accuracy.

As another example, for many years physicists have been trying to compute the total energy of the helium atom from first principles using Monte Carlo techniques. The accuracy of these computations is determined largely by the number of random trials used. As faster computers become available and computational techniques are refined, the attainable accuracy improves. The total energy is the sum of the kinetic energy and the potential energy, which are computed separately and have opposite signs. Thus, the total energy is computed as a difference and suffers cancellation. Table 1.2 gives a sequence of values obtained over a number of years (these data were kindly provided by Dr. Robert Panoff). During this span the computed values for the kinetic and potential energies changed by only 6 percent or less, yet the resulting estimate for the total energy changed by 144 percent. The one or two significant digits in the earlier computations were completely lost in the subsequent subtraction.

Year	Kinetic	Potential	Total
1971	13.0	−14.0	−1.0
1977	12.76	−14.02	−1.26
1980	12.22	−14.35	−2.13
1985	12.28	−14.65	−2.37
1988	12.40	−14.84	−2.44

Table 1.2: Computed values for total energy of helium atom

Example 1.15 Quadratic Formula. Cancellation and other numerical difficulties need not involve a long series of computations. For example, use of the standard formula for the roots of a quadratic equation is fraught with numerical pitfalls. As every schoolchild learns, the two solutions of the quadratic equation

$$ax^2 + bx + c = 0$$

are given by the *quadratic formula*

$$x = \frac{-b \pm \sqrt{b^2 - 4ac}}{2a}.$$

For some values of the coefficients, naive use of this formula in floating-point arithmetic can produce overflow, underflow, or catastrophic cancellation.

For example, if the coefficients are very large or very small, then b^2 or $4ac$ may overflow or underflow. The possibility of overflow can be avoided by rescaling the coefficients, such as dividing all three coefficients by the coefficient of largest magnitude. Such a rescaling does not change the roots of the quadratic equation, but now the largest coefficient is 1 and overflow cannot occur in computing b^2 or $4ac$. Such rescaling does not eliminate the possibility of underflow, but it does prevent *needless* underflow, which could otherwise occur when all three coefficients are very small.

Cancellation between $-b$ and the square root can be avoided by computing one of the roots using the alternative formula

$$x = \frac{2c}{-b \mp \sqrt{b^2 - 4ac}},$$

which has the opposite sign pattern from that of the standard formula. But cancellation inside the square root cannot be easily avoided without using higher precision (if the discriminant is small relative to the coefficients, then the two roots are close to each other, and the problem is inherently ill-conditioned).

As an illustration, we use four-digit decimal arithmetic, with rounding to nearest, to compute the roots of the quadratic equation having coefficients $a = 0.05010$, $b = -98.78$, and $c = 5.015$. For comparison, the correct roots, rounded to ten significant digits, are

$$1971.605916 \quad \text{and} \quad 0.05077069387.$$

Computing the discriminant in four-digit arithmetic produces

$$b^2 - 4ac = 9757 - 1.005 = 9756,$$

so that

$$\sqrt{b^2 - 4ac} = 98.77.$$

The standard quadratic formula then gives the roots

$$\frac{98.78 \pm 98.77}{0.1002} = 1972 \quad \text{and} \quad 0.09980.$$

The first root is the correctly rounded four-digit result, but the other root is completely wrong, with an error of about 100 percent. The culprit is cancellation, not in the sense that the final subtraction is wrong (indeed it is exactly correct), but in the sense that cancellation of the leading digits has left nothing remaining but previous rounding errors. The alternative quadratic formula gives the roots

$$\frac{10.03}{98.78 \mp 98.77} = 1003 \quad \text{and} \quad 0.05077.$$

Once again we have obtained one fully accurate root and one completely erroneous root, but in each case it is the opposite root from the one obtained previously. Cancellation is again the explanation, but the different sign pattern causes the opposite root to be contaminated. In general, for computing each root we should choose whichever formula avoids this cancellation, depending on the sign of b.

Example 1.16 Standard Deviation. The *mean* of a finite sequence of real values x_i, $i = 1, \ldots, n$, is defined by

$$\bar{x} = \frac{1}{n}\sum_{i=1}^{n} x_i,$$

and the *standard deviation* is defined by

$$\sigma = \left[\frac{1}{n-1}\sum_{i=1}^{n}(x_i - \bar{x})^2\right]^{1/2}.$$

Use of these formulas requires two passes through the data: one to compute the mean and another to compute the standard deviation. For better efficiency, it is tempting to use the mathematically equivalent formula

$$\sigma = \left[\frac{1}{n-1}\left(\sum_{i=1}^{n} x_i^2 - n\bar{x}^2\right)\right]^{1/2}$$

to compute the standard deviation, since both the sum and the sum of squares can be computed in a single pass through the data.

Unfortunately, the single cancellation at the end of the one-pass formula is often much more damaging numerically than all of the cancellations in the two-pass formula combined. The problem is that the two quantities being subtracted in the one-pass formula are apt to be relatively large and nearly equal, and hence the relative error in the difference may be large (indeed, the result can even be negative, causing the square root to fail).

Example 1.17 Computing Residuals. Suppose we are solving the scalar linear equation $ax = b$ for the unknown x, and we have obtained an approximate solution $\hat{x}$. As one measure of the quality of our answer, we compute the residual $r = b - a\hat{x}$. In floating-point arithmetic,

$$\mathrm{fl}(a\hat{x}) = a\hat{x}(1+\delta_1) \quad \text{with } |\delta_1| \le \epsilon_{\text{mach}},$$

so that

$$\begin{aligned} \mathrm{fl}(b - a\hat{x}) &= (b - a\hat{x}(1+\delta_1))(1+\delta_2) \quad \text{with } |\delta_2| \le \epsilon_{\text{mach}} \\ &= (r - a\hat{x}\delta_1)(1+\delta_2) \\ &= r(1+\delta_2) - a\hat{x}\delta_1 - a\hat{x}\delta_1\delta_2 \\ &\approx r(1+\delta_2) - \delta_1 b. \end{aligned}$$

But $\delta_1 b$ may be as large as $\epsilon_{\text{mach}} b$, which may be as large as r, which means that the error in computing the residual may be 100 percent or more. Thus, higher precision may be required to enable a meaningful computation of the residual r.

To illustrate, suppose we are using three-digit decimal arithmetic, and take $a = 2.78$, $b = 3.14$, and $\hat{x} = 1.13$. In three-digit arithmetic, $2.78 \times 1.13 = 3.14$, so the three-digit residual is 0. This result is comforting in that it shows we have done the best we can for the precision used, but it gives us no significant digits of the true residual, which is $3.14 - 2.78 \times 1.13 = 3.14 - 3.1414 = -0.0014$. What has happened is that, *by design*, b and $a\hat{x}$ are very nearly equal, and thus their difference contains nothing but rounding error. In terms of our previous analysis of this problem,

$$3.14 = \mathrm{fl}(a\hat{x}) = a\hat{x}(1+\delta_1) = 3.1414(1+\delta_1),$$

with $\delta_1 = -0.0014/3.1414 \approx -0.00044566$. There is no rounding error in the subsequent subtraction (as usual with cancellation), so $\delta_2 = 0$. The resulting computed residual is

$$\mathrm{fl}(b - a\hat{x}) \approx r(1+\delta_2) - \delta_1 b = r - \delta_1 b \approx -0.0014 - (-0.0014) = 0.$$

In general, up to twice the working precision may be required to compute the residual accurately.

1.3.10 Other Arithmetic Systems

Today, IEEE standard floating-point arithmetic is used for the overwhelming majority of scientific computations. Because it is built into the hardware of almost all modern microprocessors, IEEE floating-point arithmetic is extremely fast, and IEEE double precision enables more than adequate accuracy to be achieved for most practical purposes. Circumstances may occasionally arise, however, in which higher precision may be needed, for example for solving a problem that is unavoidably highly sensitive, or possibly due to the sheer volume of computation (although this usually takes a truly immense amount of computation). In such cases, there are several alternatives for extending the available precision, although we hasten to add that the use of extended precision should not be a substitute for careful problem formulation and sound solution techniques.

A few computer systems have provided *quadruple precision* in hardware, and this will likely become increasingly common as processors become ever faster and memories ever larger. Several software packages are available that provide *multiple precision* floating-point arithmetic (see Section 1.4.3). Some symbolic computing environments, such as `Maple` and `Mathematica` (see Section 1.4.2), provide *arbitrary precision* arithmetic in that the precision grows as necessary to maintain exact results throughout a computation. Such software approaches have major drawbacks in speed and memory, however, in that arithmetic performed in software may be orders of magnitude slower than the corresponding hardware floating-point operations, and a great deal of memory may be required to store the long strings of digits that result. Even when precision is arbitrary in the sense that it is allowed to vary, it is still ultimately limited by the finite amount of memory available on a given computer.

Whatever precision is used, a major issue in numerical analysis is determining the accuracy actually achieved in a given computation. As we have seen in this chapter, and will see throughout the remainder of this book, conventional error analysis is based on mathematical analysis of the problem being solved and the algorithm being used, as well as the properties of the arithmetic with which the algorithm is implemented. *Interval analysis* is an alternative approach that incorporates the propagation of uncertainties into the arithmetic system itself, thereby determining accuracy automatically, at least in principle. The basic idea is to represent each numerical quantity as a closed interval, say $[a, b]$, which is interpreted as the range of all possible values for that quantity. The length of the interval then represents the uncertainty, or possible error, in the quantity (if there is no uncertainty, then $a = b$).

The result of an arithmetic operation on two intervals is taken to be the set of all possible results for the corresponding real arithmetic operation with an operand from each of the respective intervals:

$$[a, b] \ \texttt{op} \ [c, d] = \{x \ \texttt{op} \ y : x \in [a, b] \text{ and } y \in [c, d]\},$$

where `op` is any of $+, -, \times, /$. The resulting set is itself an interval, whose endpoints can be computed using the following rules:

$$\begin{aligned}
[a,b] + [c,d] &= [a+c, b+d], \\
[a,b] - [c,d] &= [a-d, b-c], \\
[a,b] \times [c,d] &= [\min(ac,ad,bc,bd), \max(ac,ad,bc,bd)], \\
[a,b]/[c,d] &= [a,b] \times [1/d, 1/c], \quad \text{provided } 0 \notin [c,d].
\end{aligned}$$

When implemented in floating-point arithmetic, computation of the interval endpoints must be properly rounded to ensure that the computed interval contains the corresponding exact interval (the left endpoint is rounded toward $-\infty$ and the right endpoint toward $+\infty$; such *directed rounding* is provided as an option in IEEE arithmetic).

Propagating uncertainties (including those in the initial input) through a computation might appear to be an easy road to automatic error analysis, but in practice the resulting intervals are often too wide to be useful, for much the same reason that forward error analysis often produces excessively pessimistic bounds. If we view a computation as a composition of successive functions using fixed precision, then the final interval width will be proportional to the product of the condition numbers of all of the functions. If those functions are numerous or ill-conditioned, or both, then the final interval width is likely to be too wide to provide useful information. Another problem is that interval analysis may ignore dependences among computational variables—such as when the same variable appears more than once in a computation—and treat them as distinct sources of uncertainty, which again may lead to unnecessarily wide intervals. As a trivial example, $[a,b]-[a,b] = [a-b, b-a]$ rather than $[0,0]$.

The interval widths produced by interval arithmetic can be controlled if implemented using variable precision. In *range arithmetic*, for example, ordinary floating-point arithmetic is augmented in two ways: the mantissa can be of arbitrary length up to some predefined limit on precision, and an additional *range digit*, r, is maintained to indicate the uncertainty ($\pm r$) in the mantissa. Arithmetic operations on ranged numbers use the usual rules for interval arithmetic given earlier. As computations proceed, if the uncertainty in a given value grows, then the length of its mantissa is reduced accordingly. If the final result has too few digits in its mantissa to satisfy the accuracy requirement, then the precision limit is increased and the entire computation is repeated as many times as necessary until the accuracy requirement is met. In this manner, many (but not all) computational problems can be solved to any prespecified accuracy, but often with unpredictable (and potentially large) execution time and memory requirements.

Several software packages are available that implement interval and range arithmetic (see Section 1.4.3). The drawbacks we noted have limited the use of interval and range arithmetic for general purpose scientific computing, but interval methods nevertheless provide one of the few options available for certain types of problems, such as guaranteed methods for solving multidimensional systems of nonlinear equations and global optimization problems. Though detailed presentation of interval methods is beyond the scope of this book, we will note the availability of relevant interval-based software where appropriate.

1.3.11 Complex Arithmetic

Just as fractions of the form m/n, where m and n are integers, augment the integers to form the rational numbers, and algebraic numbers, such as $\sqrt{2}$, and transcendental numbers, such as π, augment the rational numbers to form the real numbers, so the real numbers can be augmented by $\sqrt{-1}$ to form the *complex* numbers. In this book, we will make explicit use of complex numbers primarily in discussing eigenvalue problems (Chapter 4) and Fourier transforms (Chapter 12). Elsewhere, for simplicity we will largely confine our discussion to the real case, but most of the algorithms we will consider are applicable to the complex case as well.

As is common in mathematics, in this book we will denote the imaginary unit $\sqrt{-1}$ by i, though some engineering disciplines use j instead. A given complex number z can be expressed as a sum

$$z = x + iy,$$

where the real numbers $x = \text{Re}(z)$ and $y = \text{Im}(z)$ are the real and imaginary parts, respectively, of z. We denote the set of all complex numbers by $\mathbb{C} = \{x + iy : x, y \in \mathbb{R}\}$. A complex number z is real if $\text{Im}(z) = 0$ and imaginary (or purely imaginary) if $\text{Re}(z) = 0$.

We can think of $\mathbb{C}$ as forming a two-dimensional Cartesian plane, called the *complex plane* (or sometimes the *Argand diagram*), whose two real coordinates are given by the real and imaginary parts of a given complex number. Conventionally, the real part is on the horizontal axis, and the imaginary part is on the vertical axis in the complex plane (see Fig. 1.5). Multiplication by $i = \sqrt{-1}$ corresponds to a rotation by $\pi/2$ in the complex plane. Similarly, multiplication by $i^2 = -1$ corresponds to a rotation by π, multiplication by $i^3 = -i$ corresponds to a rotation by $3\pi/2$, and multiplication by $i^4 = 1$ corresponds to a rotation by 2π (i.e., 1 is the multiplicative identity, as expected).

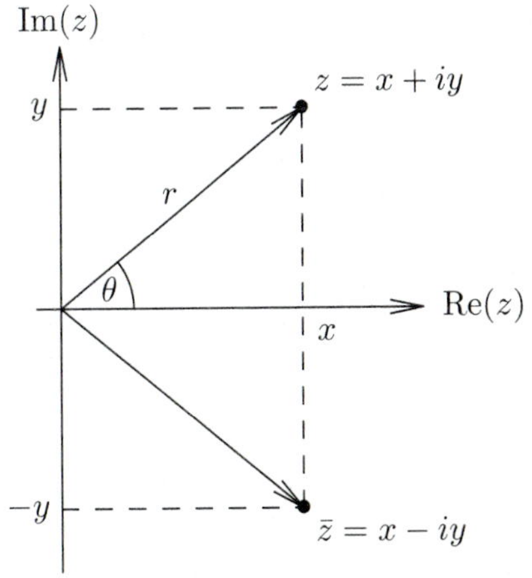

Figure 1.5: Complex plane, showing Cartesian and polar representations of complex number z and its complex conjugate $\bar{z}$.

The standard arithmetic operations on two complex numbers $z_1 = x_1 + iy_1$ and $z_2 = x_2 + iy_2$ are defined as follows:

$$\begin{aligned} z_1 + z_2 &= (x_1 + x_2) + i\,(y_1 + y_2), \\ z_1 - z_2 &= (x_1 - x_2) + i\,(y_1 - y_2), \\ z_1 \times z_2 &= (x_1x_2 - y_1y_2) + i\,(x_1y_2 + x_2y_1), \\ z_1/z_2 &= \left(\frac{x_1x_2 + y_1y_2}{x_2^2 + y_2^2}\right) + i\left(\frac{x_2y_1 - x_1y_2}{x_2^2 + y_2^2}\right), \quad \text{provided } z_2 \neq 0. \end{aligned}$$

Note that an arithmetic operation on two complex numbers requires from two to eleven real arithmetic operations, depending on the particular complex operation, so complex arithmetic can be substantially more costly than real arithmetic.

The *complex conjugate* of a complex number $z = x + iy$, denoted by $\bar{z}$, is given by

$$\bar{z} = x - iy.$$

Thus, a complex number and its complex conjugate are symmetric (mirror reflections of each other) about the real axis (see Fig. 1.5). For any complex number $z = x + iy$,

$$z\bar{z} = (x + iy)(x - iy) = x^2 + y^2$$

is always real and nonnegative, so we can define the *modulus* (or magnitude or absolute value) of a complex number $z = x + iy$ by

$$|z| = \sqrt{z\bar{z}} = \sqrt{x^2 + y^2},$$

which is just the ordinary Euclidean distance between the point (x, y) and the origin $(0, 0)$ in the complex plane.

Another useful representation of a complex number z is in polar coordinates,

$$z = x + iy = r(\cos\theta + i\sin\theta),$$

where $r = |z|$ and $\theta = \arctan(y/x)$ (see Fig. 1.5). Using *Euler's identity*,

$$e^{i\theta} = \cos\theta + i\sin\theta,$$

we obtain the exponential representation

$$z = re^{i\theta}.$$

The latter will be of particular importance in discussing Fourier transforms (see Chapter 12). Note that in the exponential representation, complex multiplication and division have the simpler form

$$\begin{aligned} z_1 \times z_2 &= r_1r_2\,e^{i(\theta_1+\theta_2)}, \\ z_1/z_2 &= (r_1/r_2)\,e^{i(\theta_1-\theta_2)}. \end{aligned}$$

In a computer, a complex number is typically represented by a pair of ordinary floating-point values corresponding to its real and imaginary parts. Support for complex arithmetic varies among computer languages and systems; for example, all versions of Fortran provide explicit support for complex data types and arithmetic, whereas C and its descendants typically do not. `MATLAB` (see Section 1.4.2) provides seamless support for complex arithmetic; indeed, the primary numeric data type in `MATLAB` is complex.

1.4 Mathematical Software

This book covers a wide range of topics in numerical analysis and scientific computing. We will discuss the essential aspects of each topic but will not have the luxury of examining any topic in great detail. To be able to solve interesting computational problems, we will often rely on mathematical software written by professionals. Leaving the algorithmic details to such software will allow us to focus on proper problem formulation and interpretation of results. We will consider only the most fundamental algorithms for each type of problem, motivated primarily by the insight to be gained into choosing an appropriate method and using it wisely. Our primary goal is to become intelligent users, rather than creators, of mathematical software.

Before citing some specific sources of good mathematical software, let us summarize the desirable characteristics that such software should possess, in no particular order of importance:

- **Reliability:** always works correctly for easy problems
- **Robustness:** usually works for hard problems, but fails gracefully and informatively when it does fail
- **Accuracy:** produces results as accurate as warranted by the problem and input data, preferably with an estimate of the accuracy achieved
- **Efficiency:** requires execution time and storage that are close to the minimum possible for the problem being solved
- **Portability:** adapts with little or no change to new computing environments
- **Maintainability:** is easy to understand and modify
- **Usability:** has a convenient and well-documented user interface
- **Applicability:** solves a broad range of problems

Obviously, these properties often conflict, and it is rare software indeed that satisfies all of them. Nevertheless, this list gives mathematical software users some idea what qualities to look for and developers some worthy goals to strive for.

1.4.1 Mathematical Software Libraries

Several widely available sources of general-purpose mathematical software are listed here. The software listed is written in Fortran unless otherwise noted. At the end of each chapter of this book, specific routines are listed for given types of problems, both from these general libraries and from more specialized packages. For additional information about available mathematical software, see `gams.nist.gov` on the World-Wide Web.

- `CMLIB`: Core Math Library compiled by the National Institute of Standards and Technology (NIST). `gams.nist.gov`
- `FMM`: Software accompanying the book *Computer Methods for Mathematical Computations*, by Forsythe, Malcolm, and Moler [127]. Available from `Netlib` (see below).
- `HSL` (Harwell Subroutine Library): Software developed at Harwell Laboratory in England. `www.cse.clrc.ac.uk/nag/hsl`
- `IMSL` (International Mathematical and Statistical Libraries): Comprehensive library of mathematical software; full library available in Fortran, subset available in C. Commercial product of Visual Numerics Inc., Houston, Texas. `www.vni.com`
- `KMN`: Software accompanying the book *Numerical Methods and Software*, by Kahaner, Moler, and Nash [220].
- `NAG` (Numerical Algorithms Group): Comprehensive library of mathematical software; full library available in Fortran, subset available in C. Commercial product of NAG Inc., Downers Grove, Illinois. `www.nag.com`
- `NAPACK`: Software accompanying the book *Applied Numerical Linear Algebra*, by Hager [178]. In addition to linear algebra, also contains routines for nonlinear equations, unconstrained optimization, and fast Fourier transforms. Available from `Netlib`.
- `NETLIB`: Free software from diverse sources. `www.netlib.org`
- `NR` (Numerical Recipes): Software accompanying the book *Numerical Recipes*, by Press, Teukolsky, Vetterling, and Flannery [315]. Available in Fortran, C, and C++ editions. `www.nr.com`
- `NUMAL`: Software developed at Mathematisch Centrum in Amsterdam. Also available in Algol and Fortran, but most readily available in C from the book *A Numerical Library in C for Scientists and Engineers*, by Lau [250].
- `NUMERALGO`: Software appearing in the journal *Numerical Algorithms*. Available from `Netlib`.
- `PORT`: Software developed at Bell Laboratories. Some routines freely available from `Netlib`, other portions available only under commercial license.
- `SLATEC`: Software compiled by consortium of U.S. government laboratories. Available from `Netlib`.
- `SOL`: Software for optimization and related problems from Systems Optimization Laboratory at Stanford University. `www.stanford.edu/~saunders/brochure/brochure.html`
- `TOMS`: Software appearing in *ACM Transactions on Mathematical Software* (formerly *Collected Algorithms of the ACM*). Algorithms identified by number (in order of appearance) as well as by name. Available from `Netlib`.

1.4.2 Scientific Computing Environments

The software libraries just listed contain subroutines that are meant to be called by user-written programs, usually in a conventional programming language such as Fortran or C. An increasingly popular alternative for scientific computing is interactive environments that provide powerful, conveniently accessible, built-in mathematical capabilities, often combined with sophisticated graphics and a very high-level programming language designed for rapid prototyping of new algorithms.

One of the most widely used such computing environments is MATLAB, which is a proprietary commercial product of The MathWorks, Inc. (www.mathworks.com). MATLAB, which stands for MATrix LABoratory, is an interactive system that integrates extensive mathematical capabilities, especially in linear algebra, with powerful scientific visualization, a high-level programming language, and a variety of optional "toolboxes" that provide specialized capabilities in particular applications, such as signal processing, image processing, control, system identification, optimization, and statistics. There is also a MATLAB interface for the NAG mathematical software library cited in Section 1.4.1. MATLAB is available for a wide variety of personal computers, workstations, and supercomputers, and comes in both professional and inexpensive student editions. If MATLAB is not available on your computer system, similar packages freely available via the World-Wide Web include octave (www.octave.org), RLaB (rlab.sourceforge.net), and Scilab (www.scilab.org). Other similar commercial products include GAUSS, HiQ, IDL, Mathcad, and PV-WAVE.

Another family of interactive computing environments is based primarily on *symbolic* (rather than numeric) computation, often called *computer algebra*. These packages, which include Axiom, Derive, Macsyma, Maple, Mathematica, MuPAD, and Reduce, provide many of the same mathematical and graphical capabilities, and in addition provide symbolic differentiation, integration, equation solving, polynomial manipulation, and the like, as well as arbitrary precision arithmetic. MATLAB also has symbolic computation capabilities via a "Symbolic Math" toolbox based on Maple.

Because MATLAB is probably the most widely used of these environments for the types of problems discussed in this book, specific MATLAB functions, either from the basic environment or from the supplementary toolboxes, are listed in the summaries of available software for each problem category, along with software from the major conventional software libraries.

1.4.3 Extended Arithmetic Packages

Software packages that provide multiple precision arithmetic include MP(#524), FM(#693), MPFUN(#719), and ZM(#786) from TOMS, as well as routines from NR [315, Section 20.6] and [316]. Software packages and systems implementing interval or range arithmetic include INTLIB(#737, #763) from TOMS, PROFIL/BIAS [234], and the software accompanying [1].

1.4.4 Practical Advice on Software

This section contains practical advice on obtaining and using the software cited throughout the book, especially for the purpose of programming assignments based on the computer problems at the end of each chapter. The computer problems do not depend on any particular software or programming language, and thus many options are available. The best choice in a given case will depend on the user's experience, resources, and objectives.

The software cited comes from a variety of sources, including large commercial libraries such as IMSL and NAG, public repositories of free software such as Netlib, and scientific computing environments such as MATLAB. Many academic and industrial computing centers and workstation laboratories will have a representative sample of such software already installed and available for use. In any case, ample software is available free via the Internet or at nominal cost from other sources (e.g., accompanying textbooks) for all of the computer problems in this book. Locating, downloading, and installing suitable software is useful real-world experience, and the skills learned in doing so are an important practical adjunct to the other skills taught in this book.

Perhaps the most important choice is that of a programming language. Fortran is the traditional language of scientific computing, and the overwhelming majority of existing software libraries and applications codes are in Fortran, although C and its variants are catching up fast with respect to available resources. In working with this book, the Fortran user will benefit from the widest variety of available software and from compatibility with the preponderance of existing application codes. In addition, since Fortran is a relatively restrictive language and compilers for it have had the benefit of many years of tuning, Fortran produces somewhat more efficient executable code on some computer systems.

C is a more versatile and expressive language than Fortran, and currently C (including its variants, such as C++ and Java) is probably the language most commonly taught in beginning programming courses. C also has the advantage of being freely available (or at nominal cost) on almost any computer system, whereas Fortran may be unavailable or considerably more expensive in some cases. C has long been used as a primary language for systems programming, but more recently it has become increasingly popular for scientific programming as well. If you desire to use C with this book, there should be plenty of software available. For example, both major commercial libraries, IMSL and NAG, have substantial subsets available in C, and the NR and NUMAL libraries are also available in C at nominal cost (see Section 1.4.1).

In addition, on many computer systems it is fairly straightforward to call Fortran routines from C programs. The main differences to watch out for are that the routine names may be slightly modified (often with an underscore before and/or after the usual name), all arguments to Fortran subroutines should be passed by address (i.e., as pointers in C), and C and Fortran have opposite array storage conventions (C matrices are stored row-wise, Fortran matrices are stored column-wise). Finally, one can automatically convert Fortran source code directly into C using the f2c converter that is available free from Bell Laboratories or from Netlib, so that Fortran routines obtained via the Internet, for example, can easily be used with C programs.

A third choice of programming language that should be seriously considered is an interactive scientific computing environment, such as MATLAB. The user of such an environment will enjoy several benefits. User programs will generally be much shorter, because of the elimination of explicit declarations, storage management, and many loops. In addition, these environments often have built-in functions for many of the problems we will encounter, which greatly simplifies the interface with such routines because much of the necessary information (array sizes, etc.) is passed implicitly by the environment. An additional bonus is built-in graphics, which avoids having to do this separately in a postprocessing phase. Even if you intend to use a standard language such as C or Fortran in the long run, you may still find it beneficial to learn a package such as MATLAB for its usefulness as a rapid prototyping environment in which new algorithms can be tried out quickly then later recoded in a standard language, if necessary, for greater efficiency or compatibility. If you wish to learn MATLAB, in addition to the tutorial and reference documentation that comes with it you might also find one of the many books on MATLAB useful (see [33, 62, 110, 144, 179, 185, 193, 231, 232, 299, 304, 314, 319, 354, 360]).

Some of the computer problems in the book call for graphical output. Depending on your computing environment, several options are available for producing the required plots. In a Unix environment, simple plots can be made using the `graph` and `plot` commands (see the corresponding `man` pages). In X-Windows, simple plots can be made on the screen with the `xgraph` tool, and then hard copies can be made using the `xwd` and `xpr` utilities, or their equivalents. Somewhat more sophisticated graphs can be made using free packages such as `gnuplot` (`www.gnuplot.info`), `pgplot` (`www.astro.caltech.edu/~tjp/pgplot`) and `plplot` (`plplot.sourceforge.net`), which are available for Unix and several other operating systems. Much more sophisticated and powerful scientific visualization systems are also available, but their capabilities go well beyond the simple plots needed for the problems in this book. If you use a PC or Mac, dozens of graphics programs are available, far too many to mention individually. Again, note that MATLAB and similar environments have built-in graphics, which is a great convenience.

Another important programming consideration is *performance*. The performance of today's microprocessor-based computer systems often depends critically on judicious exploitation of a memory hierarchy (registers, cache, RAM, disk, etc.) both by the user and by the optimizing compiler. Thus, it is important not only to choose the right algorithm but also to implement it carefully to maximize the reuse of data while they are held in the portions of the memory hierarchy with faster access times. Fortunately, the details of such programming are usually hidden from the user inside the library routines recommended in this text. This feature is just one of the many benefits of using existing, professionally written software for scientific computing whenever possible.

If you use a scientific computing environment such as MATLAB, you should be aware that there may be significant differences in performance between the built-in operations, which are generally very fast, and those you program explicitly yourself, which tend to be much slower owing to the interpreted mode of operation and to memory management overhead. Thus, one should be very careful in making performance comparisons under these circumstances. For example, one algorithm may be inferior to another in principle, yet perform better because of more effective utilization of fast built-in operations.

For general advice on many practical aspects of using workstations, Unix, X-Windows, graphics, and many other packages of interest in scientific computing, as well as performance considerations in programming, see [103, 130, 156, 244].

1.5 Historical Notes and Further Reading

The subject we now call numerical analysis or scientific computing vastly predates the advent of modern computers. Many of the concepts and methods still in use today were first formulated by pre-twentieth century giants—Newton (1642–1727), Euler (1707–1783), Lagrange (1736–1813), Laplace (1749–1827), Legendre (1752–1833), Gauss (1777–1855), Cauchy (1789–1857), Jacobi (1804–1851), Adams (1819–1892), Chebyshev (1821–1894), Hermite (1822–1901), Laguerre (1834–1886), and others—whose names recur throughout this book. The main concern then, as it is now, was finding efficient methods for obtaining approximate solutions to mathematical problems that arose in physics, astronomy, surveying, and other disciplines. Indeed, efficient use of computational resources is even more critical when using pencil, paper, and brain power (or perhaps a hand calculator) than when using a modern high-speed computer.

For the most part, modern computers have simply increased the size of problems that are feasible to tackle. They have also necessitated more careful analysis and control of rounding error, for the computation is no longer done by a human who can easily carry additional precision as needed. There is no question, however, that the development of digital computers was the impetus for the flowering of numerical analysis into the fertile and vigorously growing field that has enabled the ubiquitous role computation now plays throughout modern science and engineering. Indeed, computation has come to be regarded as an equal and indispensable partner, along with theory and experiment, in the advance of scientific knowledge and engineering practice [224].

For an account of the early history of numerical analysis, see [160]; for the more recent development of scientific computing in the computer era, see [285]. The literature of numerical analysis, from textbooks to research monographs and journals, is much too vast to be covered adequately here. In this text we will try to give appropriate credit for the major ideas presented (at least those not already obvious from the name) and cite (usually secondary) sources for further reading, but these citations and recommendations are by no means complete. There are too many excellent general textbooks on numerical analysis to mention them all, but many of these still make worthwhile reading (even some of the older ones, several of which have recently been reissued in inexpensive reprint editions). Only those of most direct relevance to our discussion will be cited.

Most numerical analysis textbooks contain a general discussion of error analysis. A seminal reference on the analysis of rounding errors is [418], which is a treasure trove of valuable insights. Its author, James H. Wilkinson, played a major role in developing and popularizing the notion of backward error analysis and was also responsible for a number of famous "computational counterexamples" that reveal various numerical instabilities in unsuspected problems and algorithms. A more recent work in a similar spirit is [196]. For various approaches to automating error analysis, including interval arithmetic, see [1, 6, 212, 271, 277]. A `MATLAB` toolbox for error analysis is discussed in [61]. An early discussion of the general notion of conditioning is given in [323].

Recent general treatments of computer arithmetic include [237, 292, 300]. The book by Sterbenz [365], though somewhat dated, remains the only book-length treatment of floating-point arithmetic. See [235] for a more concise account. The effort to standardize floating-point arithmetic and the high quality of the resulting standard were largely inspired by William Kahan, who is also responsible for many well known computational counterexamples. The IEEE floating-point standard can be found in [205]. Useful tutorials on floating-point arithmetic and the IEEE standard include [157, 297].

For an account of the emergence of mathematical software as a subdiscipline of numerical analysis and computer science, see the survey [71] and the collections [37, 78, 111, 189, 209, 324, 325]. Perhaps the earliest numerical methods textbook to feature professional quality software (not just code fragments for illustration) was [347], which is similar in tone, style, and content to the very influential book by Forsythe, Malcolm and Moler [127] that popularized this approach. In addition to the books cited in Section 1.4.1, the following numerical methods textbooks focus on the specific software libraries or packages listed: `IMSL` [326], `NAG` [198, 236], `MATLAB` [38, 118, 255, 265, 284, 339, 407], and `Mathematica` [356]. Other textbooks that provide additional discussion and examples at an introductory level include [15, 54, 55, 65, 75, 152, 220, 348, 370]. More advanced general textbooks include [81, 94, 146, 163, 183, 206, 230, 238, 294, 308, 313, 317, 342, 371, 375, 402]. Practical advice on recognizing and avoiding pitfalls in numerical computation is provided in [3, 4, 126, 364]

The book of Strang [376] provides excellent background and insights on many aspects of applied mathematics that are relevant to numerical computation in general, and in particular to almost every chapter of this book. For elementary introductions to scientific programming, see [406, 431, 432]. For advice on designing, implementing, and testing numerical software, as opposed to simply using it, see [71, 270]. Additional computer exercises and projects can be found in [79, 109, 130, 141, 144, 167, 169, 245, 360].

Review Questions

1.1. True or false: A problem is ill-conditioned if its solution is highly sensitive to small changes in the problem data.

1.2. True or false: Using higher-precision arithmetic will make an ill-conditioned problem better conditioned.

1.3. True or false: The conditioning of a problem depends on the algorithm used to solve it.

1.4. True or false: A good algorithm will produce an accurate solution regardless of the condition of the problem being solved.

1.5. True or false: The choice of algorithm for solving a problem has no effect on the propagated data error.

1.6. True or false: A stable algorithm applied to a well-conditioned problem necessarily produces an accurate solution.

1.7. True or false: If two real numbers are exactly representable as floating-point numbers, then the result of a real arithmetic operation on them will also be representable as a floating-point number.

1.8. True or false: Floating-point numbers are distributed uniformly throughout their range.

1.9. True or false: Floating-point addition is associative but not commutative.

1.10. True or false: In a floating-point number system, the underflow level is the smallest positive number that perturbs the number 1 when added to it.

1.11. True or false: The mantissa in IEEE double precision floating-point arithmetic is exactly twice the length of the mantissa in IEEE single precision.

1.12. What three properties characterize a *well-posed* problem?

1.13. List three sources of error in scientific computation.

1.14. Explain the distinction between truncation (or discretization) and rounding.

1.15. Explain the distinction between absolute error and relative error.

1.16. Explain the distinction between computational error and propagated data error.

1.17. Explain the distinction between precision and accuracy.

1.18. (*a*) What is meant by the *conditioning* of a problem?

(*b*) Is it affected by the algorithm used to solve the problem?

(*c*) Is it affected by the precision of the arithmetic used to solve the problem?

1.19. If a computational problem has a condition number of 1, is this good or bad? Why?

1.20. Explain the distinction between relative condition number and absolute condition number.

1.21. What is an inverse problem? How are the conditioning of a problem and its inverse related?

1.22. (*a*) What is meant by the *backward error* in a computed result?

(*b*) When is an approximate solution to a given problem considered to be good according to backward error analysis?

1.23. Suppose you are solving a given problem using a given algorithm. For each of the following, state whether it is affected by the *stability* of the algorithm, and why.

(*a*) Propagated data error

(*b*) Accuracy of computed result

(*c*) Conditioning of problem

1.24. (*a*) Explain the distinction between forward error and backward error.

(*b*) How are forward error and backward error related to each other quantitatively?

1.25. For a given floating-point number system, describe in words the distribution of machine numbers along the real line.

1.26. In floating-point arithmetic, which is generally more harmful, underflow or overflow? Why?

1.27. In floating-point arithmetic, which of the following operations on two positive floating-point operands can produce an overflow?

(*a*) Addition

(*b*) Subtraction

(*c*) Multiplication

(*d*) Division

1.28. In floating-point arithmetic, which of the following operations on two positive floating-point operands can produce an underflow?

(*a*) Addition

(*b*) Subtraction

(*c*) Multiplication

(*d*) Division

1.29. List two reasons why floating-point number systems are usually normalized.

1.30. In a floating-point system, what quantity determines the maximum relative error in representing a given real number by a machine number?

1.31. (*a*) Explain the difference between the rounding rules "round toward zero" and "round to nearest" in a floating-point system.

(*b*) Which of these two rounding rules is more accurate?

(*c*) What quantitative difference does this make in the unit roundoff ϵ_{mach}?

1.32. In a p-digit binary floating-point system with rounding to nearest, what is the value of the unit roundoff ϵ_{mach}?

1.33. In a floating-point system with gradual underflow (subnormal numbers), is the representation of each number still unique? Why?

1.34. In a floating-point system, is the product of two machine numbers usually exactly representable in the floating-point system? Why?

1.35. In a floating-point system, is the quotient of two nonzero machine numbers always exactly representable in the floating-point system? Why?

1.36. (*a*) Give an example to show that floating-point addition is not necessarily associative.

(*b*) Give an example to show that floating-point multiplication is not necessarily associative.

1.37. (*a*) In what circumstances does *cancellation* occur in a floating-point system?

(*b*) Does the occurrence of cancellation imply that the true result of the specific operation causing it is not exactly representable in the floating-point system? Why?

(*c*) Why is cancellation usually bad?

1.38. Give an example of a number whose decimal representation is finite (i.e., it has only a finite number of nonzero digits) but whose binary representation is not.

1.39. Give examples of floating-point arithmetic operations that would produce each of the exceptional values `Inf` and `NaN`.

1.40. In a floating-point system with base β, precision p, and rounding to nearest, what is the maximum relative error in representing any nonzero real number within the range of the system?

1.41. Explain why the cancellation that occurs when two numbers of similar magnitude are subtracted is often bad even though the result may be exactly correct for the actual operands involved.

1.42. Assume a decimal (base 10) floating-point system having machine precision $\epsilon_{\text{mach}} = 10^{-5}$ and an exponent range of ± 20. What is the result of each of the following floating-point arithmetic operations?

(*a*) $1 + 10^{-7}$

(*b*) $1 + 10^{3}$

(*c*) $1 + 10^{7}$

(*d*) $10^{10} + 10^{3}$

(*e*) $10^{10}/10^{-15}$

(*f*) $10^{-10} \times 10^{-15}$

1.43. In a floating-point number system having an underflow level of UFL $= 10^{-38}$, which of the following computations will incur an underflow?

(*a*) $a = \sqrt{b^2 + c^2}$, with $b = 1$, $c = 10^{-25}$.

(*b*) $a = \sqrt{b^2 + c^2}$, with $b = c = 10^{-25}$.

(*c*) $u = (v \times w)/(y \times z)$, with $v = 10^{-15}$, $w = 10^{-30}$, $y = 10^{-20}$, and $z = 10^{-25}$.

In each case where underflow occurs, is it reasonable simply to set to zero the quantity that underflows?

1.44. (*a*) Explain in words the difference between the unit roundoff, ϵ_{mach}, and the underflow level, UFL, in a floating-point system.

Of these two quantities,

(*b*) Which one depends only on the number of digits in the mantissa field?

(*c*) Which one depends only on the number of digits in the exponent field?

(*d*) Which one does *not* depend on the rounding rule used?

(*e*) Which one is *not* affected by allowing subnormal numbers?

1.45. Let x_k be a monotonically decreasing, finite sequence of positive numbers (i.e., $x_k > x_{k+1}$ for each k). Assuming it is practical to take the numbers in any order we choose, in what order should the sequence be summed to minimize rounding error?

1.46. Is cancellation an example of rounding error? Why?

1.47. (*a*) Explain why a divergent infinite series, such as

$$\sum_{n=1}^{\infty} \frac{1}{n},$$

can have a finite sum in floating-point arithmetic.

(*b*) At what point will the partial sums cease to change?

1.48. In floating-point arithmetic, if you are computing the sum of a convergent infinite series

$$S = \sum_{i=1}^{\infty} x_i$$

of positive terms in the natural order, what stopping criterion would you use to attain the maximum possible accuracy using the smallest number of terms?

1.49. Explain why an alternating infinite series, such as

$$e^x = 1 + x + \frac{x^2}{2!} + \frac{x^3}{3!} + \cdots$$

for $x < 0$, is difficult to evaluate accurately in floating-point arithmetic.

1.50. If f is a real-valued function of a real variable, the truncation error of the finite difference approximation to the derivative

$$f'(x) \approx \frac{f(x+h) - f(x)}{h}$$

goes to zero as $h \to 0$. If we use floating-point arithmetic, list two factors that limit how small a value of h we can use in practice.

1.51. List at least two ways in which evaluation of the quadratic formula

$$x = \frac{-b \pm \sqrt{b^2 - 4ac}}{2a}$$

may suffer numerical difficulties in floating-point arithmetic.

Exercises

1.1. The average normal human body temperature is usually quoted as 98.6 degrees Fahrenheit, which might be presumed to have been determined by computing the average over a large population and then rounding to three significant digits. In fact, however, 98.6 is simply the Fahrenheit equivalent of 37 degrees Celsius, which is accurate to only two significant digits.

(*a*) What is the maximum relative error in the accepted value, assuming it is accurate to within $\pm 0.05°$ F?

(*b*) What is the maximum relative error in the accepted value, assuming it is accurate to within $\pm 0.5°$ C?

1.2. What are the approximate absolute and relative errors in approximating π by each of the following quantities?

(*a*) 3

(*b*) 3.14

(*c*) 22/7

1.3. If a is an approximate value for a quantity whose true value is t, and a has relative error r, prove from the definitions of these terms that $a = t(1+r)$.

1.4. Consider the problem of evaluating the function $\sin(x)$, in particular, the propagated data error, i.e., the error in the function value due to a perturbation h in the argument x.

(*a*) Estimate the absolute error in evaluating $\sin(x)$.

(*b*) Estimate the relative error in evaluating $\sin(x)$.

(*c*) Estimate the condition number for this problem.

(*d*) For what values of the argument x is this problem highly sensitive?

1.5. Consider the function $f: \mathbb{R}^2 \to \mathbb{R}$ defined by $f(x,y) = x - y$. Measuring the size of the input (x,y) by $|x| + |y|$, and assuming that $|x| + |y| \approx 1$ and $x - y \approx \epsilon$, show that $\text{cond}(f) \approx 1/\epsilon$. What can you conclude about the sensitivity of subtraction?

1.6. The sine function is given by the infinite series

$$\sin(x) = x - \frac{x^3}{3!} + \frac{x^5}{5!} - \frac{x^7}{7!} + \cdots.$$

(*a*) What are the forward and backward errors if we approximate the sine function by using only the first term in the series, i.e., $\sin(x) \approx x$, for $x = 0.1$, 0.5, and 1.0?

(*b*) What are the forward and backward errors if we approximate the sine function by using the first two terms in the series, i.e., $\sin(x) \approx x - x^3/6$, for $x = 0.1$, 0.5, and 1.0?

1.7. A floating-point number system is characterized by four integers: the base β, the precision p, and the lower and upper limits L and U of the exponent range.

(*a*) If $\beta = 10$, what are the smallest values of p and U, and largest value of L, such that both 2365.27 and 0.0000512 can be represented *exactly* in a *normalized* floating-point system?

(*b*) How would your answer change if the system is not normalized, i.e., if gradual underflow is allowed?

1.8. In a floating-point system with precision $p = 6$ decimal digits, let $x = 1.23456$ and $y = 1.23579$.

(*a*) How many significant digits does the difference $y - x$ contain?

(*b*) If the floating-point system is normalized, what is the minimum exponent range for which x, y, and $y - x$ are all exactly representable?

(*c*) Is the difference $y - x$ exactly representable, regardless of exponent range, if gradual underflow is allowed? Why?

1.9. (*a*) Using four-digit decimal arithmetic and the formula given in Example 1.1, compute the surface area of the Earth, with $r = 6370$ km.

(*b*) Using the same formula and precision, compute the difference in surface area if the value for the radius is increased by 1 km.

(*c*) Since $dA/dr = 8\pi r$, the change in surface area is approximated by $8\pi rh$, where h is the change in radius. Use this formula, still with four-digit arithmetic, to compute the difference in surface area due to an increase of 1 km in radius. How does the value obtained using this approximate formula compare with that obtained from the "exact" formula in part *b*?

(*d*) Determine which of the previous two answers is more nearly correct by repeating both computations using higher precision, say, six-digit decimal arithmetic.

(*e*) Explain the results you obtained in parts *a*–*d*.

(*f*) Try this problem on a computer. How small must the change h in radius be for the same phenomenon to occur? Try both single precision and double precision, if available.

1.10. Consider the expression

$$\frac{1}{1-x} - \frac{1}{1+x},$$

assuming $x \neq \pm 1$.

(*a*) For what range of values of x is it difficult to compute this expression accurately in floating-point arithmetic?

(*b*) Give a rearrangement of the terms such that, for the range of x in part *a*, the computation is more accurate in floating-point arithmetic.

1.11. If $x \approx y$, then we would expect some cancellation in computing $\log(x) - \log(y)$. On the other hand, $\log(x) - \log(y) = \log(x/y)$, and the latter involves no cancellation. Does this mean that computing $\log(x/y)$ is likely to give a better result? (*Hint*: For what value is the log function sensitive?)

1.12. (*a*) Which of the two mathematically equivalent expressions

$$x^2 - y^2 \quad \text{and} \quad (x-y)(x+y)$$

can be evaluated more accurately in floating-point arithmetic? Why?

(*b*) For what values of x and y, relative to each other, is there a substantial difference in the accuracy of the two expressions?

1.13. The Euclidean norm of an n-dimensional vector $\boldsymbol{x}$ is defined by

$$\|\boldsymbol{x}\|_2 = \left(\sum_{i=1}^{n} x_i^2\right)^{1/2}.$$

How would you avoid overflow and harmful underflow in this computation?

1.14. For computing the midpoint m of an interval $[a, b]$, which of the following two formulas is preferable in floating-point arithmetic? Why? When? (*Hint*: Devise examples for which the "midpoint" given by the formula lies *outside* the interval $[a, b]$.)

(*a*) $m = (a + b)/2.0$

(*b*) $m = a + (b - a)/2.0$

1.15. Give specific examples to show that floating-point addition is not associative in each of the following floating-point systems:

(*a*) The toy floating-point system of Example 1.9

(*b*) IEEE single-precision floating-point arithmetic

1.16. Explain how the various definitions for the unit roundoff ϵ_{mach} given in Section 1.3.5 can differ in practice. (*Hint*: Consider the toy floating-point system of Example 1.9.)

1.17. Let x be a given nonzero floating-point number in a normalized system, and let y be an adjacent floating-point number, also nonzero.

(*a*) What is the minimum possible spacing between x and y?

(*b*) What is the maximum possible spacing between x and y?

1.18. How many normalized machine numbers are there in a single-precision IEEE floating-point system? How many additional machine numbers are gained if subnormals are allowed?

1.19. In a single-precision IEEE floating-point system, what are the values of the largest machine number, OFL, and the smallest positive normalized machine number, UFL? How do your answers change if subnormals are allowed?

1.20. What is the IEEE single-precision binary floating-point representation of the decimal fraction 0.1

(*a*) with chopping?

(*b*) with rounding to nearest?

1.21. (*a*) In a floating-point system, is the unit roundoff ϵ_{mach} necessarily a machine number?

(*b*) Is it possible to have a floating-point system in which $\epsilon_{\text{mach}} < \text{UFL}$? If so, give an example.

1.22. Assume that you are solving the quadratic equation $ax^2 + bx + c = 0$, with $a = 1.22$, $b = 3.34$, and $c = 2.28$, using a normalized floating-point system with $\beta = 10$, $p = 3$.

(*a*) What is the computed value of the discriminant $b^2 - 4ac$?

(*b*) What is the correct value of the discriminant in real (exact) arithmetic?

(*c*) What is the relative error in the computed value of the discriminant?

1.23. Assume a normalized floating-point system with $\beta = 10$, $p = 3$, and $L = -98$.

(*a*) What is the value of the underflow level UFL for this system?

(*b*) If $x = 6.87 \times 10^{-97}$ and $y = 6.81 \times 10^{-97}$, what is the result of $x - y$?

(*c*) What would be the result of $x - y$ if the system permitted gradual underflow?

1.24. Consider the following claim: if two floating-point numbers x and y with the same sign differ by a factor of at most the base β (i.e., $1/\beta \le x/y \le \beta$), then their difference, $x - y$, is exactly representable in the floating-point system. Show that this claim is true for $\beta = 2$, but give a counterexample for $\beta > 2$.

1.25. Some microprocessors have an instruction `mpyadd(a,b,c)`, for multiply-add, which takes single-length inputs and adds `c` to the double-length product of `a` and `b` before normalizing and returning a single-length result. How can such an instruction be used to compute double-precision products *without* using any double-length variables (i.e., the double-length product of `a` and `b` will be contained in two single-length variables, say, `s` and `t`)?

1.26. Verify that the alternative quadratic formula given in Example 1.15 indeed gives the correct roots to the quadratic equation (in exact arithmetic).

1.27. Give a detailed explanation of the numerical inferiority of the one-pass formula for computing the standard deviation compared with the two-pass formula given in Example 1.16.

Computer Problems

1.1. Write a program to compute the absolute and relative errors in Stirling's approximation

$$n! \approx \sqrt{2\pi n}\,(n/e)^n$$

for $n = 1, \ldots, 10$. Does the absolute error grow or shrink as n increases? Does the relative error grow or shrink as n increases?

1.2. Write a program to determine approximate values for the unit roundoff ϵ_{mach} and the underflow level UFL, and test it on a real computer. (*Optional*: Can you also determine the overflow level OFL, on your machine? This is trickier because an actual overflow may be fatal.) Print the resulting values in decimal, and also try to determine the number of bits in the mantissa and exponent fields of the floating-point system you use.

1.3. In most floating-point systems, a quick approximation to the unit roundoff can be obtained by evaluating the expression

$$\epsilon_{\text{mach}} \approx |\mathtt{3 * (4/3 - 1) - 1}|.$$

(*a*) Explain why this trick works.

(*b*) Try it on a variety of computers (in both single and double precision) and calculators to confirm that it works.

(*c*) Would this trick work in a floating-point system with base $\beta = 3$?

1.4. Write a program to compute the mathematical constant e, the base of natural logarithms, from the definition

$$e = \lim_{n\to\infty} (1 + 1/n)^n.$$

Specifically, compute $(1 + 1/n)^n$ for $n = 10^k$, $k = 1, 2, \ldots, 20$. If the programming language you use does not have an operator for exponentiation, you may use the equivalent formula

$$(1 + 1/n)^n = \exp(n \log(1 + 1/n)),$$

where exp and log are built-in functions. Determine the error in your successive approximations by comparing them with the value of exp(1). Does the error always decrease as n increases? Explain your results.

1.5. (*a*) Consider the function

$$f(x) = (e^x - 1)/x.$$

Use l'Hôpital's rule to show that

$$\lim_{x\to 0} f(x) = 1.$$

(*b*) Check this result empirically by writing a program to compute $f(x)$ for $x = 10^{-k}$, $k = 1, \ldots, 15$. Do your results agree with theoretical expectations? Explain why.

(*c*) Perform the experiment in part *b* again, this time using the mathematically equivalent formulation

$$f(x) = (e^x - 1)/\log(e^x),$$

evaluated as indicated, with no simplification. If this works any better, can you explain why?

1.6. Suppose you need to generate $n+1$ equally spaced points on the interval $[a, b]$, with spacing $h = (b - a)/n$.

(*a*) In floating-point arithmetic, which of the following methods,

$$x_0 = a, \quad x_k = x_{k-1} + h, \quad k = 1, \ldots, n$$

or

$$x_k = a + kh, \quad k = 0, \ldots, n,$$

is better, and why?

(*b*) Write a program implementing both methods and find an example, say, with $a = 0$ and $b = 1$, that illustrates the difference between them.

1.7. (*a*) Write a program to compute an approximate value for the derivative of a function using the finite-difference formula

$$f'(x) \approx \frac{f(x+h) - f(x)}{h}.$$

Test your program using the function $\tan(x)$ for $x = 1$. Determine the error by comparing with the square of the built-in function $\sec(x)$. Plot the magnitude of the error as a function of h, for $h = 10^{-k}$, $k = 0, \ldots, 16$. You should use log scale for h and for the magnitude of the error. Is there a minimum value for the magnitude of the error? How does the corresponding value for h compare with the rule of thumb $h \approx \sqrt{\epsilon_{\text{mach}}}$ derived in Example 1.3?

(*b*) Repeat the exercise using the centered difference approximation

$$f'(x) \approx \frac{f(x+h) - f(x-h)}{2h}.$$

1.8. Consider the infinite series

$$\sum_{n=1}^{\infty} \frac{1}{n}.$$

(*a*) Prove that the series is divergent. (*Hint*: Group the terms in sets containing terms $1/(2^{k-1}+1)$ down to $1/2^k$, for $k = 1, 2, \ldots$.)

(*b*) Explain why summing the series in floating-point arithmetic yields a finite sum.

(*c*) Try to predict when the partial sum will cease to change in both IEEE single-precision and double-precision floating-point arithmetic. Given the execution rate of your computer for floating-point operations, try to predict how long each computation would take to complete.

(*d*) Write two programs to compute the sum of the series, one in single precision and the other in double precision. Monitor the progress of the summation by printing out the index and partial sum periodically. What stopping criterion should you use? What result is actually produced on your computer? Compare your results with your predictions, including the execution time required. (*Caution*: Your single-precision version should terminate fairly quickly, but your double-precision version may take *much* longer, so it may not be practical to run it to completion, even if your computer budget is generous.)

1.9. (*a*) Write a program to compute the exponential function e^x using the infinite series

$$e^x = 1 + x + \frac{x^2}{2!} + \frac{x^3}{3!} + \cdots.$$

(*b*) Summing in the natural order, what stopping criterion should you use?
(*c*) Test your program for

$$x = \pm 1, \pm 5, \pm 10, \pm 15, \pm 20,$$

and compare your results with the built-in function $\exp(x)$.
(*d*) Can you use the series in this form to obtain accurate results for $x < 0$? (*Hint*: $e^{-x} = 1/e^x$.)
(*e*) Can you rearrange the series or regroup the terms in any way to obtain more accurate results for $x < 0$?

1.10. Write a program to solve the quadratic equation $ax^2 + bx + c = 0$ using the standard quadratic formula

$$x = \frac{-b \pm \sqrt{b^2 - 4ac}}{2a}$$

or the alternative formula

$$x = \frac{2c}{-b \mp \sqrt{b^2 - 4ac}}.$$

Your program should accept values for the coefficients a, b, and c as input and produce the two roots of the equation as output. Your program should detect when the roots are not real, but need not use complex arithmetic explicitly (for example, you could return the real and imaginary parts of the complex conjugate roots in this case). You should guard against unnecessary overflow, underflow, and cancellation. When should you use each of the two formulas? Try to make your program robust when given unusual input values, such as $a = 0$ or $c = 0$, which otherwise would make one of the formulas fail. Any root that is within the range of the floating-point system should be computed accurately, even if the other is out of range. Test your program using the following values for the coefficients:

a	b	c
6	5	-4
6×10^{154}	5×10^{154}	-4×10^{154}
0	1	1
1	-10^5	1
1	-4	3.999999
10^{-155}	-10^{155}	10^{155}

1.11. By dividing by its nonzero leading coefficient, any cubic equation can be put into the form

$$x^3 + ax^2 + bx + c = 0.$$

Assuming the coefficients are real, such an equation has at least one real root, which can be computed in closed form as follows. Make the substitution $y = x + a/3$. The equation then reduces to

$$y^3 + py + q = 0,$$

where

$$p = \frac{3b - a^2}{3}$$

and

$$q = \frac{2a^3}{27} - \frac{ab}{3} + c.$$

If the discriminant

$$D = (p/3)^3 + (q/2)^2$$

is positive, then there is only one real root, and it is given by

$$x = -\frac{a}{3} + \sqrt[3]{-\frac{q}{2} + \sqrt{D}} + \sqrt[3]{-\frac{q}{2} - \sqrt{D}}.$$

Write a routine using this method in real arithmetic (taking care that the cube root you use is real) to compute the real root of a real cubic equation for the case when only one root is real. If you feel ambitious, you may also want to compute the other two roots for this case, or consider the case of three real roots, but complex arithmetic will be required (or a more elaborate trigonometric solution). Try to make your routine as robust as possible, guarding against unnecessary overflow, underflow, and cancellation. What should your routine do if the leading coefficient is zero? Test your routine for various values of the coefficients, analogous to those used in the previous exercise. See also Computer Problem 5.17.

1.12. (*a*) Write a program to compute the mean $\bar{x}$ and standard deviation σ of a finite sequence x_i.

Your program should accept a vector $\boldsymbol{x}$ of dimension n as input and produce the mean and standard deviation of the sequence as output. For the standard deviation, try both the two-pass formula

$$\sigma = \left[\frac{1}{n-1}\sum_{i=1}^{n}(x_i - \bar{x})^2\right]^{1/2}$$

and the one-pass formula

$$\sigma = \left[\frac{1}{n-1}\left(\sum_{i=1}^{n}x_i^2 - n\bar{x}^2\right)\right]^{1/2}$$

and compare the results for an input sequence of your choice.

(*b*) Can you devise an input data sequence that dramatically illustrates the numerical difference between these two mathematically equivalent formulas? (*Caution*: Beware of taking the square root of a negative number.)

1.13. If an amount a is invested at interest rate r compounded n times per year, then the final value f at the end of one year is given by

$$f = a(1 + r/n)^n.$$

This is the familiar formula for *compound interest*. With simple interest, $n = 1$. Typically, compounding is done quarterly, $n = 4$, or perhaps even daily, $n = 365$. Obviously, the more frequent the compounding, the greater the final amount, because more interest is paid on previous interest. But how much difference does this frequency actually make? Write a program that implements the compound interest formula. Test your program using an initial investment of $a = 100$, an interest rate of 5 percent (i.e., $r = 0.05$), and the following values for n: 1, 4, 12, 365. Also experiment with what happens when n becomes very large. Can you find a value such that the final amount does not grow with the frequency of compounding, as it should? (This will be easy if you use single precision, but much harder if you use double precision.)

Implement the compound interest formula in two different ways:

(*a*) If the programming language you use does not have an operator for exponentiation (e.g., C), then you might implement the compound interest formula using a loop that repeatedly multiplies a by $(1 + r/n)$ for a total of n times. Even if your programming language does have an operator for exponentiation (e.g., Fortran), try implementing the compound interest formula using such a loop and print your results for the input values.

(*b*) With the functions $\exp(x)$ and $\log(x)$, the compound interest formula can also be written

$$f = a\exp(n\log(1 + r/n)).$$

Implement this formula using the corresponding built-in functions and compare your results with those for the first implementation using the loop, for the same input values.

1.14. The polynomial $(x-1)^6$ has the value zero at $x = 1$ and is positive elsewhere. The expanded form of the polynomial, $x^6 - 6x^5 + 15x^4 - 20x^3 + 15x^2 - 6x + 1$, is mathematically equivalent but may not give the same results numerically. Compute and plot the values of this polynomial, using each of the two forms, for 101 equally spaced points in the interval $[0.995, 1.005]$, i.e., with a spacing of 0.0001. Your plot should be scaled so that the values for x and for the polynomial use the full ranges of their respective axes. Can you explain this behavior?

1.15. The Euclidean norm of an n-dimensional vector $\boldsymbol{x}$ is defined by

$$\|\boldsymbol{x}\|_2 = \left(\sum_{i=1}^{n}x_i^2\right)^{1/2}.$$

Implement a robust routine for computing this quantity for any given input vector $\boldsymbol{x}$. Your routine should avoid overflow and harmful underflow. Compare both the accuracy and performance of your robust routine with a more straightforward naive implementation. Can you devise a vector that produces significantly different results from the two routines? How much performance does the robust routine sacrifice?

1.16. Write a program that sums n random, single-precision floating-point numbers x_i, uniformly distributed on the interval $[0, 1]$ (see Table 13.1 for an appropriate random number generator). Sum the numbers in each of the following ways (use only single-precision floating-point variables unless specifically indicated otherwise).

(*a*) Sum the numbers in the order in which they were generated, using a double-precision variable in which to accumulate the sum.

(*b*) Sum the numbers in the order in which they were generated, this time using a single-precision accumulator.

(*c*) Use the following *compensated summation* algorithm (due to Kahan), again using only single precision, to sum the numbers in the order in which they were generated:

$s = x_1$
$c = 0$
for $i = 2$ **to** n
    $y = x_i - c$
    $t = s + y$
    $c = (t - s) - y$
    $s = t$
end

(*d*) Sum the numbers in order of increasing magnitude (this will require that the numbers be sorted before summing, for which you may use a library sorting routine).

(*e*) Sum the numbers in order of decreasing magnitude (i.e., reverse the order of summation from part *d*).

Run your program for various values of n and compare the results for methods a through e. You may need to use a fairly large value for n to see a substantial difference. How do the methods rank in terms of accuracy, and why? How do the methods compare in cost? Can you explain why the algorithm in part c works?

1.17. Write a program to generate the first n terms in the sequence given by the difference equation

$$x_{k+1} = 2.25x_k - 0.5x_{k-1},$$

with starting values

$$x_1 = \frac{1}{3} \quad \text{and} \quad x_2 = \frac{1}{12}.$$

Use $n = 225$ if you are working in single precision, $n = 60$ if you are working in double precision. Make a semilog plot of the values you obtain as a function of k. The exact solution of the difference equation is given by

$$x_k = \frac{4^{1-k}}{3},$$

which decreases monotonically as k increases. Does your graph confirm this theoretically expected behavior? Can you explain your results? (*Hint*: Find the general solution to the difference equation.)

1.18. Write a program to generate the first n terms in the sequence given by the difference equation:

$$x_{k+1} = 111 - (1130 - 3000/x_{k-1})/x_k,$$

with starting values

$$x_1 = \frac{11}{2} \quad \text{and} \quad x_2 = \frac{61}{11}.$$

Use $n = 10$ if you are working in single precision, $n = 20$ if you are working in double precision. The exact solution is a monotonically increasing sequence converging to 6. Can you explain your results?

Chapter 2

Systems of Linear Equations

2.1 Linear Systems

Many relationships in nature are *linear*, meaning that effects are proportional to their causes. In mechanics, for example, Newton's Second Law of Motion, $F = ma$, says that force is proportional to acceleration, where the proportionality constant is the mass of the object. If we know the force and the mass, we can solve this linear equation for the acceleration. In electricity, Ohm's Law, $V = iR$, says that the voltage (potential difference) across a conductor is proportional to the current flowing through it, where the proportionality constant is the resistance. Again, if we know the voltage and resistance, we can solve for the current. In elasticity, Hooke's Law says that stress is proportional to strain, where the proportionality constant is Young's modulus.

In higher dimensions, such a linear relationship is expressed by a *linear transformation* $\boldsymbol{\mathcal{L}}$ that relates a vector of "causes" $\boldsymbol{u}$ to a vector of "effects" $\boldsymbol{f}$, so that

$$\boldsymbol{\mathcal{L}}\boldsymbol{u} = \boldsymbol{f}.$$

For example, Ohm's Law and Kirchhoff's Laws enable us to derive a whole *system* of coupled equations expressing the linear relationship between voltages and currents in an entire circuit made up of many conductors (see Example 2.1). As we learned in elementary linear algebra, a linear transformation between two finite-dimensional vector spaces is conveniently represented by a *matrix*. In matrix-vector notation, a system of linear algebraic equations has the form

$$\boldsymbol{A}\boldsymbol{x} = \boldsymbol{b},$$

where $\boldsymbol{A}$ is a known $m \times n$ matrix, $\boldsymbol{b}$ is an m-vector, and $\boldsymbol{x}$ an n-vector. If we know $\boldsymbol{x}$, then such a linear relationship enables us to predict effect $\boldsymbol{b}$ from cause

$\boldsymbol{x}$ by matrix-vector multiplication: $\boldsymbol{b} = \boldsymbol{A}\boldsymbol{x}$. More interestingly, the linear system may enable us to do "reverse engineering": if we know the vector $\boldsymbol{b}$ of effects, we would like to be able to determine the corresponding vector $\boldsymbol{x}$ of causes. Numerical methods for accomplishing this are the subject of this chapter.

Even when relationships are nonlinear, they can often be usefully approximated *locally* (i.e., for values near some specific fixed value) by a linear relationship. This is precisely what the derivative does in calculus: it provides a local linear approximation—the tangent line—to a nonlinear curve. This observation forms the basis for many numerical methods for solving nonlinear algebraic problems. Even nonalgebraic problems, such as differential or integral equations, can ultimately be approximated by a system of linear algebraic equations, as we will see later in this book. For these reasons, the solution of systems of linear equations forms the cornerstone of many numerical methods for solving a wide variety of practical computational problems, and consequently it is imperative that we be able to solve such systems accurately and efficiently.

A system of linear equations $\boldsymbol{A}\boldsymbol{x} = \boldsymbol{b}$ asks the question, "Can the vector $\boldsymbol{b}$ be expressed as a linear combination of the columns of the matrix $\boldsymbol{A}$?" (i.e., "Does $\boldsymbol{b}$ lie in $\text{span}(\boldsymbol{A}) = \{\boldsymbol{A}\boldsymbol{x} : \boldsymbol{x} \in \mathbb{R}^n\}$?"). If so, the system is said to be *consistent*, and the coefficients of this linear combination are given by the components of the solution vector $\boldsymbol{x}$. There may or may not be a solution; and if there is a solution, it may or may not be unique. In this chapter we will consider only *square* systems, which means that $m = n$, i.e., the matrix has the same number of rows and columns, or equivalently, the numbers of equations (rows of $\boldsymbol{A}$ and $\boldsymbol{b}$) and unknowns (components of $\boldsymbol{x}$) are the same. We will consider systems where $m \neq n$ in Chapter 3. For simplicity, we will focus our attention primarily on real linear systems; complex systems can be treated similarly.

Example 2.1 Electrical Circuit. Consider the electrical circuit shown in Fig. 2.1. Given voltages V and resistances R, and we wish to determine the resulting currents i in each of the three loops in the circuit. To do so we apply the following physical laws:

- **Ohm's Law:** The voltage drop across a resistance R in the direction of a current i is given by iR.
- **Kirchhoff's Law:** The net voltage drop in a closed loop is zero.

Applying these laws to each loop in the circuit, we obtain the system of three linear equations

$$\begin{aligned} i_1R_1 + (i_1 - i_2)R_2 + (i_1 - i_3)R_3 + V_1 &= 0, \\ (i_2 - i_1)R_2 + (i_2 - i_3)R_5 - V_2 &= 0, \\ (i_3 - i_1)R_3 + i_3R_4 + (i_3 - i_2)R_5 &= 0, \end{aligned}$$

which can be written in matrix form as

$$\begin{bmatrix} R_1 + R_2 + R_3 & -R_2 & -R_3 \\ -R_2 & R_2 + R_5 & -R_5 \\ -R_3 & -R_5 & R_3 + R_4 + R_5 \end{bmatrix} \begin{bmatrix} i_1 \\ i_2 \\ i_3 \end{bmatrix} = \begin{bmatrix} -V_1 \\ V_2 \\ 0 \end{bmatrix}.$$

Thus, this problem has the form $\boldsymbol{Ax} = \boldsymbol{b}$ and can be solved using the methods we will study in this chapter.

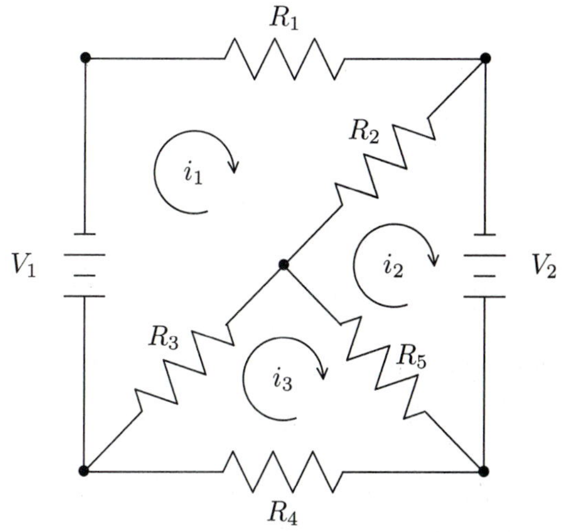

Figure 2.1: Electrical circuit with resistors and voltage sources.

2.2 Existence and Uniqueness

An $n \times n$ matrix $\boldsymbol{A}$ is said to be *nonsingular* if it satisfies any one of the following equivalent conditions:

1. $\boldsymbol{A}$ has an inverse (i.e., there is a matrix, denoted by $\boldsymbol{A}^{-1}$, such that $\boldsymbol{AA}^{-1} = \boldsymbol{A}^{-1}\boldsymbol{A} = \boldsymbol{I}$, the identity matrix).
2. $\det(\boldsymbol{A}) \neq 0$ (i.e., the determinant of $\boldsymbol{A}$ is nonzero).
3. $\text{rank}(\boldsymbol{A}) = n$ (the *rank* of a matrix is the maximum number of linearly independent rows or columns it contains).
4. For any vector $\boldsymbol{z} \neq \boldsymbol{0}$, $\boldsymbol{Az} \neq \boldsymbol{0}$ (i.e., $\boldsymbol{A}$ annihilates no nontrivial vector).

Otherwise, the matrix is *singular*. The existence and uniqueness of a solution to a system of linear equations $\boldsymbol{Ax} = \boldsymbol{b}$ depend on whether the matrix $\boldsymbol{A}$ is singular or nonsingular. If the matrix $\boldsymbol{A}$ is nonsingular, then its inverse, $\boldsymbol{A}^{-1}$, exists, and the system $\boldsymbol{Ax} = \boldsymbol{b}$ always has the unique solution $\boldsymbol{x} = \boldsymbol{A}^{-1}\boldsymbol{b}$ regardless of the value for $\boldsymbol{b}$. If, on the other hand, the matrix $\boldsymbol{A}$ is singular, then the *number* of solutions is determined by the right-hand-side vector $\boldsymbol{b}$: for a given value of $\boldsymbol{b}$ there may be no solution, but if there is a solution $\boldsymbol{x}$, so that $\boldsymbol{Ax} = \boldsymbol{b}$, then we also have $\boldsymbol{A}(\boldsymbol{x} + \gamma\boldsymbol{z}) = \boldsymbol{b}$ for any scalar γ, where $\boldsymbol{z} \neq \boldsymbol{0}$ is a vector such that $\boldsymbol{Az} = \boldsymbol{0}$ (such a $\boldsymbol{z}$ must exist, since otherwise Condition 4 in the definition implies that the matrix is nonsingular). Thus, a solution of a square, consistent, singular, linear system cannot be unique. For a given square matrix $\boldsymbol{A}$ and right-hand-side vector $\boldsymbol{b}$, the possibilities are summarized as follows:

- Unique solution: $\boldsymbol{A}$ nonsingular, $\boldsymbol{b}$ arbitrary
- Infinitely many solutions: $\boldsymbol{A}$ singular, $\boldsymbol{b} \in \operatorname{span}(\boldsymbol{A})$ (consistent)
- No solution: $\boldsymbol{A}$ singular, $\boldsymbol{b} \notin \operatorname{span}(\boldsymbol{A})$ (inconsistent)

In two dimensions, each linear equation in the system determines a straight line in the plane. The solution of the system is the intersection point of the two lines. If the two straight lines are not parallel, then they have a unique intersection point (the nonsingular case). If the two straight lines are parallel, then either they do not intersect at all (there is no solution) or the two lines coincide (any point along the line is a solution). In higher dimensions, each equation determines a hyperplane. In the nonsingular case, the unique solution is the intersection point of all the hyperplanes.

Example 2.2 Singularity and Nonsingularity. The 2×2 system

$$\begin{aligned} 2x_1 + 3x_2 &= b_1, \\ 5x_1 + 4x_2 &= b_2, \end{aligned}$$

or in matrix-vector notation

$$\boldsymbol{Ax} = \begin{bmatrix} 2 & 3 \\ 5 & 4 \end{bmatrix} \begin{bmatrix} x_1 \\ x_2 \end{bmatrix} = \begin{bmatrix} b_1 \\ b_2 \end{bmatrix} = \boldsymbol{b},$$

has a unique solution regardless of the value of $\boldsymbol{b}$, since the matrix $\boldsymbol{A}$ is nonsingular. If $\boldsymbol{b} = [8 \quad 13]^T$, for example, then the unique solution is $\boldsymbol{x} = [1 \quad 2]^T$.

The 2×2 system

$$\boldsymbol{Ax} = \begin{bmatrix} 2 & 3 \\ 4 & 6 \end{bmatrix} \begin{bmatrix} x_1 \\ x_2 \end{bmatrix} = \begin{bmatrix} b_1 \\ b_2 \end{bmatrix} = \boldsymbol{b},$$

on the other hand, has a singular matrix $\boldsymbol{A}$, and hence it may or may not have a solution, depending on the specific the value of $\boldsymbol{b}$, and it cannot have a unique solution in any case. For example, if $\boldsymbol{b} = [4 \quad 7]^T$, then there is no solution, whereas if $\boldsymbol{b} = [4 \quad 8]^T$, then

$$\boldsymbol{x} = \begin{bmatrix} \gamma \\ (4 - 2\gamma)/3 \end{bmatrix}$$

is a solution for any real number γ.

2.3 Sensitivity and Conditioning

Having stated criteria for the existence and uniqueness of a solution to a linear system $\boldsymbol{Ax} = \boldsymbol{b}$, we now consider the sensitivity of the solution $\boldsymbol{x}$ to perturbations in the input data, which for this problem are the matrix $\boldsymbol{A}$ and right-hand-side vector $\boldsymbol{b}$. To measure such perturbations, we need some notion of "size" for vectors and matrices. The scalar concept of magnitude, absolute value, or modulus can be generalized to the concept of *norms* for vectors and matrices.

2.3.1 Vector Norms

Although a more general definition is possible, all of the vector norms we will use are instances of p-norms, which for an integer $p > 0$ and an n-vector $\boldsymbol{x}$ are defined by

$$\|\boldsymbol{x}\|_p = \left(\sum_{i=1}^{n} |x_i|^p\right)^{1/p}.$$

Important special cases are:

- 1-norm:
$$\|\boldsymbol{x}\|_1 = \sum_{i=1}^{n} |x_i|,$$
sometimes called the *Manhattan norm* because in two dimensions it corresponds to the distance between two points as measured in "city blocks."
- 2-norm:
$$\|\boldsymbol{x}\|_2 = \left(\sum_{i=1}^{n} |x_i|^2\right)^{1/2},$$
which corresponds to the usual notion of distance in Euclidean space, so this is also called the *Euclidean norm*.
- ∞-norm:
$$\|\boldsymbol{x}\|_\infty = \max_{1\le i\le n} |x_i|,$$
which can be viewed as a limiting case as $p \to \infty$.

All of these norms give similar results qualitatively, but in certain circumstances a particular norm may be easiest to work with analytically or computationally. Either the 1-norm or the ∞-norm is usually used in analyzing the sensitivity of solutions to linear systems. We will make extensive use of the 2-norm later on in other contexts. The differences among these norms are illustrated for $\mathbb{R}^2$ in Fig. 2.2, which shows the unit sphere, $\{\boldsymbol{x} : \|\boldsymbol{x}\|_p = 1\}$, for $p = 1, 2, \infty$. (Note that the unit sphere, which is more accurately termed the unit circle in two dimensions, is not really "round" except in the 2-norm, from which it gets its name.) The norm of a vector is simply the factor by which the corresponding unit sphere must be expanded or shrunk to encompass the vector.

Example 2.3 Vector Norms. For the vector $\boldsymbol{x} = [-1.6,\ 1.2]^T$ shown in Fig. 2.2,

$$\|\boldsymbol{x}\|_1 = 2.8, \quad \|\boldsymbol{x}\|_2 = 2.0, \quad \|\boldsymbol{x}\|_\infty = 1.6.$$

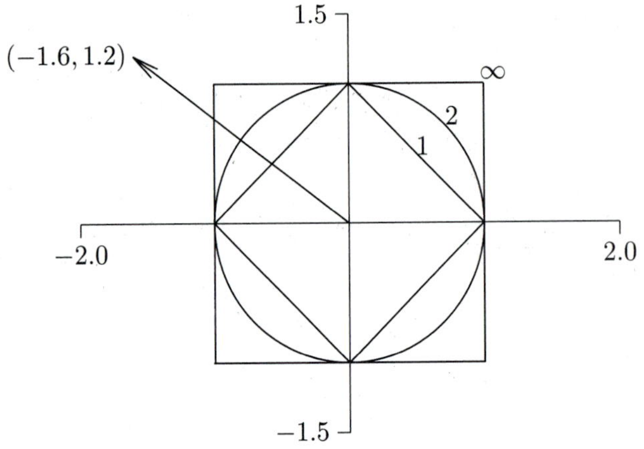

Figure 2.2: Unit spheres in various vector norms.

In general, for any n-vector $\boldsymbol{x}$, we have

$$\|\boldsymbol{x}\|_1 \geq \|\boldsymbol{x}\|_2 \geq \|\boldsymbol{x}\|_\infty.$$

On the other hand, we also have

$$\|\boldsymbol{x}\|_1 \leq \sqrt{n}\,\|\boldsymbol{x}\|_2, \quad \|\boldsymbol{x}\|_2 \leq \sqrt{n}\,\|\boldsymbol{x}\|_\infty, \quad \text{and} \quad \|\boldsymbol{x}\|_1 \leq n\,\|\boldsymbol{x}\|_\infty.$$

Thus, for a given n, any two of these norms differ by at most a constant, so they are all equivalent in the sense that if one is small, they must all be proportionally small (indeed, all p-norms are equivalent in this sense). Hence, we can choose whichever norm is most convenient in a given context. In the remainder of this book, an appropriate subscript will be used to indicate a specific norm, when necessary, but the subscript will be omitted when it does not matter which particular norm is used.

For any vector p-norm, the following important properties hold, where $\boldsymbol{x}$ and $\boldsymbol{y}$ are any vectors:

1. $\|\boldsymbol{x}\| > 0$ if $\boldsymbol{x} \neq \boldsymbol{0}$.
2. $\|\gamma\boldsymbol{x}\| = |\gamma| \cdot \|\boldsymbol{x}\|$ for any scalar γ.
3. $\|\boldsymbol{x} + \boldsymbol{y}\| \leq \|\boldsymbol{x}\| + \|\boldsymbol{y}\|$ (triangle inequality).

In a more general treatment, the *definition* of a vector norm can be taken to be any real-valued function of a vector that satisfies these three properties. Note that the first two properties together imply that $\|\boldsymbol{x}\| = 0$ if, and only if, $\boldsymbol{x} = \boldsymbol{0}$. A useful variation of the triangle inequality is

$$|\,\|\boldsymbol{x}\| - \|\boldsymbol{y}\|\,| \leq \|\boldsymbol{x} - \boldsymbol{y}\|,$$

which also shows that a vector norm is a continuous function.

2.3.2 Matrix Norms

We also need some way to measure the size or magnitude of matrices. Again, a more general definition is possible, but all of the matrix norms we will use are defined in terms of an underlying vector norm. Specifically, given a vector norm, we define the corresponding matrix norm of an $m \times n$ matrix $\boldsymbol{A}$ by

$$\|\boldsymbol{A}\| = \max_{\boldsymbol{x} \neq \boldsymbol{0}} \frac{\|\boldsymbol{A}\boldsymbol{x}\|}{\|\boldsymbol{x}\|}.$$

Such a matrix norm is said to be *induced* by or *subordinate* to the vector norm. Intuitively, the norm of a matrix measures the maximum stretching the matrix does to any vector, as measured in the given vector norm.

Some matrix norms are much easier to compute than others. For example, the matrix norm corresponding to the vector 1-norm is simply the maximum absolute column sum of the matrix,

$$\|\boldsymbol{A}\|_1 = \max_j \sum_{i=1}^{m} |a_{ij}|,$$

and the matrix norm corresponding to the vector ∞-norm is simply the maximum absolute row sum of the matrix,

$$\|\boldsymbol{A}\|_\infty = \max_i \sum_{j=1}^{n} |a_{ij}|.$$

A handy way to remember these is that the matrix norms agree with the corresponding vector norms for an $n \times 1$ matrix. Unfortunately, the matrix norm corresponding to the vector 2-norm is not so easy to compute (see Section 3.6.1).

Example 2.4 Matrix Norms. For the matrix

$$\boldsymbol{A} = \begin{bmatrix} 2 & -1 & 1 \\ 1 & 0 & 1 \\ 3 & -1 & 4 \end{bmatrix},$$

the maximum absolute column and row sums, respectively, give

$$\|\boldsymbol{A}\|_1 = 6 \quad \text{and} \quad \|\boldsymbol{A}\|_\infty = 8.$$

For the 2-norm of this matrix, see Example 3.17.

The matrix norms we have defined satisfy the following important properties, where $\boldsymbol{A}$ and $\boldsymbol{B}$ are any matrices:

1. $\|\boldsymbol{A}\| > 0$ if $\boldsymbol{A} \neq \boldsymbol{O}$.
2. $\|\gamma\boldsymbol{A}\| = |\gamma| \cdot \|\boldsymbol{A}\|$ for any scalar γ.
3. $\|\boldsymbol{A} + \boldsymbol{B}\| \leq \|\boldsymbol{A}\| + \|\boldsymbol{B}\|$.
4. $\|\boldsymbol{A}\boldsymbol{B}\| \leq \|\boldsymbol{A}\| \cdot \|\boldsymbol{B}\|$.
5. $\|\boldsymbol{A}\boldsymbol{x}\| \leq \|\boldsymbol{A}\| \cdot \|\boldsymbol{x}\|$ for any vector $\boldsymbol{x}$.

In a more general treatment, the *definition* of a matrix norm can be taken to be any real-valued function of a matrix satisfying the first three of these properties. The remaining two properties, known as *submultiplicative* or *consistency* conditions, may or may not hold for these more general matrix norms, but they always hold for the matrix norms induced by the vector p-norms. Note again that the first two properties together imply that $\|\boldsymbol{A}\| = 0$ if, and only if, $\boldsymbol{A} = \boldsymbol{O}$.

2.3.3 Matrix Condition Number

The *condition number* of a nonsingular square matrix $\boldsymbol{A}$ with respect to a given matrix norm is defined to be

$$\operatorname{cond}(\boldsymbol{A}) = \|\boldsymbol{A}\| \cdot \|\boldsymbol{A}^{-1}\|.$$

By convention, $\operatorname{cond}(\boldsymbol{A}) = \infty$ if $\boldsymbol{A}$ is singular. We will see in Section 2.3.4 that this concept is consistent with the general notion of condition number defined in Section 1.2.6 in that the condition number of the matrix bounds the ratio of the relative change in the solution of a linear system to a given relative change in the input data.

Example 2.5 Matrix Condition Number. As can easily be verified by matrix multiplication, the inverse of the matrix in Example 2.4 is given by

$$\boldsymbol{A}^{-1} = \begin{bmatrix} 0.5 & 1.5 & -0.5 \\ -0.5 & 2.5 & -0.5 \\ -0.5 & -0.5 & 0.5 \end{bmatrix},$$

so that

$$\|\boldsymbol{A}^{-1}\|_1 = 4.5 \quad \text{and} \quad \|\boldsymbol{A}^{-1}\|_\infty = 3.5.$$

Thus, we have

$$\operatorname{cond}_1(\boldsymbol{A}) = \|\boldsymbol{A}\|_1 \cdot \|\boldsymbol{A}^{-1}\|_1 = 6 \cdot 4.5 = 27$$

and

$$\operatorname{cond}_\infty(\boldsymbol{A}) = \|\boldsymbol{A}\|_\infty \cdot \|\boldsymbol{A}^{-1}\|_\infty = 8 \cdot 3.5 = 28.$$

For the condition number of this matrix using the 2-norm, see Example 3.17.

From Example 2.5 we see that the numerical value of the condition number of an $n \times n$ matrix depends on the particular norm used (indicated by the corresponding subscript), but because of the equivalence of the underlying vector norms, these values can differ by at most a fixed constant (which depends on n), and hence they are equally useful as quantitative measures of conditioning.

Since

$$\|\boldsymbol{A}\| \cdot \|\boldsymbol{A}^{-1}\| = \left(\max_{\boldsymbol{x} \neq \boldsymbol{0}} \frac{\|\boldsymbol{A}\boldsymbol{x}\|}{\|\boldsymbol{x}\|}\right) \cdot \left(\min_{\boldsymbol{x} \neq \boldsymbol{0}} \frac{\|\boldsymbol{A}\boldsymbol{x}\|}{\|\boldsymbol{x}\|}\right)^{-1},$$

the condition number of a matrix measures the ratio of the maximum relative stretching to the maximum relative shrinking that the matrix does to any nonzero vectors. Another way to say this is that the condition number of a matrix measures the amount of distortion of the unit sphere (in the corresponding vector norm) under transformation by the matrix. The larger the condition number, the more distorted (relatively long and thin) the unit sphere becomes when transformed by the matrix. In two dimensions, for example, the unit circle in the 2-norm becomes an increasingly cigar-shaped ellipse, and with the 1-norm or ∞-norm, the unit sphere is transformed from a square into an increasingly skewed parallelogram as the condition number increases.

Example 2.6 Matrix Condition Number. Fig. 2.3 illustrates the effect of four different matrices on the unit circle in $\mathbb{R}^2$ using the 2-norm. $\boldsymbol{A}_1$ rotates the unit circle clockwise by 30 degrees but does not change the Euclidean length of any vector, so $\text{cond}_2(\boldsymbol{A}_1) = 1$. $\boldsymbol{A}_2$ stretches the basis vector $\boldsymbol{e}_1$ by a factor of 2 and shrinks the basis vector $\boldsymbol{e}_2$ by a factor of 0.5, and these are both maximal, so $\text{cond}_2(\boldsymbol{A}_2) = 2/0.5 = 4$. $\boldsymbol{A}_3$ both rotates and distorts the unit circle, but the maximum ratio is still the same as with $\boldsymbol{A}_2$, so $\text{cond}_2(\boldsymbol{A}_3) = 4$. Finally, $\boldsymbol{A}_4$ is a more general transformation under which the maximum ratio no longer occurs for the basis vectors, but the value of the maximum is still the same, so $\text{cond}_2(\boldsymbol{A}_4) = 4$.

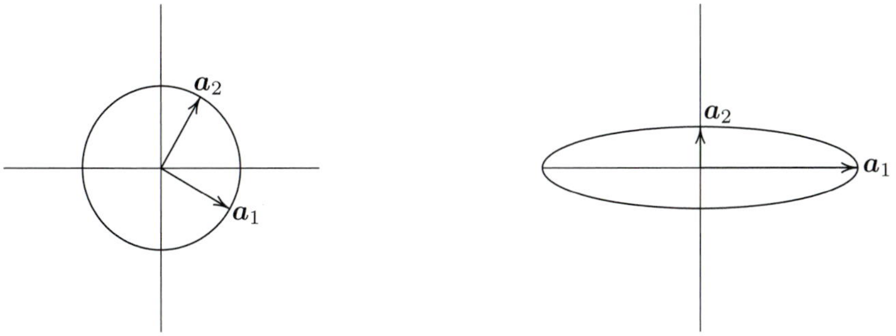

$$\boldsymbol{A}_1 = \begin{bmatrix} 0.87 & 0.5 \\ -0.5 & 0.87 \end{bmatrix}, \quad \text{cond}_2(\boldsymbol{A}_1) = 1 \qquad \boldsymbol{A}_2 = \begin{bmatrix} 2 & 0 \\ 0 & 0.5 \end{bmatrix}, \quad \text{cond}_2(\boldsymbol{A}_2) = 4$$

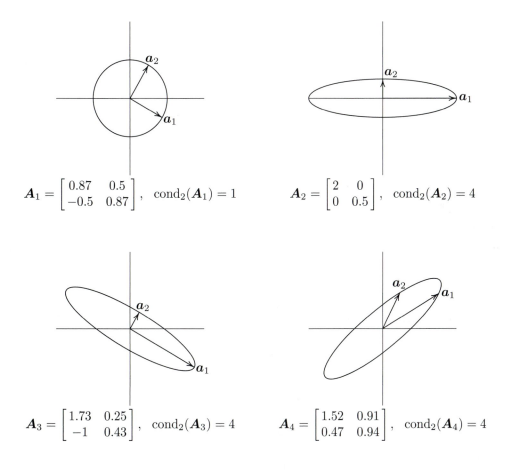

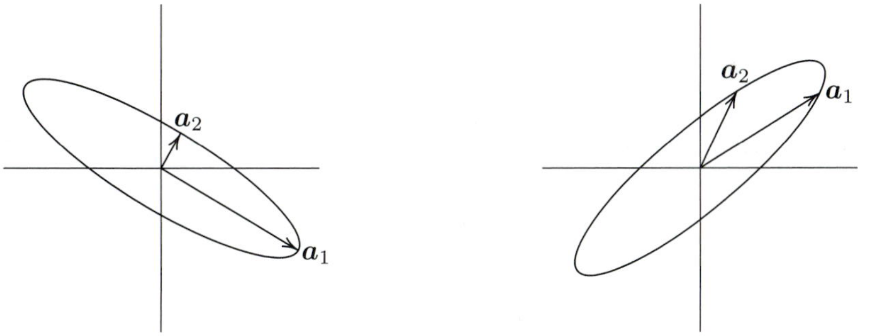

$$\boldsymbol{A}_3 = \begin{bmatrix} 1.73 & 0.25 \\ -1 & 0.43 \end{bmatrix}, \quad \text{cond}_2(\boldsymbol{A}_3) = 4 \qquad \boldsymbol{A}_4 = \begin{bmatrix} 1.52 & 0.91 \\ 0.47 & 0.94 \end{bmatrix}, \quad \text{cond}_2(\boldsymbol{A}_4) = 4$$

Figure 2.3: Transformation of unit circle in 2-norm by various matrices.

The following important properties of the condition number are easily derived from the definition and hold for any norm:

1. For any matrix $\boldsymbol{A}$, $\text{cond}(\boldsymbol{A}) \geq 1$.
2. For the identity matrix, $\text{cond}(\boldsymbol{I}) = 1$.
3. For any matrix $\boldsymbol{A}$ and nonzero scalar γ, $\text{cond}(\gamma\boldsymbol{A}) = \text{cond}(\boldsymbol{A})$.
4. For any diagonal matrix $\boldsymbol{D} = \text{diag}(d_i)$, $\text{cond}(\boldsymbol{D}) = (\max|d_i|)/(\min|d_i|)$.

The condition number is a measure of how close a matrix is to being singular: a matrix with a large condition number (which we will quantify in Section 2.3.4) is nearly singular, whereas a matrix with a condition number close to 1 is far from being singular. It is obvious from the definition that a nonsingular matrix and its inverse have the same condition number. This stands to reason, since if a matrix is nearly singular, then its inverse is equally close to being singular.

Note that the determinant of a matrix is *not* a good indicator of near singularity: although a matrix $\boldsymbol{A}$ is singular if $\det(\boldsymbol{A}) = 0$, the magnitude of a nonzero determinant, large or small, gives no information on how close to singular the matrix may be. For example, $\det(\alpha\boldsymbol{I}_n) = \alpha^n$, which can be arbitrarily small for $|\alpha| < 1$, yet the matrix is perfectly well-conditioned for any nonzero α, with a condition number of 1 in any matrix norm.

As we will see shortly, the usefulness of the condition number is in assessing the accuracy of solutions to linear systems. The definition of the condition number involves the inverse of the matrix, so computing its value is obviously a nontrivial task. In fact, to compute the condition number directly from its definition would require substantially more work than computing the solution whose accuracy is to be assessed using the condition number. In practice, therefore, the condition number is merely estimated, to perhaps within an order of magnitude, as a relatively inexpensive byproduct of the solution process.

The matrix norm $\|\boldsymbol{A}\|$ is easily computed as the maximum absolute column sum (or row sum, depending on the norm used). It is estimating $\|\boldsymbol{A}^{-1}\|$ at low cost that presents a challenge. From the properties of norms, we know that if $\boldsymbol{z}$ is the solution to $\boldsymbol{Az} = \boldsymbol{y}$, then

$$\|\boldsymbol{z}\| = \|\boldsymbol{A}^{-1}\boldsymbol{y}\| \leq \|\boldsymbol{A}^{-1}\| \cdot \|\boldsymbol{y}\|,$$

so that

$$\frac{\|\boldsymbol{z}\|}{\|\boldsymbol{y}\|} \leq \|\boldsymbol{A}^{-1}\|,$$

and this bound is achieved for some optimally chosen vector $\boldsymbol{y}$. Thus, if we can choose a vector $\boldsymbol{y}$ such that the ratio $\|\boldsymbol{z}\|/\|\boldsymbol{y}\|$ is as large as possible, then we will have a reasonable estimate for $\|\boldsymbol{A}^{-1}\|$.

Example 2.7 Condition Estimation. Consider the matrix

$$\boldsymbol{A} = \begin{bmatrix} 0.913 & 0.659 \\ 0.457 & 0.330 \end{bmatrix}.$$

If we choose $\boldsymbol{y} = [0,\ 1.5]^T$, then $\boldsymbol{z} = [-7780,\ 10780]^T$, so that

$$\|\boldsymbol{A}^{-1}\|_1 \approx \frac{\|\boldsymbol{z}\|_1}{\|\boldsymbol{y}\|_1} \approx 1.238 \times 10^4,$$

and hence

$$\text{cond}_1(\boldsymbol{A}) = \|\boldsymbol{A}\|_1 \cdot \|\boldsymbol{A}^{-1}\|_1 \approx 1.370 \times 1.238 \times 10^4 = 1.696 \times 10^4,$$

which turns out to be exact to the number of digits shown. The ramifications of this relatively large condition number will be explored in Examples 2.8 and 2.17.

The vector $\boldsymbol{y}$ in Example 2.7 was carefully chosen to produce the maximum possible ratio $\|\boldsymbol{z}\|/\|\boldsymbol{y}\|$, and hence the correct value for $\|\boldsymbol{A}^{-1}\|$. Finding such an optimal $\boldsymbol{y}$ would be prohibitively expensive, in general, but a useful approximation can be obtained much more cheaply. One heuristic is to choose $\boldsymbol{y}$ as the solution to the system $\boldsymbol{A}^T\boldsymbol{y} = \boldsymbol{c}$, where $\boldsymbol{c}$ is a vector whose components are ± 1, with the signs chosen successively to make the resulting $\boldsymbol{y}$ as large as possible. Another strategy is simply to try a few random choices for $\boldsymbol{y}$; taking the maximum ratio among them usually yields an estimate for $\|\boldsymbol{A}^{-1}\|$ that is close enough for practical purposes.

An alternative approach to condition estimation is to treat it as a convex optimization problem that can be solved very efficiently in practice using a heuristic algorithm. Still another option, when using the 2-norm, is to obtain the condition number from the singular value decomposition (see Section 3.6.1), but this is prohibitively expensive unless the SVD is already being computed anyway for other reasons. Fortunately, users need not worry about these details, as most good modern software packages for solving linear systems provide an efficient and reliable condition estimator, based on a sophisticated implementation of one of the methods outlined here (see Table 2.1).

2.3.4 Error Bounds

In addition to being a reliable indicator of near singularity, the condition number also provides a quantitative bound for the error in the computed solution to a linear system, as we will now show. Let $\boldsymbol{x}$ be the solution to the nonsingular linear system $\boldsymbol{A}\boldsymbol{x} = \boldsymbol{b}$, and let $\hat{\boldsymbol{x}}$ be the solution to the system $\boldsymbol{A}\hat{\boldsymbol{x}} = \boldsymbol{b} + \Delta\boldsymbol{b}$ with a perturbed right-hand side. If we define $\Delta\boldsymbol{x} = \hat{\boldsymbol{x}} - \boldsymbol{x}$, then we have

$$\boldsymbol{A}\hat{\boldsymbol{x}} = \boldsymbol{A}(\boldsymbol{x} + \Delta\boldsymbol{x}) = \boldsymbol{A}\boldsymbol{x} + \boldsymbol{A}\,\Delta\boldsymbol{x} = \boldsymbol{b} + \Delta\boldsymbol{b}.$$

Because $\boldsymbol{A}\boldsymbol{x} = \boldsymbol{b}$, we must have $\boldsymbol{A}\,\Delta\boldsymbol{x} = \Delta\boldsymbol{b}$, and hence $\Delta\boldsymbol{x} = \boldsymbol{A}^{-1}\Delta\boldsymbol{b}$. Taking norms, we obtain the inequalities

$$\|\boldsymbol{b}\| = \|\boldsymbol{A}\boldsymbol{x}\| \le \|\boldsymbol{A}\| \cdot \|\boldsymbol{x}\|, \quad \text{or} \quad \|\boldsymbol{x}\| \ge \|\boldsymbol{b}\|/\|\boldsymbol{A}\|,$$

and

$$\|\Delta\boldsymbol{x}\| = \|\boldsymbol{A}^{-1}\Delta\boldsymbol{b}\| \le \|\boldsymbol{A}^{-1}\| \cdot \|\Delta\boldsymbol{b}\|.$$

Combining these inequalities, we obtain

$$\frac{\|\Delta\boldsymbol{x}\|}{\|\boldsymbol{x}\|} \le \|\boldsymbol{A}^{-1}\| \cdot \|\Delta\boldsymbol{b}\| \frac{\|\boldsymbol{A}\|}{\|\boldsymbol{b}\|}.$$

By definition $\|\boldsymbol{A}\| \cdot \|\boldsymbol{A}^{-1}\| = \text{cond}(\boldsymbol{A})$, so we therefore obtain the bound

$$\frac{\|\Delta \boldsymbol{x}\|}{\|\boldsymbol{x}\|} \le \text{cond}(\boldsymbol{A}) \frac{\|\Delta \boldsymbol{b}\|}{\|\boldsymbol{b}\|}.$$

Thus, the condition number of the matrix is an "amplification factor" that bounds the maximum relative change in the solution due to a given relative change in the right-hand-side vector (compare with the general notion of condition number defined in Section 1.2.6).

A similar result holds for relative changes in the entries of the matrix $\boldsymbol{A}$. If $\boldsymbol{A}\boldsymbol{x} = \boldsymbol{b}$ and $(\boldsymbol{A} + \boldsymbol{E})\hat{\boldsymbol{x}} = \boldsymbol{b}$, then

$$\Delta \boldsymbol{x} = \hat{\boldsymbol{x}} - \boldsymbol{x} = \boldsymbol{A}^{-1}(\boldsymbol{A}\hat{\boldsymbol{x}} - \boldsymbol{b}) = -\boldsymbol{A}^{-1}\boldsymbol{E}\hat{\boldsymbol{x}}.$$

Taking norms, we obtain the inequality

$$\|\Delta \boldsymbol{x}\| \le \|\boldsymbol{A}^{-1}\| \cdot \|\boldsymbol{E}\| \cdot \|\hat{\boldsymbol{x}}\|,$$

which, upon using the definition of $\text{cond}(\boldsymbol{A})$, yields the bound

$$\frac{\|\Delta \boldsymbol{x}\|}{\|\hat{\boldsymbol{x}}\|} \le \text{cond}(\boldsymbol{A}) \frac{\|\boldsymbol{E}\|}{\|\boldsymbol{A}\|}.$$

As an alternative to the algebraic derivations just given, calculus can be used to estimate the sensitivity of linear systems. Introducing the real-valued parameter t, we define $\boldsymbol{A}(t) = \boldsymbol{A} + t\boldsymbol{E}$ and $\boldsymbol{b}(t) = \boldsymbol{b} + t\Delta\boldsymbol{b}$, and consider the solution $\boldsymbol{x}(t)$ to the linear system $\boldsymbol{A}(t)\boldsymbol{x}(t) = \boldsymbol{b}(t)$. Differentiating this equation with respect to t, we obtain

$$\boldsymbol{A}'(t)\boldsymbol{x}(t) + \boldsymbol{A}(t)\boldsymbol{x}'(t) = \boldsymbol{b}'(t),$$

or equivalently,

$$\boldsymbol{E}\boldsymbol{x}(t) + \boldsymbol{A}(t)\boldsymbol{x}'(t) = \Delta\boldsymbol{b}.$$

Rearranging, we then have

$$\boldsymbol{x}'(t) = \boldsymbol{A}(t)^{-1}(\Delta\boldsymbol{b} - \boldsymbol{E}\boldsymbol{x}(t)),$$

which gives

$$\boldsymbol{x}'(0) = \boldsymbol{A}^{-1}(\Delta\boldsymbol{b} - \boldsymbol{E}\boldsymbol{x}(0)).$$

Now by Taylor's Theorem, $\boldsymbol{x}(t) = \boldsymbol{x}(0) + t\boldsymbol{x}'(0) + \mathcal{O}(t^2)$, so that we have

$$\boldsymbol{x}(t) - \boldsymbol{x}(0) = t\boldsymbol{x}'(0) + \mathcal{O}(t^2) = t\boldsymbol{A}^{-1}(\Delta\boldsymbol{b} - \boldsymbol{E}\boldsymbol{x}(0)) + \mathcal{O}(t^2).$$

Writing $\boldsymbol{x} \equiv \boldsymbol{x}(0)$, taking norms, and dividing by $\|\boldsymbol{x}\|$, we obtain the bound

$$\begin{aligned}
\frac{\|\boldsymbol{x}(t) - \boldsymbol{x}\|}{\|\boldsymbol{x}\|} &\le \|\boldsymbol{A}^{-1}\| \left(\frac{\|\Delta\boldsymbol{b}\|}{\|\boldsymbol{x}\|} + \|\boldsymbol{E}\| \right) |t| + \mathcal{O}(t^2) \\
&\le \text{cond}(\boldsymbol{A}) \left(\frac{\|\Delta\boldsymbol{b}\|}{\|\boldsymbol{A}\| \cdot \|\boldsymbol{x}\|} + \frac{\|\boldsymbol{E}\|}{\|\boldsymbol{A}\|} \right) |t| + \mathcal{O}(t^2) \\
&\le \text{cond}(\boldsymbol{A}) \left(\frac{\|\Delta\boldsymbol{b}\|}{\|\boldsymbol{b}\|} + \frac{\|\boldsymbol{E}\|}{\|\boldsymbol{A}\|} \right) |t| + \mathcal{O}(t^2).
\end{aligned}$$

Thus, we again see that the relative change in the solution is bounded by the condition number times the relative change in the problem data.

A geometric interpretation of these sensitivity results in two dimensions is that if the straight lines defined by the two equations are nearly parallel, then their point of intersection is not sharply defined if the lines are a bit uncertain because of rounding or measurement error. If, on the other hand, the lines are far from parallel, say nearly perpendicular, then their intersection is relatively sharply defined. These two cases are illustrated in Fig. 2.4, where the dashed lines indicate the region of uncertainty for each solid line, so that the intersection point in each case could be anywhere within the shaded parallelogram. Thus, a large condition number is associated with a large uncertainty in the solution.

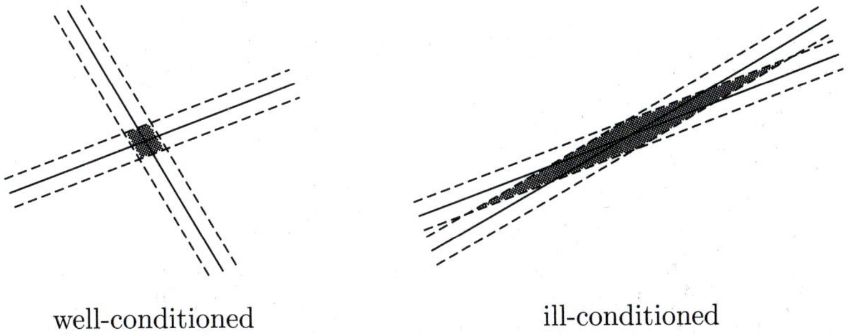

Figure 2.4: Well-conditioned and ill-conditioned linear systems.

To summarize, if the input data are accurate to machine precision, then we can expect the relative error in an approximate solution $\hat{\boldsymbol{x}}$ to a linear system $\boldsymbol{A}\boldsymbol{x} = \boldsymbol{b}$ to be bounded by

$$\frac{\|\hat{\boldsymbol{x}} - \boldsymbol{x}\|}{\|\boldsymbol{x}\|} \lessapprox \operatorname{cond}(\boldsymbol{A})\, \epsilon_{\text{mach}}.$$

Interpreting this result in terms of backward error analysis, we observe that a computed solution can be expected to lose about $\log_{10}(\operatorname{cond}(\boldsymbol{A}))$ decimal digits of accuracy relative to the accuracy of the input. The matrix in Example 2.7, for instance, has a condition number greater than 10^4, so we would expect no correct digits in the solution to a linear system with this matrix unless the input data are accurate to more than four decimal digits and the working precision carries more than four decimal digits (see Examples 2.8 and 2.17).

As a quantitative measure of sensitivity, the matrix condition number plays the same role for the problem of solving linear systems—and yields the same type of relationship between forward and backward error—as the general notion of condition number defined in Section 1.2.6. An important difference, however, is that the matrix condition number is never less than 1.

Before leaving the subject of assessing accuracy in terms of condition numbers, note these two caveats:

- The foregoing analysis using norms provides a bound on the relative error in the *largest* components of the solution vector. The *relative* error in the smaller components can be much larger, because a vector norm is dominated by the largest components of a vector. Componentwise error bounds can be obtained but are somewhat more complicated to compute, and we will not pursue this topic. Componentwise bounds are of particular interest when the system is poorly scaled (see Section 2.4.10).

- The condition number of a matrix is affected by the scaling of the matrix (see Example 2.10). A large condition number can result simply from poor scaling (see Example 2.20), as well as from near singularity. Rescaling the matrix can help the former, but not the latter (see Section 2.4.10).

2.3.5 Residual

One way to verify a solution to an equation is to substitute it into the equation and see how closely the left and right sides match. The *residual* of an approximate solution $\hat{\boldsymbol{x}}$ to a linear system $\boldsymbol{A}\boldsymbol{x} = \boldsymbol{b}$ is the difference

$$\boldsymbol{r} = \boldsymbol{b} - \boldsymbol{A}\hat{\boldsymbol{x}}.$$

If $\boldsymbol{A}$ is nonsingular, then in theory the error $\|\Delta\boldsymbol{x}\| = \|\hat{\boldsymbol{x}} - \boldsymbol{x}\| = 0$ if, and only if, $\|\boldsymbol{r}\| = 0$. In practice, however, these quantities are not necessarily small simultaneously. First, note that if the equation $\boldsymbol{A}\boldsymbol{x} = \boldsymbol{b}$ is multiplied by an arbitrary nonzero constant, then the solution is unaffected, but the residual is multiplied by the same factor. Thus, the residual can be made arbitrarily large or small, depending on the scaling of the problem, and hence the size of the residual is meaningless unless it is considered relative to the size of the problem data and the solution. For this reason, the *relative residual* for the approximate solution $\hat{\boldsymbol{x}}$ is defined to be $\|\boldsymbol{r}\|/(\|\boldsymbol{A}\|\cdot\|\hat{\boldsymbol{x}}\|)$.

To relate the error to the residual, we observe that

$$\|\Delta\boldsymbol{x}\| = \|\hat{\boldsymbol{x}} - \boldsymbol{x}\| = \|\boldsymbol{A}^{-1}(\boldsymbol{A}\hat{\boldsymbol{x}} - \boldsymbol{b})\| = \|-\boldsymbol{A}^{-1}\boldsymbol{r}\| \le \|\boldsymbol{A}^{-1}\|\cdot\|\boldsymbol{r}\|,$$

Dividing both sides by $\|\hat{\boldsymbol{x}}\|$ and using the definition of $\text{cond}(\boldsymbol{A})$, we then have

$$\frac{\|\Delta\boldsymbol{x}\|}{\|\hat{\boldsymbol{x}}\|} \le \text{cond}(\boldsymbol{A})\frac{\|\boldsymbol{r}\|}{\|\boldsymbol{A}\|\cdot\|\hat{\boldsymbol{x}}\|}.$$

Thus, a small relative residual implies a small relative error in the solution when, and only when, $\boldsymbol{A}$ is well-conditioned.

To see the implications of a large residual, on the other hand, suppose that the computed solution $\hat{\boldsymbol{x}}$ exactly satisfies

$$(\boldsymbol{A} + \boldsymbol{E})\hat{\boldsymbol{x}} = \boldsymbol{b}.$$

Then

$$\|\boldsymbol{r}\| = \|\boldsymbol{b} - \boldsymbol{A}\hat{\boldsymbol{x}}\| = \|\boldsymbol{E}\hat{\boldsymbol{x}}\| \le \|\boldsymbol{E}\|\cdot\|\hat{\boldsymbol{x}}\|,$$

so that we have the inequality

$$\frac{\|\boldsymbol{r}\|}{\|\boldsymbol{A}\|\cdot\|\hat{\boldsymbol{x}}\|} \le \frac{\|\boldsymbol{E}\|}{\|\boldsymbol{A}\|}.$$

Thus, a large relative residual implies a large backward error in the matrix, which means that the algorithm used to compute the solution is unstable. Another way of saying this is that a stable algorithm will invariably produce a solution with a small relative residual, irrespective of the conditioning of the problem, and hence a small residual, by itself, sheds little light on the quality of the approximate solution. We will comment further on this issue in Section 2.4.5.

Example 2.8 Small Residual. Consider the linear system

$$\boldsymbol{Ax} = \begin{bmatrix} 0.913 & 0.659 \\ 0.457 & 0.330 \end{bmatrix} \begin{bmatrix} x_1 \\ x_2 \end{bmatrix} = \begin{bmatrix} 0.254 \\ 0.127 \end{bmatrix} = \boldsymbol{b},$$

whose matrix we saw in Example 2.7. Consider two approximate solutions

$$\hat{\boldsymbol{x}}_1 = \begin{bmatrix} -0.0827 \\ 0.5 \end{bmatrix} \quad \text{and} \quad \hat{\boldsymbol{x}}_2 = \begin{bmatrix} 0.999 \\ -1.001 \end{bmatrix}.$$

The norms of their respective residuals are

$$\|\boldsymbol{r}_1\|_1 = 2.1 \times 10^{-4} \quad \text{and} \quad \|\boldsymbol{r}_2\|_1 = 2.4 \times 10^{-2}.$$

So which is the better solution? We are tempted to say $\hat{\boldsymbol{x}}_1$ because of its much smaller residual. But the exact solution to this system is $\boldsymbol{x} = [1, \; -1]^T$, as is easily confirmed, so $\hat{\boldsymbol{x}}_2$ is actually much more accurate than $\hat{\boldsymbol{x}}_1$. The reason for this surprising behavior is that the matrix $\boldsymbol{A}$ is ill-conditioned, as we saw in Example 2.7, and because of its large condition number, a small residual does not imply a small error in the solution. To see how $\hat{\boldsymbol{x}}_1$ was obtained, see Example 2.17.

2.4 Solving Linear Systems

2.4.1 Problem Transformations

To solve a linear system $\boldsymbol{Ax} = \boldsymbol{b}$, the general strategy outlined in Section 1.1.2 suggests that we should transform the system into one whose solution is the same as that of the original system but is easier to compute. What type of transformation of a linear system leaves the solution unchanged? The answer is that we can premultiply (i.e., multiply from the left) both sides of the linear system $\boldsymbol{Ax} = \boldsymbol{b}$ by any nonsingular matrix $\boldsymbol{M}$ without affecting the solution. To see why, note that the solution to the linear system $\boldsymbol{MAz} = \boldsymbol{Mb}$ is given by

$$\boldsymbol{z} = (\boldsymbol{MA})^{-1}\boldsymbol{Mb} = \boldsymbol{A}^{-1}\boldsymbol{M}^{-1}\boldsymbol{Mb} = \boldsymbol{A}^{-1}\boldsymbol{b} = \boldsymbol{x}.$$

Example 2.9 Permutations. An important example of such a transformation is the fact that the rows of $\boldsymbol{A}$ and corresponding entries of $\boldsymbol{b}$ can be reordered without changing the solution $\boldsymbol{x}$. This is intuitively obvious: all of the equations in the system must be satisfied simultaneously, so the order in which they happen to be written down is irrelevant; they may as well have been drawn randomly from a hat. Formally, such a reordering of the rows is accomplished by premultiplying both sides of the equation by a *permutation* matrix $\boldsymbol{P}$, which is a square matrix having exactly one 1 in each row and column and zeros elsewhere (i.e., an identity matrix with its rows and columns permuted). For example,

$$\begin{bmatrix} 0 & 0 & 1 \\ 1 & 0 & 0 \\ 0 & 1 & 0 \end{bmatrix} \begin{bmatrix} v_1 \\ v_2 \\ v_3 \end{bmatrix} = \begin{bmatrix} v_3 \\ v_1 \\ v_2 \end{bmatrix}.$$

A permutation matrix is always nonsingular; in fact, its inverse is simply its transpose, $\boldsymbol{P}^{-1} = \boldsymbol{P}^T$ (the *transpose* of a matrix $\boldsymbol{M}$, denoted by $\boldsymbol{M}^T$, is a matrix whose columns are the rows of $\boldsymbol{M}$, that is, if $\boldsymbol{N} = \boldsymbol{M}^T$, then $n_{ij} = m_{ji}$). Thus, the reordered system can be written $\boldsymbol{PAx} = \boldsymbol{Pb}$, and the solution $\boldsymbol{x}$ is unchanged.

Postmultiplying (i.e., multiplying from the right) by a permutation matrix reorders the columns of the matrix instead of the rows. Such a transformation *does* change the solution, but only in that the components of the solution are permuted. To see this, observe that the solution to the system $\boldsymbol{APz} = \boldsymbol{b}$ is given by

$$\boldsymbol{z} = (\boldsymbol{AP})^{-1}\boldsymbol{b} = \boldsymbol{P}^{-1}\boldsymbol{A}^{-1}\boldsymbol{b} = \boldsymbol{P}^T\boldsymbol{A}^{-1}\boldsymbol{b} = \boldsymbol{P}^T\boldsymbol{x},$$

and hence the solution to the original system $\boldsymbol{Ax} = \boldsymbol{b}$ is given by $\boldsymbol{x}=\boldsymbol{Pz}$.

Example 2.10 Diagonal Scaling. Another simple but important type of transformation is *diagonal scaling*. Recall that a matrix $\boldsymbol{D}$ is *diagonal* if $d_{ij} = 0$ for all $i \neq j$, that is, the only nonzero entries are $d_{ii}, i = 1, \ldots, n$, on the *main diagonal*. Premultiplying both sides of a linear system $\boldsymbol{Ax} = \boldsymbol{b}$ by a nonsingular diagonal matrix $\boldsymbol{D}$ multiplies each row of the matrix and right-hand side by the corresponding diagonal entry of $\boldsymbol{D}$, and hence is called *row scaling*. In principle, row scaling does not change the solution to the linear system, but in practice it can affect the numerical solution process and the accuracy that can be attained for a given problem, as we will see.

Column scaling—postmultiplying the matrix of a linear system by a nonsingular diagonal matrix $\boldsymbol{D}$—multiplies each column of the matrix by the corresponding diagonal entry of $\boldsymbol{D}$. Such a transformation does alter the solution, in effect changing the units in which the components of the solution are measured. The solution to the scaled system $\boldsymbol{ADz} = \boldsymbol{b}$ is given by

$$\boldsymbol{z} = (\boldsymbol{AD})^{-1}\boldsymbol{b} = \boldsymbol{D}^{-1}\boldsymbol{A}^{-1}\boldsymbol{b} = \boldsymbol{D}^{-1}\boldsymbol{x},$$

and hence the solution to the original system $\boldsymbol{Ax} = \boldsymbol{b}$ is given by $\boldsymbol{x}=\boldsymbol{Dz}$.

2.4.2 Triangular Linear Systems

The next question is what type of linear system is easy to solve. Suppose there is an equation in the system $\boldsymbol{Ax} = \boldsymbol{b}$ that involves only one of the unknown solution components (i.e., only one entry in that row of $\boldsymbol{A}$ is nonzero). Then that equation can easily be solved (by division) for that unknown. Now suppose there is another equation in the system that involves only two unknowns, one of which is the one already determined. By substituting the one solution component already determined into this second equation, we can then easily solve for its other unknown. If this pattern continues, with only one new unknown component arising per equation, then all of the solution components can be computed in succession. A matrix with this special property is called *triangular*, for reasons that will soon become apparent. Because triangular linear systems are easily solved by this successive substitution process, they are a suitable target in transforming a general linear system.

Although the general triangular form just described is all that is required to enable the system to be solved by successive substitution, it is convenient to define two specific triangular forms for computational purposes. A matrix $\boldsymbol{L}$ is *lower triangular* if all of its entries above the main diagonal are zero (i.e., if $\ell_{ij} = 0$ for $i < j$). Similarly, a matrix $\boldsymbol{U}$ is *upper triangular* if all of its entries below the main diagonal are zero (i.e., if $u_{ij} = 0$ for $i > j$). A matrix that is triangular in the more general sense defined earlier can be permuted into upper or lower triangular form by a suitable permutation of its rows or columns.

For a lower triangular system $\boldsymbol{Lx} = \boldsymbol{b}$, successive substitution is called *forward-substitution* and can be expressed mathematically as

$$x_1 = b_1/\ell_{11}, \qquad x_i = \left(b_i - \sum_{j=1}^{i-1} \ell_{ij} x_j\right) \Big/ \ell_{ii}, \quad i = 2, \ldots, n.$$

One way to implement it is shown in Algorithm 2.1.

Algorithm 2.1 Forward-Substitution for Lower Triangular System

```
for j = 1 to n                    { loop over columns }
    if ℓ_jj = 0 then stop         { stop if matrix is singular }
    x_j = b_j/ℓ_jj                { compute solution component }
    for i = j + 1 to n
        b_i = b_i − ℓ_ij x_j      { update right-hand side }
    end
end
```

Similarly, for an upper triangular system $\boldsymbol{Ux} = \boldsymbol{b}$, successive substitution is called *back-substitution* and can be expressed mathematically as

$$x_n = b_n/u_{nn}, \qquad x_i = \left(b_i - \sum_{j=i+1}^{n} u_{ij} x_j\right) \Big/ u_{ii}, \quad i = n-1, \ldots, 1.$$

One way to implement it is shown in Algorithm 2.2.

For both of these algorithms, we have chosen the ordering of the loop indices so that the matrix is accessed by columns (rather than by rows), and the inner-loop operation is a scalar times a vector plus a vector, or "saxpy" (see Section 2.7.2).

Algorithm 2.2 Back-Substitution for Upper Triangular System

```
for j = n to 1                      { loop backwards over columns }
    if u_jj = 0 then stop           { stop if matrix is singular }
    x_j = b_j / u_jj                { compute solution component }
    for i = 1 to j − 1
        b_i = b_i − u_ij x_j        { update right-hand side }
    end
end
```

We could also have chosen the opposite ordering of the loop indices, in which case the matrix would be accessed by rows, and the inner-loop operation would be an inner product of two vectors, or "sdot." These implementation choices may have a significant impact on performance, depending on the particular programming language and computer system used (see Computer Problem 2.16). Also note that a zero diagonal entry will cause either of the algorithms to fail, but this is to be expected, since a triangular matrix with a zero diagonal entry must be singular.

Example 2.11 Triangular Linear System. Consider the upper triangular linear system

$$\begin{bmatrix} 1 & 2 & 2 \\ 0 & -4 & -6 \\ 0 & 0 & -1 \end{bmatrix} \begin{bmatrix} x_1 \\ x_2 \\ x_3 \end{bmatrix} = \begin{bmatrix} 3 \\ -6 \\ 1 \end{bmatrix}.$$

The last equation, $-x_3 = 1$, can be solved directly for $x_3 = -1$. This value can then be substituted into the second equation to obtain $x_2 = 3$, and finally both x_3 and x_2 are substituted into the first equation to obtain $x_1 = -1$.

2.4.3 Elementary Elimination Matrices

Our strategy then is to devise a nonsingular linear transformation that transforms a given general linear system into a triangular linear system that we can then solve easily by successive substitution. Thus, we need a transformation that replaces selected nonzero entries of the given matrix with zeros. This can be accomplished by taking appropriate linear combinations of the rows of the matrix, as we will now show.

Consider the 2-vector $\boldsymbol{a} = [a_1 \quad a_2]^T$. If $a_1 \neq 0$, then

$$\begin{bmatrix} 1 & 0 \\ -a_2/a_1 & 1 \end{bmatrix} \begin{bmatrix} a_1 \\ a_2 \end{bmatrix} = \begin{bmatrix} a_1 \\ 0 \end{bmatrix}.$$

More generally, given an n-vector $\boldsymbol{a}$, we can annihilate *all* of its entries below the

kth position, provided that $a_k \neq 0$, by the following transformation:

$$M_k\, a = \begin{bmatrix} 1 & \cdots & 0 & 0 & \cdots & 0 \\ \vdots & \ddots & \vdots & \vdots & \ddots & \vdots \\ 0 & \cdots & 1 & 0 & \cdots & 0 \\ 0 & \cdots & -m_{k+1} & 1 & \cdots & 0 \\ \vdots & \ddots & \vdots & \vdots & \ddots & \vdots \\ 0 & \cdots & -m_n & 0 & \cdots & 1 \end{bmatrix} \begin{bmatrix} a_1 \\ \vdots \\ a_k \\ a_{k+1} \\ \vdots \\ a_n \end{bmatrix} = \begin{bmatrix} a_1 \\ \vdots \\ a_k \\ 0 \\ \vdots \\ 0 \end{bmatrix},$$

where $m_i = a_i/a_k$, $i = k+1, \ldots, n$. The divisor a_k is called the *pivot*. A matrix of this form is sometimes called an *elementary elimination matrix* or *Gauss transformation*, and its effect on a vector is to add a multiple of row k to each subsequent row, with the multipliers m_i chosen so that the result in each case is zero. Note the following facts about these elementary elimination matrices:

1. M_k is a lower triangular matrix with unit main diagonal, and hence it must be nonsingular.
2. $M_k = I - m_k e_k^T$, where $m_k = [0, \ldots, 0, m_{k+1}, \ldots, m_n]^T$ and e_k is the kth column of the identity matrix.
3. $M_k^{-1} = I + m_k e_k^T$, which means that M_k^{-1}, which we will denote by L_k, is the same as M_k except that the signs of the multipliers are reversed.
4. If M_j, $j > k$, is another elementary elimination matrix, with vector of multipliers m_j, then

$$M_k M_j = I - m_k e_k^T - m_j e_j^T + m_k e_k^T m_j e_j^T = I - m_k e_k^T - m_j e_j^T,$$

since $e_k^T m_j = 0$. Thus, their product is essentially their "union." Because they have the same form, a similar result holds for the product of their inverses, $L_k L_j$. Note that the order of multiplication is significant; these results do not hold for the reverse product.

Example 2.12 Elementary Elimination Matrices. If $a = [2 \;\; 4 \;\; -2]^T$, then

$$M_1 a = \begin{bmatrix} 1 & 0 & 0 \\ -2 & 1 & 0 \\ 1 & 0 & 1 \end{bmatrix} \begin{bmatrix} 2 \\ 4 \\ -2 \end{bmatrix} = \begin{bmatrix} 2 \\ 0 \\ 0 \end{bmatrix}, \quad M_2 a = \begin{bmatrix} 1 & 0 & 0 \\ 0 & 1 & 0 \\ 0 & 0.5 & 1 \end{bmatrix} \begin{bmatrix} 2 \\ 4 \\ -2 \end{bmatrix} = \begin{bmatrix} 2 \\ 4 \\ 0 \end{bmatrix}.$$

We also note that

$$L_1 = M_1^{-1} = \begin{bmatrix} 1 & 0 & 0 \\ 2 & 1 & 0 \\ -1 & 0 & 1 \end{bmatrix}, \quad L_2 = M_2^{-1} = \begin{bmatrix} 1 & 0 & 0 \\ 0 & 1 & 0 \\ 0 & -0.5 & 1 \end{bmatrix},$$

and

$$M_1 M_2 = \begin{bmatrix} 1 & 0 & 0 \\ -2 & 1 & 0 \\ 1 & 0.5 & 1 \end{bmatrix}, \quad L_1 L_2 = \begin{bmatrix} 1 & 0 & 0 \\ 2 & 1 & 0 \\ -1 & -0.5 & 1 \end{bmatrix}.$$

2.4.4 Gaussian Elimination and LU Factorization

Using elementary elimination matrices, it is a fairly simple matter to reduce a general linear system $\boldsymbol{Ax} = \boldsymbol{b}$ to upper triangular form. We first choose an elementary elimination matrix $\boldsymbol{M}_1$ according to the recipe given in Section 2.4.3, with the first diagonal entry a_{11} as pivot, so that the first column of $\boldsymbol{A}$ becomes zero below the first row when premultiplied by $\boldsymbol{M}_1$. Of course, all of the remaining columns of $\boldsymbol{A}$, as well as the right-hand-side vector $\boldsymbol{b}$, must also be multiplied by $\boldsymbol{M}_1$, so the new system becomes $\boldsymbol{M}_1\boldsymbol{Ax} = \boldsymbol{M}_1\boldsymbol{b}$, but by our previous discussion the solution is unchanged.

Next we use the second diagonal entry as pivot to determine a second elementary elimination matrix $\boldsymbol{M}_2$ that annihilates all of the entries of the second column of the new matrix, $\boldsymbol{M}_1\boldsymbol{A}$, below the second row. Again, $\boldsymbol{M}_2$ must be applied to the entire matrix and right-hand-side vector, so that we obtain the further modified linear system $\boldsymbol{M}_2\boldsymbol{M}_1\boldsymbol{Ax} = \boldsymbol{M}_2\boldsymbol{M}_1\boldsymbol{b}$. Note that the first column of the matrix $\boldsymbol{M}_1\boldsymbol{A}$ is not affected by $\boldsymbol{M}_2$ because all of its entries are zero in the relevant rows. This process is continued for each successive column until all of the subdiagonal entries of the matrix have been annihilated. If we define the matrix $\boldsymbol{M} = \boldsymbol{M}_{n-1}\cdots\boldsymbol{M}_1$, then the transformed linear system

$$\boldsymbol{MAx} = \boldsymbol{M}_{n-1}\cdots\boldsymbol{M}_1\boldsymbol{Ax} = \boldsymbol{M}_{n-1}\cdots\boldsymbol{M}_1\boldsymbol{b} = \boldsymbol{Mb}$$

is upper triangular and can be solved by back-substitution to obtain the solution to the original linear system $\boldsymbol{Ax} = \boldsymbol{b}$.

The process we have just described is known as *Gaussian elimination*. It is also known as *LU factorization* or *LU decomposition* because it decomposes the matrix $\boldsymbol{A}$ into a product of a unit lower triangular matrix, $\boldsymbol{L}$, and an upper triangular matrix, $\boldsymbol{U}$. To see this, recall that the product $\boldsymbol{L}_k\boldsymbol{L}_j$ is unit lower triangular if $k < j$, so that

$$\boldsymbol{L} = \boldsymbol{M}^{-1} = (\boldsymbol{M}_{n-1}\cdots\boldsymbol{M}_1)^{-1} = \boldsymbol{M}_1^{-1}\cdots\boldsymbol{M}_{n-1}^{-1} = \boldsymbol{L}_1\cdots\boldsymbol{L}_{n-1}$$

is unit lower triangular. We have already seen that, by design, the matrix $\boldsymbol{U} = \boldsymbol{MA}$ is upper triangular. Therefore, we have expressed $\boldsymbol{A}$ as a product

$$\boldsymbol{A} = \boldsymbol{LU},$$

where $\boldsymbol{L}$ is unit lower triangular and $\boldsymbol{U}$ is upper triangular. Given such a factorization, the linear system $\boldsymbol{Ax} = \boldsymbol{b}$ can be written as $\boldsymbol{LUx} = \boldsymbol{b}$ and hence can be solved by first solving the lower triangular system $\boldsymbol{Ly} = \boldsymbol{b}$ by forward-substitution, then the upper triangular system $\boldsymbol{Ux} = \boldsymbol{y}$ by back-substitution. Note that the intermediate solution $\boldsymbol{y}$ is the same as the transformed right-hand-side vector, $\boldsymbol{Mb}$, in the previous formulation. Thus, Gaussian elimination and LU factorization are simply two ways of expressing the same solution process. However, by emphasizing the forward and backward triangular solution phases as separate from the factorization, perhaps the LU formulation makes it clearer that the factorization phase need not be repeated when solving additional systems having different right-hand-side vectors but the same matrix $\boldsymbol{A}$, since the $\boldsymbol{L}$ and $\boldsymbol{U}$ factors can be reused.

The Gaussian elimination process is summarized formally in Algorithm 2.3. This algorithm also computes the LU factorization of $\boldsymbol{A}$: the subdiagonal entries of $\boldsymbol{L}$ are given by $\ell_{ik} = m_{ik}$, and the diagonal and superdiagonal entries of $\boldsymbol{U}$ replace those of $\boldsymbol{A}$. In practice, we need not bother explicitly setting the subdiagonal entries of $\boldsymbol{A}$ to zero, since all we care about are the resulting triangular matrices $\boldsymbol{U}$ and $\boldsymbol{L}$. Indeed, the subdiagonal entries of $\boldsymbol{A}$ that have been zeroed are the perfect places to store the subdiagonal entries of $\boldsymbol{L}$: Algorithm 2.3 effectively computes the factorization "in place" if we write a_{ik} instead of m_{ik} at each occurrence (see Section 2.4.6 for these and other implementation details). In solving a linear system $\boldsymbol{Ax} = \boldsymbol{b}$, the necessary transformation of the right-hand-side vector $\boldsymbol{b}$ could be included as part of the LU factorization process, or it could be done as a separate step, using Algorithm 2.1 to solve the lower triangular system $\boldsymbol{Ly} = \boldsymbol{b}$ after $\boldsymbol{L}$ has been obtained using Algorithm 2.3. In either case, Algorithm 2.2 is then used to solve the upper triangular system $\boldsymbol{Ux} = \boldsymbol{y}$ to obtain the solution $\boldsymbol{x}$.

Algorithm 2.3 LU Factorization by Gaussian Elimination

```
for k = 1 to n − 1                    { loop over columns }
    if a_kk = 0 then stop             { stop if pivot is zero }
    for i = k + 1 to n                { compute multipliers
        m_ik = a_ik / a_kk                for current column }
    end
    for j = k + 1 to n
        for i = k + 1 to n            { apply transformation to
            a_ij = a_ij − m_ik a_kj       remaining submatrix }
        end
    end
end
```

Example 2.13 Gaussian Elimination. We illustrate Gaussian elimination by solving the linear system

$$\begin{aligned} x_1 + 2x_2 + 2x_3 &= 3, \\ 4x_1 + 4x_2 + 2x_3 &= 6, \\ 4x_1 + 6x_2 + 4x_3 &= 10, \end{aligned}$$

or in matrix notation

$$\boldsymbol{Ax} = \begin{bmatrix} 1 & 2 & 2 \\ 4 & 4 & 2 \\ 4 & 6 & 4 \end{bmatrix} \begin{bmatrix} x_1 \\ x_2 \\ x_3 \end{bmatrix} = \begin{bmatrix} 3 \\ 6 \\ 10 \end{bmatrix} = \boldsymbol{b}.$$

To annihilate the subdiagonal entries of the first column of $\boldsymbol{A}$, we subtract four times the first row from each of the second and third rows:

$$\boldsymbol{M}_1\boldsymbol{A} = \begin{bmatrix} 1 & 0 & 0 \\ -4 & 1 & 0 \\ -4 & 0 & 1 \end{bmatrix} \begin{bmatrix} 1 & 2 & 2 \\ 4 & 4 & 2 \\ 4 & 6 & 4 \end{bmatrix} = \begin{bmatrix} 1 & 2 & 2 \\ 0 & -4 & -6 \\ 0 & -2 & -4 \end{bmatrix},$$

$$M_1 b = \begin{bmatrix} 1 & 0 & 0 \\ -4 & 1 & 0 \\ -4 & 0 & 1 \end{bmatrix} \begin{bmatrix} 3 \\ 6 \\ 10 \end{bmatrix} = \begin{bmatrix} 3 \\ -6 \\ -2 \end{bmatrix}.$$

Now to annihilate the subdiagonal entry of the second column of $M_1 A$, we subtract 0.5 times the second row from the third row:

$$M_2 M_1 A = \begin{bmatrix} 1 & 0 & 0 \\ 0 & 1 & 0 \\ 0 & -0.5 & 1 \end{bmatrix} \begin{bmatrix} 1 & 2 & 2 \\ 0 & -4 & -6 \\ 0 & -2 & -4 \end{bmatrix} = \begin{bmatrix} 1 & 2 & 2 \\ 0 & -4 & -6 \\ 0 & 0 & -1 \end{bmatrix},$$

$$M_2 M_1 b = \begin{bmatrix} 1 & 0 & 0 \\ 0 & 1 & 0 \\ 0 & -0.5 & 1 \end{bmatrix} \begin{bmatrix} 3 \\ -6 \\ -2 \end{bmatrix} = \begin{bmatrix} 3 \\ -6 \\ 1 \end{bmatrix}.$$

We have therefore reduced the original system to the equivalent upper triangular system

$$U x = \begin{bmatrix} 1 & 2 & 2 \\ 0 & -4 & -6 \\ 0 & 0 & -1 \end{bmatrix} \begin{bmatrix} x_1 \\ x_2 \\ x_3 \end{bmatrix} = \begin{bmatrix} 3 \\ -6 \\ 1 \end{bmatrix} = M b = y,$$

which can now be solved by back-substitution (as in Example 2.11) to obtain $x = \begin{bmatrix} -1 & 3 & -1 \end{bmatrix}^T$. To write out the LU factorization explicitly, we have

$$L_1 L_2 = \begin{bmatrix} 1 & 0 & 0 \\ 4 & 1 & 0 \\ 4 & 0 & 1 \end{bmatrix} \begin{bmatrix} 1 & 0 & 0 \\ 0 & 1 & 0 \\ 0 & 0.5 & 1 \end{bmatrix} = \begin{bmatrix} 1 & 0 & 0 \\ 4 & 1 & 0 \\ 4 & 0.5 & 1 \end{bmatrix} = L,$$

so that

$$A = \begin{bmatrix} 1 & 2 & 2 \\ 4 & 4 & 2 \\ 4 & 6 & 4 \end{bmatrix} = \begin{bmatrix} 1 & 0 & 0 \\ 4 & 1 & 0 \\ 4 & 0.5 & 1 \end{bmatrix} \begin{bmatrix} 1 & 2 & 2 \\ 0 & -4 & -6 \\ 0 & 0 & -1 \end{bmatrix} = L U.$$

2.4.5 Pivoting

There is one obvious problem with the Gaussian elimination process as we have described it, as well as another, somewhat more subtle, problem. The obvious potential difficulty is that the process breaks down if the leading diagonal entry of the remaining unreduced portion of the matrix is zero at any stage, as computing the multipliers m_i for a given column requires division by the diagonal entry in that column. The solution to this problem is almost equally obvious: if the diagonal entry is zero at stage k, then interchange row k of the system (both matrix and right-hand-side vector) with some subsequent row whose entry in column k is nonzero. We know from Example 2.9 that such an interchange does not alter the solution to the system. With a nonzero diagonal entry as pivot, the process can then proceed as usual. Interchanging rows in this manner is called *pivoting*.

Example 2.14 Pivoting and Singularity. The potential need for pivoting has nothing to do with whether the matrix is singular. For example, the matrix

$$A = \begin{bmatrix} 0 & 1 \\ 1 & 0 \end{bmatrix}$$

is nonsingular yet has no LU factorization unless we interchange rows, whereas the singular matrix

$$A = \begin{bmatrix} 1 & 1 \\ 1 & 1 \end{bmatrix}$$

has the LU factorization

$$A = \begin{bmatrix} 1 & 1 \\ 1 & 1 \end{bmatrix} = \begin{bmatrix} 1 & 0 \\ 1 & 1 \end{bmatrix} \begin{bmatrix} 1 & 1 \\ 0 & 0 \end{bmatrix} = LU.$$

But what if there is no nonzero entry on or below the diagonal in column k? Then there is nothing to do at this stage, since all the entries to be annihilated are already zero, and we can simply move on to the next column (i.e., $M_k = I$). Note that this step leaves a zero on the diagonal, and hence the resulting upper triangular matrix U is singular, but the LU factorization can still be completed. It does mean, however, that the subsequent back-substitution process will fail, since it requires a division by each diagonal entry of U, but this is not surprising because the original matrix must have been singular anyway. A more insidious problem is that in floating-point arithmetic we may not get an exact zero, but only a very small diagonal entry, which brings us to the more subtle point.

In principle, any nonzero value will do as the pivot for computing the multipliers, but in finite-precision arithmetic the choice should be made with some care to minimize propagation of numerical error. In particular, we wish to limit the magnitudes of the multipliers so that previous rounding errors will not be amplified when the remaining portion of the matrix and right-hand side are multiplied by each elementary elimination matrix. The multipliers will never exceed 1 in magnitude if for each column we choose the entry of largest magnitude on or below the diagonal as pivot. Such a policy is called *partial pivoting*, and it is essential in practice for a numerically stable implementation of Gaussian elimination for general linear systems.

Example 2.15 Small Pivots. Using finite-precision arithmetic, we must avoid not only zero pivots but also *small* pivots in order to prevent unacceptable error growth, as shown in the following example. Let

$$A = \begin{bmatrix} \epsilon & 1 \\ 1 & 1 \end{bmatrix},$$

where ϵ is a positive number smaller than the unit roundoff ϵ_{mach} in a given floating-point system. If we do not interchange rows, then the pivot is ϵ and the resulting multiplier is $-1/\epsilon$, so that we get the elimination matrix

$$\boldsymbol{M} = \begin{bmatrix} 1 & 0 \\ -1/\epsilon & 1 \end{bmatrix},$$

and hence

$$\boldsymbol{L} = \begin{bmatrix} 1 & 0 \\ 1/\epsilon & 1 \end{bmatrix} \quad \text{and} \quad \boldsymbol{U} = \begin{bmatrix} \epsilon & 1 \\ 0 & 1 - 1/\epsilon \end{bmatrix} = \begin{bmatrix} \epsilon & 1 \\ 0 & -1/\epsilon \end{bmatrix}$$

in floating-point arithmetic. But then

$$\boldsymbol{LU} = \begin{bmatrix} 1 & 0 \\ 1/\epsilon & 1 \end{bmatrix} \begin{bmatrix} \epsilon & 1 \\ 0 & -1/\epsilon \end{bmatrix} = \begin{bmatrix} \epsilon & 1 \\ 1 & 0 \end{bmatrix} \neq \boldsymbol{A}.$$

Using a small pivot, and a correspondingly large multiplier, has caused an unrecoverable loss of information in the transformed matrix. If we interchange rows, on the other hand, then the pivot is 1 and the resulting multiplier is $-\epsilon$, so that we get the elimination matrix

$$\boldsymbol{M} = \begin{bmatrix} 1 & 0 \\ -\epsilon & 1 \end{bmatrix},$$

and hence

$$\boldsymbol{L} = \begin{bmatrix} 1 & 0 \\ \epsilon & 1 \end{bmatrix} \quad \text{and} \quad \boldsymbol{U} = \begin{bmatrix} 1 & 1 \\ 0 & 1 - \epsilon \end{bmatrix} = \begin{bmatrix} 1 & 1 \\ 0 & 1 \end{bmatrix}$$

in floating-point arithmetic. We therefore have

$$\boldsymbol{LU} = \begin{bmatrix} 1 & 0 \\ \epsilon & 1 \end{bmatrix} \begin{bmatrix} 1 & 1 \\ 0 & 1 \end{bmatrix} = \begin{bmatrix} 1 & 1 \\ \epsilon & 1 \end{bmatrix},$$

which is the correct result after permutation.

Although the foregoing example is rather extreme, the principle holds in general that larger pivots produce smaller multipliers and hence smaller errors. In particular, if the largest entry on or below the diagonal in each column is used as pivot, as in Algorithm 2.4, then the multipliers are bounded in magnitude by 1. The row interchanges required by partial pivoting slightly complicate the formal description of LU factorization given earlier. In particular, each elementary elimination matrix $\boldsymbol{M}_k$ is preceded by a permutation matrix $\boldsymbol{P}_k$ that interchanges rows to bring the entry of largest magnitude on or below the diagonal in column k into the diagonal pivot position. We still have $\boldsymbol{MA} = \boldsymbol{U}$, where $\boldsymbol{U}$ is upper triangular, but now

$$\boldsymbol{M} = \boldsymbol{M}_{n-1}\boldsymbol{P}_{n-1} \cdots \boldsymbol{M}_1\boldsymbol{P}_1.$$

$\boldsymbol{M}^{-1}$ is still triangular in the general sense defined earlier, but because of the permutations, $\boldsymbol{M}^{-1}$ is not necessarily *lower* triangular, though we still denote it by $\boldsymbol{L}$. Thus, "LU" factorization no longer literally means "lower times upper" triangular, but it is still equally useful for solving linear systems by successive substitution.

Algorithm 2.4 LU Factorization by Gaussian Elimination with Partial Pivoting

```
for k = 1 to n − 1                          { loop over columns }
    Find index p such that                  { search for pivot in
        |a_pk| ≥ |a_ik| for k ≤ i ≤ n            current column }
    if p ≠ k then                           { interchange rows,
        interchange rows k and p                 if necessary }
    if a_kk = 0 then                        { skip current column
        continue with next k                     if it's already zero }
    for i = k + 1 to n                      { compute multipliers
        m_ik = a_ik / a_kk                       for current column }
    end
    for j = k + 1 to n
        for i = k + 1 to n                  { apply transformation to
            a_ij = a_ij − m_ik a_kj              remaining submatrix }
        end
    end
end
```

We note that the permutation matrix

$$\boldsymbol{P} = \boldsymbol{P}_{n-1} \cdots \boldsymbol{P}_1$$

permutes the rows of $\boldsymbol{A}$ into the order determined by partial pivoting. An alternative interpretation, therefore, is to think of partial pivoting as a way of determining a row ordering for the system in which no interchanges would be required for numerical stability (though of course there is no way to determine such an ordering in advance). Thus, we obtain the factorization

$$\boldsymbol{PA} = \boldsymbol{LU},$$

where now $\boldsymbol{L}$ really is lower triangular. To solve the linear system $\boldsymbol{Ax} = \boldsymbol{b}$, we first solve the lower triangular system $\boldsymbol{Ly} = \boldsymbol{Pb}$ by forward-substitution, then the upper triangular system $\boldsymbol{Ux} = \boldsymbol{y}$ by back-substitution.

Example 2.16 Gaussian Elimination with Partial Pivoting. In Example 2.13, we did not use row interchanges, and some of the multipliers were greater than 1. For illustration, we now repeat that example, this time using partial pivoting. The system in Example 2.13 is

$$\boldsymbol{Ax} = \begin{bmatrix} 1 & 2 & 2 \\ 4 & 4 & 2 \\ 4 & 6 & 4 \end{bmatrix} \begin{bmatrix} x_1 \\ x_2 \\ x_3 \end{bmatrix} = \begin{bmatrix} 3 \\ 6 \\ 10 \end{bmatrix} = \boldsymbol{b}.$$

The largest entry in the first column is 4, so we interchange the first two rows using the permutation matrix

$$\boldsymbol{P}_1 = \begin{bmatrix} 0 & 1 & 0 \\ 1 & 0 & 0 \\ 0 & 0 & 1 \end{bmatrix},$$

obtaining the permuted system

$$\boldsymbol{P}_1\boldsymbol{A}\boldsymbol{x} = \begin{bmatrix} 4 & 4 & 2 \\ 1 & 2 & 2 \\ 4 & 6 & 4 \end{bmatrix} \begin{bmatrix} x_1 \\ x_2 \\ x_3 \end{bmatrix} = \begin{bmatrix} 6 \\ 3 \\ 10 \end{bmatrix} = \boldsymbol{P}_1\boldsymbol{b}.$$

To annihilate the subdiagonal entries of the first column, we use the elimination matrix

$$\boldsymbol{M}_1 = \begin{bmatrix} 1 & 0 & 0 \\ -0.25 & 1 & 0 \\ -1 & 0 & 1 \end{bmatrix},$$

obtaining the transformed system

$$\boldsymbol{M}_1\boldsymbol{P}_1\boldsymbol{A}\boldsymbol{x} = \begin{bmatrix} 4 & 4 & 2 \\ 0 & 1 & 1.5 \\ 0 & 2 & 2 \end{bmatrix} \begin{bmatrix} x_1 \\ x_2 \\ x_3 \end{bmatrix} = \begin{bmatrix} 6 \\ 1.5 \\ 4 \end{bmatrix} = \boldsymbol{M}_1\boldsymbol{P}_1\boldsymbol{b}.$$

The largest entry in the second column on or below the diagonal is 2, so we interchange the last two rows using the permutation matrix

$$\boldsymbol{P}_2 = \begin{bmatrix} 1 & 0 & 0 \\ 0 & 0 & 1 \\ 0 & 1 & 0 \end{bmatrix},$$

obtaining the permuted system

$$\boldsymbol{P}_2\boldsymbol{M}_1\boldsymbol{P}_1\boldsymbol{A}\boldsymbol{x} = \begin{bmatrix} 4 & 4 & 2 \\ 0 & 2 & 2 \\ 0 & 1 & 1.5 \end{bmatrix} \begin{bmatrix} x_1 \\ x_2 \\ x_3 \end{bmatrix} = \begin{bmatrix} 6 \\ 4 \\ 1.5 \end{bmatrix} = \boldsymbol{P}_2\boldsymbol{M}_1\boldsymbol{P}_1\boldsymbol{b}.$$

To annihilate the subdiagonal entry of the second column, we use the elimination matrix

$$\boldsymbol{M}_2 = \begin{bmatrix} 1 & 0 & 0 \\ 0 & 1 & 0 \\ 0 & -0.5 & 1 \end{bmatrix},$$

obtaining the transformed system

$$\boldsymbol{M}_2\boldsymbol{P}_2\boldsymbol{M}_1\boldsymbol{P}_1\boldsymbol{A}\boldsymbol{x} = \begin{bmatrix} 4 & 4 & 2 \\ 0 & 2 & 2 \\ 0 & 0 & 0.5 \end{bmatrix} \begin{bmatrix} x_1 \\ x_2 \\ x_3 \end{bmatrix} = \begin{bmatrix} 6 \\ 4 \\ -0.5 \end{bmatrix} = \boldsymbol{M}_2\boldsymbol{P}_2\boldsymbol{M}_1\boldsymbol{P}_1\boldsymbol{b}.$$

We have therefore reduced the original system to an equivalent upper triangular system, which can now be solved by back-substitution to obtain the same solution as before, $\boldsymbol{x} = \begin{bmatrix} -1 & 3 & -1 \end{bmatrix}^T$.

To write out the LU factorization explicitly, we have

$$\boldsymbol{L} = \boldsymbol{M}^{-1} = (\boldsymbol{M}_2\boldsymbol{P}_2\boldsymbol{M}_1\boldsymbol{P}_1)^{-1} = \boldsymbol{P}_1^T\boldsymbol{L}_1\boldsymbol{P}_2^T\boldsymbol{L}_2 =$$

$$\begin{bmatrix} 0 & 1 & 0 \\ 1 & 0 & 0 \\ 0 & 0 & 1 \end{bmatrix} \begin{bmatrix} 1 & 0 & 0 \\ 0.25 & 1 & 0 \\ 1 & 0 & 1 \end{bmatrix} \begin{bmatrix} 1 & 0 & 0 \\ 0 & 0 & 1 \\ 0 & 1 & 0 \end{bmatrix} \begin{bmatrix} 1 & 0 & 0 \\ 0 & 1 & 0 \\ 0 & 0.5 & 1 \end{bmatrix} = \begin{bmatrix} 0.25 & 0.5 & 1 \\ 1 & 0 & 0 \\ 1 & 1 & 0 \end{bmatrix},$$

and hence

$$\boldsymbol{A} = \begin{bmatrix} 1 & 2 & 2 \\ 4 & 4 & 2 \\ 4 & 6 & 4 \end{bmatrix} = \begin{bmatrix} 0.25 & 0.5 & 1 \\ 1 & 0 & 0 \\ 1 & 1 & 0 \end{bmatrix} \begin{bmatrix} 4 & 4 & 2 \\ 0 & 2 & 2 \\ 0 & 0 & 0.5 \end{bmatrix} = \boldsymbol{LU}.$$

Note that $\boldsymbol{L}$ is not lower triangular, but it is triangular in the more general sense (it is a permutation of a lower triangular matrix). Alternatively, we can take

$$\boldsymbol{P} = \boldsymbol{P}_2\boldsymbol{P}_1 = \begin{bmatrix} 1 & 0 & 0 \\ 0 & 0 & 1 \\ 0 & 1 & 0 \end{bmatrix} \begin{bmatrix} 0 & 1 & 0 \\ 1 & 0 & 0 \\ 0 & 0 & 1 \end{bmatrix} = \begin{bmatrix} 0 & 1 & 0 \\ 0 & 0 & 1 \\ 1 & 0 & 0 \end{bmatrix},$$

and

$$\boldsymbol{L} = \begin{bmatrix} 1 & 0 & 0 \\ 1 & 1 & 0 \\ 0.25 & 0.5 & 1 \end{bmatrix},$$

so that

$$\boldsymbol{PA} = \begin{bmatrix} 0 & 1 & 0 \\ 0 & 0 & 1 \\ 1 & 0 & 0 \end{bmatrix} \begin{bmatrix} 1 & 2 & 2 \\ 4 & 4 & 2 \\ 4 & 6 & 4 \end{bmatrix} = \begin{bmatrix} 1 & 0 & 0 \\ 1 & 1 & 0 \\ 0.25 & 0.5 & 1 \end{bmatrix} \begin{bmatrix} 4 & 4 & 2 \\ 0 & 2 & 2 \\ 0 & 0 & 0.5 \end{bmatrix} = \boldsymbol{LU},$$

where $\boldsymbol{L}$ now really is lower triangular but $\boldsymbol{A}$ is permuted.

The name "partial" pivoting comes from the fact that only the current column is searched for a suitable pivot. A more exhaustive pivoting strategy is *complete pivoting*, in which the entire remaining unreduced submatrix is searched for the largest entry, which is then permuted into the diagonal pivot position. Note that this requires interchanging columns as well as rows, and hence it leads to a factorization of the form

$$\boldsymbol{PAQ} = \boldsymbol{LU},$$

where $\boldsymbol{L}$ is unit lower triangular, $\boldsymbol{U}$ is upper triangular, and $\boldsymbol{P}$ and $\boldsymbol{Q}$ are permutation matrices that reorder the rows and columns, respectively, of $\boldsymbol{A}$. To solve the linear system $\boldsymbol{Ax} = \boldsymbol{b}$, we first solve the lower triangular system $\boldsymbol{Ly} = \boldsymbol{Pb}$ by forward-substitution, then the upper triangular system $\boldsymbol{Uz} = \boldsymbol{y}$ by back-substitution, and finally we permute the solution components to obtain $\boldsymbol{x} = \boldsymbol{Qz}$. Although the numerical stability of complete pivoting is theoretically superior, it requires a much more expensive pivot search than partial pivoting. Because the numerical stability of partial pivoting is more than adequate in practice, it is almost universally used in solving general linear systems by Gaussian elimination.

Pivot selection depends on the magnitudes of individual matrix entries, so the particular choice obviously depends on the scaling of the matrix. A diagonal scaling of the matrix (recall Example 2.10) may result in a different sequence of pivots.

For example, any nonzero entry in a given column can be made the largest in magnitude simply by giving that row a sufficiently heavy weighting. This does not mean that an arbitrary pivot sequence is acceptable, however: a badly skewed scaling can result in an ill-conditioned system and a correspondingly inaccurate solution (see Example 2.20). A well-formulated problem should have appropriately commensurate units for measuring the unknown variables (column scaling), and a weighting of the individual equations that properly reflects their relative importance (row scaling). It should also account for the relative accuracy of the input data. Under these circumstances, the pivoting procedure will usually produce a solution that is as accurate as the problem warrants (see Section 2.3.4).

We saw in Section 2.3.5 that the relative residual for a computed solution satisfies the inequality

$$\frac{\|\boldsymbol{r}\|}{\|\boldsymbol{A}\| \cdot \|\hat{\boldsymbol{x}}\|} \leq \frac{\|\boldsymbol{E}\|}{\|\boldsymbol{A}\|},$$

where $\boldsymbol{E}$ is the backward error in the matrix $\boldsymbol{A}$. But how large is $\|\boldsymbol{E}\|$ likely to be in practice? Wilkinson [417] showed that for LU factorization by Gaussian elimination, a bound of the form

$$\frac{\|\boldsymbol{E}\|}{\|\boldsymbol{A}\|} \leq \rho\, n^2\, \epsilon_{\text{mach}}$$

holds, where ρ, called the *growth factor*, is the ratio of the largest entry of $\boldsymbol{U}$ to the largest entry of $\boldsymbol{A}$ in magnitude (technically, the growth factor depends on the largest entry produced at *any* stage of the factorization process, but this is typically the last, or $\boldsymbol{U}$). Without pivoting, ρ can be arbitrarily large, and hence Gaussian elimination without pivoting is unstable, as we have already seen. With partial pivoting, the growth factor can still be as large as 2^{n-1} (since in the worst case the size of the entries can double at each stage of elimination), but such behavior is extremely rare. In practice, there is little or no growth, and a realistic bound is given by

$$\frac{\|\boldsymbol{E}\|}{\|\boldsymbol{A}\|} \lessapprox n\, \epsilon_{\text{mach}}.$$

This relation means that solving a linear system by Gaussian elimination with partial pivoting followed by back-substitution almost always yields a very small relative residual, regardless of how ill-conditioned the system may be. Thus, a small relative residual does not necessarily indicate that a computed solution is accurate unless the system is well-conditioned. Complete pivoting yields an even smaller growth factor, both in theory and in practice, but the additional margin of stability it provides is usually not worth the extra expense.

Example 2.17 Small Residual. Consider the linear system

$$\boldsymbol{A}\boldsymbol{x} = \begin{bmatrix} 0.913 & 0.659 \\ 0.457 & 0.330 \end{bmatrix} \begin{bmatrix} x_1 \\ x_2 \end{bmatrix} = \begin{bmatrix} 0.254 \\ 0.127 \end{bmatrix} = \boldsymbol{b}$$

from Example 2.8. Using four-digit decimal arithmetic, Gaussian elimination yields the triangular system

$$\begin{bmatrix} 0.9130 & 0.6590 \\ 0 & 0.0002 \end{bmatrix} \begin{bmatrix} x_1 \\ x_2 \end{bmatrix} = \begin{bmatrix} 0.2540 \\ 0.0001 \end{bmatrix},$$

and back-substitution then gives the computed solution

$$\hat{\boldsymbol{x}} = \begin{bmatrix} -0.0827 \\ 0.5 \end{bmatrix}.$$

As we saw in Example 2.8, the residual norm for this solution is $\|\boldsymbol{r}\|_1 = 2.1 \times 10^{-4}$, which is as small as we can expect using four-digit arithmetic. Yet the exact solution to this system is easily confirmed to be $\boldsymbol{x} = [1, \; -1]^T$, so that the error is as large as the solution. The cause of this phenomenon is that the matrix $\boldsymbol{A}$ is nearly singular: as we saw in Example 2.7, its condition number is more than 10^4. The division that determines x_2 is between two quantities that are both on the order of rounding error (in four-digit arithmetic), and hence the result is essentially arbitrary. Yet, by design, when this arbitrary value for x_2 is then substituted into the first equation, a value for x_1 is computed so that the first equation is satisfied. Thus, we get a small residual but a poor solution.

As we have just seen, pivoting is generally required for Gaussian elimination to be stable. There are some classes of matrices, however, for which Gaussian elimination is stable *without* pivoting. For example, if the matrix $\boldsymbol{A}$ is *diagonally dominant* by columns, which means that each diagonal entry is larger in magnitude than the sum of the magnitudes of the other entries in its column,

$$\sum_{i=1,\, i\neq j}^{n} |a_{ij}| < |a_{jj}|, \quad j = 1, \ldots, n,$$

then pivoting is not required in computing its LU factorization by Gaussian elimination. If partial pivoting is used on such a matrix, then no row interchanges will actually occur. Another important class for which pivoting is not required is matrices that are symmetric and positive definite, which will be defined in Section 2.5. Avoiding an unnecessary pivot search can save a significant amount of time in computing the factorization.

2.4.6 Implementation of Gaussian Elimination

Gaussian elimination, or LU factorization, has the general form of a triple-nested loop, as shown schematically in Algorithm 2.5. The indices i, j, and k of the **for** loops can be taken in any order, for a total of $3! = 6$ different ways of arranging the loops. Some of the indicated arithmetic operations can be moved outside the innermost loop for greater efficiency (as in Algorithm 2.3, for example), and additional reorderings of the operations that may not have strictly nested loops are also possible. These variations of the basic algorithm have different access patterns (e.g., row-wise or column-wise), and also differ in their ability to take advantage of the architectural features of a given computer (e.g., cache, paging, vectorization, multiple processors). Thus, their performance may vary widely on a given computer or across different computers, and no single arrangement may be uniformly superior.

Algorithm 2.5 Generic Gaussian Elimination

```
for ________
    for ________
        for ________
            a_ij = a_ij - (a_ik/a_kk) a_kj
        end
    end
end
```

Numerous implementation details of the algorithm are subject to variation in this way. For example, the partial pivoting procedure we described searches along columns and interchanges rows, but alternatively, one could search along rows and interchange columns. We have also taken $\boldsymbol{L}$ to have unit diagonal, but one could instead arrange for $\boldsymbol{U}$ to have unit diagonal. Some of these variations of Gaussian elimination are of sufficient importance to have been given names, such as the Crout and Doolittle methods.

Although the many possible variations of Gaussian elimination may have a dramatic effect on performance, they all produce essentially the same factorization for a nonsingular matrix $\boldsymbol{A}$. Provided the row pivot sequence is the same, if we have two LU factorizations $\boldsymbol{PA} = \boldsymbol{LU} = \hat{\boldsymbol{L}}\hat{\boldsymbol{U}}$, then this expression implies that $\hat{\boldsymbol{L}}^{-1}\boldsymbol{L} = \hat{\boldsymbol{U}}\boldsymbol{U}^{-1} = \boldsymbol{D}$ is both lower and upper triangular, and hence diagonal. If both $\boldsymbol{L}$ and $\hat{\boldsymbol{L}}$ are assumed to be unit lower triangular, then $\boldsymbol{D}$ must in fact be the identity matrix $\boldsymbol{I}$, and hence $\boldsymbol{L} = \hat{\boldsymbol{L}}$ and $\boldsymbol{U} = \hat{\boldsymbol{U}}$, so that the factorization is unique. Even without this assumption, however, we may still conclude that that the LU factorization is unique up to diagonal scaling of the factors. This uniqueness is made explicit in the LDU factorization $\boldsymbol{PA} = \boldsymbol{LDU}$, where $\boldsymbol{L}$ is unit lower triangular, $\boldsymbol{U}$ is unit upper triangular, and $\boldsymbol{D}$ is diagonal.

Storage management is another important implementation issue. The numerous matrices we considered—the elementary elimination matrices $\boldsymbol{M}_k$, their inverses $\boldsymbol{L}_k$, and the permutation matrices $\boldsymbol{P}_k$—merely describe the factorization process formally. They are not formed explicitly in an actual implementation. To conserve storage, the $\boldsymbol{L}$ and $\boldsymbol{U}$ factors overwrite the initial storage for the input matrix $\boldsymbol{A}$, with the transformed matrix $\boldsymbol{U}$ occupying the upper triangle of $\boldsymbol{A}$ (including the diagonal), and the multipliers that make up the strict lower triangle of $\boldsymbol{L}$ occupying the (now zero) strict lower triangle of $\boldsymbol{A}$. The unit diagonal of $\boldsymbol{L}$ need not be stored.

To minimize data movement, the row interchanges required by pivoting are not usually carried out explicitly. Instead, the rows remain in their original locations, and an auxiliary integer vector is used to keep track of the new row order. Note that a single such vector suffices, because the net effect of all of the interchanges is still just a permutation of the integers $1, \ldots, n$.

2.4.7 Complexity of Solving Linear Systems

Computing the LU factorization of an $n \times n$ matrix by Gaussian elimination requires about $n^3/3$ floating-point multiplications and a similar number of additions. Solving the resulting triangular system for a single right-hand-side vector by forward- and back-substitution requires about n^2 multiplications and a similar number of additions. Thus, as the order n of the matrix grows, the LU factorization phase becomes increasingly dominant in the cost of solving linear systems.

We can also solve a linear system by explicitly inverting the matrix so that the solution is given by $\boldsymbol{x} = \boldsymbol{A}^{-1}\boldsymbol{b}$. But computing $\boldsymbol{A}^{-1}$ is tantamount to solving n linear systems: it requires an LU factorization of $\boldsymbol{A}$ followed by n forward- and back-substitutions, one for each column of the identity matrix. The total operation count is about n^3 multiplications and a similar number of additions (taking advantage of the zeros in the right-hand-side vectors for the forward-substitution). Explicit inversion is therefore three times as expensive as LU factorization.

The subsequent matrix-vector multiplication $\boldsymbol{x} = \boldsymbol{A}^{-1}\boldsymbol{b}$ to solve a linear system requires about n^2 multiplications and a similar number of additions, which is similar to the total cost of forward- and back-substitution. Hence, even for multiple right-hand-side vectors, matrix inversion is more costly than LU factorization for solving linear systems. In addition, explicit inversion gives a less accurate answer. As a simple example, if we solve the 1×1 linear system $3x = 18$ by division, we get $x = 18/3 = 6$, but explicit inversion would give $x = 3^{-1} \times 18 = 0.333 \times 18 = 5.99$ using three-digit arithmetic. In this small example, inversion requires an additional arithmetic operation and obtains a less accurate result. These disadvantages of inversion become worse as the size of the system grows.

Explicit matrix inverses often occur as a convenient notation in various formulas, but this practice does not mean that an explicit inverse is required to implement such a formula. One merely need solve a linear system with an appropriate right-hand side, which might itself be a matrix. Thus, for example, a product of the form $\boldsymbol{A}^{-1}\boldsymbol{B}$ should be computed by LU factorization of $\boldsymbol{A}$, followed by forward- and back-substitutions using each column of $\boldsymbol{B}$. It is extremely rare in practice that an explicit matrix inverse is actually needed, so whenever you see a matrix inverse in a formula, you should think "solve a system" rather than "invert a matrix."

Another method for solving linear systems that should be avoided is *Cramer's rule*, in which each component of the solution is computed as a ratio of determinants. Though often taught in elementary linear algebra courses, this method is astronomically expensive for full matrices of nontrivial size. Cramer's rule is useful mostly as a theoretical tool.

2.4.8 Gauss-Jordan Elimination

The motivation for Gaussian elimination is to reduce a general matrix to triangular form, because the resulting linear system is easy to solve. Diagonal linear systems are even easier to solve, however, so diagonal form would appear to be an even more desirable target. *Gauss-Jordan elimination* is a variation of standard Gaussian elimination in which the matrix is reduced to diagonal form rather than merely to triangular form. The same type of row combinations are used to eliminate matrix entries as in standard Gaussian elimination, but they are applied to annihilate entries above as well as below the diagonal. Thus, the elimination matrix used for a given column vector $\boldsymbol{a}$ is of the form

$$\begin{bmatrix} 1 & \cdots & 0 & -m_1 & 0 & \cdots & 0 \\ \vdots & \ddots & \vdots & \vdots & \vdots & \ddots & \vdots \\ 0 & \cdots & 1 & -m_{k-1} & 0 & \cdots & 0 \\ 0 & \cdots & 0 & 1 & 0 & \cdots & 0 \\ 0 & \cdots & 0 & -m_{k+1} & 1 & \cdots & 0 \\ \vdots & \ddots & \vdots & \vdots & \vdots & \ddots & \vdots \\ 0 & \cdots & 0 & -m_n & 0 & \cdots & 1 \end{bmatrix} \begin{bmatrix} a_1 \\ \vdots \\ a_{k-1} \\ a_k \\ a_{k+1} \\ \vdots \\ a_n \end{bmatrix} = \begin{bmatrix} 0 \\ \vdots \\ 0 \\ a_k \\ 0 \\ \vdots \\ 0 \end{bmatrix},$$

where $m_i = a_i/a_k$, $i = 1, \ldots, n$. This process requires about $n^3/2$ multiplications and a similar number of additions, which is 50 percent more expensive than standard Gaussian elimination.

During the elimination phase, the same row operations are also applied to the right-hand-side vector (or vectors) of a system of linear equations. Once the elimination phase has been completed and the matrix is in diagonal form, then the components of the solution to the linear system can be computed simply by dividing each entry of the transformed right-hand side by the corresponding diagonal entry of the matrix. This computation requires a total of only n divisions, which is significantly cheaper than solving a triangular system, but not enough to make up for the more costly elimination phase. Gauss-Jordan elimination also has the numerical disadvantage that the multipliers can exceed 1 in magnitude even if pivoting is used.

Despite its higher overall cost, Gauss-Jordan elimination may be preferred in some situations because of the extreme simplicity of its final solution phase. For example, it is sometimes advocated for implementation on parallel computers because it has a uniform workload throughout the factorization phase, and then all of the solution components can be computed simultaneously rather than one at a time as in ordinary back-substitution.

Gauss-Jordan elimination is also sometimes used to compute the inverse of a matrix explicitly, if desired. If the right-hand-side matrix is initialized to be the identity matrix $\boldsymbol{I}$ and the given matrix $\boldsymbol{A}$ is reduced to the identity matrix by Gauss-Jordan elimination, then the transformed right-hand-side matrix will be the inverse of $\boldsymbol{A}$. For computing the inverse, Gauss-Jordan elimination has about the same operation count as explicit inversion by Gaussian elimination followed by forward- and back-substitution.

Example 2.18 Gauss-Jordan Elimination. We illustrate Gauss-Jordan elimination by using it to compute the inverse of the matrix of Example 2.13. For simplicity, we omit pivoting. We begin with the matrix $\boldsymbol{A}$, augmented by the identity matrix $\boldsymbol{I}$ as right-hand side, and repeatedly apply elimination matrices to annihilate off-diagonal entries of $\boldsymbol{A}$ until we reach diagonal form, then scale by the remaining diagonal entries to produce the identity matrix on the left, and hence the inverse matrix A^{-1} on the right.

$$\begin{bmatrix} 1 & 0 & 0 \\ -4 & 1 & 0 \\ -4 & 0 & 1 \end{bmatrix} \left[\begin{array}{ccc|ccc} 1 & 2 & 2 & 1 & 0 & 0 \\ 4 & 4 & 2 & 0 & 1 & 0 \\ 4 & 6 & 4 & 0 & 0 & 1 \end{array}\right] = \left[\begin{array}{ccc|ccc} 1 & 2 & 2 & 1 & 0 & 0 \\ 0 & -4 & -6 & -4 & 1 & 0 \\ 0 & -2 & -4 & -4 & 0 & 1 \end{array}\right],$$

$$\begin{bmatrix} 1 & 0.5 & 0 \\ 0 & 1 & 0 \\ 0 & -0.5 & 1 \end{bmatrix} \left[\begin{array}{ccc|ccc} 1 & 2 & 2 & 1 & 0 & 0 \\ 0 & -4 & -6 & -4 & 1 & 0 \\ 0 & -2 & -4 & -4 & 0 & 1 \end{array}\right] = \left[\begin{array}{ccc|ccc} 1 & 0 & -1 & -1 & 0.5 & 0 \\ 0 & -4 & -6 & -4 & 1 & 0 \\ 0 & 0 & -1 & -2 & -0.5 & 1 \end{array}\right],$$

$$\begin{bmatrix} 1 & 0 & -1 \\ 0 & 1 & -6 \\ 0 & 0 & 1 \end{bmatrix} \left[\begin{array}{ccc|ccc} 1 & 0 & -1 & -1 & 0.5 & 0 \\ 0 & -4 & -6 & -4 & 1 & 0 \\ 0 & 0 & -1 & -2 & -0.5 & 1 \end{array}\right] = \left[\begin{array}{ccc|ccc} 1 & 0 & 0 & 1 & 1 & -1 \\ 0 & -4 & 0 & 8 & 4 & -6 \\ 0 & 0 & -1 & -2 & -0.5 & 1 \end{array}\right],$$

$$\begin{bmatrix} 1 & 0 & 0 \\ 0 & -0.25 & 0 \\ 0 & 0 & -1 \end{bmatrix} \left[\begin{array}{ccc|ccc} 1 & 0 & 0 & 1 & 1 & -1 \\ 0 & -4 & 0 & 8 & 4 & -6 \\ 0 & 0 & -1 & -2 & -0.5 & 1 \end{array}\right] = \left[\begin{array}{ccc|ccc} 1 & 0 & 0 & 1 & 1 & -1 \\ 0 & 1 & 0 & -2 & -1 & 1.5 \\ 0 & 0 & 1 & 2 & 0.5 & -1 \end{array}\right],$$

so that

$$A^{-1} = \begin{bmatrix} 1 & 1 & -1 \\ -2 & -1 & 1.5 \\ 2 & 0.5 & -1 \end{bmatrix}.$$

2.4.9 Solving Modified Problems

In many practical situations linear systems do not occur in isolation but as part of a sequence of related problems that change in some systematic way. For example, one may need to solve a sequence of linear systems $\boldsymbol{Ax} = \boldsymbol{b}$ having the same matrix $\boldsymbol{A}$ but different right-hand sides $\boldsymbol{b}$. After having solved the initial system by Gaussian elimination, then the $\boldsymbol{L}$ and $\boldsymbol{U}$ factors already computed can be used to solve the additional systems by forward- and back-substitution. The factorization phase need not be repeated in solving subsequent linear systems unless the matrix changes. This procedure represents a substantial savings in work, since additional triangular solutions cost only $\mathcal{O}(n^2)$ work, in contrast to the $\mathcal{O}(n^3)$ cost of a factorization.

In fact, in some important special cases a new factorization can be avoided even when the matrix does change. One such case that arises frequently is the addition or subtraction of an $n \times n$ matrix that is an outer product $\boldsymbol{uv}^T$ of two nonzero n-vectors $\boldsymbol{u}$ and $\boldsymbol{v}$. This is called a *rank-one modification* because the outer product matrix $\boldsymbol{uv}^T$ has rank one (i.e., only one linearly independent row or column), and any rank-one matrix can be expressed as such an outer product of two vectors (see Exercise 2.25). For example, if a single entry of the matrix $\boldsymbol{A}$ changes, say the (j,k) entry changes from a_{jk} to $\tilde{a}_{jk}$, then the new matrix is $\boldsymbol{A} - \alpha \boldsymbol{e}_j \boldsymbol{e}_k^T$, where $\boldsymbol{e}_j$ and $\boldsymbol{e}_k$ are the corresponding columns of the identity matrix and $\alpha = a_{jk} - \tilde{a}_{jk}$.

The *Sherman-Morrison formula*,

$$\left(\boldsymbol{A} - \boldsymbol{uv}^T\right)^{-1} = \boldsymbol{A}^{-1} + \boldsymbol{A}^{-1}\boldsymbol{u}\left(1 - \boldsymbol{v}^T\boldsymbol{A}^{-1}\boldsymbol{u}\right)^{-1}\boldsymbol{v}^T\boldsymbol{A}^{-1},$$

where $\boldsymbol{u}$ and $\boldsymbol{v}$ are n-vectors, gives the inverse of a matrix resulting from a rank-one modification of a matrix whose inverse is already known, as is easily verified by direct multiplication (see Exercise 2.27). Evaluation of this formula requires only $\mathcal{O}(n^2)$ work (for matrix-vector multiplications) rather than the $\mathcal{O}(n^3)$ work that would be required to invert the modified matrix from scratch.

For the linear system $(\boldsymbol{A} - \boldsymbol{u}\boldsymbol{v}^T)\boldsymbol{x} = \boldsymbol{b}$ with the new matrix, the Sherman-Morrison formula gives the solution

$$\boldsymbol{x} = \left(\boldsymbol{A} - \boldsymbol{u}\boldsymbol{v}^T\right)^{-1}\boldsymbol{b} = \boldsymbol{A}^{-1}\boldsymbol{b} + \boldsymbol{A}^{-1}\boldsymbol{u}\left(1 - \boldsymbol{v}^T\boldsymbol{A}^{-1}\boldsymbol{u}\right)^{-1}\boldsymbol{v}^T\boldsymbol{A}^{-1}\boldsymbol{b},$$

but we prefer to avoid explicit inverses. If we have an LU factorization for the original matrix $\boldsymbol{A}$, however, then the solution to the modified system can be obtained using Algorithm 2.6, which involves solving triangular systems and computing inner products of vectors, so that it requires no explicit inverses and only $\mathcal{O}(n^2)$ work. Note that the first step is independent of $\boldsymbol{b}$ and hence need not be repeated if there are multiple right-hand-side vectors $\boldsymbol{b}$.

Algorithm 2.6 Rank-One Updating of Solution

Solve $\boldsymbol{A}\boldsymbol{z} = \boldsymbol{u}$ for $\boldsymbol{z}$, so that $\boldsymbol{z} = \boldsymbol{A}^{-1}\boldsymbol{u}$
Solve $\boldsymbol{A}\boldsymbol{y} = \boldsymbol{b}$ for $\boldsymbol{y}$, so that $\boldsymbol{y} = \boldsymbol{A}^{-1}\boldsymbol{b}$
$\boldsymbol{x} = \boldsymbol{y} + \left((\boldsymbol{v}^T\boldsymbol{y})/(1 - \boldsymbol{v}^T\boldsymbol{z})\right)\boldsymbol{z}$

Using similar techniques, it is possible to update the factorization rather than the inverse or the solution. Caution must be exercised in using these updating formulas, however, because in general there is no guarantee of numerical stability through successive updates as the matrix changes. The *Woodbury formula*,

$$\left(\boldsymbol{A} - \boldsymbol{U}\boldsymbol{V}^T\right)^{-1} = \boldsymbol{A}^{-1} + \boldsymbol{A}^{-1}\boldsymbol{U}\left(\boldsymbol{I} - \boldsymbol{V}^T\boldsymbol{A}^{-1}\boldsymbol{U}\right)^{-1}\boldsymbol{V}^T\boldsymbol{A}^{-1},$$

where $\boldsymbol{U}$ and $\boldsymbol{V}$ are $n \times k$ matrices, generalizes the Sherman-Morrison formula to a rank-k modification of the matrix (see Exercise 2.28).

Example 2.19 Rank-One Updating of Solutions. To illustrate rank-one updating, we solve the linear system

$$\begin{bmatrix} 1 & 2 & 2 \\ 4 & 4 & 2 \\ 4 & 4 & 4 \end{bmatrix} \begin{bmatrix} x_1 \\ x_2 \\ x_3 \end{bmatrix} = \begin{bmatrix} 3 \\ 6 \\ 10 \end{bmatrix},$$

which is a rank-one modification of the system in Example 2.13, as only the $(3, 2)$ entry of the matrix $\boldsymbol{A}$ has changed, from 6 to 4. One way to choose the update vectors is

$$\boldsymbol{u} = \begin{bmatrix} 0 \\ 0 \\ 1 \end{bmatrix} \quad \text{and} \quad \boldsymbol{v} = \begin{bmatrix} 0 \\ 2 \\ 0 \end{bmatrix},$$

so that the matrix of the modified system is $\boldsymbol{A} - \boldsymbol{u}\boldsymbol{v}^T =$

$$\begin{bmatrix} 1 & 2 & 2 \\ 4 & 4 & 2 \\ 4 & 6 & 4 \end{bmatrix} - \begin{bmatrix} 0 \\ 0 \\ 1 \end{bmatrix} \begin{bmatrix} 0 & 2 & 0 \end{bmatrix} = \begin{bmatrix} 1 & 2 & 2 \\ 4 & 4 & 2 \\ 4 & 6 & 4 \end{bmatrix} - \begin{bmatrix} 0 & 0 & 0 \\ 0 & 0 & 0 \\ 0 & 2 & 0 \end{bmatrix} = \begin{bmatrix} 1 & 2 & 2 \\ 4 & 4 & 2 \\ 4 & 4 & 4 \end{bmatrix},$$

and the right-hand-side vector $\boldsymbol{b}$ has not changed.

We can use the LU factorization previously computed for $\boldsymbol{A}$ in Example 2.13 to solve $\boldsymbol{Az} = \boldsymbol{u}$, obtaining $\boldsymbol{z} = \begin{bmatrix}-1 & 1.5 & -1\end{bmatrix}^T$, and we had already solved $\boldsymbol{Ay} = \boldsymbol{b}$, obtaining $\boldsymbol{y} = \begin{bmatrix}-1 & 3 & -1\end{bmatrix}^T$. The final step is then to compute the updated solution

$$\boldsymbol{x} = \boldsymbol{y} + \frac{\boldsymbol{v}^T\boldsymbol{y}}{1 - \boldsymbol{v}^T\boldsymbol{z}}\boldsymbol{z} = \begin{bmatrix}-1\\3\\-1\end{bmatrix} + \frac{6}{1-3}\begin{bmatrix}-1\\1.5\\-1\end{bmatrix} = \begin{bmatrix}2\\-1.5\\2\end{bmatrix}.$$

We have thus computed the solution to the modified system without refactoring the modified matrix.

2.4.10 Improving Accuracy

Although the accuracy that can be expected in the solution of a linear system may seem set in concrete, accuracy can be enhanced in some cases by rescaling the system or by iteratively improving the initial computed solution. These measures are not always practicable, but they may be worth trying, especially for highly ill-conditioned systems.

Recall from Example 2.10 that *diagonal scaling* of a linear system leaves the solution either unchanged (row scaling) or changed in such a way that the solution is easily recoverable (column scaling). In practice, however, scaling affects the conditioning of the system and the selection of pivots in Gaussian elimination, both of which in turn affect the accuracy of the computed solution. Thus, row scaling and column scaling of a linear system can potentially improve (or degrade) numerical stability and accuracy.

Accuracy is usually enhanced if all the entries of the matrix have about the same order of magnitude or, better still, if the uncertainties in the matrix entries are all of about the same size. Sometimes it is obvious by inspection how to scale the matrix to accomplish such balance by the choice of measurement units for the respective variables and by weighting each equation according to its relative importance and uncertainty. No general automatic technique has ever been developed, however, that produces optimal scaling in an efficient and foolproof manner. Moreover, the scaling process itself can introduce rounding errors unless care is taken (for example, by using only powers of the arithmetic base as scaling factors).

Example 2.20 Poor Scaling. As a simple example, the linear system

$$\begin{bmatrix}1 & 0\\0 & \epsilon\end{bmatrix}\begin{bmatrix}x_1\\x_2\end{bmatrix} = \begin{bmatrix}1\\\epsilon\end{bmatrix}$$

has condition number $1/\epsilon$ and hence is very ill-conditioned if ϵ is very small. This ill-conditioning means that small perturbations in the input data can cause relatively large changes in the solution. For example, perturbing the right-hand side by the vector $\begin{bmatrix}0 & -\epsilon\end{bmatrix}^T$ changes the solution from $\begin{bmatrix}1 & 1\end{bmatrix}^T$ to $\begin{bmatrix}1 & 0\end{bmatrix}^T$. If the second row is first multiplied by $1/\epsilon$, however, then the system becomes perfectly well-conditioned, and the same perturbation now produces a commensurately small change in the solution. Thus, the apparent ill-conditioning was due purely to poor scaling. Unfortunately, how to correct poor scaling for general matrices is much less obvious.

Iterative refinement is another means of potentially improving the accuracy of a computed solution. Suppose we have computed an approximate solution $\boldsymbol{x}_0$ to the linear system $\boldsymbol{Ax} = \boldsymbol{b}$, say using some form of LU factorization, and we compute the residual

$$\boldsymbol{r}_0 = \boldsymbol{b} - \boldsymbol{A}\boldsymbol{x}_0.$$

We want the residual to be suitably small, of course, but if it isn't we can use the LU factors previously computed to solve the linear system

$$\boldsymbol{A}\boldsymbol{s}_0 = \boldsymbol{r}_0$$

for $\boldsymbol{s}_0$ and take

$$\boldsymbol{x}_1 = \boldsymbol{x}_0 + \boldsymbol{s}_0$$

as a new and "better" approximate solution, since

$$\boldsymbol{A}\boldsymbol{x}_1 = \boldsymbol{A}(\boldsymbol{x}_0 + \boldsymbol{s}_0) = \boldsymbol{A}\boldsymbol{x}_0 + \boldsymbol{A}\boldsymbol{s}_0 = (\boldsymbol{b} - \boldsymbol{r}_0) + \boldsymbol{r}_0 = \boldsymbol{b}.$$

This process can be repeated to refine the solution successively until convergence, potentially producing a solution with a residual as small as possible for the arithmetic precision used.

Unfortunately, iterative refinement requires double the storage, since both the original matrix and its LU factorization are required (to compute the residual and to solve the subsequent systems, respectively). Moreover, for iterative refinement to produce maximum benefit, the residual must usually be computed with higher precision than that used in computing the initial solution (recall Example 1.17).

For these reasons, iterative refinement is often impractical to use routinely, but it can still be useful in some circumstances. For example, iterative refinement can recover full accuracy for systems that are badly scaled, and can sometimes stabilize solution methods that are otherwise potentially unstable. Ironically, if the initial solution is relatively poor, then the residual may be large enough to be computed with sufficient accuracy without requiring extra precision. We will return to iterative refinement later in Example 11.7.

2.5 Special Types of Linear Systems

Thus far we have assumed that the linear system has a general matrix and is *dense*, meaning that essentially all of the matrix entries are nonzero. If the matrix has some special properties, then work and storage can often be saved in solving the linear system. Some examples of special properties that can be exploited include the following:

- *Symmetric*: $\boldsymbol{A} = \boldsymbol{A}^T$, i.e., $a_{ij} = a_{ji}$ for all i, j.
- *Positive definite*: $\boldsymbol{x}^T\boldsymbol{Ax} > 0$ for all $\boldsymbol{x} \neq \boldsymbol{0}$.

- *Banded*: $a_{ij} = 0$ for all $|i-j| > \beta$, where β is the *bandwidth* of $\boldsymbol{A}$. An important special case is a *tridiagonal matrix*, for which $\beta = 1$.
- *Sparse*: most entries of $\boldsymbol{A}$ are zero.

Techniques for handling symmetric and banded systems are relatively straightforward variations of Gaussian elimination for dense systems. Sparse linear systems with more general nonzero patterns, on the other hand, require more sophisticated algorithms and data structures that avoid storing or operating on the zeros in the matrix (see Section 11.4.1).

The properties just defined for real matrices have analogues for complex matrices, but in the complex case the ordinary matrix transpose is replaced by the conjugate transpose, denoted by a superscript H. If $z = \alpha + i\beta$ is a complex number, where α and β are real numbers and $i = \sqrt{-1}$, then its *complex conjugate* is defined by $\bar{z} = \alpha - i\beta$ (see Section 1.3.11). The *conjugate transpose* of a matrix $\boldsymbol{A}$ is then given by $\{\boldsymbol{A}^H\}_{ij} = \bar{a}_{ji}$. Of course, for a real matrix $\boldsymbol{A}$, $\boldsymbol{A}^H = \boldsymbol{A}^T$. A complex matrix is *Hermitian* if $\boldsymbol{A} = \boldsymbol{A}^H$, and positive definite if $\boldsymbol{x}^H\boldsymbol{A}\boldsymbol{x} > 0$ for all complex vectors $\boldsymbol{x} \neq \boldsymbol{0}$.

2.5.1 Symmetric Positive Definite Systems

If the matrix $\boldsymbol{A}$ is symmetric and positive definite, then an LU factorization can be arranged so that $\boldsymbol{U} = \boldsymbol{L}^T$, that is, $\boldsymbol{A} = \boldsymbol{L}\boldsymbol{L}^T$, where $\boldsymbol{L}$ is lower triangular and has positive diagonal entries (but not, in general, a unit diagonal). This is known as the *Cholesky factorization* of $\boldsymbol{A}$, and an algorithm for computing it can be derived by equating the corresponding entries of $\boldsymbol{A}$ and $\boldsymbol{L}\boldsymbol{L}^T$ and then generating the entries of $\boldsymbol{L}$ in the correct order. In the 2×2 case, for example, we have

$$\begin{bmatrix} a_{11} & a_{21} \\ a_{21} & a_{22} \end{bmatrix} = \begin{bmatrix} \ell_{11} & 0 \\ \ell_{21} & \ell_{22} \end{bmatrix} \begin{bmatrix} \ell_{11} & \ell_{21} \\ 0 & \ell_{22} \end{bmatrix},$$

which implies that

$$\ell_{11} = \sqrt{a_{11}}, \quad \ell_{21} = a_{21}/\ell_{11}, \quad \ell_{22} = \sqrt{a_{22} - \ell_{21}^2}.$$

One way to organize the resulting general procedure is Algorithm 2.7, in which the Cholesky factor $\boldsymbol{L}$ overwrites the original matrix $\boldsymbol{A}$.

A number of facts about the Cholesky factorization algorithm make it very attractive and popular for symmetric positive definite matrices:

- The n square roots required are all of positive numbers, so the algorithm is well-defined.
- Pivoting is not required for numerical stability.
- Only the lower triangle of $\boldsymbol{A}$ is accessed, and hence the strict upper triangular portion need not be stored.
- Only about $n^3/6$ multiplications and a similar number of additions are required.

Thus, Cholesky factorization requires only about half as much work and half as much storage as are required for LU factorization of a general matrix by Gaussian

Algorithm 2.7 Cholesky Factorization

for $k = 1$ **to** n	{ loop over columns }
$\quad a_{kk} = \sqrt{a_{kk}}$	
$\quad$ **for** $i = k+1$ **to** n	
$\qquad a_{ik} = a_{ik}/a_{kk}$	{ scale current column }
$\quad$ **end**	
$\quad$ **for** $j = k+1$ **to** n	{ from each remaining column,
$\qquad$ **for** $i = j$ **to** n	subtract multiple
$\qquad\quad a_{ij} = a_{ij} - a_{ik} \cdot a_{jk}$	of current column }
$\qquad$ **end**	
$\quad$ **end**	
end	

elimination. Unfortunately, taking advantage of this gain in storage usually requires that one triangle of the symmetric matrix be packed into a one-dimensional array, which is less convenient than the usual two-dimensional storage for a matrix. For this reason, linear algebra software packages commonly offer both packed storage and standard two-dimensional array storage versions for symmetric matrices so that the user can choose between convenience and storage conservation.

In some circumstances it may be advantageous to express the Cholesky factorization in the form $\boldsymbol{A} = \boldsymbol{L}\boldsymbol{D}\boldsymbol{L}^T$, where $\boldsymbol{L}$ is unit lower triangular and $\boldsymbol{D}$ is diagonal with positive diagonal entries. Such a factorization can be computed by a simple variant of the standard Cholesky algorithm, and it has the advantage of not requiring any square roots. The diagonal entries of $\boldsymbol{D}$ in the $\boldsymbol{L}\boldsymbol{D}\boldsymbol{L}^T$ factorization are simply the squares of the diagonal entries of $\boldsymbol{L}$ in the $\boldsymbol{L}\boldsymbol{L}^T$ factorization.

Example 2.21 Cholesky Factorization. To illustrate the algorithm, we compute the Cholesky factorization of the symmetric positive definite matrix

$$\boldsymbol{A} = \begin{bmatrix} 3 & -1 & -1 \\ -1 & 3 & -1 \\ -1 & -1 & 3 \end{bmatrix}.$$

The successive transformations of the lower triangle of the matrix will be shown, as the algorithm touches only that portion of the matrix. Dividing the first column by the square root of its diagonal entry, $\sqrt{3} \approx 1.7321$, gives

$$\begin{bmatrix} 1.7321 & & \\ -0.5774 & 3 & \\ -0.5774 & -1 & 3 \end{bmatrix}.$$

The second column is updated by subtracting from it the $(2,1)$ entry, -0.5774, times the relevant portion of the first column, and the third column is updated by subtracting from it the $(3,1)$ entry, also -0.5774, times the relevant portion of the first column, which gives

$$\begin{bmatrix} 1.7321 & & \\ -0.5774 & 2.6667 & \\ -0.5774 & -1.3333 & 2.6667 \end{bmatrix}.$$

The second column is then divided by the square root of its diagonal entry, $\sqrt{2.6667} \approx 1.6330$, to give

$$\begin{bmatrix} 1.7321 & & \\ -0.5774 & 1.6330 & \\ -0.5774 & -0.8165 & 2.6667 \end{bmatrix}.$$

The third column is updated by subtracting from it the $(3,2)$ entry, -0.8165, times the relevant portion of the second column, which gives

$$\begin{bmatrix} 1.7321 & & \\ -0.5774 & 1.6330 & \\ -0.5774 & -0.8165 & 2.0000 \end{bmatrix}.$$

Taking the square root of the third diagonal entry yields the final result

$$\boldsymbol{L} = \begin{bmatrix} 1.7321 & & \\ -0.5774 & 1.6330 & \\ -0.5774 & -0.8165 & 1.4142 \end{bmatrix}.$$

2.5.2 Symmetric Indefinite Systems

If the matrix $\boldsymbol{A}$ is symmetric but indefinite (i.e., $\boldsymbol{x}^T\boldsymbol{A}\boldsymbol{x}$ can take both positive and negative values, depending on $\boldsymbol{x}$), then Cholesky factorization is not applicable, and some form of pivoting is generally required for numerical stability. Obviously, any pivoting must be symmetric—of the form $\boldsymbol{PAP}^T$, where $\boldsymbol{P}$ is a permutation matrix—if the symmetry of the matrix is to be preserved.

We would like to obtain a factorization of the form $\boldsymbol{PAP}^T = \boldsymbol{LDL}^T$, where $\boldsymbol{L}$ is unit lower triangular and $\boldsymbol{D}$ is diagonal. Unfortunately, such a factorization, with diagonal $\boldsymbol{D}$, may not exist, and in any case it generally cannot be computed stably using only symmetric pivoting. The best we can do is to take $\boldsymbol{D}$ to be either tridiagonal or block diagonal with 1×1 and 2×2 diagonal blocks. (A *block matrix* is a matrix whose entries are partitioned into submatrices, or "blocks," of compatible dimensions. In a block diagonal matrix, all of these submatrices are zero except those on the main block diagonal.)

Efficient algorithms have been developed by Aasen for the tridiagonal factorization, and by Bunch and Parlett (with subsequent improvements in the pivoting procedure by Bunch and Kaufman and others) for the block diagonal factorization (see [164]). In either case, the pivoting procedure yields a stable factorization that requires only about $n^3/6$ multiplications and a similar number of additions. Also, in either case, the subsequent solution phase requires only $\mathcal{O}(n^2)$ work. Thus, the cost of solving symmetric indefinite systems is similar to that for positive definite systems using Cholesky factorization, and only about half the cost for nonsymmetric systems using Gaussian elimination.

2.5.3 Banded Systems

Gaussian elimination for band matrices differs little from the general case—the only algorithmic changes are in the ranges of the loops. Of course, one should also use a data structure for a band matrix that avoids storing the zero entries outside the band. A common choice when the band is dense is to store the matrix in a two-dimensional array by diagonals. If pivoting is required for numerical stability, then the algorithm becomes slightly more complicated in that the bandwidth can grow (but no more than double). Thus, a general-purpose solver for banded systems of arbitrary bandwidth is very similar to a code for Gaussian elimination for general matrices.

For a fixed small bandwidth, however, a solver for banded systems can be extremely simple, especially if pivoting is not required for stability. Consider, for example, the tridiagonal matrix

$$\boldsymbol{A} = \begin{bmatrix} b_1 & c_1 & 0 & \cdots & 0 \\ a_2 & b_2 & c_2 & \ddots & \vdots \\ 0 & \ddots & \ddots & \ddots & 0 \\ \vdots & \ddots & a_{n-1} & b_{n-1} & c_{n-1} \\ 0 & \cdots & 0 & a_n & b_n \end{bmatrix}.$$

If pivoting is not required for stability, which is often the case for tridiagonal systems arising in practice (e.g., if the matrix is diagonally dominant or positive definite), then Gaussian elimination reduces to Algorithm 2.8, and the resulting triangular factors of $\boldsymbol{A}$ are then given by

$$\boldsymbol{L} = \begin{bmatrix} 1 & 0 & \cdots & \cdots & 0 \\ m_2 & 1 & \ddots & \ddots & \vdots \\ 0 & \ddots & \ddots & \ddots & \vdots \\ \vdots & \ddots & m_{n-1} & 1 & 0 \\ 0 & \cdots & 0 & m_n & 1 \end{bmatrix}, \quad \boldsymbol{U} = \begin{bmatrix} d_1 & c_1 & 0 & \cdots & 0 \\ 0 & d_2 & c_2 & \ddots & \vdots \\ \vdots & \ddots & \ddots & \ddots & 0 \\ \vdots & \ddots & \ddots & d_{n-1} & c_{n-1} \\ 0 & \cdots & \cdots & 0 & d_n \end{bmatrix}.$$

Algorithm 2.8 Tridiagonal LU Factorization without Pivoting

```
d_1 = b_1
for i = 2 to n                  { loop over columns }
    m_i = a_i / d_{i-1}         { compute multiplier }
    d_i = b_i - m_i c_{i-1}     { apply transformation }
end
```

In general, a banded system of bandwidth β requires only $\mathcal{O}(\beta n)$ storage, and the factorization requires only $\mathcal{O}(\beta^2 n)$ work, both of which represent substantial savings over full systems if $\beta \ll n$.

2.6 Iterative Methods for Linear Systems

Gaussian elimination is an example of a *direct* method for solving linear systems, i.e., one that produces the exact solution (assuming exact arithmetic) to a linear system in a *finite* number of steps. *Iterative* methods, on the other hand, begin with an initial guess for the solution and successively improve it until the solution is as accurate as desired. In theory, an infinite number of iterations might be required to converge to the exact solution, but in practice the iterations terminate when the residual $\|\boldsymbol{b} - \boldsymbol{A}\boldsymbol{x}\|$, or some other measure of error, is as small as desired. For some types of problems, iterative methods may have significant advantages over direct methods. Consideration of iterative methods for solving linear systems will be postponed until Chapter 11, where we consider the numerical solution of partial differential equations, which leads to sparse linear systems that are often best solved by iterative methods.

2.7 Software for Linear Systems

Almost any software library for scientific computing contains routines for solving linear systems of various types. Table 2.1 is a list of appropriate routines for solving real, general, dense linear systems, and also for estimating the condition number, in some widely available software collections. Some packages use different prefixes or suffixes in the routine names to indicate the data type, typically `s` for single-precision real, `d` for double-precision real, `c` for single-precision complex, and `z` for double-precision complex; only the single-precision real versions are listed here. In most such subroutine libraries, more specialized routines are available for particular types of linear systems, such as symmetric, positive definite, banded, or combinations of these. Some of these routines are listed in Table 2.2; other routines that are more storage efficient or cater to other special tasks may also be available.

Conventional software for solving linear systems $\boldsymbol{A}\boldsymbol{x} = \boldsymbol{b}$ is sometimes implemented as a single routine, or it may be split into two routines, one for computing a factorization and another for solving the resulting triangular system. In either case, repeating the factorization should not be necessary if additional solutions are needed with the same matrix but different right-hand sides. The input typically required includes a two-dimensional array containing the matrix $\boldsymbol{A}$, a one-dimensional array containing the right-hand-side vector $\boldsymbol{b}$ (or a two-dimensional array for multiple right-hand-side vectors), the integer order n of the system, the leading dimension of the array containing $\boldsymbol{A}$ (so that the subroutine can interpret subscripts properly in the array), and possibly some work space and a flag indicating the particular task to be performed. On return, the solution $\boldsymbol{x}$ usually overwrites the storage for $\boldsymbol{b}$, and the factorization overwrites the storage for $\boldsymbol{A}$. Additional output may include a

Source	Factor	Solve	Condition estimate
FMM [127]	decomp	solve	
HSL	ma21	ma21	
IMSL	lftrg	lfsrg	lfcrg
KMN [220]	sgefs	sgefs	sgefs
LAPACK [10]	sgetrf	sgetrs	sgecon
LINPACK [98]	sgefa	sgesl	sgeco
MATLAB	lu	\	rcond/condest
NAG	f07adf	f07aef	f07agf
NAPACK [178]	fact	solve	con
NR [315]	ludcmp	lubksb	
NUMAL [250]	dec	sol	
SLATEC	sgefa	sgesl	sgeco

Table 2.1: Software for solving general linear systems

status flag to indicate any errors or warnings and an estimate of the condition number of the matrix (or sometimes the reciprocal of the condition number). Because of the additional cost of condition estimation, this feature is usually optional.

Solving linear systems using an interactive environment such as MATLAB is simpler than when using conventional software because the package keeps track internally of details such as the dimensions of vectors and matrices, and many matrix operations are built into the syntax and semantics of the language. For example, the solution to the linear system $\boldsymbol{Ax} = \boldsymbol{b}$ is given in MATLAB by the "left division" operator, denoted by backslash, so that `x = A \ b`. Internally, the solution is computed by LU factorization and forward- and back-substitution, but the user need not be aware of this. The LU factorization can be computed explicitly, if desired, by the MATLAB `lu` function, `[L, U] = lu(A)`, or, if the matrix is symmetric and positive definite, its Cholesky factorization is obtained by `L = chol(A)`.

Source	Symmetric positive definite	Symmetric indefinite	General banded
HSL	ma22	ma29	ma35
IMSL	lftds/lfsds	lftsf/lfssf	lftrb/lfsrb
LAPACK [10]	spotrf/spotrs	ssytrf/ssytrs	sgbtrf/sgbtrs
LINPACK [98]	spofa/sposl	ssifa/ssisl	sgbfa/sgbsl
NAG	f07fdf/f07fef	f07mdf/f07mef	f07bdf/f07bef
NAPACK [178]	sfact/ssolve	ifact/isolve	bfact/bsolve
NR [315]	choldc/cholsl		bandec/banbks
NUMAL [250]	chldec2/chlsol2	decsym2/solsym2	decbnd/solbnd
SLATEC	spofa/sposl	ssifa/ssisl	sgbfa/sgbsl

Table 2.2: Software for solving special linear systems

2.7.1 LINPACK and LAPACK

LINPACK is a standard software package for solving a wide variety of systems of linear equations, both general dense systems and those having various special properties, such as symmetric or banded. Solving linear systems is of such fundamental importance in scientific computing that LINPACK has become a standard benchmark for comparing the performance of computers. The LINPACK manual [98] is a useful source of practical advice on solving systems of linear equations.

A more recent package called LAPACK updates the entire LINPACK collection for higher performance on modern computer architectures, including some parallel computers. In many cases, the newer algorithms in LAPACK also achieve greater accuracy, robustness, and functionality than their predecessors in LINPACK. LAPACK includes both simple and expert drivers for all of the major computational problems in linear algebra, as well as the many underlying computational and auxiliary routines required for various factorizations, solution of triangular systems, norm estimation, scaling, and iterative refinement. Both LINPACK and LAPACK are available from Netlib, and the linear system solvers in many other libraries and packages are based directly on them.

2.7.2 Basic Linear Algebra Subprograms

The high-level routines in LINPACK and LAPACK are based on lower-level Basic Linear Algebra Subprograms (BLAS). The BLAS were originally designed to encapsulate basic operations on vectors so that they could be optimized for a given computer architecture while the high-level routines that call them remain portable. New computer architectures have prompted the development of higher-level BLAS that encapsulate matrix-vector and matrix-matrix operations for better utilization of hierarchical memory such as cache, vector registers, and virtual memory with paging. A few of the most important BLAS routines of each level are listed in Table 2.3.

Level	TOMS #	Work	Examples	Function
1	539	$\mathcal{O}(n)$	saxpy	Scalar times vector plus vector
			sdot	Inner product of two vectors
			snrm2	Euclidean norm of vector
2	656	$\mathcal{O}(n^2)$	sgemv	Matrix-vector multiplication
			strsv	Triangular solution
			sger	Rank-one update
3	679	$\mathcal{O}(n^3)$	sgemm	Matrix-matrix multiplication
			strsm	Multiple triangular solutions
			ssyrk	Rank-k update

Table 2.3: Examples of basic linear algebra subprograms (BLAS)

The key to good performance is *data reuse*, that is, performing as many arithmetic operations as possible involving a given data item while it is held in the portion of the memory hierarchy with the most rapid access. The level-3 BLAS have greater opportunity for data reuse because they perform $\mathcal{O}(n^3)$ operations on $\mathcal{O}(n^2)$ data items, whereas in the lower-level BLAS the number of operations is proportional to the number of data items. Generic versions of the BLAS are available from Netlib, and many computer vendors provide custom versions that are optimized for highest performance on their particular systems.

2.8 Historical Notes and Further Reading

Gauss formulated his elimination method in 1810, but he expressed it in terms of simplifying a quadratic form rather than factoring a matrix. Indeed, matrices were not introduced until 1855 by Cayley, and the interpretation of Gaussian elimination as a matrix factorization was not realized until the 1940s by Dwyer, von Neumann, and others (see [373]). A grave concern of the early pioneers of digital computation, such as von Neumann [410] and Turing [400] (the concept of matrix condition number is due to Turing), was whether accumulated rounding error in solving large linear systems by Gaussian elimination would render the results useless, and initially there was considerable pessimism on this score. Computational experience soon showed that the method was surprisingly stable and accurate in practice, however, and error analyses eventually followed to help explain this good fortune (see especially the work of Wilkinson [417, 418, 419]).

As it turns out, Gaussian elimination with partial pivoting has a worse than optimal operation count [381], is unstable in the worst case [417], and in a theoretical sense cannot be implemented efficiently in parallel [409]. Yet it is consistently effective in practice, even on parallel computers, and is one of the principal workhorses of scientific computing. Most numerical algorithms obey Murphy's law—"if anything can go wrong, it will"—but Gaussian elimination seems to be a happy exception. For further discussion of some of the "mysteries" of this remarkable algorithm, see [394, 397]; for "computational counterexamples," see [131, 426].

For background on linear algebra, the reader may wish to consult the excellent textbooks by Strang [377, 379]. For more advanced matrix theory, see [199, 200]. Additional examples, exercises, and practical applications of computational linear algebra can be found in [197, 262]. An encyclopedic reference on matrix computations is [164]; textbook treatments include [83, 89, 155, 178, 215, 368, 372, 396, 413]. An influential early work on solving linear systems, and one of the first to include high-quality software, is [128]. A useful tutorial handbook on matrix computations, both in Fortran and MATLAB, is [73].

For a comprehensive treatment of error analysis and perturbation theory for linear systems and many other problems in linear algebra, see [196, 374]. An overview of condition number estimation is given in [194]. A detailed survey of componentwise (as opposed to normwise) perturbation theory in linear algebra is given in [195]. LINPACK and LAPACK are documented in [98] and [10], respectively. For the BLAS (Basic Linear Algebra Subprograms) see [96, 97, 252]. One of the earliest papers to examine the effect of the computing environment on the performance of Gaussian elimination and other matrix computations was [273]. For a sample of the now large literature on this topic, see [90, 99, 100, 293].

Review Questions

2.1. True or false: If a matrix $\boldsymbol{A}$ is nonsingular, then the number of solutions to the linear system $\boldsymbol{Ax} = \boldsymbol{b}$ depends on the particular choice of right-hand-side vector $\boldsymbol{b}$.

2.2. True or false: If a matrix has a very small determinant, then the matrix is nearly singular.

2.3. For a symmetric matrix $\boldsymbol{A}$, it is always the case that $\|\boldsymbol{A}\|_1 = \|\boldsymbol{A}\|_\infty$.

2.4. True or false: If a triangular matrix has a zero entry on its main diagonal, then the matrix is necessarily singular.

2.5. True or false: If any matrix has a zero entry on its main diagonal, then the matrix is necessarily singular.

2.6. True or false: An underdetermined system of linear equations $\boldsymbol{Ax} = \boldsymbol{b}$, where $\boldsymbol{A}$ is an $m \times n$ matrix with $m < n$, always has a solution.

2.7. True or false: The product of two upper triangular matrices is upper triangular.

2.8. True or false: The product of two symmetric matrices is symmetric.

2.9. True or false: The inverse of a nonsingular upper triangular matrix is upper triangular.

2.10. True or false: If the rows of an $n \times n$ matrix $\boldsymbol{A}$ are linearly dependent, then the columns of the matrix are also linearly dependent.

2.11. True or false: A system of linear equations $\boldsymbol{Ax} = \boldsymbol{b}$ has a solution if, and only if, the $m \times n$ matrix $\boldsymbol{A}$ and the augmented $m \times (n+1)$ matrix $[\,\boldsymbol{A} \quad \boldsymbol{b}\,]$ have the same rank.

2.12. True or false: If $\boldsymbol{A}$ is any $n \times n$ matrix and $\boldsymbol{P}$ is any $n \times n$ permutation matrix, then $\boldsymbol{PA} = \boldsymbol{AP}$.

2.13. True or false: Provided row interchanges are allowed, the LU factorization always exists, even for a singular matrix $\boldsymbol{A}$.

2.14. True or false: If a linear system is well-conditioned, then pivoting is unnecessary in Gaussian elimination.

2.15. True or false: If a matrix is singular then it cannot have an LU factorization.

2.16. True or false: If a nonsingular symmetric matrix is not positive definite, then it cannot have a Cholesky factorization.

2.17. True or false: A symmetric positive definite matrix is always well-conditioned.

2.18. True or false: Gaussian elimination without pivoting fails only when the matrix is ill-conditioned or singular.

2.19. True or false: Once the LU factorization of a matrix has been computed to solve a linear system, then subsequent linear systems with the same matrix but different right-hand-side vectors can be solved without refactoring the matrix.

2.20. True or false: In explicit matrix inversion by LU factorization and triangular solution, the majority of the work is due to the factorization.

2.21. True or false: If $\boldsymbol{x}$ is any n-vector, then $\|\boldsymbol{x}\|_1 \geq \|\boldsymbol{x}\|_\infty$.

2.22. True or false: The norm of a singular matrix is zero.

2.23. True or false: If $\|\boldsymbol{A}\| = 0$, then $\boldsymbol{A} = \boldsymbol{O}$.

2.24. True or false: $\|\boldsymbol{A}\|_1 = \|\boldsymbol{A}^T\|_\infty$.

2.25. True or false: If $\boldsymbol{A}$ is any $n \times n$ nonsingular matrix, then $\text{cond}(\boldsymbol{A}) = \text{cond}(\boldsymbol{A}^{-1})$.

2.26. True or false: In solving a nonsingular system of linear equations, Gaussian elimination with partial pivoting usually yields a small residual even if the matrix is ill-conditioned.

2.27. True or false: The multipliers in Gaussian elimination with partial pivoting are bounded by 1 in magnitude, so the entries of the successive reduced matrices cannot grow in magnitude.

2.28. Can a system of linear equations $\boldsymbol{Ax} = \boldsymbol{b}$ have exactly two distinct solutions?

2.29. Can the number of solutions to a linear system $\boldsymbol{Ax} = \boldsymbol{b}$ ever be determined solely from the matrix $\boldsymbol{A}$ without knowing the right-hand-side vector $\boldsymbol{b}$?

2.30. In solving a square system of linear equations $\boldsymbol{Ax} = \boldsymbol{b}$, which would be a more serious difficulty: that the rows of $\boldsymbol{A}$ are linearly dependent, or that the columns of $\boldsymbol{A}$ are linearly dependent? Explain.

2.31. (*a*) State one defining property of a *singular* matrix $\boldsymbol{A}$.

(*b*) Suppose that the linear system $\boldsymbol{Ax} = \boldsymbol{b}$ has two distinct solutions $\boldsymbol{x}$ and $\boldsymbol{y}$. Use the property you gave in part *a* to prove that $\boldsymbol{A}$ must be singular.

2.32. Given a nonsingular system of linear equations $\boldsymbol{Ax} = \boldsymbol{b}$, what effect on the solution vector $\boldsymbol{x}$ results from each of the following actions?

(*a*) Permuting the rows of $[\boldsymbol{A} \quad \boldsymbol{b}]$

(*b*) Permuting the columns of $\boldsymbol{A}$

(*c*) Multiplying both sides of the equation from the left by a nonsingular matrix $\boldsymbol{M}$

2.33. Suppose that both sides of a system of linear equations $\boldsymbol{Ax} = \boldsymbol{b}$ are multiplied by a nonzero scalar α.

(*a*) Does this change the true solution $\boldsymbol{x}$?

(*b*) Does this change the residual vector $\boldsymbol{r} = \boldsymbol{b} - \boldsymbol{Ax}$ for a given $\boldsymbol{x}$?

(*c*) What conclusion can be drawn about assessing the quality of a computed solution?

2.34. Suppose that both sides of a system of linear equations $\boldsymbol{Ax} = \boldsymbol{b}$ are premultiplied by a nonsingular diagonal matrix.

(*a*) Does this change the true solution $\boldsymbol{x}$?

(*b*) Can this affect the conditioning of the system?

(*c*) Can this affect the choice of pivots in Gaussian elimination?

2.35. Specify an elementary elimination matrix that zeros the last two components of the vector

$$\begin{bmatrix} 3 \\ 2 \\ -1 \\ 4 \end{bmatrix}.$$

2.36. (*a*) Specify a 4×4 permutation matrix that interchanges the 2nd and 4th components of any 4-vector.

(*b*) Specify a 4×4 permutation matrix that reverses the order of the components of any 4-vector.

2.37. With a singular matrix and the use of exact arithmetic, at what point will the solution process break down in solving a linear system by Gaussian elimination

(*a*) With partial pivoting?

(*b*) Without pivoting?

2.38. (*a*) What is the difference between partial pivoting and complete pivoting in Gaussian elimination?

(*b*) State one advantage of each type of pivoting relative to the other.

2.39. Consider the following matrix $\boldsymbol{A}$, whose LU factorization we wish to compute using Gaussian elimination:

$$\boldsymbol{A} = \begin{bmatrix} 4 & -8 & 1 \\ 6 & 5 & 7 \\ 0 & -10 & -3 \end{bmatrix}.$$

What will the initial pivot element be if

(*a*) No pivoting is used?

(*b*) Partial pivoting is used?

(*c*) Complete pivoting is used?

2.40. Give two reasons why pivoting is essential for a numerically stable implementation of Gaussian elimination.

2.41. If $\boldsymbol{A}$ is an ill-conditioned matrix, and its LU factorization is computed by Gaussian elimination with partial pivoting, would you expect the ill-conditioning to be reflected in $\boldsymbol{L}$, in $\boldsymbol{U}$, or both? Why?

2.42. (*a*) What is the inverse of the following matrix?

$$\begin{bmatrix} 1 & 0 & 0 & 0 \\ 0 & 1 & 0 & 0 \\ 0 & m_1 & 1 & 0 \\ 0 & m_2 & 0 & 1 \end{bmatrix}$$

(*b*) How might such a matrix arise in computational practice?

2.43. (*a*) Can every nonsingular $n \times n$ matrix $\boldsymbol{A}$ be written as a product, $\boldsymbol{A} = \boldsymbol{LU}$, where $\boldsymbol{L}$ is a lower triangular matrix and $\boldsymbol{U}$ is an upper triangular matrix?

(*b*) If so, what is an algorithm for accomplishing this? If not, give a counterexample to illustrate.

2.44. Given an $n \times n$ nonsingular matrix $\boldsymbol{A}$ and a second $n \times n$ matrix $\boldsymbol{B}$, what is the best way to compute the $n \times n$ matrix $\boldsymbol{A}^{-1}\boldsymbol{B}$?

2.45. If $\boldsymbol{A}$ and $\boldsymbol{B}$ are $n \times n$ matrices, with $\boldsymbol{A}$ nonsingular, and $\boldsymbol{c}$ is an n-vector, how would you efficiently compute the product $\boldsymbol{A}^{-1}\boldsymbol{Bc}$?

2.46. If $\boldsymbol{A}$ is an $n\times n$ matrix and $\boldsymbol{x}$ is an n-vector, which of the following computations requires less work? Explain.

(*a*) $\boldsymbol{y} = (\boldsymbol{x}\,\boldsymbol{x}^T)\,\boldsymbol{A}$

(*b*) $\boldsymbol{y} = \boldsymbol{x}\,(\boldsymbol{x}^T\,\boldsymbol{A})$

2.47. How does the computational work in solving an $n\times n$ triangular system of linear equations compare with that for solving a general $n\times n$ system of linear equations?

2.48. Assume that you have already computed the LU factorization, $\boldsymbol{A} = \boldsymbol{LU}$, of the nonsingular matrix $\boldsymbol{A}$. How would you use it to solve the linear system $\boldsymbol{A}^T\boldsymbol{x} = \boldsymbol{b}$?

2.49. If $\boldsymbol{L}$ is a nonsingular lower triangular matrix, $\boldsymbol{P}$ is a permutation matrix, and $\boldsymbol{b}$ is a given vector, how would you solve each of the following linear systems?

(*a*) $\boldsymbol{LPx} = \boldsymbol{b}$

(*b*) $\boldsymbol{PLx} = \boldsymbol{b}$

2.50. In the plane $\mathbb{R}^2$, is it possible to have a vector $\boldsymbol{x} \neq \boldsymbol{0}$ such that $\|\boldsymbol{x}\|_1 = \|\boldsymbol{x}\|_\infty$? If so, give an example.

2.51. In the plane $\mathbb{R}^2$, is it possible to have two vectors $\boldsymbol{x}$ and $\boldsymbol{y}$ such that $\|\boldsymbol{x}\|_1 > \|\boldsymbol{y}\|_1$, but $\|\boldsymbol{x}\|_\infty < \|\boldsymbol{y}\|_\infty$? If so, give an example.

2.52. In general, which matrix norm is easier to compute, $\|\boldsymbol{A}\|_1$ or $\|\boldsymbol{A}\|_2$? Why?

2.53. (*a*) Is the magnitude of the determinant of a matrix a good indicator of whether the matrix is nearly singular?

(*b*) If so, why? If not, what is a better indicator of near singularity?

2.54. (*a*) How is the condition number of a matrix $\boldsymbol{A}$ defined for a given matrix norm?

(*b*) How is the condition number used in estimating the accuracy of a computed solution to a linear system $\boldsymbol{Ax} = \boldsymbol{b}$?

2.55. Why is computing the condition number of a general matrix a nontrivial problem?

2.56. Give an example of a 3×3 matrix $\boldsymbol{A}$, other than the identity matrix, such that $\text{cond}(\boldsymbol{A}) = 1$.

2.57. (*a*) What is the condition number of the following matrix using the 1-norm?

$$\begin{bmatrix} 4 & 0 & 0 \\ 0 & -6 & 0 \\ 0 & 0 & 2 \end{bmatrix}$$

(*b*) Does your answer differ using the ∞-norm?

2.58. Suppose that the $n\times n$ matrix $\boldsymbol{A}$ is perfectly well-conditioned, i.e., $\text{cond}(A) = 1$. Which of the following matrices would then necessarily share this same property?

(*a*) $c\boldsymbol{A}$, where c is any nonzero scalar

(*b*) $\boldsymbol{DA}$, where $\boldsymbol{D}$ is a nonsingular diagonal matrix

(*c*) $\boldsymbol{PA}$, where $\boldsymbol{P}$ is any permutation matrix

(*d*) $\boldsymbol{BA}$, where $\boldsymbol{B}$ is any nonsingular matrix

(*e*) $\boldsymbol{A}^{-1}$, the inverse of $\boldsymbol{A}$

(*f*) $\boldsymbol{A}^T$, the transpose of $\boldsymbol{A}$

2.59. Let $\boldsymbol{A} = \text{diag}(1/2)$ be an $n\times n$ diagonal matrix with all its diagonal entries equal to $1/2$.

(*a*) What is the value of $\det(\boldsymbol{A})$?

(*b*) What is the value of $\text{cond}(\boldsymbol{A})$?

(*c*) What conclusion can you draw from these results?

2.60. Suppose that the $n\times n$ matrix $\boldsymbol{A}$ is exactly singular, but its floating-point representation, $\text{fl}(\boldsymbol{A})$, is nonsingular. In this case, what would you expect the order of magnitude of the condition number $\text{cond}(\text{fl}(\boldsymbol{A}))$ to be?

2.61. Classify each of the following matrices as well-conditioned or ill-conditioned:

(*a*) $\begin{bmatrix} 10^{10} & 0 \\ 0 & 10^{-10} \end{bmatrix}$

(*b*) $\begin{bmatrix} 10^{10} & 0 \\ 0 & 10^{10} \end{bmatrix}$

(*c*) $\begin{bmatrix} 10^{-10} & 0 \\ 0 & 10^{-10} \end{bmatrix}$

(*d*) $\begin{bmatrix} 1 & 2 \\ 2 & 4 \end{bmatrix}$

2.62. Which of the following are good indicators that a matrix is nearly singular?

(*a*) Its determinant is small.

(*b*) Its norm is small.

(*c*) Its norm is large.

(*d*) Its condition number is large.

2.63. (*a*) In solving a linear system $Ax = b$, what is meant by the *residual* of an approximate solution $\hat{x}$?

(*b*) Does a small relative residual always imply that the solution is accurate? Why?

(*c*) Does a large relative residual always imply that the solution is inaccurate? Why?

2.64. In a floating-point system having 10 decimal digits of precision, if Gaussian elimination with partial pivoting is used to solve a linear system whose matrix has a condition number of 10^3, and whose input data are accurate to full machine precision, about how many digits of accuracy would you expect in the solution?

2.65. Assume that you are solving a system of linear equations $\boldsymbol{Ax} = \boldsymbol{b}$ on a computer whose floating-point number system has 12 decimal digits of precision, and that the problem data are correct to full machine precision. About how large can the condition number of the matrix $\boldsymbol{A}$ be before the computed solution x will contain no significant digits?

2.66. Under what circumstances does a small residual vector $\boldsymbol{r} = \boldsymbol{b} - \boldsymbol{Ax}$ imply that $\boldsymbol{x}$ is an accurate solution to the linear system $\boldsymbol{Ax} = \boldsymbol{b}$?

2.67. Let $\boldsymbol{A}$ be an arbitrary square matrix and c an arbitrary scalar. Which of the following statements must necessarily hold?

(*a*) $\|c\boldsymbol{A}\| = |c| \cdot \|\boldsymbol{A}\|$.

(*b*) $\text{cond}(c\boldsymbol{A}) = |c| \cdot \text{cond}(\boldsymbol{A})$.

2.68. (*a*) What is the main difference between Gaussian elimination and Gauss-Jordan elimination?

(*b*) State one advantage of each type of elimination relative to the other.

2.69. Rank the following methods according to the amount of work required for solving a general system of linear equations of order n:

(*a*) Gauss-Jordan elimination

(*b*) Gaussian elimination with partial pivoting

(*c*) Cramer's rule

(*d*) Explicit matrix inversion followed by matrix-vector multiplication

2.70. (*a*) How much storage is required to store an $n \times n$ matrix of rank one efficiently?

(*b*) How many arithmetic operations are required to multiply an n-vector by an $n \times n$ matrix of rank one efficiently?

2.71. In a comparison of ordinary Gaussian elimination with Gauss-Jordan elimination for solving a linear system $\boldsymbol{Ax} = \boldsymbol{b}$,

(*a*) Which has a more expensive factorization?

(*b*) Which has a more expensive back-substitution?

(*c*) Which has a higher overall cost?

2.72. For each of the following elimination algorithms for solving linear systems, is there any pivoting strategy that can guarantee that all of the multipliers will be at most 1 in absolute value?

(*a*) Gaussian elimination

(*b*) Gauss-Jordan elimination

2.73. What two properties of a matrix $\boldsymbol{A}$ together imply that $\boldsymbol{A}$ has a Cholesky factorization?

2.74. List three advantages of Cholesky factorization compared with LU factorization.

2.75. How many square roots are required to compute the Cholesky factorization of an $n \times n$ symmetric positive definite matrix?

2.76. Let $\boldsymbol{A} = \{a_{ij}\}$ be an $n \times n$ symmetric positive definite matrix.

(*a*) What is the $(1, 1)$ entry of its Cholesky factor?

(*b*) What is the $(n, 1)$ entry of its Cholesky factor?

2.77. What is the Cholesky factorization of the following matrix?

$$\begin{bmatrix} 4 & 2 \\ 2 & 2 \end{bmatrix}$$

2.78. (*a*) Is it possible, in general, to solve a symmetric indefinite linear system at a cost similar to that for using Cholesky factorization to solve a symmetric positive definite linear system?

(*b*) If so, what is an algorithm for accomplishing this? If not, why?

2.79. Give two reasons why iterative improvement for solutions of linear systems is often impractical to implement.

2.80. Suppose you have already solved the $n \times n$ linear system $\boldsymbol{Ax} = \boldsymbol{b}$ by LU factorization and back-substitution. What is the further cost (order of magnitude will suffice) of solving a new system

(*a*) With the same matrix but a different right-hand-side vector?

(*b*) With the matrix changed by adding a matrix of rank one?

(*c*) With the matrix changed completely?

Exercises

2.1. In Section 2.2, four defining properties are given for a singular matrix. Show that these four properties are indeed equivalent.

2.2. Suppose that each of the row sums of an $n \times n$ matrix $\boldsymbol{A}$ is equal to zero. Show that $\boldsymbol{A}$ must be singular.

2.3. Suppose that $\boldsymbol{A}$ is a singular $n \times n$ matrix. Prove that if the linear system $\boldsymbol{Ax} = \boldsymbol{b}$ has at least one solution $\boldsymbol{x}$, then it has infinitely many solutions.

2.4. (*a*) Show that the following matrix is singular.

$$\boldsymbol{A} = \begin{bmatrix} 1 & 1 & 0 \\ 1 & 2 & 1 \\ 1 & 3 & 2 \end{bmatrix}$$

(*b*) If $\boldsymbol{b} = [2 \quad 4 \quad 6]^T$, how many solutions are there to the system $\boldsymbol{Ax} = \boldsymbol{b}$?

2.5. What is the inverse of the following matrix?

$$\boldsymbol{A} = \begin{bmatrix} 1 & 0 & 0 \\ 1 & -1 & 0 \\ 1 & -2 & 1 \end{bmatrix}$$

2.6. Let $\boldsymbol{A}$ be an $n \times n$ matrix such that $\boldsymbol{A}^2 = \boldsymbol{O}$, the zero matrix. Show that $\boldsymbol{A}$ must be singular.

2.7. Let

$$\boldsymbol{A} = \begin{bmatrix} 1 & 1+\epsilon \\ 1-\epsilon & 1 \end{bmatrix}.$$

(*a*) What is the determinant of $\boldsymbol{A}$?

(*b*) In floating-point arithmetic, for what range of values of ϵ will the computed value of the determinant be zero?

(*c*) What is the LU factorization of $\boldsymbol{A}$?

(*d*) In floating-point arithmetic, for what range of values of ϵ will the computed value of $\boldsymbol{U}$ be singular?

2.8. Let $\boldsymbol{A}$ and $\boldsymbol{B}$ be any two $n \times n$ matrices.

(*a*) Prove that $(\boldsymbol{AB})^T = \boldsymbol{B}^T\boldsymbol{A}^T$.

(*b*) If $\boldsymbol{A}$ and $\boldsymbol{B}$ are both nonsingular, prove that $(\boldsymbol{AB})^{-1} = \boldsymbol{B}^{-1}\boldsymbol{A}^{-1}$.

2.9. If $\boldsymbol{A}$ is any nonsingular real matrix, show that $(\boldsymbol{A}^{-1})^T = (\boldsymbol{A}^T)^{-1}$. Consequently, the notation $\boldsymbol{A}^{-T}$ can be used unambiguously to denote this matrix. Similarly, if $\boldsymbol{A}$ is any nonsingular complex matrix, then $(\boldsymbol{A}^{-1})^H = (\boldsymbol{A}^H)^{-1}$, and the notation $\boldsymbol{A}^{-H}$ can be used unambiguously to denote this matrix.

2.10. Let $\boldsymbol{P}$ be any permutation matrix.

(*a*) Prove that $\boldsymbol{P}^{-1} = \boldsymbol{P}^T$.

(*b*) Prove that $\boldsymbol{P}$ can be expressed as a product of pairwise interchanges.

2.11. Write out a detailed algorithm for solving a lower triangular linear system $\boldsymbol{Lx} = \boldsymbol{b}$ by forward-substitution.

2.12. Verify that the dominant term in the operation count (number of multiplications or number of additions) for solving a lower triangular system of order n by forward substitution is $n^2/2$.

2.13. How would you solve a partitioned linear system of the form

$$\begin{bmatrix} \boldsymbol{L}_1 & \boldsymbol{O} \\ \boldsymbol{B} & \boldsymbol{L}_2 \end{bmatrix} \begin{bmatrix} \boldsymbol{x} \\ \boldsymbol{y} \end{bmatrix} = \begin{bmatrix} \boldsymbol{b} \\ \boldsymbol{c} \end{bmatrix},$$

where $\boldsymbol{L}_1$ and $\boldsymbol{L}_2$ are nonsingular lower triangular matrices, and the solution and right-hand-side vectors are partitioned accordingly? Show the specific steps you would perform in terms of the given submatrices and vectors.

2.14. Prove each of the four properties of elementary elimination matrices enumerated in Section 2.4.3.

2.15. (*a*) Prove that the product of two lower triangular matrices is lower triangular.

(*b*) Prove that the inverse of a nonsingular lower triangular matrix is lower triangular.

2.16. (*a*) What is the LU factorization of the following matrix?

$$\begin{bmatrix} 1 & a \\ c & b \end{bmatrix}$$

(*b*) Under what condition is this matrix singular?

2.17. Write out the LU factorization of the following matrix (show both the $\boldsymbol{L}$ and $\boldsymbol{U}$ matrices explicitly):

$$\begin{bmatrix} 1 & -1 & 0 \\ -1 & 2 & -1 \\ 0 & -1 & 1 \end{bmatrix}.$$

2.18. Prove that the matrix

$$\boldsymbol{A} = \begin{bmatrix} 0 & 1 \\ 1 & 0 \end{bmatrix}$$

has no LU factorization, i.e., no lower triangular matrix $\boldsymbol{L}$ and upper triangular matrix $\boldsymbol{U}$ exist such that $\boldsymbol{A} = \boldsymbol{LU}$.

2.19. Let $\boldsymbol{A}$ be an $n \times n$ nonsingular matrix. Consider the following algorithm:

1. Scan columns 1 through n of $\boldsymbol{A}$ in succession, and permute rows, if necessary, so that the diagonal entry is the largest entry in magnitude on or below the diagonal in each column. The result is $\boldsymbol{PA}$ for some permutation matrix $\boldsymbol{P}$.
2. Now carry out Gaussian elimination *without* pivoting to compute the LU factorization of $\boldsymbol{PA}$.

(*a*) Is this algorithm numerically stable?

(*b*) If so, explain why. If not, give a counterexample to illustrate.

2.20. Prove that if Gaussian elimination with partial pivoting is applied to a matrix $\boldsymbol{A}$ that is diagonally dominant by columns, then no row interchanges will occur.

2.21. If $\boldsymbol{A}$, $\boldsymbol{B}$, and $\boldsymbol{C}$ are $n \times n$ matrices, with $\boldsymbol{B}$ and $\boldsymbol{C}$ nonsingular, and $\boldsymbol{b}$ is an n-vector, how would you implement the formula

$$\boldsymbol{x} = \boldsymbol{B}^{-1}(2\boldsymbol{A} + \boldsymbol{I})(\boldsymbol{C}^{-1} + \boldsymbol{A})\boldsymbol{b}$$

without computing any matrix inverses?

2.22. Verify that the dominant term in the operation count (number of multiplications or number of additions) for LU factorization of a matrix of order n by Gaussian elimination is $n^3/3$.

2.23. Verify that the dominant term in the operation count (number of multiplications or number of additions) for computing the inverse of a matrix of order n by Gaussian elimination is n^3.

2.24. Verify that the dominant term in the operation count (number of multiplications or number of additions) for Gauss-Jordan elimination for a matrix of order n is $n^3/2$.

2.25. (*a*) If $\boldsymbol{u}$ and $\boldsymbol{v}$ are nonzero n-vectors, prove that the $n \times n$ outer product matrix $\boldsymbol{uv}^T$ has rank one.

(*b*) If $\boldsymbol{A}$ is an $n \times n$ matrix such that $\text{rank}(\boldsymbol{A}) = 1$, prove that there exist nonzero n-vectors $\boldsymbol{u}$ and $\boldsymbol{v}$ such that $\boldsymbol{A} = \boldsymbol{uv}^T$.

2.26. An $n \times n$ matrix $\boldsymbol{A}$ is said to be *elementary* if it differs from the identity matrix by a matrix of rank one, i.e., if $\boldsymbol{A} = \boldsymbol{I} - \boldsymbol{uv}^T$ for some n-vectors $\boldsymbol{u}$ and $\boldsymbol{v}$.

(*a*) If $\boldsymbol{A}$ is elementary, what condition on $\boldsymbol{u}$ and $\boldsymbol{v}$ ensures that $\boldsymbol{A}$ is nonsingular?

(*b*) If $\boldsymbol{A}$ is elementary and nonsingular, prove that $\boldsymbol{A}^{-1}$ is also elementary by showing that $\boldsymbol{A}^{-1} = \boldsymbol{I} - \sigma\boldsymbol{uv}^T$ for some scalar σ. What is the specific value for σ, in terms of $\boldsymbol{u}$ and $\boldsymbol{v}$?

(*c*) Is an elementary elimination matrix, as defined in Section 2.4.3, elementary? If so, what are $\boldsymbol{u}$, $\boldsymbol{v}$, and σ in this case?

2.27. Prove that the Sherman-Morrison formula

$$(\boldsymbol{A} - \boldsymbol{uv}^T)^{-1} =$$

$$\boldsymbol{A}^{-1} + \boldsymbol{A}^{-1}\boldsymbol{u}(1 - \boldsymbol{v}^T\boldsymbol{A}^{-1}\boldsymbol{u})^{-1}\boldsymbol{v}^T\boldsymbol{A}^{-1}$$

given in Section 2.4.9 is correct. (*Hint*: Multiply both sides by $\boldsymbol{A} - \boldsymbol{uv}^T$.)

2.28. Prove that the Woodbury formula

$$(\boldsymbol{A} - \boldsymbol{UV}^T)^{-1} =$$

$$\boldsymbol{A}^{-1} + \boldsymbol{A}^{-1}\boldsymbol{U}(\boldsymbol{I} - \boldsymbol{V}^T\boldsymbol{A}^{-1}\boldsymbol{U})^{-1}\boldsymbol{V}^T\boldsymbol{A}^{-1}$$

given in Section 2.4.9 is correct. (*Hint*: Multiply both sides by $\boldsymbol{A} - \boldsymbol{UV}^T$.)

2.29. For $p = 1, 2$, and ∞, prove that the vector p-norms satisfy the three properties given near the end of Section 2.3.1.

2.30. For $p = 1$ and ∞, prove that the matrix p-norms satisfy the five properties given near the end of Section 2.3.2

2.31. Let $\boldsymbol{A}$ be a symmetric positive definite matrix. Show that the function

$$\|\boldsymbol{x}\|_A = (\boldsymbol{x}^T\boldsymbol{A}\boldsymbol{x})^{1/2}$$

satisfies the three properties of a vector norm given near the end of Section 2.3.1. This vector norm is said to be *induced* by the matrix $\boldsymbol{A}$.

2.32. Show that the following functions of an $m \times n$ matrix $\boldsymbol{A}$ satisfy the first three properties of a matrix norm given near the end of Section 2.3.2 and hence are matrix norms in the more general sense mentioned there.

(*a*)

$$\|\boldsymbol{A}\|_{\max} = \max_{i,j} |a_{ij}|$$

Note that this is simply the ∞-norm of $\boldsymbol{A}$ considered as a vector in $\mathbb{R}^{mn}$.

(*b*)

$$\|\boldsymbol{A}\|_F = \left(\sum_{i,j} |a_{ij}|^2 \right)^{1/2}$$

Note that this is simply the 2-norm of $\boldsymbol{A}$ considered as a vector in $\mathbb{R}^{mn}$. It is called the *Frobenius matrix norm*.

2.33. Prove or give a counterexample: If $\boldsymbol{A}$ is a nonsingular matrix, then $\|\boldsymbol{A}^{-1}\| = \|\boldsymbol{A}\|^{-1}$.

2.34. Suppose that $\boldsymbol{A}$ is a positive definite matrix.

(*a*) Show that $\boldsymbol{A}$ must be nonsingular.

(*b*) Show that $\boldsymbol{A}^{-1}$ must be positive definite.

2.35. Suppose that the matrix $\boldsymbol{A}$ has a factorization of the form $\boldsymbol{A} = \boldsymbol{B}\boldsymbol{B}^T$, with $\boldsymbol{B}$ nonsingular. Show that $\boldsymbol{A}$ must be symmetric and positive definite.

2.36. Derive an algorithm for computing the Cholesky factorization $\boldsymbol{L}\boldsymbol{L}^T$ of an $n \times n$ symmetric positive definite matrix $\boldsymbol{A}$ by equating the corresponding entries of $\boldsymbol{A}$ and $\boldsymbol{L}\boldsymbol{L}^T$.

2.37. Suppose that the symmetric matrix

$$\boldsymbol{B} = \begin{bmatrix} \alpha & \boldsymbol{a}^T \\ \boldsymbol{a} & \boldsymbol{A} \end{bmatrix}$$

of order $n+1$ is positive definite.

(*a*) Show that the scalar α must be positive and the $n \times n$ matrix $\boldsymbol{A}$ must be positive definite.

(*b*) What is the Cholesky factorization of $\boldsymbol{B}$ in terms of the constituent submatrices?

2.38. Suppose that the symmetric matrix

$$\boldsymbol{B} = \begin{bmatrix} \boldsymbol{A} & \boldsymbol{a} \\ \boldsymbol{a}^T & \alpha \end{bmatrix}$$

of order $n+1$ is positive definite.

(*a*) Show that the scalar α must be positive and the $n \times n$ matrix $\boldsymbol{A}$ must be positive definite.

(*b*) What is the Cholesky factorization of $\boldsymbol{B}$ in terms of the constituent submatrices?

2.39. Verify that the dominant term in the operation count (number of multiplications or number of additions) for Cholesky factorization of a symmetric positive definite matrix of order n is $n^3/6$.

2.40. Let $\boldsymbol{A}$ be a band matrix with bandwidth β, and suppose that the LU factorization $\boldsymbol{PA} = \boldsymbol{LU}$ is computed using Gaussian elimination with partial pivoting. Show that the bandwidth of the upper triangular factor $\boldsymbol{U}$ is at most 2β.

2.41. Let $\boldsymbol{A}$ be a nonsingular tridiagonal matrix.

(*a*) Show that in general $\boldsymbol{A}^{-1}$ is dense.

(*b*) Compare the work and storage required in this case to solve the linear system $\boldsymbol{Ax} = \boldsymbol{b}$ by Gaussian elimination and back-substitution with those required to solve the system by explicit matrix inversion.

This example illustrates yet another reason why explicit matrix inversion is usually a bad idea.

2.42. (*a*) Devise an algorithm for computing the inverse of a nonsingular $n \times n$ triangular matrix *in place*, i.e., with no additional array storage.

(*b*) Is it possible to compute the inverse of a general nonsingular $n \times n$ matrix in place? If so, sketch an algorithm for doing so, and if not, explain why. For purposes of this exercise, you may assume that pivoting is not required.

2.43. Suppose you need to solve the linear system $\boldsymbol{Cz} = \boldsymbol{d}$, where $\boldsymbol{C}$ is a complex $n \times n$ matrix and $\boldsymbol{d}$ and $\boldsymbol{z}$ are complex n-vectors, but your linear equation solver handles only real systems. Let $\boldsymbol{C} = \boldsymbol{A} + i\boldsymbol{B}$ and $\boldsymbol{d} = \boldsymbol{b} + i\boldsymbol{c}$, where $\boldsymbol{A}$, $\boldsymbol{B}$, $\boldsymbol{b}$, and $\boldsymbol{c}$ are real and $i = \sqrt{-1}$. Show that the solution $\boldsymbol{z} = \boldsymbol{x} + i\boldsymbol{y}$ is given by the $2n \times 2n$ real linear system

$$\begin{bmatrix} \boldsymbol{A} & -\boldsymbol{B} \\ \boldsymbol{B} & \boldsymbol{A} \end{bmatrix} \begin{bmatrix} \boldsymbol{x} \\ \boldsymbol{y} \end{bmatrix} = \begin{bmatrix} \boldsymbol{b} \\ \boldsymbol{c} \end{bmatrix}.$$

Is this a good way to solve this problem? Why?

Computer Problems

2.1. (*a*) Show that the matrix

$$\boldsymbol{A} = \begin{bmatrix} 0.1 & 0.2 & 0.3 \\ 0.4 & 0.5 & 0.6 \\ 0.7 & 0.8 & 0.9 \end{bmatrix}$$

is singular. Describe the set of solutions to the system $\boldsymbol{Ax} = \boldsymbol{b}$ if

$$\boldsymbol{b} = \begin{bmatrix} 0.1 \\ 0.3 \\ 0.5 \end{bmatrix}.$$

(*b*) If we were to use Gaussian elimination with partial pivoting to solve this system using exact arithmetic, at what point would the process fail?

(*c*) Because some of the entries of $\boldsymbol{A}$ are not exactly representable in a binary floating-point system, the matrix is no longer exactly singular when entered into a computer; thus, solving the system by Gaussian elimination will not necessarily fail. Solve this system on a computer using a library routine for Gaussian elimination. Compare the computed solution with your description of the solution set in part *a*. If your software includes a condition estimator, what is the estimated value for $\text{cond}(\boldsymbol{A})$? How many digits of accuracy in the solution would this lead you to expect?

2.2. (*a*) Use a library routine for Gaussian elimination to solve the system $\boldsymbol{Ax} = \boldsymbol{b}$, where

$$\boldsymbol{A} = \begin{bmatrix} 2 & 4 & -2 \\ 4 & 9 & -3 \\ -2 & -1 & 7 \end{bmatrix}, \quad \boldsymbol{b} = \begin{bmatrix} 2 \\ 8 \\ 10 \end{bmatrix}.$$

(*b*) Use the LU factorization of $\boldsymbol{A}$ already computed to solve the system $\boldsymbol{Ay} = \boldsymbol{c}$, where

$$\boldsymbol{c} = \begin{bmatrix} 4 \\ 8 \\ -6 \end{bmatrix},$$

without refactoring the matrix.

(*c*) If the matrix $\boldsymbol{A}$ changes so that $a_{1,2} = 2$, use the Sherman-Morrison updating technique to compute the new solution $\boldsymbol{x}$ without refactoring the matrix, using the original right-hand-side vector $\boldsymbol{b}$.

2.3. The following diagram depicts a plane truss having 13 members (the numbered lines) connected by 10 joints (the numbered circles). The indicated loads, in tons, are applied at joints 2, 5, and 6, and we wish to determine the resulting force on each member of the truss.

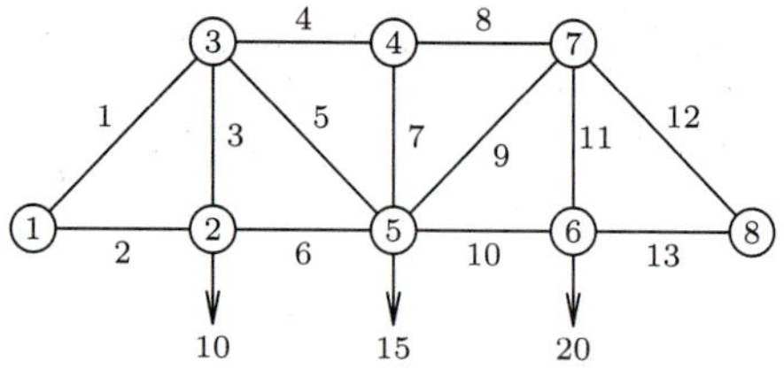

For the truss to be in static equilibrium, there must be no net force, horizontally or vertically, at any joint. Thus, we can determine the member forces by equating the horizontal forces to the left and right at each joint, and similarly equating the vertical forces upward and downward at each joint. For the eight joints, this would give 16 equations, which is more than the 13 unknown forces to be determined. For the truss to be statically determinate, that is, for there to be a unique solution, we assume that joint 1 is rigidly fixed both horizontally and vertically, and that joint 8 is fixed vertically. Resolving the member forces into horizontal and vertical components and defining $\alpha = \sqrt{2}/2$, we obtain the following system of equations for the member forces f_i:

$$\begin{aligned}
\text{Joint 2}: &\begin{cases} f_2 = f_6 \\ f_3 = 10 \end{cases} \\
\text{Joint 3}: &\begin{cases} \alpha f_1 = f_4 + \alpha f_5 \\ \alpha f_1 + f_3 + \alpha f_5 = 0 \end{cases} \\
\text{Joint 4}: &\begin{cases} f_4 = f_8 \\ f_7 = 0 \end{cases} \\
\text{Joint 5}: &\begin{cases} \alpha f_5 + f_6 = \alpha f_9 + f_{10} \\ \alpha f_5 + f_7 + \alpha f_9 = 15 \end{cases} \\
\text{Joint 6}: &\begin{cases} f_{10} = f_{13} \\ f_{11} = 20 \end{cases} \\
\text{Joint 7}: &\begin{cases} f_8 + \alpha f_9 = \alpha f_{12} \\ \alpha f_9 + f_{11} + \alpha f_{12} = 0 \end{cases} \\
\text{Joint 8}: &\{\; f_{13} + \alpha f_{12} = 0
\end{aligned}$$

Use a library routine to solve this system of linear equations for the vector $\boldsymbol{f}$ of member forces. Note that the matrix of this system is quite sparse, so you may wish to experiment with a banded system solver or more general sparse solver, although this particular problem instance is too small for these to offer significant advantage over a general solver.

2.4. Write a routine for estimating the condition number of a matrix $\boldsymbol{A}$. You may use either the 1-norm or the ∞-norm (or try both and compare the results). You will need to compute $\|\boldsymbol{A}\|$, which is easy, and estimate $\|\boldsymbol{A}^{-1}\|$, which is more challenging. As discussed in Section 2.3.3, one way to estimate $\|\boldsymbol{A}^{-1}\|$ is to choose a vector $\boldsymbol{y}$ such that the ratio $\|\boldsymbol{z}\|/\|\boldsymbol{y}\|$ is large, where $\boldsymbol{z}$ is the solution to $\boldsymbol{A}\boldsymbol{z} = \boldsymbol{y}$. Try two different approaches to choosing $\boldsymbol{y}$:

(*a*) Choose $\boldsymbol{y}$ as the solution to the system $\boldsymbol{A}^T\boldsymbol{y} = \boldsymbol{c}$, where $\boldsymbol{c}$ is a vector each of whose components is ± 1, with the sign for each component chosen by the following heuristic. Using the factorization $\boldsymbol{A} = \boldsymbol{L}\boldsymbol{U}$, the system $\boldsymbol{A}^T\boldsymbol{y} = \boldsymbol{c}$ is solved in two stages, successively solving the triangular systems $\boldsymbol{U}^T\boldsymbol{v} = \boldsymbol{c}$ and $\boldsymbol{L}^T\boldsymbol{y} = \boldsymbol{v}$. At each step of the first triangular solution, choose the corresponding component of $\boldsymbol{c}$ to be 1 or -1, depending on which will make the resulting component of $\boldsymbol{v}$ larger in magnitude. (You will need to write a custom triangular solution routine to implement this.) Then solve the second triangular system in the usual way for $\boldsymbol{y}$. The idea here is that any ill-conditioning in $\boldsymbol{A}$ will be reflected in $\boldsymbol{U}$, resulting in a relatively large $\boldsymbol{v}$. The relatively well-conditioned unit triangular matrix $\boldsymbol{L}$ will then preserve this relationship, resulting in a relatively large $\boldsymbol{y}$.

(*b*) Choose some small number, say, five, different vectors $\boldsymbol{y}$ randomly and use the one producing the largest ratio $\|\boldsymbol{z}\|/\|\boldsymbol{y}\|$. (For this you can use an ordinary triangular solution routine.)

You may use a library routine to obtain the necessary LU factorization of $\boldsymbol{A}$. Test both of the approaches on each of the following matrices:

$$\boldsymbol{A}_1 = \begin{bmatrix} 10 & -7 & 0 \\ -3 & 2 & 6 \\ 5 & -1 & 5 \end{bmatrix},$$

$$\boldsymbol{A}_2 = \begin{bmatrix} -73 & 78 & 24 \\ 92 & 66 & 25 \\ -80 & 37 & 10 \end{bmatrix}.$$

How do the results using these two methods compare? To check the quality of your estimates, compute $\boldsymbol{A}^{-1}$ explicitly to determine its true norm (this computation can also make use of the LU factorization already computed). If you have access to linear equations software that already includes a condition estimator, how do your results compare with its?

2.5. (*a*) Use a single-precision routine for Gaussian elimination to solve the system $\boldsymbol{A}\boldsymbol{x} = \boldsymbol{b}$, where

$$\boldsymbol{A} = \begin{bmatrix} 21.0 & 67.0 & 88.0 & 73.0 \\ 76.0 & 63.0 & 7.0 & 20.0 \\ 0.0 & 85.0 & 56.0 & 54.0 \\ 19.3 & 43.0 & 30.2 & 29.4 \end{bmatrix},$$

$$\boldsymbol{b} = \begin{bmatrix} 141.0 \\ 109.0 \\ 218.0 \\ 93.7 \end{bmatrix}.$$

(*b*) Compute the residual $\boldsymbol{r} = \boldsymbol{b} - \boldsymbol{A}\boldsymbol{x}$ using double-precision arithmetic, if available (but storing the final result in a single-precision vector $\boldsymbol{r}$). Note that the solution routine may destroy the array containing $\boldsymbol{A}$, so you may need to save a separate copy for computing the residual. (If only one precision is available in the computing environment you use, then do all of this problem in that precision.)

(*c*) Solve the linear system $\boldsymbol{A}\boldsymbol{z} = \boldsymbol{r}$ to obtain the "improved" solution $\boldsymbol{x} + \boldsymbol{z}$. Note that $\boldsymbol{A}$ need not be refactored.

(*d*) Repeat steps *b* and *c* until no further improvement is observed.

2.6. An $n \times n$ *Hilbert* matrix $\boldsymbol{H}$ has entries $h_{ij} = 1/(i + j - 1)$, so it has the form

$$\begin{bmatrix} 1 & 1/2 & 1/3 & \cdots \\ 1/2 & 1/3 & 1/4 & \cdots \\ 1/3 & 1/4 & 1/5 & \cdots \\ \vdots & \vdots & \vdots & \ddots \end{bmatrix}.$$

For $n = 2, 3, \ldots$, generate the Hilbert matrix of order n, and also generate the n-vector $\boldsymbol{b} = \boldsymbol{H}\boldsymbol{x}$, where $\boldsymbol{x}$ is the n-vector with all of its components equal to 1. Use a library routine for Gaussian elimination (or Cholesky factorization, since the Hilbert matrix is symmetric and positive definite) to solve the resulting linear system $\boldsymbol{Hx} = \boldsymbol{b}$, obtaining an approximate solution $\hat{\boldsymbol{x}}$. Compute the ∞-norm of the residual $\boldsymbol{r} = \boldsymbol{b} - \boldsymbol{H}\hat{\boldsymbol{x}}$ and of the error $\Delta\boldsymbol{x} = \hat{\boldsymbol{x}} - \boldsymbol{x}$, where $\boldsymbol{x}$ is the vector of all ones. How large can you take n before the error is 100 percent (i.e., there are no significant digits in the solution)? Also use a condition estimator to obtain cond($\boldsymbol{H}$) for each value of n. Try to characterize the condition number as a function of n. As n varies, how does the number of correct digits in the components of the computed solution relate to the condition number of the matrix?

2.7. (*a*) What happens when Gaussian elimination with partial pivoting is used on a matrix of the following form?

$$\begin{bmatrix} 1 & 0 & 0 & 0 & 1 \\ -1 & 1 & 0 & 0 & 1 \\ -1 & -1 & 1 & 0 & 1 \\ -1 & -1 & -1 & 1 & 1 \\ -1 & -1 & -1 & -1 & 1 \end{bmatrix}$$

Do the entries of the transformed matrix grow? What happens if complete pivoting is used instead? (Note that part *a* does not require a computer.)

(*b*) Use a library routine for Gaussian elimination with partial pivoting to solve various sizes of linear systems of this form, using right-hand-side vectors chosen so that the solution is known. How do the error, residual, and condition number behave as the systems become larger? This artificially contrived system illustrates the worst-case growth factor cited in Section 2.4.5 and is not indicative of the usual behavior of Gaussian elimination with partial pivoting.

2.8. Multiplying both sides of a linear system $\boldsymbol{Ax} = \boldsymbol{b}$ by a nonsingular diagonal matrix $\boldsymbol{D}$ to obtain a new system $\boldsymbol{DAx} = \boldsymbol{Db}$ simply rescales the rows of the system and in theory does not change the solution. Such scaling does affect the condition number of the matrix and the choice of pivots in Gaussian elimination, however, so it may affect the accuracy of the solution in finite-precision arithmetic. Note that scaling can introduce some rounding error in the matrix unless the entries of $\boldsymbol{D}$ are powers of the base of the floating-point arithmetic system being used (why?).

Using a linear system with randomly chosen matrix $\boldsymbol{A}$, and right-hand-side vector $\boldsymbol{b}$ chosen so that the solution is known, experiment with various scaling matrices $\boldsymbol{D}$ to see what effect they have on the condition number of the matrix $\boldsymbol{DA}$ and the solution given by a library routine for solving the linear system $\boldsymbol{DAx} = \boldsymbol{Db}$. Be sure to try some fairly skewed scalings, where the magnitudes of the diagonal entries of $\boldsymbol{D}$ vary widely (the purpose is to simulate a system with badly chosen units). Compare both the relative residuals and the error given by the various scalings. Can you find a scaling that gives very poor accuracy? Is the residual still small in this case?

2.9. (*a*) Use Gaussian elimination *without* pivoting to solve the linear system

$$\begin{bmatrix} \epsilon & 1 \\ 1 & 1 \end{bmatrix} \begin{bmatrix} x_1 \\ x_2 \end{bmatrix} = \begin{bmatrix} 1+\epsilon \\ 2 \end{bmatrix}$$

for $\epsilon = 10^{-2k}$, $k = 1, \ldots, 10$. The exact solution is $x = [1 \quad 1]^T$, independent of the value of ϵ. How does the accuracy of the computed solution behave as the value of ϵ decreases?

(*b*) Repeat part *a*, still using Gaussian elimination without pivoting, but this time use one iteration of iterative refinement to improve the solution, computing the residual in the same precision as the rest of the computations. Now how does the accuracy of the computed solution behave as the value of ϵ decreases?

2.10. Consider the linear system

$$\begin{bmatrix} 1 & 1+\epsilon \\ 1-\epsilon & 1 \end{bmatrix} \begin{bmatrix} x_1 \\ x_2 \end{bmatrix} = \begin{bmatrix} 1+(1+\epsilon)\epsilon \\ 1 \end{bmatrix},$$

where ϵ is a small parameter to be specified. The exact solution is obviously

$$\boldsymbol{x} = \begin{bmatrix} 1 \\ \epsilon \end{bmatrix}$$

for any value of ϵ.

Use a library routine based on Gaussian elimination to solve this system. Experiment with various values for ϵ, especially values near $\sqrt{\epsilon_{\text{mach}}}$ for your computer. For each value of ϵ you try, compute an estimate of the condition number of the matrix and the relative error in each component of the solution. How accurately is each component determined? How does the accuracy attained for each component compare with expectations based on the condition number of the matrix and the error bounds given in Section 2.3.4? What conclusions can you draw from this experiment?

2.11. (*a*) Write programs implementing Gaussian elimination with no pivoting, partial pivoting, and complete pivoting.
(*b*) Generate several linear systems with random matrices (i.e., use a random number generator to obtain the matrix entries) and right-hand sides chosen so that the solutions are known, and compare the accuracy, residuals, and performance of the three implementations.
(*c*) Can you devise a (nonrandom) matrix for which complete pivoting is significantly more accurate than partial pivoting?

2.12. Write a routine for solving tridiagonal systems of linear equations using the algorithm given in Section 2.5.3 and test it on some sample systems. Describe how your routine would change if you included partial pivoting. Describe how your routine would change if the system were positive definite and you computed the Cholesky factorization instead of the LU factorization.

2.13. The determinant of a triangular matrix is equal to the product of its diagonal entries. Use this fact to develop a routine for computing the determinant of an arbitrary $n \times n$ matrix $\boldsymbol{A}$ by using its LU factorization. You may use a library routine for Gaussian elimination with partial pivoting to obtain the LU factorization, or you may design your own routine. How can you determine the proper sign for the determinant? To avoid risk of overflow or underflow, you may wish to consider computing the logarithm of the determinant instead of the actual value of the determinant.

2.14. Write programs implementing matrix multiplication $\boldsymbol{C} = \boldsymbol{AB}$, where $\boldsymbol{A}$ is $m \times n$ and $\boldsymbol{B}$ is $n \times k$, in two different ways:
(*a*) Compute the mk inner products of rows of $\boldsymbol{A}$ with columns of $\boldsymbol{B}$,
(*b*) Form each column of $\boldsymbol{C}$ as a linear combination of columns of $\boldsymbol{A}$.
In `BLAS` terminology (see Section 2.7.2), the first implementation uses `sdot`, whereas the second uses `saxpy`. Compare the performance of these two implementations on your computer. You may need to try fairly large matrices before the differences in performance become significant. Find out as much as you can about your computer system (e.g., cache size and cache management policy), and use this information to explain the results you observe.

2.15. Implement Gaussian elimination using each of the six different orderings of the triple-nested loop and compare their performance on your computer. For purposes of this exercise, you may ignore pivoting for numerical stability, but be sure to use test matrices that do not require pivoting. You may need to try a fairly large system before the differences in performance become significant. Find out as much as you can about your computer system (e.g., cache size and cache management policy), and use this information to explain the results you observe.

2.16. Both forward- and back-substitution for solving triangular linear systems involve nested loops whose two indices can be taken in either order. Implement both forward- and back-substitution using each of the two index orderings (a total of four algorithms), and compare their performance for triangular test matrices of various sizes. You may need to try a fairly large system before the differences in performance become significant. Is the best choice of index orderings the same for both algorithms? Find out as much as you can about your computer system (e.g., cache size and cache management policy), and use this information to explain the results you observe.

2.17. Consider a horizontal cantilevered beam that is clamped at one end but free along the remainder of its length. A discrete model of the forces on the beam yields a system of linear equations $\boldsymbol{Ax} = \boldsymbol{b}$, where the $n \times n$ matrix $\boldsymbol{A}$ has the banded form

$$\begin{bmatrix} 9 & -4 & 1 & 0 & \cdots & \cdots & 0 \\ -4 & 6 & -4 & 1 & \ddots & & \vdots \\ 1 & -4 & 6 & -4 & 1 & \ddots & \vdots \\ 0 & \ddots & \ddots & \ddots & \ddots & \ddots & 0 \\ \vdots & \ddots & 1 & -4 & 6 & -4 & 1 \\ \vdots & & \ddots & 1 & -4 & 5 & -2 \\ 0 & \cdots & \cdots & 0 & 1 & -2 & 1 \end{bmatrix},$$

the n-vector $\boldsymbol{b}$ is the known load on the bar (including its own weight), and the n-vector $\boldsymbol{x}$ represents the resulting deflection of the bar that is to be determined. We will take the bar to be uniformly loaded, with $b_i = 1$ for each component of the load vector.

(*a*) Letting $n = 100$, solve this linear system using both a standard library routine for dense linear systems and a library routine designed for banded (or more general sparse) systems. How do the two routines compare in the time required to compute the solution? How well do the answers obtained agree with each other?

(*b*) Verify that the matrix $\boldsymbol{A}$ has the UL factorization $\boldsymbol{A} = \boldsymbol{R}\boldsymbol{R}^T$, where $\boldsymbol{R}$ is an upper triangular matrix of the form

$$\begin{bmatrix} 2 & -2 & 1 & 0 & \cdots & 0 \\ 0 & 1 & -2 & 1 & \ddots & \vdots \\ \vdots & \ddots & \ddots & \ddots & \ddots & 0 \\ \vdots & & \ddots & 1 & -2 & 1 \\ \vdots & & & \ddots & 1 & -2 \\ 0 & \cdots & \cdots & \cdots & 0 & 1 \end{bmatrix}.$$

Letting $n = 1000$, solve the linear system using this factorization (two triangular solves will be required). Also solve the system in its original form using a banded (or general sparse) system solver as in part *a*. How well do the answers obtained agree with each other? Which approach seems more accurate? What is the condition number of $\boldsymbol{A}$, and what accuracy does it suggest that you should expect? Try iterative refinement to see if the accuracy or residual improves for the less accurate method.

Chapter 3

Linear Least Squares

3.1 Linear Least Squares Problems

Suppose you want to know the typical monthly rainfall in Seattle. Would a single month's measurements suffice? Of course not—any given month might be unusually sunny or stormy. Instead, one would probably take readings over many months—at least a year, or perhaps ten years—and average them. The resulting average might not be exactly correct for any particular month, yet somehow we intuitively feel that it gives a far more accurate picture of typical rainfall than any single reading is likely to give. This principle—taking many measurements to smooth out measurement errors or other random variations—is almost universal in observational and experimental sciences. Land surveyors deliberately take more measurements than are strictly necessary to determine distances between reference points. Astronomers and communications engineers use this principle in extracting meaningful signals from noisy data. Even the carpenter's maxim "measure twice, cut once" is an example of the wisdom of this approach.

In the rainfall example, we sought a single number to represent, or in some sense approximate, a whole ensemble of numbers. More generally, it is common for a variety of theoretical and practical reasons to seek a lower-dimensional approximation to some higher-dimensional object. We might do this as a way of smoothing out errors or ignoring irrelevant details, as in extracting a signal or trend from noisy data, or as a way of reducing a large amount of data to a more manageable amount, or replacing some complicated function by a simple approximation. We do not expect such an approximation to be exact—indeed, for most purposes we don't want it to be exact—but nevertheless we wish to retain some resemblance to the original data. In the terminology of linear algebra, we wish to project a vector from a higher-dimensional space onto some lower-dimensional subspace. One of the most popular and computationally convenient ways of accomplishing this is the method of least squares, which we will study in this chapter.

We will restrict our attention for now to linear problems, deferring nonlinear least squares to Section 6.6. We saw in Section 2.2 that a square linear system is exactly determined: with the same number of equations and unknowns, a unique solution always exists, provided the matrix is nonsingular. In interpolation, for example, we exploit the parity between parameters and data points to fit the given data exactly by a linear combination of basis functions (see Chapter 7). In the current setting, however, we presume that the given data are noisy or contain irrelevant detail, and hence there is no particular virtue in fitting them exactly. Indeed, we can smooth out such variations by forgoing an exact fit and instead using more data points or measurements than necessary, producing an *overdetermined* system with more equations than unknowns. Writing the linear system in matrix-vector notation, we have

$$\boldsymbol{A}\boldsymbol{x} = \boldsymbol{b},$$

where $\boldsymbol{A}$ is an $m \times n$ matrix with $m > n$, $\boldsymbol{b}$ is an m-vector, and $\boldsymbol{x}$ an n-vector. In general, with only n parameters in the vector $\boldsymbol{x}$, we would not expect to be able to reproduce the m-vector $\boldsymbol{b}$ as a linear combination of the n columns of $\boldsymbol{A}$. In other words, for an overdetermined system there is usually no solution in the usual sense. Instead, we minimize the distance between the left and right sides, i.e., we minimize some norm of the *residual* vector $\boldsymbol{r} = \boldsymbol{b} - \boldsymbol{A}\boldsymbol{x}$ as a function of $\boldsymbol{x}$. In principle any norm could be used, but as we will see, there are strong reasons to prefer the Euclidean or 2-norm, including its relationship with the inner product and orthogonality, its smoothness and strict convexity, and its computational convenience. Use of the 2-norm gives the method of least squares its name: the solution is the vector $\boldsymbol{x}$ that minimizes the sum of squares of differences between the components of the left and right sides of the linear system. To reflect this lack of exact equality, we write a *linear least squares* problem as

$$\boldsymbol{A}\boldsymbol{x} \cong \boldsymbol{b},$$

where the approximation is understood to be in the 2-norm, or least squares, sense.

Example 3.1 Overdetermined System. A surveyor is to determine the heights of three hills above some reference point. Sighting first from the reference point, the surveyor measures their respective heights to be $x_1 = 1237$ ft., $x_2 = 1941$ ft., and $x_3 = 2417$ ft. To confirm these initial measurements, the surveyor climbs to the top of the first hill and measures the height of the second hill above the first to be $x_2 - x_1 = 711$ ft., and the third above the first to be $x_3 - x_1 = 1177$ ft. Finally, the surveyor climbs to the top of the second hill and measures the height of the third hill above the second to be $x_3 - x_2 = 475$ ft. Noting the inconsistency among these measurements, the surveyor uses methods we will soon demonstrate to compute the least squares solution to the overdetermined linear system

$$\boldsymbol{A}\boldsymbol{x} = \begin{bmatrix} 1 & 0 & 0 \\ 0 & 1 & 0 \\ 0 & 0 & 1 \\ -1 & 1 & 0 \\ -1 & 0 & 1 \\ 0 & -1 & 1 \end{bmatrix} \begin{bmatrix} x_1 \\ x_2 \\ x_3 \end{bmatrix} \cong \begin{bmatrix} 1237 \\ 1941 \\ 2417 \\ 711 \\ 1177 \\ 475 \end{bmatrix} = \boldsymbol{b},$$

obtaining $\boldsymbol{x} = [1236,\ 1943,\ 2416]^T$. These values, which differ slightly from the three initial height measurements, represent a compromise that best reconciles (in the least squares sense) the inconsistencies resulting from measurement errors.

Early development of the method of least squares was due largely to Gauss, who used it for solving problems in astronomy, particularly determining the orbits of celestial bodies such as asteroids and comets. The elliptical orbit of such a body is determined by five parameters (see Computer Problem 3.5), so in principle only five observations of its position should be necessary to determine the complete orbit. Owing to measurement errors, however, an orbit based on only five observations would be highly unreliable. Instead, many more observations are taken, and the method of least squares is used to smooth out the errors and obtain more accurate values for the orbital parameters. Least squares approximation reduces the dozens or hundreds of observations, which lie in a correspondingly high-dimensional space, down to the five-dimensional parameter space of the elliptical orbit model.

Example 3.2 Data Fitting. One of the most common uses for the method of least squares is in *data fitting*, or *curve fitting*, especially when the data have some random error associated with them, as do most empirical laboratory measurements or other observations of nature. Given data points (t_i, y_i), $i = 1, \dots, m$, we wish to find the n-vector $\boldsymbol{x}$ of parameters that gives the "best fit" to the data by the *model function* $f(t, \boldsymbol{x})$, with $f\colon \mathbb{R}^{n+1} \to \mathbb{R}$, where by best fit we mean in the least squares sense:

$$\min_{\boldsymbol{x}} \sum_{i=1}^{m} (y_i - f(t_i, \boldsymbol{x}))^2.$$

A data-fitting problem is *linear* if the function f is linear in the components of the parameter vector $\boldsymbol{x}$, which means that f is a linear combination

$$f(t, \boldsymbol{x}) = x_1\phi_1(t) + x_2\phi_2(t) + \cdots + x_n\phi_n(t)$$

of functions ϕ_j that depend only on t. For example, polynomial fitting, with

$$f(t, \boldsymbol{x}) = x_1 + x_2 t + x_3 t^2 + \cdots + x_n t^{n-1},$$

is a linear data-fitting problem because a polynomial is linear in its coefficients x_j, although nonlinear in the independent variable t. An example of a *nonlinear* data-fitting problem, which we will consider in Section 6.6, is a sum of exponentials

$$f(t, \boldsymbol{x}) = x_1 e^{x_2 t} + \cdots + x_{n-1} e^{x_n t}.$$

If we define the $m \times n$ matrix $\boldsymbol{A}$ with entries $a_{ij} = \phi_j(t_i)$ and m-vector $\boldsymbol{b}$ with components $b_i = y_i$, then a linear least squares data-fitting problem takes the form

$$\boldsymbol{A}\boldsymbol{x} \cong \boldsymbol{b}.$$

For example, in fitting a quadratic polynomial, which has three parameters, to five data points $(t_1, y_1), \dots, (t_5, y_5)$, the matrix $\boldsymbol{A}$ is 5×3, and the problem has the form

$$\boldsymbol{Ax} = \begin{bmatrix} 1 & t_1 & t_1^2 \\ 1 & t_2 & t_2^2 \\ 1 & t_3 & t_3^2 \\ 1 & t_4 & t_4^2 \\ 1 & t_5 & t_5^2 \end{bmatrix} \begin{bmatrix} x_1 \\ x_2 \\ x_3 \end{bmatrix} \cong \begin{bmatrix} y_1 \\ y_2 \\ y_3 \\ y_4 \\ y_5 \end{bmatrix} = \boldsymbol{b}.$$

A matrix of this particular form, whose columns (or rows) are successive powers of some independent variable, is called a *Vandermonde matrix*.

Suppose that we have the following measured data

t	0.0	0.5	1.0	1.5	2.0	2.5	3.0	3.5	4.0	4.5	5.0
y	2.9	2.7	4.8	5.3	7.1	7.6	7.7	7.6	9.4	9.0	9.6
t	5.5	6.0	6.5	7.0	7.5	8.0	8.5	9.0	9.5	10.0	
y	10.0	10.2	9.7	8.3	8.4	9.0	8.3	6.6	6.7	4.1	

These 21 data points, plotted as bullets in Fig. 3.1, apparently contain some random noise, but they seem to fall roughly along a parabolic arc (or perhaps some underlying physical process, such as the trajectory of a projectile, might suggest a parabolic model), so we decide to fit them with a quadratic polynomial. Obviously, a quadratic will not fit the data exactly, but we wish merely to determine the general trend of the data and would not want to mimic the random measurement noise anyway, so a least squares approximation seems appropriate. The resulting overdetermined 21×3 linear system we obtain has the form

$$\boldsymbol{Ax} = \begin{bmatrix} 1 & 0.0 & 0.0 \\ 1 & 0.5 & 0.25 \\ 1 & 1.0 & 1.0 \\ \vdots & \vdots & \vdots \\ 1 & 10.0 & 100.0 \end{bmatrix} \begin{bmatrix} x_1 \\ x_2 \\ x_3 \end{bmatrix} \cong \begin{bmatrix} 2.9 \\ 2.7 \\ 4.8 \\ \vdots \\ 4.1 \end{bmatrix} = \boldsymbol{b}.$$

The solution to this system, which we will see later how to compute, turns out to be $\boldsymbol{x} \approx \begin{bmatrix} 2.18 & 2.67 & -0.238 \end{bmatrix}^T$, which means that the approximating polynomial, plotted as a smooth curve in Fig. 3.1, is given by

$$p(t) = 2.18 + 2.67t - 0.238t^2.$$

This particular polynomial is the best fit to the given data among all quadratic polynomials in the sense that it minimizes the sum of squares of vertical distances between the data points and the curve over all possible quadratic polynomials.

The method of least squares is an important tool in statistics, where it is also known as *regression analysis*. We will be concerned only with numerical algorithms for solving least squares problems. For the many important statistical considerations in formulating least squares problems and properly interpreting the results, consult any book on regression analysis or multivariate statistics.

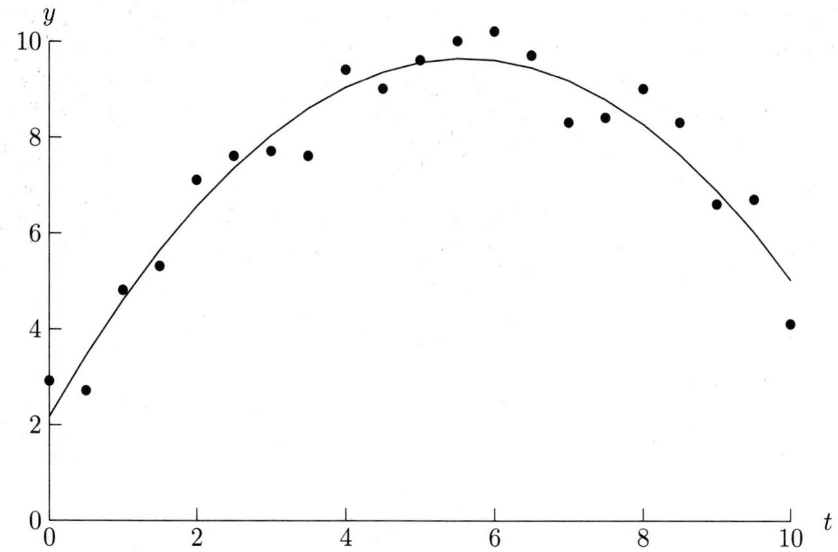

Figure 3.1: Least squares fit of quadratic polynomial to given data.

3.2 Existence and Uniqueness

Recall from Section 2.1 that an $m \times n$ linear system $\boldsymbol{Ax} = \boldsymbol{b}$ asks whether $\boldsymbol{b}$ can be expressed as a linear combination of the columns of $\boldsymbol{A}$. For square systems ($m = n$), the answer is always "yes" for nonsingular $\boldsymbol{A}$. For overdetermined systems ($m > n$), on the other hand, the answer is usually "no" unless $\boldsymbol{b}$ happens to lie in span($\boldsymbol{A}$), which is highly unlikely in most applications. In the method of least squares, however, we neither expect nor do we usually desire an exact match between the two sides of the equation, but merely the closest match possible in the 2-norm. With this different concept of a solution, the criteria for its existence and uniqueness differ somewhat from those for square linear systems, as we will see next.

First, we observe that the existence of a least squares solution is always guaranteed: the function $\phi(\boldsymbol{y}) = \|\boldsymbol{b} - \boldsymbol{y}\|_2$ is continuous and coercive on $\mathbb{R}^m$, so ϕ has a minimum on the closed, unbounded set span($\boldsymbol{A}$) (see Section 6.2), i.e., there is an m-vector $\boldsymbol{y} \in$ span($\boldsymbol{A}$) closest to $\boldsymbol{b}$ in the Euclidean norm. Moreover, ϕ is strictly convex on the convex set span($\boldsymbol{A}$), so the vector $\boldsymbol{y} \in$ span($\boldsymbol{A}$) closest to $\boldsymbol{b}$ is unique (see Section 6.2.1). This does not imply, however, that the solution $\boldsymbol{x}$ to the least squares problem is necessarily unique. Suppose $\boldsymbol{x}_1$ and $\boldsymbol{x}_2$ are such solutions, and let $\boldsymbol{z} = \boldsymbol{x}_2 - \boldsymbol{x}_1$. Then, since $\boldsymbol{Ax}_1 = \boldsymbol{y} = \boldsymbol{Ax}_2$, we have $\boldsymbol{Az} = \boldsymbol{0}$. Now if $\boldsymbol{z} \neq \boldsymbol{0}$, i.e., $\boldsymbol{x}_1 \neq \boldsymbol{x}_2$, then the columns of $\boldsymbol{A}$ must be linearly dependent (compare with Condition 4 for nonsingularity of a square matrix in Section 2.2). We conclude that the solution to an $m \times n$ least squares problem $\boldsymbol{Ax} \cong \boldsymbol{b}$ is unique if, and only if, $\boldsymbol{A}$ has full column rank, i.e., rank($\boldsymbol{A}$) $= n$ (compare with Condition 3 for nonsingularity of a square matrix in Section 2.2). If rank($\boldsymbol{A}$) $< n$, then $\boldsymbol{A}$ is said to be *rank-deficient*, and though a solution of the corresponding least squares problem must still exist, it cannot be unique in this case. We will consider the implications of rank deficiency later, but for now we will assume that $\boldsymbol{A}$ has full column rank.

The existence proof just cited is nonconstructive and gives little insight into how to characterize or compute the solution to a linear least squares problem. We next consider analytic, geometric, and algebraic perspectives that yield more insight into the nature of least squares problems and various methods for solving them.

3.2.1 Normal Equations

As a minimization problem, a least squares problem can be treated using methods of multivariate calculus, analogous to setting the derivative equal to zero in univariate calculus. We wish to minimize the squared Euclidean norm of the residual vector $\boldsymbol{r} = \boldsymbol{b} - \boldsymbol{A}\boldsymbol{x}$. Denoting this objective function by $\phi \colon \mathbb{R}^n \to \mathbb{R}$, we have

$$\phi(\boldsymbol{x}) = \|\boldsymbol{r}\|_2^2 = \boldsymbol{r}^T\boldsymbol{r} = (\boldsymbol{b} - \boldsymbol{A}\boldsymbol{x})^T(\boldsymbol{b} - \boldsymbol{A}\boldsymbol{x}) = \boldsymbol{b}^T\boldsymbol{b} - 2\boldsymbol{x}^T\boldsymbol{A}^T\boldsymbol{b} + \boldsymbol{x}^T\boldsymbol{A}^T\boldsymbol{A}\boldsymbol{x}.$$

A necessary condition for a minimum is that $\boldsymbol{x}$ be a critical point of ϕ, where the gradient vector $\nabla\phi(\boldsymbol{x})$, whose ith component is given by $\partial\phi(\boldsymbol{x})/\partial x_i$, is zero (see Section 6.2.2). Thus, we must have

$$\boldsymbol{0} = \nabla\phi(\boldsymbol{x}) = 2\boldsymbol{A}^T\boldsymbol{A}\boldsymbol{x} - 2\boldsymbol{A}^T\boldsymbol{b},$$

so any minimizer $\boldsymbol{x}$ for ϕ must satisfy the $n \times n$ symmetric linear system

$$\boldsymbol{A}^T\boldsymbol{A}\boldsymbol{x} = \boldsymbol{A}^T\boldsymbol{b}.$$

A sufficient condition that such an $\boldsymbol{x}$ is indeed a minimum is that the Hessian matrix of second partial derivatives, which in this instance is just $2\boldsymbol{A}^T\boldsymbol{A}$, is positive definite (again, see Section 6.2.2). It is easy to show that $\boldsymbol{A}^T\boldsymbol{A}$ is positive definite if, and only if, the columns of $\boldsymbol{A}$ are linearly independent, i.e., $\text{rank}(\boldsymbol{A}) = n$, which is the criterion for uniqueness of the least squares solution that we saw earlier.

The linear system $\boldsymbol{A}^T\boldsymbol{A}\boldsymbol{x} = \boldsymbol{A}^T\boldsymbol{b}$ is commonly known as the system of *normal equations*. The (i, j) entry of the matrix $\boldsymbol{A}^T\boldsymbol{A}$ is the inner product of the ith and jth columns of $\boldsymbol{A}$; for this reason $\boldsymbol{A}^T\boldsymbol{A}$ is sometimes called the *cross-product matrix* of $\boldsymbol{A}$. This square linear system suggests a method, which we will examine in more detail in Section 3.4.1, for solving overdetermined least squares problems.

Example 3.3 Normal Equations. The system of normal equations for the linear least squares problem in Example 3.1 is the symmetric positive definite system

$$\boldsymbol{A}^T\boldsymbol{A}\boldsymbol{x} = \begin{bmatrix} 3 & -1 & -1 \\ -1 & 3 & -1 \\ -1 & -1 & 3 \end{bmatrix} \begin{bmatrix} x_1 \\ x_2 \\ x_3 \end{bmatrix} = \begin{bmatrix} -651 \\ 2177 \\ 4069 \end{bmatrix} = \boldsymbol{A}^T\boldsymbol{b},$$

whose solution $\boldsymbol{x} = [1236,\ 1943,\ 2416]^T$, which can be computed using the Cholesky factorization that was obtained in Example 2.21, achieves the minimum possible sum of squares, $\|\boldsymbol{r}\|_2^2 = 35$.

3.2.2 Orthogonality and Orthogonal Projectors

For a geometric view of least squares problems, we need the notion of orthogonality. Recall that for vectors $\boldsymbol{v}_1,\ \boldsymbol{v}_2 \in \mathbb{R}^m$,

$$\boldsymbol{v}_1^T \boldsymbol{v}_2 = \|\boldsymbol{v}_1\|_2 \cdot \|\boldsymbol{v}_2\|_2 \cdot \cos(\theta),$$

where θ is the angle between $\boldsymbol{v}_1$ and $\boldsymbol{v}_2$. Thus, $\boldsymbol{v}_1$ and $\boldsymbol{v}_2$ are said to be *orthogonal* (or *perpendicular* or *normal*) to each other if $\boldsymbol{v}_1^T \boldsymbol{v}_2 = 0$.

For a least squares problem $\boldsymbol{A}\boldsymbol{x} \cong \boldsymbol{b}$, with $m > n$, the m-vector $\boldsymbol{b}$ generally does not lie in $\text{span}(\boldsymbol{A})$, a subspace of dimension at most n. The vector $\boldsymbol{y} = \boldsymbol{A}\boldsymbol{x} \in \text{span}(\boldsymbol{A})$ closest to $\boldsymbol{b}$ in the Euclidean norm occurs when the residual vector $\boldsymbol{r} = \boldsymbol{b} - \boldsymbol{A}\boldsymbol{x}$ is orthogonal to $\text{span}(\boldsymbol{A})$ (see Fig. 3.2). Thus, for the least squares solution $\boldsymbol{x}$, the residual vector $\boldsymbol{r} = \boldsymbol{b} - \boldsymbol{A}\boldsymbol{x}$ must be orthogonal to each column of $\boldsymbol{A}$, and hence we must have

$$\boldsymbol{0} = \boldsymbol{A}^T \boldsymbol{r} = \boldsymbol{A}^T(\boldsymbol{b} - \boldsymbol{A}\boldsymbol{x}),$$

or

$$\boldsymbol{A}^T \boldsymbol{A}\boldsymbol{x} = \boldsymbol{A}^T \boldsymbol{b},$$

which is the same system of normal equations we derived earlier using calculus.

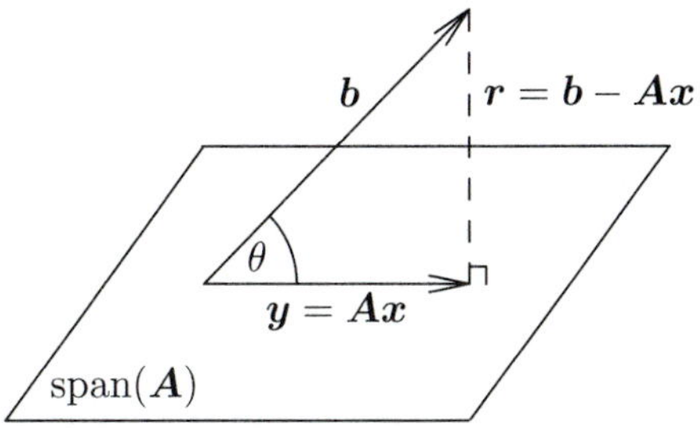

Figure 3.2: Geometric depiction of linear least squares problem. Parallelogram depicts subspace $\text{span}(\boldsymbol{A})$, in which $\boldsymbol{b}$ generally does *not* lie.

From the foregoing discussion of orthogonality, especially Fig. 3.2, we see intuitively that the vector $\boldsymbol{y} = \boldsymbol{A}\boldsymbol{x} \in \text{span}(\boldsymbol{A})$ closest to $\boldsymbol{b}$ in the Euclidean norm is the orthogonal projection of $\boldsymbol{b}$ onto $\text{span}(\boldsymbol{A})$. This observation leads to an algebraic characterization of least squares solutions, which we now examine more formally.

A square matrix $\boldsymbol{P}$ is a *projector* if it is *idempotent* (i.e., $\boldsymbol{P}^2 = \boldsymbol{P}$). Such a matrix projects any given vector onto a subspace, namely $\text{span}(\boldsymbol{P})$, but leaves unchanged any vector that is already in that subspace. If a projector $\boldsymbol{P}$ is also symmetric (i.e., $\boldsymbol{P}^T = \boldsymbol{P}$), then it is an *orthogonal projector*. If $\boldsymbol{P}$ is an orthogonal projector, then $\boldsymbol{P}_\perp = \boldsymbol{I} - \boldsymbol{P}$ is an orthogonal projector onto $\text{span}(\boldsymbol{P})^\perp$, the orthogonal complement of $\text{span}(\boldsymbol{P})$, i.e., the subspace of all vectors orthogonal to $\text{span}(\boldsymbol{P})$. Any vector $\boldsymbol{v} \in \mathbb{R}^m$ can be expressed as a sum

$$\boldsymbol{v} = (\boldsymbol{P} + (\boldsymbol{I} - \boldsymbol{P}))\, \boldsymbol{v} = \boldsymbol{P}\boldsymbol{v} + \boldsymbol{P}_\perp \boldsymbol{v}$$

of mutually orthogonal vectors, one in $\text{span}(\boldsymbol{P})$ and the other in $\text{span}(\boldsymbol{P})^{\perp}$.

To apply these concepts to the least squares problem $\boldsymbol{Ax} \cong \boldsymbol{b}$, assume that $\boldsymbol{P}$ is an orthogonal projector onto $\text{span}(\boldsymbol{A})$. Then we have

$$\begin{aligned} \|\boldsymbol{b} - \boldsymbol{Ax}\|_2^2 &= \|\boldsymbol{P}(\boldsymbol{b} - \boldsymbol{Ax}) + \boldsymbol{P}_{\perp}(\boldsymbol{b} - \boldsymbol{Ax})\|_2^2 \\ &= \|\boldsymbol{P}(\boldsymbol{b} - \boldsymbol{Ax})\|_2^2 + \|\boldsymbol{P}_{\perp}(\boldsymbol{b} - \boldsymbol{Ax})\|_2^2 \quad \text{(by Pythagorean Theorem)} \\ &= \|\boldsymbol{Pb} - \boldsymbol{Ax}\|_2^2 + \|\boldsymbol{P}_{\perp}\boldsymbol{b}\|_2^2 \quad \text{(since } \boldsymbol{PA} = \boldsymbol{A} \text{ and } \boldsymbol{P}_{\perp}\boldsymbol{A} = \boldsymbol{O}). \end{aligned}$$

The second term on the right does not depend on $\boldsymbol{x}$, so the residual norm is minimized when $\boldsymbol{x}$ is chosen so that the first term is zero. Thus, the least squares solution is given by the overdetermined, but consistent, linear system

$$\boldsymbol{Ax} = \boldsymbol{Pb}.$$

One way to obtain a square linear system from this equation is to premultiply both sides by $\boldsymbol{A}^T$ and note that $\boldsymbol{A}^T\boldsymbol{P} = \boldsymbol{A}^T\boldsymbol{P}^T = (\boldsymbol{PA})^T = \boldsymbol{A}^T$, giving

$$\boldsymbol{A}^T\boldsymbol{Ax} = \boldsymbol{A}^T\boldsymbol{b},$$

which once again is the system of normal equations derived earlier.

One way to obtain the orthogonal projector explicitly is to observe that if $\boldsymbol{A}$ has full column rank, so that $\boldsymbol{A}^T\boldsymbol{A}$ is nonsingular, then

$$\boldsymbol{P} = \boldsymbol{A}(\boldsymbol{A}^T\boldsymbol{A})^{-1}\boldsymbol{A}^T$$

is symmetric and idempotent, and hence is an orthogonal projector onto $\text{span}(\boldsymbol{A})$. Thus, the vector $\boldsymbol{y} \in \text{span}(\boldsymbol{A})$ closest to $\boldsymbol{b}$ is given by the orthogonal projection

$$\boldsymbol{y} = \boldsymbol{Pb} = \boldsymbol{A}(\boldsymbol{A}^T\boldsymbol{A})^{-1}\boldsymbol{A}^T\boldsymbol{b} = \boldsymbol{Ax},$$

where $\boldsymbol{x}$ is the least squares solution given by the normal equations. Note also that $\boldsymbol{b}$ is the sum

$$\boldsymbol{b} = \boldsymbol{Pb} + \boldsymbol{P}_{\perp}\boldsymbol{b} = \boldsymbol{Ax} + (\boldsymbol{b} - \boldsymbol{Ax}) = \boldsymbol{y} + \boldsymbol{r}$$

of two mutually orthogonal vectors, $\boldsymbol{y} \in \text{span}(\boldsymbol{A})$ and $\boldsymbol{r} \in \text{span}(\boldsymbol{A})^{\perp}$.

Another alternative is to let $\boldsymbol{Q}$ be an $m \times n$ matrix whose columns form an *orthonormal basis* (i.e., $\boldsymbol{Q}^T\boldsymbol{Q} = \boldsymbol{I}$) for $\text{span}(\boldsymbol{A})$. Then $\boldsymbol{P} = \boldsymbol{QQ}^T$ is symmetric and idempotent, so it is an orthogonal projector onto $\text{span}(\boldsymbol{Q}) = \text{span}(\boldsymbol{A})$. Using this approach we can obtain a square system from the previous consistent overdetermined system by premultiplying both sides by $\boldsymbol{Q}^T$ and noting that $\boldsymbol{Q}^T\boldsymbol{P} = \boldsymbol{Q}^T\boldsymbol{QQ}^T = \boldsymbol{Q}^T$, which gives the square system

$$\boldsymbol{Q}^T\boldsymbol{Ax} = \boldsymbol{Q}^T\boldsymbol{b}.$$

We will see later how to compute the matrix $\boldsymbol{Q}$ in such a way that this system is upper triangular and therefore easy to solve. Avoiding formation of the usual normal equations by this approach also has advantages in accuracy and stability, as we will soon see.

Example 3.4 Orthogonality and Projections. We illustrate these concepts by continuing with the least squares problem in Examples 3.1 and 3.3. At the solution $\boldsymbol{x} = [1236,\ 1943,\ 2416]^T$, the residual vector,

$$\boldsymbol{r} = \boldsymbol{b} - \boldsymbol{A}\boldsymbol{x} = \boldsymbol{b} - \boldsymbol{y} = \begin{bmatrix} 1237 \\ 1941 \\ 2417 \\ 711 \\ 1177 \\ 475 \end{bmatrix} - \begin{bmatrix} 1236 \\ 1943 \\ 2416 \\ 707 \\ 1180 \\ 473 \end{bmatrix} = \begin{bmatrix} 1 \\ -2 \\ 1 \\ 4 \\ -3 \\ 2 \end{bmatrix},$$

is orthogonal to each column of $\boldsymbol{A}$, i.e., $\boldsymbol{A}^T\boldsymbol{r} = \boldsymbol{0}$. The orthogonal projector onto span($\boldsymbol{A}$) is given by

$$\boldsymbol{P} = \boldsymbol{A}(\boldsymbol{A}^T\boldsymbol{A})^{-1}\boldsymbol{A}^T = \frac{1}{4}\begin{bmatrix} 2 & 1 & 1 & -1 & -1 & 0 \\ 1 & 2 & 1 & 1 & 0 & -1 \\ 1 & 1 & 2 & 0 & 1 & 1 \\ -1 & 1 & 0 & 2 & 1 & -1 \\ -1 & 0 & 1 & 1 & 2 & 1 \\ 0 & -1 & 1 & -1 & 1 & 2 \end{bmatrix},$$

and the orthogonal projector onto span$(\boldsymbol{A})^\perp$ is given by

$$\boldsymbol{P}_\perp = \boldsymbol{I} - \boldsymbol{P} = \frac{1}{4}\begin{bmatrix} 2 & -1 & -1 & 1 & 1 & 0 \\ -1 & 2 & -1 & -1 & 0 & 1 \\ -1 & -1 & 2 & 0 & -1 & -1 \\ 1 & -1 & 0 & 2 & -1 & 1 \\ 1 & 0 & -1 & -1 & 2 & -1 \\ 0 & 1 & -1 & 1 & -1 & 2 \end{bmatrix},$$

so that $\boldsymbol{b} = \boldsymbol{P}\boldsymbol{b} + \boldsymbol{P}_\perp\boldsymbol{b} = \boldsymbol{y} + \boldsymbol{r}$.

3.3 Sensitivity and Conditioning

We turn now to the sensitivity and conditioning of linear least squares problems. First, we must extend the notion of matrix condition number to include rectangular matrices. The definition of condition number for a square matrix given in Section 2.3.3 makes use of the matrix inverse. A nonsquare matrix $\boldsymbol{A}$ does not have an inverse in the conventional sense, but it is possible to define a *pseudoinverse*, denoted by $\boldsymbol{A}^+$, that behaves like an inverse in many respects (see Exercise 3.32). We will later see a more general definition that applies to any matrix, but for now we consider only matrices $\boldsymbol{A}$ with full column rank, in which case $\boldsymbol{A}^T\boldsymbol{A}$ is nonsingular and we define the pseudoinverse of $\boldsymbol{A}$ to be

$$\boldsymbol{A}^+ = (\boldsymbol{A}^T\boldsymbol{A})^{-1}\boldsymbol{A}^T.$$

Trivially, we see that $\boldsymbol{A}^+\boldsymbol{A} = \boldsymbol{I}$, and from Section 3.2.2 we see that $\boldsymbol{P} = \boldsymbol{A}\boldsymbol{A}^+$ is an orthogonal projector onto span($\boldsymbol{A}$), so that the solution to the least squares problem $\boldsymbol{A}\boldsymbol{x} \cong \boldsymbol{b}$ is given by

$$\boldsymbol{x} = \boldsymbol{A}^+\boldsymbol{b}.$$

We now define the condition number of an $m \times n$ matrix with $\text{rank}(\boldsymbol{A}) = n$ to be

$$\text{cond}(\boldsymbol{A}) = \|\boldsymbol{A}\|_2 \cdot \|\boldsymbol{A}^+\|_2.$$

By convention, $\text{cond}(\boldsymbol{A}) = \infty$ if $\text{rank}(\boldsymbol{A}) < n$. Just as the condition number of a square matrix measures closeness to singularity, the condition number of a rectangular matrix measures closeness to rank deficiency.

Whereas the conditioning of a square linear system $\boldsymbol{A}\boldsymbol{x} = \boldsymbol{b}$ depends only on the matrix $\boldsymbol{A}$, the conditioning of a least squares problem $\boldsymbol{A}\boldsymbol{x} \cong \boldsymbol{b}$ depends on the right-hand-side vector $\boldsymbol{b}$ as well as the matrix $\boldsymbol{A}$, and thus cond($\boldsymbol{A}$) alone does not suffice to characterize sensitivity. In particular, if $\boldsymbol{b}$ lies near span($\boldsymbol{A}$), then a small perturbation in $\boldsymbol{b}$ changes $\boldsymbol{y} = \boldsymbol{P}\boldsymbol{b}$ relatively little. But if $\boldsymbol{b}$ is nearly orthogonal to span($\boldsymbol{A}$), on the other hand, then $\boldsymbol{y} = \boldsymbol{P}\boldsymbol{b}$ itself will be relatively small, so that a small change in $\boldsymbol{b}$ can cause a relatively large change in $\boldsymbol{y}$, and hence in the least squares solution $\boldsymbol{x}$. Thus, for a given $\boldsymbol{A}$, we would expect a least squares problem with a $\boldsymbol{b}$ that yields a large residual (i.e., a poor fit to the data) to be more sensitive than one with a small residual (i.e., a good fit to the data). An appropriate measure of the closeness of $\boldsymbol{b}$ to span($\boldsymbol{A}$) is the ratio

$$\frac{\|\boldsymbol{A}\boldsymbol{x}\|_2}{\|\boldsymbol{b}\|_2} = \frac{\|\boldsymbol{y}\|_2}{\|\boldsymbol{b}\|_2} = \cos(\theta),$$

where θ is the angle between $\boldsymbol{b}$ and $\boldsymbol{y}$ (see Fig. 3.2). Thus, we expect greater sensitivity when this ratio is small, so that θ is near $\pi/2$.

We now make a more quantitative assessment of the sensitivity of the solution $\boldsymbol{x}$ of a least squares problem $\boldsymbol{A}\boldsymbol{x} \cong \boldsymbol{b}$, where $\boldsymbol{A}$ has full column rank. For simplicity, we will consider perturbations in $\boldsymbol{b}$ and $\boldsymbol{A}$ separately. For a perturbed right-hand-side vector $\boldsymbol{b} + \Delta\boldsymbol{b}$, the perturbed solution is given by the normal equations

$$\boldsymbol{A}^T\boldsymbol{A}(\boldsymbol{x} + \Delta\boldsymbol{x}) = \boldsymbol{A}^T(\boldsymbol{b} + \Delta\boldsymbol{b}).$$

Because $\boldsymbol{A}^T\boldsymbol{A}\boldsymbol{x} = \boldsymbol{A}^T\boldsymbol{b}$, we then have

$$\boldsymbol{A}^T\boldsymbol{A}\,\Delta\boldsymbol{x} = \boldsymbol{A}^T\Delta\boldsymbol{b},$$

so that

$$\Delta\boldsymbol{x} = (\boldsymbol{A}^T\boldsymbol{A})^{-1}\boldsymbol{A}^T\Delta\boldsymbol{b} = \boldsymbol{A}^+\Delta\boldsymbol{b}.$$

Taking norms, we obtain

$$\|\Delta\boldsymbol{x}\|_2 \le \|\boldsymbol{A}^+\|_2 \cdot \|\Delta\boldsymbol{b}\|_2.$$

Dividing both sides by $\|\boldsymbol{x}\|_2$, we obtain the bound

$$\begin{aligned}
\frac{\|\Delta \boldsymbol{x}\|_2}{\|\boldsymbol{x}\|_2} &\leq \|\boldsymbol{A}^+\|_2 \frac{\|\Delta \boldsymbol{b}\|_2}{\|\boldsymbol{x}\|_2} \\
&= \operatorname{cond}(\boldsymbol{A}) \frac{\|\boldsymbol{b}\|_2}{\|\boldsymbol{A}\|_2 \cdot \|\boldsymbol{x}\|_2} \frac{\|\Delta \boldsymbol{b}\|_2}{\|\boldsymbol{b}\|_2} \\
&\leq \operatorname{cond}(\boldsymbol{A}) \frac{\|\boldsymbol{b}\|_2}{\|\boldsymbol{A}\boldsymbol{x}\|_2} \frac{\|\Delta \boldsymbol{b}\|_2}{\|\boldsymbol{b}\|_2} \\
&= \operatorname{cond}(\boldsymbol{A}) \frac{1}{\cos(\theta)} \frac{\|\Delta \boldsymbol{b}\|_2}{\|\boldsymbol{b}\|_2}.
\end{aligned}$$

Thus, the condition number for the least squares solution $\boldsymbol{x}$ with respect to perturbations in $\boldsymbol{b}$ depends on $\operatorname{cond}(\boldsymbol{A})$ and also on the angle θ between $\boldsymbol{b}$ and $\boldsymbol{A}\boldsymbol{x}$ (see Fig. 3.2). In particular, the condition number is approximately $\operatorname{cond}(\boldsymbol{A})$ when the residual is small, so that $\cos(\theta) \approx 1$, but the condition number can be arbitrarily worse than $\operatorname{cond}(\boldsymbol{A})$ when the residual is large, so that $\cos(\theta) \approx 0$.

For a perturbed matrix $\boldsymbol{A} + \boldsymbol{E}$, the perturbed solution is given by the normal equations

$$(\boldsymbol{A} + \boldsymbol{E})^T(\boldsymbol{A} + \boldsymbol{E})(\boldsymbol{x} + \Delta \boldsymbol{x}) = (\boldsymbol{A} + \boldsymbol{E})^T \boldsymbol{b}.$$

Noting that $\boldsymbol{A}^T\boldsymbol{A}\boldsymbol{x} = \boldsymbol{A}^T\boldsymbol{b}$, dropping second-order terms (i.e., products of small perturbations), and rearranging, we then have

$$\begin{aligned}
\boldsymbol{A}^T\boldsymbol{A}\,\Delta\boldsymbol{x} &\approx \boldsymbol{E}^T\boldsymbol{b} - \boldsymbol{E}^T\boldsymbol{A}\boldsymbol{x} - \boldsymbol{A}^T\boldsymbol{E}\boldsymbol{x} \\
&= \boldsymbol{E}^T(\boldsymbol{b} - \boldsymbol{A}\boldsymbol{x}) - \boldsymbol{A}^T\boldsymbol{E}\boldsymbol{x} \\
&= \boldsymbol{E}^T\boldsymbol{r} - \boldsymbol{A}^T\boldsymbol{E}\boldsymbol{x},
\end{aligned}$$

so that

$$\Delta\boldsymbol{x} \approx (\boldsymbol{A}^T\boldsymbol{A})^{-1}\boldsymbol{E}^T\boldsymbol{r} - (\boldsymbol{A}^T\boldsymbol{A})^{-1}\boldsymbol{A}^T\boldsymbol{E}\boldsymbol{x} = (\boldsymbol{A}^T\boldsymbol{A})^{-1}\boldsymbol{E}^T\boldsymbol{r} - \boldsymbol{A}^+\boldsymbol{E}\boldsymbol{x}.$$

Taking norms, we obtain

$$\|\Delta\boldsymbol{x}\|_2 \lessapprox \|(\boldsymbol{A}^T\boldsymbol{A})^{-1}\|_2 \cdot \|\boldsymbol{E}\|_2 \cdot \|\boldsymbol{r}\|_2 + \|\boldsymbol{A}^+\|_2 \cdot \|\boldsymbol{E}\|_2 \cdot \|\boldsymbol{x}\|_2.$$

Dividing both sides by $\|\boldsymbol{x}\|_2$ and using the fact that $\|\boldsymbol{A}\|_2^2 \cdot \|(\boldsymbol{A}^T\boldsymbol{A})^{-1}\|_2 = [\operatorname{cond}(\boldsymbol{A})]^2$, we obtain the bound

$$\begin{aligned}
\frac{\|\Delta\boldsymbol{x}\|_2}{\|\boldsymbol{x}\|_2} &\lessapprox \|(\boldsymbol{A}^T\boldsymbol{A})^{-1}\|_2 \cdot \|\boldsymbol{E}\|_2 \frac{\|\boldsymbol{r}\|_2}{\|\boldsymbol{x}\|_2} + \|\boldsymbol{A}^+\|_2 \cdot \|\boldsymbol{E}\|_2 \\
&= [\operatorname{cond}(\boldsymbol{A})]^2 \frac{\|\boldsymbol{E}\|_2}{\|\boldsymbol{A}\|_2} \frac{\|\boldsymbol{r}\|_2}{\|\boldsymbol{A}\|_2 \cdot \|\boldsymbol{x}\|_2} + \operatorname{cond}(\boldsymbol{A}) \frac{\|\boldsymbol{E}\|_2}{\|\boldsymbol{A}\|_2} \\
&\leq \left([\operatorname{cond}(\boldsymbol{A})]^2 \frac{\|\boldsymbol{r}\|_2}{\|\boldsymbol{A}\boldsymbol{x}\|_2} + \operatorname{cond}(\boldsymbol{A})\right) \frac{\|\boldsymbol{E}\|_2}{\|\boldsymbol{A}\|_2} \\
&= \left([\operatorname{cond}(\boldsymbol{A})]^2 \tan(\theta) + \operatorname{cond}(\boldsymbol{A})\right) \frac{\|\boldsymbol{E}\|_2}{\|\boldsymbol{A}\|_2}.
\end{aligned}$$

Thus, the condition number for the least squares solution $\boldsymbol{x}$ with respect to perturbations in $\boldsymbol{A}$ depends on $\text{cond}(\boldsymbol{A})$ and also on the angle θ between $\boldsymbol{b}$ and $\boldsymbol{Ax}$ (see Fig. 3.2). In particular, the condition number is approximately $\text{cond}(\boldsymbol{A})$ when the residual is small, so that $\tan(\theta) \approx 0$, but the condition number is effectively squared for a moderate residual, and becomes arbitrarily large when the residual is larger still. These sensitivity results will not only enable us to assess the quality of least squares solutions, but will also play an important role in understanding the relative merits of the various algorithms for computing such solutions numerically.

Example 3.5 Sensitivity and Conditioning. We again illustrate these concepts by continuing with Examples 3.1, 3.3, and 3.4. The pseudoinverse is given by

$$\boldsymbol{A}^+ = (\boldsymbol{A}^T\boldsymbol{A})^{-1}\boldsymbol{A}^T = \frac{1}{4}\begin{bmatrix} 2 & 1 & 1 & -1 & -1 & 0 \\ 1 & 2 & 1 & 1 & 0 & -1 \\ 1 & 1 & 2 & 0 & 1 & 1 \end{bmatrix}.$$

The matrix norms can be computed to obtain

$$\|\boldsymbol{A}\|_2 = 2, \qquad \|\boldsymbol{A}^+\|_2 = 1,$$

so that

$$\text{cond}(\boldsymbol{A}) = \|\boldsymbol{A}\|_2 \cdot \|\boldsymbol{A}^+\|_2 = 2.$$

From the ratio

$$\cos(\theta) = \frac{\|\boldsymbol{Ax}\|_2}{\|\boldsymbol{b}\|_2} = \frac{\|\boldsymbol{y}\|_2}{\|\boldsymbol{b}\|_2} \approx \frac{3640.8761}{3640.8809} \approx 0.99999868,$$

we see that the angle θ between $\boldsymbol{b}$ and $\boldsymbol{y}$ is about 0.001625, which is very tiny, as expected for a problem with a very close fit to the data. From the small condition number and small angle θ, we conclude that this particular least squares problem is well-conditioned.

Example 3.6 Condition-Squaring Effect. Consider the matrix and perturbation

$$\boldsymbol{A} = \begin{bmatrix} 1 & 1 \\ \epsilon & -\epsilon \\ 0 & 0 \end{bmatrix}, \qquad \boldsymbol{E} = \begin{bmatrix} 0 & 0 \\ 0 & 0 \\ -\epsilon & \epsilon \end{bmatrix},$$

where $\epsilon \ll 1$, say around $\sqrt{\epsilon_{\text{mach}}}$, for which we have

$$\text{cond}(\boldsymbol{A}) = 1/\epsilon, \qquad \|\boldsymbol{E}\|_2/\|\boldsymbol{A}\|_2 = \epsilon.$$

For the right-hand-side vector $\boldsymbol{b} = [1 \;\; 0 \;\; \epsilon]^T$, we have $\|\Delta\boldsymbol{x}\|_2/\|\boldsymbol{x}\|_2 = 0.5$, so the relative perturbation in the solution is about equal to $\text{cond}(\boldsymbol{A})$ times the relative perturbation in $\boldsymbol{A}$. There is no condition-squaring effect for this right-hand side because the residual is small and $\tan(\theta) \approx \epsilon$, effectively suppressing the condition-squared term in the perturbation bound.

For the right-hand-side vector $\boldsymbol{b} = [1 \quad 0 \quad 1]^T$, on the other hand, we have $\|\Delta\boldsymbol{x}\|_2/\|\boldsymbol{x}\|_2 = 0.5/\epsilon$, so the relative perturbation in the solution is about equal to $[\text{cond}(\boldsymbol{A})]^2$ times the relative perturbation in $\boldsymbol{A}$. For this right-hand side, the norm of the residual is about 1 and $\tan(\theta) \approx 1$, so that the condition-squared term in the perturbation bound is not suppressed, and the solution is highly sensitive.

3.4 Problem Transformations

We will now consider several methods for transforming an overdetermined linear least squares problem $\boldsymbol{Ax} \cong \boldsymbol{b}$ into a square (ultimately triangular) linear system, so that it can then be solved by the methods of Chapter 2.

3.4.1 Normal Equations

As we saw in Section 3.2.1, if $\boldsymbol{A}$ has full column rank, then the $n \times n$ symmetric positive definite system of normal equations

$$\boldsymbol{A}^T\boldsymbol{Ax} = \boldsymbol{A}^T\boldsymbol{b}$$

has the same solution $\boldsymbol{x}$ as the $m \times n$ least squares problem $\boldsymbol{Ax} \cong \boldsymbol{b}$. To solve this square system, we compute the Cholesky factorization (see Section 2.5.1)

$$\boldsymbol{A}^T\boldsymbol{A} = \boldsymbol{LL}^T,$$

where $\boldsymbol{L}$ is lower triangular, and then the solution $\boldsymbol{x}$ can be computed by solving the triangular systems $\boldsymbol{Ly} = \boldsymbol{A}^T\boldsymbol{b}$ and $\boldsymbol{L}^T\boldsymbol{x} = \boldsymbol{y}$.

Using the normal equations to solve an overdetermined least squares problem is an example of the general strategy noted earlier, in which a difficult problem is converted into successively easier ones having the same solution. In this case, the sequence of problem transformations is

$$\text{Rectangular} \quad \longrightarrow \quad \text{square} \quad \longrightarrow \quad \text{triangular}.$$

Unfortunately, this method also illustrates another important fact, namely, that a problem transformation that is legitimate theoretically is not always advisable numerically. In theory the system of normal equations gives the exact solution to a linear least squares problem, but in practice this approach sometimes yields disappointingly inaccurate results. There are two reasons for this behavior:

- Information can be lost in forming the cross-product matrix and right-hand-side vector. For example, take

$$\boldsymbol{A} = \begin{bmatrix} 1 & 1 \\ \epsilon & 0 \\ 0 & \epsilon \end{bmatrix},$$

  where $0 < \epsilon < \sqrt{\epsilon_{\text{mach}}}$ in a given floating-point system. In floating-point arithmetic we then have

$$\boldsymbol{A}^T\boldsymbol{A} = \begin{bmatrix} 1+\epsilon^2 & 1 \\ 1 & 1+\epsilon^2 \end{bmatrix} = \begin{bmatrix} 1 & 1 \\ 1 & 1 \end{bmatrix},$$

which is singular to working precision.

- The condition number of the cross-product matrix, which determines the sensitivity of the solution to the normal equations (see Section 2.3), is the square of that of the original matrix $\boldsymbol{A}$:

$$\text{cond}(\boldsymbol{A}^T\boldsymbol{A}) = [\text{cond}(\boldsymbol{A})]^2.$$

  We saw in Section 3.3 that there is a potential condition-squaring effect in the sensitivity of least squares solutions, but this should be a significant factor only when the residual is large (i.e., the fit is poor). Unfortunately, the normal equations can suffer a condition-squaring effect even when the fit is good and the residual is small, making the computed solution more sensitive than warranted by the underlying least squares problem. In this sense, the normal equations method is unstable.

These shortcomings do not make the normal equations method useless, but they are cause for concern and provide motivation for seeking more numerically robust methods for linear least squares problems.

3.4.2 Augmented System

Another way to transform a least squares problem into a square linear system is to embed it in a larger system. The definition of the residual vector $\boldsymbol{r}$, together with the requirement that the residual be orthogonal to the columns of $\boldsymbol{A}$, gives the system of two equations

$$\begin{aligned} \boldsymbol{r} + \boldsymbol{A}\boldsymbol{x} &= \boldsymbol{b}, \\ \boldsymbol{A}^T\boldsymbol{r} &= \boldsymbol{0}, \end{aligned}$$

which can be written in matrix form as the $(m+n) \times (m+n)$ *augmented system*

$$\begin{bmatrix} \boldsymbol{I} & \boldsymbol{A} \\ \boldsymbol{A}^T & \boldsymbol{O} \end{bmatrix} \begin{bmatrix} \boldsymbol{r} \\ \boldsymbol{x} \end{bmatrix} = \begin{bmatrix} \boldsymbol{b} \\ \boldsymbol{0} \end{bmatrix},$$

whose solution yields both the desired solution $\boldsymbol{x}$ and the residual $\boldsymbol{r}$ at that solution.

At first glance, this method does not look promising: The augmented system is symmetric but not positive definite, it is larger than the original system, and it requires that we store two copies of $\boldsymbol{A}$. Moreover, if we simply pivot along the diagonal (equivalent to block elimination in the block 2×2 system), we reproduce the normal equations, whose potential numerical shortcomings we have already observed. The one advantage we have gained is that other pivoting strategies are now available, which can be beneficial for numerical or other reasons.

The selection of pivots in computing a symmetric indefinite (see Section 2.5.2) or LU factorization of the augmented system matrix will obviously depend on the relative magnitudes of the entries in the upper and lower block rows. The relative scales of $\boldsymbol{r}$ and $\boldsymbol{x}$ are arbitrary, so we introduce a scaling parameter α for the residual, giving the new system

$$\begin{bmatrix} \alpha\boldsymbol{I} & \boldsymbol{A} \\ \boldsymbol{A}^T & \boldsymbol{O} \end{bmatrix} \begin{bmatrix} \boldsymbol{r}/\alpha \\ \boldsymbol{x} \end{bmatrix} = \begin{bmatrix} \boldsymbol{b} \\ \boldsymbol{0} \end{bmatrix}.$$

The parameter α controls the relative weights of the entries in the two subsystems in choosing pivots from either. A reasonable rule of thumb is to take

$$\alpha = \max_{i,j} |a_{ij}|/1000,$$

but some experimentation may be required to determine the best value.

A straightforward implementation of this method can be prohibitive in cost (proportional to $(m+n)^3$), so the special structure of the augmented matrix must be carefully exploited. For example, the augmented system method is used effectively in `MATLAB` for large sparse linear least squares problems.

3.4.3 Orthogonal Transformations

In view of the potential numerical difficulties with the normal equations approach, we need an alternative that does not require formation of the cross-product matrix and right-hand-side vector. Thus, we seek a more numerically robust type of transformation that will yield a simpler problem whose solution is the same as that of the original least squares problem but is more easily computed. As with square linear systems, we will see that triangular form is a suitable target in simplifying least squares problems. Reducing a matrix to triangular form via Gaussian elimination is not appropriate in this context, however, because such a transformation does not preserve the Euclidean norm and hence does not preserve the least squares solution.

Taking a cue from our earlier discussion of orthogonality, we now define a type of linear transformation that does preserve the Euclidean norm. A square real matrix $\boldsymbol{Q}$ is said to be *orthogonal* if its columns are orthonormal, i.e., if $\boldsymbol{Q}^T\boldsymbol{Q} = \boldsymbol{I}$, the identity matrix. An orthogonal transformation $\boldsymbol{Q}$ preserves the Euclidean norm of any vector $\boldsymbol{v}$, since

$$\|\boldsymbol{Q}\boldsymbol{v}\|_2^2 = (\boldsymbol{Q}\boldsymbol{v})^T\boldsymbol{Q}\boldsymbol{v} = \boldsymbol{v}^T\boldsymbol{Q}^T\boldsymbol{Q}\boldsymbol{v} = \boldsymbol{v}^T\boldsymbol{v} = \|\boldsymbol{v}\|_2^2.$$

Orthogonal matrices can transform vectors in various ways, such as rotation or reflection, but they do not change the Euclidean length of a vector. Hence, if we multiply both sides of a linear least squares problem by an orthogonal matrix, the solution is unchanged.

Orthogonal matrices are of great importance in many areas of numerical computation because their norm-preserving property means that they do not amplify error. Thus, for example, orthogonal transformations can be used to solve square linear systems *without* the need for pivoting for numerical stability. Unfortunately, orthogonalization methods are significantly more expensive computationally than methods based on Gaussian elimination, so their superior numerical properties come at a price that may or may not be worthwhile, depending on context.

3.4.4 Triangular Least Squares Problems

Now that we have a family of transformations that preserve the least squares solution, we next need a suitable target for simplifying a least squares problem so that it becomes easy to solve. As we did with square linear systems, let us consider least squares problems having an upper triangular matrix. In the overdetermined case, $m > n$, such a problem has the form

$$\begin{bmatrix} \boldsymbol{R} \\ \boldsymbol{O} \end{bmatrix} \boldsymbol{x} \cong \begin{bmatrix} \boldsymbol{c}_1 \\ \boldsymbol{c}_2 \end{bmatrix},$$

where $\boldsymbol{R}$ is an $n \times n$ upper triangular matrix, and we have partitioned the right-hand-side vector $\boldsymbol{c}$ similarly. The least squares residual is then given by

$$\|\boldsymbol{r}\|_2^2 = \|\boldsymbol{c}_1 - \boldsymbol{R}\boldsymbol{x}\|_2^2 + \|\boldsymbol{c}_2\|_2^2.$$

Because it is independent of $\boldsymbol{x}$, we have no control over the second term, $\|\boldsymbol{c}_2\|_2^2$, in the foregoing sum, but the first term can be forced to be zero by choosing $\boldsymbol{x}$ to satisfy the triangular system

$$\boldsymbol{R}\boldsymbol{x} = \boldsymbol{c}_1,$$

which can be solved for $\boldsymbol{x}$ by back-substitution. We have therefore found the least squares solution $\boldsymbol{x}$ and can also conclude that the minimum sum of squares is

$$\|\boldsymbol{r}\|_2^2 = \|\boldsymbol{c}_2\|_2^2.$$

3.4.5 QR Factorization

Orthogonal transformation to triangular form is accomplished by the *QR factorization*, which, for an $m \times n$ matrix $\boldsymbol{A}$ with $m > n$, has the form

$$\boldsymbol{A} = \boldsymbol{Q} \begin{bmatrix} \boldsymbol{R} \\ \boldsymbol{O} \end{bmatrix},$$

where $\boldsymbol{Q}$ is an $m \times m$ orthogonal matrix and $\boldsymbol{R}$ is an $n \times n$ upper triangular matrix. Such a factorization transforms the linear least squares problem $\boldsymbol{A}\boldsymbol{x} \cong \boldsymbol{b}$ into a triangular least squares problem having the same solution, since

$$\|\boldsymbol{r}\|_2^2 = \|\boldsymbol{b} - \boldsymbol{A}\boldsymbol{x}\|_2^2 = \|\boldsymbol{b} - \boldsymbol{Q} \begin{bmatrix} \boldsymbol{R} \\ \boldsymbol{O} \end{bmatrix} \boldsymbol{x}\|_2^2 = \|\boldsymbol{Q}^T\boldsymbol{b} - \begin{bmatrix} \boldsymbol{R} \\ \boldsymbol{O} \end{bmatrix} \boldsymbol{x}\|_2^2 = \|\boldsymbol{c}_1 - \boldsymbol{R}\boldsymbol{x}\|_2^2 + \|\boldsymbol{c}_2\|_2^2,$$

where the transformed right-hand side

$$\boldsymbol{Q}^T\boldsymbol{b} = \begin{bmatrix} \boldsymbol{c}_1 \\ \boldsymbol{c}_2 \end{bmatrix}$$

is partitioned so that $\boldsymbol{c}_1$ is an n-vector. The solution $\boldsymbol{x}$ then satisfies the $n \times n$ triangular linear system $\boldsymbol{R}\boldsymbol{x} = \boldsymbol{c}_1$, and the minimum residual norm is given by $\|\boldsymbol{r}\|_2 = \|\boldsymbol{c}_2\|_2$. In the next section, we will see how to compute the QR factorization.

QR factorization has many other uses besides solving least squares problems. If we partition $\boldsymbol{Q}$ as $\boldsymbol{Q} = [\,\boldsymbol{Q}_1 \quad \boldsymbol{Q}_2\,]$, where $\boldsymbol{Q}_1$ contains the first n columns and $\boldsymbol{Q}_2$ contains the remaining $m - n$ columns of $\boldsymbol{Q}$, then we have

$$\boldsymbol{A} = \boldsymbol{Q} \begin{bmatrix} \boldsymbol{R} \\ \boldsymbol{O} \end{bmatrix} = [\,\boldsymbol{Q}_1 \quad \boldsymbol{Q}_2\,] \begin{bmatrix} \boldsymbol{R} \\ \boldsymbol{O} \end{bmatrix} = \boldsymbol{Q}_1\boldsymbol{R}.$$

A factorization of the form $\boldsymbol{A} = \boldsymbol{Q}_1\boldsymbol{R}$, with $\boldsymbol{Q}_1$ having orthonormal columns and the same dimensions as $\boldsymbol{A}$, and $\boldsymbol{R}$ square and upper triangular, is sometimes called the *reduced*, or "economy size" QR factorization of $\boldsymbol{A}$. If $\boldsymbol{A}$ has full column rank, so that $\boldsymbol{R}$ is nonsingular, then the columns of $\boldsymbol{Q}_1$ form an *orthonormal basis* for span($\boldsymbol{A}$) and the columns of $\boldsymbol{Q}_2$ form an orthonormal basis for its orthogonal complement, span$(\boldsymbol{A})^\perp$, which is the same as the *null space* of $\boldsymbol{A}^T$ (i.e., $\{\boldsymbol{z} \in \mathbb{R}^m : \boldsymbol{A}^T\boldsymbol{z} = \boldsymbol{0}\}$). Such orthonormal bases are useful not only in least squares computations, as we saw near the end of Section 3.2.2, but also in eigenvalue computations, optimization, and many other problems we will see later.

3.5 Orthogonalization Methods

Our approach to computing the QR factorization of a matrix will be similar to LU factorization using Gaussian elimination in that we will introduce zeros successively into the matrix $\boldsymbol{A}$, eventually reaching upper triangular form, but we will use orthogonal transformations rather than elementary elimination matrices so that the Euclidean norm will be preserved. A number of such orthogonalization methods are commonly used, including

- Householder transformations (elementary reflectors)
- Givens transformations (plane rotations)
- Gram-Schmidt orthogonalization

We will focus mainly on the use of Householder transformations, which is the most popular and generally the most effective approach in this context, but we will sketch the other two methods as well.

3.5.1 Householder Transformations

We seek an orthogonal transformation that annihilates desired components of a given vector. One way to accomplish this is a *Householder transformation*, or *elementary reflector*, which is a matrix of the form

$$\boldsymbol{H} = \boldsymbol{I} - 2\,\frac{\boldsymbol{v}\boldsymbol{v}^T}{\boldsymbol{v}^T\boldsymbol{v}},$$

where $\boldsymbol{v}$ is a nonzero vector. From the definition, we see that $\boldsymbol{H} = \boldsymbol{H}^T = \boldsymbol{H}^{-1}$, so that $\boldsymbol{H}$ is both orthogonal and symmetric. Given a vector $\boldsymbol{a}$, we wish to choose the vector $\boldsymbol{v}$ so that all the components of $\boldsymbol{a}$ except the first are annihilated, i.e.,

$$\boldsymbol{H}\boldsymbol{a} = \begin{bmatrix} \alpha \\ 0 \\ \vdots \\ 0 \end{bmatrix} = \alpha \begin{bmatrix} 1 \\ 0 \\ \vdots \\ 0 \end{bmatrix} = \alpha\,\boldsymbol{e}_1.$$

Using the formula for $\boldsymbol{H}$, we have

$$\alpha\,\boldsymbol{e}_1 = \boldsymbol{H}\boldsymbol{a} = \left(\boldsymbol{I} - 2\,\frac{\boldsymbol{v}\boldsymbol{v}^T}{\boldsymbol{v}^T\boldsymbol{v}}\right)\boldsymbol{a} = \boldsymbol{a} - 2\,\boldsymbol{v}\,\frac{\boldsymbol{v}^T\boldsymbol{a}}{\boldsymbol{v}^T\boldsymbol{v}},$$

and hence

$$\boldsymbol{v} = (\boldsymbol{a} - \alpha\,\boldsymbol{e}_1)\,\frac{\boldsymbol{v}^T\boldsymbol{v}}{2\boldsymbol{v}^T\boldsymbol{a}}.$$

But the scalar factor is irrelevant in determining $\boldsymbol{v}$, since it divides out in the formula for $\boldsymbol{H}$ anyway, so we can take

$$\boldsymbol{v} = \boldsymbol{a} - \alpha\,\boldsymbol{e}_1.$$

To preserve the norm, we must have $\alpha = \pm\|\boldsymbol{a}\|_2$, and the sign should be chosen to avoid cancellation (i.e., $\alpha = -\text{sign}(a_1)\|\boldsymbol{a}\|_2$). Another potential numerical difficulty is that the computation of $\|\boldsymbol{a}\|_2$ could incur unnecessary overflow or underflow if the components of $\boldsymbol{a}$ are very large or very small. Dividing $\boldsymbol{a}$ at the outset by its component of largest magnitude avoids this problem. Again, such a scale factor does not change the resulting transformation $\boldsymbol{H}$.

To gain more insight into the algebraic derivation just given, consider the geometric interpretation depicted in Fig. 3.3. We can transform the vector $\boldsymbol{a}$ onto the first coordinate axis (where its other components will become zero), while preserving its norm, by reflecting it across either of the two hyperplanes (the dashed lines in the two-dimensional drawings) bisecting the respective angles between $\boldsymbol{a}$ and the first coordinate axis. The transformed vector obtained will be either $\pm\|\boldsymbol{a}\|_2\boldsymbol{e}_1$, depending on which of the two hyperplanes we choose. Such a hyperplane is given by $\text{span}(\boldsymbol{v})^\perp = \{\boldsymbol{x} : \boldsymbol{v}^T\boldsymbol{x} = 0\}$ for some nonzero vector $\boldsymbol{v}$. It is clear from the drawings that $\boldsymbol{v}$ must be parallel to $\boldsymbol{a} - \alpha\,\boldsymbol{e}_1$, where $\alpha = \pm\|\boldsymbol{a}\|_2$, depending on the choice of hyperplane. Recall from Section 3.2.2 that the orthogonal projector onto $\text{span}(\boldsymbol{v})$ is given by $\boldsymbol{P} = \boldsymbol{v}(\boldsymbol{v}^T\boldsymbol{v})^{-1}\boldsymbol{v}^T = (\boldsymbol{v}\boldsymbol{v}^T)/(\boldsymbol{v}^T\boldsymbol{v})$, and the projector onto $\text{span}(\boldsymbol{v})^\perp$ is given by $\boldsymbol{I} - \boldsymbol{P}$. Thus, $(\boldsymbol{I} - \boldsymbol{P})\boldsymbol{a} = \boldsymbol{a} - \boldsymbol{v}(\boldsymbol{v}^T\boldsymbol{a})/(\boldsymbol{v}^T\boldsymbol{v})$ gives the projection of $\boldsymbol{a}$ onto the hyperplane, but to reach the first coordinate axis we need to go twice as far, or $\boldsymbol{a} - 2\boldsymbol{v}(\boldsymbol{v}^T\boldsymbol{a})/(\boldsymbol{v}^T\boldsymbol{v})$, so the transformation we need is $\boldsymbol{H} = \boldsymbol{I} - 2\boldsymbol{P} = \boldsymbol{I} - 2(\boldsymbol{v}\boldsymbol{v}^T)/(\boldsymbol{v}^T\boldsymbol{v})$. Either choice of hyperplane works in principle, but to avoid cancellation in computing $\boldsymbol{v}$ in finite-precision arithmetic, we should choose the sign for α that yields the point on the first coordinate axis farther away from $\boldsymbol{a}$. For the example vector $\boldsymbol{a}$ shown in the drawings, the positive sign should be chosen (i.e., the drawing on the right) because a_1 is negative.

Example 3.7 Householder Transformation. To illustrate the construction just described, we determine a Householder transformation that annihilates all but the first component of the vector

$$\boldsymbol{a} = \begin{bmatrix} 2 \\ 1 \\ 2 \end{bmatrix}.$$

Following the foregoing recipe, we choose the vector

$$\boldsymbol{v} = \boldsymbol{a} - \alpha\,\boldsymbol{e}_1 = \begin{bmatrix} 2 \\ 1 \\ 2 \end{bmatrix} - \alpha \begin{bmatrix} 1 \\ 0 \\ 0 \end{bmatrix} = \begin{bmatrix} 2 \\ 1 \\ 2 \end{bmatrix} - \begin{bmatrix} \alpha \\ 0 \\ 0 \end{bmatrix},$$

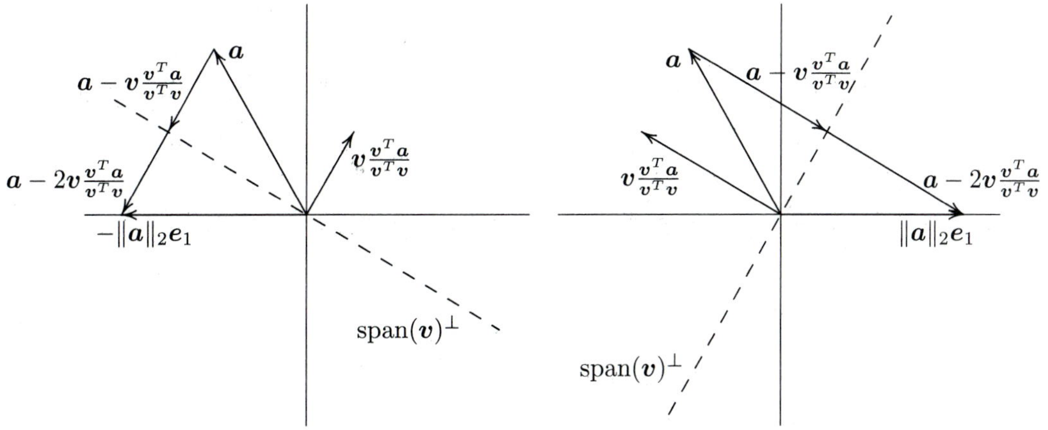

Figure 3.3: Geometric interpretation of Householder transformation as reflection.

where $\alpha = \pm\|\boldsymbol{a}\|_2 = \pm 3$. Because a_1 is positive, we can avoid cancellation by choosing the negative sign for α. We therefore have

$$\boldsymbol{v} = \begin{bmatrix} 2 \\ 1 \\ 2 \end{bmatrix} - \begin{bmatrix} -3 \\ 0 \\ 0 \end{bmatrix} = \begin{bmatrix} 5 \\ 1 \\ 2 \end{bmatrix}.$$

To confirm that the Householder transformation performs as expected, we compute

$$\boldsymbol{H}\boldsymbol{a} = \boldsymbol{a} - 2\,\frac{\boldsymbol{v}^T\boldsymbol{a}}{\boldsymbol{v}^T\boldsymbol{v}}\,\boldsymbol{v} = \begin{bmatrix} 2 \\ 1 \\ 2 \end{bmatrix} - 2\,\frac{15}{30}\begin{bmatrix} 5 \\ 1 \\ 2 \end{bmatrix} = \begin{bmatrix} -3 \\ 0 \\ 0 \end{bmatrix},$$

which shows that the zero pattern of the result is correct and that the 2-norm is preserved. Note that there is no need to form the matrix $\boldsymbol{H}$ explicitly, as the vector $\boldsymbol{v}$ is all we need to apply $\boldsymbol{H}$ to any vector.

Thus far we have shown how to construct a Householder transformation to annihilate all but the first component of a given vector. More generally, for a given m-vector $\boldsymbol{a}$, consider the partitioning

$$\boldsymbol{a} = \begin{bmatrix} \boldsymbol{a}_1 \\ \boldsymbol{a}_2 \end{bmatrix},$$

where $\boldsymbol{a}_1$ is a $(k-1)$-vector, $1 \le k < m$. If we take the Householder vector to be

$$\boldsymbol{v} = \begin{bmatrix} \boldsymbol{0} \\ \boldsymbol{a}_2 \end{bmatrix} - \alpha\,\boldsymbol{e}_k,$$

where $\alpha = -\text{sign}(a_k)\|\boldsymbol{a}_2\|_2$, then the resulting Householder transformation annihilates the last $m-k$ components of $\boldsymbol{a}$. Using a sequence of Householder transformations defined in this way for $k = 1, \ldots, n$, we can annihilate all the subdiagonal entries of an $m \times n$ matrix $\boldsymbol{A}$, proceeding column by column from left to right, thereby reducing the matrix to upper triangular form. Each Householder transformation must be applied to the remaining unreduced portion of the matrix, but it will not affect the prior columns already reduced, and hence the zeros are preserved through successive transformations. In applying a Householder transformation $\boldsymbol{H}$ to an arbitrary vector $\boldsymbol{u}$, we note that

$$\boldsymbol{H}\boldsymbol{u} = \left(\boldsymbol{I} - 2\,\frac{\boldsymbol{v}\boldsymbol{v}^T}{\boldsymbol{v}^T\boldsymbol{v}}\right)\boldsymbol{u} = \boldsymbol{u} - \left(2\,\frac{\boldsymbol{v}^T\boldsymbol{u}}{\boldsymbol{v}^T\boldsymbol{v}}\right)\boldsymbol{v},$$

which is substantially cheaper to compute than a general matrix-vector multiplication and requires only that we know the vector $\boldsymbol{v}$, but does not require explicit formation of the matrix $\boldsymbol{H}$. QR factorization of an $m \times n$ matrix $\boldsymbol{A}$ by Householder transformations is summarized in Algorithm 3.1, where we have denoted the jth column of $\boldsymbol{A}$ by $\boldsymbol{a}_j$, and for simplicity we have omitted the rescaling that would be necessary for a robust implementation. In an efficient implementation, one would avoid operations involving the leading zeros of each $\boldsymbol{v}_k$. Upon completion of the algorithm, the matrix is upper triangular.

Algorithm 3.1 Householder QR Factorization

```
for k = 1 to min(n, m − 1)                              { loop over columns }
    α_k = −sign(a_kk) sqrt(a_kk^2 + ··· + a_mk^2)       { compute Householder
    v_k = [0 ··· 0 a_kk ··· a_mk]^T − α_k e_k              vector for current col }
    β_k = v_k^T v_k
    if β_k = 0 then                                     { skip current column
        continue with next k                               if it's already zero }
    for j = k to n                                      { apply transformation
        γ_j = v_k^T a_j                                    to remaining
        a_j = a_j − (2γ_j/β_k) v_k                         submatrix }
    end
end
```

Note that if at any step k we have $\beta_k = 0$, then the subdiagonal entries to be annihilated at this step are already zero, so we can simply skip to the next column and the QR factorization can still be completed. However, by our choice of sign for α_k, β_k cannot be zero unless a_{kk} is zero, which means that column k of $\boldsymbol{A}$ must be linearly dependent on the first $k-1$ columns, and hence $\boldsymbol{A}$ is not of full column rank. In this case, the resulting upper triangular matrix $\boldsymbol{R}$ will have a zero diagonal entry and will therefore be singular. A more insidious problem is a very tiny, though nonzero, diagonal entry, indicating *near* rank deficiency. We will consider the implications of rank deficiency and near rank deficiency in Section 3.5.4.

The process just described produces a factorization of the form

$$\boldsymbol{H}_n \cdots \boldsymbol{H}_1 \boldsymbol{A} = \begin{bmatrix} \boldsymbol{R} \\ \boldsymbol{O} \end{bmatrix},$$

where $\boldsymbol{R}$ is upper triangular. The product of the successive Householder transformations $\boldsymbol{H}_n \cdots \boldsymbol{H}_1$ is itself an orthogonal matrix. Thus, if we take

$$\boldsymbol{Q}^T = \boldsymbol{H}_n \cdots \boldsymbol{H}_1, \quad \text{or equivalently,} \quad \boldsymbol{Q} = \boldsymbol{H}_1 \cdots \boldsymbol{H}_n,$$

then

$$\boldsymbol{A} = \boldsymbol{Q} \begin{bmatrix} \boldsymbol{R} \\ \boldsymbol{O} \end{bmatrix}.$$

Hence, we have indeed computed the QR factorization of the matrix $\boldsymbol{A}$, which we can now use to solve the linear least squares problem. To preserve the solution, however, we must also transform the right-hand-side vector $\boldsymbol{b}$ by the same sequence of Householder transformations. We thus solve the equivalent triangular least squares problem

$$\begin{bmatrix} \boldsymbol{R} \\ \boldsymbol{O} \end{bmatrix} \boldsymbol{x} \cong \boldsymbol{Q}^T \boldsymbol{b} = \begin{bmatrix} \boldsymbol{c}_1 \\ \boldsymbol{c}_2 \end{bmatrix}.$$

For purposes of solving the linear least squares problem, the product $\boldsymbol{Q}$ of the Householder transformations need not be explicitly formed. In most software for this problem, $\boldsymbol{R}$ is stored in the upper triangle of the array originally containing $\boldsymbol{A}$, while the nonzero portions of the Householder vectors $\boldsymbol{v}_k$ required for forming the individual Householder transformations are stored in the (now zero) lower triangular portion of $\boldsymbol{A}$. (Technically, one additional n-vector of storage is required, since each Householder vector has one more nonzero component than the subdiagonal portion of the corresponding column of $\boldsymbol{A}$ will accommodate.) As we have already seen, Householder transformations are most easily applied in this form anyway (as opposed to explicit matrix-vector multiplication), so the vectors $\boldsymbol{v}_k$ are all that is needed to solve the original least squares problem as well as any subsequent problems having the same matrix but different right-hand-side vectors. If $\boldsymbol{Q}$ is needed explicitly for some other reason, however, then it can be computed by multiplying each Householder transformation in sequence times a matrix that is initially the identity matrix $\boldsymbol{I}$, but this computation will require additional storage.

Example 3.8 Householder QR Factorization. We illustrate Householder QR factorization by using it to solve the least squares problem in Example 3.1. The Householder vector $\boldsymbol{v}_1$ for annihilating the subdiagonal entries of the first column of $\boldsymbol{A}$ is

$$\boldsymbol{v}_1 = \boldsymbol{a}_1 - \alpha\,\boldsymbol{e}_1 = \begin{bmatrix} 1 \\ 0 \\ 0 \\ -1 \\ -1 \\ 0 \end{bmatrix} - \begin{bmatrix} -1.7321 \\ 0 \\ 0 \\ 0 \\ 0 \\ 0 \end{bmatrix} = \begin{bmatrix} 2.7321 \\ 0 \\ 0 \\ -1 \\ -1 \\ 0 \end{bmatrix}.$$

Applying the resulting Householder transformation $\boldsymbol{H}_1$ yields

$$\boldsymbol{H}_1\boldsymbol{A} = \begin{bmatrix} -1.7321 & 0.5774 & 0.5774 \\ 0 & 1 & 0 \\ 0 & 0 & 1 \\ 0 & 0.7887 & -0.2113 \\ 0 & -0.2113 & 0.7887 \\ 0 & -1 & 1 \end{bmatrix}, \qquad \boldsymbol{H}_1\boldsymbol{b} = \begin{bmatrix} 376 \\ 1941 \\ 2417 \\ 1026 \\ 1492 \\ 475 \end{bmatrix}.$$

The Householder vector $\boldsymbol{v}_2$ for annihilating the subdiagonal entries of the second column of $\boldsymbol{H}_1\boldsymbol{A}$ is

$$\boldsymbol{v}_2 = \begin{bmatrix} 0 \\ 1 \\ 0 \\ 0.7887 \\ -0.2113 \\ -1 \end{bmatrix} - \begin{bmatrix} 0 \\ -1.6330 \\ 0 \\ 0 \\ 0 \\ 0 \end{bmatrix} = \begin{bmatrix} 0 \\ 2.6330 \\ 0 \\ 0.7887 \\ -0.2113 \\ -1 \end{bmatrix}.$$

Applying the resulting Householder transformation $\boldsymbol{H}_2$ yields

$$\boldsymbol{H}_2\boldsymbol{H}_1\boldsymbol{A} = \begin{bmatrix} -1.7321 & 0.5774 & 0.5774 \\ 0 & -1.6330 & 0.8165 \\ 0 & 0 & 1 \\ 0 & 0 & 0.0332 \\ 0 & 0 & 0.7231 \\ 0 & 0 & 0.6899 \end{bmatrix}, \qquad \boldsymbol{H}_2\boldsymbol{H}_1\boldsymbol{b} = \begin{bmatrix} 376 \\ -1200 \\ 2417 \\ 85 \\ 1744 \\ 1668 \end{bmatrix}.$$

The Householder vector $\boldsymbol{v}_3$ for annihilating the subdiagonal entries of the third column of $\boldsymbol{H}_2\boldsymbol{H}_1\boldsymbol{A}$ is

$$\boldsymbol{v}_3 = \begin{bmatrix} 0 \\ 0 \\ 1 \\ 0.0332 \\ 0.7231 \\ 0.6899 \end{bmatrix} - \begin{bmatrix} 0 \\ 0 \\ -1.4142 \\ 0 \\ 0 \\ 0 \end{bmatrix} = \begin{bmatrix} 0 \\ 0 \\ 2.4142 \\ 0.0332 \\ 0.7231 \\ 0.6899 \end{bmatrix}.$$

Applying the resulting Householder transformation $\boldsymbol{H}_3$ yields

$$\boldsymbol{H}_3\boldsymbol{H}_2\boldsymbol{H}_1\boldsymbol{A} = \begin{bmatrix} -1.7321 & 0.5774 & 0.5774 \\ 0 & -1.6330 & 0.8165 \\ 0 & 0 & -1.4142 \\ 0 & 0 & 0 \\ 0 & 0 & 0 \\ 0 & 0 & 0 \end{bmatrix} = \begin{bmatrix} \boldsymbol{R} \\ \boldsymbol{O} \end{bmatrix}$$

and

$$H_3 H_2 H_1 b = \begin{bmatrix} 376 \\ -1200 \\ -3417 \\ 5 \\ 3 \\ 1 \end{bmatrix} = Q^T b = \begin{bmatrix} c_1 \\ c_2 \end{bmatrix}.$$

We can now solve the upper triangular system $Rx = c_1$ by back-substitution to obtain $x = [1236,\ 1943,\ 2416]^T$. Both the solution and the minimum residual sum of squares, given by $\|r\|_2^2 = \|c_2\|_2^2 = 35$, agree with those in Example 3.3.

3.5.2 Givens Rotations

Householder transformations introduce many zeros in a column at once. Although generally good for efficiency, this approach can be too heavy-handed when greater selectivity is needed in introducing zeros. For this reason, in some situations it is better to use Givens rotations, which introduce zeros one at a time.

We seek an orthogonal matrix that annihilates a single component of a given vector. One way to accomplish this is a *plane rotation*, often called a *Givens rotation* in the context of QR factorization, which has the form

$$G = \begin{bmatrix} c & s \\ -s & c \end{bmatrix},$$

where c and s are the cosine and sine, respectively, of the angle of rotation. Orthogonality requires that $c^2 + s^2 = 1$, which of course is true of the cosine and sine of any given angle. In the current context, given a 2-vector $a = [a_1 \quad a_2]^T$, we want to choose c and s so that

$$Ga = \begin{bmatrix} c & s \\ -s & c \end{bmatrix} \begin{bmatrix} a_1 \\ a_2 \end{bmatrix} = \begin{bmatrix} \alpha \\ 0 \end{bmatrix}.$$

In effect, if we rotate a so that it is aligned with the first coordinate axis, then its second component will become zero. The previous equation can be rewritten as

$$\begin{bmatrix} a_1 & a_2 \\ a_2 & -a_1 \end{bmatrix} \begin{bmatrix} c \\ s \end{bmatrix} = \begin{bmatrix} \alpha \\ 0 \end{bmatrix}.$$

We can now perform Gaussian elimination on this system to obtain the triangular system

$$\begin{bmatrix} a_1 & a_2 \\ 0 & -a_1 - a_2^2/a_1 \end{bmatrix} \begin{bmatrix} c \\ s \end{bmatrix} = \begin{bmatrix} \alpha \\ -\alpha a_2/a_1 \end{bmatrix}.$$

Back-substitution then gives

$$s = \frac{\alpha a_2}{a_1^2 + a_2^2}, \qquad c = \frac{\alpha a_1}{a_1^2 + a_2^2}.$$

Finally, the requirement that $c^2 + s^2 = 1$, so that $\alpha = \sqrt{a_1^2 + a_2^2}$, implies that

$$c = \frac{a_1}{\sqrt{a_1^2 + a_2^2}}, \qquad s = \frac{a_2}{\sqrt{a_1^2 + a_2^2}}.$$

As with Householder transformations, unnecessary overflow or underflow can be avoided by appropriate scaling. If $|a_1| > |a_2|$, then we can work with the tangent of the angle of rotation, $t = s/c = a_2/a_1$, so that the cosine and sine are given by

$$c = 1/\sqrt{1+t^2}, \qquad s = c \cdot t.$$

If $|a_2| > |a_1|$, on the other hand, then we can use the analogous formulas involving the cotangent $\tau = c/s = a_1/a_2$, obtaining

$$s = 1/\sqrt{1+\tau^2}, \qquad c = s \cdot \tau.$$

In either case, we can avoid squaring any magnitude larger than 1. The angle of rotation need not be determined explicitly, as only its sine and cosine are needed.

Example 3.9 Givens Rotation. To illustrate the construction just described, we determine a Givens rotation that annihilates the second component of the vector

$$\boldsymbol{a} = \begin{bmatrix} 4 \\ 3 \end{bmatrix}.$$

For this problem, we can safely compute the cosine and sine directly, obtaining

$$c = \frac{a_1}{\sqrt{a_1^2 + a_2^2}} = \frac{4}{5} = 0.8, \qquad s = \frac{a_2}{\sqrt{a_1^2 + a_2^2}} = \frac{3}{5} = 0.6,$$

or, equivalently, we can use the tangent $t = a_2/a_1 = 3/4 = 0.75$ to obtain

$$c = \frac{1}{\sqrt{1 + (0.75)^2}} = \frac{1}{1.25} = 0.8, \qquad s = c \cdot t = (0.8)(0.75) = 0.6.$$

Thus, the rotation is given by

$$\boldsymbol{G} = \begin{bmatrix} c & s \\ -s & c \end{bmatrix} = \begin{bmatrix} 0.8 & 0.6 \\ -0.6 & 0.8 \end{bmatrix}.$$

To confirm that the rotation performs as expected, we compute

$$\boldsymbol{G}\boldsymbol{a} = \begin{bmatrix} 0.8 & 0.6 \\ -0.6 & 0.8 \end{bmatrix} \begin{bmatrix} 4 \\ 3 \end{bmatrix} = \begin{bmatrix} 5 \\ 0 \end{bmatrix},$$

which shows that the zero pattern of the result is correct and that the 2-norm is preserved. The value of the angle of rotation, which in this case is about 36.87 degrees, does not enter directly into the computation and need not be determined explicitly.

We have seen how to design a plane rotation to annihilate one component of a 2-vector. To annihilate any desired component of an m-vector, we can apply the same technique by rotating the target component, say j, with another component, say i. The two selected components of the vector are used as before to determine the appropriate 2×2 rotation matrix, which is then embedded as a 2×2 submatrix in rows and columns i and j of the m-dimensional identity matrix $\boldsymbol{I}_m$, as illustrated here for the case $m = 5$, $i = 2$, $j = 4$:

$$\begin{bmatrix} 1 & 0 & 0 & 0 & 0 \\ 0 & c & 0 & s & 0 \\ 0 & 0 & 1 & 0 & 0 \\ 0 & -s & 0 & c & 0 \\ 0 & 0 & 0 & 0 & 1 \end{bmatrix} \begin{bmatrix} a_1 \\ a_2 \\ a_3 \\ a_4 \\ a_5 \end{bmatrix} = \begin{bmatrix} a_1 \\ \alpha \\ a_3 \\ 0 \\ a_5 \end{bmatrix}.$$

Using a sequence of such Givens rotations, we can successively annihilate individual entries of a matrix $\boldsymbol{A}$ to reduce the matrix to upper triangular form. The only restriction on the order in which we annihilate entries is that we should avoid reintroducing nonzero values into matrix entries that have previously been annihilated, but this can be accomplished by a number of different orderings. Once again, the product of all of the rotations is itself an orthogonal matrix that gives us the desired QR factorization.

A straightforward implementation of the Givens method for solving general linear least squares problems requires about 50 percent more work than the Householder method. It also requires more storage, since each rotation requires two numbers, c and s, to define it (and hence the zeroed entry a_{ij} does not suffice for storage). These work and storage disadvantages can be overcome to make the Givens method competitive with the Householder method, but at the cost of a more complicated implementation. Therefore, the Givens method is generally reserved for situations in which its greater selectivity is of paramount importance, such as when the matrix is sparse or when some particular pattern of existing zeros must be maintained.

As with Householder transformations, the matrix $\boldsymbol{Q}$ need not be formed explicitly because multiplication by the successive rotations produces the same effect as multiplication by $\boldsymbol{Q}$. If $\boldsymbol{Q}$ is needed explicitly for some other reason, however, then it can be computed by multiplying each rotation in sequence times a matrix that is initially the identity matrix $\boldsymbol{I}$.

Example 3.10 Givens QR Factorization. We illustrate Givens QR factorization by using it to solve the least squares problem in Example 3.1. The matrix for this problem has only six nonzero entries below the diagonal, which can be annihilated selectively one at a time using Givens rotations (the Householder method cannot easily take advantage of such sparsity, as it annihilates an entire column at a time).

Working from the bottom of the first column upward, the first nonzero entry of $\boldsymbol{A}$ is in the (5,1) position, which can be annihilated using a Givens rotation based on the first and fifth entries of the first column of $\boldsymbol{A}$. An appropriate rotation is given by $c = 1/\sqrt{2}$, $s = -1/\sqrt{2}$, which, after embedding in the 6×6 identity matrix, gives

$$G_1 = \begin{bmatrix} 0.7071 & 0 & 0 & 0 & -0.7071 & 0 \\ 0 & 1 & 0 & 0 & 0 & 0 \\ 0 & 0 & 1 & 0 & 0 & 0 \\ 0 & 0 & 0 & 1 & 0 & 0 \\ 0.7071 & 0 & 0 & 0 & 0.7071 & 0 \\ 0 & 0 & 0 & 0 & 0 & 1 \end{bmatrix}.$$

Applying this rotation to $\boldsymbol{A}$ and $\boldsymbol{b}$ yields

$$G_1 A = \begin{bmatrix} 1.4142 & 0 & -0.7071 \\ 0 & 1 & 0 \\ 0 & 0 & 1 \\ -1 & 1 & 0 \\ 0 & 0 & 0.7071 \\ 0 & -1 & 1 \end{bmatrix}, \quad G_1 b = \begin{bmatrix} 42 \\ 1941 \\ 2417 \\ 711 \\ 1707 \\ 475 \end{bmatrix}.$$

We next annihilate the (4,1) entry using a Givens rotation based on the first and fourth entries of the first column. An appropriate rotation is given by $c = \sqrt{2}/\sqrt{3}$, $s = -1/\sqrt{3}$, which, after embedding in the identity matrix gives

$$G_2 = \begin{bmatrix} 0.8165 & 0 & 0 & -0.5774 & 0 & 0 \\ 0 & 1 & 0 & 0 & 0 & 0 \\ 0 & 0 & 1 & 0 & 0 & 0 \\ 0.5774 & 0 & 0 & 0.8165 & 0 & 0 \\ 0 & 0 & 0 & 0 & 1 & 0 \\ 0 & 0 & 0 & 0 & 0 & 1 \end{bmatrix}.$$

Applying this rotation yields

$$G_2 G_1 A = \begin{bmatrix} 1.7321 & -0.5744 & -0.5744 \\ 0 & 1 & 0 \\ 0 & 0 & 1 \\ 0 & 0.8165 & -0.4082 \\ 0 & 0 & 0.7071 \\ 0 & -1 & 1 \end{bmatrix}, \quad G_2 G_1 b = \begin{bmatrix} -376 \\ 1941 \\ 2417 \\ 605 \\ 1707 \\ 475 \end{bmatrix}.$$

This completes the first column, so we would next move on to the second column and annihilate its nonzero subdiagonal entries one by one in a similar manner, and then finally do likewise for the third column, eventually producing the upper triangular matrix and transformed right-hand side

$$Q^T A = \begin{bmatrix} 1.7321 & -0.5774 & -0.5774 \\ 0 & 1.6330 & -0.8165 \\ 0 & 0 & 1.4142 \\ 0 & 0 & 0 \\ 0 & 0 & 0 \\ 0 & 0 & 0 \end{bmatrix}, \quad Q^T b = \begin{bmatrix} -376 \\ 1200 \\ 3417 \\ 5.66 \\ -1.63 \\ -0.56 \end{bmatrix},$$

where $\boldsymbol{Q}^T$ is the product of all of the Givens rotations used. We can now solve the upper triangular system by back-substitution to obtain $\boldsymbol{x} = [1236,\ 1943,\ 2416]^T$.

3.5.3 Gram-Schmidt Orthogonalization

Another method for computing the QR factorization is *Gram-Schmidt orthogonalization*. Given two linearly independent m-vectors $\boldsymbol{a}_1$ and $\boldsymbol{a}_2$, we wish to determine two orthonormal m-vectors $\boldsymbol{q}_1$ and $\boldsymbol{q}_2$ that span the same subspace as $\boldsymbol{a}_1$ and $\boldsymbol{a}_2$. We first normalize $\boldsymbol{a}_1$ to obtain $\boldsymbol{q}_1 = \boldsymbol{a}_1/\|\boldsymbol{a}_1\|_2$. Next we want to subtract from $\boldsymbol{a}_2$ its component in $\boldsymbol{q}_1$, which can be accomplished by projecting $\boldsymbol{a}_2$ orthogonally onto span($\boldsymbol{q}_1$); see Fig. 3.4. The latter is equivalent to the $m \times 1$ least squares problem

$$\boldsymbol{q}_1\gamma \cong \boldsymbol{a}_2,$$

whose solution is given, via the normal equation, by

$$\gamma = \left(\boldsymbol{q}_1^T\boldsymbol{q}_1\right)^{-1}\left(\boldsymbol{q}_1^T\boldsymbol{a}_2\right) = \boldsymbol{q}_1^T\boldsymbol{a}_2.$$

We can therefore obtain the desired vector $\boldsymbol{q}_2$ by normalizing the residual vector $\boldsymbol{r} = \boldsymbol{a}_2 - (\boldsymbol{q}_1^T\boldsymbol{a}_2)\boldsymbol{q}_1$ for this $m \times 1$ least squares problem.

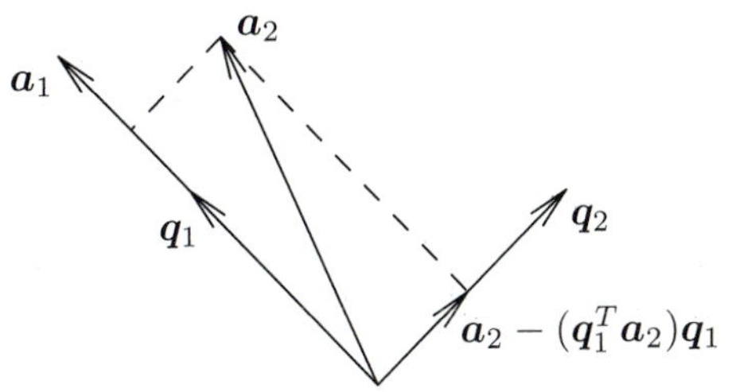

Figure 3.4: One step of Gram-Schmidt orthogonalization.

The process just described can be extended to any number of vectors $\boldsymbol{a}_1, \ldots, \boldsymbol{a}_k$, $1 \le k \le m$, by orthogonalizing each successive vector against all the preceding ones, giving the *classical* Gram-Schmidt orthogonalization procedure shown in Algorithm 3.2. If we take the $\boldsymbol{a}_k$ to be the columns of the $m \times n$ matrix $\boldsymbol{A}$, then the resulting $\boldsymbol{q}_k$ are the columns of the $m \times n$ matrix $\boldsymbol{Q}_1$ and the r_{jk} are the entries of the $n \times n$ upper triangular matrix $\boldsymbol{R}$ in the reduced QR factorization of $\boldsymbol{A}$ (see Section 3.4.5).

Unfortunately, the classical Gram-Schmidt procedure is less than satisfactory when implemented in finite-precision arithmetic, as orthogonality among the computed $\boldsymbol{q}_k$ tends to be lost due to rounding error. Moreover, the classical Gram-Schmidt procedure requires separate storage for $\boldsymbol{A}$ and $\boldsymbol{Q}_1$ (as well as $\boldsymbol{R}$) because the original $\boldsymbol{a}_k$ is used in the inner loop, and hence $\boldsymbol{q}_k$, which is updated in the inner loop, cannot overwrite it. Both of these shortcomings could be alleviated simply by using $\boldsymbol{q}_k$ instead of $\boldsymbol{a}_k$ in the inner loop, which yields an alternate Gram-Schmidt procedure that still generates $\boldsymbol{R}$ by columns. However, a more thorough rearrangement of the computation will provide an additional advantage.

Specifically, as soon as each new vector $\boldsymbol{q}_k$ has been computed we will immediately orthogonalize each of the remaining vectors against it, generating $\boldsymbol{R}$ by rows

Algorithm 3.2 Classical Gram-Schmidt Orthogonalization

```
for k = 1 to n                         { loop over columns }
    q_k = a_k
    for j = 1 to k − 1                 { subtract from current
        r_jk = q_j^T a_k                  column its components
        q_k = q_k − r_jk q_j              in preceding columns }
    end
    r_kk = ||q_k||_2
    if r_kk = 0 then stop              { stop if linearly dependent }
    q_k = q_k / r_kk                   { normalize current column }
end
```

rather than by columns. This rearrangement yields the *modified* Gram-Schmidt orthogonalization procedure shown in Algorithm 3.3, which is equivalent mathematically, but superior numerically, to classical Gram-Schmidt. With either version of Gram-Schmidt, if at any step k we have $r_{kk} = 0$, then column k of $\boldsymbol{A}$ must be linearly dependent on the first $k-1$ columns, and hence $\boldsymbol{A}$ is not of full column rank. In the form given here, neither algorithm can continue in this circumstance. However, unlike either of the column-oriented Gram-Schmidt procedures, the row-oriented modified Gram-Schmidt procedure permits the use of column pivoting to identify a maximal linearly independent set of columns of $\boldsymbol{A}$ (see Section 3.5.4). A more insidious problem is a very tiny, though nonzero, value for r_{kk}, indicating *near* rank deficiency, which again can be dealt with gracefully by using column pivoting in conjunction with the row-oriented modified Gram-Schmidt procedure.

Algorithm 3.3 Modified Gram-Schmidt Orthogonalization

```
for k = 1 to n                         { loop over columns }
    r_kk = ||a_k||_2
    if r_kk = 0 then stop              { stop if linearly dependent }
    q_k = a_k / r_kk                   { normalize current column }
    for j = k + 1 to n                 { subtract from succeeding
        r_kj = q_k^T a_j                  columns their components
        a_j = a_j − r_kj q_k              in current column }
    end
end
```

In Algorithm 3.3 we have continued to write the $\boldsymbol{a}_k$ and $\boldsymbol{q}_k$ separately for clarity, but now they can in fact share the same storage (a programmer would have formulated the algorithm this way in the first place). Unfortunately, separate storage for $\boldsymbol{Q}_1$ and $\boldsymbol{R}$ is still required, a disadvantage compared with the Householder method, for which $\boldsymbol{R}$ and the implicit representation of $\boldsymbol{Q}$ can share the space formerly occupied by $\boldsymbol{A}$. On the other hand, Gram-Schmidt provides an explicit representation for $\boldsymbol{Q}_1$, which, if desired, would require additional storage with the Householder method.

Even with the modified Gram-Schmidt procedure, cancellation can still occur when components in one vector are subtracted from another, leading to a significant loss of orthogonality among the columns of $\boldsymbol{Q}_1$ when $\boldsymbol{A}$ is ill-conditioned, though the loss is much less severe than with classical Gram-Schmidt. For this reason, when using modified Gram-Schmidt to solve a linear least squares problem $\boldsymbol{Ax} \cong \boldsymbol{b}$, it is not advisable to use the computed $\boldsymbol{Q}_1$ explicitly to compute the transformed right-hand side $\boldsymbol{c}_1 = \boldsymbol{Q}_1^T\boldsymbol{b}$. Instead, it is better numerically to treat the right-hand-side vector $\boldsymbol{b}$ as an $(n+1)$-st column, using modified Gram-Schmidt to compute the reduced QR factorization of the resulting $m \times (n+1)$ augmented matrix

$$[\,\boldsymbol{A} \quad \boldsymbol{b}\,] = [\,\boldsymbol{Q}_1 \quad \boldsymbol{q}_{n+1}\,] \begin{bmatrix} \boldsymbol{R} & \boldsymbol{c}_1 \\ \boldsymbol{0} & \rho \end{bmatrix},$$

and then the least squares solution $\boldsymbol{x}$ is given by the solution to the $n \times n$ triangular linear system $\boldsymbol{Rx} = \boldsymbol{c}_1$.

With either version of the Gram-Schmidt procedure, the orthogonality of the resulting matrix $\boldsymbol{Q}_1$ can be significantly enhanced by *reorthogonalization*: simply repeat the procedure on $\boldsymbol{Q}_1$. Such reorthogonalization could be performed repeatedly as a form of iterative refinement, but typically a single reorthogonalization produces a satisfactory result.

Example 3.11 Gram-Schmidt QR Factorization. We illustrate modified Gram-Schmidt orthogonalization by using it to solve the least squares problem in Example 3.1. Normalizing the first column of $\boldsymbol{A}$, we compute

$$r_{1,1} = \|\boldsymbol{a}_1\|_2 = 1.7321, \qquad \boldsymbol{q}_1 = \boldsymbol{a}_1/r_{1,1} = \begin{bmatrix} 0.5774 \\ 0 \\ 0 \\ -0.5774 \\ -0.5774 \\ 0 \end{bmatrix}.$$

Orthogonalizing the first column against the subsequent columns, we obtain

$$r_{1,2} = \boldsymbol{q}_1^T\boldsymbol{a}_2 = -0.5774, \qquad r_{1,3} = \boldsymbol{q}_1^T\boldsymbol{a}_3 = -0.5774.$$

Subtracting these multiples of $\boldsymbol{q}_1$ from the second and third columns, respectively, and replacing the first column with $\boldsymbol{q}_1$, we obtain the transformed matrix

$$\begin{bmatrix} 0.5774 & 0.3333 & 0.3333 \\ 0 & 1 & 0 \\ 0 & 0 & 1 \\ -0.5774 & 0.6667 & -0.3333 \\ -0.5774 & -0.3333 & 0.6667 \\ 0 & -1 & 1 \end{bmatrix}.$$

Normalizing the second column, we compute

$$r_{2,2} = \|\boldsymbol{a}_2\|_2 = 1.6330, \qquad \boldsymbol{q}_2 = \boldsymbol{a}_2/r_{2,2} = \begin{bmatrix} 0.2041 \\ 0.6124 \\ 0 \\ 0.4082 \\ -0.2041 \\ -0.6124 \end{bmatrix}.$$

Orthogonalizing the second column against the third column, we obtain

$$r_{2,3} = \boldsymbol{q}_2^T \boldsymbol{a}_3 = -0.8165.$$

Subtracting this multiple of $\boldsymbol{q}_2$ from the third column and replacing the second column with $\boldsymbol{q}_2$, we obtain the transformed matrix

$$\begin{bmatrix} 0.5774 & 0.2041 & 0.5 \\ 0 & 0.6124 & 0.5 \\ 0 & 0 & 1 \\ -0.5774 & 0.4082 & 0 \\ -0.5774 & -0.2041 & 0.5 \\ 0 & -0.6124 & 0.5 \end{bmatrix}.$$

Finally, we normalize the third column

$$r_{3,3} = \|\boldsymbol{a}_3\|_2 = 1.4142, \qquad \boldsymbol{q}_3 = \boldsymbol{a}_3/r_{3,3} = \begin{bmatrix} 0.3536 \\ 0.3536 \\ 0.7071 \\ 0 \\ 0.3536 \\ 0.3536 \end{bmatrix}.$$

Replacing the third column with $\boldsymbol{q}_3$, we have obtained the reduced QR factorization

$$\boldsymbol{A} = \begin{bmatrix} 0.5774 & 0.2041 & 0.3536 \\ 0 & 0.6124 & 0.3536 \\ 0 & 0 & 0.7071 \\ -0.5774 & 0.4082 & 0 \\ -0.5774 & -0.2041 & 0.3536 \\ 0 & -0.6124 & 0.3536 \end{bmatrix} \begin{bmatrix} 1.7321 & -0.5774 & -0.5774 \\ 0 & 1.6330 & -0.8165 \\ 0 & 0 & 1.4142 \end{bmatrix} = \boldsymbol{Q}_1 \boldsymbol{R}.$$

For this well-conditioned problem, we can safely compute the transformed right-hand side explicitly, obtaining

$$\boldsymbol{Q}_1^T \boldsymbol{b} = \begin{bmatrix} -376 \\ 1200 \\ 3417 \end{bmatrix} = \boldsymbol{c}_1.$$

We can now solve the upper triangular system $\boldsymbol{R}\boldsymbol{x} = \boldsymbol{c}_1$ by back-substitution to obtain $\boldsymbol{x} = [1236,\ 1943,\ 2416]^T$.

3.5.4 Rank Deficiency

So far we have assumed that $\boldsymbol{A}$ is of full column rank, i.e., $\text{rank}(\boldsymbol{A}) = n$. If this is not the case, i.e., if $\boldsymbol{A}$ has linearly dependent columns, then the QR factorization still exists, but the upper triangular factor $\boldsymbol{R}$ is singular (as is $\boldsymbol{A}^T\boldsymbol{A}$). Thus, many vectors $\boldsymbol{x}$ give the same minimum residual norm, and the least squares solution is not unique. This situation usually arises from a poorly designed experiment, insufficient data, or an inadequate or redundant model. Thus, the problem should probably be reformulated or rethought.

If one insists on forging ahead as is, however, then a common practice is to select the minimum residual solution $\boldsymbol{x}$ having the smallest Euclidean norm. This may be computed by QR factorization with column pivoting, which we consider next, or by the singular value decomposition (SVD), which we will consider in Section 3.6. Note that such a procedure for dealing with rank deficiency also enables us to handle underdetermined problems, where $m < n$, since the columns of $\boldsymbol{A}$ are necessarily linearly dependent in that case.

Example 3.12 Rank Deficiency. Suppose that the surveyor in Example 3.1 had measured only the relative heights of each pair of hills with respect to each other, but did not directly measure the height of any of the hills with respect to the reference point, so that we have the 3×3 linear system

$$\boldsymbol{A}\boldsymbol{x} = \begin{bmatrix} -1 & 1 & 0 \\ -1 & 0 & 1 \\ 0 & -1 & 1 \end{bmatrix} \begin{bmatrix} x_1 \\ x_2 \\ x_3 \end{bmatrix} \cong \begin{bmatrix} 711 \\ 1177 \\ 475 \end{bmatrix} = \boldsymbol{b}.$$

Would there still be enough information to determine the heights of the three hills? To answer this question, we compute the QR factorization

$$\boldsymbol{A} = \begin{bmatrix} -0.7071 & 0.4082 & 0.5774 \\ -0.7071 & -0.4082 & -0.5774 \\ 0 & -0.8165 & 0.5774 \end{bmatrix} \begin{bmatrix} 1.4142 & -0.7071 & -0.7071 \\ 0 & 1.2247 & -1.2247 \\ 0 & 0 & 0 \end{bmatrix} = \boldsymbol{QR},$$

which shows that $\boldsymbol{R}$ is singular, and hence $\boldsymbol{A}$ is rank deficient. In this simple example, we could have seen this directly from the fact that all the row sums of $\boldsymbol{A}$ are zero (i.e., $\boldsymbol{A}\boldsymbol{e} = \boldsymbol{0}$), but rank deficiency is seldom so obvious in practice.

In practice, the rank of a matrix is often not clear-cut. Thus, a relative tolerance is used to detect near rank deficiency of least squares problems, just as in detecting near singularity of square linear systems. If a least squares problem is nearly rank-deficient, then the solution will be sensitive to perturbations in the input data. We will be able to examine these issues more precisely when we introduce the singular value decomposition of a matrix in Section 3.6. Within the context of QR factorization, a reliable method for detecting and dealing with possible rank deficiency is *column pivoting*, which we consider next.

Example 3.13 Near Rank Deficiency. Consider the 3×2 matrix

$$\boldsymbol{A} = \begin{bmatrix} 0.913 & 0.659 \\ 0.780 & 0.563 \\ 0.457 & 0.330 \end{bmatrix}.$$

If we compute a QR factorization of $\boldsymbol{A}$, we find that

$$\boldsymbol{R} = \begin{bmatrix} -1.28484 & -0.92744 \\ 0 & 0.00013 \end{bmatrix}.$$

Thus, $\boldsymbol{R}$ is extremely close to being singular, and if we use $\boldsymbol{R}$ to solve a least squares problem, the result will be correspondingly sensitive to perturbations in the problem data. For practical purposes, the rank of $\boldsymbol{A}$ is only one rather than two, since its columns are nearly linearly dependent.

The columns of a matrix $\boldsymbol{A}$ can be viewed as an unordered set of vectors from which we wish to select a maximal linearly independent subset. Rather than processing the columns in the natural order in computing the QR factorization, we instead select for reduction at each stage the column of the remaining unreduced submatrix having maximum Euclidean norm. This column is interchanged (explicitly or implicitly) with the next column in the natural order and then is zeroed below the diagonal in the usual manner. The transformation required to do this must then be applied to the remaining unreduced columns, and the process is repeated. The process just described is called QR factorization with *column pivoting*. Note that in order for column pivoting to work, at each step of the QR factorization process the remaining columns must have no components in the columns already completed. This is true for the Householder, Givens, and row-oriented modified Gram-Schmidt algorithms, but not for the column-oriented Gram-Schmidt algorithms (classical or modified), and hence the latter cannot be used with column pivoting.

If $\text{rank}(\boldsymbol{A}) = k < n$, then after k steps of QR factorization with column pivoting, the norms of the remaining unreduced columns will be zero (or "negligible" in finite-precision arithmetic) below row k. Thus, we have produced an orthogonal factorization of the form

$$\boldsymbol{Q}^T\boldsymbol{A}\boldsymbol{P} = \begin{bmatrix} \boldsymbol{R} & \boldsymbol{S} \\ \boldsymbol{O} & \boldsymbol{O} \end{bmatrix},$$

where $\boldsymbol{R}$ is $k \times k$, upper triangular, and nonsingular, and $\boldsymbol{P}$ is a permutation matrix that performs the column interchanges. At this point, a *basic solution* (i.e., a solution having at most k nonzero components) to the least squares problem $\boldsymbol{Ax} \cong \boldsymbol{b}$ can be computed by solving the triangular system $\boldsymbol{Rz} = \boldsymbol{c}_1$, where $\boldsymbol{c}_1$ is a vector composed of the first k components of $\boldsymbol{Q}^T\boldsymbol{b}$, and then taking

$$\boldsymbol{x} = \boldsymbol{P} \begin{bmatrix} \boldsymbol{z} \\ \boldsymbol{0} \end{bmatrix}.$$

In the context of data fitting, this procedure amounts to ignoring components of the model that are redundant or not well-determined. If a *minimum-norm solution* is desired, however, it can be computed at the expense of some additional orthogonal transformations applied on the right to annihilate $\boldsymbol{S}$ as well.

Example 3.14 Basic and Minimum-Norm Solutions. Continuing with Example 3.12, a basic solution would assign a height of zero to one of the hills (the hill chosen would depend on the column permutation $\boldsymbol{P}$ in the QR factorization), which would then enable us to determine the heights of the other two hills with respect to it by solving a smaller system. For this example, assigning the third hill a height of zero yields the basic solution $\boldsymbol{x}^T = [-1180, \ -472, \ 0]$ (negative heights simply mean that the first two hills are below the hill assigned height zero). Note that this solution does not exactly satisfy the linear system (reflecting the fact that it is inconsistent, which is possible for a square system only if it is rank deficient), but it is a (nonunique) least squares solution. The minimum-norm solution for this rank-deficient problem is $\boldsymbol{x}^T = [-629, \ 79, \ 551]$ (see Example 3.16).

In practice, the rank of $\boldsymbol{A}$ is usually unknown, so the column pivoting process is used to discover the rank by monitoring the norms of the remaining unreduced columns and terminating the factorization when the maximum value falls below some relative tolerance. More sophisticated *rank-revealing* techniques based on QR factorization are also available, as well as the singular value decomposition, which is the most reliable (but most expensive) way to determine the rank numerically (see Section 3.6.1).

3.6 Singular Value Decomposition

As with square linear systems, a diagonal linear least squares problem is even easier to solve than a triangular one. Recall the relationship between the triangular LU factorization and the diagonal factorization produced by Gauss-Jordan elimination for a square matrix (see Section 2.4.8). Somewhat analogously, it is possible to go beyond the triangular QR factorization to achieve a diagonal factorization of a rectangular matrix using orthogonal transformations.

The *singular value decomposition* (*SVD*) of an $m \times n$ matrix $\boldsymbol{A}$ has the form

$$\boldsymbol{A} = \boldsymbol{U\Sigma V}^T,$$

where $\boldsymbol{U}$ is an $m \times m$ orthogonal matrix, $\boldsymbol{V}$ is an $n \times n$ orthogonal matrix, and $\boldsymbol{\Sigma}$ is an $m \times n$ diagonal matrix, with

$$\sigma_{ij} = \begin{cases} 0 & \text{for } i \neq j \\ \sigma_i \geq 0 & \text{for } i = j \end{cases}.$$

The diagonal entries σ_i are called the *singular values* of $\boldsymbol{A}$ and are usually ordered so that $\sigma_{i-1} \geq \sigma_i$, $i = 2, \ldots, \min\{m, n\}$. The columns $\boldsymbol{u}_i$ of $\boldsymbol{U}$ and $\boldsymbol{v}_i$ of $\boldsymbol{V}$ are the corresponding left and right *singular vectors*. Because it is closely related to algorithms for computing eigenvalues, we will postpone a discussion of how to compute the SVD until Section 4.7, but we will discuss applications of the SVD here because of its important role in solving least squares and related problems.

Example 3.15 Singular Value Decomposition. The singular value decomposition of

$$\boldsymbol{A} = \begin{bmatrix} 1 & 2 & 3 \\ 4 & 5 & 6 \\ 7 & 8 & 9 \\ 10 & 11 & 12 \end{bmatrix} \quad \text{is given by} \quad \boldsymbol{U\Sigma V}^T =$$

$$\begin{bmatrix} 0.141 & 0.825 & -0.420 & -0.351 \\ 0.344 & 0.426 & 0.298 & 0.782 \\ 0.547 & 0.028 & 0.664 & -0.509 \\ 0.750 & -0.371 & -0.542 & 0.079 \end{bmatrix} \begin{bmatrix} 25.5 & 0 & 0 \\ 0 & 1.29 & 0 \\ 0 & 0 & 0 \\ 0 & 0 & 0 \end{bmatrix} \begin{bmatrix} 0.504 & 0.574 & 0.644 \\ -0.761 & -0.057 & 0.646 \\ 0.408 & -0.816 & 0.408 \end{bmatrix}.$$

Thus, we have $\sigma_1 = 25.5$, $\sigma_2 = 1.29$, and $\sigma_3 = 0$. A singular value of zero indicates that the matrix is rank-deficient; in general, the rank of a matrix is equal to the number of nonzero singular values, which in this example is two.

The SVD provides a particularly flexible method for solving linear least squares problems of any shape or rank. Consider first the overdetermined, full-rank case. If $\boldsymbol{A}$ is $m \times n$ with $\text{rank}(\boldsymbol{A}) = n$, then

$$\boldsymbol{A} = \boldsymbol{U\Sigma V}^T = [\boldsymbol{U}_1 \quad \boldsymbol{U}_2] \begin{bmatrix} \boldsymbol{\Sigma}_1 \\ \boldsymbol{O} \end{bmatrix} \boldsymbol{V}^T = \boldsymbol{U}_1 \boldsymbol{\Sigma}_1 \boldsymbol{V}^T,$$

where $\boldsymbol{U}_1$ is $m \times n$ and $\boldsymbol{\Sigma}_1$ is $n \times n$ and nonsingular, is the *reduced*, "economy size" SVD of $\boldsymbol{A}$. The solution to the least squares problem $\boldsymbol{Ax} \cong \boldsymbol{b}$ is then given by

$$\boldsymbol{x} = \boldsymbol{V\Sigma}_1^{-1}\boldsymbol{U}_1^T\boldsymbol{b},$$

as can easily be verified by substituting the reduced SVD of $\boldsymbol{A}$ into the normal equations. More generally, for $\boldsymbol{A}$ of any shape or rank, the least squares solution to $\boldsymbol{Ax} \cong \boldsymbol{b}$ of minimum Euclidean norm is given by

$$\boldsymbol{x} = \sum_{\sigma_i \neq 0} \frac{\boldsymbol{u}_i^T \boldsymbol{b}}{\sigma_i} \boldsymbol{v}_i.$$

The SVD is especially useful for ill-conditioned or nearly rank-deficient problems, since any relatively tiny singular values can be dropped from the summation, thereby making the solution much less sensitive to perturbations in the data.

Example 3.16 Minimum-Norm Solution. The SVD of the matrix $\boldsymbol{A}$ in Example 3.12 is given by $\boldsymbol{A} = \boldsymbol{U\Sigma V}^T =$

$$\begin{bmatrix} -0.707 & 0.408 & 0.577 \\ -0.707 & -0.408 & -0.577 \\ 0 & -0.816 & 0.577 \end{bmatrix} \begin{bmatrix} 1.732 & 0 & 0 \\ 0 & 1.732 & 0 \\ 0 & 0 & 0 \end{bmatrix} \begin{bmatrix} 0.816 & -0.408 & -0.408 \\ 0 & 0.707 & -0.707 \\ -0.577 & -0.577 & -0.577 \end{bmatrix},$$

so the least squares solution of minimum Euclidean norm is given by

$$x = \frac{u_1^T b}{\sigma_1} v_1 + \frac{u_2^T b}{\sigma_2} v_2 = \frac{-1335}{1.732} \begin{bmatrix} 0.816 \\ -0.408 \\ -0.408 \end{bmatrix} + \frac{-578}{1.732} \begin{bmatrix} 0 \\ 0.707 \\ -0.707 \end{bmatrix} = \begin{bmatrix} -629 \\ 79 \\ 551 \end{bmatrix}.$$

3.6.1 Other Applications of SVD

The singular value decomposition $A = U\Sigma V^T$ has many other important applications, among which are the following:

Euclidean matrix norm. The matrix norm induced by the Euclidean vector norm is given by the largest singular value of the matrix,

$$\|A\|_2 = \max_{x \neq 0} \frac{\|Ax\|_2}{\|x\|_2} = \sigma_{\max}.$$

We are not yet prepared to see why this is true because it depends on knowledge of eigenvalues (Chapter 4) and optimization (Chapter 6).

Euclidean condition number. The condition number of an arbitrary matrix A in the Euclidean norm is given by the ratio

$$\text{cond}(A) = \sigma_{\max}/\sigma_{\min}.$$

This definition agrees with the definition of cond(A) for a square matrix given in Section 2.3.3 when using the Euclidean norm, as well as the condition number of an overdetermined matrix of full column rank as defined in Section 3.3. It generalizes both of these to rectangular matrices of arbitrary shape and rank. Note that with this definition, as before, $\text{cond}(A) = \infty$ if $\text{rank}(A) < \min(m, n)$, since in that case $\sigma_{\min} = 0$. Just as the condition number of a square matrix measures closeness to singularity, the condition number of a rectangular matrix measures closeness to rank deficiency.

Example 3.17 Euclidean Matrix Norm and Condition Number. The SVD of the matrix A in Examples 2.4 and 2.5 is given by $A = U\Sigma V^T =$

$$\begin{bmatrix} 0.392 & -0.920 & -0.021 \\ 0.240 & 0.081 & 0.967 \\ 0.888 & 0.384 & -0.253 \end{bmatrix} \begin{bmatrix} 5.723 & 0 & 0 \\ 0 & 1.068 & 0 \\ 0 & 0 & 0.327 \end{bmatrix} \begin{bmatrix} 0.645 & -0.224 & 0.731 \\ -0.567 & 0.501 & 0.653 \\ 0.513 & 0.836 & -0.196 \end{bmatrix},$$

so that

$$\|A\|_2 = 5.723, \qquad \text{cond}_2(A) = 5.723/0.327 = 17.5$$

Rank determination. The rank of a matrix is equal to the number of nonzero singular values it has (see Examples 3.15 and 3.16). In practice, however, the rank may not be well-determined in that some singular values may be very small but nonzero. For many purposes it may be better to regard any singular values falling below some threshold (relative to the largest singular value) as negligible in determining the "numerical rank" of the matrix. One way to interpret this is that the given matrix is very near to (i.e., within the given threshold of) a matrix of the rank so determined. Use of the SVD to determine the numerical rank is more reliable (though more expensive) than using QR factorization with column pivoting (see Section 3.5.4).

Example 3.18 Rank Determination. The SVD of the matrix $\boldsymbol{A}$ in Example 3.13 is given by $\boldsymbol{A} = \boldsymbol{U\Sigma V}^T =$

$$\begin{bmatrix} 0.71058 & -0.26631 & -0.65127 \\ 0.60707 & -0.23592 & 0.75882 \\ 0.35573 & 0.93457 & 0.00597 \end{bmatrix} \begin{bmatrix} 1.58460 & 0 \\ 0 & 0.00011 \\ 0 & 0 \end{bmatrix} \begin{bmatrix} 0.81083 & 0.58528 \\ -0.58528 & 0.81083 \end{bmatrix}.$$

Thus, with a threshold of about 10^{-4} or larger, the rank would be declared to be one rather than two.

Pseudoinverse. Define the pseudoinverse of a scalar σ to be $1/\sigma$ if $\sigma \neq 0$, and zero otherwise. Define the pseudoinverse of a (possibly rectangular) diagonal matrix by transposing the matrix and taking the scalar pseudoinverse of each entry. Then the pseudoinverse of a general $m \times n$ matrix $\boldsymbol{A}$ is given by

$$\boldsymbol{A}^+ = \boldsymbol{V\Sigma}^+\boldsymbol{U}^T.$$

Note that the pseudoinverse always exists regardless of whether the matrix is square or of full rank. If $\boldsymbol{A}$ is square and nonsingular, then the pseudoinverse is the same as the usual matrix inverse, $\boldsymbol{A}^{-1}$. If $\boldsymbol{A}$ has full column rank, then this definition agrees with that given in Section 3.3 (see Exercise 3.33). In all cases, the least squares solution to $\boldsymbol{Ax} \cong \boldsymbol{b}$ of minimum Euclidean norm is given by $\boldsymbol{A}^+\boldsymbol{b}$.

Example 3.19 Pseudoinverse. From the SVD shown in Example 3.16, we see that the pseudoinverse of the matrix $\boldsymbol{A}$ in Example 3.12 is given by

$$\boldsymbol{A}^+ = \frac{1}{3}\begin{bmatrix} -1 & -1 & 0 \\ 1 & 0 & -1 \\ 0 & 1 & 1 \end{bmatrix},$$

so that the least squares solution to $\boldsymbol{Ax} \cong \boldsymbol{b}$ of minimum Euclidean norm is given by

$$\boldsymbol{x} = \boldsymbol{A}^+\boldsymbol{b} = \frac{1}{3}\begin{bmatrix} -1 & -1 & 0 \\ 1 & 0 & -1 \\ 0 & 1 & 1 \end{bmatrix}\begin{bmatrix} 711 \\ 1177 \\ 475 \end{bmatrix} = \begin{bmatrix} -629 \\ 79 \\ 551 \end{bmatrix}.$$

Orthonormal bases. If $\boldsymbol{A} = \boldsymbol{U\Sigma V}^T$, then the columns of $\boldsymbol{U}$ corresponding to nonzero singular values form an *orthonormal basis* for span($\boldsymbol{A}$), and the remaining columns of $\boldsymbol{U}$ form an orthonormal basis for its orthogonal complement, span$(\boldsymbol{A})^{\perp}$. Similarly, the columns of $\boldsymbol{V}$ corresponding to zero singular values form an orthonormal basis for the *null space* of $\boldsymbol{A}$, $\{\boldsymbol{x} \in \mathbb{R}^n : \boldsymbol{Ax} = \boldsymbol{0}\}$, and the remaining columns of $\boldsymbol{V}$ form an orthonormal basis for the orthogonal complement of the null space.

Lower-rank approximation. Another way to write the SVD is

$$\boldsymbol{A} = \boldsymbol{U\Sigma V}^T = \sigma_1\boldsymbol{E}_1 + \sigma_2\boldsymbol{E}_2 + \cdots + \sigma_n\boldsymbol{E}_n,$$

where $\boldsymbol{E}_i = \boldsymbol{u}_i\boldsymbol{v}_i^T$. Each $\boldsymbol{E}_i$ is of rank one and can be stored using only $m+n$ storage locations. Moreover, the product $\boldsymbol{E}_i\boldsymbol{x}$ can be formed using only $m+n$ multiplications. Thus, a useful condensed approximation to $\boldsymbol{A}$ can be obtained by omitting from the foregoing summation those terms corresponding to the smaller singular values, since they have relatively little effect on the sum. It can be shown that this approximation using the k largest singular values is the closest matrix of rank k to $\boldsymbol{A}$ in the Frobenius norm. (The *Frobenius norm* of an $m \times n$ matrix is the Euclidean norm of the matrix considered as a vector in $\mathbb{R}^{mn}$.) Such an approximation is useful in image processing, data compression, information retrieval, cryptography, and numerous other applications.

Example 3.20 Lower-Rank Approximation. From the SVD shown in Example 3.18 for the matrix $\boldsymbol{A}$ given in Example 3.13, we see that the rank-one matrix

$$\sigma_1\boldsymbol{E}_1 = \sigma_1\boldsymbol{u}_1\boldsymbol{v}_1^T = 1.58460 \begin{bmatrix} 0.71058 \\ 0.60707 \\ 0.35573 \end{bmatrix} \begin{bmatrix} 0.81083 & 0.58528 \end{bmatrix} = \begin{bmatrix} 0.91298 & 0.65902 \\ 0.77999 & 0.56302 \\ 0.45706 & 0.32992 \end{bmatrix}$$

is an extremely close approximation to the original matrix $\boldsymbol{A}$, since σ_2 is so tiny that the term associated with it makes almost no contribution to the sum.

Total least squares. In an ordinary linear least squares problem $\boldsymbol{Ax} \cong \boldsymbol{b}$, we implicitly assume that the entries of $\boldsymbol{A}$ are known exactly, whereas the entries of $\boldsymbol{b}$ are subject to random error, and this justifies minimizing the vertical distances between the data points and the curve. When all of the variables are subject to measurement error or other uncertainty, however, it may make more sense to minimize the orthogonal distances between the data points and the curve, which yields the *total least squares* solution. Recall that in ordinary least squares we seek to minimize $\|\boldsymbol{b} - \boldsymbol{y}\|_2$ subject to the constraint that $\boldsymbol{y} \in$ span($\boldsymbol{A}$), i.e., we seek the closest compatible system, allowing only the right-hand side to vary. In total least squares, we also seek the closest compatible system, but allow *both* the matrix and the right-hand side to vary. As we saw in the previous paragraph, such a matrix approximation problem can be solved by the singular value decomposition. In particular, consider the SVD of the $m \times (n+1)$ matrix $[\,\boldsymbol{A} \;\; \boldsymbol{b}\,] = \boldsymbol{U\Sigma V}^T$. For the approximating system $[\,\hat{\boldsymbol{A}} \;\; \boldsymbol{y}\,]$ to be compatible, i.e., $\boldsymbol{y} \in$ span($\hat{\boldsymbol{A}}$), it must have rank at most n. As we have just seen, the closest approximating matrix of rank n is obtained by using the first n singular values and omitting σ_{n+1}. The solution $\boldsymbol{x}$ of the resulting compatible system must satisfy the equation

$$[\,\hat{\boldsymbol{A}} \quad \boldsymbol{y}\,]\begin{bmatrix} \boldsymbol{x} \\ -1 \end{bmatrix} = \boldsymbol{0},$$

which shows that $[\,\boldsymbol{x}^T \quad -1\,]^T$ must lie in the null space of $[\,\hat{\boldsymbol{A}} \quad \boldsymbol{y}\,]$, which in turn implies that $[\,\boldsymbol{x}^T \quad -1\,]^T$ is proportional to $\boldsymbol{v}_{n+1}$, the right singular vector corresponding to σ_{n+1}. Thus, to obtain the solution we need merely scale $\boldsymbol{v}_{n+1}$ so that its last component is -1. We conclude that, provided $\sigma_{n+1} < \sigma_n$ and $v_{n+1,n+1} \neq 0$, the total least squares solution is given by

$$\boldsymbol{x} = -\frac{1}{v_{n+1,n+1}}\begin{bmatrix} v_{1,n+1} \\ \vdots \\ v_{n,n+1} \end{bmatrix}.$$

More general problems, for example with multiple right-hand sides and with some of the variables known exactly, can be handled by a similar approach but are rather more complicated (see [404] for details).

Example 3.21 Total Least Squares. Consider the problem of fitting the model function

$$f(t, x) = x\,t$$

(i.e., a straight line through the origin, with slope x to be determined) to the following data points:

t	-2	-1	3
y	-1	3	-2

Fitting the y values as a function of t is appropriate if the y data are subject to error but the data for t are exact. The resulting ordinary least squares fit, shown in Fig. 3.5(a), minimizes the sum of squares of vertical distances between the straight line and the data points, which gives a slope of $x = -0.5$. If the data for t are equally subject to error, however, then we might just as well have fit t as a function of y. The resulting ordinary least squares fit, shown in Fig. 3.5(b), minimizes the sum of squares of horizontal distances between the straight line and the data points, which gives a slope of $x = -2$. In such a situation, a better strategy than either of these is total least squares, which treats all the data equally. The resulting fit, shown in Fig. 3.5(c), minimizes the sum of squares of shortest (i.e., perpendicular) distances between the straight line and the data points, which gives a slope of $x = -1$. To see how the latter fit was obtained, we observe that the matrix $\boldsymbol{A}$ for this problem has only one column, hence we compute the SVD

$$[\,\boldsymbol{A} \quad \boldsymbol{b}\,] = [\,\boldsymbol{t} \quad \boldsymbol{y}\,] = \begin{bmatrix} -2 & -1 \\ -1 & 3 \\ 3 & -2 \end{bmatrix} =$$

$$\begin{bmatrix} -0.154 & 0.802 & 0.577 \\ -0.617 & -0.535 & 0.577 \\ 0.772 & -0.267 & 0.577 \end{bmatrix} \begin{bmatrix} 4.583 & 0 \\ 0 & 2.646 \\ 0 & 0 \end{bmatrix} \begin{bmatrix} 0.707 & -0.707 \\ -0.707 & -0.707 \end{bmatrix} = \boldsymbol{U\Sigma V}^T,$$

so that

$$x = -(1/v_{2,2})\, v_{1,2} = -(1/(-0.707))\,(-0.707) = -1.$$

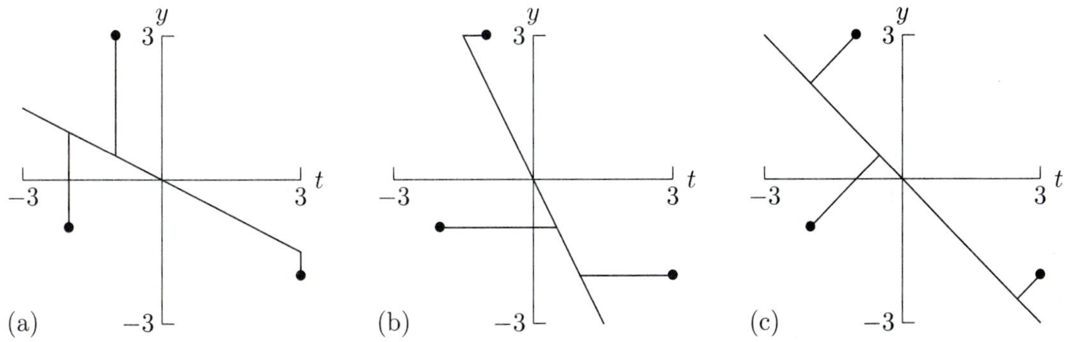

Figure 3.5: Ordinary and total least squares fits of straight line to given data.

3.7 Comparison of Methods

We have now seen a number of methods for solving least squares problems. The choice among them depends on the particular problem being solved and involves tradeoffs among efficiency, accuracy, and reliability.

The normal equations method is easy to implement: it simply requires matrix multiplication and Cholesky factorization. Moreover, reducing the problem to an $n \times n$ system is very attractive when $m \gg n$. By taking advantage of its symmetry, forming the cross-product matrix $\boldsymbol{A}^T\boldsymbol{A}$ requires about $mn^2/2$ multiplications and a similar number of additions. Solving the resulting linear system by Cholesky factorization requires about $n^3/6$ multiplications and a similar number of additions. Unfortunately, the normal equations method produces a solution whose relative error is proportional to $[\text{cond}(\boldsymbol{A})]^2$, and the required Cholesky factorization can be expected to break down if $\text{cond}(\boldsymbol{A}) \approx 1/\sqrt{\epsilon_{\text{mach}}}$ or worse.

For solving dense linear least squares problems, the Householder method is generally the most efficient and accurate of the orthogonalization methods. It requires about $mn^2 - n^3/3$ multiplications and a similar number of additions. It can be shown that the Householder method produces a solution whose relative error is proportional to $\text{cond}(\boldsymbol{A}) + \|\boldsymbol{r}\|_2[\text{cond}(\boldsymbol{A})]^2$, which is the best that can be expected since this is the inherent sensitivity of the solution to the least squares problem itself (recall Section 3.3). Moreover, the Householder method can be expected to break down (in the back-substitution phase) only if $\text{cond}(\boldsymbol{A}) \approx 1/\epsilon_{\text{mach}}$ or worse.

For nearly square problems, $m \approx n$, the normal equations and Householder methods require about the same amount of work. But for highly overdetermined problems, $m \gg n$, the Householder method requires about twice as much work as the normal equations method. On the other hand, the Householder method is more accurate and more broadly applicable than the normal equations method. These advantages may not be worth the additional cost, however, when the problem is sufficiently well-conditioned that the normal equations method provides adequate accuracy. For rank-deficient or nearly rank-deficient problems, of course, the Householder method with column pivoting can produce a useful solution when the normal equations method would fail outright.

Finally, the SVD is the most expensive method, with a cost proportional to $mn^2 + n^3$ and a proportionality constant ranging from 4 to 10 or more, depending on the particular algorithm used (see Section 4.7). Thus, the superb robustness and reliability of the SVD come at a high price, which may nevertheless be worth it in especially critical or delicate situations.

3.8 Software for Linear Least Squares

Table 3.1 is a list of appropriate routines for solving linear least squares problems, both full rank and rank-deficient. Most of the routines listed are based on QR factorization. Many packages also include software for the SVD, which can be used to solve least squares problems, although at greater computational expense. The SVD provides a particularly reliable method for determining numerical rank and dealing with possible rank deficiency (see Section 3.6). Because methods for computing the SVD are closely related to methods for eigenvalue computations (see Section 4.7), software for computing the SVD is listed along with software for eigenvalues and eigenvectors in Table 4.2. For solving total least squares problems, where all of the variables are subject to random error, `dtls` is available from `Netlib`.

Conventional software for solving linear least squares problems $\boldsymbol{Ax} \cong \boldsymbol{b}$ is sometimes implemented as a single routine, or it may be split into two routines, one for computing a factorization and another for solving the resulting triangular system. The input typically required includes a two-dimensional array containing the matrix $\boldsymbol{A}$, a one-dimensional array containing the right-hand-side vector $\boldsymbol{b}$ (or a two-dimensional array for multiple right-hand-side vectors), the number of rows m and number of columns n in the matrix, the leading dimension of the array containing $\boldsymbol{A}$ (so that the subroutine can interpret subscripts properly in the array), and possibly some work space and a flag indicating the particular task to be performed. The user may also need to supply a tolerance if column pivoting or other means of rank determination is performed. On return, the solution $\boldsymbol{x}$ usually overwrites the storage for $\boldsymbol{b}$, and the factorization overwrites the storage for $\boldsymbol{A}$.

In `MATLAB`, the backslash operator used for solving square linear systems is extended to include rectangular systems as well. Thus, the least squares solution to the overdetermined system $\boldsymbol{Ax} \cong \boldsymbol{b}$ is given by `x = A\b`. Internally, the solution

Source	Factor	Solve	Rank-deficient
FMM [127]	svd		svd
IMSL	lqrrr	lqrsl	lsqrr
KMN [220]	sqrls	sqrls	ssvdc
LAPACK [10]	sgeqrf	sormqr/strtrs	sgeqpf/stzrqf
Lawson & Hanson [251]	hft	hs1	hfti
LINPACK [98]	sqrdc	sqrsl	sqrst
MATLAB	qr	\	svd
NAG	f08aef	f08agf/f07tef	f04jgf
NAPACK [178]	qr	over	sing/rsolve
NR [315]	qrdcmp[a]	qrsolv	svdcmp/svbksb
NUMAL [250]	lsqortdec	lsqsol	solovr
SLATEC	sqrdc	sqrsl	llsia/sglss/minfit
SOL [425]	hredl	qrvslv	mnlnls

[a]As published, qrdcmp and qrsolv handle only square matrices, but they are easily modified to handle rectangular matrices.

Table 3.1: Software for linear least squares problems

is computed by QR factorization, but the user need not be aware of this. The QR factorization can be computed explicitly, if desired, by using the MATLAB qr function, [Q, R] = qr(A). The MATLAB function for computing the singular value decomposition has the form [U, S, V] = svd(A).

In addition to mathematical software libraries such as those listed in the table, many statistical packages have extensive software for solving least squares problems in various contexts, and they often include many diagnostic features for assessing the quality of the results. Well-known packages in this category include BMDP, Minitab, Omnitab, S, S-Plus, SAS, and SPSS. There is also a statistics toolbox available for MATLAB. Additional software is available for data fitting using criteria other than least squares, particularly for the 1-norm and the ∞-norm, which are preferable in some contexts.

3.9 Historical Notes and Further Reading

The method of least squares, based on the normal equations, was formulated and used by Gauss in 1795 but first published by Legendre in 1805, resulting in a priority dispute (see [311]). Gram-Schmidt orthogonalization was formulated by Gram in 1883 and in its modern algorithmic form by Schmidt in 1907. The "modified" version of Gram-Schmidt is actually older than the "classical" version, having been derived by Laplace in 1816, but its numerical superiority was not recognized until 1966 by Rice. Householder's method for computing the QR factorization was published in 1958, although elementary reflectors (now called Householder transformations) had been used for another purpose by Turnbull and Aitken in 1932. Givens' method for computing the QR factorization was also published in 1958, although plane rotations had been used a century earlier by Jacobi for computing eigenvalues (see Section 4.5.8). The use of QR factorization, particularly the Householder method, for solving least squares problems was popularized by Golub in 1965 [161]. Comprehensive references on least squares computations include [35, 115, 251]. The books on matrix computations cited in Section 2.8 also discuss linear least squares problems in some detail. Techniques for dealing with rank deficiency are the subject of [188]. For a thorough discussion of *total least squares*, which is appropriate when all of the variables are subject to random error, see [404]. For a statistical perspective on least squares computations, see [229, 389].

We have focused on the simplest type of least squares problems, in which the model function is linear and all of the data points are weighted equally. We will discuss nonlinear least squares problems in Section 6.6. Incorporating varying weights for the data points or more general cross-correlations among the variables is relatively straightforward within the framework we have discussed. Allowing varying weights for the data points, for example, simply involves multiplying both sides of the least squares system by an appropriate diagonal matrix.

The singular value decomposition was formulated independently by Beltrami in 1873 and by Jordan in 1874, both in the context of quadratic forms. The definition of the SVD in terms of matrices was formulated in the 1930s by Eckart and Young, who also proved the lower-rank approximation theorem cited in Section 3.6.1. For a detailed history of the singular value decomposition, see [369]. The singular value decomposition has a wide variety of applications beyond those discussed in the text, including image processing [12], signal processing [399], control [276], geophysics [208], information retrieval [30], and cryptography [274]. The pseudoinverse, as we have defined it, was formulated by Moore in 1920 and popularized by Penrose in 1955, spawning a vast literature on this topic.

Review Questions

3.1. True or false: A linear least squares problem always has a solution.

3.2. True or false: Fitting a straight line to a set of data points is a linear least squares problem, whereas fitting a quadratic polynomial to the data is a nonlinear least squares problem.

3.3. True or false: At the solution to a linear least squares problem $\boldsymbol{Ax} \cong \boldsymbol{b}$, the residual vector $\boldsymbol{r} = \boldsymbol{b} - \boldsymbol{Ax}$ is orthogonal to span($\boldsymbol{A}$).

3.4. True or false: An overdetermined linear least squares problem $\boldsymbol{Ax} \cong \boldsymbol{b}$ always has a unique solution $\boldsymbol{x}$ that minimizes the Euclidean norm of the residual vector $\boldsymbol{r} = \boldsymbol{b} - \boldsymbol{Ax}$.

3.5. True or false: In solving a linear least squares problem $\boldsymbol{Ax} \cong \boldsymbol{b}$, if the vector $\boldsymbol{b}$ lies in span($\boldsymbol{A}$), then the residual is $\boldsymbol{0}$.

3.6. True or false: In solving a linear least squares problem $\boldsymbol{Ax} \cong \boldsymbol{b}$, if the residual is $\boldsymbol{0}$, then the solution $\boldsymbol{x}$ must be unique.

3.7. True or false: The product of a Householder transformation and a Givens rotation is always an orthogonal matrix.

3.8. True or false: If the $n \times n$ matrix $\boldsymbol{Q}$ is a Householder transformation, and $\boldsymbol{x}$ is an arbitrary n-vector, then the last k components of the vector $\boldsymbol{Qx}$ are zero for some $k < n$.

3.9. True or false: Methods based on orthogonal factorization are generally more expensive computationally than methods based on the normal equations for solving linear least squares problems.

3.10. (*a*) In a data-fitting problem in which m data points (t_i, y_i) are fit by a model function

$f(t, \boldsymbol{x})$, where t is the independent variable and $\boldsymbol{x}$ is an n-vector of parameters to be determined, what does it mean for the function f to be *linear* in the components of $\boldsymbol{x}$?

(*b*) Give an example of a model function $f(t, \boldsymbol{x})$ that is linear in this sense.

(*c*) Give an example of a model function $f(t, \boldsymbol{x})$ that is nonlinear.

3.11. In a linear least squares problem $\boldsymbol{Ax} \cong \boldsymbol{b}$, where $\boldsymbol{A}$ is an $m \times n$ matrix, if $\text{rank}(\boldsymbol{A}) < n$, then which of the following situations are possible?

(*a*) There is no solution.

(*b*) There is a unique solution.

(*c*) There is a solution, but it is not unique.

3.12. In solving an overdetermined least squares problem $\boldsymbol{Ax} \cong \boldsymbol{b}$, which would be a more serious difficulty: that the rows of $\boldsymbol{A}$ are linearly dependent, or that the columns of $\boldsymbol{A}$ are linearly dependent? Explain.

3.13. In an overdetermined linear least squares problem with model function $f(t, \boldsymbol{x}) = x_1\phi_1(t) + x_2\phi_2(t) + x_3\phi_3(t)$, what will be the rank of the resulting least squares matrix $\boldsymbol{A}$ if we take $\phi_1(t) = 1$, $\phi_2(t) = t$, and $\phi_3(t) = 1 - t$?

3.14. What is the system of normal equations for the linear least squares problem $\boldsymbol{Ax} \cong \boldsymbol{b}$?

3.15. List two ways in which use of the normal equations for solving linear least squares problems may suffer loss of numerical accuracy.

3.16. Let $\boldsymbol{A}$ be an $m \times n$ matrix. Under what conditions on the matrix $\boldsymbol{A}$ is the matrix $\boldsymbol{A}^T\boldsymbol{A}$

(*a*) Symmetric?

(*b*) Nonsingular?

(*c*) Positive definite?

3.17. Which of the following properties of an $m \times n$ matrix $\boldsymbol{A}$, with $m > n$, indicate that the minimum residual solution of the least squares problem $\boldsymbol{Ax} \cong \boldsymbol{b}$ is *not* unique?

(*a*) The columns of $\boldsymbol{A}$ are linearly dependent.

(*b*) The rows of $\boldsymbol{A}$ are linearly dependent.

(*c*) The matrix $\boldsymbol{A}^T\boldsymbol{A}$ is singular.

3.18. (*a*) Can Gaussian elimination with pivoting be used to compute an LU factorization of a rectangular $m \times n$ matrix $\boldsymbol{A}$, where $\boldsymbol{L}$ is an $m \times k$ matrix whose entries above its main diagonal are all zero, $\boldsymbol{U}$ is a $k \times n$ matrix whose entries below its main diagonal are all zero, and $k = \min\{m, n\}$?

(*b*) If this were possible, would it provide a way to solve an overdetermined least squares problem $\boldsymbol{Ax} \cong \boldsymbol{b}$, where $m > n$? Why?

3.19. (*a*) What is meant by two vectors $\boldsymbol{x}$ and $\boldsymbol{y}$ being *orthogonal* to each other?

(*b*) Prove that if two nonzero vectors are orthogonal to each other, then they must also be linearly independent.

(*c*) Give an example of two nonzero vectors in $\mathbb{R}^2$ that are orthogonal to each other.

(*d*) Give an example of two nonzero vectors in $\mathbb{R}^2$ that are not orthogonal to each other.

(*e*) List two ways in which orthogonality is important in the context of linear least squares problems.

3.20. In Euclidean n-space, is orthogonality a transitive relation? That is, if $\boldsymbol{x}$ is orthogonal to $\boldsymbol{y}$, and $\boldsymbol{y}$ is orthogonal to $\boldsymbol{z}$, is $\boldsymbol{x}$ necessarily orthogonal to $\boldsymbol{z}$?

3.21. What is meant by an orthogonal projector? How is this concept relevant to linear least squares?

3.22. (*a*) Why are orthogonal transformations, such as Householder or Givens, often used to solve least squares problems?

(*b*) Why are such methods not often used to solve square linear systems?

(*c*) Do orthogonal transformations have any advantage over Gaussian elimination for solving square linear systems? If so, state one.

3.23. Which of the following matrices are orthogonal?

(*a*) $\begin{bmatrix} 0 & 1 \\ 1 & 0 \end{bmatrix}$

(*b*) $\begin{bmatrix} 1 & 0 \\ 0 & -1 \end{bmatrix}$

(*c*) $\begin{bmatrix} 2 & 0 \\ 0 & 1/2 \end{bmatrix}$

(*d*) $\begin{bmatrix} \sqrt{2}/2 & \sqrt{2}/2 \\ -\sqrt{2}/2 & \sqrt{2}/2 \end{bmatrix}$

3.24. Which of the following properties does an $n \times n$ orthogonal matrix necessarily have?

(*a*) It is nonsingular.

(*b*) It preserves the Euclidean vector norm when multiplied times a vector.

(*c*) Its transpose is its inverse.
(*d*) Its columns are orthonormal.
(*e*) It is symmetric.
(*f*) It is diagonal.
(*g*) Its Euclidean matrix norm is 1.
(*h*) Its Euclidean condition number 1.

3.25. Which of the following types of matrices are necessarily orthogonal?
(*a*) Permutation
(*b*) Symmetric positive definite
(*c*) Householder transformation
(*d*) Givens rotation
(*e*) Nonsingular
(*f*) Diagonal

3.26. Show that multiplication by an orthogonal matrix preserves the Euclidean norm of a vector.

3.27. What condition must a nonzero n-vector $\boldsymbol{w}$ satisfy to ensure that the matrix $\boldsymbol{H} = \boldsymbol{I} - 2\boldsymbol{w}\boldsymbol{w}^T$ is orthogonal?

3.28. If $\boldsymbol{Q}$ is a 2×2 orthogonal matrix such that

$$\boldsymbol{Q}\begin{bmatrix}1\\1\end{bmatrix} = \begin{bmatrix}\alpha\\0\end{bmatrix},$$

what must the value of α be?

3.29. How many scalar multiplications are required to multiply an arbitrary n-vector by an $n \times n$ Householder transformation matrix $\boldsymbol{H} = \boldsymbol{I} - 2\boldsymbol{w}\boldsymbol{w}^T$, where $\boldsymbol{w}$ is an n-vector with $\|\boldsymbol{w}\|_2 = 1$?

3.30. Given a vector $\boldsymbol{a}$, in designing a Householder transformation $\boldsymbol{H}$ such that $\boldsymbol{H}\boldsymbol{a} = \alpha\,\boldsymbol{e}_1$, we know that $\alpha = \pm\|\boldsymbol{a}\|_2$. On what basis should the sign be chosen?

3.31. List one advantage and one disadvantage of Givens rotations for QR factorization compared with Householder transformations.

3.32. When used to annihilate the second component of a 2-vector, does a Householder transformation always give the same result as a Givens rotation?

3.33. In addition to the input array containing the matrix $\boldsymbol{A}$, which can be overwritten, how much additional auxiliary array storage is required to compute and store the following?
(*a*) The LU factorization of $\boldsymbol{A}$ by Gaussian elimination with partial pivoting, where $\boldsymbol{A}$ is $n \times n$
(*b*) The QR factorization of $\boldsymbol{A}$ by Householder transformations, where $\boldsymbol{A}$ is $m \times n$

3.34. In solving a linear least squares problem $\boldsymbol{A}\boldsymbol{x} \cong \boldsymbol{b}$, where $\boldsymbol{A}$ is an $m \times n$ matrix with $m \geq n$ and $\text{rank}(\boldsymbol{A}) < n$, at what point will the least squares solution process break down (assuming exact arithmetic)?
(*a*) Using Cholesky factorization to solve the normal equations
(*b*) Using QR factorization by Householder transformations

3.35. Compared to the classical Gram-Schmidt procedure, which of the following are advantages of modified Gram-Schmidt orthogonalization?
(*a*) Requires less storage
(*b*) Requires less work
(*c*) Is more stable numerically

3.36. For computing the QR factorization of an $m \times n$ matrix, with $m \geq n$, how large must n be before there is a difference between the classical and modified Gram-Schmidt procedures?

3.37. Explain why the Householder method requires less storage than the modified Gram-Schmidt method for computing the QR factorization of a matrix $\boldsymbol{A}$.

3.38. Explain how QR factorization with column pivoting can be used to determine the rank of a matrix.

3.39. Explain why column pivoting can be used with the modified Gram-Schmidt orthogonalization procedure but not with the classical Gram-Schmidt procedure.

3.40. In terms of the condition number of the matrix $\boldsymbol{A}$, compare the range of applicability of the normal equations method and the Householder QR method for solving the linear least squares problem $\boldsymbol{A}\boldsymbol{x} \cong \boldsymbol{b}$ [i.e., for what values of $\text{cond}(\boldsymbol{A})$ can each method be expected to break down?].

3.41. Let $\boldsymbol{A}$ be an $m \times n$ matrix.
(*a*) What is the maximum number of nonzero singular values that $\boldsymbol{A}$ can have?
(*b*) If $\text{rank}(A) = k$, how many nonzero singular values does $\boldsymbol{A}$ have?

3.42. Let $\boldsymbol{a}$ be a nonzero column vector. Considered as an $n \times 1$ matrix, $\boldsymbol{a}$ has only one positive singular value. What is its value?

3.43. Express the Euclidean condition number of a matrix in terms of its singular values.

3.44. List two reliable methods for determining the rank of a rectangular matrix numerically.

3.45. If $\boldsymbol{A}$ is a $2n \times n$ matrix, rank the following methods according to the amount of work required to solve the linear least squares problem $\boldsymbol{Ax} \approx \boldsymbol{b}$.

(*a*) QR factorization by Householder transformations

(*b*) Normal equations

(*c*) Singular value decomposition

3.46. List at least two applications for the singular value decomposition (SVD) of a matrix other than solving least squares problems.

Exercises

3.1. If a vertical beam has a downward force applied at its lower end, the amount by which it stretches will be proportional to the magnitude of the force. Thus, the total length y of the beam is given by the equation

$$y = x_1 + x_2 t,$$

where x_1 is its original length, t is the force applied, and x_2 is the proportionality constant. Suppose that the following measurements are taken:

t	10	15	20
y	11.60	11.85	12.25

(*a*) Set up the overdetermined 3×2 system of linear equations corresponding to the data collected.

(*b*) Is this system consistent? If not, compute each possible pair of values for (x_1, x_2) obtained by selecting any two of the equations from the system. Is there any reason to prefer any one of these results?

(*c*) Set up the system of normal equations and solve it to obtain the least squares solution to the overdetermined system. Compare your result with those obtained in part *b*.

3.2. Suppose you are fitting a straight line to the three data points (0,1), (1,2), (3,3).

(*a*) Set up the overdetermined linear system for the least squares problem.

(*b*) Set up the corresponding normal equations.

(*c*) Compute the least squares solution by Cholesky factorization.

3.3. Set up the linear least squares system $\boldsymbol{Ax} \cong \boldsymbol{b}$ for fitting the model function $f(t, \boldsymbol{x}) = x_1 t + x_2 e^t$ to the three data points (1,2), (2,3), (3,5).

3.4. In fitting a straight line $y = x_0 + x_1 t$ to the three data points (t_i, y_i) = (0,0), (1,0), (1,1), is the least squares solution unique? Why?

3.5. Let $\boldsymbol{x}$ be the solution to the linear least squares problem $\boldsymbol{Ax} \cong \boldsymbol{b}$, where

$$\boldsymbol{A} = \begin{bmatrix} 1 & 0 \\ 1 & 1 \\ 1 & 2 \\ 1 & 3 \end{bmatrix}.$$

Let $\boldsymbol{r} = \boldsymbol{b} - \boldsymbol{Ax}$ be the corresponding residual vector. Which of the following three vectors is a possible value for $\boldsymbol{r}$? Why?

$$(a) \begin{bmatrix} 1 \\ 1 \\ 1 \\ 1 \end{bmatrix} \quad (b) \begin{bmatrix} -1 \\ -1 \\ 1 \\ 1 \end{bmatrix} \quad (c) \begin{bmatrix} -1 \\ 1 \\ 1 \\ -1 \end{bmatrix}$$

3.6. (*a*) What is the Euclidean norm of the minimum residual vector for the following linear least squares problem?

$$\begin{bmatrix} 1 & 1 \\ 0 & 1 \\ 0 & 0 \end{bmatrix} \begin{bmatrix} x_1 \\ x_2 \end{bmatrix} \cong \begin{bmatrix} 2 \\ 1 \\ 1 \end{bmatrix}$$

(*b*) What is the solution vector $\boldsymbol{x}$ for this problem?

3.7. Let $\boldsymbol{A}$ be an $m \times n$ matrix and $\boldsymbol{b}$ an m-vector.

(*a*) Prove that a solution to the least squares problem $\boldsymbol{Ax} \cong \boldsymbol{b}$ always exists.

(*b*) Prove that such a solution is unique if, and only if, $\text{rank}(\boldsymbol{A}) = n$.

3.8. Suppose that $\boldsymbol{A}$ is an $m \times n$ matrix of rank n. Prove that the matrix $\boldsymbol{A}^T\boldsymbol{A}$ is positive definite.

3.9. Prove that the augmented system matrix in Section 3.4.2 *cannot* be positive definite.

3.10. Let $\boldsymbol{B}$ be an $n \times n$ matrix, and assume that $\boldsymbol{B}$ is both orthogonal and triangular.
(a) Prove that $\boldsymbol{B}$ must be diagonal.
(b) What are the diagonal entries of $\boldsymbol{B}$?
(c) Let $\boldsymbol{A}$ be $n \times n$ and nonsingular. Use parts a and b to prove that the QR factorization of $\boldsymbol{A}$ is unique up to the signs of the diagonal entries of $\boldsymbol{R}$. In particular, there exist unique matrices $\boldsymbol{Q}$ and $\boldsymbol{R}$ such that $\boldsymbol{Q}$ is orthogonal, $\boldsymbol{R}$ is upper triangular with positive entries on its main diagonal, and $\boldsymbol{A} = \boldsymbol{QR}$.

3.11. Suppose that the partitioned matrix

$$\begin{bmatrix} A & B \\ O & C \end{bmatrix}$$

is orthogonal, where the submatrices $\boldsymbol{A}$ and $\boldsymbol{C}$ are square. Prove that $\boldsymbol{A}$ and $\boldsymbol{C}$ must be orthogonal, and $\boldsymbol{B} = \boldsymbol{O}$.

3.12. (a) Let $\boldsymbol{A}$ be an $n \times n$ matrix. Show that any two of the following conditions imply the other:
1. $\boldsymbol{A}^T = \boldsymbol{A}$
2. $\boldsymbol{A}^T\boldsymbol{A} = \boldsymbol{I}$
3. $\boldsymbol{A}^2 = \boldsymbol{I}$

(b) Give a specific example, other than the identity matrix $\boldsymbol{I}$ or a permutation of it, of a 3×3 matrix that has all three of these properties.
(c) Name a nontrivial class of matrices that have all three of these properties.

3.13. If $\boldsymbol{A}$ is both an orthogonal matrix and an orthogonal projector, what can you conclude about $\boldsymbol{A}$?

3.14. Show that if the vector $\boldsymbol{v} \neq \boldsymbol{0}$, then the matrix

$$\boldsymbol{H} = \boldsymbol{I} - 2\frac{\boldsymbol{v}\boldsymbol{v}^T}{\boldsymbol{v}^T\boldsymbol{v}}$$

is orthogonal and symmetric.

3.15. Let $\boldsymbol{a}$ be any nonzero vector. If $\boldsymbol{v} = \boldsymbol{a} - \alpha\,\boldsymbol{e}_1$, where $\alpha = \pm\|\boldsymbol{a}\|_2$, and

$$\boldsymbol{H} = \boldsymbol{I} - 2\frac{\boldsymbol{v}\boldsymbol{v}^T}{\boldsymbol{v}^T\boldsymbol{v}},$$

show that $\boldsymbol{Ha} = \alpha\,\boldsymbol{e}_1$.

3.16. Consider the vector $\boldsymbol{a}$ as an $n \times 1$ matrix.
(a) Write out its QR factorization, showing the matrices $\boldsymbol{Q}$ and $\boldsymbol{R}$ explicitly.
(b) What is the solution to the linear least squares problem $\boldsymbol{a}x \cong \boldsymbol{b}$, where $\boldsymbol{b}$ is a given n-vector?

3.17. Determine the Householder transformation that annihilates all but the first entry of the vector $[1 \;\; 1 \;\; 1 \;\; 1]^T$. Specifically, if

$$\left(\boldsymbol{I} - 2\frac{\boldsymbol{v}\boldsymbol{v}^T}{\boldsymbol{v}^T\boldsymbol{v}}\right)\begin{bmatrix} 1 \\ 1 \\ 1 \\ 1 \end{bmatrix} = \begin{bmatrix} \alpha \\ 0 \\ 0 \\ 0 \end{bmatrix},$$

what are the values of α and $\boldsymbol{v}$?

3.18. Suppose that you are computing the QR factorization of the matrix

$$\boldsymbol{A} = \begin{bmatrix} 1 & 1 & 1 \\ 1 & 2 & 4 \\ 1 & 3 & 9 \\ 1 & 4 & 16 \end{bmatrix}$$

by Householder transformations.
(a) How many Householder transformations are required?
(b) What does the first column of $\boldsymbol{A}$ become as a result of applying the first Householder transformation?
(c) What does the first column then become as a result of applying the second Householder transformation?
(d) How many Givens rotations would be required to compute the QR factorization of $\boldsymbol{A}$?

3.19. Consider the vector

$$\boldsymbol{a} = \begin{bmatrix} 2 \\ 3 \\ 4 \end{bmatrix}.$$

(a) Specify an elementary elimination matrix that annihilates the third component of $\boldsymbol{a}$.
(b) Specify a Householder transformation that annihilates the third component of $\boldsymbol{a}$.
(c) Specify a Givens rotation that annihilates the third component of $\boldsymbol{a}$.
(d) When annihilating a given nonzero component of any vector, is it ever possible for the corresponding elementary elimination matrix and Householder transformation to be the same? Why?
(e) When annihilating a given nonzero component of any vector, is it ever possible for the corresponding Householder transformation and Givens rotation to be the same? Why?

3.20. Suppose you want to annihilate the second component of a vector

$$\boldsymbol{a} = \begin{bmatrix} a_1 \\ a_2 \end{bmatrix}$$

using a Givens rotation, but a_1 is already zero.

(*a*) Is it still possible to annihilate a_2 with a Givens rotation? If so, specify an appropriate Givens rotation; if not, explain why.

(*b*) Under these circumstances, can a_2 be annihilated with an elementary elimination matrix? If so, how? If not, why?

3.21. A Givens rotation is defined by two parameters, c and s, and therefore would appear to require two storage locations in a computer implementation. The two parameters depend on a single angle of rotation, however, so in principle it should be possible to record the rotation by storing only one number. Devise a scheme for storing and recovering Givens rotations using only one storage location per rotation.

3.22. Let $\boldsymbol{A}$ be an $m \times n$ matrix of rank n. Let

$$\boldsymbol{A} = \boldsymbol{Q} \begin{bmatrix} \boldsymbol{R} \\ \boldsymbol{O} \end{bmatrix}$$

be the QR factorization of $\boldsymbol{A}$, with $\boldsymbol{Q}$ orthogonal and $\boldsymbol{R}$ an $n \times n$ upper triangular matrix. Let $\boldsymbol{A}^T\boldsymbol{A} = \boldsymbol{L}\boldsymbol{L}^T$ be the Cholesky factorization of $\boldsymbol{A}^T\boldsymbol{A}$.

(*a*) Show that $\boldsymbol{R}^T\boldsymbol{R} = \boldsymbol{L}\boldsymbol{L}^T$.

(*b*) Can one conclude that $\boldsymbol{R} = \boldsymbol{L}^T$? Why?

3.23. In Section 3.4.1 we observed that the cross-product matrix $\boldsymbol{A}^T\boldsymbol{A}$ is exactly singular in floating-point arithmetic if

$$\boldsymbol{A} = \begin{bmatrix} 1 & 1 \\ \epsilon & 0 \\ 0 & \epsilon \end{bmatrix},$$

where ϵ is a positive number smaller than $\sqrt{\epsilon_{\text{mach}}}$ in a given floating-point system. Show that if $\boldsymbol{A} = \boldsymbol{Q}\boldsymbol{R}$ is the reduced QR factorization for this matrix $\boldsymbol{A}$, then $\boldsymbol{R}$ is *not* singular, even in floating-point arithmetic.

3.24. Verify that the dominant term in the operation count (number of multiplications or number of additions) for solving an $m \times n$ linear least squares problem using the normal equations and Cholesky factorization is $mn^2/2 + n^3/6$.

3.25. Verify that the dominant term in the operation count (number of multiplications or number of additions) for QR factorization of an $m \times n$ matrix using Householder transformations is $mn^2 - n^3/3$.

3.26. Let $c = \cos(\theta)$ and $s = \sin(\theta)$ for some angle θ. Give a detailed geometric description of the effects on vectors in the Euclidean plane $\mathbb{R}^2$ of each the following 2×2 orthogonal matrices.

(*a*) $\boldsymbol{G} = \begin{bmatrix} c & s \\ -s & c \end{bmatrix}$ (*b*) $\boldsymbol{H} = \begin{bmatrix} -c & s \\ s & c \end{bmatrix}$

3.27. (*a*) Suppose that $\boldsymbol{Q}$ is an $n \times k$ matrix whose columns form an orthonormal basis for a subspace $\boldsymbol{\mathcal{S}}$ of $\mathbb{R}^n$. Show that $\boldsymbol{Q}\boldsymbol{Q}^T$ is an orthogonal projector onto $\boldsymbol{\mathcal{S}}$.

(*b*) If $\boldsymbol{A}$ is a matrix with linearly independent columns, show that $\boldsymbol{A}(\boldsymbol{A}^T\boldsymbol{A})^{-1}\boldsymbol{A}^T$ is an orthogonal projector onto span($\boldsymbol{A}$). How does this result relate to the linear least squares problem?

(*c*) If $\boldsymbol{P}$ is an orthogonal projector onto a subspace $\boldsymbol{\mathcal{S}}$, show that $\boldsymbol{I} - \boldsymbol{P}$ is an orthogonal projector onto the orthogonal complement of $\boldsymbol{\mathcal{S}}$.

(*d*) Let $\boldsymbol{v}$ be any nonzero n-vector. What is the orthogonal projector onto the subspace spanned by $\boldsymbol{v}$?

3.28. (*a*) In the Gram-Schmidt procedure of Section 3.5.3, if we define the orthogonal projectors $\boldsymbol{P}_k = \boldsymbol{q}_k\boldsymbol{q}_k^T$, $k = 1, \ldots, n$, where $\boldsymbol{q}_k$ is the kth column of $\boldsymbol{Q}$ in the resulting QR factorization, show that

$$(\boldsymbol{I} - \boldsymbol{P}_k)(\boldsymbol{I} - \boldsymbol{P}_{k-1}) \cdots (\boldsymbol{I} - \boldsymbol{P}_1) = \boldsymbol{I} - \boldsymbol{P}_k - \boldsymbol{P}_{k-1} - \cdots - \boldsymbol{P}_1.$$

(*b*) Show that the classical Gram-Schmidt procedure is equivalent to

$$\boldsymbol{q}_k = (\boldsymbol{I} - (\boldsymbol{P}_1 + \cdots + \boldsymbol{P}_{k-1}))\boldsymbol{a}_k,$$

(*c*) Show that the modified Gram-Schmidt procedure is equivalent to

$$\boldsymbol{q}_k = (\boldsymbol{I} - \boldsymbol{P}_{k-1}) \cdots (\boldsymbol{I} - \boldsymbol{P}_1)\boldsymbol{a}_k.$$

(*d*) An alternative way to stablize the classical procedure is to apply it more than once (i.e., iterative refinement), which is equivalent to taking

$$\boldsymbol{q}_k = (\boldsymbol{I} - (\boldsymbol{P}_1 + \cdots + \boldsymbol{P}_{k-1}))^m\boldsymbol{a}_k,$$

where $m = 2$ is typically sufficient. Show that all three of these variations are mathematically equivalent (though they may differ markedly in finite-precision arithmetic).

3.29. Let $\boldsymbol{v}$ be a nonzero n-vector. The hyperplane normal to $\boldsymbol{v}$ is the $(n-1)$-dimensional subspace of all vectors $\boldsymbol{z}$ such that $\boldsymbol{v}^T\boldsymbol{z} = 0$. A *reflector* is a linear transformation $\boldsymbol{R}$ such that $\boldsymbol{Rx} = -\boldsymbol{x}$ if $\boldsymbol{x}$ is a scalar multiple of $\boldsymbol{v}$, and $\boldsymbol{Rx} = \boldsymbol{x}$ if $\boldsymbol{v}^T\boldsymbol{x} = 0$. Thus, the hyperplane acts as a mirror: for any vector, its component within the hyperplane is invariant, whereas its component orthogonal to the hyperplane is reversed.

(*a*) Show that $\boldsymbol{R} = 2\boldsymbol{P} - \boldsymbol{I}$, where $\boldsymbol{P}$ is the orthogonal projector onto the hyperplane normal to $\boldsymbol{v}$. Draw a picture to illustrate this result.

(*b*) Show that $\boldsymbol{R}$ is symmetric and orthogonal.

(*c*) Show that the Householder transformation

$$\boldsymbol{H} = \boldsymbol{I} - 2\frac{\boldsymbol{v}\boldsymbol{v}^T}{\boldsymbol{v}^T\boldsymbol{v}},$$

is a reflector.

(*d*) Show that for any two vectors $\boldsymbol{s}$ and $\boldsymbol{t}$ such that $\boldsymbol{s} \neq \boldsymbol{t}$ and $\|\boldsymbol{s}\|_2 = \|\boldsymbol{t}\|_2$, there is a reflector $\boldsymbol{R}$ such that $\boldsymbol{Rs} = \boldsymbol{t}$.

(*e*) Show that any orthogonal matrix $\boldsymbol{Q}$ is a product of reflectors.

(*f*) Illustrate the previous result by expressing the plane rotation

$$\begin{bmatrix} c & s \\ -s & c \end{bmatrix},$$

where $c^2 + s^2 = 1$, as a product of two reflectors. For some specific angle of rotation, draw a picture to show the mirrors.

3.30. (*a*) Consider the column vector $\boldsymbol{a}$ as an $n \times 1$ matrix. Write out its reduced singular value decomposition, showing the matrices $\boldsymbol{U}$, $\boldsymbol{\Sigma}$, and $\boldsymbol{V}$ explicitly.

(*b*) Consider the row vector $\boldsymbol{a}^T$ as a $1 \times n$ matrix. Write out its reduced SVD, showing the matrices $\boldsymbol{U}$, $\boldsymbol{\Sigma}$, and $\boldsymbol{V}$ explicitly.

3.31. If $\boldsymbol{A}$ is an $m \times n$ matrix and $\boldsymbol{b}$ is an m-vector, prove that the solution $\boldsymbol{x}$ of minimum Euclidean norm to the least squares problem $\boldsymbol{Ax} \cong \boldsymbol{b}$ is given by

$$\boldsymbol{x} = \sum_{\sigma_i \neq 0} \frac{\boldsymbol{u}_i^T\boldsymbol{b}}{\sigma_i}\boldsymbol{v}_i,$$

where the σ_i, $\boldsymbol{u}_i$, and $\boldsymbol{v}_i$ are the singular values and corresponding singular vectors of $\boldsymbol{A}$.

3.32. Prove that the pseudoinverse $\boldsymbol{A}^+$ of an $m \times n$ matrix $\boldsymbol{A}$, as defined using the SVD in Section 3.6.1, satisfies the following four properties, known as the *Moore-Penrose conditions*.

(*a*) $\boldsymbol{AA}^+\boldsymbol{A} = \boldsymbol{A}$.

(*b*) $\boldsymbol{A}^+\boldsymbol{AA}^+ = \boldsymbol{A}^+$.

(*c*) $(\boldsymbol{AA}^+)^T = \boldsymbol{AA}^+$.

(*d*) $(\boldsymbol{A}^+\boldsymbol{A})^T = \boldsymbol{A}^+\boldsymbol{A}$.

3.33. Prove that the pseudoinverse $\boldsymbol{A}^+$ of an $m \times n$ matrix $\boldsymbol{A}$, as defined using the SVD in Section 3.6.1, has the value indicated for each of the following special cases.

(*a*) If $m = n$ and $\boldsymbol{A}$ is nonsingular, then $\boldsymbol{A}^+ = \boldsymbol{A}^{-1}$.

(*b*) If $m > n$ and $\boldsymbol{A}$ has rank n, then $\boldsymbol{A}^+ = (\boldsymbol{A}^T\boldsymbol{A})^{-1}\boldsymbol{A}^T$.

(*c*) If $m < n$ and $\boldsymbol{A}$ has rank m, then $\boldsymbol{A}^+ = \boldsymbol{A}^T(\boldsymbol{AA}^T)^{-1}$.

3.34. (*a*) What is the pseudoinverse of the following matrix?

$$\boldsymbol{A}_0 = \begin{bmatrix} 1 & 0 \\ 0 & 0 \end{bmatrix}$$

(*b*) If $\epsilon > 0$, what is the pseudoinverse of the following matrix?

$$\boldsymbol{A}_\epsilon = \begin{bmatrix} 1 & 0 \\ 0 & \epsilon \end{bmatrix}$$

(*c*) What do these results imply about the conditioning of the problem of computing the pseudoinverse of a given matrix?

Computer Problems

3.1. For $n = 0, 1, \ldots, 5$, fit a polynomial of degree n by least squares to the following data:

t	0.0	1.0	2.0	3.0	4.0	5.0
y	1.0	2.7	5.8	6.6	7.5	9.9

Make a plot of the original data points along with each resulting polynomial curve (you may make separate graphs for each curve or a single graph containing all of the curves). Which polynomial would you say captures the general trend of the data better? Obviously, this is a subjective question, and its answer depends on both the nature of the given data (e.g., the uncertainty of the data values) and the purpose of the fit. Explain your assumptions in answering.

3.2. A common problem in surveying is to determine the altitudes of a series of points with respect to some reference point. The measurements are subject to error, so more observations are taken than are strictly necessary to determine the altitudes, and the resulting overdetermined system is solved in the least squares sense to smooth out errors. Suppose that there are four points whose altitudes x_1, x_2, x_3, x_4 are to be determined. In addition to direct measurements of each x_i with respect to the reference point, measurements are also taken of each point with respect to all of the others. The resulting measurements are:

$$\begin{aligned} x_1 &= 2.95, & x_2 &= 1.74, \\ x_3 &= -1.45, & x_4 &= 1.32, \\ x_1 - x_2 &= 1.23, & x_1 - x_3 &= 4.45, \\ x_1 - x_4 &= 1.61, & x_2 - x_3 &= 3.21, \\ x_2 - x_4 &= 0.45, & x_3 - x_4 &= -2.75. \end{aligned}$$

Set up the corresponding least squares system $\boldsymbol{Ax} \cong \boldsymbol{b}$ and use a library routine, or one of your own design, to solve it for the best values of the altitudes. How do your computed values compare with the direct measurements?

3.3. (*a*) For a series of matrices $\boldsymbol{A}$ of order n, record the execution times for a library routine to compute the LU factorization of $\boldsymbol{A}$. Using a linear least squares routine, or one of your own design, fit a cubic polynomial to the execution times as a function of n. To obtain reliable results, use a fairly wide range of values for n, say, in increments of 100 from 100 up to several hundred, depending on the speed and available memory of the computer you use. You may obtain more accurate timings by averaging several runs for a given matrix size. The resulting cubic polynomial could be used to predict the execution time for other values of n not tried, such as very large values for n. What is the predicted execution time for a matrix of order 10,000?

(*b*) Try to determine the basic execution rate (in floating-point operations per second, or *flops*) for your computer by timing a known computation, such as matrix multiplication. You can then use this information to determine the complexity of LU factorization, based on the polynomial fit to the execution times. After converting to floating-point operations, how does the dominant term compare with the theoretically expected value of $4n^3/3$ (counting both additions and multiplications)? Try to explain any discrepancy. If you use a system that provides operation counts automatically, try this same experiment fitting the operation counts directly.

3.4. (*a*) Solve the following least squares problem using any method you like:

$$\begin{bmatrix} 0.16 & 0.10 \\ 0.17 & 0.11 \\ 2.02 & 1.29 \end{bmatrix} \begin{bmatrix} x_1 \\ x_2 \end{bmatrix} \cong \begin{bmatrix} 0.26 \\ 0.28 \\ 3.31 \end{bmatrix}.$$

(*b*) Now solve the same least squares problem again, but this time use the slightly perturbed right-hand side

$$\boldsymbol{b} = \begin{bmatrix} 0.27 \\ 0.25 \\ 3.33 \end{bmatrix}.$$

(*c*) Compare your results from parts *a* and *b*. Can you explain this difference?

3.5. A planet follows an elliptical orbit, which can be represented in a Cartesian (x, y) coordinate system by the equation

$$ay^2 + bxy + cx + dy + e = x^2.$$

(*a*) Use a library routine, or one of your own design, for linear least squares to determine the orbital parameters a, b, c, d, e, given the following observations of the planet's position:

x	1.02	0.95	0.87	0.77	0.67
y	0.39	0.32	0.27	0.22	0.18
x	0.56	0.44	0.30	0.16	0.01
y	0.15	0.13	0.12	0.13	0.15

In addition to printing the values for the orbital parameters, plot the resulting orbit and the given data points in the (x, y) plane.

(*b*) This least squares problem is nearly rank-deficient. To see what effect this has on the solution, perturb the input data slightly by adding to each coordinate of each data point a random number uniformly distributed on the interval $[-0.005, 0.005]$ (see Section 13.5) and solve the least squares problem with the perturbed data. Compare the new values for the parameters with those previously computed. What effect does this difference have on the plot of the orbit? Can you explain this behavior?

(*c*) Solve the same least squares problem again, for both the original and the perturbed data, this time using a library routine (or one of your own design) specifically designed to deal with rank deficiency (by using column pivoting, for example). Such a routine usually includes as an input parameter a tolerance to be used in determining the numerical rank of the matrix. Experiment with various values for the tolerance, say, 10^{-k}, $k = 1, \ldots, 5$. What is the resulting rank of the matrix for each value of the tolerance? Compare the behavior of the two solutions (for the original and the perturbed data) with each other as the tolerance and the resulting rank change. How well do the resulting orbits fit the data points as the tolerance and rank vary? Which solution would you regard as better: one that fits the data more closely, or one that is less sensitive to small perturbations in the data? Why?

(*d*) Use a library routine to compute the singular value decomposition of the 10×5 least squares matrix.

(*e*) Use the singular value decomposition to compute the solution to the least squares problem. With the singular values in order of decreasing magnitude, compute the solutions using the first k singular values, $k = 1, \ldots, 5$. For each of the five solutions obtained, print the values for the orbital parameters and also plot the resulting orbits along with the given data points in the (x, y) plane.

(*f*) Perturb the input data slightly by adding to each coordinate of each data point a random number uniformly distributed on the interval $[-0.005, 0.005]$ (see Section 13.5). Compute the singular value decomposition of the new least squares matrix, and solve the least squares problem with the perturbed data as in part *e*. Compare the new values for the parameters with those previously computed for each value of k. What effect does this difference have on the plot of the orbits? Can you explain this behavior? Which solution would you regard as better: one that fits the data more closely, or one that is less sensitive to small perturbations in the data? Why?

(*g*) For simplicity, we have used ordinary least squares in this problem, but in fact all of the data are equally subject to observational errors (indeed, x appears on both sides of the equation), which makes the applicability of ordinary least squares questionable. Reformulate this problem as a total least squares problem and solve the latter using the singular value decomposition as described in Section 3.6.1.

3.6. Write a routine for computing the pseudoinverse of an arbitrary $m \times n$ matrix. You may call a library routine to compute the singular value decomposition, then use its output to compute the pseudoinverse (see Section 3.6.1). Consider the use of a tolerance for declaring relatively small singular values to be zero. Test your routine on both singular and nonsingular matrices. In the latter case, of course, your results should agree with those of standard matrix inversion. What happens when the matrix is nonsingular, but severely ill-conditioned (e.g., a Hilbert matrix)?

3.7. Write a routine for solving an arbitrary, possibly rank-deficient, linear least squares problem $\boldsymbol{Ax} \cong \boldsymbol{b}$ using the singular value decomposition. You may call a library routine to compute the SVD, then use its output to compute the least squares solution (see Section 3.6). The input to your routine should include the matrix $\boldsymbol{A}$, right-hand-side vector $\boldsymbol{b}$, and a tolerance for determining the numerical rank of $\boldsymbol{A}$. Test your routine on some of the linear least squares problems in the other computer problems for this chapter.

3.8. To demonstrate how results from the normal equations method and QR factorization can differ numerically, we need a least squares problem that is ill-conditioned and also has a small residual. We can generate such a problem as follows. We will fit a polynomial of degree $n-1$,

$$p_{n-1}(t) = x_1 + x_2 t + x_3 t^2 + \cdots + x_n t^{n-1},$$

to m data points (t_i, y_i), $m > n$. We choose $t_i = (i-1)/(m-1)$, $i = 1, \ldots, m$, so that the data points are equally spaced on the interval $[0, 1]$. We will generate the corresponding values y_i by first choosing values for the x_j, say, $x_j = 1$,

$j = 1, \ldots, n$, and evaluating the resulting polynomial to obtain $y_i = p_{n-1}(t_i)$, $i = 1, \ldots, m$. We could now see whether we can recover the x_j that we used to generate the y_i, but to make it more interesting, we first randomly perturb the y_i values to simulate the data error typical of least squares problems. Specifically, we take $y_i = y_i + (2u_i - 1) * \epsilon$, $i = 1, \ldots, m$, where each u_i is a random number uniformly distributed on the interval $[0, 1)$ (see Section 13.5) and ϵ is a small positive number that determines the maximum perturbation. If you are using IEEE double precision, reasonable parameters for this problem are $m = 21$, $n = 12$, and $\epsilon = 10^{-10}$.

Having generated the data set (t_i, y_i) as just outlined, we will now compare the two methods for computing the least squares solution to this polynomial data-fitting problem. First, form the system of normal equations for this problem and solve it using a library routine for Cholesky factorization. Next, solve the least squares system using a library routine for QR factorization. Compare the two resulting solution vectors $\boldsymbol{x}$. For which method is the solution more sensitive to the perturbation we introduced into the data? Which method comes closer to recovering the $\boldsymbol{x}$ that we used to generate the data? Does the fact that the solutions differ affect our ability to fit the data points (t_i, y_i) closely by the polynomial? Why?

3.9. Use the augmented system method of Section 3.4.2 to solve the least squares problem derived in the previous exercise. The augmented system is symmetric but not positive definite, so Cholesky factorization is not applicable, but you can use a symmetric indefinite or LU factorization. Experiment with various values for the scaling parameter α. How do the accuracy and execution time of this method compare with those of the normal equations and QR factorization methods?

3.10. The *covariance matrix* for the $m \times n$ least squares problem $\boldsymbol{Ax} \cong \boldsymbol{b}$ is given by $\sigma^2(\boldsymbol{A}^T\boldsymbol{A})^{-1}$, where $\sigma^2 = \|\boldsymbol{b} - \boldsymbol{Ax}\|_2^2/(m-n)$ at the least squares solution $\boldsymbol{x}$. The entries of this matrix contain important information about the goodness of the fit and any cross-correlations among the fitted parameters. The covariance matrix is an exception to the general rule that inverses of matrices should never be computed explicitly. If an orthogonalization method is used to solve the least squares problem, then the cross-product matrix $\boldsymbol{A}^T\boldsymbol{A}$ is never formed, so we need an alternative method for computing the covariance matrix.

(*a*) Show that $(\boldsymbol{A}^T\boldsymbol{A})^{-1} = (\boldsymbol{R}^T\boldsymbol{R})^{-1}$, where $\boldsymbol{R}$ is the upper triangular factor obtained by QR factorization of $\boldsymbol{A}$.

(*b*) Based on this fact, implement a routine for computing the covariance matrix using only the already computed $\boldsymbol{R}$. (For purposes of this exercise, you may ignore the scalar factor σ^2.) Test your routine on a few example matrices to confirm that it gives the same result as computing $(\boldsymbol{A}^T\boldsymbol{A})^{-1}$.

3.11. Most library routines for computing the QR factorization of an $m \times n$ matrix $\boldsymbol{A}$ return the matrix $\boldsymbol{R}$ in the upper triangle of the storage for $\boldsymbol{A}$ and the Householder vectors in the lower triangle of $\boldsymbol{A}$, with an extra vector to accommodate the overlap on the diagonal. Write a routine that takes this output array and auxiliary vector and forms the orthogonal matrix $\boldsymbol{Q}$ explicitly by multiplying the corresponding sequence of Householder transformations times an $m \times m$ matrix that is initialized to the identity matrix $\boldsymbol{I}$. Of course, the latter will require a separate array. Test your program on several matrices and confirm that your computed $\boldsymbol{Q}$ is indeed orthogonal and that the product

$$\boldsymbol{Q}\begin{bmatrix} \boldsymbol{R} \\ \boldsymbol{O} \end{bmatrix}$$

recovers $\boldsymbol{A}$.

3.12. (*a*) Implement both the classical and modified Gram-Schmidt procedures and use each to generate an orthogonal matrix $\boldsymbol{Q}$ whose columns form an orthonormal basis for the column space of the Hilbert matrix $\boldsymbol{H}$, with entries $h_{ij} = 1/(i+j-1)$, for $n = 2, \ldots, 12$ (see Computer Problem 2.6). As a measure of the quality of the results (specifically, the potential loss of orthogonality), plot the quantity $-\log_{10}(\|\boldsymbol{I} - \boldsymbol{Q}^T\boldsymbol{Q}\|)$, which can be interpreted as "digits of accuracy," for each method as a function of n. In addition, try applying the classical procedure twice (i.e., apply your classical Gram-Schmidt routine to its own output $\boldsymbol{Q}$ to obtain a new $\boldsymbol{Q}$), and again plot the resulting departure from orthogonality. How do the three methods compare in speed, storage, and accuracy?

(*b*) Repeat the previous experiment, but this time use the Householder method, that is, use the explicitly computed orthogonal matrix $\boldsymbol{Q}$ resulting from Householder QR factorization of the Hilbert matrix. Note that if the routine you use for Householder QR factorization does not form $\boldsymbol{Q}$ explicitly, then you can obtain $\boldsymbol{Q}$ by multiplying the sequence of Householder transformations times a matrix that is initialized to the identity matrix $\boldsymbol{I}$ (see previous exercise). Again, plot the departure from orthogonality for this method and compare it with that of the previous methods.

(*c*) Repeat the previous experiment, but this time use the SVD to obtain the orthonormal basis (see Section 3.6.1).

(*d*) Yet another way to compute an orthonormal basis is to use the normal equations. If we form the cross-product matrix and compute its Cholesky factorization $\boldsymbol{A}^T\boldsymbol{A} = \boldsymbol{L}\boldsymbol{L}^T$, then we have

$$\begin{aligned} \boldsymbol{I} &= \boldsymbol{L}^{-1}(\boldsymbol{A}^T\boldsymbol{A})\boldsymbol{L}^{-T} \\ &= (\boldsymbol{A}\boldsymbol{L}^{-T})^T(\boldsymbol{A}\boldsymbol{L}^{-T}), \end{aligned}$$

which means that $\boldsymbol{Q} = \boldsymbol{A}\boldsymbol{L}^{-T}$ is orthogonal, and its column space is obviously the same as that of $\boldsymbol{A}$. Repeat the previous experiment using Hilbert matrices again, this time using the $\boldsymbol{Q}$ obtained in this way from the normal equations (the required triangular solution may be a little tricky to compute, depending on the software you use). Again, plot the resulting departure from orthogonality and compare it with that of the previous methods.

(*e*) Can you explain the relative quality of the results you obtained for the various methods used in these experiments?

3.13. What is the exact solution $\boldsymbol{x}$ to the linear least squares problem

$$\begin{bmatrix} 1 & 1 & 1 \\ \epsilon & 0 & 0 \\ 0 & \epsilon & 0 \\ 0 & 0 & \epsilon \end{bmatrix} \begin{bmatrix} x_1 \\ x_2 \\ x_3 \end{bmatrix} \cong \begin{bmatrix} 1 \\ 0 \\ 0 \\ 0 \end{bmatrix}$$

as a function of ϵ?

Solve this least squares problem using each of the following methods. For each method, experiment with the value of the parameter ϵ to see how small you can take it and still obtain an accurate solution. Pay particular attention to values around $\epsilon \approx \sqrt{\epsilon_{\text{mach}}}$ and $\epsilon \approx \epsilon_{\text{mach}}$.

(*a*) Normal equations

(*b*) Augmented system

(*c*) Householder QR

(*d*) Givens QR

(*e*) Classical Gram-Schmidt orthogonalization

(*f*) Modified Gram-Schmidt orthogonalization

(*g*) Classical Gram-Schmidt with iterative refinement (i.e., CGS applied twice)

(*h*) Singular value decomposition

Chapter 4

Eigenvalue Problems

4.1 Eigenvalues and Eigenvectors

Linear transformations on a vector space can take many different forms: expanding or shrinking a vector by a scalar multiple, rotating a vector or reflecting it in a hyperplane, permuting the components of a vector, and so on. The effect of most linear transformations is a complicated mixture of these, but a special few are much simpler in their actions. In analyzing any problem characterized by a linear transformation, insight can be gained by breaking the transformation down into its simplest constituent actions so that its overall behavior can be readily understood. This approach enables a structural engineer, for example, to determine the stability of a structure, or a numerical analyst (as we will see later) to establish the convergence of an iterative algorithm. The key issue is what happens when a given linear transformation is applied repeatedly: do the results settle down into some steady state, or oscillate, or grow uncontrollably (i.e., blow up)? This question can be answered by resolving the transformation into a set of simple actions, specifically, expansion or contraction along certain directions.

A given direction in a vector space is determined by any nonzero vector pointing in that direction. Thus, given an $n \times n$ matrix $\boldsymbol{A}$ representing a linear transformation on an n-dimensional vector space, we wish to find a nonzero vector $\boldsymbol{x}$ and a scalar λ such that

$$\boldsymbol{A}\boldsymbol{x} = \lambda \boldsymbol{x}.$$

Such a scalar λ is called an *eigenvalue*, and $\boldsymbol{x}$ is a corresponding *eigenvector*. In addition to the *right* eigenvector just defined, we could also define a nonzero *left* eigenvector $\boldsymbol{y}$ such that $\boldsymbol{y}^T\boldsymbol{A} = \lambda\boldsymbol{y}^T$. A left eigenvector of $\boldsymbol{A}$ is a right eigenvector of $\boldsymbol{A}^T$, however, so for computational purposes we will consider only right eigenvectors (nevertheless, left eigenvectors will play an important role in the theory). The set of all the eigenvalues of a matrix $\boldsymbol{A}$, denoted by $\lambda(\boldsymbol{A})$, is called the *spectrum* of $\boldsymbol{A}$. The maximum modulus of the eigenvalues, $\max\{|\lambda| : \lambda \in \lambda(\boldsymbol{A})\}$, is called the *spectral radius* of $\boldsymbol{A}$, denoted by $\rho(\boldsymbol{A})$.

An eigenvector of a matrix determines a direction in which the effect of the matrix is particularly simple: the matrix expands or shrinks any vector lying in that direction by a scalar multiple, and the expansion or contraction factor is given by the corresponding eigenvalue λ. Thus, eigenvalues and eigenvectors provide a means of understanding the complicated behavior of a general linear transformation by decomposing it into simpler actions.

Eigenvalue problems occur in many areas of science and engineering. For example, the natural modes and frequencies of vibration of a structure are determined by the eigenvectors and eigenvalues, respectively, of an appropriate matrix. The stability of the structure is determined by the eigenvalues, and thus their computation is of critical interest. We will also see later in this book that eigenvalues are useful in analyzing numerical methods, for example, convergence analysis of iterative methods for solving systems of algebraic equations and stability analysis of methods for solving differential equations.

Example 4.1 Spring-Mass System. Consider the system of springs and masses shown in Fig. 4.1, with three masses m_1, m_2, and m_3 at vertical displacements y_1, y_2, and y_3, connected by three springs having spring constants k_1, k_2, and k_3. According to *Newton's Second Law*, the motion of the system is governed by the system of ordinary differential equations

$$\boldsymbol{M}\boldsymbol{y}'' + \boldsymbol{K}\boldsymbol{y} = 0,$$

where

$$\boldsymbol{M} = \begin{bmatrix} m_1 & 0 & 0 \\ 0 & m_2 & 0 \\ 0 & 0 & m_3 \end{bmatrix}$$

is called the *mass matrix* and

$$\boldsymbol{K} = \begin{bmatrix} k_1 + k_2 & -k_2 & 0 \\ -k_2 & k_2 + k_3 & -k_3 \\ 0 & -k_3 & k_3 \end{bmatrix}$$

is called the *stiffness matrix*. Such a system exhibits simple harmonic motion with natural frequency ω, i.e., the solution components are given by

$$y_k(t) = x_k e^{i\omega t},$$

where x_k is the amplitude, $k = 1, 2$, or 3, and $i = \sqrt{-1}$. To determine the frequency ω and mode of vibration (i.e., the amplitudes x_k), we note that for each solution component,

$$y_k''(t) = -\omega^2 x_k e^{i\omega t}.$$

Substituting this relationship into the differential equation, we obtain the algebraic equation

$$\boldsymbol{K}\boldsymbol{x} = \omega^2 \boldsymbol{M}\boldsymbol{x},$$

or

$$Ax = \lambda x,$$

where $A = M^{-1}K$ and $\lambda = \omega^2$. Thus, the natural frequencies and modes of vibration of the spring-mass system can be determined by solving the resulting eigenvalue problem (see Computer Problem 4.13).

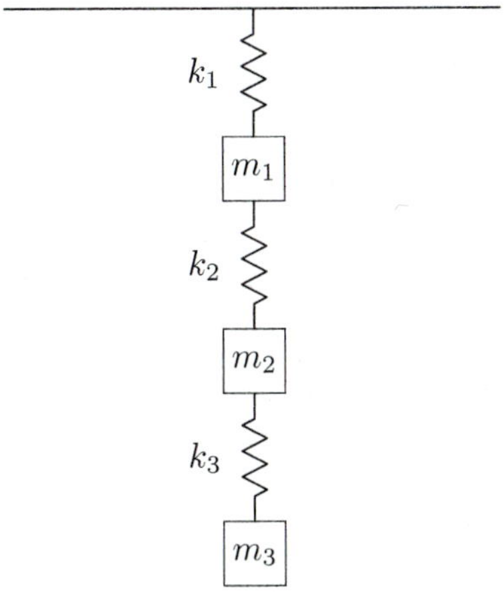

Figure 4.1: Spring-mass system.

Although most of our examples will involve only real matrices, both the theory and computational procedures we will discuss in this chapter are generally applicable to matrices with complex entries as well. Notationally, the main difference in dealing with complex matrices is that the conjugate transpose, denoted by A^H, is used instead of the usual matrix transpose, A^T (recall the definitions of transpose and conjugate transpose from Section 2.5). For example, a left eigenvector corresponding to an eigenvalue λ of a complex matrix A is a nonzero vector y such that $y^H A = \lambda y^H$. It is important to note that even for real matrices we may be forced to deal with complex numbers, since the eigenvalues of a real matrix may be complex rather than real.

Example 4.2 Eigenvalues and Eigenvectors.

1. $A = \begin{bmatrix} 2 & 0 \\ 0 & 1 \end{bmatrix}, \quad \lambda_1 = 2,\ x_1 = \begin{bmatrix} 1 \\ 0 \end{bmatrix}, \quad \lambda_2 = 1,\ x_2 = \begin{bmatrix} 0 \\ 1 \end{bmatrix}.$

2. $A = \begin{bmatrix} 2 & 1 \\ 0 & 1 \end{bmatrix}, \quad \lambda_1 = 2,\ x_1 = \begin{bmatrix} 1 \\ 0 \end{bmatrix}, \quad \lambda_2 = 1,\ x_2 = \begin{bmatrix} -1 \\ 1 \end{bmatrix}.$

3. $A = \begin{bmatrix} 3 & 1 \\ 1 & 3 \end{bmatrix}, \quad \lambda_1 = 4,\ x_1 = \begin{bmatrix} 1 \\ 1 \end{bmatrix}, \quad \lambda_2 = 2,\ x_2 = \begin{bmatrix} -1 \\ 1 \end{bmatrix}.$

4. $A = \begin{bmatrix} 0 & 1 \\ -1 & 0 \end{bmatrix}, \quad \lambda_1 = i,\ x_1 = \begin{bmatrix} 1 \\ i \end{bmatrix}, \quad \lambda_2 = -i,\ x_2 = \begin{bmatrix} i \\ 1 \end{bmatrix}$, where $i = \sqrt{-1}$.

For example matrix 1, which is diagonal, the eigenvalues are the diagonal entries, and the eigenvectors are the columns of the identity matrix $\boldsymbol{I}$. For example matrix 2, which is triangular, the eigenvalues are still the diagonal entries, but the eigenvectors are now less obvious. For example matrix 3, which is symmetric, the eigenvalues are real. Example matrix 4 shows, however, that a nonsymmetric real matrix need not have real eigenvalues.

4.2 Existence and Uniqueness

4.2.1 Characteristic Polynomial

The equation $\boldsymbol{Ax} = \lambda \boldsymbol{x}$ is equivalent to

$$(\boldsymbol{A} - \lambda \boldsymbol{I})\boldsymbol{x} = \boldsymbol{0}.$$

This homogeneous system of linear equations has a nonzero solution $\boldsymbol{x}$ if, and only if, its matrix is singular. Thus, the eigenvalues of $\boldsymbol{A}$ are the values of λ such that

$$\det(\boldsymbol{A} - \lambda \boldsymbol{I}) = 0.$$

Now $\det(\boldsymbol{A} - \lambda \boldsymbol{I})$ is a polynomial of degree n in λ, called the *characteristic polynomial* of $\boldsymbol{A}$, and its roots are the eigenvalues of $\boldsymbol{A}$.

Example 4.3 Characteristic Polynomial. The characteristic polynomial of the third example matrix in Example 4.2 is

$$\det\left(\begin{bmatrix} 3 & 1 \\ 1 & 3 \end{bmatrix} - \lambda \begin{bmatrix} 1 & 0 \\ 0 & 1 \end{bmatrix}\right) = \det\left(\begin{bmatrix} 3-\lambda & 1 \\ 1 & 3-\lambda \end{bmatrix}\right)$$

$$= (3-\lambda)(3-\lambda) - (1)(1) = \lambda^2 - 6\lambda + 8 = 0.$$

From the quadratic formula, the roots of this polynomial are given by

$$\lambda = \frac{6 \pm \sqrt{36-32}}{2} = \frac{6 \pm 2}{2},$$

so the eigenvalues are $\lambda_1 = 4$ and $\lambda_2 = 2$.

According to the *Fundamental Theorem of Algebra*, a polynomial

$$p(\lambda) = c_0 + c_1\lambda + \cdots + c_n\lambda^n$$

of positive degree n (i.e., $c_n \neq 0$), with real or complex coefficients c_k, always has a root λ_1, which may be complex even if the coefficients of the polynomial are real. The quotient $p(\lambda)/(\lambda - \lambda_1)$ is a polynomial of degree one less, so it has a root λ_2. Repeating this process as long as the degree remains positive, we see that the original polynomial can be written as a product of linear factors,

$$p(\lambda) = c_n\,(\lambda - \lambda_1)(\lambda - \lambda_2)\cdots(\lambda - \lambda_n).$$

Thus, $p(\lambda)$ has exactly n roots, counting *multiplicities* (i.e., the number of times each root appears in the expression of the polynomial as a product of linear factors). Because the eigenvalues of a matrix are the roots of its characteristic polynomial, which has degree n, we conclude that an $n \times n$ matrix $\boldsymbol{A}$ *always has n eigenvalues*, but they may not be real and may not be distinct. The latter case simply means that more than one direction may have the same expansion or contraction factor. It is often convenient to number the eigenvalues from largest to smallest in magnitude, so that $|\lambda_1| \geq |\lambda_2| \geq \cdots \geq |\lambda_n|$. Although the eigenvalues of a real matrix are not necessarily real, complex eigenvalues of a real matrix must occur in complex conjugate pairs: if $\lambda = \alpha + i\beta$, where $i = \sqrt{-1}$ and $\beta \neq 0$, is an eigenvalue of a real matrix, then so is $\bar{\lambda} = \alpha - i\beta$ (see Exercise 4.9).

We have just seen that for any matrix there is an associated polynomial whose roots are the eigenvalues of the matrix. The reverse is also true: for any polynomial, there is an associated matrix whose eigenvalues are the roots of the polynomial. First, dividing a polynomial of positive degree n by the coefficient of its nth-degree term yields a *monic* polynomial of the form $p(\lambda) = c_0 + c_1\lambda + \cdots + c_{n-1}\lambda^{n-1} + \lambda^n$ having the same roots as the original polynomial. Then $p(\lambda)$ is the characteristic polynomial of the $n \times n$ *companion matrix*

$$\boldsymbol{C}_n = \begin{bmatrix} 0 & 0 & \cdots & 0 & -c_0 \\ 1 & 0 & \cdots & 0 & -c_1 \\ 0 & 1 & \cdots & 0 & -c_2 \\ \vdots & \vdots & \ddots & \vdots & \vdots \\ 0 & 0 & \cdots & 1 & -c_{n-1} \end{bmatrix},$$

whose entries are the coefficients of the polynomial (with signs reversed) in the last column, ones on the subdiagonal, and zeros elsewhere; and thus the roots of $p(\lambda)$ are the eigenvalues of $\boldsymbol{C}_n$. Note that the correspondence between polynomials and matrices cannot be one-to-one, however, since a general matrix of order n depends on n^2 parameters (its entries), whereas a polynomial of degree n depends on only $n + 1$ parameters (its coefficients). Thus, distinct matrices can have the same characteristic polynomial.

We are now in a position to make an important theoretical observation about computing eigenvalues. Abel proved in 1824 that the roots of a polynomial of degree greater than four cannot always be expressed by a closed-form formula in the coefficients using ordinary arithmetic operations and root extractions. Thus, in general, computing the eigenvalues of matrices of order greater than four requires a (theoretically infinite) iterative process. Otherwise, if eigenvalues could always be computed in a finite number of steps, then we could compute the roots of any polynomial in a finite number of steps simply by computing the eigenvalues of its companion matrix, which would contradict Abel's theorem. Fortunately, as we will soon see, the best iterative algorithms for computing eigenvalues converge very rapidly, so that the number of iterations required to attain reasonable accuracy is usually quite small in practice.

Though it is extremely useful for theoretical purposes, the characteristic polynomial turns out not to be useful as a means of actually computing eigenvalues for matrices of nontrivial size. There are several reasons for this:

- Computing the coefficients of the characteristic polynomial for a given matrix is, in general, a substantial task (see Computer Problem 4.15).
- The coefficients of the characteristic polynomial can be highly sensitive to perturbations in the matrix, and hence their computation is unstable.
- Rounding error incurred in forming the characteristic polynomial can destroy the accuracy of the roots subsequently computed.
- Computing the roots of a polynomial of high degree is another substantial task (indeed, one of the better ways of computing the roots of a polynomial is to compute the eigenvalues of its companion matrix using the methods we will consider in this chapter; see Section 5.5.8).

Thus, the transformation

$$\text{Matrix} \longrightarrow \text{characteristic polynomial} \longrightarrow \text{eigenvalues}$$

does not produce a significantly easier intermediate problem and in practice does not preserve the eigenvalues numerically, even though it preserves them in theory.

Example 4.4 Characteristic Polynomial. To illustrate one of the potential numerical difficulties associated with the characteristic polynomial, consider the matrix

$$\boldsymbol{A} = \begin{bmatrix} 1 & \epsilon \\ \epsilon & 1 \end{bmatrix},$$

where ϵ is a positive number slightly smaller than $\sqrt{\epsilon_{\text{mach}}}$ in a given floating-point system. The exact eigenvalues of $\boldsymbol{A}$ are $1+\epsilon$ and $1-\epsilon$. Computing the characteristic polynomial of $\boldsymbol{A}$ in floating-point arithmetic, we obtain

$$\det(\boldsymbol{A} - \lambda \boldsymbol{I}) = \lambda^2 - 2\lambda + (1 - \epsilon^2) = \lambda^2 - 2\lambda + 1,$$

which has 1 as a double root. Thus, we cannot resolve the two eigenvalues by this method even though they are quite distinct in the working precision. We would need up to twice the precision in the coefficients of the characteristic polynomial to compute the eigenvalues to the same precision as that of the input matrix.

4.2.2 Multiplicity and Diagonalizability

The *algebraic multiplicity* of an eigenvalue is its multiplicity as a root of the characteristic polynomial. An eigenvalue of algebraic multiplicity 1 is said to be *simple*. The *geometric multiplicity* of an eigenvalue is the number of linearly independent eigenvectors corresponding to that eigenvalue. For example, 1 is an eigenvalue of both algebraic and geometric multiplicity n for the $n \times n$ identity matrix $\boldsymbol{I}$. The geometric multiplicity of an eigenvalue cannot exceed the algebraic multiplicity, but it can be less than the algebraic multiplicity. An eigenvalue with the latter property is said to be *defective*. Similarly, an $n \times n$ matrix that has fewer than n linearly independent eigenvectors is said to be defective.

If an $n \times n$ matrix $\boldsymbol{A}$ is *nondefective*, then it has a full set of linearly independent eigenvectors $\boldsymbol{x}_1, \ldots, \boldsymbol{x}_n$ corresponding to the eigenvalues $\lambda_1, \ldots, \lambda_n$. If we let $\boldsymbol{D} = \text{diag}(\lambda_1, \ldots, \lambda_n)$ and $\boldsymbol{X} = [\boldsymbol{x}_1 \cdots \boldsymbol{x}_n]$, then $\boldsymbol{X}$ is nonsingular and we have

$$\boldsymbol{AX} = \boldsymbol{XD},$$

so that

$$\boldsymbol{X}^{-1}\boldsymbol{AX} = \boldsymbol{D},$$

and hence $\boldsymbol{A}$ is said to be *diagonalizable*. This is an example of a *similarity transformation*, which we will consider in detail in Section 4.4. In particular, if the eigenvalues of a matrix are all distinct, then the eigenvalues must all be simple, and the matrix is necessarily nondefective and hence diagonalizable.

4.2.3 Eigenspaces and Invariant Subspaces

Eigenvectors are not unique in that they can be scaled arbitrarily: if $\boldsymbol{Ax} = \lambda\boldsymbol{x}$, then for any scalar $\gamma \neq 0$, $\gamma\boldsymbol{x}$ is also an eigenvector corresponding to λ, since $\boldsymbol{A}(\gamma\boldsymbol{x}) = \lambda(\gamma\boldsymbol{x})$. For example, for the second matrix in Example 4.2,

$$\boldsymbol{A} = \begin{bmatrix} 2 & 1 \\ 0 & 1 \end{bmatrix}, \qquad \gamma\boldsymbol{x}_2 = \gamma\begin{bmatrix} -1 \\ 1 \end{bmatrix} = \begin{bmatrix} -\gamma \\ \gamma \end{bmatrix}$$

is an eigenvector corresponding to the eigenvalue $\lambda_2 = 1$ for any nonzero scalar γ. Consequently, eigenvectors are usually *normalized* by requiring some norm of the vector to be 1.

When viewed in this way, it becomes clear that the fundamental object of interest is not really any particular eigenvector, but rather the set $\mathcal{S}_\lambda = \{\boldsymbol{x} : \boldsymbol{Ax} = \lambda\boldsymbol{x}\}$, which contains the zero vector as well as all eigenvectors corresponding to an eigenvalue λ. $\mathcal{S}_\lambda$ is easily shown to be a subspace of $\mathbb{R}^n$ (or $\mathbb{C}^n$ in the complex case), called the *eigenspace* corresponding to the eigenvalue λ (see Exercise 4.21). Any particular eigenvector $\boldsymbol{x}$ can be regarded as representative of the corresponding eigenspace. Note that the dimension of the eigenspace $\mathcal{S}_\lambda$ can be greater than 1 if the associated eigenvalue λ has geometric multiplicity greater than 1.

For a given matrix $\boldsymbol{A}$, a subspace $\mathcal{S}$ of $\mathbb{R}^n$ (or $\mathbb{C}^n$ in the complex case) is said to be an *invariant subspace* if $\boldsymbol{A}\mathcal{S} \subseteq \mathcal{S}$, i.e., if $\boldsymbol{x} \in \mathcal{S}$ implies $\boldsymbol{Ax} \in \mathcal{S}$. Note that an eigenspace is an invariant subspace. More generally, if $\boldsymbol{x}_1, \ldots, \boldsymbol{x}_p$ are eigenvectors of $\boldsymbol{A}$, then $\text{span}([\boldsymbol{x}_1 \cdots \boldsymbol{x}_p])$ is an invariant subspace.

4.2.4 Properties of Matrices and Eigenvalue Problems

In preparation for further discussion of eigenvalue problems, we note here some relevant properties that an $n \times n$ real or complex matrix $\boldsymbol{A}$ may have, some of which we have already seen (see especially Section 2.5):

- *Diagonal*: $a_{ij} = 0$ for $i \neq j$
- *Tridiagonal*: $a_{ij} = 0$ for $|i - j| > 1$

- *Triangular*: $a_{ij} = 0$ for $i > j$ (upper triangular) or $a_{ij} = 0$ for $i < j$ (lower triangular)
- *Hessenberg*: $a_{ij} = 0$ for $i > j+1$ (upper Hessenberg) or $a_{ij} = 0$ for $i < j-1$ (lower Hessenberg)
- *Orthogonal*: $\boldsymbol{A}^T\boldsymbol{A} = \boldsymbol{A}\boldsymbol{A}^T = \boldsymbol{I}$
- *Unitary*: $\boldsymbol{A}^H\boldsymbol{A} = \boldsymbol{A}\boldsymbol{A}^H = \boldsymbol{I}$
- *Symmetric*: $\boldsymbol{A} = \boldsymbol{A}^T$
- *Hermitian*: $\boldsymbol{A} = \boldsymbol{A}^H$
- *Normal*: $\boldsymbol{A}^H\boldsymbol{A} = \boldsymbol{A}\boldsymbol{A}^H$

Note that some of these properties come in pairs, where one is relevant primarily for real matrices and the other is the appropriate analogue for complex matrices (e.g., symmetric/Hermitian, orthogonal/unitary). As we will see, the eigenvalues of diagonal and triangular matrices are simply their diagonal entries; tridiagonal and Hessenberg matrices are useful intermediate forms in computing eigenvalues; orthogonal and unitary matrices are useful in transforming general matrices into simpler forms; symmetric and Hermitian matrices have only real eigenvalues; and normal matrices always have a full set of orthonormal eigenvectors (i.e., they are unitarily diagonalizable).

Example 4.5 Matrix Properties. The following examples illustrate some matrix properties and operations that are relevant to eigenvalue problems:

$$\text{Transpose:} \quad \begin{bmatrix} 1 & 2 \\ 3 & 4 \end{bmatrix}^T = \begin{bmatrix} 1 & 3 \\ 2 & 4 \end{bmatrix},$$

$$\text{Conjugate transpose:} \quad \begin{bmatrix} 1+i & 1+2i \\ 2-i & 2-2i \end{bmatrix}^H = \begin{bmatrix} 1-i & 2+i \\ 1-2i & 2+2i \end{bmatrix},$$

$$\text{Symmetric:} \quad \begin{bmatrix} 1 & 2 \\ 2 & 3 \end{bmatrix}, \qquad \text{nonsymmetric:} \quad \begin{bmatrix} 1 & 3 \\ 2 & 4 \end{bmatrix},$$

$$\text{Hermitian:} \quad \begin{bmatrix} 1 & 1+i \\ 1-i & 2 \end{bmatrix}, \qquad \text{nonHermitian:} \quad \begin{bmatrix} 1 & 1+i \\ 1+i & 2 \end{bmatrix},$$

$$\text{Orthogonal:} \quad \begin{bmatrix} 0 & 1 \\ 1 & 0 \end{bmatrix}, \quad \begin{bmatrix} -1 & 0 \\ 0 & -1 \end{bmatrix}, \qquad \text{nonorthogonal:} \quad \begin{bmatrix} 1 & 1 \\ 1 & 2 \end{bmatrix},$$

$$\text{Orthogonal:} \quad \begin{bmatrix} \sqrt{2}/2 & \sqrt{2}/2 \\ -\sqrt{2}/2 & \sqrt{2}/2 \end{bmatrix}, \qquad \text{unitary:} \quad \begin{bmatrix} i\sqrt{2}/2 & \sqrt{2}/2 \\ -\sqrt{2}/2 & -i\sqrt{2}/2 \end{bmatrix},$$

$$\text{Normal:} \quad \begin{bmatrix} 1 & 2 & 0 \\ 0 & 1 & 2 \\ 2 & 0 & 1 \end{bmatrix}, \qquad \text{nonnormal:} \quad \begin{bmatrix} 1 & 1 \\ 0 & 1 \end{bmatrix}.$$

Important questions whose answers materially affect the choice of algorithm and software for solving an eigenvalue problem include:

- Is the matrix real, or complex?
- Is the matrix relatively small and dense, or large and sparse?
- Does the matrix have any special properties, such as symmetry, or is it a general matrix?
- Are all of the eigenvalues needed, or only a few (for example, perhaps only the largest or smallest in magnitude)?
- Are only the eigenvalues needed, or are the corresponding eigenvectors required as well?

4.2.5 Localizing Eigenvalues

For some purposes, we may not need high accuracy in determining the eigenvalues of a matrix, but only relatively crude information about their location in the complex plane. For example, we might merely need to know that all of the eigenvalues lie within a given disk or half plane, or simply that none of them is zero (i.e., the matrix is nonsingular). The simplest such "localization" result is that if λ is an eigenvalue of $\boldsymbol{A}$, then

$$|\lambda| \leq \|\boldsymbol{A}\|,$$

which holds for any matrix norm induced by a vector norm. Thus, the eigenvalues of $\boldsymbol{A}$ all lie in a disk in the complex plane of radius $\|\boldsymbol{A}\|$ centered at the origin. A sharper estimate is given by *Gershgorin's Theorem*, which says that the eigenvalues of an $n \times n$ matrix $\boldsymbol{A}$ are all contained within the union of n disks, with the kth disk centered at a_{kk} and having radius $\sum_{j \neq k} |a_{kj}|$. To see why this is true, let λ be any eigenvalue, with corresponding eigenvector $\boldsymbol{x}$, normalized so that $\|\boldsymbol{x}\|_\infty = 1$. Let x_k be an entry of $\boldsymbol{x}$ such that $|x_k| = 1$ (at least one component has magnitude 1, by definition of the ∞-norm). Because $\boldsymbol{A}\boldsymbol{x} = \lambda\boldsymbol{x}$, we have

$$(\lambda - a_{kk})x_k = \sum_{j \neq k} a_{kj}x_j,$$

so that

$$|\lambda - a_{kk}| \leq \sum_{j \neq k} |a_{kj}| \cdot |x_j| \leq \sum_{j \neq k} |a_{kj}|.$$

Applying this theorem to $\boldsymbol{A}^T$ shows that a similar result holds for disks defined by off-diagonal absolute column sums. In addition to being useful in its own right, a number of other useful results follow from Gershgorin's Theorem. For example, a strictly diagonally dominant matrix must be nonsingular, since zero cannot lie in any of its Gershgorin disks.

Example 4.6 Gershgorin Disks. The Gershgorin disks for the real matrix

$$\boldsymbol{A}_1 = \begin{bmatrix} 4.0 & -0.5 & 0.0 \\ 0.6 & 5.0 & -0.6 \\ 0.0 & 0.5 & 3.0 \end{bmatrix}$$

are plotted in the complex plane in Fig 4.2. The three eigenvalues of this matrix, indicated by $\times$ in the figure, lie within the union of the disks. Note that two of the eigenvalues are complex conjugates. The matrix

$$\boldsymbol{A}_2 = \begin{bmatrix} 4.0 & 0.5 & 0.0 \\ 0.6 & 5.0 & 0.6 \\ 0.0 & 0.5 & 3.0 \end{bmatrix}$$

has the same Gershgorin disks, but all three of its eigenvalues, indicated by • in the figure, are real and hence lie on the real axis of the complex plane.

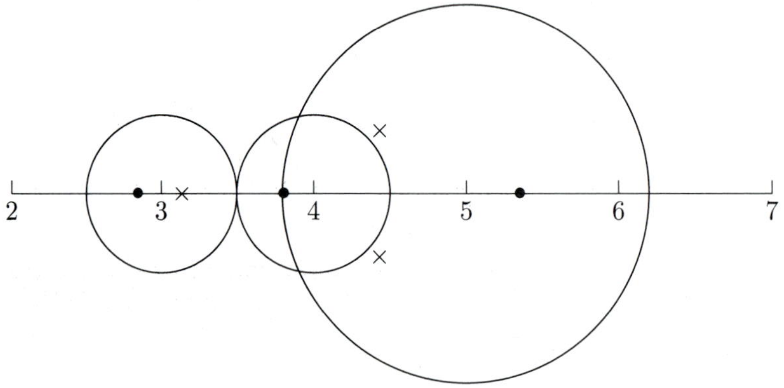

Figure 4.2: Gershgorin disks and eigenvalues for example matrices.

4.3 Sensitivity and Conditioning

The conditioning of an eigenvalue problem measures the sensitivity of the eigenvalues and eigenvectors to small changes in the matrix. As we will see, the condition number of a matrix eigenvalue problem is *not* the condition number of the same matrix with respect to solving linear equations. Moreover, different eigenvalues or eigenvectors of a given matrix are not necessarily equally sensitive to perturbations in the matrix.

Suppose that the $n \times n$ matrix $\boldsymbol{A}$, with eigenvalues $\lambda_1, \ldots, \lambda_n$, is nondefective, so that it has a full set of n linearly independent eigenvectors, $\boldsymbol{x}_1, \ldots, \boldsymbol{x}_n$, which form the columns of a nonsingular matrix $\boldsymbol{X} = [\boldsymbol{x}_1 \cdots \boldsymbol{x}_n]$ such that $\boldsymbol{X}^{-1}\boldsymbol{A}\boldsymbol{X} = \boldsymbol{D} = \text{diag}(\lambda_1, \ldots, \lambda_n)$ (i.e., $\boldsymbol{A}$ is diagonalizable; see Section 4.2.2). Let μ be an eigenvalue of the perturbed matrix $\boldsymbol{A} + \boldsymbol{E}$, and let $\boldsymbol{F} = \boldsymbol{X}^{-1}\boldsymbol{E}\boldsymbol{X}$. Then

$$\boldsymbol{X}^{-1}(\boldsymbol{A} + \boldsymbol{E})\boldsymbol{X} = \boldsymbol{X}^{-1}\boldsymbol{A}\boldsymbol{X} + \boldsymbol{X}^{-1}\boldsymbol{E}\boldsymbol{X} = \boldsymbol{D} + \boldsymbol{F},$$

so that $\boldsymbol{A} + \boldsymbol{E}$ and $\boldsymbol{D} + \boldsymbol{F}$ are similar and hence have the same eigenvalues (see Section 4.4). Thus, there is an eigenvector $\boldsymbol{v}$ such that $(\boldsymbol{D} + \boldsymbol{F})\boldsymbol{v} = \mu\boldsymbol{v}$, which can be rewritten

$$\boldsymbol{v} = (\mu\boldsymbol{I} - \boldsymbol{D})^{-1}\boldsymbol{F}\boldsymbol{v},$$

provided μ is not an eigenvalue of $\boldsymbol{D}$ (and hence of $\boldsymbol{A}$, in which case the eigenvalue is unperturbed), so that $\mu\boldsymbol{I} - \boldsymbol{D}$ is nonsingular. Taking norms, we have

$$\|\boldsymbol{v}\|_2 \le \|(\mu\boldsymbol{I} - \boldsymbol{D})^{-1}\|_2 \cdot \|\boldsymbol{F}\|_2 \cdot \|\boldsymbol{v}\|_2,$$

which, after dividing both sides by $\|\boldsymbol{v}\|_2$ and $\|(\mu\boldsymbol{I} - \boldsymbol{D})^{-1}\|_2$, yields

$$\|(\mu\boldsymbol{I} - \boldsymbol{D})^{-1}\|_2^{-1} \le \|\boldsymbol{F}\|_2.$$

Because $(\mu\boldsymbol{I} - \boldsymbol{D})^{-1}$ is diagonal, $\|(\mu\boldsymbol{I} - \boldsymbol{D})^{-1}\|_2 = 1/|\mu - \lambda_k|$, where λ_k is the eigenvalue of $\boldsymbol{D}$ (and hence of $\boldsymbol{A}$) closest to μ. Thus, we have the bound

$$\begin{aligned} |\mu - \lambda_k| &= \|(\mu\boldsymbol{I} - \boldsymbol{D})^{-1}\|_2^{-1} \\ &\le \|\boldsymbol{F}\|_2 = \|\boldsymbol{X}^{-1}\boldsymbol{E}\boldsymbol{X}\|_2 \\ &\le \|\boldsymbol{X}^{-1}\|_2 \cdot \|\boldsymbol{E}\|_2 \cdot \|\boldsymbol{X}\|_2 \\ &= \text{cond}_2(\boldsymbol{X})\, \|\boldsymbol{E}\|_2, \end{aligned}$$

i.e., a perturbation of size $\|\boldsymbol{E}\|_2$ to $\boldsymbol{A}$ changes each of its eigenvalues by at most $\text{cond}_2(\boldsymbol{X})$ times as much, where $\boldsymbol{X}$ is the matrix of eigenvectors. This result, due to Bauer and Fike, says that the absolute condition number of the eigenvalues of a matrix is given by the condition number of its matrix of eigenvectors with respect to solving linear equations (there is no point in using a relative condition number here because the eigenvalues already reflect the scale of the matrix). We can conclude that the eigenvalues may be sensitive if the eigenvectors are nearly linearly dependent (i.e., the matrix is nearly defective), but are insensitive if the eigenvectors are far from being linearly dependent. In particular, if $\boldsymbol{A}$ is a *normal* matrix (i.e., $\boldsymbol{A}^H\boldsymbol{A} = \boldsymbol{A}\boldsymbol{A}^H$), then the eigenvectors can be chosen to be orthonormal (see Section 4.4), so that $\text{cond}_2(\boldsymbol{X}) = 1$. Thus, the eigenvalues of normal matrices, which includes all real symmetric and complex Hermitian matrices, are always well-conditioned.

The result just derived is applicable only if the matrix is nondefective. Moreover, the bound it provides depends on *all* of the eigenvectors, and hence may significantly overestimate the sensitivities of some of the eigenvalues, which can vary substantially. Thus, we now consider the sensitivity of an individual eigenvalue of a (possibly defective) matrix $\boldsymbol{A}$. Let $\boldsymbol{x}$ and $\boldsymbol{y}$ be right and left eigenvectors, respectively, corresponding to a simple eigenvalue λ of $\boldsymbol{A}$, and consider the perturbed eigenvalue problem

$$(\boldsymbol{A} + \boldsymbol{E})(\boldsymbol{x} + \Delta\boldsymbol{x}) = (\lambda + \Delta\lambda)(\boldsymbol{x} + \Delta\boldsymbol{x}).$$

Expanding both sides, dropping second-order terms (i.e., products of small perturbations, such as $\boldsymbol{E}\Delta\boldsymbol{x}$), and using the fact that $\boldsymbol{A}\boldsymbol{x} = \lambda\boldsymbol{x}$, we obtain the approximation

$$\boldsymbol{A}\Delta\boldsymbol{x} + \boldsymbol{E}\boldsymbol{x} \approx \Delta\lambda\,\boldsymbol{x} + \lambda\Delta\boldsymbol{x}.$$

Premultiplying both sides by $\boldsymbol{y}^H$, we obtain

$$\boldsymbol{y}^H\boldsymbol{A}\Delta\boldsymbol{x} + \boldsymbol{y}^H\boldsymbol{E}\boldsymbol{x} \approx \Delta\lambda\,\boldsymbol{y}^H\boldsymbol{x} + \lambda\boldsymbol{y}^H\Delta\boldsymbol{x}.$$

Because $\boldsymbol{y}$ is a left eigenvector, $\boldsymbol{y}^H \boldsymbol{A} = \lambda \boldsymbol{y}^H$, and using this fact yields

$$\boldsymbol{y}^H \boldsymbol{E}\boldsymbol{x} \approx \Delta\lambda\, \boldsymbol{y}^H \boldsymbol{x}.$$

By assumption λ is a simple eigenvalue, so $\boldsymbol{y}^H \boldsymbol{x} \neq 0$ (see Exercise 4.20) and hence we can divide by $\boldsymbol{y}^H \boldsymbol{x}$ to obtain

$$\Delta\lambda \approx \frac{\boldsymbol{y}^H \boldsymbol{E}\boldsymbol{x}}{\boldsymbol{y}^H \boldsymbol{x}},$$

which, upon taking norms yields the bound

$$|\Delta\lambda| \lessapprox \frac{\|\boldsymbol{y}\|_2 \cdot \|\boldsymbol{x}\|_2}{|\boldsymbol{y}^H \boldsymbol{x}|} \|\boldsymbol{E}\|_2 = \frac{1}{\cos(\theta)} \|\boldsymbol{E}\|_2,$$

where θ is the angle between $\boldsymbol{x}$ and $\boldsymbol{y}$. Thus, the absolute condition number of a simple eigenvalue is given by the reciprocal of the cosine of the angle between its corresponding right and left eigenvectors. We can conclude that a simple eigenvalue is sensitive if its right and left eigenvectors are nearly orthogonal, so that $\cos(\theta) \approx 0$, but is insensitive if the angle between its right and left eigenvectors is small, so that $\cos(\theta) \approx 1$. In particular, the eigenvalues of real symmetric and complex Hermitian matrices are always well-conditioned, since the right and left eigenvectors are the same, so that $\cos(\theta) = 1$.

The sensitivity of a multiple eigenvalue is much more complicated to analyze, and we will not pursue it here. We can get a hint of what can go wrong, however, from the fact that the right and left eigenvectors for a multiple eigenvalue can be orthogonal, so that the denominator of the condition number we derived in the simple case goes to zero, and hence the condition number becomes arbitrarily large. Suffice it to say that multiple or close eigenvalues can be poorly conditioned, especially if the matrix is defective. The sensitivity of eigenvectors is also relatively complicated to analyze, as the sensitivity of an eigenvector depends on both the sensitivity of the corresponding eigenvalue and the distance between that eigenvalue and the other eigenvalues. If a matrix has well-conditioned and well-separated eigenvalues, then its eigenvectors will also be well-conditioned, but if the eigenvalues are ill-conditioned or closely clustered, then the eigenvectors may be poorly conditioned. *Balancing*—rescaling by a diagonal similarity transformation—can improve the conditioning of an eigenvalue problem, and many software packages for eigenvalue problems offer such an option.

Example 4.7 Eigenvalue Sensitivity. Consider the matrix

$$\boldsymbol{A} = \begin{bmatrix} -149 & -50 & -154 \\ 537 & 180 & 546 \\ -27 & -9 & -25 \end{bmatrix},$$

whose eigenvalues are $\lambda_1 = 1$, $\lambda_2 = 2$, and $\lambda_3 = 3$. Because $\boldsymbol{A}$ has distinct eigenvalues, it is necessarily nondefective and hence diagonalizable, but $\boldsymbol{A}$ is not normal (i.e., $\boldsymbol{A}^T\boldsymbol{A} \neq \boldsymbol{A}\boldsymbol{A}^T$). The right and left eigenvectors of $\boldsymbol{A}$, respectively, normalized to have 2-norm 1, are given by the columns of the matrices

$$\boldsymbol{X} = \begin{bmatrix} 0.316 & 0.404 & 0.139 \\ -0.949 & -0.909 & -0.974 \\ 0.000 & -0.101 & 0.179 \end{bmatrix} \quad \text{and} \quad \boldsymbol{Y} = \begin{bmatrix} 0.681 & -0.676 & -0.688 \\ 0.225 & -0.225 & -0.229 \\ 0.697 & -0.701 & -0.688 \end{bmatrix}.$$

The overall condition number for the eigenvalues is given by $\text{cond}_2(\boldsymbol{X}) = 1289$, so we would expect the eigenvalues to be sensitive to perturbations in the matrix $\boldsymbol{A}$. Moreover, since

$$\boldsymbol{y}_1^T\boldsymbol{x}_1 = 0.0017, \quad \boldsymbol{y}_2^T\boldsymbol{x}_2 = 0.0025, \quad \text{and} \quad \boldsymbol{y}_3^T\boldsymbol{x}_3 = 0.0046,$$

we see that the right and left eigenvectors corresponding to each eigenvalue are almost orthogonal, again suggesting that the eigenvalues are ill-conditioned. To demonstrate this sensitivity, the eigenvalues of the same matrix except with the a_{22} entry changed to 180.01 are $\lambda_1 = 0.207$, $\lambda_2 = 2.301$, and $\lambda_3 = 3.502$, which differ substantially from the original eigenvalues, considering the tiny perturbation made in a single entry of $\boldsymbol{A}$. The eigenvalues of the same matrix except with the a_{22} entry changed to 179.99 are $\lambda_1 = 1.664 + 1.054i$, $\lambda_2 = 1.664 - 1.054i$, and $\lambda_3 = 2.662$, so that a similarly tiny perturbation has caused two well-separated real eigenvalues of the original matrix to become a complex conjugate pair.

4.4 Problem Transformations

Many numerical methods for computing eigenvalues and eigenvectors are based on reducing the original matrix to a simpler form whose eigenvalues and eigenvectors are easily determined. Thus, we need to identify what types of transformations leave eigenvalues either unchanged or easily recoverable, and for what types of matrices the eigenvalues are easily determined.

Shift. A *shift* subtracts a constant scalar from each diagonal entry of a matrix, effectively shifting the origin of the real line or complex plane. If $\boldsymbol{Ax} = \lambda\boldsymbol{x}$ and σ is any scalar, then $(\boldsymbol{A} - \sigma\boldsymbol{I})\boldsymbol{x} = (\lambda - \sigma)\boldsymbol{x}$. Thus, the eigenvalues of the matrix $\boldsymbol{A} - \sigma\boldsymbol{I}$ are translated, or shifted, from those of $\boldsymbol{A}$ by σ, but the eigenvectors are unaffected.

Inversion. If $\boldsymbol{A}$ is nonsingular and $\boldsymbol{Ax} = \lambda\boldsymbol{x}$ with $\boldsymbol{x} \neq \boldsymbol{0}$, then λ is necessarily nonzero, and $\boldsymbol{A}^{-1}\boldsymbol{x} = (1/\lambda)\boldsymbol{x}$. Thus, the eigenvalues of $\boldsymbol{A}^{-1}$ are the reciprocals of the eigenvalues of $\boldsymbol{A}$, and the eigenvectors of the two matrices are the same.

Powers. If $\boldsymbol{Ax} = \lambda\boldsymbol{x}$, then $\boldsymbol{A}^2\boldsymbol{x} = \lambda^2\boldsymbol{x}$. Thus, squaring a matrix squares its eigenvalues, but the eigenvectors are unchanged. More generally, if k is any positive integer, then $\boldsymbol{A}^k\boldsymbol{x} = \lambda^k\boldsymbol{x}$. Thus, taking the kth power of a matrix also takes the kth power of its eigenvalues, and again the eigenvectors remain unchanged.

Polynomials. More generally still, if

$$p(t) = c_0 + c_1t + c_2t^2 + \cdots c_kt^k$$

is any polynomial of degree k, then we can define

$$p(\boldsymbol{A}) = c_0\boldsymbol{I} + c_1\boldsymbol{A} + c_2\boldsymbol{A}^2 + \cdots + c_k\boldsymbol{A}^k.$$

Now if $\boldsymbol{Ax} = \lambda\boldsymbol{x}$, then $p(\boldsymbol{A})\boldsymbol{x} = p(\lambda)\boldsymbol{x}$. Thus, the eigenvalues of a polynomial in a matrix $\boldsymbol{A}$ are given by the same polynomial evaluated at the eigenvalues of $\boldsymbol{A}$, and the corresponding eigenvectors of $p(\boldsymbol{A})$ are the same as those of $\boldsymbol{A}$.

Similarity. The transformations we have considered thus far alter the eigenvalues of a matrix in a systematic way but leave the eigenvectors unchanged. We next consider a general type of transformation that leaves the eigenvalues unchanged, but transforms the eigenvectors in a systematic way. A matrix $\boldsymbol{B}$ is *similar* to a matrix $\boldsymbol{A}$ if there is a nonsingular matrix $\boldsymbol{T}$ such that

$$\boldsymbol{B} = \boldsymbol{T}^{-1}\boldsymbol{AT}.$$

Then

$$\boldsymbol{By} = \lambda\boldsymbol{y} \quad \Rightarrow \quad \boldsymbol{T}^{-1}\boldsymbol{ATy} = \lambda\boldsymbol{y} \quad \Rightarrow \quad \boldsymbol{ATy} = \lambda\boldsymbol{Ty},$$

so that $\boldsymbol{A}$ and $\boldsymbol{B}$ have the same eigenvalues, and if $\boldsymbol{y}$ is an eigenvector of $\boldsymbol{B}$, then $\boldsymbol{x} = \boldsymbol{Ty}$ is an eigenvector of $\boldsymbol{A}$. Thus, similarity transformations preserve eigenvalues, and, although they do not preserve eigenvectors, the eigenvectors are still easily recoverable. Note that the converse is not true: two matrices that are similar must have the same eigenvalues, but two matrices that have the same eigenvalues are not necessarily similar (see Example 4.9).

Example 4.8 Similarity Transformation. From the eigenvalues and eigenvectors of the third example matrix in Example 4.2, we see that

$$\boldsymbol{AT} = \begin{bmatrix} 3 & 1 \\ 1 & 3 \end{bmatrix} \begin{bmatrix} 1 & -1 \\ 1 & 1 \end{bmatrix} = \begin{bmatrix} 1 & -1 \\ 1 & 1 \end{bmatrix} \begin{bmatrix} 4 & 0 \\ 0 & 2 \end{bmatrix} = \boldsymbol{TD},$$

where $\boldsymbol{D} = \text{diag}(\lambda_1, \lambda_2)$, and hence

$$\boldsymbol{T}^{-1}\boldsymbol{AT} = \begin{bmatrix} 0.5 & 0.5 \\ -0.5 & 0.5 \end{bmatrix} \begin{bmatrix} 3 & 1 \\ 1 & 3 \end{bmatrix} \begin{bmatrix} 1 & -1 \\ 1 & 1 \end{bmatrix} = \begin{bmatrix} 4 & 0 \\ 0 & 2 \end{bmatrix} = \boldsymbol{D},$$

so that the original matrix $\boldsymbol{A}$ is similar to the diagonal matrix $\boldsymbol{D}$, and the eigenvectors of $\boldsymbol{A}$ form the columns of the transformation matrix $\boldsymbol{T}$.

The definition of a similarity transformation requires only that the transformation matrix $\boldsymbol{T}$ be nonsingular, but it could be arbitrarily ill-conditioned (i.e., nearly singular). Thus, whenever possible, orthogonal or unitary similarity transformations are strongly preferred for numerical computations so that the transformation matrix is perfectly well-conditioned.

4.4.1 Diagonal, Triangular, and Block Triangular Forms

We next need to establish suitable targets in transforming eigenvalue problems so that they are more easily solved. If $\boldsymbol{A}$ is diagonal and λ is equal to any of its diagonal entries, then the diagonal matrix $\boldsymbol{A} - \lambda\boldsymbol{I}$ necessarily has a zero diagonal entry and hence is singular. Thus, the eigenvalues of a diagonal matrix are its diagonal entries, and the eigenvectors are the corresponding columns of the identity matrix $\boldsymbol{I}$. Diagonal form is therefore a desirable target in simplifying an eigenvalue problem for a general matrix by a similarity transformation. This form can often be achieved, for example when all the eigenvalues are distinct, but unfortunately, some matrices cannot be transformed into diagonal form by a similarity transformation. The closest we can come, in general, is *Jordan form*, in which the matrix is reduced nearly to diagonal form but may yet have a few nonzero entries on the first superdiagonal, corresponding to one or more multiple eigenvalues. The Jordan form is not useful for numerical computation, however, because it is not a continuous function of the matrix entries, and it cannot be computed stably, in general.

Example 4.9 Nondiagonalizable Matrix. The matrix

$$\boldsymbol{A} = \begin{bmatrix} 1 & 1 \\ 0 & 1 \end{bmatrix},$$

which is already in Jordan form, cannot be diagonalized by any similarity transformation. The problem is that the matrix is defective: the eigenvalue 1 has multiplicity two, but there is only one linearly independent corresponding eigenvector. To see this, note that if

$$\begin{bmatrix} 1 & 1 \\ 0 & 1 \end{bmatrix} \begin{bmatrix} x_1 \\ x_2 \end{bmatrix} = 1 \begin{bmatrix} x_1 \\ x_2 \end{bmatrix},$$

then $x_1 + x_2 = x_1$, so that $x_2 = 0$, and hence every eigenvector is a multiple of $\boldsymbol{e}_1 = [1 \quad 0]^T$. Thus, there is no 2×2 nonsingular matrix of linearly independent eigenvectors with which to diagonalize $\boldsymbol{A}$ by a similarity transformation. In particular, this shows that $\boldsymbol{A}$ is *not* similar to the 2×2 identity matrix even though they have the same eigenvalues.

Fortunately, every matrix *can* be transformed into triangular form—called *Schur form* in this context—by a similarity transformation (in fact, by a unitary similarity transformation), and the eigenvalues of a triangular matrix are also the diagonal entries, for $\boldsymbol{A} - \lambda \boldsymbol{I}$ must have a zero on its diagonal if $\boldsymbol{A}$ is triangular and λ is any diagonal entry of $\boldsymbol{A}$. The eigenvectors of a triangular matrix are not quite so obvious but are still straightforward to compute. If

$$\boldsymbol{A} - \lambda \boldsymbol{I} = \begin{bmatrix} \boldsymbol{U}_{11} & \boldsymbol{u} & \boldsymbol{U}_{13} \\ \boldsymbol{0} & 0 & \boldsymbol{v}^T \\ \boldsymbol{O} & \boldsymbol{0} & \boldsymbol{U}_{33} \end{bmatrix}$$

is triangular, then the system $\boldsymbol{U}_{11}\boldsymbol{y} = \boldsymbol{u}$ can be solved for $\boldsymbol{y}$, so that

$$\boldsymbol{x} = \begin{bmatrix} \boldsymbol{y} \\ -1 \\ \boldsymbol{0} \end{bmatrix}$$

is an eigenvector. (We have assumed here that $\boldsymbol{U}_{11}$ is nonsingular, which means that we are working with the *first* occurrence of λ on the diagonal.)

For any matrix, the triangular Schur form is always attainable by a unitary similarity transformation, but the Schur form of a real matrix will have complex entries if the matrix has any complex eigenvalues. An alternative with only real entries is *real Schur form*, which is block triangular with 1×1 and 2×2 diagonal blocks corresponding to real eigenvalues and complex conjugate pairs of eigenvalues, respectively, and is attainable by an orthogonal similarity transformation.

Real Schur form is an example of the more general *block triangular form*

$$\boldsymbol{A} = \begin{bmatrix} \boldsymbol{A}_{11} & \boldsymbol{A}_{12} & \cdots & \boldsymbol{A}_{1p} \\ & \boldsymbol{A}_{22} & \cdots & \boldsymbol{A}_{2p} \\ & & \ddots & \vdots \\ & & & \boldsymbol{A}_{pp} \end{bmatrix},$$

where each diagonal block is *square* and all subdiagonal blocks are zero. The determinant of a matrix of this form is the product of the determinants of the diagonal blocks, so its spectrum is the union of the spectra of the diagonal blocks, i.e., $\lambda(\boldsymbol{A}) = \bigcup_{j=1}^{p} \lambda(\boldsymbol{A}_{jj})$. Moreover, the eigenvectors of $\boldsymbol{A}$ are easily recoverable from those of the diagonal blocks (see Exercise 4.22). Thus, the eigenvalue problem for a matrix in block triangular form breaks into smaller subproblems that can be solved more easily, and many algorithms for computing eigenvalues exploit this feature. If a matrix $\boldsymbol{A}$ can be symmetrically permuted into block triangular form with at least two blocks, i.e., there is a permutation matrix $\boldsymbol{P}$ such that

$$\boldsymbol{PAP}^T = \begin{bmatrix} \boldsymbol{A}_{11} & \boldsymbol{A}_{12} \\ \boldsymbol{O} & \boldsymbol{A}_{22} \end{bmatrix},$$

then $\boldsymbol{A}$ is said to be *reducible*.

One way of transforming a given $n \times n$ matrix $\boldsymbol{A}$ into block triangular form is by finding an invariant subspace $\mathcal{S}$ such that $\boldsymbol{A}\mathcal{S} \subseteq \mathcal{S}$ (see Section 4.2.3). If $\boldsymbol{X}_1$ is an $n \times p$ matrix whose columns are a basis for such an invariant subspace $\mathcal{S}$, then by definition each column of $\boldsymbol{AX}_1$ is a linear combination of the columns of $\boldsymbol{X}_1$, and hence there is a $p \times p$ matrix $\boldsymbol{B}_{11}$ such that $\boldsymbol{AX}_1 = \boldsymbol{X}_1\boldsymbol{B}_{11}$. Now let $\boldsymbol{X}_2$ be an $n \times (n-p)$ matrix whose columns are a basis for the complementary subspace, so that the matrix $\boldsymbol{X} = [\boldsymbol{X}_1 \;\; \boldsymbol{X}_2]$ is nonsingular, and write its inverse in partitioned form

$$\boldsymbol{X}^{-1} = \begin{bmatrix} \boldsymbol{Y}_1 \\ \boldsymbol{Y}_2 \end{bmatrix},$$

so that

$$\boldsymbol{I}_n = \boldsymbol{X}^{-1}\boldsymbol{X} = \begin{bmatrix} \boldsymbol{Y}_1 \\ \boldsymbol{Y}_2 \end{bmatrix} [\,\boldsymbol{X}_1 \;\; \boldsymbol{X}_2\,] = \begin{bmatrix} \boldsymbol{Y}_1\boldsymbol{X}_1 & \boldsymbol{Y}_1\boldsymbol{X}_2 \\ \boldsymbol{Y}_2\boldsymbol{X}_1 & \boldsymbol{Y}_2\boldsymbol{X}_2 \end{bmatrix} = \begin{bmatrix} \boldsymbol{I}_p & \boldsymbol{O} \\ \boldsymbol{O} & \boldsymbol{I}_{n-p} \end{bmatrix}.$$

Then

$$\begin{aligned} \boldsymbol{X}^{-1}\boldsymbol{AX} &= \begin{bmatrix} \boldsymbol{Y}_1 \\ \boldsymbol{Y}_2 \end{bmatrix} \boldsymbol{A}\,[\,\boldsymbol{X}_1 \;\; \boldsymbol{X}_2\,] = \begin{bmatrix} \boldsymbol{Y}_1\boldsymbol{AX}_1 & \boldsymbol{Y}_1\boldsymbol{AX}_2 \\ \boldsymbol{Y}_2\boldsymbol{AX}_1 & \boldsymbol{Y}_2\boldsymbol{AX}_2 \end{bmatrix} \\ &= \begin{bmatrix} \boldsymbol{Y}_1\boldsymbol{X}_1\boldsymbol{B}_{11} & \boldsymbol{Y}_1\boldsymbol{AX}_2 \\ \boldsymbol{Y}_2\boldsymbol{X}_1\boldsymbol{B}_{11} & \boldsymbol{Y}_2\boldsymbol{AX}_2 \end{bmatrix} = \begin{bmatrix} \boldsymbol{B}_{11} & \boldsymbol{B}_{12} \\ \boldsymbol{O} & \boldsymbol{B}_{22} \end{bmatrix}, \end{aligned}$$

which is block triangular.

The simplest form attainable by a similarity transformation, as well as the type of similarity transformation required, depends on the properties of the given matrix. The simpler diagonal form is obviously preferred whenever possible, and, for both theoretical and numerical reasons, orthogonal or unitary similarity transformations are also preferred whenever possible. Unfortunately, not all matrices are unitarily diagonalizable, and some matrices, as Example 4.9 shows, are not diagonalizable at all. Table 4.1 indicates what form is attainable for a given type of matrix and a given type of similarity transformation. Given a matrix $\boldsymbol{A}$ with one of the properties indicated, there exist matrices $\boldsymbol{B}$ and $\boldsymbol{T}$ having the indicated properties such that $\boldsymbol{B} = \boldsymbol{T}^{-1}\boldsymbol{A}\boldsymbol{T}$. In the first four cases, where $\boldsymbol{B}$ is diagonal, the columns of $\boldsymbol{T}$ are the eigenvectors of $\boldsymbol{A}$. In all cases, the diagonal entries of $\boldsymbol{B}$ are the eigenvalues, except for real Schur form, where complex eigenvalues occur in conjugate pairs corresponding to the 2×2 diagonal blocks of $\boldsymbol{B}$. Note that the eigenvalues of a real symmetric or complex Hermitian matrix are always real (see Exercise 4.10).

$\boldsymbol{A}$	$\boldsymbol{T}$	$\boldsymbol{B}$
Distinct eigenvalues	Nonsingular	Diagonal
Real symmetric	Orthogonal	Real diagonal
Complex Hermitian	Unitary	Real diagonal
Normal	Unitary	Diagonal
Arbitrary real	Orthogonal	Real block triangular (real Schur)
Arbitrary	Unitary	Triangular (Schur)
Arbitrary	Nonsingular	Almost diagonal (Jordan)

Table 4.1: Forms attainable by similarity transformation for various types of matrices

4.5 Computing Eigenvalues and Eigenvectors

4.5.1 Power Iteration

A simple method for computing a single eigenvalue and corresponding eigenvector of an $n \times n$ matrix $\boldsymbol{A}$ is Algorithm 4.1, known as *power iteration*, which multiplies an arbitrary nonzero vector repeatedly by the matrix, in effect multiplying the initial starting vector by successively higher powers of the matrix.

Algorithm 4.1 Power Iteration

```
x_0 = arbitrary nonzero vector
for k = 1, 2, ...
    x_k = A x_{k-1}                { generate next vector }
end
```

Assuming that $\boldsymbol{A}$ has a unique eigenvalue λ_1 of maximum modulus, with corresponding eigenvector $\boldsymbol{v}_1$, power iteration converges to a multiple of $\boldsymbol{v}_1$. To see why, assume we can express the starting vector $\boldsymbol{x}_0$ as a linear combination, $\boldsymbol{x}_0 = \sum_{j=1}^{n} \alpha_j \boldsymbol{v}_j$, where the $\boldsymbol{v}_j$ are eigenvectors of $\boldsymbol{A}$. We then have

$$\begin{aligned} \boldsymbol{x}_k &= \boldsymbol{A}\boldsymbol{x}_{k-1} = \boldsymbol{A}^2\boldsymbol{x}_{k-2} = \cdots = \boldsymbol{A}^k\boldsymbol{x}_0 \\ &= \boldsymbol{A}^k \sum_{j=1}^{n} \alpha_j \boldsymbol{v}_j = \sum_{j=1}^{n} \alpha_j \boldsymbol{A}^k \boldsymbol{v}_j = \sum_{j=1}^{n} \lambda_j^k \alpha_j \boldsymbol{v}_j \\ &= \lambda_1^k \left(\alpha_1 \boldsymbol{v}_1 + \sum_{j=2}^{n} (\lambda_j/\lambda_1)^k \alpha_j \boldsymbol{v}_j \right). \end{aligned}$$

For $j > 1$, $|\lambda_j/\lambda_1| < 1$, so that $(\lambda_j/\lambda_1)^k \to 0$, leaving only the term corresponding to $\boldsymbol{v}_1$ nonvanishing.

Example 4.10 Power Iteration. In the sequence of vectors produced by power iteration, the ratio of the values of a given component of $\boldsymbol{x}_k$ from one iteration to the next converges to the dominant eigenvalue λ_1. If we apply power iteration to the third example matrix in Example 4.2,

$$\boldsymbol{A} = \begin{bmatrix} 3 & 1 \\ 1 & 3 \end{bmatrix},$$

with starting vector

$$\boldsymbol{x}_0 = \begin{bmatrix} 0 \\ 1 \end{bmatrix},$$

then we obtain the following sequence.

k	$\boldsymbol{x}_k^T$		Ratio
0	0	1	
1	1	3	3.000
2	6	10	3.333
3	28	36	3.600
4	120	136	3.778
5	496	528	3.882
6	2016	2080	3.939
7	8128	8256	3.969
8	32640	32896	3.984
9	130816	131328	3.992

The sequence of vectors $\boldsymbol{x}_k$ is converging to a multiple of the eigenvector $[1 \quad 1]^T$. In addition, the table shows the ratio of the values of a given nonzero component of $\boldsymbol{x}_k$ from one iteration to the next, which is converging to the dominant eigenvalue, $\lambda_1 = 4$.

Power iteration usually works in practice, but it can fail for a number of reasons:

- The starting vector $\boldsymbol{x}_0$ may have *no* component in the dominant eigenvector $\boldsymbol{v}_1$ (i.e., $\alpha_1 = 0$). This possibility is extremely unlikely if $\boldsymbol{x}_0$ is chosen randomly, and in any case it is not a problem in practice because rounding error usually introduces such a component.

- There may be more than one eigenvalue having the same (maximum) modulus, in which case the iteration may converge to a vector that is a linear combination of the corresponding eigenvectors. This possibility cannot be discounted in practice; for example, the dominant eigenvalue(s) of a real matrix may be a complex conjugate pair, which of course have the same modulus.
- For a real matrix and real starting vector, the iteration cannot converge to a complex vector.

Geometric growth of the components at each iteration risks eventual overflow (or underflow if the dominant eigenvalue is less than 1 in magnitude), so in practice the approximate eigenvector is rescaled at each iteration to have norm 1, typically using the ∞-norm, yielding Algorithm 4.2. With this normalization, $\boldsymbol{x}_k \to \boldsymbol{v}_1/\|\boldsymbol{v}_1\|_\infty$, and $\|\boldsymbol{y}_k\|_\infty \to |\lambda_1|$.

Algorithm 4.2 Normalized Power Iteration

$\boldsymbol{x}_0$ = arbitrary nonzero vector
for $k = 1, 2, \ldots$
  $\boldsymbol{y}_k = \boldsymbol{A}\boldsymbol{x}_{k-1}$ { generate next vector }
  $\boldsymbol{x}_k = \boldsymbol{y}_k/\|\boldsymbol{y}_k\|_\infty$ { normalize }
end

Example 4.11 Normalized Power Iteration. Repeating Example 4.10 with this normalized scheme, we obtain the following sequence:

k	$\boldsymbol{x}_k^T$		$\|\boldsymbol{y}_k\|_\infty$
0	0.000	1.0	
1	0.333	1.0	3.000
2	0.600	1.0	3.333
3	0.778	1.0	3.600
4	0.882	1.0	3.778
5	0.939	1.0	3.882
6	0.969	1.0	3.939
7	0.984	1.0	3.969
8	0.992	1.0	3.984
9	0.996	1.0	3.992

The eigenvalue approximations have not changed, but now the approximate eigenvector is normalized at each iteration, thereby avoiding geometric growth or decay of its components. The behavior of normalized power iteration is depicted graphically in Fig. 4.3. The eigenvectors of the example matrix are shown by dashed arrows. The initial vector

$$\boldsymbol{x}_0 = \begin{bmatrix} 0 \\ 1 \end{bmatrix} = 1/2 \begin{bmatrix} 1 \\ 1 \end{bmatrix} + 1/2 \begin{bmatrix} -1 \\ 1 \end{bmatrix} = \alpha_1 \boldsymbol{v}_1 + \alpha_2 \boldsymbol{v}_2$$

contains equal components in the two eigenvectors. Repeated multiplication by the matrix $\boldsymbol{A}$ causes the component in $\boldsymbol{v}_1$ (the eigenvector corresponding to the larger

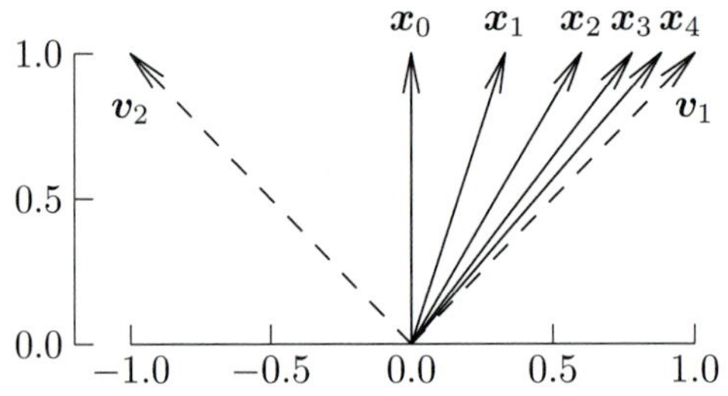

Figure 4.3: Geometric interpretation of power iteration.

eigenvalue, $\lambda_1 = 4$) to dominate as the other component decays like $(\lambda_2/\lambda_1)^k = (1/2)^k$, and hence the sequence of approximate eigenvectors converges to $\boldsymbol{v}_1$.

The convergence rate of power iteration depends on the ratio $|\lambda_2/\lambda_1|$, where λ_2 is the eigenvalue having second-largest modulus: the smaller this ratio, the faster the convergence. (In the terminology and notation of Section 5.4, the convergence rate of power iteration is *linear*, with rate $r = 1$ and constant $C = |\lambda_2/\lambda_1|$.) It may be possible to choose a shift σ (see Section 4.4) such that this ratio is more favorable for the shifted matrix $\boldsymbol{A} - \sigma \boldsymbol{I}$, i.e.,

$$\left|\frac{\lambda_2 - \sigma}{\lambda_1 - \sigma}\right| < \left|\frac{\lambda_2}{\lambda_1}\right|,$$

and thus convergence is accelerated. Of course, the shift must then be added to the result to obtain the eigenvalue of the original matrix. In Example 4.11, for instance, if we use a shift of $\sigma = 1$ (which is equal to the other eigenvalue), then the ratio becomes zero and the method converges in a single iteration, though we would not usually be able to make such a fortuitous choice in practice. In general, if the eigenvalues are all real and ordered from leftmost, λ_1, to rightmost, λ_n, on the real line, then the optimal convergence rate for power iteration is attained with the value of the shift either $(\lambda_2 + \lambda_n)/2$, in which case the method converges to a multiple of $\boldsymbol{v}_1$, or $(\lambda_1 + \lambda_{n-1})/2$, in which case it converges to a multiple of $\boldsymbol{v}_n$. Regardless of the value of the shift, however, power iteration can converge only to an eigenvector corresponding to one of the extreme eigenvalues. Though shifts have limited usefulness in simple power iteration, we will see that they can have a much greater effect in other contexts.

4.5.2 Inverse Iteration

For some applications, the smallest eigenvalue of a matrix in magnitude is required rather than the largest. We can make use of the fact that the eigenvalues of $\boldsymbol{A}^{-1}$ are the reciprocals of those of $\boldsymbol{A}$ (see Section 4.4), and hence the smallest eigenvalue of $\boldsymbol{A}$ is the reciprocal of the largest eigenvalue of $\boldsymbol{A}^{-1}$. This suggests applying power iteration to $\boldsymbol{A}^{-1}$, but as usual the inverse of $\boldsymbol{A}$ need not be computed explicitly. Instead, the equivalent system of linear equations is solved at each iteration using the triangular factors resulting from LU or Cholesky factorization of $\boldsymbol{A}$, which need be done only once, before iterations begin. The result is Algorithm 4.3, known as *inverse iteration*. Inverse iteration converges to the eigenvector corresponding to the smallest eigenvalue of $\boldsymbol{A}$. The eigenvalue obtained is the dominant eigenvalue of $\boldsymbol{A}^{-1}$, and hence its reciprocal is the smallest eigenvalue of $\boldsymbol{A}$ in modulus.

Algorithm 4.3 Inverse Iteration

```
x_0 = arbitrary nonzero vector
for k = 1, 2, ...
    Solve A y_k = x_{k-1} for y_k        { generate next vector }
    x_k = y_k / ||y_k||_∞                { normalize }
end
```

Example 4.12 Inverse Iteration. To illustrate inverse iteration, we use it to compute the smallest eigenvalue of the matrix in Example 4.10, obtaining the sequence

k	$\boldsymbol{x}_k^T$		$\|\boldsymbol{y}_k\|_\infty$
0	0.000	1.0	
1	−0.333	1.0	0.375
2	−0.600	1.0	0.417
3	−0.778	1.0	0.450
4	−0.882	1.0	0.472
5	−0.939	1.0	0.485
6	−0.969	1.0	0.492
7	−0.984	1.0	0.496
8	−0.992	1.0	0.498
9	−0.996	1.0	0.499

which is converging to an eigenvector $[-1 \quad 1]^T$ corresponding to the dominant eigenvalue of $\boldsymbol{A}^{-1}$, which is 0.5. This same vector is an eigenvector corresponding to the smallest eigenvalue of $\boldsymbol{A}$, $\lambda_2 = 2$, which is the reciprocal of the largest eigenvalue of $\boldsymbol{A}^{-1}$.

Employing a shift offers far more potential for accelerating convergence, as well as greater flexibility in which eigenvalue is obtained, when used in conjunction with inverse iteration than with power iteration. In particular, the eigenvalue of $\boldsymbol{A} - \sigma\boldsymbol{I}$ of smallest magnitude is simply $\lambda - \sigma$, where λ is the eigenvalue of $\boldsymbol{A}$ *closest* to σ. Thus, with an appropriate choice of shift, inverse iteration can be used to compute *any* eigenvalue of $\boldsymbol{A}$, not just the extreme eigenvalues. Moreover, if the shift is very close to an eigenvalue of $\boldsymbol{A}$, then convergence will be very rapid. For this reason, inverse iteration is particularly useful for computing the eigenvector corresponding to an approximate eigenvalue that has already been obtained by some other means, since it converges extremely rapidly when applied to the matrix $\boldsymbol{A} - \lambda\boldsymbol{I}$, where λ is an approximate eigenvalue. In the terminology and notation of Section 5.4, the convergence rate of inverse iteration remains linear, but the constant C becomes extremely small when the shift is an approximate eigenvalue of $\boldsymbol{A}$.

4.5.3 Rayleigh Quotient Iteration

If $\boldsymbol{x}$ is an approximate eigenvector for a real matrix $\boldsymbol{A}$, then determining the best estimate for the corresponding eigenvalue λ can be considered as an $n \times 1$ linear least squares approximation problem

$$\boldsymbol{x}\lambda \cong \boldsymbol{A}\boldsymbol{x}.$$

From the normal equation $\boldsymbol{x}^T\boldsymbol{x}\lambda = \boldsymbol{x}^T\boldsymbol{A}\boldsymbol{x}$, we see that the least squares solution is given by

$$\lambda = \frac{\boldsymbol{x}^T\boldsymbol{A}\boldsymbol{x}}{\boldsymbol{x}^T\boldsymbol{x}}.$$

The latter quantity, known as the *Rayleigh quotient*, has many useful properties (see, for example, Computer Problem 6.10). In particular, it can be used to accelerate the convergence of a method such as power iteration, since at iteration k the Rayleigh quotient $\boldsymbol{x}_k^T\boldsymbol{A}\boldsymbol{x}_k/\boldsymbol{x}_k^T\boldsymbol{x}_k$ gives a better approximation to an eigenvalue than that provided by the basic method alone.

Example 4.13 Rayleigh Quotient. Repeating Example 4.11 using normalized power iteration, the value of the Rayleigh quotient at each iteration is shown in the following table.

k	$\boldsymbol{x}_k^T$		$\|\boldsymbol{y}_k\|_\infty$	$\boldsymbol{x}_k^T\boldsymbol{A}\boldsymbol{x}_k/\boldsymbol{x}_k^T\boldsymbol{x}_k$
0	0.000	1.0		3.000
1	0.333	1.0	3.000	3.600
2	0.600	1.0	3.333	3.882
3	0.778	1.0	3.600	3.969
4	0.882	1.0	3.778	3.992
5	0.939	1.0	3.882	3.998
6	0.969	1.0	3.939	4.000

Note that the Rayleigh quotient converges to the dominant eigenvalue, $\lambda_1 = 4$, much faster than the successive approximations produced by power iteration alone.

Given an approximate eigenvector, the Rayleigh quotient provides a good estimate for the corresponding eigenvalue. Conversely, inverse iteration converges very rapidly to an eigenvector if an approximate eigenvalue is used as shift, with a single iteration often sufficing. It is natural, therefore, to combine these two ideas in Algorithm 4.4, known as *Rayleigh quotient iteration*.

Algorithm 4.4 Rayleigh Quotient Iteration

$\boldsymbol{x}_0$ = arbitrary nonzero vector
for $k = 1, 2, \ldots$
  $\sigma_k = \boldsymbol{x}_{k-1}^T\boldsymbol{A}\boldsymbol{x}_{k-1}/\boldsymbol{x}_{k-1}^T\boldsymbol{x}_{k-1}$ { compute shift }
  Solve $(\boldsymbol{A} - \sigma_k\boldsymbol{I})\,\boldsymbol{y}_k = \boldsymbol{x}_{k-1}$ for $\boldsymbol{y}_k$ { generate next vector }
  $\boldsymbol{x}_k = \boldsymbol{y}_k/\|\boldsymbol{y}_k\|_\infty$ { normalize }
end

As one might expect, Rayleigh quotient iteration converges very rapidly: its convergence rate is at least quadratic for any nondefective eigenvalue, and cubic for any normal matrix, which includes the symmetric matrices to which it is most frequently applied. Thus, asymptotically, the number of correct digits in the approximate eigenvector is at least doubled, and usually tripled, for each iteration (see Section 5.4), so that very few iterations are required to achieve maximum accuracy. On the other hand, using a different shift at each iteration means that the matrix must be refactored each time to solve the linear system, so that the cost per iteration is relatively high unless the matrix has some special form, such as tridiagonal, that makes the factorization easy. Rayleigh quotient iteration also works for complex matrices, for which the transpose is replaced by the conjugate transpose, so that the Rayleigh quotient becomes $\boldsymbol{x}^H\boldsymbol{A}\boldsymbol{x}/\boldsymbol{x}^H\boldsymbol{x}$.

Example 4.14 Rayleigh Quotient Iteration. Using the matrix from Example 4.10 and a randomly chosen starting vector $\boldsymbol{x}_0$, Rayleigh quotient iteration converges to the accuracy shown in only two iterations:

k	$\boldsymbol{x}_k^T$		σ_k
0	0.807	0.397	3.792
1	0.924	1.000	3.997
2	1.000	1.000	4.000

4.5.4 Deflation

Suppose that an eigenvalue λ_1 and corresponding eigenvector $\boldsymbol{x}_1$ for a matrix $\boldsymbol{A}$ have been computed. We now consider how to compute a second eigenvalue λ_2 of $\boldsymbol{A}$, if needed, by a process called *deflation*, which effectively removes the known eigenvalue. This process is analogous to removing a known root λ_1 from a polynomial $p(\lambda)$ by dividing it out to obtain a polynomial $p(\lambda)/(\lambda - \lambda_1)$ of degree one less.

Let $\boldsymbol{H}$ be any nonsingular matrix such that $\boldsymbol{H}\boldsymbol{x}_1 = \alpha\boldsymbol{e}_1$, a scalar multiple of the first column of the identity matrix $\boldsymbol{I}$ (a Householder transformation is a good choice for $\boldsymbol{H}$). Then the similarity transformation determined by $\boldsymbol{H}$ transforms $\boldsymbol{A}$ into the block triangular form

$$\boldsymbol{H}\boldsymbol{A}\boldsymbol{H}^{-1} = \begin{bmatrix} \lambda_1 & \boldsymbol{b}^T \\ \boldsymbol{0} & \boldsymbol{B} \end{bmatrix},$$

where $\boldsymbol{B}$ is a matrix of order $n-1$ having eigenvalues $\lambda_2, \ldots, \lambda_n$. Thus, we can work with $\boldsymbol{B}$ to compute the next eigenvalue λ_2. Moreover, if $\boldsymbol{y}_2$ is an eigenvector of $\boldsymbol{B}$ corresponding to λ_2, then

$$\boldsymbol{x}_2 = \boldsymbol{H}^{-1}\begin{bmatrix} \gamma \\ \boldsymbol{y}_2 \end{bmatrix}, \quad \text{where} \quad \gamma = \frac{\boldsymbol{b}^T\boldsymbol{y}_2}{\lambda_2 - \lambda_1},$$

is an eigenvector corresponding to λ_2 for the original matrix $\boldsymbol{A}$, provided $\lambda_1 \neq \lambda_2$. An alternative approach to deflation is to let $\boldsymbol{u}_1$ be any vector such that $\boldsymbol{u}_1^T\boldsymbol{x}_1 = \lambda_1$.

Then the matrix $\boldsymbol{A} - \boldsymbol{x}_1\boldsymbol{u}_1^T$ has eigenvalues $0, \lambda_2, \ldots, \lambda_n$. Possible choices for $\boldsymbol{u}_1$ include

- $\boldsymbol{u}_1 = \lambda_1\boldsymbol{x}_1$, if $\boldsymbol{A}$ is symmetric and $\boldsymbol{x}_1$ is normalized so that $\|\boldsymbol{x}_1\|_2 = 1$
- $\boldsymbol{u}_1 = \lambda_1\boldsymbol{y}_1$, where $\boldsymbol{y}_1$ is the corresponding left eigenvector (i.e., $\boldsymbol{A}^T\boldsymbol{y}_1 = \lambda_1\boldsymbol{y}_1$) normalized so that $\boldsymbol{y}_1^T\boldsymbol{x}_1 = 1$
- $\boldsymbol{u}_1 = \boldsymbol{A}^T\boldsymbol{e}_k$, if $\boldsymbol{x}_1$ is normalized so that $\|\boldsymbol{x}_1\|_\infty = 1$, and the kth component of $\boldsymbol{x}_1$ is 1

With either approach, the deflation process can be repeated to compute additional eigenvalues and eigenvectors, but it becomes increasingly cumbersome and may lose accuracy numerically, so this explicit deflation technique is not recommended for computing many eigenvalues and eigenvectors of a matrix; we will soon see much better alternatives for this purpose. To enhance accuracy, any additional eigenvalues and eigenvectors found from deflated matrices should be refined using inverse iteration on the original matrix with shift equal to the approximate eigenvalue already found.

4.5.5 Simultaneous Iteration

Each of the methods we have considered thus far is designed to compute a single eigenvalue/eigenvector pair for a given matrix. As we have just seen, explicit deflation can be used to enable subsequent computation of additional eigenvalue/eigenvector pairs one at a time, but this approach is less than ideal. We will now consider methods for computing several eigenvalue/eigenvector pairs at once. The simplest way to accomplish this is to use power iteration with several different starting vectors. Let $\boldsymbol{x}_1^{(0)}, \ldots, \boldsymbol{x}_p^{(0)}$ be p linearly independent starting vectors, which form the columns of an $n \times p$ matrix $\boldsymbol{X}_0$ of rank p. Applying power iteration to each of these vectors, we obtain Algorithm 4.5, known as *simultaneous iteration*.

Algorithm 4.5 Simultaneous Iteration

$\boldsymbol{X}_0$ = arbitrary $n \times p$ matrix of rank p
for $k = 1, 2, \ldots$
  $\boldsymbol{X}_k = \boldsymbol{A}\boldsymbol{X}_{k-1}$ { generate next matrix }
end

Let $\mathcal{S}_0 = \text{span}(\boldsymbol{X}_0)$, and let $\mathcal{S}$ be the invariant subspace spanned by the eigenvectors $\boldsymbol{v}_1, \ldots, \boldsymbol{v}_p$ corresponding to the p largest eigenvalues of $\boldsymbol{A}$ in magnitude, $\lambda_1, \ldots, \lambda_p$ (recall Section 4.2.3). Suppose that no nonzero vector in $\mathcal{S}$ is orthogonal to $\mathcal{S}_0$. Then for any $k > 0$, the columns of $\boldsymbol{X}_k = \boldsymbol{A}^k\boldsymbol{X}_0$ form a basis for the p-dimensional subspace $\mathcal{S}_k = \boldsymbol{A}^k\mathcal{S}_0$, and, provided that $|\lambda_p| > |\lambda_{p+1}|$, a proof analogous to that for simple power iteration shows that the subspaces $\mathcal{S}_k$ converge to $\mathcal{S}$. For this reason, simultaneous iteration is also called *subspace iteration*.

There are a number of problems with the iteration scheme just outlined. For one thing, as with simple power iteration, the columns of $\boldsymbol{X}_k$ will need to be rescaled at each iteration to avoid eventual overflow or underflow. More insidiously, since the effect of this scheme is to carry out power iteration on each column of $\boldsymbol{X}_0$ individually, each column of $\boldsymbol{X}_k$ converges to a multiple of the dominant eigenvector of $\boldsymbol{A}$, and hence the columns of $\boldsymbol{X}_k$ form an increasingly ill-conditioned basis for the subspace $\mathcal{S}_k$. We can address both of these problems by orthonormalizing the columns of $\boldsymbol{X}_k$ at each iteration, using any of the methods for QR factorization from Chapter 3. This produces Algorithm 4.6, known as *orthogonal iteration*.

Algorithm 4.6 Orthogonal Iteration

$\boldsymbol{X}_0$ = arbitrary $n \times p$ matrix of rank p
for $k = 1, 2, \ldots$
  Compute reduced QR factorization { normalize }
    $\hat{\boldsymbol{Q}}_k \boldsymbol{R}_k = \boldsymbol{X}_{k-1}$
  $\boldsymbol{X}_k = \boldsymbol{A}\hat{\boldsymbol{Q}}_k$ { generate next matrix }
end

In this algorithm, $\hat{\boldsymbol{Q}}_k \boldsymbol{R}_k$ is the *reduced* QR factorization of $\boldsymbol{X}_{k-1}$ (see Section 3.4.5), with $\hat{\boldsymbol{Q}}_k$ an $n \times p$ matrix having orthonormal columns and $\boldsymbol{R}_k$ a $p \times p$ upper triangular matrix. Under the same conditions as before, the matrices $\boldsymbol{X}_k$ produced by this orthogonal version of simultaneous iteration converge to an $n \times p$ matrix $\boldsymbol{X}$ whose columns form a basis for the invariant subspace corresponding to the p largest eigenvalues of $\boldsymbol{A}$ in magnitude, $\lambda_1, \ldots, \lambda_p$. Because $\text{span}(\hat{\boldsymbol{Q}}_k) = \text{span}(\boldsymbol{X}_{k-1})$, the matrices $\hat{\boldsymbol{Q}}_k$ converge to an $n \times p$ matrix $\hat{\boldsymbol{Q}}$ whose columns form an orthonormal basis for this same invariant subspace.

Recall from Section 4.4.1 that there is a $p \times p$ matrix $\boldsymbol{B}$ such that $\boldsymbol{A}\hat{\boldsymbol{Q}} = \hat{\boldsymbol{Q}}\boldsymbol{B}$. Note, however, that for any j, $1 \le j \le p$, the first j columns of $\hat{\boldsymbol{Q}}$ (or $\boldsymbol{X}$) are the same as if the iterations had been executed on only the first j columns of $\boldsymbol{A}$, and the remaining $p - j$ columns of $\hat{\boldsymbol{Q}}$ can be expanded into a basis for the complementary subspace, yielding a block triangular form. Thus, if $|\lambda_j| > |\lambda_{j+1}|$, $j = 1, \ldots, p$, then $\boldsymbol{B}$ must be triangular. If the eigenvalues are not all distinct in modulus, then $\boldsymbol{B}$ will be merely block triangular; for example, any pair of complex conjugate eigenvalues of a real matrix will yield a corresponding 2×2 diagonal block. Thus, we see that orthogonal simultaneous iteration produces a triangular (or block triangular) matrix, from which the p largest eigenvalues of $\boldsymbol{A}$ can be obtained, along with corresponding orthonormal eigenvectors. Note, however, that the orthogonalization required at each iteration is expensive, and the convergence of the iterations may be quite slow, depending on the ratios of magnitudes of consecutive eigenvalues. We will address these and other issues in the next section.

4.5.6 QR Iteration

In principle, by taking $p = n$, we can use simultaneous iteration to compute *all* of the eigenvalues and eigenvectors of a given $n \times n$ matrix $\boldsymbol{A}$. Thus, we now consider what happens when orthogonal iteration is applied to an orthonormal set of basis vectors for $\mathbb{R}^n$ (or $\mathbb{C}^n$), for which we may as well use the columns of the identity matrix, i.e., $\boldsymbol{X}_0 = \boldsymbol{I}$. If we define

$$\boldsymbol{A}_k = \hat{\boldsymbol{Q}}_k^H \boldsymbol{A} \hat{\boldsymbol{Q}}_k,$$

then, based on our observations in Section 4.5.5, we expect the sequence of matrices $\boldsymbol{A}_k$ to converge to triangular, or at least block triangular, form. Thus, both for monitoring convergence and for (eventually) recovering the eigenvalues of $\boldsymbol{A}$, the matrices $\boldsymbol{A}_k$, each of which is unitarily similar to $\boldsymbol{A}$, are of primary interest. We will therefore develop a recurrence for computing each successive $\boldsymbol{A}_k$ directly from its immediate predecessor in the sequence, rather than by explicitly forming the product $\hat{\boldsymbol{Q}}_k^H \boldsymbol{A} \hat{\boldsymbol{Q}}_k$ using the original matrix $\boldsymbol{A}$ at each step.

If we begin with $\boldsymbol{X}_0 = \boldsymbol{I}$, then the QR factorization $\hat{\boldsymbol{Q}}_0 \boldsymbol{R}_0 = \boldsymbol{X}_0$ gives $\hat{\boldsymbol{Q}}_0 = \boldsymbol{R}_0 = \boldsymbol{I}$, so that $\boldsymbol{X}_1 = \boldsymbol{A}\hat{\boldsymbol{Q}}_0 = \boldsymbol{A}$. For the next iteration, we compute the QR factorization $\hat{\boldsymbol{Q}}_1 \boldsymbol{R}_1 = \boldsymbol{X}_1 = \boldsymbol{A}$, from which we can directly compute

$$\boldsymbol{A}_1 = \hat{\boldsymbol{Q}}_1^H \boldsymbol{A} \hat{\boldsymbol{Q}}_1 = \hat{\boldsymbol{Q}}_1^H (\hat{\boldsymbol{Q}}_1 \boldsymbol{R}_1) \hat{\boldsymbol{Q}}_1 = \boldsymbol{R}_1 \hat{\boldsymbol{Q}}_1,$$

i.e., $\boldsymbol{A}_1$ is just the product of the QR factors of $\boldsymbol{A}$ in reverse order. The next step in orthogonal simultaneous iteration requires the formation of $\boldsymbol{X}_2 = \boldsymbol{A}\hat{\boldsymbol{Q}}_1$ and its QR factorization $\hat{\boldsymbol{Q}}_2 \boldsymbol{R}_2 = \boldsymbol{X}_2$, but we can achieve the same effect by computing the QR factorization $\boldsymbol{Q}_2 \boldsymbol{R}_2 = \boldsymbol{A}_1$, so that

$$\boldsymbol{X}_2 = \boldsymbol{A}\hat{\boldsymbol{Q}}_1 = \hat{\boldsymbol{Q}}_1 \hat{\boldsymbol{Q}}_1^H \boldsymbol{A} \hat{\boldsymbol{Q}}_1 = \hat{\boldsymbol{Q}}_1 \boldsymbol{A}_1 = \hat{\boldsymbol{Q}}_1 (\boldsymbol{Q}_2 \boldsymbol{R}_2) = (\hat{\boldsymbol{Q}}_1 \boldsymbol{Q}_2) \boldsymbol{R}_2 = \hat{\boldsymbol{Q}}_2 \boldsymbol{R}_2.$$

Thus, rather than forming and factoring $\boldsymbol{X}_2$, we can compute $\boldsymbol{A}_2 = \boldsymbol{R}_2 \boldsymbol{Q}_2$ directly from the reverse product of the QR factors of $\boldsymbol{A}_1$. Clearly we can continue the iterations in this manner, generating the matrices $\boldsymbol{A}_k$ successively without any need to form the matrices $\boldsymbol{X}_k$ or compute their QR factorizations explicitly. This simple and elegant reorganization of simultaneous iteration is summarized in Algorithm 4.7, known as *QR iteration*.

Algorithm 4.7 QR Iteration

$\boldsymbol{A}_0 = \boldsymbol{A}$
for $k = 1, 2, \ldots$
    Compute QR factorization   { normalize }
        $\boldsymbol{Q}_k \boldsymbol{R}_k = \boldsymbol{A}_{k-1}$
    $\boldsymbol{A}_k = \boldsymbol{R}_k \boldsymbol{Q}_k$ { generate next matrix }
end

The equivalence of orthogonal subspace iteration (with $p = n$ and $\boldsymbol{X}_0 = \boldsymbol{I}$) and QR iteration is embodied in the relationship

$$\hat{\boldsymbol{Q}}_k = \boldsymbol{Q}_1 \boldsymbol{Q}_2 \cdots \boldsymbol{Q}_k$$

between the sequences of unitary matrices they generate. Let us similarly define the triangular matrices

$$\hat{\boldsymbol{R}}_k = \boldsymbol{R}_k \boldsymbol{R}_{k-1} \cdots \boldsymbol{R}_1.$$

Now since $\boldsymbol{A} = \boldsymbol{Q}_1\boldsymbol{R}_1$, we have

$$\boldsymbol{A}^2 = \boldsymbol{Q}_1\boldsymbol{R}_1\boldsymbol{Q}_1\boldsymbol{R}_1 = \boldsymbol{Q}_1\boldsymbol{Q}_2\boldsymbol{R}_2\boldsymbol{R}_1 = \hat{\boldsymbol{Q}}_2\hat{\boldsymbol{R}}_2.$$

A simple induction shows that

$$\boldsymbol{A}^k = \hat{\boldsymbol{Q}}_k\hat{\boldsymbol{R}}_k,$$

which says that QR iteration in effect produces QR factorizations of successive powers of $\boldsymbol{A}$, and hence the columns of $\hat{\boldsymbol{Q}}_k$ form an orthonormal basis for the subspace spanned by the columns of $\boldsymbol{A}^k$, which in turn result from applying simultaneous iteration to $\boldsymbol{A}$ starting with the columns of the identity matrix. A similar induction shows that

$$\boldsymbol{A}_k = \hat{\boldsymbol{Q}}_k^H\boldsymbol{A}\hat{\boldsymbol{Q}}_k,$$

which confirms that the $\boldsymbol{A}_k$ generated by the QR recurrence are indeed the same as if defined directly in terms of the initial matrix $\boldsymbol{A}$. We are now in a position to conclude that under the same conditions as for subspace iteration, the matrices $\boldsymbol{A}_k$ generated by QR iteration converge at least to block triangular form, and to triangular form when the eigenvalues of $\boldsymbol{A}$ are distinct in modulus. Obviously, the matrices $\boldsymbol{A}_k$ are unitarily similar to each other and to the initial matrix $\boldsymbol{A}$, and hence QR iteration effectively converges to the Schur form of $\boldsymbol{A}$, with the eigenvalues of $\boldsymbol{A}$ given by the diagonal entries (or diagonal blocks) and the eigenvectors obtained from the product of the unitary matrices $\boldsymbol{Q}_k$ generated by the algorithm. Note that if $\boldsymbol{A}$ is real symmetric (or complex Hermitian), then the symmetry is preserved by QR iteration. Thus, QR iteration converges in this case to a matrix that is both symmetric and triangular, and hence is diagonal.

Example 4.15 QR Iteration. To illustrate QR iteration, we will apply it to the real symmetric matrix

$$\boldsymbol{A} = \begin{bmatrix} 2.9766 & 0.3945 & 0.4198 & 1.1159 \\ 0.3945 & 2.7328 & -0.3097 & 0.1129 \\ 0.4198 & -0.3097 & 2.5675 & 0.6079 \\ 1.1159 & 0.1129 & 0.6079 & 1.7231 \end{bmatrix},$$

which has eigenvalues $\lambda_1 = 4$, $\lambda_2 = 3$, $\lambda_3 = 2$, $\lambda_4 = 1$. Computing its QR factorization and then forming the reverse product, we obtain

$$\boldsymbol{A}_1 = \begin{bmatrix} 3.7703 & 0.1745 & 0.5126 & -0.3934 \\ 0.1745 & 2.7675 & -0.3872 & 0.0539 \\ 0.5126 & -0.3872 & 2.4019 & -0.1241 \\ -0.3934 & 0.0539 & -0.1241 & 1.0603 \end{bmatrix}.$$

Most of the off-diagonal entries are now smaller in magnitude, and the diagonal entries are somewhat closer to the eigenvalues. Continuing for a couple more iterations, we obtain

$$\boldsymbol{A}_2 = \begin{bmatrix} 3.9436 & 0.0143 & 0.3046 & 0.1038 \\ 0.0143 & 2.8737 & -0.3362 & -0.0285 \\ 0.3046 & -0.3362 & 2.1785 & 0.0083 \\ 0.1038 & -0.0285 & 0.0083 & 1.0042 \end{bmatrix}$$

and

$$A_3 = \begin{bmatrix} 3.9832 & -0.0356 & 0.1611 & -0.0262 \\ -0.0356 & 2.9421 & -0.2432 & 0.0098 \\ 0.1611 & -0.2432 & 2.0743 & 0.0047 \\ -0.0262 & 0.0098 & 0.0047 & 1.0003 \end{bmatrix}.$$

The off-diagonal entries are now fairly small, and the diagonal entries are quite close to the eigenvalues. Only a few more iterations would be required to compute the eigenvalues to the full accuracy shown.

The reformulation of simultaneous iteration as QR iteration leads to a convenient and elegant implementation, but it does not by itself address the two major drawbacks noted earlier, slow convergence and high cost per iteration. We will now see that both of these shortcomings can be overcome effectively in the context of QR iteration to produce a highly efficient algorithm for computing all the eigenvalues and corresponding eigenvectors of any matrix.

As with any variant of power iteration, the convergence rate of QR iteration depends on the ratio of magnitudes of successive eigenvalues, and we have already seen that the value of this ratio can be made more favorable by using a shift. For each QR iteration, a shift is subtracted off before the QR factorization and then added back to the reverse product so that the resulting matrix will still be similar to the initial matrix. This process yields Algorithm 4.8.

Algorithm 4.8 QR Iteration with Shifts

$A_0 = A$
for $k = 1, 2, \ldots$
  Choose shift σ_k
  Compute QR factorization { normalize }
    $Q_k R_k = A_{k-1} - \sigma_k I$
  $A_k = R_k Q_k + \sigma_k I$ { generate next matrix }
end

Before discussing how to choose an appropriate value for the shift, we first make the important observation that QR iteration not only implements simultaneous iteration with A, but it also implicitly carries out simultaneous iteration with A^{-H} (i.e., inverse iteration with A^H) as well (see Exercise 2.9 for an explanation of this notation). To see this, we recall that

$$Q_k R_k = A_{k-1},$$

and if we invert and (Hermitian) transpose both sides, then we have

$$Q_k R_k^{-H} = A_{k-1}^{-H}.$$

Similarly, the subsequent reverse product gives

$$A_k^{-H} = R_k^{-H} Q_k,$$

and from

$$\boldsymbol{A}^k = \hat{\boldsymbol{Q}}_k \hat{\boldsymbol{R}}_k$$

we have

$$(\boldsymbol{A}^{-H})^k = \hat{\boldsymbol{Q}}_k \hat{\boldsymbol{R}}_k^{-H}.$$

Note that $\boldsymbol{R}_k^{-H}$ is a *lower* triangular matrix, which simply means that this dual "QL" orthogonalization procedure proceeds from right to left (i.e., starting with column n and working backward) instead of left to right. We can conclude that the columns of $\hat{\boldsymbol{Q}}_k$ produced by QR iteration are the same as would be produced by inverse iteration with $\boldsymbol{A}_k^H$.

We now know that QR iteration is just an implicit form of inverse iteration, and we had already seen that inverse iteration converges extremely rapidly when the shift is approximately equal to an eigenvalue, so this suggests that we should choose the shift σ_k at each iteration to approximate an eigenvalue. Now the lower right corner entry of $\boldsymbol{A}_{k-1}$, $a_{nn}^{(k-1)}$, is just such an approximate eigenvalue, since it is the Rayleigh quotient corresponding to the last column of $\hat{\boldsymbol{Q}}_k$, which as we have just seen is the result of applying inverse iteration with $\boldsymbol{A}^H$ to $\boldsymbol{e}_n$, and hence it converges to the eigenvector of $\boldsymbol{A}^H$ corresponding to the smallest eigenvalue in modulus, λ_n. Note that if $\sigma_k = a_{nn}^{(k-1)}$ were actually equal to λ_n, then $\boldsymbol{A}_{k-1} - \sigma_k \boldsymbol{I}$ would be singular, and the entire last row of the resulting $\boldsymbol{R}_k$, and hence also of the reverse product $\boldsymbol{R}_k \boldsymbol{Q}_k$, would be zero, so that $\boldsymbol{A}_k = \boldsymbol{R}_k \boldsymbol{Q}_k + \sigma_k \boldsymbol{I}$ would be block upper triangular, with its last row all zeros except for the eigenvalue in the last column. This suggests that we can declare convergence of the iterations to an eigenvalue when the magnitudes of the off-diagonal entries of the last row of $\boldsymbol{A}_k$ are sufficiently small (e.g., less than $\epsilon_{\text{mach}}\|\boldsymbol{A}\|$), at which point, due to the block triangular form, we can then restrict attention to the leading submatrix of dimension $n-1$. Continuing in this manner, eigenvalues of successively smaller matrices are deflated out until all the eigenvalues have been obtained.

Example 4.16 QR Iteration with Shifts. To illustrate the QR algorithm with shifts, we repeat Example 4.15 using the Rayleigh quotient shift (i.e., the (n, n) entry) at each iteration. Thus, with

$$\boldsymbol{A}_0 = \begin{bmatrix} 2.9766 & 0.3945 & 0.4198 & 1.1159 \\ 0.3945 & 2.7328 & -0.3097 & 0.1129 \\ 0.4198 & -0.3097 & 2.5675 & 0.6079 \\ 1.1159 & 0.1129 & 0.6079 & 1.7231 \end{bmatrix},$$

we use $\sigma_1 = 1.7231$ as shift for the first iteration. Computing the QR factorization of the resulting shifted matrix $\boldsymbol{A}_0 - \sigma_1 \boldsymbol{I}$, forming the reverse product, and then adding back the shift, we obtain

$$\boldsymbol{A}_1 = \begin{bmatrix} 3.8816 & -0.0178 & 0.2355 & 0.5065 \\ -0.0178 & 2.9528 & -0.2134 & -0.1602 \\ 0.2355 & -0.2134 & 2.0404 & -0.0951 \\ 0.5065 & -0.1602 & -0.0951 & 1.1253 \end{bmatrix},$$

which is noticeably closer to diagonal form and to the correct eigenvalues than after one iteration of the unshifted algorithm (compare with Example 4.15). Our next shift will be the current corner entry, $\sigma_2 = 1.1253$, which gives

$$A_2 = \begin{bmatrix} 3.9946 & -0.0606 & 0.0499 & 0.0233 \\ -0.0606 & 2.9964 & -0.0882 & -0.0103 \\ 0.0499 & -0.0882 & 2.0081 & -0.0252 \\ 0.0233 & -0.0103 & -0.0252 & 1.0009 \end{bmatrix}.$$

Our next shift, $\sigma_3 = 1.0009$, is very close to an eigenvalue and gives

$$A_3 = \begin{bmatrix} 3.9980 & -0.0426 & 0.0165 & 0.0000 \\ -0.0426 & 3.0000 & -0.0433 & 0.0000 \\ 0.0165 & -0.0433 & 2.0020 & 0.0000 \\ 0.0000 & 0.0000 & 0.0000 & 1.0000 \end{bmatrix},$$

which is very close to diagonal form. As expected for inverse iteration with a shift close to an eigenvalue, the smallest eigenvalue has been determined to the full accuracy shown. The last row of A_3 is all zeros (to the accuracy shown), so we can reduce the problem to the leading 3×3 submatrix for further iterations. Because the diagonal entries are already very close to the eigenvalues, only one or two additional iterations will be required to obtain full accuracy for the remaining eigenvalues.

As one might expect from its kinship with Rayleigh quotient iteration, the shifted QR iteration we have just described almost always converges very rapidly, at least quadratically and often cubically. However, there are some instances, for example when the shift is exactly halfway between two eigenvalues and hence favors neither, in which the simple Rayleigh quotient shift fails. A more robust alternative is the *Wilkinson shift*, which uses the eigenvalue of the 2×2 submatrix in the lower right corner of A_{k-1} that is closest to $a_{nn}^{(k-1)}$. Another complication we have glossed over is what to do for a real matrix when an eigenvalue is complex, which would appear to necessitate the use of complex arithmetic. It turns out, however, that two successive iterations, one with shift σ and the other with shift $\bar{\sigma}$, produce a real result, and they can be combined and implemented using only real arithmetic. An appropriate choice in this case is the *Francis shift*, which uses *both* of the eigenvalues of the 2×2 submatrix in the lower right corner of A_{k-1}, which will either both be real or else will be complex conjugates, so that a double shift can be performed using only real arithmetic.

There are extremely rare instances in which none of the systematic shifts yields convergence, so practical implementations of QR iteration usually include "exceptional" shifts, chosen essentially randomly, in cases where the usual shifts fail to yield convergence in a reasonable number of iterations. Yet another refinement of QR iteration is an implicit implementation that applies a sequence of similarity transformations directly to A, thereby avoiding the (rare) possibility of cancellation due to explicit subtraction of σI and also avoiding explicit computation of QR factorizations. Sophisticated, "industrial-strength" implementations of QR iteration, such as the implicit double-shift algorithm with a robust repertoire of shifting strategies, are so rapidly and reliably convergent that for practical purposes they can be considered essentially "direct" methods, as typically only two or three iterations are required per eigenvalue, so that the total cost of computing all the eigenvalues is only a small constant times n times the cost per iteration.

As we saw in Chapter 3, the QR factorization of a general $n \times n$ matrix that must be performed for each QR iteration requires $\mathcal{O}(n^3)$ work. This work could be substantially reduced, however, if the matrix were already nearly triangular before iterations begin. To obtain some insight into how to proceed, it is instructive to look more closely at what happens when we perform the QR factorization $\boldsymbol{A} = \boldsymbol{QR}$, typically using Householder transformations, and then form the reverse product to obtain a similarity transformation. We begin by annihilating the entries of the first column of $\boldsymbol{A}$ below the first row using a Householder transformation $\boldsymbol{H}_1$ whose corresponding Householder vector has a nonzero first component. Thus, when we postmultiply the resulting reduced matrix on the right by $\boldsymbol{H}_1^H = \boldsymbol{H}_1$, the first column will fill back in with nonzeros. If we are a bit less aggressive, however, and annihilate the entries in the first column of $\boldsymbol{A}$ only below the *second* row, then the resulting Householder vector will have zero as its first component, and hence when we subsequently postmultiply by the corresponding Householder transformation on the right, the zeros just introduced into the first column will be preserved. Continuing in this manner, annihilating the entries in each successive column below the first subdiagonal and then postmultiplying by the same transformation on the right, we arrive after $n-2$ steps at an upper Hessenberg matrix (i.e., zero below its first subdiagonal; see Section 4.2.4) that is similar to $\boldsymbol{A}$.

The initial reduction to Hessenberg form requires $\mathcal{O}(n^3)$ work, but what we have gained is that the QR factorization of an upper Hessenberg matrix, typically using Givens rotations, requires only $\mathcal{O}(n^2)$ work. Furthermore, Hessenberg form is preserved by QR iteration; that is, if $\boldsymbol{A}_{k-1}$ is an upper Hessenberg matrix, then, since $\boldsymbol{A}_{k-1} = \boldsymbol{Q}_k\boldsymbol{R}_k$,

$$\boldsymbol{A}_k = \boldsymbol{R}_k\boldsymbol{Q}_k = \boldsymbol{R}_k\boldsymbol{A}_{k-1}\boldsymbol{R}_k^{-1}$$

is also an upper Hessenberg matrix, since upper Hessenberg form is preserved under pre- or post-multiplication by an upper triangular matrix. Note that a symmetric or Hermitian Hessenberg matrix is tridiagonal, so for a real symmetric or complex Hermitian matrix, the initial reduction is to tridiagonal form, which is also preserved by QR iteration and is even more advantageous because the QR factorization of a tridiagonal matrix requires only $\mathcal{O}(n)$ work. The advantages of preliminary reduction to upper Hessenberg or tridiagonal form are summarized as follows:

- The work per QR iteration is reduced to $\mathcal{O}(n^2)$ for a general matrix, and to $\mathcal{O}(n)$ for a real symmetric or complex Hermitian matrix.
- Fewer QR iterations are required, since the matrix is already nearly triangular (or nearly diagonal in the symmetric or Hermitian case).
- If there are any zero entries on the first subdiagonal, then the Hessenberg matrix is block triangular, and hence the problem can be broken into smaller subproblems.

For these reasons, QR iteration is implemented as a two-stage process:

Symmetric	$\longrightarrow$	tridiagonal	$\longrightarrow$	diagonal
		or		
General	$\longrightarrow$	Hessenberg	$\longrightarrow$	triangular

The preliminary reduction requires a definite number of steps, whereas the subsequent iterative stage continues until convergence. In practice, however, only a small number of iterations is usually required, so the $\mathcal{O}(n^3)$ cost of the preliminary reduction actually dominates the cost of computing the eigenvalues. The total cost is strongly affected by whether the eigenvectors are needed, since their computation determines whether the orthogonal transformations must be accumulated. For the real symmetric case, the overall cost is roughly $\frac{4}{3}n^3$ arithmetic operations (counting both additions and multiplications) if only the eigenvalues are needed, and about $9n^3$ operations if the eigenvectors are also desired. For the general real case, the overall cost is roughly $10n^3$ operations if only the eigenvalues are needed, and about $25n^3$ operations if the eigenvectors are also desired.

QR iteration is a remarkably effective method for computing all the eigenvalues, and optionally the eigenvectors, of a full $n \times n$ matrix, but it does have some disadvantages, which accrue largely from the fact that we manipulate the *entire* matrix, both during the initial reduction and the subsequent iterative stage:

- It becomes prohibitively expensive for very large values of n.
- It takes no significant advantage when we need only a few of the eigenvalues and eigenvectors, as is often the case, especially when n is large.
- It requires an excessive amount of computer storage when the matrix is large and sparse, as the similarity transformations employed introduce many new nonzero entries that must be stored.

We will next consider an approach that enables the exploitation and preservation of sparsity by using the matrix only for matrix-vector multiplications, and solves only relatively small eigenvalue problems when only a few eigenvalues are needed.

4.5.7 Krylov Subspace Methods

QR iteration is based on simultaneous iteration starting with an orthonormal set of basis vectors—namely, the columns of the identity matrix—that span the entire space $\mathbb{R}^n$ (or $\mathbb{C}^n$). An alternative is to build up a subspace *incrementally*, one vector at a time. Let $\boldsymbol{A}$ be an $n \times n$ matrix, $\boldsymbol{x}_0$ an arbitrary nonzero starting vector, and for $k > 0$ define the *Krylov sequence* $\boldsymbol{x}_k = \boldsymbol{A}\boldsymbol{x}_{k-1}$ (i.e., the sequence generated by simple power iteration starting with $\boldsymbol{x}_0$). For each $k = 1, \ldots, n$, we then define the $n \times k$ *Krylov matrix*

$$\boldsymbol{K}_k = [\,\boldsymbol{x}_0 \quad \boldsymbol{x}_1 \quad \cdots \quad \boldsymbol{x}_{k-1}\,] = [\,\boldsymbol{x}_0 \quad \boldsymbol{A}\boldsymbol{x}_0 \quad \cdots \quad \boldsymbol{A}^{k-1}\boldsymbol{x}_0\,]$$

and the corresponding *Krylov subspace* $\mathcal{K}_k = \text{span}(\boldsymbol{K}_k)$. Observe that for $k = n$,

$$\boldsymbol{A}\boldsymbol{K}_n \quad = \quad [\,\boldsymbol{A}\boldsymbol{x}_0 \quad \cdots \quad \boldsymbol{A}\boldsymbol{x}_{n-2} \quad \boldsymbol{A}\boldsymbol{x}_{n-1}\,]$$

$$\begin{aligned} &= [\boldsymbol{x}_1 \quad \cdots \quad \boldsymbol{x}_{n-1} \quad \boldsymbol{x}_n] \\ &= \boldsymbol{K}_n [\boldsymbol{e}_2 \quad \cdots \quad \boldsymbol{e}_n \quad \boldsymbol{a}] \equiv \boldsymbol{K}_n \boldsymbol{C}_n, \end{aligned}$$

where $\boldsymbol{a} = \boldsymbol{K}_n^{-1}\boldsymbol{x}_n$, assuming $\boldsymbol{K}_n$ is nonsingular. We therefore have

$$\boldsymbol{K}_n^{-1}\boldsymbol{A}\boldsymbol{K}_n = \boldsymbol{C}_n,$$

so that $\boldsymbol{A}$ is similar to $\boldsymbol{C}_n$, which is an upper Hessenberg matrix (in fact, it is a companion matrix; see Section 4.2.1). We have thus derived a method for similarity reduction to Hessenberg form using only matrix-vector multiplication.

Unfortunately, the convergence of the successive columns of $\boldsymbol{K}_k$ to the dominant eigenvector of $\boldsymbol{A}$ means that $\boldsymbol{K}_n$ is likely to be an exceedingly ill-conditioned basis for $\mathcal{K}_n$, but we can remedy this by computing the QR factorization

$$\boldsymbol{Q}_n\boldsymbol{R}_n = \boldsymbol{K}_n,$$

so that the columns of the $n \times n$ matrix $\boldsymbol{Q}_n$ form an orthonormal basis for $\mathcal{K}_n$. We then have

$$\boldsymbol{Q}_n^H\boldsymbol{A}\boldsymbol{Q}_n = (\boldsymbol{K}_n\boldsymbol{R}_n^{-1})^{-1}\boldsymbol{A}\boldsymbol{K}_n\boldsymbol{R}_n^{-1} = \boldsymbol{R}_n\boldsymbol{K}_n^{-1}\boldsymbol{A}\boldsymbol{K}_n\boldsymbol{R}_n^{-1} = \boldsymbol{R}_n\boldsymbol{C}_n\boldsymbol{R}_n^{-1} \equiv \boldsymbol{H},$$

which, since the upper Hessenberg form of $\boldsymbol{C}_n$ is preserved under pre- or post-multiplication by an upper triangular matrix, is an upper Hessenberg matrix that is unitarily similar to $\boldsymbol{A}$.

For these developments to be useful, we still need to show that the columns of

$$\boldsymbol{Q}_n = [\boldsymbol{q}_1 \quad \boldsymbol{q}_2 \quad \cdots \quad \boldsymbol{q}_n]$$

can be computed one at a time. Equating the kth columns on each side of the equation $\boldsymbol{A}\boldsymbol{Q}_n = \boldsymbol{Q}_n\boldsymbol{H}$ yields the recurrence

$$\boldsymbol{A}\boldsymbol{q}_k = h_{1k}\boldsymbol{q}_1 + \cdots + h_{kk}\boldsymbol{q}_k + h_{k+1,k}\boldsymbol{q}_{k+1}$$

relating $\boldsymbol{q}_{k+1}$ to the preceding vectors $\boldsymbol{q}_1, \ldots, \boldsymbol{q}_k$. Premultiplying this equation by $\boldsymbol{q}_j^H$ and using orthonormality, we see that $h_{jk} = \boldsymbol{q}_j^H\boldsymbol{A}\boldsymbol{q}_k$, $j = 1, \ldots, k$. With appropriate normalization, these relationships yield Algorithm 4.9, due to Arnoldi, which is analogous to the Gram-Schmidt orthogonalization procedure given in Section 3.5.3. Note that this is the numerically superior modified version of Gram-Schmidt, because the "updated" vector $\boldsymbol{u}_k$ is used at each step of the inner loop, rather than the "original" $\boldsymbol{u}_k$ as in classical Gram-Schmidt. Even so, additional measures, such as iterative refinement, may be required to ensure that the computed vectors are orthogonal to working precision.

We can obtain eigenvalue and eigenvector approximations at a given step k of the Arnoldi process using a generalization of the Rayleigh quotient known as the *Rayleigh-Ritz procedure*, which in effect projects the matrix $\boldsymbol{A}$ onto the Krylov subspace $\mathcal{K}_k$. Let the $n \times k$ matrix

$$\boldsymbol{Q}_k = [\boldsymbol{q}_1 \quad \cdots \quad \boldsymbol{q}_k]$$

Algorithm 4.9 Arnoldi Iteration

$\boldsymbol{x}_0$ = arbitrary nonzero starting vector
$\boldsymbol{q}_1 = \boldsymbol{x}_0/\|\boldsymbol{x}_0\|_2$ { normalize }
for $k = 1, 2, \ldots$
  $\boldsymbol{u}_k = \boldsymbol{A}\boldsymbol{q}_k$ { generate next vector }
  for $j = 1$ **to** k { subtract from new vector its components in all preceding vectors }
    $h_{jk} = \boldsymbol{q}_j^H \boldsymbol{u}_k$
    $\boldsymbol{u}_k = \boldsymbol{u}_k - h_{jk}\boldsymbol{q}_j$
  end
  $h_{k+1,k} = \|\boldsymbol{u}_k\|_2$
  if $h_{k+1,k} = 0$ **then** stop { stop if matrix is reducible }
  $\boldsymbol{q}_{k+1} = \boldsymbol{u}_k/h_{k+1,k}$ { normalize }
end

contain the first k Arnoldi vectors $\boldsymbol{q}_j$, and let the $n \times (n-k)$ matrix

$$\boldsymbol{U}_k = [\,\boldsymbol{q}_{k+1} \quad \cdots \quad \boldsymbol{q}_n\,]$$

contain the remaining Arnoldi vectors yet to be computed, so that $\boldsymbol{Q}_n = [\boldsymbol{Q}_k \ \ \boldsymbol{U}_k]$. Then we have

$$\boldsymbol{H} = \boldsymbol{Q}_n^H \boldsymbol{A} \boldsymbol{Q}_n = \begin{bmatrix} \boldsymbol{Q}_k^H \\ \boldsymbol{U}_k^H \end{bmatrix} \boldsymbol{A}\,[\,\boldsymbol{Q}_k \quad \boldsymbol{U}_k\,] = \begin{bmatrix} \boldsymbol{Q}_k^H\boldsymbol{A}\boldsymbol{Q}_k & \boldsymbol{Q}_k^H\boldsymbol{A}\boldsymbol{U}_k \\ \boldsymbol{U}_k^H\boldsymbol{A}\boldsymbol{Q}_k & \boldsymbol{U}_k^H\boldsymbol{A}\boldsymbol{U}_k \end{bmatrix} = \begin{bmatrix} \boldsymbol{H}_k & \boldsymbol{M} \\ \tilde{\boldsymbol{H}}_k & \boldsymbol{N} \end{bmatrix},$$

where $\boldsymbol{M}$ and $\boldsymbol{N}$ are matrices yet to be computed. Because $\boldsymbol{H}$ is upper Hessenberg, we can conclude that $\boldsymbol{H}_k$ is also upper Hessenberg and that $\tilde{\boldsymbol{H}}_k$ has at most one nonzero entry, $h_{k+1,k}$, in its upper right corner. The eigenvalues of $\boldsymbol{H}_k$ are called *Ritz values*, and the vectors $\boldsymbol{Q}_k\boldsymbol{y}$, where $\boldsymbol{y}$ is an eigenvector of $\boldsymbol{H}_k$, are called *Ritz vectors*. It can be shown that the Ritz values converge to eigenvalues of $\boldsymbol{A}$, and the corresponding Ritz vectors usually converge to the corresponding eigenvectors of $\boldsymbol{A}$. Of course, one must still compute the eigenvalues and eigenvectors of the Hessenberg matrix $\boldsymbol{H}_k$ by some other method, such as QR iteration, but this is a much easier problem if $k \ll n$, and in practice the Rayleigh-Ritz procedure usually produces good approximations to the extreme eigenvalues of $\boldsymbol{A}$ after a relatively small number of iterations of the Arnoldi process.

Arnoldi iteration appears to break down if $h_{k+1,k} = 0$ at any step k, but in fact this is beneficial in that it implies that $\tilde{\boldsymbol{H}}_k = \boldsymbol{O}$, which means that $\boldsymbol{H}$ is block triangular, $\mathcal{K}_k$ is an invariant subspace, and the corresponding Ritz values and vectors obtained from $\boldsymbol{H}_k$ are eigenvalues and eigenvectors of $\boldsymbol{A}$.

The amount of work required by the Arnoldi process grows rapidly with the number of iterations: the kth iteration requires a matrix-vector multiplication by $\boldsymbol{A}$ plus $\mathcal{O}(kn)$ additional work to orthogonalize the kth Arnoldi vector against all of the previous ones, and computation of Ritz values and vectors (eigenvalues and eigenvectors of $\boldsymbol{H}_k$) would require another $\mathcal{O}(k^3)$ work. One must also store the matrix $\boldsymbol{Q}_k$ of Arnoldi vectors and the Hessenberg matrix $\boldsymbol{H}_k$. For this reason, in practical implementations the Arnoldi process is typically run for only a few iterations and then restarted with a new starting vector that is carefully constructed, based on information already generated, to be relatively rich in components of the desired eigenvectors. A few repetitions of the restarted Arnoldi process usually produces excellent approximations to the extreme eigenvalues and corresponding eigenvectors of $\boldsymbol{A}$ with a reasonable amount of work.

All of the computational and storage costs associated with the Arnoldi process drop dramatically if the matrix is symmetric (or Hermitian). In particular, the matrix $\boldsymbol{H}_k$ is then tridiagonal (and therefore is usually denoted instead by $\boldsymbol{T}_k$), and the relation between the vectors $\boldsymbol{q}_k$ becomes a three-term recurrence, which greatly reduces both the work and the storage required. This symmetric version yields Algorithm 4.10, due to Lanczos.

Algorithm 4.10 Lanczos Iteration

$\boldsymbol{q}_0 = \boldsymbol{0}$	{ initialize }
$\beta_0 = 0$	
$\boldsymbol{x}_0 =$ arbitrary nonzero starting vector	
$\boldsymbol{q}_1 = \boldsymbol{x}_0/\|\boldsymbol{x}_0\|_2$	{ normalize }
for $k = 1, 2, \ldots$	
$\boldsymbol{u}_k = \boldsymbol{A}\boldsymbol{q}_k$	{ generate next vector }
$\alpha_k = \boldsymbol{q}_k^H \boldsymbol{u}_k$	{ subtract off its components
$\boldsymbol{u}_k = \boldsymbol{u}_k - \beta_{k-1}\boldsymbol{q}_{k-1} - \alpha_k \boldsymbol{q}_k$	in two preceding vectors }
$\beta_k = \|\boldsymbol{u}_k\|_2$	
if $\beta_k = 0$ **then** stop	{ stop if matrix is reducible }
$\boldsymbol{q}_{k+1} = \boldsymbol{u}_k/\beta_k$	{ normalize }
end	

The α_k and β_k generated by Lanczos iteration are the diagonal and subdiagonal entries, respectively, of the Hermitian tridiagonal matrix $\boldsymbol{T}_k$, whose eigenvalues and eigenvectors must be determined by some other method, but again this is relatively easy if $k \ll n$, and in practice excellent approximations to the extreme eigenvalues of $\boldsymbol{A}$ are obtained after a relatively small number of iterations. Lanczos iteration appears to break down if $\beta_k = 0$ at any step k, but in that case an invariant subspace has already been identified, and the Ritz values and Ritz vectors obtained from $\boldsymbol{T}_k$ are eigenvalues and eigenvectors of $\boldsymbol{A}$. A potential pitfall in finite-precision arithmetic is a loss of orthogonality among the computed Lanczos vectors $\boldsymbol{q}_k$ due to rounding errors. This problem can be overcome by reorthogonalizing the vectors as needed, but the expense of doing so can be substantial. Alternatively, one can ignore the problem, in which case the algorithm still tends to produce good eigenvalue approximations, but multiple copies of some eigenvalues may be generated.

Example 4.17 Lanczos Iteration. The behavior of Lanczos iteration is illustrated in Fig. 4.4, where the algorithm is applied to a matrix of order 29 whose eigenvalues are $1, \ldots, 29$. The iteration count is plotted on the vertical axis, and the corresponding Ritz values γ_j are on the horizontal axis. At each iteration k, the points (γ_j, k), $j = 1, \ldots, k$, are plotted. We see that the extreme eigenvalues are closely approximated by Ritz values after only a few iterations, but the interior eigenvalues take much longer to appear. For this small matrix with well-separated eigenvalues, the Ritz values are identical to the eigenvalues after 29 iterations, as theory predicts, but for more realistic problems this cannot be relied upon owing to rounding error. Moreover, running the algorithm for a full n iterations is generally infeasible if n is very large. The main point, however, is the relatively rapid convergence to the extreme eigenvalues, which is typical of Lanczos iteration in general.

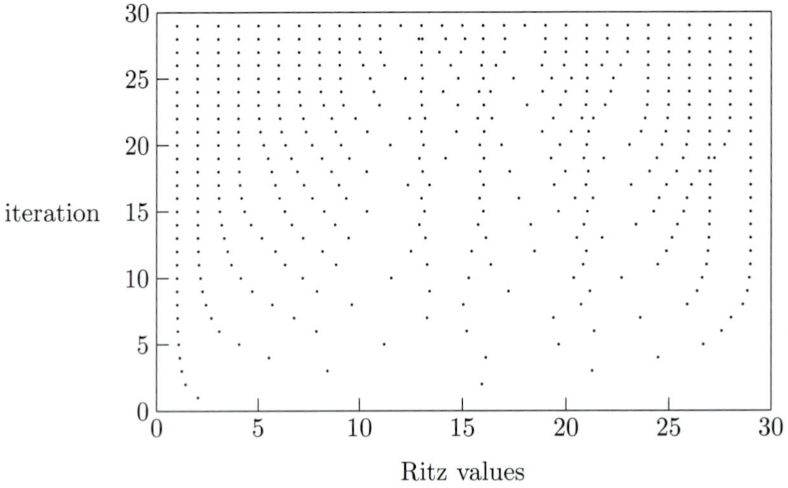

Figure 4.4: Convergence of Ritz values to eigenvalues in Lanczos method.

The Arnoldi and Lanczos iterations most quickly produce approximate eigenvalues near the ends of the spectrum. If eigenvalues are needed from the middle of the spectrum, say, near the value σ, then these iterations can be applied to the matrix $(\boldsymbol{A} - \sigma \boldsymbol{I})^{-1}$, assuming that it is practical to solve systems of the form $(\boldsymbol{A} - \sigma \boldsymbol{I})\boldsymbol{x} = \boldsymbol{y}$. Such a "shift-and-invert" strategy enables much more rapid convergence to interior eigenvalues, since they correspond to extreme eigenvalues of the shifted matrix.

4.5.8 Jacobi Method

One of the oldest methods for computing all the eigenvalues of a real symmetric (or complex Hermitian) matrix is due to Jacobi. Starting with a real symmetric matrix $\boldsymbol{A}_0 = \boldsymbol{A}$, each iteration has the form

$$\boldsymbol{A}_{k+1} = \boldsymbol{J}_k^T \boldsymbol{A}_k \boldsymbol{J}_k,$$

where $\boldsymbol{J}_k$ is a plane rotation chosen to annihilate a symmetric pair of entries in the matrix $\boldsymbol{A}_k$ (so that the symmetry of the original matrix is preserved). Recall from Section 3.5.2 that a plane rotation is an orthogonal matrix that differs from the identity matrix $\boldsymbol{I}$ in only four entries, and this 2×2 submatrix has the form

$$\begin{bmatrix} c & s \\ -s & c \end{bmatrix},$$

with c and s the cosine and sine of the angle of rotation, respectively, so that $c^2 + s^2 = 1$. The choice of c and s is slightly more complicated in this context than in the Givens method for QR factorization because we are annihilating a symmetric pair of matrix entries by a similarity transformation, as opposed to annihilating a single entry by a one-sided transformation. As before, it suffices to consider only the 2×2 case,

$$\begin{aligned} \boldsymbol{J}^T \boldsymbol{A} \boldsymbol{J} &= \begin{bmatrix} c & -s \\ s & c \end{bmatrix} \begin{bmatrix} a & b \\ b & d \end{bmatrix} \begin{bmatrix} c & s \\ -s & c \end{bmatrix} \\ &= \begin{bmatrix} c^2 a - 2csb + s^2 d & c^2 b + cs(a-d) - s^2 b \\ c^2 b + cs(a-d) - s^2 b & c^2 d + 2csb + s^2 a \end{bmatrix}, \end{aligned}$$

where $b \neq 0$ (else there is nothing to do). The transformed matrix will be diagonal if

$$c^2 b + cs(a-d) - s^2 b = 0.$$

Dividing both sides of this equation by $c^2 b$, we obtain

$$1 + \frac{s}{c}\,\frac{(a-d)}{b} - \frac{s^2}{c^2} = 0.$$

Making the substitution $t = s/c$, we obtain a quadratic equation

$$1 + t\,\frac{(a-d)}{b} - t^2 = 0$$

for t, the tangent of the angle of rotation, from which we can recover $c = 1/\sqrt{1+t^2}$ and $s = c \cdot t$. It is advantageous numerically to use the root of smaller magnitude of the equation for t.

Example 4.18 Jacobi Rotation. To illustrate the use of a plane rotation to annihilate a symmetric pair of off-diagonal entries, we consider the 2×2 matrix

$$\boldsymbol{A} = \begin{bmatrix} 1 & 2 \\ 2 & 1 \end{bmatrix}.$$

The quadratic equation for the tangent reduces to $t^2 = 1$ in this case, so we have $t = \pm 1$. The two roots are of the same magnitude, so we arbitrarily choose $t = -1$, which yields $c = 1/\sqrt{2}$ and $s = -1/\sqrt{2}$. The resulting plane rotation $\boldsymbol{J}$ gives

$$\boldsymbol{J}^T \boldsymbol{A} \boldsymbol{J} = \begin{bmatrix} 1/\sqrt{2} & 1/\sqrt{2} \\ -1/\sqrt{2} & 1/\sqrt{2} \end{bmatrix} \begin{bmatrix} 1 & 2 \\ 2 & 1 \end{bmatrix} \begin{bmatrix} 1/\sqrt{2} & -1/\sqrt{2} \\ 1/\sqrt{2} & 1/\sqrt{2} \end{bmatrix} = \begin{bmatrix} 3 & 0 \\ 0 & -1 \end{bmatrix}.$$

For an $n \times n$ symmetric matrix, the classical Jacobi method uses a plane rotation to annihilate the largest symmetric pair of off-diagonal entries of $\boldsymbol{A}_k$ at iteration k, but this requires an expensive search to find the largest entry. More modern implementations instead make cyclic sweeps through the matrix, annihilating symmetric off-diagonal entries in a systematic row-wise or column-wise order. With an appropriate ordering for the successive annihilations, the sum of squares of the off-diagonal entries decreases by at least a constant factor for each sweep, and thus the resulting sequence of matrices converges at least linearly to a diagonal matrix (in fact, convergence is ultimately quadratic). In practice, convergence is declared when all of the off-diagonal entries of the matrix have been reduced below some small tolerance. The resulting approximately diagonal matrix is orthogonally similar to the original matrix, so its diagonal entries are approximate eigenvalues, and the product of all the plane rotations gives the corresponding eigenvectors, if needed.

The Jacobi method is reliable, simple to program, capable of very high accuracy, and its asymptotic convergence rate is quadratic. However, a single Jacobi sweep requires almost as much work as computing the eigenvalues and eigenvectors using tridiagonal reduction followed by QR iteration. Thus, since it typically requires five to ten sweeps to converge, the Jacobi method usually requires five to ten times more work than QR iteration to compute the eigenvalues and eigenvectors of a symmetric matrix. The main source of inefficiency in the Jacobi method is that matrix entries that have previously been annihilated can subsequently become nonzero again, thereby requiring repeated annihilation. The main computational advantage of more modern methods such as QR iteration is that they are carefully designed to preserve zero entries once they have been introduced into the matrix. Recently, however, the Jacobi method has regained some popularity because it is relatively easy to implement efficiently on parallel computers.

Example 4.19 Jacobi Method. Let

$$\boldsymbol{A}_0 = \boldsymbol{A} = \begin{bmatrix} 1 & 0 & 2 \\ 0 & 2 & 1 \\ 2 & 1 & 1 \end{bmatrix}.$$

The cyclic Jacobi method repeatedly sweeps through the matrix annihilating successive off-diagonal entries. We first annihilate the symmetrically placed (1, 3) and (3, 1) entries using the plane rotation

$$\boldsymbol{J}_0 = \begin{bmatrix} 0.707 & 0 & -0.707 \\ 0 & 1 & 0 \\ 0.707 & 0 & 0.707 \end{bmatrix}$$

to obtain

$$\boldsymbol{A}_1 = \boldsymbol{J}_0^T \boldsymbol{A}_0 \boldsymbol{J}_0 = \begin{bmatrix} 3 & 0.707 & 0 \\ 0.707 & 2 & 0.707 \\ 0 & 0.707 & -1 \end{bmatrix}.$$

We next annihilate the symmetrically placed (1, 2) and (2, 1) entries using the plane rotation

$$J_1 = \begin{bmatrix} 0.888 & -0.460 & 0 \\ 0.460 & 0.888 & 0 \\ 0 & 0 & 1 \end{bmatrix}$$

to obtain

$$A_2 = J_1^T A_1 J_1 = \begin{bmatrix} 3.366 & 0 & 0.325 \\ 0 & 1.634 & 0.628 \\ 0.325 & 0.628 & -1 \end{bmatrix}.$$

We next annihilate the symmetrically placed (2, 3) and (3, 2) entries using the plane rotation

$$J_2 = \begin{bmatrix} 1 & 0 & 0 \\ 0 & 0.975 & -0.221 \\ 0 & 0.221 & 0.975 \end{bmatrix}$$

to obtain

$$A_3 = J_2^T A_2 J_2 = \begin{bmatrix} 3.366 & 0.072 & 0.317 \\ 0.072 & 1.776 & 0 \\ 0.317 & 0 & -1.142 \end{bmatrix}.$$

Beginning a new sweep, we again annihilate the symmetrically placed (1, 3) and (3, 1) entries using the plane rotation

$$J_3 = \begin{bmatrix} 0.998 & 0 & -0.070 \\ 0 & 1 & 0 \\ 0.070 & 0 & 0.998 \end{bmatrix}$$

to obtain

$$A_4 = J_3^T A_3 J_3 = \begin{bmatrix} 3.388 & 0.072 & 0 \\ 0.072 & 1.776 & -0.005 \\ 0 & -0.005 & -1.164 \end{bmatrix}.$$

This process continues until the off-diagonal entries are reduced to as small a magnitude as desired. The result is an approximately diagonal matrix that is orthogonally similar to the original matrix, with the orthogonal similarity transformation given by the product of the plane rotations.

4.5.9 Bisection or Spectrum-Slicing

Another family of methods is based on *counting* eigenvalues. For a real symmetric (or complex Hermitian) matrix, there are various methods for determining the number of eigenvalues that are less than a given real number σ. By systematically choosing various values for σ (slicing the spectrum at σ) and monitoring the resulting count, any eigenvalue can be isolated as accurately as desired. We sketch such methods briefly here.

Let $\boldsymbol{A}$ be a real symmetric matrix. The *inertia* of $\boldsymbol{A}$ is a triple of integers consisting of the numbers of positive, negative, and zero eigenvalues. A *congruence transformation* has the form $\boldsymbol{SAS}^T$, where $\boldsymbol{S}$ is any nonsingular matrix. Unless $\boldsymbol{S}^T = \boldsymbol{S}^{-1}$ (i.e., $\boldsymbol{S}$ is orthogonal), a congruence is not a similarity transformation and hence does not preserve the eigenvalues of $\boldsymbol{A}$. However, by *Sylvester's Law of Inertia*, a congruence transformation does preserve the inertia of $\boldsymbol{A}$, i.e., the numbers of positive, negative, and zero eigenvalues are invariant under congruence transformations.

If we can find a congruence transformation that makes the inertia easy to determine, then we can apply it to the matrix $\boldsymbol{A} - \sigma\boldsymbol{I}$ to determine the numbers of eigenvalues to the right or left of σ. An obvious candidate is the $\boldsymbol{LDL}^T$ factorization discussed in Section 2.5.2, where $\boldsymbol{D}$ is a matrix whose inertia is easily determined. By computing the $\boldsymbol{LDL}^T$ factorization, and hence the inertia, of $\boldsymbol{A} - \sigma\boldsymbol{I}$ for any desired value of σ, individual eigenvalues can be isolated as accurately as desired using an interval bisection technique (see Section 5.5.1).

The most commonly used spectrum-slicing method for computing individual eigenvalues is based on the *Sturm sequence property* of symmetric matrices. Let $\boldsymbol{A}$ be a symmetric matrix and let $p_k(\sigma)$ denote the determinant of the leading principal submatrix of order k of $\boldsymbol{A} - \sigma\boldsymbol{I}$. Then the zeros of $p_k(\sigma)$ strictly separate (i.e., are interleaved with) those of $p_{k-1}(\sigma)$. Furthermore, the number of agreements in sign of successive members of the sequence $p_k(\sigma)$, for $k = 1, \ldots, n$, is equal to the number of eigenvalues of $\boldsymbol{A}$ that are strictly greater than σ. This property allows the determination of the number of eigenvalues lying in a given interval, and again bisection can be used to isolate a given eigenvalue as accurately as desired. The determinants $p_k(\sigma)$ are especially easy to compute if $\boldsymbol{A}$ is tridiagonal, in which case the successive determinants are related by a three-term recurrence, so $\boldsymbol{A}$ is usually reduced to tridiagonal form by a similarity transformation before applying the Sturm sequence technique. This is currently the standard method for computing eigenvalues of dense symmetric matrices when only a few eigenvalues are needed, say the largest, or smallest, or all the eigenvalues lying in a specified interval. Once the desired eigenvalues have been computed, the corresponding eigenvectors can be computed, if needed, using inverse iteration with the computed eigenvalues as shifts.

4.5.10 Divide-and-Conquer

Yet another method for computing eigenvalues and eigenvectors of real symmetric matrices is based on a divide-and-conquer approach. Let $\boldsymbol{T}$ be an $n \times n$ real symmetric tridiagonal matrix (which may have resulted from preliminary reduction of a general real symmetric matrix). We begin by expressing $\boldsymbol{T}$ as a sum of two matrices, the first block diagonal with tridiagonal blocks and the second of rank one. Specifically, we take

$$\boldsymbol{T} = \begin{bmatrix} \boldsymbol{T}_1 & \boldsymbol{O} \\ \boldsymbol{O} & \boldsymbol{T}_2 \end{bmatrix} + \beta\, \boldsymbol{u}\boldsymbol{u}^T,$$

where the $k \times k$ matrix $\boldsymbol{T}_1$ and the $(n-k) \times (n-k)$ matrix $\boldsymbol{T}_2$ are tridiagonal, $\beta = t_{k+1,k} = t_{k,k+1}$, and $\boldsymbol{u} = \boldsymbol{e}_k + \boldsymbol{e}_{k+1}$ (i.e., $\boldsymbol{u}$ has all components 0 except for components k and $k+1$, both of which are 1). We then compute the eigenvalues and eigenvectors of the smaller symmetric tridiagonal matrices $\boldsymbol{T}_1$ and $\boldsymbol{T}_2$, obtaining

$$\boldsymbol{Q}_1^T \boldsymbol{T}_1 \boldsymbol{Q}_1 = \boldsymbol{D}_1 \quad \text{and} \quad \boldsymbol{Q}_2^T \boldsymbol{T}_2 \boldsymbol{Q}_2 = \boldsymbol{D}_2,$$

where $\boldsymbol{D}_1$ and $\boldsymbol{D}_2$ are diagonal and $\boldsymbol{Q}_1$ and $\boldsymbol{Q}_2$ are orthogonal. Letting $\boldsymbol{D} = \text{diag}(\boldsymbol{D}_1, \boldsymbol{D}_2)$ and $\boldsymbol{Q} = \text{diag}(\boldsymbol{Q}_1, \boldsymbol{Q}_2)$, we then have

$$\begin{aligned}
\boldsymbol{Q}^T \boldsymbol{T} \boldsymbol{Q} &= \begin{bmatrix} \boldsymbol{Q}_1^T & \boldsymbol{O} \\ \boldsymbol{O} & \boldsymbol{Q}_2^T \end{bmatrix} \left(\begin{bmatrix} \boldsymbol{T}_1 & \boldsymbol{O} \\ \boldsymbol{O} & \boldsymbol{T}_2 \end{bmatrix} + \beta\, \boldsymbol{u}\boldsymbol{u}^T \right) \begin{bmatrix} \boldsymbol{Q}_1 & \boldsymbol{O} \\ \boldsymbol{O} & \boldsymbol{Q}_2 \end{bmatrix} \\
&= \begin{bmatrix} \boldsymbol{Q}_1^T \boldsymbol{T}_1 \boldsymbol{Q}_1 & \boldsymbol{O} \\ \boldsymbol{O} & \boldsymbol{Q}_2^T \boldsymbol{T}_2 \boldsymbol{Q}_2 \end{bmatrix} + \beta \begin{bmatrix} \boldsymbol{Q}_1^T & \boldsymbol{O} \\ \boldsymbol{O} & \boldsymbol{Q}_2^T \end{bmatrix} \boldsymbol{u}\boldsymbol{u}^T \begin{bmatrix} \boldsymbol{Q}_1 & \boldsymbol{O} \\ \boldsymbol{O} & \boldsymbol{Q}_2 \end{bmatrix} \\
&= \boldsymbol{D} + \beta\, \boldsymbol{v}\boldsymbol{v}^T,
\end{aligned}$$

where

$$\boldsymbol{v} = \boldsymbol{Q}^T \boldsymbol{u} = \begin{bmatrix} \boldsymbol{Q}_1^T & \boldsymbol{O} \\ \boldsymbol{O} & \boldsymbol{Q}_2^T \end{bmatrix} \boldsymbol{u} = \begin{bmatrix} \boldsymbol{v}_1 \\ \boldsymbol{v}_2 \end{bmatrix}.$$

Because of the special form of $\boldsymbol{u}$, $\boldsymbol{v}_1$ is just the last column of $\boldsymbol{Q}_1^T$ and $\boldsymbol{v}_2$ is the first column of $\boldsymbol{Q}_2^T$.

At this point we have reduced the original eigenvalue problem for a symmetric tridiagonal matrix to that of computing the eigenvalues and eigenvectors of a rank-one modification of a diagonal matrix. To solve the latter eigenvalue problem, we consider its characteristic polynomial, $p(\lambda)$. Assuming λ is not an eigenvalue of $\boldsymbol{D}$, then $\boldsymbol{D} - \lambda \boldsymbol{I}$ is nonsingular, and we have

$$\boldsymbol{D} + \beta\, \boldsymbol{v}\boldsymbol{v}^T - \lambda \boldsymbol{I} = (\boldsymbol{D} - \lambda \boldsymbol{I}) \left(\boldsymbol{I} + \beta\, (\boldsymbol{D} - \lambda \boldsymbol{I})^{-1} \boldsymbol{v}\boldsymbol{v}^T \right).$$

Thus,

$$p(\lambda) = \det\left(\boldsymbol{D} + \beta\, \boldsymbol{v}\boldsymbol{v}^T - \lambda \boldsymbol{I} \right) = \det(\boldsymbol{D} - \lambda \boldsymbol{I}) \cdot \det\left(\boldsymbol{I} + \beta\, (\boldsymbol{D} - \lambda \boldsymbol{I})^{-1} \boldsymbol{v}\boldsymbol{v}^T \right).$$

By assumption $\det(\boldsymbol{D} - \lambda \boldsymbol{I}) \neq 0$, so we conclude that $p(\lambda) = 0$ precisely when $\det\left(\boldsymbol{I} + \beta\, (\boldsymbol{D} - \lambda \boldsymbol{I})^{-1} \boldsymbol{v}\boldsymbol{v}^T \right) = 0$. By Exercise 4.25, the determinant of this rank-one modification of the identity matrix has the value

$$\det\left(\boldsymbol{I} + \beta\, (\boldsymbol{D} - \lambda \boldsymbol{I})^{-1} \boldsymbol{v}\boldsymbol{v}^T \right) = 1 + \beta\, \boldsymbol{v}^T (\boldsymbol{D} - \lambda \boldsymbol{I})^{-1} \boldsymbol{v} = 1 + \beta \sum_{j=1}^{n} \frac{v_j^2}{d_j - \lambda} \equiv f(\lambda).$$

Thus, the roots of the characteristic polynomial $p(\lambda)$ are given by the zeros of the rational function $f(\lambda)$. The roots of $f(\lambda) = 0$, which is called the *secular equation*, can be computed efficiently and reliably using a one-dimensional nonlinear equation solver such as Newton's method (see Section 5.5). Once an eigenvalue λ has been found, then a corresponding eigenvector of $\boldsymbol{D} + \beta \boldsymbol{v}\boldsymbol{v}^T$ is given by $(\boldsymbol{D} - \lambda \boldsymbol{I})^{-1} \boldsymbol{v}$, as can be verified by direct multiplication. Unfortunately, when two eigenvalues are very close, the cancellation incurred in $\boldsymbol{D} - \lambda \boldsymbol{I}$ may cause the resulting eigenvectors to be inaccurate and far from orthogonal, so a more sophisticated approach is required. These difficulties with numerical stability and eigenvector orthogonality remained unsolved for several years after the divide-and-conquer method was initially proposed, but these obstacles were ultimately overcome—though we omit the details—to produce accurate and reliable implementations of the method that have found a place in standard software packages, such as LAPACK, alongside routines based on tried and true methods such as QR iteration.

Another issue we have glossed over is what happens when the diagonal entries of $\boldsymbol{D}$ are not all distinct or some $v_j = 0$. In such cases the secular equation has fewer than n roots, which may seem problematic, but such a situation is actually beneficial because then the relevant diagonal entries d_j are in fact eigenvalues of $\boldsymbol{D} + \beta \boldsymbol{v}\boldsymbol{v}^T$. Such deflation tends to occur quite frequently in practice, thereby speeding up the algorithm substantially.

Having shown how to solve a symmetric tridiagonal eigenvalue problem by breaking it into two smaller symmetric tridiagonal eigenvalue problems, we can apply this technique recursively at each level to obtain a divide-and-conquer algorithm for computing the eigenvalues and eigenvectors of the original matrix. For maximum advantage, each problem should be split approximately in half (i.e., $k \approx n/2$) at each level. In principle, recursion can be carried out all the way down to the bottom, but in practice it is more efficient to switch to another method, such as QR iteration, when the matrices become sufficiently small. For larger matrices, divide-and-conquer offers no significant advantage over QR iteration if only the eigenvalues are required, but it reduces the total work for a general real symmetric matrix (including the preliminary reduction to tridiagonal form) by more than half if the eigenvectors are also needed, and often does much better still due to substantial deflation. Thus, divide-and-conquer is often significantly faster than QR iteration for computing all the eigenvalues and eigenvectors of a symmetric matrix.

4.5.11 Relatively Robust Representation

We have seen several methods that can effectively compute the eigenvalues of a real symmetric tridiagonal matrix in $\mathcal{O}(n^2)$ floating-point operations. But every method we have seen thus far generally requires $\mathcal{O}(n^3)$ work to compute the corresponding mutually orthogonal eigenvectors. Can we do better? In QR iteration, orthogonal eigenvectors are computed by accumulating the orthogonal transformations along the way, which inevitably requires $\mathcal{O}(n^3)$ work. The divide-and-conquer method can do better if the amount of deflation is sufficiently favorable, but $\mathcal{O}(n^3)$ work is still required in the worst case. Both of these algorithms produce the eigenvectors as an integral part of the overall algorithm. Another possibility would be first to compute the eigenvalues by a separate $\mathcal{O}(n^2)$ algorithm, and then determine the eigenvectors using inverse iteration with the computed eigenvalues as shifts. With such good shifts, only a very small number of iterations should be required per eigenvector, and since the matrix is tridiagonal, each iteration costs only $\mathcal{O}(n)$ work, for an effective total cost of $\mathcal{O}(n^2)$ work for computing all of the eigenvectors. Unfortunately, there are several flaws in such a scheme:

- The starting vector for computing a given eigenvector must have a nonzero component in that eigenvector. A random starting vector would satisfy this requirement with high probability, but for quick and sure convergence, the starting vector needs to be relatively rich in the corresponding eigenvector.
- With an approximate eigenvalue as shift, the linear system to be solved will be highly ill-conditioned, and hence the right-hand-side vector may need to be scaled to prevent overflow.
- The eigenvectors computed independently for different eigenvalues, especially for close eigenvalues, may not be orthogonal. Of course, the computed eigenvectors could be explicitly orthogonalized, but this would incur the $\mathcal{O}(n^3)$ work we are trying to avoid.

All of these obstacles are addressed in the recently developed *relatively robust representation* (RRR) method. The name of the method comes from the fact that the eigenvalues of a tridiagonal matrix can be relatively sensitive to perturbations in its diagonal and off-diagonal entries (thereby limiting the accuracy with which the eigenvalues can be computed), but there are alternative representations of the matrix for which the eigenvalues are much less sensitive to perturbations. For example, it can be shown that the eigenvalues are much less sensitive to perturbations in the entries of the bidiagonal Cholesky or LDL^T factors of the (possibly shifted) tridiagonal matrix. Such alternative representations enable computation of the eigenvalues, even tightly clustered ones, to high relative accuracy, with the help of a shift that makes the gaps between clustered eigenvalues relatively large. High accuracy turns out to be the key, because if the eigenvalues and corresponding eigenvectors are computed with sufficiently high accuracy, then the eigenvectors will *automatically* be orthogonal, and thus will not require explicit, and expensive, orthogonalization.

Another key feature of the RRR algorithm is the systematic choice of a good starting vector for inverse iteration with the shifted tridiagonal matrix $\boldsymbol{T} - \lambda \boldsymbol{I}$, where λ is an approximate eigenvalue. This is accomplished by means of a *twisted factorization*, which is a combination of two partial triangular factorizations of the tridiagonal matrix obtained by eliminating successive subdiagonal entries starting from the upper left, and also eliminating successive superdiagonal entries starting from the lower right, until the eliminations meet, say at row k, which is then zero except for the diagonal entry, say d_k. Schematically, the sequence of annihilations for $n = 5$ and $k = 3$ has the form

$$\begin{bmatrix} \times & \times & & & \\ \times & \times & \times & & \\ & \times & \times & \times & \\ & & \times & \times & \times \\ & & & \times & \times \end{bmatrix} \rightarrow \begin{bmatrix} \times & \times & & & \\ & \times & \times & & \\ & \times & \times & \times & \\ & & \times & \times & \\ & & & \times & \times \end{bmatrix} \rightarrow \begin{bmatrix} \times & \times & & & \\ & \times & \times & & \\ & & \times & & \\ & & \times & \times & \\ & & & \times & \times \end{bmatrix},$$

where $\times$ indicates a nonzero entry and blank indicates a zero entry. It turns out that $d_k \boldsymbol{e}_k$ is a good starting vector for inverse iteration, where $|d_k|$ is as small as possible over all choices of k, $1 \le k \le n$. All n possible twisted factorizations can be computed with only $\mathcal{O}(n)$ work, and there are heuristics for choosing an appropriate value for k even more cheaply.

The final piece of the puzzle is the use of differential variants of the *qd* (*quotient-difference*) algorithm (which is beyond the scope of this book), both for computing the eigenvalues accurately (via the singular values of the bidiagonal factors of the tridiagonal matrix) and for computing the twisted factorizations used in computing the eigenvectors. All of these features combine to yield an algorithm for computing all of the eigenvalues and orthogonal eigenvectors for a real symmetric tridiagonal matrix at a cost of $\mathcal{O}(n^2)$ work, which is much faster than other algorithms for matrices of significant size. When the RRR algorithm is applied to a real symmetric tridiagonal matrix resulting from preliminary reduction of a general real symmetric matrix, this means that the $\mathcal{O}(n^3)$ cost of the preliminary reduction dominates the cost of the subsequent computation of both the eigenvalues and the eigenvectors. The RRR algorithm has not yet undergone the many years of development and testing of older competing algorithms, such as QR iteration, but its speed and low workspace requirements may well cause this approach to become the standard for symmetric eigenproblems. Another advantage of the RRR approach is that the eigenvectors are computed independently, which means that they can be computed selectively only as needed or in parallel, although this potential advantage is not yet exploited in the implementation currently available in `LAPACK`.

4.5.12 Comparison of Methods

We have discussed a wide variety of algorithms for computing eigenvalues and eigenvectors, so a summary and comparison is perhaps in order. For computing all the eigenvalues (and optionally eigenvectors) of a general real or complex matrix, the standard approach is preliminary reduction to Hessenberg form, followed by QR iteration. For a real symmetric or complex Hermitian matrix, far more options are available, but almost all of them involve preliminary reduction to tridiagonal form. Until just a few years ago, QR iteration was the standard method for computing all of the eigenvalues (and optionally eigenvectors) of the resulting tridiagonal matrix. More recently, however, first divide-and-conquer and then relatively robust representation (RRR) methods have surpassed QR iteration in speed for computing all the eigenvectors. Implementations of both of these newer methods are available in `LAPACK`, but neither can be considered fully mature at this point, nor do they have the decades-long record of reliability enjoyed by QR iteration. Thus, for now, the choice is between the speed of the newer methods, especially RRR, and the more proven dependability of QR iteration. The Jacobi method is even more reliable, but its very slow speed restricts its usefulness to special situations.

When only a few eigenvalues and eigenvectors are needed, a different set of choices is available. For symmetric matrices of modest size, tridiagonal reduction followed by bisection for the eigenvalues and inverse iteration for the corresponding eigenvectors remains the standard approach, though this role may eventually be taken over by RRR methods. For very large matrices, especially when the matrix is sparse, the standard algorithms for preliminary reduction to Hessenberg or tridiagonal form are prohibitively expensive, both in work and storage. In such cases, the matrix is best considered as a linear operator with which one can form matrix-vector products. In this context, the current methods of choice are Arnoldi iteration for general matrices and Lanczos iteration for symmetric or Hermitian matrices, though orthogonal simultaneous iteration can also be useful in either case.

4.6 Generalized Eigenvalue Problems

Many eigenvalue problems occurring in practice have the form of a *generalized eigenvalue problem*

$$\boldsymbol{A}\boldsymbol{x} = \lambda \boldsymbol{B}\boldsymbol{x},$$

where $\boldsymbol{A}$ and $\boldsymbol{B}$ are given $n \times n$ matrices. In structural vibration problems, for example, $\boldsymbol{A}$ represents the *stiffness matrix* and $\boldsymbol{B}$ the *mass matrix*, and the eigenvalues and eigenvectors determine the natural frequencies and modes of vibration of the structure (see Example 4.1). A detailed study of the theory and algorithms for this and other generalized eigenvalue problems is beyond the scope of this book, but the basic methods available for their solution are briefly outlined next.

If either of the matrices $\boldsymbol{A}$ or $\boldsymbol{B}$ is nonsingular, then the generalized eigenvalue problem can be converted to a standard eigenvalue problem, either

$$(\boldsymbol{B}^{-1}\boldsymbol{A})\,\boldsymbol{x} = \lambda \boldsymbol{x} \quad \text{or} \quad (\boldsymbol{A}^{-1}\boldsymbol{B})\,\boldsymbol{x} = (1/\lambda)\,\boldsymbol{x}.$$

Such a transformation is not generally recommended, however, since it may cause

- Loss of accuracy due to rounding error in forming the product matrix, especially when $\boldsymbol{A}$ or $\boldsymbol{B}$ is ill-conditioned
- Loss of symmetry when $\boldsymbol{A}$ and $\boldsymbol{B}$ are symmetric

If $\boldsymbol{A}$ and $\boldsymbol{B}$ are symmetric, and one of them is positive definite, then symmetry can still be retained by using the Cholesky factorization. For example, if $\boldsymbol{B} = \boldsymbol{L}\boldsymbol{L}^T$, then the generalized eigenvalue problem can be rewritten as the standard symmetric eigenvalue problem

$$(\boldsymbol{L}^{-1}\boldsymbol{A}\boldsymbol{L}^{-T})\,\boldsymbol{y} = \lambda \boldsymbol{y},$$

and $\boldsymbol{x}$ can be recovered from the triangular linear system $\boldsymbol{L}^T\boldsymbol{x} = \boldsymbol{y}$. Transformation to a standard eigenvalue problem may still incur unnecessary rounding error, however, and it offers no help if both $\boldsymbol{A}$ and $\boldsymbol{B}$ are singular.

A numerically superior approach, which is applicable even when the matrices are singular or indefinite, is the *QZ algorithm*. Note that if $\boldsymbol{A}$ and $\boldsymbol{B}$ are both triangular, then the eigenvalues are given by $\lambda_i = a_{ii}/b_{ii}$ for $b_{ii} \neq 0$. This fact motivates the QZ algorithm, which reduces $\boldsymbol{A}$ and $\boldsymbol{B}$ simultaneously to upper triangular form by orthogonal transformations. First, $\boldsymbol{B}$ is reduced to upper triangular form by an orthogonal transformation $\boldsymbol{Q}_0$ applied on the left, and the same orthogonal transformation is also applied to $\boldsymbol{A}$. Then a sequence of orthogonal transformations $\boldsymbol{Q}_k$ is applied to both matrices from the left to reduce $\boldsymbol{A}$ to upper Hessenberg form, and these alternate with orthogonal transformations $\boldsymbol{Z}_k$ applied on the right to restore $\boldsymbol{B}$ to upper triangular form. Finally, in a process analogous to QR iteration for the standard eigenvalue problem, additional orthogonal transformations are applied, alternating on the left and right, so that $\boldsymbol{A}$ converges to upper triangular form while maintaining the upper triangular form of $\boldsymbol{B}$. The product of all the transformations on the left is denoted by $\boldsymbol{Q}$, and the product of those on the right is denoted by $\boldsymbol{Z}$, giving the algorithm its name. The eigenvalues can now be determined from the mutually triangular form, and the eigenvectors can be recovered via $\boldsymbol{Q}$ and $\boldsymbol{Z}$.

4.7 Computing the Singular Value Decomposition

Recall from Section 3.6 that the *singular value decomposition* (*SVD*) of an $m \times n$ real matrix has the form

$$\boldsymbol{A} = \boldsymbol{U}\boldsymbol{\Sigma}\boldsymbol{V}^T,$$

where $\boldsymbol{U}$ is an $m \times m$ orthogonal matrix, $\boldsymbol{V}$ is an $n \times n$ orthogonal matrix, and $\boldsymbol{\Sigma}$ is an $m \times n$ diagonal matrix, with

$$\sigma_{ij} = \begin{cases} 0 & \text{for } i \neq j \\ \sigma_i \geq 0 & \text{for } i = j \end{cases}.$$

The diagonal entries σ_i are called the *singular values* of $\boldsymbol{A}$ and are usually ordered so that $\sigma_i \geq \sigma_{i+1}$, $i = 1, \ldots, n-1$. The columns $\boldsymbol{u}_i$ of $\boldsymbol{U}$ and $\boldsymbol{v}_i$ of $\boldsymbol{V}$ are the corresponding left and right *singular vectors*. For some of the many ways in which the SVD is used in practice, see Section 3.6.1.

Singular values and vectors are intimately related to eigenvalues and eigenvectors: the singular values of $\boldsymbol{A}$ are the nonnegative square roots of the eigenvalues of $\boldsymbol{A}^T\boldsymbol{A}$, and the columns of $\boldsymbol{U}$ and $\boldsymbol{V}$ are orthonormal eigenvectors of $\boldsymbol{A}\boldsymbol{A}^T$ and $\boldsymbol{A}^T\boldsymbol{A}$, respectively. Stable algorithms for computing the SVD work directly with $\boldsymbol{A}$, however, without forming $\boldsymbol{A}\boldsymbol{A}^T$ or $\boldsymbol{A}^T\boldsymbol{A}$, thereby avoiding any loss of information associated with forming these matrix products explicitly.

For a dense matrix, the SVD is usually computed by a variant of QR iteration. First, $\boldsymbol{A}$ is reduced to bidiagonal form by a finite sequence of orthogonal transformations, then the remaining off-diagonal entries are annihilated iteratively. The SVD can also be computed by a variant of the Jacobi method (see Computer Problem 4.16), which can be useful on parallel computers or if the matrix has some special structure. The total number of arithmetic operations required to compute the SVD of an $m \times n$ dense matrix is proportional to $mn^2 + n^3$, with the proportionality constants ranging from 4 to 10 or more, depending on the particular algorithm used and the combination of singular values and right or left singular vectors desired. If the matrix is large and sparse, then bidiagonalization is most effectively performed by a variant of the Lanczos algorithm, which is especially suitable if only a few of the extreme singular values and corresponding singular vectors are needed.

4.8 Software for Eigenvalue Problems

Table 4.2 is a list of some of the software available for eigenvalue and singular value problems. The routines listed are in most cases high-level drivers whose underlying routines can also be called directly if greater user control is required. Only the most comprehensive and commonly occurring cases are listed, and only for real matrices. There are many additional routines available in these packages, including routines for complex matrices and for various special situations, such as when only the eigenvalues and not the eigenvectors are needed, or when only a few eigenvalues are needed, or when the matrix has some special property, such as being banded. Routines are also available for both symmetric and nonsymmetric generalized eigenvalue problems. EISPACK and its successor LAPACK are the standards in software for dense eigenvalue problems, and the eigenvalue routines in most other libraries are based on them.

Source	Eigenvalues/eigenvectors General	Symmetric	Singular value decomposition
EISPACK [143, 358]	rg	rs	svd
FMM [127]			svd
HSL	eb06	ea06	eb10
IMSL	evcrg	evcsf	lsvrr
LAPACK [10]	sgeev	ssyev	sgesvd
Lawson & Hanson [251]			svdrs
LINPACK [98]			ssvdc
MATLAB	eig	eig	svd
NAG	f02ebf	f02faf	f02wef
NAPACK [178]	diag	sdiag	sing
NR [315]	elmhes/hqr	tred2/tqli	svdcmp
NUMAL [250]	comeig1	qrisym	qrisngvaldec
SLATEC	rg	rs	ssvdc

Table 4.2: Software for standard dense eigenvalue and singular value problems

Conventional software for computing eigenvalues is fairly complicated, especially if eigenvectors are also computed. The standard approach, QR iteration, is typically broken into separate routines for the preliminary reduction to tridiagonal or Hessenberg form, and then QR iteration for computing the eigenvalues. The orthogonal or unitary similarity transformations may or may not be accumulated, depending on whether eigenvectors are also desired. Because of the complexity of the underlying routines, higher-level drivers are often provided for applications that do not require fine control. Typically, the input required is a two-dimensional array containing the matrix, together with information about the size of the matrix and the array containing it. The eigenvalues are returned in one or two one-dimensional arrays, depending on whether they are real or complex; and normalized eigenvectors, if requested, are similarly returned in one or two two-dimensional arrays. Similar remarks apply to software for computing the singular value decomposition except that arrays must be provided for both left and right singular vectors, if requested, and the decomposition is always real if the input matrix is real.

As usual, life is simpler using an interactive environment such as MATLAB, in which functions for eigenvalue and singular value computations are built in. A diagonal matrix $\boldsymbol{D}$ of eigenvalues and full matrix $\boldsymbol{V}$ of eigenvectors of a (real or complex) matrix $\boldsymbol{A}$ are provided by the MATLAB function `[V, D] = eig(A)`. Internally, the eigenvalues and eigenvectors are computed by Hessenberg reduction and then QR iteration to obtain the Schur form of the matrix, but the user need not be aware of this. If the Hessenberg or Schur forms are desired explicitly, they can be computed by the MATLAB functions `hess` and `schur`. The MATLAB function for computing the singular value decomposition has the form `[U, S, V] = svd(A)`.

For software implementing the Lanczos algorithm for large sparse symmetric eigenvalue problems, see `laso` from `Netlib`, `ea15` from the Harwell library, `lancz` from `napack`, or the software published in [80]. The Arnoldi method for large sparse nonsymmetric eigenvalue problems is implemented in ARPACK (see [253]), which is available from `Netlib` and also serves as the basis for the MATLAB function `eigs` for computing a few eigenvalues and eigenvectors and `svds` for computing a few singular values and singular vectors of a matrix. The Lanczos and subspace iteration methods for computing singular values and vectors of large sparse matrices are implemented in SVDPACK from `Netlib`.

4.9 Historical Notes and Further Reading

The concept of eigenvalues predates the formal notion of matrices, which was introduced by Cayley in 1855. The name *eigenvalues* did not become standard, however, until the mid twentieth century; previously they had been called characteristic values, proper values, or latent roots. The notion of similarity can be traced back as far as Cauchy, but Weierstrass first showed in 1868 that similar matrices have equivalent eigenstructures. Jordan formulated his canonical form under similarity transformations in 1870. Schur proved in 1909 that any matrix is unitarily similar to a triangular matrix, but the significance of his result was not fully realized until the invention fifty years later of QR iteration, which produces this Schur form.

The Jacobi method for computing eigenvalues of symmetric matrices dates from 1845. Power iteration is sufficiently obvious to have been rediscovered repeatedly, but as a practical method its use dates from early in the twentieth century, for example by Müntz in 1913. In 1931 Krylov used the sequence generated by the power method (now called a *Krylov sequence*) to determine the characteristic polynomial of a matrix (see Computer Problem 4.15). Inverse iteration was proposed by Wielandt in 1944. The Lanczos method for symmetric matrices was first published in 1950, and was followed soon thereafter by the Arnoldi method for nonsymmetric matrices in 1951. The method of bisection using the Sturm sequence property was proposed by Givens in 1954. Givens also suggested preliminary reduction to tridiagonal form using plane rotations, a method whose efficiency was subsequently improved upon by Householder in 1958 using the elementary reflections that now bear his name. QR iteration was devised independently by Francis and by Kublanovskaya in 1961, based on the earlier LR method of Rutishauser (1958), which uses elementary eliminations instead of orthogonal transformations (and hence is less stable). The direct precursors of much of the modern software for eigenvalue and related problems were collected in [420], published in 1971.

The divide-and-conquer method for symmetric tridiagonal matrices was proposed by Cuppen in 1981, but its first stable implementation was published by Gu and Eisenstat in 1995. The various ingredients in the relatively robust representation method were developed by Dhillon, Fernando, Parlett, and others, and were combined into a complete algorithm for the tridiagonal eigenproblem in Dhillon's thesis in 1997. The QZ algorithm for generalized eigenvalue problems was published by Moler and Stewart in 1973. A Jacobi-like algorithm for computing the singular value decomposition was published by Kogbetliantz in 1955. Bidiagonal reduction followed by a variant of QR iteration for computing the SVD was proposed by Golub and Kahan in 1965, and the basic algorithm that is still in use today was published by Businger and Golub in 1969.

The classic reference on eigenvalue computations is [419]. Other general references on this topic include [63, 168, 302]. For more insights into QR iteration, see [303, 412]. For detailed discussion of methods for large eigenvalue problems, see [80, 335]. A comprehensive, up-to-date guide is [18]. Most of the books on matrix computations cited in Section 2.8 also discuss eigenvalue and singular value computations in some detail, and again [164] can be singled out for its comprehensiveness. `EISPACK` is documented in [143, 358], and its successor `LAPACK` is documented in [10].

Review Questions

4.1. True or false: The eigenvalues of a matrix are not necessarily all distinct.

4.2. True or false: All the eigenvalues of a real matrix are necessarily real.

4.3. True or false: An eigenvector corresponding to a given eigenvalue of a matrix is unique.

4.4. True or false: Every $n \times n$ matrix $\boldsymbol{A}$ has n linearly independent eigenvectors.

4.5. True or false: If an $n \times n$ matrix is singular, then it does not have a full set of n linearly independent eigenvectors.

4.6. True or false: A square matrix $\boldsymbol{A}$ is singular if, and only if, 0 is one of its eigenvalues.

4.7. True or false: If $\lambda = 0$ for every eigenvalue λ of a matrix $\boldsymbol{A}$, then $\boldsymbol{A} = \boldsymbol{O}$.

4.8. True or false: The diagonal elements of a complex Hermitian matrix must be real.

4.9. True or false: The eigenvalues of a complex Hermitian matrix must be real.

4.10. True or false: If two matrices have the same eigenvalues, then the two matrices are similar.

4.11. True or false: If two matrices are similar, then they have the same eigenvectors.

4.12. True or false: Given any arbitrary square matrix, there is some diagonal matrix that is similar to it.

4.13. True or false: Given any arbitrary square matrix, there is some triangular matrix that is unitarily similar to it.

4.14. True or false: The condition number of a matrix with respect to solving linear systems also determines the conditioning of its eigenvalues.

4.15. True or false: The eigenvalues of a real symmetric or complex Hermitian matrix are always well-conditioned.

4.16. True or false: A matrix that is both symmetric and Hessenberg must be tridiagonal.

4.17. True or false: If an $n \times n$ matrix $\boldsymbol{A}$ has distinct eigenvalues, then QR iteration applied to $\boldsymbol{A}$ necessarily converges to a diagonal matrix.

4.18. True or false: For a square matrix, the eigenvalues and the singular values are the same.

4.19. Explain the distinction between a right eigenvector and a left eigenvector.

4.20. What is meant by the *spectral radius* of a matrix?

4.21. For a given matrix $\boldsymbol{A}$,

(*a*) Can the same eigenvalue correspond to two different eigenvectors?

(*b*) Can the same eigenvector correspond to two different eigenvalues?

4.22. What is meant by the *characteristic polynomial* of a matrix? What does it have to do with eigenvalues?

4.23. Explain the distinction between algebraic multiplicity and geometric multiplicity of an eigenvalue.

4.24. What is meant by an *invariant subspace* for a given matrix $\boldsymbol{A}$?

4.25. What are the eigenvalues and eigenvectors of a diagonal matrix? Give an example.

4.26. Which of the following conditions necessarily imply that an $n \times n$ real matrix $\boldsymbol{A}$ is diagonalizable (i.e., is similar to a diagonal matrix)?

(*a*) $\boldsymbol{A}$ has n distinct eigenvalues.

(*b*) $\boldsymbol{A}$ has only real eigenvalues.

(*c*) $\boldsymbol{A}$ is nonsingular.

(*d*) $\boldsymbol{A}$ is equal to its transpose.

(*e*) $\boldsymbol{A}$ commutes with its transpose.

4.27. Which of the following classes of matrices necessarily have all real eigenvalues?

(*a*) Real symmetric

(*b*) Real triangular

(*c*) Arbitrary real

(*d*) Complex symmetric

(*e*) Complex Hermitian

(*f*) Complex triangular with real diagonal

(*g*) Arbitrary complex

4.28. Let $\boldsymbol{A}$ and $\boldsymbol{B}$ be similar square matrices, i.e., $\boldsymbol{B} = \boldsymbol{T}^{-1}\boldsymbol{A}\boldsymbol{T}$ for some nonsingular matrix $\boldsymbol{T}$. If $\boldsymbol{y}$ is an eigenvector of $\boldsymbol{B}$, then exhibit an eigenvector of $\boldsymbol{A}$.

4.29. Give an example of a matrix that is not diagonalizable, i.e., that is not similar to any diagonal matrix.

4.30. The eigenvalues of a matrix are the roots of its characteristic polynomial. Does this fact provide a generally effective numerical method for computing the eigenvalues? Why?

4.31. Before applying QR iteration to compute the eigenvalues of a matrix, the matrix is usually first transformed to a simpler form. For each type of matrix listed below, what intermediate form is appropriate?

(*a*) A general real matrix

(*b*) A real symmetric matrix

4.32. A general matrix can be reduced to triangular form by a single QR factorization, and the eigenvalues of a triangular matrix are its diagonal entries. Does this procedure suffice to compute the eigenvalues of the original matrix? Why?

4.33. Gauss-Jordan elimination reduces a matrix to diagonal form. Does this make the eigenvalues of the matrix obvious? Why?

4.34. (*a*) Why is the Jacobi method for computing all the eigenvalues of a real symmetric matrix relatively slowly convergent?

(*b*) Name a method that is faster, and explain briefly why it is faster.

4.35. For which of the following classes of matrices of order n can the eigenvalues be computed in a finite number of steps for arbitrary n?

(*a*) Diagonal

(*b*) Tridiagonal

(*c*) Triangular

(*d*) Hessenberg

(*e*) General real matrix with distinct eigenvalues

(*f*) General real matrix with eigenvalues that are not necessarily distinct

4.36. In using QR iteration for computing the eigenvalues of a matrix, why is the matrix usually first reduced to some simpler form, such as Hessenberg or tridiagonal?

4.37. Applied to a given matrix $\boldsymbol{A}$, QR iteration for computing eigenvalues converges to either diagonal or triangular form. What property of $\boldsymbol{A}$ determines which of these two forms is obtained?

4.38. As a preliminary step before computing its eigenvalues, a matrix $\boldsymbol{A}$ is often first reduced to Hessenberg form by a unitary similarity transformation. Why stop there? If such a preliminary reduction to Hessenberg form is good, wouldn't triangular form be even better? What is wrong with this argument?

4.39. If you had a routine for computing all the eigenvalues of a nonsymmetric matrix, how could you use it to compute the roots of any polynomial?

4.40. Order the following algorithms 1 through 4, from least work required to most work required, for a square nonsingular matrix $\boldsymbol{A}$:

(*a*) LU factorization by Gaussian elimination with partial pivoting

(*b*) Computing all of the eigenvalues and eigenvectors

(*c*) Solving an upper triangular system by back-substitution

(*d*) Computing the inverse of the matrix

4.41. Power iteration converges to which eigenvector of a matrix?

4.42. (*a*) If a matrix $\boldsymbol{A}$ has a simple dominant eigenvalue λ_1, what quantity determines the convergence rate of the power method for computing λ_1?

(*b*) How can the convergence rate of power iteration be improved?

4.43. Given an approximate eigenvector $\boldsymbol{x}$ for a matrix $\boldsymbol{A}$, what is the best estimate (in the least squares sense) for the corresponding eigenvalue?

4.44. List three conditions under which power iteration may fail.

4.45. Inverse iteration converges to which eigenvector of a matrix?

4.46. In power iteration or inverse iteration, why are the vector iterates normalized at each iteration?

4.47. What is the main reason that shifts are used in iterative methods for computing eigenvalues, such as the power, inverse iteration, and QR iteration methods?

4.48. Given a general square matrix $\boldsymbol{A}$, what method would you use to compute the following?

(*a*) The smallest eigenvalue of $\boldsymbol{A}$

(*b*) The largest eigenvalue of $\boldsymbol{A}$

(*c*) The eigenvalue of $\boldsymbol{A}$ closest to some specified scalar β

(*d*) All of the eigenvalues of $\boldsymbol{A}$

4.49. (*a*) Given an approximate eigenvalue λ for a matrix, how can one obtain a good approximate eigenvector?

(*b*) Given an approximate eigenvector $\boldsymbol{x}$ for a matrix, how can one obtain a good approximate eigenvalue?

4.50. What is a Krylov sequence, and for what purpose is it useful?

4.51. Why is the Lanczos method faster than power iteration for computing a few eigenvalues of a real symmetric matrix?

4.52. What features make the Lanczos method suitable for large sparse symmetric eigenvalue problems?

4.53. What is meant by the *inertia* of a real symmetric matrix?

4.54. (*a*) What is meant by a *congruence* transformation of a real symmetric matrix?

(*b*) What properties of the matrix, if any, are preserved by such a transformation.

4.55. Explain briefly how spectrum-slicing methods work for computing individual eigenvalues of a real symmetric matrix.

4.56. (*a*) List two reasons why converting a generalized eigenvalue problem $\boldsymbol{Ax} = \lambda \boldsymbol{Bx}$ to the standard eigenvalue problem $(\boldsymbol{B}^{-1}\boldsymbol{A})\boldsymbol{x} = \lambda \boldsymbol{x}$ might not be a good idea.

(*b*) What is a better approach?

4.57. (*a*) How are the singular values of an $m \times n$ real matrix $\boldsymbol{A}$ related to the eigenvalues of the $n \times n$ matrix $\boldsymbol{A}^T\boldsymbol{A}$?

(*b*) Is forming $\boldsymbol{A}^T\boldsymbol{A}$ and computing its eigenvalues a good way to compute the singular values of a matrix $\boldsymbol{A}$? Why?

Exercises

4.1. (*a*) Prove that 5 is an eigenvalue of the matrix

$$A = \begin{bmatrix} 6 & 3 & 3 & 1 \\ 0 & 7 & 4 & 5 \\ 0 & 0 & 5 & 4 \\ 0 & 0 & 0 & 8 \end{bmatrix}.$$

(*b*) Exhibit an eigenvector of A corresponding to the eigenvalue 5.

4.2. What are the eigenvalues and corresponding eigenvectors of the following matrix?

$$\begin{bmatrix} 1 & 2 & -4 \\ 0 & 2 & 1 \\ 0 & 0 & 3 \end{bmatrix}$$

4.3. Let

$$A = \begin{bmatrix} 1 & 4 \\ 1 & 1 \end{bmatrix}.$$

Your answers to the following questions should be numeric and specific to this particular matrix, not just the general definitions.

(*a*) What is the characteristic polynomial of A?

(*b*) What are the roots of the characteristic polynomial of A?

(*c*) What are the eigenvalues of A?

(*d*) What are the eigenvectors of A?

(*e*) Perform one iteration of power iteration on A, using $x_0 = [1 \quad 1]^T$ as starting vector.

(*f*) To what eigenvector of A will power iteration ultimately converge?

(*g*) What eigenvalue estimate is given by the Rayleigh quotient, using the vector $x = [1 \quad 1]^T$?

(*h*) To what eigenvector of A would inverse iteration ultimately converge?

(*i*) What eigenvalue of A would be obtained if inverse iteration were used with shift $\sigma = 2$?

(*j*) If QR iteration were applied to A, to what form would it converge: diagonal or triangular? Why?

4.4. Give an example of a 2×2 matrix A and a nonzero starting vector x_0 such that power iteration fails to converge to the eigenvector corresponding to the dominant eigenvalue of A.

4.5. Suppose that all of the row sums of an $n \times n$ matrix A have the same value, say, α.

(*a*) Show that α is an eigenvalue of A.

(*b*) What is the corresponding eigenvector?

4.6. Show that an $n \times n$ matrix A is singular if, and only if, zero is one of its eigenvalues.

4.7. Let A be a complex $n \times n$ matrix.

(*a*) Show that A and A^T have the same eigenvalues.

(*b*) Show that the eigenvalues of A^H are complex conjugates of the eigenvalues of A.

4.8. Prove that an $n \times n$ matrix A is diagonalizable by a similarity transformation if, and only if, it has a complete set of n linearly independent eigenvectors.

4.9. (*a*) Let $p(\lambda) = c_0 + c_1\lambda + \cdots + c_n\lambda^n$ be a polynomial with real coefficients. Show that any complex roots of $p(\lambda) = 0$ must occur in conjugate pairs, i.e., if $p(\alpha + i\beta) = 0$, then $p(\alpha - i\beta) = 0$. (*Hint*: Show that for any $z \in \mathbb{C}$, $p(\bar{z}) = \overline{p(z)}$.)

(*b*) Let A be any real matrix. By applying the result of part *a* to the characteristic polynomial $\det(A - \lambda I)$, we can conclude that complex eigenvalues of a real matrix must occur in conjugate pairs. This result can also be proved directly: Let λ be a complex eigenvalue with corresponding eigenvector x. Show that $\bar{\lambda}$ is an eigenvalue with corresponding eigenvector $\bar{x}$.

4.10. (*a*) Prove that all the eigenvalues of a complex Hermitian matrix A are real (*Hint*: Consider $x^H A x$).

(*b*) Prove that all the eigenvalues of a real symmetric matrix A are real.

4.11. Give an example of a symmetric complex matrix (not Hermitian) that has complex eigenvalues (i.e., with nonzero imaginary parts).

4.12. Prove that the eigenvalues of a positive definite matrix A are all positive.

4.13. Prove that for any matrix norm induced by a vector norm, $\rho(A) \leq \|A\|$.

4.14. Is there any real value for the parameter α such that the matrix

$$\begin{bmatrix} 1 & 0 & \alpha \\ 4 & 2 & 0 \\ 6 & 5 & 3 \end{bmatrix}$$

(*a*) Has all real eigenvalues?

(*b*) Has all complex eigenvalues with nonzero imaginary parts?

In each case, either give such a value for α or give a reason why none exists.

4.15. If $\boldsymbol{A}$ and $\boldsymbol{B}$ are $n \times n$ matrices and $\boldsymbol{A}$ is nonsingular, show that the matrices $\boldsymbol{AB}$ and $\boldsymbol{BA}$ are similar.

4.16. Assume that $\boldsymbol{A}$ is a nonsingular $n \times n$ matrix.

(*a*) What is the relationship between the eigenvalues of $\boldsymbol{A}$ and those of $\boldsymbol{A}^{-1}$? Prove your answer.

(*b*) What is the relationship between the eigenvectors of $\boldsymbol{A}$ and those of $\boldsymbol{A}^{-1}$? Prove your answer.

4.17. If λ is an eigenvalue of an $n \times n$ matrix $\boldsymbol{A}$, show that λ^2 is an eigenvalue of $\boldsymbol{A}^2$.

4.18. A matrix $\boldsymbol{A}$ is said to be *nilpotent* if $\boldsymbol{A}^k = \boldsymbol{O}$ for some positive integer k.

(*a*) Show that if $\boldsymbol{A}$ is nilpotent, then all of the eigenvalues of $\boldsymbol{A}$ are zero.

(*b*) Show that if $\boldsymbol{A}$ is both nilpotent and normal (i.e., $\boldsymbol{A}^H\boldsymbol{A} = \boldsymbol{A}\boldsymbol{A}^H$), then $\boldsymbol{A} = \boldsymbol{O}$.

4.19. A matrix $\boldsymbol{A}$ is said to be *idempotent* if $\boldsymbol{A}^2 = \boldsymbol{A}$. If $\boldsymbol{A}$ is idempotent, characterize its eigenvalues.

4.20. (*a*) Suppose that $\boldsymbol{A}$ is an $n \times n$ Hermitian matrix. Let λ and μ, $\lambda \neq \mu$, be eigenvalues of $\boldsymbol{A}$ with corresponding eigenvectors $\boldsymbol{x}$ and $\boldsymbol{y}$, respectively. Show that $\boldsymbol{y}^H\boldsymbol{x} = 0$ (i.e., eigenvectors corresponding to distinct eigenvalues of a Hermitian matrix are orthogonal).

(*b*) More generally, suppose now that $\boldsymbol{A}$ is not Hermitian. If $\boldsymbol{Ax} = \lambda\boldsymbol{x}$ and $\boldsymbol{y}^H\boldsymbol{A} = \mu\boldsymbol{y}^H$, with $\lambda \neq \mu$, show that $\boldsymbol{y}^H\boldsymbol{x} = 0$ (i.e., right and left eigenvectors corresponding to distinct eigenvalues are orthogonal).

(*c*) Finally, suppose that $\boldsymbol{Ax} = \lambda\boldsymbol{x}$ and $\boldsymbol{y}^H\boldsymbol{A} = \lambda\boldsymbol{y}^H$, where $\boldsymbol{A}$ is nonHermitian and λ is a simple eigenvalue. Show that $\boldsymbol{y}^H\boldsymbol{x} \neq 0$ (i.e., right and left eigenvectors corresponding to the same simple eigenvalue cannot be orthogonal).

4.21. (*a*) Let $\boldsymbol{A}$ be an $n \times n$ real or complex matrix. Prove that for any real or complex scalar λ, the set $\mathcal{S}_\lambda = \{\boldsymbol{x} : \boldsymbol{Ax} = \lambda\boldsymbol{x}\}$ is a *subspace* of either $\mathbb{R}^n$ or $\mathbb{C}^n$.

(*b*) Show that λ is an eigenvalue of $\boldsymbol{A}$ if, and only if, $\mathcal{S}_\lambda \neq \{\boldsymbol{0}\}$.

4.22. Suppose the $n \times n$ matrix $\boldsymbol{A}$ has the block upper triangular form

$$\boldsymbol{A} = \begin{bmatrix} \boldsymbol{A}_{11} & \boldsymbol{A}_{12} \\ \boldsymbol{O} & \boldsymbol{A}_{22} \end{bmatrix},$$

where $\boldsymbol{A}_{11}$ is $k \times k$ and $\boldsymbol{A}_{22}$ is $(n-k) \times (n-k)$.

(*a*) If λ is an eigenvalue of $\boldsymbol{A}_{11}$ with corresponding eigenvector $\boldsymbol{u}$, show that λ is an eigenvalue of $\boldsymbol{A}$. (*Hint*: Find an $(n-k)$-vector $\boldsymbol{v}$ such that $\begin{bmatrix} \boldsymbol{u} \\ \boldsymbol{v} \end{bmatrix}$ is an eigenvector of $\boldsymbol{A}$ corresponding to λ.)

(*b*) If λ is an eigenvalue of $\boldsymbol{A}_{22}$ (but not of $\boldsymbol{A}_{11}$) with corresponding eigenvector $\boldsymbol{v}$, show that λ is an eigenvalue of $\boldsymbol{A}$. (*Hint*: Find a k-vector $\boldsymbol{u}$ such that $\begin{bmatrix} \boldsymbol{u} \\ \boldsymbol{v} \end{bmatrix}$ is an eigenvector of $\boldsymbol{A}$ corresponding to λ.)

(*c*) If λ is an eigenvalue of $\boldsymbol{A}$ with corresponding eigenvector $\begin{bmatrix} \boldsymbol{u} \\ \boldsymbol{v} \end{bmatrix}$, where $\boldsymbol{u}$ is a k-vector, show that λ is either an eigenvalue of $\boldsymbol{A}_{11}$ with corresponding eigenvector $\boldsymbol{u}$ or an eigenvalue of $\boldsymbol{A}_{22}$ with corresponding eigenvector $\boldsymbol{v}$.

(*d*) Combine the previous parts of this exercise to show that λ is an eigenvalue of $\boldsymbol{A}$ if, and only if, it is an eigenvalue of either $\boldsymbol{A}_{11}$ or $\boldsymbol{A}_{22}$.

4.23. Let $\boldsymbol{A}$ be an $n \times n$ matrix with eigenvalues $\lambda_1, \ldots, \lambda_n$.

(*a*) Show that the determinant of $\boldsymbol{A}$ is equal to the product of its eigenvalues, i.e., $\det(\boldsymbol{A}) = \Pi_{j=1}^n \lambda_j$. (*Hint*: Consider the characteristic polynomial of $\boldsymbol{A}$.)

(*b*) The *trace* of a matrix is defined to be the sum of its diagonal entries, i.e., $\text{trace}(\boldsymbol{A}) = \sum_{j=1}^n a_{jj}$. Show that the trace of $\boldsymbol{A}$ is equal to the sum of its eigenvalues, i.e., $\text{trace}(\boldsymbol{A}) = \sum_{j=1}^n \lambda_j$. (*Hint*: Consider the characteristic polynomial of $\boldsymbol{A}$.)

4.24. Let $\boldsymbol{A}$ be an $n \times n$ real matrix of rank one.

(*a*) Show that $\boldsymbol{A} = \boldsymbol{uv}^T$ for some nonzero real vectors $\boldsymbol{u}$ and $\boldsymbol{v}$.

(*b*) Show that $\boldsymbol{u}^T\boldsymbol{v}$ is an eigenvalue of $\boldsymbol{A}$.

(*c*) What are the other eigenvalues of $\boldsymbol{A}$?

(*d*) If power iteration is applied to $\boldsymbol{A}$, how many iterations are required for it to converge exactly to the eigenvector corresponding to the dominant eigenvalue?

4.25. Show that for any two real vectors $\boldsymbol{u}$ and $\boldsymbol{v}$, $\det(\boldsymbol{I}+\boldsymbol{u}\boldsymbol{v}^T) = 1+\boldsymbol{u}^T\boldsymbol{v}$. (*Hint*: Combine results of Exercises 4.23 and 4.24.)

4.26. Recall that a matrix $\boldsymbol{A}$ is *normal* if it commutes with its conjugate transpose, i.e., $\boldsymbol{A}^H\boldsymbol{A} = \boldsymbol{A}\boldsymbol{A}^H$.

(*a*) Show that if a matrix $\boldsymbol{T}$ is both triangular and normal, then it must be diagonal.

(*b*) Show that a matrix $\boldsymbol{A}$ is normal if, and only if, it is unitarily diagonalizable, i.e., there is a unitary matrix $\boldsymbol{Q}$ and a diagonal matrix $\boldsymbol{D}$ such that $\boldsymbol{Q}^H\boldsymbol{A}\boldsymbol{Q} = \boldsymbol{D}$. (*Hint*: Consider the Schur form of $\boldsymbol{A}$ and apply the result of part *a*.)

4.27. Let $\boldsymbol{A}$ be an $n \times n$ matrix with $\rho(\boldsymbol{A}) < 1$.

(*a*) Show that $\boldsymbol{I} - \boldsymbol{A}$ is nonsingular.

(*b*) Show that

$$(\boldsymbol{I}-\boldsymbol{A})^{-1} = \sum_{k=0}^{\infty} \boldsymbol{A}^k.$$

4.28. Let $\lambda_1 \le \lambda_2 \le \cdots \le \lambda_n$ be the (real) eigenvalues of an $n \times n$ real symmetric matrix $\boldsymbol{A}$.

(*a*) To which of the eigenvalues of $\boldsymbol{A}$ is it possible for power iteration to converge by using an appropriately chosen shift σ?

(*b*) In each such case, what value for the shift gives the most rapid convergence?

(*c*) Answer the same two questions for inverse iteration.

4.29. Let the $n \times n$ complex Hermitian matrix $\boldsymbol{C}$ be written as $\boldsymbol{C} = \boldsymbol{A}+i\boldsymbol{B}$ (i.e., the matrices $\boldsymbol{A}$ and $\boldsymbol{B}$ are its real and imaginary parts, respectively). Define the $2n \times 2n$ real matrix $\tilde{\boldsymbol{C}}$ by

$$\tilde{\boldsymbol{C}} = \begin{bmatrix} \boldsymbol{A} & -\boldsymbol{B} \\ \boldsymbol{B} & \boldsymbol{A} \end{bmatrix}.$$

(*a*) Show that $\tilde{\boldsymbol{C}}$ is symmetric.

(*b*) Let λ be an eigenvalue of $\boldsymbol{C}$ with corresponding eigenvector $\boldsymbol{x}+i\boldsymbol{y}$. Show that λ is an eigenvalue of $\tilde{\boldsymbol{C}}$, with both

$$\begin{bmatrix} \boldsymbol{x} \\ \boldsymbol{y} \end{bmatrix} \quad \text{and} \quad \begin{bmatrix} -\boldsymbol{y} \\ \boldsymbol{x} \end{bmatrix}$$

as corresponding eigenvectors.

(*c*) The previous results show that a routine for real symmetric eigenvalue problems can be used to solve complex Hermitian eigenvalue problems. Is this a good approach? Why?

4.30. (*a*) What are the eigenvalues of the following complex symmetric matrix?

$$\begin{bmatrix} 2i & 1 \\ 1 & 0 \end{bmatrix}$$

(*b*) How many linearly independent eigenvectors does it have?

(*c*) Contrast this situation with that for a real symmetric or complex Hermitian matrix.

4.31. (*a*) If λ is an eigenvalue of an orthogonal matrix $\boldsymbol{Q}$, show that $|\lambda| = 1$.

(*b*) What are the singular values of an orthogonal matrix?

4.32. (*a*) What are the eigenvalues of the Householder transformation

$$\boldsymbol{H} = \boldsymbol{I} - 2\frac{\boldsymbol{v}\boldsymbol{v}^T}{\boldsymbol{v}^T\boldsymbol{v}},$$

where $\boldsymbol{v}$ is any nonzero vector?

(*b*) What are the eigenvalues of the plane rotation

$$\boldsymbol{G} = \begin{bmatrix} c & s \\ -s & c \end{bmatrix},$$

where $c^2 + s^2 = 1$?

4.33. Let $\boldsymbol{A}$ be a real symmetric tridiagonal matrix having no zero entries on its subdiagonal. Show that $\boldsymbol{A}$ must have distinct eigenvalues.

4.34. Let $\boldsymbol{A}$ be a *singular* upper Hessenberg matrix having no zero entries on its subdiagonal. Show that the QR method applied to $\boldsymbol{A}$ produces an exact eigenvalue after only one iteration. This result suggests that the convergence of the QR method will be very rapid if we use a shift that is approximately equal to an eigenvalue.

4.35. Verify that the successive orthogonal vectors produced by the Lanczos algorithm (Section 4.5.7) satisfy a three-term recurrence. For example, $\boldsymbol{A}\boldsymbol{q}_3$ is already orthogonal to $\boldsymbol{q}_1$ and hence need be orthogonalized only against $\boldsymbol{q}_2$ and $\boldsymbol{q}_3$.

4.36. Let $\boldsymbol{A}$ be an $m \times n$ real matrix. Consider the real symmetric eigenvalue problem

$$\begin{bmatrix} \boldsymbol{O} & \boldsymbol{A} \\ \boldsymbol{A}^T & \boldsymbol{O} \end{bmatrix} \begin{bmatrix} \boldsymbol{u} \\ \boldsymbol{v} \end{bmatrix} = \lambda \begin{bmatrix} \boldsymbol{u} \\ \boldsymbol{v} \end{bmatrix}.$$

(*a*) Show that if λ, $\boldsymbol{u}$, and $\boldsymbol{v}$ satisfy this relationship, with $\boldsymbol{u}$ and $\boldsymbol{v}$ suitably normalized, then $|\lambda|$ is a singular value of $\boldsymbol{A}$ with corresponding left and right singular vectors $\boldsymbol{u}$ and $\boldsymbol{v}$, respectively.

(*b*) Is solving this eigenvalue problem a good way to compute the SVD of the matrix $\boldsymbol{A}$? Why?

Computer Problems

4.1. (*a*) Compute the eigenvalues and eigenvectors of the matrix

$$A = \begin{bmatrix} 1 & 1000 \\ 0.001 & 1 \end{bmatrix}.$$

(*b*) Compute the condition number of the matrix of eigenvectors and also the absolute condition number of each eigenvalue (see Section 4.3).

(*c*) What are the eigenvalues of the matrix

$$B = \begin{bmatrix} 1 & 1000 \\ 0 & 1 \end{bmatrix}?$$

How do the changes in the eigenvalues resulting from this perturbation of A compare with expectations?

4.2. (*a*) Implement power iteration to compute the dominant eigenvalue and a corresponding normalized eigenvector of the matrix

$$A = \begin{bmatrix} 2 & 3 & 2 \\ 10 & 3 & 4 \\ 3 & 6 & 1 \end{bmatrix}.$$

As starting vector, take $x_0 = [0 \quad 0 \quad 1]^T$.

(*b*) Using any of the methods for deflation given in Section 4.5.4, deflate out the eigenvalue found in part *a* and apply power iteration again to compute the second largest eigenvalue of the same matrix.

(*c*) Use a general real eigensystem library routine to compute all of the eigenvalues and eigenvectors of the matrix, and compare the results with those obtained in parts *a* and *b*.

4.3. (*a*) Implement inverse iteration with a shift to compute the eigenvalue nearest to 2, and a corresponding normalized eigenvector, of the matrix

$$A = \begin{bmatrix} 6 & 2 & 1 \\ 2 & 3 & 1 \\ 1 & 1 & 1 \end{bmatrix}.$$

You may use an arbitrary starting vector.

(*b*) Use a real symmetric eigensystem library routine to compute all of the eigenvalues and eigenvectors of the matrix, and compare the results with those obtained in part *a*.

4.4. Write a program implementing Rayleigh quotient iteration for computing an eigenvalue and corresponding eigenvector of a matrix. Test your program on the matrix in the previous exercise, using a random starting vector.

4.5. (*a*) Use a library routine to compute the eigenvalues of the matrix

$$A = \begin{bmatrix} 9 & 4.5 & 3 \\ -56 & -28 & -18 \\ 60 & 30 & 19 \end{bmatrix}.$$

(*b*) Compute the eigenvalues of the same matrix again, except with the a_{33} entry changed to 18.95. What is the relative change in magnitudes of the eigenvalues?

(*c*) Compute the eigenvalues of the same matrix again, except with the a_{33} entry changed to 19.05. What is the relative change in magnitudes of the eigenvalues?

(*d*) What conclusion can you draw about the conditioning of the eigenvalues of A? Compute an appropriate condition number or condition numbers to explain this behavior.

4.6. Implement the following simple version of QR iteration with shifts for computing the eigenvalues of a general real matrix A.

Repeat until convergence:

1. $\sigma = a_{n,n}$ (use corner entry as shift)
2. Compute QR factorization $QR = A - \sigma I$
3. $A = RQ + \sigma I$

(These steps will be easy if you use a package such as `MATLAB` but more involved if you use a library routine for the QR factorization or write your own.)

What convergence test should you use? Test your program on the matrices in Computer Problems 4.2 and 4.3.

4.7. Write a program implementing Lanczos iteration as given in Section 4.5.7. Test your program using a random real symmetric matrix A of order n having eigenvalues $1, 2, \ldots, n$. To generate such a matrix, first generate an $n \times n$ matrix B with random entries uniformly distributed on the interval $[0, 1)$ (see Section 13.5), and then compute the QR factorization $B = QR$. Now take $A = QDQ^T$, where $D = \text{diag}(1, \ldots, n)$.

The Lanczos algorithm generates only the tridiagonal matrix $\boldsymbol{T}_k$ at iteration k, so you will need to compute its eigenvalues (i.e., the Ritz values γ_i, $i = 1, \ldots, k$) at each iteration, say, by using a library routine based on QR iteration. For the purpose of this exercise, run the Lanczos algorithm for a full n iterations.

To see graphically how the Ritz values behave as iterations proceed, construct a plot with the iteration number on the vertical axis and the Ritz values at each iteration on the horizontal axis. Plot each pair (γ_i, k), $i = 1, \ldots, k$, as a discrete point at each iteration k (see Fig. 4.4). As iterations proceed and the number of Ritz values grows correspondingly, you should see vertical "trails" of Ritz values converging on the true eigenvalues. Try several values for n, say, $n = 10, 20, \ldots, 50$, making a separate plot for each.

4.8. Compute all the roots of the polynomial

$$p(t) = 24 - 40t + 35t^2 - 13t^3 + t^4$$

by forming the companion matrix (see Section 4.2.1) and then calling an eigenvalue routine to compute its eigenvalues. Note that the companion matrix is already in Hessenberg form, which you may be able to take advantage of, depending on the specific software you use. Compare the speed and accuracy of the companion matrix method with those of a library routine designed specifically for computing roots of polynomials (see Table 5.2). You may need to experiment with polynomials of larger degree to see a significant difference.

4.9. Compute the eigenvalues of the Hilbert matrix of order n (see Computer Problem 2.6) for several values of n, say, up to $n = 20$. Can you characterize the range of magnitudes of the eigenvalues as a function of n?

4.10. A singular matrix must have a zero eigenvalue, but must a nearly singular matrix have a "small" eigenvalue? Consider a matrix of the form

$$\begin{bmatrix} 1 & -1 & -1 & -1 & -1 \\ 0 & 1 & -1 & -1 & -1 \\ 0 & 0 & 1 & -1 & -1 \\ 0 & 0 & 0 & 1 & -1 \\ 0 & 0 & 0 & 0 & 1 \end{bmatrix},$$

whose eigenvalues are obviously all ones. Use a library routine to compute the singular values of such a matrix for various dimensions. How does the ratio $\sigma_{\max}/\sigma_{\min}$ behave as the order of the matrix grows? What conclusions can you draw?

4.11. A real symmetric tridiagonal matrix with a multiple eigenvalue must have a zero on its subdiagonal, but do a close pair of eigenvalues imply that some subdiagonal element must be small? Consider the symmetric tridiagonal matrix of order $n = 2k + 1$ having $k, k-1, \ldots, 1, 0, 1, \ldots, k$ as its diagonal entries and all ones as its subdiagonal and superdiagonal entries. Compute the eigenvalues of this matrix for various values of n. Does it have any multiple or nearly multiple eigenvalues? What conclusions can you draw?

4.12. A *Markov chain* is a system that has n possible states and passes through a series of transitions from one state to another. The probability of a transition from state j to state i is given by a_{ij}, where $0 \le a_{ij} \le 1$ and $\sum_{i=1}^{n} a_{ij} = 1$. Let $\boldsymbol{A}$ denote the matrix of transition probabilities, and let $x_i^{(k)}$ denote the probability that the system is in state i after transition k. If the initial probability distribution vector is $\boldsymbol{x}^{(0)}$, then the probability distribution vector after k steps is given by

$$\boldsymbol{x}^{(k)} = \boldsymbol{A}\boldsymbol{x}^{(k-1)} = \boldsymbol{A}^k \boldsymbol{x}^{(0)}.$$

The long-term behavior of the system is therefore determined by the value of $\lim_{k\to\infty} \boldsymbol{A}^k$.

Consider a system with three states and transition matrix

$$\boldsymbol{A} = \begin{bmatrix} 0.8 & 0.2 & 0.1 \\ 0.1 & 0.7 & 0.3 \\ 0.1 & 0.1 & 0.6 \end{bmatrix},$$

and suppose that the system is initially in state 1.

(*a*) What is the probability distribution vector after three steps?

(*b*) What is the long-term value of the probability distribution vector?

(*c*) Does the long-term value of the probability distribution vector depend on the particular starting value $\boldsymbol{x}^{(0)}$?

(*d*) What is the value of $\lim_{k\to\infty} \boldsymbol{A}^k$, and what is the rank of this matrix?

(*e*) Explain your previous results in terms of the eigenvalues and eigenvectors of $\boldsymbol{A}$.

(*f*) Must 1 *always* be an eigenvalue of the transition matrix of a Markov chain? Why?

(*g*) A probability distribution vector $\boldsymbol{x}$ is said to be *stationary* if $\boldsymbol{Ax} = \boldsymbol{x}$. How can you determine such a stationary value $\boldsymbol{x}$ using the eigenvalues and eigenvectors of $\boldsymbol{A}$?

(*h*) How can you determine a stationary value $\boldsymbol{x}$ *without* knowledge of the eigenvalues and eigenvectors of $\boldsymbol{A}$?

(*i*) In this particular example, is it possible for a previous distribution vector to recur, other than a stationary distribution? For Markov chains in general, is such nontrivial cyclic behavior possible? If not, why? If so, give an example. (*Hint*: Think about the location of the eigenvalues of $\boldsymbol{A}$ in the complex plane.)

(*j*) Can there be more than one stationary distribution vector for a given Markov chain? If not, why? If so, give an example.

(*k*) Of what numerical method does this problem remind you?

4.13. Consider the generalized eigenvalue problem $\boldsymbol{Kx} = \lambda \boldsymbol{Mx}$ derived from the spring-mass system given in Example 4.1 and illustrated in Fig. 4.1. For purposes of this problem, assume the values $k_1 = k_2 = k_3 = 1$, $m_1 = 2$, $m_2 = 3$, and $m_3 = 4$, in arbitrary units.

(*a*) For this particular problem, the mass matrix $\boldsymbol{M}$ is diagonal, so there is no harm in converting the generalized eigenvalue problem to a standard eigenvalue problem. Taking this approach, determine all three natural frequencies and modes of vibration for the system, using any combination you choose of the power and inverse iteration methods (you may use shifts, or deflation, or both).

(*b*) Use a library routine for solving generalized eigenvalue problems to solve this problem directly in its original form, and compare the results with those obtained in part *a*.

4.14. (*a*) The *matrix exponential* function of an $n \times n$ matrix $\boldsymbol{A}$ is defined by the infinite series

$$\exp(\boldsymbol{A}) = \boldsymbol{I} + \boldsymbol{A} + \frac{\boldsymbol{A}^2}{2!} + \frac{\boldsymbol{A}^3}{3!} + \cdots.$$

Write a program to evaluate $\exp(\boldsymbol{A})$ using the foregoing series definition.

(*b*) An alternative way to compute the matrix exponential uses the eigenvalue-eigenvector decomposition

$$\boldsymbol{A} = \boldsymbol{U} \operatorname{diag}(\lambda_1, \ldots, \lambda_n) \boldsymbol{U}^{-1},$$

where $\lambda_1, \ldots, \lambda_n$ are the eigenvalues of $\boldsymbol{A}$ and $\boldsymbol{U}$ is a matrix whose columns are corresponding eigenvectors. Then the matrix exponential is given by

$$\exp(\boldsymbol{A}) = \boldsymbol{U} \operatorname{diag}(e^{\lambda_1}, \ldots, e^{\lambda_n}) \boldsymbol{U}^{-1}.$$

Write a second program to evaluate $\exp(\boldsymbol{A})$ using this method.

Test both methods using each of the following test matrices:

$$\boldsymbol{A}_1 = \begin{bmatrix} 2 & -1 \\ -1 & 2 \end{bmatrix},$$

$$\boldsymbol{A}_2 = \begin{bmatrix} -49 & 24 \\ -64 & 31 \end{bmatrix}.$$

Compare your results with those for a library routine for computing the matrix exponential. Which of your two routines is more accurate and robust? Try to explain why. See [275] for several additional methods for computing the matrix exponential.

4.15. In this exercise we will consider several methods for determining the coefficients of the characteristic polynomial of a matrix $\boldsymbol{A}$. As we have previously observed, the coefficients of the characteristic polynomial may be very sensitive to perturbations in the matrix, so these methods are *not* recommended as a means of computing eigenvalues. Implement each of the following methods and compare their accuracy and efficiency on a variety of test matrices. After verifying that your implementations work correctly for some simple test matrices, try to devise matrices for which the sensitivity of the polynomial coefficients becomes obvious. With each method, after determining the coefficients of the characteristic polynomial, use a polynomial root finder (see Table 5.2) to compute its roots. How does their accuracy compare with that of the eigenvalues of $\boldsymbol{A}$ computed by a standard eigenvalue routine?

(*a*) *Krylov method.* According to the *Cayley-Hamilton Theorem*, an $n \times n$ matrix $\boldsymbol{A}$ satisfies its own characteristic equation, that is, if $p(\lambda) = c_0 + c_1\lambda + \cdots + c_{n-1}\lambda^{n-1} + \lambda^n$ is the characteristic polynomial of $\boldsymbol{A}$, then

$$p(\boldsymbol{A}) = c_0 + c_1\boldsymbol{A} + \cdots + c_{n-1}\boldsymbol{A}^{n-1} + \boldsymbol{A}^n = \boldsymbol{O}.$$

If we multiply this equation on the right by an arbitrary nonzero vector $\boldsymbol{x}_0$, and for $k = 1, \ldots, n$ let $\boldsymbol{x}_k = \boldsymbol{A}\boldsymbol{x}_{k-1}$ (i.e., the sequence generated by power iteration starting with $\boldsymbol{x}_0$), then we obtain the system of linear equations

$$c_0\boldsymbol{x}_o + c_1\boldsymbol{x}_1 + \cdots + c_{n-1}\boldsymbol{x}_{n-1} = -\boldsymbol{x}_n,$$

or $\boldsymbol{Kc} = -\boldsymbol{x}_n$, where $\boldsymbol{K} = [\,\boldsymbol{x}_0 \quad \boldsymbol{x}_1 \quad \cdots \quad \boldsymbol{x}_{n-1}\,]$ is the $n \times n$ Krylov matrix generated from $\boldsymbol{x}_0$ by $\boldsymbol{A}$. The solution to this system gives the coefficients $c_0, \ldots, c_{n-1}$ of the characteristic polynomial of $\boldsymbol{A}$, and $c_n = 1$.

(*b*) *Leverrier method.* This method employs a recurrence involving the *trace* for a sequence of matrices (see Exercise 4.23 for the definition).

$c_n = 1$
$\boldsymbol{B}_{n-1} = \boldsymbol{A}$
$c_{n-1} = -\text{trace}(\boldsymbol{B}_{n-1})$
for $k = n-2$ **to** 0
  $\boldsymbol{B}_k = \boldsymbol{A}(\boldsymbol{B}_{k+1} + c_{k+1}\boldsymbol{I})$
  $c_k = -\text{trace}(\boldsymbol{B}_k)/(n-k)$
end

(*c*) *Danilevsky method.* This method reduces $\boldsymbol{A}$ to a companion matrix by a similarity transformation using a sequence of elimination matrices analogous to those used in Gauss-Jordan elimination (see Section 2.4.8). At step k, $k = 1, \ldots, n-1$, we define a matrix $\boldsymbol{T}_k$ that is the identity matrix except that its $(k+1)$st column is the same as the kth column of $\boldsymbol{A}$. Observe that $\boldsymbol{T}_k^{-1}$ is the identity matrix except that its $(k+1)$st column is

$$\frac{1}{a_{k+1,k}}\begin{bmatrix} -a_{1,k} \\ \vdots \\ -a_{k,k} \\ 1 \\ -a_{k+2,k} \\ \vdots \\ -a_{n,k} \end{bmatrix}.$$

Premultiplication of $\boldsymbol{A}$ on the left by $\boldsymbol{T}_k^{-1}$ does not affect the first $k-1$ columns of $\boldsymbol{A}$, but it transforms column k into companion matrix form, i.e., column k has all zero entries except for a 1 in the subdiagonal entry. Postmultiplication on the right by $\boldsymbol{T}_k$, which is necessary to maintain similarity, does not disturb the first k columns. Thus, if we let $\boldsymbol{A}_0 = \boldsymbol{A}$ and compute $\boldsymbol{A}_k = \boldsymbol{T}_k^{-1}\boldsymbol{A}_{k-1}\boldsymbol{T}_k$, $k = 1, \ldots, n-1$, then after $n-1$ steps, $\boldsymbol{A}_{n-1}$ will be a companion matrix similar to $\boldsymbol{A}$, and hence the last column of $\boldsymbol{A}_{n-1}$ must contain the coefficients $c_0, \ldots, c_{n-1}$ (with signs reversed) of the characteristic polynomial of $\boldsymbol{A}$ (see Section 4.2.1). As with any elimination method, pivoting may be required to avoid division by zero, and in any case it is advisable to minimize error growth. At step k, the row containing the entry of largest magnitude in column k below row k is interchanged with row $k+1$, if necessary, to yield the largest possible pivot $|a_{k+1,k}|$. To maintain similarity, the corresponding columns must also be interchanged. If at some step there is no nonzero entry below the diagonal in the pivot column, then the algorithm cannot be continued, but in that case the matrix is block triangular, so the algorithm can be applied to the diagonal blocks separately.

(*d*) The Danilevsky method simplifies considerably for an upper Hessenberg matrix. In particular, no pivot search is necessary, since at step k, $a_{k+1,k}$ is the only nonzero candidate for the pivot. (If $a_{k+1,k} = 0$ in a Hessenberg matrix, then the matrix is block triangular, and the algorithm can be applied to the diagonal blocks separately.) This suggests a two-phase approach: first reduce $\boldsymbol{A}$ to upper Hessenberg form, say by a sequence of Householder similarity transformations, resulting in an upper Hessenberg matrix $\boldsymbol{H} = \boldsymbol{Q}^H\boldsymbol{AQ}$ similar to $\boldsymbol{A}$, and then apply the Danilevsky method to $\boldsymbol{H}$, ultimately producing a companion matrix similar to $\boldsymbol{A}$ whose last column contains the coefficients of the characteristic polynomial of $\boldsymbol{A}$.

(*e*) The original motivation for the classical methods we have just seen for computing the coefficients of the characteristic polynomial was to use the resulting polynomial to compute eigenvalues. Such methods have been superseded by modern algorithms for computing eigenvalues, such as QR iteration, that are much more accurate, reliable, and efficient. The availability of the latter algorithms suggests yet another way to obtain the coefficients of the characteristic polynomial of a matrix (though it turns the traditional motivation on its head): compute the eigenvalues $\lambda_1, \ldots, \lambda_n$ of the matrix first, and then compute the characteristic polynomial $p(\lambda) = (\lambda-\lambda_1)(\lambda-\lambda_2)\cdots(\lambda-\lambda_n)$ from them. This is the method used in the `poly` function of `MATLAB`.

4.16. (*a*) Write a routine that uses a one-sided plane rotation to symmetrize an arbitrary 2×2

real matrix. That is, given a 2×2 real matrix $\boldsymbol{A}$, choose c and s so that

$$\begin{bmatrix} c & s \\ -s & c \end{bmatrix} \begin{bmatrix} a_{11} & a_{12} \\ a_{21} & a_{22} \end{bmatrix} = \begin{bmatrix} b_{11} & b_{12} \\ b_{12} & b_{22} \end{bmatrix}$$

is real symmetric.

(*b*) Write a routine that uses a two-sided plane rotation to annihilate the off-diagonal entries of an arbitrary 2×2 real symmetric matrix. That is, given a real symmetric 2×2 matrix $\boldsymbol{B}$, choose c and s so that

$$\begin{bmatrix} c & -s \\ s & c \end{bmatrix} \begin{bmatrix} b_{11} & b_{12} \\ b_{12} & b_{22} \end{bmatrix} \begin{bmatrix} c & s \\ -s & c \end{bmatrix} = \begin{bmatrix} d_{11} & 0 \\ 0 & d_{22} \end{bmatrix}$$

is diagonal.

(*c*) Combine the two routines developed in parts *a* and *b* to obtain a routine for computing the singular value decomposition $\boldsymbol{A} = \boldsymbol{U\Sigma V}^T$ of an arbitrary 2×2 real matrix $\boldsymbol{A}$. Note that $\boldsymbol{U}$ will be a product to two plane rotations, whereas $\boldsymbol{V}$ will be a single plane rotation. Test your routine on several 2×2 real matrices and compare the results with those for a library SVD routine.

By systematically solving successive 2×2 subproblems, the module you have just developed can be used to compute the SVD of an arbitrary $m \times n$ real matrix in a manner analogous to the Jacobi method for real symmetric eigenvalue problems.

Chapter 5

Nonlinear Equations

5.1 Nonlinear Equations

Some relationships in nature are linear, as we saw in Chapter 2, but many others are inherently *nonlinear* in that effects are not in direct proportion to their causes. For example, the force on a moving object due to air resistance is proportional to the *square* of its velocity, where the proportionality constant is called the *drag coefficient*. Thus, drag grows rapidly with velocity, which accounts for why fuel economy of an automobile is poor if you drive too fast: you are expending most of the energy pushing air out of the way. If you want to know the drag for a given velocity, you simply evaluate this quadratic function; but if you want to know what velocity would yield a given drag, then you must solve a quadratic equation.

Another example of a nonlinear equation is the familiar *ideal gas law*,

$$pV = nRT,$$

relating pressure p, volume V, and temperature T, where n is the amount of gas present and R is a universal constant. As the name suggests, the ideal gas law is only a crude approximation to reality because it ignores important physical effects, such as the nonzero size of the gas molecules and the forces between them, so that it is reasonably accurate only at relatively high temperatures and low pressures. A better approximation that takes some of these effects into account is the *van der Waals equation of state*,

$$\left(p + \frac{a}{v^2}\right)(v - b) = RT,$$

where $v = V/n$ is the specific volume and a and b are constants that depend on the particular gas. This example is typical in that the relationship becomes more nonlinear as more physical features are included.

By analogy with a general system of linear equations $\boldsymbol{Ax} = \boldsymbol{b}$, perhaps the most natural way to write a general nonlinear equation would be $\boldsymbol{f}(\boldsymbol{x}) = \boldsymbol{y}$, which asks the question, "For what value of $\boldsymbol{x}$ does the nonlinear function $\boldsymbol{f}(\boldsymbol{x})$ take on the value $\boldsymbol{y}$?" It is more customary, however, to subtract $\boldsymbol{y}$ from both sides of the equation and incorporate it into $\boldsymbol{f}$, so that the equation to be solved is expressed as $\boldsymbol{f}(\boldsymbol{x}) = \boldsymbol{0}$. In one dimension, this simply means that we seek the intersection of the curve defined by f with the x axis rather than the horizontal line $y =$ constant.

Thus, a general system of m nonlinear equations in n unknowns has the form

$$\boldsymbol{f}(\boldsymbol{x}) = \boldsymbol{0},$$

where $\boldsymbol{f}\colon \mathbb{R}^n \to \mathbb{R}^m$, and we seek an n-vector $\boldsymbol{x}$ such that all m component functions of $\boldsymbol{f}(\boldsymbol{x})$ are zero *simultaneously*. If the system is overdetermined, $m > n$, then usually there is no solution in this strict sense, and one seeks instead an approximate solution in the least squares sense (see Section 6.6). If the system is underdetermined, $m < n$, then usually there are infinitely many solutions; this case is mainly of interest as a constraint for an optimization problem (see Section 6.7). In this chapter we will be concerned only with the case $m = n$, nonlinear systems having the same number of equations as unknowns. For $m = n = 1$, we have a single nonlinear equation in one unknown, an important special case we will discuss at some length.

A solution value $\boldsymbol{x}$ such that $\boldsymbol{f}(\boldsymbol{x}) = \boldsymbol{0}$ is called a *root* of the equation, and a *zero* of the function $\boldsymbol{f}$. Though technically they have distinct meanings, these two terms are informally used more or less interchangeably, with the obvious meaning. Thus, this problem is often referred to as *root finding* or *zero finding*.

Example 5.1 Nonlinear Equations. An example of a nonlinear equation in one dimension is

$$f(x) = x^2 - 4\sin(x) = 0,$$

for which one approximate solution is $x = 1.93375$. An example of a system of two nonlinear equations in two unknowns is

$$\boldsymbol{f}(\boldsymbol{x}) = \begin{bmatrix} f_1(\boldsymbol{x}) \\ f_2(\boldsymbol{x}) \end{bmatrix} = \begin{bmatrix} x_1^2 - x_2 + 0.25 \\ -x_1 + x_2^2 + 0.25 \end{bmatrix} = \begin{bmatrix} 0 \\ 0 \end{bmatrix},$$

for which the solution vector is $\boldsymbol{x} = \begin{bmatrix} 0.5 & 0.5 \end{bmatrix}^T$.

5.2 Existence and Uniqueness

A general geometric description of solutions to systems of nonlinear equations is analogous to that for systems of linear equations. Each nonlinear equation in a system defines a "curved" hypersurface (as opposed to a "flat" hyperplane for a linear equation) in $\mathbb{R}^n$, and a solution to the system is any point where all these hypersurfaces intersect. But curved surfaces can intersect, or fail to intersect, in many more ways than flat surfaces can. For example, unlike flat surfaces, two curved surfaces can be tangent without being coincident. As a result, it is often difficult to determine the existence or number of solutions of nonlinear equations. Whereas for systems of linear equations the number of solutions must be either zero, one, or infinitely many, nonlinear equations can have any number of solutions.

Example 5.2 Solutions of Nonlinear Systems. Consider the system of nonlinear equations in two dimensions

$$\boldsymbol{f}(\boldsymbol{x}) = \begin{bmatrix} x_1^2 - x_2 + \gamma \\ -x_1 + x_2^2 + \gamma \end{bmatrix} = \begin{bmatrix} 0 \\ 0 \end{bmatrix},$$

where γ is a parameter to be specified. Each of the two component equations defines a parabola, and any point where the two parabolas intersect is a solution to the system. Depending on the particular value for γ, this system can have either zero, one, two, or four solutions, as illustrated in Fig. 5.1.

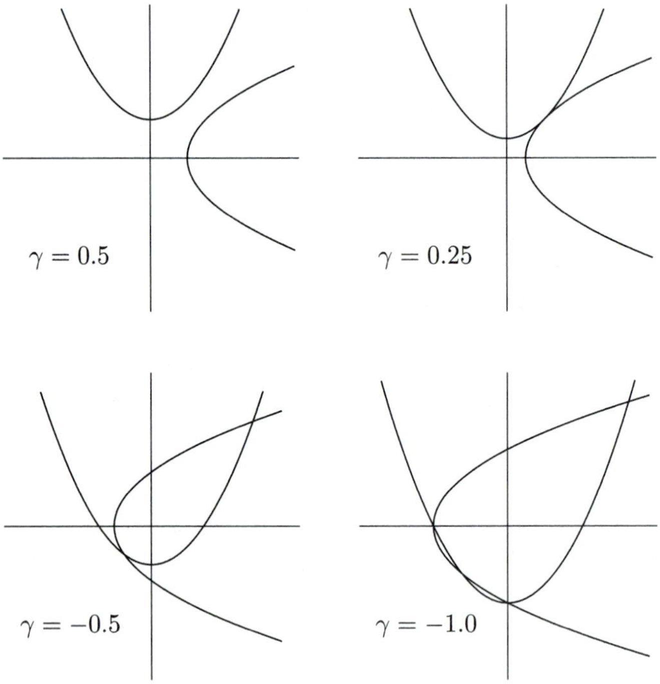

Figure 5.1: Systems of nonlinear equations with various numbers of solutions.

Example 5.3 Solutions of Nonlinear Equations. Even in one dimension, a wide variety of behavior is possible, as shown by these examples.

- $e^x + 1 = 0$ has no solution.

- $e^{-x} - x = 0$ has one solution.
- $x^2 - 4\sin(x) = 0$ has two solutions.
- $x^3 + 6x^2 + 11x - 6 = 0$ has three solutions.
- $\sin(x) = 0$ has infinitely many solutions.

Although it is difficult to make any global assertions about solutions of nonlinear equations, there are nevertheless some useful local criteria that guarantee existence of a solution. The simplest of these is for one-dimensional problems, for which a sufficient condition for a solution is provided by the *Intermediate Value Theorem*, which says that if f is continuous on a closed interval $[a, b]$, and c lies between $f(a)$ and $f(b)$, then there is a value $x^* \in [a, b]$ such that $f(x^*) = c$. Thus, if $f(a)$ and $f(b)$ differ in sign, then by taking $c = 0$ in the theorem we can conclude that there must be a root within the interval $[a, b]$. Such an interval $[a, b]$ for which the sign of f differs at its endpoints is called a *bracket* for a solution of the one-dimensional nonlinear equation $f(x) = 0$. As we will see later, refining such a bracket plays an important part in some algorithms for finding a solution. Identifying such a bracket in the first place, however, is often a matter of trial and error.

The bracket criterion just given can be generalized to n dimensions. For motivation, we first note that in one dimension the condition $f(a) \leq 0$ and $f(b) \geq 0$ is equivalent to $(x - z)f(x) \geq 0$ for $x = a$ and $x = b$, where z is any point in the open interval (a, b). Now if $\boldsymbol{f}: \mathbb{R}^n \to \mathbb{R}^n$ is continuous on the closure of an open, bounded set $S \subseteq \mathbb{R}^n$, and $(\boldsymbol{x} - \boldsymbol{z})^T \boldsymbol{f}(\boldsymbol{x}) \geq 0$ for any $\boldsymbol{z} \in S$ and any $\boldsymbol{x}$ in the boundary of S, then $\boldsymbol{f}(\boldsymbol{x}) = \boldsymbol{0}$ has a solution in S. Unfortunately, this generalization of the bracket criterion is usually impractical to apply in n dimensions.

Another relevant theorem from calculus in this context is the *Inverse Function Theorem*, which says that for a continuously differentiable function $\boldsymbol{f}$, if the Jacobian matrix $\boldsymbol{J}_f$ defined by $\{\boldsymbol{J}_f(\boldsymbol{x})\}_{ij} = \partial f_i(\boldsymbol{x})/\partial x_j$ is nonsingular at a point $\boldsymbol{x}^*$, then there is a neighborhood of $\boldsymbol{f}(\boldsymbol{x}^*)$ in which $\boldsymbol{f}$ is invertible, that is, the equation $\boldsymbol{f}(\boldsymbol{x}) = \boldsymbol{y}$ has a solution for any $\boldsymbol{y}$ in that neighborhood of $\boldsymbol{f}(\boldsymbol{x}^*)$. Unfortunately, even if $\boldsymbol{J}_f(\boldsymbol{x})$ is nonsingular for all $\boldsymbol{x} \in \mathbb{R}^n$, so that $\boldsymbol{f}$ is locally invertible everywhere, it still may not be globally invertible on all of $\mathbb{R}^n$ unless some additional condition holds, such as $\|\boldsymbol{J}_f^{-1}(\boldsymbol{x})\|$ being bounded above by some finite constant. Such strong sufficient conditions may seem unlikely to hold in practice, but keep in mind that they are far from necessary for a solution to exist, so one should not be deterred from seeking a solution in any particular instance just because one may not be able to ensure the existence of a solution in advance.

Yet another approach to verifying the existence of solutions to nonlinear systems is provided by the theory of fixed points and contractive mappings. A function $\boldsymbol{g}: \mathbb{R}^n \to \mathbb{R}^n$ is *contractive* on a set $S \subseteq \mathbb{R}^n$ if there is a constant γ, with $0 < \gamma < 1$, such that

$$\|\boldsymbol{g}(\boldsymbol{x}) - \boldsymbol{g}(\boldsymbol{z})\| \leq \gamma \|\boldsymbol{x} - \boldsymbol{z}\|$$

for all $\boldsymbol{x}, \boldsymbol{z} \in S$. A *fixed point* of $\boldsymbol{g}$ is any value $\boldsymbol{x}$ such that $\boldsymbol{g}(\boldsymbol{x}) = \boldsymbol{x}$. The *Contraction Mapping Theorem* says that if $\boldsymbol{g}$ is contractive on a closed set $S \subseteq \mathbb{R}^n$ and $\boldsymbol{g}(S) \subseteq S$, then $\boldsymbol{g}$ has a unique fixed point in S. Thus, if $\boldsymbol{f}$ has the form $\boldsymbol{f}(\boldsymbol{x}) = \boldsymbol{x} - \boldsymbol{g}(\boldsymbol{x})$, where $\boldsymbol{g}$ is contractive on a closed set $S \subseteq \mathbb{R}^n$, with $\boldsymbol{g}(S) \subseteq S$, then $\boldsymbol{f}(\boldsymbol{x}) = \boldsymbol{0}$ has a unique solution in S, namely the fixed point of $\boldsymbol{g}$. The general applicability of this approach may not be obvious now, but we will soon see that it provides the basis for useful iterative algorithms for computing solutions to nonlinear systems.

Finally, we mention another powerful theoretical tool, the *topological degree* of a function $\boldsymbol{f}$ on a given closed and bounded set $S \subseteq \mathbb{R}^n$. Its formal definition is too complicated to state here, but we can think of the degree informally as the number of zeros $\boldsymbol{x}^*$ of $\boldsymbol{f}$ in S, counted by positive or negative orientation, i.e.,

$$\sum_{\boldsymbol{x}^* \in S} \text{sign}(\det(\boldsymbol{J}_f(\boldsymbol{x}^*))).$$

It turns out that the degree can be defined analytically in terms of a certain integral, the numerical evaluation of which is involved and expensive, but it can be computed reliably using methods based on interval arithmetic (see Section 1.3.10). Though the topological degree is an important theoretical tool, it is of limited practical utility in ordinary numerical computations.

Thus far we have focused primarily on existence, rather than uniqueness, of solutions to nonlinear equations because one generally takes it for granted that a nonlinear equation may have more than one solution, at least globally. One may still be concerned, however, about local uniqueness. Recall from Section 2.2 that an $n \times n$ system of linear equations $\boldsymbol{Ax} = \boldsymbol{b}$ always has a unique solution whenever the matrix $\boldsymbol{A}$ is nonsingular. The analogous regularity condition for a nonlinear function $\boldsymbol{f}$, at least locally, is that the Jacobian matrix $\boldsymbol{J}_f(\boldsymbol{x}^*)$ is nonsingular at a given point $\boldsymbol{x}^*$, and in that case the *Inverse Function Theorem* cited earlier establishes the existence of a neighborhood U of $\boldsymbol{x}^*$ that $\boldsymbol{f}$ maps one-to-one onto some neighborhood of $\boldsymbol{y} = \boldsymbol{f}(\boldsymbol{x}^*)$, which implies that U contains no other solution to $\boldsymbol{f}(\boldsymbol{x}) = \boldsymbol{y}$. Thus, in the "normal" situation, where $\boldsymbol{J}_f$ is nonsingular, solutions are isolated. Degeneracy can occur, however, when $\boldsymbol{J}_f(\boldsymbol{x}^*)$ is singular at a solution $\boldsymbol{x}^*$, and we will see that such degeneracy affects the conditioning of the solution as well as the convergence properties of iterative algorithms for computing it.

For a nonlinear equation in one dimension, such degeneracy at a solution x^* means that both the function *and* its derivative are zero, i.e., $f(x^*) = 0$ and $f'(x^*) = 0$; such a solution is called a *multiple root*. Geometrically, this property means that the curve defined by f has a horizontal tangent on the x axis. More generally, for a smooth function f, if $f(x^*) = f'(x^*) = f''(x^*) = \cdots = f^{(m-1)}(x^*) = 0$ but $f^{(m)}(x^*) \neq 0$, then x^* is said to be a root of *multiplicity* m. If $m = 1$, i.e., $f(x^*) = 0$ and $f'(x^*) \neq 0$, then x^* is said to be a *simple root*.

Example 5.4 Multiple Root. Examples of equations having a multiple root include the quadratic equation $x^2 - 2x + 1 = 0$, for which $x = 1$ is a root of multiplicity two, and the cubic equation $x^3 - 3x^2 + 3x - 1 = 0$, for which $x = 1$ is a root of multiplicity three. Each of these functions is tangent to the horizontal axis at the root, as can be seen in Fig. 5.2. Note that the quadratic on the left touches the horizontal axis but does not cross it, and hence the bracket criterion (which requires a sign change in the function) would fail to identify this solution.

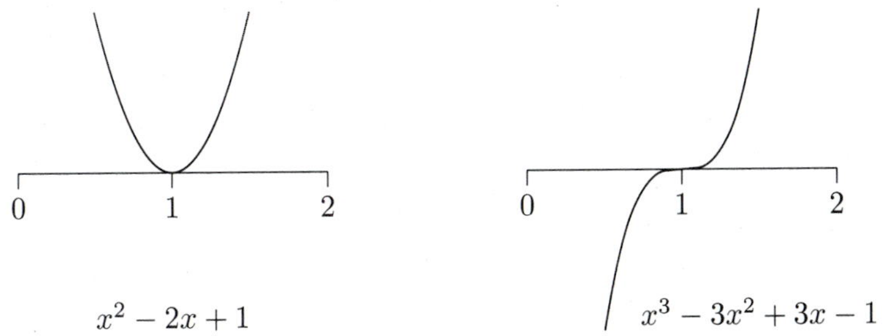

Figure 5.2: Two nonlinear functions, each having a multiple root.

5.3 Sensitivity and Conditioning

As was already discussed in Section 1.2.6, the sensitivity of the root-finding problem for a given function is opposite to that for *evaluating* the function: if the function value is insensitive to the value of the argument, then the root will be sensitive, whereas if the function value is sensitive to the argument, then the root will be insensitive. This property makes sense, because the two problems are inverses of each other: if $\boldsymbol{f}(\boldsymbol{x}) = \boldsymbol{y}$, then finding $\boldsymbol{x}$ given $\boldsymbol{y}$ has the opposite conditioning from finding $\boldsymbol{y}$ given $\boldsymbol{x}$.

For a quantitative measure of sensitivity for the root-finding problem, we must use an *absolute* (as opposed to relative) condition number, since the function value at the solution is zero by definition. Recall from Section 1.2.6 that in one dimension the absolute condition number for evaluating a smooth function f near a root x^* is $|f'(x^*)|$, and the root-finding problem for f at x^* has absolute condition number $1/|f'(x^*)|$. This means that when we have found a point $\hat{x}$ at which $|f(\hat{x})| \leq \epsilon$, the error $|\hat{x} - x^*|$ in the solution may be as large as $\epsilon/|f'(x^*)|$, which can be quite large if $|f'(x^*)|$ is very small. The corresponding absolute condition numbers for function evaluation and root-finding problems in n-dimensions are $\|\boldsymbol{J}_f(\boldsymbol{x}^*)\|$ and $\|\boldsymbol{J}_f^{-1}(\boldsymbol{x}^*)\|$, respectively.

These results are illustrated in Fig. 5.3, which is analogous to Fig. 2.4 for linear systems, except the lines are now curved and we seek the intersection points of those curves with the horizontal axis. The dashed curves indicate the region of uncertainty about each solid curve, so that the root in each case could be anywhere between the points at which the dashed curves intersect the horizontal axis. The small interval of uncertainty for the root on the left is due to the steep slope (and hence small reciprocal of that slope), whereas the large interval of uncertainty for the root on the right is due to the shallow slope (and hence large reciprocal of that slope).

In one dimension, $f'(x^*) = 0$ at a multiple root x^*, so the condition number of a multiple root is infinite. This makes sense because a slight perturbation can cause a multiple root to become more than one root or not a root at all (see Example 5.4). Similarly, for a solution $\boldsymbol{x}^*$ to an n-dimensional nonlinear system, the condition number is infinite if $\boldsymbol{J}_f(\boldsymbol{x}^*)$ is singular. Again this makes sense, because the existence and number of roots may be discontinuous at such a point.

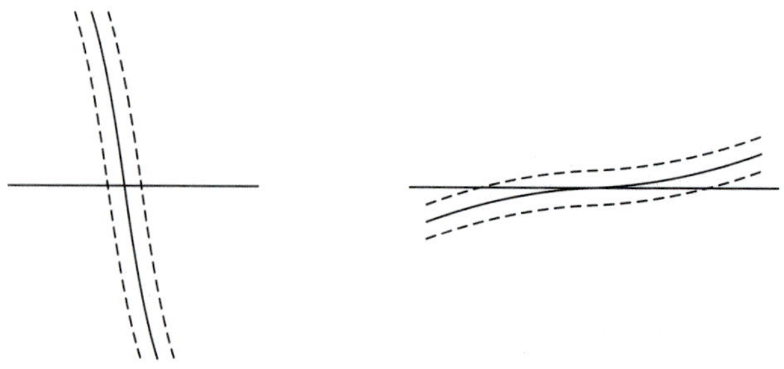

Figure 5.3: Conditioning of roots of nonlinear equations.

Example 5.5 Singular Jacobian. For the nonlinear system of Example 5.2, with $\gamma = 0.25$ (the upper right case in Fig.5.1), the Jacobian matrix

$$\boldsymbol{J}_f(\boldsymbol{x}) = \begin{bmatrix} 2x_1 & -1 \\ -1 & 2x_2 \end{bmatrix}$$

is singular at the unique solution $\boldsymbol{x}^* = [0.5, 0.5]^T$. For a slightly smaller value of γ there are two solutions, and for a slightly larger value of γ there is no solution.

The conditioning of a nonlinear equation affects our expectations of an approximate solution $\hat{\boldsymbol{x}}$: should we expect $\|\boldsymbol{f}(\hat{\boldsymbol{x}})\| \approx 0$, which corresponds to having a small residual, or $\|\hat{\boldsymbol{x}} - \boldsymbol{x}^*\| \approx 0$, which measures closeness to the (usually unknown) true solution $\boldsymbol{x}^*$? As with linear systems, these two criteria for a solution are not necessarily "small" simultaneously, depending on the conditioning. For an ill-conditioned problem, $\|\boldsymbol{f}(\hat{\boldsymbol{x}})\|$ can be small without $\hat{\boldsymbol{x}}$ being close to the true solution. As with linear systems, a small residual implies an accurate solution only if the problem is well-conditioned. These considerations, along with several others, affect the choice of stopping criteria for iterative solution methods, which we will consider next.

5.4 Convergence Rates and Stopping Criteria

Unlike linear equations, most nonlinear equations cannot be solved in a finite number of steps. Thus, we must usually resort to an iterative method that produces increasingly accurate approximations to a solution, and we terminate the iterations when the result is sufficiently accurate. The total cost of solving the problem depends on both the cost per iteration and the number of iterations required for convergence, and there is often a tradeoff between these two factors.

To compare the effectiveness of iterative methods, we need to characterize their convergence rates. The error at iteration k, which we denote by $\boldsymbol{e}_k$, is usually given by $\boldsymbol{e}_k = \boldsymbol{x}_k - \boldsymbol{x}^*$, where $\boldsymbol{x}_k$ is the approximate solution at iteration k and $\boldsymbol{x}^*$ is the true solution. Some methods for one-dimensional problems do not produce a specific approximate solution x_k, however, but merely an interval known to contain the solution, with the length of the interval decreasing as iterations proceed. For such methods, we take e_k to be the length of this interval at iteration k. In either case, an iterative method is said to converge with rate r if

$$\lim_{k\to\infty} \frac{\|\boldsymbol{e}_{k+1}\|}{\|\boldsymbol{e}_k\|^r} = C$$

for some finite constant $C > 0$. Some particular cases of interest are:

- If $r = 1$ and $C < 1$, the convergence rate is *linear.*
- If $r > 1$, the convergence rate is *superlinear.*
- If $r = 2$, the convergence rate is *quadratic.*
- If $r = 3$, the convergence rate is *cubic*, and so on.

One way to interpret the distinction between linear and superlinear convergence is that, asymptotically, a linearly convergent sequence gains a constant number of additional correct digits per iteration, whereas a superlinearly convergent sequence gains an increasing number of additional correct digits with each iteration. Specifically, a linearly convergent sequence gains $-\log_\beta(C)$ base-β digits per iteration, but a superlinearly convergent sequence has r times as many correct digits after each iteration as it had the previous iteration. In particular, a quadratically convergent method doubles the number of correct digits with each iteration.

Example 5.6 Convergence Rates. If the members of each of the following sequences are the magnitudes of the errors at successive iterations of an iterative method, then the convergence rate is as indicated.

1. $10^{-2}, 10^{-3}, 10^{-4}, 10^{-5}, \ldots$ linear, with $C = 10^{-1}$
2. $10^{-2}, 10^{-4}, 10^{-6}, 10^{-8}, \ldots$ linear, with $C = 10^{-2}$
3. $10^{-2}, 10^{-3}, 10^{-5}, 10^{-8}, \ldots$ superlinear, but not quadratic
4. $10^{-2}, 10^{-4}, 10^{-8}, 10^{-16}, \ldots$ quadratic

A convergence theorem may tell us that an iterative scheme will converge for a given problem, and how rapidly it will do so, but that does not specifically address the issue of when to stop iterating and declare the resulting approximate solution to be "good enough." Devising a suitable stopping criterion is a complex and subtle issue for a number of reasons. We may know in principle that the error $\|\boldsymbol{e}_k\|$ is becoming small, but since we do not know the true solution, we have no way of knowing $\|\boldsymbol{e}_k\|$ directly. A reasonable surrogate is the relative change in successive iterates, $\|\boldsymbol{x}_{k+1} - \boldsymbol{x}_k\|/\|\boldsymbol{x}_k\|$. When the latter quantity becomes sufficiently small, then the approximate solutions have ceased changing significantly and there is little point in continuing. On the other hand, to ensure that the problem has actually been solved, one may also want to verify that the residual $\|\boldsymbol{f}(\boldsymbol{x}_k)\|$ is suitably small. As we have already observed, however, these two quantities are not necessarily small simultaneously, depending on the conditioning of the problem. In addition, all of these criteria are affected by the relative scaling of the components of both the argument $\boldsymbol{x}$ and the function $\boldsymbol{f}$, and possibly other problem-dependent features as well. For all these reasons, a foolproof stopping criterion can be difficult to achieve and complicated to state. In stating iterative algorithms in this book, we will usually omit any explicit convergence test and instead merely indicate an indefinite number of iterations, with the understanding that the iterative process is to be terminated when a suitable stopping criterion is met. This avoids cluttering an otherwise clean algorithm statement with a complicated convergence test, or else using a misleadingly simplistic one.

5.5 Nonlinear Equations in One Dimension

We first consider solution methods for nonlinear equations in one dimension: given a continuous function $f: \mathbb{R} \to \mathbb{R}$, we seek a point $x^* \in \mathbb{R}$ such that $f(x^*) = 0$.

5.5.1 Interval Bisection

In finite-precision arithmetic, there may be no machine number x^* such that $f(x^*)$ is exactly zero. An alternative is to seek a very short interval $[a, b]$ in which f has a change of sign. As we saw in Section 5.2, such a *bracket* ensures that the corresponding continuous function must take on the value zero somewhere within the interval. The *bisection* method begins with an initial bracket and successively reduces its length until the solution has been isolated as accurately as desired (or the arithmetic precision will permit). At each iteration, the function is evaluated at the *midpoint* of the current interval, and half of the interval can then be discarded, depending on the sign of the function at the midpoint. The bisection method is stated formally in Algorithm 5.1, for which the initial input is a function f, an interval $[a, b]$ such that $\text{sign}(f(a)) \neq \text{sign}(f(b))$, and an error tolerance *tol* for the length of the final interval.

Algorithm 5.1 Interval Bisection

while $((b - a) > tol)$ **do**
    $m = a + (b - a)/2$
    if $\text{sign}(f(a)) = \text{sign}(f(m))$ **then**
        $a = m$
    else
        $b = m$
    end
end

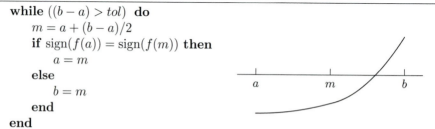

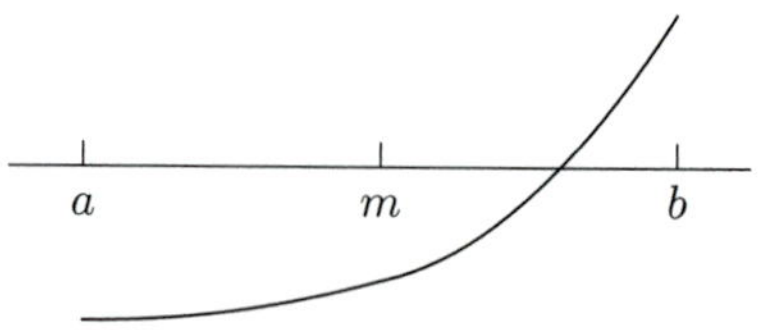

We note a couple of details in Algorithm 5.1 that are designed to avoid potential pitfalls when it is implemented in finite-precision, floating-point arithmetic. First, perhaps the most obvious formula for computing the midpoint m of the interval $[a, b]$ is $m = (a + b)/2$. However, with this formula the result in finite-precision arithmetic is not even guaranteed to fall within the interval $[a, b]$ (in two-digit, decimal arithmetic, for example, this formula gives a "midpoint" of 0.7 for the interval $[0.67, 0.69]$). Moreover, the intermediate quantity $a+b$ could overflow in an extreme case, even though the midpoint is well defined and should be computable. A better alternative is the formula $m = a + (b - a)/2$, which cannot overflow and is guaranteed to fall within the interval $[a, b]$, provided a and b have the same sign (as will normally be the case unless the root happens to be near zero). Second, testing whether two function values $f(x_1)$ and $f(x_2)$ agree in sign is mathematically equivalent to testing whether the product $f(x_1) \cdot f(x_2)$ is positive or negative. In floating-point arithmetic, however, such an implementation is risky because the product could easily underflow when the function values are small, which they will be as we approach the root. A safer alternative is to use the sign function explicitly, where $\text{sign}(x) = 1$ if $x \geq 0$ and $\text{sign}(x) = -1$ if $x < 0$.

Example 5.7 Interval Bisection. We illustrate the bisection method by finding a root of the equation

$$f(x) = x^2 - 4\sin(x) = 0.$$

For the initial bracketing interval $[a, b]$, we take $a = 1$ and $b = 3$. All that really matters is that the function values differ in sign at the two points. We evaluate the function at the midpoint $m = a + (b - a)/2 = 2$ and find that $f(m)$ has the opposite sign from $f(a)$, so we retain the first half of the initial interval by setting $b = m$. We then repeat the process until the bracketing interval isolates the root of the equation as accurately as desired. The sequence of iterations is shown here.

a	$f(a)$	b	$f(b)$
1.000000	−2.365884	3.000000	8.435520
1.000000	−2.365884	2.000000	0.362810
1.500000	−1.739980	2.000000	0.362810
1.750000	−0.873444	2.000000	0.362810
1.875000	−0.300718	2.000000	0.362810
1.875000	−0.300718	1.937500	0.019849
1.906250	−0.143255	1.937500	0.019849
1.921875	−0.062406	1.937500	0.019849
1.929688	−0.021454	1.937500	0.019849
1.933594	−0.000846	1.937500	0.019849
1.933594	−0.000846	1.935547	0.009491
1.933594	−0.000846	1.934570	0.004320
1.933594	−0.000846	1.934082	0.001736
1.933594	−0.000846	1.933838	0.000445
1.933716	−0.000201	1.933838	0.000445
1.933716	−0.000201	1.933777	0.000122
1.933746	−0.000039	1.933777	0.000122
1.933746	−0.000039	1.933762	0.000041
1.933746	−0.000039	1.933754	0.000001
1.933750	−0.000019	1.933754	0.000001
1.933752	−0.000009	1.933754	0.000001
1.933753	−0.000004	1.933754	0.000001

The bisection method makes no use of the magnitudes of the function values, only their signs. As a result, bisection is certain to converge but does so rather slowly. Specifically, at each successive iteration the length of the interval containing the solution, and hence a bound on the possible error, is reduced by half. This means that the bisection method is linearly convergent, with $r = 1$ and $C = 0.5$. Another way of stating this is that we gain one additional correct bit in the approximate solution for each iteration of bisection. Given a starting interval $[a, b]$, the length of the interval after k iterations is $(b - a)/2^k$, so that achieving an error tolerance of *tol* requires

$$\left\lceil \log_2\left(\frac{b-a}{tol}\right)\right\rceil$$

iterations, regardless of the particular function f involved.

5.5.2 Fixed-Point Iteration

We now consider an alternative problem that will help us solve our original problem. Given a function $g\colon \mathbb{R} \to \mathbb{R}$, a value x such that

$$x = g(x)$$

is called a *fixed point* of the function g, since x is unchanged when g is applied to it. Whereas with a nonlinear equation $f(x) = 0$ we seek a point where the curve defined by f intersects the x-axis (i.e., the line $y = 0$), with a fixed-point problem $x = g(x)$ we seek a point where the curve defined by g intersects the diagonal line $y = x$. Fixed-point problems often arise directly in practice, but they are also important because a nonlinear equation can usually be recast as a fixed-point problem for a related nonlinear function. Indeed, many iterative algorithms for solving nonlinear equations are based on iteration schemes of the form

$$x_{k+1} = g(x_k),$$

where g is a function chosen so that its fixed points are solutions for $f(x) = 0$. Such a scheme is called *fixed-point iteration* or sometimes *functional iteration*, since the function g is applied repeatedly to an initial starting value x_0.

For a given equation $f(x) = 0$, there may be many equivalent fixed-point problems $x = g(x)$ with different choices for the function g. But not all fixed-point formulations are equally useful in deriving an iteration scheme for solving a given nonlinear equation. The resulting iteration schemes may differ not only in their convergence rates but also in whether they converge at all.

Example 5.8 Fixed-Point Problems. The nonlinear equation

$$f(x) = x^2 - x - 2 = 0$$

has roots $x^* = 2$ and $x^* = -1$. Equivalent fixed-point problems include

1. $g(x) = x^2 - 2$,
2. $g(x) = \sqrt{x + 2}$,

3. $g(x) = 1 + 2/x$,
4. $g(x) = (x^2 + 2)/(2x - 1)$.

Each of these functions is plotted near $x = 2$ in Fig. 5.4, along with the line $y = x$. By design, each of the functions intersects the line $y = x$ at the fixed point $(2, 2)$.

The corresponding fixed-point iteration schemes are depicted graphically in Fig. 5.5. A vertical arrow corresponds to evaluation of the function at a point, and a horizontal arrow pointing to the line $y = x$ indicates that the result of the previous function evaluation is used as the argument for the next. For the first of these functions, even with a starting point very near the solution, the successive iterates diverge. For the other three functions, the successive iterates converge to the fixed point even if started at a point relatively far from the solution, although the rates of convergence appear to vary somewhat.

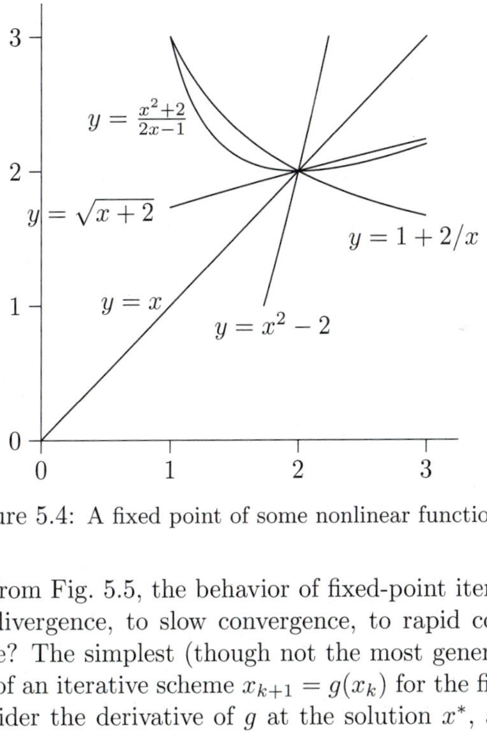

Figure 5.4: A fixed point of some nonlinear functions.

As one can see from Fig. 5.5, the behavior of fixed-point iteration schemes can vary widely, from divergence, to slow convergence, to rapid convergence. What makes the difference? The simplest (though not the most general) way to characterize the behavior of an iterative scheme $x_{k+1} = g(x_k)$ for the fixed-point problem $x = g(x)$ is to consider the derivative of g at the solution x^*, assuming that g is smooth. In particular, if $x^* = g(x^*)$ and $|g'(x^*)| < 1$, then the iterative scheme is *locally convergent*, i.e., there is an interval containing x^* such that fixed-point iteration with g converges if started at a point within that interval. If $|g'(x^*)| > 1$, on the other hand, then fixed-point iteration with g diverges for any starting point other than x^*.

The proof of this result is simple and instructive, so we sketch it here. If x^* is a fixed point, then for the error at the kth iteration we have

$$e_{k+1} = x_{k+1} - x^* = g(x_k) - g(x^*).$$

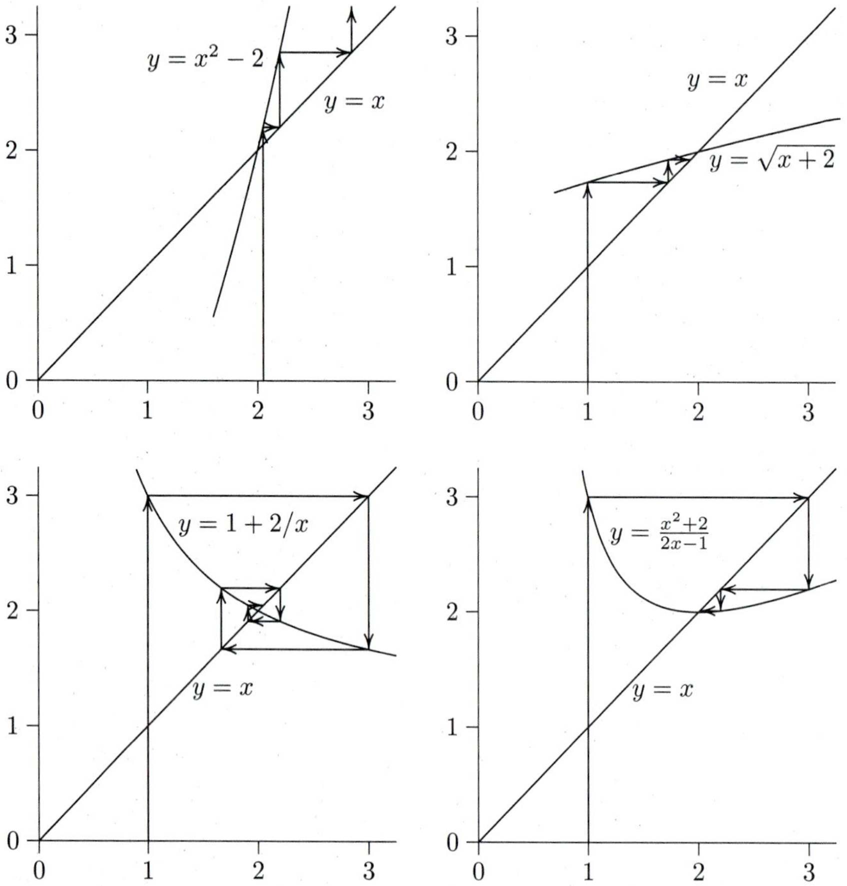

Figure 5.5: Fixed-point iterations for some nonlinear functions.

By the *Mean Value Theorem*, there is a point θ_k between x_k and x^* such that

$$g(x_k) - g(x^*) = g'(\theta_k)(x_k - x^*),$$

so that

$$e_{k+1} = g'(\theta_k)e_k.$$

We do not know the value of θ_k, but if $|g'(x^*)| < 1$, then by starting the iterations close enough to x^*, we can be assured that there is a constant C such that $|g'(\theta_k)| \leq C < 1$, for $k = 0, 1, \ldots$. Thus, we have

$$|e_{k+1}| \leq C|e_k| \leq \cdots \leq C^k|e_0|,$$

but $C < 1$ implies $C^k \to 0$, so $|e_k| \to 0$ and the sequence converges.

As we can see from the proof, when fixed-point iteration converges the asymptotic convergence rate is linear, with constant $C = |g'(x^*)|$. The smaller the constant, the faster the convergence, so ideally we would like to have $g'(x^*) = 0$, in which case Taylor's Theorem shows that

$$g(x_k) - g(x^*) = g''(\xi_k)(x_k - x^*)^2/2$$

for some ξ_k between x_k and x^*. Thus,

$$\lim_{k\to\infty} \frac{|e_{k+1}|}{|e_k|^2} = \left|\frac{g''(x^*)}{2}\right|,$$

and hence the convergence rate is at least quadratic. In Section 5.5.3, we will see a systematic way of choosing g so that this occurs.

Example 5.9 Convergence of Fixed-Point Iteration. For the four fixed-point problems in Example 5.8, we have

1. $g'(x) = 2x$, so $g'(2) = 4$, and hence fixed-point iteration diverges.
2. $g'(x) = 1/(2\sqrt{x+2})$, so $g'(2) = 1/4$, and hence fixed-point iteration converges linearly with $C = 1/4$. The positive sign of $g'(2)$ causes the iterates to approach the fixed-point from one side.
3. $g'(x) = -2/x^2$, so $g'(2) = -1/2$, and hence fixed-point iteration converges linearly with $C = 1/2$. The negative sign of $g'(2)$ causes the iterates to spiral around the fixed-point, alternating sides.
4. $g'(x) = (2x^2 - 2x - 4)/(2x-1)^2$, so $g'(2) = 0$, and hence fixed-point iteration converges quadratically.

5.5.3 Newton's Method

The bisection technique makes no use of the function values other than their signs, which results in slow but sure convergence. More rapidly convergent methods can be derived by using the function values to obtain a more accurate approximation to the solution at each iteration. In particular, the truncated Taylor series

$$f(x+h) \approx f(x) + f'(x)h$$

is a linear function of h that approximates f near a given x. We can therefore replace the nonlinear function f with this linear function, whose zero is easily determined to be $h = -f(x)/f'(x)$, assuming that $f'(x) \neq 0$. Of course, the zeros of the two functions are not identical in general, so we repeat the process. This motivates the iteration scheme, known as *Newton's method*, shown in Algorithm 5.2. As illustrated in Fig. 5.6, Newton's method can be interpreted as approximating the function f near x_k by the tangent line at $f(x_k)$. We can then take the next approximate solution to be the zero of this linear function, and repeat the process.

Example 5.10 Newton's Method. We illustrate Newton's method by again finding a root of the equation

$$f(x) = x^2 - 4\sin(x) = 0.$$

Algorithm 5.2 Newton's Method for One-Dimensional Nonlinear Equation

$x_0 =$ initial guess
for $k = 0, 1, 2, \ldots$
  $x_{k+1} = x_k - f(x_k)/f'(x_k)$
end

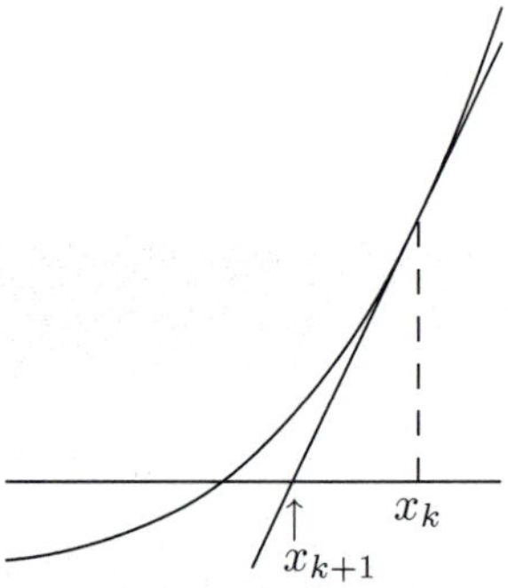

Figure 5.6: Newton's method for solving nonlinear equation.

The derivative of this function is given by

$$f'(x) = 2x - 4\cos(x),$$

so that the iteration scheme is given by

$$x_{k+1} = x_k - \frac{x_k^2 - 4\sin(x_k)}{2x_k - 4\cos(x_k)}.$$

Taking $x_0 = 3$ as initial guess, we obtain the sequence of iterations shown next, where $h_k = -f(x_k)/f'(x_k)$ denotes the change in x_k at each iteration. The iteration can be terminated when $|h_k|/|x_k|$ or $|f(x_k)|$, or both, are as small as desired.

k	x_k	$f(x_k)$	$f'(x_k)$	h_k
0	3.000000	8.435520	9.959970	−0.846942
1	2.153058	1.294772	6.505771	−0.199019
2	1.954039	0.108438	5.403795	−0.020067
3	1.933972	0.001152	5.288919	−0.000218
4	1.933754	0.000000	5.287670	0.000000

We can view Newton's method as a systematic way of transforming a nonlinear equation $f(x) = 0$ into a fixed-point problem $x = g(x)$, where

$$g(x) = x - f(x)/f'(x).$$

To study the convergence of this scheme, we therefore determine the derivative

$$g'(x) = f(x)f''(x)/(f'(x))^2.$$

If x^* is a simple root (i.e., $f(x^*) = 0$ and $f'(x^*) \neq 0$), then $g'(x^*) = 0$. Thus, the asymptotic convergence rate of Newton's method for a simple root is quadratic, i.e., $r = 2$. We have already seen an illustration of this: the fourth fixed-point iteration scheme in Example 5.8 is Newton's method for solving that example equation (note that the fourth iteration function in Fig. 5.5 has a horizontal tangent at the fixed point).

The quadratic convergence rate of Newton's method for a simple root means that asymptotically the error is squared at each iteration. Another way of stating this is that the number of correct digits in the approximate solution is doubled at each iteration of Newton's method. For a multiple root, on the other hand, Newton's method is only linearly convergent, with constant $C = 1 - (1/m)$, where m is the multiplicity. It is important to remember, however, that these convergence results are only local, and Newton's method may not converge at all unless started close enough to the solution. For example, a relatively small value for $f'(x_k)$ (i.e., a nearly horizontal tangent of f) tends to cause the next iterate to lie far away from the current approximation.

Example 5.11 Newton's Method for Multiple Root. Both types of behavior are shown in the following examples, where the first shows quadratic convergence to a simple root and the second shows linear convergence to a multiple root. The multiplicity of the root for the second problem is 2, so $C = 1/2$.

	$f(x) = x^2 - 1$	$f(x) = x^2 - 2x + 1$
k	x_k	x_k
0	2.0	2.0
1	1.25	1.5
2	1.025	1.25
3	1.0003	1.125
4	1.00000005	1.0625
5	1.0	1.03125

5.5.4 Secant Method

One drawback of Newton's method is that both the function and its derivative must be evaluated at each iteration. The derivative may be inconvenient or expensive to evaluate, so we might consider replacing it by a finite difference approximation using some small step size h, as in Example 1.3, but this would require a second evaluation of the function at each iteration purely for the purpose of obtaining derivative information. A better idea is to base the finite difference approximation on successive iterates,

$$f'(x_k) \approx \frac{f(x_k) - f(x_{k-1})}{x_k - x_{k-1}},$$

where the function must be evaluated anyway. This approach gives the *secant method*, shown in Algorithm 5.3. As illustrated in Fig. 5.7, the secant method can be interpreted as approximating the function f by the secant line through the previous two iterates, and taking the zero of the resulting linear function to be the next approximate solution.

Algorithm 5.3 Secant Method

$x_0, x_1 =$ initial guesses
for $k = 1, 2, \ldots$
$\quad x_{k+1} = x_k - f(x_k)(x_k - x_{k-1})/(f(x_k) - f(x_{k-1}))$
end

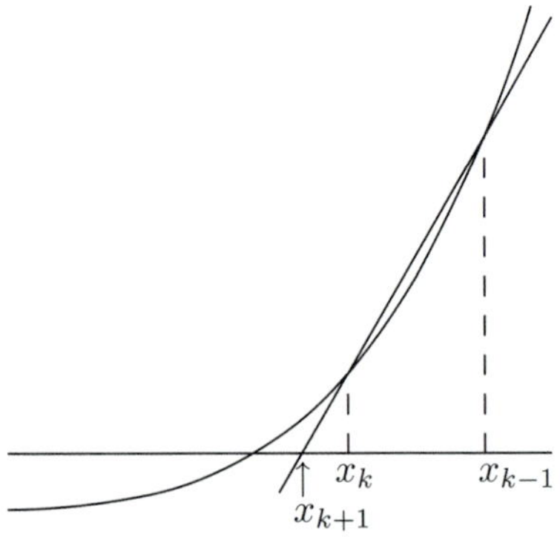

Figure 5.7: Secant method for solving nonlinear equation.

Example 5.12 Secant Method. We illustrate the secant method by again finding a root of the equation

$$f(x) = x^2 - 4\sin(x) = 0.$$

We evaluate the function at each of two starting guesses, $x_0 = 1$ and $x_1 = 3$, and take the next approximate solution to be the zero of the straight line fitting the two function values. We then repeat the process using this new value and the more recent of our two previous values, so only one new function evaluation is needed per iteration. The sequence of iterations is shown next, where h_k denotes the change in x_k at each iteration.

k	x_k	$f(x_k)$	h_k
0	1.000000	−2.365884	
1	3.000000	8.435520	−1.561930
2	1.438070	−1.896774	0.286735
3	1.724805	−0.977706	0.305029
4	2.029833	0.534305	−0.107789
5	1.922044	−0.061523	0.011130
6	1.933174	−0.003064	0.000583
7	1.933757	0.000019	−0.000004
8	1.933754	0.000000	0.000000

Because each new approximate solution produced by the secant method depends on two previous iterates, its convergence behavior is somewhat more complicated to analyze, so we omit most of the details. It can be shown that the errors satisfy

$$\lim_{k\to\infty} \frac{|e_{k+1}|}{|e_k| \cdot |e_{k-1}|} = c$$

for some finite constant $c > 0$, which implies that the sequence is locally convergent and suggests that the rate is superlinear. For each k we define

$$s_k = |e_{k+1}|/|e_k|^r,$$

where r is the convergence rate to be determined. Thus, we have

$$|e_{k+1}| = s_k |e_k|^r = s_k (s_{k-1} |e_{k-1}|^r)^r = s_k s_{k-1}^r |e_{k-1}|^{r^2},$$

so that

$$\frac{|e_{k+1}|}{|e_k| \cdot |e_{k-1}|} = \frac{s_k s_{k-1}^r |e_{k-1}|^{r^2}}{s_{k-1} |e_{k-1}|^r \, |e_{k-1}|} = s_k s_{k-1}^{r-1} \, |e_{k-1}|^{r^2 - r - 1}.$$

But $|e_k| \to 0$, whereas the foregoing ratio on the left tends to a nonzero constant; so we must have $r^2 - r - 1 = 0$, which implies that the convergence rate is given by the positive solution to this quadratic equation, $r = (1 + \sqrt{5}\,)/2 \approx 1.618$. Thus, the secant method is normally superlinearly convergent, but, like Newton's method, it must be started close enough to the solution in order to converge.

Compared with Newton's method, the secant method has the advantage of requiring only one new function evaluation per iteration, but it has the disadvantages of requiring two starting guesses and converging somewhat more slowly, though still superlinearly. The lower cost per iteration of the secant method often more than offsets the larger number of iterations required for convergence, however, so that the total cost of finding a root is often less for the secant method than for Newton's method.

5.5.5 Inverse Interpolation

At each iteration of the secant method, a straight line is fit to two values of the function whose zero is sought. A higher convergence rate (but not exceeding $r = 2$) can be obtained by fitting a higher-degree polynomial to the appropriate number of function values. For example, one could fit a quadratic polynomial to three successive iterates and use one of its roots as the next approximate solution. There are several difficulties with this idea, however: the polynomial may not have any real roots, and even if it does they may not be easy to compute, and it may not be easy to choose which root to use as the next iterate. (On the other hand, if one seeks a *complex root*, then a polynomial having complex roots is desirable; in *Muller's method*, for example, a quadratic polynomial is used in approximating complex roots.)

An answer to these difficulties is provided by *inverse interpolation*, in which one fits the values x_k as a function of the values $y_k = f(x_k)$ by a polynomial $p(y)$, so that the next approximate solution is simply $p(0)$. This idea is illustrated in Fig. 5.8, where a parabola fitting y as a function of x has no real root (i.e., it fails to cross the x axis), but a parabola fitting x as a function of y is merely evaluated at $y = 0$ to obtain the next iterate.

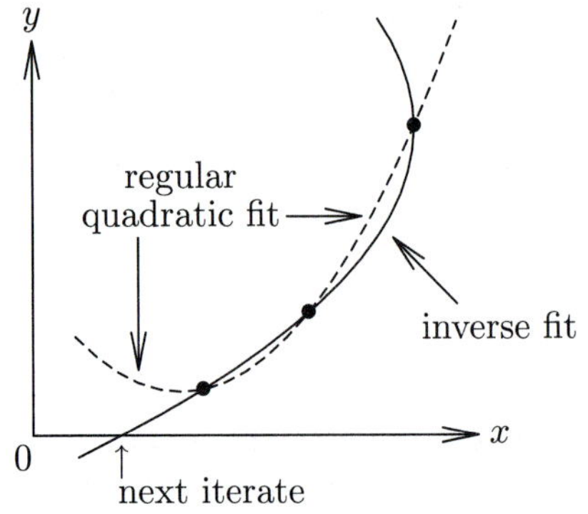

Figure 5.8: Inverse interpolation for approximating root. Dashed line is regular quadratic fit, solid line is inverse quadratic fit.

Using inverse quadratic interpolation, at each iteration we have three approximate solution values, which we denote by a, b, and c, with corresponding function values f_a, f_b, and f_c, respectively. The next approximate solution is found by fitting a quadratic polynomial to a, b, and c as a function of f_a, f_b, and f_c, and then evaluating the polynomial at 0. This task is accomplished by the following formulas, whose derivation will become clearer after we study Lagrange interpolation in Section 7.3.2:

$$u = f_b/f_c, \qquad v = f_b/f_a, \qquad w = f_a/f_c,$$

$$p = v(w(u-w)(c-b) - (1-u)(b-a)), \qquad q = (w-1)(u-1)(v-1).$$

The new approximate solution is given by $b + p/q$. The process is then repeated with b replaced by the new approximation, a replaced by the old b, and c replaced by the old a. Note that only one new function evaluation is needed per iteration. The convergence rate of inverse quadratic interpolation for root finding is $r \approx 1.839$, which is the same as for regular quadratic interpolation (Muller's method). Again this result is local, and the iterations must be started close enough to the solution to obtain convergence.

Example 5.13 Inverse Quadratic Interpolation. We illustrate inverse quadratic interpolation by again finding a root of the equation

$$f(x) = x^2 - 4\sin(x) = 0.$$

Taking $a = 1$, $b = 2$, and $c = 3$ as starting values, the sequence of iterations is shown next, where $h_k = p/q$ denotes the change in x_k at each iteration.

k	x_k	$f(x_k)$	h_k
0	1.000000	−2.365884	
1	2.000000	0.362810	
2	3.000000	8.435520	
3	1.886318	−0.244343	−0.113682
4	1.939558	0.030786	0.053240
5	1.933742	−0.000060	−0.005815
6	1.933754	0.000000	0.000011

5.5.6 Linear Fractional Interpolation

The zero-finding methods we have considered thus far may have difficulty if the function whose zero is sought has a horizontal or vertical asymptote. A horizontal asymptote may yield a tangent or secant line that is almost horizontal, causing the next approximate solution to be far afield, and a vertical asymptote may be skipped over, placing the approximation on the wrong branch of the function. *Linear fractional interpolation*, which uses a rational fraction of the form

$$\phi(x) = \frac{x-u}{vx-w},$$

is a useful alternative in such cases. This function has a zero at $x = u$, a vertical asymptote at $x = w/v$, and a horizontal asymptote at $y = 1/v$.

In seeking a zero of a nonlinear function $f(x)$, suppose that we have three approximate solution values, which we denote by a, b, and c, with corresponding function values f_a, f_b, and f_c, respectively. Fitting the linear fraction ϕ to the three data points yields a 3×3 system of linear equations

$$\begin{bmatrix} 1 & af_a & -f_a \\ 1 & bf_b & -f_b \\ 1 & cf_c & -f_c \end{bmatrix} \begin{bmatrix} u \\ v \\ w \end{bmatrix} = \begin{bmatrix} a \\ b \\ c \end{bmatrix},$$

whose solution determines the coefficients u, v, and w. We now replace a and b with b and c, respectively, and take the next approximate solution to be the zero of the linear fraction, $c = u$. Because v and w play no direct role, the solution to the foregoing system is most conveniently implemented as a single formula for the change h in c, which is given by

$$h = \frac{(a-c)(b-c)(f_a-f_b)f_c}{(a-c)(f_c-f_b)f_a-(b-c)(f_c-f_a)f_b}.$$

Linear fractional interpolation is also effective as a general-purpose one-dimensional zero finder, as the following example illustrates. Its asymptotic convergence rate is the same as that given by quadratic interpolation (inverse or regular), $r \approx 1.839$. Once again this result is local, and the iterations must be started close enough to the solution to obtain convergence.

Example 5.14 Linear Fractional Interpolation. We illustrate linear fractional interpolation by again finding a root of the equation

$$f(x) = x^2 - 4\sin(x) = 0.$$

Taking $a = 1$, $b = 2$, and $c = 3$ as starting values, the sequence of iterations is shown next.

k	x_k	$f(x_k)$	h_k
0	1.000000	−2.365884	
1	2.000000	0.362810	
2	3.000000	8.435520	
3	1.906953	−0.139647	−1.093047
4	1.933351	−0.002131	0.026398
5	1.933756	0.000013	−0.000406
6	1.933754	0.000000	−0.000003

5.5.7 Safeguarded Methods

Rapidly convergent methods for solving nonlinear equations, such as Newton's method, the secant method, and other types of methods based on interpolation, are unsafe in that they may not converge unless they are started close enough to the solution. Safe methods such as bisection, on the other hand, are slow and therefore costly. Which should one choose?

A solution to this dilemma is provided by hybrid methods that combine features of both types of methods. For example, one could use a rapidly convergent method but maintain a bracket around the solution. If the next approximate solution given by the rapid algorithm falls outside the bracketing interval, one would fall back on a safe method, such as bisection, for one iteration. Then one can try the rapid method again on a smaller interval with a greater chance of success. Ultimately, the fast convergence rate should prevail. This approach seldom does worse than the slow method and usually does much better.

A popular implementation of such a hybrid approach was originally developed by Dekker, van Wijngaarden, and others, and later improved by Brent. This method, which is found in a number of subroutine libraries, combines the safety of bisection with the faster convergence of inverse quadratic interpolation. By avoiding Newton's method, derivatives of the function are not required. A careful implementation must address a number of potential pitfalls in floating-point arithmetic, such as underflow, overflow, or an unrealistically tight user-supplied error tolerance.

5.5.8 Zeros of Polynomials

Thus far we have discussed methods for finding a single zero of an arbitrary function in one dimension. For the special case of a polynomial $p(x)$ of degree n, one often may need to find all n of its zeros, which may be complex even if the coefficients of the polynomial are real. Several approaches are available:

- Use one of the methods we have discussed, such as Newton's method or Muller's method, to find a single root x_1 (keeping in mind that the root may be complex), then consider the deflated polynomial $p(x)/(x - x_1)$ of degree one less. Repeat until all roots have been found. It is a good idea to go back and refine each root using the original polynomial $p(x)$ to avoid contamination due to rounding error in forming the deflated polynomials.
- Form the *companion matrix* (see Section 4.2.1) of the given polynomial and use an eigenvalue routine to compute its eigenvalues, which are the roots of the polynomial. This method, which is used by the `roots` function in `MATLAB`, is reliable but is less efficient in both work and storage than methods tailored specifically for this problem.
- Use a method designed specifically for finding all the roots of a polynomial. Some of these methods are based on classical techniques for isolating the roots of a polynomial in a region of the complex plane, typically a union of disks, and then refining it in a manner similar in spirit to bisection until the roots have been localized as accurately as desired. Like bisection, such methods are guaranteed to work but are only linearly convergent. More rapidly convergent methods are available, however, including the methods of Laguerre, of Bairstow, and of Jenkins and Traub. The latter is probably the most effective method currently available for finding all of the roots of a polynomial.

The first two of these approaches are relatively simple to implement since they make use of other software for the primary subtasks. The third approach is rather complicated, but fortunately good software implementations are available (see Section 5.7).

5.6 Systems of Nonlinear Equations

Systems of nonlinear equations tend to be more difficult to solve than single nonlinear equations for a number of reasons:

- A much wider range of behavior is possible, so that a theoretical analysis of the existence and number of solutions is much more complex, as we saw in Section 5.2.
- With conventional numerical methods, there is no simple way, in general, of bracketing a desired solution to produce an absolutely safe method with guaranteed convergence. Using homotopy methods (see Computer Problem 9.10) or interval methods (see Section 1.3.10), global convergence guarantees are possible, but detailed discussion of these methods is beyond the scope of this book (we will, however, cite available software based on such methods in Section 5.7).
- As we will soon see, computational overhead increases rapidly with the dimension of the problem.

5.6.1 Fixed-Point Iteration

Just as for one dimension, a system of nonlinear equations can be converted into a fixed-point problem, so we now briefly consider the multidimensional case. If

$\boldsymbol{g}: \mathbb{R}^n \to \mathbb{R}^n$, then a fixed-point problem for $\boldsymbol{g}$ is to find an $\boldsymbol{x} \in \mathbb{R}^n$ such that

$$\boldsymbol{x} = \boldsymbol{g}(\boldsymbol{x}).$$

The corresponding fixed-point iteration is simply

$$\boldsymbol{x}_{k+1} = \boldsymbol{g}(\boldsymbol{x}_k),$$

given some starting vector $\boldsymbol{x}_0$.

In one dimension, we saw that the convergence (and convergence rate) of fixed-point iteration is determined by $|g'(x^*)|$, where x^* is the solution. In higher dimensions the analogous condition is that the spectral radius

$$\rho(\boldsymbol{G}(\boldsymbol{x}^*)) < 1,$$

where $\boldsymbol{G}(\boldsymbol{x})$ denotes the *Jacobian matrix* of $\boldsymbol{g}$ evaluated at $\boldsymbol{x}$,

$$\{\boldsymbol{G}(\boldsymbol{x})\}_{ij} = \frac{\partial g_i(\boldsymbol{x})}{\partial x_j}.$$

If the foregoing condition is satisfied, then the fixed-point iteration converges if started close enough to the solution. (Note that testing this condition does not necessarily require computing eigenvalues, since $\rho(\boldsymbol{A}) \le \|\boldsymbol{A}\|$ for any matrix $\boldsymbol{A}$ and any matrix norm induced by a vector norm; see Exercise 4.13.) As with one-dimensional problems, the smaller the spectral radius the faster the convergence rate. In particular, if $\boldsymbol{G}(\boldsymbol{x}^*) = \boldsymbol{O}$, then the convergence rate is at least quadratic. We will next see that the n-dimensional version of Newton's method is a systematic way of choosing $\boldsymbol{g}$ so that this happens.

5.6.2 Newton's Method

Many methods for solving nonlinear equations in one-dimension do not generalize directly to n dimensions. The most popular and powerful method that does generalize is *Newton's method*, which for a differentiable function $\boldsymbol{f}: \mathbb{R}^n \to \mathbb{R}^n$ is based on the truncated Taylor series

$$\boldsymbol{f}(\boldsymbol{x} + \boldsymbol{s}) \approx \boldsymbol{f}(\boldsymbol{x}) + \boldsymbol{J}_f(\boldsymbol{x})\,\boldsymbol{s},$$

where $\boldsymbol{J}_f(\boldsymbol{x})$ is the Jacobian matrix of $\boldsymbol{f}$, $\{\boldsymbol{J}_f(\boldsymbol{x})\}_{ij} = \partial f_i(\boldsymbol{x})/\partial x_j$. If $\boldsymbol{s}$ satisfies the linear system $\boldsymbol{J}_f(\boldsymbol{x})\,\boldsymbol{s} = -\boldsymbol{f}(\boldsymbol{x})$, then $\boldsymbol{x} + \boldsymbol{s}$ is taken as an approximate zero of $\boldsymbol{f}$. In this sense, Newton's method replaces a system of nonlinear equations with a system of linear equations, but since the solutions of the two systems are not identical in general, the process must be repeated, as shown in Algorithm 5.4, until the approximate solution is as accurate as desired.

Example 5.15 Newton's Method. We illustrate Newton's method by solving the nonlinear system

$$\boldsymbol{f}(\boldsymbol{x}) = \begin{bmatrix} x_1 + 2x_2 - 2 \\ x_1^2 + 4x_2^2 - 4 \end{bmatrix} = \begin{bmatrix} 0 \\ 0 \end{bmatrix},$$

Algorithm 5.4 Newton's Method for System of Nonlinear Equations

$\boldsymbol{x}_0$ = initial guess
for $k = 0, 1, 2, \ldots$
  Solve $\boldsymbol{J}_f(\boldsymbol{x}_k)\,\boldsymbol{s}_k = -\boldsymbol{f}(\boldsymbol{x}_k)$ for $\boldsymbol{s}_k$ { compute Newton step }
  $\boldsymbol{x}_{k+1} = \boldsymbol{x}_k + \boldsymbol{s}_k$ { update solution }
end

for which the Jacobian matrix is given by

$$\boldsymbol{J}_f(\boldsymbol{x}) = \begin{bmatrix} 1 & 2 \\ 2x_1 & 8x_2 \end{bmatrix}.$$

If we take $\boldsymbol{x}_0 = [1 \quad 2]^T$, then

$$\boldsymbol{f}(\boldsymbol{x}_0) = \begin{bmatrix} 3 \\ 13 \end{bmatrix}, \qquad \boldsymbol{J}_f(\boldsymbol{x}_0) = \begin{bmatrix} 1 & 2 \\ 2 & 16 \end{bmatrix}.$$

Solving the system

$$\boldsymbol{J}_f(\boldsymbol{x}_0)\,\boldsymbol{s}_0 = \begin{bmatrix} 1 & 2 \\ 2 & 16 \end{bmatrix} \boldsymbol{s}_0 = \begin{bmatrix} -3 \\ -13 \end{bmatrix} = -\boldsymbol{f}(\boldsymbol{x}_0)$$

gives $\boldsymbol{s}_0 = [-1.83 \quad -0.58]^T$, and hence

$$\boldsymbol{x}_1 = \boldsymbol{x}_0 + \boldsymbol{s}_0 = \begin{bmatrix} -0.83 \\ 1.42 \end{bmatrix}, \qquad \boldsymbol{f}(\boldsymbol{x}_1) = \begin{bmatrix} 0 \\ 4.72 \end{bmatrix}, \qquad \boldsymbol{J}_f(\boldsymbol{x}_1) = \begin{bmatrix} 1 & 2 \\ -1.67 & 11.3 \end{bmatrix}.$$

Solving the system

$$\boldsymbol{J}_f(\boldsymbol{x}_1)\,\boldsymbol{s}_1 = \begin{bmatrix} 1 & 2 \\ -1.67 & 11.3 \end{bmatrix} \boldsymbol{s}_1 = \begin{bmatrix} 0 \\ -4.72 \end{bmatrix} = -\boldsymbol{f}(\boldsymbol{x}_1)$$

gives $\boldsymbol{s}_1 = [0.64 \quad -0.32]^T$, and hence

$$\boldsymbol{x}_2 = \boldsymbol{x}_1 + \boldsymbol{s}_1 = \begin{bmatrix} -0.19 \\ 1.10 \end{bmatrix}, \qquad \boldsymbol{f}(\boldsymbol{x}_2) = \begin{bmatrix} 0 \\ 0.83 \end{bmatrix}, \qquad \boldsymbol{J}_f(\boldsymbol{x}_2) = \begin{bmatrix} 1 & 2 \\ -0.38 & 8.76 \end{bmatrix}.$$

Iterations continue until convergence to the solution $\boldsymbol{x}^* = [0 \quad 1]^T$.

We can determine the convergence rate of Newton's method in n dimensions by differentiating the corresponding fixed-point operator (assuming it is smooth) and evaluating the resulting Jacobian matrix at the solution $\boldsymbol{x}^*$:

$$\boldsymbol{g}(\boldsymbol{x}) = \boldsymbol{x} - \boldsymbol{J}_f(\boldsymbol{x})^{-1}\boldsymbol{f}(\boldsymbol{x}),$$

$$\boldsymbol{G}(\boldsymbol{x}^*) = \boldsymbol{I} - \boldsymbol{J}_f(\boldsymbol{x}^*)^{-1}\boldsymbol{J}_f(\boldsymbol{x}^*) + \sum_{i=1}^{n} f_i(\boldsymbol{x}^*)\boldsymbol{H}_i(\boldsymbol{x}^*) = \boldsymbol{O},$$

where $\boldsymbol{H}_i(\boldsymbol{x})$ denotes a component matrix of the derivative of $\boldsymbol{J}_f(\boldsymbol{x})^{-1}$ (which is a tensor). Thus, the convergence rate of Newton's method for solving a nonlinear system is normally quadratic, provided that the Jacobian matrix $\boldsymbol{J}_f(\boldsymbol{x}^*)$ is nonsingular, but the algorithm may have to be started close to the solution in order to converge.

The arithmetic overhead per iteration for Newton's method in n dimensions can be substantial:

- Computing the Jacobian matrix $\boldsymbol{J}_f(\boldsymbol{x}_k)$, either in closed form or by finite differences, requires the equivalent of n^2 scalar function evaluations for a dense problem (i.e., if every component function of $\boldsymbol{f}$ depends on every component of $\boldsymbol{x}$). Computation of the Jacobian may be much cheaper if it is sparse or has some special structure. Another alternative for computing derivatives is automatic differentiation (see Section 8.6.2).
- Solving the linear system $\boldsymbol{J}_f(\boldsymbol{x}_k)\boldsymbol{s}_k = -\boldsymbol{f}(\boldsymbol{x}_k)$ by LU factorization costs $\mathcal{O}(n^3)$ arithmetic operations, again assuming the Jacobian matrix is dense.

Many variations on Newton's method, sometimes called *quasi-Newton methods*, have been designed to reduce these relatively high costs. One of these is simply to reuse the same Jacobian matrix for several consecutive iterations, which avoids both recomputing it and refactoring it at every iteration. The convergence rate suffers accordingly, of course, so there is a tradeoff between the average cost per iteration and the number of iterations required for convergence. Another option is to solve the linear system at each iteration to only a rough approximation, say by an iterative method with a loose convergence tolerance, since computing the Newton step to high accuracy is of dubious value anyway when far from the solution to the nonlinear system. For more on this approach, see Section 6.5.7. Among the most successful variations on Newton's method are the secant updating methods, which we consider next. Still other variations on Newton's method attempt to improve its reliability when far from a solution; some of these will be addressed in Sections 5.6.4 and 6.5.3.

5.6.3 Secant Updating Methods

The partial derivatives that make up the Jacobian matrix could be replaced by finite difference approximations along each coordinate direction, but this would entail additional function evaluations purely for the purpose of obtaining derivative information. Instead, we take our cue from the secant method for nonlinear equations in one dimension, which avoids explicitly computing derivatives by approximating the derivative based on the change in function values between successive iterates. An analogous approach for problems in n dimensions is gradually to build up an approximation to the Jacobian matrix based on function values at successive iterates, where the function would have to be evaluated anyway. Moreover, these methods save further on computational overhead by updating a factorization of the approximate Jacobian matrix at each iteration (using techniques similar to the Sherman-Morrison formula) rather than refactoring it each time. Because of these two features, such methods are usually called *secant updating methods*.

These savings in computational overhead per iteration are offset, however, by a slower rate of convergence, which is generally superlinear for secant updating methods but not quadratic. Nevertheless, as with the secant method in one dimension, there is often a net reduction in the overall cost of finding a solution, especially when the problem function and its derivatives are expensive to evaluate.

One of the simplest and most effective secant updating methods for solving nonlinear systems is *Broyden's method*, shown in Algorithm 5.5, which begins with an approximate Jacobian matrix and updates it (or a factorization of it) at each iteration. The initial Jacobian approximation $\boldsymbol{B}_0$ can be taken as the true Jacobian (or a finite difference approximation to it) at the starting point $\boldsymbol{x}_0$, or, to avoid computing derivatives altogether, $\boldsymbol{B}_0$ can simply be initialized to be the identity matrix $\boldsymbol{I}$.

Algorithm 5.5 Broyden's Method

$\boldsymbol{x}_0$ = initial guess
$\boldsymbol{B}_0$ = initial Jacobian approximation
for $k = 0, 1, 2, \ldots$
  Solve $\boldsymbol{B}_k\,\boldsymbol{s}_k = -\boldsymbol{f}(\boldsymbol{x}_k)$ for $\boldsymbol{s}_k$ { compute Newton-like step }
  $\boldsymbol{x}_{k+1} = \boldsymbol{x}_k + \boldsymbol{s}_k$ { update solution }
  $\boldsymbol{y}_k = \boldsymbol{f}(\boldsymbol{x}_{k+1}) - \boldsymbol{f}(\boldsymbol{x}_k)$
  $\boldsymbol{B}_{k+1} = \boldsymbol{B}_k + ((\boldsymbol{y}_k - \boldsymbol{B}_k\boldsymbol{s}_k)\boldsymbol{s}_k^T)/(\boldsymbol{s}_k^T\boldsymbol{s}_k)$ { update approx Jacobian }
end

The motivation for the formula for the updated Jacobian approximation $\boldsymbol{B}_{k+1}$ is that it gives the least change to $\boldsymbol{B}_k$ subject to satisfying the *secant equation*

$$\boldsymbol{B}_{k+1}(\boldsymbol{x}_{k+1} - \boldsymbol{x}_k) = \boldsymbol{f}(\boldsymbol{x}_{k+1}) - \boldsymbol{f}(\boldsymbol{x}_k).$$

In this way, the sequence of matrices $\boldsymbol{B}_k$ gains and maintains information about the behavior of the function $\boldsymbol{f}$ along the various directions generated by the algorithm, without the need for the function to be sampled purely for the purpose of obtaining derivative information.

Updating $\boldsymbol{B}_k$ as just indicated would still leave one needing to solve a linear system at each iteration at a cost of $\mathcal{O}(n^3)$ arithmetic. Therefore, in practice a factorization of $\boldsymbol{B}_k$ is updated instead of updating $\boldsymbol{B}_k$ directly, so that the total cost per iteration is only $\mathcal{O}(n^2)$.

Example 5.16 Broyden's Method. We illustrate Broyden's method by again solving the nonlinear system of Example 5.15,

$$\boldsymbol{f}(\boldsymbol{x}) = \begin{bmatrix} x_1 + 2x_2 - 2 \\ x_1^2 + 4x_2^2 - 4 \end{bmatrix} = \begin{bmatrix} 0 \\ 0 \end{bmatrix}.$$

Again we let $\boldsymbol{x}_0 = [1 \quad 2]^T$, so $\boldsymbol{f}(\boldsymbol{x}_0) = [3 \quad 13]^T$, and we let

$$\boldsymbol{B}_0 = \boldsymbol{J}_f(\boldsymbol{x}_0) = \begin{bmatrix} 1 & 2 \\ 2 & 16 \end{bmatrix}.$$

Solving the system

$$\boldsymbol{B}_0\,\boldsymbol{s}_0 = \begin{bmatrix} 1 & 2 \\ 2 & 16 \end{bmatrix} \boldsymbol{s}_0 = \begin{bmatrix} -3 \\ -13 \end{bmatrix} = -\boldsymbol{f}(\boldsymbol{x}_0)$$

gives $\boldsymbol{s}_0 = [\,-1.83 \quad -0.58\,]^T$, and hence

$$\boldsymbol{x}_1 = \boldsymbol{x}_0 + \boldsymbol{s}_0 = \begin{bmatrix} -0.83 \\ 1.42 \end{bmatrix}, \qquad \boldsymbol{f}(\boldsymbol{x}_1) = \begin{bmatrix} 0 \\ 4.72 \end{bmatrix}, \qquad \boldsymbol{y}_0 = \begin{bmatrix} -3 \\ -8.28 \end{bmatrix}.$$

From the updating formula, we therefore have

$$\boldsymbol{B}_1 = \begin{bmatrix} 1 & 2 \\ 2 & 16 \end{bmatrix} + \begin{bmatrix} 0 & 0 \\ -2.34 & -0.74 \end{bmatrix} = \begin{bmatrix} 1 & 2 \\ -0.34 & 15.3 \end{bmatrix}.$$

Solving the system

$$\boldsymbol{B}_1\,\boldsymbol{s}_1 = \begin{bmatrix} 1 & 2 \\ -0.34 & 15.3 \end{bmatrix} \boldsymbol{s}_1 = \begin{bmatrix} 0 \\ -4.72 \end{bmatrix} = -\boldsymbol{f}(\boldsymbol{x}_1)$$

gives $\boldsymbol{s}_1 = [\,0.59 \quad -0.30\,]^T$, and hence

$$\boldsymbol{x}_2 = \boldsymbol{x}_1 + \boldsymbol{s}_1 = \begin{bmatrix} -0.24 \\ 1.120 \end{bmatrix}, \qquad \boldsymbol{f}(\boldsymbol{x}_2) = \begin{bmatrix} 0 \\ 1.08 \end{bmatrix}, \qquad \boldsymbol{y}_1 = \begin{bmatrix} 0 \\ -3.64 \end{bmatrix}.$$

From the updating formula, we therefore have

$$\boldsymbol{B}_2 = \begin{bmatrix} 1 & 2 \\ -0.34 & 15.3 \end{bmatrix} + \begin{bmatrix} 0 & 0 \\ 1.46 & -0.73 \end{bmatrix} = \begin{bmatrix} 1 & 2 \\ 1.12 & 14.5 \end{bmatrix}.$$

Iterations continue until convergence to the solution $\boldsymbol{x}^* = [\,0 \quad 1\,]^T$.

5.6.4 Robust Newton-Like Methods

Newton's method and its variants may fail to converge when started far from a solution. Unfortunately, in n dimensions there is no simple analogue of bisection in one dimension that can provide a fail-safe hybrid method. Nevertheless, safeguards can be taken that may substantially widen the region of convergence for Newton-like methods.

The simplest of these precautions is the *damped Newton method*, in which the Newton (or Newton-like) step $\boldsymbol{s}_k$ is computed as usual at each iteration, but then the new iterate is taken to be

$$\boldsymbol{x}_{k+1} = \boldsymbol{x}_k + \alpha_k \boldsymbol{s}_k,$$

where α_k is a scalar parameter to be chosen. The motivation is that far from a solution the full Newton step is likely to be unreliable—often much too large—and so α_k can be adjusted to ensure that $\boldsymbol{x}_{k+1}$ is a better approximation to the solution than $\boldsymbol{x}_k$. One way to enforce this condition is to monitor $\|\boldsymbol{f}(\boldsymbol{x}_k)\|_2$ and ensure that it decreases sufficiently with each iteration. One could even minimize $\|\boldsymbol{f}(\boldsymbol{x}_k + \alpha_k \boldsymbol{s}_k)\|_2$ with respect to α_k at each iteration (see the discussion of line searches in Chapter 6). Whatever the strategy for choosing α_k, when the iterates become close enough to a solution of the nonlinear system, the value $\alpha_k = 1$ should suffice, and indeed the α_k must approach 1 in order to maintain the usual convergence rate. Although this damping technique can improve the robustness of Newton-like methods, it is not foolproof. For example, there may be no value for α_k that produces sufficient decrease, or the iterations may converge to a local minimum of $\|\boldsymbol{f}(\boldsymbol{x})\|_2$ having a value other than 0.

A somewhat more complicated but often more effective approach to making Newton-like methods more robust is to maintain an estimate of the radius of a *trust region* within which the Taylor series approximation upon which Newton's method is based is sufficiently accurate for the resulting computed step to be reliable. By adjusting the size of the trust region as necessary to constrain the step size, these methods can usually make progress toward a solution even when started far away, yet still converge rapidly once near a solution, since the trust radius should then be large enough to permit full Newton steps to be taken. Again, however, the point to which such a method converges may be a nonzero local minimum of $\|\boldsymbol{f}(\boldsymbol{x})\|_2$. Unlike damped Newton methods, trust region methods may modify the direction as well as the length of the Newton step when necessary, and hence they are generally more robust. See Section 6.5.3 for further discussion and a graphical illustration.

5.7 Software for Nonlinear Equations

Table 5.1 is a list of some of the software available for solving general nonlinear equations. In the multidimensional case, we distinguish between routines that do or do not require the user to supply derivatives for the functions, although in some cases the routines cited offer both options.

Software for solving a nonlinear equation $\boldsymbol{f}(\boldsymbol{x}) = \boldsymbol{0}$ typically requires the user to supply the name of a routine that computes the value of the function $\boldsymbol{f}$ for any given value of $\boldsymbol{x}$. The user must also supply absolute or relative error tolerances that are used in the stopping criterion for the iterative solution process. Additional input for one-dimensional problems usually includes the endpoints of an interval in which the function has a change of sign. Additional input for multidimensional problems includes the number of functions and variables in the system and a starting guess for the solution, and may also include the name of a routine for computing the Jacobian of the function and a workspace array for storing the Jacobian matrix or an approximation to it. In addition to the computed solution $\boldsymbol{x}^*$, the output typically includes a status flag indicating any warnings or errors.

For both single equations and systems, it is highly advisable to make a preliminary plot, or at least a rough sketch, of the function(s) involved to determine a good starting guess or bracketing interval. Some trial and error may be required to determine an initial guess for which a zero finder converges, or finds the desired root in cases with more than one solution.

	One-dimensional	Multidimensional	
Source	No derivatives	No derivatives	Derivatives
Brent [47]	zero		
FMM [127]	zeroin		
HSL	nb01/nb02	ns11	
IMSL	zbren	neqbf	neqnj
Dennis & Schnabel [92]		nedriver	nedriver
KMN [220]	fzero	snsqe	snsqe
MATLAB	fzero	fsolve	
MINPACK [279]		hybrd1	hybrj1
NAG	c05adf	c05nbf	c05pbf
NAPACK	root	quasi	
NR [315]	zbrent	broydn	newt
NUMAL [250]	zeroin	quanewbnd	
SLATEC	fzero	snsq/sos	
TOMS	zero1(#631)	brentm(#554)	tensolve(#768)

Table 5.1: Software for nonlinear equations

Some additional packages for solving systems of nonlinear equations are based on methods (not covered in this book) that can guarantee global convergence to a solution. One such approach is *homotopy* and *continuation* methods, which parameterize the problem space and then follow a path from a trivial problem instance to the actual problem to be solved. See Computer Problem 9.10 for an example of this approach, which can be especially useful for very difficult nonlinear problems for which a good starting guess for the solution is unavailable. Software implementing such methods includes `fixpt(#555)`, `dafne(#617)`, and `hompack(#652, #777)`, all available from TOMS. Yet another "guaranteed" approach is *generalized bisection*, which is based on interval methods and is implemented in the routines `chabis(#666)` and `intbis(#681)` available from TOMS.

Table 5.2 is a list of specialized software for finding all the zeros of a polynomial with real or complex coefficients.

5.8 Historical Notes and Further Reading

Iterative methods for finding roots of specific nonlinear equations appear in ancient Greek, Babylonian, Arabic, and Indian texts. These methods far predated the invention of calculus and were based on algebraic or geometric reasoning. Newton's method has an interesting history and is only partially due to Newton himself (see [430]). Although he had used a method equivalent to the secant method as early as 1665, Newton first formulated in 1669 a method that is roughly equivalent to what we now call Newton's method. Surprisingly, however, Newton's own version did not use derivatives (which he introduced elsewhere in the same publication), but instead was based on binomial expansions and was initially applied

Source	Real	Complex
HSL	pa17	pa16
IMSL	zporc/zplrc	zpocc
MATLAB	roots	roots
NAG	c02agf	c02aff
NAPACK		czero
NR [315]	zrhqr	zroots
NUMERALGO		polzeros(na10)
SLATEC	rpzero/rpqr79	cpzero/cpqr79
TOMS	rpoly(#493)	cpoly(#419)

Table 5.2: Software for finding zeros of polynomials

only to polynomials. Newton's approach was strongly influenced by a closely related method that had been published by Vieta in 1600. Raphson simplified and improved on Newton's approach in 1690, giving rise to the name *Newton-Raphson method*, by which it is still often called today. The first expression of what we now call Newton's method using derivatives was published in 1740 by Simpson, who was also first to extend the method to more than one dimension. The simple and elegant modern formulation of Newton's method was published by Lagrange in 1798 and popularized by Fourier in 1831, by which time the contributions of Vieta and Simpson had been forgotten, leaving only the name of Newton (and sometimes Raphson) associated with the method. Ironically, Simpson probably deserves more credit for "Newton's" method than for "Simpson's" rule (see Section 8.9).

Muller published his method based on successive quadratic interpolation in 1956, Jarratt and Nudds proposed using linear fractional interpolation in 1965, and Cox suggested inverse interpolation in 1970. Hybrid, safeguarded methods were developed by Dekker, van Wijngaarden, and others in the 1960s and improved and popularized in 1973 by Brent through software published in the book [47].

For systems of nonlinear equations, Newton's method has served to motivate most other methods, and it is the standard by which they are measured. Indeed, "Newton's method" has become as much a paradigm as a specific algorithm, synonymous with local linear approximations to nonlinear problems of many different types. Secant updating methods were first developed for optimization problems in 1959, but analogous methods were soon developed for solving systems of nonlinear equations; Broyden's method was published in 1965.

The basic methods for solving nonlinear equations in one dimension are discussed in almost every general textbook on numerical methods. More detailed treatment of the classical methods can be found in [202, 296, 393]. For zero finding using linear fractional interpolation, see [211]; more general rational functions for this purpose are discussed in [249]. For finding the zeros of a polynomial via the eigenvalues of its companion matrix, see [106]; for the Jenkins-Traub method, see [213, 214]. Comprehensive references on solving systems of nonlinear equations are [92, 295]. For more recent surveys, see [227, 322]. An incisive overview of the theory and convergence analysis of secant updating methods appears in [91]. The

MINPACK software for nonlinear equations is documented in [279]. Continuation and homotopy methods are the subject of [7, 8, 125], and interval methods for solving systems of equations are surveyed in [287].

Review Questions

5.1. True or false: A small residual $\|\boldsymbol{f}(\boldsymbol{x})\|$ guarantees an accurate solution of a system of nonlinear equations $\boldsymbol{f}(\boldsymbol{x}) = \boldsymbol{0}$.

5.2. True or false: Newton's method is an example of a fixed-point iteration scheme.

5.3. True or false: If an iterative method for solving a nonlinear equation gains more than one bit of accuracy per iteration, then it is said to have a superlinear convergence rate.

5.4. True or false: For a given fixed level of accuracy, a superlinearly convergent iterative method always requires fewer iterations than a linearly convergent method to find a solution to that level of accuracy.

5.5. Suppose you are using an iterative method to solve a nonlinear equation $f(x) = 0$ for a root that is ill-conditioned, and you need to choose a convergence test. Would it be better to terminate the iteration when you find an iterate x_k for which $|f(x_k)|$ is small, or when $|x_k - x_{k-1}|$ is small? Why?

5.6. (*a*) What is meant by a *bracket* for a nonlinear function in one dimension?

(*b*) What does this concept have to do with zero finding?

5.7. For root finding problems, why must we use an absolute rather than a relative condition number in assessing sensitivity?

5.8. (*a*) What is the definition of the convergence rate r of an iterative method?

(*b*) Is it possible to have a cubically convergent method ($r = 3$) for finding a zero of a function?

(*c*) If not, why, and if so, how might such a scheme be derived?

5.9. If the errors at successive iterations of an iterative method are as follows, how would you characterize the convergence rate?

(*a*) 10^{-2}, 10^{-4}, 10^{-8}, 10^{-16}, ...

(*b*) 10^{-2}, 10^{-4}, 10^{-6}, 10^{-8}, ...

5.10. What condition ensures that the bisection method will find a zero of a continuous nonlinear function f in the interval $[a, b]$?

5.11. (*a*) If the bisection method for finding a zero of a function $f: \mathbb{R} \to \mathbb{R}$ starts with an initial bracket of length 1, what is the length of the interval containing the root after six iterations?

(*b*) Do you need to know the particular function f to answer the question in part *a*?

(*c*) If we assume that it is started with a bracket for the solution in which there is a sign change, is the convergence rate of the bisection method dependent on whether the solution sought is a simple root or a multiple root? Why?

5.12. Suppose you are using the bisection method to find a zero of a nonlinear function, starting with an initial bracketing interval $[a, b]$. Give a general expression for the number of iterations that will be required to achieve an error tolerance of *tol* for the length of the final bracketing interval.

5.13. What is meant by a *quadratic* convergence rate for an iterative method?

5.14. If an iterative method squares the error every *two* iterations, what is its convergence rate r?

5.15. (*a*) What does it mean for a root of an equation to be a *multiple* root?

(*b*) What is the effect of a multiple root on the convergence rate of the bisection method?

(*c*) What is the effect of a multiple root on the convergence rate of Newton's method?

5.16. Which of the following behaviors are possible in using Newton's method for solving a nonlinear equation?

(*a*) It may converge linearly.

(*b*) It may converge quadratically.

(*c*) It may not converge at all.

5.17. What is the convergence rate for Newton's method for finding the root $x = 2$ of each of the following equations?

(*a*) $f(x) = (x-1)(x-2)^2 = 0$

(*b*) $f(x) = (x-1)^2(x-2) = 0$

5.18. (*a*) What is meant by a *fixed point* of a function $g(x)$?

(*b*) Given a nonlinear equation $f(x) = 0$, how can you determine an equivalent fixed-point problem, that is, a function $g(x)$ such that a fixed point x of g is a solution to the nonlinear equation $f(x) = 0$?

(*c*) Specifically, what function $g(x)$ results from this approach?

5.19. In using the secant method for solving a one-dimensional nonlinear equation,

(*a*) How many starting guesses for the solution are required?

(*b*) How many new function evaluations are required per iteration?

5.20. Let $g: \mathbb{R} \to \mathbb{R}$ be a smooth function having a fixed point x^*.

(*a*) What condition determines whether the iteration scheme $x_{k+1} = g(x_k)$ is locally convergent to x^*?

(*b*) Wh[illegible]nvergence rate?

(*c*) [illegible]l condition implies that the [illegible]uadratic?

[illegible]od for finding a zero of a [illegible]$\to \mathbb{R}$ an example of such a [illegible]eme? If so, what is the [illegible] If not, then explain why [illegible]

[illegible]o of a nonlinear func-[illegible]rmine if two function val-[illegible]nd $f(b)$, differ in sign. Is the fol-[illegible] good way to test for this condition: **if** $(f(a) * f(b) < 0) \ldots$? Why?

5.22. Let $g: \mathbb{R} \to \mathbb{R}$ be a smooth function, and let x^* be a point such that $g(x^*) = x^*$.

(*a*) State a general condition under which the iteration scheme $x_{k+1} = g(x_k)$ converges quadratically to x^*, assuming that the starting guess x_0 is close enough to x^*.

(*b*) Use this condition to prove that Newton's method is locally quadratically convergent to a simple zero x^* of a smooth function $f: \mathbb{R} \to \mathbb{R}$.

5.23. List one advantage and one disadvantage of the secant method compared with the bisection method for finding a simple zero of a single nonlinear equation.

5.24. List one advantage and one disadvantage of the secant method compared with Newton's method for solving a nonlinear equation in one dimension.

5.25. The secant method for solving a one-dimensional nonlinear equation uses linear interpolation of the given function at two points. Interpolation at more points by a higher-degree polynomial would increase the convergence rate of the iteration.

(*a*) Give three reasons why such an approach might not work well.

(*b*) What alternative approach using higher-degree interpolation in this context avoids these difficulties?

5.26. For solving a one-dimensional nonlinear equation, how many function or derivative evaluations are required per iteration of each of the following methods?

(*a*) Newton's method

(*b*) Secant method

5.27. Rank the following methods 1 through 3, from slowest convergence rate to fastest convergence rate, for finding a simple root of a nonlinear equation in one dimension:

(*a*) Bisection method

(*b*) Newton's method

(*c*) Secant method

5.28. In solving a nonlinear equation in one dimension, how many bits of accuracy are gained per iteration of

(*a*) Bisection method?

(*b*) Newton's method?

5.29. In solving a nonlinear equation $f(x) = 0$, if you assume that the cost of evaluating the derivative $f'(x)$ is about the same as the cost of evaluating $f(x)$, how does the cost of Newton's method compare with the cost of the secant method per iteration?

5.30. What is meant by *inverse* interpolation? Why is it useful for root finding problems in one dimension?

5.31. Suppose that you are using fixed-point iteration based on the fixed-point problem $x = g(x)$ to find a solution x^* to a nonlinear equation $f(x) = 0$. Which would be more favorable for the convergence rate: a horizontal tangent of g at x^* or a horizontal tangent of f at x^*? Why?

5.32. Suggest a procedure for safeguarding the secant method for solving a one-dimensional nonlinear equation so that it will still converge even if started far from a root.

5.33. For what type of function is linear fractional interpolation a particularly good choice of zero finder?

5.34. Each of the following methods for computing a root of a nonlinear equation has the same asymptotic convergence rate. For each method, specify a situation in which that method is particularly appropriate.

(*a*) Regular quadratic interpolation

(*b*) Inverse quadratic interpolation

(*c*) Linear fractional interpolation

5.35. State at least one method for finding all the zeros of a polynomial, and discuss its advantages and disadvantages.

5.36. Does the bisection method generalize to finding zeros of multidimensional functions? Why?

5.37. For solving an n-dimensional nonlinear equation, how many scalar function evaluations are required per iteration of Newton's method?

5.38. Relative to Newton's method, which of the following factors motivate secant updating methods for solving systems of nonlinear equations?

(*a*) Lower cost per iteration

(*b*) Faster convergence rate

(*c*) Greater robustness far from solution

(*d*) Avoidance of computing derivatives

5.39. Give two reasons why secant updating methods for solving systems of nonlinear equations are often more efficient than Newton's method despite converging more slowly.

Exercises

5.1. Consider the nonlinear equation

$$f(x) = x^2 - 2 = 0.$$

(*a*) With $x_0 = 1$ as a starting point, what is the value of x_1 if you use Newton's method for solving this problem?

(*b*) With $x_0 = 1$ and $x_1 = 2$ as starting points, what is the value of x_2 if you use the secant method for the same problem?

5.2. Write out Newton's iteration for solving each of the following nonlinear equations:

(*a*) $x^3 - 2x - 5 = 0$.

(*b*) $e^{-x} = x$.

(*c*) $x \sin(x) = 1$.

5.3. Newton's method is sometimes used to implement the built-in square root function on a computer, with the initial guess supplied by a lookup table.

(*a*) What is the Newton iteration for computing the square root of a positive number y (i.e., for solving the equation $f(x) = x^2 - y = 0$, given y)?

(*b*) If we assume that the starting guess has an accuracy of 4 bits, how many iterations would be necessary to attain 24-bit accuracy? 53-bit accuracy?

5.4. On a computer with no functional unit for floating-point division, one might instead use multiplication by the reciprocal of the divisor. Apply Newton's method to produce an iterative scheme for approximating the reciprocal of a number $y > 0$ (i.e., to solve the equation $f(x) = (1/x) - y = 0$, given y). Considering the intended application, your formula should contain no divisions!

5.5. (*a*) Show that the iterative method

$$x_{k+1} = \frac{x_{k-1} f(x_k) - x_k f(x_{k-1})}{f(x_k) - f(x_{k-1})}$$

is mathematically equivalent to the secant method for solving a scalar nonlinear equation $f(x) = 0$.

(*b*) When implemented in finite-precision floating-point arithmetic, what advantages or disadvantages does the formula given in part *a* have compared with the formula for the secant method given in Section 5.5.4)?

5.6. Suppose we wish to develop an iterative method to compute the square root of a given positive number y, i.e., to solve the nonlinear equation $f(x) = x^2 - y = 0$ given the value of y. Each of the functions g_1 and g_2 listed next gives a fixed-point problem that is equivalent to the equation $f(x) = 0$. For each of these functions, determine whether the corresponding fixed-point iteration scheme $x_{k+1} = g_i(x_k)$ is locally convergent to $\sqrt{y}$ if $y = 3$. Explain your reasoning in each case.
(*a*) $g_1(x) = y + x - x^2$.
(*b*) $g_2(x) = 1 + x - x^2/y$.
(*c*) What is the fixed-point iteration *function* given by Newton's method for this particular problem?

5.7. The gamma function has the following known values: $\Gamma(0.5) = \sqrt{\pi}$, $\Gamma(1) = 1$, $\Gamma(1.5) = \sqrt{\pi}/2$. From these three values, determine the approximate value x for which $\Gamma(x) = 1.5$, using one step of each of the following methods.
(*a*) Quadratic interpolation
(*b*) Inverse quadratic interpolation
(*c*) Linear fractional interpolation

5.8. Using the various criteria given in Section 5.2, investigate the existence and uniqueness of solutions to the system of nonlinear equations in Example 5.2. How do your results change as γ varies through the range of values given in the example?

5.9. Express the Newton iteration for solving each of the following systems of nonlinear equations.
(*a*)

$$\begin{aligned} x_1^2 + x_2^2 &= 1, \\ x_1^2 - x_2 &= 0. \end{aligned}$$

(*b*)

$$\begin{aligned} x_1^2 + x_1 x_2^3 &= 9, \\ 3x_1^2 x_2 - x_2^3 &= 4. \end{aligned}$$

(*c*)

$$\begin{aligned} x_1 + x_2 - 2x_1 x_2 &= 0, \\ x_1^2 + x_2^2 - 2x_1 + 2x_2 &= -1. \end{aligned}$$

(*d*)

$$\begin{aligned} x_1^3 - x_2^2 &= 0, \\ x_1 + x_1^2 x_2 &= 2. \end{aligned}$$

(*e*)

$$\begin{aligned} 2\sin(x_1) + \cos(x_2) - 5x_1 &= 0, \\ 4\cos(x_1) + 2\sin(x_2) - 5x_2 &= 0. \end{aligned}$$

5.10. Carry out one iteration of Newton's method applied to the system of nonlinear equations

$$\begin{aligned} x_1^2 - x_2^2 &= 0, \\ 2x_1 x_2 &= 1, \end{aligned}$$

with starting value $\boldsymbol{x}_0 = [0 \quad 1]^T$.

5.11. Suppose you are using the secant method to find a root x^* of a nonlinear equation $f(x) = 0$. Show that if at any iteration it happens to be the case that either $x_k = x^*$ or $x_{k-1} = x^*$ (but not both), then it will also be true that $x_{k+1} = x^*$.

5.12. Newton's method for solving a scalar nonlinear equation $f(x) = 0$ requires computation of the derivative of f at each iteration. Suppose that we instead replace the true derivative with a constant value d, that is, we use the iteration scheme

$$x_{k+1} = x_k - f(x_k)/d.$$

(*a*) Under what condition on the value of d will this scheme be locally convergent?
(*b*) What will be the convergence rate, in general?
(*c*) Is there any value for d that would still yield quadratic convergence?

5.13. Consider the system of equations

$$\begin{aligned} x_1 - 1 &= 0, \\ x_1 x_2 - 1 &= 0. \end{aligned}$$

For what starting point or points, if any, will Newton's method for solving this system fail? Why?

5.14. Supply the details of a proof that if x^* is a fixed point of the smooth function $g: \mathbb{R} \to \mathbb{R}$, and $g'(x^*) = 0$, then the convergence rate of the fixed-point iteration scheme $x_{k+1} = g(x_k)$ is at least quadratic if started close enough to x^*.

5.15. Verify the formula given in Section 5.5.6 for the change h in c when using linear fractional interpolation to find a zero of a nonlinear function.

Computer Problems

5.1. (*a*) How many zeros does the function

$$f(x) = \sin(10x) - x$$

have? (*Hint*: Sketching the graph of the function will be very helpful.)

(*b*) Use a library routine or one of your own design to find all of the zeros of this function. (*Hint*: You will need a different starting point or initial bracketing interval for each root.)

5.2. For the equation

$$f(x) = x^2 - 3x + 2 = 0,$$

each of the following functions yields an equivalent fixed-point problem:

$$\begin{aligned} g_1(x) &= (x^2+2)/3, \\ g_2(x) &= \sqrt{3x-2}, \\ g_3(x) &= 3 - 2/x, \\ g_4(x) &= (x^2-2)/(2x-3). \end{aligned}$$

(*a*) Analyze the convergence properties of each of the corresponding fixed-point iteration schemes for the root $x = 2$ by considering $|g_i'(2)|$.

(*b*) Confirm your analysis by implementing each of the schemes and verifying its convergence (or lack thereof) and approximate convergence rate.

5.3. Implement the bisection, Newton, and secant methods for solving nonlinear equations in one dimension, and test your implementations by finding at least one root for each of the following equations. What termination criterion should you use? What convergence rate is achieved in each case? Compare your results (solutions and convergence rates) with those for a library routine for solving nonlinear equations.

(*a*) $x^3 - 2x - 5 = 0$.

(*b*) $e^{-x} = x$.

(*c*) $x \sin(x) = 1$.

(*d*) $x^3 - 3x^2 + 3x - 1 = 0$.

5.4. Repeat the previous exercise, this time implementing the inverse quadratic interpolation and linear fractional interpolation methods, and answer the same questions as before.

5.5. Consider the function

$$f(x) = (((x - 0.5) + x) - 0.5) + x,$$

evaluated as indicated (i.e., without any simplification). On your computer, is there any floating-point value x such that $f(x)$ is *exactly* zero? If you use a zero-finding routine on this function, what result is returned, and what is the value of f for this argument? Experiment with the error tolerance to determine its effect on the results obtained.

5.6. Compute the first several iterations of Newton's method for solving each of the following equations, starting with the given initial guess.

(*a*) $x^2 - 1 = 0, \quad x_0 = 10^6$.

(*b*) $(x-1)^4 = 0, \quad x_0 = 10$.

For each equation, answer the following questions: What is the apparent convergence rate of the sequence initially? What should the asymptotic convergence rate of Newton's method be for this equation? How many iterations are required before the asymptotic range is reached? Give an analytical explanation of the behavior you observe empirically.

5.7. (*a*) How does Newton's method behave when you apply it to find a solution to the nonlinear equation

$$x^5 - x^3 - 4x = 0,$$

with $x_0 = 1$ as starting point?

(*b*) What are the real roots of the foregoing equation? Is there anything pathological about them?

5.8. Consider the problem of finding the smallest positive root of the nonlinear equation

$$\cos(x) + 1/(1 + e^{-2x}) = 0.$$

Investigate, both theoretically and empirically, the following iterative schemes for solving this problem using the starting point $x_0 = 3$. For each scheme, you should show that it is indeed an equivalent fixed-point problem, determine analytically whether it is locally convergent and its expected convergence rate, and then implement the method to confirm your results.

(*a*) $x_{k+1} = \arccos(-1/(1 + e^{-2x_k}))$.

(*b*) $x_{k+1} = 0.5 \log(-1/(1 + 1/\cos(x_k)))$.

(*c*) Newton's method.

5.9. In celestial mechanics, *Kepler's equation*

$$M = E - e\sin(E)$$

relates the mean anomaly M to the eccentric anomaly E of an elliptical orbit of eccentricity e, where $0 < e < 1$.

(a) Prove that fixed-point iteration using the iteration function

$$g(E) = M + e\sin(E)$$

is locally convergent.

(b) Use the fixed-point iteration scheme in part a to solve Kepler's equation for the eccentric anomaly E corresponding to a mean anomaly of $M = 1$ (radians) and an eccentricity of $e = 0.5$.

(c) Use Newton's method to solve the same problem.

(d) Use a library zero finder to solve the same problem.

5.10. In neutron transport theory, the critical length of a fuel rod is determined by the roots of the equation

$$\cot(x) = (x^2 - 1)/(2x).$$

Use a zero finder to determine the smallest positive root of this equation.

5.11. The natural frequencies of vibration of a uniform beam of unit length, clamped on one end and free on the other, satisfy the equation

$$\tan(x)\tanh(x) = -1.$$

Use a zero finder to determine the smallest positive root of this equation.

5.12. The vertical distance y that a parachutist falls before opening the parachute is given by the equation

$$y = \log(\cosh(t\sqrt{gk}))/k,$$

where t is the elapsed time in seconds, $g = 9.8065$ m/s^2 is the acceleration due to gravity, and $k = 0.00341$ m^{-1} is a constant related to air resistance. Use a zero finder to determine the elapsed time required to fall a distance of 1 km.

5.13. Use a zero finder to determine the depth (relative to its radius) to which a sphere of density 0.4 (relative to water) sinks. (*Hint*: The volume of a sphere of radius r is $4\pi r^3/3$, and the volume of a spherical "cap" of height h is $\pi h^2(3r - h)/3$).

5.14. The *van der Waals equation of state*,

$$\left(p + \frac{a}{v^2}\right)(v - b) = RT,$$

relates the pressure p, specific volume v, and temperature T of a gas, where R is a universal constant and a and b are constants that depend on the particular gas. In appropriate units, $R = 0.082054$, and for carbon dioxide, $a = 3.592$ and $b = 0.04267$. Use a zero finder to compute the specific volume v for a temperature of 300 K and for pressures of 1 atm, 10 atm, and 100 atm. Compare your results to those for the *ideal gas law*, $pv = RT$. The latter can be used as a starting guess for an iterative method to solve the van der Waals equation.

5.15. If an amount a is borrowed at interest rate r for n years, then the total amount to be repaid is given by

$$a(1 + r)^n.$$

Yearly payments of p each would reduce this amount by

$$\sum_{0}^{n-1} p(1 + r)^i = p\,\frac{(1 + r)^n - 1}{r}.$$

The loan will be repaid when these two quantities are equal.

(a) For a loan of a = \$100,000 and yearly payments of p = \$10,000, how long will it take to pay off the loan if the interest rate is 6 percent, i.e., $r = 0.06$?

(b) For a loan of a = \$100,000 and yearly payments of p = \$10,000, what interest rate r would be required for the loan to be paid off in $n = 20$ years?

(c) For a loan of a = \$100,000, how large must the yearly payments p be for the loan to be paid off in $n = 20$ years at 6 percent interest?

You may use any method you like to solve the given equation in each case. For the purpose of this problem, we will treat n as a continuous variable (i.e., it can have fractional values).

5.16. (*a*) Write a program using Newton's method to compute the nth root of a given number y, that is, to solve the nonlinear equation $f(x) = x^n - y = 0$ for x, given y and n. We want to be able to compute any nth root, so your program should work for complex as well as real roots. Test your program by computing the complex cube root of 3 lying in the upper left quadrant of the complex plane, using $x_0 = -1+i$ as starting guess.

(*b*) Repeat part *a*, but this time use Muller's method (i.e., successive quadratic polynomial interpolation). For this method, you will need two additional starting guesses.

5.17. By dividing by its nonzero leading coefficient, any cubic equation can be put into the form

$$x^3 + ax^2 + bx + c = 0.$$

According to *Vieta's Theorem*, the three roots of such a cubic equation satisfy the system of nonlinear equations

$$\begin{aligned} -(x_1 + x_2 + x_3) &= a, \\ x_1x_2 + x_2x_3 + x_1x_3 &= b, \\ -x_1x_2x_3 &= c. \end{aligned}$$

Write a program based on Newton's method, or any other method of your choice, to solve this system for any given cubic polynomial. Note that two of the roots may be complex even if the coefficients are real, so you will need to use a complex starting guess and complex arithmetic to find the complex roots. Test your program on a variety of cubic equations and compare your results with the roots computed by a library routine for computing roots of cubic (or more general) polynomials. See also Computer Problem 1.11.

5.18. (*a*) Write a program based on Newton's method to solve the system of nonlinear equations

$$\begin{aligned} (x_1 + 3)(x_2^3 - 7) + 18 &= 0, \\ \sin(x_2 e^{x_1} - 1) &= 0 \end{aligned}$$

with starting point $\boldsymbol{x}_0 = [-0.5 \quad 1.4]^T$.

(*b*) Write a program based on Broyden's method to solve the same system with the same starting point.

(*c*) Compare the convergence rates of the two methods by computing the error at each iteration, given that the exact solution is $\boldsymbol{x}^* = [0 \quad 1]^T$. How many iterations does each method require to attain full machine precision?

5.19. Bioremediation involves the use of bacteria to consume toxic wastes. At steady state, the bacterial density x and nutrient concentration y satisfy the system of nonlinear equations

$$\begin{aligned} \gamma xy - x(1+y) &= 0, \\ -xy + (\delta - y)(1+y) &= 0, \end{aligned}$$

where γ and δ are parameters that depend on various physical features of the system; typical values are $\gamma = 5$ and $\delta = 1$. Solve this system numerically using Newton's method. You should find at least one solution with a nonzero bacterial density ($x \neq 0$), and one solution in which the bacterial population has died out ($x = 0$).

5.20. (*a*) According to quantum mechanics, the ground state of a particle in a spherical well is determined by the system of nonlinear equations

$$\begin{aligned} \frac{x}{\tan(x)} &= -y, \\ x^2 + y^2 &= s^2, \end{aligned}$$

where s depends on the mass and radius of the particle and the strength of the potential. In appropriate units, $s = 3.5$. Use any method of your choice to solve this nonlinear system.

(*b*) The first excited state of the particle is determined by the nonlinear system

$$\begin{aligned} \frac{1}{x\tan(x)} - \frac{1}{x^2} &= \frac{1}{y} + \frac{1}{y^2}, \\ x^2 + y^2 &= s^2. \end{aligned}$$

Again, use any method of your choice to solve this nonlinear system.

5.21. Lorenz derived a simple system of ordinary differential equations describing buoyant convection in a fluid as a crude model for atmospheric circulation. At steady state, the convective velocity x, temperature gradient y, and heat flow z satisfy the system of nonlinear equations

$$\begin{aligned} \sigma(y - x) &= 0, \\ rx - y - xz &= 0, \\ xy - bz &= 0, \end{aligned}$$

where σ (the Prandtl number), r (the Rayleigh number), and b are positive constants that depend on the properties of the fluid, the applied temperature gradient, and the geometry of the problem. Typical values Lorenz used are $\sigma = 10$, $r = 28$, and $b = 8/3$. Write a program using Newton's method to solve this system of equations. You should find three different solutions.

5.22. (*a*) Solve the following nonlinear system by the obvious fixed-point iteration scheme.

$$\begin{aligned} x_1 &= -\frac{\cos(x_1)}{81} + \frac{x_2^2}{9} + \frac{\sin(x_3)}{3}, \\ x_2 &= \frac{\sin(x_1)}{3} + \frac{\cos(x_3)}{3}, \\ x_3 &= -\frac{\cos(x_1)}{9} + \frac{x_2}{3} + \frac{\sin(x_3)}{6}. \end{aligned}$$

(*b*) At the fixed point, what is the value of the constant C in the linear convergence rate? How does this compare with your observation of the actual convergence behavior?

(*c*) Solve the same system using Newton's method and compare the convergence behavior with that for fixed-point iteration.

5.23. Write a program to solve the system of nonlinear equations

$$\begin{aligned} 16x^4 + 16y^4 + z^4 &= 16, \\ x^2 + y^2 + z^2 &= 3, \\ x^3 - y &= 0 \end{aligned}$$

using Newton's method. You may solve the resulting linear system at each iteration either by a library routine or by a linear system solver of your own design. As starting guess, you may take each variable to be 1. In addition, try nonlinear solvers from a subroutine library, based on both Newton and secant updating methods, and compare the solutions obtained and the convergence rates with those for your program.

5.24. The derivation of a two-point Gaussian quadrature rule (which we will consider in Section 8.3.3) on the interval $[-1, 1]$ using the method of undetermined coefficients leads to the following system of nonlinear equations for the nodes x_1, x_2 and weights w_1, w_2:

$$\begin{aligned} w_1 + w_2 &= 2, \\ w_1 x_1 + w_2 x_2 &= 0, \\ w_1 x_1^2 + w_2 x_2^2 &= 2/3, \\ w_1 x_1^3 + w_2 x_2^3 &= 0. \end{aligned}$$

Solve this system for x_1, x_2, w_1, and w_2 using a library routine or one of your own design. How many different solutions can you find?

5.25. Use a library routine, or one of your own design, to solve the following system of nonlinear equations:

$$\begin{aligned} \sin(x) + y^2 + \log(z) &= 3, \\ 3x + 2^y - z^3 &= 0, \\ x^2 + y^2 + z^3 &= 6. \end{aligned}$$

Try to find as many different solutions as you can. You should find at least four real solutions (there are also complex solutions).

5.26. A model for combustion of propane in air yields the system of nonlinear equations

$$\begin{aligned} x_1 + x_4 &= 3, \\ 2x_1 + x_2 + x_4 + x_7 + x_8 + x_9 + 2x_{10} &= R + 10, \\ 2x_2 + 2x_5 + x_6 + x_7 &= 8, \\ 2x_3 + x_5 &= 4R, \\ x_1 x_5 - 0.193\, x_2 x_4 &= 0, \\ x_6\sqrt{x_2} - 0.002597\sqrt{x_2 x_4 S} &= 0, \\ x_7\sqrt{x_4} - 0.003448\sqrt{x_1 x_4 S} &= 0, \\ x_4 x_8 - 0.00001799\, x_2 S &= 0, \\ x_4 x_9 - 0.0002155\, x_1\sqrt{x_3 S} &= 0, \\ x_4^2(x_{10} - 0.00003846\, S) &= 0, \end{aligned}$$

where $R = 4.056734$ and $S = \sum_{i=1}^{10} x_i$. Use a library routine to solve this nonlinear system. (*Hint*: If any square root should fail because a variable becomes negative, replace that variable by its absolute value.)

5.27. Each of the following systems of nonlinear equations may present some difficulty in computing a solution. Use a library routine, or one of your own design, to solve each of the systems from the given starting point. In some cases, the nonlinear solver may fail to converge or may converge to a point other than a solution. When this happens, try to explain the reason for the observed behavior. Also note the convergence rate attained, and if it is slower than expected, try to explain why.

(*a*)

$$\begin{aligned} x_1 + x_2(x_2(5 - x_2) - 2) &= 13, \\ x_1 + x_2(x_2(1 + x_2) - 14) &= 29, \end{aligned}$$

starting from $x_1 = 15$, $x_2 = -2$.

(*b*)

$$\begin{aligned} x_1^2 + x_2^2 + x_3^2 &= 5, \\ x_1 + x_2 &= 1, \\ x_1 + x_3 &= 3, \end{aligned}$$

starting from $x_1 = (1 + \sqrt{3})/2$, $x_2 = (1 - \sqrt{3})/2$, $x_3 = \sqrt{3}$.

(*c*)

$$\begin{aligned} x_1 + 10x_2 &= 0, \\ \sqrt{5}\,(x_3 - x_4) &= 0, \\ (x_2 - x_3)^2 &= 0, \\ \sqrt{10}\,(x_1 - x_4)^2 &= 0, \end{aligned}$$

starting from $x_1 = 1$, $x_2 = 2$, $x_3 = 1$, $x_4 = 1$.

(*d*)

$$\begin{aligned} x_1 &= 0, \\ 10x_1/(x_1 + 0.1) + 2x_2^2 &= 0, \end{aligned}$$

starting from $x_1 = 1.8$, $x_2 = 0$.

(*e*)

$$\begin{aligned} 10^4 x_1 x_2 &= 1, \\ e^{-x_1} + e^{-x_2} &= 1.0001, \end{aligned}$$

starting from $x_1 = 0$, $x_2 = 1$.

5.28. Newton's method can be used to compute the inverse of a nonsingular $n \times n$ matrix $\boldsymbol{A}$. If we define the function $\boldsymbol{F}: \mathbb{R}^{n \times n} \to \mathbb{R}^{n \times n}$ by

$$\boldsymbol{F}(\boldsymbol{X}) = \boldsymbol{I} - \boldsymbol{A}\boldsymbol{X},$$

where $\boldsymbol{X}$ is an $n \times n$ matrix, then $\boldsymbol{F}(\boldsymbol{X}) = \boldsymbol{O}$ precisely when $\boldsymbol{X} = \boldsymbol{A}^{-1}$. Because $\boldsymbol{F}'(\boldsymbol{X}) = -\boldsymbol{A}$, Newton's method for solving this equation has the form

$$\begin{aligned} \boldsymbol{X}_{k+1} &= \boldsymbol{X}_k - [\boldsymbol{F}'(\boldsymbol{X}_k)]^{-1}\boldsymbol{F}(\boldsymbol{X}_k) \\ &= \boldsymbol{X}_k + \boldsymbol{A}^{-1}(\boldsymbol{I} - \boldsymbol{A}\boldsymbol{X}_k). \end{aligned}$$

But $\boldsymbol{A}^{-1}$ is what we are trying to compute, so instead we use the current approximation to $\boldsymbol{A}^{-1}$, namely $\boldsymbol{X}_k$. Thus, the iteration scheme takes the form

$$\boldsymbol{X}_{k+1} = \boldsymbol{X}_k + \boldsymbol{X}_k(\boldsymbol{I} - \boldsymbol{A}\boldsymbol{X}_k).$$

(*a*) If we define the residual matrix

$$\boldsymbol{R}_k = \boldsymbol{I} - \boldsymbol{A}\boldsymbol{X}_k$$

and the error matrix

$$\boldsymbol{E}_k = \boldsymbol{A}^{-1} - \boldsymbol{X}_k,$$

show that

$$\boldsymbol{R}_{k+1} = \boldsymbol{R}_k^2 \quad \text{and} \quad \boldsymbol{E}_{k+1} = \boldsymbol{E}_k\boldsymbol{A}\boldsymbol{E}_k,$$

from which we can conclude that the convergence rate is quadratic, despite using only an approximate derivative.

(*b*) Write a program to compute the inverse of a given input matrix $\boldsymbol{A}$ using this iteration scheme. A reasonable starting guess is to take

$$\boldsymbol{X}_0 = \frac{\boldsymbol{A}^T}{\|\boldsymbol{A}\|_1 \cdot \|\boldsymbol{A}\|_\infty}.$$

Test your program on some random matrices and compare its accuracy and efficiency with conventional methods for computing the inverse, such as LU factorization or Gauss-Jordan elimination.

5.29. Newton's method can be used to compute an eigenvalue λ and corresponding eigenvector $\boldsymbol{x}$ of an $n \times n$ matrix $\boldsymbol{A}$. If we define the function $\boldsymbol{f}: \mathbb{R}^{n+1} \to \mathbb{R}^{n+1}$ by

$$\boldsymbol{f}(\boldsymbol{x}, \lambda) = \begin{bmatrix} \boldsymbol{A}\boldsymbol{x} - \lambda\boldsymbol{x} \\ \boldsymbol{x}^T\boldsymbol{x} - 1 \end{bmatrix},$$

then $\boldsymbol{f}(\boldsymbol{x}, \lambda) = \boldsymbol{0}$ precisely when λ is an eigenvalue and $\boldsymbol{x}$ is a corresponding normalized eigenvector. Because

$$\boldsymbol{J}_f(\boldsymbol{x}, \lambda) = \begin{bmatrix} \boldsymbol{A} - \lambda\boldsymbol{I} & -\boldsymbol{x} \\ 2\boldsymbol{x}^T & 0 \end{bmatrix},$$

Newton's method for solving this equation has the form

$$\begin{bmatrix} \boldsymbol{x}_{k+1} \\ \lambda_{k+1} \end{bmatrix} = \begin{bmatrix} \boldsymbol{x}_k \\ \lambda_k \end{bmatrix} + \begin{bmatrix} \boldsymbol{s}_k \\ \delta_k \end{bmatrix},$$

where $[\,\boldsymbol{s}_k \quad \delta_k\,]^T$ is the solution to the linear system

$$\begin{bmatrix} \boldsymbol{A} - \lambda_k\boldsymbol{I} & -\boldsymbol{x}_k \\ 2\boldsymbol{x}_k^T & 0 \end{bmatrix} \begin{bmatrix} \boldsymbol{s}_k \\ \delta_k \end{bmatrix} = -\begin{bmatrix} \boldsymbol{A}\boldsymbol{x}_k - \lambda_k\boldsymbol{x}_k \\ \boldsymbol{x}_k^T\boldsymbol{x}_k - 1 \end{bmatrix}.$$

Write a program to compute an eigenvalue-eigenvector pair of a given input matrix $\boldsymbol{A}$ using this iteration scheme. A reasonable starting guess is to take $\boldsymbol{x}_0$ to be an arbitrary normalized nonzero vector (i.e., $\boldsymbol{x}_0^T\boldsymbol{x}_0 = 1$) and take $\lambda_0 = \boldsymbol{x}_0^T\boldsymbol{A}\boldsymbol{x}_0$ (Why?). Test your program on some random matrices and compare its accuracy and efficiency with those of conventional methods for computing a single eigenvalue-eigenvector pair, such as the power method. Note, however, that Newton's method does not necessarily converge to the dominant eigenvalue.

Chapter 6

Optimization

6.1 Optimization Problems

Optimization problems arise in all areas of science and engineering, and are perhaps even more common in business and industry. Any *design* problem usually involves optimizing some figure of merit, such as cost or efficiency. Among all configurations in some space of possible designs, we want the one that best achieves some desired *objective*. Of course, the result will depend on the particular objective. For example, an automobile engine designed to maximize power will differ greatly from one designed to maximize fuel efficiency.

Examples of optimization problems abound. A structural engineer might minimize the weight of a bridge subject to a constraint on its strength. A dietitian might minimize the cost of a diet subject to meeting nutritional requirements. These examples illustrate two important features about optimization problems. The first is that in most optimization problems the choices in design space are not totally unfettered: the solution must satisfy some restrictions or *constraints*. The lightest possible bridge might be made of string and balsa wood, and would not support much of a load. The cheapest possible diet might starve its victims. For this reason, the bridge must meet a minimum strength requirement, and the diet must meet minimum nutritional requirements. Among all such *feasible* choices, however, we want one that minimizes the weight or cost, respectively.

The second important feature is the duality that pervades optimization. For example, the structural engineer might instead maximize the strength of the bridge subject to a constraint on its weight, and the dietitian might maximize the nutritional value of a diet subject to a constraint on its cost. In each case the constraint has become the objective and vice versa, and minimization has become maximization. There is an intimate relationship between such dual problems, whose solutions are often identical.

Example 6.1 Energy Minimization. People are not the only optimizers. Many physical systems, from molecules to galaxies, naturally seek a configuration having minimum energy. A simple example is the spring-mass system shown in Fig. 6.1, where an object of mass m is suspended at position (x, y) from two springs with spring constants k_1 and k_2 and rest lengths L_1 and L_2, and whose upper ends are fixed at a distance D apart. The *potential energy* of the system is given by

$$V(x, y) = \tfrac{1}{2}\, k_1 \left(\sqrt{x^2 + y^2} - L_1\right)^2 + \tfrac{1}{2}\, k_2 \left(\sqrt{(D - x)^2 + y^2} - L_2\right)^2 - mgy,$$

where g is the acceleration due to gravity. The system is in equilibrium when the mass is at the position (x, y) that minimizes the potential energy $V(x, y)$. Thus, this and many other physical systems can be analyzed using optimization techniques.

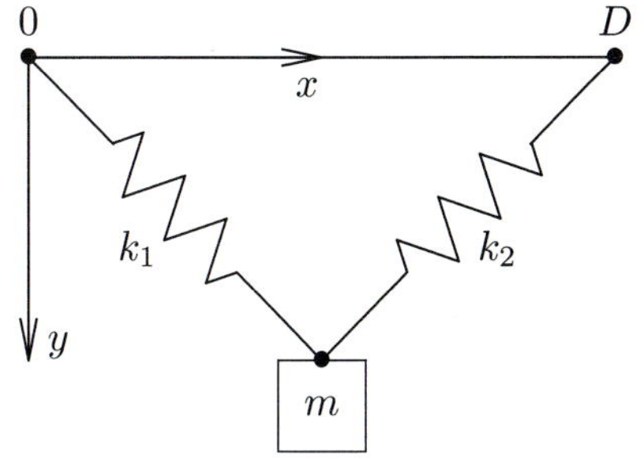

Figure 6.1: Spring-mass system.

An optimization problem can be expressed mathematically as the problem of determining an argument for which a given function has an extreme value (minimum or maximum) on a given domain. More formally, given a function $f: \mathbb{R}^n \to \mathbb{R}$, and a set $S \subseteq \mathbb{R}^n$, we seek $\boldsymbol{x}^* \in S$ such that f attains a minimum on S at $\boldsymbol{x}^*$, i.e., $f(\boldsymbol{x}^*) \le f(\boldsymbol{x})$ for all $\boldsymbol{x} \in S$. Such a point $\boldsymbol{x}^*$ is called a *minimizer*, or simply a *minimum*, of f. A maximum of f is a minimum of $-f$, so it suffices to consider only minimization.

The *objective function* f may be linear or nonlinear, and it is usually assumed to be differentiable. The set S is usually defined by a set of equations and inequalities, called *constraints*, which may be linear or nonlinear. Any vector $\boldsymbol{x} \in S$, i.e., that satisfies the constraints, is called a *feasible point*, and S is called the *feasible set*. If $S = \mathbb{R}^n$, then the problem is *unconstrained*.

A general *continuous* optimization problem has the form

$$\min_{\boldsymbol{x}} f(\boldsymbol{x}) \quad \text{subject to} \quad \boldsymbol{g}(\boldsymbol{x}) = \boldsymbol{0} \quad \text{and} \quad \boldsymbol{h}(\boldsymbol{x}) \le \boldsymbol{0},$$

where $f: \mathbb{R}^n \to \mathbb{R}$, $\boldsymbol{g}: \mathbb{R}^n \to \mathbb{R}^m$, and $\boldsymbol{h}: \mathbb{R}^n \to \mathbb{R}^p$. Optimization problems are classified by the properties of the functions involved. For example, if f, $\boldsymbol{g}$, and $\boldsymbol{h}$ are all linear (or affine), then we have a *linear programming* problem. If any of the functions involved are nonlinear, then we have a *nonlinear programming* problem.

(The use of the term *programming* in optimization has nothing to do with computer programming, but instead refers to planning activities in the sense of operations research or management science.)

Example 6.2 Constrained Optimization. A simple example with $n = 2$ and $m = 1$, i.e., two variables and one constraint, is to minimize the surface area of a cylinder subject to a constraint on its volume:

$$\min_{\boldsymbol{x}} f(x_1, x_2) = 2\pi x_1(x_1 + x_2) \quad \text{subject to} \quad g(x_1, x_2) = \pi x_1^2 x_2 - V = 0,$$

where x_1 and x_2 are the radius and height of the cylinder and V is the required volume. The objective function f and constraint function g are both nonlinear in this instance. The solution to this problem, which we will compute in Example 6.6, minimizes the amount of material required to make a container of the given volume.

Before proceeding, we need to be a bit more precise about what we mean by a solution to an optimization problem. The concept of a minimum defined earlier is more properly called a *global minimum*, in that $f(\boldsymbol{x}^*) \le f(\boldsymbol{x})$ for *any* feasible point $\boldsymbol{x}$. Finding such a global minimum, or even verifying that a point is a global minimum after it has been found, is difficult unless the problem has special properties. Most optimization methods use local information, such as derivatives and Taylor series expansions, and consequently are designed to find only a *local minimum*, i.e., a feasible point $\boldsymbol{x}^*$ such that $f(\boldsymbol{x}^*) \le f(\boldsymbol{x})$ for any feasible point $\boldsymbol{x}$ *in some neighborhood* of $\boldsymbol{x}^*$. These concepts are illustrated for a one-dimensional problem in Fig. 6.2.

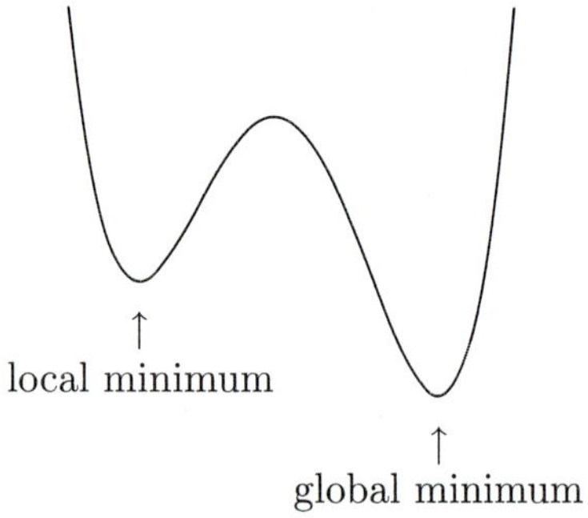

Figure 6.2: Local and global minima.

Unless the problem has special properties, there is usually no way to guarantee that a specific local minimum, or in particular a global minimum, will be found using conventional numerical methods. Often the best one can do is to start with an initial guess that is as close to the desired minimum as possible and hope that the iterative solution process will then converge to it. For some purposes, any local minimum may suffice. If a global minimum is required, however, then one might try several different starting points, widely scattered throughout the feasible set. If they all produce the same result, then there is a good chance that a global minimum has been found. If they produce different results, then taking the lowest of the local minima is the best one can do, but there may still be unexplored regions with even smaller values of the objective function.

For some important categories of problems, global optimization is much more tractable. For example, global solutions to linear programming problems, or more generally *convex* programming problems (defined later), are routinely obtained by very efficient methods. Global optimization for more general problems is an active area of research in which significant progress has been made in recent years, but the techniques employed are beyond the scope of this book; see Section 6.9 for references.

We also will not address *discrete* optimization problems—such as *integer programming*, in which the variables can take on only integer values—because such problems usually require combinatorial rather than numerical techniques. In addition to traditional combinatorial techniques, such as branch-and-bound, there has been a great deal of research in recent years on new approaches to discrete optimization, such as simulated annealing and genetic algorithms, but these topics are beyond the scope of this book.

6.2 Existence and Uniqueness

It is difficult to say anything conclusive about the existence or uniqueness of a solution to an optimization problem without making some assumptions about the objective function f and the feasible set S. A basic result from analysis is that if f is continuous on a *closed* and *bounded* set $S \subseteq \mathbb{R}^n$, then f has a global minimum on S. But if S is not closed or is unbounded, then f may have no local or global minimum on S. For example, the continuous function $f(x) = x$ has no minimum on any open interval $S = (a, b)$ or on the closed but unbounded set $S = \mathbb{R}$. We will next consider some properties that ensure the existence of a global minimum even when the feasible set is unbounded, which includes the important case of unconstrained optimization.

A continuous function f on an unbounded set $S \subseteq \mathbb{R}^n$ is said to be *coercive* if

$$\lim_{\|\boldsymbol{x}\| \to \infty} f(\boldsymbol{x}) = +\infty,$$

i.e., for any constant M, there is an $r > 0$ (depending on M) such that $f(\boldsymbol{x}) \geq M$ for any $\boldsymbol{x} \in S$ such that $\|\boldsymbol{x}\| \geq r$. The importance of this concept, which says that $f(\boldsymbol{x})$ must be large whenever $\|\boldsymbol{x}\|$ is large, is that if f is coercive on a closed, unbounded set $S \subseteq \mathbb{R}^n$, then f has a global minimum on S (see Exercise 6.10).

Example 6.3 Coercive and Noncoercive Functions.

- $f(x) = x^2$ is coercive on $\mathbb{R}$ because it has arbitrarily large positive values for arbitrarily large positive or negative arguments. It has a global minimum at $x = 0$.
- $f(x) = x^3$ is *not* coercive on $\mathbb{R}$ because it has arbitrarily large negative (rather than positive) values for arbitrarily large negative arguments. It has no global minimum.

- $f(x) = e^x$ is *not* coercive on $\mathbb{R}$ because it does not have arbitrarily large positive values for arbitrarily large negative arguments. Though bounded below by 0, it has no global minimum.
- $f(x, y) = x^4 - 4xy + y^4$ is coercive on $\mathbb{R}^2$. This is less obvious because of the $4xy$ term, but observe that $f(x, y) = (x^4 + y^4)(1 - 4xy/(x^4 + y^4))$, and $4xy/(x^4 + y^4) \to 0$ as $\|(x, y)\| \to +\infty$. It has global minima at $(-1, -1)$ and $(1, 1)$.
- $f(x, y) = ax + by + c$, where at least one of the real numbers a and b is nonzero, is *not* coercive on $\mathbb{R}^2$, because it has the constant value c on the unbounded line $ax + by = 0$. It has no global minimum.

A *level set* for a function $f: S \subseteq \mathbb{R}^n \to \mathbb{R}$ is the set of all points in S for which the function has some given constant value. In $\mathbb{R}^2$ level sets are sometimes called *contour lines* or simply *contours* (familiar from topographic maps and weather maps), and in $\mathbb{R}^n$ they are sometimes called *isosurfaces* of the function (the ellipses in Fig. 6.5 are an illustrative example in $\mathbb{R}^2$). We are also interested in the interior of the region whose boundary is a level set, i.e., the set of all points for which the function is less than or equal to a given constant value, so we define the *sublevel set* for a given $\gamma \in \mathbb{R}$ to be

$$L_\gamma = \{\boldsymbol{x} \in S : f(\boldsymbol{x}) \le \gamma\}.$$

Level and sublevel sets have many uses in optimization and elsewhere, but of most immediate interest here is the fact that if f is continuous on a set $S \subseteq \mathbb{R}^n$ and has a nonempty sublevel set that is closed and bounded, then f has a global minimum on S (see Exercise 6.11). We note that if S is unbounded, then f is coercive on S if, and only if, *all* of its sublevel sets are bounded.

6.2.1 Convexity

We have now seen some useful existence results for optimization problems, but we have said nothing about uniqueness of solutions or the relationship between local and global minima. Little can be said about these issues, in general, without some additional assumptions. The most important of these is *convexity*. A set $S \subseteq \mathbb{R}^n$ is *convex* if it contains the line segment between any two of its points, i.e.,

$$\{\alpha\boldsymbol{x} + (1 - \alpha)\boldsymbol{y} : 0 \le \alpha \le 1\} \subseteq S$$

for all $\boldsymbol{x}, \boldsymbol{y} \in S$. Examples of some convex and nonconvex sets are shown in Fig. 6.3. A function $f: S \subseteq \mathbb{R}^n \to \mathbb{R}$ is *convex* on a convex set S if its graph along any line segment in S lies *on or below* the chord connecting the function values at the endpoints of the segment, i.e., if

$$f(\alpha\boldsymbol{x} + (1 - \alpha)\boldsymbol{y}) \le \alpha f(\boldsymbol{x}) + (1 - \alpha)f(\boldsymbol{y})$$

for all $\alpha \in [0, 1]$ and all $\boldsymbol{x}, \boldsymbol{y} \in S$. In the preceding definition, if strict inequality holds for all $\alpha \in (0, 1)$, then f is said to be *strictly convex*. A convex function is

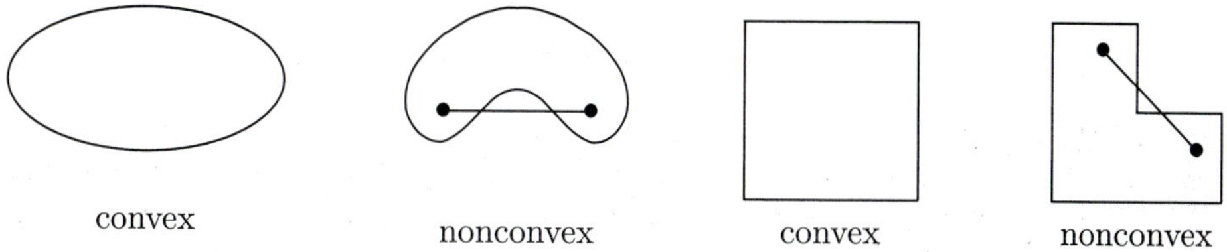

Figure 6.3: Examples of convex and nonconvex sets in $\mathbb{R}^2$. Each set includes interior of region bounded by closed curve.

strictly convex if its graph in $\mathbb{R}^n \times \mathbb{R}$ contains no straight line segment. Examples of nonconvex, convex, and strictly convex functions in one dimension are shown in Fig. 6.4.

A number of important results follow from convexity. For example, if f is a convex function on a convex set S, then f is necessarily continuous at any interior point of S. Also, any sublevel set of a convex function is convex. But the most important such result is that any local minimum of a convex function f on a convex set $S \subseteq \mathbb{R}^n$ is a global minimum of f on S. Moreover, any local minimum of a *strictly* convex function f on a convex set $S \subseteq \mathbb{R}^n$ is the *unique* global minimum of f on S (see Exercise 6.12). Note that the latter result guarantees uniqueness but not the existence of a global minimum. If S is closed and bounded, of course, then existence is already assured. It turns out that if f is strictly convex on an unbounded set $S \subseteq \mathbb{R}^n$, then f has a (necessarily unique) minimum on S if, and only if, f is coercive on S.

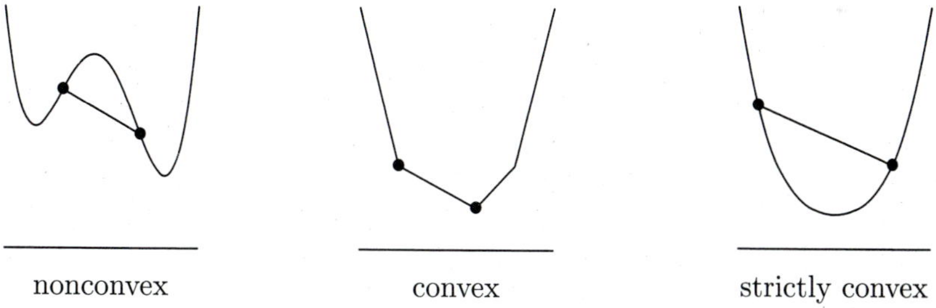

Figure 6.4: Examples of nonconvex, convex, and strictly convex functions in one dimension.

6.2.2 Unconstrained Optimality Conditions

The existence and uniqueness results we have cited thus far give no hint how to *find* a minimum or to verify that a point is indeed a minimum once it has been found. To do that, we will assume that the objective function f is smooth and then generalize to n dimensions the standard approach from one-dimensional calculus: set the first derivative equal to zero and then use the sign of the second derivative to determine whether the resulting solution is a minimum, a maximum, or an inflection point.

If $f\colon \mathbb{R}^n \to \mathbb{R}$ is differentiable, then the vector-valued function $\nabla f\colon \mathbb{R}^n \to \mathbb{R}^n$ defined by

$$\nabla f(\boldsymbol{x}) = \begin{bmatrix} \dfrac{\partial f(\boldsymbol{x})}{\partial x_1} \\ \dfrac{\partial f(\boldsymbol{x})}{\partial x_2} \\ \vdots \\ \dfrac{\partial f(\boldsymbol{x})}{\partial x_n} \end{bmatrix}$$

is called the *gradient* of f. An important fact about the gradient vector of a continuously differentiable function f is that it points "uphill" from $f(\boldsymbol{x})$, and the negative gradient, $-\nabla f(\boldsymbol{x})$, points "downhill," i.e., toward points having lower function values than $f(\boldsymbol{x})$. To see why this is true, recall from *Taylor's Theorem* that for any $\boldsymbol{s} \in \mathbb{R}^n$ we have

$$f(\boldsymbol{x}+\boldsymbol{s}) = f(\boldsymbol{x}) + \nabla f(\boldsymbol{x}+\alpha\boldsymbol{s})^T\boldsymbol{s}$$

for some $\alpha \in (0,1)$. Taking $\boldsymbol{s} = -\nabla f(\boldsymbol{x})$ and using the continuity of ∇f then shows that f decreases along $-\nabla f(\boldsymbol{x})$ in some neighborhood of $\boldsymbol{x}$, provided $\nabla f(\boldsymbol{x}) \neq \boldsymbol{0}$. But if $\boldsymbol{x}^*$ is a local minimum of f, then by definition there can be no such downhill direction, so we must have $\nabla f(\boldsymbol{x}^*) = \boldsymbol{0}$. Such an $\boldsymbol{x}^*$ where $\nabla f(\boldsymbol{x}^*) = \boldsymbol{0}$ is called a *critical point* of f (also sometimes called a *stationary point* or *equilibrium point*). We can conclude that if $f\colon S \subseteq \mathbb{R}^n \to \mathbb{R}$ is continuously differentiable and $\boldsymbol{x}^*$ is an interior point of S at which f has a local minimum, then $\boldsymbol{x}^*$ must be a critical point of f. This is called a *first-order necessary condition* for a minimum, because it involves only first derivatives of the objective function.

Example 6.4 Equilibrium. Continuing with Example 6.1, a minimum of the potential energy must occur at a critical point of V, i.e., when $\nabla V(x,y) = 0$. We recall from mechanics that the force (a vector) is equal to the negative gradient of the potential energy (a scalar), i.e.,

$$\boldsymbol{F}(x,y) = -\nabla V(x,y).$$

Thus, the potential energy is minimized and the system is in equilibrium when the net force from the springs and gravity is zero. Such a physical interpretation explains the synonyms stationary point or equilibrium point for a critical point.

We have just seen that a necessary condition for an interior point $\boldsymbol{x}$ of S to be a local minimum of f is that $\boldsymbol{x}$ be a critical point, i.e., $\nabla f(\boldsymbol{x}) = \boldsymbol{0}$. The latter is a system of (usually nonlinear) equations, so we can use the methods of Chapter 5 to seek a critical point. If f is convex, then any critical point must be a global minimum, and we are done. In general, however, this necessary condition is not sufficient to guarantee even a local minimum: a critical point may be a minimum, a maximum, or neither (e.g., a saddle point, from which some directions are downhill and others are uphill). Thus, we need a criterion for classifying critical points and checking their optimality.

If $f: \mathbb{R}^n \to \mathbb{R}$ is twice differentiable, then the matrix-valued function $\boldsymbol{H}_f: \mathbb{R}^n \to \mathbb{R}^{n\times n}$ defined by

$$\boldsymbol{H}_f(\boldsymbol{x}) = \begin{bmatrix} \dfrac{\partial^2 f(\boldsymbol{x})}{\partial x_1^2} & \dfrac{\partial^2 f(\boldsymbol{x})}{\partial x_1 \partial x_2} & \cdots & \dfrac{\partial^2 f(\boldsymbol{x})}{\partial x_1 \partial x_n} \\ \dfrac{\partial^2 f(\boldsymbol{x})}{\partial x_2 \partial x_1} & \dfrac{\partial^2 f(\boldsymbol{x})}{\partial x_2^2} & \cdots & \dfrac{\partial^2 f(\boldsymbol{x})}{\partial x_2 \partial x_n} \\ \vdots & \vdots & \ddots & \vdots \\ \dfrac{\partial^2 f(\boldsymbol{x})}{\partial x_n \partial x_1} & \dfrac{\partial^2 f(\boldsymbol{x})}{\partial x_n \partial x_2} & \cdots & \dfrac{\partial^2 f(\boldsymbol{x})}{\partial x_n^2} \end{bmatrix}$$

is called the *Hessian matrix* of f. Note that the Hessian matrix of f is simply the Jacobian matrix of the gradient, ∇f. If the second partial derivatives of f are continuous, then $\partial^2 f/\partial x_i \partial x_j = \partial^2 f/\partial x_j \partial x_i$, and hence the Hessian matrix of f is symmetric.

Assume that $f: \mathbb{R}^n \to \mathbb{R}$ is twice continuously differentiable, and let $\boldsymbol{x}^*$ be a critical point of f. According to Taylor's Theorem, for $\boldsymbol{s} \in \mathbb{R}^n$ we have

$$f(\boldsymbol{x}^* + \boldsymbol{s}) = f(\boldsymbol{x}^*) + \nabla f(\boldsymbol{x}^*)^T \boldsymbol{s} + \tfrac{1}{2}\, \boldsymbol{s}^T \boldsymbol{H}_f(\boldsymbol{x}^* + \alpha \boldsymbol{s})\, \boldsymbol{s}$$

for some $\alpha \in (0, 1)$. Since $\boldsymbol{x}^*$ is a critical point, we have $\nabla f(\boldsymbol{x}^*) = \boldsymbol{0}$, so the term involving the Hessian matrix determines whether $f(\boldsymbol{x}^* + \boldsymbol{s})$ is larger or smaller than $f(\boldsymbol{x}^*)$. If $\boldsymbol{H}_f(\boldsymbol{x}^*)$ is positive definite at $\boldsymbol{x}^*$, then by continuity $\boldsymbol{H}_f(\boldsymbol{x}^* + \alpha\boldsymbol{s})$ is also positive definite in some neighborhood of $\boldsymbol{x}^*$, and hence the value of f must *increase* near $\boldsymbol{x}^*$. We can conclude that if the Hessian matrix is positive definite at a critical point $\boldsymbol{x}^*$, then $\boldsymbol{x}^*$ must be a local minimum of f. This is called a *second-order sufficient condition* for a minimum because it involves second derivatives of the objective function. By similar reasoning, we can classify critical points as follows. At a critical point $\boldsymbol{x}^*$, where $\nabla f(\boldsymbol{x}^*) = \boldsymbol{0}$, if $\boldsymbol{H}_f(\boldsymbol{x}^*)$ is

- Positive definite, then $\boldsymbol{x}^*$ is a minimum of f.
- Negative definite, then $\boldsymbol{x}^*$ is a maximum of f.
- Indefinite, then $\boldsymbol{x}^*$ is a saddle point of f.
- Singular, then various pathological situations can occur.

The Hessian matrix also provides a practical test for convexity of a function. If $f: S \subseteq \mathbb{R}^n \to \mathbb{R}$ is twice continuously differentiable on a convex set S and $\boldsymbol{H}_f(\boldsymbol{x})$ is positive definite at a point $\boldsymbol{x} \in S$, then f is convex on some convex neighborhood of $\boldsymbol{x}$. Moreover, if $\boldsymbol{H}_f(\boldsymbol{x})$ is positive definite at every $\boldsymbol{x} \in S$, then f is convex on S.

There are a number of ways to test a symmetric matrix for positive definiteness. One of the simplest and cheapest is to try to compute its Cholesky factorization: the Cholesky algorithm will succeed if, and only if, the matrix is positive definite (this approach requires a Cholesky factorization routine that fails gracefully when given an input matrix that is not positive definite). Another good method is to compute the inertia of the matrix (see Section 4.5.9) using a symmetric factorization of the form $\boldsymbol{LDL}^T$, as in Section 2.5.2. A much more expensive approach is to compute the eigenvalues of the matrix and check whether they are all positive.

Example 6.5 Classifying Critical Points. Consider the function $f: \mathbb{R}^2 \to \mathbb{R}$,

$$f(\boldsymbol{x}) = 2x_1^3 + 3x_1^2 + 12x_1x_2 + 3x_2^2 - 6x_2 + 6,$$

whose gradient is given by

$$\nabla f(\boldsymbol{x}) = \begin{bmatrix} 6x_1^2 + 6x_1 + 12x_2 \\ 12x_1 + 6x_2 - 6 \end{bmatrix}.$$

Solving the nonlinear system $\nabla f(\boldsymbol{x}) = \boldsymbol{0}$ using any of the methods from Chapter 5, we obtain two critical points, $[1 \quad -1]^T$ and $[2 \quad -3]^T$. To test them for optimality, we determine the Hessian matrix,

$$\boldsymbol{H}_f(\boldsymbol{x}) = \begin{bmatrix} 12x_1 + 6 & 12 \\ 12 & 6 \end{bmatrix}.$$

Note that $\boldsymbol{H}_f$ is symmetric, as expected. Evaluating $\boldsymbol{H}_f$ at each of the critical points, we obtain

$$\boldsymbol{H}_f(1, -1) = \begin{bmatrix} 18 & 12 \\ 12 & 6 \end{bmatrix},$$

which is *not* positive definite (its eigenvalues are approximately 25.4 and -1.4), and

$$\boldsymbol{H}_f(2, -3) = \begin{bmatrix} 30 & 12 \\ 12 & 6 \end{bmatrix},$$

which is positive definite (its eigenvalues are approximately 35.0 and 1.0). We conclude that $[2 \quad -3]^T$ is a local minimum of f, whereas $[1 \quad -1]^T$ is a saddle point.

6.2.3 Constrained Optimality Conditions

Thus far we have considered only minima that occur at an interior point of the feasible set, which of course is always the case for an unconstrained problem. But for constrained optimization, the solution often occurs on the boundary of the feasible set. When constraints are present, the fundamental principle remains the same: a minimum occurs at a point $\boldsymbol{x}^*$ when there is no downhill direction starting from $\boldsymbol{x}^*$, but now we require that $\boldsymbol{x}^* \in S$, where S is the feasible set, and we need consider only *feasible* directions, i.e., directions for which the constraints continue to be satisfied. More precisely, a nonzero vector $\boldsymbol{s}$ is a *feasible direction* at a point $\boldsymbol{x}^* \in S$ if there is an $r > 0$ such that $\boldsymbol{x}^* + \alpha\boldsymbol{s} \in S$ for all $\alpha \in [0, r]$. A first-order necessary optimality condition is that for any feasible direction $\boldsymbol{s}$,

$$\nabla f(\boldsymbol{x}^*)^T \boldsymbol{s} \geq 0,$$

which says that f is nondecreasing near $\boldsymbol{x}^*$ along any feasible direction. Note that at an interior point of S any direction is feasible, so this inequality must hold for both $\boldsymbol{s}$ and $-\boldsymbol{s}$, which implies that $\nabla f(\boldsymbol{x}^*) = \boldsymbol{0}$, which is the first-order necessary condition for an interior minimum that we saw previously. Similarly, a second-order necessary optimality condition is that in addition to the first-order condition,

$$\boldsymbol{s}^T \boldsymbol{H}_f(\boldsymbol{x}^*)\, \boldsymbol{s} \geq 0$$

for any feasible direction $\boldsymbol{s}$, which says that $\boldsymbol{H}_f(\boldsymbol{x}^*)$ is positive semidefinite for any feasible direction.

A convenient means of dealing with constraints, both theoretically and computationally, is provided by Lagrange multipliers. Consider the problem of minimizing a nonlinear function subject to nonlinear equality constraints,

$$\min_{\boldsymbol{x}} f(\boldsymbol{x}) \quad \text{subject to} \quad \boldsymbol{g}(\boldsymbol{x}) = \boldsymbol{0},$$

where $f: \mathbb{R}^n \to \mathbb{R}$ and $\boldsymbol{g}: \mathbb{R}^n \to \mathbb{R}^m$, with $m \leq n$. A necessary condition for a feasible point $\boldsymbol{x}^*$ to be a solution to this problem is that the negative gradient of f lie in the space spanned by the constraint normals, i.e., that

$$-\nabla f(\boldsymbol{x}^*) = \boldsymbol{J}_g^T(\boldsymbol{x}^*)\, \boldsymbol{\lambda}^*$$

for some $\boldsymbol{\lambda}^* \in \mathbb{R}^m$, where $\boldsymbol{J}_g(\boldsymbol{x})$ is the Jacobian matrix of $\boldsymbol{g}(\boldsymbol{x})$. The components of $\boldsymbol{\lambda}^*$ are called *Lagrange multipliers*. This necessary condition says that we cannot reduce the objective function without violating the constraints, and it motivates the definition of the *Lagrangian function*, $\mathcal{L}: \mathbb{R}^{n+m} \to \mathbb{R}$, given by

$$\mathcal{L}(\boldsymbol{x}, \boldsymbol{\lambda}) = f(\boldsymbol{x}) + \boldsymbol{\lambda}^T \boldsymbol{g}(\boldsymbol{x}),$$

whose gradient and Hessian are given by

$$\nabla \mathcal{L}(\boldsymbol{x}, \boldsymbol{\lambda}) = \begin{bmatrix} \nabla_x \mathcal{L}(\boldsymbol{x}, \boldsymbol{\lambda}) \\ \nabla_\lambda \mathcal{L}(\boldsymbol{x}, \boldsymbol{\lambda}) \end{bmatrix} = \begin{bmatrix} \nabla f(\boldsymbol{x}) + \boldsymbol{J}_g^T(\boldsymbol{x})\boldsymbol{\lambda} \\ \boldsymbol{g}(\boldsymbol{x}) \end{bmatrix}$$

and

$$\boldsymbol{H}_{\mathcal{L}}(\boldsymbol{x}, \boldsymbol{\lambda}) = \begin{bmatrix} \boldsymbol{B}(\boldsymbol{x}, \boldsymbol{\lambda}) & \boldsymbol{J}_g^T(\boldsymbol{x}) \\ \boldsymbol{J}_g(\boldsymbol{x}) & \boldsymbol{O} \end{bmatrix},$$

where

$$\boldsymbol{B}(\boldsymbol{x}, \boldsymbol{\lambda}) = \nabla_{xx} \mathcal{L}(\boldsymbol{x}, \boldsymbol{\lambda}) = \boldsymbol{H}_f(\boldsymbol{x}) + \sum_{i=1}^{m} \lambda_i \boldsymbol{H}_{g_i}(\boldsymbol{x}).$$

Together, the necessary condition and the requirement of feasibility say that we are looking for a critical point of the Lagrangian function, which is expressed by the system of $n+m$ nonlinear equations in $n+m$ unknowns

$$\nabla \mathcal{L}(\boldsymbol{x}, \boldsymbol{\lambda}) = \begin{bmatrix} \nabla f(\boldsymbol{x}) + \boldsymbol{J}_g^T(\boldsymbol{x})\boldsymbol{\lambda} \\ \boldsymbol{g}(\boldsymbol{x}) \end{bmatrix} = \boldsymbol{0}.$$

It is important to note that the block 2×2 matrix $\boldsymbol{H}_{\mathcal{L}}(\boldsymbol{x}, \boldsymbol{\lambda})$ is symmetric but cannot be positive definite, even if the matrix $\boldsymbol{B}(\boldsymbol{x}, \boldsymbol{\lambda})$ is positive definite (in general, $\boldsymbol{B}(\boldsymbol{x}, \boldsymbol{\lambda})$ is not positive definite, but the Lagrangian function is sometimes augmented by a "penalty" term so that its Hessian matrix will be positive definite). Thus, a critical point of $\mathcal{L}(\boldsymbol{x}, \boldsymbol{\lambda})$ is necessarily a saddle point rather than a minimum or maximum.

If the Hessian of the Lagrangian is never positive definite, even at a constrained minimum, then how can we check a critical point of the Lagrangian for optimality? It turns out that a sufficient condition for a constrained minimum is that the matrix $\boldsymbol{B}(\boldsymbol{x}^*, \boldsymbol{\lambda}^*)$ at the critical point be positive definite on the *tangent space* to the constraint surface, which is simply the *null space* of $\boldsymbol{J}_g(\boldsymbol{x}^*)$ (i.e., the set of all vectors orthogonal to the rows of $\boldsymbol{J}_g(\boldsymbol{x}^*)$). If $\boldsymbol{Z}$ is a matrix whose columns form a basis for this subspace, then we check whether the symmetric matrix $\boldsymbol{Z}^T\boldsymbol{B}\boldsymbol{Z}$, called the *projected* (or *reduced*) Hessian, is positive definite. This condition says that we need positive definiteness only with respect to locally feasible directions (i.e., parallel to the constraint surface), for movement orthogonal to the constraint surface would violate the constraints. A suitable matrix $\boldsymbol{Z}$ can be obtained from an orthogonal factorization of $\boldsymbol{J}_g(\boldsymbol{x}^*)^T$ (see Section 3.4.5).

Example 6.6 Equality-Constrained Optimality. To illustrate the concepts just introduced, we apply them to the equality-constrained optimization problem in Example 6.2. For

$$f(x_1, x_2) = 2\pi x_1(x_1 + x_2) \quad \text{and} \quad g(x_1, x_2) = \pi x_1^2 x_2 - V,$$

we have

$$\nabla f(\boldsymbol{x}) = 2\pi \begin{bmatrix} 2x_1 + x_2 \\ x_1 \end{bmatrix} \quad \text{and} \quad \boldsymbol{J}_g(\boldsymbol{x}) = \pi \begin{bmatrix} 2x_1x_2 & x_1^2 \end{bmatrix}.$$

Thus, the system of equations to be solved is

$$\nabla\mathcal{L}(\boldsymbol{x}, \boldsymbol{\lambda}) = \begin{bmatrix} \nabla f(\boldsymbol{x}) + \boldsymbol{J}_g^T(\boldsymbol{x})\boldsymbol{\lambda} \\ g(\boldsymbol{x}) \end{bmatrix} = \pi \begin{bmatrix} 2(2x_1 + x_2 + x_1x_2\lambda) \\ 2x_1 + x_1^2\lambda \\ x_1^2x_2 - V/\pi \end{bmatrix} = \boldsymbol{0}.$$

Assuming the container is to hold one liter, or $V = 1000\ \text{cm}^3$, we solve this nonlinear system by any of the methods in Section 5.6 to obtain the approximate solution $x_1 = 5.4$ cm, $x_2 = 10.8$ cm, $\lambda = -0.37$. To confirm the optimality of this solution, we compute

$$\boldsymbol{H}_f(\boldsymbol{x}) = 2\pi \begin{bmatrix} 2 & 1 \\ 1 & 0 \end{bmatrix} \quad \text{and} \quad \boldsymbol{H}_g(\boldsymbol{x}) = 2\pi \begin{bmatrix} x_2 & x_1 \\ x_1 & 0 \end{bmatrix},$$

so that

$$\boldsymbol{B}(\boldsymbol{x}^*, \boldsymbol{\lambda}^*) = 2\pi \begin{bmatrix} 2 + x_2\lambda & 1 + x_1\lambda \\ 1 + x_1\lambda & 0 \end{bmatrix} = \begin{bmatrix} -12.6 & -6.3 \\ -6.3 & 0 \end{bmatrix}.$$

This matrix is not positive definite (its eigenvalues are approximately -15.2 and 2.6), but that is to be expected, since the solution must be a saddle point of $\mathcal{L}$. To consider the appropriate subspace, we compute a null vector $\boldsymbol{z}$ (i.e., a basis for the one-dimensional null space) for $\boldsymbol{J}_g(\boldsymbol{x}^*) = \begin{bmatrix} 369 & 92.3 \end{bmatrix}$ and obtain $\boldsymbol{z} = \begin{bmatrix} -0.243 & 0.970 \end{bmatrix}^T$, so that

$$\boldsymbol{z}^T\boldsymbol{B}\boldsymbol{z} = 2.23,$$

which is positive, confirming that the point found is indeed a constrained minimum. The optimal function value is $f(\boldsymbol{x}^*) = 554$ cm^2 of surface area.

When there are inequality constraints, i.e., when the problem has the form

$$\min_{\boldsymbol{x}} f(\boldsymbol{x}) \quad \text{subject to} \quad \boldsymbol{g}(\boldsymbol{x}) = \boldsymbol{0} \quad \text{and} \quad \boldsymbol{h}(\boldsymbol{x}) \le \boldsymbol{0},$$

where $f: \mathbb{R}^n \to \mathbb{R}$, $\boldsymbol{g}: \mathbb{R}^n \to \mathbb{R}^m$, and $\boldsymbol{h}: \mathbb{R}^n \to \mathbb{R}^p$ are suitably smooth, the optimality conditions become more complicated. We can still define the Lagrangian function as before, including both the equality constraints $\boldsymbol{g}$ and inequality constraints $\boldsymbol{h}$, but some of the inequality constraints may be irrelevant to the solution. A given inequality constraint $h_i(\boldsymbol{x}) \le 0$ is said to be *active* (or *binding*) at a feasible point $\boldsymbol{x}$ if $h_i(\boldsymbol{x}) = 0$; an equality constraint is always active. If a given inequality constraint h_i is inactive at a constrained local minimum $\boldsymbol{x}^*$, then the corresponding Lagrange multiplier λ_i^* must be zero. Thus, either $h_i(\boldsymbol{x}^*) = 0$ or $\lambda_i^* = 0$, which is conveniently stated as a *complementarity condition* $h_i(\boldsymbol{x}^*)\lambda_i^* = 0$. We will assume the *constraint qualification* that the Jacobian matrix of the set of active constraints has full row rank. Under these assumptions, if $\boldsymbol{x}^*$ is a constrained local minimum, then there exists a vector of Lagrange multipliers $\boldsymbol{\lambda}^* \in \mathbb{R}^{m+p}$ such that the following conditions hold:

1. $\nabla_x \mathcal{L}(\boldsymbol{x}^*, \boldsymbol{\lambda}^*) = \boldsymbol{0}$,
2. $\boldsymbol{g}(\boldsymbol{x}^*) = \boldsymbol{0}$,
3. $\boldsymbol{h}(\boldsymbol{x}^*) \le \boldsymbol{0}$,
4. $\lambda_i^* \ge 0, \quad i = m+1, \ldots, m+p$,
5. $h_i(\boldsymbol{x}^*)\lambda_i^* = 0, \quad i = m+1, \ldots, m+p$.

These first-order necessary conditions are known as the *Karush-Kuhn-Tucker* (or *KKT*) conditions for a constrained local minimum. Second-order necessary and sufficient conditions analogous to those for the equality-constrained case can be defined by focusing on the active constraints, but we will not go into these details.

Example 6.7 Inequality-Constrained Optimality. As a simple illustration of inequality-constrained optimization, we minimize quadratic function

$$f(\boldsymbol{x}) = 0.5x_1^2 + 2.5x_2^2$$

subject to the inequality constraint

$$h(\boldsymbol{x}) = x_2 - x_1 + 1 \le 0.$$

The unconstrained minimum of f occurs at the origin, which is infeasible, so the constraint must be active at the solution. The Lagrangian function is given by

$$\mathcal{L}(\boldsymbol{x}, \lambda) = f(\boldsymbol{x}) + \lambda^T h(\boldsymbol{x}) = 0.5x_1^2 + 2.5x_2^2 + \lambda(x_2 - x_1 + 1),$$

where the Lagrange multiplier λ is a scalar in this instance because there is only one constraint. Now

$$\nabla f(\boldsymbol{x}) = \begin{bmatrix} x_1 \\ 5x_2 \end{bmatrix} \quad \text{and} \quad \boldsymbol{J}_h(\boldsymbol{x}) = [\,-1 \quad 1\,],$$

so we have

$$\nabla_x \mathcal{L}(\boldsymbol{x}, \lambda) = \nabla f(\boldsymbol{x}) + \boldsymbol{J}_h^T(\boldsymbol{x})\lambda = \begin{bmatrix} x_1 \\ 5x_2 \end{bmatrix} + \lambda \begin{bmatrix} -1 \\ 1 \end{bmatrix}.$$

The optimality conditions require that the solution must satisfy the system of equations

$$\begin{bmatrix} \nabla_x \mathcal{L}(\boldsymbol{x}, \lambda) \\ h(\boldsymbol{x}) \end{bmatrix} = \begin{bmatrix} x_1 - \lambda \\ 5x_2 + \lambda \\ x_2 - x_1 + 1 \end{bmatrix} = \mathbf{0},$$

which in this case is a linear system whose matrix formulation is

$$\begin{bmatrix} 1 & 0 & -1 \\ 0 & 5 & 1 \\ -1 & 1 & 0 \end{bmatrix} \begin{bmatrix} x_1 \\ x_2 \\ \lambda \end{bmatrix} = \begin{bmatrix} 0 \\ 0 \\ -1 \end{bmatrix}.$$

Solving this system, we obtain the solution

$$x_1 = 0.833, \quad x_2 = -0.167, \quad \lambda = 0.833.$$

The solution is illustrated in Fig. 6.5. The necessary conditions for optimality require that the negative gradient of the objective function be in alignment with the gradient of the constraint (as indicated by the two sets of arrows in the drawing), and that the point lie on the line $x_2 - x_1 + 1 = 0$. The only point satisfying both requirements is the solution we computed, indicated by a bullet in the diagram. Note that λ is positive, as required.

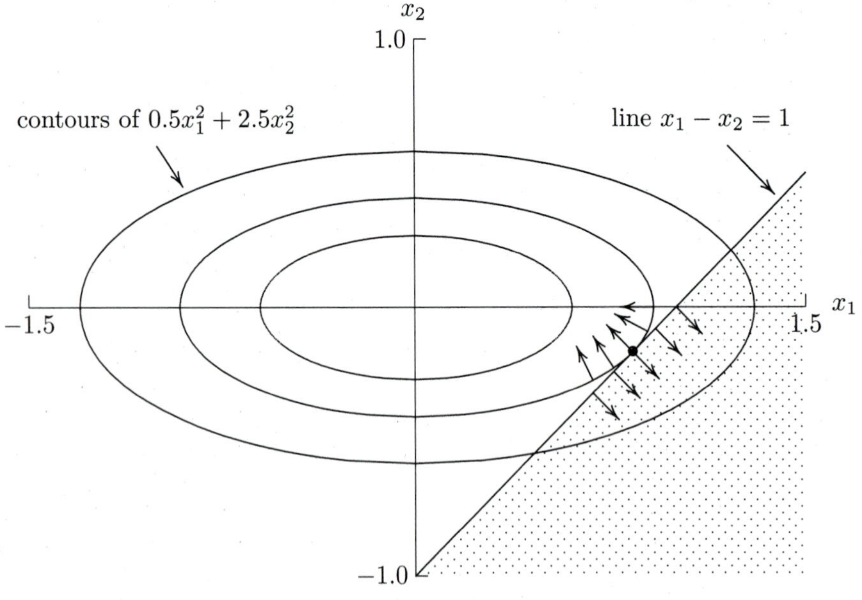

Figure 6.5: Solution to constrained optimization problem. Feasible region is shaded.

6.3 Sensitivity and Conditioning

We have just seen that minimizing a function and solving an equation are intimately related, but the solution to an optimization problem is inherently more sensitive than the solution to an equation. We observed in Sections 1.2.6 and 5.3 that a simple root x^* of an equation $f(x) = 0$ in one dimension has absolute condition number $1/|f'(x^*)|$, which means that for a point $\hat{x}$ at which $|f(\hat{x})| \leq \epsilon$, the error $|\hat{x} - x^*|$ in the solution may be as large as $\epsilon/|f'(x^*)|$. To derive a comparable result for minimizing a function in one dimension, we consider the Taylor series

$$f(\hat{x}) = f(x^* + h) = f(x^*) + f'(x^*)h + \tfrac{1}{2} f''(x^*)h^2 + \mathcal{O}(h^3).$$

At a minimum of f we have $f'(x^*) = 0$, so that $f(\hat{x}) \approx f(x^*) + \frac{1}{2}f''(x^*)h^2$, and hence $h^2 \approx 2(f(\hat{x}) - f(x^*))/f''(x^*)$, provided that $f''(x^*) \neq 0$. This means that for a point $\hat{x}$ at which $|f(\hat{x}) - f(x^*)| \leq \epsilon$, the error $|\hat{x} - x^*|$ in the solution may be as large as $\sqrt{2\epsilon/|f''(x^*)|}$. If ϵ represents the accuracy with which the function can be computed, then having $|f(\hat{x}) - f(x^*)| \leq \epsilon$ is as good a result as we can expect, yet the error $|\hat{x} - x^*|$ can be much larger, even if $|f''(x^*)|$ is of reasonable size. If $\epsilon = \epsilon_{\text{mach}}$, for example, and $|f''(x^*)|$ is of order 1, then the error is about $\sqrt{\epsilon_{\text{mach}}}$. Thus, based on function values alone, the solution can be computed to only about half as many digits of accuracy as the underlying machine precision.

This result should not be surprising because a minimum of a function is analogous to a multiple root of a nonlinear equation: in either case a horizontal tangent implies that the function is locally approximately parallel to the x axis, so that the function values are relatively insensitive, and accordingly the solution is poorly determined. This fact should be kept in mind when selecting an error tolerance for an optimization problem: an unrealistically tight tolerance may drive up the cost of computing a solution without producing a concomitant gain in accuracy.

Greater accuracy may be attainable, however, if derivatives of the objective function are available, since we can then directly solve the nonlinear equation $f'(x) = 0$, which usually does *not* have a horizontal tangent. The absolute condition number of a simple root x^* of $f'(x) = 0$ is $1/|f''(x^*)|$, which means that for a point $\hat{x}$ at which $|f'(\hat{x})| \leq \epsilon$, the error $|\hat{x} - x^*|$ in the solution may be as large as $\epsilon/|f''(x^*)|$. The latter is likely to be much smaller than our previous bound on the error unless $|f''(x^*)|$ is extremely small.

All of these observations generalize to unconstrained minimization in n dimensions. If $f: \mathbb{R}^n \to \mathbb{R}$ is suitably smooth, then we have the Taylor series

$$f(\hat{\boldsymbol{x}}) = f(\boldsymbol{x}^* + h\boldsymbol{s}) = f(\boldsymbol{x}^*) + h\nabla f(\boldsymbol{x}^*)^T\boldsymbol{s} + \tfrac{1}{2} h^2\boldsymbol{s}^T\boldsymbol{H}_f(\boldsymbol{x}^*)\,\boldsymbol{s} + \mathcal{O}(h^3),$$

where $|h| = \|\hat{\boldsymbol{x}} - \boldsymbol{x}^*\|$ and $\|\boldsymbol{s}\| = 1$. At a minimum $\boldsymbol{x}^*$ of f we have $\nabla f(\boldsymbol{x}^*) = \boldsymbol{0}$ and $\boldsymbol{H}_f(\boldsymbol{x}^*)$ positive definite, so that

$$h^2 \approx \frac{2\,(f(\hat{\boldsymbol{x}}) - f(\boldsymbol{x}^*))}{\boldsymbol{s}^T\boldsymbol{H}_f(\boldsymbol{x}^*)\,\boldsymbol{s}},$$

and hence if $\hat{\boldsymbol{x}}$ is a point such that $|f(\hat{\boldsymbol{x}}) - f(\boldsymbol{x}^*)| \leq \epsilon$, then a bound on the error is given by

$$\|\hat{\boldsymbol{x}} - \boldsymbol{x}^*\|^2 \lessapprox \frac{2\,\epsilon}{\boldsymbol{s}^T\boldsymbol{H}_f(\boldsymbol{x}^*)\,\boldsymbol{s}} \leq \frac{2\,\epsilon}{\lambda_{\min}},$$

where $\lambda_{\min}$ is the smallest eigenvalue of $\boldsymbol{H}_f(\boldsymbol{x}^*)$. That the sensitivity of the solution $\boldsymbol{x}^*$ depends on the Hessian matrix $\boldsymbol{H}_f(\boldsymbol{x}^*)$ is not surprising, since this matrix determines the shape of the contours (level sets) of f near $\boldsymbol{x}^*$. If $\boldsymbol{H}_f(\boldsymbol{x}^*)$ is ill-conditioned, then the contours of f will be relatively long and thin along some directions (namely eigenvectors of $\boldsymbol{H}_f(\boldsymbol{x}^*)$ corresponding to relatively small eigenvalues), and the solution $\boldsymbol{x}^*$ will be highly sensitive, and the value of f correspondingly insensitive, to perturbations in those directions.

Analyzing the sensitivity of a solution to a constrained optimization problem is significantly more complicated, and we will merely highlight the main issues. For an equality-constrained problem, $\min f(\boldsymbol{x})$ subject to $\boldsymbol{g}(\boldsymbol{x}) = \boldsymbol{0}$, the error in the solution can be resolved into two components, one parallel to the constraint surface and the other orthogonal to the constraint surface. The sensitivity of the component parallel to the constraints depends on the conditioning of the projected Hessian matrix $\boldsymbol{Z}^T\boldsymbol{B}(\boldsymbol{x}^*, \boldsymbol{\lambda}^*)\boldsymbol{Z}$ (see Section 6.2.3), much as in the unconstrained case just considered. The sensitivity of the component orthogonal to the constraints depends on the magnitudes of the Lagrange multipliers, which in turn depend on the conditioning of the Jacobian matrix $\boldsymbol{J}_g^T(\boldsymbol{x}^*)$ of the constraint function $\boldsymbol{g}$. In particular, the larger a given Lagrange multiplier, the more influential the corresponding constraint is on the solution. If the Jacobian matrix $\boldsymbol{J}_g^T(\boldsymbol{x}^*)$ is nearly rank deficient, then the Lagrange multipliers will be highly sensitive and the resulting solution will likely be inaccurate.

6.4 Optimization in One Dimension

We begin with methods for optimization in one dimension, which is an important problem in its own right, and will also be a key subproblem in many algorithms for optimization in higher dimensions. First, we need a way of bracketing a minimum in an interval, analogous to the way we used a sign change for bracketing solutions to nonlinear equations in one dimension. A function $f: \mathbb{R} \to \mathbb{R}$ is *unimodal* on an interval $[a, b]$ if there is a unique value $x^* \in [a, b]$ such that $f(x^*)$ is the minimum of f on $[a, b]$, and for any $x_1, x_2 \in [a, b]$ with $x_1 < x_2$,

$$x_2 < x^* \text{ implies } f(x_1) > f(x_2) \quad \text{and} \quad x_1 > x^* \text{ implies } f(x_1) < f(x_2).$$

Thus, $f(x)$ is strictly decreasing for $x \le x^*$ and strictly increasing for $x \ge x^*$. The significance of this property is that it will enable us to refine an interval containing a solution by computing sample values of the function within the interval and discarding portions of the interval according to the function values obtained, analogous to bisection for solving nonlinear equations.

6.4.1 Golden Section Search

Suppose f is unimodal on $[a, b]$, and let $x_1, x_2 \in [a, b]$ with $x_1 < x_2$. Comparing the function values $f(x_1)$ and $f(x_2)$ and using the unimodality property allows us to discard a subinterval, either $(x_2, b]$ or $[a, x_1)$, and know that the minimum of the function lies within the remaining subinterval. In particular, if $f(x_1) < f(x_2)$, then the minimum cannot lie in the interval $(x_2, b]$, and if $f(x_1) > f(x_2)$, then the minimum cannot lie in the interval $[a, x_1)$. Thus, we are left with a shorter interval, either $[a, x_2]$ or $[x_1, b]$, within which we already have one function value, either $f(x_1)$ or $f(x_2)$, respectively. Hence, we will need to compute only one new function evaluation to repeat this process.

To make consistent progress in reducing the length of the interval containing the minimum, each new pair of points should have the same relative positions within the new interval that the previous pair had within the previous interval. Such an arrangement will enable us to reduce the length of the interval by a fixed fraction at each iteration, much as we reduced the length by half at each iteration of the bisection method for computing a zero of a function.

To accomplish this objective, we choose the relative positions of the two points within the current interval to be τ and $1-\tau$, where $\tau^2 = 1-\tau$, so that $\tau = (\sqrt{5}-1)/2 \approx 0.618$ and $1-\tau \approx 0.382$. With this choice, no matter which subinterval is retained, its length will be τ relative to the previous interval, and the interior point retained will be at position either τ or $1-\tau$ relative to the new interval. Thus, we will need to compute only one new function value, at the complementary point, to continue the iteration. This choice of sample points is called *golden section search*, after the "golden ratio," $(1+\sqrt{5})/2 \approx 1.618$, of antiquity. The complete procedure is shown in Algorithm 6.1, for which the initial input is a function f, an interval $[a, b]$ on which f is unimodal, and an error tolerance *tol*. For a unimodal function, golden section search is safe but slowly convergent. Specifically, its convergence rate is linear, with $r = 1$ and $C \approx 0.618$.

Algorithm 6.1 Golden Section Search

$\tau = (\sqrt{5}-1)/2$
$x_1 = a + (1-\tau)(b-a)$
$f_1 = f(x_1)$
$x_2 = a + \tau(b-a)$
$f_2 = f(x_2)$
while $((b-a) > tol)$ **do**
  if $(f_1 > f_2)$ **then**
    $a = x_1$
    $x_1 = x_2$
    $f_1 = f_2$
    $x_2 = a + \tau(b-a)$
    $f_2 = f(x_2)$
  else
    $b = x_2$
    $x_2 = x_1$
    $f_2 = f_1$
    $x_1 = a + (1-\tau)(b-a)$
    $f_1 = f(x_1)$
  end
end

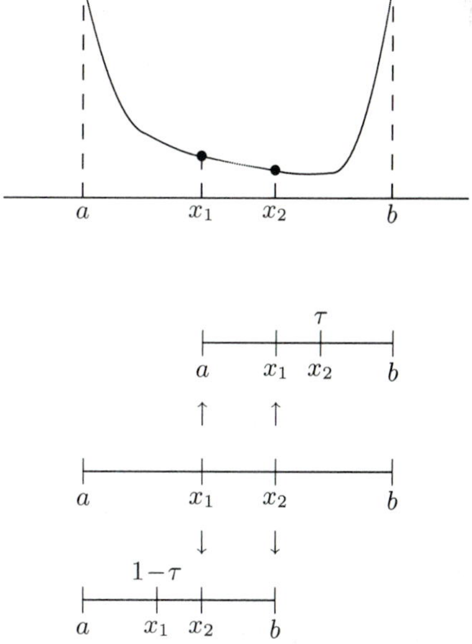

Example 6.8 Golden Section Search. We illustrate golden section search by using it to minimize the function

$$f(x) = 0.5 - xe^{-x^2}.$$

Starting with the initial interval $[0, 2]$, we evaluate the function at points $x_1 = 0.764$ and $x_2 = 1.236$, obtaining $f(x_1) = 0.074$ and $f(x_2) = 0.232$. Because $f(x_1) < f(x_2)$, we know that the minimum must lie in the interval $[a, x_2]$, and thus we may replace b by x_2 and repeat the process. The first iteration is depicted in Fig. 6.6, and the full sequence of iterates is given next.

x_1	$f(x_1)$	x_2	$f(x_2)$
0.763932	0.073809	1.236068	0.231775
0.472136	0.122204	0.763932	0.073809
0.763932	0.073809	0.944272	0.112868
0.652476	0.073740	0.763932	0.073809
0.583592	0.084857	0.652476	0.073740
0.652476	0.073740	0.695048	0.071243
0.695048	0.071243	0.721360	0.071291
0.678787	0.071815	0.695048	0.071243
0.695048	0.071243	0.705098	0.071122
0.705098	0.071122	0.711310	0.071133
0.701260	0.071147	0.705098	0.071122
0.705098	0.071122	0.707471	0.071118
0.707471	0.071118	0.708937	0.071121
0.706565	0.071118	0.707471	0.071118

Note that the function values are relatively insensitive near the minimum, as expected (see Section 6.3).

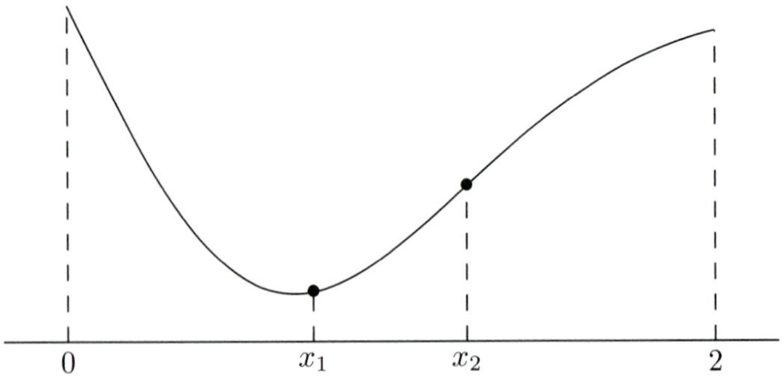

Figure 6.6: First iteration of golden section search for example problem.

Although unimodality plays a role in one-dimensional optimization similar to that played by a sign change in root finding, there are important practical differences. A sign change brackets a root of an equation regardless of how large the bracketing interval may be. The same is true of unimodality, but in practice most functions cannot be expected to be unimodal unless both endpoints of the interval are reasonably near a minimum, or unless the function has a special property such as convexity. Thus, more trial and error may be required to find a suitable starting interval for one-dimensional optimization than is typically required for root finding. In practice, one might simply search for three points such that the value of the objective function is greater at the two outer points than at the intermediate point. Although golden section search always converges, it is not guaranteed to find the global minimum, or even a local minimum, unless the objective function is unimodal on the starting interval.

6.4.2 Successive Parabolic Interpolation

As we have seen, golden section search for optimization is analogous in a number of ways to bisection for solving a nonlinear equation; in particular, golden section search makes no use of the function values other than to compare them. As with nonlinear equations, faster methods can be obtained by making greater use of the function values, such as fitting them with some simpler function. Fitting a straight line to two points, as in the secant method, is of no value for optimization because the resulting linear function has no minimum. Instead, we must use a polynomial of degree at least two.

The simplest example of this approach is *successive parabolic interpolation*. Initially, the function f to be minimized is evaluated at three points and a quadratic polynomial is fit to the three resulting function values. The minimum of the resulting parabola, assuming it has one, is then taken as a new approximate minimum of the function. One of the previous points is then dropped and the process repeated until convergence. At a given iteration, we have three points, say u, v, and w, with corresponding function values f_u, f_v, and f_w, respectively, where v is the best approximate minimum thus far. The minimum of the parabola interpolating the three function values is given by $v + p/q$, where

$$\begin{aligned} p &= \pm(v-u)^2(f_v - f_w) - (v-w)^2(f_v - f_u), \\ q &= \mp 2((v-u)(f_v - f_w) - (v-w)(f_v - f_u)). \end{aligned}$$

We now replace u by w, w by v, and v by the new approximate minimum $v+p/q$ and repeat until convergence. This process is illustrated in Fig. 6.7. Successive parabolic interpolation is not guaranteed to converge, but under normal circumstances if started close enough to a minimum it converges superlinearly with convergence rate $r \approx 1.324$.

Example 6.9 Successive Parabolic Interpolation. We illustrate successive parabolic interpolation by using it to minimize the function from Example 6.8,

$$f(x) = 0.5 - xe^{-x^2}.$$

We evaluate the function at three points, say, $x_0 = 0$, $x_1 = 1.2$, and $x_2 = 0.6$, obtaining $f(x_0) = 0.5$, $f(x_1) = 0.216$, $f(x_2) = 0.081$. We fit a parabola to these three points and take its minimizer, $x_3 = 0.754$, to be the next approximation to

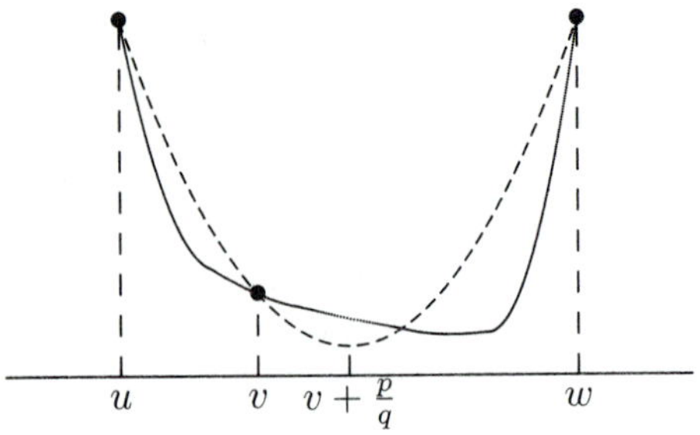

Figure 6.7: Successive parabolic iteration for minimizing a function.

the solution. We then discard x_0 and repeat the process with the three remaining points. The first iteration is depicted in Fig. 6.8, and the full sequence of iterates is given next.

k	x_k	$f(x_k)$
0	0.000000	0.500000
1	1.200000	0.215687
2	0.600000	0.081394
3	0.754267	0.072981
4	0.720797	0.071278
5	0.708374	0.071119
6	0.706920	0.071118
7	0.707103	0.071118

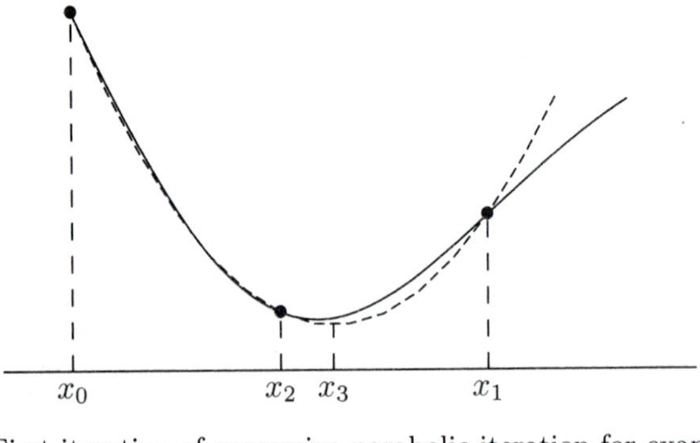

Figure 6.8: First iteration of successive parabolic iteration for example problem.

6.4.3 Newton's Method

A local quadratic approximation to the objective function is useful because the minimum of a quadratic is easy to compute. Another way to obtain a local quadratic approximation is to use a truncated Taylor series expansion,

$$f(x+h) \approx f(x) + f'(x)h + \tfrac{1}{2} f''(x)h^2.$$

By differentiation, we find that the minimum of this quadratic function of h is given by $h = -f'(x)/f''(x)$. This result suggests the iteration scheme shown in Algorithm 6.2, which is equivalent to Newton's method for solving the nonlinear equation $f'(x) = 0$ (compare with Algorithm 5.2). As usual, Newton's method for finding a minimum normally has a quadratic convergence rate. Unless it is started near the desired minimum, however, Newton's method may fail to converge, or it may converge to a maximum or to an inflection point of the function.

Algorithm 6.2 Newton's Method for One-Dimensional Optimization

x_0 = initial guess
for $k = 0, 1, 2, \ldots$
    $x_{k+1} = x_k - f'(x_k)/f''(x_k)$
end

Example 6.10 Newton's Method. We illustrate Newton's method by using it to minimize the function from Example 6.8,

$$f(x) = 0.5 - xe^{-x^2}.$$

The first and second derivatives of f are given by

$$f'(x) = (2x^2 - 1)e^{-x^2} \quad \text{and} \quad f''(x) = 2x(3 - 2x^2)e^{-x^2},$$

so the Newton iteration for finding a minimum of f is given by

$$x_{k+1} = x_k - (2x_k^2 - 1)/(2x_k(3 - 2x_k^2)).$$

Using $x_0 = 1$ as starting guess, we obtain the sequence of iterates shown next.

k	x_k	$f(x_k)$
0	1.000000	0.132121
1	0.500000	0.110600
2	0.700000	0.071162
3	0.707072	0.071118
4	0.707107	0.071118

6.4.4 Safeguarded Methods

As with solving nonlinear equations in one dimension, slow-but-sure and fast-but-risky optimization methods can be combined to provide both safety and efficiency. A fast method is tried at each iteration, but an interval bracketing the solution is also maintained so that a safe method can be used instead whenever the fast method generates an iterate that lies outside the interval. Once close enough to the solution, rapid convergence should be attained by the fast method. Most library routines for one-dimensional optimization are based on such a hybrid approach. One popular combination, which requires no derivatives of the objective function, is golden section search and successive parabolic interpolation.

6.5 Unconstrained Optimization

We next consider multidimensional unconstrained optimization, which has a number of features in common with both one-dimensional optimization and with solving systems of nonlinear equations in n dimensions.

6.5.1 Direct Search

Recall that golden section search for one-dimensional optimization makes no use of the objective function values other than to compare them. Direct search methods for multidimensional optimization share this property, although they do not retain the convergence guarantee of golden section search. Perhaps the best known of these is the method of Nelder and Mead, which is implemented in the `fminsearch` function of `MATLAB`. To seek a minimum of a function $f: \mathbb{R}^n \to \mathbb{R}$, the function is first evaluated at each of $n+1$ starting points, no three of which are collinear (i.e., the points form a *simplex* in $\mathbb{R}^n$). A new point is generated along the straight line from the worst current point through the centroid of the other points. This new point then replaces the worst point, and the process is repeated until convergence. The algorithm involves several parameters that determine how far to move along the line and how much to expand or contract the simplex, depending on whether a given iteration is successful in generating a point with a still-lower function value. Direct search methods are especially useful for nonsmooth objective functions, for which few other methods are applicable, and they can be effective when n is small, but they tend to be quite expensive when n is larger than two or three. There has been renewed interest in direct search methods in recent years, however, because they are relatively easily parallelized.

6.5.2 Steepest Descent

As expected, greater use of the objective function and its derivatives leads to faster methods. Recall from Section 6.2.2 that the negative gradient of a differentiable function $f: \mathbb{R}^n \to \mathbb{R}$ points downhill, i.e., toward points having lower function values, from any point $\boldsymbol{x}$ such that $\nabla f(\boldsymbol{x}) \neq \boldsymbol{0}$. In fact, $-\nabla f(\boldsymbol{x})$ is locally the direction of *steepest descent* for the function f in the sense that the value of the function initially decreases more rapidly along the direction of the negative gradient than along any other direction. Thus, the negative gradient is a potentially fruitful direction in which to seek points having lower function values, but it gives no indication how far to go in that direction.

The maximum possible benefit from movement in any downhill direction would be to attain the minimum of the objective function along that direction. For any fixed $\boldsymbol{x}$ and direction $\boldsymbol{s}$, we can define a function $\phi: \mathbb{R} \to \mathbb{R}$ by

$$\phi(\alpha) = f(\boldsymbol{x} + \alpha \boldsymbol{s}).$$

In this way the problem of minimizing the objective function f along direction $\boldsymbol{s}$ from $\boldsymbol{x}$ is seen to be a one-dimensional optimization problem that can be solved by one of the methods discussed in Section 6.4. Because we are minimizing the objective function only along a fixed line in $\mathbb{R}^n$, such a procedure is called a *line search*. Taking $\boldsymbol{s} = -\nabla f(\boldsymbol{x})$ as the direction for such a line search yields one of the oldest and simplest methods for multidimensional optimization, the *steepest descent method*, shown in Algorithm 6.3. Once the minimum is found in a given direction, the negative gradient is computed at the new point and the process is repeated until convergence.

Algorithm 6.3 Steepest Descent

$\boldsymbol{x}_0$ = initial guess
for $k = 0, 1, 2, \ldots$
  $\boldsymbol{s}_k = -\nabla f(\boldsymbol{x}_k)$ { compute negative gradient }
  Choose α_k to minimize $f(\boldsymbol{x}_k + \alpha_k \boldsymbol{s}_k)$ { perform line search }
  $\boldsymbol{x}_{k+1} = \boldsymbol{x}_k + \alpha_k \boldsymbol{s}_k$ { update solution }
end

The steepest descent method is very reliable in that it can always make progress provided the gradient is nonzero. But as Example 6.11 demonstrates, the method is rather myopic in its view of the behavior of the function, and the resulting iterates can zigzag back and forth, making very slow progress toward a solution. In general, the convergence rate of steepest descent is only linear, with a constant factor that can be arbitrarily close to 1, depending on the specific objective function f.

Example 6.11 Steepest Descent. We illustrate the steepest descent method by using it to minimize the function

$$f(\boldsymbol{x}) = 0.5x_1^2 + 2.5x_2^2,$$

whose gradient is given by

$$\nabla f(\boldsymbol{x}) = \begin{bmatrix} x_1 \\ 5x_2 \end{bmatrix}.$$

If we take $\boldsymbol{x}_0 = \begin{bmatrix} 5 & 1 \end{bmatrix}^T$ as starting point, the gradient is $\nabla f(\boldsymbol{x}_0) = \begin{bmatrix} 5 & 5 \end{bmatrix}^T$. One-dimensional minimization of f as a function of α along the negative gradient direction gives $\alpha_0 = 1/3$, so that the next approximation is

$$\boldsymbol{x}_1 = \boldsymbol{x}_0 + \alpha_0 \boldsymbol{s}_0 = \boldsymbol{x}_0 - \alpha_0 \nabla f(\boldsymbol{x}_0) = \begin{bmatrix} 5 \\ 1 \end{bmatrix} - \frac{1}{3}\begin{bmatrix} 5 \\ 5 \end{bmatrix} = \begin{bmatrix} 3.333 \\ -0.667 \end{bmatrix}.$$

We then evaluate the gradient at this new point to determine the next search direction and repeat the process. The resulting sequence of iterates is shown numerically in the following table and graphically in Fig. 6.9, where the ellipses represent contours on which the function f has a constant value. The gradient direction at any given point is always normal to the level curve passing through that point. Note that the minimum along a given search direction occurs when the gradient at the new point is orthogonal to the search direction. The sequence of iterates given by steepest descent is converging slowly toward the solution, which for this problem is at the origin, where the minimum function value is zero.

k	$\boldsymbol{x}_k^T$		$f(\boldsymbol{x}_k)$	$\nabla f(\boldsymbol{x}_k)^T$	
0	5.000	1.000	15.000	5.000	5.000
1	3.333	−0.667	6.667	3.333	−3.333
2	2.222	0.444	2.963	2.222	2.222
3	1.481	−0.296	1.317	1.481	−1.481
4	0.988	0.198	0.585	0.988	0.988
5	0.658	−0.132	0.260	0.658	−0.658
6	0.439	0.088	0.116	0.439	0.439
7	0.293	−0.059	0.051	0.293	−0.293
8	0.195	0.039	0.023	0.195	0.195
9	0.130	−0.026	0.010	0.130	−0.130

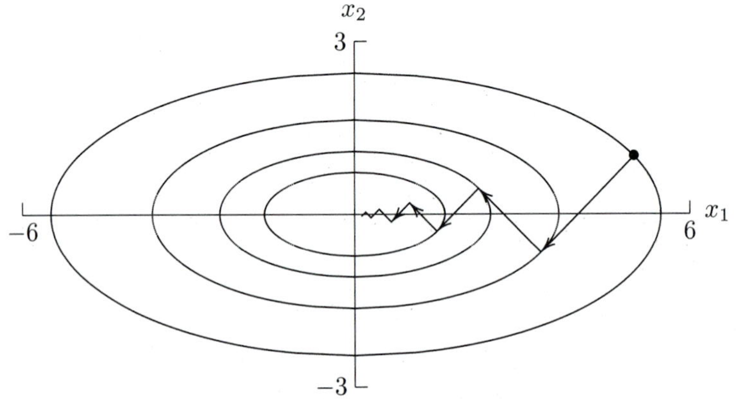

Figure 6.9: Convergence of steepest descent.

6.5.3 Newton's Method

A broader view of the objective function can be gained from a local quadratic approximation, which can be obtained from the truncated Taylor series expansion

$$f(\boldsymbol{x}+\boldsymbol{s}) \approx f(\boldsymbol{x}) + \nabla f(\boldsymbol{x})^T \boldsymbol{s} + \tfrac{1}{2}\, \boldsymbol{s}^T \boldsymbol{H}_f(\boldsymbol{x})\, \boldsymbol{s},$$

where $\boldsymbol{H}_f(\boldsymbol{x})$ is the *Hessian matrix* of second partial derivatives of f, $\{\boldsymbol{H}_f(\boldsymbol{x})\}_{ij} = \partial^2 f(\boldsymbol{x})/\partial x_i \partial x_j$. This quadratic function in $\boldsymbol{s}$ is minimized when

$$\boldsymbol{H}_f(\boldsymbol{x})\, \boldsymbol{s} = -\nabla f(\boldsymbol{x}),$$

which suggests the iterative scheme shown in Algorithm 6.4. The Hessian matrix is the Jacobian matrix of the gradient, so this approach is equivalent to Newton's method for solving the nonlinear system $\nabla f(\boldsymbol{x}) = \boldsymbol{0}$ (compare with Algorithm 5.4). The convergence rate of Newton's method for unconstrained optimization is normally quadratic. As usual, however, Newton's method is unreliable unless started close enough to the solution.

Algorithm 6.4 Newton's Method for Unconstrained Optimization

$\boldsymbol{x}_0$ = initial guess
for $k = 0, 1, 2, \ldots$
  Solve $\boldsymbol{H}_f(\boldsymbol{x}_k)\, \boldsymbol{s}_k = -\nabla f(\boldsymbol{x}_k)$ for $\boldsymbol{s}_k$ { compute Newton step }
  $\boldsymbol{x}_{k+1} = \boldsymbol{x}_k + \boldsymbol{s}_k$ { update solution }
end

Example 6.12 Newton's Method. We illustrate Newton's method by using it to minimize the function from Example 6.11,

$$f(\boldsymbol{x}) = 0.5x_1^2 + 2.5x_2^2,$$

whose gradient and Hessian are given by

$$\nabla f(\boldsymbol{x}) = \begin{bmatrix} x_1 \\ 5x_2 \end{bmatrix} \quad \text{and} \quad \boldsymbol{H}_f(\boldsymbol{x}) = \begin{bmatrix} 1 & 0 \\ 0 & 5 \end{bmatrix}.$$

If we take $\boldsymbol{x}_0 = [\,5 \quad 1\,]^T$ as starting point, the gradient is $\nabla f(\boldsymbol{x}_0) = [\,5 \quad 5\,]^T$. The linear system to be solved for the Newton step is therefore

$$\begin{bmatrix} 1 & 0 \\ 0 & 5 \end{bmatrix} \boldsymbol{s}_0 = \begin{bmatrix} -5 \\ -5 \end{bmatrix},$$

whose solution is $\boldsymbol{s}_0 = [\,-5 \quad -1\,]$, and hence the next approximate solution is

$$\boldsymbol{x}_1 = \boldsymbol{x}_0 + \boldsymbol{s}_0 = \begin{bmatrix} 5 \\ 1 \end{bmatrix} + \begin{bmatrix} -5 \\ -1 \end{bmatrix} = \begin{bmatrix} 0 \\ 0 \end{bmatrix},$$

which is the exact solution for this problem. That Newton's method has converged in a single iteration in this case should not be surprising, since the function being minimized is a quadratic. Of course, the quadratic model used by Newton's method is not exact in general, but nevertheless it enables Newton's method to take a more global view of the problem, yielding much more rapid asymptotic convergence than the steepest descent method.

Intuitively, unconstrained minimization is like finding the bottom of a bowl by rolling a marble down the side. If the bowl is oblong, then the marble will rock back and forth along the valley before eventually settling at the bottom, analogous to the zigzagging path taken by the steepest descent method. With Newton's method, the metric of the space is redefined so that the bowl becomes circular, and hence the marble rolls directly to the bottom.

Unlike the steepest descent method, Newton's method does not require a line search parameter because the quadratic model determines an appropriate length as well as direction for the step to the next approximate solution. When started far from a solution, however, it may still be advisable to perform a line search along the direction of the Newton step s_k in order to make the method more robust (this procedure is sometimes called the *damped Newton method*). Once the iterates are near the solution, then the value $\alpha_k = 1$ for the line search parameter should suffice for subsequent iterations.

An alternative to a line search is a *trust-region method*, in which an estimate is maintained of the radius of a sphere within which the quadratic model is sufficiently accurate for the computed Newton step to be reliable (see Section 5.6.4), and the next approximate solution is constrained to lie within that trust region. If the current trust radius is binding, minimizing the quadratic model function subject to this constraint may modify the direction as well as the length of the Newton step, as illustrated in Fig. 6.10. The accuracy of the quadratic model at a given step is assessed by comparing the actual decrease in the objective function value with the decrease predicted by the quadratic model, and the trust radius is then increased or decreased accordingly. Once near a solution, the trust radius should be large enough to permit full Newton steps, yielding rapid local convergence.

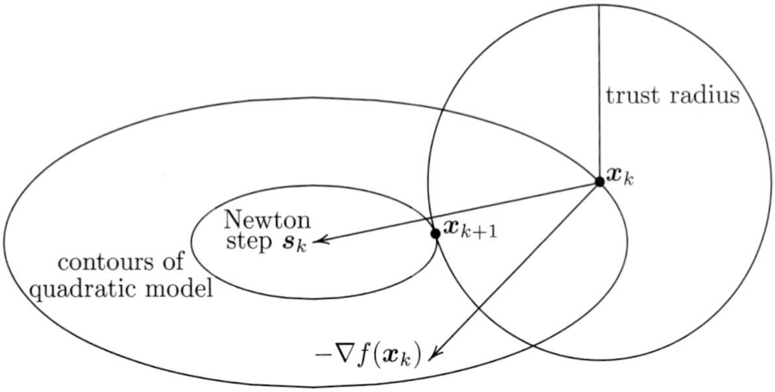

Figure 6.10: Modification of Newton step in trust-region method.

If the objective function f has continuous second partial derivatives, then the Hessian matrix H_f is symmetric; and near a minimum it is positive definite (see Section 6.2.2). Thus, the linear system for the Newton step s_k can be solved by Cholesky factorization, requiring only about half of the work required by LU factorization. Far from a minimum, however, $H_f(x_k)$ may not be positive definite and thus a symmetric indefinite factorization (see Section 2.5.2) may be required. If H_f is not positive definite, then the resulting Newton step s_k is not necessarily a *descent direction* for the function, i.e., we may not have

$$\nabla f(x_k)^T s_k < 0.$$

In this case, an alternative descent direction can be used, such as the negative gradient or a *direction of negative curvature* (i.e., a vector p_k such that $p_k^T H_f(x_k) p_k < 0$, which can be obtained readily from a symmetric indefinite factorization of $H_f(x_k)$), along which a line search can be performed. Another alternative is to modify the Hessian matrix so that it becomes positive definite, e.g., replace $\boldsymbol{H}_f(\boldsymbol{x}_k)$ with $\boldsymbol{H}_f(\boldsymbol{x}_k) + \mu\boldsymbol{I}$, where μ is a scalar chosen so that the modified matrix is positive definite. As μ varies, the resulting computed step varies between the usual Newton step $\boldsymbol{s}_k$ and the steepest descent direction $-\nabla f(\boldsymbol{x}_k)$. Such alternative measures should become unnecessary once the approximate solution is sufficiently close to the desired minimum, so that the ultimate quadratic convergence rate of Newton's method can still be attained.

6.5.4 Quasi-Newton Methods

Newton's method usually converges very rapidly once it nears a solution, but it requires a substantial amount of work per iteration; specifically, for a problem with a dense Hessian matrix, each iteration requires $\mathcal{O}(n^2)$ scalar function evaluations to form the gradient vector and Hessian matrix and $\mathcal{O}(n^3)$ arithmetic operations to solve the linear system for the Newton step. Many variants of Newton's method have been developed to reduce its overhead or improve its reliability, or both. These *quasi-Newton methods* have the general form

$$\boldsymbol{x}_{k+1} = \boldsymbol{x}_k - \alpha_k \boldsymbol{B}_k^{-1} \nabla f(\boldsymbol{x}_k),$$

where α_k is a line search parameter and $\boldsymbol{B}_k$ is some approximation to the Hessian matrix obtained in any of a number of ways, including secant updating, finite differences, periodic reevaluation, or neglecting some terms in the true Hessian of the objective function.

Many quasi-Newton methods are more robust than the pure Newton method and have considerably lower overhead per iteration, yet remain superlinearly (though not quadratically) convergent. For example, *secant updating* methods for optimization, which we will consider next, require no second derivative evaluations, require only one gradient evaluation per iteration, and solve the necessary linear system at each iteration by updating methods that require only $\mathcal{O}(n^2)$ work rather than the $\mathcal{O}(n^3)$ work that would be required by a matrix factorization at each step. These substantial savings in work per iteration more than offset the somewhat slower convergence rate (generally superlinear but not quadratic), so that these methods usually take less total time to compute a solution.

6.5.5 Secant Updating Methods

As with secant updating methods for solving nonlinear equations, the motivation for secant updating methods for optimization is to reduce the work per iteration of Newton's method and possibly improve its robustness. One could simply use Broyden's method (see Section 5.6.3) to seek a zero of the gradient, but this approach would not preserve the symmetry of the Hessian matrix. Several secant updating formulas for unconstrained minimization have been developed that not only preserve symmetry in the approximate Hessian matrix but also preserve positive definiteness. Symmetry reduces the amount of work and storage required by about half, and positive definiteness guarantees that the resulting quasi-Newton step will be a descent direction.

One of the most effective of these secant updating methods for optimization, called *BFGS* after the initials of its four co-inventors, is shown in Algorithm 6.5. In practice, a factorization of $\boldsymbol{B}_k$ is updated rather than $\boldsymbol{B}_k$ itself, so that the linear system for the quasi-Newton step $\boldsymbol{s}_k$ can be solved at a cost per iteration of $\mathcal{O}(n^2)$ rather than $\mathcal{O}(n^3)$ operations. Note that unlike Newton's method for optimization, no second derivatives are required. These methods are often started with $\boldsymbol{B}_0 = \boldsymbol{I}$, which means that the initial step is along the negative gradient (i.e., the direction of steepest descent), and then second derivative information is gradually built up in the approximate Hessian matrix by updating over successive iterations.

Algorithm 6.5 BFGS Method for Unconstrained Optimization

$\boldsymbol{x}_0$ = initial guess
$\boldsymbol{B}_0$ = initial Hessian approximation
for $k = 0, 1, 2, \ldots$
  Solve $\boldsymbol{B}_k\, \boldsymbol{s}_k = -\nabla f(\boldsymbol{x}_k)$ for $\boldsymbol{s}_k$ { compute quasi-Newton step }
  $\boldsymbol{x}_{k+1} = \boldsymbol{x}_k + \boldsymbol{s}_k$ { update solution }
  $\boldsymbol{y}_k = \nabla f(\boldsymbol{x}_{k+1}) - \nabla f(\boldsymbol{x}_k)$
  $\boldsymbol{B}_{k+1} = \boldsymbol{B}_k + (\boldsymbol{y}_k \boldsymbol{y}_k^T)/(\boldsymbol{y}_k^T \boldsymbol{s}_k)$ { update approximate Hessian }
  $\quad - (\boldsymbol{B}_k \boldsymbol{s}_k \boldsymbol{s}_k^T \boldsymbol{B}_k)/(\boldsymbol{s}_k^T \boldsymbol{B}_k \boldsymbol{s}_k)$
end

Like most secant updating methods, BFGS normally has a superlinear convergence rate, even though the approximate Hessian does not necessarily converge to the true Hessian. A line search can also be used to enhance the effectiveness of the method. Indeed, for a quadratic objective function, if an exact line search is performed at each iteration, then the BFGS method terminates at the exact solution in at most n iterations, where n is the dimension of the problem.

Example 6.13 BFGS Method. We illustrate the BFGS method by using it to minimize the function from Example 6.11,

$$f(\boldsymbol{x}) = 0.5x_1^2 + 2.5x_2^2,$$

whose gradient is given by

$$\nabla f(\boldsymbol{x}) = \begin{bmatrix} x_1 \\ 5x_2 \end{bmatrix}.$$

Starting with $\boldsymbol{x}_0 = \begin{bmatrix} 5 & 1 \end{bmatrix}^T$ and $\boldsymbol{B}_0 = \boldsymbol{I}$, the initial step is simply the negative gradient, so

$$\boldsymbol{x}_1 = \boldsymbol{x}_0 + \boldsymbol{s}_0 = \begin{bmatrix} 5 \\ 1 \end{bmatrix} + \begin{bmatrix} -5 \\ -5 \end{bmatrix} = \begin{bmatrix} 0 \\ -4 \end{bmatrix}.$$

Updating the approximate Hessian according to the BFGS formula, we obtain

$$\boldsymbol{B}_1 = \begin{bmatrix} 0.667 & 0.333 \\ 0.333 & 0.667 \end{bmatrix}.$$

A new step is now computed and the process continued. The resulting sequence of iterates is shown next.

k	$\boldsymbol{x}_k^T$		$f(\boldsymbol{x}_k)$	$\nabla f(\boldsymbol{x}_k)^T$	
0	5.000	1.000	15.000	5.000	5.000
1	0.000	−4.000	40.000	0.000	−20.000
2	−2.222	0.444	2.963	−2.222	2.222
3	0.816	0.082	0.350	0.816	0.408
4	−0.009	−0.015	0.001	−0.009	−0.077
5	−0.001	0.001	0.000	−0.001	0.005

The increase in function value on the first iteration could have been avoided by using a line search.

6.5.6 Conjugate Gradient Method

The conjugate gradient method is another alternative to Newton's method that does not require explicit second derivatives. Indeed, unlike secant updating methods, the conjugate gradient method does not even store an approximation to the Hessian matrix, which makes it especially suitable for very large problems.

As we saw in Section 6.5.2, the steepest descent method tends to search in the same directions repeatedly, leading to very slow convergence. As its name suggests, the *conjugate gradient method*, shown in Algorithm 6.6, also uses gradients, but it avoids repeatedly searching the same directions by modifying the new gradient at each step to remove components in previous directions. The resulting sequence of *conjugate* (i.e., orthogonal in the inner product $(\boldsymbol{x}, \boldsymbol{y}) = \boldsymbol{x}^T \boldsymbol{H}_f \, \boldsymbol{y}$) search directions implicitly accumulates information about the Hessian matrix as iterations proceed. Details of the motivation for this method are discussed in Section 11.5.5.

Algorithm 6.6 Conjugate Gradient Method for Unconstrained Optimization

---

$\boldsymbol{x}_0$ = initial guess
$\boldsymbol{g}_0 = \nabla f(\boldsymbol{x}_0)$
$\boldsymbol{s}_0 = -\boldsymbol{g}_0$
for $k = 0, 1, 2, \ldots$
    Choose α_k to minimize $f(\boldsymbol{x}_k + \alpha_k \boldsymbol{s}_k)$ { perform line search }
    $\boldsymbol{x}_{k+1} = \boldsymbol{x}_k + \alpha_k \boldsymbol{s}_k$ { update solution }
    $\boldsymbol{g}_{k+1} = \nabla f(\boldsymbol{x}_{k+1})$ { compute new gradient }
    $\beta_{k+1} = (\boldsymbol{g}_{k+1}^T \boldsymbol{g}_{k+1}) / (\boldsymbol{g}_k^T \boldsymbol{g}_k)$
    $\boldsymbol{s}_{k+1} = -\boldsymbol{g}_{k+1} + \beta_{k+1} \boldsymbol{s}_k$ { modify gradient }
end

The formula for β_{k+1} used in Algorithm 6.6 is due to Fletcher and Reeves. An alternative formula due to Polak and Ribiere,

$$\beta_{k+1} = ((\boldsymbol{g}_{k+1} - \boldsymbol{g}_k)^T \boldsymbol{g}_{k+1}) / (\boldsymbol{g}_k^T \boldsymbol{g}_k),$$

is equivalent for quadratic functions with exact line searches but tends to perform better than the Fletcher-Reeves formula for general nonlinear functions with inexact line searches. Theoretically, the conjugate gradient method is exact after at most n iterations for a quadratic objective function in n dimensions, but it is usually quite effective for more general unconstrained optimization problems as well. It is common to restart the algorithm after every n iterations by reinitializing to use the negative gradient at the current point.

Example 6.14 Conjugate Gradient Method. We illustrate the conjugate gradient method by using it to minimize the function from Example 6.11,

$$f(\boldsymbol{x}) = 0.5x_1^2 + 2.5x_2^2,$$

whose gradient is given by

$$\nabla f(\boldsymbol{x}) = \begin{bmatrix} x_1 \\ 5x_2 \end{bmatrix}.$$

Starting with $\boldsymbol{x}_0 = [\,5 \quad 1\,]^T$, the initial search direction is the negative gradient,

$$\boldsymbol{s}_0 = -\boldsymbol{g}_0 = -\nabla f(\boldsymbol{x}_0) = \begin{bmatrix} -5 \\ -5 \end{bmatrix}.$$

The exact minimum along this line is given by $\alpha_0 = 1/3$, so that the next approximation is $\boldsymbol{x}_1 = [\,3.333 \quad -0.667\,]^T$, at which point we compute the new gradient,

$$\boldsymbol{g}_1 = \nabla f(\boldsymbol{x}_1) = \begin{bmatrix} 3.333 \\ -3.333 \end{bmatrix}.$$

So far there is no difference from the steepest descent method. At this point, however, rather than search along the new negative gradient, we compute instead the quantity

$$\beta_1 = (\boldsymbol{g}_1^T \boldsymbol{g}_1)/(\boldsymbol{g}_0^T \boldsymbol{g}_0) = 0.444,$$

which gives as the next search direction

$$\boldsymbol{s}_1 = -\boldsymbol{g}_1 + \beta_1 \boldsymbol{s}_0 = \begin{bmatrix} -3.333 \\ 3.333 \end{bmatrix} + 0.444 \begin{bmatrix} -5 \\ -5 \end{bmatrix} = \begin{bmatrix} -5.556 \\ 1.111 \end{bmatrix}.$$

The minimum along this direction is given by $\alpha_1 = 0.6$, which gives the exact solution at the origin. Thus, as expected for a quadratic function, the conjugate gradient method converges in $n = 2$ steps in this case.

6.5.7 Truncated or Inexact Newton Methods

Another way of potentially reducing the work per iteration of Newton's method or its variants is to use an iterative method (see Section 11.5) to solve the linear system for the Newton or quasi-Newton step,

$$\boldsymbol{B}_k \boldsymbol{s}_k = -\nabla f(\boldsymbol{x}_k),$$

where $\boldsymbol{B}_k$ is the true or approximate Hessian matrix, rather than using a direct method based on factorization of $\boldsymbol{B}_k$. One advantage is that only a few iterations of the iterative method may suffice to produce a step that is just as useful as the true Newton step. Indeed, far from a minimum the true Newton step may offer no special advantage, yet can be very costly to compute accurately. Such an approach is called an *inexact* or *truncated* Newton method, because the linear system for the Newton step is solved inexactly by terminating the iterative linear solver before convergence.

If $\boldsymbol{B}_k$ is positive definite, then a good choice for the iterative linear solver is the conjugate gradient method (see Section 11.5.5). The conjugate gradient method begins with the negative gradient vector and eventually converges to the true Newton step, so truncating the iterations produces a step that is intermediate between these two vectors and is always a descent direction when $\boldsymbol{B}_k$ is positive definite. Moreover, since the conjugate gradient method requires only matrix-vector products, the Hessian matrix need not be formed explicitly, which can mean a substantial savings in storage. To supply the product $\boldsymbol{B}_k\boldsymbol{v}$, for example, the finite difference approximation

$$\boldsymbol{B}_k\boldsymbol{v} \approx \frac{\nabla f(\boldsymbol{x}_k + h\boldsymbol{v}) - \nabla f(\boldsymbol{x}_k)}{h}$$

can be computed instead, without ever forming $\boldsymbol{B}_k$.

In implementing a truncated Newton method, the termination criterion for the inner iteration must be chosen carefully to preserve the superlinear (or quadratic) convergence rate of the outer iteration. In addition, special measures may be required if the matrix $\boldsymbol{B}_k$ is not positive definite. Nevertheless, truncated Newton methods are usually very effective in practice and are among the best methods available for large sparse problems.

6.6 Nonlinear Least Squares

Least squares data fitting can be viewed as an optimization problem. Given data points (t_i, y_i), $i = 1, \ldots, m$, we wish to find the vector $\boldsymbol{x} \in \mathbb{R}^n$ of parameters that gives the best fit in the least squares sense to the model function $f(t, \boldsymbol{x})$, where $f\colon \mathbb{R}^{n+1} \to \mathbb{R}$. In Chapter 3 we considered only the case in which the model function f is linear in the components of $\boldsymbol{x}$; we are now in a position to consider *nonlinear least squares* as a special case of nonlinear optimization.

If we define the components of the *residual* function $\boldsymbol{r}\colon \mathbb{R}^n \to \mathbb{R}^m$ by

$$r_i(\boldsymbol{x}) = y_i - f(t_i, \boldsymbol{x}), \quad i = 1, ..., m,$$

then we wish to minimize the function

$$\phi(\boldsymbol{x}) = \tfrac{1}{2}\, \boldsymbol{r}(\boldsymbol{x})^T \boldsymbol{r}(\boldsymbol{x}),$$

i.e., the sum of squares of the residual components (the factor $\frac{1}{2}$ is inserted for later convenience and has no effect on the optimal value for $\boldsymbol{x}$). The gradient vector and Hessian matrix of ϕ are given by

$$\nabla\phi(\boldsymbol{x}) = \boldsymbol{J}^T(\boldsymbol{x})\, \boldsymbol{r}(\boldsymbol{x})$$

and

$$\boldsymbol{H}_\phi(\boldsymbol{x}) = \boldsymbol{J}^T(\boldsymbol{x})\,\boldsymbol{J}(\boldsymbol{x}) + \sum_{i=1}^{m} r_i(\boldsymbol{x})\,\boldsymbol{H}_{r_i}(\boldsymbol{x}),$$

where $\boldsymbol{J}(\boldsymbol{x})$ is the Jacobian matrix of $\boldsymbol{r}(\boldsymbol{x})$, and $\boldsymbol{H}_{r_i}(\boldsymbol{x})$ denotes the Hessian matrix of the component function $r_i(\boldsymbol{x})$. Thus, if we apply Newton's method and $\boldsymbol{x}_k$ is an approximate solution, then the Newton step $\boldsymbol{s}_k$ is given by the linear system

$$\left(\boldsymbol{J}^T(\boldsymbol{x}_k)\,\boldsymbol{J}(\boldsymbol{x}_k) + \sum_{i=1}^{m} r_i(\boldsymbol{x}_k)\,\boldsymbol{H}_{r_i}(\boldsymbol{x}_k)\right)\boldsymbol{s}_k = -\boldsymbol{J}^T(\boldsymbol{x}_k)\,\boldsymbol{r}(\boldsymbol{x}_k).$$

The m Hessian matrices $\boldsymbol{H}_{r_i}$ of the residual components are usually inconvenient and expensive to compute. Fortunately, we can exploit the special structure of this problem to avoid computing them in most cases, as we will see next.

6.6.1 Gauss-Newton Method

Note that in $\boldsymbol{H}_\phi$ each of the Hessian matrices $\boldsymbol{H}_{r_i}$ is multiplied by the corresponding residual component function r_i, which should be small at a solution if the model function fits the data reasonably well. This feature motivates the *Gauss-Newton method* for nonlinear least squares, in which the terms involving $\boldsymbol{H}_{r_i}$ are dropped from the Hessian and the linear system

$$\left(\boldsymbol{J}^T(\boldsymbol{x}_k)\,\boldsymbol{J}(\boldsymbol{x}_k)\right)\boldsymbol{s}_k = -\boldsymbol{J}^T(\boldsymbol{x}_k)\,\boldsymbol{r}(\boldsymbol{x}_k)$$

determines an approximate Newton step $\boldsymbol{s}_k$ at each iteration. We recognize this system as the normal equations (see Section 3.2.1) for the $m \times n$ linear least squares problem

$$\boldsymbol{J}(\boldsymbol{x}_k)\,\boldsymbol{s}_k \cong -\boldsymbol{r}(\boldsymbol{x}_k),$$

which can be solved more reliably by orthogonal factorization of $\boldsymbol{J}(\boldsymbol{x}_k)$ (see Section 3.5). The next approximate solution is then given by

$$\boldsymbol{x}_{k+1} = \boldsymbol{x}_k + \boldsymbol{s}_k,$$

and the process is repeated until convergence. In effect, the Gauss-Newton method replaces a nonlinear least squares problem by a sequence of linear least squares problems whose solutions converge to the solution of the original nonlinear problem.

Example 6.15 Gauss-Newton Method. We illustrate the Gauss-Newton method for nonlinear least squares by fitting the nonlinear model function

$$f(t, \boldsymbol{x}) = x_1 e^{x_2 t}$$

to the four data points

t	0.0	1.0	2.0	3.0
y	2.0	0.7	0.3	0.1

For this model function, the entries of the Jacobian matrix of the residual function $\boldsymbol{r}$ are given by

$$\{\boldsymbol{J}(\boldsymbol{x})\}_{i,1} = \frac{\partial r_i(\boldsymbol{x})}{\partial x_1} = -e^{x_2 t_i}, \qquad \{\boldsymbol{J}(\boldsymbol{x})\}_{i,2} = \frac{\partial r_i(\boldsymbol{x})}{\partial x_2} = -x_1 t_i e^{x_2 t_i},$$

$i = 1, \ldots, 4$. If we take $\boldsymbol{x}_0 = [\,1 \quad 0\,]^T$ as starting point, then the linear least squares problem to be solved for the Gauss-Newton step $\boldsymbol{s}_0$ is

$$\boldsymbol{J}(\boldsymbol{x}_0)\,\boldsymbol{s}_0 = \begin{bmatrix} -1 & 0 \\ -1 & -1 \\ -1 & -2 \\ -1 & -3 \end{bmatrix} \boldsymbol{s}_0 \cong \begin{bmatrix} -1 \\ 0.3 \\ 0.7 \\ 0.9 \end{bmatrix} = -\boldsymbol{r}(\boldsymbol{x}_0).$$

The least squares solution to this system is $\boldsymbol{s}_0 = [\,0.69 \quad -0.61\,]^T$. We then take $\boldsymbol{x}_1 = \boldsymbol{x}_0 + \boldsymbol{s}_0 = [\,1.69 \quad -0.61\,]^T$ as the next approximate solution and repeat the process until convergence. The resulting sequence of iterates is shown next.

k	$\boldsymbol{x}_k^T$		$\\|\boldsymbol{r}(\boldsymbol{x}_k)\\|_2^2$
0	1.000	0.000	2.390
1	1.690	−0.610	0.212
2	1.975	−0.930	0.007
3	1.994	−1.004	0.002
4	1.995	−1.009	0.002
5	1.995	−1.010	0.002

Like all methods based on Newton's method, the Gauss-Newton method for solving nonlinear least squares problems may fail to converge unless it is started close enough to the solution. A line search can be used to improve its robustness, but additional modifications may be necessary to ensure that the computed step $\boldsymbol{s}_k$ is a descent direction when far from the solution. In addition, if the residual components at the solution are relatively large, then the terms omitted from the Hessian matrix may not be negligible, in which case the Gauss-Newton approximation may be inaccurate, so that the method converges slowly at best and may not converge at all. In such "large-residual" cases, it may be best to use a general nonlinear optimization method that takes into account the full Hessian matrix.

6.6.2 Levenberg-Marquardt Method

The *Levenberg-Marquardt method* is a useful alternative when the Gauss-Newton approximation yields an ill-conditioned or rank-deficient linear least squares subproblem. At each iteration of this method, the linear system for the step $\boldsymbol{s}_k$ is of the form

$$\left(\boldsymbol{J}^T(\boldsymbol{x}_k)\,\boldsymbol{J}(\boldsymbol{x}_k) + \mu_k \boldsymbol{I}\right)\boldsymbol{s}_k = -\boldsymbol{J}^T(\boldsymbol{x}_k)\,\boldsymbol{r}(\boldsymbol{x}_k),$$

where μ_k is a nonnegative scalar parameter chosen by some strategy. The corresponding linear least squares problem to be solved is

$$\begin{bmatrix} \boldsymbol{J}(\boldsymbol{x}_k) \\ \sqrt{\mu_k}\,\boldsymbol{I} \end{bmatrix} \boldsymbol{s}_k \cong \begin{bmatrix} -\boldsymbol{r}(\boldsymbol{x}_k) \\ \boldsymbol{0} \end{bmatrix}.$$

This method, which is an example of a general technique known as *regularization* (see Section 8.5), can be variously interpreted as replacing the terms omitted from the true Hessian by a scalar multiple of the identity matrix, or as shifting the spectrum of the approximate Hessian to make it positive definite (or equivalently, as boosting the rank of the corresponding least squares problem), or as using a weighted combination of the Gauss-Newton step and the steepest descent direction. With a suitable strategy for choosing the parameter μ_k, typically based on a *trust-region* approach, the Levenberg-Marquardt method can be very robust in practice, and it forms the basis for several effective software packages for solving nonlinear least squares problems.

6.7 Constrained Optimization

We turn now to methods for constrained optimization, first considering equality-constrained problems, which have the form

$$\min_{\boldsymbol{x}} f(\boldsymbol{x}) \quad \text{subject to} \quad \boldsymbol{g}(\boldsymbol{x}) = \boldsymbol{0},$$

where $f\colon \mathbb{R}^n \to \mathbb{R}$ and $\boldsymbol{g}\colon \mathbb{R}^n \to \mathbb{R}^m$, with $m \le n$.

6.7.1 Sequential Quadratic Programming

As we saw in Section 6.2.3, a constrained local minimum must be a critical point of the *Lagrangian function*

$$\mathcal{L}(\boldsymbol{x}, \boldsymbol{\lambda}) = f(\boldsymbol{x}) + \boldsymbol{\lambda}^T \boldsymbol{g}(\boldsymbol{x}),$$

where $\boldsymbol{\lambda} \in \mathbb{R}^m$ is a vector of *Lagrange multipliers*. Thus, one way to compute a constrained minimum is to solve the system of $n+m$ equations in $n+m$ unknowns

$$\nabla \mathcal{L}(\boldsymbol{x}, \boldsymbol{\lambda}) = \begin{bmatrix} \nabla f(\boldsymbol{x}) + \boldsymbol{J}_g^T(\boldsymbol{x})\,\boldsymbol{\lambda} \\ \boldsymbol{g}(\boldsymbol{x}) \end{bmatrix} = \boldsymbol{0}.$$

From a starting guess $(\boldsymbol{x}_0, \boldsymbol{\lambda}_0)$, we can apply Newton's method to solve this nonlinear system. The linear system to be solved at iteration k for the Newton step $(\boldsymbol{s}_k, \boldsymbol{\delta}_k)$ is

$$\begin{bmatrix} \boldsymbol{B}(\boldsymbol{x}_k, \boldsymbol{\lambda}_k) & \boldsymbol{J}_g^T(\boldsymbol{x}_k) \\ \boldsymbol{J}_g(\boldsymbol{x}_k) & \boldsymbol{O} \end{bmatrix} \begin{bmatrix} \boldsymbol{s}_k \\ \boldsymbol{\delta}_k \end{bmatrix} = - \begin{bmatrix} \nabla f(\boldsymbol{x}_k) + \boldsymbol{J}_g^T(\boldsymbol{x}_k)\,\boldsymbol{\lambda}_k \\ \boldsymbol{g}(\boldsymbol{x}_k) \end{bmatrix},$$

where

$$\boldsymbol{B}(\boldsymbol{x}, \boldsymbol{\lambda}) = \boldsymbol{H}_f(\boldsymbol{x}) + \sum_{i=1}^{m} \lambda_i\, \boldsymbol{H}_{g_i}(\boldsymbol{x}).$$

We recognize this block 2×2 system of equations as the first-order optimality conditions for the constrained optimization problem

$$\min_{\boldsymbol{s}} \tfrac{1}{2}\, \boldsymbol{s}^T \boldsymbol{B}(\boldsymbol{x}_k, \boldsymbol{\lambda}_k)\, \boldsymbol{s} + \boldsymbol{s}^T \left(\nabla f(\boldsymbol{x}_k) + \boldsymbol{J}_g^T(\boldsymbol{x}_k)\,\boldsymbol{\lambda}_k\right)$$

subject to

$$J_g(\boldsymbol{x}_k)\, \boldsymbol{s} + \boldsymbol{g}(\boldsymbol{x}_k) = \boldsymbol{0}.$$

The latter is a *quadratic programming* problem, i.e., a problem with a quadratic objective function and linear constraints, so this approach is known as *sequential quadratic programming*. Just as Newton's method replaces a nonlinear system of equations by a sequence of linear systems, or an unconstrained nonlinear optimization problem by a sequence of unconstrained quadratic problems, so Newton's method replaces a constrained nonlinear optimization problem by a sequence of quadratic programming problems.

Because of its relationship to the constrained optimality conditions, the block 2×2 matrix of the Newton system is sometimes called the *KKT matrix*; for convenience we will write the $(n+m) \times (n+m)$ KKT system more compactly as

$$\begin{bmatrix} \boldsymbol{B} & \boldsymbol{J}^T \\ \boldsymbol{J} & \boldsymbol{O} \end{bmatrix} \begin{bmatrix} \boldsymbol{s} \\ \boldsymbol{\delta} \end{bmatrix} = - \begin{bmatrix} \boldsymbol{w} \\ \boldsymbol{g} \end{bmatrix}.$$

There are a number of ways to solve such quadratic programming problems:

Direct solution. The KKT matrix is symmetric but not positive definite, so Cholesky factorization is not applicable, but a symmetric indefinite factorization (see Section 2.5.2) can be used, preferably with a pivoting strategy that takes advantage of sparsity, to solve directly for $(\boldsymbol{s}, \boldsymbol{\delta})$. Alternatively, a suitable iterative solution method could be used.

Range-space method. Assuming $\boldsymbol{B}$ is nonsingular and $\boldsymbol{J}$ has full row rank, block elimination in the KKT system yields the $m \times m$ symmetric (but not necessarily positive definite) system

$$\left(\boldsymbol{J}\boldsymbol{B}^{-1}\boldsymbol{J}^T\right) \boldsymbol{\delta} = \boldsymbol{g} - \boldsymbol{J}\boldsymbol{B}^{-1}\boldsymbol{w},$$

which can be solved for $\boldsymbol{\delta}$, and then $\boldsymbol{s}$ can be determined by solving the system

$$\boldsymbol{B}\, \boldsymbol{s} = -\boldsymbol{w} - \boldsymbol{J}^T \boldsymbol{\delta},$$

which follows from the first block row of the KKT system. Both of these systems require a factorization of the $n \times n$ matrix $\boldsymbol{B}$, which is symmetric but not necessarily positive definite. The range-space method is most attractive when the number of constraints m is relatively small. Unfortunately, as in the normal equations method for least squares problems (see Section 3.4.1), explicit formation of the product $\boldsymbol{J}\boldsymbol{B}^{-1}\boldsymbol{J}^T$ may cause loss of information and may degrade the conditioning of the problem, so this method must be used with caution.

Null-space method. Compute the QR factorization

$$\boldsymbol{J}^T = \boldsymbol{Q} \begin{bmatrix} \boldsymbol{R} \\ \boldsymbol{O} \end{bmatrix}$$

and partition

$$\boldsymbol{Q} = [\,\boldsymbol{Y} \quad \boldsymbol{Z}\,],$$

where $\boldsymbol{Y}$ is $n \times m$ and $\boldsymbol{Z}$ is $n \times (n-m)$. Assuming $\boldsymbol{J}$ has full row rank, the $m \times m$ upper triangular matrix $\boldsymbol{R}$ will be nonsingular. As we saw in Section 3.4.5, the columns of $\boldsymbol{Y}$ form an orthonormal basis for the range space of $\boldsymbol{J}^T$ (i.e., span($\boldsymbol{J}^T$)), and the columns of $\boldsymbol{Z}$ form an orthonormal basis for the null space of $\boldsymbol{J}$. Thus, $\boldsymbol{s}$ can be written as a sum of components in these two mutually orthogonal subspaces,

$$\boldsymbol{s} = \boldsymbol{Y}\boldsymbol{u} + \boldsymbol{Z}\boldsymbol{v},$$

where $\boldsymbol{u} \in \mathbb{R}^m$ and $\boldsymbol{v} \in \mathbb{R}^{n-m}$. Because $\boldsymbol{J}\boldsymbol{Y} = \boldsymbol{R}^T$ and $\boldsymbol{J}\boldsymbol{Z} = \boldsymbol{O}$, the second block row of the KKT system yields the $m \times m$ lower triangular system

$$\boldsymbol{J}\boldsymbol{s} = \boldsymbol{J}(\boldsymbol{Y}\boldsymbol{u} + \boldsymbol{Z}\boldsymbol{v}) = \boldsymbol{R}^T\boldsymbol{u} = -\boldsymbol{g},$$

which can be solved for $\boldsymbol{u}$. Similarly, premultiplying the first block row of the KKT system by $\boldsymbol{Z}^T$ yields the $(n-m) \times (n-m)$ symmetric system

$$\left(\boldsymbol{Z}^T\boldsymbol{B}\boldsymbol{Z}\right)\boldsymbol{v} = -\boldsymbol{Z}^T(\boldsymbol{w} - \boldsymbol{B}\boldsymbol{Y}\boldsymbol{u}),$$

which can be solved for $\boldsymbol{v}$, so that $\boldsymbol{s}$ is now completely determined. Note that the projected Hessian matrix $\boldsymbol{Z}^T\boldsymbol{B}\boldsymbol{Z}$ should be positive definite near a constrained minimum (see Section 6.2.3), so that Cholesky factorization can be used to solve the latter system. Finally, premultiplying the first block row of the KKT system by $\boldsymbol{Y}^T$ yields the triangular system

$$\boldsymbol{Y}^T\boldsymbol{J}^T\boldsymbol{\delta} = \boldsymbol{R}\boldsymbol{\delta} = -\boldsymbol{Y}^T(\boldsymbol{w} + \boldsymbol{B}\boldsymbol{s}),$$

which can be solved for $\boldsymbol{\delta}$. The null-space method is most attractive when the number of constraints m is relatively large, so that $n-m$ is small. The use of orthogonal matrices in the null-space method avoids the potential loss of information and degradation of conditioning associated with the range-space method. Moreover, the null-space method does not require $\boldsymbol{B}$ to be nonsingular, so it is more broadly applicable than the range-space method.

We have now seen several methods for computing the Newton step $(\boldsymbol{s}_k, \boldsymbol{\delta}_k)$ at each iteration of the sequential quadratic programming method for solving a constrained nonlinear optimization problem. As usual, however, Newton's method may be unreliable unless it is started close to the solution. We have seen that Newton's method can be made more robust by using a line search or trust-region strategy, but for a constrained problem it is no longer clear how we should measure progress toward a solution: should we focus on minimizing the objective function f or on satisfying the constraints $\boldsymbol{g}$? A suitable *merit function* for measuring progress is a weighted combination of these two objectives, such as

$$\phi_\rho(\boldsymbol{x}) = f(\boldsymbol{x}) + \tfrac{1}{2}\,\rho\,\boldsymbol{g}(\boldsymbol{x})^T\boldsymbol{g}(\boldsymbol{x}),$$

where ρ is a nonnegative real parameter. This type of merit function is called a *penalty function* because it penalizes violation of the constraints, with the relative severity of the penalty determined by ρ. Another type of merit function is an *augmented Lagrangian function*, such as

$$\mathcal{L}_\rho(\boldsymbol{x}, \boldsymbol{\lambda}) = f(\boldsymbol{x}) + \boldsymbol{\lambda}^T\boldsymbol{g}(\boldsymbol{x}) + \tfrac{1}{2}\,\rho\,\boldsymbol{g}(\boldsymbol{x})^T\boldsymbol{g}(\boldsymbol{x}),$$

where again ρ is a nonnegative real parameter. With an appropriate choice of the weighting parameter ρ, which may need to be adjusted adaptively, either type of merit function can be used in conjunction with a line search or trust-region strategy to make sequential quadratic programming more robust for solving constrained optimization problems.

Even if a good starting guess $\boldsymbol{x}_0$ for the solution is available, the user is unlikely to have any basis for choosing a starting guess $\boldsymbol{\lambda}_0$ for the Lagrange multipliers. At a constrained minimum $\boldsymbol{x}^*$, the first-order optimality conditions say that $\boldsymbol{J}_g^T(\boldsymbol{x}^*)\boldsymbol{\lambda}^* = -\nabla f(\boldsymbol{x}^*)$. Thus, given a starting guess $\boldsymbol{x}_0$ for the solution, a reasonable starting guess for the corresponding Lagrange multipliers can be obtained by solving the $n \times m$ linear least squares problem

$$\boldsymbol{J}_g^T(\boldsymbol{x}_0)\,\boldsymbol{\lambda}_0 \cong -\nabla f(\boldsymbol{x}_0),$$

which projects the negative gradient of the objective function onto the span of the constraint normals.

The sequential quadratic programming method can be extended to problems with inequality constraints by using an *active set strategy*, in which the inequality constraints are provisionally divided into those that are already strictly satisfied (and can therefore be disregarded temporarily) and those that are violated (and are therefore treated as equality constraints temporarily). This division of the constraints is revised as iterations proceed until eventually the constraints that are binding at the solution are identified. When there are inequality constraints, the merit function must be modified so that only the violated constraints are penalized.

6.7.2 Penalty and Barrier Methods

We have just seen how to solve a constrained nonlinear optimization problem by solving a sequence of quadratic programming problems. Another family of methods is based on converting a constrained optimization problem into an unconstrained optimization problem or a sequence of such problems. One way to accomplish this is by using a *penalty function method*, which attempts to attain feasibility while simultaneously minimizing the objective function by minimizing a weighted combination of the two. We have already seen a penalty function used as a merit function in Section 6.7.1. For the equality-constrained problem

$$\min_{\boldsymbol{x}} f(\boldsymbol{x}) \quad \text{subject to} \quad \boldsymbol{g}(\boldsymbol{x}) = \boldsymbol{0},$$

if $\boldsymbol{x}_\rho^*$ is the solution to the unconstrained problem

$$\min_{\boldsymbol{x}} \phi_\rho(\boldsymbol{x}) = f(\boldsymbol{x}) + \tfrac{1}{2}\,\rho\,\boldsymbol{g}(\boldsymbol{x})^T\boldsymbol{g}(\boldsymbol{x}),$$

then under appropriate conditions it can be shown that

$$\lim_{\rho\to\infty} \boldsymbol{x}_\rho^* = \boldsymbol{x}^*,$$

where $\boldsymbol{x}^*$ is the solution to the original constrained problem. For any finite value of ρ, we can apply an unconstrained optimization method from Section 6.5 to find a minimum of $\phi_\rho(\boldsymbol{x})$, and in principle the solution $\boldsymbol{x}_\rho^*$ will be as close as desired to $\boldsymbol{x}^*$ for large enough ρ.

This approach has a compelling simplicity about it, but it comes with some significant drawbacks. Perhaps the most serious of these is that the Hessian matrix of ϕ_ρ becomes increasingly ill-conditioned as ρ becomes larger, and hence the solutions $\boldsymbol{x}_\rho^*$ are increasingly poorly determined, with the result that even a very good unconstrained optimization method will find it increasingly difficult to compute an accurate solution. For this reason, this method is usually implemented so that a sequence of unconstrained optimization problems is solved for increasing values of ρ, with the solution for each serving as starting guess for the next. Another way to lessen the effect of ill-conditioning is to use an *augmented Lagrangian function*, such as

$$\mathcal{L}_\rho(\boldsymbol{x}, \boldsymbol{\lambda}) = f(\boldsymbol{x}) + \boldsymbol{\lambda}^T \boldsymbol{g}(\boldsymbol{x}) + \tfrac{1}{2}\,\rho\, \boldsymbol{g}(\boldsymbol{x})^T \boldsymbol{g}(\boldsymbol{x}),$$

instead of a simple penalty function. The necessary Lagrange multiplier estimates can be obtained in a variety of ways, including the least squares approximation we saw in Section 6.7.1.

Example 6.16 Penalty Method. We illustrate the penalty method by using it to solve the constrained optimization problem from Example 6.7, taking the constraint as an equality. For this problem, we have

$$\phi_\rho(\boldsymbol{x}) = f(\boldsymbol{x}) + \tfrac{1}{2}\,\rho\, \boldsymbol{g}(\boldsymbol{x})^T \boldsymbol{g}(\boldsymbol{x}) = 0.5x_1^2 + 2.5x_2^2 + 0.5\,\rho\,(x_2 - x_1 + 1)^2.$$

Starting with $\boldsymbol{x}_0 = \begin{bmatrix} 1 & 1 \end{bmatrix}^T$ as initial guess and taking $\rho = 1$, we use an unconstrained optimization routine to compute a minimum $\boldsymbol{x}_\rho^*$ of ϕ_ρ. We then increase ρ, say by a factor of ten, and compute a new unconstrained minimum using the previous solution as starting guess. The resulting sequence of unconstrained minima is shown next. For $\rho = 1000$, the solution is accurate to the number of digits shown.

ρ	$\boldsymbol{x}_\rho^{*T}$	
1	0.454	−0.091
10	0.769	−0.154
100	0.826	−0.165
1000	0.833	−0.167

The constrained optimization methods we have considered thus far attain feasibility only in the limit at the solution: penalty methods penalize constraint violations, but they do not avoid them altogether. For some problems, the objective function may not be defined except at feasible points (for example, an infeasible point might require taking the square root of a negative number). In such cases, one must not only start with an initial guess that is feasible, but all intermediate points at which the objective function is evaluated must remain feasible. One way to accomplish this is by using a *barrier function*, which increasingly penalizes *feasible* points as they approach the boundary of the feasible region. Consider the inequality-constrained problem

$$\min_{\boldsymbol{x}} f(\boldsymbol{x}) \quad \text{subject to} \quad \boldsymbol{h}(\boldsymbol{x}) \le \boldsymbol{0},$$

where $f: \mathbb{R}^n \to \mathbb{R}$ and $\boldsymbol{h}: \mathbb{R}^n \to \mathbb{R}^p$. Two examples of barrier functions for this problem are the *inverse barrier function*

$$\phi_\mu(\boldsymbol{x}) = f(\boldsymbol{x}) - \mu \sum_{i=1}^{p} \frac{1}{h_i(\boldsymbol{x})}$$

and the *logarithmic barrier function*

$$\phi_\mu(\boldsymbol{x}) = f(\boldsymbol{x}) - \mu \sum_{i=1}^{p} \log(-h_i(\boldsymbol{x})).$$

For any $\mu > 0$, the unconstrained minimum $\boldsymbol{x}_\mu^*$ of ϕ_μ is necessarily feasible, and $\boldsymbol{x}_\mu^* \to \boldsymbol{x}^*$, the constrained minimum, as $\mu \to 0$. We can apply an unconstrained optimization method from Section 6.5 to find a minimum of $\phi_\mu(\boldsymbol{x})$, and in principle the solution $\boldsymbol{x}_\mu^*$ will be as close as desired to $\boldsymbol{x}^*$ for small enough μ, but again these problems become increasingly ill-conditioned as μ becomes smaller, so typically a sequence of problems is solved for a decreasing sequence of values of μ. In recent years, such *interior-point methods* have had a major impact in constrained optimization, including linear programming, which we consider next.

6.7.3 Linear Programming

One of the most important and commonly occurring constrained optimization problems is *linear programming*, in which both the objective function and the constraints are all linear. One of several standard forms for such problems is

$$\min_{\boldsymbol{x}} f(\boldsymbol{x}) = \boldsymbol{c}^T \boldsymbol{x} \quad \text{subject to} \quad \boldsymbol{A}\boldsymbol{x} = \boldsymbol{b} \quad \text{and} \quad \boldsymbol{x} \geq \boldsymbol{0},$$

where $m < n$, $\boldsymbol{A} \in \mathbb{R}^{m \times n}$, $\boldsymbol{b} \in \mathbb{R}^m$, and $\boldsymbol{c}, \boldsymbol{x} \in \mathbb{R}^n$. The feasible region for such a problem is a convex polyhedron in $\mathbb{R}^n$, and the global minimum must occur at one of its vertices. The standard method for solving linear programming problems, called the *simplex method*, systematically examines a sequence of these vertices to find a vertex yielding the minimum.

A detailed description of the simplex method is beyond the scope of this book, but the main procedures, which we merely sketch here, make use of a number of tools we have already seen. Phase 1 of the simplex method is to find a vertex of the feasible region. A vertex of the feasible region is a point where all of the constraints are satisfied, and $n - m$ of the inequality constraints are binding (i.e., $x_i = 0$). If we choose any subset of $n - m$ variables, called *nonbasic variables*, and set them to zero, then we can use the equality constraints to solve for the m remaining *basic variables*. If the resulting values for the basic variables are nonnegative, then we have found a feasible vertex. Otherwise, we must choose a different set of nonbasic variables and try again. There are systematic procedures, which involve adding new artificial variables and constraints, to ensure that a feasible vertex is found rapidly and efficiently.

Phase 2 of the simplex method moves systematically from vertex to vertex until the minimum point is found. Starting from the feasible vertex found in Phase 1, a neighboring vertex that has a smaller value for the objective function is selected. The specific new vertex chosen is obtained by exchanging one of the current nonbasic variables for the basic variable that produces the greatest reduction in the value of the objective function, subject to remaining feasible. This process is then repeated until no vertex has a lower function value than the current point, which must therefore be optimal.

The linear system solutions required at each step of the simplex method use matrix factorization and updating techniques similar to those in Chapter 2. In particular, much of the efficiency of the method depends on updating the factorization at each step as variables are added or deleted one at a time.

In this brief sketch of the simplex method, we have glossed over many details, such as the various degeneracies that can arise, the detection of infeasible or unbounded problems, the updating of the factorization, and the optimality test. Suffice it to say that all of these can be addressed effectively, so that the method is very reliable and efficient in practice, able to solve problems having thousands of variables and constraints.

The efficiency of the simplex method in practice is somewhat surprising, since the number of vertices that must potentially be examined is

$$\binom{n}{m} = \frac{n!}{m!\,(n-m)!},$$

which is enormous for problems of realistic size. Yet in practice, the number of iterations required is usually only a small multiple of the number of constraints m, essentially independent of the number of variables n (the value of n affects the cost per iteration, but not the number of iterations).

Although the simplex method is extremely effective in practice, in principle it can require in the worst case a solution time that is exponential in the size of the problem, and there are contrived examples for which such behavior actually occurs. In recent years, new methods for linear programming have been developed, such as those of Khachiyan and of Karmarkar, whose worst-case solution time is polynomial in the size of the problem. These methods move through the interior of the feasible region, not restricting themselves to investigating only its vertices. Although such *interior-point methods* have had significant practical impact, the simplex method remains the predominant method in standard packages for linear programming, and its effectiveness in practice is excellent.

Example 6.17 Linear Programming. To illustrate linear programming we consider a graphical solution of the problem

$$\min_{\boldsymbol{x}} f(\boldsymbol{x}) = \boldsymbol{c}^T\boldsymbol{x} = -8x_1 - 11x_2$$

subject to the linear inequality constraints

$$5x_1 + 4x_2 \le 40, \quad -x_1 + 3x_2 \le 12, \quad x_1 \ge 0, \quad x_2 \ge 0.$$

The feasible region, which is bounded by the coordinate axes and the other two straight lines, is shaded in Fig. 6.11. Contour lines of the objective function are drawn, with corresponding values of the objective function shown along the bottom of the graph. The minimum value necessarily occurs at one of the vertices of the feasible region, in this case the point $\boldsymbol{x}^* = [3.79 \quad 5.26]^T$ indicated by a bullet in the graph, where the objective function has the value −88.2.

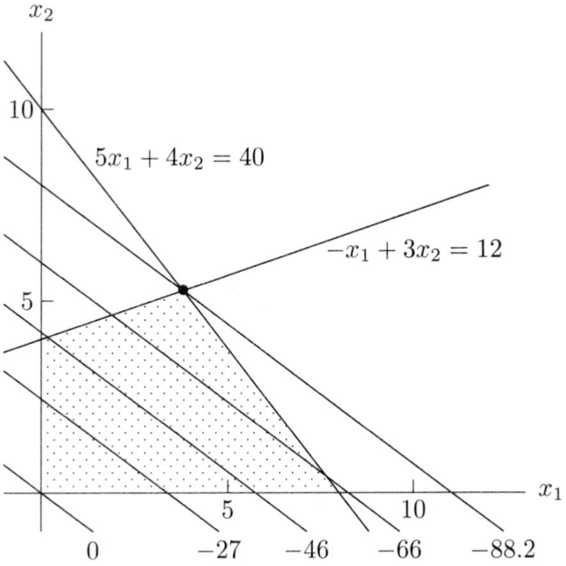

Figure 6.11: Linear programming problem from Example 6.17.

6.8 Software for Optimization

Table 6.1 is a list of some of the software available for solving one-dimensional and unconstrained optimization problems. In the multidimensional case, we distinguish between routines that do or do not require the user to supply derivatives for the functions, although in some cases the routines cited offer both options.

Software for minimizing a function $f(\boldsymbol{x})$ typically requires the user to supply the name of a routine that computes the value of the objective function f for any given value of $\boldsymbol{x}$. The user must also supply absolute or relative error tolerances that are used in the stopping criterion for the iterative solution process. Additional input for one-dimensional problems usually includes the endpoints of an interval in which the function is unimodal. (If the function is not unimodal, then the routine often will still find a local minimum, but it may not be the global minimum on the interval.) Additional input for multidimensional problems includes the dimension of the problem and a starting guess for the solution, and may also include the name of a routine for computing the gradient (and possibly the Hessian) of the objective function and a workspace array for storing the Hessian or an approximation to it. In addition to the computed solution $\boldsymbol{x}^*$, the output typically includes a status flag

	One-dimensional	Multidimensional	
Source	No derivatives	No derivatives	Derivatives
Brent [47]	localmin	praxis	
FMM [127]	fmin		
HSL	vd01/vd04	va08/va10/va24	va06/va09/va13
IMSL	uvmif	uminf	umiah
KMN [220]	fmin	uncmin	
MATLAB	fminbnd	fminsearch	fminunc
NAG	e04abf	e04jyf	e04lyf
NAPACK			cg
NR [315]	brent	powell	dfpmin
NUMAL [250]	minin	praxis	flemin/rnk1min
PORT		mnf	mng
Schnabel, et al. [340]		uncmin	uncmin
TOMS			mini(#500)
TOMS		smsno(#611)	sumsl(#611)
TOMS		bbvscg(#630)	bbvscg(#630)
TOMS			tnpack(#702)
TOMS		tensor(#739)	tensor(#739)

Table 6.1: Software for one-dimensional and unconstrained optimization

indicating any warnings or errors. A preliminary plot of the functions involved can help greatly in determining a suitable starting guess.

Table 6.2 is a list of some of the software available for solving nonlinear least squares problems, linear programming problems, and general nonlinear constrained optimization problems. Good software is also available from a number of sources for solving many other types of optimization problems, including quadratic programming, linear or simple bounds constraints, network flow problems, etc. There is an optimization toolbox for MATLAB in which some of the software listed in the tables can be found, along with numerous additional routines for various other optimization problems. For the nonlinear analogue of total least squares, called *orthogonal distance regression*, odrpack(#676) is available from TOMS. A comprehensive survey of optimization software can be found in [281].

6.9 Historical Notes and Further Reading

Optimality conditions for unconstrained optimization are as old as calculus. For equality-constrained optimization, optimality conditions based on what are now called Lagrange multipliers were formulated in the eighteenth century, initially by Euler and then further developed by Lagrange. The Karush-Kuhn-Tucker conditions for inequality-constrained optimization appeared in Karush's thesis in 1939 but did not become widely known until their independent publication in the open literature by Kuhn and Tucker in 1951.

Source	Nonlinear least squares	Linear programming	Nonlinear programming
HSL	ns13/va27/vb01/vb13	la01/la04	vf01/vf04/vf13
IMSL	unlsf	dlprs	nconf/ncong
MATLAB	lsqnonlin/lsqcurvefit	linprog	fmincon
MINPACK	lmdif1		
NAG	e04fyf	e04mff	e04ucf
Netlib	varpro/dqed		
NR [315]	mrqmin	simplx	
NUMAL [250]	gssnewton/marquardt		
PORT	n2f/n2g/nsf/nsg		
SLATEC	snls1	splp	
SOL		minos	npsol
TOMS	nl2sol(#573)		
TOMS	tensolve(#768)		

Table 6.2: Software for nonlinear least squares and constrained optimization

As with nonlinear equations in one dimension, the one-dimensional optimization methods based on Newton's method or interpolation are classical. A theory of optimal one-dimensional search methods using only function value comparisons was initiated in the 1950s by Kiefer, who showed that Fibonacci search, in which successive evaluation points are determined by ratios of Fibonacci numbers, is optimal in the sense that it produces the minimum interval of uncertainty for a given number of function evaluations. What we usually want, however, is to fix the error tolerance rather than the number of function evaluations, so golden section search, which can be viewed as a limiting case of Fibonacci search, turns out to be more practical. See [416] for a detailed discussion of these methods. As with nonlinear equations, hybrid safeguarded methods for one-dimensional optimization were popularized by Brent [47].

For multidimensional optimization, most of the basic direct search methods were proposed in the 1960s. The method of Nelder and Mead is based on an earlier method of Spendley, Hext, and Himsworth. Another popular direct search method is that of Hooke and Jeeves. For a survey of these methods, see [386, 424].

Steepest descent and Newton's method for multidimensional optimization were analyzed as practical algorithms by Cauchy. Secant updating methods were originated by Davidon (who used the term *variable metric method*) in 1959. In 1963, Fletcher and Powell published an improved implementation, which came to be known as the DFP method. Continuing this trend of initialisms, the BFGS method was developed independently by Broyden, Fletcher, Goldfarb, and Shanno in 1970. Many other secant updates have been proposed, but these two have been the most successful, with BFGS having a slight edge. The conjugate gradient method was originally developed by Hestenes and Stiefel in the early 1950s to solve symmetric linear systems by minimizing a quadratic function. It was later adapted to minimize general nonlinear functions by Fletcher and Reeves in 1964.

The Levenberg-Marquardt method for nonlinear least squares was originally developed by Levenberg in 1944 and improved by Marquardt in 1963. A modern implementation of this method, due to Moré [278], can be found in `MINPACK` [279].

Penalty function methods for constrained optimization originated with Courant in the early 1940s and were popularized by Fiacco and McCormick in the 1960s. The sequential quadratic programming method was first described by Wilson in his 1963 thesis. The simplex method for linear programming, which is still a workhorse for such problems, was originated by Dantzig in the late 1940s. The first polynomial-time algorithm for linear programming, the ellipsoid algorithm published by Khachiyan in 1979, was based on earlier work in the 1970s by Shor and by Judin and Nemirovskii (Khachiyan's main contribution was to show that the algorithm indeed has polynomial complexity). A much more practical polynomial-time algorithm is the interior-point method of Karmarkar, published in 1984, which is related to earlier barrier methods popularized by Fiacco and McCormick [120].

For a detailed treatment of optimality conditions and other theoretical background on optimization, see [223, 263, 305]. There are many good general references on optimization with an emphasis on numerical algorithms, including [16, 27, 31, 68, 123, 154, 258, 267, 286, 291]. References focusing primarily on methods for unconstrained optimization include [92, 158, 228, 290]. The theory and convergence analysis of Newton's method and quasi-Newton methods are summarized in [280] and [91], respectively. Trust-region methods are exhaustively covered in [74]. For detailed discussion of nonlinear least squares, see [24, 343]. For detailed treatment of penalty and barrier methods, see [120]. A survey of sequential quadratic programming methods is given in [36]. The classic account of the simplex method for linear programming is [82]. More recent treatments of the simplex method can be found in [155, 258, 286, 291]. For an overview of linear programming including polynomial-time algorithms, see [159]. For a review of interior-point methods in constrained optimization, see [423, 427]. A general reference on global optimization is [201]; global optimization using interval methods is the subject of [186, 225, 318].

Review Questions

6.1. True or false: Points that minimize a nonlinear function are inherently less accurately determined than points for which a nonlinear function has a zero value.

6.2. True or false: If a function is unimodal on a closed interval, then it has exactly one minimum on the interval.

6.3. True or false: In minimizing a unimodal function of one variable by golden section search, the point discarded at each iteration is always the point having the largest function value.

6.4. True or false: For minimizing a real-valued function of several variables, the steepest descent method is usually more rapidly convergent than Newton's method.

6.5. True or false: The solution to a linear programming problem must occur at one of the vertices of the feasible region.

6.6. True or false: The approximate solution produced at each step of the simplex method for linear programming is a feasible point.

6.7. Suppose that the real-valued function f is unimodal on the interval $[a, b]$. Let x_1 and x_2 be two points in the interval, with $a < x_1 < x_2 < b$. If $f(x_1) = 1.232$ and $f(x_2) = 3.576$, then which of the following statements is valid?

1. The minimum of f must lie in the subinterval $[x_1, b]$.

2. The minimum of f must lie in the subinterval $[a, x_2]$.
3. One can't tell which of these two subintervals the minimum must lie in without knowing the values of $f(a)$ and $f(b)$.

6.8. (*a*) In minimizing a unimodal function of one variable on the interval $[0, 1]$ by golden section search, at what two points in the interval is the function initially evaluated?

(*b*) Why are those particular points chosen?

6.9. If the real-valued function f is monotonic on the interval $[a, b]$, will golden section search to find a minimum of f still converge? If not, why, and if so, to what point?

6.10. Suppose that the real-valued function f is unimodal on the interval $[a, b]$, and x_1 and x_2 are points in the interval such that $x_1 < x_2$ and $f(x_1) < f(x_2)$.

(*a*) What is the shortest interval in which you know that the minimum of f must lie?

(*b*) How would your answer change if we happened to have $f(x_1) = f(x_2)$?

6.11. List one advantage and one disadvantage of golden section search compared with successive parabolic interpolation for minimizing a function of one variable.

6.12. (*a*) Why is linear interpolation of a function $f: \mathbb{R} \to \mathbb{R}$ not useful for finding a minimum of f?

(*b*) In using quadratic interpolation for one-dimensional problems, why would one use inverse quadratic interpolation for finding a zero but regular quadratic interpolation for finding a minimum?

6.13. For minimizing a function $f: \mathbb{R} \to \mathbb{R}$, successive parabolic interpolation and Newton's method both fit a quadratic polynomial to the function f and then take its minimum as the next approximate solution.

(*a*) How do these two methods differ in choosing the quadratic polynomials they use?

(*b*) What difference does this make in their respective convergence rates?

6.14. Explain why Newton's method minimizes a quadratic function in one iteration but does not solve a quadratic equation in one iteration.

6.15. Suppose you want to minimize a function of one variable, $f: \mathbb{R} \to \mathbb{R}$. For each convergence rate given, name a method that normally has that convergence rate for this problem:

(*a*) Linear but not superlinear

(*b*) Superlinear but not quadratic

(*c*) Quadratic

6.16. Suppose you want to minimize a function of several variables, $f: \mathbb{R}^n \to \mathbb{R}$. For each convergence rate given, name a method that normally has that convergence rate for this problem:

(*a*) Linear but not superlinear

(*b*) Superlinear but not quadratic

(*c*) Quadratic

6.17. Which of the following iterative methods have a superlinear convergence rate under normal circumstances?

(*a*) Successive parabolic interpolation for minimizing a function

(*b*) Golden section search for minimizing a function

(*c*) Interval bisection for finding a zero of a function

(*d*) Secant updating methods for minimizing a function of n variables

(*e*) Steepest descent method for minimizing a function of n variables

6.18. (*a*) For minimizing a real-valued function f of n variables, what is the initial search direction in the conjugate gradient method?

(*b*) Under what condition will the BFGS method for minimization use this same initial search direction?

6.19. For minimizing a quadratic function of n variables, what is the maximum number of iterations required to converge to the exact solution (assuming exact arithmetic) from an arbitrary starting point for each of the following algorithms?

(*a*) Conjugate gradient method

(*b*) Newton's method

(*c*) BFGS secant updating method with exact line search

6.20. (*a*) What is meant by a *critical point* of a smooth nonlinear function $f: \mathbb{R}^n \to \mathbb{R}$?

(*b*) Is a critical point always a minimum or maximum of the function?

(*c*) How can you test a given critical point to determine which type it is?

6.21. Let $f: \mathbb{R}^2 \to \mathbb{R}$ be a real-valued function of two variables. What is the geometrical interpretation of the gradient vector

$$\nabla f(\boldsymbol{x}) = \begin{bmatrix} \partial f(\boldsymbol{x})/\partial x_1 \\ \partial f(\boldsymbol{x})/\partial x_2 \end{bmatrix}?$$

Specifically, explain the meaning of the direction and magnitude of $\nabla f(\boldsymbol{x})$.

6.22. (*a*) If $f: \mathbb{R}^n \to \mathbb{R}$, what do we call the Jacobian matrix of the gradient $\nabla f(\boldsymbol{x})$?

(*b*) What special property does this matrix have, assuming f is twice continuously differentiable?

(*c*) What additional special property does this matrix have near a local minimum of f?

6.23. The steepest descent method for minimizing a function of several variables is usually slow but reliable. However, it can sometimes fail, and it can also sometimes converge rapidly. Under what conditions would each of these two types of behavior occur?

6.24. Consider Newton's method for minimizing a function of n variables:

(*a*) When might the use of a line search parameter be beneficial?

(*b*) When might the use of a line search parameter *not* be beneficial?

6.25. Many iterative methods for solving multidimensional nonlinear problems replace the given nonlinear problem by a sequence of linear problems, each of which can be solved by some matrix factorization. For each method listed, what is the most appropriate matrix factorization for solving the linear subproblems? (Assume that we start close enough to a solution to avoid any potential difficulties.)

(*a*) Newton's method for solving a system of nonlinear equations

(*b*) Newton's method for minimizing a function of several variables

(*c*) Gauss-Newton method for solving a nonlinear least squares problem

6.26. Let $\boldsymbol{f}: \mathbb{R}^n \to \mathbb{R}^n$ be a nonlinear function. Since $\|\boldsymbol{f}(\boldsymbol{x})\| = 0$ if, and only if, $\boldsymbol{f}(\boldsymbol{x}) = \boldsymbol{0}$, does this relation mean that searching for a minimum of $\|\boldsymbol{f}(\boldsymbol{x})\|$ is equivalent to solving the nonlinear system $\boldsymbol{f}(\boldsymbol{x}) = \boldsymbol{0}$? Why?

6.27. (*a*) Why is a line search parameter *always* used in the steepest descent method for minimizing a general function of several variables?

(*b*) Why might one use a line search parameter in Newton's method for minimizing a function of several variables?

(*c*) Asymptotically, as the solution is approached, what should be the value of this line search parameter for Newton's method?

6.28. What is a good way to test a symmetric matrix to determine whether it is positive definite?

6.29. Suppose we want to minimize a function $f: \mathbb{R}^n \to \mathbb{R}$ using a secant updating method. Why would one *not* just apply Broyden's method for finding a zero of the gradient of f?

6.30. To what method does the first iteration of the BFGS method for minimization reduce if the initial approximate Hessian is

(*a*) The identity matrix $\boldsymbol{I}$?

(*b*) The exact Hessian at the starting point?

6.31. In secant updating methods for solving systems of nonlinear equations or minimizing a function of several variables, why is it preferable to update a factorization of the approximate Jacobian or Hessian matrix rather than update the matrix itself?

6.32. For solving a very large unconstrained optimization problem whose objective function has a sparse Hessian matrix, which type of method would be better, a secant updating method such as BFGS or the conjugate gradient method? Why?

6.33. How does the conjugate gradient method for minimizing an unconstrained nonlinear function differ from a truncated Newton method for the same problem, assuming the conjugate gradient method is used in the latter as the iterative solver for the Newton linear system?

6.34. For what type of nonlinear least squares problem, if any, would you expect the Gauss-Newton method to converge quadratically?

6.35. For what type of nonlinear least squares problem may the Gauss-Newton method converge very slowly or not at all? Why?

6.36. For what two general classes of least squares problems is the Gauss-Newton approximation to the Hessian exact at the solution?

6.37. The Levenberg-Marquardt method adds an extra term to the Gauss-Newton approximation to the Hessian. Give a geometric or algebraic interpretation of this additional term.

6.38. What are Lagrange multipliers, and what is their relevance to constrained optimization problems?

6.39. Consider the optimization problem $\min f(\boldsymbol{x})$ subject to $\boldsymbol{g}(\boldsymbol{x}) = \boldsymbol{0}$, where $f: \mathbb{R}^n \to \mathbb{R}$ and $\boldsymbol{g}: \mathbb{R}^n \to \mathbb{R}^m$.

(*a*) What is the Lagrangian function for this problem?

(*b*) What is a necessary condition for optimality for this problem?

6.40. Explain the difference between range space methods and null space methods for solving constrained optimization problems.

6.41. What is meant by an *active set strategy* for inequality-constrained optimization problems?

6.42. (*a*) Is it possible, in general, to solve linear programming problems by an algorithm whose computational complexity is polynomial in the size of the problem data?

(*b*) Does the simplex method have this property?

Exercises

6.1. Determine whether each of the following functions is coercive on $\mathbb{R}^2$.

(*a*) $f(x, y) = x + y + 2$.

(*b*) $f(x, y) = x^2 + y^2 + 2$.

(*c*) $f(x, y) = x^2 - 2xy + y^2$.

(*d*) $f(x, y) = x^4 - 2xy + y^4$.

6.2. Determine whether each of the following functions is convex, strictly convex, or nonconvex on $\mathbb{R}$.

(*a*) $f(x) = x^2$.

(*b*) $f(x) = x^3$.

(*c*) $f(x) = e^{-x}$.

(*d*) $f(x) = |x|$.

6.3. For each of the following functions, what do the first- and second-order optimality conditions say about whether 0 is a minimum on $\mathbb{R}$?

(*a*) $f(x) = x^2$.

(*b*) $f(x) = x^3$.

(*c*) $f(x) = x^4$.

(*d*) $f(x) = -x^4$.

6.4. Determine the critical points of each of the following functions and characterize each as a minimum, maximum, or inflection point. Also determine whether each function has a global minimum or maximum on $\mathbb{R}$.

(*a*) $f(x) = x^3 + 6x^2 - 15x + 2$.

(*b*) $f(x) = 2x^3 - 25x^2 - 12x + 15$.

(*c*) $f(x) = 3x^3 + 7x^2 - 15x - 3$.

(*d*) $f(x) = x^2 e^x$.

6.5. Determine the critical points of each of the following functions and characterize each as a minimum, maximum, or saddle point. Also determine whether each function has a global minimum or maximum on $\mathbb{R}^2$.

(*a*) $f(x, y) = x^2 - 4xy + y^2$.

(*b*) $f(x, y) = x^4 - 4xy + y^4$.

(*c*) $f(x, y) = 2x^3 - 3x^2 - 6xy(x - y - 1)$.

(*d*) $f(x, y) = (x - y)^4 + x^2 - y^2 - 2x + 2y + 1$.

6.6. Determine the critical points of the Lagrangian function for each of the following problems and determine whether each is a constrained minimum, a constrained maximum, or neither.

(*a*)

$$f(x, y) = x^2 + y^2$$

subject to

$$g(x, y) = x + y - 1 = 0.$$

(*b*)

$$f(x, y) = x^3 + y^3$$

subject to

$$g(x, y) = x + y - 1 = 0.$$

(*c*)

$$f(x, y) = 2x + y$$

subject to

$$g(x, y) = x^2 + y^2 - 1 = 0.$$

(*d*)

$$f(x, y) = x^2 + y^2$$

subject to

$$g(x, y) = xy^2 - 1 = 0.$$

6.7. Use the first- and second-order optimality conditions to show that $\boldsymbol{x}^* = [2.5 \quad -1.5 \quad -1]^T$ is a constrained local minimum for the function

$$f(\boldsymbol{x}) = x_1^2 - 2x_1 + x_2^2 - x_3^2 + 4x_3$$

subject to

$$g(\boldsymbol{x}) = x_1 - x_2 + 2x_3 - 2 = 0.$$

6.8. Consider the function $f\colon \mathbb{R}^2 \to \mathbb{R}$ defined by

$$f(\boldsymbol{x}) = \tfrac{1}{2}\,(x_1^2 - x_2)^2 + \tfrac{1}{2}\,(1 - x_1)^2.$$

(*a*) At what point does f attain a minimum?

(*b*) Perform one iteration of Newton's method for minimizing f using as starting point $\boldsymbol{x}_0 = [2 \quad 2]^T$.

(*c*) In what sense is this a good step?

(*d*) In what sense is this a bad step?

6.9. Let $f\colon \mathbb{R}^n \to \mathbb{R}$ be given by

$$f(\boldsymbol{x}) = \tfrac{1}{2}\,\boldsymbol{x}^T \boldsymbol{A}\boldsymbol{x} - \boldsymbol{x}^T\boldsymbol{b} + c,$$

where $\boldsymbol{A}$ is an $n \times n$ symmetric positive definite matrix, $\boldsymbol{b}$ is an n-vector, and c is a scalar.

(*a*) Show that Newton's method for minimizing this function converges in one iteration from any starting point $\boldsymbol{x}_0$.

(*b*) If the steepest descent method is used on this problem, what happens if the starting value $\boldsymbol{x}_0$ is such that $\boldsymbol{x}_0 - \boldsymbol{x}^*$ is an eigenvector of $\boldsymbol{A}$, where $\boldsymbol{x}^*$ is the solution?

6.10. (*a*) Prove that if a continuous function $f\colon \mathbb{R}^n \to \mathbb{R}$ is coercive on $\mathbb{R}^n$ (see Section 6.2), then f has a global minimum on $\mathbb{R}^n$. (*Hint*: In the definition of coercive, let $M = f(\boldsymbol{0})$ and consider the resulting closed and bounded set $\{\boldsymbol{x} \in \mathbb{R}^n : \|\boldsymbol{x}\| \leq r\}$.)

(*b*) Adapt your proof to obtain the same result for any closed, unbounded set $S \subseteq \mathbb{R}^n$.

6.11. Prove that if a continuous function $f\colon S \subseteq \mathbb{R}^n \to \mathbb{R}$ has a nonempty sublevel set that is closed and bounded, then f has a global minimum on S.

6.12. (*a*) Prove that any local minimum of a convex function f on a convex set $S \subseteq \mathbb{R}^n$ is a global minimum of f on S. (*Hint*: If a local minimum $\boldsymbol{x}$ is not a global minimum, then let $\boldsymbol{y}$ be a point in S such that $f(\boldsymbol{y}) < f(\boldsymbol{x})$ and consider the line segment between $\boldsymbol{x}$ and $\boldsymbol{y}$ to obtain a contradiction.)

(*b*) Prove that any local minimum of a strictly convex function f on a convex set $S \subseteq \mathbb{R}^n$ is the unique global minimum of f on S. (*Hint*: Assume there are two distinct minima $\boldsymbol{x}, \boldsymbol{y} \in S$ and consider the line segment between $\boldsymbol{x}$ and $\boldsymbol{y}$ to obtain a contradiction.)

6.13. A function $f\colon \mathbb{R}^n \to \mathbb{R}$ is said to be *quasiconvex* on a convex set $S \subseteq \mathbb{R}^n$ if for any $\boldsymbol{x}, \boldsymbol{y} \in S$,

$$f(\alpha\boldsymbol{x} + (1-\alpha)\boldsymbol{y}) \leq \max\{f(\boldsymbol{x}), f(\boldsymbol{y})\}$$

for all $\alpha \in (0, 1)$, and f is *strictly quasiconvex* if strict inequality holds when $\boldsymbol{x} \neq \boldsymbol{y}$. If $f\colon \mathbb{R} \to \mathbb{R}$ has a minimum on an interval $[a, b]$, show that f is unimodal on $[a, b]$ if, and only if, f is strictly quasiconvex on $[a, b]$.

6.14. Prove that the block 2×2 Hessian matrix of the Lagrangian function for equality-constrained optimization (see Section 6.2.3) cannot be positive definite.

6.15. Consider the problem

$$\min_{x,y} f(x, y) = x^2 + y^2$$

subject to

$$g(x, y) = x + y - 1 = 0.$$

Show that if the penalty method given in Section 6.7.2 is applied to this problem, then $\boldsymbol{x}_\rho^* \to \boldsymbol{x}^*$ as $\rho \to \infty$.

6.16. Consider the problem

$$\min_{x,y} f(x, y) = x^2 + y^2$$

subject to

$$g(x, y) = y^2 - (x-1)^3 = 0.$$

(*a*) First try to solve this problem using the method of Lagrange multipliers. Explain why this method fails for this problem.

(b) Next try the penalty method given in Section 6.7.2 to solve this problem, i.e., solve

$$\min_{x,y} f(x,y) + \tfrac{1}{2}\,\rho\, g(x,y)^2.$$

Derive an expression for the solution to the latter problem as a function of ρ and then take the limit as $\rho \to \infty$.

6.17. Consider the linear programming problem

$$\min_{\boldsymbol{x}} f(\boldsymbol{x}) = -3x_1 - 2x_2$$

subject to

$$5x_1 + x_2 \le 6, \quad 3x_1 + 4x_2 \le 6,$$

$$4x_1 + 3x_2 \le 6, \quad x_1 \ge 0, \quad x_2 \ge 0.$$

(a) How many vertices does the feasible region have?

(b) Since the solution must occur at a vertex, solve the problem by evaluating the objective function at each vertex and choosing the one that gives the lowest value.

(c) Obtain a graphical solution to the problem by drawing the feasible region and contours of the objective function, as in Fig. 6.11.

6.18. How can the linear programming problem given in Example 6.17 be stated in the standard form given at the beginning of Section 6.7.3? (*Hint*: Additional variables may be needed.)

Computer Problems

6.1. (a) The function

$$f(x) = x^2 - 2x + 2$$

has a minimum at $x^* = 1$. On your computer, for what range of values of x near x^* is $f(x) = f(x^*)$? Can you explain this phenomenon? What are the implications regarding the accuracy with which a minimum can be computed?

(b) Repeat the preceding exercise, this time using the function

$$f(x) = 0.5 - xe^{-x^2},$$

which has a minimum at $x^* = \sqrt{2}/2$.

6.2. Consider the function f defined by

$$f(x) = \begin{cases} 0.5 & \text{if } x = 0 \\ (1 - \cos(x))/x^2 & \text{if } x \ne 0 \end{cases}.$$

(a) Use l'Hôpital's rule to show that f is continuous at $x = 0$.

(b) Use differentiation to show that f has a local maximum at $x = 0$.

(c) Use a library routine, or one of your own design, to find a maximum of f on the interval $[-2\pi, 2\pi]$, on which $-f$ is unimodal. Experiment with the error tolerance to determine how accurately the routine can approximate the known solution at $x = 0$.

(d) If you have difficulty in obtaining a highly accurate result, try to explain why. (*Hint*: Make a plot of f in the vicinity of $x = 0$, say on the interval $[-0.001, 0.001]$ with a spacing of 0.00001 between points.)

(e) Can you devise an alternative formulation of f such that the maximum can be determined more accurately? (*Hint*: Consider a double angle formula.)

6.3. Use a library routine, or one of your own design, to find a minimum of each of the following functions on the interval $[0, 3]$. Draw a plot of each function to confirm that it is unimodal.

(a) $f(x) = x^4 - 14x^3 + 60x^2 - 70x$.

(b) $f(x) = 0.5x^2 - \sin(x)$.

(c) $f(x) = x^2 + 4\cos(x)$.

(d) $f(x) = \Gamma(x)$. (The *gamma function*, defined by

$$\Gamma(x) = \int_0^\infty t^{x-1} e^{-t}\, dt, \quad x > 0,$$

is a built-in function on many computer systems.)

6.4. Try using a library routine for one-dimensional optimization on a function that is *not* unimodal and see what happens. Does it find the global minimum on the given interval, merely a local minimum, or neither? Experiment with various functions and different intervals to determine the range of behavior that is possible.

6.5. If a water hose with initial water velocity v is aimed at angle α with respect to the ground to hit a target of height h, then the horizontal distance x from nozzle to target satisfies the quadratic equation

$$(g/(2v^2\cos^2\alpha))x^2 - (\tan\alpha)x + h = 0,$$

where $g = 9.8065$ m/s^2 is the acceleration due to gravity. How do you interpret the two roots of this quadratic equation? Assuming that $v = 20$ m/s and $h = 13.5$ m, use a one-dimensional optimization routine to find the maximum distance x at which the target can still be hit, and the angle α for which the maximum occurs.

6.6. Write a general-purpose line search routine. Your routine should take as input a vector defining the starting point, a second vector defining the search direction, the name of a routine defining the objective function, and a convergence tolerance. For the resulting one-dimensional optimization problem, you may call a library routine or one of your own design. In any case, you will need to determine a bracket for the minimum along the search direction using some heuristic procedure. Test your routine for a variety of objective functions and search directions. This routine will be useful in some of the other computer exercises in this section.

6.7. Consider the function $f\colon \mathbb{R}^2 \to \mathbb{R}$ defined by

$$f(x, y) = 2x^3 - 3x^2 - 6xy(x - y - 1).$$

(*a*) Determine all of the critical points of f analytically (i.e., without using a computer).

(*b*) Classify each critical point found in part *a* as a minimum, a maximum, or a saddle point, again working analytically.

(*c*) Verify your analysis graphically by creating a contour plot or three-dimensional surface plot of f over the region $-2 \le x \le 2$, $-2 \le y \le 2$.

(*d*) Use a library routine for minimization to find the minima of both f and $-f$. Experiment with various starting points to see how well the routine gets around other types of critical points to find minima and maxima. You may find it instructive to plot the sequence of iterates generated by the routine.

6.8. Consider the function $f\colon \mathbb{R}^2 \to \mathbb{R}$ defined by

$$f(x, y) = 2x^2 - 1.05x^4 + x^6/6 + xy + y^2.$$

Using any method or routine you like, how many critical points can you find for this function? Classify each critical point you find as a local minimum, a local maximum, or a saddle point. What is the global minimum of this function?

6.9. Write a program to find a minimum of Rosenbrock's function,

$$f(x, y) = 100(y - x^2)^2 + (1 - x)^2$$

using each of the following methods:

(*a*) Steepest descent

(*b*) Newton

(*c*) Damped Newton (Newton's method with a line search)

You should try each of the methods from each of the three starting points $[-1 \quad 1]^T$, $[0 \quad 1]^T$, and $[2 \quad 1]^T$. For any line searches and linear system solutions required, you may use either library routines or routines of your own design. Plot the path taken in the plane by the approximate solutions for each method from each starting point.

6.10. Let $\boldsymbol{A}$ be an $n \times n$ real symmetric matrix with eigenvalues $\lambda_1 \le \cdots \le \lambda_n$. It can be shown that the critical points of the Rayleigh quotient (see Section 4.5.3) are eigenvectors of $\boldsymbol{A}$, and in particular

$$\lambda_1 = \min_{\boldsymbol{x} \ne \boldsymbol{0}} \frac{\boldsymbol{x}^T \boldsymbol{A} \boldsymbol{x}}{\boldsymbol{x}^T \boldsymbol{x}}$$

and

$$\lambda_n = \max_{\boldsymbol{x} \ne \boldsymbol{0}} \frac{\boldsymbol{x}^T \boldsymbol{A} \boldsymbol{x}}{\boldsymbol{x}^T \boldsymbol{x}},$$

with the minimum and maximum occurring at the corresponding eigenvectors. Thus, we can in principle compute the extreme eigenvalues and corresponding eigenvectors of $\boldsymbol{A}$ using any suitable method for optimization.

(*a*) Use an unconstrained optimization routine to compute the extreme eigenvalues and corresponding eigenvectors of the matrix

$$\boldsymbol{A} = \begin{bmatrix} 6 & 2 & 1 \\ 2 & 3 & 1 \\ 1 & 1 & 1 \end{bmatrix}.$$

Is the solution unique in each case? Why?

(*b*) The foregoing characterization of λ_1 and λ_n remains valid if we restrict the vector $\boldsymbol{x}$ to be normalized by taking $\boldsymbol{x}^T\boldsymbol{x} = 1$. Repeat part *a*, but use a constrained optimization routine to impose this normalization constraint. What is the significance of the Lagrange multiplier in this context?

6.11. Write a program implementing the BFGS method of Section 6.5.5 for unconstrained minimization. For the purpose of this exercise, you may refactor the resulting matrix $\boldsymbol{B}$ at each iteration, whereas in a real implementation you would update either $\boldsymbol{B}^{-1}$ or a factorization of $\boldsymbol{B}$ to reduce the amount of work per iteration. You may use an initial value of $\boldsymbol{B}_0 = \boldsymbol{I}$, but you might also wish to include an option to compute a finite difference approximation to the Hessian of the objective function to use as the initial $\boldsymbol{B}_0$. You may wish to include a line search to enhance the robustness of your program. Test your program on some of the other computer problems in this chapter, and compare its robustness and convergence rate with those of Newton's method and the method of steepest descent.

6.12. Write a program implementing the conjugate gradient method of Section 6.5.6 for unconstrained minimization. You will need a line search routine to determine the parameter α_k at each iteration. Try both the Fletcher-Reeves and Polak-Ribiere formulas for computing β_{k+1} to see how much difference this makes. Test your program on both quadratic and nonquadratic objective functions. For a reasonable error tolerance, does your program terminate in at most n steps for a quadratic function of n variables?

6.13. Using a library routine or one of your own design, find least squares solutions to the following overdetermined systems of nonlinear equations:

(*a*)

$$\begin{aligned} x_1^2 + x_2^2 &= 2, \\ (x_1 - 2)^2 + x_2^2 &= 2, \\ (x_1 - 1)^2 + x_2^2 &= 9. \end{aligned}$$

(*b*)

$$\begin{aligned} x_1^2 + x_2^2 + x_1x_2 &= 0, \\ \sin^2(x_1) &= 0, \\ \cos^2(x_2) &= 0. \end{aligned}$$

6.14. The concentration of a drug in the bloodstream is expected to diminish exponentially with time. We will fit the model function

$$y = f(t, \boldsymbol{x}) = x_1 e^{x_2 t}$$

to the following data:

t	0.5	1.0	1.5	2.0
y	6.80	3.00	1.50	0.75
t	2.5	3.0	3.5	4.0
y	0.48	0.25	0.20	0.15

(*a*) Perform the exponential fit using nonlinear least squares. You may use a library routine or one of your own design, perhaps using the Gauss-Newton method.

(*b*) Taking the logarithm of the model function gives $\log(x_1) + x_2 t$, which is now linear in x_2. Thus, an exponential fit can also be done using linear least squares, assuming that we also take logarithms of the data points y_i. Use linear least squares to compute x_1 and x_2 in this manner. Do the values obtained agree with those determined in part *a*? Why?

6.15. A bacterial population P grows according to the geometric progression

$$P_k = rP_{k-1},$$

where r is the growth rate. The following population counts (in billions) are observed:

k	1	2	3	4
P_k	0.19	0.36	0.69	1.3
k	5	6	7	8
P_k	2.5	4.7	8.5	14

(*a*) Perform a nonlinear least squares fit of the growth function to these data to estimate the initial population P_0 and the growth rate r.

(*b*) By using logarithms, a fit to these data can also be done by linear least squares (see previous exercise). Perform such a linear least squares fit to obtain estimates for P_0 and r, and compare your results with those for the nonlinear fit.

6.16. The *Michaelis-Menten equation* describes the chemical kinetics of enzyme reactions. According to this equation, if v_0 is the initial velocity, V is the maximum velocity, K_m is the Michaelis constant, and S is the substrate concentration, then

$$v_0 = \frac{V}{1 + K_m/S}.$$

In a typical experiment, v_0 is measured as S is varied, and then V and K_m are to be determined from the resulting data.

(*a*) Given the measured data,

S	2.5	5.0	10.0
v_0	0.024	0.036	0.053
S	15.0	20.0	
v_0	0.060	0.064	

determine V and K_m by performing a nonlinear least squares fit of v_0 as a function of S. You may use a library routine or one of your own design, perhaps using the Gauss-Newton method.

(*b*) To avoid a nonlinear fit, a number of researchers have rearranged the Michaelis-Menten equation so that a linear least squares fit will suffice. For example, Lineweaver and Burk used the rearrangement

$$\frac{1}{v_o} = \frac{1}{V} + \frac{K_m}{V} \cdot \frac{1}{S}$$

and performed a linear fit of $1/v_o$ as a function of $1/S$ to determine $1/V$ and K_m/V, from which the values of V and K_m can then be derived. Similarly, Dixon used the rearrangement

$$\frac{S}{v_0} = \frac{K_m}{V} + \frac{1}{V} \cdot S$$

and performed a linear fit of S/v_0 as a function of S to determine K_m/V and $1/V$, from which the values of V and K_m can then be derived. Finally, Eadie and Hofstee used the rearrangement

$$v_0 = V - K_m \cdot \frac{v_0}{S}$$

and performed a linear fit of v_0 as a function of v_0/S to determine V and K_m.

Verify the algebraic validity of each of these rearrangements. Perform the indicated linear least squares fit in each case, using the same data as in part *a*, and determine the resulting values for V and K_m. Compare the results with those obtained in part *a*. Why do they differ? For which of these linear fits are the resulting parameter values closest to those determined by the true nonlinear fit for these data?

6.17. We wish to fit the model function

$$f(t, \boldsymbol{x}) = x_1 + x_2 t + x_3 t^2 + x_4 e^{x_5 t}$$

to the following data:

t	0.00	0.25	0.50
y	20.00	51.58	68.73
t	0.75	1.00	1.25
y	75.46	74.36	67.09
t	1.50	1.75	2.00
y	54.73	37.98	17.28

We must determine the values for the five parameters x_i that best fit the data in the least squares sense. The model function is linear in the first four parameters, but it is a nonlinear function of the fifth parameter, x_5. We will solve this problem in five different ways:

(*a*) Use a general multidimensional unconstrained minimization routine with $\phi(\boldsymbol{x}) = \frac{1}{2}\boldsymbol{r}^T(\boldsymbol{x})\boldsymbol{r}(\boldsymbol{x})$ as objective function, where $\boldsymbol{r}$ is the residual function defined by $r_i(x) = y_i - f(t_i, \boldsymbol{x})$. This method will determine all five parameters (i.e., the five components of $\boldsymbol{x}$) simultaneously.

(*b*) Use a multidimensional nonlinear equation solver to solve the system of nonlinear equations $\nabla\phi(\boldsymbol{x}) = \boldsymbol{0}$.

(*c*) Given a value for x_5, the best values for the remaining four parameters can be determined by linear least squares. Thus, we can view the problem as a one-dimensional nonlinear minimization problem with an objective function whose input is x_5 and whose output is the residual sum of squares of the resulting linear least squares problem. Use a one-dimensional minimization routine to solve the problem in this manner. (*Hint*: Your routine for computing the objective function will in turn call a linear least squares routine.)

(*d*) Solve the problem in the same manner as *c*, except use a one-dimensional nonlinear equation solver to find a zero of the derivative of the objective function in part *c*.

(*e*) Use the Gauss-Newton method for nonlinear least squares to solve the problem. You will need to call a linear least squares routine to solve the linear least squares subproblem at each iteration.

In each of the five methods, you may compute any derivatives required either analytically or by finite differences. You may need to do some experimentation to find a suitable starting value for which each method converges. Of course, after you have solved the problem once, you will know the correct answer, but try to use "fair" starting guesses for the remaining methods. You may need to use global variables in MATLAB or C, or common blocks in Fortran, to pass information to subroutines in some cases.

6.18. An empirical model of a chemical processing plant yields the following constrained optimization problem:

$$\max_{\boldsymbol{x}} f(\boldsymbol{x}) = 5\,x_1 x_2 x_4 - 4\,x_1 x_2^{1.4} - 0.75\,x_3^{0.6}$$

subject to

$$x_1 x_4 - 8.4\,x_2 x_3 (1 - x_4)^2 = 0,$$

$$x_1 \geq 0,\ x_2 \geq 0,\ x_3 \geq 0, \text{ and } 0 \leq x_4 \leq 1,$$

where the variables are defined as follows:

x_1	feed rate in liters/hr
x_2	concentration of reactant in g mole/liter
x_3	volume of reactor in liters
x_4	fraction of reactant converted into product
f	profit in \$/hr

The equality constraint comes from a material balance. Solve this problem using a library routine or one of your own design, based on any method of your choice.

6.19. According to *Fermat's Principle of Least Time*, a light ray takes the path that requires the least time in going from one point to another. Many laws of geometrical optics, such as the laws of reflection and refraction, can be derived from this principle. Refraction is the "bending" of a light ray when it passes between two media in which the velocity of light differs, such as air and glass.

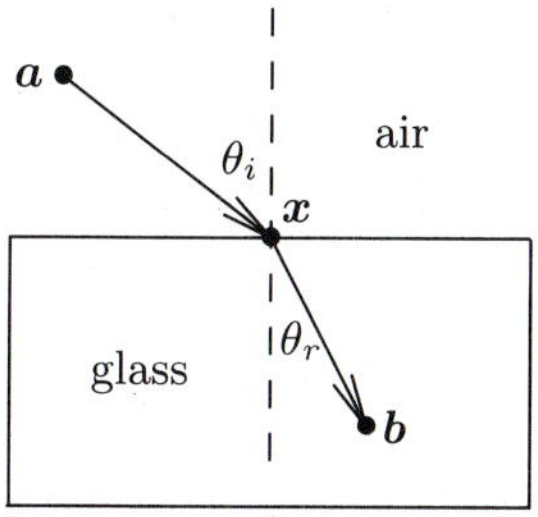

The ratio of velocities is called the *refractive index*; for air and glass, $v_a/v_g = 1.5$.

(*a*) For given points $\boldsymbol{a}$ in the air and $\boldsymbol{b}$ in the glass, and taking the surface of the glass to be the line $x_2 = 0$, formulate an optimization problem whose solution is the point (x_1, x_2) on the surface of the glass at which a light ray enters the glass in going from $\boldsymbol{a}$ to $\boldsymbol{b}$.

(*b*) For $\boldsymbol{a} = (-1, 1)$ and $\boldsymbol{b} = (1, -1)$, solve the optimization problem in part *a* to determine $\boldsymbol{x}$.

(*c*) Check the consistency of your results from part *b* with *Snell's Law of Refraction*, which says that

$$\frac{\sin(\theta_i)}{\sin(\theta_r)} = \frac{v_a}{v_g},$$

where the angle of incidence θ_i and angle of refraction θ_r are measured with respect to the normal to the surface at $\boldsymbol{x}$ (the dashed line in the drawing).

(*d*) How do your results for parts *b* and *c* change if instead of glass the ray strikes water, for which the refractive index is $v_a/v_w = 1.33$?

6.20. (*a*) A lifeguard sees a swimmer in distress, with the two positioned as shown in the drawing. If the lifeguard runs at a speed of 5 m/s and swims at 1 m/s, what is the optimal path for the lifeguard to reach the swimmer in the shortest time? Formulate an optimization problem whose solution is the point along the shoreline at which the lifeguard should enter the water. Using the optimal path, how long will it take the lifeguard to reach the swimmer?

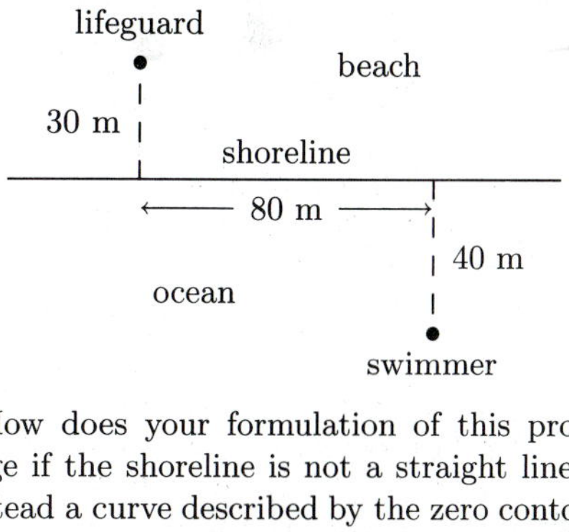

(*b*) How does your formulation of this problem change if the shoreline is not a straight line, but is instead a curve described by the zero contour of some function g? Try solving the modified problem with some simple curve, such as a portion of an ellipse, representing the shoreline.

6.21. Use a library routine for linear programming to solve the following problem:

$$\max_{\boldsymbol{x}} f(\boldsymbol{x}) = 2x_1 + 4x_2 + x_3 + x_4$$

subject to

$$\begin{aligned} x_1 + 3x_2 + x_4 &\le 4 \\ 2x_1 + x_2 &\le 3 \\ x_2 + 4x_3 + x_4 &\le 3 \end{aligned}$$

and

$$x_i \ge 0, \quad i = 1, 2, 3, 4.$$

6.22. Use the method of Lagrange multipliers to solve each of the following constrained optimization problems. To solve the resulting system of nonlinear equations, you may use a library routine or one of your own design. Once you find a critical point of the Lagrangian function, check it for optimality using the second-order optimality condition and by sampling the objective at nearby feasible points. You may also wish to compare your results with those of a library routine designed for constrained optimization.

(*a*) Quadratic objective function and linear constraints:

$$\begin{aligned} \min_{\boldsymbol{x}} f(\boldsymbol{x}) &= (4x_1 - x_2)^2 + (x_2 + x_3 - 2)^2 \\ &\quad + (x_4 - 1)^2 + (x_5 - 1)^2 \end{aligned}$$

subject to

$$\begin{aligned} x_1 + 3x_2 &= 0, \\ x_3 + x_4 - 2x_5 &= 0, \\ x_2 - x_5 &= 0. \end{aligned}$$

(*b*) Quadratic objective function and nonlinear constraints:

$$\begin{aligned} \min_{\boldsymbol{x}} f(\boldsymbol{x}) &= 4x_1^2 + 2x_2^2 + 2x_3^2 \\ &\quad - 33x_1 + 16x_2 - 24x_3 \end{aligned}$$

subject to

$$\begin{aligned} 3x_1 - 2x_2^2 &= 7, \\ 4x_1 - x_3^2 &= 11. \end{aligned}$$

(*c*) Nonquadratic objective function and nonlinear constraints:

$$\begin{aligned} \min_{\boldsymbol{x}} f(\boldsymbol{x}) &= (x_1 - 1)^2 + (x_1 - x_2)^2 \\ &\quad + (x_2 - x_3)^2 + (x_3 - x_4)^4 \\ &\quad + (x_4 - x_5)^4 \end{aligned}$$

subject to

$$\begin{aligned} x_1 + x_2^2 + x_3^3 &= 3\sqrt{2} + 2, \\ x_2 - x_3^2 + x_4 &= 2\sqrt{2} - 2, \\ x_1 x_5 &= 2. \end{aligned}$$

Chapter 7

Interpolation

7.1 Interpolation

Consider the following set of data:

t	1.0	2.0	3.0	4.0	5.0	6.0
y	1.9	2.7	4.8	5.3	7.1	9.4

Such data might be the results of a sequence of laboratory measurements, where t might represent time or temperature and y might represent distance or pressure. Or the data might represent measurements of some natural phenomenon, such as the population of an endangered species or a supernova light curve over time. Or the data might represent stock prices at various times or sales figures over successive periods. Or the data might represent values of some mathematical function for various arguments.

There are many different things we might want to do with such data. We might want to draw a smooth curve through the data points when plotting them on a graph. We might want to infer data values between the points, or predict values beyond the range of the available data. If the data represent some physical phenomenon, such as population, we might want to determine some important parameters, such as the birth and death rates. If the data represent some underlying function, we might want to approximate its derivative or integral, or evaluate the function quickly for a given argument.

In this chapter we will learn how to represent such discrete data in terms of relatively simple functions that are then easily manipulated. We have already seen one way to do this in Example 3.2, namely, fitting a function to the data by least squares approximation. We will adopt a similar approach here, but we will insist that the function not just capture the general trend of the data, but actually pass through the data points, i.e., the function must match the given data values exactly. Such a function is called an *interpolant.* Interpolation simply means fitting some function to given data so that the function has the same values as the given data. We have already seen several instances of interpolation in various numerical methods, such as the secant method for nonlinear equations, where we fit a straight line to two function values, and successive parabolic interpolation for minimization, where we fit a quadratic function to three function values. We will now make a more general and systematic study of interpolation.

In general, the simplest interpolation problem in one dimension is of the following form: for given data

$$(t_i, y_i), \quad i = 1, \dots, m,$$

with $t_1 < t_2 < \cdots < t_m$, we seek a function $f: \mathbb{R} \to \mathbb{R}$ such that

$$f(t_i) = y_i, \quad i = 1, \dots, m.$$

We call f an *interpolating function*, or simply an *interpolant*, for the given data. It is often desirable for $f(t)$ to have "reasonable" values for t between the data points, but such a requirement may be difficult to quantify. In more complicated interpolation problems, additional data might be prescribed, such as the slope of the interpolant at given points, or additional constraints might be imposed on the interpolant, such as monotonicity, convexity, or the degree of smoothness required. One could also consider higher-dimensional interpolation in which f is a function of more than one variable, but we will not do so in this book.

We have already mentioned several purposes for interpolation, which include

- Plotting a smooth curve through discrete data points
- Reading between the lines of a table
- Differentiating or integrating tabular data
- Evaluating a mathematical function quickly and easily
- Replacing a complicated function by a simple one

Traditionally, one of the most common uses for interpolation was in computing approximate values of mathematical functions, such as square roots and trigonometric functions, for arguments between those appearing in published tables. The advent of computers and powerful calculators that can compute such functions rapidly for any argument has virtually eliminated this application for interpolation, yet interpolation remains one of the cornerstones of numerical analysis. The reason for its continuing central role is that interpolation is much more than just a technique for manipulating data. The alternate representation of discrete data as a function rather than a table of values (and vice versa) is a key concept in bridging the gap between finite- and infinite-dimensional problems. Two of the main issues in numerical computation are (1) accurately approximating infinite-dimensional problems by finite-dimensional problems, and (2) developing methods for solving the resulting finite-dimensional problems accurately and efficiently. Thus far in this book we have focused on the second of these issues; this chapter marks our transition to the first, which will occupy us for most of the remainder of the book.

To give a very simple example, suppose we fit a linear function $y = x_1 + x_2 t$ to two data points (t_1, y_1), (t_2, y_2), which are sample values of some function, whether evaluated analytically or measured empirically. If we regard t_1 and t_2 as fixed, then each of these representations has two "parameters": y_1 and y_2 for the original data, and the intercept x_1 and slope x_2 for the linear fit. Thus, either representation is a two-dimensional object that can be interpreted as a point in $\mathbb{R}^2$. In many ways, however, the linear function is much more useful: we can evaluate it anywhere in the interval $[t_1, t_2]$ or even outside that interval. Moreover, the slope of the linear fit provides a direct approximation of the derivative of the underlying function. Of course, all of this information is implicit in the original two data points, but not in such a convenient explicit form. To generalize on this example, an arbitrary continuous function can be represented (approximately) using a finite number of parameters either by a table of its values at a finite, discrete set of points or by a function that depends on a finite number of parameters. For many purposes, the latter type of representation is more immediately useful, and one way to obtain such a representation is by interpolation (we will see others later).

Although interpolation is a powerful tool, fitting the data exactly is not always appropriate. For example, if the data points are subject to experimental errors or other sources of significant error, it is usually preferable to smooth out the noise by a technique such as least squares approximation (see Chapter 3). Another context in which approximation is generally more appropriate than interpolation is in the design of library routines for computing special functions, such as those usually supplied by the math libraries for most programming languages. In this case, it is important that the approximating function be close to the exact underlying mathematical function for arguments throughout some domain, but it is not essential that the function values match exactly at any particular points. An appropriate type of approximation in this case is to minimize the maximum deviation between the given function and the approximating function over some interval. This approach is variously known as uniform, Chebyshev, or minimax approximation. A general study of approximation theory and algorithms is beyond the scope of this book, however, and we will confine our attention to interpolation.

It is important to realize that there is some arbitrariness in most interpolation problems, since there are arbitrarily many functions that interpolate any given set of data points. Simply requiring that some mathematical function fit the data points leaves open such questions as:

- What form should the function have? There may be relevant mathematical or physical considerations that suggest a particular form of interpolant.
- How should the function behave between data points?
- Should the function inherit properties of the data, such as monotonicity, convexity, or periodicity?
- Are we interested primarily in the values of the parameters that define the interpolating function, or simply in evaluating the function at various points for plotting or other purposes?
- If the function and data are plotted, should the results be visually pleasing?

The choice of interpolating function depends on the answers to these questions as well as the data to be fit. The selection of a function for interpolation is usually based on:

- How easy the interpolant is to work with (determining the parameters of the interpolant from the data, evaluating the interpolant at a given point, differentiating or integrating the interpolant, etc.)
- How well the properties of the interpolant match the properties of the data to be fit (smoothness, monotonicity, convexity, periodicity, etc.)

Some families of functions commonly used for interpolation include:

- Polynomials
- Piecewise polynomials
- Trigonometric functions
- Exponential functions
- Rational functions

In this chapter we will focus on interpolation by polynomials and piecewise polynomials. We will consider trigonometric interpolation in Chapter 12. We have already seen an example of interpolation by a rational function, namely, linear fractional interpolation, in Section 5.5.6. The use of more general rational functions, as in *Padé approximation*, is an important topic, but it is beyond the scope of this book.

7.2 Existence, Uniqueness, and Conditioning

The question of existence and uniqueness of an interpolant comes down to matching the number of parameters in the interpolant to the number of data points to be fit: if there are too few parameters, then the interpolant does not exist; if there are too many parameters, then the interpolant is not unique. We now make these notions more precise.

For a given set of data points (t_i, y_i), $i = 1, \ldots, m$, an interpolant is chosen from the space of functions spanned by a suitable set of *basis functions* $\phi_1(t), \ldots, \phi_n(t)$. The interpolating function f is therefore expressed as a linear combination of these basis functions,

$$f(t) = \sum_{j=1}^{n} x_j \phi_j(t),$$

where the parameters x_j are to be determined. Requiring that f interpolate the data (t_i, y_i) means that

$$f(t_i) = \sum_{j=1}^{n} x_j \phi_j(t_i) = y_i, \quad i = 1, \ldots, m,$$

which is a system of linear equations that we can write in matrix form as

$$\boldsymbol{A}\boldsymbol{x} = \boldsymbol{y},$$

where the entries of the $m \times n$ *basis matrix* $\boldsymbol{A}$ are given by $a_{ij} = \phi_j(t_i)$ (i.e., a_{ij} is the value of the jth basis function evaluated at the ith data point), the components of the right-hand-side m-vector $\boldsymbol{y}$ are the known data values y_i, and the components of the n-vector $\boldsymbol{x}$ to be determined are the unknown parameters x_j.

If we choose the number of basis functions n to be equal to the number of data points m, then we obtain a square linear system, and hence the data points can be fit exactly, provided the basis matrix $\boldsymbol{A}$ is nonsingular. In other contexts, these two values would not necessarily be the same. In least squares approximation, for example, the number of basis functions, and thus the number of parameters to be determined, is deliberately chosen to be smaller than the number of data points (i.e., the system is overdetermined in that there are more equations than unknowns), so that the data usually cannot be fit exactly. In some circumstances, on the other hand, it is beneficial if the linear system is underdetermined, so that the resulting nonuniqueness of the interpolant will allow the freedom necessary to satisfy additional properties that might be desired, such as monotonicity, convexity, or a specified degree of smoothness.

In summary, the existence and uniqueness of the interpolant to a given set of data points depend on the nonsingularity of the basis matrix $\boldsymbol{A}$. Moreover, the sensitivity of the parameters $\boldsymbol{x}$ to perturbations in the data depends on the conditioning of $\boldsymbol{A}$. For a given family of functions, there may be many different choices of basis functions. The particular choice of basis functions affects the conditioning of the linear system $\boldsymbol{Ax} = \boldsymbol{y}$, the amount of work required to solve it, and the ease with which the resulting interpolant can be evaluated or otherwise manipulated. We will comment further on the issues of existence, uniqueness, and sensitivity for interpolation problems in the context of specific types of interpolating functions.

7.3 Polynomial Interpolation

The simplest and most common type of interpolation uses polynomials. For a given integer $k \geq 0$, we denote by $\mathbb{P}_k$ the set of all polynomials of degree at most k, defined on a given interval. With addition and scalar multiplication defined in the obvious way, $\mathbb{P}_k$ forms a vector space of dimension $k + 1$. As we will see, the choice of basis functions for this vector space has a dramatic effect on the cost of computing and manipulating the interpolant, as well as the sensitivity of the parameters that define it.

7.3.1 Monomial Basis

To interpolate n data points, we choose $k = n - 1$ so that the dimension of the space will match the number of data points. The most natural basis for $\mathbb{P}_{n-1}$, the vector space of polynomials of degree at most $n - 1$, is composed of the first n *monomials*,

$$\phi_j(t) = t^{j-1}, \quad j = 1, \ldots, n,$$

for which a given polynomial $p_{n-1} \in \mathbb{P}_{n-1}$ has the form

$$p_{n-1}(t) = x_1 + x_2 t + \cdots + x_n t^{n-1}.$$

In the monomial basis, the vector $\boldsymbol{x}$ of coefficients of the polynomial interpolating the data points (t_i, y_i), $i = 1, \ldots, n$, is given by the $n \times n$ linear system

$$\boldsymbol{Ax} = \begin{bmatrix} 1 & t_1 & \cdots & t_1^{n-1} \\ 1 & t_2 & \cdots & t_2^{n-1} \\ \vdots & \vdots & \ddots & \vdots \\ 1 & t_n & \cdots & t_n^{n-1} \end{bmatrix} \begin{bmatrix} x_1 \\ x_2 \\ \vdots \\ x_n \end{bmatrix} = \begin{bmatrix} y_1 \\ y_2 \\ \vdots \\ y_n \end{bmatrix} = \boldsymbol{y}.$$

A matrix of this form, whose columns are successive powers of some independent variable t, is called a *Vandermonde matrix*. Suppose that the t_i, $i = 1, \ldots n$, are all distinct and that $\boldsymbol{A}$ is the corresponding Vandermonde matrix. Now if $\boldsymbol{Az} = \boldsymbol{0}$ for some $\boldsymbol{z} \in \mathbb{R}^n$, then the polynomial whose coefficients are given by $\boldsymbol{z}$, which is of degree at most $n-1$, has n zeros and therefore must be the zero polynomial, i.e., $\boldsymbol{z} = \boldsymbol{0}$. We conclude that a Vandermonde matrix is necessarily nonsingular provided the t_i are all distinct, and hence the polynomial interpolant exists.

Example 7.1 Monomial Basis. To illustrate polynomial interpolation using the monomial basis, we will determine the polynomial of degree two interpolating the three data points $(-2, -27)$, $(0, -1)$, $(1, 0)$. In general, there is a unique polynomial

$$p_2(t) = x_1 + x_2 t + x_3 t^2$$

of degree two interpolating three points (t_1, y_1), (t_2, y_2), (t_3, y_3). With the monomial basis, the coefficients of the polynomial are given by the system of linear equations

$$\boldsymbol{Ax} = \begin{bmatrix} 1 & t_1 & t_1^2 \\ 1 & t_2 & t_2^2 \\ 1 & t_3 & t_3^2 \end{bmatrix} \begin{bmatrix} x_1 \\ x_2 \\ x_3 \end{bmatrix} = \begin{bmatrix} y_1 \\ y_2 \\ y_3 \end{bmatrix} = \boldsymbol{y}.$$

For this particular set of data, this system becomes

$$\begin{bmatrix} 1 & -2 & 4 \\ 1 & 0 & 0 \\ 1 & 1 & 1 \end{bmatrix} \begin{bmatrix} x_1 \\ x_2 \\ x_3 \end{bmatrix} = \begin{bmatrix} -27 \\ -1 \\ 0 \end{bmatrix}.$$

Solving this system by Gaussian elimination yields the solution $\boldsymbol{x} = \begin{bmatrix} -1 & 5 & -4 \end{bmatrix}^T$, so that the interpolating polynomial is

$$p_2(t) = -1 + 5t - 4t^2.$$

Polynomial interpolation and polynomial evaluation are inverses of each other in the following sense: if $\boldsymbol{A}$ is a Vandermonde matrix as just defined, then computing the matrix-vector product $\boldsymbol{Ax}$ evaluates at n points the polynomial whose coefficients are given by the components of $\boldsymbol{x}$, whereas computing the matrix-vector product $\boldsymbol{A}^{-1}\boldsymbol{y}$ (by solving the linear system $\boldsymbol{Ax} = \boldsymbol{y}$) determines the coefficients of the polynomial whose values at n points are given by the components of $\boldsymbol{y}$.

Solving the system $\boldsymbol{Ax} = \boldsymbol{y}$ using a standard linear equation solver to determine the coefficients of the interpolating polynomial requires $\mathcal{O}(n^3)$ work. [Solvers for Vandermonde systems with $\mathcal{O}(n^2)$ complexity are possible, but they are based on other polynomial representations that we will see shortly.] Moreover, when using the monomial basis, the resulting Vandermonde matrix $\boldsymbol{A}$ is often ill-conditioned, especially for high-degree polynomials. The reason for this is illustrated in Fig. 7.1, in which the first several monomials are plotted on the interval $[0, 1]$ (any other interval would show the same relative effect). These functions are progressively less distinguishable as the degree increases, which makes the columns of the Vandermonde matrix nearly linearly dependent. For most choices of data points t_i, the condition number of the Vandermonde matrix grows at least exponentially with the number of data points n. Thus, although the Vandermonde matrix is necessarily nonsingular in theory, it becomes arbitrarily ill-conditioned as n grows, and hence the resulting polynomial coefficients become highly sensitive; for sufficiently large n, the Vandermonde matrix becomes singular to within the working precision.

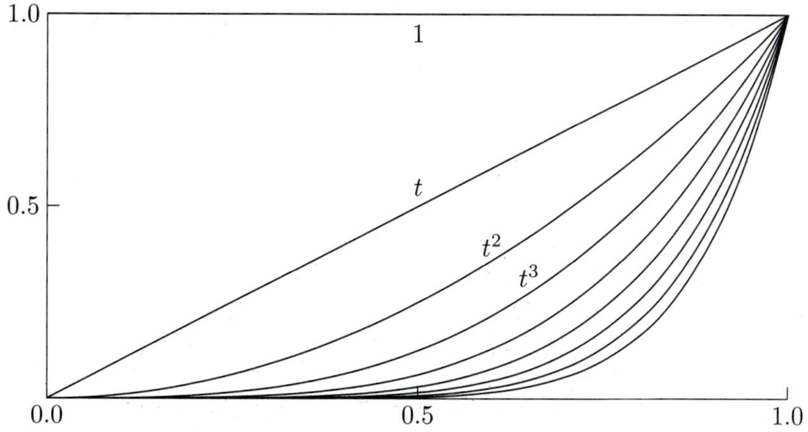

Figure 7.1: Monomial basis functions.

This ill-conditioning does not prevent the computed polynomial from fitting the data points well, since Gaussian elimination with partial pivoting will produce a small residual for the solution to the linear system in any case, but it does mean that the values of the coefficients will be poorly determined. Both the conditioning of the linear system and the amount of computational work required to solve it can be improved by using a different basis. A change of basis still gives the same unique interpolating polynomial for a given data set (simple proof: if there were two interpolating polynomials, then their difference would be a polynomial of degree at most $n-1$ having n zeros, which must therefore be the zero polynomial.) What does change is the *representation* of that polynomial in a different basis.

The conditioning of the monomial basis can be improved somewhat by shifting and scaling the independent variable t so that

$$\phi_j(t) = \left(\frac{t-c}{d}\right)^{j-1},$$

where, for example, $c = (t_1 + t_n)/2$ is the midpoint and $d = (t_n - t_1)/2$ is half the range of the data, so that the new independent variable lies in the interval $[-1, 1]$. Such a transformation also helps avoid overflow or harmful underflow in computing the entries of the basis matrix or evaluating the resulting polynomial. Even with optimal shifting and scaling, however, the monomial basis is usually still poorly conditioned, and we must seek superior alternatives.

In addition to the cost of determining the interpolating function, the cost of evaluating it at a given point is an important factor in choosing an interpolation method. When represented in the monomial basis, a polynomial

$$p_{n-1}(t) = x_1 + x_2 t + \cdots + x_n t^{n-1}$$

can be evaluated very efficiently using *Horner's method*, also known as *nested evaluation* or *synthetic division*:

$$p_{n-1}(t) = x_1 + t(x_2 + t(x_3 + t(\cdots (x_{n-1} + x_n t) \cdots))),$$

which requires only n additions and n multiplications. For example,

$$1 - 4t + 5t^2 - 2t^3 + 3t^4 = 1 + t(-4 + t(5 + t(-2 + 3t))).$$

The same principle applies in forming a Vandermonde matrix:

$$a_{i,j} = \phi_j(t_i) = t_i^{j-1} = t_i\, \phi_{j-1}(t_i) = t_i\, a_{i,j-1}, \quad j = 2, \ldots, n,$$

which is superior to using explicit exponentiation. Other manipulations of the interpolating polynomial, such as differentiation or integration, are also relatively easy with the monomial basis representation.

7.3.2 Lagrange Interpolation

For a given set of data points (t_i, y_i), $i = 1, \ldots, n$, the *Lagrange* basis functions for $\mathbb{P}_{n-1}$, also called *fundamental polynomials* or *cardinal functions*, are given by

$$\ell_j(t) = \frac{\prod_{k=1,\, k\neq j}^{n} (t - t_k)}{\prod_{k=1,\, k\neq j}^{n} (t_j - t_k)}, \quad j = 1, \ldots, n.$$

From the definition, we see that $\ell_j(t)$ is a polynomial of degree $n - 1$ and

$$\ell_j(t_i) = \begin{cases} 1 & \text{if } i = j \\ 0 & \text{if } i \neq j \end{cases}, \quad i, j = 1, \ldots, n,$$

which means that for this basis the matrix of the linear system $\boldsymbol{Ax} = \boldsymbol{y}$ is the identity matrix $\boldsymbol{I}$. Thus, using the Lagrange basis, the polynomial interpolating the data points (t_i, y_i) is given by

$$p_{n-1}(t) = y_1 \ell_1(t) + y_2 \ell_2(t) + \cdots + y_n \ell_n(t).$$

Fig. 7.2 shows the Lagrange basis functions for five equally spaced points on the interval $[0, 1]$. Compare this graph with the corresponding graph for the monomial basis functions in Fig. 7.1. Using the Lagrange basis makes it easy to determine the interpolating polynomial for a given set of data points, and the resulting parameters are perfectly conditioned. But the Lagrange form of the polynomial is more expensive to evaluate for a given argument compared with the monomial basis representation, and it is also more difficult to differentiate, integrate, etc.

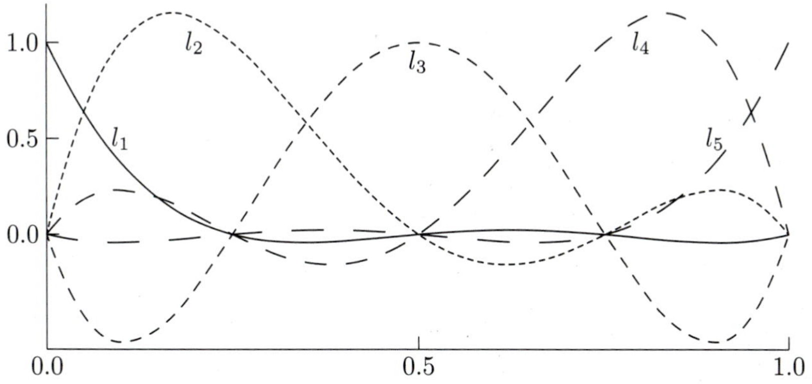

Figure 7.2: Lagrange basis functions.

Example 7.2 Lagrange Interpolation. To illustrate Lagrange interpolation, we use it to determine the interpolating polynomial for the three data points from Example 7.1. The Lagrange form for the polynomial of degree two interpolating three points (t_1, y_1), (t_2, y_2), (t_3, y_3) is

$$p_2(t) = y_1 \frac{(t-t_2)(t-t_3)}{(t_1-t_2)(t_1-t_3)} + y_2 \frac{(t-t_1)(t-t_3)}{(t_2-t_1)(t_2-t_3)} + y_3 \frac{(t-t_1)(t-t_2)}{(t_3-t_1)(t_3-t_2)}.$$

For the data from Example 7.1, this formula becomes

$$\begin{aligned} p_2(t) &= -27\frac{(t-0)(t-1)}{(-2-0)(-2-1)} + (-1)\frac{(t-(-2))(t-1)}{(0-(-2))(0-1)} + 0\frac{(t-(-2))(t-0)}{(1-(-2))(1-0)} \\ &= -27\frac{t(t-1)}{6} + \frac{(t+2)(t-1)}{2}. \end{aligned}$$

Depending on the use to be made of it, the polynomial can be evaluated in this form for any t, or it can be simplified to produce the same result we obtained in Example 7.1 using the monomial basis (as expected, since the interpolating polynomial is unique).

7.3.3 Newton Interpolation

We have thus far seen two methods for polynomial interpolation, one for which the basis matrix $\boldsymbol{A}$ is full (Vandermonde) and the other for which it is diagonal (Lagrange). As a result, these two methods have very different tradeoffs between the cost of computing the interpolant and the cost of evaluating it for a given argument. We will now consider *Newton interpolation*, for which the basis matrix is between these two extremes.

For a given set of data points (t_i, y_i), $i = 1, \ldots, n$, the *Newton* basis functions for $\mathbb{P}_{n-1}$ are given by

$$\pi_j(t) = \prod_{k=1}^{j-1}(t - t_k), \quad j = 1, \ldots, n,$$

where we take the value of the product to be 1 when the limits make it vacuous. In the Newton basis, a given polynomial has the form

$$\begin{aligned} p_{n-1}(t) \quad &= \quad x_1 + x_2(t - t_1) + x_3(t - t_1)(t - t_2) + \cdots \\ &\quad + x_n(t - t_1)(t - t_2)\cdots(t - t_{n-1}). \end{aligned}$$

From the definition, we see that $\pi_j(t_i) = 0$ for $i < j$, so that the basis matrix $\boldsymbol{A}$, with $a_{ij} = \pi_j(t_i)$, is lower triangular. Hence, the solution $\boldsymbol{x}$ to the system $\boldsymbol{A}\boldsymbol{x} = \boldsymbol{y}$, which determines the coefficients of the basis functions in the interpolant, can be computed by forward-substitution (see Section 2.4.2) in $\mathcal{O}(n^2)$ arithmetic operations. In practice, the triangular matrix need not be formed explicitly, since its entries can be computed as needed during the forward-substitution process. Fig. 7.3 shows the Newton basis functions for five equally spaced points on the interval $[0, 2]$. Compare this graph with the corresponding graphs for the monomial and Lagrange basis functions given earlier.

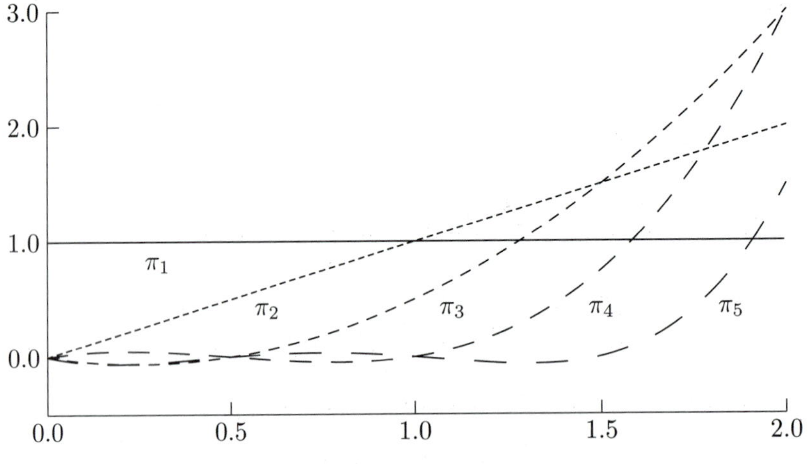

Figure 7.3: Newton basis functions.

Example 7.3 Newton Interpolation. To illustrate Newton interpolation, we use it to determine the interpolating polynomial for the three data points from

Example 7.1. With the Newton basis, we have the lower triangular linear system

$$\begin{bmatrix} 1 & 0 & 0 \\ 1 & t_2 - t_1 & 0 \\ 1 & t_3 - t_1 & (t_3 - t_1)(t_3 - t_2) \end{bmatrix} \begin{bmatrix} x_1 \\ x_2 \\ x_3 \end{bmatrix} = \begin{bmatrix} y_1 \\ y_2 \\ y_3 \end{bmatrix}.$$

For the data from Example 7.1, this system becomes

$$\begin{bmatrix} 1 & 0 & 0 \\ 1 & 2 & 0 \\ 1 & 3 & 3 \end{bmatrix} \begin{bmatrix} x_1 \\ x_2 \\ x_3 \end{bmatrix} = \begin{bmatrix} -27 \\ -1 \\ 0 \end{bmatrix},$$

whose solution, obtained by forward-substitution, is $\boldsymbol{x} = \begin{bmatrix} -27 & 13 & -4 \end{bmatrix}^T$. Thus, the interpolating polynomial is

$$p(t) = -27 + 13(t+2) - 4(t+2)t,$$

which reduces to the same polynomial we obtained earlier by either of the other two methods.

Once the coefficients x_j have been determined, the resulting Newton polynomial interpolant can be evaluated efficiently for any argument using Horner's nested evaluation scheme:

$$p_{n-1}(t) = x_1 + (t - t_1)(x_2 + (t - t_2)(x_3 + (t - t_3)(\cdots(x_{n-1} + x_n(t - t_{n-1}))\cdots))).$$

Thus, Newton interpolation has a better balance between the cost of computing the interpolant and the cost of evaluating it for a given argument than the previous two methods.

The Newton basis functions can be derived by considering the problem of building a polynomial interpolant *incrementally* as successive new data points are added. If $p_j(t)$ is a polynomial of degree $j-1$ interpolating j given points, then for any constant x_{j+1}

$$p_{j+1}(t) = p_j(t) + x_{j+1}\,\pi_{j+1}(t)$$

is a polynomial of degree j that also interpolates the same j points. The free parameter x_{j+1} can then be chosen so that $p_{j+1}(t)$ interpolates the $(j+1)$st point, y_{j+1}. Specifically,

$$x_{j+1} = \frac{y_{j+1} - p_j(t_{j+1})}{\pi_{j+1}(t_{j+1})}.$$

In this manner, Newton interpolation begins with the constant polynomial $p_1(t) = y_1$ interpolating the first data point and builds successively from there to incorporate the remaining data points into the interpolant.

Example 7.4 Incremental Newton Interpolation. We illustrate by building the Newton interpolant for the previous example incrementally as new data points are added. We begin with the first data point, $(t_1, y_1) = (-2, -27)$, which is interpolated by the constant polynomial

$$p_1(t) = y_1 = -27.$$

Incorporating the second data point, $(t_2, y_2) = (0, -1)$, we modify the previous polynomial so that it interpolates the new data point as well:

$$\begin{aligned} p_2(t) &= p_1(t) + x_2\,\pi_2(t) = p_1(t) + \frac{y_2 - p_1(t_2)}{\pi_2(t_2)}\,\pi_2(t) \\ &= p_1(t) + \frac{y_2 - y_1}{t_2 - t_1}(t - t_1) = -27 + 13(t+2). \end{aligned}$$

Finally, we incorporate the third data point, $(t_3, y_3) = (1, 0)$, modifying the previous polynomial so that it interpolates the new data point as well:

$$\begin{aligned} p_3(t) &= p_2(t) + x_3\,\pi_3(t) = p_2(t) + \frac{y_3 - p_2(t_3)}{\pi_3(t_3)}\,\pi_3(t) \\ &= p_2(t) + \frac{y_3 - p_2(t_3)}{(t_3 - t_1)(t_3 - t_2)}(t - t_1)(t - t_2) \\ &= -27 + 13(t+2) - 4(t+2)t. \end{aligned}$$

Given a set of data points (t_i, y_i), $i = 1, \ldots, n$, an alternative method for computing the coefficients x_j of the Newton polynomial interpolant is via quantities known as *divided differences*, which are usually denoted by $f[\;]$ and are defined recursively by the formula

$$f[t_1, t_2, \ldots, t_k] = \frac{f[t_2, t_3, \ldots, t_k] - f[t_1, t_2, \ldots, t_{k-1}]}{t_k - t_1},$$

where the recursion begins with $f[t_k] = y_k$, $k = 1, \ldots, n$. It turns out that the coefficient of the jth basis function in the Newton interpolant is given by $x_j = f[t_1, t_2, \ldots, t_j]$. Like forward-substitution, use of this recursion requires only $\mathcal{O}(n^2)$ arithmetic operations to compute the coefficients of the Newton interpolant, but it is less prone to overflow or underflow than is direct formation of the entries of the triangular Newton basis matrix.

Example 7.5 Divided Differences. We illustrate divided differences by using this approach to determine the Newton interpolant for the same data points as in the previous examples.

$$\begin{aligned} f[t_1] &= y_1 = -27, \quad f[t_2] = y_2 = -1, \quad f[t_3] = y_3 = 0, \\ f[t_1, t_2] &= \frac{f[t_2] - f[t_1]}{t_2 - t_1} = \frac{-1 - (-27)}{0 - (-2)} = 13, \\ f[t_2, t_3] &= \frac{f[t_3] - f[t_2]}{t_3 - t_2} = \frac{0 - (-1)}{1 - 0} = 1, \\ f[t_1, t_2, t_3] &= \frac{f[t_2, t_3] - f[t_1, t_2]}{t_3 - t_1} = \frac{1 - 13}{1 - (-2)} = -4. \end{aligned}$$

Thus, the Newton polynomial is given by

$$\begin{aligned} p(t) &= f[t_1]\,\pi_1(t) + f[t_1,t_2]\,\pi_2(t) + f[t_1,t_2,t_3]\,\pi_3(t) \\ &= f[t_1] + f[t_1,t_2](t-t_1) + f[t_1,t_2,t_3](t-t_1)(t-t_2) \\ &= -27 + 13(t+2) - 4(t+2)t. \end{aligned}$$

Note that the validity of Newton interpolation does not depend on any particular ordering of the points $t_1, \ldots, t_n$: in principle any ordering gives the same polynomial. However, the conditioning of the triangular basis matrix $\boldsymbol{A}$ does depend on the ordering of the points. Thus, the sensitivity of the coefficients to perturbations in the data depends on the particular ordering chosen, and the "left-to-right" ordering is not necessarily the best. For example, it is often better to take the points in order of their distances from their mean or their distances from a specific point at which the resulting interpolant will be evaluated.

7.3.4 Orthogonal Polynomials

Orthogonal polynomials are yet another useful type of basis for $\mathbb{P}_{n-1}$. The inner product $\langle p, q\rangle$ of two polynomials p and q on an interval $[a,b]$ is defined by

$$\langle p, q\rangle = \int_a^b p(t)\,q(t)\,w(t)\,dt,$$

where $w(t)$ is a nonnegative *weight function*, and p and q are said to be *orthogonal* if $\langle p, q\rangle = 0$. A set of polynomials $\{p_i\}$ is said to be *orthonormal* if

$$\langle p_i, p_j\rangle = \begin{cases} 1 & \text{for } i = j \\ 0 & \text{for } i \neq j \end{cases}.$$

Given a set of polynomials, the Gram-Schmidt orthogonalization process (see Section 3.5.3) can be used to generate an orthonormal set spanning the same space. For example, with the inner product given by the weight function $w(t) \equiv 1$ on the interval $[-1,1]$, if we apply the Gram-Schmidt process to the set of monomials, 1, t, t^2, t^3, ..., and scale the results so that $P_k(1) = 1$ for each k, we obtain the *Legendre polynomials*

$$1,\ t,\ (3t^2-1)/2,\ (5t^3-3t)/2,\ (35t^4-30t^2+3)/8,\ (63t^5-70t^3+15t)/8,\ \ldots,$$

the first n of which form an orthogonal basis for $\mathbb{P}_{n-1}$, the space of polynomials of degree at most $n-1$. The first few Legendre polynomials are plotted in Fig. 7.4. Other choices of interval and weight function similarly yield other well-known sets of orthogonal polynomials, some of which are listed in Table 7.1.

Orthogonal polynomials have many useful properties and are the subject of an elegant theory, which we cannot discuss in detail here. One of their most important properties is that they satisfy a *three-term recurrence* of the form

$$p_{k+1}(t) = (\alpha_k\, t + \beta_k)\, p_k(t) - \gamma_k\, p_{k-1}(t),$$

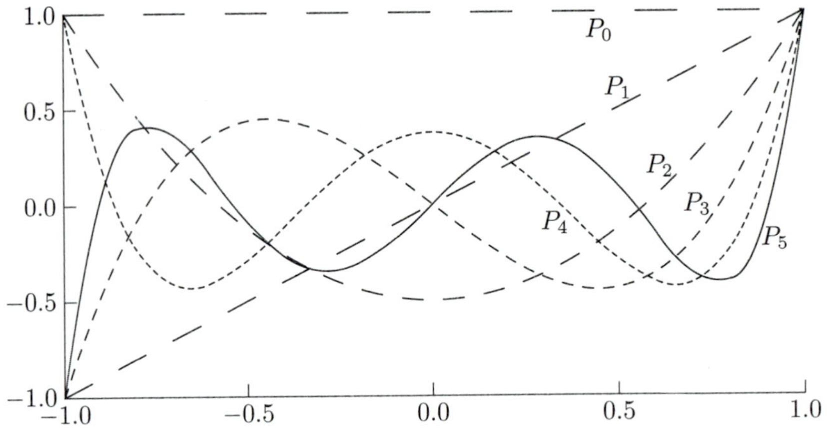

Figure 7.4: First six Legendre polynomials.

Name	Symbol	Interval	Weight function
Legendre	P_k	$[-1, 1]$	1
Chebyshev, 1st kind	T_k	$[-1, 1]$	$(1-t^2)^{-1/2}$
Chebyshev, 2nd kind	U_k	$[-1, 1]$	$(1-t^2)^{1/2}$
Jacobi	J_k	$[-1, 1]$	$(1-t)^{\alpha}(1+t)^{\beta}, \quad \alpha, \beta > -1$
Laguerre	L_k	$[0, \infty)$	e^{-t}
Hermite	H_k	$(-\infty, \infty)$	e^{-t^2}

Table 7.1: Commonly occurring families of orthogonal polynomials

which makes them very efficient to generate and evaluate. The Legendre polynomials, for example, satisfy the recurrence

$$(k+1)\, P_{k+1}(t) = (2k+1)\, t\, P_k(t) - k\, P_{k-1}(t).$$

Orthogonality makes such polynomials very convenient for least squares approximation of a given function by a polynomial of any desired degree, since the matrix of the resulting system of normal equations is diagonal. Orthogonal polynomials are also useful in generating Gaussian quadrature rules, a topic considered in Section 8.3.3.

In the next section we will consider interpolation of continuous functions, a topic for which the Chebyshev polynomials play an important role. The kth Chebyshev polynomial of the first kind is defined on the interval $[-1, 1]$ by

$$T_k(t) = \cos(k \arccos(t)).$$

From this definition it is not obvious that T_k is a polynomial. Using appropriate trigonometric identities, we could show this by deriving its coefficients explicitly, but a simpler approach is to observe that $T_0(t) = 1$ and $T_1(t) = t$, and from the multiple angle formula for cosines we have the three-term recurrence

$$T_{k+1}(t) = 2\,t\,T_k(t) - T_{k-1}(t).$$

The first few Chebyshev polynomials, which are plotted in Fig. 7.5, are given by

$$1, \quad t, \quad 2t^2 - 1, \quad 4t^3 - 3t, \quad 8t^4 - 8t^2 + 1, \quad 16t^5 - 20t^3 + 5t, \quad \ldots.$$

Observe that T_k is a polynomial of degree k, contains only terms of even degree if k is even and only terms of odd degree if k is odd, its coefficients alternate in sign, and its term of highest degree has a coefficient of 2^{k-1}. Perhaps the most important property of the Chebyshev polynomials, however, is the *equi-alternation* or *equi-oscillation* property, which is evident from the definition and from Fig. 7.5: successive extrema of T_k are equal in magnitude and alternate in sign. This property tends to distribute the error uniformly when these polynomials are used for approximating an arbitrary continuous function.

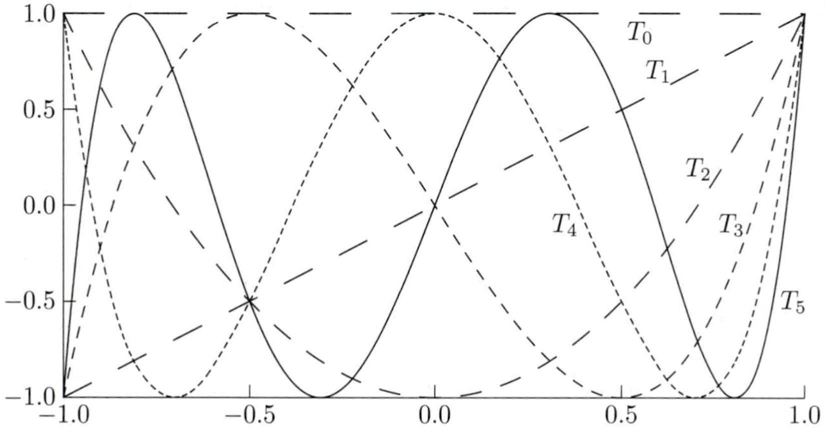

Figure 7.5: First six Chebyshev polynomials.

The *equi-alternation* property also has useful implications for polynomial interpolation of a continuous function in that the maximum error over the interval is minimized (within a small constant factor) when the interpolation points are chosen to be the roots or the extrema of a Chebyshev polynomial of appropriate degree. From the trigonometric definition of T_k, it is easy to see that its k zeros are given by

$$t_i = \cos\left(\frac{(2i-1)\pi}{2k}\right), \quad i = 1, \ldots, k,$$

and its $k+1$ extrema (including the endpoints) are given by

$$t_i = \cos\left(\frac{i\pi}{k}\right), \quad i = 0, 1, \ldots, k.$$

The $k-1$ interior extrema are in fact the zeros of U_{k-1}, the Chebyshev polynomial of the second kind of degree $k-1$. Either of these sets of points is known as the

Chebyshev points, and we will see that they play an important role in interpolation, numerical integration, and numerical solution of differential equations. The Chebyshev points are the abscissas of points in the plane that are equally spaced around the unit circle but have abscissas bunched near the ends of the interval $[-1, 1]$, as illustrated in Fig. 7.6.

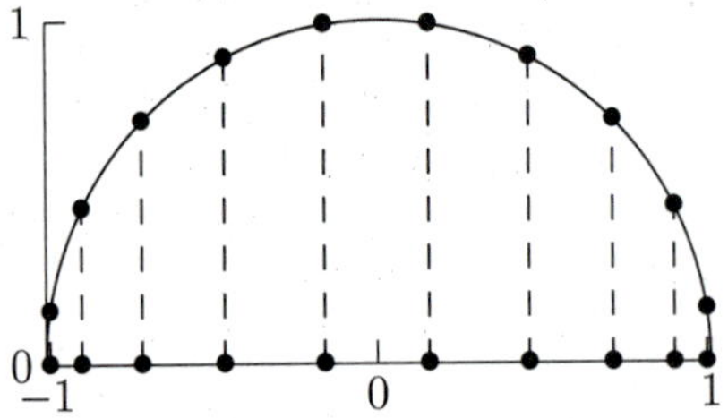

Figure 7.6: Chebyshev points for interpolation.

7.3.5 Interpolating Continuous Functions

Thus far we have considered interpolation of discrete data without worrying about the behavior of the interpolant between the data points. If the data points represent a discrete sample of an underlying continuous function, then we may wish to know how closely the interpolant approximates the given function between the sample points. For polynomial interpolation, an answer to this question is given by the following result. If f is a sufficiently smooth function and p_{n-1} is the polynomial of degree at most $n-1$ that interpolates f at n points $t_1, \ldots, t_n$, then for each $t \in [t_1, t_n]$ there is a $\theta \in (t_1, t_n)$ such that

$$f(t) - p_{n-1}(t) = \frac{f^{(n)}(\theta)}{n!}(t - t_1)(t - t_2)\cdots(t - t_n).$$

Unfortunately, the point θ is unknown, so this result is not particularly useful unless we have a bound on the appropriate derivative of f. If such a bound is known, say $|f^{(n)}(t)| \le M$ for all $t \in [t_1, t_n]$, and $h = \max\{t_{i+1} - t_i : i = 1, \ldots, n-1\}$, then the previous result leads to a somewhat coarse but easily applied bound

$$\max_{t \in [t_1, t_n]} |f(t) - p_{n-1}(t)| \le \frac{Mh^n}{4n}.$$

This result shows that the error diminishes as n increases (and hence h decreases), as one would expect, but only if $|f^{(n)}(t)|$ does not grow too rapidly with n. We will next see that such bad behavior can indeed occur.

We have already seen that, depending on the basis chosen, a polynomial interpolant of high degree can be expensive to determine or to evaluate, and its coefficients can be poorly determined. In addition to these undesirable computational properties, the use of a polynomial interpolant of high degree can have undesirable theoretical consequences as well. Because its derivative has $n-1$ zeros, a polynomial of degree n has $n-1$ extrema or inflection points. Thus, simply put, a high-degree polynomial necessarily has many "wiggles," which may bear no relation to the data to be fit. Although a polynomial interpolant passes through the required data points, it may oscillate wildly between data points and thus be useless for many of the purposes for which interpolation is done in the first place.

One manifestation of this feature is potential lack of uniform convergence of polynomial interpolants to an underlying continuous function as the number of equally spaced points (and hence the polynomial degree) increases. This phenomenon is illustrated by Runge's function $f(t) = 1/(1 + 25t^2)$, shown graphically in Fig. 7.7, where we see that polynomial interpolants of increasing degree converge to the function in the middle of the interval, but diverge near the endpoints.

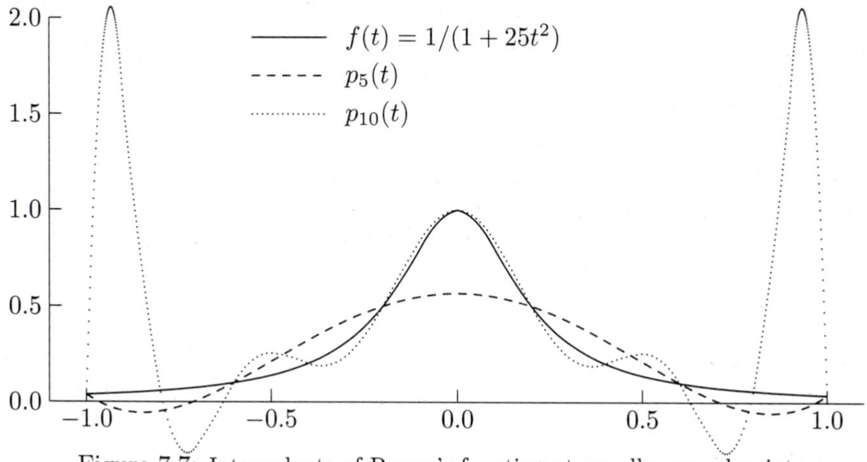

Figure 7.7: Interpolants of Runge's function at equally spaced points.

We have just seen that equally spaced interpolation points may give unsatisfactory results, especially near the ends of the interval. More satisfactory results are likely to be obtained with polynomial interpolation if the points are bunched near the ends of the interval instead of being equally spaced. One way to accomplish this is to use the *Chebyshev points*, which were defined in Section 7.3.4 on the interval $[-1, 1]$, and can be suitably transformed to an arbitrary interval. Use of the Chebyshev points for polynomial interpolation distributes the error more evenly and yields convergence throughout the interval for any sufficiently smooth underlying function, as illustrated for Runge's function in Fig. 7.8. Of course, one may have no choice in placing the interpolation points, either because of existing measured data or because a particular distribution (such as equally spaced) is required for other reasons. But when one does have the freedom to choose interpolation points, which is often the case in numerical integration or in solving differential equations, the Chebyshev points are an excellent choice.

Before leaving this topic, we note that another useful form of polynomial interpolation for an underlying smooth function f is the *Taylor polynomial* given by the truncated Taylor series

$$p_n(t) = f(a) + f'(a)(t - a) + \frac{f''(a)}{2}(t - a)^2 + \cdots + \frac{f^{(n)}(a)}{n!}(t - a)^n,$$

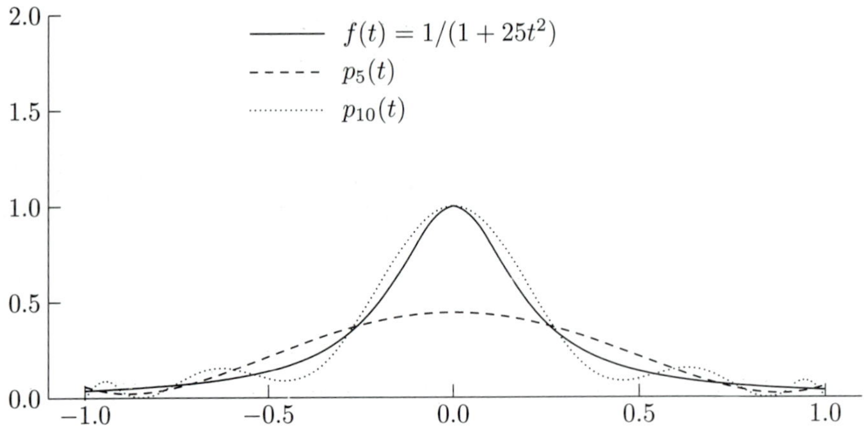

Figure 7.8: Interpolants of Runge's function at Chebyshev points.

which interpolates f in the sense that the values of p_n and its first n derivatives match those of f and its first n derivatives evaluated at $t = a$, so that $p_n(t)$ is a good approximation to $f(t)$ for t near a. We have seen the usefulness of this type of polynomial interpolant in Newton's method for root finding (where we used a linear polynomial) and for minimization (where we used a quadratic polynomial).

7.4 Piecewise Polynomial Interpolation

An appropriate choice of basis functions and interpolation points can mitigate some of the difficulties associated with interpolation by a polynomial of high degree. Nevertheless, fitting a single polynomial to a large number of data points is still likely to yield unsatisfactory oscillating behavior in the interpolant. Piecewise polynomial interpolation provides an alternative to the practical and theoretical difficulties associated with high-degree polynomial interpolation. The main advantage of piecewise polynomial interpolation is that a large number of data points can be fit with low-degree polynomials.

In piecewise polynomial interpolation of a given set of data points (t_i, y_i), $i = 1, \ldots, n$, with $t_1 < t_2 < \cdots < t_n$, a *different* polynomial is used in each subinterval $[t_i, t_{i+1}]$. For this reason the abscissas t_i, at which the interpolant changes from one polynomial to another, are called *knots*, or *breakpoints*, or *control points*. The simplest example is piecewise linear interpolation, in which successive data points are connected by straight lines.

Although piecewise polynomial interpolation eliminates the problems of excessive oscillation and nonconvergence, it appears to sacrifice smoothness of the interpolating function. There are many degrees of freedom in choosing a piecewise polynomial interpolant, however, which can be exploited to obtain a smooth interpolating function despite its piecewise nature.

7.4.1 Hermite Cubic Interpolation

In *Hermite*, or *osculatory*, interpolation the derivatives as well as the values of the interpolating function are specified at the data points. Specifying derivative values simply adds more equations to the linear system that determines the parameters of the interpolating function. To have a well-defined solution, the number of equations and the number of parameters to be determined must be equal.

To provide adequate flexibility while maintaining simplicity and computational efficiency, piecewise cubic polynomials are the most common choice of function for Hermite interpolation. A *Hermite cubic* interpolant is a piecewise cubic polynomial interpolant with a continuous first derivative. A piecewise cubic polynomial with n knots has $4(n-1)$ parameters to be determined, since there are $n-1$ different cubics and each has four parameters. Interpolating the given data gives $2(n-1)$ equations, because each of the $n-1$ cubics must match the two data points at either end of its subinterval. Requiring the derivative to be continuous gives $n-2$ additional equations, because the derivatives of the cubics on either side must match at each of the $n-2$ interior data points. We therefore have a total of $3n-4$ equations, which still leaves n free parameters. Thus, a Hermite cubic interpolant is not unique, and the remaining free parameters can be chosen so that the result is visually pleasing or satisfies additional constraints, such as monotonicity or convexity.

7.4.2 Cubic Spline Interpolation

In general, a *spline* is a piecewise polynomial of degree k that is continuously differentiable $k-1$ times. For example, a linear spline is a piecewise linear polynomial that has degree one and is continuous but not differentiable (it could be described as a "broken line"). A *cubic spline* is a piecewise cubic polynomial that is twice continuously differentiable. As with a Hermite cubic, interpolating the given data and requiring continuity of the first derivative imposes $3n-4$ constraints on the cubic spline. Requiring a continuous second derivative imposes $n-2$ additional constraints, leaving two remaining free parameters. The final two parameters can be fixed in a number of ways, such as:

- Specifying the first derivative at the endpoints t_1 and t_n, based either on desired boundary conditions or on estimates of the derivative from the data
- Forcing the second derivative to be zero at the endpoints, which gives the so-called *natural* spline
- Enforcing a "not-a-knot" condition, which effectively forces two consecutive cubic pieces to be the same, at t_2 and at t_{n-1}
- Forcing equality of the first derivatives as well as equality of the second derivatives at the endpoints t_1 and t_n (if the spline is to be periodic)

Example 7.6 Cubic Spline Interpolation. To illustrate spline interpolation, we will determine the natural cubic spline interpolating three data points (t_i, y_i), $i = 1, 2, 3$. The required interpolant is a piecewise cubic function defined by separate cubic polynomials in each of the two intervals $[t_1, t_2]$ and $[t_2, t_3]$. Denote these two polynomials by

$$p_1(t) = \alpha_1 + \alpha_2 t + \alpha_3 t^2 + \alpha_4 t^3, \qquad p_2(t) = \beta_1 + \beta_2 t + \beta_3 t^2 + \beta_4 t^3.$$

Eight parameters are to be determined, and we will therefore need eight equations. Requiring the first cubic to interpolate the data at the endpoints of the first interval gives the two equations

$$\alpha_1 + \alpha_2 t_1 + \alpha_3 t_1^2 + \alpha_4 t_1^3 = y_1, \qquad \alpha_1 + \alpha_2 t_2 + \alpha_3 t_2^2 + \alpha_4 t_2^3 = y_2.$$

Requiring the second cubic to interpolate the data at the endpoints of the second interval gives the two equations

$$\beta_1 + \beta_2 t_2 + \beta_3 t_2^2 + \beta_4 t_2^3 = y_2, \qquad \beta_1 + \beta_2 t_3 + \beta_3 t_3^2 + \beta_4 t_3^3 = y_3.$$

Requiring the first derivative of the interpolating function to be continuous at t_2 gives the equation

$$\alpha_2 + 2\alpha_3 t_2 + 3\alpha_4 t_2^2 = \beta_2 + 2\beta_3 t_2 + 3\beta_4 t_2^2.$$

Requiring the second derivative of the interpolating function to be continuous at t_2 gives the equation

$$2\alpha_3 + 6\alpha_4 t_2 = 2\beta_3 + 6\beta_4 t_2.$$

Finally, by definition a natural spline has second derivative equal to zero at the endpoints, which gives the two equations

$$2\alpha_3 + 6\alpha_4 t_1 = 0, \qquad 2\beta_3 + 6\beta_4 t_3 = 0.$$

Writing out the system of equations in full, we have

$$\begin{bmatrix} 1 & t_1 & t_1^2 & t_1^3 & 0 & 0 & 0 & 0 \\ 1 & t_2 & t_2^2 & t_2^3 & 0 & 0 & 0 & 0 \\ 0 & 0 & 0 & 0 & 1 & t_2 & t_2^2 & t_2^3 \\ 0 & 0 & 0 & 0 & 1 & t_3 & t_3^2 & t_3^3 \\ 0 & 1 & 2t_2 & 3t_2^2 & 0 & -1 & -2t_2 & -3t_2^2 \\ 0 & 0 & 2 & 6t_2 & 0 & 0 & -2 & -6t_2 \\ 0 & 0 & 2 & 6t_1 & 0 & 0 & 0 & 0 \\ 0 & 0 & 0 & 0 & 0 & 0 & 2 & 6t_3 \end{bmatrix} \begin{bmatrix} \alpha_1 \\ \alpha_2 \\ \alpha_3 \\ \alpha_4 \\ \beta_1 \\ \beta_2 \\ \beta_3 \\ \beta_4 \end{bmatrix} = \begin{bmatrix} y_1 \\ y_2 \\ y_2 \\ y_3 \\ 0 \\ 0 \\ 0 \\ 0 \end{bmatrix}.$$

When particular data values are substituted for the t_i and y_i, this system of eight linear equations can be solved for the eight unknown parameters α_i and β_i. We have used a standard polynomial representation of the spline in this example for simplicity; there are other representations for splines in which the linear system for the spline coefficients has a highly regular, banded structure and therefore can be solved more efficiently (see Section 7.4.3).

The choice between Hermite cubic and spline interpolation depends on the data to be fit and on the purpose of the interpolation. If a high degree of smoothness is of paramount importance, then spline interpolation may be most appropriate. On the other hand, a Hermite cubic interpolant may have a more pleasing visual appearance, and it allows the flexibility to preserve monotonicity if the original data are monotonic. These issues are illustrated in Figs. 7.9 and 7.10, where a monotone Hermite cubic and a cubic spline interpolate the same monotonic data points (indicated by the bullets in the figures). We see that the additional degree of smoothness required of the cubic spline causes it to overshoot, and the resulting interpolant is not monotonic. The Hermite cubic, on the other hand, is clearly less smooth, but visually it seems to reflect the behavior of the data better. In any case, it is advisable to plot the interpolant and the original data to help assess how well the interpolating function captures the behavior of the data.

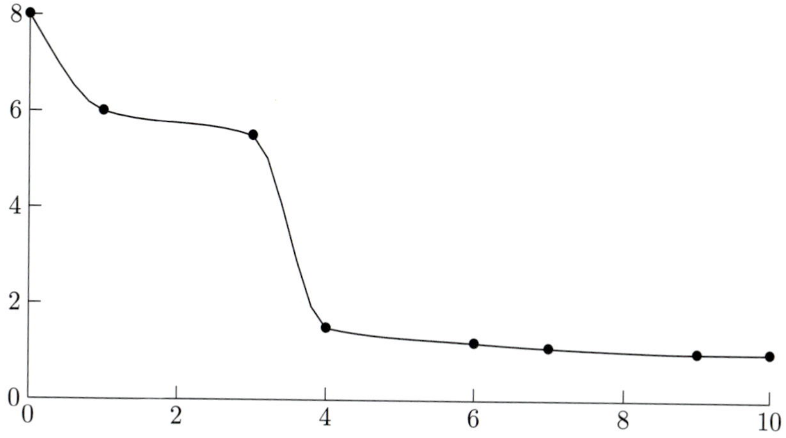

Figure 7.9: Monotone Hermite cubic interpolation of monotonic data.

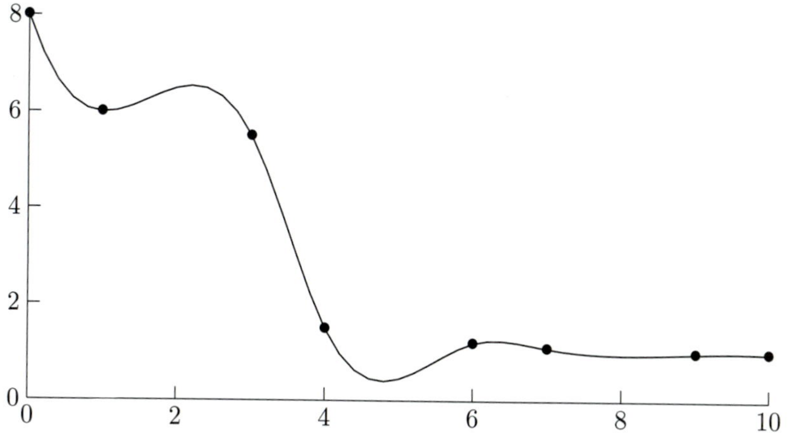

Figure 7.10: Cubic spline interpolation of monotonic data.

7.4.3 B-splines

One might wonder if an arbitrary spline can be represented as a linear combination of basis functions, which we have already seen can be done in various ways for polynomials. An elegant answer to this question is provided by *B-splines*, which take their name from the fact that they form a *basis* for the family of spline functions of a given degree.

B-splines can be defined in a number of ways, including recursion, convolution, and divided differences. Here we will define them recursively. Although in practice we use only the finite set of knots $t_1, \ldots, t_n$, for notational convenience we will assume an infinite set of knots

$$\cdots < t_{-2} < t_{-1} < t_0 < t_1 < t_2 < \cdots$$

The additional knots can be taken to be arbitrarily defined points outside the interval $[t_1, t_n]$. Again for notational convenience, we will also make use of the linear functions

$$v_i^k(t) = \frac{t - t_i}{t_{i+k} - t_i}.$$

To start the recursion, we define B-splines of degree 0 by

$$B_i^0(t) = \begin{cases} 1 & \text{if } t_i \le t < t_{i+1} \\ 0 & \text{otherwise} \end{cases},$$

and then for $k > 0$ we define B-splines of degree k by

$$B_i^k(t) = v_i^k(t) B_i^{k-1}(t) + (1 - v_{i+1}^k(t)) B_{i+1}^{k-1}(t).$$

Since B_i^0 is piecewise constant and v_i^k is linear, we see from the definition that B_i^1 is piecewise linear. Similarly, B_i^2 is in turn piecewise quadratic, and in general, B_i^k is a piecewise polynomial of degree k. The first few B-splines are pictured in Fig. 7.11. Another motivation for their name is their bell shape. For $k = 1$, they are often called "hat" functions.

We note the following important properties of the B-spline functions B_i^k:

1. For $t < t_i$ or $t > t_{i+k+1}$, $B_i^k(t) = 0$.
2. For $t_i < t < t_{i+k+1}$, $B_i^k(t) > 0$.
3. For all t, $\sum_{i=-\infty}^{\infty} B_i^k(t) = 1$.
4. For $k \ge 1$, B_i^k is $k-1$ times continuously differentiable.
5. The set of functions $\{B_{1-k}^k, \ldots, B_{n-1}^k\}$ is linearly independent on the interval $[t_1, t_n]$.
6. The set of functions $\{B_{1-k}^k, \ldots, B_{n-1}^k\}$ spans the set of all splines of degree k having knots t_i.

Properties 1 and 2 together say that the B-spline functions have local support. Property 3 indicates how the functions are normalized, and Property 4 says that they are indeed splines. Properties 5 and 6 together say that for a given k, these functions form a basis for the set of all splines of degree k having the same set of knots. Thus, if we use the B-spline basis, the linear system to be solved for the spline coefficients will be nonsingular and banded. The locality of the B-spline

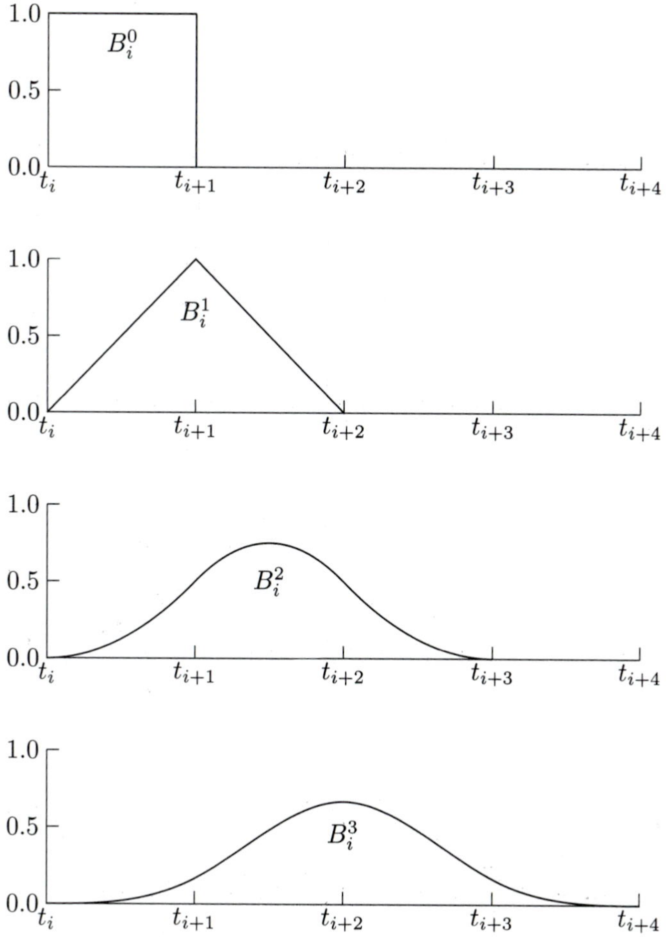

Figure 7.11: First four B-splines.

representation also means that if the data value at a given knot changes, then the coefficients of only a few basis functions are affected, which is in marked contrast to the standard polynomial representation, for which changing a single data point changes all of the coefficients of the spline interpolant.

The use of the B-spline basis yields efficient and stable methods for determining and evaluating spline interpolants, and many library routines for spline interpolation are based on this approach. B-splines are also useful in many other contexts, such as the numerical solution of differential equations, as we will see later.

7.5 Software for Interpolation

Table 7.2 is a list of some of the software available for polynomial interpolation and for cubic spline interpolation in one dimension. Some of the spline packages offer the option of Hermite cubic interpolation as well. For monotonicity-preserving Hermite cubic interpolation, `pchip` is available as a package from `Netlib` and is also a function in `MATLAB`. A separate spline toolbox is also available for `MATLAB`. Tension splines—a particularly flexible approach to spline curve fitting that conveniently allows smoothing and shape preservation, if desired—are implemented in `tspack(#716)` from `TOMS`. We note that software is also available from many of these same sources for interpolation in two or more dimensions, both for regularly spaced and for irregularly scattered data. For generating orthogonal polynomials of various types, the software package `orthpol(#726)` is available from `TOMS`.

Source	Polynomial interpolation	Compute spline	Evaluate spline
`FITPACK` [95]		`curfit`	`curev/splev`
`FMM` [127]		`spline`	`seval`
`HSL`	`tb02`	`tb04`	`tg01`
`IMSL`		`csint/csdec/csher`	`csval`
`KMN` [220]		`pchez`	`pchev`
`MATLAB`	`polyfit`	`spline`	`ppval`
`NAG`	`e01aef`	`e01baf/e01bef`	`e01bff`
`NR` [315]	`polint`	`spline`	`splint`
`NUMAL` [250]	`newton`		
`PPPACK` [87]		`cubspl`	`ppvalu`
Shikin & Plis [353]		`spline`	`spline`
`SLATEC`	`polint`	`bint4/bintk`	`bvalu/bspev`
Späth [362]	`newdia/newsol`	`cub1r5/cub2r7`	`cubval`

Table 7.2: Software for polynomial and piecewise cubic interpolation

Software for interpolation often consists of two routines: one for computing an interpolant and another for evaluating it at any given point or set of points. The input to the first routine includes the number of data points and two one-dimensional arrays containing the values of the independent variable and corresponding function values to be fit, and the output includes one or more arrays containing the coefficients of the interpolant. The input to the second routine includes one or more values at which the interpolant is to be evaluated, together with the arrays containing the coefficients previously determined, and the output is the corresponding value(s) of the interpolant (and possibly its derivative) at the desired point(s).

7.5.1 Software for Special Functions

A number of functions that have proved useful in applied mathematics have become known as *special functions*. Examples include elementary functions such as exponential, logarithmic, and trigonometric functions, as well as functions that commonly occur in mathematical physics (among other areas), such as the gamma and beta functions, Bessel functions, hypergeometric functions, elliptic integrals, and many others. The specialized techniques used in approximating these functions are beyond the scope of this book, but good software is available for evaluating almost any standard function of interest. The most frequently occurring functions are typically supplied as built-in functions in most programming languages used for scientific computing. Software for many additional functions can be found in most of the general-purpose libraries listed in Section 1.4.1. In addition, `Netlib` contains several collections of special function routines, including `amos`, `cephes`, `elefunt`, `fdlibm`, `fn`, `specfun`, and `vfnlib`, and routines for numerous individual functions can be found in `TOMS`. Of particular note is the portable elementary function library `fdlibm`, available from `Netlib`, which is better than the default libraries supplied by many system vendors. An extensive survey of available software for special functions can be found in [257].

7.6 Historical Notes and Further Reading

As the names associated with it—Newton, Lagrange, Hermite, and many others—suggest, polynomial interpolation has long been an important part of applied mathematics. The term *interpolation* is due to Wallis, an older contemporary of Newton, who was also first to use the symbol ∞ for infinity. A comprehensive reference on polynomial interpolation, approximation, orthogonal polynomials, and related topics is [85]. Additional references on approximation include [64, 312, 329, 414]. For Padé approximation, see [20, 21, 49]. General references on orthogonal polynomials include [28, 66, 134, 145, 337, 388]. For more details specifically on Chebyshev polynomials, see [133, 330]. Spline functions were first formulated by Schoenberg in 1946. The theory of splines is presented in detail in [5, 233, 341]. More computationally oriented references on splines are [87, 95, 353, 362], all of which include software. The use of splines in computer graphics and geometric modeling is detailed in [26, 116, 428]. For monotone piecewise cubic interpolation, see [136, 137, 204]. In addition to their use for interpolation, splines can also be used for more general approximation. For example, least squares fitting by cubic splines is a good method for smoothing noisy data; see [320, 321]. The literature on special functions is vast; recent references on computing special functions, many of which include software, include [22, 72, 283, 392, 433].

Review Questions

7.1. True or false: There are arbitrarily many different mathematical functions that interpolate a given set of data points.

7.2. True or false: If an interpolating function accurately reproduces the given data values, then this fact implies that the coefficients in the linear combination of basis functions are well-determined.

7.3. True or false: If the polynomial interpolating a given set of data points is unique, then so is the representation of that polynomial.

7.4. True or false: When interpolating a continuous function by a polynomial at equally spaced points on a given interval, the polynomial interpolant always converges to the function as the number of interpolation points increases.

7.5. What is the basic distinction between interpolation and approximation of a function?

7.6. State at least two different applications for interpolation.

7.7. Give two examples of numerical methods (for problems other than interpolation itself) that are based on polynomial interpolation.

7.8. Is it ever possible for two distinct polynomials to interpolate the same n data points? If so, under what conditions, and if not, why?

7.9. State at least two important criteria for choosing a particular set of basis functions for use in interpolation.

7.10. Determining the parameters of an interpolant can be interpreted as solving a linear system $\boldsymbol{Ax} = \boldsymbol{y}$, where the matrix $\boldsymbol{A}$ depends on the basis functions used and the vector $\boldsymbol{y}$ contains the function values to be fit. Describe in words the pattern of nonzero entries in the matrix $\boldsymbol{A}$ for polynomial interpolation using each of the following bases:

(*a*) Monomial basis

(*b*) Lagrange basis

(*c*) Newton basis

7.11. (*a*) Is interpolation an appropriate procedure for fitting a function to noisy data?

(*b*) If so, why, and if not, what is a good alternative?

7.12. (*a*) For a given set of data points (t_i, y_i), $i = 1, \ldots, n$, rank the following three methods for polynomial interpolation according to the cost of determining the interpolant (i.e., determining the coefficients of the basis functions), from 1 for the cheapest to 3 for the most expensive:

Monomial basis

Lagrange basis

Newton basis

(*b*) Which of the three methods has the best-conditioned basis matrix $\boldsymbol{A}$, where $a_{ij} = \phi_j(t_i)$?

(*c*) For which of the three methods is evaluating the resulting interpolant at a given point the most expensive?

7.13. (*a*) What is a Vandermonde matrix?

(*b*) In what context does such a matrix arise?

(*c*) Why is such a matrix often ill-conditioned when its order is relatively large?

7.14. Given a set of n data points, (t_i, y_i), $i = 1, \ldots, n$, determining the coefficients x_i of the interpolating polynomial requires the solution of an $n \times n$ system of linear equations $\boldsymbol{Ax} = \boldsymbol{y}$.

(*a*) If we use the monomial basis $1, t, t^2, \ldots,$ give an expression for the entries a_{ij} of the matrix $\boldsymbol{A}$ that is efficient to evaluate.

(*b*) Does the condition of $\boldsymbol{A}$ tend to become better, or worse, or stay about the same as n grows?

(*c*) How does this change affect the accuracy with which the interpolating polynomial fits the given data points?

7.15. For Lagrange polynomial interpolation of n data points (t_i, y_i), $i = 1, \ldots, n$,

(*a*) What is the degree of each polynomial function $\ell_j(t)$ in the Lagrange basis?

(*b*) What function results if we sum the n functions in the Lagrange basis (i.e., if we take $g(t) = \sum_{j=1}^{n} \ell_j(t)$, what function $g(t)$ results)?

7.16. List one advantage and one disadvantage of Lagrange interpolation compared with using the monomial basis for polynomial interpolation.

7.17. What is the computational cost (number of additions and multiplications) of evaluating a polynomial of degree n using Horner's method?

7.18. Why is interpolation by a polynomial of high degree often unsatisfactory?

7.19. (*a*) In interpolating a continuous function by a polynomial, what key features determine the error in approximating the function by the resulting interpolant?

(*b*) Under what circumstances can the error be large even though the number of interpolation points is large?

7.20. How should the interpolation points be placed in an interval in order to guarantee convergence of the polynomial interpolant to sufficiently smooth functions on the interval as the number of points increases?

7.21. What does it mean for two polynomials p and q to be *orthogonal* to each other on an interval $[a, b]$?

7.22. (*a*) What is meant by a *Taylor* polynomial?

(*b*) In what sense does it interpolate a given function?

7.23. In fitting a large number of data points, what is the main advantage of piecewise polynomial interpolation over interpolation by a single polynomial?

7.24. (*a*) How does Hermite interpolation differ from ordinary interpolation?

(*b*) How does a cubic spline interpolant differ from a Hermite cubic interpolant?

7.25. In choosing between Hermite cubic and cubic spline interpolation, which should one choose

(*a*) If maximum smoothness of the interpolant is desired?

(*b*) If the data are monotonic and this property is to be preserved?

7.26. (*a*) How many times is a Hermite cubic interpolant continuously differentiable?

(*b*) How many times is a cubic spline interpolant continuously differentiable?

7.27. The continuity and smoothness requirements on a cubic spline interpolant still leave two free parameters. Give at least two examples of additional constraints that might be imposed to determine the cubic spline interpolant to a set of data points.

7.28. (*a*) How many parameters are required to define a piecewise cubic polynomial with n knots?

(*b*) Obviously, a similar number of equations is required to determine those parameters. Assuming the interpolating function is to be a natural cubic spline, explain how the requirements on the function account for the necessary number of equations in the linear system to be solved for the parameters.

7.29. Which of the following interpolants to n data points are unique?

(*a*) Polynomial of degree at most $n-1$

(*b*) Hermite cubic

(*c*) Cubic spline

7.30. For which of the following types of interpolation is it possible, in general, to preserve monotonicity in a set of n data points (i.e., the interpolant is increasing or decreasing if the data points are increasing or decreasing)?

(*a*) Polynomial of degree at most $n-1$

(*b*) Hermite cubic

(*c*) Cubic spline

7.31. Why is it advantageous if the basis functions used for interpolation are localized (i.e., each basis function involves only a few data points)?

Exercises

7.1. Given the three data points $(-1, 1)$, $(0, 0)$, $(1, 1)$, determine the interpolating polynomial of degree two:

(*a*) Using the monomial basis

(*b*) Using the Lagrange basis

(*c*) Using the Newton basis

Show that the three representations give the same polynomial.

7.2. Express the following polynomial in the correct form for evaluation by Horner's method: $p(t) = 5t^3 - 3t^2 + 7t - 2$.

7.3. Write a formal algorithm for evaluating a polynomial at a given argument using Horner's nested evaluation scheme

(*a*) For a polynomial expressed in terms of the monomial basis

(*b*) For a polynomial expressed in Newton form

7.4. How many multiplications are required to evaluate a polynomial $p(t)$ of degree $n-1$ at a given point t

(*a*) Represented in the monomial basis?

(*b*) Represented in the Lagrange basis?

(*c*) Represented in the Newton basis?

7.5. (*a*) Determine the polynomial interpolant to the data

t	1	2	3	4
y	11	29	65	125

using the monomial basis.

(*b*) Determine the Lagrange polynomial interpolant to the same data and show that the resulting polynomial is equivalent to that obtained in part *a*.

(*c*) Compute the Newton polynomial interpolant to the same data using each of the three methods given in Section 7.3.3 (triangular matrix, incremental interpolation, and divided differences) and show that each produces the same result as the previous two methods.

7.6. Use the error bound from Section 7.3.5 to estimate the maximum error in interpolating the function $\sin(t)$ by a polynomial of degree four using five equally spaced points on the interval $[0, \pi/2]$. Check your bound by comparing a few sample values of the function and the interpolant. How many points would be required to achieve a maximum error of 10^{-10}?

7.7. Reconcile the error bound given in Section 7.3.5 with the behavior shown in Fig. 7.7 of polynomial interpolants to Runge's function, $f(t) = 1/(1 + 25t^2)$, for equally spaced points on $[-1, 1]$.

7.8. Compare the cost of forming a Vandermonde matrix inductively, as in Section 7.3.1, with the cost using explicit exponentiation.

7.9. Use Lagrange interpolation to derive the formulas given in Section 5.5.5 for inverse quadratic interpolation.

7.10. (*a*) For a given set of data points, $t_1, \ldots, t_n$, define the function $\pi(t)$ by

$$\pi(t) = (t - t_1)(t - t_2) \cdots (t - t_n).$$

Show that

$$\pi'(t_j) = (t_j - t_1) \cdots (t_j - t_{j-1})(t_j - t_{j+1}) \cdots (t_j - t_n).$$

(*b*) Use the result of part *a* to show that the jth Lagrange basis function can be expressed as

$$\ell_j(t) = \frac{\pi(t)}{(t - t_j)\,\pi'(t_j)}.$$

7.11. Prove that the formula using divided differences given in Section 7.3.3,

$$x_j = f[t_1, t_2, \ldots, t_j],$$

indeed gives the coefficient of the jth basis function in the Newton polynomial interpolant.

7.12. (*a*) Verify directly that the first six Legendre polynomials given in Section 7.3.4 are indeed mutually orthogonal.

(*b*) Verify directly that they satisfy the three-term recurrence given in Section 7.3.4.

(*c*) Express each of the first six monomials, 1, t, $\ldots$, t^5, as a linear combination of the first six Legendre polynomials, $p_0, \ldots, p_5$.

7.13. (*a*) Verify that the Chebyshev polynomials of the first kind, as defined in Section 7.3.4, satisfy the three-term recurrence given there.

(*b*) Verify that the first six Chebyshev polynomials are as listed in Section 7.3.4.

(*c*) Verify that the expressions for the roots and extrema of T_k given in Section 7.3.4 are correct.

7.14. Derive a formula for transforming the Chebyshev points from the interval $[-1, 1]$ to an arbitrary interval $[a, b]$.

7.15. In general, is it possible to interpolate n data points by a piecewise *quadratic* polynomial, with knots at the given data points, such that the interpolant is

(*a*) Once continuously differentiable?

(*b*) Twice continuously differentiable?

In each case, if the answer is "yes," explain why, and if the answer is "no," give the maximum value for n for which it *is* possible.

7.16. Verify the properties of B-splines enumerated in Section 7.4.3.

Computer Problems

7.1. (*a*) Write a routine that uses Horner's rule to evaluate a polynomial $p(t)$ given its degree n, an array $\boldsymbol{x}$ containing its coefficients, and the value t of the independent variable at which it is to be evaluated.

(*b*) Add options to your routine to evaluate the derivative $p'(t)$ or the integral $\int_a^b p(t)\,dt$, given a and b.

7.2. (*a*) Write a routine for computing the Newton polynomial interpolant for a given set of data points, and a second routine for evaluating the Newton interpolant at a given argument value using Horner's rule.

(*b*) Write a routine for computing the new Newton polynomial interpolant when a new data point is added.

(*c*) If your programming language supports recursion, write a recursive routine that implements part *a* by calling your routine for part *b* recursively. Compare its performance with that of your original implementation.

7.3. (*a*) Use a library routine, or one of your own design, to solve the 8×8 linear system in Example 7.6 using the data given in Example 7.1.

(*b*) Plot the resulting natural cubic spline, along with the given data points. Also plot the first and second derivatives of the cubic spline and confirm that all of the required conditions are met.

7.4. Compute both polynomial and cubic spline interpolants to Runge's function, $f(t) = 1/(1 + 25t^2)$, using both $n = 11$ and 21 equally spaced points on the interval $[-1, 1]$. Compare your results graphically by plotting both interpolants and the original function for each value of n.

7.5. An experiment has produced the following data:

t	0.0	0.5	1.0	6.0	7.0	9.0
y	0.0	1.6	2.0	2.0	1.5	0.0

We wish to interpolate the data with a smooth curve in the hope of obtaining reasonable values of y for values of t between the points at which measurements were taken.

(*a*) Using any method you like, determine the polynomial of degree five that interpolates the given data, and make a smooth plot of it over the range $0 \le t \le 9$.

(*b*) Similarly, determine a cubic spline that interpolates the given data, and make a smooth plot of it over the same range.

(*c*) Which interpolant seems to give more reasonable values between the given data points? Can you explain why each curve behaves the way it does?

(*d*) Might piecewise linear interpolation be a better choice for these particular data? Why?

7.6. Interpolating the data points

t	0	1	4	9	16
y	0	1	2	3	4
t	25	36	49	64	
y	5	6	7	8	

should give an approximation to the square root function.

(*a*) Compute the polynomial of degree eight that interpolates these nine data points. Plot the resulting polynomial as well as the corresponding values given by the built-in `sqrt` function over the domain $[0, 64]$.

(*b*) Use a cubic spline routine to interpolate the same data and again plot the resulting curve along with the built-in `sqrt` function.

(*c*) Which of the two interpolants is more accurate over most of the domain?

(*d*) Which of the two interpolants is more accurate between 0 and 1?

7.7. The *gamma function* is defined by

$$\Gamma(x) = \int_0^\infty t^{x-1} e^{-t}\, dt, \quad x > 0.$$

For an integer argument n, the gamma function has the value

$$\Gamma(n) = (n-1)!\,,$$

so interpolating the data points

t	1	2	3	4	5
y	1	1	2	6	24

should yield an approximation to the gamma function over the given range.

(*a*) Compute the polynomial of degree four that interpolates these five data points. Plot the resulting polynomial as well as the corresponding values given by the built-in `gamma` function over the domain $[1, 5]$.

(*b*) Use a cubic spline routine to interpolate the same data and again plot the resulting curve along with the built-in `gamma` function.

(*c*) Which of the two interpolants is more accurate over most of the domain?

(*d*) Which of the two interpolants is more accurate between 1 and 2?

7.8. Consider the following population data for the United States:

Year	Population
1900	76,212,168
1910	92,228,496
1920	106,021,537
1930	123,202,624
1940	132,164,569
1950	151,325,798
1960	179,323,175
1970	203,302,031
1980	226,542,199

There is a unique polynomial of degree eight that interpolates these nine data points, but of course that polynomial can be represented in many different ways. Consider the following possible sets of basis functions $\phi_j(t)$, $j = 1, \ldots, 9$:

1. $\phi_j(t) = t^{j-1}$
2. $\phi_j(t) = (t - 1900)^{j-1}$
3. $\phi_j(t) = (t - 1940)^{j-1}$
4. $\phi_j(t) = ((t - 1940)/40)^{j-1}$

(*a*) For each of these four sets of basis functions, generate the corresponding Vandermonde matrix and compute its condition number using a library routine for condition estimation. How do the condition numbers compare? Explain your results.

(*b*) Using the best-conditioned basis found in part *a*, compute the polynomial interpolant to the population data. Plot the resulting polynomial, using Horner's nested evaluation scheme to evaluate the polynomial at one-year intervals to obtain a smooth curve. Also plot the original data points on the same graph.

(*c*) Use a routine for Hermite cubic interpolation, such as `pchip` from `MATLAB` or `Netlib`, to compute a monotone Hermite cubic interpolant to the population data and again plot the resulting curve on the same graph.

(*d*) Use a cubic spline routine to interpolate the population data and again plot the resulting curve on the same graph.

(*e*) Extrapolate the population to 1990 using each of the polynomial, Hermite cubic, and cubic spline interpolants and compare the values obtained. How close are these to the true value of 248,709,873 according to the 1990 census?

(*f*) Determine the Lagrange interpolant to the same nine data points and evaluate it at the same yearly intervals as in parts *b* and *c*. Compare the total execution time with those for Horner's nested evaluation scheme and for evaluating the cubic spline.

(*g*) Determine the Newton form of the polynomial interpolating the same nine data points. Now determine the Newton polynomial of one degree higher that also interpolates the additional data point for 1990 given in part *d*, without starting over from scratch (i.e., use the Newton polynomial of degree eight already computed to determine the new Newton polynomial). Plot both of the resulting polynomials (of degree eight and nine) over the interval from 1900 to 1990.

(*h*) Round the population data for each year to the nearest million and compute the corresponding polynomial interpolant of degree eight using the same basis as in part *b*. Compare the resulting coefficients with those determined in part *b*. Explain your results.

Chapter 8

Numerical Integration and Differentiation

8.1 Integration

In elementary geometry one learns how to calculate the area of simple figures such as rectangles, triangles, and circles, and similarly the volume of cubes, spheres, etc. One of the motivating problems for the invention of integral calculus was calculating areas and volumes of irregularly shaped regions, which is a central problem in classical mechanics. One of the fundamental principles of classical mechanics is that for many purposes a rigid body can be treated as a point mass located at its centroid, and similarly a distributed force is equivalent to a concentrated force applied at an appropriate point. For example, consider a beam of length L supporting a distributed load, as shown in Fig. 8.1. If $\rho(x)$ represents the density of the load as a function of the horizontal coordinate x, then the total load W on the beam is simply the area under the curve $\rho(x)$, which is given by the integral

$$W = \int_0^L \rho(x)\, dx.$$

Moreover, the point of application of the equivalent concentrated load is the centroid C of the region under the curve, whose horizontal coordinate $\bar{x}$ is given by the integral

$$\bar{x} = \frac{1}{W} \int_0^L x\, \rho(x)\, dx.$$

Methods for approximating the area of such an irregular region were known to the ancients, including Archimedes, whose approach was to tile the region with small squares of known size and then count the number of squares within the region.

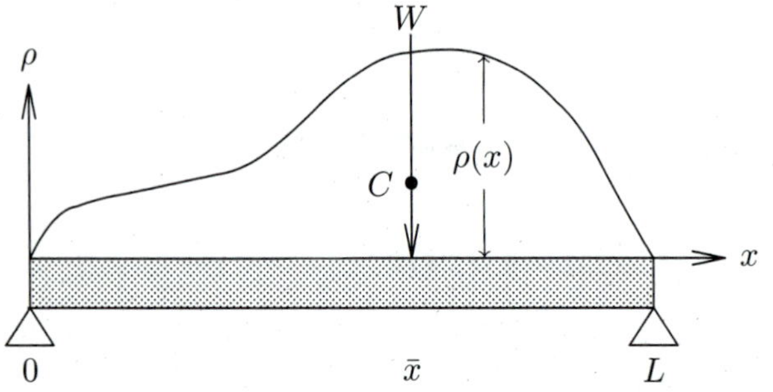

Figure 8.1: Concentrated load equivalent to distributed load on beam.

Though they lacked a strong theoretical underpinning, such as a rigorous notion of limit, in spirit these methods are not unlike the numerical methods in use today for approximating integrals. For a function $f: \mathbb{R} \to \mathbb{R}$ on an interval $[a, b]$, the modern definition of the integral

$$I(f) = \int_a^b f(x)\, dx$$

is based on *Riemann sums* of the form

$$R_n = \sum_{i=1}^{n} (x_{i+1} - x_i)\, f(\xi_i),$$

where $a = x_1 < x_2 < \cdots < x_n < x_{n+1} = b$ and $\xi \in [x_i, x_{i+1}]$, $i = 1, \ldots, n$. Let $h_n = \max\{x_{i+1} - x_i : i = 1, \ldots, n-1\}$. If for any choice of x_i such that $h_n \to 0$ and any choice of ξ_i we have $\lim_{n\to\infty} R_n = R$, where R is finite, then f is said to be *Riemann integrable* on $[a, b]$, and the value of the integral is R. This definition already suggests a method for approximating an integral: just use a finite Riemann sum with n chosen large enough to achieve the desired accuracy. This idea works, but unless the points x_i and ξ_i are chosen carefully, it requires evaluation of the integrand function f at far more points than the minimum number necessary to achieve a given accuracy. In this chapter we will see efficient methods that produce high accuracy at relatively low cost, which for integration is measured by the number of function evaluations required.

There are more general concepts of integration, such as Lebesgue integration, that are invaluable as theoretical tools, but their nonconstructive nature makes them unsuitable for numerical computation, so we will restrict our attention to Riemann integrals. The usefulness of integration goes far beyond the applications in geometry and mechanics that initially motivated it, and includes

- Integral transforms, such as the Laplace, Fourier, and Hankel transforms
- Special functions of applied mathematics and mathematical physics, many of which have integral representations, including the gamma, beta, Bessel, and error functions, and Fresnel and elliptic integrals
- Finite element and boundary element methods for partial differential equations
- Integral equations and variational methods

- Probability and statistics, in which many fundamental concepts, such as probability distributions, moments, and expectations, are defined by integrals
- Classical and quantum physics, in which the potential or free energy of many systems is given by an integral, for example the electrostatic potential due to a given charge distribution

8.2 Existence, Uniqueness, and Conditioning

If $f: \mathbb{R} \to \mathbb{R}$ is bounded and continuous almost everywhere (i.e., continuous except on a set of measure zero, which is a set that can be contained in the union of a countable number of open intervals of arbitrarily small total length) on an interval $[a, b]$, then the Riemann integral $I(f)$ exists. This sufficient condition is also necessary, so unbounded functions are not properly Riemann integrable. For practical purposes, integrable functions are bounded functions with at most a finite number of points of discontinuity within the interval of integration. Since all the Riemann sums defining the Riemann integral of a given function on a given interval must have the same limit, uniqueness of the Riemann integral is built into the definition.

The conditioning of an integration problem is a measure of the sensitivity of the result to perturbations in the input data, which in this case are the integrand function f and the interval of integration $[a, b]$. To quantify this sensitivity, we will need a norm for functions defined on a given interval. By analogy with the ∞-norm for finite-dimensional vectors, for a function f on a closed interval $[a, b]$ we define

$$\|f\|_\infty = \max_{x \in [a,b]} |f(x)|.$$

Now suppose that $\hat{f}$ is a perturbation of the integrand function f. Then we have

$$\begin{aligned} |I(\hat{f}) - I(f)| &= \left| \int_a^b \hat{f}(x)\,dx - \int_a^b f(x)\,dx \right| \\ &\le \int_a^b |\hat{f}(x) - f(x)|\,dx \\ &\le (b-a)\,\|\hat{f} - f\|_\infty, \end{aligned}$$

which says that the absolute condition number of the integration problem is at most $b - a$. This bound is attained for $\hat{f}(x) = f(x) + c$, where c is any positive constant, so the absolute condition number is in fact equal to $b - a$. This is a very satisfactory result in that the effect of a perturbation of the integrand is at worst proportional to the length of the interval of integration. For the relative condition number, from the preceding inequality we see that

$$\frac{|I(\hat{f}) - I(f)|/|I(f)|}{\|\hat{f} - f\|_\infty / \|f\|_\infty} \le \frac{(b-a)\,\|f\|_\infty}{|I(f)|}.$$

The latter quantity is always greater than or equal to 1, and can be arbitrarily large for some integrands, since $|I(f)|$ can be small (or even zero) without $\|f\|_\infty$

being small, but in that event we should use the absolute condition number instead. Thus, in either case, the modest size of the relevant condition number tells us that integration problems are generally well-conditioned with respect to perturbations in the integrand. This should not be surprising, since integration is an averaging or smoothing process that tends to dampen the effect of small changes in the integrand.

Now suppose that $\hat{b}$ is a perturbation of b, with $\hat{b} > b$ (a similar analysis applies if $\hat{b} < b$, or to analogous perturbations of a). Then we have

$$\left| \int_a^{\hat{b}} f(x)\,dx - \int_a^b f(x)\,dx \right| = \left| \int_b^{\hat{b}} f(x)\,dx \right| \le (\hat{b} - b) \max_{x \in [b,\hat{b}]} |f(x)|.$$

Thus, the absolute condition number with respect to perturbations in the limits of integration is usually of modest size, but it can be arbitrarily large if the integrand has a singularity nearby.

8.3 Numerical Quadrature

In elementary calculus one learns to evaluate a definite integral

$$I(f) = \int_a^b f(x)\,dx$$

analytically by finding an *antiderivative* F of the integrand function f (i.e., a function F such that $F'(x) = f(x)$), and then using the *Fundamental Theorem of Calculus* to evaluate

$$I(f) = F(b) - F(a).$$

Unfortunately, some integrals cannot be evaluated in such a closed form (e.g., $f(x) = \exp(-x^2)$), and many integrals arising in practice are too complicated to evaluate analytically even if this were possible in principle. Thus, we are often forced to employ numerical methods to evaluate definite integrals approximately.

The numerical approximation of definite integrals is known as *numerical quadrature*. This name, which derives from ancient methods for approximating areas of irregular or curved figures by tiling them with small squares, helps distinguish this topic from the numerical integration of differential equations, which we will consider later in this book. In approximating integrals, we will take our cue from the Riemann sums that define the integral: the integral will be approximated by a weighted sum of integrand values at a finite number of sample points in the interval of integration. Specifically, the integral $I(f)$ is approximated by an n-point *quadrature rule*, which has the form

$$Q_n(f) = \sum_{i=1}^{n} w_i\, f(x_i),$$

where $a \le x_1 < x_2 < \cdots < x_n \le b$. The points x_i at which the integrand f is evaluated are called *nodes* or *abscissas*, and the multipliers w_i are called *weights* or *coefficients.* A quadrature rule is said to be *open* if $a < x_1$ and $x_n < b$, and *closed* if $a = x_1$ and $x_n = b$. Our main objective will be to choose the nodes and weights so that we obtain a desired level of accuracy at a reasonable computational cost in terms of the number of integrand evaluations required.

Quadrature rules can be derived using polynomial interpolation. In effect, the integrand function f is evaluated at the points x_i, $i = 1, \ldots, n$, the polynomial of degree $n-1$ that interpolates the function values at those points is determined (see Section 7.3), and the integral of the interpolant is then taken as an approximation to the integral of the original function. In practice, the interpolating polynomial is not determined explicitly each time a particular integral is to be evaluated. Instead, polynomial interpolation is used to determine the nodes and weights for a given quadrature rule, which can then be used in approximating the integral of any function over the interval. In particular, if Lagrange interpolation is used (see Section 7.3.2), then the weights are given by the integrals of the corresponding Lagrange basis functions for the given set of points x_i, $i = 1, \ldots, n$,

$$w_i = \int_a^b \ell_i(x)\, dx, \quad i = 1, \ldots, n,$$

and these are the same for any integrand. For obvious reasons, the resulting quadrature rule is said to be *interpolatory*.

An alternative method for deriving interpolatory quadrature rules, called the *method of undetermined coefficients*, is to choose the weights so that the rule integrates the first n polynomial basis functions exactly, which results in a system of n equations in n unknowns. With the monomial basis, for example, this strategy results in the system of *moment equations*

$$\begin{aligned}
w_1 \cdot 1 + w_2 \cdot 1 + \cdots + w_n \cdot 1 &= \int_a^b 1\, dx = b - a, \\
w_1 \cdot x_1 + w_2 \cdot x_2 + \cdots + w_n \cdot x_n &= \int_a^b x\, dx = (b^2 - a^2)/2, \\
&\ \ \vdots \\
w_1 \cdot x_1^{n-1} + w_2 \cdot x_2^{n-1} + \cdots + w_n \cdot x_n^{n-1} &= \int_a^b x^{n-1}\, dx = (b^n - a^n)/n.
\end{aligned}$$

Writing this system in matrix form, we have

$$\begin{bmatrix} 1 & 1 & \cdots & 1 \\ x_1 & x_2 & \cdots & x_n \\ \vdots & \vdots & \ddots & \vdots \\ x_1^{n-1} & x_2^{n-1} & \cdots & x_n^{n-1} \end{bmatrix} \begin{bmatrix} w_1 \\ w_2 \\ \vdots \\ w_n \end{bmatrix} = \begin{bmatrix} b - a \\ (b^2 - a^2)/2 \\ \vdots \\ (b^n - a^n)/n \end{bmatrix}.$$

The matrix of this system is a *Vandermonde matrix*, which is nonsingular because the nodes x_i are assumed to be distinct (see Section 7.3.1). The unique solution of this system yields the weights $w_1, \ldots, w_n$, which are the same as those given by integrating the Lagrange basis functions.

Example 8.1 Method of Undetermined Coefficients. We illustrate the method of undetermined coefficients by deriving a three-point quadrature rule

$$Q_3(f) = w_1 f(x_1) + w_2 f(x_2) + w_3 f(x_3)$$

for the interval $[a, b]$ using the monomial basis. We take the two endpoints and midpoint as the three nodes, i.e., $x_1 = a$, $x_2 = (a+b)/2$, and $x_3 = b$. Written in matrix form, the moment equations give the Vandermonde system

$$\begin{bmatrix} 1 & 1 & 1 \\ a & (a+b)/2 & b \\ a^2 & ((a+b)/2)^2 & b^2 \end{bmatrix} \begin{bmatrix} w_1 \\ w_2 \\ w_3 \end{bmatrix} = \begin{bmatrix} b-a \\ (b^2-a^2)/2 \\ (b^3-a^3)/3 \end{bmatrix}.$$

Solving this system by Gaussian elimination, we obtain the weights

$$w_1 = (b-a)/6, \qquad w_2 = 2(b-a)/3, \qquad w_3 = (b-a)/6.$$

The resulting quadrature rule is known as *Simpson's rule*.

By construction, an n-point interpolatory quadrature rule integrates each of the first $n-1$ monomial basis functions exactly, and hence by linearity it integrates any polynomial of degree at most $n-1$ exactly. A quadrature rule is said to be of *degree* d if it is exact (i.e., the error is zero) for every polynomial of degree d but is not exact for some polynomial of degree $d+1$. As we have just seen, an n-point interpolatory quadrature rule is of degree at least $n-1$. Conversely, any quadrature rule with degree at least $n-1$ must be interpolatory, since it satisfies the moment equations.

The significance of the degree is that it conveniently characterizes the accuracy of a given rule. If Q_n is an interpolatory quadrature rule, and p_{n-1} is the polynomial of degree at most $n-1$ interpolating a sufficiently smooth integrand f at the nodes $x_1, \ldots, x_n$, then the error bound for the polynomial interpolant from Section 7.3.5 yields the following rough error bound for the approximate integral:

$$\begin{aligned} |I(f) - Q_n(f)| &= |I(f) - I(p_{n-1})| = |I(f - p_{n-1})| \\ &\le (b-a)\, \|f - p_{n-1}\|_\infty \\ &\le \frac{b-a}{4n}\, h^n\, \|f^{(n)}\|_\infty \\ &\le \frac{1}{4}\, h^{n+1}\, \|f^{(n)}\|_\infty, \end{aligned}$$

where $h = \max\{x_{i+1} - x_i : i = 1, \ldots, n-1\}$.

We will be able to make sharper error estimates when we consider specific quadrature rules, but the preceding general bound already indicates that we can obtain higher accuracy by taking n larger, or h smaller, or both. Indeed, the bound shows that $Q_n(f) \to I(f)$ as $n \to \infty$, as well as the minimum convergence rate we can expect, provided $f^{(n)}$ remains well behaved. In the absence of the latter assumption, however, convergence may not obtain or the rate may be arbitrarily slow. That some regularity assumptions on the integrand function are necessary to obtain satisfactory results should not be surprising, as otherwise *any* method based on sampling the integrand at only a finite number of points can be completely wrong. When the number of sample points is increased, say from n to m, an important factor affecting efficiency is whether the n function values already computed can be reused in the new rule, so that only $m - n$ new function values need be computed. A sequence of quadrature rules is said to be *progressive* if the nodes of Q_{n_1} are a subset of those of Q_{n_2} for $n_2 > n_1$.

Instead of (or in addition to) increasing the number of points (and hence the degree), the preceding bound also suggests that the error can be reduced by subdividing the interval of integration into smaller subintervals and applying the quadrature rule separately in each, since this will reduce h. This approach, which is equivalent to using piecewise polynomial interpolation on the original interval, leads to *composite* (or *compound*) quadrature rules, which we will consider in Section 8.3.5. For now, we will focus on *simple* quadrature rules, in which a single rule is applied over the entire given interval.

The error bound just given, and others we will see later based on Taylor series expansions, depend on higher derivatives of the integrand function for which we may have no convenient bound. In practice, therefore, error estimates for quadrature rules are usually based on the difference between the results obtained when two different rules are used to approximate the same integral. The second rule may be obtained from the base rule either by increasing the number of points (and hence the degree) or by subdividing the interval of integration and applying the base rule in each subinterval. We will see examples of both of these approaches. To save on function evaluations, it is highly desirable for the two rules to be progressive.

In addition to its accuracy, we must also be concerned with the stability of a quadrature rule. If $\hat{f}$ is a perturbation to the integrand function f, then we have

$$\begin{aligned}
|Q_n(\hat{f}) - Q_n(f)| &= |Q_n(\hat{f} - f)| \\
&= \left| \sum_{i=1}^{n} w_i \left(\hat{f}(x_i) - f(x_i)\right) \right| \\
&\le \sum_{i=1}^{n} \left(|w_i| \cdot |\hat{f}(x_i) - f(x_i)| \right) \\
&\le \left(\sum_{i=1}^{n} |w_i| \right) \|\hat{f} - f\|_\infty,
\end{aligned}$$

which says that the absolute condition number of the quadrature rule is at most $\sum_{i=1}^{n} |w_i|$. The preceding bound is attainable for an appropriately chosen perturbation, so the absolute condition number is in fact equal to $\sum_{i=1}^{n} |w_i|$. Recall from the first moment equation that for an interpolatory quadrature rule we have $\sum_{i=1}^{n} w_i = b - a$. If the weights are all nonnegative, then the absolute condition number of the quadrature rule is $b - a$, which the same as that of the underlying integration problem (see Section 8.2), and thus the quadrature rule is stable. If some of the weights are negative, however, then the absolute condition number can be much larger and the quadrature rule can be unstable.

8.3.1 Newton-Cotes Quadrature

The simplest placement of nodes for an interpolatory quadrature rule is to choose equally spaced points in the interval $[a, b]$, which is the defining property of *Newton-Cotes* quadrature. An n-point *open* Newton-Cotes rule has nodes

$$x_i = a + i\,(b-a)/(n+1), \quad i = 1, \ldots, n,$$

and an n-point *closed* Newton-Cotes rule has nodes

$$x_i = a + (i-1)\,(b-a)/(n-1), \quad i = 1, \ldots, n.$$

The following are some of the simplest and best known examples of Newton-Cotes quadrature rules:

- Interpolating the function value at the midpoint of the interval by a polynomial of degree zero (i.e., a constant) gives the one-point open Newton-Cotes rule known as the *midpoint rule*:
$$M(f) = (b-a)\, f\left(\frac{a+b}{2}\right).$$
- Interpolating the function values at the two endpoints of the interval by a polynomial of degree one (i.e., a straight line) gives the two-point closed Newton-Cotes rule known as the *trapezoid rule*:
$$T(f) = \frac{b-a}{2}\,(f(a) + f(b)).$$
- Interpolating the function values at the two endpoints and the midpoint by a polynomial of degree two (i.e., a quadratic) gives the three-point closed Newton-Cotes rule known as *Simpson's rule*:
$$S(f) = \frac{b-a}{6}\left(f(a) + 4\,f\left(\frac{a+b}{2}\right) + f(b)\right),$$
which we derived in Example 8.1.

Example 8.2 Newton-Cotes Quadrature. To illustrate the application of Newton-Cotes quadrature rules, we approximate the integral

$$I(f) = \int_0^1 e^{-x^2}\, dx$$

using each of the three Newton-Cotes quadrature rules just given.

$$\begin{aligned} M(f) &= (1-0)\exp(-0.25) \approx 0.778801 \\ T(f) &= \frac{1}{2}\,(\exp(0) + \exp(-1)) \approx 0.683940 \\ S(f) &= \frac{1}{6}\,(\exp(0) + 4\exp(-0.25) + \exp(-1)) \approx 0.747180 \end{aligned}$$

The integrand and the interpolating polynomial for each rule are shown in Fig. 8.2. The correctly rounded result for this problem is 0.746824. It is somewhat surprising to see that the magnitude of the error from the trapezoid rule (0.062884) is about twice that from the midpoint rule (0.031977), and that Simpson's rule, with an error of only 0.000356, seems remarkably accurate considering the size of the interval over which it is applied. We will soon see explanations for these phenomena.

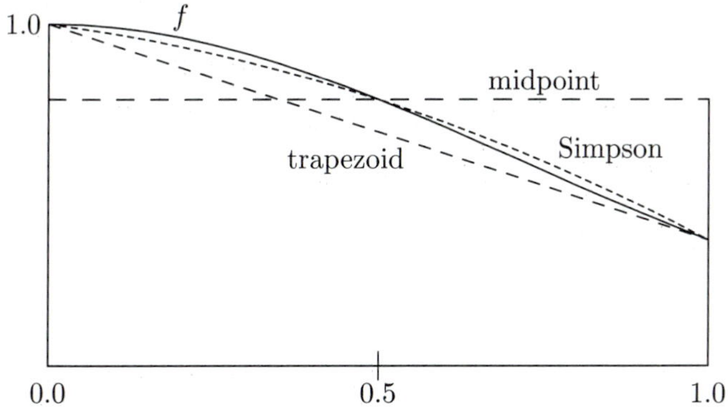

Figure 8.2: Integration of $f(x) = e^{-x^2}$ by Newton-Cotes quadrature rules.

The error in the midpoint quadrature rule can be estimated using a Taylor series expansion about the midpoint $m = (a+b)/2$ of the interval $[a, b]$:

$$\begin{aligned} f(x) &= f(m) + f'(m)(x-m) + \frac{f''(m)}{2}(x-m)^2 \\ &+ \frac{f^{(3)}(m)}{6}(x-m)^3 + \frac{f^{(4)}(m)}{24}(x-m)^4 + \cdots. \end{aligned}$$

Integrating this expression from a to b, the odd-order terms drop out, yielding

$$\begin{aligned} I(f) &= f(m)(b-a) + \frac{f''(m)}{24}(b-a)^3 + \frac{f^{(4)}(m)}{1920}(b-a)^5 + \cdots \\ &= M(f) + E(f) + F(f) + \cdots, \end{aligned}$$

where $E(f)$ and $F(f)$ represent the first two terms in the error expansion for the midpoint rule.

To derive a comparable error expansion for the trapezoid quadrature rule, we substitute $x = a$ and $x = b$ into the Taylor series, add the two resulting series together, observe once again that the odd-order terms drop out, solve for $f(m)$, and substitute into the midpoint expansion to obtain

$$I(f) = T(f) - 2E(f) - 4F(f) - \cdots.$$

Note that

$$T(f) - M(f) = 3E(f) + 5F(f) + \cdots,$$

and hence the difference between the two quadrature rules provides an estimate for the dominant term in their error expansions,

$$E(f) \approx \frac{T(f) - M(f)}{3},$$

provided that the length of the interval is sufficiently small that $(b-a)^5 \ll (b-a)^3$, and the integrand f is such that $f^{(4)}$ is well-behaved. Under these assumptions, we may draw several conclusions from the preceding derivations:

- The midpoint rule is about twice as accurate as the trapezoid rule (as we saw in Example 8.2), despite being based on a polynomial interpolant of degree one less.
- The difference between the midpoint rule and the trapezoid rule can be used to estimate the error in either of them.
- Halving the length of the interval decreases the error in either rule by a factor of about 1/8.

An appropriately weighted combination of the midpoint and trapezoid rules eliminates the leading term, $E(f)$, from the error expansion,

$$\begin{aligned} I(f) &= \frac{2}{3}M(f) + \frac{1}{3}T(f) - \frac{2}{3}F(f) + \cdots \\ &= S(f) - \frac{2}{3}F(f) + \cdots, \end{aligned}$$

which provides an alternative derivation for Simpson's rule as well as an expression for its dominant error term.

Example 8.3 Error Estimation. We illustrate these error estimates by computing the approximate value for the integral $\int_0^1 x^2\,dx$. Using the midpoint rule, we obtain

$$M(f) = (1-0)\left(\frac{1}{2}\right)^2 = \frac{1}{4},$$

and using the trapezoid rule we obtain

$$T(f) = \frac{1-0}{2}\left(0^2 + 1^2\right) = \frac{1}{2}.$$

Thus, we have the estimate

$$E(f) \approx \frac{T(f) - M(f)}{3} = \frac{1/4}{3} = \frac{1}{12}.$$

We conclude that the error in $M(f)$ is about $\frac{1}{12}$, and the error in $T(f)$ is about $-\frac{1}{6}$. In addition, we can now compute the approximate value given by Simpson's rule for this integral,

$$S(f) = \frac{2}{3}M(f) + \frac{1}{3}T(f) = \frac{2}{3}\cdot\frac{1}{4} + \frac{1}{3}\cdot\frac{1}{2} = \frac{1}{3},$$

which is exact for this integral (as is to be expected since, by design, Simpson's rule is exact for quadratic polynomials). Thus, the error estimates for $M(f)$ and $T(f)$ are exact for this integrand (though this would not be true in general).

We observed previously that an n-point interpolatory quadrature has degree at least $n-1$. Thus, we would expect the midpoint rule to have degree zero, the trapezoid rule degree one, Simpson's rule degree two, and so on. We saw from the Taylor series expansion, however, that the error for the midpoint rule depends on the second and higher derivatives of the integrand, which vanish for linear as well as for constant polynomials. This implies that the midpoint rule integrates linear polynomials exactly, and hence its degree is one rather than zero. Similarly, the error for Simpson's rule depends on the fourth and higher derivatives, which vanish for cubic as well as quadratic polynomials, so that Simpson's rule is of degree three rather than two (which explains the surprisingly high accuracy obtained in Example 8.2).

In general, for any odd value of n, an n-point Newton-Cotes rule has degree one greater than that of the polynomial interpolant on which it is based. This phenomenon is due to cancellation of positive and negative errors, as illustrated for the midpoint and Simpson rules in Fig. 8.3, which, on the left, shows a linear polynomial and the constant function interpolating it at the midpoint and, on the right, a cubic and the quadratic interpolating it at the midpoint and endpoints. Integration of the linear polynomial by the midpoint rule yields two congruent triangles of equal area. The inclusion of one of the triangles compensates exactly for the omission of the other. A similar phenomenon occurs for the cubic polynomial, where the two shaded regions also have equal areas, so that the addition of one compensates for the subtraction of the other. Such cancellation does not occur, however, for an n-point Newton-Cotes rule if n is even. Thus, in general, an n-point Newton-Cotes rule is of degree $n-1$ if n is even, but of degree n if n is odd.

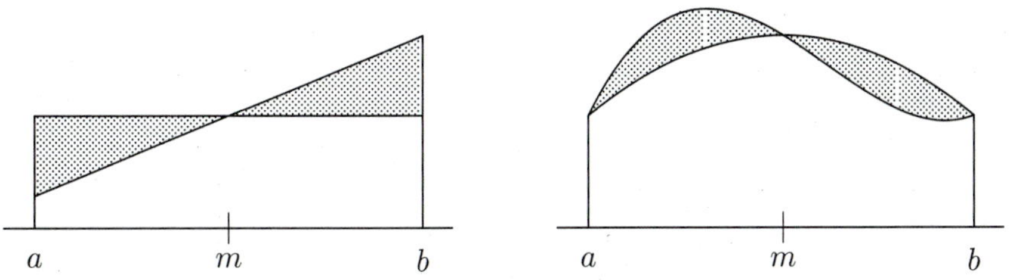

Figure 8.3: Cancellation of errors in midpoint (left) and Simpson (right) rules.

Newton-Cotes quadrature rules are relatively easy to derive and to apply, but they have some serious drawbacks. Recall from Section 7.3.5 that interpolation of a continuous function at equally spaced points by a high-degree polynomial may suffer from unwanted oscillation, and as the number of interpolation points grows, convergence to the underlying function is not guaranteed. The consequence for quadrature rules based on such interpolation is that every n-point Newton-Cotes rule with $n \geq 11$ has at least one negative weight. Indeed, it can be shown that $\sum_{i=1}^{n} |w_i| \to \infty$ as $n \to \infty$, which means that Newton-Cotes rules become arbitrarily ill-conditioned, and hence unstable, as the number of points grows. The presence of large positive and negative weights also means that the value of the integral is computed as a sum of large quantities of differing sign, and hence substantial cancellation is likely in finite-precision arithmetic.

For the reasons just given, we cannot expect to attain arbitrarily high accuracy on a given interval by using a Newton-Cotes rule with a large number of points. In practice, therefore, Newton-Cotes rules are usually restricted to a modest number of points, and if higher accuracy is required, then the interval is subdivided and the rule is applied in each subinterval separately (such strategies will be discussed in Section 8.3.5). In this regard, a positive feature of Newton-Cotes rules is that they are progressive, but on the other hand, Newton-Cotes rules do not have the highest possible degree (and hence accuracy) for the number of points used (and hence the number of function evaluations required), and we will soon see that we can do much better.

8.3.2 Clenshaw-Curtis Quadrature

We saw in Section 7.3.5 that the *Chebyshev points*, suitably transformed from $[-1, 1]$ to a given interval of interest, have distinct advantages over equally spaced points for interpolating a continuous function by a polynomial. In particular, the maximum error over the interval is generally much smaller with the Chebyshev points, and the resulting interpolants converge to any sufficiently smooth function as the number of points $n \to \infty$. One might conjecture, therefore, that the Chebyshev points would also be a better choice of nodes for interpolatory quadrature rules, as was first suggested by Fejér, and indeed this expectation turns out to be the case.

With the Chebyshev points as nodes for a given n, the corresponding weights could be computed in the usual manner by integrating the Lagrange basis functions or by the method of undetermined coefficients. It can be shown that the resulting weights are always positive for any n, and that the resulting approximate values converge to the exact integral as $n \to \infty$. Thus, quadrature rules based on the Chebyshev points are extremely attractive in that they are always stable and significantly more accurate than Newton-Cotes rules for the same number of nodes.

Another attractive feature of such quadrature rules is that they can be implemented in a self-contained manner: as Clenshaw and Curtis first observed, the weights corresponding to the Chebyshev points need not be tabulated in advance or even computed explicitly at all. Instead, based on the trigonometric definition of the Chebyshev polynomials, they developed remarkably simple and efficient procedures for expressing the polynomial interpolant to the integrand function as a linear combination of Chebyshev polynomials, and then integrating the resulting approximation in closed form to arrive at an approximate value for the integral. Alternatively, techniques based on the fast Fourier transform (see Chapter 12) can be used to implement this type of quadrature rule. These efficient, self-contained implementations of quadrature rules based on the Chebyshev points have become known as *Clenshaw-Curtis* quadrature.

Although the zeros and extrema of the Chebyshev polynomials have similar properties in terms of the stability and accuracy of the resulting quadrature rules, the Chebyshev extrema, unlike the Chebyshev zeros, have the advantage of yielding *progressive* quadrature rules. If the number of Chebyshev extrema is increased from n to $2n-1$, then only $n-1$ new points are added, so that only $n-1$ new function evaluations are required. For this reason, use of the Chebyshev extrema is sometimes called *practical* Clenshaw-Curtis quadrature, whereas use of the Chebyshev zeros is called *classical* Clenshaw-Curtis quadrature or Fejér quadrature.

We have seen that Clenshaw-Curtis quadrature rules have many virtues: stability, accuracy, simplicity, self-containment, and progressiveness. Nevertheless, they are still not optimal in that the degree of an n-point rule is only $n-1$, which is well below the maximum possible. Next we will see that quadrature rules of optimal degree can be derived by exploiting all of the available degrees of freedom.

8.3.3 Gaussian Quadrature

In the quadrature rules we have seen thus far, the n nodes were prespecified and the n corresponding weights were then optimally chosen to maximize the degree of the resulting quadrature rule. With only n parameters free to be chosen, the resulting degree is generally $n-1$. If the locations of the nodes were also freely chosen, however, then there would be $2n$ free parameters, so that a degree of $2n-1$ should be achievable. In *Gaussian* quadrature, both the nodes and the weights are optimally chosen to maximize the degree of the resulting quadrature rule. In general, for each n there is a unique n-point Gaussian rule, and it is of degree $2n-1$. Gaussian quadrature rules therefore have the highest possible accuracy for the number of nodes used, but they are significantly more difficult to derive than Newton-Cotes rules. The nodes and weights can still be determined by the method of undetermined coefficients, but the resulting system of equations is nonlinear.

Example 8.4 Gaussian Quadrature Rule. To illustrate the derivation of a Gaussian quadrature rule, we will derive a two-point rule on the interval $[-1,1]$,

$$I(f) = \int_{-1}^{1} f(x)\,dx \approx w_1 f(x_1) + w_2 f(x_2) = G_2(f),$$

where the nodes x_1, x_2 as well as the weights w_1, w_2 are to be chosen to maximize the resulting degree. Requiring that the rule integrate the first four monomials exactly gives the system of four moment equations

$$\begin{aligned}
w_1 + w_2 &= \int_{-1}^{1} 1\,dx = 2, \\
w_1 x_1 + w_2 x_2 &= \int_{-1}^{1} x\,dx = 0, \\
w_1 x_1^2 + w_2 x_2^2 &= \int_{-1}^{1} x^2\,dx = \frac{2}{3}, \\
w_1 x_1^3 + w_2 x_2^3 &= \int_{-1}^{1} x^3\,dx = 0.
\end{aligned}$$

One solution for this nonlinear system is given by

$$x_1 = -1/\sqrt{3}, \qquad x_2 = 1/\sqrt{3}, \qquad w_1 = 1, \qquad w_2 = 1,$$

and the other solution is obtained by reversing the signs of x_1 and x_2 (see Computer Problem 5.24). Thus, the two-point Gaussian quadrature rule has the form

$$G_2(f) = f(-1/\sqrt{3}\,) + f(1/\sqrt{3}\,),$$

and by construction it has degree three.

Alternatively, the nodes of a Gaussian quadrature rule can be obtained by using orthogonal polynomials. If p is a polynomial of degree n such that

$$\int_a^b p(x)x^k\,dx = 0, \quad k = 0, \ldots, n-1,$$

and hence p is orthogonal to all polynomials on $[a, b]$ of degree less than n, then it is fairly easy to show (see Exercise 8.9) that

1. The n zeros of p are real, simple, and lie in the open interval (a, b).
2. The n-point interpolatory quadrature rule on $[a, b]$ whose nodes are the zeros of p has degree $2n - 1$; i.e., it is the unique n-point Gaussian rule.

The Legendre polynomial P_n (see Section 7.3.4) is just such a polynomial. For this reason, the resulting rule is often called a Gauss-Legendre quadrature rule. Of course, the zeros of the Legendre polynomial must still be computed, and then the corresponding weights for the quadrature rule can be determined in the usual way. This method also extends naturally to various other weight functions and intervals corresponding to other families of orthogonal polynomials. The nodes and weights for a Gaussian quadrature rule can also be computed by solving an eigenvalue problem for a tridiagonal matrix associated with the corresponding orthogonal polynomials and weight function (see [165]).

Example 8.4 is typical in that for any n the Gaussian nodes are symmetrically placed about the midpoint of the interval; for odd values of n the midpoint itself is always a node. Example 8.4 is also typical in that the nodes are usually irrational numbers even when the endpoints a and b are rational. This feature makes Gaussian rules relatively inconvenient for hand computation, compared with simple Newton-Cotes rules. When using a computer, however, the nodes and weights are usually tabulated in advance and contained in a subroutine that can be called when needed, so the user need not compute or even know their actual values. The nodes and weights for many Gaussian quadrature rules are tabulated in [2, 385, 435].

Gaussian quadrature rules are also more difficult to apply than Newton-Cotes rules because the weights and nodes are derived for some specific interval, such as $[-1, 1]$, and thus any other interval of integration $[a, b]$ must be transformed into the standard interval for which the nodes and weights have been tabulated. If we wish to use a quadrature rule that is tabulated on the interval $[\alpha, \beta]$,

$$\int_\alpha^\beta f(x)\,dx \approx \sum_{i=1}^n w_i f(x_i),$$

to approximate an integral on the interval $[a, b]$,

$$I(g) = \int_a^b g(t)\,dt,$$

then we must use a change of variable from x in $[\alpha, \beta]$ to t in $[a, b]$. Many such transformations are possible, but a simple linear transformation

$$t = \frac{(b-a)x + a\beta - b\alpha}{\beta - \alpha}$$

has the advantage of preserving the degree of the quadrature rule. The integral is then given by

$$\begin{aligned} I(g) &= \frac{b-a}{\beta-\alpha} \int_\alpha^\beta g\left(\frac{(b-a)x + a\beta - b\alpha}{\beta - \alpha}\right) dx \\ &\approx \frac{b-a}{\beta-\alpha} \sum_{i=1}^n w_i g\left(\frac{(b-a)x_i + a\beta - b\alpha}{\beta - \alpha}\right). \end{aligned}$$

Example 8.5 Change of Interval. To illustrate a change of interval, we use the two-point Gaussian quadrature rule G_2 derived for the interval $[-1, 1]$ in Example 8.4 to approximate the integral

$$I(g) = \int_0^1 e^{-t^2}\,dt$$

from Example 8.2. Using the linear transformation of variable just given, we have

$$t = \frac{x+1}{2},$$

so that the integral is approximated by $G_2(g) =$

$$\frac{1}{2}\left[\exp\left(-\left(\frac{(-1/\sqrt{3})+1}{2}\right)^2\right) + \exp\left(-\left(\frac{(1/\sqrt{3})+1}{2}\right)^2\right)\right] \approx 0.746595,$$

which is slightly more accurate than the result given by Simpson's rule for this integral (see Example 8.2), despite using only two points instead of three.

By design, Gaussian quadrature rules have maximal degree, and hence optimal accuracy, for the number of points used. Moreover, it can be shown that the resulting weights are always positive for any n, so that Gaussian quadrature rules are always stable and the resulting approximate values converge to the exact integral as $n \to \infty$. Unfortunately, Gaussian quadrature rules also have a serious drawback: for $m \neq n$, G_m and G_n have no nodes in common (except for the midpoint when m and n are both odd). Thus, Gaussian rules are *not* progressive, which means that when the number of nodes is increased, say from n to m, m new evaluations of the integrand are required rather than $m - n$. We will see next how this deficiency can be remedied, but at some cost in the degree attainable.

8.3.4 Progressive Gaussian Quadrature

We have just observed that Gaussian quadrature rules are not progressive: if all the nodes and weights are freely chosen to maximize the degree for any given number of nodes, then rules with different numbers of nodes will have essentially no nodes in common, which means that integrand values computed for one set of nodes cannot be reused in evaluating another rule with a different number of nodes.

Avoiding this additional work is the motivation for *Kronrod* quadrature rules. Such rules come in pairs: an n-point Gaussian rule G_n and a $(2n+1)$-point Kronrod rule K_{2n+1} whose nodes are optimally chosen subject to the constraint that all of the nodes of G_n are reused in K_{2n+1}. Thus, n of the nodes used in K_{2n+1} are prespecified, leaving the remaining $n+1$ nodes, as well as all $2n+1$ of the weights (including those corresponding to the nodes of G_n), free to be chosen to maximize the degree of the resulting rule. The rule K_{2n+1} is therefore of degree $3n+1$, whereas a true $(2n+1)$-point Gaussian rule would be of degree $4n+1$. Thus, there is a tradeoff between accuracy and efficiency.

One of the main reasons for using two quadrature rules with different numbers of points is to obtain an error estimate for the approximate value of the integral based on the difference between the values given by the two rules. In using a Gauss-Kronrod pair, the value of K_{2n+1} is taken as the approximation to the integral, and a realistic but conservative estimate for the error, based partly on theory and partly on experience, is given by

$$(200\,|G_n - K_{2n+1}|)^{1.5}.$$

Because they efficiently provide both high accuracy and a reliable error estimate, Gauss-Kronrod rules are among the most effective quadrature methods available, and they form the basis for many of the quadrature routines in major software libraries. The pair of rules (G_7, K_{15}), in particular, has become a commonly used standard.

This approach of adding optimally chosen new nodes to a prespecified set from another rule is taken a step further in *Patterson* quadrature rules. In particular, adding $2n+2$ optimally chosen nodes to the $2n+1$ nodes of the Kronrod rule K_{2n+1} yields a quadrature rule with degree $6n+4$ that reuses all of the $2n+1$ integrand values already computed for G_n and K_{2n+1}. For certain values of n, further extensions of this type are possible, and some of these have been tabulated for rules of up to 511 points.

Before we leave this topic, we note that much more modest extensions of Gaussian quadrature rules are sometimes useful. A true Gaussian quadrature rule is always *open*, i.e., the nodes never include the endpoints of the interval of integration. But for some purposes, it is useful if one or both endpoints are included. In *Gauss-Radau* quadrature, one of the endpoints of the interval of integration is prespecified as a node, leaving the remaining $n-1$ nodes, as well as all n weights, free to be chosen to maximize the degree of the resulting rule. There are $2n-1$ free parameters, so an n-point Gauss-Radau rule has degree $2n-2$. Similarly, in *Gauss-Lobatto* quadrature, both endpoints of the interval of integration are prespecified as nodes, leaving the remaining $n-2$ nodes, as well as all n weights, free to be chosen to maximize the degree of the resulting rule. There are $2n-2$ free parameters, so an n-point Gauss-Lobatto rule has degree $2n-3$.

8.3.5 Composite Quadrature

Thus far we have considered simple quadrature rules obtained by interpolating the integrand function by a single polynomial over the entire interval of integration. The accuracy of such a rule can be increased, and the error estimated, by increasing the number of interpolation points, and hence the corresponding degree of the polynomial interpolant. Another alternative is to subdivide the original interval into two or more subintervals and apply a simple quadrature rule in each subinterval. Summing these partial results then yields an approximation to the overall integral. Such an approach is equivalent to using piecewise polynomial interpolation on the original interval and then integrating the piecewise interpolant to approximate the integral.

A *composite*, or *compound*, quadrature rule on a given interval $[a, b]$ results from subdividing the interval into k subintervals, typically of uniform length $h = (b-a)/k$, applying an n-point simple quadrature rule Q_n in each subinterval, and then taking the sum of these results as the approximate value of the integral. If the rule Q_n is open, then evaluating the composite rule will require kn evaluations of the integrand function. If Q_n is closed, on the other hand, then some of the points are repeated, so that only $k(n-1)+1$ evaluations of the integrand are required.

Example 8.6 Composite Quadrature Rules. If the interval $[a, b]$ is subdivided into k subintervals of length $h = (b-a)/k$ and $x_j = a + jh$, $j = 0, \ldots, k$, then the *composite midpoint rule* is given by

$$M_k(f) = \sum_{j=1}^{k} (x_j - x_{j-1})\, f\left(\frac{x_{j-1}+x_j}{2}\right) = h \sum_{j=1}^{k} f\left(\frac{x_{j-1}+x_j}{2}\right),$$

and the *composite trapezoid rule* is given by

$$\begin{aligned} T_k(f) &= \sum_{j=1}^{k} \frac{(x_j - x_{j-1})}{2}\,(f(x_{j-1}) + f(x_j)) \\ &= h\left(\tfrac{1}{2}f(a) + f(x_1) + \cdots + f(x_{k-1}) + \tfrac{1}{2}f(b)\right). \end{aligned}$$

A composite rule is always stable provided the underlying rule Q_n is stable. Convergence to the exact integral as the number of subintervals $k \to \infty$ is guaranteed, provided the underlying rule Q_n has degree at least zero (i.e., it integrates constants exactly). To see why, let the composite rule be given by

$$C_k(f) = \sum_{j=1}^{k} \left(\sum_{i=1}^{n} w_i\, f(x_{ij}) \right),$$

where w_i is the ith weight of Q_n and x_{ij} is the ith node of Q_n in the jth subinterval. Interchanging the order of summation, we have

$$C_k(f) = \sum_{i=1}^{n}\left(\sum_{j=1}^{k} w_i\, f(x_{ij})\right) = \sum_{i=1}^{n} w_i \left(\sum_{j=1}^{k} f(x_{ij})\right) = \frac{1}{h}\sum_{i=1}^{n} w_i \left(\sum_{j=1}^{k} h\, f(x_{ij})\right).$$

The latter expression in parentheses is a Riemann sum, which by definition has limit $I(f)$ as $k \to \infty$ (see Section 8.1). Thus, we have

$$\lim_{k\to\infty} C_k(f) = \frac{1}{h}\sum_{i=1}^{n} w_i \lim_{k\to\infty}\left(\sum_{j=1}^{k} h\, f(x_{ij})\right) = I(f)\,\frac{1}{h}\sum_{i=1}^{n} w_i = I(f).$$

The last equality follows from the fact that Q_n integrates constants exactly, so that the sum of the weights is equal to h, the subinterval length. Thus, in principle, by taking k sufficiently large it is possible to achieve arbitrarily high accuracy (up to the limit of the arithmetic precision) using a composite rule, even with an underlying rule Q_n of low degree, although this may not be the most efficient way to attain a given level of accuracy. Indeed, the general error bound in Section 8.3 suggests that more can usually be gained by increasing n than by decreasing h. In practice, a compromise between these is usually most appropriate.

Composite quadrature rules offer a particularly simple means of estimating the error by using different levels of subdivision, which can easily be made progressive. We observed in Section 8.3.1 that halving the interval length reduces the error in the midpoint or trapezoid rules by a factor of about 1/8. Halving their length doubles the number of subintervals, however, so the overall reduction in the error is by a factor of about 1/4. If the number of subintervals is k, and hence the subinterval length is $h = (b-a)/k$, then the dominant term in the remainder for the composite midpoint or trapezoid rules is $\mathcal{O}(kh^3) = \mathcal{O}(h^2)$, so the accuracy of these rules is said to be of second order. Similarly, the composite Simpson's rule is of fourth-order accuracy, meaning that the dominant term in its remainder is $\mathcal{O}(h^4)$, and hence halving the subinterval length reduces the overall error by a factor of about 1/16.

8.3.6 Adaptive Quadrature

A composite quadrature rule with an error estimate suggests a simple *automatic* quadrature procedure: continue subdividing all the subintervals until the estimated overall error meets the desired accuracy tolerance. Maintaining uniform subdivisions is grossly inefficient for many integrands, however, as large numbers of function evaluations may be expended in regions where the integrand function is well behaved and the accuracy tolerance is easily met. A more intelligent approach is *adaptive* quadrature, in which the interval of integration is selectively refined to reflect the behavior of any particular integrand function.

A typical adaptive quadrature strategy works as follows. First we need a pair of quadrature rules, say Q_{n_1} and Q_{n_2}, whose difference provides an error estimate. A simple example is the trapezoid and midpoint rules, whose difference overestimates the error in the more accurate rule by a factor of three, as we saw in Section 8.3.1. Greater efficiency is usually obtained with rules of higher degree, however, such as the Gauss-Kronrod pair (G_7,K_{15}). Another alternative is to use a single rule at two different levels of subdivision; Simpson's rule is a popular choice in this approach. In any case, to minimize the number of function evaluations required, the pair of rules should be progressive.

The adaptive procedure is now conceptually simple: apply both rules Q_{n_1} and Q_{n_2} on the initial interval of integration $[a, b]$. If the resulting approximate values for the integral differ by more than the desired tolerance, divide the interval into two or more subintervals and repeat the procedure on each subinterval. If the tolerance is met on a given subinterval, then no further subdivision of that subinterval will be required. If the tolerance is not met on a given subinterval, then the subdivision process is repeated again, and so on until the tolerance is met on all subintervals. Such a strategy leads to a nonuniform sampling of the integrand function that places many sample points in regions where the function is difficult to integrate and relatively few points where the function is easily integrated, as illustrated in Fig. 8.4.

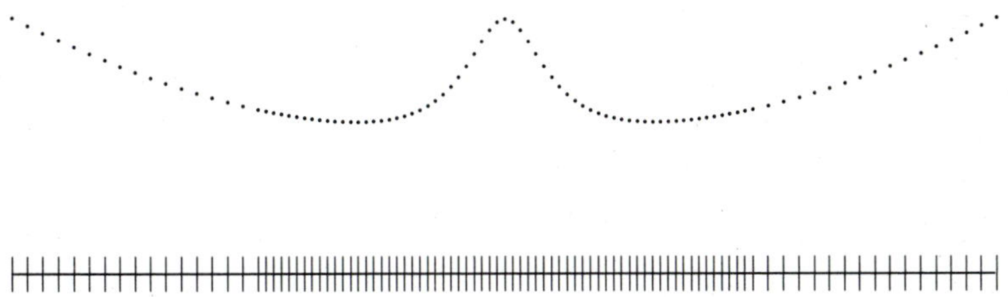

Figure 8.4: Typical placement of evaluation points by adaptive quadrature routine.

The high-level description just given glosses over a number of important implementation issues, including

- How should the stopping criterion be implemented? For example, should the error tolerance be relative (usually preferable), or absolute (in case the value of the integral is near zero), or a combination of the two?
- Can the error tolerance always eventually be met? Will the recursion always terminate?
- How can we avoid wasting time subdividing unconverged subintervals that make a negligible contribution to the total integral?
- How should we allow for the effects of finite-precision arithmetic? For example, what if the length of a subinterval becomes so small that it contains no machine numbers other than its endpoints?

In many adaptive quadrature routines these issues are addressed by using some combination of relative and absolute error tests involving machine-dependent parameters (such as the machine precision ϵ_{mach}), together with an upper limit on the number of levels of subdivision allowed. When confronted with a difficult problem, such as a noisy or unsmooth integrand or an unrealistically tight error tolerance, such routines may expend a large number of function evaluations before returning an inaccurate answer accompanied by a warning message that the subdivision limit was exceeded.

Gander and Gautschi suggested an alternative approach that often does considerably better. The key idea is to develop a termination criterion that is robust, machine independent, and avoids arbitrary limits on the depth of the recursion. An important ingredient in such a criterion is a rough prior estimate of the magnitude of the integral, call it $\hat{I}$. Such a rough estimate, which need merely be of the correct order of magnitude, can be obtained in various ways, such as sampling the integrand f at a few randomly chosen points within the interval of integration $[a, b]$. For a given subinterval, relative (or absolute) agreement of the quadrature rules Q_{n_1} and Q_{n_2} to within machine precision can then be checked by testing whether $\hat{I} + (Q_{n_2} - Q_{n_1})$ differs from $\hat{I}$. A user-supplied tolerance $\epsilon \geq \epsilon_{\text{mach}}$ can be implemented by increasing $\hat{I}$ by a factor of $\epsilon/\epsilon_{\text{mach}}$. Finally, an arbitrary limit on subdivision levels can be avoided in a similarly machine-independent way by testing whether the computed midpoint of a subinterval lies strictly within the subinterval. A generic adaptive quadrature procedure with these features is summarized in Algorithm 8.1.

Algorithm 8.1 Adaptive Quadrature

```
procedure adaptquad(f, a, b, Î)
    I1 = Qn1(f, a, b)                    { evaluate quadrature rules }
    I2 = Qn2(f, a, b)
    m = a + (b − a)/2                    { compute midpoint of interval }
    if (m ≤ a or m ≥ b) then             { if no more machine numbers,
        issue warning                        tolerance may not be met }
        return I2                        { return best result }
    end
    if Î + (I2 − I1) = Î then            { if convergence tolerance met,
        return I2                            return converged result }
    else                                 { if convergence tolerance not met,
        return (adaptquad(f, a, m, Î) +      subdivide recursively}
                adaptquad(f, m, b, Î))
    end
```

Although adaptive quadrature procedures tend to be very effective in practice, they can be fooled: both the approximate integral and the error estimate can be completely wrong. The reason is that the integrand function is sampled at only a finite number of points, so it is possible that significant features of the integrand may be missed. For example, it may happen that the interval of integration is very wide, but all of the "interesting" behavior of the integrand is confined to a very narrow range. In this case, sampling by the adaptive routine may completely miss the interesting part of the integrand's behavior, and the resulting value for the integral may be completely wrong. This situation may seem unlikely, but it can happen, for example, if we are trying to evaluate an integral over an unbounded interval and have truncated it unwisely (see Section 8.4.2).

Another potential difficulty with adaptive quadrature routines is that they may be very inefficient in handling discontinuities (finite jumps) in the integrand or its derivatives. For example, an adaptive routine may expend a great many function evaluations in refining the region around a discontinuity of the integrand because it assumes that the integrand is smooth (but very steep) at such a point. A good way to avoid such behavior is to split the interval at the point of discontinuity into two subintervals and call the quadrature routine separately in each, thereby obviating the need for the routine to resolve the discontinuity.

8.4 Other Integration Problems

8.4.1 Tabular Data

Thus far we have assumed that the integrand function can be evaluated at any desired point within the interval of integration. This assumption may not be valid if the integrand is defined only by a table of its values at selected discrete points, as is typical of empirical measurements, for example. A reasonable approach to integrating such tabular data is by piecewise interpolation. For example, integrating the piecewise linear interpolant to tabular data gives a composite trapezoid rule. An excellent method for integrating tabular data is provided by Hermite cubic or cubic spline interpolation. In effect, the overall integral is computed by integrating analytically each of the cubic pieces that make up the interpolant. This facility is provided by some of the spline interpolation packages cited in Section 7.5.

8.4.2 Improper Integrals

Boundedness of both the integrand function and the interval of integration are inherent in the definition of the Riemann integral. If either the integrand or the interval is unbounded, then it may still be possible to define an *improper integral*. For an unbounded interval, say $[a, \infty)$, the improper integral is defined as

$$\int_a^\infty f(x)\,dx = \lim_{b\to\infty} \int_a^b f(x)\,dx,$$

provided f is integrable on $[a, b]$ for any finite b, and the indicated limit exists and is finite. Unbounded intervals of the form $(-\infty, b]$ or $(-\infty, \infty)$ are treated similarly. For an integrand that is unbounded at a point $c \in [a, b]$, i.e., a *vertical asymptote* or *singularity* of the integrand, the improper integral is defined as

$$\int_a^b f(x)\,dx = \lim_{\gamma\to c-} \int_a^\gamma f(x)\,dx + \lim_{\gamma\to c+} \int_\gamma^b f(x)\,dx,$$

provided that f is integrable on any subinterval $[a, \gamma] \subseteq [a, c)$ and $[\gamma, b] \subseteq (c, b]$, and the indicated limits exist and are finite. There are a number of ways of computing such improper integrals, assuming of course that the integral exists.

For an unbounded interval of integration, one may be able to compute the improper integral using a standard quadrature routine for a finite interval. A number of approaches are possible:

- Replace any infinite limit of integration by a finite value. Such a finite limit should be chosen carefully so that the omitted tail is negligible or its contribution to the integral can be estimated. But the remaining finite interval should not be so wide that an adaptive quadrature routine will be fooled into sampling the integrand badly.
- Transform the variable of integration so that the new interval is finite. Typical transformations include $x = -\log t$ or $x = t/(1-t)$. Care must be taken not to introduce singularities or other difficulties by such a transformation.

Another alternative is to use a quadrature rule, such as Gauss-Laguerre or Gauss-Hermite, that is designed for an unbounded interval.

For an integrand having an integrable singularity within the interval of integration, one may be tempted simply to try an adaptive quadrature routine and hope that it will work, but such an approach is unlikely to prove satisfactory. Outright failure will result if the integrand happens to be evaluated at the singularity, which will likely occur if the singularity lies at one of the endpoints, as singularities often do. Even if the routine is lucky enough to avoid evaluating the integrand at the singularity, an adaptive quadrature routine will generally be extremely inefficient for an integrand having a singularity because polynomials, which never have vertical asymptotes, cannot efficiently approximate functions that do (recall that our error bounds depend on higher derivatives of the integrand, which will inevitably be large near a singularity).

A better approach for dealing with a singularity in the integrand is to remove the singularity either by transforming the variable of integration or by dividing out or subtracting off an analytically integrable function having the same singularity. As an example of the first approach, the integral

$$\int_0^{\pi/2} \frac{\cos(x)}{\sqrt{x}}\, dx$$

has a singularity at $x = 0$, but under the transformation $x = t^2$ it becomes the innocuous integral

$$\int_0^{\pi/2} \frac{\cos(x)}{\sqrt{x}}\, dx = \int_0^{\sqrt{\pi/2}} \frac{\cos(t^2)}{t}\, 2t\, dt = 2\int_0^{\sqrt{\pi/2}} \cos(t^2)\, dt,$$

which has no singularity and is easily integrable by an adaptive routine. As an example of the second approach, the integral

$$\int_0^{\pi/2} \frac{1}{\sqrt{\sin x}}\, dx$$

has a singularity at $x = 0$, but by subtracting off $1/\sqrt{x}$ we have

$$\int_0^{\pi/2} \frac{1}{\sqrt{\sin x}}\, dx = \int_0^{\pi/2} \left(\frac{1}{\sqrt{\sin x}} - \frac{1}{\sqrt{x}}\right) dx + \int_0^{\pi/2} \frac{1}{\sqrt{x}}\, dx.$$

The first of the two resulting integrands is now well behaved near 0 and can safely be replaced by 0 at 0, and the second is analytically integrable to give the value

$2\sqrt{2\pi}$. There is often some art involved in finding such transformations, and not all singularities are removable in this manner. If there is more than one singularity, then the transformations required to remove them may conflict, in which case a remedy is to break the interval of integration into subintervals, each of which contains at most one singularity, typically at one endpoint.

8.4.3 Double Integrals

Thus far we have considered only one-dimensional integrals, where we wish to determine the area under a curve over an interval. In evaluating a two-dimensional, or *double integral*, we wish to compute the volume under a surface over a planar region. For a rectangular region $[a, b] \times [c, d] \subseteq \mathbb{R}^2$, a double integral has the form

$$\int_a^b \int_c^d f(x, y)\, dx\, dy.$$

For a more general domain $\Omega \subseteq \mathbb{R}^2$, the integral takes the form

$$\iint_\Omega f(x, y)\, dA.$$

By analogy with numerical quadrature for one-dimensional integrals, the numerical approximation of two-dimensional integrals is sometimes called *numerical cubature*.

To evaluate a double integral, a number of approaches are available, including the following:

- Use a pair of adaptive one-dimensional quadrature routines, one for the outer integral and the other for the inner integral. Each time the outer routine calls its integrand function, the latter in turn calls the inner quadrature routine. This approach requires some care in setting the error tolerances for the respective quadrature routines.
- Use a Cartesian product rule. Such rules result from applying one-dimensional quadrature rules in successive dimensions. This approach is limited to regions that can be decomposed into rectangles.
- Use a nonproduct interpolatory cubature rule. Such rules, with error estimates, are available for a number of standard regions, the most important of which for adaptive use is triangles, since many two-dimensional regions can be efficiently triangulated to any desired level of refinement.

8.4.4 Multiple Integrals

To evaluate a multiple integral in dimensions higher than two, the options just listed for double integrals still work in principle, but their cost grows rapidly with the number of dimensions. The only generally viable approach for computing integrals in higher dimensions is the *Monte Carlo method*. The function is sampled at n points distributed randomly in the domain of integration, and then the mean of these function values is multiplied by the area (or volume, etc.) of the domain to obtain an estimate for the integral. The error in this estimate goes to zero as $1/\sqrt{n}$, which means, for example, that to gain an additional decimal digit of accuracy the number of sample points must be increased by a factor of 100. For this reason, it is not unusual for Monte Carlo calculations of integrals to require millions of evaluations of the integrand.

The Monte Carlo method is not competitive for integrals in one or two dimensions, but the beauty of the method is that its convergence rate is independent of the number of dimensions. Thus, for example, one million points in six dimensions amounts to only ten points per dimension, which is much better than any type of conventional quadrature rule would require for the same level of accuracy. The efficiency of Monte Carlo integration can be enhanced by various methods for biasing the sampling, either to achieve more uniform coverage of the sampled volume (e.g., by avoiding undesirable random clumping of the sample points; see Section 13.4) or to concentrate sampling in regions where the integrand is largest in magnitude (importance sampling) or in variability (stratified sampling), in a spirit similar to adaptive quadrature. See Chapter 13 for further information on the use of random sampling for numerical integration as well as other types of problems.

8.5 Integral Equations

An *integral equation* is an equation in which the unknown to be determined is a *function* inside an integral sign. An integral equation can be thought of as a continuous analogue, or limiting case, of a system of algebraic equations. For example, the analogue of a linear system $\boldsymbol{Ax} = \boldsymbol{y}$ is a *Fredholm integral equation of the first kind*, which has the form

$$\int_a^b K(s,t)\,u(t)\,dt = f(s),$$

where the functions K, called the *kernel*, and f are known, and the function u is to be determined. Integral equations arise naturally in many fields of science and engineering, particularly observational sciences (e.g., astronomy, seismology, spectrometry, tomography), where the kernel K represents the response function of an instrument (determined by calibration with known signals), f represents measured data, and u represents the underlying signal that is sought. In effect, we are trying to *resolve* the measured data f as a (continuous) linear combination of standard signals. Integral equations also result from Green's function methods [331] or boundary element methods [241] for solving differential equations (topics beyond the scope of this book).

Establishing the existence and uniqueness of solutions to integral equations is much more problematic than with algebraic equations. Moreover, when a solution does exist, it may be extremely sensitive to perturbations in the input data, which are often subject to random experimental or measurement errors. The reason for this sensitivity is that integration is a smoothing process, so its inverse (i.e., determining the integrand from the integral) is just the opposite. Integrating an arbitrary function u against a smooth kernel K dampens any high-frequency oscillation, so solving for u tends to *introduce* high-frequency oscillation in the result.

According to the *Riemann-Lebesgue Lemma*,

$$\lim_{n\to\infty} \int_a^b K(s,t)\sin(nt)\,dt = 0$$

for any integrable kernel K, which implies that an arbitrarily high-frequency component of u has an arbitrarily small effect on f. Thus, integral equations of the first kind with smooth kernels are always ill-conditioned.

A standard technique for solving integral equations numerically is to use a quadrature rule to replace the integral by an approximating finite sum. Denote the nodes and weights of the quadrature rule by t_j and w_j, $j = 1, \ldots, n$. We also choose n points s_i for the variable s, often the same as the t_j, but not necessarily so. Then the approximation to the integral equation becomes

$$\sum_{j=1}^{n} w_j K(s_i, t_j)\, u(t_j) = f(s_i), \quad i = 1, \ldots n.$$

This is a system of linear algebraic equations $\boldsymbol{Ax} = \boldsymbol{y}$, where $a_{ij} = w_j K(s_i, t_j)$, $y_i = f(s_i)$, and $x_j = u(t_j)$, which can be solved for $\boldsymbol{x}$ to obtain a discrete sample of approximate values of the function u.

Example 8.7 Integral Equation. Consider the integral equation

$$\int_{-1}^{1} (1 + \alpha st)\, u(t)\, dt = 1,$$

i.e., $K(s,t) = 1 + \alpha st$ and $f(s) = 1$, where α is a known positive constant whose value is unspecified for now. Using the composite midpoint quadrature rule with two subintervals, taking $t_1 = -\frac{1}{2}$, $t_2 = \frac{1}{2}$, and $w_1 = w_2 = 1$, and also taking $s_1 = -\frac{1}{2}$ and $s_2 = \frac{1}{2}$, we obtain the linear system

$$\boldsymbol{Ax} = \begin{bmatrix} 1+\alpha/4 & 1-\alpha/4 \\ 1-\alpha/4 & 1+\alpha/4 \end{bmatrix} \begin{bmatrix} x_1 \\ x_2 \end{bmatrix} = \begin{bmatrix} 1 \\ 1 \end{bmatrix} = \boldsymbol{y}.$$

It is easily verified that the solution to this linear system is $\boldsymbol{x} = \begin{bmatrix} \frac{1}{2} & \frac{1}{2} \end{bmatrix}^T$, independent of the value of α.

Now suppose that the errors in the measured values of $y_1 = f(s_1)$ and $y_2 = f(s_2)$ are ϵ_1 and ϵ_2, respectively. Then by linearity, the change in the solution $\boldsymbol{x}$ is given by the same linear system, but with a right-hand side of $\begin{bmatrix} \epsilon_1 & \epsilon_2 \end{bmatrix}^T$. The resulting change in $\boldsymbol{x}$ is therefore given by

$$\Delta\boldsymbol{x} = \begin{bmatrix} \Delta x_1 \\ \Delta x_2 \end{bmatrix} = \begin{bmatrix} (\epsilon_1 - \epsilon_2)/\alpha + (\epsilon_1 + \epsilon_2)/4 \\ (\epsilon_2 - \epsilon_1)/\alpha + (\epsilon_1 + \epsilon_2)/4 \end{bmatrix}.$$

Thus, if α is sufficiently small, the relative error in the computed value for $\boldsymbol{x}$ can be arbitrarily large. A very small value for α in this particular kernel corresponds to a very insensitive instrument with a very flat response. This is reflected in the conditioning of the matrix $\boldsymbol{A}$, whose columns become more nearly linearly dependent as α decreases in magnitude. This simple example is typical of integral equations with smooth kernels.

Note that the sensitivity in the previous example is inherent in the problem and is not due to the method of solving it. In general, such an integral operator with a smooth kernel has zero as an eigenvalue (i.e., there are nonzero functions that it annihilates), and hence using a more accurate quadrature rule makes the conditioning of the linear system worse and the resulting solution more erratic. Because of this behavior, additional information may be required to obtain a physically meaningful solution. Such techniques include:

- *Truncated singular value decomposition.* The solution to the system $\boldsymbol{Ax} = \boldsymbol{y}$ is computed using the SVD of $\boldsymbol{A}$; but the small singular values of $\boldsymbol{A}$, which reflect the ill-conditioning, are omitted from the solution (see Section 3.6).
- *Regularization.* A damped solution is obtained by solving the minimization problem
$$\min_{\boldsymbol{x}}(\|\boldsymbol{y} - \boldsymbol{Ax}\|_2^2 + \mu\|\boldsymbol{x}\|_2^2),$$
where the nonnegative parameter μ determines the relative weight given to the norm of the residual and the norm of the solution. This minimization problem is equivalent to the linear least squares problem
$$\begin{bmatrix} \boldsymbol{A} \\ \sqrt{\mu}\boldsymbol{I} \end{bmatrix} \boldsymbol{x} \cong \begin{bmatrix} \boldsymbol{y} \\ \boldsymbol{0} \end{bmatrix},$$
which can be solved by the methods discussed in Chapter 3. More generally, other norms, usually based on first or second differences between its components, can also be used to weight the smoothness of the solution. The Levenberg-Marquardt method for nonlinear least squares problems (see Section 6.6.2) is another example of regularization.
- *Constrained optimization.* Some norm of the residual $\|\boldsymbol{y} - \boldsymbol{Ax}\|$ is minimized subject to constraints on $\boldsymbol{x}$ that disallow nonphysical solutions. In many applications, for example, the components of the solution $\boldsymbol{x}$ are required to be nonnegative or monotonic. The resulting constrained optimization problem can then be solved using the methods discussed in Section 6.7.

Several such methods are implemented in the `MATLAB` toolbox documented in [187].

We have considered only Fredholm integral equations of the first kind. Many other types arise in practice, including integral equations of the second kind (eigenvalue problems), Volterra integral equations (which differ from Fredholm integral equations in that the upper limit of integration is the variable s instead of the fixed value b), singular integral equations (in which one or both of the limits of integration are infinite), and nonlinear integral equations. All types of integral equations can be discretized by means of numerical quadrature, yielding a system of algebraic equations. Alternatively, the unknown function u can be approximated by a linear combination $u(t) \approx \sum_{j=1}^{n} c_j\phi_j(t)$ of suitably chosen basis functions ϕ_j, which leads to a system of algebraic equations for the coefficients c_j. This type of approach will be examined in more detail in Chapter 10, where we consider similar methods for boundary value problems for differential equations.

8.6 Numerical Differentiation

We now turn briefly to numerical differentiation. It is important to realize that differentiation is an inherently sensitive problem, as small perturbations in the data can cause large changes in the result. Integration, on the other hand, is a smoothing process and is inherently stable in this respect. The contrast between differentiation and integration should not be surprising, since they are inverse processes to each other. The difference between them is illustrated in Fig. 8.5, which shows two functions that have equal definite integrals but very different derivatives.

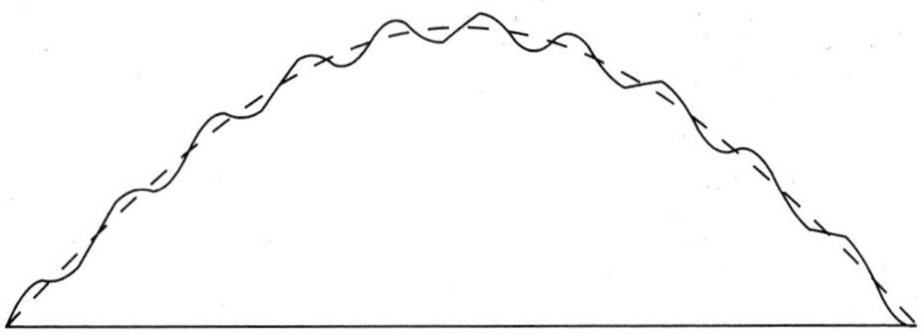

Figure 8.5: Two functions whose integrals are equal but whose derivatives are not.

When approximating the derivative of a function whose values are known only at a discrete set of points, a good approach is to fit some smooth function to the given discrete data and then differentiate the approximating function to approximate the derivatives of the original function. If the given data are sufficiently smooth, then interpolation may be appropriate; but if the given data are noisy, then a smoothing approximating function, such as a least squares polynomial or spline, is more appropriate. Consider the example shown in Fig. 3.1. If the 21 data points were fit exactly by a polynomial of degree 20, then the derivative of that polynomial would be quite erratic, changing sign many times, and moreover the derivative would be highly sensitive to small changes in the data. In sharp contrast, the derivative of the approximating quadratic polynomial (the solid curve in the figure) is well behaved and relatively insensitive to changes in the data.

8.6.1 Finite Difference Approximations

Although finite difference formulas are generally inappropriate for discrete or noisy data, they are very useful for approximating derivatives of a smooth function that is known analytically, or can be evaluated accurately for any given argument, or is defined implicitly by a differential equation. We now develop some finite difference formulas that will be useful in our study of the numerical solution of differential equations.

Given a smooth function $f: \mathbb{R} \to \mathbb{R}$, we wish to approximate its first and second derivatives at a point x. For a given step size h, consider the Taylor series expansions

$$f(x+h) = f(x) + f'(x)h + \frac{f''(x)}{2}h^2 + \frac{f'''(x)}{6}h^3 + \cdots$$

and

$$f(x-h) = f(x) - f'(x)h + \frac{f''(x)}{2}h^2 - \frac{f'''(x)}{6}h^3 + \cdots.$$

Solving for $f'(x)$ in the first series, we obtain the *forward difference formula*

$$\begin{aligned} f'(x) &= \frac{f(x+h)-f(x)}{h} - \frac{f''(x)}{2}h + \cdots \\ &\approx \frac{f(x+h)-f(x)}{h}, \end{aligned}$$

which gives an approximation that is first-order accurate since the dominant term in the remainder of the series is $\mathcal{O}(h)$. Similarly, from the second series we derive the *backward difference formula*

$$\begin{aligned} f'(x) &= \frac{f(x)-f(x-h)}{h} + \frac{f''(x)}{2}h + \cdots \\ &\approx \frac{f(x)-f(x-h)}{h}, \end{aligned}$$

which is also first-order accurate. Subtracting the second series from the first gives the *centered difference formula*

$$\begin{aligned} f'(x) &= \frac{f(x+h)-f(x-h)}{2h} - \frac{f'''(x)}{6}h^2 + \cdots \\ &\approx \frac{f(x+h)-f(x-h)}{2h}, \end{aligned}$$

which is second-order accurate. Finally, adding the two series together gives a centered difference formula for the second derivative

$$\begin{aligned} f''(x) &= \frac{f(x+h)-2f(x)+f(x-h)}{h^2} - \frac{f^{(4)}(x)}{12}h^2 + \cdots \\ &\approx \frac{f(x+h)-2f(x)+f(x-h)}{h^2}, \end{aligned}$$

which is also second-order accurate. By using function values at additional points, $x \pm 2h$, $x \pm 3h$, $\ldots$, we can derive similar finite difference approximations with still higher accuracy or for higher-order derivatives.

Note that higher-accuracy difference formulas require more function values. Whether these translate into higher overall cost depends on the particular situation, since a more accurate formula may permit the use of a larger step size h and correspondingly fewer steps. In choosing a value for h, rounding error must also be considered in addition to the truncation error given by the series expansion (see Example 1.3).

Using Taylor series expansions to derive finite difference formulas becomes increasingly cumbersome for approximations of increasingly high accuracy or higher-order derivatives. We next consider an alternative method based on polynomial interpolation that is not only more convenient, but will also more readily permit later generalization, for example to unequally spaced points. Let t_i, $i = 1, \ldots, n$ be equally spaced points in $\mathbb{R}$, with step size $h = t_{i+1} - t_i$, $i = 1, \ldots, n-1$. Let $y_i = f(t_i)$, $i = 1, \ldots, n$, where $f\colon \mathbb{R} \to \mathbb{R}$ is a smooth function.

For $i = 1, \ldots, n-1$, the polynomial of degree one interpolating the two data points $(t_i, y_i), (t_{i+1}, y_{i+1})$ is given by the Lagrange interpolant (see Section 7.3.2)

$$p(t) = y_i \frac{t - t_{i+1}}{t_i - t_{i+1}} + y_{i+1} \frac{t - t_i}{t_{i+1} - t_i} = y_i \frac{t - t_{i+1}}{-h} + y_{i+1} \frac{t - t_i}{h}.$$

Differentiating this polynomial with respect to t, we have

$$p'(t) = \frac{y_{i+1} - y_i}{h},$$

which is the same as the first-order, forward difference formula for the first derivative that we derived earlier using Taylor series. The first-order, backward difference formula for the first derivative can be derived similarly by interpolating $(t_{i-1}, y_{i-1}), (t_i, y_i)$.

For $i = 2, \ldots, n-1$, the polynomial of degree two interpolating the three data points $(t_{i-1}, y_{i-1}), (t_i, y_i), (t_{i+1}, y_{i+1})$ is given by the Lagrange interpolant

$$\begin{aligned} p(t) &= y_{i-1} \frac{(t - t_i)(t - t_{i+1})}{(t_{i-1} - t_i)(t_{i-1} - t_{i+1})} + y_i \frac{(t - t_{i-1})(t - t_{i+1})}{(t_i - t_{i-1})(t_i - t_{i+1})} \\ &\quad + y_{i+1} \frac{(t - t_{i-1})(t - t_i)}{(t_{i+1} - t_{i-1})(t_{i+1} - t_i)} \\ &= y_{i-1} \frac{(t - t_i)(t - t_{i+1})}{2h^2} + y_i \frac{(t - t_{i-1})(t - t_{i+1})}{-h^2} + y_{i+1} \frac{(t - t_{i-1})(t - t_i)}{2h^2}. \end{aligned}$$

Differentiating this polynomial with respect to t, we have

$$p'(t) = y_{i-1} \frac{(t - t_i) + (t - t_{i+1})}{2h^2} + y_i \frac{(t - t_{i-1}) + (t - t_{i+1})}{-h^2} + y_{i+1} \frac{(t - t_{i-1}) + (t - t_i)}{2h^2},$$

and evaluating the derivative at $t = t_i$ then gives

$$p'(t_i) = \frac{y_{i+1} - y_{i-1}}{2h},$$

which is the same as the second-order, centered difference formula for the first derivative that we derived earlier using Taylor series. Finally, differentiating a second time gives

$$p''(t) = y_{i-1} \frac{2}{2h^2} + y_i \frac{2}{-h^2} + y_{i+1} \frac{2}{2h^2} = \frac{y_{i+1} - 2y_i + y_{i-1}}{h^2},$$

which is the same as the second-order, centered difference formula for the second derivative that we derived earlier using Taylor series.

We can continue in this manner to compute approximate derivatives of higher accuracy or higher order by interpolating more points and using correspondingly higher degree polynomials. Indeed, we can achieve the highest possible accuracy or order for a given number of data points by interpolating *all* of the data points with a single polynomial. Moreover, this interpolatory approach is easily generalized. We could use other representations of the interpolating polynomial. We could use unequally spaced points, for example the Chebyshev points to achieve higher accuracy. We could use interpolating functions other than polynomials, for example trigonometric functions for periodic data.

8.6.2 Automatic Differentiation

A number of alternatives are available for computing derivatives of a function, including finite difference approximations or closed-form formulas determined either by hand or by a computer algebra package. Each of these methods has significant drawbacks, however: manual differentiation is tedious and error-prone; symbolic derivatives tend to be unwieldy for complicated functions; finite difference approximations require a sometimes delicate choice of step size, and their accuracy is limited by discretization error.

Another alternative, at least for any function expressed by a computer program, is *automatic differentiation*, often abbreviated as *AD*. The basic idea of AD is simple: a computer program consists of basic arithmetic operations and elementary functions, each of whose derivatives is easily computed. Thus, the function computed by the program is, in effect, a composite of many simple functions whose derivatives can be propagated through the program by repeated use of the chain rule, effectively computing the derivative of the function step by step along with the function itself. The result is the true derivative of the original function, subject only to rounding error but suffering no discretization error.

Though AD is conceptually simple, its practical implementation is more complicated, requiring careful analysis of the input program and clever strategies for reducing the potentially explosive complexity of the resulting derivative code. Fortunately, most of these practical impediments have been successfully overcome, and a number of effective software packages are now available for automatic differentiation. Some of these packages accept a Fortran or C input program and then output a second program for computing the desired derivatives, whereas other packages use operator overloading to perform derivative computations automatically along with the function evaluation. When applicable, AD can be much easier, more efficient, and more accurate than other methods for computing derivatives. AD can also be useful for determining the sensitivity of the output of a program to perturbations in its input parameters. Such information might otherwise be obtainable only through many repeated runs of the program, which could be prohibitively expensive for a large, complex program.

8.7 Richardson Extrapolation

In many problems, such as numerical integration or differentiation, we compute an approximate value for some quantity based on some step size. Ideally, we would like to obtain the limiting value as the step size goes to zero, but we cannot take the step size to be arbitrarily small because of excessive cost or rounding error. Based on values for nonzero step sizes, however, we may be able to estimate what the value would be for a step size of zero.

Let $F(h)$ denote the value obtained with step size h. If we compute the value of F for some nonzero step sizes, and if we know the theoretical behavior of $F(h)$ as $h \to 0$, then we can *extrapolate* from the known values to obtain an approximate value for $F(0)$. This extrapolated value should have a higher-order accuracy than the values on which it is based. We emphasize, however, that the extrapolated value, though an improvement, is still only an approximation, not the exact solution, and its accuracy is still limited by the step size and arithmetic precision used.

To be more specific, suppose that

$$F(h) = a_0 + a_1 h^p + \mathcal{O}(h^r)$$

as $h \to 0$ for some p and r, with $r > p$. We assume that we know the values of p and r, but not a_0 or a_1. Indeed, $F(0) = a_0$ is the quantity we seek. Suppose that we have computed F for two step sizes, say, h and h/q for some positive integer q. Then we have

$$F(h) = a_0 + a_1 h^p + \mathcal{O}(h^r)$$

and

$$F(h/q) = a_0 + a_1 (h/q)^p + \mathcal{O}(h^r) = a_0 + a_1 q^{-p} h^p + \mathcal{O}(h^r).$$

This system of two linear equations in the two unknowns a_0 and a_1 is easily solved to obtain

$$a_0 = F(h) + \frac{F(h) - F(h/q)}{q^{-p} - 1} + \mathcal{O}(h^r).$$

Thus, the accuracy of the improved value, a_0, is $\mathcal{O}(h^r)$ rather than $\mathcal{O}(h^p)$.

If $F(h)$ is known for several values of h, then the extrapolation process can be repeated to produce still more accurate approximations, up to the limitations imposed by finite-precision arithmetic. For example, if we have computed F for the values h, $h/2$, and $h/4$, then the extrapolated value based on h and $h/2$ can be combined with the extrapolated value based on $h/2$ and $h/4$ in a further extrapolation to produce a still more accurate estimate for $F(0)$.

Example 8.8 Richardson Extrapolation. To illustrate Richardson extrapolation, we use it to improve the accuracy of a finite difference approximation to the derivative of the function $\sin(x)$ at the point $x = 1$. Using the first-order accurate, forward difference formula derived in Section 8.6.1, we have for this problem

$$F(h) = a_0 + a_1 h + \mathcal{O}(h^2),$$

which means that $p = 1$ and $r = 2$ in this case. Using step sizes of $h = 0.5$ and $h/2 = 0.25$ (i.e., $q = 2$), we obtain

$$F(h) = \frac{\sin(1.5) - \sin(1)}{0.5} = 0.312048$$

and

$$F(h/2) = \frac{\sin(1.25) - \sin(1)}{0.25} = 0.430055.$$

The extrapolated value is then given by

$$F(0) = a_0 = F(h) + \frac{F(h) - F(h/2)}{(1/2) - 1} = 2F(h/2) - F(h) = 0.548061.$$

For comparison, the correctly rounded result is given by $\cos(1) = 0.540302$. In this example the extrapolation is linear, as can be seen on the left in Fig. 8.6, because the lowest-order term in h is linear.

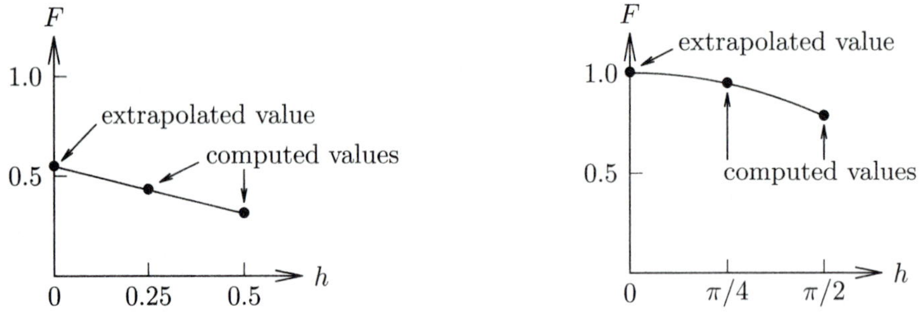

Figure 8.6: Richardson extrapolation in Examples 8.8 (left) and 8.9 (right).

Example 8.9 Romberg Integration. As another example of Richardson extrapolation, we evaluate the integral

$$\int_0^{\pi/2} \sin(x)\,dx.$$

If we use the composite trapezoid quadrature rule, we recall from Section 8.3.5 that

$$F(h) = a_0 + a_1 h^2 + \mathcal{O}(h^4),$$

which means that $p = 2$ and $r = 4$ in this case. With $h = \pi/2$, we obtain the value $F(h) = 0.785398$. Taking $q = 2$, we obtain the value $F(h/2) = F(\pi/4) = 0.948059$. The extrapolated value is then given by

$$F(0) = a_0 = F(h) + \frac{F(h) - F(h/2)}{2^{-2} - 1} = \frac{4F(h/2) - F(h)}{3} = 1.002280,$$

which is substantially more accurate than either value previously computed (the exact answer is 1). In this example the extrapolation is quadratic, as can be seen on the right in Fig. 8.6, because the lowest-order term in h is quadratic.

For any integer $k \geq 0$, let $T_{k,0}$ denote the approximation to the integral $\int_a^b f(x)\,dx$ given by the composite trapezoid rule with step size $h_k = (b-a)/2^k$. Then for any integer j, $j = 1, \ldots, k$, we can recursively define the successive extrapolated values

$$T_{k,j} = \frac{4^j\, T_{k,j-1} - T_{k-1,j-1}}{4^j - 1},$$

which form a triangular array

$$\begin{array}{lllll} T_{0,0} & & & & \\ T_{1,0} & T_{1,1} & & & \\ T_{2,0} & T_{2,1} & T_{2,2} & & \\ T_{3,0} & T_{3,1} & T_{3,2} & T_{3,3} & \\ \vdots & \vdots & \vdots & \vdots & \ddots \end{array}.$$

In this example we have already computed $T_{0,0} = 0.785398$, $T_{1,0} = 0.948059$, and the extrapolated value $T_{1,1} = 1.002280$. If we reduce the step size by another factor of two in the composite trapezoid rule, we obtain $T_{2,0} = F(h/4) = F(\pi/8) = 0.987116$. We can now combine the results for $h/2$ and $h/4$ to obtain the extrapolated value

$$T_{2,1} = F(h/2) + \frac{F(h/2) - F(h/4)}{2^{-2} - 1} = \frac{4\,T_{2,0} - T_{1,0}}{4 - 1} = 1.000135.$$

Because we have eliminated the leading $\mathcal{O}(h^2)$ error term for the composite trapezoid rule, the accuracy of the first level of extrapolated values is $\mathcal{O}(h^4)$. Thus, we can further extrapolate on these values, but now with $q = 4$, to obtain

$$T_{2,2} = \frac{4^2\, T_{2,1} - T_{1,1}}{4^2 - 1} = \frac{16 \times 1.000135 - 1.002280}{15} = 0.999992,$$

which is still more accurate than any of the values computed previously.

Recursive computation of extrapolated values in this manner, based on the composite trapezoid rule with successively halved step sizes, is called *Romberg integration*. It is capable of producing very high accuracy (up to the limit imposed by the arithmetic precision) for very smooth integrands. It is often implemented in an automatic (though nonadaptive) fashion, with the recurrence continuing until the difference in successive diagonal entries of the triangular array falls below a specified error tolerance.

8.8 Software for Integration and Differentiation

Table 8.1 is a list of some of the software available for numerical quadrature. Most of the one-dimensional quadrature routines listed are adaptive routines based on

Gauss-Kronrod quadrature rules. We note that software for solving initial value problems for ordinary differential equations, which will be covered in Chapter 9, can also be used for computing definite integrals (see Computer Problem 9.9). Available software for computing quadrature rules includes `iqpack(#655)` from `TOMS` for computing the weights corresponding to a given set of nodes; `gaussq` from `Netlib` and `gauss` (the latter is part of the `orthpol(#726)` package) and `gqrat(#793)` from `TOMS` for computing the nodes and weights for various Gaussian quadrature rules; and `extend(#672)` from `TOMS` for computing optimal extensions of quadrature rules having some preassigned nodes (i.e., progressive Gaussian rules).

Source	One-dimensional	Two-dimensional	Multidimensional
FMM [127]	quanc8		
Gander & Gautschi [140]	adaptsim/ adaptlob		
HSL	qa02/qa04/qa05		qb01/qm01
IMSL	qdag/qdags	twodq	qand
MATLAB	quad/quadl	dblquad	
KMN [220]	q1da		
NAG	d01ajf	d01daf	d01fcf
NR [315]		vegas/miser	dfridr
NUMAL [250]	quadrat	tricub	
QUADPACK [310]	qag/qags		
SLATEC	qag/qnc/qng/gaus8		
TOMS	squank(#379)	cubtri(#584)	dcuhre(#698)
TOMS	qxg/qxgs(#691)	triex(#612)	dcutet(#720)
TOMS	quad(#699)	dcutri(#706)	
TOMS		cubpack(#764)	

Table 8.1: Software for numerical integration

Software for numerical integration typically requires the user to supply the name of a routine that computes the value of the integrand function for any argument. The user must also supply the endpoints of the interval of integration, as well as absolute or relative error tolerances. In addition to the approximate value of the integral, the output usually includes an estimate of the error, a status flag indicating any warnings or error conditions, and possibly a count of the number of function evaluations that were required.

Although adaptive quadrature routines can often be used as black boxes, they can be ineffective for integrals having discontinuities, singularities, or other such difficulties. In such cases, it may be advantageous to transform the problem to enable the adaptive routine to arrive at an accurate result more efficiently. For practical advice on handling such problematic integrals, see [3, 4, 363].

Software available for numerical differentiation includes `td01` from `HSL`, `deriv` from `IMSL`, `diff` from `MATLAB`, and `d04aaf` from `NAG`. In addition, a number of packages are available that implement automatic differentiation (see Section 8.6.2), including `ADIC`, `ADIFOR`, `ADOL-C`, `ADOL-F`, `AMC`, `GRESS`, `Odyssée`, and `PADRE2`. See `www.mcs.anl.gov/adifor` for further information.

8.9 Historical Notes and Further Reading

The idea of a quadrature rule based on polynomial interpolation at equally-spaced points appears in a letter from Newton to Leibniz in 1676. Cotes systematized Newton's approach and published weights for all rules with $n \leq 10$ points in 1711. Simpson published his quadrature rule in 1743, but it was known much earlier to Cavalieri (1639), to Gregory (1668), and obviously to Cotes. Gauss realized that greater accuracy could be obtained by optimizing the placement of the interpolation points, and published the first such quadrature rules in 1814. The Chebyshev points were suggested as nodes for quadrature rules by Fejér in 1933; an efficient implementation was published by Clenshaw and Curtis in 1960. Kronrod published his quadrature rules in 1964, and Patterson's further extensions were published in 1968. One of the first adaptive quadrature routines was published by McKeeman in 1962. Richardson published his extrapolation technique in 1927; its application to numerical integration was published by Romberg in 1955.

General references on numerical integration include [86, 107, 112, 153, 239, 240]. The nodes and weights for many Gaussian quadrature rules are tabulated in [2, 385, 435]. Our discussion of adaptive quadrature is based in part on [140]. The `quadpack` package is documented in [310]; see also [119]. For cautionary advice on using adaptive quadrature routines, see [259, 261]. Computing double integrals using one-dimensional adaptive quadrature routines is discussed in [138]. General references on computing multiple integrals include [76, 175, 260, 357, 384]. The use of interval techniques in integration is discussed in [59]. For comprehensive coverage of extrapolation techniques, see [48, 219, 421]. For more details on the numerical solution of integral equations, see [88, 422]. Various techniques for dealing with rank-deficient and ill-posed problems, such as those resulting from discretization of integral equations or numerical differentiation, are the subject of [188]. A comprehensive reference on automatic differentiation is [172].

Review Questions

8.1. True or false: Evaluating a definite integral is always a well-conditioned problem.

8.2. True or false: Because it is based on polynomial interpolation of degree one higher, the trapezoid rule is generally more accurate than the midpoint rule.

8.3. True or false: The degree of a quadrature rule is the degree of the interpolating polynomial on which the rule is based.

8.4. True or false: An n-point Newton-Cotes quadrature rule is always of degree $n - 1$.

8.5. True or false: Gaussian quadrature rules of different orders never have any points in common.

8.6. What conditions are both necessary and sufficient for a Riemann integral to exist?

8.7. (*a*) Under what conditions is a definite integral likely to be sensitive to small perturbations in the integrand?

(*b*) Under what conditions is a definite integral likely to be sensitive to small perturbations in the limits of integration?

8.8. What is the difference between an open quadrature rule and a closed quadrature rule?

8.9. Name two different methods for computing the weights corresponding to a given set of nodes of a quadrature rule.

8.10. How can you estimate the error in a quadrature rule without computing the derivatives of the integrand function that would be required by a Taylor series expansion?

8.11. (*a*) How does the node placement differ between Newton-Cotes quadrature and Clenshaw-Curtis quadrature?

(*b*) Which would you expect to be more accurate for the same number of nodes? Why?

8.12. (*a*) How does the node placement differ between Newton-Cotes quadrature and Gaussian quadrature?

(*b*) Which would you expect to be more accurate for the same number of nodes? Why?

8.13. (*a*) If a quadrature rule for an interval $[a, b]$ is based on polynomial interpolation at n equally spaced points in the interval, what is the highest degree such that the rule integrates all polynomials of that degree exactly?

(*b*) How would your answer change if the points were optimally placed to integrate the highest possible degree polynomials exactly?

8.14. (*a*) Would you expect an n-point Newton-Cotes quadrature rule to work well for integrating Runge's function, $\int_{-1}^{1}(1+25x^2)^{-1}\,dx$, if n is very large? Why?

(*b*) Would you expect an n-point Clenshaw-Curtis quadrature rule to work well for integrating Runge's function, $\int_{-1}^{1}(1+25x^2)^{-1}\,dx$, if n is very large? Why?

8.15. (*a*) What is the degree of Simpson's rule for numerical quadrature?

(*b*) What is the degree of an n-point Gaussian quadrature rule?

8.16. Newton-Cotes and Gaussian quadrature rules are both based on polynomial interpolation.

(*a*) What specific property characterizes a Newton-Cotes quadrature rule for a given number of nodes?

(*b*) What specific property characterizes a Gaussian quadrature rule for a given number of nodes?

8.17. (*a*) Explain how the midpoint rule, which is based on interpolation by a polynomial of degree zero, can nevertheless integrate polynomials of degree one exactly.

(*b*) Is the midpoint rule a Gaussian quadrature rule? Explain your answer.

8.18. Suppose that the quadrature rule

$$\int_a^b f(x)\,dx \approx \sum_{i=1}^{n} w_i f(x_i)$$

is exact for all constant functions. What does this imply about the weights w_i or the nodes x_i?

8.19. Why is it important for all of the weights of a quadrature rule to be nonnegative?

8.20. If the integrand has an integrable singularity at one endpoint of the interval of integration, which type of quadrature rule would be better to use, a closed Newton-Cotes rule or a Gaussian rule? Why?

8.21. What is the degree of each of the following types of numerical quadrature rules?

(*a*) An n-point Newton-Cotes rule, where n is odd

(*b*) An n-point Newton-Cotes rule, where n is even

(*c*) An n-point Gaussian rule

(*d*) What accounts for the difference between the answers to parts *a* and *b*?

(*e*) What accounts for the difference between the answers to parts *b* and *c*?

8.22. For each of the following properties, state which type of quadrature, Newton-Cotes or Gaussian, more accurately fits the description:

(*a*) Easier to compute nodes and weights

(*b*) Easier to apply for a general interval $[a, b]$

(*c*) More accurate for the same number of nodes

(*d*) Has maximal degree for the number of nodes

(*e*) Nodes easy to reuse as order of rule changes

8.23. What is the relationship between Gaussian quadrature and orthogonal polynomials?

8.24. (*a*) What does it mean for a sequence of quadrature rules to be *progressive*?

(*b*) Why is this property important?

8.25. (*a*) What is the advantage of using a Gauss-Kronrod pair of quadrature rules, such as G_7 and K_{15}, compared with using two Gaussian rules, such as G_7 and G_{15}, to obtain an approximate integral with error estimate?

(*b*) How many evaluations of the integrand function are required to evaluate *both* of the rules G_7 and K_{15} in a given interval?

8.26. Rank the following types of quadrature rules in order of their degree for the same number of nodes (1 for highest degree, etc.):

(*a*) Newton-Cotes

(*b*) Gaussian

(*c*) Kronrod

8.27. (*a*) What is a composite quadrature rule?

(*b*) Why is a composite quadrature rule preferable to a simple quadrature rule for achieving high accuracy in numerically computing a definite integral on a given interval?

(*c*) In using the composite trapezoid quadrature rule to approximate a definite integral on an interval $[a, b]$, by what factor is the overall error reduced if the mesh size (i.e., subinterval length) h is halved?

8.28. (*a*) Describe in general terms how adaptive quadrature works.

(*b*) How can one obtain the error estimate needed?

(*c*) Under what circumstances might such a procedure produce a result that is seriously in error?

(*d*) Under what circumstances might such a procedure be very inefficient?

8.29. What is the most efficient way to use an adaptive quadrature routine for computing a definite integral whose integrand has a known discontinuity within the interval of integration?

8.30. What is a good way to integrate tabular data (i.e., an integrand whose value is known only at a discrete set of points)?

8.31. (*a*) How might one use a standard quadrature routine, designed for integrating over a finite interval, to integrate a function over an unbounded interval?

(*b*) What precautions would need to be taken to ensure a good result?

8.32. How might one use a standard one-dimensional quadrature routine to compute the value of a double integral over a rectangular region?

8.33. Why is Monte Carlo *not* a practical method for computing one-dimensional integrals?

8.34. Relative to other methods for numerical quadrature, why is the Monte Carlo method more effective in higher dimensions than in low dimensions?

8.35. Explain why integral equations of the first kind with smooth kernels are always ill-conditioned.

8.36. Explain how a quadrature rule can be used to solve an integral equation numerically. What type of computational problem results?

8.37. In solving an integral equation of the first kind by numerical quadrature, does the solution always improve if the order of the quadrature rule is increased or the mesh size is decreased? Why?

8.38. List three approaches for obtaining a meaningful solution to an ill-conditioned linear system approximating an integral equation of the first kind.

8.39. Consider the problem of approximating the derivative of a function that is measured or sampled at only a finite number of points.

(*a*) One way to obtain an approximate derivative is to interpolate the discrete data points and then differentiate the interpolant. Is this a good method for approximating the derivative? Why?

(*b*) Similarly, one can approximate the integral of a function given by such discrete data by integrating the interpolant. Is this a good method for computing the integral? Why?

8.40. Comparing integration and differentiation, which problem is inherently better conditioned? Why?

8.41. (*a*) Suggest a good method for numerically approximating the derivative of a function whose value is given only at a discrete set of data points.

(*b*) For this problem, what would be the effect of noisy data, and how would you cope with it in your numerical method?

8.42. List two methods for deriving finite difference approximations to the derivatives of a given function.

8.43. Briefly describe the basic idea of automatic differentiation. What basic result from calculus does it depend heavily on?

8.44. (*a*) Explain the basic idea of Richardson extrapolation.

(*b*) Does it give a more accurate answer than the values on which it is based?

(*c*) Does extrapolation to step size zero mean that the result is exact (i.e., the error is zero)?

8.45. What is meant by Romberg integration?

Exercises

8.1. (*a*) Compute the approximate value of the integral $\int_0^1 x^3\,dx$, first by the midpoint rule and then by the trapezoid rule.

(*b*) Use the difference between these two results to estimate the error in each of them.

(*c*) Combine the two results to obtain the Simpson's rule approximation to the integral.

(*d*) Would you expect the latter to be exact for this problem? Why?

8.2. (*a*) Using the composite midpoint quadrature rule, compute the approximate value for the integral $\int_0^1 x^3\,dx$, using a mesh size (subinterval length) of $h = 1$ and also using a mesh size of $h = 0.5$.

(*b*) Based on the two approximate values computed in part *a*, use Richardson extrapolation to compute a more accurate approximation to the integral.

(*c*) Would you expect the extrapolated result computed in part *b* to be exact in this case? Why?

8.3. If $Q(f) = \sum_{i=1}^{n} w_i f(x_i)$ is an interpolatory quadrature rule (i.e., based on polynomial interpolation) on the interval $[0, 1]$, then is it true that $\sum_{i=1}^{n} w_i = 1$? Prove your answer.

8.4. Fill in the details of the derivation of the error estimates for the midpoint and trapezoid quadrature rules given in Section 8.3.1. In particular, show that the odd-order terms drop out in both cases, as claimed.

8.5. (*a*) If the integrand f is twice continuously differentiable and $f''(x) \geq 0$ on $[a, b]$, show that the composite midpoint and trapezoid quadrature rules satisfy the bracketing property

$$M_k(f) \leq \int_a^b f(x)\,dx \leq T_k(f).$$

(*b*) If the integrand f is convex on $[a, b]$ (see Section 6.2.1), show that the composite midpoint and trapezoid quadrature rules satisfy the bracketing property in part *a*.

8.6. Suppose that Lagrange interpolation at a given set of nodes $x_1, \ldots, x_n$ is used to derive a quadrature rule. Prove that the corresponding weights are given by the integrals of the Lagrange basis functions, $w_i = \int_a^b \ell_i(x)\,dx$, $i = 1, \ldots, n$.

8.7. Derive an open two-point Newton-Cotes quadrature rule for the interval $[a, b]$. What are the resulting nodes and weights? What is the degree of the resulting rule?

8.8. To answer the following questions, you may consult a book of tables such as [2] to find the relevant weights, or else compute them yourself.

(*a*) What is the largest value of n for which all of the weights of an n-point closed Newton-Cotes quadrature rule are positive?

(*b*) What is the smallest value of n for which at least one of the weights of an n-point closed Newton-Cotes quadrature rule is negative?

(*c*) What is the largest value of n for which all of the weights of an n-point open Newton-Cotes quadrature rule are positive?

(*d*) What is the smallest value of n for which at least one of the weights of an n-point open Newton-Cotes quadrature rule is negative?

8.9. Let p be a real polynomial of degree n such that

$$\int_a^b p(x)\,x^k\,dx = 0, \quad k = 0, \ldots, n-1.$$

(*a*) Show that the n zeros of p are real, simple, and lie in the open interval (a, b). (*Hint*: Consider the polynomial $q_k(x) = (x - x_1)(x - x_2)\cdots(x - x_k)$, where x_i, $i = 1, \ldots, k$, are the roots of p in $[a, b]$.)

(*b*) Show that the n-point interpolatory quadrature rule on $[a, b]$ whose nodes are the zeros of p has degree $2n - 1$. (*Hint*: Consider the quotient and remainder polynomials when a given polynomial is divided by p.)

8.10. Newton-Cotes quadrature rules are derived by fixing the nodes and then determining the corresponding weights by the method of undetermined coefficients so that the degree is maximized for the given nodes. The opposite approach could also be taken, with the weights constrained and the nodes to be determined. In a *Chebyshev* quadrature rule, for example, all of the weights are taken to have the same value, w, thereby eliminating n multiplications in evaluating the resulting quadrature rule, since the single weight can be factored out of the summation.

(*a*) Use the method of undetermined coefficients to determine the nodes and weight for a three-point Chebyshev quadrature rule on the interval $[-1, 1]$.
(*b*) What is the degree of the resulting rule?

8.11. (*a*) Suppose you are using the trapezoid rule to approximate an integral over an interval $[a, b]$. If you wish to obtain a more accurate approximation of the integral, which will gain more accuracy: (1) dividing the interval in half and using the trapezoid rule on each subinterval, or (2) using Simpson's rule on the original interval? Note that either approach will use the same three function values, at the endpoints and the midpoint of the original interval. Support your answer with an error analysis. Test your conclusions experimentally with a few sample integrals.
(*b*) Suppose you are using Simpson's rule to approximate an integral over an interval $[a, b]$. If you wish to obtain a more accurate approximation of the integral, which will gain more accuracy: (1) dividing the interval in half and using Simpson's rule on each subinterval, or (2) using a closed Newton-Cotes rule with the same five points as nodes? Support your answer with an error analysis. Test your conclusions experimentally with a few sample integrals.
(*c*) In general, for a closed n-point quadrature rule Q_n, is more accuracy gained by halving the step size and using Q_n on each subinterval, or using the rule Q_{2n-1} on the original interval? Use the general error bound from Section 8.3 to support your conclusion.

8.12. The forward difference formula

$$f'(x) \approx \frac{f(x+h) - f(x)}{h}$$

and the backward difference formula

$$f'(x) \approx \frac{f(x) - f(x-h)}{h}$$

are both first-order accurate approximations to the first derivative of a function $f: \mathbb{R} \to \mathbb{R}$. What order accuracy results if we average these two approximations? Support your answer with an error analysis.

8.13. Given a sufficiently smooth function $f: \mathbb{R} \to \mathbb{R}$, use Taylor series to derive a second-order accurate, one-sided difference approximation to $f'(x)$ in terms of the values of $f(x)$, $f(x+h)$, and $f(x+2h)$.

8.14. Suppose that the first-order accurate, forward difference approximation to the derivative of a function at a given point produces the value -0.8333 for $h = 0.2$ and the value -0.9091 for $h = 0.1$. Use Richardson extrapolation to obtain a better approximate value for the derivative.

8.15. Archimedes approximated the value of π by computing the perimeter of a regular polygon inscribing or circumscribing a circle of diameter 1. The perimeter of an inscribed polygon with n sides is given by

$$p_n = n \sin(\pi/n),$$

and that of a circumscribed polygon by

$$q_n = n \tan(\pi/n),$$

and these values provide lower and upper bounds, respectively, on the value of π.
(*a*) Using the power series expansions for the sine and tangent functions, show that p_n and q_n can be expressed in the form

$$p_n = a_0 + a_1 h^2 + a_2 h^4 + \cdots$$

and

$$q_n = b_0 + b_1 h^2 + b_2 h^4 + \cdots,$$

where $h = 1/n$. What are the true values of a_0 and b_0?
(*b*) Given the values $p_6 = 3.0000$ and $p_{12} = 3.1058$, use Richardson extrapolation to produce a better estimate for π. Similarly, given the values $q_6 = 3.4641$ and $q_{12} = 3.2154$, use Richardson extrapolation to produce a better estimate for π.

Computer Problems

8.1. Since

$$\int_0^1 \frac{4}{1+x^2}\, dx = \pi,$$

one can compute an approximate value for π using numerical integration of the given function.

(*a*) Use the midpoint, trapezoid, and Simpson composite quadrature rules to compute the approximate value for π in this manner for various step sizes h. Try to characterize the error as a function of h for each rule, and also compare the accuracy of the rules with each other (based on the known value of π). Is there any point beyond which decreasing h yields no further improvement? Why?

(*b*) Implement Romberg integration and repeat part *a* using it.

(*c*) Compute π again by the same method, this time using a library routine for adaptive quadrature and various error tolerances. How reliable is the error estimate it produces? Compare the work required (integrand evaluations and elapsed time) with that for parts *a* and *b*. Make a plot analogous to Fig. 8.4 to show graphically where the integrand is sampled by the adaptive routine.

(*d*) Compute π again by the same method, this time using Monte Carlo integration with various numbers n of sample points. Try to characterize the error as a function of n, and also compare the work required with that for the previous methods. For a suitable random number generator, see Section 13.5.

8.2. The integral in the previous problem is rather easy. Repeat the problem, this time computing the more difficult integral

$$\int_0^1 \sqrt{x}\, \log(x)\, dx = -\frac{4}{9}.$$

8.3. Evaluate each of the following integrals.

(*a*)

$$\int_{-1}^1 \cos(x)\, dx$$

(*b*)

$$\int_{-1}^1 \frac{1}{1+100x^2}\, dx$$

(*c*)

$$\int_{-1}^1 \sqrt{|x|}\, dx$$

Try several composite quadrature rules for various fixed mesh sizes and compare their efficiency and accuracy. Also, try one or more adaptive quadrature routines using various error tolerances, and again compare efficiency for a given accuracy. Make a plot analogous to Fig. 8.4 to show graphically where the integrand is sampled by the adaptive routine.

8.4. Use numerical integration to verify or refute each of the following conjectures.

(*a*)

$$\int_0^1 \sqrt{x^3}\, dx = 0.4$$

(*b*)

$$\int_0^1 \frac{1}{1+10x^2}\, dx = 0.4$$

(*c*)

$$\int_0^1 \frac{e^{-9x^2} + e^{-1024(x-1/4)^2}}{\sqrt{\pi}}\, dx = 0.2$$

(*d*)

$$\int_0^{10} \frac{50}{\pi(2500x^2+1)}\, dx = 0.5$$

(*e*)

$$\int_{-9}^{100} \frac{1}{\sqrt{|x|}}\, dx = 26$$

(*f*)

$$\int_0^{10} 25e^{-25x}\, dx = 1$$

(*g*)

$$\int_0^1 \log(x)\, dx = -1$$

8.5. Each of the following integrands is defined piecewise over the indicated interval. Use an adaptive quadrature routine to evaluate each integral over the given interval. For the same overall accuracy requirement, compare the cost of evaluating the integral using a single subroutine call over the whole interval with the cost when the routine is called separately in each appropriate subinterval.

Experiment with both loose and strict error tolerances. Make a plot analogous to Fig. 8.4 to show graphically where the integrand is sampled by the adaptive routine.

(*a*)

$$f(x) = \begin{cases} 0 & 0 \le x < 0.3 \\ 1 & 0.3 \le x \le 1 \end{cases}$$

(*b*)

$$f(x) = \begin{cases} 1/(x+2) & 0 \le x < e-2 \\ 0 & e-2 \le x \le 1 \end{cases}$$

(*c*)

$$f(x) = \begin{cases} e^x & -1 \le x < 0 \\ e^{1-x} & 0 \le x \le 2 \end{cases}$$

(*d*)

$$f(x) = \begin{cases} e^{10x} & -1 \le x < 0.5 \\ e^{10(1-x)} & 0.5 \le x \le 1.5 \end{cases}$$

(*e*)

$$f(x) = \begin{cases} \sin(\pi x) & 0 \le x < 0.5 \\ \sin^2(\pi x) & 0.5 \le x \le 1.0 \end{cases}$$

8.6. Evaluate the following quantities using each of the given methods:

(*a*) Use an adaptive quadrature routine to evaluate each of the integrals

$$I_k = e^{-1} \int_0^1 x^k e^x \, dx$$

for $k = 0, 1, \ldots, 20$.

(*b*) Verify that the integrals just defined satisfy the recurrence

$$I_k = 1 - kI_{k-1},$$

and use it to generate the same quantities, starting with $I_0 = 1 - e^{-1}$.

(*c*) Generate the same quantities using the backward recurrence

$$I_{k-1} = (1 - I_k)/k,$$

beginning with $I_n = 0$ for some chosen value $n > 20$. Experiment with different values of n to see the effect on the accuracy of the values generated.

(*d*) Compare the three methods with respect to accuracy, stability, and execution time. Can you explain these results?

8.7. The surface area of an ellipsoid obtained by rotating an ellipse about its major axis is given by the integral

$$I(f) = 4\pi\sqrt{\alpha} \int_0^{1/\sqrt{\beta}} \sqrt{1 - Kx^2} \, dx,$$

where $\beta = 100$, $\alpha = (3 - 2\sqrt{2})/\beta$, and $K = \beta\sqrt{1 - \alpha\beta}$. Use an adaptive quadrature routine to compute this integral. Make a plot analogous to Fig. 8.4 to show graphically where the integrand is sampled by the adaptive routine. Compare your results with the exact integral, which is given by

$$\pi\sqrt{\alpha/K}\,(\pi + \sin(2\theta) - 2\theta),$$

where $\theta = \arccos(\sqrt{K/\beta})$.

8.8. The intensity of diffracted light near a straight edge is determined by the values of the *Fresnel integrals*

$$C(x) = \int_0^x \cos\left(\frac{\pi t^2}{2}\right) dt$$

and

$$S(x) = \int_0^x \sin\left(\frac{\pi t^2}{2}\right) dt.$$

Use an adaptive quadrature routine to evaluate these integrals for enough values of x to draw a smooth plot of $C(x)$ and $S(x)$ over the range $0 \le x \le 5$. You may wish to check your results by obtaining a routine for computing Fresnel integrals from a special function library (see Section 7.5.1).

8.9. The period of a simple pendulum is determined by the *complete elliptic integral* of the first kind

$$K(x) = \int_0^{\pi/2} \frac{d\theta}{\sqrt{1 - x^2 \sin^2\theta}}.$$

Use an adaptive quadrature routine to evaluate this integral for enough values of x to draw a smooth plot of $K(x)$ over the range $0 \le x \le 1$. You may wish to check your results by obtaining a routine for computing elliptic integrals from a special function library (see Section 7.5.1).

8.10. The *gamma function* is defined by

$$\Gamma(x) = \int_0^\infty t^{x-1} e^{-t}\, dt, \quad x > 0.$$

Write a program to compute the value of this function from the definition using each of the following approaches:

(*a*) Truncate the infinite interval of integration and use a composite quadrature rule, such as trapezoid or Simpson. You will need to do some experimentation or analysis to determine where to truncate the interval, based on the usual tradeoff between efficiency and accuracy.

(*b*) Truncate the interval and use a standard adaptive quadrature routine. Again, explore the tradeoff between accuracy and efficiency.

(*c*) Gauss-Laguerre quadrature is designed for the interval $[0, \infty]$ and the weight function e^{-t}, so it is ideal for approximating this integral. Look up the nodes and weights for Gauss-Laguerre quadrature rules of various orders (see [2, 385, 435], for example) and compute the resulting estimates for the integral.

(*d*) If available, use an adaptive quadrature routine designed for an unbounded interval of integration.

For each method, compute the approximate value of the integral for several values of x in the range 1 to 10. Compare your results with the values given by the built-in `gamma` function or with the known values for integer arguments,

$$\Gamma(n) = (n-1)!\,.$$

How do the various methods compare in efficiency for a given level of accuracy?

8.11. Planck's theory of blackbody radiation leads to the integral

$$\int_0^\infty \frac{x^3}{e^x - 1}\, dx.$$

Evaluate this integral using each of the methods in the previous exercise, and compare their efficiency and accuracy.

8.12. (*a*) Evaluate the integral

$$\int_{-\infty}^\infty \exp(-x^2)\cos(x)\, dx$$

by truncating the interval of integration and using a composite quadrature rule. Experiment with both the limits of integration and the step size of the composite rule. Compare your results with the exact value of the integral, which is $\sqrt{\pi}\exp(-1/4)$.

(*b*) Repeat part *a*, but this time use an adaptive quadrature routine.

(*c*) Gauss-Hermite quadrature is designed for the interval $[-\infty, \infty]$ and the weight function $\exp(-x^2)$, so it is ideal for approximating this integral. Look up the nodes and weights for Gauss-Hermite quadrature rules of various orders (see [2, 385, 435], for example) and compute the resulting estimates for the integral.

8.13. In two dimensions, suppose that there is a uniform charge distribution in the region $-1 \le x \le 1$, $-1 \le y \le 1$. Then, with suitably chosen units, the electrostatic potential at a point $(\hat{x}, \hat{y})$ outside the region is given by the double integral

$$\Phi(\hat{x}, \hat{y}) = \int_{-1}^1 \int_{-1}^1 \frac{dx\, dy}{\sqrt{(\hat{x} - x)^2 + (\hat{y} - y)^2}}.$$

Evaluate this integral for enough points $(\hat{x}, \hat{y})$ to plot the $\Phi(\hat{x}, \hat{y})$ surface over the region $2 \le \hat{x} \le 10$, $2 \le \hat{y} \le 10$.

8.14. Using any method you choose, evaluate the double integral

$$\iint e^{-xy}\, dx\, dy$$

over each of the following regions:

(*a*) The unit square, i.e., $0 \le x \le 1$, $0 \le y \le 1$.

(*b*) The quarter of the unit disk lying in the first quadrant, i.e., $x^2 + y^2 \le 1$, $x \ge 0$, $y \ge 0$.

8.15. (*a*) Write an automatic quadrature routine using the composite Simpson rule. Successively refine uniformly until a given error tolerance is met. Estimate the error at each stage by comparing the values obtained for consecutive mesh sizes. What kind of data structure is needed for reusing previously computed function values?

(*b*) Write an adaptive quadrature routine using the composite Simpson rule. Successively refine only those subintervals that have not yet met an error tolerance. What kind of data structure is needed for keeping track of which subintervals have converged?

After debugging, test your routines using some of the integrals in the previous problems and compare the results with those previously obtained. How does the efficiency of your adaptive routine compare with that of your nonadaptive routine?

8.16. Select an adaptive quadrature routine and try to devise an integrand function for which it gives an answer that is completely wrong. (*Hint*: This problem may require at least one round of trial and error.) Can you devise a *smooth* function for which the adaptive routine is seriously in error?

8.17. (*a*) Solve the integral equation

$$\int_0^1 (s^2+t^2)^{1/2} u(t)\, dt = \frac{(s^2+1)^{3/2} - s^3}{3}$$

on the interval $[0,1]$ by discretizing the integral using the composite Simpson quadrature rule with n equally spaced points t_j, and also using the same n points for the s_i. Solve the resulting linear system $\boldsymbol{Ax} = \boldsymbol{y}$ using a library routine for Gaussian elimination with partial pivoting. Experiment with various values for n in the range from 3 to 15, comparing your results with the known unique solution, $u(t) = t$. Which value of n gives the best results? Can you explain why?

(*b*) For each value of n in part *a*, compute the condition number of the matrix $\boldsymbol{A}$. How does it behave as a function of n?

(*c*) Repeat part *a*, this time solving the linear system using the singular value decomposition, but omit any "small" singular values. Try various thresholds for truncating the singular values, and again compare your results with the known true solution.

(*d*) Repeat part *a*, this time using the method of regularization. Experiment with various values for the regularization parameter μ to determine which value yields the best results for a given value of n. For each value of μ, plot a point on a two-dimensional graph whose axes are the norm of the solution and the norm of the residual. What is the shape of the curve traced out as μ varies? Does this shape suggest an optimal value for μ?

(*e*) Repeat part *a*, this time using an optimization routine to minimize $\|\boldsymbol{y} - \boldsymbol{Ax}\|_2^2$ subject to the constraint that the components of the solution must be nonnegative. Again, compare your results with the known true solution.

(*f*) Repeat part *e*, this time imposing the additional constraint that the solution be monotonically increasing, i.e., $x_1 \geq 0$ and $x_i - x_{i-1} \geq 0$, $i = 2, \ldots, n$. How much difference does this make in approximating the true solution?

8.18. In this exercise we will experiment with numerical differentiation using data from Computer Problem 3.1:

t	0.0	1.0	2.0	3.0	4.0	5.0
y	1.0	2.7	5.8	6.6	7.5	9.9

For each of the following methods for estimating the derivative, compute the derivative of the original data and also experiment with randomly perturbing the y values to determine the sensitivity of the resulting derivative estimates. For each method, comment on both the reasonableness of the derivative estimates and their sensitivity to perturbations. Note that the data are monotonically increasing, so one might expect the derivative always to be positive.

(*a*) For $n = 0, 1, \ldots, 5$, fit a polynomial of degree n by least squares to the data, then differentiate the resulting polynomial and evaluate the derivative at each of the given t values.

(*b*) Interpolate the data with a cubic spline, differentiate the resulting piecewise cubic polynomial, and evaluate the derivative at each of the given t values (some spline routines provide the derivative automatically, but it can be done manually if necessary).

(*c*) Repeat part *b*, this time using a smoothing spline routine. Experiment with various levels of smoothing, using whatever mechanism for controlling the degree of smoothing that the routine provides.

(*d*) Interpolate the data with a monotonic Hermite cubic, differentiate the resulting piecewise cubic polynomial, and evaluate the derivative at each of the given t values.

Chapter 9

Initial Value Problems for Ordinary Differential Equations

9.1 Ordinary Differential Equations

Most physical systems change over time. From an orbiting satellite to a cooling cup of coffee, from a swinging pendulum to a decaying radioisotope, from reacting chemical species to competing biological species, a state of flux is the norm. One of the motivating problems for the invention of differential calculus was to characterize the motion of celestial bodies and earthly projectiles so that their future locations could be predicted. Differential equations provide a mathematical language for describing *continuous* change. Beginning with Newton's laws of motion, most of the fundamental laws of science are expressed as differential equations. Even a system that is *not* changing is often best understood as being in an equilibrium state of a relevant differential equation.

Suppose that the state of a system at any given time t is described by some vector function $\boldsymbol{y}(t)$, where $\boldsymbol{y}\colon \mathbb{R} \to \mathbb{R}^n$. For example, the components of $\boldsymbol{y}(t)$ might represent the spatial coordinates of a projectile or concentrations of various chemical species. A *differential equation* prescribes a relationship between this unknown state function $\boldsymbol{y}(t)$ and one or more of its derivatives with respect to t that must hold at any given time. In solving a differential equation the objective is to determine a differentiable function $\boldsymbol{y}(t)$ that satisfies the prescribed relationship. Finding such a solution of the differential equation is important because it will enable us to predict the future evolution of the system over time.

Example 9.1 Newton's Second Law of Motion. Perhaps the most famous differential equation, as well as the most important both historically and practically, is *Newton's Second Law of Motion*, $F = ma$, or force equals mass times acceleration. This differential equation relates the state of an object, in this case its position in space, to the second derivative of that state function. In one dimension, the differential equation looks like this:

$$F(t, y(t), dy(t)/dt) = m\, d^2y(t)/dt^2,$$

where the force F in general depends on the time t, the position $y(t)$, and the velocity $dy(t)/dt$, and the acceleration is the second derivative of the position, $d^2y(t)/dt^2$. If F is the force on an object due to Earth's gravity, then $F = -mg$, where g is a known constant. The solution to the differential equation is then given by

$$y(t) = -\tfrac{1}{2}gt^2 + c_1t + c_2,$$

where c_1 and c_2 are constants that depend on the initial position and velocity of the object. This solution function describes the trajectory of the object over time under the force of gravity.

When there is only one independent variable, such as time, then all derivatives of the dependent variables are with respect to that independent variable, and we have an *ordinary* differential equation, or *ODE*. In Chapter 11 we will consider systems with more than one independent variable, so that partial derivatives are required and we have a *partial* differential equation, or *PDE*. To make ODEs less cumbersome to express, we will use the notation $\boldsymbol{y}'(t) = d\boldsymbol{y}(t)/dt$ to indicate the first derivative with respect to the independent variable t, and we will often suppress the explicit dependence on t, for example writing $\boldsymbol{y}' = d\boldsymbol{y}/dt$, with the dependence on t understood. For example, with these conventions Newton's Second Law can be written $F = m\,y''$.

The highest-order derivative appearing in an ODE determines the *order* of the ODE. For example, Newton's Second Law is a second-order ODE. If a system has n dependent variables, then to express an arbitrary relationship between the state vector $\boldsymbol{y}(t) \in \mathbb{R}^n$ and its first k derivatives, the most general kth order ODE has the *implicit* form

$$\boldsymbol{f}(t, \boldsymbol{y}, \boldsymbol{y}', \boldsymbol{y}'', \ldots, \boldsymbol{y}^{(k)}) = \boldsymbol{0},$$

where $\boldsymbol{f}: \mathbb{R}^{kn+n+1} \to \mathbb{R}^n$ is a known function and $\boldsymbol{y}(t)$ is to be determined. A kth order ODE is said to be *explicit* if it can be written in the form

$$\boldsymbol{y}^{(k)} = \boldsymbol{f}(t, \boldsymbol{y}, \boldsymbol{y}', \boldsymbol{y}'', \ldots, \boldsymbol{y}^{(k-1)}),$$

where $\boldsymbol{f}: \mathbb{R}^{kn+1} \to \mathbb{R}^n$. Many ODEs arise naturally in this form, and many others can be transformed into it. For example, Newton's Second Law is technically implicit, but it can be made explicit by dividing both sides by the mass m, so that it becomes $y'' = F/m$. When $\boldsymbol{y}^{(k)}$ cannot be isolated on one side in this manner, then solving the ODE requires a combination of techniques from Chapter 5 and the present chapter, but such problems are beyond the scope of this book, and we will consider only explicit ODEs.

We will also consider only first-order ODEs. This is not a real restriction because a higher-order ODE can always be transformed into an equivalent first-order system as follows. For an explicit kth order ODE of the form just given, define the k new unknowns $\boldsymbol{u}_1(t) = \boldsymbol{y}(t)$, $\boldsymbol{u}_2(t) = \boldsymbol{y}'(t)$, ... , $\boldsymbol{u}_k(t) = \boldsymbol{y}^{(k-1)}(t)$, so that the original kth order equation becomes a *system* of kn first-order equations

$$\boldsymbol{u}' = \begin{bmatrix} \boldsymbol{u}_1' \\ \boldsymbol{u}_2' \\ \vdots \\ \boldsymbol{u}_{k-1}' \\ \boldsymbol{u}_k' \end{bmatrix} = \begin{bmatrix} \boldsymbol{u}_2 \\ \boldsymbol{u}_3 \\ \vdots \\ \boldsymbol{u}_k \\ \boldsymbol{f}(t, \boldsymbol{u}_1, \boldsymbol{u}_2, \dots, \boldsymbol{u}_k) \end{bmatrix} = \boldsymbol{g}(t, \boldsymbol{u}).$$

Again, Newton's Second Law, which is of second order, is a good example. If we define the new unknowns $u_1(t) = y(t)$ and $u_2(t) = y'(t)$, then Newton's Second Law becomes a system of two first-order equations

$$\begin{bmatrix} u_1' \\ u_2' \end{bmatrix} = \begin{bmatrix} u_2 \\ F/m \end{bmatrix}.$$

This system says that the velocity $u_2(t)$ is the first derivative of the position $u_1(t)$, and the acceleration is the first derivative of the velocity.

In this chapter, therefore, we will focus on explicit, first-order ODEs, which have the form

$$\boldsymbol{y}' = \boldsymbol{f}(t, \boldsymbol{y}),$$

where $\boldsymbol{f}: \mathbb{R}^{n+1} \to \mathbb{R}^n$. Written out in full, such an ODE looks like this:

$$\boldsymbol{y}' = \boldsymbol{y}'(t) = \begin{bmatrix} y_1'(t) \\ y_2'(t) \\ \vdots \\ y_n'(t) \end{bmatrix} = \begin{bmatrix} dy_1(t)/dt \\ dy_2(t)/dt \\ \vdots \\ dy_n(t)/dt \end{bmatrix} = \begin{bmatrix} f_1(t, \boldsymbol{y}) \\ f_2(t, \boldsymbol{y}) \\ \vdots \\ f_n(t, \boldsymbol{y}) \end{bmatrix} = \boldsymbol{f}(t, \boldsymbol{y}(t)) = \boldsymbol{f}(t, \boldsymbol{y}).$$

When $n > 1$, we have a *system* of *coupled* ODEs. For simplicity, we will often take $n = 1$, i.e., a single scalar ODE $y' = f(t, y)$.

Example 9.2 Ordinary Differential Equations. The simplest possible ODE is $\boldsymbol{y}' = \boldsymbol{0}$, i.e., $\boldsymbol{f}(t, \boldsymbol{y}) \equiv \boldsymbol{0}$, which says, ironically, that nothing is changing! A solution to this ODE is given by $\boldsymbol{y}(t) = \boldsymbol{c}$, for any constant $\boldsymbol{c} \in \mathbb{R}^n$. With its infinite family of solutions (one for each choice of $\boldsymbol{c}$), this example already shows that the solution to an ODE is not unique.

The next simplest ODE is $\boldsymbol{y}' = \boldsymbol{b}$, where $\boldsymbol{b} \in \mathbb{R}^n$ is a constant. A solution to this ODE is given by $\boldsymbol{y}(t) = \boldsymbol{b}t + \boldsymbol{c}$, for any constant $\boldsymbol{c} \in \mathbb{R}^n$. Some of these solutions are sketched in Fig 9.1 for $n = 1$, $b = 1/2$, and various values of c.

A number of special cases of the general explicit first-order ODE arise often in practice. If $\boldsymbol{f}$ does not depend explicitly on t, then the ODE is *autonomous* and

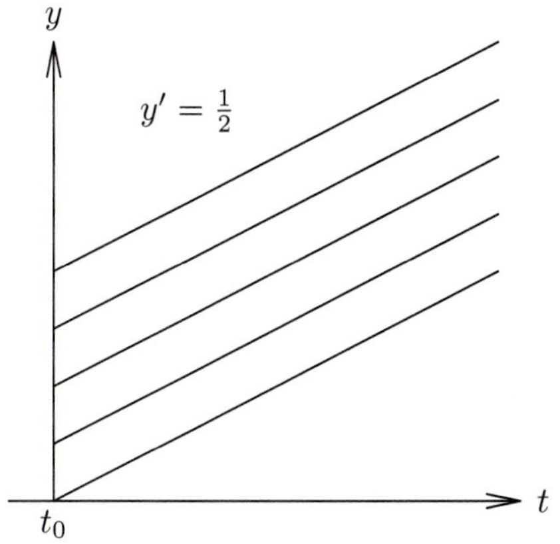

Figure 9.1: Some solutions for $y' = 1/2$.

can be written in the form $\boldsymbol{y}' = \boldsymbol{f}(\boldsymbol{y})$. A nonautonomous ODE $\boldsymbol{y}' = \boldsymbol{f}(t, \boldsymbol{y})$ can always be converted to autonomous form by introducing an additional dependent variable $y_{n+1}(t) = t$, yielding the autonomous ODE

$$\begin{bmatrix} \boldsymbol{y}' \\ y'_{n+1} \end{bmatrix} = \begin{bmatrix} \boldsymbol{f}(y_{n+1}, \boldsymbol{y}) \\ 1 \end{bmatrix}.$$

If $\boldsymbol{f}$ has the form $\boldsymbol{f}(t, \boldsymbol{y}) = \boldsymbol{A}(t)\boldsymbol{y} + \boldsymbol{b}(t)$, where $\boldsymbol{A}(t)$ and $\boldsymbol{b}(t)$ are matrix-valued and vector-valued functions of t, respectively, then the ODE is said to be *linear*. In the linear ODE just given, if the matrix $\boldsymbol{A}$ does not depend on t, then the ODE is said to have *constant coefficients*, and if $\boldsymbol{b}(t) \equiv \boldsymbol{0}$, then the ODE is said to be *homogeneous*. Thus, a first-order, linear, homogeneous ODE with constant coefficients has the simple form $\boldsymbol{y}' = \boldsymbol{A}\boldsymbol{y}$, where $\boldsymbol{A} \in \mathbb{R}^{n \times n}$.

Example 9.3 Chemical Reaction Kinetics. Suppose the concentrations as a function of time for three chemical species are given by $y_1(t)$, $y_2(t)$, and $y_3(t)$. If the rate of the reaction $y_1 \to y_2$ is proportional to y_1, and the rate of the reaction $y_2 \to y_3$ is proportional to y_2, then the concentrations are governed by the linear, homogeneous, constant-coefficient ODE

$$\boldsymbol{y}' = \begin{bmatrix} y'_1 \\ y'_2 \\ y'_3 \end{bmatrix} = \begin{bmatrix} -k_1 y_1 \\ k_1 y_1 - k_2 y_2 \\ k_2 y_2 \end{bmatrix} = \begin{bmatrix} -k_1 & 0 & 0 \\ k_1 & -k_2 & 0 \\ 0 & k_2 & 0 \end{bmatrix} \begin{bmatrix} y_1 \\ y_2 \\ y_3 \end{bmatrix} = \boldsymbol{A}\boldsymbol{y},$$

where k_1 and k_2 are the rate constants for the two reactions. If there were a *source* term $\boldsymbol{b}(t)$ replenishing one or more of the species, then the ODE would not be homogeneous.

Example 9.4 Predator-Prey Population Dynamics. The populations of two species, a prey denoted by y_1 and a predator denoted by y_2, can be modeled by the autonomous, nonlinear ODE

$$\boldsymbol{y}' = \begin{bmatrix} y_1' \\ y_2' \end{bmatrix} = \begin{bmatrix} y_1(\alpha_1 - \beta_1 y_2) \\ y_2(-\alpha_2 + \beta_2 y_1) \end{bmatrix} = \boldsymbol{f}(\boldsymbol{y})$$

used by Volterra in 1926 to describe fish and shark populations and earlier by Lotka to describe oscillations in chemical reactions. The parameters α_1 and α_2 are the natural birth and death rates in isolation of prey and predators, respectively, and the parameters β_1 and β_2 determine the effect of interactions between the two populations, where the probability of interaction is proportional to the product of the populations.

An ODE $\boldsymbol{y}' = \boldsymbol{f}(t, \boldsymbol{y})$ does not by itself determine a unique solution function because only the slopes $\boldsymbol{y}'(t)$ of the solution components are prescribed by the ODE for any value of t, not the solution value $\boldsymbol{y}(t)$ itself, so there is usually an infinite family of functions that satisfy the ODE. To single out a particular solution, we must specify the value of the solution function, denoted by $\boldsymbol{y}_0$, for some value of t, denoted by t_0. Thus, part of the given problem data is the requirement that

$$\boldsymbol{y}(t_0) = \boldsymbol{y}_0.$$

Under reasonable assumptions (see Section 9.2), this additional requirement determines a unique solution to the given ODE. Because the independent variable t often represents time, we think of t_0 as the initial time and $\boldsymbol{y}_0$ as the initial value of the state vector. Accordingly, the requirement that $\boldsymbol{y}(t_0) = \boldsymbol{y}_0$ is called an *initial condition*, and an ODE together with an initial condition is called an *initial value problem*, or *IVP*. Starting from its initial state $\boldsymbol{y}_0$ at time t_0, the ODE governs the dynamic evolution of the system for $t \geq t_0$, and we seek a function $\boldsymbol{y}(t)$ that satisfies the initial condition and describes the state of the system as a function of time.

Example 9.5 Initial Value Problem. Consider the scalar ODE $y' = y$. The infinite family of solutions is given by $y(t) = ce^t$, where c is any real constant. If we impose the initial condition $y(t_0) = y_0$, then this will single out the unique solution that satisfies the initial condition. If $t_0 = 0$, for example, then we have $y(t_0) = y(0) = ce^0 = c$, so that we must have $c = y_0$, which means that the unique solution satisfying both the ODE and the initial condition is $y(t) = y_0 \, e^t$. Some solutions for this ODE are sketched in Fig. 9.2, including the particular solution that satisfies the given initial condition.

If we integrate the ODE $\boldsymbol{y}' = \boldsymbol{f}(t, \boldsymbol{y})$ and use the initial condition $\boldsymbol{y}(t_0) = \boldsymbol{y}_0$, we obtain the *integral equation*

$$\boldsymbol{y}(t) = \boldsymbol{y}_0 + \int_{t_0}^{t} \boldsymbol{f}(s, \boldsymbol{y}(s)) \, ds,$$

which must be satisfied by the solution $\boldsymbol{y}(t)$ of the IVP. Although it is useful for theoretical purposes, in practice this equivalent integral equation is usually no easier

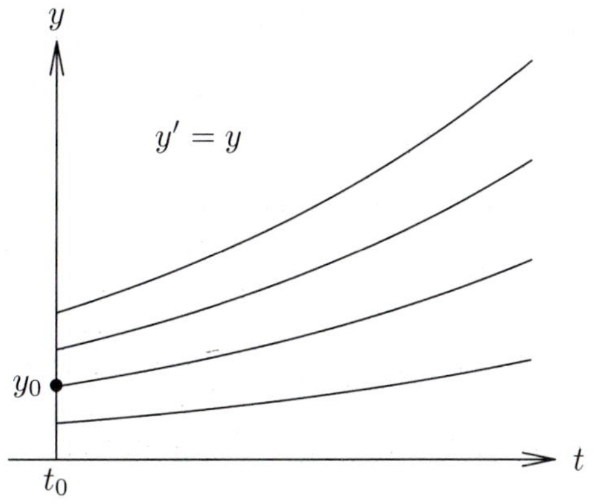

Figure 9.2: Some solutions for $y' = y$.

to solve than the original ODE. It does explain, however, why solving an ODE, by whatever means, is often referred to as *integrating* the ODE. In the special case when $\boldsymbol{f}$ does not depend on $\boldsymbol{y}$, i.e., the ODE has the form $\boldsymbol{y}' = \boldsymbol{f}(t)$, then the solution is given by the integral

$$\boldsymbol{y}(t) = \boldsymbol{y}_0 + \int_{t_0}^{t} \boldsymbol{f}(s)\, ds,$$

which can be evaluated analytically or by numerical quadrature (see Section 8.3).

9.2 Existence, Uniqueness, and Conditioning

We have seen that an initial condition is necessary for the solution of an ODE to be unique. But is this condition sufficient? Moreover, does a solution always exist? Without some restrictions on the problem, the answer to both questions is "no," but under reasonable assumptions that usually hold, both answers are "yes." First, we must be more precise about the problem domain, which we assume to be a closed and bounded set $D = [a, b] \times \Omega \subseteq \mathbb{R}^{n+1}$. Now suppose that $\boldsymbol{f}: \mathbb{R}^{n+1} \to \mathbb{R}^n$ is continuous in t on $[a, b]$ and *Lipschitz continuous* in $\boldsymbol{y}$ on D, i.e., there is a constant L such that for any $t \in [a, b]$ and any $\boldsymbol{y}$ and $\hat{\boldsymbol{y}} \in \Omega$,

$$\|\boldsymbol{f}(t, \hat{\boldsymbol{y}}) - \boldsymbol{f}(t, \boldsymbol{y})\| \leq L \, \|\hat{\boldsymbol{y}} - \boldsymbol{y}\|.$$

Then it can be shown that for any interior point $(t_0, \boldsymbol{y}_0)$ of D, there is a subinterval of $[a, b]$ containing t_0 in which there is a unique solution $\boldsymbol{y}$ of the IVP $\boldsymbol{y}' = \boldsymbol{f}(t, \boldsymbol{y})$ with initial condition $\boldsymbol{y}(t_0) = \boldsymbol{y}_0$, and moreover this solution can be uniquely continued to the boundary of D. Lipschitz continuity of $\boldsymbol{f}$ is ensured if $\boldsymbol{f}$ is differentiable, in which case we can take $L = \max_{(t,\boldsymbol{y}) \in D} \|\boldsymbol{J}_f(t, \boldsymbol{y})\|$, where $\boldsymbol{J}_f$ is the $n \times n$ Jacobian matrix of $\boldsymbol{f}$ with respect to $\boldsymbol{y}$, $\{\boldsymbol{J}_f(t, \boldsymbol{y})\}_{ij} = \partial f_i(t, \boldsymbol{y}) / \partial y_j$.

Under the assumption of Lipschitz continuity on a closed and bounded domain D, we can also assess the sensitivity of the solution to perturbations in the problem data, which for an IVP are the initial value $\boldsymbol{y}_0$ and the function $\boldsymbol{f}$. Let $\hat{\boldsymbol{y}}(t)$ be the solution to the IVP $\hat{\boldsymbol{y}}' = \boldsymbol{f}(t, \hat{\boldsymbol{y}})$ with perturbed initial condition $\hat{\boldsymbol{y}}(t_0) = \hat{\boldsymbol{y}}_0$. Then it can be shown that for any $t \geq t_0$,

$$\|\hat{\boldsymbol{y}}(t) - \boldsymbol{y}(t)\| \leq e^{L(t-t_0)} \|\hat{\boldsymbol{y}}_0 - \boldsymbol{y}_0\|.$$

If the function $\boldsymbol{f}$ is also perturbed, so that we have the IVP $\hat{\boldsymbol{y}}' = \hat{\boldsymbol{f}}(t, \hat{\boldsymbol{y}})$, then for any $t \geq t_0$,

$$\|\hat{\boldsymbol{y}}(t) - \boldsymbol{y}(t)\| \leq e^{L(t-t_0)} \|\hat{\boldsymbol{y}}_0 - \boldsymbol{y}_0\| + \frac{e^{L(t-t_0)} - 1}{L} \|\hat{\boldsymbol{f}} - \boldsymbol{f}\|,$$

where $\|\hat{\boldsymbol{f}} - \boldsymbol{f}\| = \max_{(t,\boldsymbol{y}) \in D} \|\hat{\boldsymbol{f}}(t, \boldsymbol{y}) - \boldsymbol{f}(t, \boldsymbol{y})\|$. These perturbation bounds show that the unique solution to the IVP is a continuous function of the problem data, and hence the problem is well-posed. But exponential divergence of the perturbed solutions over time, which is allowed by the $e^{L(t-t_0)}$ term in the bounds and is realized in the worst case, means that the solution can still be highly sensitive to such perturbations. We next consider this issue in greater detail.

Previously in this book we have used the term *conditioning* to refer to the sensitivity of the solution of a problem to perturbations in the input, and *stability* to refer to the sensitivity of an algorithm to perturbations that occur during computation. In the study of differential equations, however, there is a long-standing tradition of using the term stability for both of these concepts, an ambiguity that obviously invites confusion. In discussing the numerical solution of differential equations, we will conform to this tradition, but we will try to make clear at all times whether we are referring to the stability of the problem or of a numerical method for solving it. As we will soon see, however, these two meanings of stability tend to be intertwined for differential equations anyway, so perhaps the ambiguity is only natural.

A solution of the ODE $\boldsymbol{y}' = \boldsymbol{f}(t, \boldsymbol{y})$ is said to be *stable* if for every $\epsilon > 0$ there is a $\delta > 0$ such that if $\hat{\boldsymbol{y}}(t)$ satisfies the ODE and $\|\hat{\boldsymbol{y}}(t_0) - \boldsymbol{y}(t_0)\| \leq \delta$, then $\|\hat{\boldsymbol{y}}(t) - \boldsymbol{y}(t)\| \leq \epsilon$ for all $t \geq t_0$. Thus, for a stable solution, if the initial value is perturbed, then the perturbed solution remains close to the original solution, which rules out the exponential divergence of perturbed solutions allowed by the perturbation bound cited earlier. A stable solution is said to be *asymptotically stable* if $\|\hat{\boldsymbol{y}}(t) - \boldsymbol{y}(t)\| \to 0$ as $t \to \infty$. This stronger form of stability means that the original and perturbed solutions not only remain close to each other, they converge toward each other over time. As we will soon see in detail, the significance of these concepts for the numerical solution of ODEs is that any errors introduced during the computation can be either amplified or diminished over time, depending on the stability of the solution sought. But first we consider how to determine when a solution is stable.

Example 9.6 Stability of Solutions. For the ODE from Example 9.2 with $n = 1$, i.e., $y' = b$ for a given constant b, the solutions are parallel straight lines with slope b, as illustrated in Fig. 9.1, so the solutions of this ODE are stable but not asymptotically stable. More interesting is the scalar ODE

$$y' = \lambda y,$$

where λ is a constant. The solution is given by

$$y(t) = y_0 \, e^{\lambda t},$$

where $t_0 = 0$ is the initial time and $y(0) = y_0$ is the initial value. We saw a particular instance of this ODE with $\lambda = 1$ in Example 9.5, and some of its solutions are sketched in Fig. 9.2. If $\lambda > 0$, then all nonzero solutions grow exponentially, so that any two solutions diverge away from each other, as illustrated in Fig. 9.2, and hence every solution is unstable. If $\lambda < 0$, on the other hand, then all nonzero solutions decay exponentially, so that any two solutions converge toward each other, as illustrated in Fig. 9.3. In this case, therefore, every solution is not only stable, but asymptotically stable. If λ is complex, say $\lambda = a + ib$, then from Section 1.3.11 we see that

$$e^{\lambda t} = e^{(a+ib)t} = e^{at} e^{ibt} = e^{at}(\cos(bt) + i \sin(bt)),$$

so whether the solutions grow or decay exponentially is determined by the sign of $\mathrm{Re}(\lambda)$. In particular, the solutions are unstable if $\mathrm{Re}(\lambda) > 0$ and asymptotically stable if $\mathrm{Re}(\lambda) < 0$. If $\mathrm{Re}(\lambda) = 0$, then the solutions oscillate, but any two solutions remain a bounded distance apart, and hence the solutions are stable but not asymptotically stable.

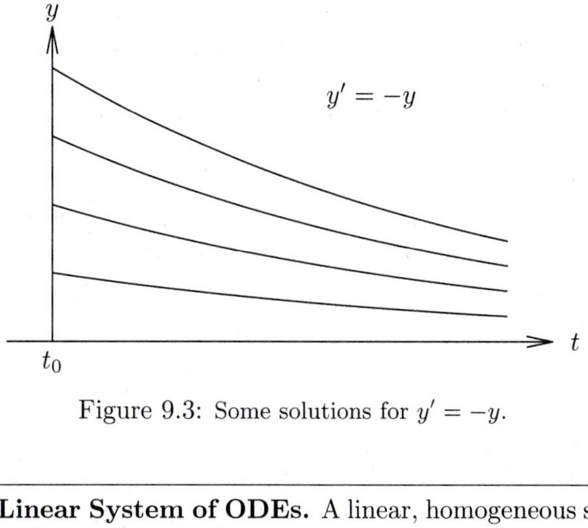

Figure 9.3: Some solutions for $y' = -y$.

Example 9.7 Linear System of ODEs. A linear, homogeneous system of ODEs with constant coefficients has the form

$$\boldsymbol{y}' = \boldsymbol{A}\boldsymbol{y},$$

where $\boldsymbol{A}$ is an $n \times n$ matrix. Suppose we have the initial condition $\boldsymbol{y}(0) = \boldsymbol{y}_0$. Let the eigenvalues of $\boldsymbol{A}$ be denoted by λ_i, and the corresponding eigenvectors by $\boldsymbol{v}_i$, $i = 1, \ldots, n$. Assume, for the moment, that $\boldsymbol{A}$ is diagonalizable, so that the eigenvectors are linearly independent and we can express $\boldsymbol{y}_0$ as a linear combination

$$\boldsymbol{y}_0 = \sum_{i=1}^{n} \alpha_i \boldsymbol{v}_i.$$

Then it is easily confirmed that

$$\boldsymbol{y}(t) = \sum_{i=1}^{n} \alpha_i \boldsymbol{v}_i e^{\lambda_i t}$$

is a solution to the ODE that satisfies the initial condition. By the same reasoning as for the scalar case in Example 9.6, we see that eigenvalues of $\boldsymbol{A}$ with positive real parts yield exponentially growing solution components, eigenvalues with negative real parts yield exponentially decaying solution components, and eigenvalues with zero real parts yield oscillating solution components. Thus, the solutions of this ODE are stable if $\mathrm{Re}(\lambda_i) \leq 0$ for every eigenvalue, and asymptotically stable if $\mathrm{Re}(\lambda_i) < 0$ for every eigenvalue, but unstable if there is any eigenvalue such that $\mathrm{Re}(\lambda_i) > 0$. The situation is more complicated if $\boldsymbol{A}$ is not diagonalizable, in which case stability requires not only that $\mathrm{Re}(\lambda_i) \leq 0$ for every eigenvalue, but $\mathrm{Re}(\lambda_i) < 0$ for any eigenvalue that is not simple.

As we have just seen, for a linear ODE with constant coefficients, eigenvalue analysis can be used to determine the stability not only of a particular solution, but of *all* solutions of the ODE. For a linear ODE with variable coefficients, $\boldsymbol{y}'(t) = \boldsymbol{A}(t)\boldsymbol{y}(t)$, eigenvalue analysis of the matrix $\boldsymbol{A}(t)$ for a particular value of t may give some indication of the behavior of solutions in the short run, but the signs of the eigenvalues (or their real parts) may change as t varies, so that unless $\boldsymbol{A}(t)$ has some special property such as being periodic, little can be established via eigenvalue analysis about long term stability of solutions.

For a general nonlinear ODE $\boldsymbol{y}' = \boldsymbol{f}(t, \boldsymbol{y})$, determining the stability of solutions is more complicated still. For a given solution $\boldsymbol{y}(t)$, the ODE can be linearized locally by means of a truncated Taylor series expansion, yielding a linear ODE of the form

$$\boldsymbol{z}' = \boldsymbol{J_f}(t, \boldsymbol{y}(t))\, \boldsymbol{z},$$

where $\boldsymbol{J_f}$ is the $n \times n$ Jacobian matrix of $\boldsymbol{f}$ with respect to $\boldsymbol{y}$, $\{\boldsymbol{J_f}(t, \boldsymbol{y})\}_{ij} = \partial f_i(t, \boldsymbol{y})/\partial y_j$. If the original nonlinear ODE is autonomous, then the linearized ODE has constant coefficients, and hence its eigenvalues determine the stability of its solutions as in Example 9.7. If the original nonlinear ODE is not autonomous, then the linearized ODE has variable coefficients, and the same comments apply as in the previous paragraph. In either case, since the Jacobian matrix is evaluated for a particular solution, its eigenvalues provide stability information only about that solution. Thus, the stability information given by the eigenvalues of the Jacobian matrix may have only limited, local validity in $\boldsymbol{y}$ as well as in t.

9.3 Numerical Solution of ODEs

There are many analytical techniques for solving ODEs, such as separation of variables, integrating factors, series solutions, and so on. Unfortunately, most ODEs arising in practice are not susceptible to being solved by any of these analytical methods, and usually the only viable alternative is to compute a numerical approximation to the desired solution. Although either type of solution usually suffices for most purposes, there are basic differences between them. Whereas an analytical solution of an ODE is a closed-form formula for the solution function at any time, a numerical solution is a table of approximate values of the solution function at a discrete set of points. Whereas the true solution is a continuous function in an infinite-dimensional space, a numerical solution is a discrete vector in a finite-dimensional space.

Our approach to solving differential equations numerically will be based on finite-dimensional approximations, a process called *discretization*. We will replace differential equations by algebraic equations whose solutions approximate those of the given differential equations. For an initial value problem, approximate solution values are generated step by step in discrete increments across the interval in which the solution is sought. For this reason, numerical methods for solving ODEs are sometimes called *discrete variable methods*. In stepping from one discrete point to the next, we will in general incur some error, which means that our new approximate solution value will lie on a *different* solution of the ODE from the one on which we started. The stability or instability of the solutions determines in part whether such errors are amplified or diminished with time.

9.3.1 Euler's Method

A numerical solution of an IVP is obtained by starting at time t_0 with the given initial value $\boldsymbol{y}_0$ and attempting to track the solution trajectory dictated by the ODE. We can determine the initial slope $\boldsymbol{y}_0'$ of each component of the solution by evaluating $\boldsymbol{f}$ at the given initial data, i.e., $\boldsymbol{y}_0' = \boldsymbol{f}(t_0, \boldsymbol{y}_0)$. We use this information to predict the value $\boldsymbol{y}_1$ of the solution at some future time $t_1 = t_0 + h_0$ for some suitably chosen increment h_0. We can then evaluate $\boldsymbol{y}_1' = \boldsymbol{f}(t_1, \boldsymbol{y}_1)$ and repeat the process to take another step forward, and so on until we reach the final desired time.

The simplest example of this approach is *Euler's method*, for which the approximate solution at time $t_{k+1} = t_k + h_k$ is given by

$$\boldsymbol{y}_{k+1} = \boldsymbol{y}_k + h_k\, \boldsymbol{f}(t_k, \boldsymbol{y}_k).$$

For reasons we will soon see, Euler's method is generally inefficient, so it is seldom used in practice, but it is of fundamental importance in understanding the basic concepts and principles in solving differential equations numerically. Moreover, Euler's method is the simplest instance of several different families of ODE methods that we will consider later. We will therefore examine Euler's method in some detail, including several different ways of deriving it.

Taylor series. Consider the Taylor series

$$\boldsymbol{y}(t+h) = \boldsymbol{y}(t) + h\, \boldsymbol{y}'(t) + \tfrac{1}{2} h^2\, \boldsymbol{y}''(t) + \cdots.$$

Euler's method results from taking $t = t_k$, $h = h_k$, $\boldsymbol{y}'(t_k) = \boldsymbol{f}(t_k, \boldsymbol{y}_k)$, and dropping terms of second and higher order.

Finite difference approximation. If we replace the derivative $\boldsymbol{y}'(t)$ in the ODE $\boldsymbol{y}' = \boldsymbol{f}(t, \boldsymbol{y})$ by a first-order forward difference approximation (see Section 8.6.1), we obtain an algebraic equation

$$\frac{\boldsymbol{y}_{k+1} - \boldsymbol{y}_k}{h_k} = \boldsymbol{f}(t_k, \boldsymbol{y}_k),$$

which gives Euler's method when solved for $\boldsymbol{y}_{k+1}$.

Polynomial interpolation. Using Hermite interpolation, we can fit a polynomial of degree one to the solution function by matching both the solution components $\boldsymbol{y}_k$ and the derivative components $\boldsymbol{f}(t_k, \boldsymbol{y}_k)$ at t_k. The resulting polynomial in h is $\boldsymbol{p}(h) = \boldsymbol{y}_k + h\,\boldsymbol{f}(t_k, \boldsymbol{y}_k)$, which gives Euler's method when evaluated at $h = h_k$. Thus, Euler's method advances the solution at each step by extrapolating along the tangent line from $(t_k, \boldsymbol{y}_k)$ with slope $\boldsymbol{f}(t_k, \boldsymbol{y}_k)$.

Numerical quadrature. From the integral characterization of the ODE solution in Section 9.1, we have

$$\boldsymbol{y}(t_{k+1}) = \boldsymbol{y}(t_k) + \int_{t_k}^{t_{k+1}} \boldsymbol{f}(s, \boldsymbol{y}(s))\, ds.$$

If we approximate this integral using the *rectangle rule* $\int_a^b g(s)\, ds \approx (b-a)\, g(a)$, then we obtain Euler's method.

Method of undetermined coefficients. At step k, we know $\boldsymbol{y}_k$ and $\boldsymbol{y}'_k = \boldsymbol{f}(t_k, \boldsymbol{y}_k)$, and based on these values we want to predict the value $\boldsymbol{y}_{k+1}$ at the next step. If we take a linear combination of the known data, then our predictor will have the form

$$\boldsymbol{y}_{k+1} = \alpha\, \boldsymbol{y}_k + \beta\, \boldsymbol{y}'_k,$$

where α and β are coefficients to be determined. With two parameters to be determined, we can force the predictor to be exact for the first two monomials. If $\boldsymbol{y}(t) = \boldsymbol{e}$, the vector whose components are all ones (the first monomial), then $\boldsymbol{y}'(t) = \boldsymbol{0}$, and we have the equation

$$\boldsymbol{e} = \alpha\, \boldsymbol{e} + \beta\, \boldsymbol{0},$$

which implies that $\alpha = 1$. If $\boldsymbol{y}(t) = t\,\boldsymbol{e}$, then $\boldsymbol{y}'(t) = \boldsymbol{e}$, and we have the equation

$$t_{k+1}\boldsymbol{e} = \alpha\, t_k \boldsymbol{e} + \beta\, \boldsymbol{e} = (t_k + \beta)\, \boldsymbol{e},$$

which implies that $\beta = t_{k+1} - t_k = h_k$. Thus, our predictor is

$$\boldsymbol{y}_{k+1} = \boldsymbol{y}_k + h_k\, \boldsymbol{y}'_k,$$

which is Euler's method.

Example 9.8 Euler's Method. In Example 9.5 we considered the IVP $y' = y$ with initial value y_0 at initial time $t_0 = 0$. This simple problem is easily solved

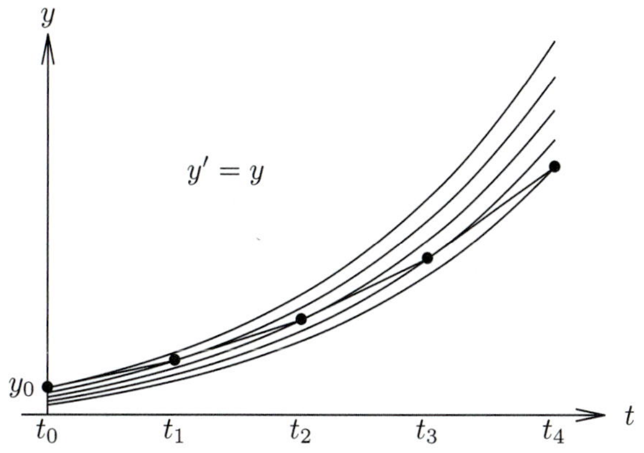

Figure 9.4: Euler's method for $y' = y$.

analytically, but for illustration let us apply Euler's method to solve it numerically. For simplicity, we will use a fixed step size h. We first advance the solution from time $t_0 = 0$ to time $t_1 = t_0 + h$,

$$y_1 = y_0 + h\, y_0' = y_0 + h\, y_0 = (1 + h)\, y_0.$$

Note that the approximate solution value y_1 we obtain at t_1 is not exact (i.e., $y_1 \neq y(t_1)$). For example, if $t_0 = 0$, $y_0 = 1$, and $h = 0.5$, then $y_1 = 1.5$, whereas the exact solution for this initial value is $y(0.5) = \exp(0.5) \approx 1.649$. Thus, the value y_1 lies on a *different* solution of the ODE from the one on which we started, as shown in Fig. 9.4.

To continue the numerical solution process, we take another step from t_1 to $t_2 = t_1 + h = 1.0$, obtaining $y_2 = y_1 + h\, y_1 = 1.5 + (0.5)(1.5) = 2.25$. Note that y_2 differs not only from the true solution of the original problem at $t = 1$, namely, $y(1) = \exp(1) \approx 2.718$, but it also differs from the solution passing through the previous point (t_1, y_1), which has the approximate value 2.473 at $t = 1$. Thus, we have moved to still another solution of the ODE. We can continue to take additional steps, generating a table of discrete values of the approximate solution over whatever interval we desire. As we do so, we will hop from one solution to another at each step. The solutions of this ODE are unstable, so the errors we make at each step are amplified with time as a result of the divergence of the solutions, as can be seen in Fig. 9.4. For an equation with stable solutions, on the other hand, the errors in the numerical solution do not grow, and for an equation with asymptotically stable solutions, such as $y' = -y$, the errors diminish with time, as shown in Fig. 9.5.

Euler's method is an example of a *one-step*, or *single-step*, method in that the next approximate solution value depends only on the current values of t_k, $\boldsymbol{y}_k$, and h_k. Such methods have the general form

$$\boldsymbol{y}_{k+1} = \boldsymbol{y}_k + h_k\, \boldsymbol{\phi}(t_k, \boldsymbol{y}_k, h_k)$$

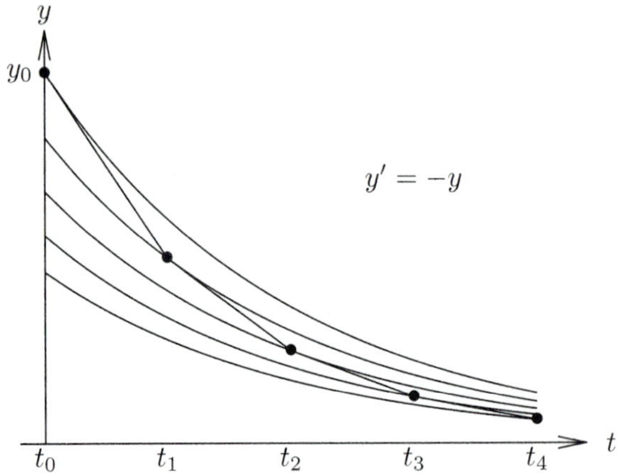

Figure 9.5: Euler's method for $y' = -y$.

for some function $\phi: \mathbb{R}^{n+2} \to \mathbb{R}^n$. We will see several additional one-step methods, as well as *multistep* methods for which the next approximate solution value depends on solution and derivative values at several steps.

9.3.2 Accuracy and Stability

Like other methods that approximate derivatives by finite differences, a numerical procedure for solving an ODE suffers from two distinct sources of error:

- *Rounding error*, which is due to the finite precision of floating-point arithmetic
- *Truncation error* (or discretization error), which is due to the method used, and which would remain, even if all arithmetic were performed exactly

Although they arise from different sources, these two types of errors are not independent of each other. For example, the truncation error can usually be reduced by using a smaller step size h, but doing so may incur greater rounding error (see Example 1.3). In most practical situations, however, truncation error is the dominant factor in determining the accuracy of numerical solutions of ODEs, so we will henceforth ignore rounding error in this context.

The truncation error at the kth step comes in two distinct but related flavors:

- *Global error* is the cumulative overall error

$$\boldsymbol{e}_k = \boldsymbol{y}_k - \boldsymbol{y}(t_k),$$

  where $\boldsymbol{y}_k$ is the computed solution at t_k and $\boldsymbol{y}(t)$ is the true solution of the ODE passing through the initial point $(t_0, \boldsymbol{y}_0)$.
- *Local error* is the error made in one step of the numerical method,

$$\boldsymbol{\ell}_k = \boldsymbol{y}_k - \boldsymbol{u}_{k-1}(t_k),$$

  where $\boldsymbol{u}_{k-1}(t)$ is the solution of the ODE passing through the previous point $(t_{k-1}, \boldsymbol{y}_{k-1})$.

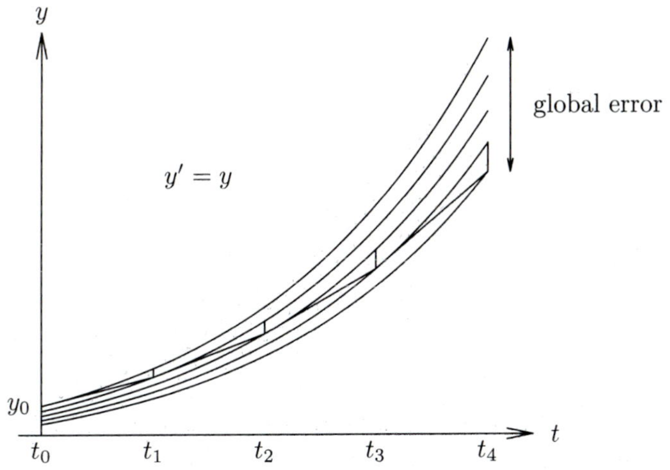

Figure 9.6: Local and global errors in Euler's method for $y' = y$.

Since

$$\begin{aligned} \boldsymbol{y}_k &= \boldsymbol{y}_{k-1} + h_{k-1}\,\boldsymbol{\phi}(t_{k-1}, \boldsymbol{y}_{k-1}, h_{k-1}) \\ &= \boldsymbol{u}_{k-1}(t_{k-1}) + h_{k-1}\,\boldsymbol{\phi}(t_{k-1}, \boldsymbol{u}_{k-1}(t_{k-1}), h_{k-1}), \end{aligned}$$

we see that the local error at a given step is simply the amount by which the solution of the ODE fails to satisfy the finite difference equation. The global error is obviously of primary interest, but only the local error can be readily estimated and controlled, so we need to understand the relationship between the two.

In a bank savings account earning compound interest, early deposits have more time to grow than later ones, and this growth means that the total value of the account is not simply the sum of the individual deposits. Similarly, the global error of an approximate solution to an ODE at a given step reflects not only the local error at that step, but also the compounded effects of the local errors at all previous steps. Thus, the global error is not simply the sum of the local errors. If the solutions of the ODE are diverging, then the local errors at each step are magnified over time, so that the global error is greater than the sum of the local errors, as shown in Fig. 9.6, where the local errors are indicated by small vertical bars between solutions and the global error is indicated by a bar at the end. If the solutions of the ODE are converging, on the other hand, then the global error may be less than the sum of the local errors, as shown in Fig. 9.7. In order to assess the effectiveness of a numerical method, we need to characterize both its local error (accuracy) and the compounding effects over multiple steps (stability).

The *accuracy* of a numerical method is said to be of order p if

$$\boldsymbol{\ell}_k = \mathcal{O}(h_k^{p+1}).$$

The motivation for this definition, with the order of accuracy one less than the exponent of the step size in the local error, is that if the local error is $\mathcal{O}(h_k^{p+1})$,

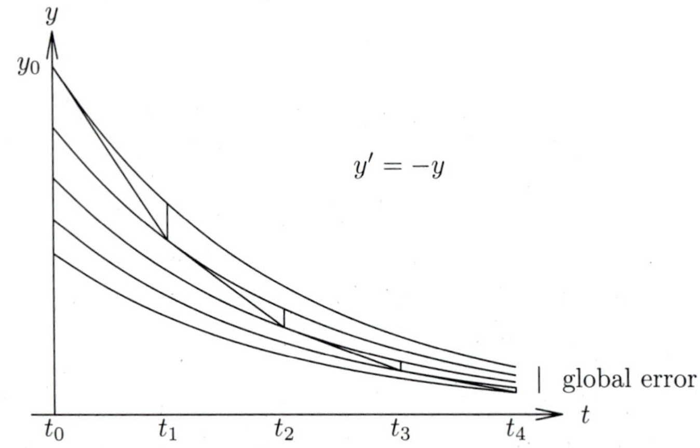

Figure 9.7: Local and global errors in Euler's method for $y' = -y$.

then the local error per unit step, $\boldsymbol{\ell}_k/h_k$, is $\mathcal{O}(h_k^p)$, and it can be shown that under reasonable conditions the global error $\boldsymbol{e}_k$ is $\mathcal{O}(h^p)$, where h is the average step size.

The concept of *stability* of a numerical method for an ODE is analogous to the stability of solutions to an ODE. Recall that a solution to an ODE is stable if perturbations of the solution do not diverge away from it over time. Similarly, a numerical method is said to be *stable* if small perturbations do not cause the resulting numerical solution to diverge away without bound. Such divergence of numerical solutions could be caused by instability of the solution to the ODE, but as we will see, it can also be caused by the numerical method itself, even when the solutions to the ODE are stable. To focus specifically on instability due to the numerical method, an alternate definition of stability requires that the numerical solution at any arbitrary but fixed time t remain bounded as $h \to 0$. The two definitions are effectively equivalent, however, as either definition prohibits excessive growth as the number of steps becomes arbitrarily large.

Let us first examine stability and accuracy in the simple context of Euler's method applied to the scalar ODE that we considered in Example 9.6, $y' = \lambda y$, where λ is a (possibly complex) constant. With initial condition $y(0) = y_0$, the exact solution to the IVP is given by $y(t) = y_0 e^{\lambda t}$. Applying Euler's method to this ODE using a fixed step size h, we have the recurrence

$$y_{k+1} = y_k + h\,\lambda\,y_k = (1 + h\,\lambda)\,y_k,$$

which implies that

$$y_k = (1 + h\,\lambda)^k\,y_0.$$

The quantity $1 + h\lambda$ is called the *growth factor*. If $\text{Re}(\lambda) < 0$, then the exact solution of the ODE decays to zero as t increases, as will the successive computed solution values if $|1+h\lambda| < 1$. If $|1+h\lambda| > 1$, on the other hand, then the computed solution values grow without bound regardless of the sign of $\text{Re}(\lambda)$, which means that Euler's method can be unstable even when the exact solution is stable. In order for Euler's method to be stable, the step size h must satisfy the inequality

$$|1 + h\,\lambda| \leq 1,$$

which says that $h\lambda$ must lie inside a circle in the complex plane of radius 1 centered at -1. If λ is real, then $h\lambda$ must lie in the interval $(-2, 0)$, which means that for $\lambda < 0$, we must have $h \leq -2/\lambda$ for Euler's method to be stable. We also note that the growth factor $1 + h\lambda$ agrees with the series expansion

$$e^{h\lambda} = 1 + h\lambda + \frac{(h\lambda)^2}{2} + \frac{(h\lambda)^3}{6} + \cdots$$

through terms of first order in h, so the accuracy of Euler's method is of first order.

To determine the accuracy and stability of Euler's method for a general system of ODEs $\boldsymbol{y}' = \boldsymbol{f}(t, \boldsymbol{y})$, consider the Taylor series

$$\boldsymbol{y}(t+h) = \boldsymbol{y}(t) + h\,\boldsymbol{y}'(t) + \mathcal{O}(h^2) = \boldsymbol{y}(t) + h\,\boldsymbol{f}(t, \boldsymbol{y}(t)) + \mathcal{O}(h^2).$$

If we take $t = t_k$ and $h = h_k$, we obtain

$$\boldsymbol{y}(t_{k+1}) = \boldsymbol{y}(t_k) + h_k\,\boldsymbol{f}(t_k, \boldsymbol{y}(t_k)) + \mathcal{O}(h_k^2).$$

If we now subtract this from the expression for $\boldsymbol{y}_{k+1}$ given by Euler's method we obtain

$$\boldsymbol{y}_{k+1} - \boldsymbol{y}(t_{k+1}) = [\boldsymbol{y}_k - \boldsymbol{y}(t_k)] + h_k\,[\boldsymbol{f}(t_k, \boldsymbol{y}_k) - \boldsymbol{f}(t_k, \boldsymbol{y}(t_k))] - \mathcal{O}(h_k^2).$$

The difference on the left side is the global error $\boldsymbol{e}_{k+1}$. If there were no prior errors, then we would have $\boldsymbol{y}_k = \boldsymbol{y}(t_k)$, and the first two differences in brackets on the right side would be zero, leaving only the $\mathcal{O}(h_k^2)$ term, which is the local error. This result means that Euler's method is first-order accurate.

From the preceding derivation, we see that the global error at a given step is the sum of the local error at that step and what might be termed the *propagated error* from previous steps. To characterize the latter, by the *Mean Value Theorem* for a vector-valued function of a vector we can write

$$\boldsymbol{f}(t_k, \boldsymbol{y}_k) - \boldsymbol{f}(t_k, \boldsymbol{y}(t_k)) = \bar{\boldsymbol{J}}_f\,(\boldsymbol{y}_k - \boldsymbol{y}(t_k)),$$

where $\bar{\boldsymbol{J}}_f = \int_0^1 \boldsymbol{J}_f(t_k, \alpha\,\boldsymbol{y}_k + (1-\alpha)\,\boldsymbol{y}(t_k))\,d\alpha$ and $\boldsymbol{J}_f$ is the Jacobian matrix of $\boldsymbol{f}$ with respect to $\boldsymbol{y}$, so that we can express the global error at step $k+1$ as

$$\boldsymbol{e}_{k+1} = (\boldsymbol{I} + h_k \bar{\boldsymbol{J}}_f)\,\boldsymbol{e}_k + \boldsymbol{\ell}_{k+1}.$$

Thus, the global error is multiplied at each step by the factor $\boldsymbol{I} + h_k \bar{\boldsymbol{J}}_f$, which is called the *growth factor* or *amplification factor*. The errors do not grow if the spectral radius

$$\rho(\boldsymbol{I} + h_k \bar{\boldsymbol{J}}_f) \leq 1,$$

which is satisfied if all the eigenvalues of $h_k \bar{\boldsymbol{J}}_f$ lie inside a circle in the complex plane of radius 1 centered at -1. If this is not the case, then the errors grow and the method is unstable, regardless of whether the solution to the ODE is stable. We will see a dramatic example of such numerical instability for a stable solution in Example 9.10.

Note that this more general analysis produced the same stability and accuracy results as we obtained using the simple scalar test equation $y' = \lambda y$. Especially for more complicated numerical methods, this simple scalar test ODE is far easier to work with than a general ODE, and it produces essentially the same stability results if we equate the complex coefficient λ with the eigenvalues of the Jacobian matrix $\boldsymbol{J}_f$ at a given point. An important caveat, however, is that λ is constant, whereas the Jacobian $\boldsymbol{J}_f$ varies for a nonlinear equation, and hence the stability can potentially change. Also note that in general the amplification factor depends on the particular ODE being solved (which determines the Jacobian $\boldsymbol{J}_f$), the particular numerical method used (which determines the form of the amplification factor), and the step size h.

In choosing a step size h_k for advancing the numerical solution of an ODE at step k, we would like to minimize computational cost by taking as large a step as possible, but we must take into account both stability and accuracy. To yield a meaningful solution, the step size must obey any stability restrictions imposed by the method being used. In addition, a local error estimate is needed to ensure that the desired accuracy is attained. With Euler's method, for example, a Taylor series expansion shows that the local error is approximately $(h_k^2/2)\boldsymbol{y}_k''$, so the step size should satisfy

$$h_k \le \sqrt{2\,tol/\|\boldsymbol{y}_k''\|},$$

where tol is a specified local error tolerance. Of course, we do not know the value of $\boldsymbol{y}_k''$, but we can estimate it by a difference quotient of the form

$$\boldsymbol{y}_k'' \approx \frac{\boldsymbol{y}_k' - \boldsymbol{y}_{k-1}'}{t_k - t_{k-1}}.$$

Other methods of obtaining local error estimates are based on the difference between results obtained using methods of different orders of accuracy or different step sizes.

9.3.3 Implicit Methods

Euler's method is an *explicit* method in that it uses only information at time t_k to advance the solution to time t_{k+1}. This may appear to be a virtue, but we saw that Euler's method has a rather limited stability region. A larger stability region can be obtained by using information at time t_{k+1}, which makes the method *implicit*. The simplest example is the *backward Euler method*,

$$\boldsymbol{y}_{k+1} = \boldsymbol{y}_k + h_k\,\boldsymbol{f}(t_{k+1}, \boldsymbol{y}_{k+1}),$$

which can easily be derived by any of the methods given in Section 9.3.1 for deriving Euler's method, for example numerical quadrature using the "other" rectangle rule, $\int_a^b g(s)\,ds \approx (b-a)g(b)$.

The backward Euler method is implicit because we must evaluate $\boldsymbol{f}$ with the argument $\boldsymbol{y}_{k+1}$ before we know its value. This statement simply means that a value for $\boldsymbol{y}_{k+1}$ that satisfies the preceding equation must be determined, and if $\boldsymbol{f}$ is a nonlinear function of $\boldsymbol{y}$, as is often the case, then an iterative solution method, such as fixed-point iteration or Newton's method, must be used. A good starting guess for the iteration can be obtained from an explicit method, such as Euler's method, or from the solution at the previous time step.

Example 9.9 Backward Euler Method. Consider the nonlinear scalar ODE

$$y' = -y^3$$

with initial condition $y(0) = 1$. Using the backward Euler method with a step size of $h = 0.5$, we obtain the equation

$$y_1 = y_0 + h\, f(t_1, y_1) = 1 - 0.5\, y_1^3$$

for the solution value at the next step. This nonlinear equation for y_1 is already set up to solve by fixed-point iteration, repeatedly substituting successive values for y_1 on the right-hand side, or we could use any other method from Chapter 5, such as Newton's method. In any case, we need a starting guess for y_1, for which we could simply use the previous solution value, $y_0 = 1$, or we could use an explicit method to produce a starting guess for the implicit method. Using Euler's method, for example, we would obtain $y_1 = y_0 - 0.5\, y_0^3 = 0.5$ as a starting guess for the iterative solution of the implicit equation. The iterations eventually converge to the final value $y_1 \approx 0.7709$.

Given the extra trouble and computation in using an implicit method, one might wonder why we would bother. The answer is that implicit methods generally have a significantly larger stability region than comparable explicit methods. To determine the stability and accuracy of the backward Euler method, we apply it to the scalar test ODE $y' = \lambda y$, obtaining

$$y_{k+1} = y_k + h\,\lambda\, y_{k+1},$$

or

$$(1 - h\,\lambda)\, y_{k+1} = y_k,$$

so that

$$y_k = \left(\frac{1}{1 - h\,\lambda}\right)^k y_0.$$

Thus, for the backward Euler method to be stable we must have

$$\left|\frac{1}{1 - h\,\lambda}\right| \le 1,$$

which holds for *any* $h > 0$ when $\mathrm{Re}(\lambda) < 0$. Thus, the stability region for the backward Euler method includes the entire left half of the complex plane, or the interval $(-\infty, 0)$ if λ is real, and there is no stability restriction on the step size when computing a stable solution. The growth factor

$$\frac{1}{1 - h\lambda} = 1 + h\lambda + (h\lambda)^2 + \cdots$$

agrees with the expansion for $e^{h\lambda}$ through terms of order h, so the backward Euler method is first-order accurate.

More generally, the amplification factor for the backward Euler method for a general ODE is $(\boldsymbol{I} - h\boldsymbol{J}_f)^{-1}$, whose spectral radius is less than 1 provided the eigenvalues of $h\boldsymbol{J}_f$ lie outside a circle in the complex plane of radius 1 centered at 1. Thus, the stability region for the backward Euler method includes the entire left half of the complex plane, and hence for computing a stable solution the method is stable for any positive step size. Such a method is said to be *unconditionally stable*. The great virtue of an unconditionally stable method is that the desired local accuracy places the only constraint on our choice of step size. Thus, we may be able to take much larger steps than for an explicit method of comparable order and attain much higher overall efficiency despite requiring more computation per step because of having to solve an equation at each step of the implicit method.

Although the backward Euler method is unconditionally stable, its first-order accuracy severely limits its usefulness. We can obtain a method of higher-order accuracy by combining the Euler and backward Euler methods. In particular, averaging these two methods yields the implicit *trapezoid method*

$$\boldsymbol{y}_{k+1} = \boldsymbol{y}_k + h_k\left(\boldsymbol{f}(t_k, \boldsymbol{y}_k) + \boldsymbol{f}(t_{k+1}, \boldsymbol{y}_{k+1})\right)/2,$$

which can also be derived directly by any of the usual methods, for example numerical quadrature using the trapezoid quadrature rule.

To determine the stability and accuracy of the trapezoid method, we apply it to the scalar test ODE $y' = \lambda y$, obtaining

$$y_{k+1} = y_k + h\left(\lambda y_k + \lambda y_{k+1}\right)/2,$$

which implies that

$$y_k = \left(\frac{1 + h\lambda/2}{1 - h\lambda/2}\right)^k y_0.$$

Thus, the method is stable if

$$\left|\frac{1 + h\lambda/2}{1 - h\lambda/2}\right| < 1,$$

which holds for any $h > 0$ when $\text{Re}(\lambda) < 0$, so that the trapezoid method is unconditionally stable. In addition, the growth factor

$$\begin{aligned}\frac{1 + h\lambda/2}{1 - h\lambda/2} &= \left(1 + \frac{h\lambda}{2}\right)\left(1 + \frac{h\lambda}{2} + \left(\frac{h\lambda}{2}\right)^2 + \left(\frac{h\lambda}{2}\right)^3 + \cdots\right) \\ &= 1 + h\lambda + \frac{(h\lambda)^2}{2} + \frac{(h\lambda)^3}{4} + \cdots\end{aligned}$$

agrees with the expansion of $e^{h\lambda}$ through terms of order h^2, and hence the trapezoid method is second-order accurate. More generally, the trapezoid method has amplification factor $(\boldsymbol{I} + \frac{1}{2}h\boldsymbol{J}_f)(\boldsymbol{I} - \frac{1}{2}h\boldsymbol{J}_f)^{-1}$, whose spectral radius is less than 1 provided the eigenvalues of $h\boldsymbol{J}_f$ lie in the left half of the complex plane. Thus, the trapezoid method is unconditionally stable as well as second-order accurate.

We have now seen two examples of implicit methods that are unconditionally stable, but not all implicit methods have this property. Implicit methods generally have larger stability regions than explicit methods, but the allowable step size is not always unlimited. Implicitness alone is not sufficient to guarantee stability.

9.3.4 Stiffness

Asymptotically stable solutions converge toward each other over time. This convergence has the favorable property of tending to damp out errors in a numerical solution, but if the convergence of solutions is too rapid, then difficulties of a different type may arise. A typical instance is illustrated in Fig. 9.8, where a slowly varying solution is surrounded by other solutions with rapidly decaying transients. Such an ODE is said to be *stiff*.

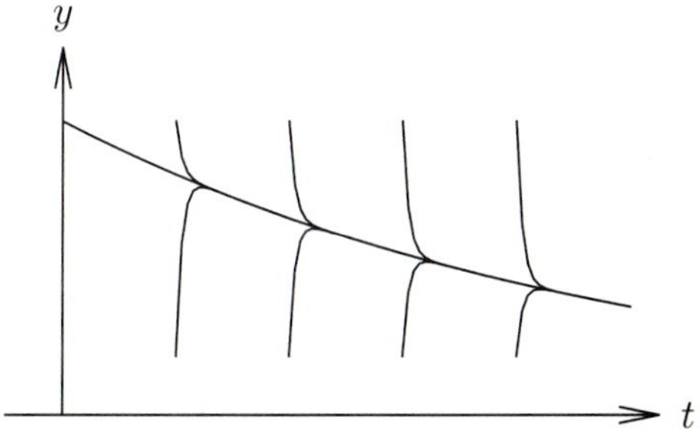

Figure 9.8: Solutions for typical stiff ODE.

Stiffness can be defined in a number of different ways. Physically, stiffness corresponds to a process whose components have highly disparate time scales or a process whose time scale is very short compared to the interval over which it is being studied. Mathematically, a stable ODE $\boldsymbol{y}' = \boldsymbol{f}(t, \boldsymbol{y})$ is stiff if its Jacobian matrix $\boldsymbol{J}_f$ has eigenvalues that differ greatly in magnitude. There may be eigenvalues with relatively large negative real parts (corresponding to strongly damped components of the solution) or relatively large imaginary parts (corresponding to rapidly oscillating components of the solution). Pragmatically, an ODE is stiff if an explicit method such as Euler's method is highly inefficient because the step size required to maintain stability is far smaller than the step size required to maintain the desired accuracy. Thus, stiffness is a relative concept that depends on the stability region of the method used, the accuracy required, and the length of the interval of integration, as well as the ODE.

For the scalar test ODE $y' = \lambda y$ over the interval $[a, b]$, the IVP is stiff if

$$(b - a)\,\mathrm{Re}(\lambda) \ll -1$$

because the stability restriction on the step size h in Euler's method is relatively severe. More generally, an ODE over the interval $[a, b]$ is stiff near a solution $\boldsymbol{y}(t)$ if

$$(b-a)\min_j(\mathrm{Re}(\lambda_j)) \ll -1,$$

where the λ_j are the eigenvalues of the Jacobian matrix $\boldsymbol{J}_f(t, \boldsymbol{y}(t))$. Some numerical methods are very inefficient for stiff equations because the rapidly varying component of the solution forces very small step sizes to be used to maintain stability. Since the stability restriction depends on the rapidly varying component of the solution, whereas the accuracy restriction depends on the slowly varying component, the step size may be much more severely restricted by stability than by the required accuracy. Euler's method, for example, is extremely inefficient for solving a stiff equation because of its small stability region. The unconditional stability of the implicit backward Euler method, on the other hand, makes it suitable for stiff problems. Stiff ODEs need not be difficult to solve numerically provided a suitable method, generally implicit, is chosen.

Example 9.10 Stiffness. To illustrate the numerical solution of a stiff ODE, consider the IVP

$$y' = -100y + 100t + 101$$

with initial condition $y(0) = 1$. The general solution of this ODE is $y(t) = 1 + t + ce^{-100t}$, and the particular solution satisfying the initial condition is $y(t) = 1 + t$ (i.e., $c = 0$). Since the solution is linear, Euler's method is theoretically exact for this problem. However, to illustrate the effect of truncation or rounding errors, let us perturb the initial value slightly. With a step size $h = 0.1$, the first few steps for the given initial values are:

t	0.0	0.1	0.2	0.3	0.4
Exact solution	1.00	1.10	1.20	1.30	1.40
Euler solution	0.99	1.19	0.39	8.59	−64.2
Euler solution	1.01	1.01	2.01	−5.99	67.0

The computed solution is incredibly sensitive to the initial value, as each tiny perturbation results in a wildly different solution. An explanation for this behavior is shown in Fig. 9.9. Any point deviating from the desired particular solution, even by only a small amount, lies on a different solution, for which $c \neq 0$, and therefore the rapid transient of the general solution is present. Euler's method bases its projection on the derivative at the current point, and the resulting large value causes the numerical solution to diverge radically from the desired solution. This behavior should not surprise us. The Jacobian for this equation is $J_f = -100$, so the stability condition for Euler's method requires a step size $h < 0.02$, which we are violating.

By contrast, the backward Euler method has no trouble solving this problem. In fact, the backward Euler solution is extremely *insensitive* to the initial value, as shown in the following table,

t	0.0	0.1	0.2	0.3	0.4
Exact solution	1.00	1.10	1.20	1.30	1.40
BE solution	0.00	1.01	1.19	1.30	1.40
BE solution	2.00	1.19	1.21	1.30	1.40

and illustrated in Fig. 9.10. Even with a very large perturbation in the initial value, by using the derivative at the next point rather than the current point, the transient is quickly damped out and the backward Euler solution converges to the desired solution after only a few steps. This behavior is consistent with the unconditional stability of the backward Euler method for a stable equation.

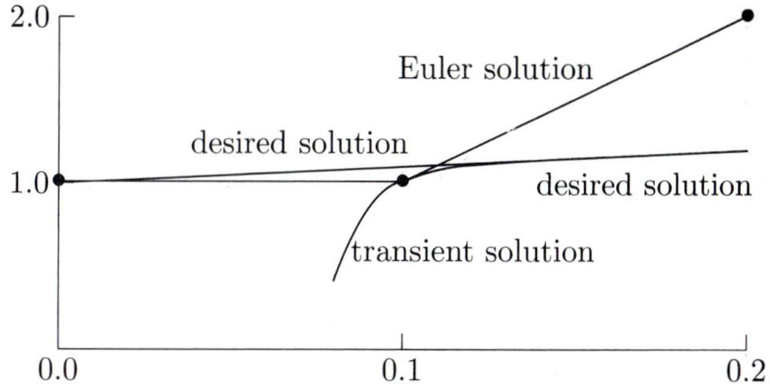

Figure 9.9: Unstable solution of stiff ODE using Euler's method.

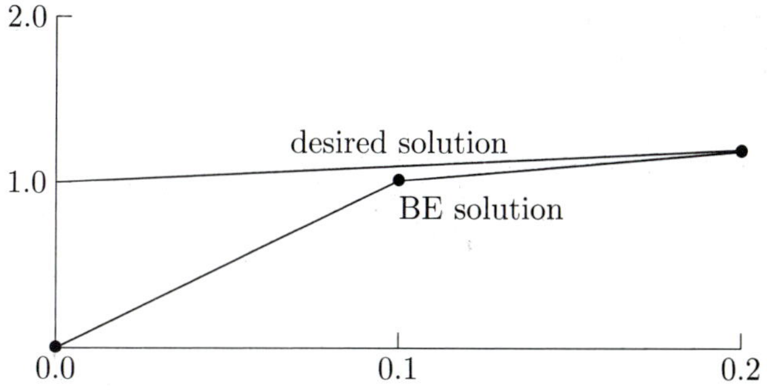

Figure 9.10: Stable solution of stiff ODE using backward Euler method.

We have seen that implicit methods are required for stiff ODEs, and thus a (generally nonlinear) equation must be solved at each step. Although fixed-point iteration is a natural choice for solving this equation in other contexts, it is not a viable option when the ODE is stiff. The problem is that in order for fixed-point iteration to converge, the step size h must be very small, which would defeat the purpose of using an implicit method in the first place. As a result, Newton's method or some variant of it is the standard approach for solving the nonlinear equation at each step of methods designed for stiff ODEs. This introduces significant overhead for computing or approximating the Jacobian matrix and solving the resulting linear system at each step, but the much larger step size allowed generally makes it worthwhile. Another caveat concerning stiffness is that our discussion has focused on stiffness due to rapidly decaying transients. Stiffness due to rapidly oscillating components requires a somewhat different approach that we will not go into here.

9.3.5 Taylor Series Methods

We have seen that Euler's method can be derived from a Taylor series expansion. By retaining more terms in the Taylor series, we can generate higher-order single-step methods. For example, retaining one additional term in the Taylor series

$$\boldsymbol{y}(t+h) = \boldsymbol{y}(t) + h\,\boldsymbol{y}'(t) + \frac{h^2}{2}\,\boldsymbol{y}''(t) + \frac{h^3}{6}\,\boldsymbol{y}'''(t) + \cdots$$

gives the second-order method

$$\boldsymbol{y}_{k+1} = \boldsymbol{y}_k + h_k\,\boldsymbol{y}_k' + \frac{h_k^2}{2}\,\boldsymbol{y}_k''.$$

Note, however, that this approach requires the computation of higher derivatives of $\boldsymbol{y}$. These can be obtained by differentiating $\boldsymbol{y}' = \boldsymbol{f}(t, \boldsymbol{y})$ using the chain rule, e.g.,

$$\boldsymbol{y}'' = \boldsymbol{f}_t(t, \boldsymbol{y}) + \boldsymbol{f}_y(t, \boldsymbol{y})\,\boldsymbol{y}' = \boldsymbol{f}_t(t, \boldsymbol{y}) + \boldsymbol{f}_y(t, \boldsymbol{y})\,\boldsymbol{f}(t, \boldsymbol{y}),$$

where the subscripts indicate partial derivatives with respect to the given variable. As the order increases, such expressions for the derivatives rapidly become too complicated to be practical to compute, so Taylor series methods of higher order have not often been used in practice. Recently, however, the availability of symbolic manipulation and automatic differentiation systems has made these methods more feasible.

Example 9.11 Taylor Series Method. To illustrate the second-order Taylor series method, we use it to solve the nonlinear scalar ODE

$$y'(t) = f(t, y) = -2ty^2,$$

with initial value $y(0) = 1$. We differentiate f to obtain for this problem

$$y'' = f_t(t, y) + f_y(t, y)f(t, y) = -2y^2 + (-4ty)(-2ty^2) = 2y^2(4t^2y - 1).$$

Taking a step from $t_0 = 0$ to $t_1 = 0.25$ using step size $h = 0.25$, we obtain

$$y_1 = y_0 + h\,y_0' + \frac{h^2}{2}\,y_0'' = 1 + 0 - 0.0625 = 0.9375.$$

Continuing with another step from $t_1 = 0.25$ to $t_2 = 0.5$, we obtain

$$y_2 = y_1 + h\,y_1' + \frac{h^2}{2}\,y_1'' = 0.9375 - 0.1099 - 0.0421 = 0.7856.$$

For comparison, the exact solution for this problem is $y(t) = 1/(1+t^2)$, and hence the true solution at the integration points is $y(0.25) = 0.9412$ and $y(0.5) = 0.8$.

9.3.6 Runge-Kutta Methods

Runge-Kutta methods are single-step methods that are similar in motivation to Taylor series methods but do not involve explicit computation of higher derivatives. Instead, Runge-Kutta methods replace higher derivatives by finite difference approximations based on values of $\boldsymbol{f}$ at points between t_k and t_{k+1}. Alternatively, Runge-Kutta methods can be derived by applying numerical quadrature rules to evaluate the integral

$$\boldsymbol{y}_{k+1} - \boldsymbol{y}_k = \int_{t_k}^{t_{k+1}} \boldsymbol{f}(t, \boldsymbol{y}(t))\, dt.$$

In either case, some bootstrapping will be required to obtain the necessary values of $\boldsymbol{f}$, since we do not know the second argument of $\boldsymbol{f}$, namely the solution $\boldsymbol{y}(t)$, for t between t_k and t_{k+1}.

To demonstrate the derivation of a Runge-Kutta method, recall from Section 9.3.5 that the second derivative of $\boldsymbol{y}$ is given by

$$\boldsymbol{y}'' = \boldsymbol{f}_t + \boldsymbol{f}_y \boldsymbol{f},$$

where each function is evaluated at $(t, \boldsymbol{y})$. We can approximate the term on the right by expanding $\boldsymbol{f}$ in a Taylor series in two variables

$$\boldsymbol{f}(t+h, \boldsymbol{y}+h\boldsymbol{f}) = \boldsymbol{f} + h\boldsymbol{f}_t + h\boldsymbol{f}_y\boldsymbol{f} + \mathcal{O}(h^2),$$

from which we obtain

$$\boldsymbol{f}_t + \boldsymbol{f}_y\boldsymbol{f} = \frac{\boldsymbol{f}(t+h, \boldsymbol{y}+h\boldsymbol{f}) - \boldsymbol{f}(t, \boldsymbol{y})}{h} + \mathcal{O}(h).$$

With this approximation to the second derivative, the second-order Taylor series method given in Section 9.3.5 becomes

$$\begin{aligned} \boldsymbol{y}_{k+1} &= \boldsymbol{y}_k + h_k\, \boldsymbol{f}(t_k, \boldsymbol{y}_k) + \frac{h_k^2}{2}\, \frac{\boldsymbol{f}(t_k + h_k, \boldsymbol{y}_k + h_k \boldsymbol{f}(t_k, \boldsymbol{y}_k)) - \boldsymbol{f}(t_k, \boldsymbol{y}_k)}{h_k} \\ &= \boldsymbol{y}_k + \frac{h_k}{2}\left(\boldsymbol{f}(t_k, \boldsymbol{y}_k) + \boldsymbol{f}(t_k + h_k, \boldsymbol{y}_k + h_k \boldsymbol{f}(t_k, \boldsymbol{y}_k))\right), \end{aligned}$$

which is known as *Heun's method* and can be implemented in the form

$$\boldsymbol{y}_{k+1} = \boldsymbol{y}_k + \frac{h_k}{2}(\boldsymbol{k}_1 + \boldsymbol{k}_2),$$

where $\boldsymbol{k}_1 = \boldsymbol{f}(t_k, \boldsymbol{y}_k)$ and $\boldsymbol{k}_2 = \boldsymbol{f}(t_k + h_k, \boldsymbol{y}_k + h_k \boldsymbol{k}_1)$. Alternatively, Heun's method can be derived by applying the trapezoid quadrature rule on the interval $[t_k, t_{k+1}]$, but with the unknown value $\boldsymbol{y}(t_{k+1})$ replaced by the Euler prediction $\boldsymbol{y}_k + h_k \boldsymbol{k}_1$ in evaluating $\boldsymbol{f}$ at t_{k+1}.

Example 9.12 Heun's Method. To illustrate the use of Heun's method, we use it to solve the nonlinear scalar ODE from Example 9.11,

$$y' = -2ty^2,$$

with initial value $y(0) = 1$. Taking a step from $t_0 = 0$ to $t_1 = 0.25$ using step size $h = 0.25$, we obtain

$$k_1 = f(t_0, y_0) = 0, \qquad k_2 = f(t_0 + h, y_0 + hk_1) = -0.5,$$

so that

$$y_1 = y_0 + \frac{h}{2}(k_1 + k_2) = 1 + (0.125)(-0.5) = 0.9375.$$

Continuing with another step from $t_1 = 0.25$ to $t_2 = 0.5$, we obtain

$$k_1 = f(t_1, y_1) = -0.4395, \qquad k_2 = f(t_1 + h, y_1 + hk_1) = -0.6850,$$

so that

$$y_2 = y_1 + \frac{h}{2}(k_1 + k_2) = 0.9375 + (0.125)(-1.1245) = 0.7969.$$

For comparison, the exact solution for this problem is $y(t) = 1/(1 + t^2)$, and hence the true solution at the integration points is $y(0.25) = 0.9412$ and $y(0.5) = 0.8$.

The best-known Runge-Kutta method is the classical fourth-order scheme

$$\boldsymbol{y}_{k+1} = \boldsymbol{y}_k + \frac{h_k}{6}(\boldsymbol{k}_1 + 2\boldsymbol{k}_2 + 2\boldsymbol{k}_3 + \boldsymbol{k}_4),$$

where

$$\begin{aligned}
\boldsymbol{k}_1 &= \boldsymbol{f}(t_k, \boldsymbol{y}_k), \\
\boldsymbol{k}_2 &= \boldsymbol{f}(t_k + h_k/2, \boldsymbol{y}_k + (h_k/2)\boldsymbol{k}_1), \\
\boldsymbol{k}_3 &= \boldsymbol{f}(t_k + h_k/2, \boldsymbol{y}_k + (h_k/2)\boldsymbol{k}_2), \\
\boldsymbol{k}_4 &= \boldsymbol{f}(t_k + h_k, \boldsymbol{y}_k + h_k\boldsymbol{k}_3).
\end{aligned}$$

This method is analogous to Simpson's rule; indeed it *is* Simpson's rule if $\boldsymbol{f}$ depends only on t. For an illustration of the use of the classical fourth-order Runge-Kutta method for solving a system of ODEs, see Example 10.6.

Runge-Kutta methods have a number of virtues. To proceed to time t_{k+1}, they require no history of the solution prior to time t_k, which makes them *self-starting* at the beginning of the integration, and also makes it easy to change the step size during the integration. These features also make Runge-Kutta methods relatively easy to program, which accounts in part for their popularity.

On the other hand, classical Runge-Kutta methods provide no error estimate on which to base the choice of step size. More recently, however, *embedded* Runge-Kutta methods have been developed in which an error estimate is based on the difference between a pair of methods of different order, but which share function evaluations for efficiency. For example, *Fehlberg's method* uses six function evaluations per step to produce both fourth- and fifth-order accurate approximations to the solution. Another effective 4(5) embedded pair was developed by Dormand and Prince.

This approach has led to automatic Runge-Kutta solvers that are effective for many problems but relatively inefficient for stiff problems or when very high accuracy is required. It is possible, however, to define *implicit* Runge-Kutta methods with superior stability properties that are suitable for solving stiff equations.

9.3.7 Extrapolation Methods

Extrapolation methods are based on the use of a single-step method to integrate the ODE over a given interval, $t_k \le t \le t_{k+1}$, using several different step sizes h_i and yielding results denoted by $\boldsymbol{Y}(h_i)$. This gives a discrete approximation to a function $\boldsymbol{Y}(h)$, where $\boldsymbol{Y}(0) = \boldsymbol{y}(t_{k+1})$. An interpolating polynomial or rational function $\hat{\boldsymbol{Y}}(h)$ is fit to these data, and $\hat{\boldsymbol{Y}}(0)$ is then taken as the approximation to $\boldsymbol{Y}(0)$. We saw another example of this approach in Richardson extrapolation for numerical differentiation and integration in Section 8.7. Extrapolation methods are capable of achieving very high accuracy, but they tend to be much less efficient and less flexible than other methods for ODEs, so they are used mainly when extremely high accuracy is required and cost is not a significant factor.

9.3.8 Multistep Methods

Multistep methods use information at more than one previous point to estimate the solution at the next point. For this reason, they are sometimes called *methods with memory*. *Linear* multistep methods have the form

$$\boldsymbol{y}_{k+1} = \sum_{i=1}^{m} \alpha_i \boldsymbol{y}_{k+1-i} + h \sum_{i=0}^{m} \beta_i \boldsymbol{f}(t_{k+1-i}, \boldsymbol{y}_{k+1-i}).$$

If $\beta_0 = 0$, then the method is explicit, but if $\beta_0 \ne 0$, then the method is implicit. The parameters α_i and β_i can be determined by polynomial interpolation. *Adams* methods, for example, are derived by interpolating derivative values $\boldsymbol{y}' = \boldsymbol{f}$ at m previous points and then integrating the resulting interpolating polynomial to obtain

$$\boldsymbol{y}_{k+1} = \boldsymbol{y}_k + \int_{t_k}^{t_{k+1}} \boldsymbol{f}(t, \boldsymbol{y}(t))\, dt \approx \boldsymbol{y}_k + \int_{t_k}^{t_{k+1}} \boldsymbol{p}(t)\, dt.$$

BDF (backward differentiation formula) methods, on the other hand, are derived by interpolating the solution values $\boldsymbol{y}$ at m previous points, differentiating the resulting interpolating polynomial, and setting the derivative equal to $\boldsymbol{f}(t_{k+1}, \boldsymbol{y}_{k+1})$ at t_{k+1} to obtain $\boldsymbol{y}_{k+1}$.

Example 9.13 Derivation of Multistep Methods. To illustrate another derivation of multistep methods, we derive an *explicit* two-step method of the form

$$y_{k+1} = \alpha_1 y_k + h\,(\beta_1 y_k' + \beta_2 y_{k-1}'),$$

where three parameters α_1, β_1, and β_2 are to be determined. To simplify notation, we consider only the scalar case; the resulting method can be applied componentwise to systems of ODEs. Using the method of undetermined coefficients, we will force the formula to be exact for the first three monomials. If $y(t) = 1$, then $y'(t) = 0$, so that we have the equation

$$1 = \alpha_1 \cdot 1 + h\,(\beta_1 \cdot 0 + \beta_2 \cdot 0).$$

If $y(t) = t$, then $y'(t) = 1$, so that we have the equation

$$t_{k+1} = \alpha_1 t_k + h\,(\beta_1 \cdot 1 + \beta_2 \cdot 1).$$

If $y(t) = t^2$, then $y'(t) = 2t$, so that we have the equation

$$t_{k+1}^2 = \alpha_1 t_k^2 + h\,(\beta_1 \cdot 2t_k + \beta_2 \cdot 2t_{k-1}).$$

All three of these equations must hold for any values of the t_i, so we make the convenient choice $t_{k-1} = 0$, $h = 1$ (hence $t_k = 1$ and $t_{k+1} = 2$) and solve the resulting 3×3 linear system to obtain the values $\alpha_1 = 1$, $\beta_1 = \frac{3}{2}$, $\beta_2 = -\frac{1}{2}$. Thus, the resulting explicit two-step method is

$$y_{k+1} = y_k + \frac{h}{2}\,(3y_k' - y_{k-1}'),$$

and by construction it is of order two.

Similarly, we can derive a three-parameter *implicit* method of the form

$$y_{k+1} = \alpha_1 y_k + h\,(\beta_0 y_{k+1}' + \beta_1 y_k').$$

Again using the method of undetermined coefficients, we force the formula to be exact for the first three monomials, obtaining the three equations

$$\begin{aligned} 1 &= \alpha_1 \cdot 1 + h\,(\beta_0 \cdot 0 + \beta_1 \cdot 0), \\ t_{k+1} &= \alpha_1 t_k + h\,(\beta_0 \cdot 1 + \beta_1 \cdot 1), \\ t_{k+1}^2 &= \alpha_1 t_k^2 + h\,(\beta_0 \cdot 2t_{k+1} + \beta_1 \cdot 2t_k). \end{aligned}$$

Making the convenient choice $t_k = 0$, $h = 1$ (hence, $t_{k+1} = 1$), we solve the resulting 3×3 linear system to obtain the values $\alpha_1 = 1$, $\beta_0 = \frac{1}{2}$, $\beta_1 = \frac{1}{2}$. Thus, the resulting implicit method is

$$y_{k+1} = y_k + \frac{h}{2}\,(y_{k+1}' + y_k'),$$

which we recognize as the *trapezoid method*, and by construction it is of order two. Higher-order multistep methods can be derived in this same manner, forcing the desired formula to be exact for as many monomials as there are parameters to be determined and then solving the resulting system of equations for those parameters.

Since multistep methods require several previous solution values and derivative values, how do we get started initially, before we have any past history to use? One strategy is to use a single-step method, which requires no past history, to generate solution values at enough points to begin using a multistep method. Another option is to use a low-order method initially and gradually increase the order as additional solution values become available.

As we saw with single-step methods, implicit multistep methods are usually more accurate and stable than explicit multistep methods, but they require an initial guess to solve the resulting (usually nonlinear) equation for $\boldsymbol{y}_{k+1}$. A good initial guess is conveniently supplied by an explicit method, so the explicit and implicit methods are used as a *predictor-corrector* pair. One could use the corrector repeatedly (i.e., fixed-point iteration) until some convergence tolerance is met, but doing so may not be worth the expense. So, a fixed number of corrector steps, often only one, may be used instead, giving a *PECE* (predict, evaluate, correct, evaluate) scheme. Although it has no effect on the value of $\boldsymbol{y}_{k+1}$, the second evaluation of $\boldsymbol{f}$ in a PECE scheme yields an improved value of $\boldsymbol{y}'_{k+1}$ for future use.

Alternatively, the nonlinear equation for $\boldsymbol{y}_{k+1}$ given by an implicit multistep method can be solved by Newton's method or other similar iterative method, again with a good starting guess supplied by the solution at the previous step or by an explicit multistep method. In particular, Newton's method or a close variant of it is essential when using an implicit multistep method designed for stiff ODEs, as fixed-point iteration will fail to converge for reasonable step sizes.

Example 9.14 Predictor-Corrector Method. To illustrate the use of a predictor-corrector pair, we use the two multistep methods derived in Example 9.13 to solve the nonlinear scalar ODE from Examples 9.11 and 9.12,

$$y' = -2ty^2,$$

with initial value $y(0) = 1$. The second-order explicit method requires two starting values, so in addition to the initial value $y_0 = 1$ at $t_0 = 0$, we will also use the value $y_1 = 0.9375$ at $t_1 = 0.25$ obtained using the single-step Heun method in Example 9.12. We can now use the second-order explicit method with step size $h = 0.25$ to take a step from $t_1 = 0.25$ to $t_2 = 0.5$, obtaining the *predicted* value

$$\hat{y}_2 = y_1 + \frac{h}{2}(3y'_1 - y'_0) = 0.9375 + 0.125(-1.3184 + 0) = 0.7727.$$

We *evaluate* f at this predicted value $\hat{y}_2$ to obtain the corresponding derivative value $\hat{y}'_2 = -0.5971$. We can now use these predicted values in the corresponding implicit method (in this case the trapezoid method) to obtain the *corrected* solution value

$$y_2 = y_1 + \frac{h}{2}(y'_2 + y'_1) = 0.9375 + 0.125(-0.5971 - 0.4395) = 0.8079.$$

We *evaluate* f again using this new value y_2 to obtain the improved value $y'_2 = -0.6528$, which would be needed in taking further steps. At this point we have completed the PECE procedure for this step. The corrector could be repeated, if desired, until convergence is obtained. For comparison, the exact solution for this problem is $y(t) = 1/(1 + t^2)$, and hence the true solution at the integration points is $y(0.25) = 0.9412$ and $y(0.5) = 0.8$.

One of the most popular pairs of multistep methods is the explicit fourth-order *Adams-Bashforth predictor*

$$\boldsymbol{y}_{k+1} = \boldsymbol{y}_k + \frac{h}{24}(55\,\boldsymbol{y}'_k - 59\,\boldsymbol{y}'_{k-1} + 37\,\boldsymbol{y}'_{k-2} - 9\,\boldsymbol{y}'_{k-3})$$

and the implicit fourth-order *Adams-Moulton corrector*

$$y_{k+1} = y_k + \frac{h}{24}(9\,y'_{k+1} + 19\,y'_k - 5\,y'_{k-1} + y'_{k-2}).$$

BDF (backward differentiation formula) methods, typified by the third-order method

$$y_{k+1} = \frac{1}{11}(18\,y_k - 9\,y_{k-1} + 2\,y_{k-2}) + \frac{6h}{11}\,y'_{k+1},$$

have relatively large stability regions that make them particularly effective for solving stiff ODEs.

The general properties of multistep methods can be summarized as follows:

- They are not self-starting, because several previous solution values are required. Thus, a special starting procedure must be used initially, such as a single-step method, until enough values have been generated to begin using a multistep method of the desired order.
- Changing step size is complicated, since the interpolation formulas are most conveniently based on equally spaced intervals for several consecutive points.
- A good local error estimate can be determined from the difference between the predictor and the corrector.
- They are relatively complicated to program.
- Being based on interpolation, they can efficiently provide solution values at output points other than the integration points.
- Implicit methods have a much greater region of stability than explicit methods but must be iterated to convergence to realize this benefit fully (e.g., a PECE scheme is actually explicit, albeit in a somewhat complicated way).
- Although implicit methods are more stable than explicit methods, they are still not necessarily unconditionally stable. Indeed, no multistep method of greater than second order is unconditionally stable, even if it is implicit.
- A properly designed implicit multistep method can be very effective for solving stiff equations.

The stability and accuracy of some of the most popular multistep methods are summarized in Table 9.1, where "stability threshold" indicates the left endpoint of the stability interval for a scalar equation, and "error constant" indicates the coefficient of the h^{p+1} term in the local error, where p is the order of the method. All of these Adams methods have $\alpha_1 = 1$, and $\alpha_i = 0$ for $i > 1$, so we list only the β_i. We observe that the implicit methods are both more stable and more accurate than the corresponding explicit methods of the same order.

9.3.9 Multivalue Methods

As we have seen, changing step size is difficult with multistep methods because the past history of the solution is most easily maintained at equally spaced intervals. Like multistep methods, *multivalue methods* are based on polynomial interpolation, but they avoid many of the implementation difficulties associated with multistep methods.

9.4 Software for ODE Initial Value Problems

Table 9.2 is a list of some of the software available for numerical solution of initial value problems for ordinary differential equations. Many of these routines have additional variants for special situations, such as root finding or sparse Jacobians. Another important category that we have not discussed is differential-algebraic systems, in which the solution must satisfy a system containing both differential and algebraic equations. The best-known routine for solving such problems is `dassl`, which is available from `Netlib`.

Source	Runge-Kutta	Adams	Stiff
FMM [127]	rkf45		
Hairer et al. [180, 181]	dopri5		radau5
HSL	da02		dc03
IMSL	ivprk	ivpag	ivpag
KMN [220]		sdriv2	sdriv2
MATLAB	ode23/ode45	ode113	ode15s/ode23s
NAG	d02bjf	d02cjf	d02ejf
Netlib	dverk	ode	vode/vodpk
NR [315]	odeint		stiff
NUMAL [250]	rke	multistep	gms
ODEPACK		lsode	lsode
SLATEC	derkf	deabm/sdriv1	debdf/sdriv2
TOMS	gerk(#504)		stint(#534)
TOMS	brk45(#669)/rkn(#670)		mebdf(#703)
TOMS	rksuite(#771)		

Table 9.2: Software for ODE initial value problems

Software for solving an ODE $\boldsymbol{y}' = \boldsymbol{f}(t, \boldsymbol{y})$ typically requires the user to supply the name of a routine that computes the value of the function $\boldsymbol{f}$ for any given values of t and $\boldsymbol{y}$. Additional input includes the number of equations in the system; the initial values of the independent variable t_0 and the vector $\boldsymbol{y}_0$ of dependent variables at the start of the integration; the value t_{out} of the independent variable at which the integration is to stop; and absolute or relative error tolerances, or both. Additional input, especially for a stiff ODE solver, may include the name of a routine for computing the Jacobian $\boldsymbol{J}_f$ of $\boldsymbol{f}$ and the name of a workspace array for storing such matrices. Output typically includes the solution vector $\boldsymbol{y}$ at t_{out}, a status flag indicating any warnings or error conditions, and possibly some measures of the quality and cost of the solution. Usually such software is set up so that it can be called repeatedly, with the new initial t equal to the previous t_{out}, in order to obtain output at desired points across the overall interval of integration.

9.5 Historical Notes and Further Reading

Finite difference approximations were used for various purposes by Newton, Leibniz, and other early developers of the calculus. The first systematic study of difference equations was published by Taylor (of Taylor series fame) in 1715. Euler proposed his method for initial value problems in 1768, and it was first analyzed in detail by Cauchy in 1840. Much of the early impetus for the numerical solution of ordinary differential equations came from celestial mechanics. In 1846 while still a student, Adams—who would later publish the Adams-Bashforth and Adams-Moulton methods in 1883—finished in a dead heat with LeVerrier in predicting the location at which the planet Neptune would be discovered. Their orbital calculations were based on known but previously unexplained perturbations in the orbit of Uranus.

Runge-Kutta methods were formulated with increasing levels of generality by Runge (1895), Heun (1900), and Kutta (1901). The embedded Runge-Kutta method of Fehlberg was published in 1970, and that of Dormand and Prince in 1980. The modern stability theory for numerical methods for ODEs was developed by Dahlquist in the 1950s. BDF methods for solving stiff ODEs were formulated by Curtis and Hirschfelder in 1952 and popularized by Gear in 1971 through a very influential book [147] and a computer program `difsub (TOMS #407)` implementing the methods. Other influential codes for solving ODEs were developed by Hindmarsh, Krogh, Shampine, and others. Multivalue methods were proposed by Nordsieck in 1962 to address the implementation difficulties of multistep methods. For the equivalence of multistep and multivalue methods, see Skeel [355]. A practical ODE method based on extrapolation was pioneered by Gragg in the early 1960s, and an effective implementation was published by Bulirsch and Stoer in 1966.

Relevant background material on ordinary differential equations can be found in standard textbooks, such as [34, 40, 44]. A classic treatment of the more advanced theory is [70]; a recent text oriented toward numerical methods is [266]. Recent books on the numerical solution of initial value problems for ODEs include [14, 101, 180, 181, 207, 243, 346]. Earlier books and monographs on this topic include [57, 117, 147, 190, 191, 242, 248, 350, 366]. In addition, see the surveys [58, 93, 148, 173, 349, 352, 367]. Practical advice on using ODE software can be found in [345]. See [351] for details on the ODE solvers in `MATLAB`. For solving highly oscillatory ODEs see [307], and for solving differential-algebraic systems see [14, 45, 181].

Review Questions

9.1. True or false: An ODE solution that is unbounded as time increases is necessarily unstable.

9.2. True or false: In approximating a solution of an ODE numerically, the global error grows only if the solution sought is unstable.

9.3. True or false: In solving an ODE numerically, the roundoff error and the truncation error are independent of each other.

9.4. True or false: In solving an IVP for an ODE numerically, the global error is always at least as large as the sum of the local errors.

9.5. True or false: For approximating a stable solution of an ODE numerically, an implicit method is always stable.

9.6. True or false: In numerically approximating a stable solution of an ODE, one can take arbitrarily large time steps using an unconditionally stable method and still achieve any required accuracy.

9.7. True or false: Stiff ODEs are always difficult and expensive to solve.

9.8. (*a*) In general, does a differential equation, by itself, determine a unique solution?

(*b*) If so, why, and if not, what additional information must be specified to determine a solution uniquely?

9.9. (*a*) What is meant by a *first-order* ODE?

(*b*) Why are higher-order ODEs usually transformed into equivalent first-order ODEs before solving them numerically?

9.10. (*a*) Describe in words the distinction between a stable and an unstable solution of an ODE.

(*b*) State a mathematical criterion for determining the stability of a solution of an ODE.

(*c*) Can the stability or instability of an ODE solution change with time?

9.11. Which of the following types of first-order ODEs have stable solutions?

(*a*) An ODE whose solutions converge toward each other

(*b*) An ODE whose Jacobian matrix has only eigenvalues with negative real parts

(*c*) A stiff ODE

(*d*) An ODE with exponentially decaying solutions

9.12. Classify each of the following ODEs as having unstable, stable, or asymptotically stable solutions.

(*a*) $y' = y + t$.

(*b*) $y' = y - t$.

(*c*) $y' = t - y$.

(*d*) $y' = 1$.

9.13. How does a typical numerical solution of an ODE differ from an analytical solution?

9.14. (*a*) What is Euler's method for solving an ODE?

(*b*) Show at least one way it can be derived.

9.15. In solving an ODE numerically, which is usually more significant, rounding error or truncation error?

9.16. Describe in words the difference between the local error and the global error in solving an IVP for an ODE numerically.

9.17. Under what condition is the global error in solving an IVP for an ODE likely to be smaller than the sum of the local errors at each step?

9.18. (*a*) Define in words the error amplification or growth factor for one step of a numerical method for solving an IVP for an ODE.

(*b*) Does the amplification factor depend only on the equation, only on the method of solution, or on both?

(*c*) What is the value of the amplification factor for one step of Euler's method?

(*d*) What stability region does this imply for Euler's method?

9.19. (*a*) What is the basic difference between an explicit method and an implicit method for solving an ODE numerically?

(*b*) Comparing these two types of methods, list one relative advantage for each.

(*c*) Name a specific example of a method (or family of methods) of each type.

9.20. The use of an implicit method for solving a nonlinear ODE requires the iterative solution of a nonlinear equation. How can one get a good starting guess for this iteration?

9.21. Is it possible for a numerical solution method to be unstable when applied to a stable ODE?

9.22. What does it mean for the accuracy of a numerical method for solving ODEs to be of order p?

9.23. (*a*) For solving ODEs, what is the highest-order accuracy that a linear multistep method can have and still be unconditionally stable?

(*b*) Give an example of a method having these properties (by name or by formula).

9.24. Compare the stability regions (i.e., the stability constraints on the step size) for the Euler and backward Euler methods for solving a scalar ODE.

9.25. For the backward Euler method, which factor places a stronger restriction on the choice of step size: stability or accuracy?

9.26. Which of the following numerical methods for solving a stable ODE numerically are unconditionally stable?

(*a*) Euler's method

(*b*) Backward Euler method

(*c*) Trapezoid method

9.27. (*a*) What is meant by a *stiff* ODE?

(*b*) Why may a stiff ODE be difficult to solve numerically?

(*c*) What type of method is appropriate for solving stiff ODEs?

9.28. Suppose one is using the backward Euler method to solve a nonlinear ODE numerically. The resulting nonlinear algebraic equation at each step must be solved iteratively. If a fixed number of iterations are performed at each step, is the resulting method unconditionally stable? Why?

9.29. Explain why implicit methods are better than explicit methods for solving stiff ODEs numerically.

9.30. What is the simplest numerical method that is stable for solving a stiff ODE?

9.31. For solving ODEs numerically, why is it usually impractical to generate methods of very high accuracy by using many terms in a Taylor series expansion?

9.32. In solving an ODE numerically, with which type of method, Runge-Kutta or multistep, is it easier to supply values for the numerical solution at arbitrary output points within each step?

9.33. (*a*) What is the basic difference between a single-step method and a multistep method for solving an ODE numerically?

(*b*) Comparing these two types of methods, list one relative advantage for each.

(*c*) Name a specific example of a method (or family of methods) of each type.

9.34. List two advantages and two disadvantages of multistep methods compared with classical Runge-Kutta methods for solving ODEs numerically.

9.35. What is the principal drawback of a Taylor series methods compared with Runge-Kutta methods for solving ODEs numerically?

9.36. (*a*) What is the principal advantage of extrapolation methods for solving ODEs numerically?

(*b*) What are the disadvantages of such methods?

9.37. In using a multistep method to solve an ODE numerically, why might one still need to have a single-step method available?

9.38. Why are multistep methods for solving ODEs numerically often used in predictor-corrector pairs?

9.39. If a predictor-corrector method for solving an ODE is implemented as a PECE scheme, does the second evaluation affect the value obtained for the solution at the point being computed? If so, what is the effect, and if not, then why is the second evaluation done?

9.40. List two reasons why multivalue methods are easier to implement than multistep methods for solving ODEs adaptively with automatic error control.

9.41. For each of the following properties, state which type of ODE method, multistep or classical Runge-Kutta, more accurately fits the description:

(*a*) Self starting

(*b*) More efficient in attaining high accuracy

(*c*) Can be efficient for stiff problems

(*d*) Easier to program

(*e*) Easier to change step size

(*f*) Easier to obtain a local error estimate

(*g*) Easier to produce output at arbitrary intermediate points within each step

9.42. Give two approaches to starting a multistep method initially when past solution history is not yet available.

Exercises

9.1. Write each of the following ODEs as an equivalent first-order system of ODEs:

(*a*) $y'' = t + y + y'$.

(*b*) $y''' = y'' + ty$.

(*c*) $y''' = y'' - 2y' + y - t + 1$.

9.2. Write each of the following ODEs as an equivalent first-order system of ODEs:

(*a*) Van der Pol equation:

$$y'' = y'(1 - y^2) - y.$$

(*b*) Blasius equation:

$$y''' = -y\,y''.$$

(*c*) Newton's Second Law of Motion for two-body problem:

$$\begin{aligned} y_1'' &= -GMy_1/(y_1^2 + y_2^2)^{3/2}, \\ y_2'' &= -GMy_2/(y_1^2 + y_2^2)^{3/2}. \end{aligned}$$

9.3. Are solutions of the following system of ODEs stable?

$$\begin{aligned} y_1' &= -y_1 + y_2, \\ y_2' &= -2y_2. \end{aligned}$$

Explain your answer.

9.4. Consider the ODE $y' = -5y$ with initial condition $y(0) = 1$. We will solve this ODE numerically using a step size of $h = 0.5$.

(*a*) Are solutions to this ODE stable?

(*b*) Is Euler's method stable for this ODE using this step size?

(*c*) Compute the numerical value for the approximate solution at $t = 0.5$ given by Euler's method.

(*d*) Is the backward Euler method stable for this ODE using this step size?

(*e*) Compute the numerical value for the approximate solution at $t = 0.5$ given by the backward Euler method.

9.5. With an initial value of $y_0 = 1$ at $t_0 = 0$ and a time step of $h = 1$, compute the approximate solution value y_1 at time $t_1 = 1$ for the ODE $y' = -y$ using each of the following two numerical methods. (Your answers should be numbers, not formulas.)

(*a*) Euler's method

(*b*) Backward Euler method

9.6. For the ODE, initial value, and step size given in Example 9.9, prove that fixed-point iteration for solving the implicit equation for y_1 is in fact convergent. What is the convergence rate?

9.7. Consider the IVP

$$y'' = y$$

for $t \geq 0$, with initial values $y(0) = 1$ and $y'(0) = 2$.

(*a*) Express this second-order ODE as an equivalent system of two first-order ODEs.

(*b*) What are the corresponding initial conditions for the system of ODEs in part *a*?

(*c*) Are solutions of this system stable?

(*d*) Perform one step of Euler's method for this ODE system using a step size of $h = 0.5$.

(*e*) Is Euler's method stable for this problem using this step size?

(*f*) Is the backward Euler method stable for this problem using this step size?

9.8. Consider the IVP for the ODE $y' = -y^2$ with the initial condition $y(0) = 1$. We will use the backward Euler method to compute the approximate value of the solution y_1 at time $t_1 = 0.1$ (i.e., take one step using the backward Euler method with step size $h = 0.1$ starting from $y_0 = 1$ at $t_0 = 0$). Since the backward Euler method is implicit, and the ODE is nonlinear, we will need to solve a nonlinear algebraic equation for y_1.

(*a*) Write out that nonlinear algebraic equation for y_1.

(*b*) Write out the Newton iteration for solving the nonlinear algebraic equation.

(*c*) Obtain a starting guess for the Newton iteration by using one step of Euler's method for the ODE.

(*d*) Finally, compute an approximate value for the solution y_1 by using one iteration of Newton's method for the nonlinear algebraic equation.

9.9. For each property listed below, state which of the following three ODE methods has or have the given property.

(1)

$$y_{k+1} = y_k + \frac{h}{2}(f(t_k, y_k) + f(t_{k+1}, y_k + hf(t_k, y_k)))$$

(2)

$$y_{k+1} = y_k + \frac{h}{2}(3f(t_k, y_k) - f(t_{k-1}, y_{k-1}))$$

(3)

$$y_{k+1} = y_k + \frac{h}{2}(f(t_k, y_k) + f(t_{k+1}, y_{k+1}))$$

(*a*) Second-order accurate
(*b*) Single-step method
(*c*) Implicit method
(*d*) Self-starting
(*e*) Unconditionally stable
(*f*) Runge-Kutta type method
(*g*) Good for solving stiff ODEs

9.10. Use the linear ODE $y' = \lambda y$ to analyze the accuracy and stability of Heun's method (see Section 9.3.6). In particular, verify that this method is second-order accurate, and describe or plot its stability region in the complex plane.

9.11. Applying the midpoint quadrature rule on the interval $[t_k, t_{k+1}]$ leads to the implicit *midpoint method*

$$y_{k+1} = y_k + h_k f(t_k + h_k/2, (y_k + y_{k+1})/2)$$

for solving the ODE $y' = f(t, y)$. Determine the order of accuracy and the stability region of this method.

9.12. The centered difference approximation

$$y' \approx \frac{y_{k+1} - y_{k-1}}{2h}$$

leads to the explicit, two-step, *leapfrog method*

$$y_{k+1} = y_{k-1} + 2hf(t_k, y_k)$$

for solving the ODE $y' = f(t, y)$. Determine the order of accuracy and the stability region of this method.

9.13. Let $\boldsymbol{A}$ be an $n \times n$ matrix. Compare and contrast the behavior of the linear difference equation

$$\boldsymbol{x}_{k+1} = \boldsymbol{A}\boldsymbol{x}_k$$

with that of the linear differential equation

$$\boldsymbol{x}' = \boldsymbol{A}\boldsymbol{x}.$$

What is the general solution in each case? In each case, what property of the matrix $\boldsymbol{A}$ would imply that the solution remains bounded for any starting vector $\boldsymbol{x}_0$? You may assume that the matrix $\boldsymbol{A}$ is diagonalizable.

9.14. Give a criterion for stability or asymptotic stability of the solutions to the kth order, scalar, homogeneous, constant-coefficient ODE

$$u^{(k)} + c_{k-1}u^{(k-1)} + \cdots + c_1 u' + c_0 u = 0.$$

(*Hint*: Transform to a first-order system $\boldsymbol{y}' = \boldsymbol{A}\boldsymbol{y}$ and observe that $\boldsymbol{A}$ is a *companion matrix*; see Section 4.2.1.)

Computer Problems

9.1. (*a*) Use a library routine to solve the *Lotka-Volterra model* of predator-prey population dynamics given in Example 9.4, integrating from $t = 0$ to $t = 25$. Use the parameter values $\alpha_1 = 1$, $\beta_1 = 0.1$, $\alpha_2 = 0.5$, $\beta_2 = 0.02$, and initial populations $y_1(0) = 100$ and $y_2(0) = 10$. Plot each of the two populations as a function of time, and on a separate graph plot the trajectory of the point $(y_1(t), y_2(t))$ in the plane as a function of time. The latter is sometimes called a "phase portrait." Give a physical interpretation of the behavior you observe. Try other initial populations and observe the results using the same type of graphs. Can you find nonzero initial populations such that either of the populations eventually becomes extinct? Can you find nonzero initial populations that never change? (*Hint*: You can find such a *stationary point* without solving the differential equation.)

(*b*) Repeat part *a*, but this time use the *Leslie-Gower model*

$$\begin{aligned} y_1' &= y_1(\alpha_1 - \beta_1 y_2), \\ y_2' &= y_2(\alpha_2 - \beta_2 y_2/y_1). \end{aligned}$$

Use the same parameter values except take $\beta_2 = 10$. How does the behavior of the solutions differ between the two models?

9.2. The *Kermack-McKendrick model* for the course of an epidemic in a population is given by the system of ODEs

$$\begin{aligned} y_1' &= -cy_1y_2, \\ y_2' &= cy_1y_2 - dy_2, \\ y_3' &= dy_2, \end{aligned}$$

where y_1 represents susceptibles, y_2 represents infectives in circulation, and y_3 represents infectives removed by isolation, death, or recovery and immunity. The parameters c and d represent the infection rate and removal rate, respectively. Use a library routine to solve this system numerically, with the parameter values $c = 1$ and $d = 5$, and initial values $y_1(0) = 95$, $y_2(0) = 5$, $y_3(0) = 0$. Integrate from $t = 0$ to $t = 1$. Plot each solution component on the same graph as a function of t. As expected with an epidemic, you should see the number of infectives grow at first, then diminish to zero. Experiment with other values for the parameters and initial conditions. Can you find values for which the epidemic does not grow, or for which the entire population is wiped out?

9.3. Experiment with several different library routines having automatic step-size selection to solve the ODE

$$y' = -200ty^2$$

numerically. Consider two different initial conditions, $y(0) = 1$ and $y(-3) = 1/901$, and in each case compute the solution until $t = 1$. Monitor the step size used by the routines and discuss how and why it changes as the solution progresses. Explain the difference in behavior for the two different initial conditions. Compare the different routines with respect to efficiency for a given accuracy requirement.

9.4. Consider the system of ODEs modeling chemical reaction kinetics given in Example 9.3.

(*a*) What is the Jacobian matrix for this ODE system, and what are its eigenvalues? If the rate constants are positive, are the solutions of this system stable? Under what conditions will the system be stiff?

(*b*) Solve the ODE system numerically, assuming initial concentrations $y_1(0) = y_2(0) = y_3(0) = 1$. Take $k_1 = 1$ and experiment with values of k_2 of varying magnitude, specifically, $k_2 = 10$, 100, and 1000. For each value of k_2, solve the system using a Runge-Kutta method, an Adams method, and a method designed for stiff systems, such as a backward differentiation formula. You may use library routines for this purpose, or you may wish to develop your own routines, perhaps using the classical fourth-order Runge-Kutta method, the fourth-order Adams-Bashforth predictor and Adams-Moulton corrector, and the BDF formula given in Sections 9.3.6 and 9.3.8. If you develop your own codes, a fixed step size will suffice for this exercise. If you use library routines, compare the different methods with respect to their efficiency, as measured by function evaluations or execution time, for a given accuracy. If you develop you own codes, compare the different methods with respect to accuracy and stability for a given step size. In each instance, integrate the ODE system from $t = 0$ until the solution is approximately in steady state, or until the method is clearly unstable or grossly inefficient.

9.5. The following system of ODEs models nonlinear chemical reactions

$$\begin{aligned} y_1' &= -\alpha y_1 + \beta y_2 y_3, \\ y_2' &= \alpha y_1 - \beta y_2 y_3 - \gamma y_2^2, \\ y_3' &= \gamma y_2^2, \end{aligned}$$

where $\alpha = 4 \times 10^{-2}$, $\beta = 10^4$, and $\gamma = 3 \times 10^7$. Starting with initial conditions $y_1(0) = 1$ and $y_2(0) = y_3(0) = 0$, integrate this ODE from $t = 0$ to $t = 3$. You may use either a library routine or an ODE solver of your own design. Try both stiff and nonstiff methods, and experiment with various error tolerances. Compare the efficiencies of the stiff and nonstiff methods as a function of the error tolerance.

9.6. The following system of ODEs, formulated by Lorenz, represents a crude model of atmospheric circulation:

$$\begin{aligned} y_1' &= \sigma(y_2 - y_1), \\ y_2' &= ry_1 - y_2 - y_1 y_3, \\ y_3' &= y_1 y_2 - by_3. \end{aligned}$$

Taking $\sigma = 10$, $b = 8/3$, $r = 28$, and initial values $y_1(0) = y_3(0) = 0$ and $y_2(0) = 1$, integrate this ODE from $t = 0$ to $t = 100$. Plot each of y_1, y_2, and y_3 as a function of t, and also plot each of the trajectories $(y_1(t), y_2(t))$, $(y_1(t), y_3(t))$, and $(y_2(t), y_3(t))$ as a function of t, each on a separate plot. Try perturbing the initial values by a tiny amount and see how much difference this makes in the final value of $\boldsymbol{y}(100)$.

9.7. An important problem in classical mechanics is to determine the motion of two bodies under mutual gravitational attraction. Suppose that a body of mass m is orbiting a second body of much larger mass M, such as the earth orbiting the sun.

From Newton's laws of motion and gravitation, the orbital trajectory $(x(t), y(t))$ is described by the system of second-order ODEs

$$x'' = -GMx/r^3,$$
$$y'' = -GMy/r^3,$$

where G is the gravitational constant and $r = (x^2 + y^2)^{1/2}$ is the distance of the orbiting body from the center of mass of the two bodies. For this exercise, we choose units such that $GM = 1$.

(*a*) Use a library routine to solve this system of ODEs with the initial conditions

$$x(0) = 1 - e, \qquad y(0) = 0,$$
$$x'(0) = 0, \qquad y'(0) = \left(\frac{1+e}{1-e}\right)^{1/2},$$

where e is the eccentricity of the resulting elliptical orbit, which has period 2π. Try the values $e = 0$ (which should give a circular orbit), $e = 0.5$, and $e = 0.9$. For each case, solve the ODE for at least one period and obtain output at enough intermediate points to draw a smooth plot of the orbital trajectory. Make separate plots of x versus t, y versus t, and y versus x. Experiment with different error tolerances to see how they affect the cost of the integration and how close the orbit comes to being closed. If you trace the trajectory through several periods, does the orbit tend to wander or remain steady?

(*b*) Check your numerical solutions in part *a* to see how well they conserve the following quantities, which should remain constant:

Conservation of energy:

$$\frac{(x')^2 + (y')^2}{2} - \frac{1}{r},$$

Conservation of angular momentum:

$$x\,y' - y\,x'.$$

9.8. Consider a restricted form of the three-body problem in which a body of small mass orbits two other bodies with much larger masses, such as an Apollo spacecraft orbiting the earth-moon system. We will use a two-dimensional coordinate system in the plane determined by the three bodies, with the origin at the center of mass of the two larger bodies, and the coordinate system rotating so that the two larger bodies appear fixed. The coordinate system is shown in the accompanying diagram,

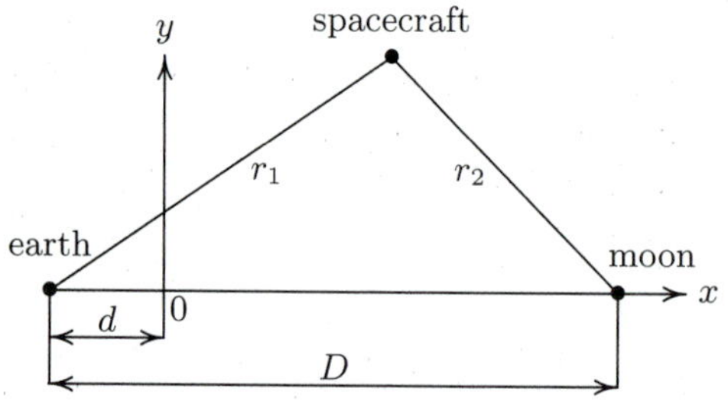

where D is the distance from earth to moon, d is the distance from the center of earth to the center of mass, r_1 is the distance from earth to spacecraft, and r_2 is the distance from moon to spacecraft. The mass of the spacecraft is assumed to be negligible compared with the other masses.

By using Newton's laws of motion and gravitation, and allowing for the centrifugal and Coriolis forces due to the rotating coordinate system, the motion of the spacecraft is described by the system of second-order ODEs

$$\begin{aligned} x'' &= -G\,[M(x+\mu D)/r_1^3 \\ &\quad + m(x-\mu^* D)/r_2^3] \\ &\quad + \Omega^2 x + 2\Omega y', \\ y'' &= -G\,[My/r_1^3 + my/r_2^3] \\ &\quad + \Omega^2 y - 2\Omega x', \end{aligned}$$

where G is the gravitational constant, M and m are the masses of earth and moon, μ^* and μ are the mass fractions of earth and moon, and Ω is the angular velocity of rotation of the moon about the earth (and hence of the coordinate system). The numerical values of these quantities are given in the following table:

G	$6.67259 \times 10^{-11}\text{m}^3/(\text{kg s}^2)$
M	5.974×10^{24} kg
m	7.348×10^{22} kg
μ^*	$M/(m+M)$
μ	$m/(m+M)$
D	3.844×10^{8} m
d	4.669×10^{6} m
r_1	$[(x+d)^2 + y^2]^{1/2}$
r_2	$[(D-d-x)^2 + y^2]^{1/2}$
Ω	2.661×10^{-6}/s

Use a library routine to solve this system of ODEs with the initial conditions

$$x(0) = 4.613 \times 10^8, \qquad y(0) = 0,$$
$$x'(0) = 0, \qquad y'(0) = -1074.$$

Plot the resulting solution trajectory $(x(t), y(t))$ in the plane as a function of time. Indicate the positions of earth and moon on the graph. Compute the solution for at least one complete orbit (i.e., until the spacecraft returns to its original location), which is from $t = 0$ until approximately $t = 2.4 \times 10^6$ s. Experiment with various error tolerances to see how much difference they make in whether the orbit is actually closed. Try to monitor the step size used by the ODE routine as the integration progresses. When does the step size become smaller or larger? How close does the spacecraft come to the surface of earth? (Earth's radius is 6.378×10^6 m, so the center of mass of the earth-moon system is actually *inside* the earth.)

9.9. A definite integral $\int_a^b f(t)\,dt$ can be evaluated by solving the equivalent ODE $y'(t) = f(t)$, $a \le t \le b$, with initial condition $y(a) = 0$. The value of the integral is then simply $y(b)$. Use a library ODE solver to evaluate each definite integral in the first several Computer Problems for Chapter 8, and compare its efficiency with that of an adaptive quadrature routine for the same accuracy.

9.10. Homotopy methods for solving systems of nonlinear algebraic equations parameterize the solution space $\boldsymbol{x}(t)$ and then follow a trajectory from an initial guess to the final solution. As one example of this approach, for solving a system of nonlinear equations $\boldsymbol{f}(\boldsymbol{x}) = \boldsymbol{0}$, where $\boldsymbol{f}: \mathbb{R}^n \to \mathbb{R}^n$, with initial guess $\boldsymbol{x}_0$, the following ODE initial value problem is a continuous analogue of Newton's method:

$$\boldsymbol{x}' = -\boldsymbol{J}_f^{-1}(\boldsymbol{x})\boldsymbol{f}(\boldsymbol{x}), \qquad \boldsymbol{x}(0) = \boldsymbol{x}_0,$$

where $\boldsymbol{J}_f$ is the Jacobian matrix of $\boldsymbol{f}$, and of course the inverse need not be computed explicitly. Use this method to solve the nonlinear system given in Computer Problem 5.23. Starting from the given initial guess, integrate the resulting system of ODEs from $t = 0$ until a steady state is reached. Compare the resulting solution with that obtained by a conventional nonlinear system solver. Plot the trajectory of the components of $\boldsymbol{x}(t)$ from $t = 0$ to the final solution. You may also want to try this technique on some of the other Computer Problems from Chapter 5.

Chapter 10

Boundary Value Problems for Ordinary Differential Equations

10.1 Boundary Value Problems

By itself, a differential equation does not uniquely determine a solution; additional side conditions must be imposed on the solution to make it unique. These side conditions prescribe values that the solution or its derivatives must have at some specified point or points. If all of the side conditions are specified at the same point, say t_0, then we have an initial value problem, which we considered in Chapter 9. If the side conditions are specified at more than one point, then we have a *boundary value problem*, or *BVP*. For an ordinary differential equation, the side conditions are typically specified at two points, namely the endpoints of some interval $[a, b]$, which is why the side conditions are called *boundary conditions* or *boundary values*. This chapter is concerned with numerical methods for solving such *two-point boundary value problems*.

Example 10.1 Newton's Second Law of Motion. In Example 9.1 we saw that the general solution to *Newton's Second Law of Motion*, $F = ma$, which is a second-order ODE, involves two constants of integration, and hence two side conditions must be specified in order to determine a unique solution over the interval of integration, say $[a, b]$. In an initial value problem, both the position $y(a)$ and velocity $y'(a)$ would be specified at the initial point a, and this would uniquely determine the solution $y(t)$ over the entire interval. Other side conditions could be specified, however, such as the initial position $y(a)$ and final position $y(b)$, or the initial position $y(a)$ and final velocity $y'(b)$. Indeed, any linear (or even nonlinear) combination of solution and derivative values at the endpoints could be specified, each giving a different two-point boundary value problem for this ODE.

In the example just given, a second-order scalar ODE required two side conditions to determine a unique solution, and this pattern holds in general: a kth order ODE requires k side conditions. As we saw in Section 9.1, however, a higher-order ODE can always be transformed to a first-order system of ODEs, so it suffices to consider only the first-order case. A general first-order two-point boundary value problem for an ODE has the form

$$\boldsymbol{y}' = \boldsymbol{f}(t, \boldsymbol{y}), \qquad a < t < b,$$

with boundary conditions

$$\boldsymbol{g}(\boldsymbol{y}(a), \boldsymbol{y}(b)) = \boldsymbol{0},$$

where $\boldsymbol{f}: \mathbb{R}^{n+1} \to \mathbb{R}^n$ and $\boldsymbol{g}: \mathbb{R}^{2n} \to \mathbb{R}^n$. The boundary conditions are said to be *separated* if any given component of $\boldsymbol{g}$ involves solution values only at a or at b, but not both. The boundary conditions are said to be *linear* if they have the form

$$\boldsymbol{B}_a \, \boldsymbol{y}(a) + \boldsymbol{B}_b \, \boldsymbol{y}(b) = \boldsymbol{c},$$

where $\boldsymbol{B}_a, \boldsymbol{B}_b \in \mathbb{R}^{n \times n}$ and $\boldsymbol{c} \in \mathbb{R}^n$. If the boundary conditions are both separated and linear, then for each $i, 1 \le i \le n$, either the ith row of $\boldsymbol{B}_a$ or the ith row of $\boldsymbol{B}_b$ contains only zero entries. The BVP is said to be linear if both the ODE and the boundary conditions are linear.

Example 10.2 Separated Linear Boundary Conditions. The two-point boundary value problem for the second-order scalar ODE

$$u'' = f(t, u, u'), \qquad a < t < b,$$

with boundary conditions

$$u(a) = \alpha, \qquad u(b) = \beta,$$

is equivalent to the first-order system of ODEs

$$\begin{bmatrix} y_1' \\ y_2' \end{bmatrix} = \begin{bmatrix} y_2 \\ f(t, y_1, y_2) \end{bmatrix}, \qquad a < t < b,$$

with separated linear boundary conditions

$$\begin{bmatrix} 1 & 0 \\ 0 & 0 \end{bmatrix} \begin{bmatrix} y_1(a) \\ y_2(a) \end{bmatrix} + \begin{bmatrix} 0 & 0 \\ 1 & 0 \end{bmatrix} \begin{bmatrix} y_1(b) \\ y_2(b) \end{bmatrix} = \begin{bmatrix} \alpha \\ \beta \end{bmatrix}.$$

Our primary focus will be on second-order scalar BVPs (and equivalent first-order systems) of the type given in Example 10.2. Many important physical problems have this form, including

- The bending of an elastic beam under a distributed transverse load
- The distribution of electrical potential between two flat electrodes
- The temperature distribution in an internally heated homogeneous wall whose surfaces are maintained at fixed temperatures
- The steady-state concentration of a pollutant in porous soil

The one-dimensional version of Poisson's equation, a partial differential equation we will study in Chapter 11, is also of this form.

10.2 Existence, Uniqueness, and Conditioning

There is a fundamental difference between initial value problems and boundary value problems that profoundly affects both their theoretical analysis and their numerical solution. For initial value problems, the availability of complete state information about the solution at a single point in time enables the establishment (under suitable assumptions) of a small subinterval in which a unique solution exists, and then that local solution can be extended to successive nearby points to prove existence of a global solution. As we saw in Chapter 9, numerical methods for IVPs work the same way, beginning with an initial state and then stepping in small time increments to generate successive approximate solution values. With a boundary value problem, on the other hand, there is no single point at which complete state information is given, and hence no point at which local existence of a solution can be established, and likewise no point with sufficient data to initiate a time stepping procedure for generating a numerical solution. For this reason, existence and uniqueness are generally much more difficult to establish for BVPs than for IVPs, and indeed existence or uniqueness may not hold.

Example 10.3 Existence and Uniqueness. Consider the two-point BVP

$$u'' = -u, \qquad 0 < t < b,$$

with boundary conditions

$$u(0) = 0, \qquad u(b) = \beta.$$

The general solution of the ODE satisfying $u(0) = 0$ is $u(t) = c\sin(t)$ for any constant c. If b is an integer multiple of π, then $c\sin(b) = 0$ for any c, so there are infinitely many solutions of the BVP if $\beta = 0$, but there is no solution if $\beta \neq 0$.

For the general first-order two-point boundary value problem

$$\boldsymbol{y}' = \boldsymbol{f}(t, \boldsymbol{y}), \qquad a < t < b,$$

with boundary conditions

$$\boldsymbol{g}(\boldsymbol{y}(a), \boldsymbol{y}(b)) = \boldsymbol{0},$$

let $\boldsymbol{y}(t; \boldsymbol{x})$ denote the solution to the ODE with initial condition $\boldsymbol{y}(a) = \boldsymbol{x}$ for $\boldsymbol{x} \in \mathbb{R}^n$. For a given $\boldsymbol{x}$, the solution $\boldsymbol{y}(t; \boldsymbol{x})$ of the IVP is a solution of the BVP if

$$\boldsymbol{g}(\boldsymbol{x}, \boldsymbol{y}(b; \boldsymbol{x})) = \boldsymbol{0}.$$

The solvability of the BVP therefore depends on the existence and uniqueness of solutions to the system of nonlinear algebraic equations $\boldsymbol{h}(\boldsymbol{x}) \equiv \boldsymbol{g}(\boldsymbol{x}, \boldsymbol{y}(b; \boldsymbol{x})) = \boldsymbol{0}$, which, as we saw in Section 5.2, is often a highly nontrivial question. Thus, we cannot expect the general type of existence and uniqueness theorem for BVPs that was given for IVPs in Section 9.2, and existence and uniqueness of solutions for nonlinear BVPs usually must be determined on a case-by-case basis.

For a *linear* BVP, however, we can say more. Let $\boldsymbol{y}_i(t)$ be the solution to the homogeneous ODE $\boldsymbol{y}' = \boldsymbol{A}(t)\boldsymbol{y}$ with initial condition $\boldsymbol{y}(a) = \boldsymbol{e}_i$, where $\boldsymbol{e}_i$ is the ith column of the identity matrix $\boldsymbol{I}$. Let $\boldsymbol{Y}(t)$ denote the matrix whose ith column is $\boldsymbol{y}_i(t)$; $\boldsymbol{Y}$ is called the *fundamental solution matrix* for the ODE, and its columns are called solution *modes*. Then the linear BVP

$$\boldsymbol{y}' = \boldsymbol{A}(t)\,\boldsymbol{y} + \boldsymbol{b}(t), \qquad a < t < b,$$

where $\boldsymbol{A}(t)$ and $\boldsymbol{b}(t)$ are continuous, with boundary conditions

$$\boldsymbol{B}_a\,\boldsymbol{y}(a) + \boldsymbol{B}_b\,\boldsymbol{y}(b) = \boldsymbol{c},$$

has a unique solution if, and only if, the matrix

$$\boldsymbol{Q} \equiv \boldsymbol{B}_a \boldsymbol{Y}(a) + \boldsymbol{B}_b \boldsymbol{Y}(b)$$

is nonsingular.

Example 10.4 Existence and Uniqueness. The second-order two-point BVP from Example 10.3 is equivalent to the linear first-order system of ODEs

$$\begin{bmatrix} y_1' \\ y_2' \end{bmatrix} = \begin{bmatrix} 0 & 1 \\ -1 & 0 \end{bmatrix} \begin{bmatrix} y_1 \\ y_2 \end{bmatrix}, \qquad 0 < t < b,$$

with linear boundary conditions

$$\begin{bmatrix} 1 & 0 \\ 0 & 0 \end{bmatrix} \begin{bmatrix} y_1(0) \\ y_2(0) \end{bmatrix} + \begin{bmatrix} 0 & 0 \\ 1 & 0 \end{bmatrix} \begin{bmatrix} y_1(b) \\ y_2(b) \end{bmatrix} = \begin{bmatrix} 0 \\ \beta \end{bmatrix}.$$

The fundamental solution matrix for this ODE is

$$\boldsymbol{Y}(t) = \begin{bmatrix} \cos(t) & \sin(t) \\ -\sin(t) & \cos(t) \end{bmatrix},$$

so that

$$\boldsymbol{Q} = \begin{bmatrix} 1 & 0 \\ 0 & 0 \end{bmatrix} \begin{bmatrix} 1 & 0 \\ 0 & 1 \end{bmatrix} + \begin{bmatrix} 0 & 0 \\ 1 & 0 \end{bmatrix} \begin{bmatrix} \cos(b) & \sin(b) \\ -\sin(b) & \cos(b) \end{bmatrix} = \begin{bmatrix} 1 & 0 \\ \cos(b) & \sin(b) \end{bmatrix},$$

which is singular precisely when b is an integer multiple of π.

A basic result from the theory of linear ODEs is that if the matrix $\boldsymbol{Q}$ just defined is nonsingular, then the unique solution of the BVP is given by

$$\boldsymbol{y}(t) = \boldsymbol{Y}(t)\,\boldsymbol{Q}^{-1}\left(\boldsymbol{c} - \boldsymbol{B}_b \boldsymbol{Y}(b) \int_a^b \boldsymbol{Y}^{-1}(s)\,\boldsymbol{b}(s)\,ds\right) + \boldsymbol{Y}(t) \int_a^t \boldsymbol{Y}^{-1}(s)\,\boldsymbol{b}(s)\,ds.$$

This result can be expressed more compactly if we rescale the fundamental solution matrix more appropriately for the BVP by defining

$$\boldsymbol{\Phi}(t) = \boldsymbol{Y}(t)\,\boldsymbol{Q}^{-1},$$

and then define the *Green's function*

$$\boldsymbol{G}(t,s) = \begin{cases} \boldsymbol{\Phi}(t)\boldsymbol{B}_a\boldsymbol{\Phi}(a)\boldsymbol{\Phi}^{-1}(s), & a \le s \le t \\ -\boldsymbol{\Phi}(t)\boldsymbol{B}_b\,\boldsymbol{\Phi}(b)\boldsymbol{\Phi}^{-1}(s), & t < s \le b \end{cases}.$$

The previous result then becomes

$$\boldsymbol{y}(t) = \boldsymbol{\Phi}(t)\,\boldsymbol{c} + \int_a^b \boldsymbol{G}(t,s)\,\boldsymbol{b}(s)\,ds,$$

and we can bound the solution by taking norms,

$$\|\boldsymbol{y}\|_\infty \le \kappa\left(|\boldsymbol{c}| + \int_a^b |\boldsymbol{b}(s)|\,ds\right),$$

where

$$\kappa = \max\{\|\boldsymbol{\Phi}\|_\infty, \|\boldsymbol{G}\|_\infty\}.$$

Consider now the perturbed problem

$$\hat{\boldsymbol{y}}' = \boldsymbol{A}(t)\,\hat{\boldsymbol{y}} + \hat{\boldsymbol{b}}(t), \qquad a < t < b,$$

with boundary conditions

$$\boldsymbol{B}_a\,\hat{\boldsymbol{y}}(a) + \boldsymbol{B}_b\,\hat{\boldsymbol{y}}(b) = \hat{\boldsymbol{c}}.$$

The perturbation in the solution, $\boldsymbol{z}(t) = \hat{\boldsymbol{y}}(t) - \boldsymbol{y}(t)$, satisfies the BVP

$$\boldsymbol{z}' = \boldsymbol{A}(t)\,\boldsymbol{z} + \Delta\boldsymbol{b}(t), \qquad a < t < b,$$

with boundary conditions

$$\boldsymbol{B}_a\,\boldsymbol{y}(a) + \boldsymbol{B}_b\,\boldsymbol{y}(b) = \Delta\boldsymbol{c},$$

where $\Delta\boldsymbol{b}(t) = \hat{\boldsymbol{b}}(t) - \boldsymbol{b}(t)$ and $\Delta\boldsymbol{c} = \hat{\boldsymbol{c}} - \boldsymbol{c}$, and therefore we can bound the perturbation in the solution as before,

$$\|\boldsymbol{z}\|_\infty \le \kappa\left(|\Delta\boldsymbol{c}| + \int_a^b |\Delta\boldsymbol{b}(s)|\,ds\right).$$

Thus, the quantity κ is an absolute condition number for the BVP with respect to perturbations in the inhomogeneous terms in the ODE and the boundary conditions. The situation is more complicated for perturbations in the matrices $\boldsymbol{A}(t)$, $\boldsymbol{B}_a$, and $\boldsymbol{B}_b$, but comparable results hold for these as well.

The condition number we have just derived provides theoretical insight into the conditioning of linear BVPs, but it is often impractical to compute. Its intuitive content is fairly clear, however: the conditioning (or stability) of BVPs depends on the interplay between the growth of solution modes and the boundary conditions. For an IVP, instability is associated with modes that grow exponentially as time increases. For a BVP, on the other hand, the solution is determined everywhere simultaneously, so there is no notion of a "direction" of integration in the interval $[a, b]$, and we must be concerned with both growing and decaying solution modes. In particular, the growth of a solution mode that increases as time increases is limited if such a mode must satisfy a boundary condition on the right (i.e., at b), and similarly the "growth" of a decaying mode (i.e, a mode that increases as time decreases) is limited by a boundary condition on the left (i.e., at a). Thus, for a BVP to be well-conditioned, the growing and decaying modes must be controlled appropriately by the boundary conditions imposed. These considerations can be formalized in the concept of *dichotomy* for BVPs, but we will not do so here.

Example 10.5 Stable Boundary Value Problem. Solutions of the intial value problem for the ODE

$$\begin{bmatrix} y_1' \\ y_2' \end{bmatrix} = \begin{bmatrix} \lambda & 0 \\ 0 & -\lambda \end{bmatrix} \begin{bmatrix} y_1 \\ y_2 \end{bmatrix}, \qquad \boldsymbol{y}(0) = \boldsymbol{y}_0,$$

where $\text{Re}(\lambda) \neq 0$, are unstable due to exponential growth in one of the two modes. But if $\text{Re}(\lambda) < 0$, say, and we impose the boundary conditions

$$y_1(0) = 1, \qquad y_2(b) = 1$$

on the interval $[0, b]$, then the BVP is stable, even if b is very large, since growth in the solution that would otherwise be possible is limited by the boundary conditions.

Many of the concepts and results we have given on existence, uniqueness, and conditioning for linear BVPs can be extended to general nonlinear BVPs by local linearization of the ODE and the boundary conditions, but the conclusions must be applied with caution because their region of validity may be severely limited.

10.3 Shooting Method

The *shooting method* replaces a given boundary value problem by a sequence of initial value problems. We saw in Section 10.2 that the general first-order two-point boundary value problem

$$\boldsymbol{y}' = \boldsymbol{f}(t, \boldsymbol{y}), \qquad a < t < b,$$

with boundary conditions

$$\boldsymbol{g}(\boldsymbol{y}(a), \boldsymbol{y}(b)) = \boldsymbol{0},$$

is equivalent to the system of nonlinear algebraic equations

$$\boldsymbol{h}(\boldsymbol{x}) \equiv \boldsymbol{g}(\boldsymbol{x}, \boldsymbol{y}(b; \boldsymbol{x})) = \boldsymbol{0},$$

where $\boldsymbol{y}(t; \boldsymbol{x})$ denotes the solution to the associated IVP with initial condition $\boldsymbol{y}(a) = \boldsymbol{x}$ for $\boldsymbol{x} \in \mathbb{R}^n$. One way to solve the BVP, therefore, is to solve the nonlinear system $\boldsymbol{h}(\boldsymbol{x}) = \boldsymbol{0}$ using any suitable method from Chapter 5. Evaluation of $\boldsymbol{h}(\boldsymbol{x})$ for any given value $\boldsymbol{x}$ will require solving an IVP to determine $\boldsymbol{y}(b; \boldsymbol{x})$, for which we can use any suitable method from Chapter 9.

To make this approach more concrete, consider the two-point BVP for a scalar second-order ODE given in Example 10.2, where we are given the initial value $u(a)$ and final value $u(b)$ of the solution, but not the initial slope $u'(a)$. If we knew the latter, then we would have an IVP. We lack that information, but we can guess a value for the initial slope, solve the resulting IVP, and then check to see if the computed solution value at $t = b$ matches the desired boundary value, $u(b) = \beta$. The basic idea is illustrated in Fig. 10.1. Each curve represents a solution of the same second-order ODE, with different values for the initial slope $u'(a)$ giving different solutions for the ODE. All of the solutions start with the given initial value $u(a) = \alpha$, but for only one value of the initial slope does the resulting solution curve hit the desired boundary condition $u(b) = \beta$. The motivation for the name *shooting* method should now be obvious: we keep adjusting our aim until we hit the target.

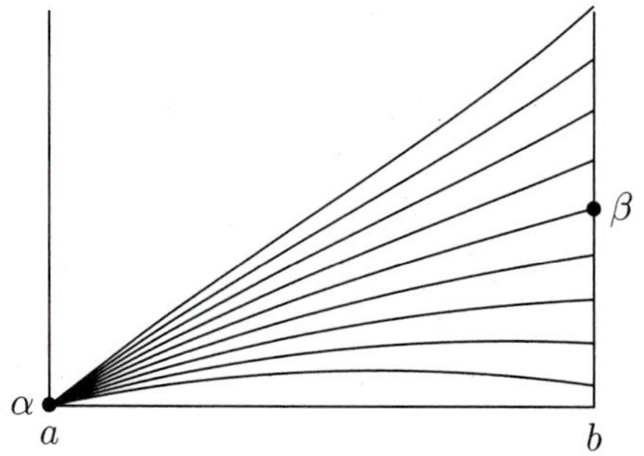

Figure 10.1: Shooting method for two-point boundary value problem.

After transforming into a first-order system, the boundary conditions for Example 10.2 become

$$\boldsymbol{g}(\boldsymbol{y}(a), \boldsymbol{y}(b)) = \begin{bmatrix} y_1(a) - \alpha \\ y_1(b) - \beta \end{bmatrix} = \boldsymbol{0}.$$

Thus, the nonlinear system to be solved is

$$\boldsymbol{h}(\boldsymbol{x}) = \begin{bmatrix} y_1(a; \boldsymbol{x}) - \alpha \\ y_1(b; \boldsymbol{x}) - \beta \end{bmatrix} = \boldsymbol{0},$$

where $\boldsymbol{x}$ is the initial value. The first component of $\boldsymbol{h}(\boldsymbol{x})$ will be zero if $x_1 = \alpha$, and the initial slope x_2 remains to be determined so that the second component of $\boldsymbol{h}(\boldsymbol{x})$ will be zero. In effect, therefore, we must solve the scalar nonlinear equation in x_2,

$$h_2(\alpha, x_2) = y_1(b; \alpha, x_2) = 0,$$

for which we can use a one-dimensional zero finder from Section 5.5.

Example 10.6 Shooting Method. We illustrate the shooting method on the two-point BVP for the second-order scalar ODE

$$u'' = 6t, \qquad 0 < t < 1,$$

with boundary conditions

$$u(0) = 0, \qquad u(1) = 1.$$

For each guess for $u'(0)$, we will integrate the ODE using the classical fourth-order Runge-Kutta method (see Section 9.3.6) to determine how close we come to hitting the desired solution value at $t = 1$. Before doing so, however, we must first transform the second-order ODE into a system of two first-order ODEs

$$\begin{bmatrix} y_1' \\ y_2' \end{bmatrix} = \begin{bmatrix} y_2 \\ 6t \end{bmatrix},$$

where $y_1(t) = u(t)$ and $y_2(t) = u'(t)$. We first try an initial slope of $y_2(0) = 1$. Using a step size of $h = 0.5$, we first step from $t_0 = 0$ to $t_1 = 0.5$. The classical fourth-order Runge-Kutta method gives the approximate solution value at t_1

$$\begin{aligned} \boldsymbol{y}_1 &= \boldsymbol{y}_0 + \frac{h}{6}(\boldsymbol{k}_1 + 2\boldsymbol{k}_2 + 2\boldsymbol{k}_3 + \boldsymbol{k}_4) \\ &= \begin{bmatrix} 0 \\ 1 \end{bmatrix} + \frac{0.5}{6}\left(\begin{bmatrix} 1 \\ 0 \end{bmatrix} + 2\begin{bmatrix} 1.0 \\ 1.5 \end{bmatrix} + 2\begin{bmatrix} 1.375 \\ 1.500 \end{bmatrix} + \begin{bmatrix} 1.75 \\ 3.00 \end{bmatrix} \right) = \begin{bmatrix} 0.625 \\ 1.750 \end{bmatrix}. \end{aligned}$$

Next we step from $t_1 = 0.5$ to $t_2 = 1$, obtaining

$$\boldsymbol{y}_2 = \begin{bmatrix} 0.625 \\ 1.750 \end{bmatrix} + \frac{0.5}{6}\left(\begin{bmatrix} 1.75 \\ 3.00 \end{bmatrix} + 2\begin{bmatrix} 2.5 \\ 4.5 \end{bmatrix} + 2\begin{bmatrix} 2.875 \\ 4.500 \end{bmatrix} + \begin{bmatrix} 4 \\ 6 \end{bmatrix} \right) = \begin{bmatrix} 2 \\ 4 \end{bmatrix},$$

so we have hit the value $y_1(1) = 2$ instead of the desired value $y_1(1) = 1$. We try again, this time with an initial slope of $y_2(0) = -1$, obtaining

$$\boldsymbol{y}_1 = \begin{bmatrix} 0 \\ -1 \end{bmatrix} + \frac{0.5}{6}\left(\begin{bmatrix} -1 \\ 0 \end{bmatrix} + 2\begin{bmatrix} -1.0 \\ 1.5 \end{bmatrix} + 2\begin{bmatrix} -0.625 \\ 1.500 \end{bmatrix} + \begin{bmatrix} -0.25 \\ 3.00 \end{bmatrix} \right) = \begin{bmatrix} -0.375 \\ -0.250 \end{bmatrix}$$

and

$$\boldsymbol{y}_2 = \begin{bmatrix} -0.375 \\ -0.250 \end{bmatrix} + \frac{0.5}{6}\left(\begin{bmatrix} -0.25 \\ 3.00 \end{bmatrix} + 2\begin{bmatrix} 0.5 \\ 4.5 \end{bmatrix} + 2\begin{bmatrix} 0.875 \\ 4.500 \end{bmatrix} + \begin{bmatrix} 2 \\ 6 \end{bmatrix} \right) = \begin{bmatrix} 0 \\ 2 \end{bmatrix},$$

so we have hit the value $y_1(1) = 0$ instead of the desired value $y_1(1) = 1$. We now have the initial slope bracketed between -1 and 1. We omit the further iterations necessary to identify the correct initial slope, which turns out to be $y_2(0) = 0$:

$$\boldsymbol{y}_1 = \begin{bmatrix} 0 \\ 0 \end{bmatrix} + \frac{0.5}{6}\left(\begin{bmatrix} 0 \\ 0 \end{bmatrix} + 2\begin{bmatrix} 0.0 \\ 1.5 \end{bmatrix} + 2\begin{bmatrix} 0.375 \\ 1.500 \end{bmatrix} + \begin{bmatrix} 0.75 \\ 3.00 \end{bmatrix} \right) = \begin{bmatrix} 0.125 \\ 0.750 \end{bmatrix}$$

and

$$y_2 = \begin{bmatrix} 0.125 \\ 0.750 \end{bmatrix} + \frac{0.5}{6}\left(\begin{bmatrix} 0.75 \\ 3.00 \end{bmatrix} + 2\begin{bmatrix} 1.5 \\ 4.5 \end{bmatrix} + 2\begin{bmatrix} 1.875 \\ 4.500 \end{bmatrix} + \begin{bmatrix} 3 \\ 6 \end{bmatrix} \right) = \begin{bmatrix} 1 \\ 3 \end{bmatrix},$$

so we have indeed hit the target solution value, $y_1(1) = 1$. These results are illustrated in Fig. 10.2.

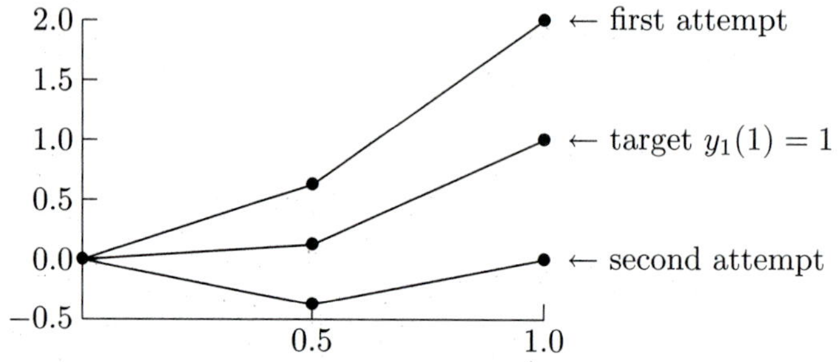

Figure 10.2: Shooting method for two-point boundary value problem in Example 10.6.

The shooting method is conceptually simple and is easy to implement using existing software for initial value problems and for nonlinear equations. It has serious drawbacks, however. Chief among these is that the shooting method inherits the stability (or instability) of the associated IVP, which as we have seen may be unstable even when the BVP is stable. This potential ill-conditioning of the IVP may make it extremely difficult to achieve convergence of the iterative method for the nonlinear equation. Moreover, for some values of the starting guess for the initial value, the solution of the IVP may not exist over the entire interval of integration in that the solution may become unbounded before reaching the right-hand endpoint of the BVP.

A potential remedy for the difficulties associated with simple shooting is provided by *multiple shooting*, in which the interval of integration $[a, b]$ is divided into subintervals and shooting is carried out on each subinterval separately. Requiring continuity at the internal mesh points provides boundary conditions for the individual subproblems. Restricting the length of its interval of integration improves the conditioning of each IVP, but it also results in a larger system of nonlinear equations to solve. Specifically, the new system of ODEs is of size mn, where m is the number of subintervals and n is the size of the original system. Multiple shooting requires starting guesses for the initial values and slopes at the mesh points, and it also requires some new choices, such as the number of subintervals to use. Although it is more robust than simple shooting, multiple shooting is hardly foolproof and must be used with considerable care.

10.4 Finite Difference Method

In solving a boundary value problem, the shooting method approximately satisfies the ODE from the outset (by using an IVP solver) and iterates until the boundary conditions are satisfied. An alternative is to satisfy the boundary conditions from the outset and iterate until the ODE is approximately satisfied. The latter approach is taken in finite difference methods, which convert a BVP directly into a system of algebraic equations rather than a sequence of IVPs as in the shooting method.

In a finite difference method, a set of mesh of points is introduced within the interval of integration and then any derivatives appearing in the ODE or boundary conditions are replaced by finite difference approximations at the mesh points. For a scalar two-point boundary value problem

$$u'' = f(t, u, u'), \qquad a < t < b,$$

with boundary conditions

$$u(a) = \alpha, \qquad u(b) = \beta,$$

we introduce mesh points $t_i = a + ih$, $i = 0, \ldots, n+1$, where $h = (b-a)/(n+1)$, and we seek approximate solution values $y_i \approx u(t_i)$, $i = 1, \ldots, n$. We already have $y_0 = u(a) = \alpha$ and $y_{n+1} = u(b) = \beta$. Next we replace the derivatives appearing in the ODE by finite difference approximations (see Section 8.6.1), such as

$$u'(t_i) \approx \frac{y_{i+1} - y_{i-1}}{2h} \qquad \text{and} \qquad u''(t_i) \approx \frac{y_{i+1} - 2y_i + y_{i-1}}{h^2},$$

choosing the finite difference formulas so that they have the same order truncation error, in this case $\mathcal{O}(h^2)$, since the accuracy will be limited by the least accurate formula. This replacement yields a system of algebraic equations

$$\frac{y_{i+1} - 2y_i + y_{i-1}}{h^2} = f\left(t_i, y_i, \frac{y_{i+1} - y_{i-1}}{2h}\right), \qquad i = 1, \ldots, n,$$

to be solved for the unknowns y_i. This system of equations determines the approximate solution at all mesh points *simultaneously*, in contrast to finite difference methods for initial value problems, which determine the solution sequentially, step by step from one mesh point to the next.

The system of algebraic equations resulting from a finite difference method for a two-point BVP may be linear or nonlinear, depending on whether f is linear or nonlinear in u and u'. If the system is nonlinear, then an iterative method, such as Newton's method, will be required to solve it, in which case a reasonable starting guess for the iterative method is to choose values on a straight line between (a, α) and (b, β). In the example just given, each equation in the system involves only three adjacent unknowns, which means that the matrix of the linear system—or the Jacobian matrix in the nonlinear case—is tridiagonal, thereby saving on both work and storage compared with a general system of equations. Such savings are typical of finite difference methods: they yield sparse matrices because each equation involves only a few variables at nearby mesh points.

Example 10.7 Finite Difference Method. We illustrate the finite difference method on the two-point BVP from Example 10.6,

$$u'' = 6t, \qquad 0 < t < 1,$$

with boundary conditions

$$u(0) = 0, \qquad u(1) = 1.$$

To keep computation to a minimum, we will compute an approximate solution at a single interior mesh point, at the midpoint of the interval $[0, 1]$. Including the boundary points, we therefore have three mesh points, $t_0 = 0$, $t_1 = 0.5$, and $t_2 = 1$. From the boundary conditions, we know that $y_0 = u(t_0) = 0$ and $y_2 = u(t_2) = 1$, and we seek an approximate solution value $y_1 \approx u(t_1)$. Replacing the derivatives by finite difference approximations at the point t_1 gives the equation

$$\frac{y_2 - 2y_1 + y_0}{h^2} = f\left(t_1, y_1, \frac{y_2 - y_0}{2h}\right)$$

Substituting the boundary data, mesh size, and right-hand side function for this example, we obtain

$$\frac{1 - 2y_1 + 0}{(0.5)^2} = 6t_1,$$

or

$$4 - 8y_1 = 6(0.5) = 3,$$

so that

$$u(0.5) \approx y_1 = \frac{1}{8} = 0.125,$$

which agrees with the approximate solution at $t = 0.5$ that we computed by the shooting method in Example 10.6.

In practice, achieving acceptable accuracy with a finite difference method requires many more mesh points, and we would expect convergence to the true solution in the limit as the number of mesh points goes to infinity. This will indeed be the case if the finite difference method is both *consistent* (i.e., its truncation error goes to zero with the mesh spacing h) and *stable* (i.e., the effect of small perturbations is bounded). We will consider these issues in more detail in Chapter 11 on partial differential equations.

10.5 Collocation Method

In Chapter 7, we saw that one way to approximate a given continuous function is to interpolate values of the function at a finite set of points. If the function is known explicitly, then we can evaluate the function at the desired points and fit some linear combination of basis functions to the resulting function values. If the function is defined implicitly by a differential equation, then a similar approach still works, but we must modify the sense in which the approximating function "fits" the unknown function. This is the motivation for the *collocation method*, whose name comes from the fact that the approximate and true solutions share a common property (namely, satisfying the differential equation) at certain specified locations.

For a scalar two-point boundary value problem

$$u'' = f(t, u, u'), \qquad a < t < b,$$

with boundary conditions

$$u(a) = \alpha, \qquad u(b) = \beta,$$

we seek an approximate solution of the form

$$u(t) \approx v(t, \boldsymbol{x}) = \sum_{i=1}^{n} x_i \phi_i(t),$$

where the ϕ_i are basis functions defined on $[a, b]$ and $\boldsymbol{x}$ is an n-vector of parameters to be determined. Popular choices of basis functions include polynomials, B-splines, and trigonometric functions. If the boundary conditions are homogeneous (i.e., $\alpha = \beta = 0$), then by choosing basis functions that already satisfy the boundary conditions, any linear combination of the basis functions will also satisfy the boundary conditions. Or, more generally, we can enforce satisfaction of the boundary conditions as part of the process of determining $\boldsymbol{x}$.

To determine the vector of parameters $\boldsymbol{x}$, we define a set of n points $a = t_1 < \cdots < t_n = b$, called *collocation points*, and we will force the approximate solution $v(t, \boldsymbol{x})$ to satisfy the ODE at the interior collocation points and the boundary conditions at the endpoints (the latter are omitted if the basis functions already satisfy the boundary conditions). The simplest choice of collocation points is to use an equally-spaced mesh. If the basis functions are polynomials, however, then the Chebyshev points will provide greater accuracy, as we saw in Chapter 7. Having chosen collocation points and suitably smooth basis functions that we can differentiate analytically, we can now substitute the approximate solution and its derivatives into the ODE at each interior collocation point to obtain a set of algebraic equations

$$v''(t_i, \boldsymbol{x}) = f\left(t_i, v(t_i, \boldsymbol{x}), v'(t_i, \boldsymbol{x})\right), \quad i = 2, \dots, n-1,$$

while enforcing the boundary conditions yields two additional equations

$$v(t_1, \boldsymbol{x}) = \alpha, \qquad v(t_n, \boldsymbol{x}) = \beta.$$

This entire system of n equations in n unknowns, which may be linear or nonlinear, depending on whether f is linear or nonlinear in u and u', is then solved for the vector of parameters $\boldsymbol{x}$ that determines the approximate solution function v.

Example 10.8 Collocation Method. We illustrate the collocation method on the two-point BVP from Examples 10.6 and 10.7,

$$u'' = 6t, \qquad 0 < t < 1,$$

with boundary conditions

$$u(0) = 0, \qquad u(1) = 1.$$

To keep computation to a minimum, we will use a single interior collocation point, at the midpoint of the interval $[0, 1]$. Including the boundary points, we therefore have three collocation points, $t_1 = 0$, $t_2 = 0.5$, and $t_3 = 1$, so we will be able to determine three parameters. As basis functions we will use the first three monomials, so the approximate solution will have the form

$$v(t, \boldsymbol{x}) = x_1 + x_2 t + x_3 t^2.$$

The derivatives of this function with respect to t are given by

$$v'(t, \boldsymbol{x}) = x_2 + 2x_3 t, \qquad v''(t, \boldsymbol{x}) = 2x_3.$$

Requiring the ODE to be satisfied at the interior collocation point $t_2 = 0.5$ gives the equation

$$v''(t_2, \boldsymbol{x}) = f(t_2, v(t_2, \boldsymbol{x}), v'(t_2, \boldsymbol{x})),$$

or

$$2x_3 = 6t_2 = 6(0.5) = 3.$$

Requiring the left boundary condition to be satisfied at $t_1 = 0$ gives the equation

$$x_1 + x_2 t_1 + x_3 t_1^2 = x_1 = 0,$$

and requiring the right boundary condition to be satisfied at $t_3 = 1$ gives the equation

$$x_1 + x_2 t_3 + x_3 t_3^2 = x_1 + x_2 + x_3 = 1.$$

This system of three equations in three unknowns is trivially solved to obtain

$$x_1 = 0, \qquad x_2 = -0.5, \qquad x_3 = 1.5,$$

so that the approximate solution function is given by the quadratic polynomial

$$u(t) \approx v(t, \boldsymbol{x}) = -0.5t + 1.5t^2.$$

At the interior collocation point, $t_2 = 0.5$, where we forced v to satisfy the ODE, we have the approximate solution value

$$u(0.5) \approx v(0.5, \boldsymbol{x}) = (-0.5)(0.5) + (1.5)(0.25) = 0.125,$$

which agrees with the solution value at $t = 0.5$ that we obtained previously by both the shooting method (Example 10.6) and the finite difference method (Example 10.7). In general, these three methods would not produce exactly the same results, but they do so here because of the nature of the particular problem. The true solution is easily seen to be $u(t) = t^3$, so that the value $u(0.5) = (0.5)^3 = 0.125$ is in fact exact. We note that the quadratic polynomial produced by the collocation method agrees with the true solution at the three points $t_1 = 0$, $t_2 = 0.5$, and $t_3 = 1$ but does not agree with the true solution at any other points (Why?). The approximate and exact solutions are plotted in Fig. 10.3.

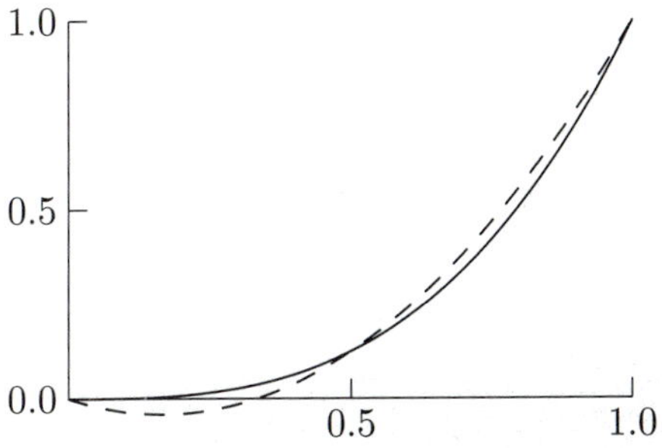

Figure 10.3: True solution (solid line) and collocation solution (dashed line) for Example 10.8.

The nature of an approximate solution resulting from the collocation method is quite different from that produced by a finite difference method. In both types of methods the approximate solution is chosen from a finite-dimensional space, in that each depends on a finite number of parameters. But the parameters in a collocation solution are the coefficients of a linear combination of basis functions, whereas the parameters in a finite difference solution are approximate values of the solution itself. In particular, the collocation solution is a continuous function from a finite-dimensional subspace of the infinite-dimensional space of continuous functions that contains the true solution, whereas the finite difference solution is not a continuous function but rather a discrete sample of approximate solution values from the finite-dimensional space of all possible values at the given sample points.

It is important to understand that satisfying the differential equation at a given point is *not* the same as agreeing with the exact solution to the differential equation at that point, since two functions can have the same slope at a point without having the same value there. Thus, in general, we do not expect the approximate solution to be exact at the collocation points (or anywhere else). As with finite difference methods, however, we do expect the accuracy to improve, and convergence to the true solution to occur, as the number of collocation points increases, and again this depends on the consistency and stability of the method.

The name collocation refers to a criterion for determining the coefficients of the basis functions, but does not by itself imply any particular choice of basis functions or collocation points. Nevertheless, certain choices of basis functions and collocation points have become so strongly associated with collocation that they have become practically synonymous with it. Basis functions such as polynomials or trigonometric functions, where each basis function is nonzero over essentially the entire problem domain (i.e., global support), yield a *spectral method* or *pseudospectral method*, whose name comes from the fact that the basis functions are eigenfunctions of a differential operator (e.g., sines and cosines for the second derivative operator). Basis functions such as B-splines, where each basis function is nonzero on only a small portion of the problem domain (i.e., highly localized support) yield a *finite element method*, whose name comes from the small subdomains (called *elements* for historical reasons) on which individual basis functions have their support.

There are a number of tradeoffs between spectral methods and finite element methods. Spectral methods provide very high accuracy for the number of points used, but the global support of the basis functions yields a dense system of equations that potentially requires a relatively large amount of work and storage to solve. Moreover, for some choices of basis functions, such as the monomials, the resulting system of equations becomes very ill-conditioned as the number of basis functions grows. Both of these difficulties can be alleviated, however, by using basis functions that are *orthogonal*, such as orthogonal polynomials or trigonometric polynomials, in which case accurate solutions can often be computed very efficiently using methods based on the fast Fourier transform.

For finite element methods, on the other hand, the highly localized support of the basis functions automatically makes them "nearly" orthogonal, which tends to yield a relatively well-conditioned system of equations, and it also makes the system sparse, so that much less work and storage are required to solve it. The overall size of the finite element system tends to be much larger, however, because a relatively large number of points may be required to attain acceptable accuracy. In principle, the accuracy of a finite element method can be increased either by reducing the mesh spacing (*h-refinement*) or increasing the degree of the B-splines used (*p-refinement*), or both, but the former is most often used in practice. By contrast, the accuracy of a spectral method can be increased only by using more basis functions, of higher degree. The local nature of finite element methods also makes them much more flexible than spectral methods in dealing with complicated domains and boundary conditions, an advantage that becomes much more significant for partial differential equations, where there are two or more independent variables.

10.6 Galerkin Method

As we have just seen, the collocation method forces the approximate solution to satisfy the differential equation at a finite number of points, which means that the residual is zero at those selected points when the approximate solution is substituted into the differential equation. An alternative is to minimize the residual, in some appropriate sense, over the entire interval of integration. Consider the scalar *Poisson equation* in one dimension,

$$u'' = f(t), \qquad a < t < b,$$

with homogeneous boundary conditions

$$u(a) = 0, \qquad u(b) = 0.$$

Again, we seek an approximate solution in the form of a linear combination of basis functions,

$$u(t) \approx v(t, \boldsymbol{x}) = \sum_{i=1}^{n} x_i \phi_i(t).$$

Substituting the approximate solution into the differential equation, we define the residual

$$r(t, \boldsymbol{x}) = v''(t, \boldsymbol{x}) - f(t) = \sum_{i=1}^{n} x_i \phi_i''(t) - f(t).$$

Using the *least squares method*, we minimize the function

$$F(\boldsymbol{x}) = \tfrac{1}{2} \int_a^b r(t, \boldsymbol{x})^2 \, dt$$

by setting each component of its gradient to zero, i.e., for $i = 1, \ldots, n$,

$$\begin{aligned} 0 &= \frac{\partial F}{\partial x_i} = \int_a^b r(t, \boldsymbol{x}) \frac{\partial r}{\partial x_i} \, dt = \int_a^b r(t, \boldsymbol{x}) \phi_i''(t) \, dt \\ &= \int_a^b \left(\sum_{j=1}^{n} x_j \phi_j''(t) - f(t) \right) \phi_i''(t) \, dt \\ &= \sum_{j=1}^{n} \left(\int_a^b \phi_j''(t) \phi_i''(t) \, dt \right) x_j - \int_a^b f(t) \phi_i''(t) \, dt, \end{aligned}$$

which is a symmetric system of linear algebraic equations $\boldsymbol{Ax} = \boldsymbol{b}$, where

$$a_{ij} = \int_a^b \phi_j''(t) \phi_i''(t) \, dt, \qquad b_i = \int_a^b f(t) \phi_i''(t) \, dt,$$

whose solution gives the vector of parameters $\boldsymbol{x}$. The integrals that define $\boldsymbol{A}$ and $\boldsymbol{b}$ can be evaluated either analytically or by numerical quadrature.

More generally, a *weighted residual method* forces the residual to be orthogonal to each of a given set of *weight functions* (or *test functions*), w_i, i.e.,

$$\int_a^b r(t, \boldsymbol{x}) w_i(t) \, dt = 0, \quad i = 1, \ldots, n,$$

which similarly yields a linear system $\boldsymbol{Ax} = \boldsymbol{b}$, where now

$$a_{ij} = \int_a^b \phi_j''(t) w_i(t) \, dt, \qquad b_i = \int_a^b f(t) w_i(t) \, dt,$$

whose solution gives the vector of parameters $\boldsymbol{x}$. The least squares method is obviously a method of this type, with $w_i = \phi_i''$. The collocation method can also be considered such a method, with $w_i(t) \equiv \delta(t - t_i)$, where t_i is the ith collocation point and δ is the *Dirac delta function*, which satisfies $\delta(s) = 0$ for $s \neq 0$ and

$$\int_a^b f(t) \delta(t - s) \, dt = f(s).$$

The matrix $\boldsymbol{A}$ resulting from a weighted residual method is generally not symmetric. Moreover, the entries of the matrix involve second derivatives of the basis functions. Both of these drawbacks are overcome in the *Galerkin method*, in which the weight functions are chosen to be the same as the basis functions, i.e., $w_i = \phi_i$, $i = 1, \ldots, n$. With this choice of weight functions, the orthogonality condition becomes

$$\int_a^b r(t, \boldsymbol{x})\phi_i(t)\, dt = 0, \quad i = 1, \ldots, n,$$

or

$$\int_a^b v''(t, \boldsymbol{x})\phi_i(t)\, dt = \int_a^b f(t)\phi_i(t)\, dt, \quad i = 1, \ldots, n.$$

The degree of differentiability can be reduced using integration by parts, which gives

$$\begin{aligned}\int_a^b v''(t, \boldsymbol{x})\phi_i(t)\, dt &= v'(t, \boldsymbol{x})\phi_i(t)\Big|_a^b - \int_a^b v'(t, \boldsymbol{x})\phi_i'(t)\, dt \\ &= v'(b, \boldsymbol{x})\phi_i(b) - v'(a, \boldsymbol{x})\phi_i(a) - \int_a^b v'(t, \boldsymbol{x})\phi_i'(t)\, dt,\end{aligned}$$

$i = 1, \ldots, n$. Assuming the basis functions ϕ_i satisfy the homogeneous boundary conditions, so that $\phi_i(a) = \phi_i(b) = 0$, the orthogonality condition then becomes

$$-\int_a^b v'(t, \boldsymbol{x})\phi_i'(t)\, dt = \int_a^b f(t)\phi_i(t)\, dt, \quad i = 1, \ldots, n,$$

or

$$-\int_a^b \left(\sum_{j=1}^n x_j\phi_j'(t)\right)\phi_i'(t)\, dt = -\sum_{j=1}^n \left(\int_a^b \phi_j'(t)\phi_i'(t)\, dt\right) x_j = \int_a^b f(t)\phi_i(t)\, dt,$$

$i = 1, \ldots, n$, which again is a system of linear equations $\boldsymbol{A}\boldsymbol{x} = \boldsymbol{b}$, where now

$$a_{ij} = -\int_a^b \phi_j'(t)\phi_i'(t)\, dt, \qquad b_i = \int_a^b f(t)\phi_i(t)\, dt,$$

whose solution gives the vector of parameters $\boldsymbol{x}$. Note that $\boldsymbol{A}$ is now symmetric and involves only first derivatives of the basis functions. Again, the integrals that define $\boldsymbol{A}$ and $\boldsymbol{b}$ can be evaluated either analytically or by numerical quadrature. For historical reasons owing to the origin of this method in structural analysis, $\boldsymbol{A}$ is called the *stiffness matrix* and $\boldsymbol{b}$ is called the *load vector*.

Approximating the solution to a boundary value problem in this manner by a continuous function from a finite-dimensional subspace is analogous to the situation depicted in Fig. 3.2: the true solution to the differential equation usually does not lie in the subspace spanned by the basis functions, but the approximate solution (a linear combination of basis functions) will be optimal when the residual is orthogonal to the subspace spanned by the basis functions, where the inner product of two functions is defined by the integral of their pointwise product.

Like collocation, the Galerkin method can be used with basis functions having global support (i.e., a spectral method) or local support (i.e., a finite element method); the tradeoffs between these two approaches have already been discussed near the end of Section 10.5. Unlike collocation, the approximate solution resulting from the Galerkin method may have a lower order of differentiability than the true solution. For example, the solution to the Poisson equation we considered must be twice differentiable by definition, but only the first derivative of the approximate solution enters into the Galerkin method, and it need not even be continuous, but merely integrable. This failure of the approximate solution to mimic all the properties of the true solution should not concern us; all that matters for practical purposes is that the approximate solution should be close to the true solution at any point. By comparison, the approximate solution resulting from a finite difference method is defined only at discrete points, and therefore it cannot be differentiable or even continuous.

Example 10.9 Galerkin Method. We illustrate the Galerkin method on the two-point BVP from Examples 10.6, 10.7, and 10.8,

$$y'' = 6t, \qquad 0 < t < 1,$$

with boundary conditions

$$y(0) = 0, \qquad y(1) = 1.$$

We will approximate the solution by a piecewise linear polynomial, for which the B-splines of degree 1 form a suitable set of basis functions. To keep computation to a minimum, we again use the same three mesh points, but now they become the knots in the piecewise linear polynomial approximation. The resulting basis of "hat" functions is shown in Fig. 10.4 (see also Fig. 7.11).

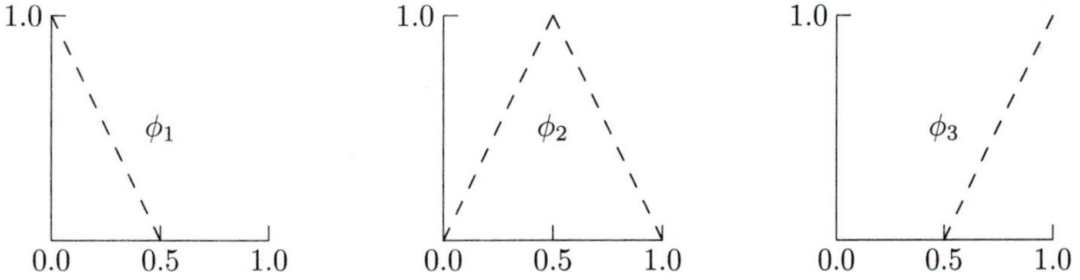

Figure 10.4: Basis of "hat" functions for piecewise linear approximate solution.

Thus, we seek an approximate solution of the form

$$u(t) \approx v(t, \boldsymbol{x}) = x_1\phi_1(t) + x_2\phi_2(t) + x_3\phi_3(t).$$

From the boundary conditions, we must have $x_1 = 0$ and $x_3 = 1$. To determine the remaining parameter x_2, we impose the Galerkin orthogonality condition on the interior basis function ϕ_2 and obtain the equation

$$-\sum_{j=1}^{3}\left(\int_0^1 \phi_j'(t)\phi_2'(t)\,dt\right)x_j = \int_0^1 6t\phi_2(t)\,dt,$$

or, upon evaluating these simple integrals analytically,

$$2x_1 - 4x_2 + 2x_3 = 3/2.$$

Substituting the known values for x_1 and x_3 then gives $x_2 = 1/8$ for the remaining unknown parameter. Thus, the piecewise linear approximate solution is

$$u(t) \approx v(t, \boldsymbol{x}) = 0.125\phi_2(t) + \phi_3(t),$$

which is plotted in Fig. 10.5 along with the exact solution. We note that $v(0.5, \boldsymbol{x}) = 0.125$, which again is exact for this particular problem.

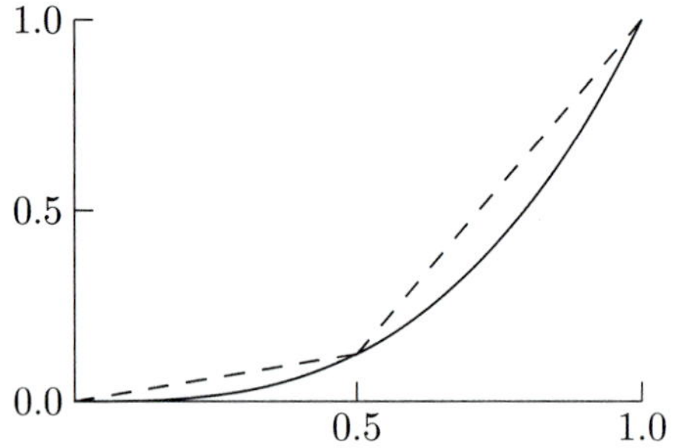

Figure 10.5: True solution (solid line) and piecewise linear Galerkin solution (dashed line) for Example 10.9.

10.7 Eigenvalue Problems

A standard eigenvalue problem for a second-order scalar BVP has the form

$$u'' = \lambda\, f(t, u, u'), \qquad a < t < b,$$

with homogeneous boundary conditions

$$u(a) = 0, \qquad u(b) = 0,$$

and we seek to determine not only the solution function u, but the parameter λ as well. The (possibly complex) scalar λ is called an *eigenvalue* and the solution u an *eigenfunction* for this two-point boundary value problem. More general eigenvalue problems may involve higher-order systems, implicit equations, more general boundary conditions, or nonlinear dependence on λ.

Discretization of an eigenvalue problem for an ODE, which can be done using a finite difference, finite element, or spectral method, results in an algebraic eigenvalue problem whose solution approximates that of the original problem. For example, consider the linear two-point boundary value problem

$$u'' = \lambda\, g(t)\, u, \qquad a < t < b,$$

with homogeneous boundary conditions

$$u(a) = 0, \qquad u(b) = 0.$$

If we introduce mesh points $t_i = a + ih$, $i = 0, \ldots, n+1$, where $h = (b-a)/(n+1)$, and replace the second derivative by a standard finite difference approximation, then we obtain a system of algebraic equations

$$\frac{y_{i+1} - 2y_i + y_{i-1}}{h^2} = \lambda\, g_i\, y_i, \quad i = 1, \ldots, n,$$

where $y_i = u(t_i)$ and $g_i = g(t_i)$, and from the boundary conditions, $y_0 = u(a) = 0$ and $y_{n+1} = u(b) = 0$. If $g_i \neq 0$ for $i = 1, \ldots, n$, so that we can divide the ith equation by g_i, then we obtain a standard algebraic eigenvalue problem $\boldsymbol{Ay} = \lambda \boldsymbol{y}$, where the $n \times n$ matrix $\boldsymbol{A}$ has the tridiagonal form

$$\boldsymbol{A} = \frac{1}{h^2} \begin{bmatrix} -2/g_1 & 1/g_1 & 0 & \cdots & 0 \\ 1/g_2 & -2/g_2 & 1/g_2 & \ddots & \vdots \\ 0 & \ddots & \ddots & \ddots & 0 \\ \vdots & \ddots & 1/g_{n-1} & -2/g_{n-1} & 1/g_{n-1} \\ 0 & \cdots & 0 & 1/g_n & -2/g_n \end{bmatrix},$$

which can be solved by the methods discussed in Chapter 4. Alternatively, the discretized system can be treated directly in its original form as a generalized eigenvalue problem (see Section 4.6).

10.8 Software for ODE Boundary Value Problems

Table 10.1 is a list of software for numerical solution of boundary value problems for ordinary differential equations. For a survey of software available for two-point boundary value problems, see [67].

Source	Shooting	Finite difference	Collocation	Galerkin
`IMSL`	`bvpms`	`bvpfd`		
`HSL`		`dd04/dd11/dd12`		
`MATLAB`			`bvp4c`	
`NAG`	`d02haf`	`d02gaf`	`d02jaf`	
`Netlib`	`musl/musn`	`twpbvp`	`colnew`	
`NR` [315]	`shoot`	`solvde`		
`NUMAL` [250]				`femlag`
`SLATEC`	`bvsup`			
`TOMS`			`colsys(#569)`	

Table 10.1: Software for ODE boundary value problems

10.9 Historical Notes and Further Reading

For historical notes relevant to the problems and methods considered in this chapter, see Sections 9.5 and 11.8. For relevant background material on ordinary differential equations and boundary value problems, see the general textbooks cited in Section 9.5. A comprehensive modern treatment of numerical solution methods for boundary value problems for ordinary differential equations can be found in [13]. Other useful references on this topic, focusing mainly on shooting and finite difference methods, include [14, 19, 132, 226, 306, 332]. Most references on spectral methods or finite element methods are primarily concerned with partial differential equations, but many of them discuss two-point boundary value problems for ODEs as an introductory illustration; for spectral methods see [41, 124, 139, 166, 268, 395], and for finite element methods see [108, 113, 218, 246, 380].

Review Questions

10.1. What specific feature distinguishes a boundary value problem from an initial value problem for an ordinary differential equation?

10.2. What is meant by *separated* boundary conditions?

10.3. Does a boundary value problem for an ODE always have a unique solution?

10.4. Is the stability of a boundary value problem always the same as that of the associated initial value problem for the same ODE? Why?

10.5. Explain how a one-dimensional zero finder can be used to solve a two-point BVP $u'' = f(t, u, u')$ with boundary conditions $u(a) = \alpha$ and $u(b) = \beta$.

10.6. For solving a two-point BVP for a *nonlinear* ODE, both the finite difference method and the shooting method are iterative. One of these approximately satisfies the ODE at each iteration, but satisfies the boundary conditions only upon convergence, whereas the other satisfies the boundary conditions at each iteration, but approximately satisfies the ODE only upon convergence. Which is which?

10.7. (*a*) In solving a two-point BVP, for what type of problem is the multiple shooting method likely to be more effective than the ordinary shooting method?

(*b*) What disadvantage does the multiple shooting method have, compared with the ordinary shooting method?

10.8. When a finite difference method is used to convert a BVP for a differential equation into a system of algebraic equations, what property determines whether the algebraic system will be linear or nonlinear?

10.9. Finite difference and finite element methods for solving BVPs convert the original differential equation into a system of algebraic equations. Why does the resulting linear system usually require far less work to solve than the usual $\mathcal{O}(n^3)$ that might be expected?

10.10. Finite difference methods and collocation methods for solving BVPs both require the solution of a system of algebraic equations, but the solutions to the respective algebraic systems differ in their meanings and how they are used.

(*a*) How do the quantities being solved for differ between the two types of methods?

(*b*) How do the resulting approximate solutions to the BVP differ in nature?

10.11. Why is it advantageous if the basis functions used in a collocation or Galerkin method have localized support (i.e., each basis function is nonzero on only a small portion of the problem domain)?

10.12. In solving a BVP, what requirement does the collocation method impose on the approximate solution?

10.13. Suppose you are solving a two-point BVP for a linear second-order ODE using the standard second-order centered finite-difference approximations to the derivatives. Describe the nonzero pattern of the matrix of the resulting system of linear algebraic equations.

10.14. Suppose you are using the shooting method to solve a two-point BVP for an ODE on an interval $[a, b]$. If solutions of the ODE are unstable on some portion of the interval, then the resulting sequence of initial value problems may be very sensitive to initial conditions, making it difficult to hit the required boundary condition.

(*a*) How could you cope with such ill-conditioning?

(*b*) How would this affect the nonlinear algebraic equation to be solved?

10.15. In solving a two-point BVP numerically, does the approximate solution produced by collocation at a finite set of points always agree with the exact solution at those points?

Exercises

10.1. Consider the two-point BVP

$$u'' = f(t), \qquad 0 < t < 1,$$

with boundary conditions

$$u(0) = 0, \qquad u(1) = 0.$$

(*a*) Use the Fundamental Theorem of Calculus and the ODE to show that the general solution to the ODE is given by

$$u(t) = c_1 + c_2 t + \int_0^t F(s)\, ds,$$

where c_1 and c_2 are arbitrary constants and

$$F(s) = \int_0^s f(x)\, dx.$$

(*b*) Use integration by parts to show that the general solution to the ODE can be written as

$$u(t) = c_1 + c_2 t + \int_0^t (t - s) f(s)\, ds.$$

(*c*) Use the boundary conditions to show that

$$c_1 = 0, \qquad c_2 = \int_0^1 (s - 1) f(s)\, ds,$$

so that the solution to the BVP is

$$u(t) = \int_0^t (t - s) f(s)\, ds + t \int_0^1 (s - 1) f(s)\, ds.$$

(*d*) Use the previous result to show that the solution to the BVP is given by

$$u(t) = \int_0^1 G(t, s) f(s)\, ds,$$

where the Green's function $G(t, s)$ is given by

$$G(t, s) = \begin{cases} s(t - 1), & 0 \le s \le t \\ t(s - 1), & t < s \le 1 \end{cases}.$$

(*e*) Use the Green's function to determine the solution to the BVP for $f(t) = 1$.

(*f*) Use the Green's function to determine the solution to the BVP for $f(t) = t$.

(*g*) Use the Green's function to determine the solution to the BVP for $f(t) = t^2$.

10.2. Consider the two-point BVP for the second-order scalar ODE

$$u'' = u, \qquad 0 < t < b,$$

with boundary conditions

$$u(0) = \alpha, \qquad u(b) = \beta.$$

(*a*) Rewrite the problem as a first-order system of ODEs with separated boundary conditions.

(*b*) Show that the fundamental solution matrix for the resulting linear system of ODEs is given by

$$\boldsymbol{Y}(t) = \begin{bmatrix} \cosh(t) & \sinh(t) \\ \sinh(t) & \cosh(t) \end{bmatrix}.$$

(*c*) Are the solutions to this ODE stable?

(*d*) Determine the matrix $\boldsymbol{Q} \equiv \boldsymbol{B}_0 \boldsymbol{Y}(0) + \boldsymbol{B}_b \boldsymbol{Y}(b)$ for this problem.

(*e*) Determine the rescaled solution matrix $\boldsymbol{\Phi}(t) = \boldsymbol{Y}(t)\, \boldsymbol{Q}^{-1}$.

(*f*) What can you say about the conditioning of $\boldsymbol{Q}$, the norm of $\boldsymbol{\Phi}(t)$, and the stability of solutions to this BVP as the right endpoint b grows?

10.3. Consider the two-point BVP

$$u'' = u^3 + t, \qquad a < t < b,$$

with boundary conditions

$$u(a) = \alpha, \qquad u(b) = \beta.$$

To use the shooting method to solve this problem, one needs a starting guess for the initial slope $u'(a)$. One way to obtain such a starting guess for the initial slope is, in effect, to do a "preliminary shooting" in which we take a single step of Euler's method with $h = b - a$.

(*a*) Using this approach, write out the resulting algebraic equation for the initial slope.

(*b*) What starting value for the initial slope results from this approach?

10.4. Suppose that the altitude of the trajectory of a projectile is described by the second-order ODE $u'' = -4$. Suppose that the projectile is fired from position $t = 0$ and height $u(0) = 1$ and is to strike a target at position $t = 1$, also of height $u(1) = 1$.

(*a*) Solve this BVP by the shooting method:

1. To determine the initial slope at $t = 0$ required to hit the desired target at $t = 1$, use the trapezoid method with step size $h = 1$ to derive a system of two equations for the unknown initial slope $s_0 = u'(0)$ and final slope $s_1 = u'(1)$.
2. What are the resulting values for the initial and final slopes?
3. Using the initial slope just determined and a step size of $h = 0.5$, use the trapezoid method once again to compute the approximate height of the projectile at $t = 0.5$.

(*b*) Solve the same BVP again, this time using a finite difference method with $h = 0.5$. What is the resulting approximate height of the projectile at the point $t = 0.5$?

(*c*) Solve the same BVP once again, this time using collocation at the point $t = 0.5$, together with the boundary values, to determine a quadratic polynomial $u(t)$ approximating the solution. What is the resulting approximate height of the projectile at the point $t = 0.5$?

Computer Problems

10.1. Solve the two-point BVP

$$u'' = 10u^3 + 3u + t^2, \qquad 0 < t < 1,$$

with boundary conditions

$$u(0) = 0, \qquad u(1) = 1,$$

by each of the following methods.

(*a*) *Shooting method.* Use a one-dimensional nonlinear equation solver to find an initial slope $u'(0)$ such that the solution of the resulting initial value problem hits the target value for $u(1)$. Solve each required initial value problem using a library ODE solver or one of your own design. Plot the sequence of solutions you obtain.

(*b*) *Finite difference method.* Divide the given interval $0 \le t \le 1$ into $n + 1$ equal subintervals,

$$0 = t_0 < t_1 < \cdots < t_n < t_{n+1} = 1,$$

with each subinterval of length $h = 1/(n + 1)$. Let y_i, $i = 1, \ldots, n$, represent the approximate solution values at the n interior points. Obtain a system of n algebraic equations for the y_i by replacing the second derivative in the differential equation by the finite difference approximation

$$y_i''(t) \approx \frac{y_{i+1} - 2y_i + y_{i-1}}{h^2},$$

$i = 1, \ldots, n$. Use a library routine, or one of your own design, to solve the resulting system of nonlinear equations. A reasonable starting guess for the nonlinear solver is a straight line between the boundary values. Plot the sequences of solutions you obtain for $n = 1$, 3, 7, and 15.

(*c*) *Collocation method.* Divide the given interval $0 \le t \le 1$ into $n - 1$ equal subintervals,

$$0 = t_1 < t_2 < \cdots < t_{n-1} < t_n = 1,$$

with each subinterval of length $h = 1/(n-1)$. Take the approximate solution $v(t, \boldsymbol{x})$ to be a polynomial of degree $n - 1$ with coefficients $\boldsymbol{x}$. Forcing $v(t, \boldsymbol{x})$ to satisfy the boundary conditions at the endpoints and to satisfy the ODE at the $n - 2$ interior points yields a system of n equations that determine the n coefficients $\boldsymbol{x}$ of the polynomial $v(t, \boldsymbol{x})$. Use a library routine, or one of your own design, to solve this system of nonlinear algebraic equations. The resulting polynomial can then be evaluated at any point in the interval to obtain an approximate solution value at that point. Print the polynomial coefficients and plot the solutions you obtain for $n = 3$, 4, 5, and 6.

10.2. Solve the two-point BVP

$$u'' = -(1 + e^u), \qquad 0 < t < 1,$$

with boundary conditions

$$u(0) = 0, \qquad u(1) = 1,$$

using each method in Computer Problem 10.1.

10.3. Using any method of your choice, find two distinct solutions to the two-point BVP

$$u'' = -|u|, \qquad 0 < t < 4,$$

with boundary conditions

$$u(0) = 0, \qquad u(4) = -2.$$

(*Hint*: One solution has positive initial slope and the other has negative initial slope.)

10.4. Using any method of your choice, find two distinct solutions to the two-point BVP

$$u'' = -e^{u+1}, \qquad 0 < t < 1,$$

with boundary conditions

$$u(0) = 0, \qquad u(1) = 0.$$

(*Hint*: Both solutions have positive initial slope.)

10.5. The curve of a hanging cable is described by the system of ODEs

$$\begin{aligned} y_1' &= \cos(y_3), \\ y_2' &= \sin(y_3), \\ y_3' &= (\cos(y_3) - \sin(y_3)|\sin(y_3)|)/y_4, \\ y_4' &= \sin(y_3) - \cos(y_3)|\cos(y_3)|, \end{aligned}$$

where $y_1(t)$ and $y_2(t)$ are the horizontal and vertical coordinates of the cable, $y_3(t)$ is the angle between the tangent to the cable and the horizontal axis, $y_4(t)$ is the tension in the cable, and t is the arc length along the cable, with the length of the cable normalized so that $0 \le t \le 1$.

(*a*) Use both the shooting and finite difference methods to determine the curve of the cable when the boundary conditions are

$$\begin{aligned} y_1(0) &= 0, \qquad & y_1(1) &= 0.75, \\ y_2(0) &= 0, \qquad & y_2(1) &= 0. \end{aligned}$$

These conditions correspond to a slack cable. Plot the solution curve $(y_1(t), y_2(t))$ you obtain for each method. Reasonable starting guesses for "missing" initial conditions are $y_3(0) = 0$ and $y_4(0) = 1$.

(*b*) Use both the shooting and finite difference methods to determine the curve of the cable when the boundary conditions are

$$\begin{aligned} y_1(0) &= 0, \qquad & y_1(1) &= 0.85, \\ y_2(0) &= 0, \qquad & y_2(1) &= 0.50. \end{aligned}$$

These conditions correspond to a taut cable. Plot the solution curve you obtain for each method.

10.6. The deflection of a horizontal beam supported at both ends and subjected to axial and transverse loads can be described by the second-order ODE

$$u'' = \lambda(-t^2 - 1)u, \qquad -1 < t < 1,$$

with boundary conditions

$$u(-1) = 0, \qquad u(1) = 0.$$

The eigenvalues and eigenfunctions for this two-point BVP determine the frequencies and modes of vibration of the beam. Use a finite difference discretization of the ODE to derive an algebraic eigenvalue problem whose eigenvalues and eigenvectors approximate those of the ODE, then compute the eigenvalues and eigenvectors using a library routine (see Section 4.8). Experiment with various mesh sizes and observe how the eigenvalues behave.

10.7. The time-independent *Schrödinger equation* in one dimension,

$$-\psi''(x) + V(x)\psi(x) = E\psi(x),$$

where we have chosen units so that the quantities are dimensionless, describes the wave function ψ of a particle of energy E subject to a potential function V. The square of the wave function, $|\psi(x)|^2$, can be interpreted as the probability of finding the particle at position x.

Assume that the particle is confined to a one-dimensional box, say, the interval $[0, 1]$, within which it can move freely. Thus, the potential is zero within the unit interval and infinite elsewhere. Since there is zero probability of finding the particle outside the box, the wave function must be zero at its boundaries. Thus, we have an eigenvalue problem for the second-order ODE

$$-\psi''(x) = E\psi(x), \qquad 0 < x < 1,$$

subject to the boundary conditions

$$\psi(0) = 0, \qquad \psi(1) = 0.$$

Note that the discrete eigenvalues E are the only energy levels permitted; this feature gives quantum mechanics its name.

Use a finite difference discretization of the ODE to derive an algebraic eigenvalue problem whose eigenvalues and eigenvectors approximate those of the ODE, then compute the eigenvalues and eigenvectors using a library routine (see Section 4.8). Experiment with various mesh sizes and observe how the eigenvalues behave.

An analytical solution to this problem is easily obtained, which gives the eigenvalues

$$E_k = k^2\pi^2$$

and corresponding eigenfunctions

$$\psi_k(x) = \sin(k\pi x), \quad k = 1, 2, \ldots.$$

How do your computed eigenvalues and eigenvectors compare with these analytical values as the mesh size of your discretization decreases? Try to characterize the error as a function of the mesh size.

Note that a nonzero potential V would not seriously complicate the numerical solution of the Schrödinger equation, but would generally make an analytical solution much more difficult to obtain.

Chapter 11

Partial Differential Equations

11.1 Partial Differential Equations

A *partial differential equation*, or *PDE*, is an equation involving partial derivatives of an unknown function with respect to more than one independent variable. PDEs are of fundamental importance in modeling all types of continuous phenomena in nature. Many of the basic laws of science are expressed as PDEs, including

- Maxwell's equations, which describe the behavior of an electromagnetic field by prescribing the relationships among the electric and magnetic field strengths, magnetic flux density, and electric charge and current densities
- Navier-Stokes equations, which describe the behavior of a fluid by prescribing the relationships among its velocity, density, pressure, and viscosity
- Linear elasticity equations, which describe vibrations in an elastic solid with given material properties by prescribing the relationship between stress and strain
- Schrödinger's equation of quantum mechanics, which describes the wave function of a particle by prescribing the relationships among its mass, potential energy, and total energy
- Einstein's equations of general relativity, which describe a gravitational field by prescribing the relationship between the curvature of spacetime and the energy density of the matter it contains

We will confine our attention to PDEs that are much simpler than those just listed, as the general theory of PDEs is far beyond the scope of this book. We will consider some basic concepts and methods in relatively simple settings, but most of these are applicable more generally. Many of these ideas carry over from ordinary differential equations, such as the need to specify initial or boundary conditions, but the situation is more complex with PDEs, in part because a problem domain in two or more dimensions can be much more irregular, and the boundary conditions much more complicated, than in one dimension. Many of the numerical solution techniques we saw in Chapters 9 and 10 also carry over to PDEs, but the computational cost increases substantially with the number of independent variables because the system of algebraic equations resulting from discretization becomes much larger.

Before proceeding, we establish some notation. For simplicity, we will deal only with single PDEs (as opposed to systems of several coupled PDEs) with only two independent variables, either one space variable denoted by x and a time variable denoted by t (such PDEs are analogous to the initial value problems for ODEs we considered in Chapter 9), or two space variables denoted by x and y (analogous to the boundary value problems for ODEs we considered in Chapter 10). We denote the unknown solution function by u, and we denote its partial derivatives with respect to the independent variables by appropriate subscripts: $u_t = \partial u/\partial t$, $u_{xy} = \partial^2 u/\partial x \partial y$, etc. We seek to determine a function $u: \mathbb{R}^2 \to \mathbb{R}$ whose partial derivatives with respect to the independent variables satisfy the relationship prescribed by a given PDE on a given domain, and which also satisfies whatever initial or boundary conditions may have been imposed. Such a solution function u can be visualized as a surface over the relevant two-dimensional domain in the (t, x) or (x, y) plane.

Example 11.1 Advection Equation. The simplest true PDE is the *advection equation*, also known as the *one-way wave equation*,

$$u_t = -c\, u_x,$$

where c is a nonzero constant. For now we take the spatial domain for x to be the entire real line. To specify a unique solution, we prescribe initial data for all x at some initial time t_0, say $t_0 = 0$. A suitable initial condition therefore has the form

$$u(0, x) = u_0(x), \qquad -\infty < x < \infty,$$

where u_0 is a given function defined on the real line, and we seek a solution $u(t, x)$ for $t \geq 0$ and all $x \in \mathbb{R}$. Such a pure initial value problem is called a *Cauchy problem*. From the chain rule, it is obvious that a solution to the advection equation with the given initial data is given by

$$u(t, x) = u_0(x - c\,t).$$

This means that for any fixed time $t > 0$, the solution is simply the initial function u_0 shifted by an amount $c\,t$ to the right if $c > 0$, or similarly to the left if $c < 0$. Another way of saying this is that the initial function u_0 is propagated to the right (or left) with velocity c, as shown in Fig. 11.1 for $c = 1$.

Note that for any $x_0 \in \mathbb{R}$, the solution function for the advection equation has the constant value $u_0(x_0)$ along the line $x - c\,t = x_0$ in the (t, x) plane. More generally, consider the advection equation with variable coefficient,

$$u_t = -a(t, x)\, u_x,$$

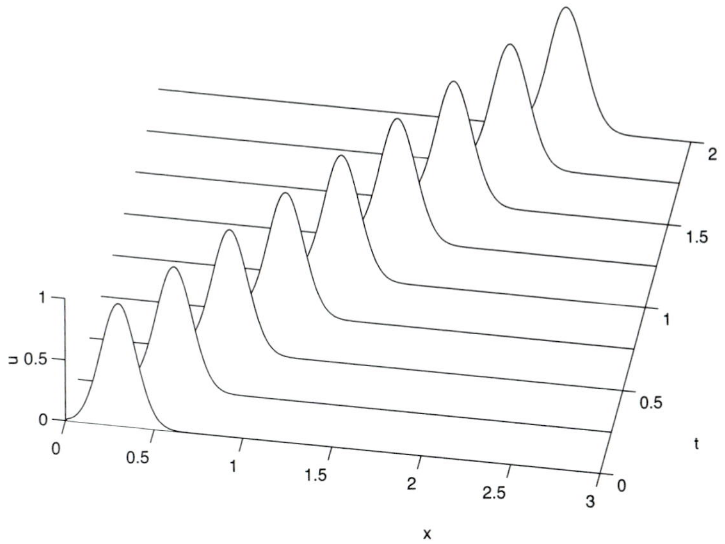

Figure 11.1: Typical solution of advection equation.

where $a\colon \mathbb{R}^2 \to \mathbb{R}$ is a smooth function, with the same initial condition as in Example 11.1. The solution to the initial value problem for the ODE

$$\frac{dx(t)}{dt} = a(t, x(t)), \qquad t \geq 0,$$

with initial condition $x(0) = x_0$, where $x_0 \in \mathbb{R}$, is a curve $x(t)$ in the (t, x) plane along which the solution u of the PDE is constant, since

$$\frac{d}{dt}\, u(t, x(t)) = u_t + u_x \frac{dx(t)}{dt} = u_t + a(t, x)\, u_x = 0.$$

Such a *level curve* (see Section 6.2) for the solution is called a *characteristic* for the PDE. Characteristics are of both theoretical and computational importance. In particular, they determine where boundary conditions can or must be imposed to obtain a well-posed problem.

Consider, for example, the advection equation with constant coefficient c on the finite spatial interval $0 \leq x \leq 1$, so that we have the problem domain shown in Fig. 11.2. Specifying initial values for $0 \leq x \leq 1$ at $t = 0$ determines the solution on only a portion of the problem domain (the shaded region in Fig. 11.2), so additional boundary conditions are needed to determine the solution fully. With $c > 0$, the characteristics go from lower left to upper right as t increases, so specifying boundary values along the vertical line $x = 0$ determines the solution on the remainder of the problem domain. Specifying boundary values along the line $x = 1$ would make the problem overdetermined, and in general no function could then satisfy both the PDE and the boundary conditions. With $c < 0$, on the other hand, the characteristics go from lower right to upper left, so we must specify boundary values along the line $x = 1$, but specifying boundary values along the line $x = 0$ would make the problem overdetermined. Although the characteristics in this example are parallel straight lines, in general they are neither straight nor parallel if the PDE has variable coefficients or is nonlinear. Indeed, the characteristics can even cross each other for some PDEs, leading to a *shock*, or discontinuity, in the solution.

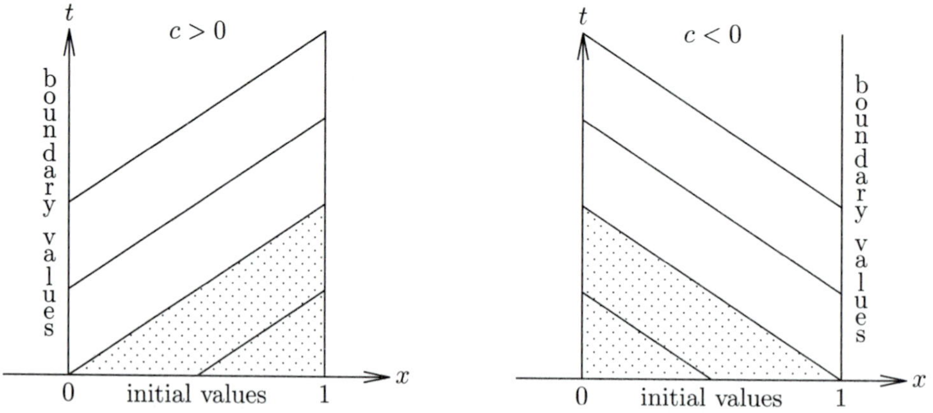

Figure 11.2: Characteristics of advection equation with positive and negative velocities.

As with ODEs, the *order* of a PDE is determined by the highest-order partial derivative appearing in the PDE. We have thus far considered only first-order PDEs, the advection equation with constant or variable coefficient. Some of the most important PDEs in practical applications are of second order, including

- *Heat equation*, $u_t = u_{xx}$
- *Wave equation*, $u_{tt} = u_{xx}$
- *Laplace equation*, $u_{xx} + u_{yy} = 0$

It turns out that these three equations are general prototypes in that any second-order linear PDE of the form

$$a u_{xx} + b u_{xy} + c\, u_{yy} + d u_x + e u_y + f u + g = 0$$

can be transformed by a change of variables into one of these three canonical equations (plus terms of lower order), provided a, b, and c are not all zero. The quantity $b^2 - 4ac$, called the *discriminant*, determines which of the canonical forms is obtained by such a transformation. Therefore, second-order linear PDEs can be classified according to the value of the discriminant into three families whose names derive from the analogous conic sections:

$b^2 - 4ac > 0$:	*hyperbolic*, typified by the wave equation
$b^2 - 4ac = 0$:	*parabolic*, typified by the heat equation
$b^2 - 4ac < 0$:	*elliptic*, typified by the Laplace equation

The classification of more general PDEs is not so clean or clear-cut. If the coefficients are variable, then the type of the equation can vary from one region to another, and if there is more than one equation in a system, then each equation can be of a different type. And of course, the problem may be nonlinear or of higher order or dimension. Nevertheless, these terms are often used to describe PDEs even when the meaning is not so precise. Roughly speaking,

- *Hyperbolic* PDEs describe time-dependent, conservative physical processes, such as convection, that *are not* evolving toward a steady state.
- *Parabolic* PDEs describe time-dependent, dissipative physical processes, such as diffusion, that *are* evolving toward a steady state.
- *Elliptic* PDEs describe systems that have already reached a steady state, or equilibrium, and hence are time-independent.

The concept of characteristics remains valid for second-order PDEs, but the situation is more complicated in that hyperbolic PDEs have two independent families of characteristics, parabolic PDEs have a single family of characteristics, and elliptic PDEs have no real characteristics. The characteristics for a given PDE determine what initial and boundary conditions result in a well-posed problem.

Systems governed by hyperbolic PDEs are *conservative* in that the "energy" of the system, as measured by an appropriate norm of the solution, is conserved over time. Hyperbolic PDEs are analogous to a linear system of ODEs whose matrix has purely imaginary eigenvalues, yielding a purely oscillatory solution that neither grows nor decays with time. Systems governed by parabolic PDEs, on the other hand, are *dissipative* in that the "energy" of the solution diminishes over time. Parabolic PDEs are analogous to a linear system of ODEs whose matrix has only eigenvalues with negative real parts, yielding an exponentially decaying solution. Another important difference is that hyperbolic PDEs propagate information at a finite speed, whereas parabolic PDEs propagate information instantaneously.

These differences between the two types of time-dependent PDEs have important theoretical and practical implications. For example, parabolic PDEs have a smoothing effect that over time damps out any lack of smoothness in the initial conditions, whereas hyperbolic PDEs propagate steep fronts or shocks undiminished, and discontinuities can develop in the solution even with smooth initial data. Systems governed by hyperbolic PDEs are in principle reversible in time, whereas parabolic systems are not. The heat equation integrated backward in time is ill-posed, for example, which corresponds physically to the fact that one cannot determine details of the thermal history of a system from its current temperature distribution. The challenges in solving parabolic or hyperbolic PDEs numerically are analogous to those in solving ODEs that are stiff because of eigenvalues with large negative real parts (parabolic) or large imaginary parts (hyperbolic).

We now consider the exemplars of each of the three types of PDEs in slightly more detail. The *heat equation* in one space dimension has the form

$$u_t = c\,u_{xx}, \qquad 0 \le x \le L, \qquad t \ge 0,$$

with given initial condition

$$u(0, x) = f(x), \qquad 0 \le x \le L,$$

and boundary conditions

$$u(t,0)=\alpha, \qquad u(t,L)=\beta, \qquad t\geq 0,$$

and c a positive constant. The problem domain is shown in Fig. 11.3. This equation models, for example, the diffusion of heat in a bar of length L whose ends are maintained at temperatures specified by the boundary conditions and whose initial temperature distribution is given by the function $f(x)$. The constant c, which governs the rate of diffusion, depends on material properties of the bar, such as its thermal conductivity, specific heat, and density. The solution u to this equation gives the subsequent temperature distribution as a function of both space and time.

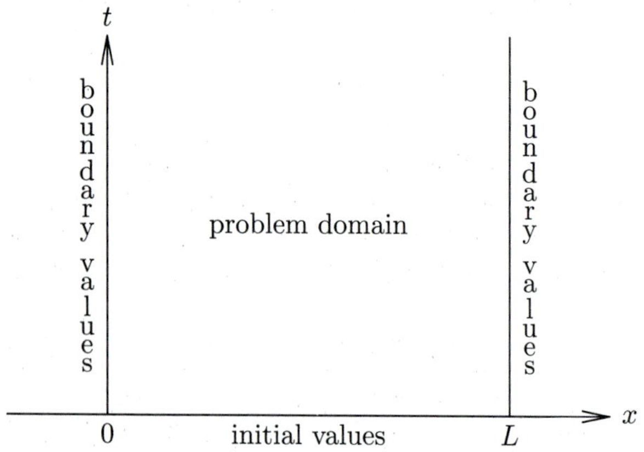

Figure 11.3: Initial-boundary value problem for time-dependent PDE in one space dimension.

The *wave equation* in one space dimension has the form

$$u_{tt}=c\,u_{xx}, \qquad 0\leq x\leq L, \qquad t\geq 0,$$

with given initial conditions

$$u(0,x)=f(x), \qquad u_t(0,x)=g(x), \qquad 0\leq x\leq L,$$

and boundary conditions

$$u(t,0)=\alpha, \qquad u(t,L)=\beta, \qquad t\geq 0,$$

and c a positive constant. This equation models, for example, vibrations of a violin string of length L whose initial profile and velocity are given by the functions $f(x)$ and $g(x)$, respectively, and whose ends are anchored as prescribed by the boundary conditions. Because it is second-order in time, this equation requires initial conditions for both the solution function and its first derivative with respect to time. The solution consists of waves propagating both to the left and the right with speed $\sqrt{c}$.

The *Laplace equation* is a special case of the *Poisson equation*, which in two space dimensions has the form

$$u_{xx} + u_{yy} = f(x, y),$$

where f is a given function defined on a domain whose boundary is typically a closed curve in $\mathbb{R}^2$, such as a square or circle. If $f \equiv 0$, then we have the Laplace equation. There are numerous possibilities for the boundary conditions that must be specified on the boundary of the domain or portions thereof:

- *Dirichlet* boundary conditions, sometimes called *essential* boundary conditions, in which the solution u is specified
- *Neumann* boundary conditions, sometimes called *natural* boundary conditions, in which one of the derivatives u_x or u_y is specified
- *Robin* boundary conditions, or *mixed* boundary conditions, in which a combination of solution values and derivative values is specified.

The Laplace equation models, for example, the electrostatic potential within a charge-free region given the potential on the boundary of the region. The Poisson equation models the electrostatic potential when there is also a known charge density within the region, represented by the function f. For this reason, the Laplace equation or the Poisson equation is also sometimes called the *potential equation*.

11.2 Time-Dependent Problems

Numerical methods for time-dependent PDEs typically use discrete time-stepping procedures to generate an approximate solution step-by-step in time, analogous to the methods for ODE initial value problems we considered in Chapter 9. The corresponding spatial discretization can be accomplished in a number of ways, some of the most common of which we will consider in this section. We will see that the relationship between the temporal and spatial discretizations is a crucial issue in producing meaningful results.

11.2.1 Semidiscrete Methods

One way to approximate the solution to a time-dependent PDE numerically is to discretize in space but leave the time variable continuous. This approach results in a system of ODEs, which can then be solved by the methods discussed in Chapter 9. For example, consider the heat equation

$$u_t = c\, u_{xx}, \qquad 0 \leq x \leq 1, \qquad t \geq 0,$$

with initial condition

$$u(0, x) = f(x), \qquad 0 \leq x \leq 1,$$

and boundary conditions

$$u(t, 0) = 0, \qquad u(t, 1) = 0, \qquad t \geq 0.$$

If we introduce spatial mesh points $x_i = i\Delta x$, $i = 0, \ldots, n+1$, where $\Delta x = 1/(n+1)$, and replace the second derivative u_{xx} with the finite difference approximation

$$u_{xx}(t, x_i) \approx \frac{u(t, x_{i+1}) - 2u(t, x_i) + u(t, x_{i-1})}{(\Delta x)^2}, \quad i = 1, \ldots, n,$$

but leave the time variable continuous, then we obtain a system of ODEs

$$y_i'(t) = \frac{c}{(\Delta x)^2} \left(y_{i+1}(t) - 2y_i(t) + y_{i-1}(t) \right), \quad i = 1, \ldots, n,$$

where $y_i(t) \approx u(t, x_i)$. From the boundary conditions, $y_0(t)$ and $y_{n+1}(t)$ are identically zero, and from the initial conditions, $y_i(0) = f(x_i)$, $i = 1, \ldots, n$. We can therefore use an ODE method to solve the initial value problem for this system. This approach is sometimes called the *method of lines*. If we think of the solution $u(t, x)$ as a surface over the (t, x) plane, this method computes cross sections of that surface along a series of lines, each of which passes through one of the discrete spatial mesh points and runs parallel to the time axis (see Fig. 11.4).

The foregoing semidiscrete system of ODEs can be written in matrix form as

$$\boldsymbol{y}' = \frac{c}{(\Delta x)^2} \begin{bmatrix} -2 & 1 & 0 & \cdots & 0 \\ 1 & -2 & 1 & \cdots & 0 \\ 0 & 1 & -2 & \cdots & 0 \\ \vdots & \ddots & \ddots & \ddots & \vdots \\ 0 & \cdots & 0 & 1 & -2 \end{bmatrix} \boldsymbol{y} = \boldsymbol{A}\boldsymbol{y}.$$

The Jacobian matrix $\boldsymbol{A}$ of this system has eigenvalues between $-4c/(\Delta x)^2$ and 0, which makes the ODE very stiff as the spatial mesh size Δx becomes small. This stiffness, which is typical of ODEs derived from PDEs in this manner, must be taken into account in choosing an appropriate ODE method for solving the semidiscrete system (see Section 9.3.4).

Spatial discretization to convert a PDE into a system of ODEs can also be done by a spectral or finite element approach. As we did for two-point boundary problems for ODEs, we approximate the solution by a linear combination of basis functions, except that now the coefficients are time dependent. Thus, we seek an approximate solution of the form

$$u(t, x) \approx v(t, x, \boldsymbol{\alpha}(t)) = \sum_{j=1}^{n} \alpha_j(t)\phi_j(x),$$

where the $\phi_j(x)$, $j = 1, \ldots, n$, are a chosen set of basis functions defined on the spatial domain, and the $\alpha_j(t)$ are time-dependent coefficients to be determined. Using the method of collocation, we substitute this approximation into the PDE and require that the equation be satisfied exactly at a discrete set of collocation points x_i, $i = 1, \ldots, n$, within the spatial domain. For the heat equation, for example, this yields a system of ODEs

$$\sum_{j=1}^{n} \alpha_j'(t)\phi_j(x_i) = c \sum_{j=1}^{n} \alpha_j(t)\phi_j''(x_i), \quad i = 1, \ldots, n,$$

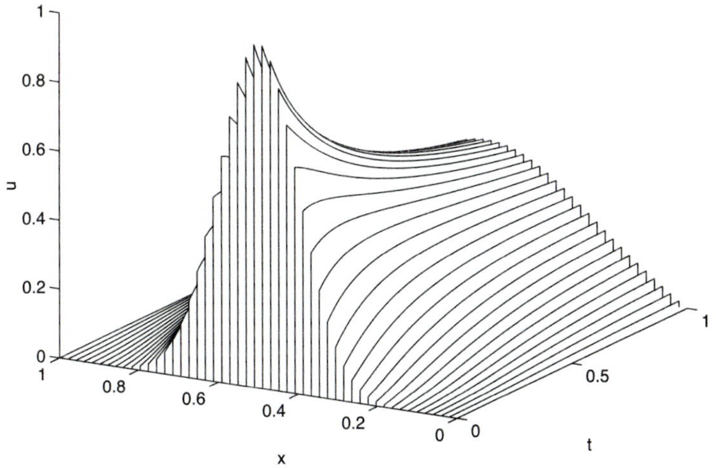

Figure 11.4: Method of lines solution of heat equation.

whose solution is the set of coefficient functions $\alpha_j(t)$, $j = 1, \ldots, n$, that determine the approximate solution v of the PDE. The implicit form of the foregoing system of ODEs is not the explicit form required by standard ODE methods, however, so we define the $n \times n$ matrices $\boldsymbol{M}$ and $\boldsymbol{N}$ by

$$m_{ij} = \phi_j(x_i), \qquad n_{ij} = \phi_j''(x_i), \qquad i, j = 1, \ldots, n.$$

Assuming the matrix $\boldsymbol{M}$ is nonsingular, we then obtain the system of ODEs

$$\boldsymbol{\alpha}'(t) = c\,\boldsymbol{M}^{-1}\boldsymbol{N}\boldsymbol{\alpha}(t),$$

which is in a form suitable for standard ODE software (as usual, the matrix $\boldsymbol{M}$ need not be inverted explicitly, but merely used to solve linear systems). We need an initial condition for this ODE, which we can obtain by requiring that the solution satisfy the given initial condition for the PDE at the spatial collocation points x_i, $i = 1, \ldots, n$.

The matrices arising in this method will be sparse if the basis functions are *local*, such as B-splines, which gives a *finite element method*. Alternatively, we could use basis functions with global support, such as Legendre or Chebyshev polynomials or trigonometric functions, which would give a *spectral* or *pseudospectral method*. With any choice of basis functions, we could also use a Galerkin method rather than collocation to determine the coefficients of the basis function expansion. In either case, as with finite difference methods, systems of ODEs arising from semidiscretization of a PDE in this manner tend to be stiff, which should be taken into account in choosing an appropriate ODE method for solving them.

Unlike the finite difference method, a spectral or finite element method does not produce approximate values of the solution u directly, but rather it generates a representation of the approximate solution as a linear combination of basis functions. The basis functions depend only on the spatial variable, but the coefficients of the linear combination (given by the solution to the system of ODEs) are time dependent. Thus, for any given time t, the corresponding linear combination of basis functions generates a cross section of the solution surface parallel to the spatial axis.

11.2.2 Fully Discrete Methods

In a fully discrete method, all of the independent variables in the PDE are discretized, including time. In a fully discrete finite difference method, we introduce a grid of mesh points throughout the problem domain in space and time, we replace all the derivatives in the PDE by finite difference approximations, and we seek an approximate value for the solution at each of the mesh points. The resulting array of approximate solution values represents a discrete sample of points on the solution surface over the problem domain in the (t, x) plane. The accuracy of such an approximate solution depends on the step sizes in both space and time.

Replacement of all partial derivatives by finite difference approximations results in a system of algebraic equations for the unknown solution values at the discrete set of mesh points. This system may be linear or nonlinear, depending on the underlying PDE. With an initial-value problem, the solution is obtained by beginning with the initial values along an appropriate boundary of the problem domain and then marching forward step by step in time, generating successive rows in the solution array. Such a time-stepping procedure may be explicit or implicit, depending on whether the formula for the solution values at the next time step involves only current and past information.

Example 11.2 Heat Equation. Consider the *heat equation*

$$u_t = c\,u_{xx}, \qquad 0 \le x \le 1, \qquad t \ge 0,$$

with initial condition

$$u(0,x) = f(x), \qquad 0 \le x \le 1,$$

and boundary conditions

$$u(t,0) = \alpha, \qquad u(t,1) = \beta, \qquad t \ge 0.$$

We define spatial mesh points $x_i = i\Delta x$, $i = 0, 1, \ldots, n+1$, where $\Delta x = 1/(n+1)$, and temporal mesh points $t_k = k\Delta t$, $k = 0, 1, \ldots$, where Δt is chosen appropriately. We denote the approximate solution at mesh point (t_k, x_i) by u_i^k, where we have used both a subscript and a superscript (the latter is *not* an exponent) to distinguish clearly between increments in space and time, respectively. Replacing u_t by a forward difference approximation and u_{xx} by a centered difference approximation in the heat equation yields a system of algebraic equations

$$\frac{u_i^{k+1} - u_i^k}{\Delta t} = c\,\frac{u_{i+1}^k - 2u_i^k + u_{i-1}^k}{(\Delta x)^2}, \quad i = 1, \ldots, n,$$

which can be rearranged to give the recurrence

$$u_i^{k+1} = u_i^k + c\,\frac{\Delta t}{(\Delta x)^2}\left(u_{i+1}^k - 2u_i^k + u_{i-1}^k\right), \quad i = 1, \ldots, n.$$

The initial conditions provide starting values $u_i^0 = f(x_i)$, $i = 1, \ldots, n$, from which we can march the approximate solution forward step by step in time using the foregoing recurrence, with the boundary conditions providing the necessary values $u_0^k = \alpha$ and $u_{n+1}^k = \beta$ for each k. The local truncation error of this scheme is $\mathcal{O}(\Delta t) + \mathcal{O}((\Delta x)^2)$, so we say that the scheme is first-order accurate in time and second-order accurate in space.

This time-stepping scheme is *explicit* because the approximate solution values at any given time step depend only on values that are available from the previous time step. The pattern of mesh points involved in computing u_i^{k+1} is illustrated in Fig. 11.5a, where lines connect the relevant mesh points and an arrow indicates the mesh point at which the approximate solution is being computed. Such a pattern is called the *stencil* of a given finite difference scheme.

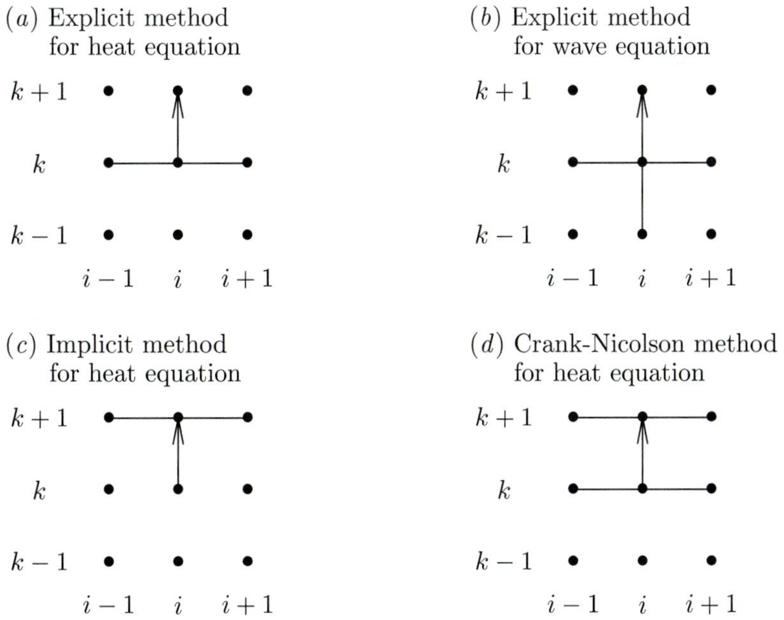

Figure 11.5: Stencils of finite difference methods for time-dependent problems.

Example 11.3 Wave Equation. Next consider the *wave equation*

$$u_{tt} = c\,u_{xx}, \qquad 0 \le x \le 1, \qquad t \ge 0,$$

with initial conditions

$$u(0,x) = f(x), \qquad u_t(0,x) = g(x), \qquad 0 \le x \le 1,$$

and boundary conditions

$$u(t,0) = \alpha, \qquad u(t,1) = \beta, \qquad t \ge 0.$$

Defining spatial and temporal mesh points as in Example 11.2, and using centered difference approximations for both u_{tt} and u_{xx} yields a system of algebraic equations

$$\frac{u_i^{k+1} - 2u_i^k + u_i^{k-1}}{(\Delta t)^2} = c\,\frac{u_{i+1}^k - 2u_i^k + u_{i-1}^k}{(\Delta x)^2}, \qquad i = 1, \dots, n,$$

which can be rearranged to give the explicit recurrence

$$u_i^{k+1} = 2u_i^k - u_i^{k-1} + c\left(\frac{\Delta t}{\Delta x}\right)^2 \left(u_{i+1}^k - 2u_i^k + u_{i-1}^k\right), \qquad i = 1, \dots, n,$$

whose stencil is shown in Fig. 11.5*b*. This scheme is second-order accurate in both space and time, but it requires data at two successive time levels, which means that additional storage is required, and it also means that we need both u_i^0 and u_i^1 initially to get started. These values can be obtained from the initial conditions

$$u_i^0 = f(x_i), \qquad u_i^1 = u_i^0 + \Delta t\, g(x_i), \qquad i = 1, \dots, n,$$

where in the latter we have used a forward difference approximation to the initial condition $u_t(0,x) = g(x)$, $0 \le x \le 1$.

In principle, there is no real distinction between discrete and semidiscrete methods for time-dependent PDEs, since the time variable is ultimately discretized in either case. There is an important practical distinction, however, in that with a semidiscrete method we entrust to a sophisticated, adaptive ODE software package the responsibility for choosing time step sizes that will maintain stability and attain the desired accuracy, whereas with a fully discrete method, the user must explicitly choose time step sizes to achieve these same goals. For example, the fully discrete finite difference scheme for the heat equation given in Example 11.2 is simply Euler's method applied to the semidiscrete system of ODEs derived for this problem using finite difference spatial discretization in Section 11.2.1. The stability region for Euler's method (see Section 9.3.2) requires for this particular problem that the eigenvalues of $\Delta t \boldsymbol{A}$ must lie inside a circle in the complex plane of radius 1 centered at -1, where the matrix $\boldsymbol{A}$ is as defined in Section 11.2.1, and therefore we must have

$$\Delta t \le \frac{(\Delta x)^2}{2\,c}$$

in order for this finite difference scheme to be stable. We conclude that in general the step sizes in time and space cannot be chosen independently of each other, and in this particular instance the stability restriction on the time step size is quite severe.

As with ODEs, a larger stability region that permits larger time steps can be obtained by using implicit methods. For the heat equation, for example, applying the backward Euler method to the semidiscrete system from Section 11.2.1 yields the implicit finite difference scheme

$$u_i^{k+1} = u_i^k + c\,\frac{\Delta t}{(\Delta x)^2}\left(u_{i+1}^{k+1} - 2u_i^{k+1} + u_{i-1}^{k+1}\right), \quad i = 1, \ldots, n,$$

whose stencil is shown in Fig. 11.5*c*. This scheme inherits the unconditional stability of the backward Euler method, which means that there is no stability restriction on the relative sizes of Δt and Δx. Accuracy is still a consideration, however, and the fact that this particular method is only first-order accurate in time still strongly limits the time step. If instead we apply the trapezoid method we obtain the implicit finite difference scheme

$$u_i^{k+1} = u_i^k + c\,\frac{\Delta t}{2(\Delta x)^2}\left(u_{i+1}^{k+1} - 2u_i^{k+1} + u_{i-1}^{k+1} + u_{i+1}^k - 2u_i^k + u_{i-1}^k\right), \quad i = 1, \ldots, n,$$

whose stencil is shown in Fig. 11.5*d*. This scheme, called the *Crank-Nicolson method*, is unconditionally stable and is second-order accurate in time as well as in space.

The greater stability of implicit finite difference methods enables them to take much larger time steps than are permissible with explicit methods, but they require more work per step because we must solve a system of equations at each step to determine the approximate solution values. For both the backward Euler and Crank-Nicolson methods for the heat equation in one space dimension, the linear system to be solved at each step is tridiagonal, and thus both the work and the storage required are modest. In higher dimensions the matrix of the linear system does not have such a simple form, but it is still very sparse, with nonzeros in a very regular pattern. We will discuss methods for solving such linear systems in Sections 11.4 and 11.5.

We have now seen a variety of finite difference schemes for the heat and wave equations, but how do we know that the approximate solutions they produce bear any relation to the true solutions of the corresponding PDEs? We do not expect an approximate solution to be exactly correct, of course, but we would hope to obtain arbitrarily good accuracy by taking sufficiently small step sizes in time and space. The finite difference scheme must have the following two important properties in order for the approximate solution to converge to the true solution of the PDE as the step sizes in time and space jointly go to zero:

- *Consistency*: the local truncation error goes to zero
- *Stability*: the approximate solution at any fixed time t remains bounded

Note that stability in this context concerns what happens as $\Delta t \to 0$, not as $t \to \infty$. The *Lax Equivalence Theorem* says that for a well-posed linear PDE, consistency and stability are together a necessary and sufficient condition for a finite difference scheme to converge to the true solution of the PDE. Neither condition alone is sufficient to guarantee convergence.

The consistency of a finite difference scheme is usually fairly easy to verify using a Taylor series expansion, but stability can be more challenging to establish. One approach to stability analysis, the *matrix method*, is based on the locations of the eigenvalues of the matrix representation of the finite difference scheme (provided the matrix is normal). We used this method in Section 11.2.1 to determine the stability of Euler's method for the heat equation. Another approach is the *Fourier method*, in which a Fourier series (complex exponential) representation of the solution error is substituted into the difference equation and then analyzed for growth or decay.

A useful stability criterion for explicit finite difference schemes for hyperbolic PDEs is based on the relationship between the *domains of dependence* of the PDE and of the finite difference scheme. The domain of dependence of the PDE for a given point is that portion of the problem domain that influences the solution at the given point, which in turn is determined by the characteristics of the PDE. For the advection equation, for example, the characteristic line through the origin in Fig. 11.2 (left) is the domain of dependence for the point at the apex of the shaded triangle. Similarly, the domain of dependence of a finite difference scheme for a given mesh point is the set of all other mesh points that affect the approximate solution at the given mesh point. A necessary condition for an explicit finite difference scheme for a hyperbolic PDE to be stable is the *CFL condition* (named for its originators, Courant, Friedrichs, and Lewy), which says that for each mesh point the domain of dependence of the PDE must lie *within* the domain of dependence of the finite difference scheme.

Example 11.4 CFL Condition. Consider the explicit finite difference scheme for the wave equation given in Example 11.3, whose stencil is shown in Fig. 11.5*b*. Use of the chain rule shows that $\psi(x + \sqrt{c}\,t)$ and $\psi(x - \sqrt{c}\,t)$ are solutions to the wave equation for any twice differentiable function ψ, so the characteristics of the wave equation are the straight lines in the (t, x) plane along which either $x + \sqrt{c}\,t$ or $x - \sqrt{c}\,t$ is constant. The domain of dependence of the wave equation for a given point is therefore a triangle with apex at the given point and with sides of slope $1/\sqrt{c}$ and $-1/\sqrt{c}$, as shown in Fig. 11.6*a*. According to the CFL condition, in order for the finite difference scheme to be stable, its domain of dependence (the shaded regions and below in Fig. 11.6*b* and *c*) must contain the domain of dependence of the PDE, which in this instance means that the step sizes must satisfy the inequality

$$\Delta t \leq \frac{\Delta x}{\sqrt{c}}.$$

The choice of step sizes shown in Fig. 11.6*b* violates this constraint, making the scheme unstable. In Fig. 11.6*c* a smaller value of Δt for the same Δx satisfies the CFL condition and yields a stable scheme.

Finally, note that centered finite difference approximations, though preferred in many contexts for their higher accuracy, may not be appropriate when the solution

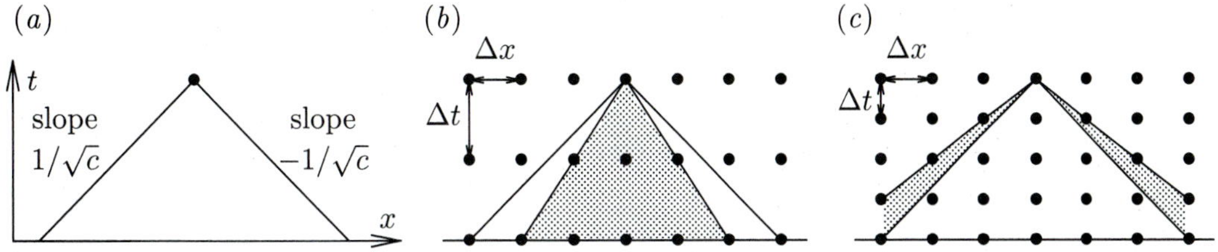

Figure 11.6: Domains of dependence for wave equation (a) and unstable (b) and stable (c) finite difference schemes.

of a PDE has a strong directional orientation and a potential for sharp fronts or shocks, as in the one-way propagation of the advection equation, for example. In such circumstances, centered finite difference schemes tend to produce unwanted oscillations in the numerical solution, and a better choice is *upwind differencing*, using a one-sided difference scheme whose sample points lie on the side from which the front is coming.

11.3 Time-Independent Problems

Just as time-dependent parabolic and hyperbolic PDEs are analogous to the initial-value problems for ODEs we considered in Chapter 9, time-independent elliptic PDEs are analogous to the boundary-value problems for ODEs we considered in Chapter 10, and most of the solution methods we saw for ODE BVPs carry over to elliptic PDEs as well. For an elliptic boundary value problem, the solution at every point in the problem domain depends on *all* of the boundary data (in contrast to the limited domain of dependence for time-dependent problems), and consequently an approximate solution must be computed everywhere simultaneously, rather than being generated step by step using a recurrence, as in Section 11.2.2. Consequently, discretization of an elliptic boundary value problem results in a single system of algebraic equations to be solved for some finite-dimensional approximation to the solution.

11.3.1 Finite Difference Methods

Finite difference methods for elliptic boundary value problems proceed as we have seen before: we define a discrete mesh of points within the problem domain and replace the derivatives in the PDE by finite difference approximations, but then we seek a numerical solution at all of the mesh points simultaneously by solving a single system of algebraic equations.

Example 11.5 Laplace Equation. Consider the *Laplace equation* on the unit square

$$u_{xx} + u_{yy} = 0, \qquad 0 \le x \le 1, \qquad 0 \le y \le 1,$$

with boundary conditions as shown on the left in Fig. 11.7. We define a discrete mesh in the domain, including boundaries, as shown on the right in Fig. 11.7. The interior grid points where we will compute the approximate solution are given by

$$(x_i, y_j) = (ih, jh), \quad i, j = 1, \dots, n,$$

where in our example $n = 2$ and $h = 1/(n+1) = 1/3$. Next we replace the second derivatives in the equation with the standard second-order centered difference approximation at each interior mesh point to obtain the finite difference equations

$$\frac{u_{i+1,j} - 2u_{i,j} + u_{i-1,j}}{h^2} + \frac{u_{i,j+1} - 2u_{i,j} + u_{i,j-1}}{h^2} = 0, \quad i, j = 1, \dots, n,$$

where $u_{i,j}$ is an approximation to the true solution $u(x_i, y_j)$ and represents one of the given boundary values if i or j is 0 or $n+1$. Simplifying and writing out the resulting four equations explicitly, we obtain

$$\begin{aligned}
4u_{1,1} - u_{0,1} - u_{2,1} - u_{1,0} - u_{1,2} &= 0, \\
4u_{2,1} - u_{1,1} - u_{3,1} - u_{2,0} - u_{2,2} &= 0, \\
4u_{1,2} - u_{0,2} - u_{2,2} - u_{1,1} - u_{1,3} &= 0, \\
4u_{2,2} - u_{1,2} - u_{3,2} - u_{2,1} - u_{2,3} &= 0.
\end{aligned}$$

Writing these four equations in matrix form, we obtain

$$\boldsymbol{Ax} = \begin{bmatrix} 4 & -1 & -1 & 0 \\ -1 & 4 & 0 & -1 \\ -1 & 0 & 4 & -1 \\ 0 & -1 & -1 & 4 \end{bmatrix} \begin{bmatrix} u_{1,1} \\ u_{2,1} \\ u_{1,2} \\ u_{2,2} \end{bmatrix} = \begin{bmatrix} u_{0,1} + u_{1,0} \\ u_{3,1} + u_{2,0} \\ u_{0,2} + u_{1,3} \\ u_{3,2} + u_{2,3} \end{bmatrix} = \begin{bmatrix} 0 \\ 0 \\ 1 \\ 1 \end{bmatrix} = \boldsymbol{b}.$$

This symmetric positive definite system of linear equations can be solved either by Cholesky factorization or by an iterative method, yielding the solution

$$\boldsymbol{x} = \begin{bmatrix} u_{1,1} \\ u_{2,1} \\ u_{1,2} \\ u_{2,2} \end{bmatrix} = \begin{bmatrix} 0.125 \\ 0.125 \\ 0.375 \\ 0.375 \end{bmatrix}.$$

Note the symmetry in the solution, which reflects the symmetry in the problem, which we could have taken advantage of and solved a problem only half as large.

In a practical problem, the mesh size h would need to be much smaller to achieve acceptable accuracy in the approximate solution of the PDE, and the resulting linear system would be much larger than in the preceding example. The matrix would be very sparse, however, since each equation would still involve at most only five of the variables, thereby saving substantially on work and storage. We can be a bit more specific about the nonzero pattern of the matrix of such a linear system. We have already seen in Section 10.4 how this type of finite difference method on a one-dimensional grid yields a tridiagonal system. A rectangular two-dimensional grid

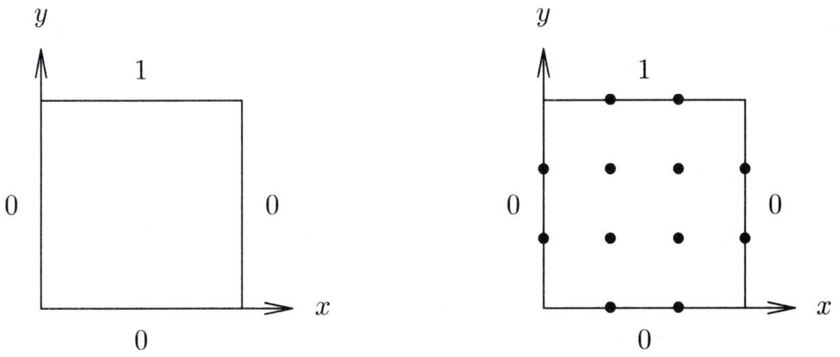

Figure 11.7: Boundary conditions (left) and mesh (right) for Laplace equation example.

can be thought of as a one-dimensional grid of one-dimensional grids. Thus, with a row- or column-wise ordering of the grid points, the corresponding matrix will be *block tridiagonal*, with each nonzero block being tridiagonal or diagonal. Such a pattern is barely evident in the matrix of the previous example, where the blocks are only 2×2; for a slightly larger example, where the pattern is more evident, see Fig. 11.8. This pattern generalizes to a three-dimensional grid, which can be viewed as a one-dimensional grid of two-dimensional grids, so that the matrix would be block tridiagonal, with the nonzero blocks again being block tridiagonal, and their nonzero subblocks in turn being tridiagonal. Of course, for a less regular grid or mesh, or a more complicated finite difference stencil, the pattern would not be so simple, but sparsity would still prevail owing to the local connectivity among the grid points.

11.3.2 Finite Element Methods

In Chapter 10 we considered finite element methods for solving boundary value problems for ODEs. Finite element methods are also applicable to boundary value problems for PDEs as well. There is no change conceptually in going from one dimension to two or three dimensions: the solution is still represented as a linear combination of basis functions, and some criterion (e.g., Galerkin) is applied to derive a system of equations that determines the coefficients of the linear combination.

The main practical difference is that instead of subintervals in one dimension, the elements become triangles or quadrilaterals in two dimensions, and tetrahedra or hexahedra in three dimensions. Additional complications can occur, such as dealing with curved boundaries. Typical basis functions include bilinear or bicubic functions in two dimensions and trilinear or tricubic functions in three dimensions, analogous to "hat" functions and piecewise cubics in one dimension. Increasing dimensionality means that the linear system to be solved will be much larger, but it is still sparse owing to the local support of the basis functions. Finite element methods for PDEs are extremely flexible and powerful, but a detailed treatment of them is beyond the scope of this book. Spectral and pseudospectral methods are also applicable in two or more space dimensions, but again we will not go into details.

11.4 Direct Methods for Sparse Linear Systems

All types of boundary value problems, as well as implicit methods for time-dependent PDEs, give rise to systems of linear algebraic equations to solve. The use of finite difference schemes involving only a few variables each, or the use of localized basis functions in a finite element approach, causes the matrix of the linear system to be sparse. This sparsity can be exploited to reduce the storage and work required for solving the linear system to much less than the $\mathcal{O}(n^2)$ and $\mathcal{O}(n^3)$, respectively, that might be expected in a more naive approach. In this section we briefly consider direct methods for solving large sparse linear systems, and then in the following section we will discuss iterative methods for such systems in somewhat more detail.

11.4.1 Sparse Factorization Methods

Gaussian elimination and its variants such as Cholesky factorization for symmetric positive definite matrices are applicable to solving large sparse systems, but a great deal of care must be exercised to achieve reasonable efficiency in both solution time and storage requirements. The key to this efficiency is to store and operate on only the nonzero entries of the matrix. Thus, special data structures are required rather than the simple two-dimensional arrays that are so natural for storing dense matrices.

For one-dimensional problems, the equations and unknowns can usually be ordered so that the nonzeros are concentrated in a relatively narrow band, which can be stored efficiently in a rectangular two-dimensional array by diagonals. Algorithms are available for reducing the bandwidth, if necessary, by reordering the rows and columns of the matrix. But for problems in two or more dimensions, even the narrowest possible band often contains mostly zeros, and hence any type of two-dimensional array storage would be prohibitively wasteful. In general, sparse systems require data structures in which individual nonzero entries are stored, along with the indices required to identify their locations in the matrix. Explicitly storing the indices not only incurs additional storage overhead but also makes arithmetic operations on the nonzeros less efficient owing to the indirect addressing required to access the operands. Thus, such a representation is worthwhile only if the matrix is sufficiently sparse, which is often the case for very large problems arising from PDEs and many other applications.

When applied to a sparse matrix, LU or Cholesky factorization can be carried out in the usual manner, but taking linear combinations of rows or columns to annihilate nonzero entries can introduce new nonzeros into locations in the matrix that were initially zero. Such new nonzeros, called *fill*, must then be stored and, depending on their locations, may eventually be annihilated themselves in order to obtain the triangular factors. In any case, the resulting triangular factors can be expected to contain at least as many nonzeros as the original matrix and usually a significant amount of fill as well. The amount of fill incurred is very sensitive to the order in which the rows and columns of the matrix are processed, so one of the central problems in sparse factorization is to reorder the original matrix to limit the amount of fill that the matrix suffers during factorization. Exact minimization of fill turns out to be a very hard combinatorial problem (NP-complete), but heuristic algorithms are available, such as minimum degree and nested dissection, that do a good job of limiting fill for many types of problems. We sketch these algorithms briefly in the following example; see [104, 151] for further details.

Example 11.6 Sparse Factorization. To illustrate sparse factorization, we consider a matrix arising from a typical two-dimensional elliptic boundary value problem, the Laplace equation on the unit square (see Example 11.5). A 3×3 grid of interior mesh points is shown on the left in Fig. 11.8, with the points, or *nodes*, numbered in a natural, row-wise order. The Laplace equation is then approximated by a system of linear equations using the standard second-order centered finite difference approximation to the second derivatives. In the diagram, a pair of nodes is connected by a line, or *edge*, if both appear in the same equation in this system. We say that two nodes are *neighbors* if they are connected by an edge.

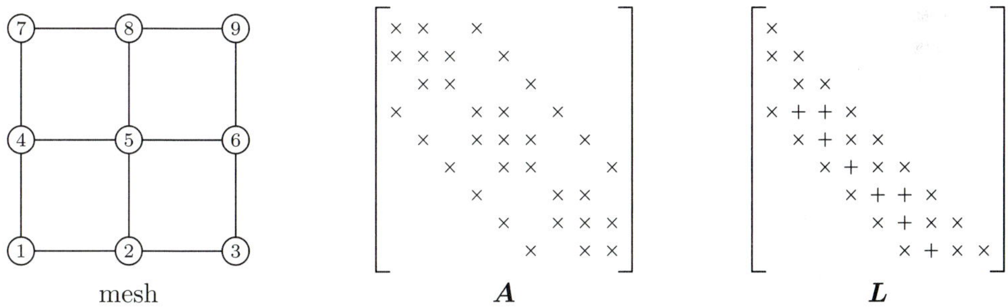

Figure 11.8: Finite difference mesh and nonzero patterns of corresponding sparse matrix $\boldsymbol{A}$ and its Cholesky factor $\boldsymbol{L}$.

The nonzero pattern of the 9×9 symmetric positive definite matrix $\boldsymbol{A}$ of this linear system is shown in the center of Fig. 11.8, where a nonzero entry of the matrix is indicated by $\times$ and zero entries are blank. The diagonal entries of the matrix correspond to the nodes in the mesh, and the nonzero off-diagonal entries correspond to the edges in the mesh (i.e., $a_{ij} \neq 0 \Leftrightarrow$ nodes i and j are neighbors). Note that the matrix is banded, but it also has many zero entries inside the band. More specifically, the matrix is block tridiagonal, with each nonzero block being either tridiagonal or diagonal, as expected for a row- or column-wise ordering of a two-dimensional grid. Cholesky factorization of the matrix in this ordering fills in the band almost completely, as shown on the right in Fig. 11.8, where fill entries (new nonzeros) are indicated by $+$. We will see that there are other orderings in which the matrix suffers considerably less fill.

Each step in the factorization process corresponds to the elimination of a node from the mesh. Eliminating a node causes all of its neighboring nodes to become connected to each other. If any such neighbors were not already connected, then *fill* results (i.e., new edges in the mesh and new nonzeros in the matrix). Thus, a good heuristic for limiting fill is to eliminate first those nodes having fewest neighbors. The number of neighbors of a given node is called its *degree*, so this heuristic is known as *minimum degree*. At each step, the minimum degree algorithm selects for elimination a node of smallest degree, breaking ties arbitrarily. After the node has been eliminated, its former neighbors all become connected to each other, so the degrees of some nodes may change. The process is then repeated, with a new node of minimum degree eliminated next, and so on until all nodes have been eliminated. A minimum degree ordering for our example problem is shown in Fig. 11.9, along with the correspondingly permuted matrix and resulting Cholesky factor. Although there is no obvious pattern to the nonzeros in the reordered matrix, the Cholesky factor suffers much less fill than with the band ordering. This difference is much more pronounced in larger problems, and more sophisticated variants of the minimum degree algorithm are among the most effective general-purpose ordering algorithms known.

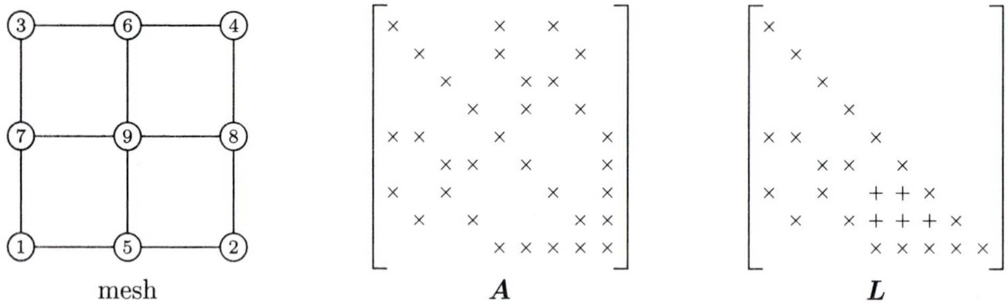

Figure 11.9: Finite difference mesh reordered by minimum degree, with nonzero patterns of correspondingly permuted sparse matrix $\boldsymbol{A}$ and its Cholesky factor $\boldsymbol{L}$.

Nested dissection is a divide-and-conquer strategy for determining a good ordering to limit fill in sparse factorization. First, a small set of nodes whose removal splits the mesh into two pieces of roughly equal size is selected, and these *separator* nodes are numbered *last*. Then the process is repeated recursively on each remaining piece of the mesh until all nodes have been numbered. A nested dissection ordering for our example problem is shown in Fig. 11.10, along with the correspondingly permuted matrix and resulting Cholesky factor. Separating the mesh into two pieces means that no node in either piece is connected to any node in the other, and hence no fill can occur in either piece as a consequence of the elimination of a node in the other. In other words, dissection induces blocks of zeros in the matrix (indicated by the squares in Fig. 11.10) that are automatically preserved during factorization, thereby limiting fill. The recursive nature of the algorithm can be seen in the hierarchical block structure of the matrix, which would involve many more levels in a larger problem.

Sparse factorization methods are accurate, reliable, and robust. They are the methods of choice for one-dimensional problems and are usually competitive for two-dimensional problems, but they can be prohibitively expensive in both work and storage for very large three-dimensional problems. We will see that iterative methods provide a viable alternative in these cases.

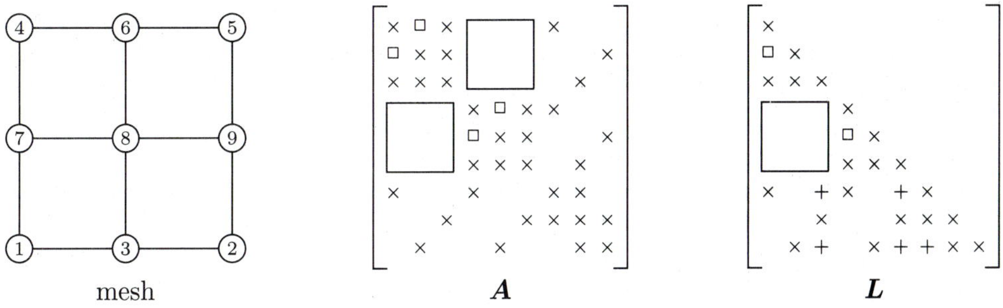

Figure 11.10: Finite difference mesh reordered by nested dissection, with nonzero patterns of correspondingly permuted sparse matrix $\boldsymbol{A}$ and its Cholesky factor $\boldsymbol{L}$.

11.4.2 Fast Direct Methods

For certain types of PDEs, special techniques can be used to solve the resulting discretized linear system much faster than would be expected. For example, for certain elliptic boundary value problems having constant coefficients and simple boundaries (e.g., the Poisson equation on a rectangular domain), the fast Fourier transform, or FFT (see Chapter 12), can be used to compute the solution to the discrete system very efficiently, provided that the number of mesh points in each dimension is a power of two. This technique is the basis for several "fast Poisson solver" software packages. For a problem with n mesh points, such a fast Poisson solver computes the solution in $\mathcal{O}(n \log_2 n)$ operations, which is nearly optimal since the cost of simply writing the output is $\mathcal{O}(n)$.

Somewhat more generally, for separable elliptic PDEs the method of *cyclic reduction* permits similarly fast solutions. Cyclic reduction is a divide-and-conquer technique in which the even-numbered equations in the system are solved in terms of the odd-numbered ones, and so on recursively until reaching the bottom of the recursion, where single equations can be solved trivially. This idea obviously works best when the order of the system is a power of two, but it can be adapted to handle systems of arbitrary order. These ideas—FFT and cyclic reduction—can be combined, for example using FFT in one dimension and cyclic reduction in the other. A more subtle combination results in the FACR (Fourier analysis/cyclic reduction) method, which is even faster than either the FFT method or the cyclic reduction method alone. The computational complexity of the FACR method is $\mathcal{O}(n \log \log n)$, which is effectively optimal, since log log is essentially constant for problems of any reasonable size.

11.5 Iterative Methods for Linear Systems

The direct methods for solving linear systems that we considered in Chapter 2 and Section 11.4.1 compute the exact solution, subject only to the effects of rounding error, in a finite number of steps. This seems a desirable property, but the price paid in work and storage can be prohibitive for very large linear systems. By contrast, iterative methods for solving linear systems begin with an initial estimate for the solution and successively improve it until the solution is as accurate as desired. In theory, an infinite number of iterations might be required to converge to the exact solution, but in practice the iteration terminates when some measure of the error, typically some norm of the residual, is as small as desired. Provided they converge rapidly enough, iterative methods have several significant advantages over direct methods, as we will see.

11.5.1 Stationary Iterative Methods

Perhaps the simplest type of iterative method for solving a linear system $\boldsymbol{A}\boldsymbol{x} = \boldsymbol{b}$ has the form

$$\boldsymbol{x}_{k+1} = \boldsymbol{G}\boldsymbol{x}_k + \boldsymbol{c},$$

where the matrix $\boldsymbol{G}$ and vector $\boldsymbol{c}$ are chosen so that a fixed point of the function $\boldsymbol{g}(\boldsymbol{x}) = \boldsymbol{G}\boldsymbol{x} + \boldsymbol{c}$ is a solution to $\boldsymbol{A}\boldsymbol{x} = \boldsymbol{b}$. Such a method is said to be *stationary* if $\boldsymbol{G}$ and $\boldsymbol{c}$ are constant over all iterations.

One way to obtain a suitable matrix $\boldsymbol{G}$ is by a *splitting*, in which the matrix $\boldsymbol{A}$ is written as

$$\boldsymbol{A} = \boldsymbol{M} - \boldsymbol{N},$$

with $\boldsymbol{M}$ nonsingular. We can then take $\boldsymbol{G} = \boldsymbol{M}^{-1}\boldsymbol{N}$ and $\boldsymbol{c} = \boldsymbol{M}^{-1}\boldsymbol{b}$, so that the iteration scheme becomes

$$\boldsymbol{x}_{k+1} = \boldsymbol{M}^{-1}\boldsymbol{N}\boldsymbol{x}_k + \boldsymbol{M}^{-1}\boldsymbol{b},$$

which is implemented as

$$\boldsymbol{M}\boldsymbol{x}_{k+1} = \boldsymbol{N}\boldsymbol{x}_k + \boldsymbol{b},$$

so that we solve a linear system with matrix $\boldsymbol{M}$ at each iteration. Formally, this splitting scheme is a fixed-point iteration with iteration function

$$\boldsymbol{g}(\boldsymbol{x}) = \boldsymbol{M}^{-1}\boldsymbol{N}\boldsymbol{x} + \boldsymbol{M}^{-1}\boldsymbol{b},$$

whose Jacobian matrix is

$$\boldsymbol{G}(\boldsymbol{x}) = \boldsymbol{M}^{-1}\boldsymbol{N}.$$

Thus, the iteration scheme is convergent if the spectral radius

$$\rho(\boldsymbol{G}) = \rho(\boldsymbol{M}^{-1}\boldsymbol{N}) < 1,$$

and the smaller $\rho(\boldsymbol{G})$, the faster the convergence (see Section 5.6.1).

For rapid convergence, we should choose $\boldsymbol{M}$ and $\boldsymbol{N}$ so that $\rho(\boldsymbol{M}^{-1}\boldsymbol{N})$ is as small as possible. There is a tradeoff, however, as the cost per iteration is determined by the cost of solving a linear system with matrix $\boldsymbol{M}$. As an extreme example, if $\boldsymbol{M} = \boldsymbol{A}$, then the scheme converges in a single iteration (i.e., we have a direct method), but that one iteration may be prohibitively expensive. In practice, $\boldsymbol{M}$ is chosen to approximate $\boldsymbol{A}$ in some sense, but is usually constrained to have some simple form, such as diagonal or triangular, so that the linear system at each iteration is easy to solve.

Example 11.7 Iterative Refinement. We have already seen one example of a stationary iterative method, namely, *iterative refinement* of a solution already computed by Gaussian elimination (see Section 2.4.10). Forward- and back-substitution using the LU factorization in effect provide an approximation, call it $\boldsymbol{B}^{-1}$, to the inverse of $\boldsymbol{A}$ (i.e., for any right-hand-side vector $\boldsymbol{y}$, the solution $\boldsymbol{B}^{-1}\boldsymbol{y}$ can be computed by forward- and back-substitution using the LU factors already computed). Iterative refinement then has the form

$$\boldsymbol{x}_{k+1} = \boldsymbol{x}_k + \boldsymbol{B}^{-1}(\boldsymbol{b} - \boldsymbol{A}\boldsymbol{x}_k),$$

which can be rewritten

$$\boldsymbol{x}_{k+1} = (\boldsymbol{I} - \boldsymbol{B}^{-1}\boldsymbol{A})\boldsymbol{x}_k + \boldsymbol{B}^{-1}\boldsymbol{b}.$$

Thus, iterative refinement is a stationary iterative method with $\boldsymbol{G} = \boldsymbol{I} - \boldsymbol{B}^{-1}\boldsymbol{A}$ and $\boldsymbol{c} = \boldsymbol{B}^{-1}\boldsymbol{b}$. The scheme therefore converges if $\rho(\boldsymbol{I} - \boldsymbol{B}^{-1}\boldsymbol{A}) < 1$, which should be the case if $\boldsymbol{B}^{-1}$ is a good approximation to $\boldsymbol{A}^{-1}$, such as the use of forward- and back-substitution with the LU factors obtained by Gaussian elimination with partial pivoting. Indeed, the convergence condition may be satisfied even by a rather poor approximation to the inverse. For example, iterative refinement can sometimes be used to stabilize "fast but risky" algorithms, such as Gaussian elimination without pivoting.

11.5.2 Jacobi Method

The simplest choice for $\boldsymbol{M}$ in the matrix splitting $\boldsymbol{A} = \boldsymbol{M} - \boldsymbol{N}$ is a diagonal matrix, specifically the diagonal of $\boldsymbol{A}$. Let $\boldsymbol{D}$ be a diagonal matrix with the same diagonal entries as $\boldsymbol{A}$, and let $\boldsymbol{L}$ and $\boldsymbol{U}$ be the strict lower and upper triangular portions of $\boldsymbol{A}$, respectively, so that

$$\boldsymbol{M} = \boldsymbol{D}, \qquad \boldsymbol{N} = -(\boldsymbol{L} + \boldsymbol{U})$$

gives a splitting of $\boldsymbol{A}$. If $\boldsymbol{A}$ has no zero diagonal entries, so that $\boldsymbol{D}$ is nonsingular, then we obtain the iterative scheme known as the *Jacobi method*:

$$\boldsymbol{x}^{(k+1)} = \boldsymbol{D}^{-1}\left(\boldsymbol{b} - (\boldsymbol{L} + \boldsymbol{U})\boldsymbol{x}^{(k)}\right).$$

(We use parenthesized superscripts for the iteration index when we need to reserve subscripts to refer to individual components of a vector.) Writing out this scheme for each individual solution component, we see that, beginning with an initial guess $\boldsymbol{x}^{(0)}$, the Jacobi method computes the next iterate by solving for each component of $\boldsymbol{x}$ in terms of the others:

$$x_i^{(k+1)} = \frac{b_i - \sum_{j \neq i} a_{ij} x_j^{(k)}}{a_{ii}}, \qquad i = 1, \ldots, n.$$

Note that the Jacobi method requires double storage for the vector $\boldsymbol{x}$ because all of the old component values are needed throughout the sweep, and therefore the new component values cannot overwrite them until the sweep has been completed.

To illustrate the Jacobi method, if we apply it to the system of finite difference equations approximating the Laplace equation in Example 11.5, we obtain

$$u_{i,j}^{(k+1)} = \frac{u_{i-1,j}^{(k)} + u_{i,j-1}^{(k)} + u_{i+1,j}^{(k)} + u_{i,j+1}^{(k)}}{4},$$

which means that at each grid point the new approximate solution is simply the average of the previous solution components at the four neighboring grid points. In this sense, solving the elliptic problem by an iterative method adds a timelike dimension (analogous to a parabolic problem, in this case the heat equation) in which the initial guess for the solution "diffuses" until a steady state is reached at the final solution.

The Jacobi method does not always converge, but it is guaranteed to converge under conditions that are often satisfied in practice (e.g., if the matrix is diagonally dominant by rows). Unfortunately, the convergence rate of the Jacobi method is usually unacceptably slow (see Section 11.5.6).

11.5.3 Gauss-Seidel Method

One reason for the slow convergence of the Jacobi method is that it does not make use of the latest information available: new component values are used only after the entire sweep has been completed. The *Gauss-Seidel method* remedies this drawback by using each new component of the solution as soon as it has been computed:

$$x_i^{(k+1)} = \frac{b_i - \sum_{j<i} a_{ij} x_j^{(k+1)} - \sum_{j>i} a_{ij} x_j^{(k)}}{a_{ii}}, \qquad i = 1, \ldots, n.$$

Using the same notation as in Section 11.5.2, the Gauss-Seidel method can be written in matrix terms as

$$\begin{aligned} \boldsymbol{x}^{(k+1)} &= \boldsymbol{D}^{-1}(\boldsymbol{b} - \boldsymbol{L}\boldsymbol{x}^{(k+1)} - \boldsymbol{U}\boldsymbol{x}^{(k)}) \\ &= (\boldsymbol{D} + \boldsymbol{L})^{-1}(\boldsymbol{b} - \boldsymbol{U}\boldsymbol{x}^{(k)}), \end{aligned}$$

and hence corresponds to the splitting

$$\boldsymbol{M} = \boldsymbol{D} + \boldsymbol{L}, \qquad \boldsymbol{N} = -\boldsymbol{U}.$$

In addition to faster convergence, another benefit of the Gauss-Seidel method is that duplicate storage is not needed for the vector $\boldsymbol{x}$, since the newly computed component values can overwrite the old ones immediately (a programmer would have used this method in the first place because of its more natural and convenient implementation). On the other hand, the updating of the unknowns must now be done successively, in contrast to the Jacobi method, in which the unknowns can be updated in any order or even simultaneously. The latter feature may make the Jacobi method preferable on a parallel computer.

To illustrate the Gauss-Seidel method, if we apply it to the system of finite difference equations approximating the Laplace equation in Example 11.5, we obtain

$$u_{i,j}^{(k+1)} = \frac{u_{i-1,j}^{(k+1)} + u_{i,j-1}^{(k+1)} + u_{i+1,j}^{(k)} + u_{i,j+1}^{(k)}}{4},$$

assuming that we sweep from left to right and bottom to top in the grid. Thus, we again average the solution values at the four surrounding grid points, but we always use each new component value as soon as it becomes available, rather than wait until the current iteration has been completed.

The Gauss-Seidel method does not always converge, but it is guaranteed to converge under conditions that are often satisfied in practice and are somewhat weaker than those for the Jacobi method (e.g., if the matrix is symmetric and positive definite). Although the Gauss-Seidel method converges more rapidly than the Jacobi method, it is often still too slow to be practical (see Section 11.5.6).

11.5.4 Successive Over-Relaxation

The convergence rate of the Gauss-Seidel method can be accelerated by a technique called *successive over-relaxation (SOR)*, which in effect uses the step to the next Gauss-Seidel iterate as a search direction, but with a fixed search parameter denoted by ω. Starting with $\boldsymbol{x}^{(k)}$, we first compute the next iterate that would be given by the Gauss-Seidel method, $\boldsymbol{x}_{GS}^{(k+1)}$, then instead take the next iterate to be

$$\boldsymbol{x}^{(k+1)} = \boldsymbol{x}^{(k)} + \omega\,(\boldsymbol{x}_{GS}^{(k+1)} - \boldsymbol{x}^{(k)}).$$

Equivalently, we can think of this scheme as taking a weighted average of the current iterate and the next Gauss-Seidel iterate:

$$\boldsymbol{x}^{(k+1)} = (1-\omega)\,\boldsymbol{x}^{(k)} + \omega\,\boldsymbol{x}_{GS}^{(k+1)}.$$

In either case, ω is a fixed *relaxation parameter* chosen to accelerate convergence. A value $\omega > 1$ gives *over*-relaxation, whereas $\omega < 1$ gives *under*-relaxation ($\omega = 1$ simply gives the Gauss-Seidel method). We always have $0 < \omega < 2$ (otherwise the method diverges), but choosing a specific value of ω to attain the best possible convergence rate is a difficult problem in general and is the subject of an elaborate theory for special classes of matrices.

Using the same notation as in Section 11.5.2, the SOR method can be written in matrix terms as

$$\begin{aligned}\boldsymbol{x}^{(k+1)} &= \boldsymbol{x}^{(k)} + \omega\left(\boldsymbol{D}^{-1}(\boldsymbol{b} - \boldsymbol{L}\boldsymbol{x}^{(k+1)} - \boldsymbol{U}\boldsymbol{x}^{(k)}) - \boldsymbol{x}^{(k)}\right)\\ &= (\boldsymbol{D} + \omega\,\boldsymbol{L})^{-1}\left((1-\omega)\,\boldsymbol{D} - \omega\,\boldsymbol{U}\right)\boldsymbol{x}^{(k)} + \omega\,(\boldsymbol{D} + \omega\,\boldsymbol{L})^{-1}\boldsymbol{b},\end{aligned}$$

and hence corresponds to the splitting

$$\boldsymbol{M} = \frac{1}{\omega}\boldsymbol{D} + \boldsymbol{L}, \qquad \boldsymbol{N} = \left(\frac{1}{\omega} - 1\right)\boldsymbol{D} - \boldsymbol{U}.$$

Like the Gauss-Seidel method, the SOR method makes repeated forward sweeps through the unknowns, updating them successively. A variant of SOR, known as *SSOR* (symmetric SOR), alternates forward and backward sweeps through the unknowns. SSOR is not necessarily faster than SOR (indeed SSOR is often slower), but it has the theoretical advantage that its iteration matrix, $\boldsymbol{G} = \boldsymbol{M}^{-1}\boldsymbol{N}$, which is too complicated to express here, is similar to a symmetric matrix when $\boldsymbol{A}$ is symmetric (which is not true of the iteration matrix for SOR). This feature makes SSOR useful as a preconditioner, for example (see Section 11.5.5).

11.5.5 Conjugate Gradient Method

We now turn from stationary iterative methods to methods based on optimization. If $\boldsymbol{A}$ is an $n \times n$ symmetric positive definite matrix, then the quadratic function

$$\phi(\boldsymbol{x}) = \tfrac{1}{2}\boldsymbol{x}^T\boldsymbol{A}\boldsymbol{x} - \boldsymbol{x}^T\boldsymbol{b}$$

attains a minimum precisely when $\boldsymbol{A}\boldsymbol{x} = \boldsymbol{b}$. Thus, we can apply any of the optimization methods discussed in Section 6.5 to obtain a solution to the corresponding linear system. Recall from Section 6.5 that most multidimensional optimization methods progress from one iteration to the next by performing a one-dimensional search along some search direction $\boldsymbol{s}_k$, so that

$$\boldsymbol{x}_{k+1} = \boldsymbol{x}_k + \alpha\boldsymbol{s}_k,$$

where α is a line search parameter that is chosen to minimize the objective function $\phi(\boldsymbol{x}_k + \alpha\boldsymbol{s}_k)$ along $\boldsymbol{s}_k$.

We note some special features of such a quadratic optimization problem. First, the negative gradient is simply the residual vector:

$$-\nabla\phi(\boldsymbol{x}) = \boldsymbol{b} - \boldsymbol{A}\boldsymbol{x} = \boldsymbol{r}.$$

Second, for any search direction $\boldsymbol{s}_k$, we need not perform a line search, because the optimal choice for α can be determined analytically. Specifically, the minimum over α occurs when the new residual is orthogonal to the search direction:

$$0 = \frac{d}{d\alpha}\phi(\boldsymbol{x}_{k+1}) = \nabla\phi(\boldsymbol{x}_{k+1})^T\frac{d}{d\alpha}\boldsymbol{x}_{k+1} = (\boldsymbol{A}\boldsymbol{x}_{k+1} - \boldsymbol{b})^T\frac{d}{d\alpha}(\boldsymbol{x}_k + \alpha\boldsymbol{s}_k) = -\boldsymbol{r}_{k+1}^T\boldsymbol{s}_k.$$

Since the new residual can be expressed in terms of the old residual and the search direction,

$$\boldsymbol{r}_{k+1} = \boldsymbol{b} - \boldsymbol{A}\boldsymbol{x}_{k+1} = \boldsymbol{b} - \boldsymbol{A}(\boldsymbol{x}_k + \alpha\boldsymbol{s}_k) = (\boldsymbol{b} - \boldsymbol{A}\boldsymbol{x}_k) - \alpha\boldsymbol{A}\boldsymbol{s}_k = \boldsymbol{r}_k - \alpha\boldsymbol{A}\boldsymbol{s}_k,$$

we can thus solve for

$$\alpha = \frac{\boldsymbol{r}_k^T\boldsymbol{s}_k}{\boldsymbol{s}_k^T\boldsymbol{A}\boldsymbol{s}_k}.$$

If we take advantage of these properties in specializing Algorithm 6.6 for this problem, then we obtain the *conjugate gradient method*, or *CG method*, for solving symmetric positive definite linear systems given in Algorithm 11.1, which should be compared with the nonlinear version given in Algorithm 6.6. Each iteration of Algorithm 11.1 requires only a single matrix-vector multiplication, $\boldsymbol{A}\boldsymbol{s}_k$, plus a small number of inner products. The storage requirements are also very modest, since the vectors $\boldsymbol{x}$, $\boldsymbol{r}$, and $\boldsymbol{s}$ can be overwritten on successive iterations.

Algorithm 11.1 Conjugate Gradient Method for Linear Systems

$\boldsymbol{x}_0$ = initial guess
$\boldsymbol{r}_0 = \boldsymbol{b} - \boldsymbol{A}\boldsymbol{x}_0$
$\boldsymbol{s}_0 = \boldsymbol{r}_0$
for $k = 0, 1, 2, \ldots$
  $\alpha_k = \boldsymbol{r}_k^T\boldsymbol{r}_k / \boldsymbol{s}_k^T\boldsymbol{A}\boldsymbol{s}_k$ { compute search parameter }
  $\boldsymbol{x}_{k+1} = \boldsymbol{x}_k + \alpha_k\boldsymbol{s}_k$ { update solution }
  $\boldsymbol{r}_{k+1} = \boldsymbol{r}_k - \alpha_k\boldsymbol{A}\boldsymbol{s}_k$ { compute new residual }
  $\beta_{k+1} = \boldsymbol{r}_{k+1}^T\boldsymbol{r}_{k+1} / \boldsymbol{r}_k^T\boldsymbol{r}_k$
  $\boldsymbol{s}_{k+1} = \boldsymbol{r}_{k+1} + \beta_{k+1}\boldsymbol{s}_k$ { compute new search direction }
end

Although the CG method is not terribly difficult to derive, we content ourselves here with the following intuitive motivation. The features noted earlier for the quadratic optimization problem would make it extremely easy to apply the steepest descent method, using the negative gradient—in this case the residual—as search direction at each iteration. Unfortunately, we have already observed that the convergence rate of steepest descent is often very poor owing to repeated searches in the same directions (see Fig. 6.9). We could avoid this repetition by orthogonalizing each new search direction against all of the previous ones (see Section 3.5.3), leaving only components in "new" directions, but this would appear to be prohibitively expensive computationally and would also require excessive storage to save all of the search directions. However, if instead of using the standard inner product we make the search directions mutually $\boldsymbol{A}$-orthogonal (vectors $\boldsymbol{y}$ and $\boldsymbol{z}$ are $\boldsymbol{A}$-orthogonal if $\boldsymbol{y}^T\boldsymbol{A}\boldsymbol{z} = 0$), or *conjugate*, then it can be shown that the successive $\boldsymbol{A}$-orthogonal search directions satisfy a three-term recurrence (this is the role played by β in the algorithm). This short recurrence makes the computation very cheap, and, most important, it means that we do not need to save all of the previous gradients, only the most recent two, which makes a huge difference in storage requirements.

The CG method is intimately related to Lanczos iteration, given in Algorithm 4.10. Like Lanczos iteration, CG uses repeated multiplication by $\boldsymbol{A}$ to generate a Krylov subspace, for which an orthogonal basis is obtained by means of a three-term recurrence. In fact, either algorithm can be derived from the other, so they are two ways of expressing the same basic process, but with one specialized to compute eigenvalues while the other is adapted to solve linear systems.

In addition to the other special properties already noted, it turns out that in the quadratic case the error at each step of CG is minimal (with respect to the norm induced by $\boldsymbol{A}$) over the space spanned by the search directions generated so far. Since the search directions are $\boldsymbol{A}$-orthogonal, and hence linearly independent, this property implies that after at most n steps the solution is exact, because the n search directions must span the whole space. Thus, in theory, CG is a direct method, but in practice rounding error causes a loss of orthogonality that spoils this finite termination property. As a result, CG is usually used in an iterative manner and halted when the residual, or some other measure of error, is sufficiently small. In practice, the method often converges in far fewer than n iterations. We will consider its convergence rate in Section 11.5.6.

Although it is a significant improvement over steepest descent, CG can still converge very slowly if the matrix $\boldsymbol{A}$ is ill-conditioned. Convergence can often be substantially accelerated by *preconditioning*, which can be thought of as implicitly multiplying $\boldsymbol{A}$ by $\boldsymbol{M}^{-1}$, where $\boldsymbol{M}$ is a matrix for which systems of the form $\boldsymbol{M}\boldsymbol{z} = \boldsymbol{y}$ are easily solved, and whose inverse approximates that of $\boldsymbol{A}$, so that $\boldsymbol{M}^{-1}\boldsymbol{A}$ is relatively well-conditioned. Technically, to preserve symmetry, we should apply CG to $\boldsymbol{L}^{-1}\boldsymbol{A}\boldsymbol{L}^{-T}$ instead of $\boldsymbol{M}^{-1}\boldsymbol{A}$, where $\boldsymbol{M} = \boldsymbol{L}\boldsymbol{L}^T$. However, the algorithm can be suitably rearranged so that only $\boldsymbol{M}$ is used and the corresponding matrix $\boldsymbol{L}$ is not required explicitly. The resulting preconditioned conjugate gradient method is shown in Algorithm 11.2 . In addition to one matrix-vector multiplication, $\boldsymbol{A}\boldsymbol{s}_k$, per iteration, we must also apply the preconditioner, $\boldsymbol{M}^{-1}\boldsymbol{r}_k$, once per iteration.

Algorithm 11.2 Preconditioned Conjugate Gradient Method

$\boldsymbol{x}_0 =$ initial guess
$\boldsymbol{r}_0 = \boldsymbol{b} - \boldsymbol{A}\boldsymbol{x}_0$
$\boldsymbol{s}_0 = \boldsymbol{M}^{-1}\boldsymbol{r}_0$
for $k = 0, 1, 2, \ldots$
    $\alpha_k = \boldsymbol{r}_k^T\boldsymbol{M}^{-1}\boldsymbol{r}_k / \boldsymbol{s}_k^T\boldsymbol{A}\boldsymbol{s}_k$ { compute search parameter }
    $\boldsymbol{x}_{k+1} = \boldsymbol{x}_k + \alpha_k\boldsymbol{s}_k$ { update solution }
    $\boldsymbol{r}_{k+1} = \boldsymbol{r}_k - \alpha_k\boldsymbol{A}\boldsymbol{s}_k$ { compute new residual }
    $\beta_{k+1} = \boldsymbol{r}_{k+1}^T\boldsymbol{M}^{-1}\boldsymbol{r}_{k+1} / \boldsymbol{r}_k^T\boldsymbol{M}^{-1}\boldsymbol{r}_k$
    $\boldsymbol{s}_{k+1} = \boldsymbol{M}^{-1}\boldsymbol{r}_{k+1} + \beta_{k+1}\boldsymbol{s}_k$ { compute new search direction }
end

The choice of an appropriate preconditioner depends on the usual tradeoff between the gain in the convergence rate and the increased cost per iteration that results from applying the preconditioner. A wide variety of preconditioners have been proposed, and this topic is an active area of research. Some of the most commonly used types of preconditioners are:

- *Diagonal* (also called *Jacobi*): $\boldsymbol{M}$ is taken to be a diagonal matrix with diagonal entries equal to those of $\boldsymbol{A}$.
- *Block diagonal* (or block Jacobi): If the indices $1, \ldots, n$ are partitioned into mutually disjoint subsets, then $m_{ij} = a_{ij}$ if i and j are in the same subset, and $m_{ij} = 0$ otherwise. Natural choices include partitioning along lines or planes in two- or three-dimensional grids, respectively, or grouping together physical variables that correspond to a common node, as in many finite element problems.
- *SSOR*: Using a matrix splitting of the form $\boldsymbol{A} = \boldsymbol{L} + \boldsymbol{D} + \boldsymbol{L}^T$ as in Section 11.5.2, we can take $\boldsymbol{M} = (\boldsymbol{D} + \boldsymbol{L})\boldsymbol{D}^{-1}(\boldsymbol{D} + \boldsymbol{L})^T$, or, introducing the SSOR relaxation

parameter ω,

$$M(\omega) = \frac{1}{2-\omega}\left(\frac{1}{\omega}D + L\right)\left(\frac{1}{\omega}D\right)^{-1}\left(\frac{1}{\omega}D + L\right)^{T}.$$

With the optimal choice of ω, the SSOR preconditioner is capable of reducing the condition number to $\text{cond}(M^{-1}A) = \mathcal{O}(\sqrt{\text{cond}(A)}\,)$, but determining this optimal value may be impractical.

- *Incomplete factorization*: Ideally, one would like to solve the linear system directly using the Cholesky factorization $A = LL^T$, but this may incur unacceptable fill (see Section 11.4.1). One may instead compute an approximate factorization $A \approx \hat{L}\hat{L}^T$ that allows little or no fill (e.g., restricting the nonzero entries of $\hat{L}$ to be in the same positions as those of the lower triangle of A), then use $M = \hat{L}\hat{L}^T$ as a preconditioner.
- *Polynomial*: M^{-1} is taken to be a polynomial in A that approximates A^{-1}. One way to obtain a suitable polynomial is to use a fixed number of steps of a stationary iterative method to solve the preconditioning system $Mz_k = r_k$ at each conjugate gradient iteration.
- *Approximate inverse*: M^{-1} is determined by using an optimization algorithm to minimize the residual

$$\|I - AM^{-1}\| \quad \text{or} \quad \|I - M^{-1}A\|$$

in some norm, with M^{-1} restricted to have a prescribed pattern of nonzero entries.

A significant amount of work is required to compute some of these preconditioners, and this work must also be included in the cost tradeoff mentioned earlier. The conjugate gradient method is rarely used without some form of preconditioning. Since diagonal preconditioning requires almost no extra work or storage, at least this much preconditioning is always advisable, and more sophisticated preconditioners are often worthwhile.

The conjugate gradient method is generally applicable only to symmetric positive definite systems. If the matrix A is indefinite or nonsymmetric, then the algorithm may break down both theoretically (e.g., the corresponding optimization problem may not have a minimum) and practically (e.g., the formula for α may fail). The method can be generalized to symmetric indefinite systems, as in the SYMMLQ algorithm of Paige and Saunders [298], for example. The conjugate gradient method cannot be generalized to nonsymmetric systems, however, without sacrificing at least one of the two properties—the short recurrence property and the minimal error property—that largely account for its effectiveness. Nevertheless, in recent years a number of related algorithms have been formulated for solving nonsymmetric linear systems, including GMRES, QMR, CGS, BiCG, Bi-CGSTAB, and others. Like CG, these algorithms are based on Krylov subspaces, but they are analogous to the nonsymmetric Arnoldi iteration (Algorithm 4.9) rather than to the symmetric Lanczos iteration. Iterative methods for nonsymmetric systems tend to be significantly less robust or require considerably more storage or work than CG, but in many cases they are still the most effective methods available for solving very large nonsymmetric systems.

Example 11.8 Iterative Methods for Linear Systems. We illustrate various iterative methods by using them to solve the 4×4 linear system for the Laplace equation on the unit square in Example 11.5. In each case we take $\boldsymbol{x}^{(0)} = \boldsymbol{0}$ as starting guess.

The Jacobi method gives the following sequence of iterates for this problem:

k	x_1	x_2	x_3	x_4
0	0.000	0.000	0.000	0.000
1	0.000	0.000	0.250	0.250
2	0.062	0.062	0.312	0.312
3	0.094	0.094	0.344	0.344
4	0.109	0.109	0.359	0.359
5	0.117	0.117	0.367	0.367
6	0.121	0.121	0.371	0.371
7	0.123	0.123	0.373	0.373
8	0.124	0.124	0.374	0.374
9	0.125	0.125	0.375	0.375

As expected, the Gauss-Seidel method converges somewhat faster, giving the following sequence of iterates for this problem:

k	x_1	x_2	x_3	x_4
0	0.000	0.000	0.000	0.000
1	0.000	0.000	0.250	0.312
2	0.062	0.094	0.344	0.359
3	0.109	0.117	0.367	0.371
4	0.121	0.123	0.373	0.374
5	0.124	0.125	0.375	0.375
6	0.125	0.125	0.375	0.375

The optimal acceleration parameter in the SOR method turns out to be $\omega = 1.072$ for this problem, which is so close to 1 that it converges only slightly faster than Gauss-Seidel, giving the following sequence of iterates:

k	x_1	x_2	x_3	x_4
0	0.000	0.000	0.000	0.000
1	0.000	0.000	0.268	0.335
2	0.072	0.108	0.356	0.365
3	0.119	0.121	0.371	0.373
4	0.123	0.124	0.374	0.375
5	0.125	0.125	0.375	0.375

Finally, the conjugate gradient method converges in only two iterations for this problem, giving the following sequence of iterates:

k	x_1	x_2	x_3	x_4
0	0.000	0.000	0.000	0.000
1	0.000	0.000	0.333	0.333
2	0.125	0.125	0.375	0.375

11.5.6 Rate of Convergence

Example 11.8 is too small for the results to be representative of the relative performance of the methods for problems of practical size. Recall from the discussion of convergence rates in Section 5.4 that, asymptotically, a linearly convergent sequence with constant C gains $-\log_{10}(C)$ decimal digits per iteration. Thus, the quantity $R = -\log_{10}(\rho(\boldsymbol{G}))$ serves as a useful quantitative measure of the speed of convergence of a stationary iterative method with iteration matrix $\boldsymbol{G}$. In this context, R is sometimes called the *rate of convergence*, but this term should not be confused the convergence rate r defined in Section 5.4.

If we use the same five-point finite difference approximation as in the previous example for the Laplace equation on the unit square, but with an arbitrary $k \times k$ grid of interior mesh points with mesh size $h = 1/(k+1)$, then the spectral radius $\rho(\boldsymbol{G})$ and approximate rate of convergence R for the stationary iterative methods are as shown in Table 11.1. We see that the rates of convergence for Jacobi and Gauss-Seidel are proportional to the square of the mesh size, or equivalently, that the number of iterations per digit of accuracy gained is proportional to the number of mesh points. The constants of proportionality also tell us that Gauss-Seidel is asymptotically twice as fast as Jacobi for this model problem. Optimal SOR, on the other hand, is an order of magnitude faster than either of the other methods, as its rate of convergence is proportional to the mesh size, and hence the number of iterations per digit gained is proportional to the number of mesh points along one side of the grid.

Method	$\rho(\boldsymbol{G})$	R
Jacobi	$\cos(\pi h)$	$(\pi^2/\log 10)h^2/2$
Gauss-Seidel	$\cos^2(\pi h)$	$(\pi^2/\log 10)h^2$
Optimal SOR	$(1-\sin(\pi h))/(1+\sin(\pi h))$	$(2\pi/\log 10)h$

Table 11.1: Spectral radius and rate of convergence for $k \times k$ grid with mesh spacing h

To make these results more concrete, the spectral radius and rate of convergence for each method are given in Table 11.2 for a range of values of k. We see that the spectral radius is extremely close to 1 for large values of k, and hence all three methods converge very slowly. From the rate of convergence R, we see that for $k = 10$ (a linear system of order 100), Jacobi requires more than 50 iterations to gain a single decimal digit of accuracy, Gauss-Seidel requires more than 25 iterations, and optimal SOR requires about 4 iterations. For $k = 100$ (a linear system of order 10,000), to gain a single decimal digit of accuracy Jacobi requires about 5000 iterations, Gauss-Seidel about 2500, and optimal SOR about 37. Thus, the Jacobi and Gauss-Seidel methods are impractical for a problem of this size, and optimal SOR, though perhaps reasonable for this problem, also becomes prohibitively slow for still larger problems. Moreover, the performance of SOR depends on knowledge of the optimal value for the relaxation parameter ω, which is known analytically for this simple model problem to be $\omega = 2/(1+\sin(\pi h))$, but which is much harder to determine in general.

	Jacobi		Gauss-Seidel		Optimal SOR	
k	$\rho(\boldsymbol{G})$	R	$\rho(\boldsymbol{G})$	R	$\rho(\boldsymbol{G})$	R
10	0.9595	0.018	0.9206	0.036	0.5604	0.252
50	0.9981	0.0008	0.9962	0.0016	0.8840	0.0535
100	0.9995	0.0002	0.9990	0.0004	0.9397	0.0270
500	0.99998	0.0000085	0.99996	0.000017	0.98754	0.005447

Table 11.2: Spectral radius of iteration matrix and rate of convergence for $k \times k$ grid

The convergence behavior of the nonstationary conjugate gradient method is more complicated, but roughly speaking the error is reduced at each iteration by a factor of

$$\frac{\sqrt{\kappa}-1}{\sqrt{\kappa}+1}$$

on average, where

$$\kappa = \text{cond}(\boldsymbol{A}) = \|\boldsymbol{A}\|_2 \cdot \|\boldsymbol{A}^{-1}\|_2 = \frac{\lambda_{\max}(\boldsymbol{A})}{\lambda_{\min}(\boldsymbol{A})}.$$

When the matrix $\boldsymbol{A}$ is well-conditioned ($\kappa \approx 1$), convergence is rapid; but if $\boldsymbol{A}$ is very ill-conditioned ($\kappa \gg 1$), then convergence can be arbitrarily slow. For this reason, a preconditioner is usually used with the conjugate gradient method. The hope is that the preconditioned matrix $\boldsymbol{M}^{-1}\boldsymbol{A}$ will have a much smaller condition number than $\boldsymbol{A}$, and hence the convergence rate will be greatly improved. The foregoing estimate is conservative, however, and the algorithm may do much better than this. For example, if the matrix $\boldsymbol{A}$ has only m distinct eigenvalues, then theoretically, conjugate gradients converges in at most m iterations. Thus, the detailed convergence behavior depends on all of the spectrum of $\boldsymbol{A}$, not just on its extreme eigenvalues, and in practice the convergence is often superlinear.

11.5.7 Multigrid Methods

We have seen that stationary iterative methods often have very poor rates of convergence. There are various techniques for accelerating convergence, but these methods generally remain impractical for problems of realistic size. These convergence results are *asymptotic*, however, and such methods may make rapid early progress before eventually settling into a slow asymptotic phase. In particular, some stationary iterative methods tend to reduce high-frequency (i.e., oscillatory) components of the error rapidly but reduce low-frequency (i.e., smooth) components of the error much more slowly, which causes the poor asymptotic rate of convergence (see Computer Problems 11.13 and 12.14 for examples). For this reason, such a method is called a *smoother*. This observation provides the motivation for *multigrid methods*, which we now outline very briefly.

The notions of smooth and oscillatory components of the error are relative to the mesh on which the solution is defined; a component that appears smooth on a fine grid may appear oscillatory when sampled on a coarser grid. If we apply a smoother on the coarser grid, then we may make rapid progress in reducing this (now oscillatory) component of the error. After a few iterations of the smoother, the results can then be interpolated back to the fine grid to produce a solution in which the low-frequency components of the error have been reduced. It may then be desirable to use a few more iterations of the smoother on the fine grid to ensure that the high-frequency components of the error remain small. The net result is an approximate solution on the fine grid for which both the high-frequency and low-frequency components of the error have been reduced. The process can then be repeated, if desired, until some convergence criterion is met.

This idea can be extended to multiple levels of grids, so that error components of various frequencies can be reduced rapidly, each at the appropriate level. Transition from a finer grid to a coarser grid involves *restriction* (sometimes called *injection*), whereas transition from a coarser grid to a finer grid involves *interpolation* (sometimes called *prolongation*).

If $\hat{\boldsymbol{x}}$ is an approximate solution to $\boldsymbol{Ax} = \boldsymbol{b}$, with residual $\boldsymbol{r} = \boldsymbol{b} - \boldsymbol{A}\hat{\boldsymbol{x}}$, then the error $\boldsymbol{e} = \boldsymbol{x} - \hat{\boldsymbol{x}}$ satisfies the equation $\boldsymbol{Ae} = \boldsymbol{r}$. Thus, in improving the approximate solution we can work with just this "residual equation" involving the error and the residual, rather than the solution and original right-hand side. One advantage of the residual equation is that zero is a reasonable starting guess for its solution. A two-grid method then takes the following form:

1. On the fine grid, use a few iterations of a smoother to compute an approximate solution $\hat{\boldsymbol{x}}$ for the system $\boldsymbol{Ax} = \boldsymbol{b}$.
2. Compute the residual $\boldsymbol{r} = \boldsymbol{b} - \boldsymbol{A}\hat{\boldsymbol{x}}$.
3. Restrict the residual to the coarse grid.
4. On the coarse grid, use a few iterations of a smoother on the residual equation to obtain a coarse-grid approximation to the error.
5. Interpolate the coarse grid correction to the fine grid to obtain an improved approximate solution on the fine grid.
6. Apply a few iterations of a smoother to the corrected solution on the fine grid.

A multigrid method results from recursion in Step 4, that is, the coarse grid correction is itself improved by using a still coarser grid, and so on down to some bottom level. The computations become cheaper as one moves to coarser and coarser grids because the systems become successively smaller. In particular, a direct method may be feasible on the coarsest grid if the system is small enough.

There are many possible strategies for cycling through the various grid levels, the most common of which are depicted schematically in Fig. 11.11. The *V-cycle* starts with the finest grid and goes down through successive levels to the coarsest grid and then back up again to the finest grid. To obtain more benefit from the coarser grids, where computations are cheaper, the *W-cycle* zigzags among the lower-level grids before moving back up to the finest grid. *Full multigrid* starts at the coarsest level, where a good initial solution is easier to come by (perhaps by direct solution), then bootstraps this solution up through the grid levels, ultimately reaching the finest grid.

By exploiting the strengths of the underlying iterative smoothers and avoiding their weaknesses, multigrid methods are capable of extraordinarily good performance. In particular, at each level the smoother rapidly reduces the oscillatory

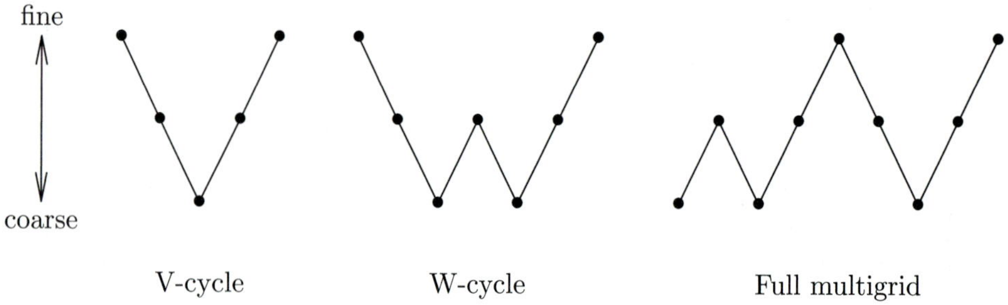

Figure 11.11: Cycling schemes for multigrid methods.

component of the error at a rate that is independent of the mesh size, since only a few iterations of the smoother, often only one, are performed at each level. All components of the error appear oscillatory at some level, so it follows that the convergence rate of the entire multigrid scheme should be rapid and independent of the mesh size, which is in stark contrast to the other iterative methods we have considered. Moreover, the cost of an entire cycle of multigrid is only a modest multiple of the cost of a single sweep on the finest grid. As a result, multigrid methods are among the most powerful methods available for solving sparse linear systems arising from PDEs and are capable of converging to within the truncation error of the discretization at a cost comparable to fast direct methods of the type discussed in Section 11.4.2, although the latter are much less broadly applicable.

11.6 Comparison of Methods

Now that we have examined both direct and iterative methods in some detail, we can summarize their relative advantages and disadvantages for solving linear systems:

- Direct methods require no initial estimate for the solution, but they take no advantage of it if a good estimate happens to be available.
- Direct methods are good at producing high accuracy, but they take no advantage if only low accuracy is needed.
- Iterative methods are often dependent on special properties, such as the matrix being symmetric positive definite, and are subject to very slow convergence for badly conditioned systems. Direct methods are more robust in both senses.
- Iterative methods usually require less work if convergence is rapid but often require the computation or estimation of various parameters or preconditioners to accelerate convergence, which at least partially offsets this advantage.
- Many iterative methods do not require explicit storage of the matrix entries and hence are good when the matrix can be produced easily on demand or is most easily implemented as a linear operator.
- Iterative methods are less readily embodied in standard software packages, since the best representation of the matrix is often problem dependent and "hard

coded" in an application program, whereas direct methods employ more standard storage schemes.

To make a more quantitative comparison, Table 11.3 shows the order of magnitude of the computational cost for solving a discretized elliptic boundary value problem in two or three dimensions (2-D or 3-D) by each of the methods we have discussed (and also a few methods that we have not discussed). These results should be taken as only a rough guide, as they depend on several assumptions:

- The discretization is by a finite difference scheme on a regular grid ($k \times k$ in two dimensions, $k \times k \times k$ in three dimensions) with mesh size $h = 1/k$. For the divide-and-conquer methods, k is assumed to be a power of two (and all logarithms are base two).
- The resulting matrix is symmetric, positive definite, and sparse, with a constant number of nonzeros per row and a condition number that is $\mathcal{O}(1/h^2)$.
- For the iterative methods that depend on various parameters, optimal values are known and used in all cases.
- For the band Cholesky method, the bandwidth is $\mathcal{O}(k)$ in two dimensions and $\mathcal{O}(k^2)$ in three dimensions.
- For the sparse Cholesky method, an optimal nested dissection ordering is used.
- For the preconditioned conjugate gradient method, the preconditioner is assumed to reduce the condition number to $\mathcal{O}(1/h)$.
- The iterative methods are iterated to convergence within the truncation error of the discretization, i.e., until the initial error is reduced by a factor of h^2.

Method	2-D	3-D
Dense Cholesky	k^6	k^9
Jacobi	$k^4 \log k$	$k^5 \log k$
Gauss-Seidel	$k^4 \log k$	$k^5 \log k$
Band Cholesky	k^4	k^7
Optimal SOR	$k^3 \log k$	$k^4 \log k$
Sparse Cholesky	k^3	k^6
Conjugate gradient	k^3	k^4
Optimal SSOR	$k^{2.5} \log k$	$k^{3.5} \log k$
Preconditioned CG	$k^{2.5}$	$k^{3.5}$
Optimal ADI	$k^2 \log^2 k$	$k^3 \log^2 k$
Cyclic reduction	$k^2 \log k$	$k^3 \log k$
FFT	$k^2 \log k$	$k^3 \log k$
Multigrid V-cycle	$k^2 \log k$	$k^3 \log k$
FACR	$k^2 \log \log k$	$k^3 \log \log k$
Full Multigrid	k^2	k^3

Table 11.3: Computational cost of solving elliptic boundary value problems as a function of the number of points k along each dimension in a regular two- or three-dimensional grid

In interpreting these results, several caveats should be kept in mind:

- We have omitted the proportionality constants. In theory these are irrelevant asymptotically, but they may matter a great deal for a specific problem of practical interest, even quite a large one. Also, the value of the proportionality constant for a given method depends on the specific discretization used.
- The methods listed are not equally applicable. For the Poisson equation on the unit square with the standard five-point difference scheme, for example, all of the foregoing assumptions hold and all of the methods listed are applicable. But for more complicated PDEs, domains, boundary conditions, and discretization schemes, some of the methods listed may not be viable options.
- The methods listed are not equally reliable or robust. Many of the iterative methods depend on judicious choices of parameters or preconditioners that may be difficult to determine in advance, and their performance may degrade significantly with choices that are less than optimal.
- The methods listed are not equally easy to implement—some are relatively straightforward, but others involve complicated algorithms and data structures. Because of such differences, the methods may also vary significantly in the relative speeds with which they perform an equivalent amount of computation.
- In practice the work may depend on implementation details. For example, the cost of multigrid is sensitive to the particular strategy used for cycling through grid levels. The figures given in the table assume the best possible case.
- Computational complexity alone does not necessarily determine the shortest time to a solution. For example, a method with high-order accuracy usually requires more work per grid point than a low-order method but may be able to use far *fewer* grid points to achieve equivalent accuracy.

In Table 11.3 the computational work is stated in terms of the number of grid points per dimension in a regular finite difference grid. In Table 11.4 the equivalent value for the work in terms of n, the order of the matrix, is given for those methods that remain viable choices for finite element discretizations with less regular meshes. The table gives the exponent of n in the dominant term of the cost estimate. These results are applicable to many finite element discretizations and are also consistent with the estimates in Table 11.3 for finite difference discretizations (with $n = k^2$ or $n = k^3$, depending on the dimension of the problem).

Method	2-D	3-D
Dense Cholesky	3	3
Band Cholesky	2	2.33
Sparse Cholesky	1.5	2
Conjugate gradient	1.5	1.33
Preconditioned CG	1.25	1.17
Multigrid	1	1

Table 11.4: Exponent of n, the order of the matrix, in the computational cost of solving elliptic boundary value problems in two or three dimensions

In Table 11.3 the methods are listed in decreasing order of cost for 2-D problems. Note that the ranking is somewhat different for 3-D problems. The reason is that factorization methods suffer a much greater penalty in going from two dimensions to three than do other methods. Although factorization methods are much less competitive in terms of the work required for three-dimensional problems, they are still useful in some cases because of their greater robustness. This is especially true for nonsymmetric matrices, since iterative methods tend to be significantly less reliable in that case. In addition, methods akin to factorization are often used to compute effective preconditioners.

The tables show that multigrid methods can be optimal, in the sense that the cost of computing the solution is of the same order as the cost of reading the input or writing the output. The FACR method is also optimal for all practical purposes, since $\log \log k$ is effectively constant for any reasonable value of k. The other fast direct methods are almost as effective in practice unless k is very large. Clearly these methods should be seriously considered whenever they are applicable, and good software is available implementing them. Unfortunately, their robustness and applicability can be quite limited, so these optimal or nearly optimal methods, though they can be quite useful in the right context, are not a panacea, and more conventional methods must often be relied upon in practice.

11.7 Software for Partial Differential Equations

Most of the problem categories we have studied previously are amenable to reasonably efficient solution by general-purpose software. Methods for the numerical solution of partial differential equations, on the other hand, tend to be much more problem-dependent, so that in practice PDEs are most often solved using custom-written software to take maximum advantage of the particular features of a given problem. Nevertheless, some software does exist for a few general classes of problems that occur often in practice. Table 11.5 is a list of some of the software for the numerical solution of PDEs available from major libraries. General problem-solving environments for partial differential equations are also available, including a PDE toolbox for `MATLAB`.

Source	2-D Poisson	3-D Poisson	Method of lines
`IMSL`	`fps2h`	`fps3h`	`molch`
`MATLAB`	`poisolv`		
`NAG`	`d03eaf`	`d03faf`	`d03pcf`
`NUMAL` [250]	`richardson`		`ark/arkmat`
`SLATEC`	`hwscrt`		

Table 11.5: Library software for partial differential equations

In addition, we list next several individual routines and software packages, many of which are available from `Netlib`, for solving various types of PDEs and also for solving sparse linear systems.

11.7.1 Software for Initial Value Problems

- CLAWPACK: 1-D and 2-D hyperbolic systems
- MATLAB: pdepe for 1-D parabolic equations
- TOMS: numerous routines and packages for solving various time-dependent problems in one or two space dimensions, including
  - pdeone(#494): 1-D systems using method of lines
  - pdecol(#540): 1-D systems using collocation
  - m3rk(#553): three-step Runge-Kutta method for parabolic equations
  - pdetwo(#565): 2-D systems using method of lines
  - bdmg(#621): 2-D nonlinear parabolic equations
  - epdcol(#688): 1-D systems using collocation
  - pdecheb(#690): Chebyshev polynomial method for parabolic equations
  - cwres(#731): moving-grid interface for 1-D systems

11.7.2 Software for Boundary Value Problems

- ELLPACK: general framework and specific algorithms for solving various elliptic boundary value problems on two- and three-dimensional domains [327]
- FISHPACK: fast 2-D Helmholtz solvers using various coordinate systems
- MATLAB: pdepe for 1-D elliptic equations
- MGGHAT: second-order linear elliptic PDEs using finite element method with adaptive mesh refinement and a multigrid solver
- PLTMG: elliptic PDEs with grid generation, adaptive mesh refinement, and a multigrid solver [23]
- TOMS: numerous routines and packages for solving various elliptic boundary value problems (e.g., Poisson, Helmholtz) in two- or three-dimensional domains, including
  - gma(#527): generalized marching algorithm for elliptic problems
  - pwscrt(#541): fast 2-D Helmholtz solvers using various coordinate systems
  - fft9(#543): fast 2-D Helmholtz solver
  - helm3d(#572): fast 3-D Helmholtz solver
  - cmmimp(#593): fast Helmholtz solver on nonrectangular planar region
  - gencol(#637): collocation method for general 2-D domain
  - intcol/hermcol(#638): collocation method for rectangular domain
  - hfft(#651): high-order fast 3-D Helmholtz solver
  - serrg2/b2eval(#685): separable elliptic equations on rectangular domain
  - capc/reccn(#732): elliptic equations on irregular 2-D domain

11.7.3 Software for Sparse Linear Systems

- HSL: chapter MA contains numerous routines for solving sparse linear systems
- MATLAB: as of Version 4.0, sparse matrices are supported, including reorderings, factorizations, and iterative solvers
- PCGPAK: preconditioned conjugate gradient methods for linear systems
- QMRPACK: quasi-minimal residual methods for nonsymmetric linear systems

- `SLAP`: iterative methods for symmetric and nonsymmetric linear systems
- `SPARSKIT`: iterative methods for sparse linear systems and utilities for manipulating sparse matrices
- `SPARSPAK`: reorderings and factorizations for sparse linear systems and least squares problems
- `SUPERLU`: Gaussian elimination with partial pivoting for sparse linear systems
- `SYMMLQ`: iterative method for symmetric indefinite linear systems
- `TEMPLATES`: iterative methods documented in [25]
- `TOMS`:
  - `gpskca(#582)`: reordering sparse matrices for reduced bandwidth
  - `lsqr(#583)`: iterative method for linear systems and least squares problems
  - `itpack/nspcg(#586)`: stationary and nonstationary iterative methods for symmetric and nonsymmetric linear systems
  - `sblas(#692)`: basic linear algebra subprograms for sparse matrices
  - `jpicc/jpicr(#740)`: incomplete Cholesky factorization preconditioner
- `UMFPACK`: unsymmetric multifrontal method for sparse linear systems
- `YSMP`: Yale Sparse Matrix Package, direct methods for linear systems
- `Y12M`: direct method for sparse linear systems

11.8 Historical Notes and Further Reading

The study of partial differential equations can be said to have begun with the formulation and solution of the wave equation by d'Alembert in 1747. Fourier's derivation and solution of the heat equation came in 1807, for which purpose he used the trigonometric series that are now known as Fourier series. The Laplace and Poisson equations were formulated by their namesakes around 1787 and 1813, respectively. Finite difference approximations were used for various purposes by Newton, Leibniz, Taylor, and other early developers of the calculus. Leibniz also used piecewise linear approximations in one dimension, faintly foreshadowing one aspect of finite element methods. In 1851 Schellbach proposed representing the solution to an elliptic boundary value problem in two dimensions by piecewise linear functions defined on a mesh of triangles, but his method for determining the coefficients differed from the criteria used today. Toward the end of the nineteenth century, Rayleigh used function expansions to obtain approximate solutions to PDEs, culminating in the work of Ritz (1908), Galerkin (1915), and Lanczos (1938) that laid the foundation for the finite element and spectral methods that would come to fruition several decades later. Finite difference methods were also in use for numerical computations early in the twentieth century, typified by Richardson's 1910 publication of a paper in which he used finite difference methods to calculate the stresses in a masonry dam on the Nile. The paper by Courant, Friedrichs, and Lewy in which the CFL condition first appeared was published in 1928. Their interest at the time was in establishing the existence of solutions for PDEs by proving the convergence of approximate solutions.

The advent of digital computers in the late 1940s enabled numerical methods for PDEs to become a truly viable option for practical problems, which led to a surge of interest in finite difference methods in the late 1940s (e.g., the Crank-Nicolson method, published in 1947) and 1950s. Stability analysis of finite difference schemes by von Neumann and others, culminating in the formulation of the Lax Equivalence Theorem in 1953, was a cornerstone of this work. Meanwhile, Courant published a paper in 1943 containing most of the essential features of the modern finite element method, although that name was not coined until 1960. Among engineers, from modest beginnings in the 1950s based largely on physical analogies, the finite element method came into full flower in the 1960s. Finally, spectral and pseudospectral methods came into prominence in the 1970s. All three approaches continue to flourish, and some of the most promising future directions combine features from all of them.

Jacobi proposed his iterative method for solving linear systems in 1845. A form of the Gauss-Seidel method was described by Gauss as early as 1823, but its systematic expression and convergence analysis were supplied by Seidel, a student of Jacobi, in 1874. Further iterative or "relaxation" methods were developed early in the twentieth century by Liebmann, Richardson, Southwell, and others. The successive over-relaxation method was published by Young in 1950, and the conjugate gradient method by Hestenes and Stiefel in 1952. The conjugate gradient method proved ineffective as a direct method owing to the effects of rounding error, so it was temporarily discarded until the early 1970s, when its use as an iterative method was popularized by Reid, Golub, and others (see [162]). For a negative result on the existence of a true analogue of the conjugate gradient method for nonsymmetric systems, see [114]. Fast direct methods were proposed by Hockney in 1965. The multigrid method was popularized in the late 1970s by Brandt and numerous others.

Classic references on the theory of partial differential equations are [142, 217]. Among dozens of more recent textbooks on partial differential equations, [32, 77, 256, 382, 401] focus more on applications and computation than most. The literature on numerical solution of partial differential equations is vast. Two early classics on finite difference methods are [129, 328]. More recent treatments focusing mainly on finite difference methods include [9, 149, 174, 254, 272, 282, 359, 383, 390, 391]. Both finite difference and finite element methods are discussed in [60, 113, 182, 207, 247, 344, 376]. For a detailed discussion of the method of lines, see [338]. For an introduction to finite element methods from a numerical point of view, see [39, 84, 108, 218, 246, 411]. Deeper mathematical treatment of the finite element method is given in [46, 380]. A classic engineering text on finite elements is [434]. For spectral and pseudospectral methods for partial differential equations, see [41, 124, 139, 166, 268, 395].

Direct methods for solving sparse linear systems are discussed in detail in [104, 151]. Fast direct methods are surveyed in [192, 309, 387]. Classic references on iterative methods for linear systems are [177, 408, 429]. More recent treatments of iterative methods include the surveys [25, 135, 227] and the comprehensive references [17, 121, 171, 176, 269, 293, 336]. For a tutorial overview of Krylov subspace methods, see [403]. For an introduction to multigrid methods, see [42, 51, 102, 216, 398, 415].

Review Questions

11.1. True or false: For solving a time-dependent partial differential equation, a finite difference method that is both consistent and stable converges to the true solution as the step sizes in time and in space go to zero.

11.2. True or false: The Gauss-Seidel iterative method for solving a system of linear equations $\boldsymbol{Ax} = \boldsymbol{b}$ always converges.

11.3. True or false: The Gauss-Seidel method is a special case of SOR (successive over-relaxation) for solving a system of linear equations.

11.4. How does a semidiscrete method differ from a fully discrete method for solving a time-dependent partial differential equation?

11.5. (*a*) Explain briefly the method of lines for solving an initial value problem for a time-dependent partial differential equation in one space dimension.

(*b*) How might the method of lines be used to solve a pure boundary value problem for a time-independent PDE in two space dimensions?

11.6. Other than the usual concerns of stability and accuracy, what additional important consideration enters into the choice of a numerical method for solving a system of ODEs arising from semidiscretization of a PDE using the method of lines?

11.7. In using a fully discrete finite difference method for solving a time-dependent partial differential equation with one space dimension, can the sizes of the time step and space step be chosen independently of each other? Why?

11.8. Fully discrete finite difference and finite element methods for solving boundary value problems convert the original differential equation into a system of algebraic equations. Why does the resulting $n \times n$ linear system usually require far less work to solve than the usual $\mathcal{O}(n^3)$ that might be expected?

11.9. Which of the following types of partial differential equations are time-dependent?

(*a*) Elliptic

(*b*) Parabolic

(*c*) Hyperbolic

11.10. Classify each of the following partial differential equations as hyperbolic, parabolic, or elliptic. Also, state whether each equation is time-dependent or time-independent.

(*a*) Laplace equation

(*b*) Wave equation

(*c*) Heat equation

(*d*) Poisson equation

11.11. What is meant by the *stencil* of a finite difference method for solving a PDE numerically?

11.12. The heat equation $u_t = c\,u_{xx}$ with appropriate initial and boundary conditions can be solved numerically by using a second-order, centered finite difference approximation for u_{xx} and then solving the resulting system of ordinary differential equations in time by some numerical method.

(*a*) On what ODE method in time is the Crank-Nicolson method based?

(*b*) What advantage does the Crank-Nicolson method have over the use of the backward Euler method?

(*c*) What fundamental advantage do both of these methods have over the use of Euler's method?

11.13. In solving the Laplace equation on the unit square using the standard second-order centered finite difference scheme in both space dimensions, what is the maximum number of unknown solution variables that are involved in any one equation of the resulting linear algebraic system?

11.14. Consider the numerical solution of the heat equation, $u_t = c\,u_{xx}$, by a fully discrete finite difference method. For the spatial discretization, suppose that we approximate the second derivative by the standard second-order centered difference formula.

(*a*) Why is Euler's method impractical for the time integration?

(*b*) Name a method for numerically solving the heat equation that is unconditionally stable and second-order accurate in both space and time.

(*c*) On what ODE method is the time integration in this method based?

11.15. Implicit finite difference methods for solving time-dependent PDEs require the solution of a system of equations at each time step. In using the backward Euler or trapezoid method to solve the heat equation in one space dimension, what is the nonzero pattern of the matrix of the linear system to be solved at each time step?

11.16. (*a*) For a finite difference method for solving a PDE numerically, what is meant by the terms *consistency*, *stability*, and *convergence*?

(*b*) How does the Lax Equivalence Theorem relate these terms to each other?

11.17. Suppose you are solving the heat equation $u_t = u_{xx}$ by applying an ODE method to solve the semidiscrete system of ODEs resulting from spatial discretization using the standard second-order centered difference approximation to the second derivative. Each of the following ODE methods then gives a time-stepping procedure that may or may not be consistent, stable, or convergent. State which of these three properties, if any, apply for each method listed (note that none, one, or more than one of the properties may apply in a given case).

(*a*) Euler's method with $\Delta t = \Delta x$

(*b*) Backward Euler method with $\Delta t = \Delta x$

(*c*) The "zero method," which produces the answer 0 at every time step

11.18. List two advantages and two disadvantages of iterative methods compared with direct methods for solving large sparse systems of linear algebraic equations.

11.19. What principal feature limits the usefulness of direct methods based on matrix factorization for solving very large sparse systems of linear equations?

11.20. What is the computational complexity of a fast Poisson solver for a problem with n mesh points?

11.21. What is meant by *fill* in the factorization of a sparse matrix?

11.22. Explain briefly the minimum degree algorithm for reordering a symmetric positive definite sparse matrix to limit fill in its Cholesky factor.

11.23. Explain briefly the nested dissection algorithm for reordering a symmetric positive definite sparse matrix to limit fill in its Cholesky factor.

11.24. What is the general form of a stationary iterative method for solving a system of linear equations $\boldsymbol{Ax} = \boldsymbol{b}$?

11.25. (*a*) What is meant by a *splitting* of a matrix $\boldsymbol{A}$?

(*b*) What form of iterative method for solving a linear system $\boldsymbol{Ax} = \boldsymbol{b}$ results from such a splitting?

(*c*) What condition on the splitting guarantees that the resulting iterative scheme is locally convergent?

(*d*) For the matrix

$$\boldsymbol{A} = \begin{bmatrix} 4 & 1 \\ 1 & 4 \end{bmatrix},$$

what is the splitting for the Jacobi method?

(*e*) For the same matrix as in part *d*, what is the splitting for the Gauss-Seidel method?

11.26. In solving a nonsingular system of linear equations $\boldsymbol{Ax} = \boldsymbol{b}$, what property of the matrix $\boldsymbol{A}$ would *necessarily* cause the Jacobi iterative method to fail outright?

11.27. Which of the following methods for solving a linear system are stationary iterative methods?

(*a*) Jacobi method

(*b*) Steepest descent method

(*c*) Iterative refinement

(*d*) Gauss-Seidel method

(*e*) Conjugate gradient method

(*f*) SOR method

11.28. (*a*) In words (or formulas if you prefer), describe the difference between the Jacobi and Gauss-Seidel iterative methods for solving a system of linear algebraic equations.

(*b*) Which method is more rapidly convergent?

(*c*) Which method requires less storage for the successive approximate solutions?

11.29. Listed below are several properties that may pertain to various methods for solving systems of linear equations. For each of the properties listed, state whether this quality more accurately describes direct or iterative methods.

(*a*) The entries of the matrix are not altered during the computation.

(*b*) A prior estimate for the solution is helpful.

(*c*) The matrix entries are stored explicitly, using a standard storage scheme such as an array.

(*d*) The work required depends on the conditioning of the problem.

(*e*) Once a given system has been solved, another system with the same matrix but a different right-hand side is easily solved.

(*f*) Acceleration parameters or preconditioners are usually employed.

(*g*) The maximum possible accuracy is relatively easy to attain.

(*h*) "Black box" software is relatively easy to implement.

(*i*) The matrix can be defined implicitly by its action on an arbitrary vector.

(*j*) A factorization of the matrix is usually performed.

(*k*) The amount of work required can often be determined in advance.

11.30. Let $\boldsymbol{A}$ be a nonsingular matrix. Denote the strict lower triangular portion of $\boldsymbol{A}$ by $\boldsymbol{L}$, the diagonal of $\boldsymbol{A}$ by $\boldsymbol{D}$, and the strict upper triangle of $\boldsymbol{A}$ by $\boldsymbol{U}$.

(*a*) Express the Jacobi iteration scheme for solving the linear system $\boldsymbol{Ax} = \boldsymbol{b}$ in terms of $\boldsymbol{L}$, $\boldsymbol{D}$, and $\boldsymbol{U}$.

(*b*) Express the Gauss-Seidel iteration scheme for solving the linear system $\boldsymbol{Ax} = \boldsymbol{b}$ in terms of $\boldsymbol{L}$, $\boldsymbol{D}$, and $\boldsymbol{U}$.

11.31. What are the usual bounds on the relaxation parameter ω in the SOR method?

11.32. Rank the following iterative methods for solving systems of linear equations in order of their usual speed of convergence, from fastest to slowest:

(*a*) Gauss-Seidel

(*b*) Jacobi

(*c*) SOR with optimal relaxation parameter ω

11.33. The conjugate gradient method for solving a symmetric positive definite system of linear equations is in principle a direct method. Why is it used in practice as an iterative method instead?

11.34. What two key features largely account for the effectiveness of the conjugate gradient method for solving large sparse symmetric positive definite linear systems?

11.35. When using the conjugate gradient method to solve a system of linear algebraic equations $\boldsymbol{Ax} = \boldsymbol{b}$, how can you accelerate its convergence rate?

11.36. (*a*) What is meant by *preconditioning* in the conjugate gradient method?

(*b*) List at least two types of preconditioners used with the conjugate gradient method.

11.37. Why are some stationary iterative methods for solving linear systems sometimes called *smoothers*?

11.38. Explain briefly the basic idea of multigrid methods.

11.39. (*a*) Explain the difference between the V-cycle and the W-cycle in multigrid methods.

(*b*) How does *full* multigrid differ from either of these?

11.40. For solving linear systems arising from elliptic boundary value problems, which type of method, iterative or direct, suffers a greater increase in work as the dimension of the problem increases? Why?

11.41. Is any type of method capable of solving linear systems arising from elliptic boundary value problems in time proportional to the number of grid points? If so, name one, and if not, why not?

Exercises

11.1. Suppose you are given a general-purpose subroutine for solving initial value problems for systems of n first-order ODEs $\boldsymbol{y}' = \boldsymbol{f}(t, \boldsymbol{y})$, and this is the only software tool you have available. For each type of problem in parts *a*, *b*, and *c* to follow, describe how you could use this routine to solve it. In each case, your answer should address the following points:

1. What is the function $\boldsymbol{f}$ for the ODE subproblem?
2. How would you obtain the necessary initial

conditions?

3. What special properties, if any, would the ODE subproblem have that would affect the choice of ODE method?

(*a*) Compute the definite integral

$$\int_a^b g(s)\, ds.$$

(*b*) Solve the two-point boundary value problem

$$y'' = y^2 + t, \qquad 0 \le t \le 1,$$

with boundary conditions

$$y(0) = 0, \qquad y(1) = 1.$$

(*c*) Solve the heat equation

$$u_t = c\,u_{xx}, \qquad 0 \le x \le 1, \qquad t \ge 0,$$

with initial condition

$$u(0, x) = g(x), \qquad 0 \le x \le 1,$$

and boundary conditions

$$u(t, 0) = 0, \qquad u(t, 1) = 0, \qquad t \ge 0.$$

11.2. Consider a finite difference solution of the Poisson equation $u_{xx} + u_{yy} = x + y$ on the unit square using the boundary conditions and mesh points shown in the drawing. Use a second-order accurate, centered finite difference scheme to compute the approximate value of the solution at the center of the square.

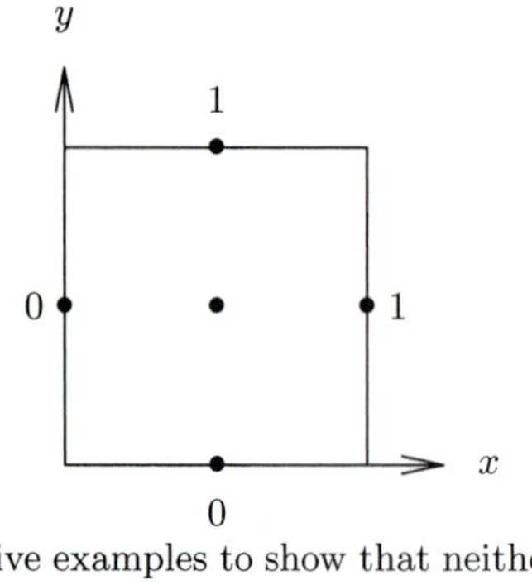

11.3. Give examples to show that neither consistency nor stability alone is sufficient to guarantee convergence of a finite difference scheme for solving a partial differential equation numerically.

11.4. Draw pictures to illustrate the nonzero pattern of the matrix resulting from a finite difference discretization of the Laplace equation on a d-dimensional grid, with k grid points in each dimension, for $d = 1$, 2, and 3, as described at the end of Section 11.3.1. Use a value of k that is large enough to show the general pattern clearly. In each case, what are the numerical values of the nonzero entries?

11.5. (*a*) For the matrix of Example 11.6, verify that the nonzero pattern of the Cholesky factor, including fill, is as shown in Figs. 11.8–11.10.

(*b*) Verify that the reorderings given in Figs. 11.9–11.10 are indeed minimum degree and nested dissection orderings, respectively. In each case, write out the permutation matrix $\boldsymbol{P}$ corresponding to the reordering, such that the reordered matrix is given by $\boldsymbol{PAP}^T$, where $\boldsymbol{A}$ is the matrix in the original natural ordering.

11.6. Prove that the Jacobi iterative method for solving the linear system $\boldsymbol{Ax} = \boldsymbol{b}$ converges if the matrix $\boldsymbol{A}$ is diagonally dominant by rows. (*Hint*: Use the ∞-norm.)

11.7. Prove that the SOR method diverges if ω does not lie in the interval $(0, 2)$.

11.8. Prove that the successive $\boldsymbol{A}$-orthogonal search directions generated by the conjugate gradient method satisfy a three-term recurrence, so that each new gradient need be orthogonalized only against the previous two.

11.9. Show that the subspace spanned by the first m search directions in the conjugate gradient method is the same as the Krylov subspace generated by the sequence $\boldsymbol{r}_0$, $\boldsymbol{Ar}_0$, $\boldsymbol{A}^2\boldsymbol{r}_0$, ..., $\boldsymbol{A}^{m-1}\boldsymbol{r}_0$.

11.10. On the basis of the background facts and motivation outlined in Section 11.5.5, fill in the details of the derivation of the conjugate gradient algorithm stated there. You will probably find it easiest first to derive a straightforward version of the algorithm, then try to improve its efficiency by reducing the number of matrix-vector multiplications and other arithmetic required.

Computer Problems

11.1. Consider the heat equation

$$u_t = u_{xx}, \qquad 0 \le x \le 1, \qquad t \ge 0,$$

with initial condition

$$u(0,x) = \begin{cases} 2x, & 0 \le x \le 0.5 \\ 2-2x, & 0.5 \le x \le 1 \end{cases},$$

and boundary conditions

$$u(t,0) = 0, \qquad u(t,1) = 0, \qquad t \ge 0.$$

(*a*) Using the full discretization given in Example 11.2, with $\Delta x = 0.05$ and $\Delta t = 0.0012$, evolve the solution from $t = 0$ to $t = 0.06$. Plot the solution at the initial time, the final time, and periodically in between (say, every ten time steps or so). If you use interactive graphics, you may prefer to plot the solution at every time step, giving the effect of an animated movie.

(*b*) Repeat part *a*, but use a time step of $\Delta t = 0.0013$. Plot the solution in the same manner as before. Can you explain the difference in results?

(*c*) Solve the same equation again, this time using the implicit method given in Section 11.2.2 based on the backward Euler method. Again use $\Delta x = 0.05$, but try a much larger time step, say, $\Delta t = 0.005$ to advance the solution from $t = 0$ to $t = 0.06$. Plot the solution at each time step. How do the results compare with those in parts *a* and *b*? Explain.

(*d*) Solve the same equation again, this time using the Crank-Nicolson method given in Section 11.2.2. Again use $\Delta x = 0.05$ and $\Delta t = 0.005$ to advance the solution from $t = 0$ to $t = 0.06$. Plot the solution at each time step. How do the results compare with your previous results? Explain.

(*e*) Form the semidiscrete system for this equation given in Section 11.2.1, using a finite difference spatial discretization with $\Delta x = 0.05$, and use an ODE solver to integrate it from $t = 0$ to $t = 0.06$. Plot the solution as before. How do the results compare with your previous results?

11.2. (*a*) Use the method of lines and an ODE solver of your choice to solve the heat equation

$$u_t = u_{xx}, \qquad 0 \le x \le 1, \qquad t \ge 0,$$

with initial condition

$$u(0,x) = \sin(\pi x), \qquad 0 \le x \le 1,$$

and Dirichlet boundary conditions

$$u(t,0) = 0, \qquad u(t,1) = 0, \qquad t \ge 0.$$

Integrate from $t = 0$ to $t = 0.1$. Plot the computed solution, preferably as a three-dimensional surface over the (t,x) plane. If you do not have three-dimensional plotting capability, plot the solution as a function of x for a few values of t, including the initial and final times. Determine the maximum error in the computed solution by comparing with the exact solution

$$u(t,x) = \exp(-\pi^2 t)\sin(\pi x).$$

Experiment with various spatial mesh sizes Δx, and try to characterize the error as a function of Δx. On a log-log scale, plot the maximum error as a function of Δx.

(*b*) Repeat part *a*, but this time with initial condition

$$u(0,x) = \cos(\pi x), \qquad 0 \le x \le 1,$$

and Neumann boundary conditions

$$u_x(t,0) = 0, \qquad u_x(t,1) = 0, \qquad t \ge 0,$$

and compare with the exact solution

$$u(t,x) = \exp(-\pi^2 t)\cos(\pi x).$$

11.3. Use the method of lines and an ODE solver of your choice to solve the wave equation

$$u_{tt} = u_{xx}, \qquad 0 \le x \le 1, \qquad t \ge 0,$$

with initial conditions

$$u(0,x) = \sin(\pi x), \quad u_t(0,x) = 0, \quad 0 \le x \le 1,$$

and boundary conditions

$$u(t,0) = 0, \quad u(t,1) = 0, \quad t \ge 0.$$

Integrate from $t = 0$ to $t = 2$. Plot the computed solution, preferably as a three-dimensional surface over the (t, x) plane. If you do not have three-dimensional plotting capability, plot the solution as a function of x for a few values of t, including the initial and final times. Determine the maximum error in the computed solution by comparing with the exact solution

$$u(t, x) = \cos(\pi t)\sin(\pi x).$$

Note that the solution is periodic with period 2, so the solution should be the same at $t = 0$ and $t = 2$. Is this true for your computed solution? Experiment with various spatial mesh sizes Δx, and try to characterize the error as a function of Δx. On a log-log scale, plot the maximum error as a function of Δx.

11.4. Use the method of lines and an ODE solver of your choice to solve the advection equation

$$u_t = -u_x, \qquad 0 \le x \le 1, \qquad t \ge 0,$$

with initial condition

$$u(0, x) = 0, \qquad 0 \le x \le 1,$$

and boundary condition

$$u(t, 0) = 1, \qquad t \ge 0.$$

Integrate from $t = 0$ to $t = 2$, and plot the computed solution, preferably as a three-dimensional surface over the (t, x) plane. If you do not have three-dimensional plotting capability, plot the solution at $x = 1$ as a function of t. Try both one-sided (upwind) and centered finite difference schemes for the spatial discretization. The exact solution is a step function of height 1 moving to the right with velocity 1. Does either difference scheme come close to this ideal? How would you describe the difference between the computed solutions given by the two schemes? Which computed solution is smoother? Which is more accurate?

11.5. Use the method of lines and an ODE solver of your choice to solve the nonlinear *Burgers' equation*

$$u_t = -uu_x + vu_{xx}, \quad 0 \le x \le 1, \quad t \ge 0,$$

with initial condition

$$u(0, x) = 1/(1 + \exp(x/(2v))), \quad 0 \le x \le 1,$$

and boundary conditions

$$u(t, x) = 1/(1 + \exp(x/(2v) - t/(4v))), \quad t \ge 0,$$

for $x = 0$ and $x = 1$, where v is a scalar parameter representing viscosity. Note that this equation has both a nonlinear convective (hyperbolic) term, $-uu_x$, and a linear diffusion (parabolic) term, vu_{xx}, and the balance between them is determined by the relative value of v.

Integrate from $t = 0$ to $t = 2$, and plot the computed solution, preferably as a three-dimensional surface over the (t, x) plane. If you do not have three-dimensional plotting capability, plot the solution at $x = 1$ as a function of t. Experiment with various values for v, say, $v = 1$, 0.5, 0.1, and 0.01. Try both one-sided (upwind) and centered finite difference schemes for the spatial discretization, and experiment with various mesh sizes. Compare your solutions with the exact solution, which is the function used previously to define the boundary conditions. Compare the accuracy and smoothness of the solutions computed by the two schemes as v varies. What can you say about the effect of changing the spatial step size for the various values of v?

11.6. Use the standard five-point finite difference discretization to solve the Poisson equation

$$-u_{xx} - u_{yy} = 2$$

on the L-shaped region in the accompanying diagram, with boundary conditions $u(x, y) = 0$ on all boundaries.

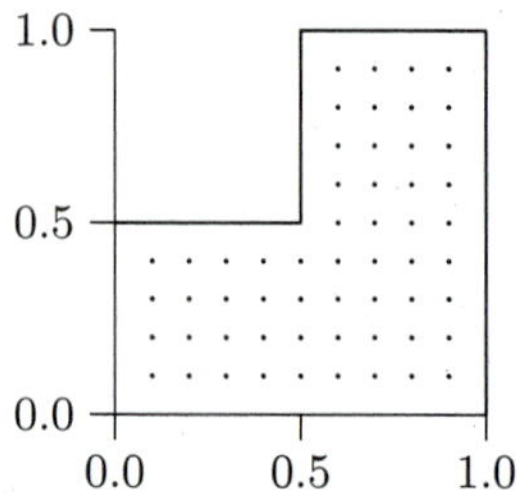

(a) Choose a mesh size h (for example, $h = 0.1$ in the diagram) and set up the appropriate matrix and right-hand-side vector. Solve the resulting linear system by a direct method and plot the resulting solution, preferably as a three-dimensional surface over the (x, y) plane. Experiment with various values for the mesh size h and observe the effect on the solution.

(*b*) Repeat part *a*, but this time use the SOR method to solve the linear system. Note that with an iterative method you need not set up the matrix explicitly but can work directly with the approximate solution at each mesh point, updating the values at each iteration. For a given mesh size h, experiment with various values for the SOR parameter ω in the range $0 < \omega < 2$. Can you find an optimal value for ω? Does the optimal ω become larger or smaller as h decreases?

11.7. The time-independent *Schrödinger equation* in two dimensions,

$$-(\psi_{xx}(x,y) + \psi_{yy}(x,y)) + V(x,y)\psi(x,y) = E\psi(x,y),$$

where we have chosen units so that the quantities are dimensionless, describes the wave function ψ of a particle of energy E subject to a potential V. The square of the wave function, $|\psi(x,y)|^2$, can be interpreted as the probability of finding the particle at position (x, y).

Assume that the particle is confined to a two-dimensional box, say, the unit square, within which it can move freely. Thus, the potential is zero within the unit square and infinite elsewhere. Since there is zero probability of finding the particle outside the box, the wave function must be zero at its boundaries. Thus, we have an eigenvalue problem for the elliptic PDE

$$-(\psi_{xx}(x,y) + \psi_{yy}(x,y)) = E\psi(x,y),$$

on the unit square, subject to the boundary condition $\psi(x, y) = 0$ on all boundaries. Note that the discrete eigenvalues E are the only energy levels permitted; this feature gives quantum mechanics its name.

Use a finite difference discretization of the PDE to derive an algebraic eigenvalue problem whose eigenvalues and eigenvectors approximate those of the PDE, then compute the eigenvalues and eigenvectors using a library routine (see Section 4.8). Experiment with various mesh sizes and observe how the eigenvalues behave.

An analytical solution to this problem is easily obtained, which gives the eigenvalues

$$E_{k,j} = (k^2 + j^2)\pi^2$$

and corresponding eigenfunctions

$$\psi_{k,j}(x,y) = \sin(k\pi x)\sin(j\pi y), \quad k,j = 1,2,\ldots.$$

How do your computed eigenvalues and eigenvectors compare with these analytical values as the mesh size of your discretization decreases? Try to characterize the error as a function of the mesh size.

Note that a nonzero potential V would not seriously complicate the numerical solution of the Schrödinger equation but would generally make an analytical solution much more difficult to obtain.

11.8. Verify empirically that the Jacobian of the semidiscrete system of ODEs given in Section 11.2.1 has eigenvalues between $-4c/(\Delta x)^2$ and 0. For this exercise, you may take $c = 1$. Experiment with several different mesh sizes Δx. How do the eigenvalues behave as $\Delta x \to 0$?

11.9. Consider the semidiscrete system of ODEs obtained from a centered spatial discretization of the advection equation. Examine the stability of Euler's method for this system of ODEs by computing the eigenvalues of its Jacobian matrix. Is there any value for the size of the time step that yields a stable method? Answer the same question for the semidiscrete system obtained from one-sided upwind differencing.

11.10. For the standard five-point approximation to Laplace's equation on a $k \times k$ grid, experiment with various values of the relaxation parameter ω in the SOR method to see how much difference this makes in the spectral radius of the resulting iteration matrix $\boldsymbol{G}$ and the rate of convergence of the algorithm. Draw a plot of $\rho(\boldsymbol{G})$ as a function of ω for $0 < \omega < 2$. How does the minimum of this curve compare with the theoretical minimum given by

$$\rho(\boldsymbol{G}) = \frac{1 - \sin(\pi h)}{1 + \sin(\pi h)},$$

which occurs for

$$\omega = \frac{2}{1 + \sin(\pi h)},$$

where $h = 1/(k + 1)$? Experiment with various values of k, say, $k = 5$, 10, 20.

11.11. Verify empirically the spectral radius and rate of convergence data given in Tables 11.1 and 11.2.

11.12. Implement the steepest descent and conjugate gradient methods for solving symmetric positive definite linear systems. Compare their performance, both in rate of convergence and in total time required, in solving a representative sample of test problems, both well-conditioned and ill-conditioned. How does the rate of convergence of the conjugate gradient method compare with the theoretical estimate given in Section 11.5.6?

11.13. (*a*) Implement the Gauss-Seidel method for solving the $n \times n$ linear system $\boldsymbol{A}\boldsymbol{x} = \boldsymbol{b}$, where $\boldsymbol{A}$ is the matrix resulting from a finite difference approximation to the one-dimensional Laplace equation on an interval, with boundary values of zero at the endpoints. Thus, $\boldsymbol{A}$ is tridiagonal with diagonal elements equal to 2 and subdiagonal and superdiagonal elements equal to -1, and $\boldsymbol{x}$ represents the solution values at the interior mesh points. Take $\boldsymbol{b} = \boldsymbol{0}$, so that the exact solution is $\boldsymbol{x} = \boldsymbol{0}$, and therefore at any iteration the error is equal to the current value for $\boldsymbol{x}$.
For the initial starting guess, take

$$x_j = \sin\left(\frac{jk\pi}{n+1}\right), \quad j = 1, \ldots, n.$$

For any given value of k, the resulting vector $\boldsymbol{x}$ represents a discrete sample of a sine wave whose frequency depends on k. Thus, by choosing various values for k and then observing the resulting Gauss-Seidel iterations, we can determine the relative speeds with which components of the error of various frequencies are damped out.

With $n = 50$, perform this experiment for $k = 1, 5, 10, \ldots, 25$. For each value of k, make a plot of the solution $\boldsymbol{x}$ at the starting value and for each of the first ten iterations of the Gauss-Seidel method. For what values of k is the error damped out most rapidly and most slowly? It turns out that frequencies beyond $k = n/2$ (called the Nyquist frequency; see Section 12.1.1), simply repeat the previous frequencies, as you may wish to verify. Do your results suggest that the Gauss-Seidel method is a *smoother*, as discussed in Section 11.5.7? Try the same experiment using a starting value for $\boldsymbol{x}$ with all entries equal to 1. Does the error decay rapidly or slowly, compared with your previous experiments?

(*b*) Repeat part *a*, but this time using the Jacobi method instead of Gauss-Seidel, and answer the same questions.

11.14. Implement a two-grid version of the multigrid algorithm, as outlined in Section 11.5.7. If recursion is supported in the computing environment you use, you may find it almost as easy to implement multiple grid levels. Test your program on a simple elliptic boundary value problem, such as the Laplace equation in one dimension on the unit interval or in two dimensions on the unit square with given boundary conditions.

11.15. Using the standard five-point discretization of the Laplace equation on a $k \times k$ grid in two dimensions, and systematically varying k, verify empirically as many of the results given in Table 11.3 as you can. Try to determine the approximate proportionality constant for the dominant term in each case.

Chapter 12

Fast Fourier Transform

12.1 Trigonometric Interpolation

Measurements of the amount of carbon dioxide in the Earth's atmosphere are an important indicator of the possibility of global warming. But the amount of CO_2 changes constantly due to seasonal effects on biological and industrial activity, so how can one determine the true overall trend? Many other phenomena—from sunspots to stock prices, from pulsars to telecommunication lines, from glacier movement to breakers on a beach—exhibit such cyclic behavior. In modeling cyclic data, it is more appropriate and informative to use trigonometric functions—specifically, sines and cosines—as basis functions rather than the polynomials and piecewise polynomials we considered in Chapter 7.

Representing a function as a linear combination of sines and cosines decomposes the function into its components of various frequencies, much as a prism resolves a light beam into its constituent colors. The resulting coefficients of the trigonometric basis functions reveal which frequencies are present in the function and in what amounts. Moreover, representing the function in *frequency space* enables various manipulations of the function required in many applications, such as in signal processing or in solving differential equations, to be performed much more efficiently than in the original time or space domain. In this chapter we will see that *trigonometric interpolation* of a sampled function can be done remarkably efficiently using an algorithm known as the *fast Fourier transform.*

It will be convenient to use complex exponential notation, which is related to ordinary trigonometric functions by *Euler's identity* (see Section 1.3.11),

$$e^{i\theta} = \cos\theta + i\sin\theta,$$

where $i = \sqrt{-1}$. Since

$$e^{-i\theta} = \cos(-\theta) + i\sin(-\theta) = \cos\theta - i\sin\theta,$$

we see that for cosine and sine waves of frequency k we have

$$\cos(2\pi kt) = \frac{e^{2\pi ikt} + e^{-2\pi ikt}}{2} \quad \text{and} \quad \sin(2\pi kt) = i\,\frac{e^{-2\pi ikt} - e^{2\pi ikt}}{2},$$

which means that a pure cosine or sine wave of frequency k is equivalent to a sum or difference, respectively, of complex exponentials of half the amplitude and of frequencies k and $-k$. For a given integer n, we will use the notation

$$\omega_n = \cos(2\pi/n) - i\sin(2\pi/n) = e^{-2\pi i/n}$$

for the given nth root of unity, meaning that $\omega_n^n = 1$. All of the nth roots of unity, sometimes called *twiddle factors* in this context, are then given by ω_n^k or by ω_n^{-k}, $k = 0, \ldots, n-1$, and are illustrated for the case $n = 4$ in Fig. 12.1. For simplicity, we will sometimes omit the subscript n from ω when its value is clear.

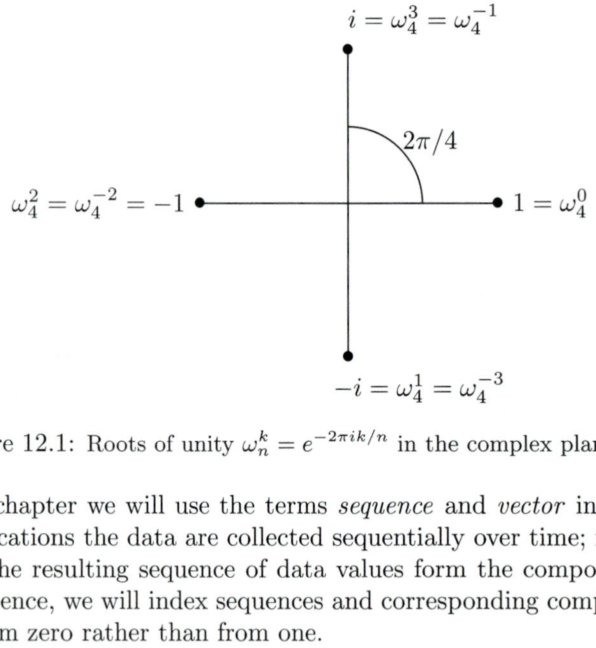

Figure 12.1: Roots of unity $\omega_n^k = e^{-2\pi ik/n}$ in the complex plane for $n = 4$.

In this chapter we will use the terms *sequence* and *vector* interchangeably. In many applications the data are collected sequentially over time; for computational purposes, the resulting sequence of data values form the components of a vector. For convenience, we will index sequences and corresponding components of vectors starting from zero rather than from one.

12.1.1 Discrete Fourier Transform

Given a sequence $\boldsymbol{x} = [x_0, \ldots, x_{n-1}]^T$, its *discrete Fourier transform*, or *DFT*, is the sequence $\boldsymbol{y} = [y_0, \ldots, y_{n-1}]^T$ given by

$$y_m = \sum_{k=0}^{n-1} x_k\,\omega_n^{mk}, \quad m = 0, 1, \ldots, n-1.$$

We can write the DFT more succinctly in matrix notation as

$$\boldsymbol{y} = \boldsymbol{F}_n\,\boldsymbol{x},$$

where the entries of the Fourier matrix $\boldsymbol{F}_n$ are given by

$$\{\boldsymbol{F}_n\}_{mk} = \omega_n^{mk}.$$

Here is how this matrix looks for the case $n = 4$:

$$\boldsymbol{F}_4 = \begin{bmatrix} 1 & 1 & 1 & 1 \\ 1 & \omega^1 & \omega^2 & \omega^3 \\ 1 & \omega^2 & \omega^4 & \omega^6 \\ 1 & \omega^3 & \omega^6 & \omega^9 \end{bmatrix} = \begin{bmatrix} 1 & 1 & 1 & 1 \\ 1 & -i & -1 & i \\ 1 & -1 & 1 & -1 \\ 1 & i & -1 & -i \end{bmatrix}.$$

In general, $\boldsymbol{F}_n$ is a complex symmetric Vandermonde matrix, but not Hermitian. Even more interesting, however, is that its inverse is easily written explicitly, e.g.,

$$\frac{1}{4}\begin{bmatrix} 1 & 1 & 1 & 1 \\ 1 & \omega^{-1} & \omega^{-2} & \omega^{-3} \\ 1 & \omega^{-2} & \omega^{-4} & \omega^{-6} \\ 1 & \omega^{-3} & \omega^{-6} & \omega^{-9} \end{bmatrix}\begin{bmatrix} 1 & 1 & 1 & 1 \\ 1 & \omega^1 & \omega^2 & \omega^3 \\ 1 & \omega^2 & \omega^4 & \omega^6 \\ 1 & \omega^3 & \omega^6 & \omega^9 \end{bmatrix} = \begin{bmatrix} 1 & 0 & 0 & 0 \\ 0 & 1 & 0 & 0 \\ 0 & 0 & 1 & 0 \\ 0 & 0 & 0 & 1 \end{bmatrix},$$

so that $\boldsymbol{F}_n^{-1} = (1/n)\boldsymbol{F}_n^H$. We therefore have the *inverse DFT*

$$x_k = \frac{1}{n}\sum_{m=0}^{n-1} y_m\, \omega_n^{-mk}, \quad k = 0, 1, \ldots, n-1,$$

which represents the components of $\boldsymbol{x}$ as a linear combination of sines and cosines, with coefficients given by the components of $\boldsymbol{y}$. Thus, if the components of $\boldsymbol{x}$ are sample values of a function, then the DFT solves the trigonometric interpolation problem with nothing more than a matrix-vector multiplication, which costs $\mathcal{O}(n^2)$ as opposed to the usual $\mathcal{O}(n^3)$ cost of solving a linear system. The main point of this chapter is that with the fast Fourier transform we can do better still, reducing the cost of trigonometric interpolation to $\mathcal{O}(n \log_2 n)$.

The DFT of a sequence, even a purely real sequence, is in general complex. This property may seem counterintuitive, but it is in essence only a notational artifact and should not alarm us, as the inverse DFT will take us back into the real domain. How can the inverse DFT of a complex sequence yield a purely real result? Obviously, through cancellation of the imaginary parts. Note that the DFT of a real sequence of length n, though it has a total of $2n$ real and imaginary parts, still contains only n independent pieces of information because the components of the second half of the transformed sequence are complex conjugates of those in the first half. (More precisely, y_k and y_{n-k} are complex conjugates for $k = 1, \ldots, (n/2)-1$). This fact can be used to save on storage if the input sequence is known to be real.

The DFT resolves an input sequence $\boldsymbol{x}$ into its underlying fundamental frequency components, whose individual contributions are given by the elements of the transformed sequence $\boldsymbol{y}$. Two components of special interest are y_0, which corresponds to zero frequency (i.e., a constant function), and $y_{n/2}$, which corresponds to the *Nyquist frequency*—the highest frequency representable at the given sampling rate. The component y_0 is sometimes called the DC component, by analogy with non-oscillating direct electrical current, and its value is simply the sum of the components of $\boldsymbol{x}$. Because the DFT is periodic in frequency, the components of $\boldsymbol{y}$ beyond the Nyquist frequency correspond to frequencies that are the negatives of those below the Nyquist frequency.

Example 12.1 Discrete Fourier Transform. To illustrate the DFT, we transform two sequences, one chosen randomly, the other chosen to have a definite cyclic character. For the random sequence, we have

$$\boldsymbol{F}_8\,\boldsymbol{x} = \boldsymbol{F}_8 \begin{bmatrix} 4 \\ 0 \\ 3 \\ 6 \\ 2 \\ 9 \\ 6 \\ 5 \end{bmatrix} = \begin{bmatrix} 35 \\ -5.07 + 8.66i \\ -3 + 2i \\ 9.07 + 2.66i \\ -5 \\ 9.07 - 2.66i \\ -3 - 2i \\ -5.07 - 8.66i \end{bmatrix} = \boldsymbol{y}.$$

We see that the transformed sequence is complex, but y_0 and y_4 are real, while y_5, y_6, and y_7 are complex conjugates of y_3, y_2, and y_1, respectively, as expected for a real input sequence. There appears to be no discernible pattern to the frequencies present, as expected for a random sequence. And y_0 is indeed equal to the sum of the elements of $\boldsymbol{x}$.

To illustrate the DFT of a cyclic sequence, we have

$$\boldsymbol{F}_8\,\boldsymbol{x} = \boldsymbol{F}_8 \begin{bmatrix} 1 \\ -1 \\ 1 \\ -1 \\ 1 \\ -1 \\ 1 \\ -1 \end{bmatrix} = \begin{bmatrix} 0 \\ 0 \\ 0 \\ 0 \\ 8 \\ 0 \\ 0 \\ 0 \end{bmatrix} = \boldsymbol{y}.$$

This sequence was chosen deliberately to have the highest possible rate of oscillation (between 1 and -1) for this sampling rate. In the transformed sequence we see a nonzero component at the Nyquist frequency (in this case y_4), and no other component is present. Again, y_0 is equal to the sum of the elements of $\boldsymbol{x}$.

12.2 FFT Algorithm

By taking advantage of certain symmetries and redundancies in the definition of the DFT, a shortcut algorithm can be developed for evaluating the DFT very efficiently. For illustration, consider the case $n = 4$. From the definition of the DFT we have

$$y_m = \sum_{k=0}^{3} x_k\,\omega_n^{mk}, \quad m = 0, \ldots, 3.$$

Writing out the four equations in full, we have

$$\begin{aligned} y_0 &= x_0\omega_n^0 + x_1\omega_n^0 + x_2\omega_n^0 + x_3\omega_n^0, \\ y_1 &= x_0\omega_n^0 + x_1\omega_n^1 + x_2\omega_n^2 + x_3\omega_n^3, \\ y_2 &= x_0\omega_n^0 + x_1\omega_n^2 + x_2\omega_n^4 + x_3\omega_n^6, \\ y_3 &= x_0\omega_n^0 + x_1\omega_n^3 + x_2\omega_n^6 + x_3\omega_n^9. \end{aligned}$$

Noting that

$$\omega_n^0 = \omega_n^4 = 1, \qquad \omega_n^2 = \omega_n^6 = -1, \qquad \omega_n^9 = \omega_n^1$$

and regrouping, we obtain the four equations

$$\begin{aligned} y_0 &= (x_0 + \omega_n^0 x_2) + \omega_n^0(x_1 + \omega_n^0 x_3), \\ y_1 &= (x_0 - \omega_n^0 x_2) + \omega_n^1(x_1 - \omega_n^0 x_3), \\ y_2 &= (x_0 + \omega_n^0 x_2) + \omega_n^2(x_1 + \omega_n^0 x_3), \\ y_3 &= (x_0 - \omega_n^0 x_2) + \omega_n^3(x_1 - \omega_n^0 x_3). \end{aligned}$$

We now observe that the transform can be computed with only 8 additions or subtractions and 6 multiplications, instead of the expected $(4-1)*4 = 12$ additions and $4^2 = 16$ multiplications. Actually, even fewer multiplications are required for this small case, since $\omega_n^0 = 1$, but we have tried to illustrate how the algorithm works in general. The main point is that computing the DFT of the original 4-point sequence has been reduced to computing the DFT of its two 2-point even and odd subsequences. This property holds in general: the DFT of an n-point sequence can be computed by breaking it into two DFTs of half the length, provided n is even.

The general pattern becomes clearer when viewed in terms of the first few Fourier matrices

$$\boldsymbol{F}_1 = 1, \qquad \boldsymbol{F}_2 = \begin{bmatrix} 1 & 1 \\ 1 & -1 \end{bmatrix}, \qquad \boldsymbol{F}_4 = \begin{bmatrix} 1 & 1 & 1 & 1 \\ 1 & -i & -1 & i \\ 1 & -1 & 1 & -1 \\ 1 & i & -1 & -i \end{bmatrix}.$$

Let $\boldsymbol{P}_4$ be the permutation matrix

$$\boldsymbol{P}_4 = \begin{bmatrix} 1 & 0 & 0 & 0 \\ 0 & 0 & 1 & 0 \\ 0 & 1 & 0 & 0 \\ 0 & 0 & 0 & 1 \end{bmatrix}$$

and $\boldsymbol{D}_2$ the diagonal matrix

$$\boldsymbol{D}_2 = \mathrm{diag}(1, \omega_4) = \begin{bmatrix} 1 & 0 \\ 0 & -i \end{bmatrix}.$$

Then we have

$$\boldsymbol{F}_4\boldsymbol{P}_4 = \left[\begin{array}{cc|cc} 1 & 1 & 1 & 1 \\ 1 & -1 & -i & i \\ \hline 1 & 1 & -1 & -1 \\ 1 & -1 & i & -i \end{array}\right] = \begin{bmatrix} \boldsymbol{F}_2 & \boldsymbol{D}_2\boldsymbol{F}_2 \\ \boldsymbol{F}_2 & -\boldsymbol{D}_2\boldsymbol{F}_2 \end{bmatrix},$$

i.e., $\boldsymbol{F}_4$ can be rearranged so that each block is a diagonally scaled version of $\boldsymbol{F}_2$. Such a hierarchical decomposition can be carried out at each level, provided the number of points is even. In general, $\boldsymbol{P}_n$ is the permutation that groups the even-numbered columns of $\boldsymbol{F}_n$ before the odd-numbered columns, and

$$\boldsymbol{D}_{n/2} = \mathrm{diag}\left(1, \omega_n, \ldots, \omega_n^{(n/2)-1}\right).$$

Thus, to apply $\boldsymbol{F}_n$ to a sequence of length n, we need merely apply $\boldsymbol{F}_{n/2}$ to its even and odd subsequences and scale the results, where necessary, by $\pm\boldsymbol{D}_{n/2}$. This recursive divide-and-conquer approach to computing the DFT, called the *fast Fourier transform*, or *FFT*, is formalized in Algorithm 12.1, where it is assumed that n is a power of two.

Algorithm 12.1 Fast Fourier Transform

```
procedure fft(x, y, n, ω)
    if n = 1 then
        y[0] = x[0]                              { bottom of recursion }
    else
        for k = 0 to (n/2) − 1
            p[k] = x[2k]                         { split into even and
            s[k] = x[2k + 1]                       odd subsequences }
        end
        fft(p, q, n/2, ω²)                       { call fft procedure
        fft(s, t, n/2, ω²)                         recursively }
        for k = 0 to n − 1
            y[k] = q[k mod (n/2)] +              { combine results }
                   ω^k t[k mod (n/2)]
        end
    end
```

We note the following points about Algorithm 12.1:

- There are $\log_2 n$ levels of recursion, each of which involves $\mathcal{O}(n)$ arithmetic operations, so the total cost is $\mathcal{O}(n \log_2 n)$. If the weights ω^k are precomputed, the total number of *real* floating-point operations required by the FFT algorithm is $5n \log_2 n$, compared with $8n^2$ real floating-point operations for an ordinary complex matrix-vector product.
- For clarity, separate arrays are used for the subsequences, but in fact the transform can be computed in place using no additional storage.
- The input sequence is assumed to be complex. If the input sequence is real, then additional symmetries in the DFT can be exploited to reduce the storage and operation count by half.
- The output sequence is not produced in the natural order. Most FFT routines automatically allow for this by appropriately rearranging either the input or output sequence. This additional step does not affect the overall computational complexity, because the necessary rearrangement (analogous to a sort) also costs $\mathcal{O}(n \log_2 n)$.

- The FFT algorithm can be formulated using iteration rather than recursion, which is often desirable for greater efficiency or when using a programming language that does not support recursion.

Despite its name, the fast Fourier transform is an algorithm, not a transform. It is a particular way (or family of ways) of computing the discrete Fourier transform of a sequence in a very efficient manner. As we have seen, the DFT is defined in terms of a matrix-vector product, whose straightforward evaluation would appear to require $\mathcal{O}(n^2)$ arithmetic operations. Use of the FFT algorithm reduces the work to only $\mathcal{O}(n \log_2 n)$, which makes an enormous practical difference in the time required to transform large sequences, as illustrated in Table 12.1.

n	$n \log_2 n$	n^2
64	384	4096
128	896	16384
256	2048	65536
512	4608	262144
1024	10240	1048576

Table 12.1: Complexity of FFT algorithm versus matrix-vector multiplication

Owing to the similar form of the DFT and its inverse (they differ only in the sign of the exponent), the FFT algorithm can also be used to compute the inverse DFT efficiently. This ability to transform back and forth quickly between the time or space domain and the frequency domain makes it practical to perform any computation or analysis that may be required in whichever domain is more convenient or efficient.

12.2.1 Limitations of FFT

Although the FFT algorithm has revolutionized many aspects of numerical computation, it is not always applicable or maximally efficient. In particular, the input sequence is assumed to be:

- Equally spaced
- Periodic
- A power of two in length

The first two of these properties follow from the definition of the DFT, whereas the third is required for maximal efficiency of the FFT algorithm. The interpolant given by the DFT, as a linear combination of sines and cosines, will necessarily be periodic, which means that for a sequence of length n, we must have $x_0 = x_n$ or, more generally, $x_k = x_{n+k}$ for any integer k (note that only x_0 through x_{n-1} are actually specified). Thus, some care must be taken in applying the FFT algorithm to produce the most meaningful results as efficiently as possible. For instance, transforming a sequence that is not really periodic, or padding a sequence to make its length a power of two may introduce spurious noise and complicate the interpretation of the results.

It is possible to define a "mixed-radix" FFT algorithm that does not require the number of points n to be a power of two. The more general algorithm is still based on divide-and-conquer; the sequence is not necessarily split exactly in half at each level, however, but rather by the smallest prime factor of the remaining sequence length. For example, a sequence of length 45 would be split into three subsequences of length 15, each of which in turn would be split into three subsequences of length five. When a subsequence can be split no further (i.e., when its length is prime), then its transform must be computed by conventional matrix-vector multiplication. The efficiency of such an algorithm depends on whether n is a product of small primes (ideally a power of two, of course). If this is not the case, then much of the computational advantage of the FFT may be lost. For example, if n itself is a prime, then the original sequence cannot be split at all, and the "fast" algorithm then becomes standard $\mathcal{O}(n^2)$ matrix-vector multiplication.

12.3 Applications of DFT

The DFT is often of direct interest itself and is also useful as a computational tool that provides an efficient means for computing other quantities. The DFT is of direct interest in detecting periodicities or cycles in discrete data. Moreover, it can be used to *remove* unwanted periodicities. For example, to remove high-frequency noise from a sequence, one can compute its DFT, set the high-frequency components of the transformed sequence to zero, then compute the inverse DFT of the modified sequence to go back to the original domain.

As another example, weather data often contain two distinct cycles, diurnal and annual. One might want to remove one of these in order to study the other in isolation. Economic data are also often "seasonally adjusted," removing unwanted periodicities to reveal secular trends. Because of such uses, the DFT is of vital importance in many aspects of signal processing, such as digital filtering.

Some computations are simpler or more efficient in the frequency domain than in the time or space domain. Examples include the discrete circular convolution of two sequences $\boldsymbol{u}$ and $\boldsymbol{v}$ of length n,

$$\{\boldsymbol{u} \star \boldsymbol{v}\}_m = \sum_{k=0}^{n-1} v_k\, u_{m-k}, \quad m = 0, 1, \ldots, n-1,$$

and related quantities such as the cross-correlation of two sequences or the auto-correlation of a sequence with itself. In each case, the equivalent operation in the frequency domain is simply pointwise multiplication (in some cases with complex conjugation).

For example, convolution is equivalent to multiplication by a *circulant matrix*, and such a matrix is diagonalized by the DFT. Thus, if the convolution $\boldsymbol{z}$ of $\boldsymbol{u}$ and

$\boldsymbol{v}$ is given by

$$\begin{bmatrix} z_0 \\ z_1 \\ \vdots \\ z_{n-2} \\ z_{n-1} \end{bmatrix} = \begin{bmatrix} u_0 & u_{n-1} & u_{n-2} & \cdots & u_1 \\ u_1 & u_0 & u_{n-1} & \cdots & u_2 \\ \vdots & \ddots & \ddots & \ddots & \vdots \\ u_{n-2} & \cdots & u_1 & u_0 & u_{n-1} \\ u_{n-1} & \cdots & u_2 & u_1 & u_0 \end{bmatrix} \begin{bmatrix} v_0 \\ v_1 \\ \vdots \\ v_{n-2} \\ v_{n-1} \end{bmatrix},$$

then the corresponding transformed sequences $\hat{\boldsymbol{z}}$, $\hat{\boldsymbol{u}}$, and $\hat{\boldsymbol{v}}$ are related by

$$\begin{bmatrix} \hat{z}_0 \\ \hat{z}_1 \\ \vdots \\ \hat{z}_{n-2} \\ \hat{z}_{n-1} \end{bmatrix} = n \begin{bmatrix} \hat{u}_0 & 0 & \cdots & \cdots & 0 \\ 0 & \hat{u}_1 & 0 & \cdots & 0 \\ \vdots & \ddots & \ddots & \ddots & \vdots \\ 0 & \cdots & 0 & \hat{u}_{n-2} & 0 \\ 0 & \cdots & \cdots & 0 & \hat{u}_{n-1} \end{bmatrix} \begin{bmatrix} \hat{v}_0 \\ \hat{v}_1 \\ \vdots \\ \hat{v}_{n-2} \\ \hat{v}_{n-1} \end{bmatrix}.$$

For this reason, when computing the convolution of two sequences it is often advantageous to use the FFT algorithm to compute the DFT of each sequence, compute their pointwise product in the frequency domain, then compute the inverse DFT to go back to the time or space domain, again via the FFT algorithm.

The FFT algorithm forms the basis for some exceptionally efficient methods for solving certain elliptic boundary value problems, such as Poisson's equation on a regular domain with periodic boundary conditions (see Section 11.4.2). It also provides a similarly efficient approach for implementing spectral or pseudospectral methods for time-dependent partial differential equations with periodic boundary conditions.

12.3.1 Fast Polynomial Multiplication

The FFT algorithm also provides a fast method for some computations that might not at first glance seem related to it. Consider, for example, the problem of multiplying two polynomials $p(t)$ and $q(t)$, whose complexity by straightforward multiplication, using the coefficients of the polynomials, is proportional to the product of their degrees. Suppose that the product polynomial whose coefficients we wish to determine is of degree $n-1$. A polynomial of degree $n-1$ is uniquely determined by its values at n distinct points. Moreover, the value of the product polynomial at a particular point t is equal to the product of the factor polynomials at that point, i.e., $(p \cdot q)(t) = p(t)q(t)$. The product polynomial is therefore uniquely determined by the values of the pointwise product of p and q at n distinct points.

Thus, one way to compute the product polynomial is to evaluate p and q at n distinct points, compute their pointwise product, and then obtain the product polynomial by interpolation from these values. Since the pointwise product requires only $\mathcal{O}(n)$ arithmetic operations, the overall efficiency of this method will depend on how efficiently we can evaluate the given polynomials and then interpolate to obtain the product polynomial.

Recall that evaluating a polynomial at a set of points is equivalent to multiplying the vector of its coefficients by a Vandermonde matrix, and interpolation is equivalent to multiplying by the inverse of a Vandermonde matrix. These steps would appear to require at least $\mathcal{O}(n^2)$ arithmetic operations each, but they can be made much more efficient if we choose the evaluation points carefully. In particular, if we choose the nth roots of unity, then the necessary polynomial evaluations and interpolations become simply the DFT and its inverse. For example, if

$$p(t) = \sum_{k=0}^{n-1} x_k t^k,$$

then

$$p(\omega_n^m) = \sum_{k=0}^{n-1} x_k (\omega_n^m)^k = \sum_{k=0}^{n-1} x_k \omega_n^{mk} = y_m.$$

Thus, if the number of points n is a power of two and the FFT algorithm is used in this manner, then the complexity of polynomial multiplication can be reduced to $\mathcal{O}(n \log_2 n)$. Restricting n to be a power of two is not a serious limitation, since we can always consider any polynomial to have degree one less than the next higher power of two by taking the remaining coefficients to be zero. This result may seem to be of largely theoretical interest because the savings are insignificant unless the polynomial degrees are fairly large, but it turns out to be useful in some applications. For example, the response of a linear, time invariant system to a unit impulse signal is given by a convolution that is a product of polynomials. This is merely one illustration of how the FFT can crop up in unexpected ways.

12.4 Wavelets

The sine and cosine functions used in Fourier analysis have many useful features of great practical importance in a wide array of applications, but they are not ideal for all purposes. In particular, these functions are very smooth (infinitely differentiable) and very broad (nonzero almost everywhere on the real line). As a result, they are not very effective for representing functions that change abruptly or have highly localized support. The Gibbs phenomenon in the Fourier representation of a square wave (the "ringing" at the corners) is one manifestation of this.

In response to this shortcoming, there has been intense interest in recent years in a new type of basis functions called *wavelets*. A given wavelet basis is generated from a single function $\phi(x)$, called a *mother wavelet* or *scaling function*, by dilation and translation, i.e., $\phi((x-b)/a)$, where a and b are real numbers with $a \neq 0$. There are many different ways of choosing the mother wavelet. The main issue is the tradeoff between smoothness and compactness. A member of one of the most commonly used families of wavelets, due to Daubechies, is illustrated in Fig. 12.2.

Typical choices for the dilation and translation parameters are $a = 2^{-j}$ and $b = k2^j$, where j and k are integers, so that $\phi_{jk}(x) = \phi(2^j x - k)$. If the mother wavelet $\phi(x)$ has sufficiently localized support, then

$$\int \phi_{jk} \phi_{mn} = 0$$

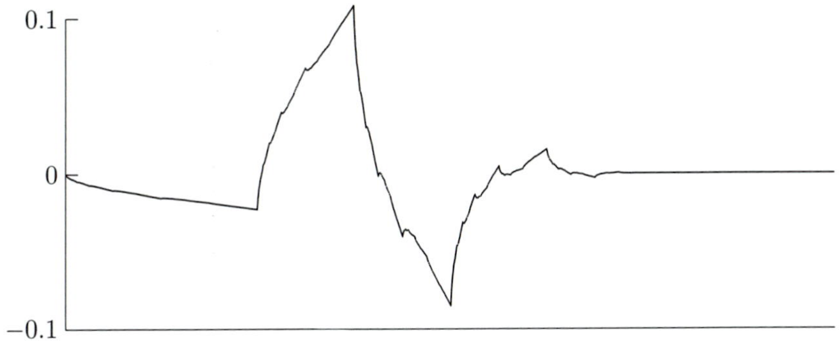

Figure 12.2: Daubechies' D_4 mother wavelet.

whenever the indices do not both match, i.e., the doubly-indexed basis functions $\phi_{jk}(x)$ are orthogonal. By replicating the mother wavelet at many different scales, it is possible to mimic the behavior of any function at many different scales; this property of wavelets is called *multiresolution*. The Fourier basis functions are localized in frequency, but not in time: small changes in frequency produce changes everywhere in the time domain. Wavelets are localized in both frequency (by dilation) and time (by translation). This localization tends to make the wavelet representation of a given function very sparse.

As with the Fourier transform, there is an analogous *discrete wavelet transform*, or *DWT*. The DWT and its inverse can be computed very efficiently by a pyramidal, or hierarchical, algorithm. In fact, the sparsity of the wavelet basis makes computation of the DWT even faster than the FFT—it requires only $\mathcal{O}(n)$ work instead of $\mathcal{O}(n \log_2 n)$ for a sequence of length n. Because of their efficiency, both in computation and in compactness of representation, wavelets are playing an increasingly important role in many areas of signal and image processing, such as data compression, noise removal, and computer vision, and are even beginning to be used as basis functions for the solution of differential equations.

12.5 Software for FFT

Table 12.2 is a list of some of the software available for computing the DFT using the FFT algorithm. Some of the routines compute both the transform and its inverse, whereas others are used as a pair, one for the transform and the other for the inverse. We distinguish between routines that transform only real sequences and those that transform complex sequences. All of the routines listed are for one-dimensional transforms; software is also available for transforms in two dimensions and higher. Software for wavelet transforms is available from `NR` [315] and `TOMS (#735)`. There is also a wavelet toolbox available for `MATLAB`. For pointers to additional wavelet software, see [170, 203].

Source	Real DFT	Complex DFT
FFTPACK	rfftf/rfftb	cfftf/cfftb
FFTW	rfftw	fftw
HSL		ft01
IMSL	fftrf/fftrb	fftcf/fftcb
KMN [220]	ezfftf/ezfftb	cfftf/cfftb
MATLAB	fft/ifft	fft/ifft
NAG	c06eaf/c06faf	c06ecf/c06fcf
NAPACK		fft/ffc
Netlib	realtr	fft
NR [315]	realft	four1
SLATEC	rfftf1/rfftb1	cfftf1/cfftb1

Table 12.2: FFT software

12.6 Historical Notes and Further Reading

The work of Fourier on the continuous integral transform and the series that now bear his name dates from early in the nineteenth century. The discrete Fourier transform is a more recent invention whose current popularity was prompted by the advent of digital computation and communication. Although it had a number of precursors going all the way back to Gauss, the modern form of the FFT algorithm for computing the DFT was published by Cooley and Tukey in 1965. Their version of the algorithm quickly revolutionized many practical computations, including signal processing, convolutions, and time series analysis. It also inspired the development of fast, divide-and-conquer algorithms for many other computations.

An accessible yet comprehensive introduction to the DFT can be found in [50]. For tutorial overviews of FFT algorithms, see [105, 333]. The FFT is elegantly presented from a matrix point of view in [405]. For a detailed discussion of the FFT algorithm and its many variants, including parallel algorithms, see [69]. For a comprehensive discussion of the FFT and its applications, see [52, 53]. For a brief tutorial introduction to wavelets, see [170, 378]; for a more comprehensive but still readable introduction, see [56, 203, 221].

Review Questions

12.1. True or false: The fast Fourier transform (FFT) algorithm can compute both the discrete Fourier transform and its inverse with equal efficiency.

12.2. (*a*) Why is the discrete Fourier transform of a sequence said to be in the *frequency* domain? (*b*) Give two reasons why such a transformation into the frequency domain can be useful.

12.3. What is meant by an nth root of unity?

12.4. For what type of function would trigonometric interpolation be more appropriate than polynomial or piecewise polynomial interpolation?

12.5. List two applications for the discrete Fourier transform (DFT).

12.6. What two assumptions are implicitly made in applying the DFT to a sequence (i.e., what two properties are the data assumed to satisfy)?

12.7. (*a*) What property must the number of points, n, satisfy for the FFT algorithm to be maximally efficient relative to straightforward evaluation of the DFT by matrix-vector multiplication?

(*b*) What is the arithmetic complexity of the FFT algorithm in this case?

12.8. Explain why the inverse DFT can be computed just as efficiently as the forward DFT using the FFT algorithm.

12.9. The DFT of a sequence of length n can be interpreted as interpolation by a set of n trigonometric basis functions.

(*a*) Why does computing the DFT *not* require the solution of an $n \times n$ linear system by matrix factorization in order to determine the coefficients of the basis functions?

(*b*) What is the worst-case computational complexity for computing the DFT? For what values of n is this the case?

(*c*) What is the best-case computational complexity for computing the DFT? For what values of n is this the case?

(*d*) Explain briefly the reason for the difference, or the lack of it, between the complexities in parts *b* and *c*.

12.10. (*a*) Why might one consider padding a sequence with zeros, if necessary, to make its length a power of two before computing its DFT via the FFT algorithm?

(*b*) Why might this *not* be a good idea?

12.11. Why is the FFT algorithm useful for computing the convolution of two sequences?

12.12. (*a*) Explain briefly how the FFT algorithm can be used to multiply two polynomials.

(*b*) How does the computational complexity of this method compare with the conventional approach to polynomial multiplication?

12.13. What advantages do wavelets have over the trigonometric functions used in Fourier analysis?

12.14. What two operations are used to generate a wavelet basis from a single mother wavelet?

12.15. What is the computational complexity of the discrete wavelet transform?

Exercises

12.1. Express each of the following trigonometric functions in complex exponential notation.

(*a*) $4\cos(2\pi kt)$

(*b*) $6\sin(2\pi kt)$

12.2. (*a*) Assuming that time is measured in seconds, give an expression for a sine wave that oscillates at a frequency of two complete cycles per second.

(*b*) What values will you obtain if you sample this function once per second?

(*c*) How often would you have to sample to obtain an accurate value for the true frequency?

12.3. (*a*) What is the DFT of a pure cosine wave $\cos(t)$ sampled at n equally spaced points on the interval $[0, 2\pi)$?

(*b*) What is the DFT of a pure sine wave $\sin(t)$ sampled at n equally spaced points on the interval $[0, 2\pi)$?

(*c*) What is the DFT of the sum of the two previous functions sampled at n equally spaced points on the interval $[0, 2\pi)$?

12.4. For a given input sequence $\boldsymbol{x}$, why is the first component of its DFT, y_0, always equal to the sum of the components of $\boldsymbol{x}$?

12.5. The Fourier matrix $\boldsymbol{F}_n$ defined by $\{\boldsymbol{F}_n\}_{mk} = \omega_n^{mk}$ is obviously symmetric. For what values of n, if any, is $\boldsymbol{F}_n$ Hermitian?

12.6. (*a*) Show that the matrix $(1/\sqrt{n})\boldsymbol{F}_n$ is unitary, where $\boldsymbol{F}_n$ is the Fourier matrix of order n.

(*b*) Using this result, prove the discrete form of *Parseval's Theorem*,

$$\|\boldsymbol{y}\|_2^2 = n\,\|\boldsymbol{x}\|_2^2,$$

where $\boldsymbol{y} = \mathrm{DFT}(\boldsymbol{x})$.

12.7. If $\boldsymbol{y}$ is the DFT of a real sequence $\boldsymbol{x}$ of length n, where n is a power of two, show that y_0 and $y_{n/2}$ must be real.

12.8. Verify the operation count given in Section 12.2 for computing the DFT of a sequence of length n, where n is a power of two, using the FFT algorithm.

12.9. If

$$y = \text{DFT}(x),$$

show that

$$x = \frac{1}{n}\overline{\text{DFT}(\overline{y})},$$

where the overbar indicates complex conjugation of each element of the sequence. This result shows that a separate routine or option for computing the inverse DFT is unnecessary, although one is often supplied for convenience in many mathematical software libraries.

12.10. The standard second-order centered finite difference approximation to the Poisson equation in one dimension with periodic Dirichlet boundary conditions yields an $n \times n$ matrix of the form

$$A = \begin{bmatrix} 2 & -1 & 0 & \cdots & -1 \\ -1 & 2 & -1 & \cdots & 0 \\ 0 & -1 & 2 & \cdots & 0 \\ \vdots & \ddots & \ddots & \ddots & \vdots \\ -1 & \cdots & 0 & -1 & 2 \end{bmatrix}.$$

Show that each column of the Fourier matrix F_n is an eigenvector of A, which implies that $F_n^{-1}AF_n$ is diagonal. This fact forms the basis for fast direct methods for the Poisson equation called "fast Poisson solvers."

Computer Problems

12.1. (*a*) For each value of m, $m = 1, \ldots, 5$, compute the DFT of the sequence $x_k = \cos(mk\pi)$, $k = 0, \ldots, 7$. Explain your results.

(*b*) Draw a plot of the two functions $\cos(\pi t)$ and $\cos(3t)$ over the interval $0 \le t \le 7$. Compute the DFT of each of the sequences $x_k = \cos(\pi k)$ and $x_k = \cos(3k)$, $k = 0, \ldots, 7$, and compare the results. Explain why the DFTs can be so different when the functions are so similar.

12.2. Gauss analyzed the orbit of the asteroid Pallas based on the observational data

θ	0	30	60	90
x	408	89	−66	10
θ	120	150	180	210
x	338	807	1238	1511
θ	240	270	300	330
x	1583	1462	1183	804

where θ is the ascension in degrees and x is the declination in minutes.

(*a*) Fit the given data to the function

$$f(\theta) = a_0 + \sum_{k=1}^{5}[a_k \cos(2\pi k\theta/360) +$$

$$b_k \sin(2\pi k\theta/360)] + a_6 \cos(2\pi 6\theta/360),$$

where a_k, $k = 0, \ldots, 6$, and b_k, $k = 1, \ldots, 5$ are parameters to be determined by the fit. Since there are twelve parameters and twelve data points, the linear system to be solved is square, and the result should interpolate the data. As a matter of historical interest, Gauss performed this computation by a divide-and-conquer method closely related to the FFT algorithm; see [160].

(*b*) Plot the original data points along with a smooth curve of the function determined by the parameters computed in part *a*.

(*c*) Use an FFT routine to compute the DFT y of the sequence x.

(*d*) What relationship can you determine between the real and imaginary parts of y and the parameters a_k and b_k computed in part *a*? (*Hint*: You may need to scale by the sequence length or its square root, depending on the particular FFT routine you use.)

12.3. Let x be a random sequence of length n, say, $n = 8$. Use an FFT routine to compute the DFT of x. Now shift the sequence x circularly (i.e., end-around) one place to the right and compute the DFT of the shifted sequence. How do the resulting transformed sequences compare? Take the modulus of each component of each of the two sequences (called the *amplitude spectrum*) and compare them as well. Try other values for the shift distance, again comparing both the transformed sequence and its amplitude spectrum to those of the original unshifted sequence. What conclusion can you draw?

12.4. (*a*) Let $\boldsymbol{x}$ be the sequence $x_k = 1$, $k = 0, \ldots, n-1$, where n is *not* a power of two. Let $\hat{\boldsymbol{x}}$ be the same sequence padded with zeros to make its length a power of two (i.e., $\hat{x}_k = 1$, $k = 0, \ldots, n-1$ and $\hat{x}_k = 0$, $k = n, \ldots, m-1$, where m is the smallest power of two greater than n). Taking $n = 5$ and $m = 8$, use a mixed-radix FFT routine (i.e., one that allows arbitrary sequence length) to compute the DFT of both $\boldsymbol{x}$ and $\hat{\boldsymbol{x}}$ and compare the results. Do the transformed sequences agree? What can you conclude about padding with zeros in order to make the sequence length a power of two? Try other other values for n and m to determine whether your findings are consistent.

(*b*) Try other sequences (e.g., nonconstant, nonperiodic) for $\boldsymbol{x}$, and other methods for padding (e.g., linear interpolation between x_n and the replication of x_0) and compare the resulting transformed sequences. Can you find any method for padding that does not alter the transformed sequence?

12.5. Using a mixed-radix FFT routine (i.e., one that allows arbitrary sequence length), measure the elapsed time to compute the DFT of a sequence of length n for $n = 1, 2, 3, \ldots, 1024$ (i.e., for each integer value from 1 to 1024). Plot the resulting execution times as a function of n, using a logarithmic scale for vertical axis. Are the upper and lower envelopes of the resulting data consistent with the theoretical complexity range of $\mathcal{O}(n \log_2 n)$ to $\mathcal{O}(n^2)$?

12.6. (*a*) Create two-dimensional plots of the n basis functions for the DFT of length n. On the vertical axis plot the real and imaginary parts of the discrete components of a given basis function (using different colors or dash patterns to distinguish them), and on the horizontal axis plot the index of each component. Although the DFT uses only discrete points, you can connect those points to make continuous curves, which will become smoother as n increases. Try a fairly large value of n to see smooth plots on your screen, but since there will be n separate frames, don't waste paper by printing all of them.

(*b*) Create three-dimensional plots of the n basis functions for the DFT of length n. On two of the axes plot the real and imaginary parts of the discrete components of a given basis function, and on the third axis plot the index of each component. Connect the points for a given function to make a continuous curve; it will become smoother as n increases. Try a fairly large value of n to see smooth plots on your screen, but again use discretion in making hard copies.

12.7. Use an eigenvalue routine to compute all of the eigenvalues of the scaled DFT matrix $(1/\sqrt{n})\boldsymbol{F}_n$ for $n = 1, 2, 3, \ldots, 16$. How many different eigenvalues do you find? Do you observe any pattern in the multiplicities of the eigenvalues? Try to devise a formula for the multiplicity of each eigenvalue as a function of n and then test it for some values of n not already computed.

12.8. Show empirically that the DFT matrix diagonalizes a circulant matrix by generating a random circulant matrix $\boldsymbol{C}$ of order n and then computing $(1/n)\boldsymbol{F}_n\boldsymbol{C}\boldsymbol{F}_n^H$, which should be diagonal. What does this result imply about the eigenvectors of $\boldsymbol{C}$? A value of $n = 8$ is reasonable for your experiment, although you may wish to try additional values.

12.9. If your programming environment supports recursion, implement a recursive version of the FFT algorithm, as given in Section 12.2. Compare its performance to a standard (presumably nonrecursive) FFT routine for input sequences of various sizes (powers of two).

12.10. Implement the DFT using standard matrix-vector multiplication by the appropriate Vandermonde matrix. Compare its performance to that of a standard FFT routine for input sequences of various sizes, both powers of two and nonpowers of two (assuming that the standard FFT routine permits a nonpower of two sequence length). In particular, try some fairly large prime values for the input sequence length and compare the performance of the two routines.

12.11. Implement a routine for digital filtering of a sequence. Use an FFT routine to transform into the frequency domain, truncate or otherwise attenuate the frequencies above a given threshold, and then return to the original domain via the inverse transform. Test your routine for some representative noisy signals.

12.12. Implement a routine for computing the convolution of two sequences. Use an FFT routine to transform the sequences, compute the pointwise product of the transformed sequences, and then transform them back into the original domain using the inverse transform.

12.13. Implement a routine for fast polynomial multiplication using the FFT algorithm, as outlined in Section 12.3.1. Test your routine on polynomials of various degrees, both powers of two and nonpowers of two.

12.14. (*a*) In this exercise we will use the DFT to study properties of iterative methods for solving a system of linear equations. Implement the Gauss-Seidel method for solving the $n \times n$ linear system $\boldsymbol{Ax} = \boldsymbol{b}$, where $\boldsymbol{A}$ is the matrix resulting from a finite difference approximation to the one-dimensional Laplace equation on an interval, with boundary values of zero at the endpoints. Thus, $\boldsymbol{A}$ is tridiagonal with diagonal elements equal to 2 and subdiagonal and superdiagonal elements equal to -1; and $\boldsymbol{x}$ represents the solution values at the interior mesh points.

Take $\boldsymbol{b} = \boldsymbol{0}$, so that the exact solution is $\boldsymbol{x} = \boldsymbol{0}$, and therefore at any iteration the error is equal to the current value for $\boldsymbol{x}$. As initial starting value, take all of the entries of $\boldsymbol{x}$ equal to 1. Using a value for n that is a power of two ($n = 64$ is a reasonable choice), perform a few iterations of the Gauss-Seidel method, say, ten or so. After each iteration, use an FFT routine to compute the DFT of the approximate solution vector, $\boldsymbol{y} = \text{DFT}(\boldsymbol{x})$. Next compute the *power spectrum*, which is a vector whose entries are the elementwise product of $\boldsymbol{y}$ and its complex conjugate. Now plot the first half of the power spectrum vector (i.e., up to the Nyquist frequency), which shows the amount of "energy" present at each frequency. Thus, your plot will show the decay rate of the components of the error of various frequencies. Which frequency components are damped out most rapidly and which most slowly? Do your results suggest that the Gauss-Seidel method is a *smoother*, as discussed in Section 11.5.7?

You might find it interesting to repeat this experiment with a two-dimensional problem using a two-dimensional FFT.

(*b*) Repeat part *a*, but this time using the Jacobi method instead of Gauss-Seidel, and answer the same questions.

Chapter 13

Random Numbers and Stochastic Simulation

13.1 Stochastic Simulation

We have thus far considered only deterministic numerical methods for solving mathematical problems. An alternative approach, which is often very powerful for certain types of problems, is *stochastic simulation*. A serious study of stochastic simulation methods is beyond the scope of this book, but we will give a brief overview of these methods and the random number generators on which they depend.

Stochastic simulation methods attempt to mimic or replicate the behavior of a system by exploiting randomness to obtain a statistical sample of possible outcomes. Because of the randomness involved, simulation methods are also commonly known in some contexts as Monte Carlo methods. Such methods are useful for studying:

- Nondeterministic (stochastic) processes
- Deterministic systems that are too complicated to model analytically
- Deterministic problems whose high dimensionality makes standard discretizations infeasible (e.g., Monte Carlo integration; see Section 8.4.4)

The two main requirements for using stochastic simulation methods are:

- Knowledge of relevant probability distributions
- A supply of random numbers for making random choices

Knowledge of the relevant probability distributions depends on theoretical or empirical information about the physical system being simulated. As a simple example, in simulating a baseball game the known batting average of a player might determine the probability that the player gets a hit in a given turn at bat. A more practical example is simulating the diffusion of particles (e.g., neutrons) through a medium (e.g., a shielding material). One must know the "cross section" or "mean free path," which are measures of the probability of a particle collision occurring, and also the probabilities of each possible outcome of a collision. The path of a single particle through the medium is then simulated by a sequence of random choices, each of which is weighted by the appropriate probability. By simulating a large number of such particle trajectories, the probability distribution of the overall results can be approximated, with the accuracy attained depending on the number of trials.

13.2 Randomness and Random Numbers

The concept of *randomness* is somewhat difficult to define. Physical processes that we usually think of as random, such as flipping a coin or tossing dice, are actually deterministic if we know enough about the equations governing their motion and the appropriate initial conditions. In recent years, the distinction between deterministic and random behavior has become blurred by such concepts as chaotic behavior of dynamical systems. Owing to their extreme sensitivity to initial conditions, the behavior of such systems can be unpredictable in practice even though it is deterministic in principle. For example, detailed weather predictions are impossible beyond approximately two weeks, even though we have a good understanding of the physical processes involved.

One way of characterizing the unpredictability that we associate with randomness is to say that a sequence of numbers is *random* if it has no shorter description than itself. In other words, there is no more economical way to convey the sequence than simply listing its members. Thus, for example, though each of the sequences $\{1, 2, 3, 4, 5\}$, $\{1, 1, 1, 1, 1\}$, and $\{4, 1, 5, 3, 2\}$ may be equally likely to occur, only the latter would be considered random. In some cases, even when variables are not really random, such as the arrival times and service times for a queue, they may be so complicated or imprecisely known that they are best treated as random variables, and the study of such systems is often tractable only by stochastic simulation methods.

In addition to unpredictability, another distinguishing characteristic of true randomness is a lack of *repeatability*: one would not expect the same long random sequence of numbers or coin tosses to occur twice. However, lack of repeatability could make testing algorithms or debugging computer programs difficult, if not impossible. Thus, there are advantages to generating random numbers by a repeatable process, but repeatability is a two-edged sword. The statistical significance of a stochastic simulation depends on the independence of the trials, which in turn depends on using *different* random sequences for each trial. In 1955, before computers were so common, the RAND Corporation published a book entitled *A Million Random Digits*. It was used in selecting random trials for experimental designs and simulations (and perhaps as bedtime reading for insomniacs?). It was soon realized, however, that if everyone always started on page one, then all trials and simulations by all the book's users would depend on the quirks of the same random sequence. This generated much debate on how to select a random starting point in the table of random numbers.

13.3 Random Number Generators

Although random numbers were once supplied by physical processes or tables, they are now produced by computers. Computer algorithms for generating random numbers are in fact deterministic, although the sequence generated may *appear* random in that it exhibits no apparent pattern. However, an algorithm for generating random numbers is a short description of the sequence it yields, which therefore by definition is not truly random, so such a sequence is more accurately called *pseudorandom*. Although a pseudorandom sequence may appear random, it is in fact quite predictable and reproducible, which is important for debugging simulation programs and verifying results. Moreover, because only finitely many numbers are representable on a computer, any sequence must eventually repeat.

A good random number generator should have as many of the following properties as possible:

- *Random pattern.* It should pass statistical tests of randomness.
- *Long period.* It should go as long as possible before repeating.
- *Efficiency.* It should execute rapidly and require little storage, since many simulations require millions of random numbers.
- *Repeatability.* It should always produce the same sequence if started with the same initial conditions.
- *Portability.* It should run on different kinds of computers and be capable of producing the same sequence on each.

It is very difficult to satisfy all of these requirements in a single random number generator. For example, some random number generators in common use produce highly correlated sequences, which may become visually evident when consecutive pairs or triples of members of the sequence are plotted in space. This phenomenon has prompted the remark "random numbers fall mainly in the planes" [264] and can invalidate simulation results obtained using such a generator.

Early attempts at producing random number generators on computers often relied on highly complicated procedures whose very complexity was felt to ensure randomness. An example is the "midsquare" method, which squares each member of the sequence and takes the middle digits of the result as the next member of the sequence. The lack of a theoretical understanding of such methods proved disastrous, however, and it was soon recognized that simple methods with a well-understood theoretical basis are far preferable.

13.3.1 Congruential Generators

Congruential random number generators have the form

$$x_k = (ax_{k-1} + b) \pmod{M},$$

where a and b are given integers, the starting integer x_0 is known as the *seed*, and the integer M is approximately (often equal to) the largest integer representable on a given computer.

The quality of such a generator depends on the choices of a and b, and in any case its period cannot exceed M. It is possible to obtain a reasonably good random number generator using this method, but the values of a and b must be chosen *very* carefully. Many random number generators supplied with computer systems are of the congruential type, and some of them are notoriously poor.

A congruential generator produces random integers between 0 and $M-1$. In order to produce random floating-point numbers, say uniformly distributed on the interval $[0, 1)$, the random integers must be divided by M (but *not* using integer division!).

13.3.2 Fibonacci Generators

Alternative methods that produce floating-point random numbers on the interval $[0, 1)$ directly are the Fibonacci generators, which generate the new value as a difference, sum, or product of previous values. A typical example is the subtractive generator

$$x_k = x_{k-17} - x_{k-5}.$$

We say that this generator has *lags* of 17 and 5. Not surprisingly, the lags must be chosen carefully to produce a good subtractive generator. Note that such a formula may produce a negative result, in which case the usual remedy is to add 1 to get back into the interval $[0, 1)$.

A Fibonacci generator requires more storage than a congruential generator and also requires a special procedure to get started (analogous to a multistep method for solving an ODE). On the other hand, Fibonacci generators require no division to produce floating-point results, and well-designed Fibonacci generators have very good statistical properties. Another advantage of Fibonacci generators is that they can have a much longer period than congruential generators. The reason for this is that the repetition of a single member of the sequence does not entail that all subsequent members will also repeat in the same order.

13.3.3 Nonuniform Distributions

Thus far we have discussed generating random numbers only from a uniform distribution on the interval $[0, 1)$. If we need a uniform distribution on some other interval $[a, b)$, then we can simply modify the values x_k generated on $[0, 1)$ by the transformation $(b - a)x_k + a$ to obtain random numbers that are uniformly distributed on the desired interval.

A more difficult problem is to sample from nonuniform distributions. If the cumulative distribution function of the desired probability density function is easily invertible, then we can generate random samples with the desired distribution by generating uniform random numbers and then inverting them. For example, the exponential distribution with rate λ has the density function

$$f(t) = \lambda e^{-\lambda t}, \qquad t > 0,$$

and cumulative distribution function

$$F(x) = \int_0^x f(t)\,dt = 1 - e^{-\lambda x}.$$

Given $y = F(x)$, we can easily solve for x, obtaining

$$x = -\frac{\log(1-y)}{\lambda}.$$

Hence, to sample from the exponential distribution, we can take

$$x_k = -\frac{\log(y_k)}{\lambda},$$

where y_k is uniform on $[0, 1)$.

Unfortunately, many important distributions are not easily invertible, and special methods must be employed to generate random numbers efficiently for these distributions. An important example is the generation of random numbers that are normally distributed with a given mean and variance. Some methods for generating normally distributed random numbers are explored in Computer Problem 13.8. Available routines for normal random numbers often assume a mean of 0 and variance of 1. If some other mean μ and variance σ^2 are desired, then each value x_k produced by the routine can be modified by the transformation $\sigma x_k + \mu$ to achieve the desired normal distribution.

13.4 Quasi-Random Sequences

Despite the quest to develop algorithms for generating perfectly random numbers, true randomness is not always a virtue. For some applications, such as Monte Carlo integration, achieving reasonably uniform coverage of the sampled volume can be more important than whether the sample points are truly random. The problem is that random sequences tend to exhibit random clumping (lightning may indeed strike in nearly the same place twice if it is truly random), leading to rather uneven coverage of the sampled volume for a given number of points. At the other extreme, perfectly uniform coverage can be achieved by using a regular grid of sample points, but as we saw in Section 8.4.4, such an approach does not scale well to higher dimensions.

A compromise between these extremes of coverage and randomness is provided by *quasi-random sequences*. Such sequences are in fact not random at all but are carefully constructed to give uniform coverage of the sampled volume while maintaining a reasonably random appearance. By design the points tend to avoid each other, so the clumping associated with true randomness is eliminated. The differences among these three sampling techniques are illustrated in Fig. 13.1. Such quasi-random sequences, also called *low-discrepancy sequences*, are finding increasing use in Monte Carlo integration and other applications, such as optimization by random search, where uniform coverage of the sampled volume is more important than the statistical properties of the sampling procedure.

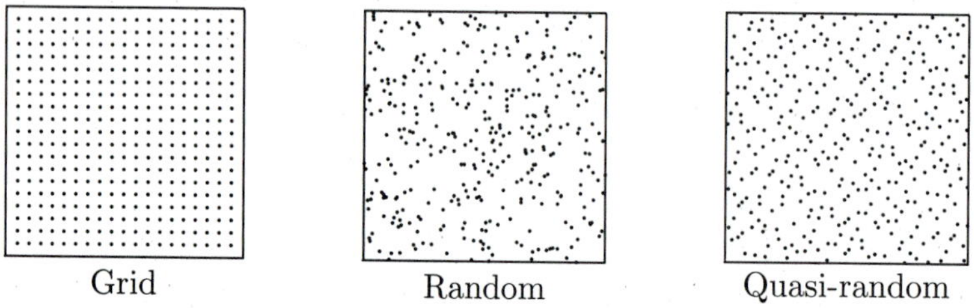

Figure 13.1: Three methods for sampling the unit square using the same number of points.

13.5 Software for Generating Random Numbers

Table 13.1 is a list of some of the random number generators available in standard software libraries. Generators are listed only for uniform and normal distributions. Some of these sources contain generators for several additional distributions, both continuous and discrete. Software for generating quasi-random sequences is available from NR [315, Section 7.7] and TOMS (#647, #659, #738). Although stochastic simulation programs can be written in any general-purpose programming language, the particular needs of this field have motivated the development of special-purpose languages and software systems for simulation, including GPSS, Simscript, Simula, and SLAM.

Source	Uniform distribution	Normal distribution
FMM [127]	urand	
HSL	fa04	fa05
IMSL	rnunf	rnnof
KMN [220]	uni	rnor
MATLAB	rand	randn
NAG	g05caf	g05ddf
Netlib	zufall	normalen
NR [315]	ran1/ran2/ran3	gasdev
RANLIB	ranf/genunf	gennor
SLATEC	rand/runif	rgauss
TOMS	sprng(#806)	grand(#488)/randn(#712)

Table 13.1: Software for generating random numbers

13.6 Historical Notes and Further Reading

Monte Carlo methods were developed in the 1940s by von Neumann, Ulam, Metropolis, and others, primarily motivated by problems in nuclear physics such as neutron transport. For a philosophical discussion of the concept of randomness, see [29]. For a brief overview of randomness, random number generators, and simulation, see [167, 289]. For a detailed treatment of stochastic simulation and Monte Carlo methods, see [43, 122, 184, 222, 334, 361]. Congruential random number generators were proposed by Lehmer in 1948. Volume 2 of the series by Knuth [235] contains a detailed discussion of random number generators and their analysis. For a survey of random number generators, see [11, 150, 210, 301]. The development of quasi-random sequences dates to the work of Halton and of Sobol' in the 1960s. For a recent review of quasi-random sequences and their applications, see [288].

Review Questions

13.1. True or false: Stochastic simulation methods are useful only for nondeterministic systems.

13.2. True or false: A very complicated algorithm for generating random numbers tends to be better than a simple one.

13.3. What two requirements are essential for stochastic simulation methods?

13.4. In using stochastic simulation methods, why is repeatability desirable in practice, even if undesirable in theory?

13.5. List at least three desirable properties of a good random number generator.

13.6. What is meant by a *congruential* random number generator?

13.7. What is meant by a *Fibonacci* random number generator?

13.8. List two advantages and two disadvantages of a Fibonacci generator compared with a congruential generator for generating random floating-point numbers uniformly distributed on the interval $[0, 1)$.

13.9. If you have a random number generator for a uniform distribution on $[0, 1)$, how can you use it to generate random numbers uniformly distributed on the interval $[a, b)$ for given real numbers a and b?

13.10. If you have a random number generator for a normal distribution with mean 0 and variance 1, how can you use it to generate random numbers uniformly normally distributed with mean μ and variance σ^2?

13.11. Why are *quasi-random* sequences sometimes more useful than truly random (or pseudo-random) sequences?

Exercises

13.1. Consider a congruential random number generator

$$x_k = (ax_{k-1} + b) \pmod M,$$

with $b = 0$, $M = 8192$, and the seed $x_0 = 1$.
(*a*) What is the period of this generator if $a = 2$?
(*b*) What is the period if $a = 125$?
(*c*) What is the longest possible period, given these values for b, M, and x_0?

13.2. (*a*) Choose a well-structured sport, such as baseball or football, and discuss how you would simulate a typical game. What type of information would be required to perform a fairly detailed and realistic simulation? Where would random choices enter into the simulation?
(*b*) Would it be feasible to simulate a sport like basketball, soccer, or hockey in this manner? Try to characterize the differences from the previous case.

Computer Problems

13.1. (*a*) In this exercise we will perform a *chi-square test* of the randomness of the sequence generated by a random number generator. Divide the interval $[0, 1)$ into n equal subintervals. Choose a library routine for generating uniformly distributed random numbers on $[0, 1)$. Generate k random numbers and count the number n_i that fall into each subinterval, $i = 1, \ldots, n$. Compute the chi-square statistic

$$\chi^2 = \sum_{i=1}^{n} \frac{(n_i - k/n)^2}{k/n}.$$

In a table for the chi-square distribution (see [435], for example, or a book on statistics), look up the probability that the chi-square statistic has the value you obtained for $n - 1$ degrees of freedom. Carry out this experiment for $n = 10$ and 20, and for $k = 100, 200, \ldots, 1000$.

(*b*) Implement your own random number generator, using either the congruential or Fibonacci method, and again perform the chi-square test as outlined in part *a*. Experiment with various choices for the parameters of the generator to see what effect these have on the randomness test. Can you find choices of parameters that produce particularly good or bad results in the randomness test (without being obviously bad, such as having a very short period)?

13.2. Monte Carlo integration requires random sampling of a region in n-dimensional space. If the sequence of random numbers one is using exhibits any serial correlation, then the sampling may systematically miss a portion of the region and may possibly even be confined to a subregion of lower dimension, which would obviously make the estimate for the integral erroneous. One way to detect such serial correlation is to plot pairs or triples of consecutive random numbers in two or three dimensions, so that any nonrandom pattern becomes apparent visually.

(*a*) Use the congruential random number generator

$$x_k = (a x_{k-1} + b) (\text{mod } M),$$

with $a = 125$, $b = 0$, $M = 8192$, and the seed $x_0 = 1$, to generate a sequence of random integers, and convert each to a floating-point number f_k on $[0, 1)$ by taking $f_k = x_k/M$. Plot 100 pairs of consecutive members of the sequence, i.e., $(f_1, f_2), (f_3, f_4), \ldots, (f_{199}, f_{200})$, as points in the unit square. Do you notice any obvious pattern? Make a second plot using 1000 pairs. Now do you notice any obvious pattern?

(*b*) Repeat the previous experiment, but try various values for the parameters a, b, and M. Can you find values that show no obvious pattern when plotted, even when you increase the number of points further?

(*c*) Repeat the same experiment again, this time using a library routine for generating uniform random numbers on $[0, 1)$.

13.3. For each random number generator used in the previous exercise, generate a sequence of n random numbers, where n is a power of two. Use an FFT routine to compute the DFT of each sequence (see Chapter 12). In each case, does the transformed sequence appear to be biased toward any particular frequencies, or does it appear to be "white noise," with all frequencies represented approximately equally? You may need to use a fairly large value of n, say, $n = 1024$, to draw any significant conclusions. How do the results of this "Fourier test" compare with your other tests (i.e., do the same generators fare well or poorly)?

13.4. A sequence of random numbers distributed uniformly on $[0, 1)$ should have mean

$$\mu = \int_0^1 x\, dx = \frac{1}{2}$$

and variance

$$\sigma^2 = \int_0^1 (x - \mu)^2\, dx = \frac{1}{12},$$

where σ is the standard deviation. Check each of the random number generators used in the previous exercise to see how close they come to these values for a sequence of length 1000. Do all of the generators pass this test?

13.5. (*a*) Suppose that you are given five independent random decimal digits. The possible outcomes can be classified much like poker hands. Show analytically that the probability of each possible outcome is given by the following table:

Hand	Pattern	Probability
Five of a kind	aaaaa	0.0001
Four of a kind	aaaab	0.0045
Full house	aaabb	0.0090
Three of a kind	aaabc	0.0720
Two pairs	aabbc	0.1080
One pair	aabcd	0.5040
Bust	abcde	0.3024

(*b*) Use a library routine for generating random numbers to determine the probability of each possible outcome by random sampling. Experiment with various numbers of trials. How do your results compare with the analytical results in part *a*? What is the effect of taking more trials?

(*c*) The ability to match the correct theoretical distribution of poker hands (called the *poker test*) is sometimes used as a measure of quality of random number generators. Try a poor random number generator from one of the previous exercises and see if it passes this test, for the same number of trials used in part *b*.

13.6. The *birthday paradox*: Use random trials to determine the smallest number of persons required for the probability to be greater than 0.5 that two persons in a group have the same birthday. Also try to justify your result analytically.

13.7. Use random sampling to determine the probability that the quadratic equation

$$ax^2 + bx + c = 0$$

will have only real roots, if each of its real coefficients a, b, and c is randomly chosen from the interval $[-1, 1]$. Also try to justify your result analytically.

13.8. In this exercise, we will consider three different ways of generating random numbers that are normally distributed with zero mean and unit variance.

(*a*) According to the *Central Limit Theorem*, if x_k, $k = 1, \ldots, n$ is a sequence of independent random numbers from a distribution with mean μ and variance σ^2, then as n increases,

$$y = \frac{\sum_{k=1}^{n} x_k - n\mu}{\sigma\sqrt{n}}$$

approaches a normal distribution with a mean of 0 and a variance of 1. If the x_k are uniformly distributed on $[0, 1)$, then $\mu = 1/2$ and $\sigma^2 = 1/12$, which implies that

$$y = \frac{\sum_{k=1}^{n} x_k - n/2}{\sqrt{n/12}}$$

approaches a normal distribution with a mean of 0 and a variance of 1. The choice $n = 12$ makes the foregoing formula particularly simple:

$$y = \sum_{k=1}^{12} x_k - 6,$$

i.e., we just sum up a dozen uniform random numbers and subtract 6, and the result should be approximately normally distributed with a mean of 0 and a variance of 1. You might also experiment with other values for n to examine the tradeoff between cost and accuracy.

(*b*) Generate two random numbers x_1 and x_2, uniformly distributed on $[0, 1)$. Then it can be shown that both

$$y_1 = \sin(2\pi x_1)\sqrt{-2\log(x_2)}$$

and

$$y_2 = \cos(2\pi x_1)\sqrt{-2\log(x_2)}$$

are normally distributed with a mean of 0 and a variance of 1.

(*c*) Generate two random numbers x_1 and x_2 uniformly distributed on $[-1, 1)$, and let $r = x_1^2 + x_2^2$. If $r > 1$, reject this pair and generate a new uniform pair x_1 and x_2. If $r \le 1$, then it can be shown that both

$$y_1 = x_1\sqrt{-2\log(r)/r}$$

and

$$y_2 = x_2\sqrt{-2\log(r)/r}$$

are normally distributed with a mean of 0 and a variance of 1.

Implement each of these three methods for generating normally distributed random numbers. To test each routine, generate $n = 1000$ normal random numbers, compute a frequency histogram with bin size $\sigma = 1$, and compare the values obtained with the known values for a true normal distribution: ..., 2.14%, 13.59%, 34.13%, 34.13%, 13.59%, 2.14%, ... Also compare your results with a histogram similarly obtained using a library routine for generating normally distributed random numbers. You may find it instructive to plot the histograms, perhaps superimposed with a suitably scaled normal density curve. Compare the methods with respect to accuracy and efficiency. You may also wish to experiment with other values for n.

13.9. One of the earliest examples of using randomness to compute a deterministic quantity is the *Buffon needle problem*, in which an approximate value for π is determined by repeatedly throwing a needle onto a plane surface ruled with equally spaced parallel lines, such as the seams in a hardwood floor. We introduce an (x, y) coordinate system to describe the position of the center of the needle, with the x axis parallel to the lines. Clearly, the probability that the needle intersects a line is independent of x, and depends only on y and the angle θ between the needle and the x axis. For simplicity, assume that the length of the needle, as well as the distance between any two adjacent lines, is 1.

By symmetry, we need be concerned only with values for θ in the interval $[0, \pi/2)$, and for y in the interval $[0, \frac{1}{2})$. To determine the proportion of this rectangle in (θ, y) for which the needle intersects a line, we choose random values for θ and y, uniformly distributed on $[0, \pi/2)$ and $[0, \frac{1}{2})$, respectively. Now a needle with its center at (x, y) will intersect a line precisely when $y \leq \sin(\theta)/2$. Therefore, the probability that the needle will intersect a line is simply the ratio of the area under the curve $\sin(\theta)/2$ over the interval $[0, \pi/2]$ to the total area of the rectangle, which is just $\pi/4$. Thus, the approximate value for π will simply be $2n/m$, where n is the total number of trials and m is the number of trials for which $y \leq \sin(\theta)/2$.

Use a library routine for generating uniform random numbers to implement this method for approximating π. How many trials are required to obtain k correct digits of π, where $k = 1, 2, 3, 4$?

13.10. (*a*) Use the Monte Carlo method to compute the area of a circle of diameter 1 inscribed in the unit square, $0 \leq x, y \leq 1$. Generate a sequence (x_k, y_k) of n pairs of random numbers uniformly distributed on $[0, 1)$, and count the number m falling within the circle. Since the area of the square is 1, the area of the circle should be approximated by m/n. Compare your result with the known area, which is given by $A = \pi r^2 = \pi/4$. Use various values for n, and try to characterize the size of the error as a function of the number of random trials.

(*b*) Use the Monte Carlo method to compute the volume of a sphere of diameter 1 inscribed in the unit cube, $0 \leq x, y, z \leq 1$. Generate a sequence (x_k, y_k, z_k) of n triples of random numbers uniformly distributed on $[0, 1)$, and count the number m falling within the sphere. Since the volume of the cube is 1, the volume of the sphere should be approximated by m/n. Compare your result with the known volume, which is given by $V = 4\pi r^3/3 = \pi/6$. Use various values for n, and try to characterize the size of the error as a function of the number of random trials.

(*c*) Compare your results for parts *a* and *b* in terms of the accuracy attained as a function of the number of trials. Explain any relationship you may observe.

13.11. Use random trials to simulate the behavior of the Markov chain given in Computer Problem 4.12. For the same transition probabilities and initial state given there, perform m trials, taking k steps for each trial. Experiment with the values for m and k, and compare the resulting probability distribution vectors with the results obtained by the methods in Chapter 4.

13.12. (*a*) Radioactive decay is an inherently nondeterministic process that can be simulated very naturally using the Monte Carlo method. Suppose that the probability of any given atom decaying over a time interval Δt is given by λ, $0 < \lambda < 1$. Then the history of a single atom can be simulated by choosing a sequence of random numbers x_k, $k = 1, \ldots$, uniformly distributed on $[0, 1)$. The atom survives until the first value x_k for which $x_k < \lambda$. Use this approach to simulate an ensemble of n atoms. Make a plot of the number of atoms remaining after k time increments, $k = 1, \ldots, m$. Take $\lambda = 0.1$ and $m = 50$, and try the values $n = 10$, 100, 1000, and 10,000, making a separate graph for each value of n. How does the value of n affect the smoothness of the resulting curve? Experiment with other values for λ, n, and m to see the range of possible behaviors.

(*b*) We can also develop a continuous, deterministic model of radioactive decay for an ensemble of atoms. The change in the number of atoms Δn over time interval Δt is proportional to the number of atoms present and the length of the time interval. Specifically,

$$\Delta n(t) = -\lambda n(t)\,\Delta t.$$

In the limit, this gives the ODE

$$n'(t) = -\lambda n(t),$$

whose solution is

$$n(t) = n(0)e^{-\lambda t},$$

the familiar decaying exponential model for radioactivity. For the same values of λ and initial number of atoms n as in part *a*, plot the resulting solution for $t = 1, \ldots, m$ on the same graph with the results from part *a*. How do the two models compare? How is their agreement affected by the initial number of atoms n? Which model do you think is closer to the way nature actually behaves? Why?

13.13. A *random walk* is a sequence of fixed-length steps, each taken in a randomly (and independently) chosen direction. A random walk can be used to model various physical phenomena, such as Brownian motion of small particles suspended in a fluid. In this exercise we will consider only the one-dimensional case in which the walk begins at 0. The walk proceeds by successive steps of unit length, with the direction—positive or negative—chosen randomly with equal probability. Write a program to implement a random walk of n steps, using a uniform random number generator to choose the direction for each step, and compute the distance from the origin at the end of the walk. Run your program for $n = 10$, 100, 1000, and 10,000, averaging the distance from the origin at the end of the walk over several trials for each value of n. Characterize the average distance from the origin as a function of n.

13.14. In a two-dimensional random walk, steps are taken randomly on a two-dimensional lattice of points, with the direction—up, down, left, or right—chosen randomly with equal probability. It turns out that such a random walk can be used to solve the Laplace equation. Impose a grid of points on the domain of the equation, including the boundary, then start n trials of a random walk from a given interior grid point, terminating each trial when some boundary point of the domain is hit. The solution at the starting grid point is then given by the average over all the trials of the solution values at the boundary points that were hit. Implement this two-dimensional random walk approach to solve the Laplace equation, using the same grid and boundary values as in Example 11.5. Compute the solution at each of the interior grid points by averaging over n trials from each point. How many trials are required to obtain results comparable to those in Example 11.5? Because of the large number of trials required, the random walk method is not competitive with other numerical methods for computing the solution over the entire domain. The random walk method does have the advantage, however, that it can compute the solution at a single point without having to compute it anywhere else, which is in contrast with most other numerical methods. Moreover, the random walk method can easily accommodate very complicated boundaries that may be difficult to deal with using conventional numerical methods.

13.15. A polymer can be modeled as a sequence of n segments (monomers) of fixed length joined by $n-1$ universal joints, so that each angle between adjacent segments can take any value from 0 to 360 degrees with equal probability.

(*a*) Use a uniform random number generator to implement this model of a polymer in two dimensions. Assume that the units chosen are such that the length of each segment is 1. The $n-1$ angles θ_k between successive segments should be uniformly distributed on the interval $[0, 2\pi)$. Try several different values for n, say 10, 100, or more if your computer budget allows (real polymers may have thousands of segments). Make several trials for each value of n and compute the average overall length of the polymer (i.e., the distance between the endpoints of the first and last segments in Cartesian coordinates). Try to characterize the average length of the polymer as a function of n. You may find it interesting to draw a picture of the polymer in two dimensions. Note that the result is simply a kind of random walk.

(*b*) Repeat part *a*, but this time in three dimensions. To generate the direction of each new segment, you will probably find it most convenient to use spherical coordinates, with both the azimuth and zenith angles, θ and ϕ, chosen as random numbers uniformly distributed on the interval $[0, 2\pi)$.

To draw a picture and compute the length of the polymer, however, you will find it easiest to use three-dimensional Cartesian coordinates. Again, run several trials for each value of n and try to characterize the average length of the polymer as a function of n. Does the increase in dimensionality make a significant difference in the length of the polymer for the same number of segments?
(c) The previous model is unrealistic in part because chemical bonds are not universal joints, and they prefer certain bond angles over others. Assume that instead we have swivel joints in three dimensions, with a fixed angle θ and free angle ϕ. Use this new model to simulate polyethylene, which has a favored bond angle of $\theta = 109°$. Again, run several trials for the same values of n and characterize the average length of the polymer as a function of n. Does this model give significantly different results from the previous model? When plotted in three dimensions, do the simulated polymers given by the two models look appreciably different?

13.16. Suppose that neutrons enter one side of a lead shielding wall that is four units thick. Each neutron enters at a random angle and travels a distance of one unit before colliding with a lead nucleus. Such a collision causes the neutron to bounce off in a random direction to travel another unit distance before another collision, and so on. After eight collisions, a given neutron has lost all of its energy and therefore stops. Use Monte Carlo simulation to determine the percentage of neutrons that exit from the other side of the wall. Does it make a significant difference whether the wall is modeled as two-dimensional or three-dimensional?

13.17. Repeat one or more of the preceding exercises using a quasi-random sequence generator (see Section 13.5 for appropriate software) instead of a standard random number generator. Does the quasi-random sequence pass any of the randomness tests given in the first few exercises? Does the quasi-random sequence make a significant difference in accuracy or efficiency for any of your simulation results?

13.18. Evaluate the double integral given in Computer Problem 8.14 using Monte Carlo integration. Try both a standard uniform random number generator and a quasi-random sequence generator and compare their efficiency in attaining a given level of accuracy.

Bibliography

[1] O. Aberth. *Precise Numerical Methods Using C++*. Academic, San Diego, CA, 1998.

[2] M. Abramowitz and I. A. Stegun. *Handbook of Mathematical Functions*. Dover, New York, 1965.

[3] F. S. Acton. *Numerical Methods That Work*. Math. Assoc. Amer., Washington, DC, 1990. (Reprint of 1970 edition).

[4] F. S. Acton. *Real Computing Made Real*. Princeton University Press, Princeton, NJ, 1996.

[5] J. H. Ahlberg, E. N. Nilson, and J. L. Walsh. *The Theory of Splines and Their Applications*. Academic, New York, 1967.

[6] G. Alefeld and J. Herzberger. *Introduction to Interval Computations*. Academic, New York, 1983.

[7] E. L. Allgower and K. Georg. *Numerical Continuation Methods*. Springer-Verlag, New York, 1990.

[8] E. L. Allgower and K. Georg. Continuation and path following. *Acta Numerica*, 2:1–64, 1993.

[9] W. F. Ames. *Numerical Methods for Partial Differential Equations*. Academic, San Diego, CA, 3d edition, 1992.

[10] E. Anderson, Z. Bai, C. Bischof, S. Blackford, J. Demmel, J. Dongarra, J. Du Croz, A. Greenbaum, S. Hammarling, A. McKenney, and D. Sorensen. *LAPACK Users' Guide*. SIAM, Philadelphia, PA, 3d edition, 1999.

[11] S. Anderson. Random number generators. *SIAM Review*, 32:221–251, 1990.

[12] H. C. Andrews and C. L. Patterson. Outer product expansions and their uses in digital image processing. *Amer. Math. Monthly*, 82:1–13, 1975.

[13] U. M. Ascher, R. M. Mattheij, and R. D. Russell. *Numerical Solution of Boundary Value Problems for Ordinary Differential Equations.* SIAM, Philadelphia, PA, 1995. (Reprint of 1988 edition).

[14] U. M. Ascher and L. R. Petzold. *Computer Methods for Ordinary Differential Equations and Differential-Algebraic Equations.* SIAM, Philadelphia, PA, 1998.

[15] K. Atkinson. *Elementary Numerical Analysis.* John Wiley & Sons, New York, 2d edition, 1993.

[16] M. Avriel. *Nonlinear Programming: Analysis and Methods.* Prentice Hall, Englewood Cliffs, NJ, 1976.

[17] O. Axelsson. *Iterative Solution Methods.* Cambridge University Press, New York, 1994.

[18] Z. Bai, J. Demmel, J. Dongarra, A. Ruhe, and H. van der Vorst, editors. *Templates for the Solution of Algebraic Eigenvalue Problems: A Practical Guide.* SIAM, Philadelphia, PA, 2000.

[19] P. B. Bailey, L. F. Shampine, and P. E. Waltman. *Nonlinear Two Point Boundary Value Problems.* Academic, New York, 1968.

[20] G. A. Baker. *Essentials of Padé Approximants.* Academic, New York, 1975.

[21] G. A. Baker and P. R. Graves-Morris. *Padé Approximants.* Cambridge University Press, New York, 2d edition, 1996.

[22] L. Baker. *C Mathematical Function Handbook.* McGraw-Hill, New York, 1992.

[23] R. E. Bank. *PLTMG: A Software Package for Solving Elliptic Partial Differential Equations.* SIAM, Philadelphia, PA, 1998.

[24] Y. Bard. *Nonlinear Parameter Estimation.* Academic, New York, 1970.

[25] R. Barrett, M. Berry, T. Chan, J. Demmel, J. Donato, J. Dongarra, V. Eijkhout, R. Pozo, C. Romine, and H. van der Vorst. *Templates for the Solution of Linear Systems: Building Blocks for Iterative Methods.* SIAM, Philadelphia, PA, 1994.

[26] R. Bartels, J. Beatty, and B. Barsky. *An Introduction to Splines for Use in Computer Graphics and Geometric Modeling.* Morgan Kaufmann, Los Altos, CA, 1987.

[27] M. S. Bazaraa, H. D. Sherali, and C. M. Shetty. *Nonlinear Programming: Theory and Algorithms.* John Wiley & Sons, New York, 2d edition, 1993.

[28] P. Beckmann. *Orthogonal Polynomials for Engineers and Scientists.* Golem Press, Boulder, CO, 1973.

[29] E. J. Beltrami. *What Is Random?* Springer-Verlag, New York, 1999.

[30] M. W. Berry, Z. Drmač, and E. R. Jessup. Matrices, vector spaces, and information retrieval. *SIAM Review*, 41:335–362, 1999.

[31] D. P. Bertsekas. *Nonlinear Programming.* Athena Scientific, Belmont, MA, 2d edition, 1999.

[32] D. Betounes. *Partial Differential Equations for Computational Science.* Springer-Verlag, New York, 1998.

[33] A. Biran and M. Breiner. *MATLAB 5 for Engineers.* Addison-Wesley, Reading, MA, 1999.

[34] G. Birkhoff and G.-C. Rota. *Ordinary Differential Equations.* John Wiley & Sons, New York, 4th edition, 1989.

[35] Å. Björck. *Numerical Methods for Least Squares Problems.* SIAM, Philadelphia, PA, 1996.

[36] P. T. Boggs and J. W. Tolle. Sequential quadratic programming. *Acta Numerica*, 4:1–51, 1995.

[37] R. F. Boisvert, editor. *Quality of Numerical Software: Assessment and Enhancement.* Chapman & Hall, New York, 1997.

[38] G. J. Borse. *Numerical Methods with MATLAB.* PWS Publishing Co., Boston, 1997.

[39] J. F. Botha and G. F. Pinder. *Fundamental Concepts in the Numerical Solution of Partial Differential Equations.* John Wiley & Sons, New York, 1983.

[40] W. E. Boyce and R. C. DiPrima. *Elementary Differential Equations and Boundary Value Problems.* John Wiley & Sons, New York, 7th edition, 2000.

[41] J. P. Boyd. *Chebyshev and Fourier Spectral Methods.* Dover, New York, 2d edition, 2001.

[42] J. H. Bramble. *Multigrid Methods.* John Wiley & Sons, New York, 1993.

[43] P. Bratley, B. L. Fox, and L. E. Schrage. *A Guide to Simulation.* Springer-Verlag, New York, 2d edition, 1987.

[44] M. Braun. *Differential Equations and Their Applications.* Springer-Verlag, New York, 4th edition, 1993.

[45] K. E. Brenan, S. L. Campbell, and L. R. Petzold. *Numerical Solution of Initial-Value Problems in Differential-Algebraic Equations.* SIAM, Philadelphia, PA, 1996. (Reprint of 1989 edition).

[46] S. C. Brenner and L. R. Scott. *The Mathematical Theory of Finite Element Methods.* Springer-Verlag, New York, 2d edition, 2002.

[47] R. P. Brent. *Algorithms for Minimization without Derivatives.* Dover, New York, 2002. (Reprint of 1973 edition).

[48] C. Brezinski and M. Redivo Zaglia. *Extrapolation Methods: Theory and Practice.* Elsevier, New York, 1991.

[49] C. Brezinski and J. Van Iseghem. A taste of Padé approximation. *Acta Numerica*, 4:53–103, 1995.

[50] W. L. Briggs and V. E. Henson. *The DFT: An Owner's Manual for the Discrete Fourier Transform.* SIAM, Philadelphia, PA, 1995.

[51] W. L. Briggs, V. E. Henson, and S. F. McCormick. *A Multigrid Tutorial.* SIAM, Philadelphia, PA, 2d edition, 2000.

[52] E. O. Brigham. *The Fast Fourier Transform.* Prentice Hall, Englewood Cliffs, NJ, 1974.

[53] E. O. Brigham. *The Fast Fourier Transform and Its Applications.* Prentice Hall, Englewood Cliffs, NJ, 1988.

[54] J. L. Buchanan and P. R. Turner. *Numerical Methods and Analysis.* McGraw-Hill, New York, 1992.

[55] R. L. Burden and J. D. Faires. *Numerical Analysis.* Brooks/Cole, Pacific Grove, CA, 7th edition, 2001.

[56] C. S. Burrus, R. A. Gopinath, and H. Guo. *Introduction to Wavelets and Wavelet Transforms.* Prentice Hall, Upper Saddle River, NJ, 1998.

[57] J. C. Butcher. *Numerical Methods for Ordinary Differential Equations.* John Wiley & Sons, New York, 2d edition, 2003.

[58] G. D. Byrne and A. C. Hindmarsh. Stiff ODE solvers: A review of current and coming attractions. *J. Comput. Phys.*, 70:1–62, 1987.

[59] O. Caprani, K. Madsen, and L. B. Rall. Integration of interval functions. *SIAM J. Math. Anal.*, 12:321–341, 1981.

[60] M. A. Celia and W. G. Gray. *Numerical Methods for Differential Equations.* Prentice Hall, Englewood Cliffs, NJ, 1992.

[61] F. Chaitin-Chatelin and V. Frayssé. *Lectures on Finite Precision Computations.* SIAM, Philadelphia, PA, 1996.

[62] S. J. Chapman. *MATLAB Programming for Engineers.* Brooks/Cole, Pacific Grove, CA, 2d edition, 2002.

[63] F. Chatelin. *Eigenvalues of Matrices.* John Wiley & Sons, New York, 1993. (Translation of 1988–89 French edition).

[64] W. Cheney. *Introduction to Approximation Theory.* AMS Chelsea Publishing, Providence, RI, 2d edition, 1998. (Reprint of 1982 edition).

[65] W. Cheney and D. Kincaid. *Numerical Mathematics and Computing.* Brooks/Cole, Pacific Grove, CA, 4th edition, 1999.

[66] T. S. Chihara. *An Introduction to Orthogonal Polynomials.* Gordon and Breach, New York, 1978.

[67] B. Childs, M. Scott, J. W. Daniel, E. Denman, and P. Nelson, editors. *Codes for Boundary Value Problems in ODEs.* Springer-Verlag, New York, 1979.

[68] E. Chong and S. Żak. *An Introduction to Optimization.* John Wiley & Sons, New York, 2d edition, 2001.

[69] E. Chu and A. George. *Inside the FFT Black Box.* CRC Press, Boca Raton, FL, 1999.

[70] E. A. Coddington and N. Levinson. *Theory of Ordinary Differential Equations.* McGraw-Hill, New York, 1955.

[71] W. J. Cody. The construction of numerical subroutine libraries. *SIAM Review*, 16:36–46, 1974.

[72] W. J. Cody and W. Waite, editors. *Software Manual for the Elementary Functions.* Prentice Hall, Englewood Cliffs, NJ, 1980.

[73] T. F. Coleman and C. Van Loan. *Handbook for Matrix Computations.* SIAM, Philadelphia, PA, 1988.

[74] A. R. Conn, N. I. M. Gould, and P. L. Toint. *Trust-Region Methods.* SIAM, Philadelphia, PA, 2000.

[75] S. D. Conte and C. de Boor. *Elementary Numerical Analysis.* McGraw-Hill, New York, 3d edition, 1980.

[76] R. Cools. Constructing cubature formulae: The science behind the art. *Acta Numerica*, 6:1–54, 1997.

[77] J. M. Cooper. *Introduction to Partial Differential Equations with MATLAB.* Birkhäuser, Boston, 1998.

[78] W. R. Cowell, editor. *Sources and Development of Mathematical Software.* Prentice Hall, Englewood Cliffs, NJ, 1984.

[79] R. E. Crandall. *Projects in Scientific Computation.* Springer-Verlag, New York, 1994.

[80] J. K. Cullum and R. A. Willoughby. *Lanczos Algorithms for Large Symmetric Eigenvalue Computations.* SIAM, Philadelphia, PA, 2002. (Reprint of 1985 edition).

[81] G. Dahlquist and Å. Björck. *Numerical Methods.* Dover, New York, 2003. (Reprint of 1974 edition).

[82] G. B. Dantzig. *Linear Programming and Extensions.* Princeton University Press, Princeton, NJ, 1963.

[83] B. N. Datta. *Numerical Linear Algebra and Applications.* Brooks/Cole, Pacific Grove, CA, 1995.

[84] A. J. Davies. *The Finite Element Method: A First Approach.* Oxford University Press, New York, 1980.

[85] P. J. Davis. *Interpolation and Approximation.* Dover, New York, 1975. (Reprint of 1963 edition).

[86] P. J. Davis and P. Rabinowitz. *Methods of Numerical Integration.* Academic, New York, 2d edition, 1984.

[87] C. de Boor. *A Practical Guide to Splines.* Springer-Verlag, New York, 2d edition, 1984.

[88] L. M. Delves and J. L. Mohamed. *Computational Methods for Integral Equations.* Cambridge University Press, New York, 1985.

[89] J. W. Demmel. *Applied Numerical Linear Algebra.* SIAM, Philadelphia, PA, 1997.

[90] J. W. Demmel, M. T. Heath, and H. A. van der Vorst. Parallel numerical linear algebra. *Acta Numerica*, 2:111–197, 1993.

[91] J. E. Dennis and J. J. Moré. Quasi-Newton methods, motivation and theory. *SIAM Review*, 19:46–89, 1977.

[92] J. E. Dennis and R. B. Schnabel. *Numerical Methods for Unconstrained Optimization and Nonlinear Equations.* SIAM, Philadelphia, PA, 1996. (Reprint of 1983 edition).

[93] P. Deuflhard. Recent progress in extrapolation methods for ordinary differential equations. *SIAM Review*, 27:505–535, 1985.

[94] P. Deuflhard and A. Hohmann. *Numerical Analysis in Modern Scientific Computing.* Springer-Verlag, New York, 2d edition, 2002.

[95] P. Dierckx. *Curve and Surface Fitting with Splines.* Oxford University Press, New York, 1993.

[96] J. Dongarra, J. DuCroz, I. S. Duff, and S. Hammarling. A set of level-3 basic linear algebra subprograms. *ACM Trans. Math. Software*, 16:1–28, 1990.

[97] J. Dongarra, J. DuCroz, S. Hammarling, and R. J. Hanson. An extended set of Fortran basic linear algebra subprograms. *ACM Trans. Math. Software*, 14:1–32, 1988.

[98] J. J. Dongarra, J. R. Bunch, C. B. Moler, and G. W. Stewart. *LINPACK User's Guide*. SIAM, Philadelphia, PA, 2d edition, 1979.

[99] J. J. Dongarra, I. S. Duff, D. C. Sorensen, and H. A. van der Vorst. *Numerical Linear Algebra for High-Performance Computers*. SIAM, Philadelphia, PA, 1998.

[100] J. J. Dongarra, F. G. Gustavson, and A. Karp. Implementing linear algebra algorithms for dense matrices on a vector pipeline machine. *SIAM Review*, 26:91–112, 1984.

[101] J. R. Dormand. *Numerical Methods for Differential Equations*. CRC Press, Boca Raton, FL, 1996.

[102] C. C. Douglas. Multigrid methods in science and engineering. *IEEE Comput. Sci. Engr.*, 3(4):55–68, 1996.

[103] K. Dowd and C. Severance. *High Performance Computing*. O'Reilly & Associates, Sebastopol, CA, 2d edition, 1998.

[104] I. S. Duff, A. M. Erisman, and J. K. Reid. *Direct Methods for Sparse Matrices*. Oxford University Press, New York, 1986.

[105] P. Duhamel and M. Vetterli. Fast Fourier transforms: A tutorial review and a state of the art. *Signal Processing*, 19:259–299, 1990.

[106] A. Edelman and H. Murakami. Polynomial roots from companion matrix eigenvalues. *Math. Comp.*, 64(210):763–776, 1995.

[107] H. Engels. *Numerical Quadrature and Cubature*. Academic, New York, 1980.

[108] K. Eriksson, D. Estep, P. Hansbo, and C. Johnson. *Computational Differential Equations*. Cambridge University Press, New York, 1996.

[109] D. M. Etter. *Engineering Problem Solving with MATLAB*. Prentice Hall, Upper Saddle River, NJ, 2d edition, 1997.

[110] D. M. Etter, D. C. Kuncicky, and H. Moore. *Introduction to MATLAB 7*. Prentice Hall, Upper Saddle River, NJ, 2005.

[111] D. J. Evans, editor. *Software for Numerical Mathematics*. Academic, New York, 1974.

[112] G. Evans. *Practical Numerical Integration*. John Wiley & Sons, New York, 1993.

[113] G. Evans, J. Blackledge, and P. Yardley. *Numerical Methods for Partial Differential Equations*. Springer-Verlag, New York, 2000.

[114] V. Faber and T. Manteuffel. Necessary and sufficient conditions for the existence of a conjugate gradient method. *SIAM J. Numer. Anal.*, 21:315–339, 1984.

[115] R. W. Farebrother. *Linear Least Squares Computations.* Marcel Dekker, New York, 1988.

[116] G. Farin. *Curves and Surfaces for Computer Aided Geometric Design.* Academic, New York, 2d edition, 1990.

[117] S. O. Fatunla. *Numerical Methods for Initial Value Problems in Ordinary Differential Equations.* Academic, New York, 1988.

[118] L. V. Fausett. *Applied Numerical Analysis Using MATLAB.* Prentice Hall, Upper Saddle River, NJ, 1999.

[119] P. Favati, G. Lotti, and F. Romani. Improving QUADPACK automatic integration routines. *ACM Trans. Math. Software*, 17:218–232, 1991.

[120] A. V. Fiacco and G. P. McCormick. *Nonlinear Programming: Sequential Unconstrained Minimization Techniques.* SIAM, Philadelphia, PA, 1990. (Reprint of 1968 edition).

[121] B. Fischer. *Polynomial Based Iteration Methods for Symmetric Linear Systems.* John Wiley & Sons, New York, 1996.

[122] G. S. Fishman. *Monte Carlo: Concepts, Algorithms, and Applications.* Springer-Verlag, New York, 1996.

[123] R. Fletcher. *Practical Methods of Optimization.* John Wiley & Sons, New York, 2d edition, 1987.

[124] B. Fornberg. *A Practical Guide to Pseudospectral Methods.* Cambridge University Press, New York, 1996.

[125] W. Forster. Homotopy methods. In R. Horst and P. M. Pardalos, editors, *Handbook of Global Optimization*, pages 669–750. Kluwer, Boston, 1995.

[126] G. E. Forsythe. Pitfalls in computation, or why a math book isn't enough. *Amer. Math. Monthly*, 77:931–956, 1970.

[127] G. E. Forsythe, M. A. Malcolm, and C. B. Moler. *Computer Methods for Mathematical Computations.* Prentice Hall, Englewood Cliffs, NJ, 1977.

[128] G. E. Forsythe and C. B. Moler. *Computer Solution of Linear Algebraic Systems.* Prentice Hall, Englewood Cliffs, NJ, 1967.

[129] G. E. Forsythe and W. R. Wasow. *Finite Difference Methods for Partial Differential Equations.* John Wiley & Sons, New York, 1960.

[130] L. Fosdick, E. Jessup, C. Schauble, and G. Domik. *An Introduction to High-Performance Scientific Computing.* The MIT Press, Cambridge, MA, 1995.

[131] L. V. Foster. Gaussian elimination with partial pivoting can fail in practice. *SIAM J. Matrix Anal. Appl.*, 15:1354–1362, 1994.

[132] L. Fox. *The Numerical Solution of Two-Point Boundary Problems.* Dover, New York, 1990. (Reprint of 1957 edition).

[133] L. Fox and I. B. Parker. *Chebyshev Polynomials in Numerical Analysis.* Oxford University Press, New York, 1968.

[134] G. Freud. *Orthogonal Polynomials.* Pergamon, New York, 1971.

[135] R. W. Freund, G. H. Golub, and N. M. Nachtigal. Iterative solution of linear systems. *Acta Numerica*, 1:57–100, 1992.

[136] F. N. Fritsch and J. Butland. A method for constructing local monotone piecewise cubic interpolants. *SIAM J. Sci. Stat. Comput.*, 5:300–304, 1984.

[137] F. N. Fritsch and R. E. Carlson. Monotone piecewise cubic interpolation. *SIAM J. Numer. Anal.*, 17:238–246, 1980.

[138] F. N. Fritsch, D. K. Kahaner, and J. N. Lyness. Double integration using one-dimensional adaptive quadrature routines: A software interface problem. *ACM Trans. Math. Software*, 7:46–75, 1981.

[139] D. Funaro. *Polynomial Approximation of Differential Equations.* Springer-Verlag, New York, 1992.

[140] W. Gander and W. Gautschi. Adaptive quadrature—revisited. *BIT*, 40:84–101, 2000.

[141] W. Gander and J. Hřebiček. *Solving Problems in Scientific Computing Using Maple and MATLAB.* Springer-Verlag, New York, 4th edition, 2004.

[142] P. R. Garabedian. *Partial Differential Equations.* Chelsea Publishing Co., New York, 2d edition, 1986. (Reprint of 1964 edition).

[143] B. S. Garbow, J. M. Boyle, J. J. Dongarra, and C. B. Moler. *Matrix Eigensystem Routines: EISPACK Guide Extension.* Springer-Verlag, New York, 1972.

[144] A. L. Garcia and C. Penland. *MATLAB Projects for Scientists and Engineers.* Prentice Hall, Upper Saddle River, NJ, 1996.

[145] W. Gautschi. Orthogonal polynomials: Applications and computation. *Acta Numerica*, 5:45–119, 1996.

[146] W. Gautschi. *Numerical Analysis: An Introduction.* Birkhäuser, Boston, 1997.

[147] C. W. Gear. *Numerical Initial Value Problems in Ordinary Differential Equations.* Prentice Hall, Englewood Cliffs, NJ, 1971.

[148] C. W. Gear. Numerical solution of ordinary differential equations: Is there anything left to do? *SIAM Review*, 23:10–24, 1981.

[149] E. Gekeler. *Discretization Methods for Stable Initial Value Problems*. Springer-Verlag, New York, 1984.

[150] J. E. Gentle. *Random Number Generation and Monte Carlo Methods*. Springer-Verlag, New York, 2d edition, 2003.

[151] A. George and J. W.-H. Liu. *Computer Solution of Large Sparse Positive Definite Systems*. Prentice Hall, Englewood Cliffs, NJ, 1981.

[152] C. F. Gerald and P. O. Wheatley. *Applied Numerical Analysis*. Pearson, Boston, 7th edition, 2004.

[153] A. Ghizzetti and A. Ossicini. *Quadrature Formulae*. Academic, New York, 1970.

[154] P. E. Gill, W. Murray, and M. H. Wright. *Practical Optimization*. Academic, New York, 1981.

[155] P. E. Gill, W. Murray, and M. H. Wright. *Numerical Linear Algebra and Optimization*, volume 1. Addison-Wesley, Reading, MA, 1991.

[156] S. Goedecker and A. Hoisie. *Performance Optimization of Numerically Intensive Codes*. SIAM, Philadelphia, PA, 2001.

[157] D. Goldberg. What every computer scientist should know about floating-point arithmetic. *ACM Computing Surveys*, 18(1):5–48, March 1991.

[158] D. Goldfarb. Algorithms for unconstrained optimization: A review of recent developments. In W. Gautschi, editor, *Mathematics of Computation 1943–1993: A Half Century of Computational Mathematics*, volume 48 of *Proc. Symp. Appl. Math.*, pages 33–48. Amer. Math. Soc., 1993.

[159] D. Goldfarb and M. J. Todd. Linear programming. In G. Nemhauser et al., editors, *Optimization*, pages 73–170. Elsevier, New York, 1989.

[160] H. H. Goldstine. *A History of Numerical Analysis from the 16th through the 19th Century*. Springer-Verlag, New York, 1977.

[161] G. H. Golub. Numerical methods for solving linear least squares problems. *Numer. Math.*, 7:206–216, 1965.

[162] G. H. Golub and D. P. O'Leary. Some history of the conjugate gradient and Lanczos methods. *SIAM Review*, 31:50–102, 1989.

[163] G. H. Golub and J. M. Ortega. *Scientific Computing and Differential Equations*. Academic, San Diego, CA, 2d edition, 1992.

[164] G. H. Golub and C. F. Van Loan. *Matrix Computations*. Johns Hopkins University Press, Baltimore, MD, 3d edition, 1996.

[165] G. H. Golub and J. H. Welsch. Calculation of Gauss quadrature rules. *Math. Comp.*, 23:221–230, 1969.

[166] D. Gottlieb and S. A. Orszag. *Numerical Analysis of Spectral Methods.* SIAM, Philadelphia, PA, 1977.

[167] H. Gould and J. Tobochnik. *An Introduction to Computer Simulation Methods.* Addison-Wesley, Reading, MA, 2d edition, 1996.

[168] A. R. Gourlay and G. A. Watson. *Computational Methods for Matrix Eigenproblems.* John Wiley & Sons, New York, 1973.

[169] T. A. Grandine. *The Numerical Methods Programming Projects Book.* Oxford University Press, New York, 1990.

[170] A. Graps. An introduction to wavelets. *IEEE Comput. Sci. Engr.*, 2(2):50–61, 1995.

[171] A. Greenbaum. *Iterative Methods for Solving Linear Systems.* SIAM, Philadelphia, PA, 1997.

[172] A. Griewank. *Evaluating Derivatives: Principles and Techniques of Algorithmic Differentiation.* SIAM, Philadelphia, PA, 2000.

[173] G. K. Gupta, R. Sacks-Davis, and P. E. Tischer. A review of recent developments in solving ODEs. *ACM Computing Surveys*, 17:5–47, 1985.

[174] B. Gustafsson, H.-O. Kreiss, and J. Oliger. *Time Dependent Problems and Difference Methods.* John Wiley & Sons, New York, 1995.

[175] S. Haber. Numerical evaluation of multiple integrals. *SIAM Review*, 12:481–526, 1970.

[176] W. Hackbusch. *Iterative Solution of Large Sparse Systems of Equations.* Springer-Verlag, New York, 1994.

[177] L. A. Hageman and D. M. Young. *Applied Iterative Methods.* Academic, New York, 1981.

[178] W. Hager. *Applied Numerical Linear Algebra.* Prentice Hall, Englewood Cliffs, NJ, 1988.

[179] B. D. Hahn. *Essential MATLAB for Scientists and Engineers.* Elsevier, New York, 2d edition, 2002.

[180] E. Hairer, S. Nørsett, and G. Wanner. *Solving Ordinary Differential Equations I: Nonstiff Problems.* Springer-Verlag, New York, 2d edition, 1993.

[181] E. Hairer and G. Wanner. *Solving Ordinary Differential Equations II: Stiff and Differential-Algebraic Problems.* Springer-Verlag, New York, 2d edition, 1996.

[182] C. A. Hall and T. A. Porsching. *Numerical Analysis of Partial Differential Equations.* Prentice Hall, Englewood Cliffs, NJ, 1990.

[183] G. Hämmerlin and K.-H. Hoffmann. *Numerical Mathematics.* Springer-Verlag, New York, 1991. (Translation of 1989 German edition).

[184] J. M. Hammersley and D. C. Handscomb. *Monte Carlo Methods.* Chapman & Hall, New York, 1965.

[185] D. Hanselman and B. Littlefield. *Mastering MATLAB 6.* Prentice Hall, Upper Saddle River, NJ, 2001.

[186] E. Hansen. *Global Optimization Using Interval Analysis.* Marcel Dekker, New York, 1992.

[187] P. C. Hansen. Regularization tools: A MATLAB package for analysis and solution of discrete ill-posed problems. *Numerical Algorithms*, 6:1–35, 1994.

[188] P. C. Hansen. *Rank-Deficient and Discrete Ill-Posed Problems: Numerical Aspects of Linear Inversion.* SIAM, Philadelphia, PA, 1998.

[189] M. A. Hennell and L. M. Delves, editors. *Production and Assessment of Numerical Software.* Academic, New York, 1980.

[190] P. Henrici. *Discrete Variable Methods in Ordinary Differential Equations.* John Wiley & Sons, New York, 1962.

[191] P. Henrici. *Error Propagation for Difference Methods.* John Wiley & Sons, New York, 1963.

[192] P. Henrici. Fast Fourier methods in computational complex analysis. *SIAM Review*, 21:481–527, 1979.

[193] D. J. Higham and N. J. Higham. *MATLAB Guide.* SIAM, Philadelphia, PA, 2000.

[194] N. J. Higham. A survey of condition number estimation for triangular matrices. *SIAM Review*, 29:575–596, 1987.

[195] N. J. Higham. A survey of componentwise perturbation theory in numerical linear algebra. In W. Gautschi, editor, *Mathematics of Computation 1943–1993: A Half Century of Computational Mathematics*, volume 48 of *Proc. Symp. Appl. Math.*, pages 49–77. Amer. Math. Soc., 1993.

[196] N. J. Higham. *Accuracy and Stability of Numerical Algorithms.* SIAM, Philadelphia, PA, 2d edition, 2002.

[197] D. R. Hill. *Experiments in Computational Matrix Algebra.* Random House, New York, 1988.

[198] T. Hopkins and C. Phillips. *Numerical Methods in Practice.* Addison-Wesley, Reading, MA, 1988.

[199] R. A. Horn and C. R. Johnson. *Matrix Analysis.* Cambridge University Press, New York, 1985.

[200] R. A. Horn and C. R. Johnson. *Topics in Matrix Analysis.* Cambridge University Press, New York, 1991.

[201] R. Horst, P. M. Pardalos, and N. V. Thoai. *Introduction to Global Optimization.* Kluwer, Boston, 2d edition, 2000.

[202] A. S. Householder. *The Numerical Treatment of a Single Nonlinear Equation.* McGraw-Hill, New York, 1970.

[203] B. B. Hubbard. *The World According to Wavelets.* A K Peters, Natick, MA, 2d edition, 1998.

[204] J. M. Hyman. Accurate monotonicity preserving cubic interpolation. *SIAM J. Sci. Stat. Comput.*, 4:645–654, 1983.

[205] IEEE. IEEE standard 754-1985 for binary floating-point arithmetic. *SIGPLAN Notices*, 22(2):9–25, 1987. (See also *IEEE Computer*, March 1981).

[206] E. Isaacson and H. B. Keller. *Analysis of Numerical Methods.* Dover, New York, 1994. (Reprint of 1966 edition).

[207] A. Iserles. *A First Course in the Numerical Analysis of Differential Equations.* Cambridge University Press, New York, 1996.

[208] D. D. Jackson. Interpretation of inaccurate, insufficient, and inconsistent data. *Geophys. J. Royal Astron. Soc.*, 28:97–109, 1972.

[209] D. Jacobs, editor. *Numerical Software: Needs and Availability.* Academic, New York, 1978.

[210] F. James. A review of pseudorandom number generators. *Comput. Phys. Comm.*, 60:329–344, 1990.

[211] P. Jarratt and D. Nudds. The use of rational functions in the iterative solution of equations on a digital computer. *Computer J.*, 8:62–65, 1965.

[212] L. Jaulin, M. Kieffer, O. Didrit, and E. Walter. *Applied Interval Analysis.* Springer-Verlag, New York, 2001.

[213] M. A. Jenkins and J. F. Traub. Zeros of a complex polynomial. *Comm. ACM*, 15:97–99, 1972.

[214] M. A. Jenkins and J. F. Traub. Zeros of a real polynomial. *ACM Trans. Math. Software*, 1:178–189, 1975.

[215] A. Jennings and J. J. McKeown. *Matrix Computation.* John Wiley & Sons, New York, 2d edition, 1992.

[216] D. C. Jespersen. Multigrid methods for partial differential equations. In G. H. Golub, editor, *Studies in Numerical Analysis*, pages 270–318. Math. Assoc. Amer., Washington, DC, 1984.

[217] F. John. *Partial Differential Equations.* Springer-Verlag, New York, 4th edition, 1982.

[218] C. Johnson. *Numerical Solution of Partial Differential Equations by the Finite Element Method.* Cambridge University Press, New York, 1987.

[219] D. C. Joyce. Survey of extrapolation processes in numerical analysis. *SIAM Review*, 13:435–488, 1971.

[220] D. Kahaner, C. Moler, and S. Nash. *Numerical Methods and Software.* Prentice Hall, Englewood Cliffs, NJ, 1989.

[221] G. Kaiser. *A Friendly Guide to Wavelets.* Birkhäuser, Boston, 1994.

[222] M. H. Kalos and P. A. Whitlock. *Monte Carlo Methods.* John Wiley & Sons, New York, 1986.

[223] W. Kaplan. *Maxima and Minima with Applications: Practical Optimization and Duality.* John Wiley & Sons, New York, 1999.

[224] W. J. Kaufmann and L. L. Smarr. *Supercomputing and the Transformation of Science.* Scientific American Library, New York, 1993.

[225] R. B. Kearfott. *Rigorous Global Search: Continuous Problems.* Kluwer, Boston, 1996.

[226] H. B. Keller. *Numerical Methods for Two-Point Boundary-Value Problems.* Dover, New York, 1992. (Reprint of 1968 edition).

[227] C. T. Kelley. *Iterative Methods for Linear and Nonlinear Equations.* SIAM, Philadelphia, PA, 1995.

[228] C. T. Kelley. *Iterative Methods for Optimization.* SIAM, Philadelphia, PA, 1999.

[229] W. J. Kennedy and J. E. Gentle. *Statistical Computing.* Marcel Dekker, New York, 1980.

[230] D. Kincaid and W. Cheney. *Numerical Analysis: Mathematics of Scientific Computing.* Brooks/Cole, Pacific Grove, CA, 3d edition, 2002.

[231] J. King. *MATLAB 6 for Engineers: Hands-on Tutorial.* R. T. Edwards, Philadelphia, PA, 2001.

[232] A. Knight. *Basics of MATLAB and Beyond.* CRC Press, Boca Raton, FL, 2000.

[233] G. D. Knott. *Interpolating Cubic Splines.* Birkhäuser, Boston, 2000.

[234] O. Knüppel. PROFIL/BIAS – a fast interval library. *Computing*, 53:277–287, 1994.

[235] D. E. Knuth. *The Art of Computer Programming: Seminumerical Algorithms*, volume 2. Addison-Wesley, Reading, MA, 3d edition, 1998.

[236] N. Köckler. *Numerical Methods and Scientific Computing.* Oxford University Press, New York, 1994.

[237] I. Koren. *Computer Arithmetic Algorithms.* A K Peters, Natick, MA, 2d edition, 2002.

[238] R. Kress. *Numerical Analysis.* Springer-Verlag, New York, 1998.

[239] A. R. Krommer and C. W. Ueberhuber. *Computational Integration.* SIAM, Philadelphia, PA, 1998.

[240] V. I. Krylov. *Approximate Calculation of Integrals.* Macmillan, New York, 1962.

[241] P. K. Kythe. *An Introduction to Boundary Element Methods.* CRC Press, Boca Raton, FL, 1995.

[242] J. D. Lambert. *Computational Methods in Ordinary Differential Systems.* John Wiley & Sons, New York, 1973.

[243] J. D. Lambert. *Numerical Methods for Ordinary Differential Systems.* John Wiley & Sons, New York, 1991.

[244] R. H. Landau and P. J. Fink. *A Scientist's and Engineer's Guide to Workstations and Supercomputers.* John Wiley & Sons, New York, 1993.

[245] R. H. Landau and M. J. Páez. *Computational Physics: Problem Solving with Computers.* John Wiley & Sons, New York, 1997.

[246] H. P. Langtangen. *Computational Partial Differential Equations.* Springer-Verlag, New York, 2d edition, 2003.

[247] L. Lapidus and G. F. Pinder. *Numerical Solution of Partial Differential Equations in Science and Engineering.* John Wiley & Sons, New York, 1982.

[248] L. Lapidus and J. Seinfeld. *Numerical Solution of Ordinary Differential Equations.* Academic, New York, 1971.

[249] F. M. Larkin. Root-finding by fitting rational functions. *Math. Comp.*, 35:803–816, 1980.

[250] H. T. Lau. *A Numerical Library in C for Scientists and Engineers.* CRC Press, Boca Raton, FL, 1995.

[251] C. L. Lawson and R. J. Hanson. *Solving Least Squares Problems.* SIAM, Philadelphia, PA, 1995. (Updated reprint of 1974 edition).

[252] C. L. Lawson, R. J. Hanson, D. R. Kincaid, and F. T. Krogh. Basic linear algebra subprograms for Fortran usage. *ACM Trans. Math. Software*, 5:308–325, 1979.

[253] R. B. Lehoucq, D. C. Sorensen, and C. Yang. *ARPACK Users' Guide: Solution of Large-Scale Eigenvalue Problems with Implicitly Restarted Arnoldi Methods.* SIAM, Philadelphia, PA, 1998.

[254] R. J. LeVeque. *Finite Volume Methods for Hyperbolic Problems.* Cambridge University Press, New York, 2002.

[255] G. Lindfield and J. Penny. *Numerical Methods Using MATLAB.* Prentice Hall, Upper Saddle River, NJ, 2d edition, 2000.

[256] J. D. Logan. *Applied Partial Differential Equations.* Springer-Verlag, New York, 1998.

[257] D. W. Lozier and F. W. J. Olver. Numerical evaluation of special functions. In W. Gautschi, editor, *Mathematics of Computation 1943–1993: A Half Century of Computational Mathematics*, volume 48 of *Proc. Symp. Appl. Math.*, pages 79–125. Amer. Math. Soc., 1993.

[258] D. G. Luenberger. *Linear and Nonlinear Programming.* Addison-Wesley, Reading, MA, 2d edition, 1984.

[259] J. N. Lyness. When not to use an automatic quadrature routine. *SIAM Review*, 25:63–88, 1983.

[260] J. N. Lyness and R. Cools. A survey of numerical cubature over triangles. In W. Gautschi, editor, *Mathematics of Computation 1943–1993: A Half Century of Computational Mathematics*, volume 48 of *Proc. Symp. Appl. Math.*, pages 127–150. Amer. Math. Soc., 1993.

[261] J. N. Lyness and J. J. Kaganove. Comments on the nature of automatic quadrature routines. *ACM Trans. Math. Software*, 2:65–81, 1976.

[262] A. R. Magid. *Applied Matrix Models.* John Wiley & Sons, New York, 1985.

[263] O. L. Mangasarian. *Nonlinear Programming.* McGraw-Hill, New York, 1969.

[264] G. Marsaglia. Random numbers fall mainly in the planes. *Proc. Nat. Acad. Sci.*, 61:25–28, 1968.

[265] J. H. Mathews and K. D. Fink. *Numerical Methods Using MATLAB.* Prentice Hall, Upper Saddle River, NJ, 4th edition, 2004.

[266] R. M. M. Mattheij and J. Molenaar. *Ordinary Differential Equations in Theory and Practice.* SIAM, Philadelphia, PA, 2002. (Reprint of 1996 edition).

[267] G. P. McCormick. *Nonlinear Programming: Theory, Algorithms, and Applications.* John Wiley & Sons, New York, 1983.

[268] B. Mercier. *An Introduction to the Numerical Analysis of Spectral Methods.* Springer-Verlag, New York, 1989.

[269] G. Meurant. *Computer Solution of Large Linear Systems.* Elsevier, New York, 1999.

[270] W. Miller. *The Engineering of Numerical Software.* Prentice Hall, Englewood Cliffs, NJ, 1984.

[271] W. Miller and C. Wrathall. *Software for Roundoff Analysis of Matrix Algorithms.* Academic, New York, 1980.

[272] A. R. Mitchell and D. F. Griffiths. *The Finite Difference Method in Partial Differential Equations.* John Wiley & Sons, New York, 1980.

[273] C. B. Moler. Matrix computations with Fortran and paging. *Comm. ACM,* 15:268–270, 1972.

[274] C. B. Moler and D. Morrison. Singular value analysis of cryptograms. *Amer. Math. Monthly,* 90:78–87, 1983.

[275] C. B. Moler and C. F. Van Loan. Nineteen dubious ways to compute the exponential of a matrix. *SIAM Review,* 20:801–836, 1978.

[276] B. C. Moore. Principal component analysis in linear systems: Contollability, observability, and model reduction. *IEEE Trans. Automatic Control,* AC-26:17–32, 1981.

[277] R. E. Moore. *Methods and Applications of Interval Analysis.* SIAM, Philadelphia, PA, 1979.

[278] J. J. Moré. The Levenberg-Marquardt algorithm: Implementation and theory. In G. A. Watson, editor, *Numerical Analysis,* pages 105–116. Springer-Verlag, New York, 1977.

[279] J. J. Moré, B. S. Garbow, and K. E. Hillstrom. User guide for MINPACK-1. Technical Report ANL-80-74, Argonne National Laboratory, Argonne, IL, 1980.

[280] J. J. Moré and D. C. Sorensen. Newton's method. In G. H. Golub, editor, *Studies in Numerical Analysis,* pages 29–82. Math. Assoc. Amer., Washington, DC, 1984.

[281] J. J. Moré and Stephen J. Wright. *Optimization Software Guide.* SIAM, Philadelphia, PA, 1993.

[282] K. W. Morton and D. F. Mayers. *Numerical Solution of Partial Differential Equations.* Cambridge University Press, New York, 2d edition, 2005.

[283] J.-M. Müller. *Elementary Functions: Algorithms and Implementation.* Birkhäuser, Boston, 2d edition, 2005.

[284] S. Nakamura. *Numerical Analysis and Graphic Visualization with MATLAB.* Prentice Hall, Upper Saddle River, NJ, 2d edition, 2002.

[285] S. G. Nash, editor. *A History of Scientific Computing.* ACM Press, New York, 1990.

[286] S. G. Nash and A. Sofer. *Linear and Nonlinear Programming.* McGraw-Hill, New York, 1996.

[287] A. Neumaier. *Interval Methods for Systems of Equations.* Cambridge University Press, New York, 1990.

[288] H. Niederreiter. *Random Number Generation and Quasi-Monte Carlo Methods.* SIAM, Philadelphia, PA, 1992.

[289] J. Nievergelt, J. C. Farrar, and E. M. Reingold. *Computer Approaches to Mathematical Problems.* Prentice Hall, Englewood Cliffs, NJ, 1974.

[290] J. Nocedal. Theory of algorithms for unconstrained optimization. *Acta Numerica*, 1:199–242, 1992.

[291] J. Nocedal and S. J. Wright. *Numerical Optimization.* Springer-Verlag, New York, 1999.

[292] A. R. Omondi. *Computer Arithmetic Systems.* Prentice Hall, Englewood Cliffs, NJ, 1994.

[293] J. M. Ortega. *Introduction to Parallel and Vector Solution of Linear Systems.* Plenum, New York, 1988.

[294] J. M. Ortega. *Numerical Analysis: A Second Course.* SIAM, Philadelphia, PA, 1990. (Reprint of 1972 edition).

[295] J. M. Ortega and W. C. Rheinboldt. *Iterative Solution of Nonlinear Equations in Several Variables.* Academic, New York, 1970.

[296] A. M. Ostrowski. *Solution of Equations and Systems of Equations.* Academic, New York, 2d edition, 1966.

[297] M. L. Overton. *Numerical Computing with IEEE Floating Point Arithmetic.* SIAM, Philadelphia, PA, 2001.

[298] C. C. Paige and M. A. Saunders. Solution of sparse indefinite systems of linear equations. *SIAM J. Numer. Anal.*, 12:617–629, 1975.

[299] W. J. Palm. *Introduction to MATLAB 6 for Engineers.* McGraw-Hill, New York, 2001.

[300] B. Parhami. *Computer Arithmetic: Algorithms and Hardware Designs.* Oxford University Press, New York, 1999.

[301] S. K. Park and K. W. Miller. Random number generators: Good ones are hard to find. *Comm. ACM*, 31:1192–1201, 1990.

[302] B. N. Parlett. *The Symmetric Eigenvalue Problem.* SIAM, Philadelphia, PA, 1998. (Updated reprint of 1980 edition).

[303] B. N. Parlett. The QR algorithm. *Computing in Science & Engineering*, 2(1):38–42, 2000.

[304] E. Pärt-Enander, A. Sjöberg, B. Melin, and P. Isaksson. *The MATLAB Handbook.* Addison-Wesley, Reading, MA, 1996.

[305] A. L. Peressini, F. E. Sullivan, and J. J. Uhl. *The Mathematics of Nonlinear Programming.* Springer-Verlag, New York, 1988.

[306] V. Pereyra. Finite difference solution of boundary value problems in ordinary differential equations. In G. H. Golub, editor, *Studies in Numerical Analysis*, pages 243–269. Math. Assoc. Amer., Washington, DC, 1984.

[307] L. R. Petzold, L. O. Jay, and J. Yen. Numerical solution of highly oscillatory ordinary differential equations. *Acta Numerica*, 6:437–484, 1997.

[308] G. M. Phillips and P. J. Taylor. *Theory and Applications of Numerical Analysis.* Academic, San Diego, CA, 2d edition, 1996.

[309] M. Pickering. *An Introduction to Fast Fourier Transform Methods for Partial Differential Equations, with Applications.* John Wiley & Sons, New York, 1986.

[310] R. Piessens, E. deDoncker, C. Ueberhuber, and D. Kahaner. *QUADPACK: A Subroutine Package for Automatic Integration.* Springer-Verlag, New York, 1983.

[311] R. L. Plackett. The discovery of the method of least squares. *Biometrika*, 59:239–251, 1972.

[312] M. J. D. Powell. *Approximation Theory and Methods.* Cambridge University Press, New York, 1981.

[313] C. Pozrikidis. *Numerical Computation in Science and Engineering.* Oxford University Press, New York, 1998.

[314] R. Pratap. *Getting Started with MATLAB 5.* Oxford University Press, New York, 1999.

[315] W. H. Press, S. A. Teukolsky, W. T. Vetterling, and B. P. Flannery. *Numerical Recipes.* Cambridge University Press, New York, 2d edition, 1992.

[316] D. M. Priest. Algorithms for arbitrary precision floating point arithmetic. In P. Kornerup and D. Matula, editors, *Proc. 10th Symp. Comput. Arith.*, pages 132–143. IEEE Computer Society Press, 1991.

[317] A. Quarteroni, R. Sacco, and F. Saleri. *Numerical Mathematics.* Springer-Verlag, New York, 2000.

[318] H. Ratschek and J. Rokne. *New Computer Methods for Global Optimization.* John Wiley & Sons, New York, 1988.

[319] D. Redfern and C. Campbell. *The MATLAB 5 Handbook.* Springer-Verlag, New York, 1998.

[320] C. H. Reinsch. Smoothing by spline functions. *Numer. Math.*, 10:177–183, 1967.

[321] C. H. Reinsch. Smoothing by spline functions II. *Numer. Math.*, 16:451–454, 1971.

[322] W. C. Rheinboldt. *Methods for Solving Systems of Nonlinear Equations.* SIAM, Philadelphia, PA, 2d edition, 1998.

[323] J. R. Rice. A theory of condition. *SIAM J. Numer. Anal.*, 3:287–310, 1966.

[324] J. R. Rice, editor. *Mathematical Software.* Academic, New York, 1971.

[325] J. R. Rice, editor. *Mathematical Software III.* Academic, New York, 1977.

[326] J. R. Rice. *Numerical Methods, Software, and Analysis.* Academic, San Diego, CA, 2d edition, 1993.

[327] J. R. Rice and R. F. Boisvert. *Solving Elliptic Problems Using ELLPACK.* Springer-Verlag, New York, 1985.

[328] R. Richtmyer and K. W. Morton. *Difference Methods for Initial-Value Problems.* John Wiley & Sons, New York, 2d edition, 1967.

[329] T. J. Rivlin. *An Introduction to the Approximation of Functions.* Dover, New York, 1981. (Reprint of 1969 edition).

[330] T. J. Rivlin. *Chebyshev Polynomials.* John Wiley & Sons, New York, 2d edition, 1990.

[331] G. F. Roach. *Green's Functions.* Cambridge University Press, New York, 2d edition, 1982.

[332] S. Roberts and J. Shipman. *Two-Point Boundary Value Problems: Shooting Methods.* Elsevier, New York, 1972.

[333] D. N. Rockmore. The FFT: An algorithm the whole family can use. *Computing in Science & Engineering*, 2(1):60–64, 2000.

[334] R. Rubinstein. *Simulation and the Monte Carlo Method.* John Wiley & Sons, New York, 1981.

[335] Y. Saad. *Numerical Methods for Large Eigenvalue Problems.* John Wiley & Sons, New York, 1992.

[336] Y. Saad. *Iterative Methods for Sparse Linear Systems.* SIAM, Philadelphia, PA, 2d edition, 2003.

[337] G. Sansone. *Orthogonal Functions.* Krieger, Huntington, NY, 1977. (Reprint of 1959 edition).

[338] W. E. Schiesser. *The Numerical Method of Lines Integration of Partial Differential Equations.* Academic, San Diego, CA, 1991.

[339] R. J. Schilling and S. L. Harris. *Applied Numerical Methods for Engineers Using MATLAB and C.* Brooks/Cole, Pacific Grove, CA, 2000.

[340] R. B. Schnabel, J. E. Koontz, and B. E. Weiss. A modular system of algorithms for unconstrained minimization. *ACM Trans. Math. Software*, 11:419–440, 1985.

[341] L. L. Schumaker. *Spline Functions.* John Wiley & Sons, New York, 1981.

[342] H. R. Schwarz. *Numerical Analysis: A Comprehensive Introduction.* John Wiley & Sons, New York, 1989.

[343] G. A. F. Seber and C. J. Wild. *Nonlinear Regression.* John Wiley & Sons, New York, 1989.

[344] G. Sewell. *The Numerical Solution of Ordinary and Partial Differential Equations.* John Wiley & Sons, New York, 2d edition, 2005.

[345] L. F. Shampine. What everyone solving differential equations numerically should know. In I. Gladwell and D. K. Sayers, editors, *Computational Techniques for Ordinary Differential Equations*, pages 1–17. Academic, New York, 1980.

[346] L. F. Shampine. *Numerical Solution of Ordinary Differential Equations.* Chapman & Hall, New York, 1994.

[347] L. F. Shampine and R. C. Allen. *Numerical Computing: An Introduction.* W. B. Saunders, Philadelphia, PA, 1973.

[348] L. F. Shampine, R. C. Allen, and S. Pruess. *Fundamentals of Numerical Computing.* John Wiley & Sons, New York, 1997.

[349] L. F. Shampine and C. W. Gear. A user's view of solving stiff ordinary differential equations. *SIAM Review*, 21:1–17, 1979.

[350] L. F. Shampine and M. K. Gordon. *Computer Solution of Ordinary Differential Equations.* W. H. Freeman, San Francisco, 1975.

[351] L. F. Shampine and M. W. Reichelt. The MATLAB ODE suite. *SIAM J. Sci. Comput.*, 18:1–22, 1997.

[352] L. F. Shampine, H. A. Watts, and S. M. Davenport. Solving nonstiff ordinary differential equations—the state of the art. *SIAM Review*, 18:376–411, 1976.

[353] E. V. Shikin and A. I. Plis. *Handbook on Splines for the User.* CRC Press, Boca Raton, FL, 1995.

[354] K. Sigmon and T. Davis. *MATLAB Primer.* CRC Press, Boca Raton, FL, 6th edition, 2002.

[355] R. D. Skeel. Equivalent forms of multistep methods. *Math. Comp.*, 33:1229–1250, 1979.

[356] R. D. Skeel and J. B. Keiper. *Elementary Numerical Computing with Mathematica.* McGraw-Hill, New York, 1993.

[357] I. H. Sloan and S. Joe. *Lattice Methods for Multiple Integration.* Oxford University Press, New York, 1994.

[358] B. T. Smith, J. M. Boyle, Y. Ikebe, V. C. Klema, and C. B. Moler. *Matrix Eigensystem Routines: EISPACK Guide.* Springer-Verlag, New York, 2d edition, 1970.

[359] G. D. Smith. *Numerical Solution of Partial Differential Equations.* Oxford University Press, New York, 3d edition, 1985.

[360] R. L. Smith. *The MATLAB Project Book.* Prentice Hall, Upper Saddle River, NJ, 1997.

[361] I. M. Sobol'. *A Primer for the Monte Carlo Method.* CRC Press, Boca Raton, FL, 1994.

[362] H. Späth. *One Dimensional Spline Interpolation Algorithms.* A K Peters, Wellesley, MA, 1995.

[363] W. Squire. *Integration for Engineers and Scientists.* Elsevier, New York, 1970.

[364] I. A. Stegun and M. Abramowitz. Pitfalls in computation. *J. SIAM*, 4:207–219, 1956.

[365] P. H. Sterbenz. *Floating-Point Computation.* Prentice Hall, Englewood Cliffs, NJ, 1974.

[366] H. J. Stetter. *Analysis of Discretization Methods for Ordinary Differential Equations.* Springer-Verlag, New York, 1973.

[367] H. J. Stetter. Initial value problems for ordinary differential equations: Development of ideas, techniques, and implementation. In W. Gautschi, editor, *Mathematics of Computation 1943–1993: A Half Century of Computational Mathematics*, volume 48 of *Proc. Symp. Appl. Math.*, pages 205–224. Amer. Math. Soc., 1993.

[368] G. W. Stewart. *Introduction to Matrix Computations.* Academic, New York, 1973.

[369] G. W. Stewart. On the early history of the singular value decomposition. *SIAM Review*, 35:551–566, 1993.

[370] G. W. Stewart. *Afternotes on Numerical Analysis.* SIAM, Philadelphia, PA, 1996.

[371] G. W. Stewart. *Afternotes Goes to Graduate School.* SIAM, Philadelphia, PA, 1998.

[372] G. W. Stewart. *Matrix Algorithms, Volume I: Basic Decompositions.* SIAM, Philadelphia, PA, 1998.

[373] G. W. Stewart. The decompositional approach to matrix computation. *Computing in Science & Engineering*, 2(1):50–59, 2000.

[374] G. W. Stewart and T. G. Sun. *Matrix Perturbation Theory.* Academic, New York, 1990.

[375] J. Stoer and R. Bulirsch. *Introduction to Numerical Analysis.* Springer-Verlag, New York, 3d edition, 2002.

[376] G. Strang. *Introduction to Applied Mathematics.* Wellesley-Cambridge Press, Wellesley, MA, 1986.

[377] G. Strang. *Linear Algebra and Its Applications.* Harcourt, New York, 3d edition, 1988.

[378] G. Strang. Wavelets. *Amer. Scientist*, 82:250–255, 1992.

[379] G. Strang. *Introduction to Linear Algebra.* Wellesley-Cambridge Press, Wellesley, MA, 3d edition, 2003.

[380] G. Strang and G. Fix. *An Analysis of the Finite Element Method.* Prentice Hall, Englewood Cliffs, NJ, 1973.

[381] V. Strassen. Gaussian elimination is not optimal. *Numer. Math.*, 13:354–356, 1969.

[382] W. A. Strauss. *Partial Differential Equations, An Introduction.* John Wiley & Sons, New York, 1992.

[383] J. C. Strikwerda. *Finite Difference Schemes and Partial Differential Equations.* SIAM, Philadelphia, PA, 2d edition, 2004.

[384] A. H. Stroud. *Approximate Calculation of Multiple Integrals.* Prentice Hall, Englewood Cliffs, NJ, 1972.

[385] A. H. Stroud and D. Secrest. *Gaussian Quadrature Formulas.* Prentice Hall, Englewood Cliffs, NJ, 1966.

[386] W. H. Swann. Direct search methods. In W. Murray, editor, *Numerical Methods for Unconstrained Optimization*, pages 13–28. Academic, New York, 1972.

[387] P. N. Swarztrauber. Fast Poisson solvers. In G. H. Golub, editor, *Studies in Numerical Analysis*, pages 319–370. Math. Assoc. Amer., Washington, DC, 1984.

[388] G. Szegö. *Orthogonal Polynomials.* American Mathematical Society, Providence, RI, 4th edition, 1975.

[389] R. A. Thisted. *Elements of Statistical Computing.* Chapman & Hall, New York, 1988.

[390] J. W. Thomas. *Numerical Partial Differential Equations: Finite Difference Methods.* Springer-Verlag, New York, 1995.

[391] J. W. Thomas. *Numerical Partial Differential Equations: Conservation Laws and Elliptic Equations.* Springer-Verlag, New York, 1999.

[392] W. J. Thompson. *Atlas for Computing Mathematical Functions.* John Wiley & Sons, New York, 1996.

[393] J. F. Traub. *Iterative Methods for the Solution of Equations.* Prentice Hall, Englewood Cliffs, NJ, 1964.

[394] L. N. Trefethen. Three mysteries of Gaussian elimination. *SIGNUM Newsletter*, 20(4):2–5, October 1985.

[395] L. N. Trefethen. *Spectral Methods in MATLAB.* SIAM, Philadelphia, PA, 2000.

[396] L. N. Trefethen and D. Bau. *Numerical Linear Algebra.* SIAM, Philadelphia, PA, 1997.

[397] L. N. Trefethen and R. S. Schreiber. Average-case stability of Gaussian elimination. *SIAM J. Matrix Anal. Appl.*, 11:335–360, 1990.

[398] U. Trottenberg, C. W. Oosterlee, and A. Schüller. *Multigrid: Basics, Parallelism and Adaptivity.* Academic, San Diego, CA, 2000.

[399] D. W. Tufts and R. Kumaresan. Singular value decomposition and improved frequency estimation using linear prediction. *IEEE Trans. Acoustics, Speech, and Signal Processing*, ASSP-30:671–675, 1982.

[400] A. M. Turing. Rounding-off errors in matrix processes. *Quart. J. Mech. Appl. Math.*, 1:287–308, 1948.

[401] A. Tveito and R. Winther. *Introduction to Partial Differential Equations: A Computational Approach.* Springer-Verlag, New York, 1998.

[402] C. W. Ueberhuber. *Numerical Computation: Methods, Software, and Analysis.* Springer-Verlag, New York, 1997. Two volumes.

[403] H. A. van der Vorst. Krylov subspace iteration. *Computing in Science & Engineering*, 2(1):32–37, 2000.

[404] S. Van Huffel and J. Vandewalle. *The Total Least Squares Problem.* SIAM, Philadelphia, PA, 1991.

[405] C. F. Van Loan. *Computational Frameworks for the Fast Fourier Transform.* SIAM, Philadelphia, PA, 1992.

[406] C. F. Van Loan. *An Introduction to Computational Science and Mathematics.* Jones and Bartlett, Sudbury, MA, 1996.

[407] C. F. Van Loan. *Introduction to Scientific Computing.* Prentice Hall, Upper Saddle River, NJ, 2d edition, 2000.

[408] R. S. Varga. *Matrix Iterative Analysis.* Prentice Hall, Englewood Cliffs, NJ, 1962.

[409] S. A. Vavasis. Gaussian elimination with pivoting is P-complete. *SIAM J. Disc. Math.*, 2:413–423, 1989.

[410] J. von Neumann and H. H. Goldstine. Numerical inverting of matrices of high order. *Bull. Amer. Math. Soc.*, 53:1021–1099, 1947.

[411] R. Wait and A. R. Mitchell. *Finite Element Analysis and Applications.* John Wiley & Sons, New York, 1985.

[412] D. S. Watkins. Understanding the QR algorithm. *SIAM Review*, 24:427–440, 1982.

[413] D. S. Watkins. *Fundamentals of Matrix Computations.* John Wiley & Sons, New York, 2d edition, 2002.

[414] G. A. Watson. *Approximation Theory and Numerical Methods.* John Wiley & Sons, New York, 1980.

[415] P. Wesseling. *An Introduction to Multigrid Methods.* John Wiley & Sons, New York, 1992.

[416] D. J. Wilde. *Optimum Seeking Methods.* Prentice Hall, Englewood Cliffs, NJ, 1964.

[417] J. H. Wilkinson. Error analysis of direct methods of matrix inversion. *J. ACM*, 8:281–330, 1961.

[418] J. H. Wilkinson. *Rounding Errors in Algebraic Processes.* Prentice Hall, Englewood Cliffs, NJ, 1963.

[419] J. H. Wilkinson. *The Algebraic Eigenvalue Problem.* Oxford University Press, New York, 1965.

[420] J. H. Wilkinson and C. Reinsch, editors. *Handbook for Automatic Computation, Linear Algebra*, volume 2. Springer-Verlag, New York, 1971.

[421] J. Wimp. *Sequence Transformations and Their Applications.* Academic, New York, 1981.

[422] G. M. Wing. *A Primer on Integral Equations of the First Kind.* SIAM, Philadelphia, PA, 1991.

[423] M. H. Wright. Interior methods for constrained optimization. *Acta Numerica*, 1:341–407, 1992.

[424] M. H. Wright. Direct search methods: Once scorned, now respectable. In D. F. Griffiths and G. A. Watson, editors, *Numerical Analysis 1995*, pages 191–208. Addison-Wesley Longman, Reading, MA, 1996.

[425] M. H. Wright and S. Glassman. Fortran subroutines to solve linear least squares problems and compute the complete orthogonal factorization. Technical Report SOL-78-8, Systems Optimization Laboratory, Stanford University, Stanford, CA, April 1978.

[426] S. J. Wright. A collection of problems for which Gaussian elimination with partial pivoting is unstable. *SIAM J. Sci. Comput.*, 14:231–238, 1993.

[427] S. J. Wright. *Primal-Dual Interior-Point Methods.* SIAM, Philadelphia, PA, 1997.

[428] F. Yamaguchi. *Curves and Surfaces in Computer-Aided Geometric Design.* Springer-Verlag, New York, 1988.

[429] D. M. Young. *Iterative Solution of Large Linear Systems.* Academic, New York, 1971.

[430] T. J. Ypma. Historical development of the Newton-Raphson method. *SIAM Review*, 37:531–551, 1995.

[431] J. L. Zachary. *Introduction to Scientific Programming: Computational Problem Solving Using Maple and C.* Springer-Verlag, New York, 1996.

[432] J. L. Zachary. *Introduction to Scientific Programming: Computational Problem Solving Using Mathematica and C.* Springer-Verlag, New York, 1998.

[433] S. Zhang and J. Jin. *Computation of Special Functions.* John Wiley & Sons, New York, 1996.

[434] O. C. Zienkiewicz and R. L. Taylor. *The Finite Element Method.* McGraw-Hill, New York, 4th edition, 1989.

[435] D. Zwillinger, editor. *Standard Mathematical Tables and Formulae.* CRC Press, Boca Raton, FL, 30th edition, 1996.

Index